THE ENCYCLOPEDIA OF

AIRCRAFT
OF WWII

THE ENCYCLOPEDIA OF
AIRCRAFT
OF WWII

GENERAL EDITOR: PAUL EDEN

Published in 2004 by Silverdale Books
an imprint of Bookmart Ltd
Registered Number 2372865
Trading as Bookmart Ltd
Blaby Road
Wigston
Leicester LE18 4SE

ISBN 1-84509-013-6

Produced by
Amber Books Ltd
Bradley's Close
74-77 White Lion Street
London N1 9PF
www.amberbooks.co.uk

PICTURE CREDITS

Printed in Singapore

Contents

This 1946 photograph shows B-29 Superfortresses stored at the 15th Air Base in Davis-Monthan Field, Tucson, Arizona, following the end of hostilities the previous year.

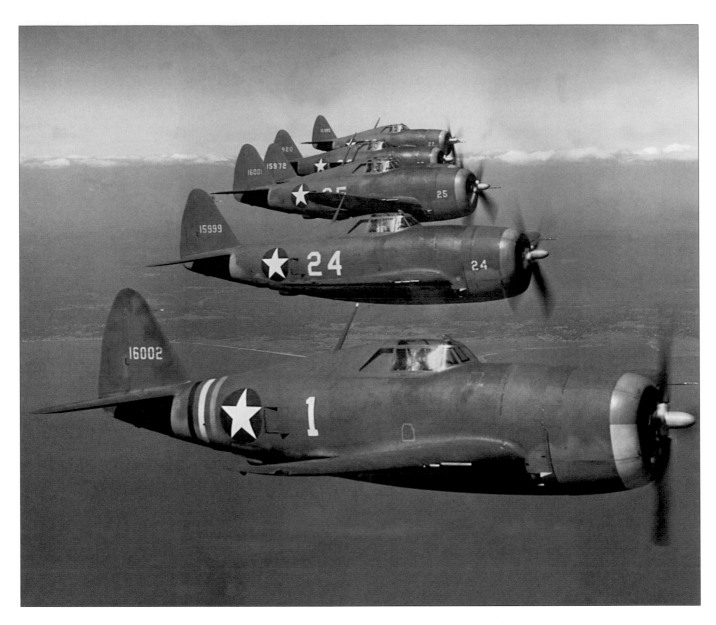

A flight of United States Army Air Force (USAAF) P-47B Thunderbolts patrols off the coast of southern England in 1943. The P-47B was lacking in performance and manoeuvrability at low levels, and was soon upgraded to the P47C, which included rudder and elevator changes to increase manoeuvrability and water injection to increase power.

Above: A Spitfire Mk XIX takes part in an air show in the UK as part of the 'Battle of Britain' flight in 1973.

Below: Soviet airmen take a well-earned rest in an interval between missions on the Eastern Front in September 1944. Standing in the background is a Polikarpov I-16 fighter.

A British Royal Air Force recovery team examine the fuselage and cockpit of a Luftwaffe Junkers Ju 88 shot down during the Battle of Britain, July 1940.

Introduction

As Europe moved inexorably towards war, the majority of combat aircraft in service were little developed beyond those used in World War I. In Britain, the new generation of monoplane fighters was just beginning to enter service in the form of the Hurricane and Spitfire. These sleek new aircraft were the first Royal Air Force (RAF) machines to show any real improvement in armament over the Sopwith Camel of 1917. A new breed of bomber was also in British service, although the onset of combat operations soon demonstrated just how vulnerable aircraft like the Blenheim and Hampden were. In France, an over-complicated aircraft acquisition system led to a number of promising types falling by the wayside. Elsewhere in Europe, the defending nations were equipped with a motley collection of obsolescent types, with the Gladiator and a few Hurricanes among the most effective.

For the Axis powers, the Spanish Civil War had provided an excellent proving ground for their latest combat types. In the case of Italy, this experience led to a mistaken belief that there was still a place for the biplane fighter in modern air warfare and while the resulting Fiat CR.42 was possibly the ultimate biplane fighter, it really belonged to an earlier era. For Germany, the fighting in Spain allowed it to prove not only its new aircraft, but also to devise tactics allowing their use to greatest advantage.

Although officially banned from producing military aircraft after its defeat in World War I, Germany had begun a covert programme of aircraft development during the early 1930s. By 1935, this was well enough developed not only for Hitler's Nazi Germany to unveil a fleet of indigenous warplanes, but also a fully-fledged *Luftwaffe*. Soon the Messerschmitt Bf 109, Junkers Ju 87 Stuka and Heinkel He 111 became available, boasting performance that was second to none.

Aided by its overwhelming superiority in the air, the German war machine swept through Europe, only coming up short at the Channel when faced with the determined, but limited might of the RAF's Fighter Command. Equipped mostly with Hurricanes, Fighter Command was barely able to stave off the Germans, but when the Luftwaffe turned its back on Britain's air defences and looked instead to attacking its cities, the battle was won. Thereafter, the RAF turned to offence with an ever improving series of Spitfire and Hurricane developments, not to mention the superlative de Havilland Mosquito and Hawker Typhoon. The Luftwaffe countered with its own new developments, including the formidable Focke-Wulf Fw 190, but the combined might of the RAF and, from late 1942, the US Army Air Force, eventually proved unassailable.

In no small part this was due to the Allies' strategic bombing campaign, founded on the Lancaster, Halifax, B-17 and B-24 bombers, which steadily took its toll on Germany's ability to produce war materiel, while the continued tactical air offensive also reaped its rewards. Pushed to ever greater achievement by this constant pressure, the German aircraft industry produced some of the most advanced aircraft of the war, including the Me 163 and Me 262 rocket-powered aircraft.

In June 1941 the German army launched its all-out assault on Stalin's Soviet Russia. Germany's initial foray into the Soviet Union was easily won, but as the Soviets moved their industry further east out of the reach of Hitler's bombers, a new wave of weaponry was developed. This included some of the finest bomber and fighter aircraft of the war, machines such as the Lavochkin and Yakovlev fighters, which were able to take on the best *Luftwaffe* fighters on equal terms.

In the Pacific, Japan's preemptive strike against the US fleet at Pearl Harbor marked America's entry into the war. In this theatre more than any other, the aircraft carrier was of primary importance and here the Japanese initially had the upper hand. Among the most feared aircraft in the world, the Mitsubishi A6M Zero remained invincible until the US Navy began producing the Grumman F4F Wildcat; even then no true match for the Zero was found until the F6F Hellcat had been perfected. Allied advances saw the Japanese pushed back towards their home islands, much of the latter part of the Pacific campaign being aimed at providing bases for the mighty Boeing B-29 Superfortress. These huge bombers flew against Japan from 1944, frequently relying on the P-51 Mustang for escort, just as their B-17 cousins did over Europe. Eventually, as Japan's defence became more desperate in the face of overwhelming odds, it fell to the B-29 to fly the missions that ended the war – the atomic raids against Hiroshima and Nagasaki.

The Encyclopedia of Aircraft of World War II describes the many warplanes involved in World War II in detail. Contemporary photography and detailed artworks bring each type to life, while descriptions of the origins and development of the key types bring you a greater appreciation and understanding of these classic machines.

Two Luftwaffe Messerschmitt Bf 109 fighters patrol above the Libyan desert in 1941, supporting ground troops in the push to capture Tobruk.

Aichi D3A 'Val'

Pearl Harbor attacker

One of the outstanding Japanese warplanes of World War II, the D3A 'Val' played a crucial role in the attack on Pearl Harbor and sank more tonnage of Allied shipping than any other Axis type.

In the mid-1930s the standard dive bomber (or Tokushu Bakugekiki 'Special Bomber' in the contemporary Japanese classification system) aboard Japanese carriers (then the IJNS *Akagi, Hosho, Kaga, Ryujo* and *Soryu*, with IJNS *Hiryu* following in 1939) were the Navy Type 94 and Type 96 Special Bombers. Also known by their shortened designations D1A1 and D1A2, these two-seat biplanes had been developed by Aichi Tokei Denki KK (Aichi Watch and Electric Machinery Co Ltd) from the German Heinkel He 66 (export version of the Luftwaffe He 50). Even though the D1A2 was more powerful and cleaner than the D1A1, it still lacked the necessary performance for contemporary combat.

After preliminary work on a cleaner biplane (D2A1, company designation AB-11) with manually retractable undercarriage was suspended, Aichi developed its AM-17 in answer to the Japanese Navy 11-Shi specification for a Kanjo Bakugekiki (carrier bomber) issued in 1936. Of monoplane design with low-mounted elliptical wings, trousered main undercarriage, and enclosed tandem cockpits for a pilot and a radio operator/gunner, the AM-17 was powered by a 710-hp (529-kW) Nakajima Hikari (Splendour) 1 radial engine.

Completed in December 1937, the AM-17, however, ran into teething troubles. After the second prototype was fitted with an 840-hp (626-kW) Mitsubishi Kinsei (Golden Star) 3 radial, enlarged vertical tail surfaces, and strengthened dive brakes under the wings, the Aichi design proved superior to the competing Nakajima D3N1. Accordingly, in December 1939, the Aichi aircraft was ordered into production as the Navy Type 99 Carrier Bomber Model 11 (shortened designation D3A1) with the 1,000-hp (746-kW) Kinsei 43 (later the 1,070-hp; 798-kW Kinsei 44) radial engine.

First combat

After carrier qualification trials aboard the *Kaga* and the *Akagi* in 1940, D3A1s saw limited combat operations in China from land bases and carriers. At the onset of the Pacific War, 135 D3A1s were embarked aboard the six carriers which attacked the US Fleet at Pearl Harbor in the morning of 7 December 1941. Fifteen D3A1s were lost in the two strikes but, along with the B5N2 torpedo and level bombers, the Aichi dive bombers succeeded in putting the battleship force of the US Pacific Fleet out of action for six months. D3A1s next gained acclaim when the First Koku Kantai forayed into the Indian Ocean. The six carriers of that Air Fleet never caught up with the two armoured carriers of the Eastern Fleet (HMS *Formidable* and *Indomitable*). However,

Above: The second of two prototype D3As is pictured here fitted with the Mitsubishi Kinsei 3 14-cylinder radial engine. Other improvements included an increase in wingspan of 16 in (40 cm).

Top: Operating in concert with Nakajima B5N2 torpedo bombers with Mitsubishi A6Ms as fighter cover, the D3A wrought havoc on Allied shipping. This example served with the 33rd Kokutai.

between April 4 and 9, 1942, their D3A1s sank not only the cruisers HMS *Cornwall, Dorsetshire*, and the aircraft-carrier *Hermes* but also two destroyers, a corvette, an auxiliary vessel, and two oilers from the Royal Navy as well as 11 merchant vessels. No Japanese ships were hit and only 16 aircraft were lost. During attacks against manoeuvring warships at sea, the Japanese dive bombers had placed more than 80 per cent of their bombs on

Although it looked ungainly with its fixed spatted undercarriage, the D3A was, in its heyday, a highly effective aircraft capable of carrying a single 551-lb (250-kg) bomb under the fusealge and two 132-lb (60-kg) bombs beneath the wings.

Above: Carrying their principal weapon (a 551-lb; 250-kg bomb) beneath each fuselage, a Kokutai of D3A2s was photographed en route for a strike on Allied shipping in mid-1942. Empty bomb racks are visible outboard of the dive brakes beneath the wing.

Serving with Admiral Nagumo's Strike Force, the D3A acquitted itself well during the early stages of the Pacific war. However, with effective air cover the Allies could have exposed the aircraft's weaknesses in aerial combat and saved many of the vessels which were sunk by dive-bomb attacks.

the targets (with 40 bombs sinking *Hermes*).

D3A1 crews still performed superbly during operations in the Aleutians, the Coral Sea battle (when they contributed three bombs to the sinking of the USS *Yorktown* and, without assistance, sank a US destroyer and a tanker), and the Battle of Midway. Nevertheless, the tide of war turned in favour of the Allies. From then on, while fighting gallantly to the end, D3A crews never achieved the level of success obtained during the first six months of the war.

Improved model

In July 1942, the Navy Type 99 Carrier Bomber was assigned the name 'Val' under the code system developed by the Allied Air Technical Intelligence Unit (ATIU) to replace cumbersome, and then poorly known, Japanese designations. During that same month, the prototype of an improved model, the D3A2 with the 1,300-hp (969-kW) Kinsei 54 and increased fuel tankage, was flown. As the Navy Type 99 Carrier Bomber Model 22, this version entered service in the autumn of 1942. By then, however, its intended successor, the Yokosuka D4Y1, was under development. Known to the Allies as the 'Judy,' that type soon replaced the 'Val' aboard Japanese carriers. The D3A's last participation in a major carrier battle was in June 1944, when 27 D3A2s of the 652nd Kokutai (Naval Air Corps) were embarked aboard the three carriers of the Second Koku Sentai (Carrier Division). Along with other carrier- and land-based Japanese aircraft they were butchered during the 'Marianas Turkey Shoot' without scoring a single hit.

Navy Type 99 Carrier Bombers, however, remained in front-line service with land-based units until the war's end and also served with operational training units (with which some aircraft were redesignated D3A2-Ks, the suffix K standing for Koshiki or School Type). Many were finally expanded in *kamikaze* attacks during the last year of the war. Production had totalled 1,495 aircraft, including 201 D3A-2s by Showa Hikoki KK (Showa Aeroplane Co Ltd).

Desperation measures

In late 1943, with Japan running out of light alloys, the D3A2-K was selected for redesign using non-strategic materials. That task was assigned to the Dai-Ichi Kaigun Koku Gijitsusho (First Naval Air Technical Arsenal). The original elliptical wings and rounded tail surfaces, judged too complex for wooden construction and assembly by semi-skilled workers, were replaced by straight tapered surfaces. Two D3Y-1K prototypes were built at the Navy arsenal and production of the Navy Type 99 Bomber Trainer was entrusted to Matsushita Koku Kogyo KK (Matsushita Air Industries Co Ltd). Named Myojo (Venus), three of these aircraft were completed before the Japanese surrender. Development of a single-seat *kamikaze* variant was initiated as the D3Y2-K and production was to have been undertaken under the D5Y1 Special Attacker designation.

This was the last D3A 'Val' in flying condition – none is currently airworthy. However, three replicas constructed from Vultee BT-15s and a further nine constructed from Vultee BT-13s have been built, many of which are used in aerial reconstructions of the attack on Pearl Harbor.

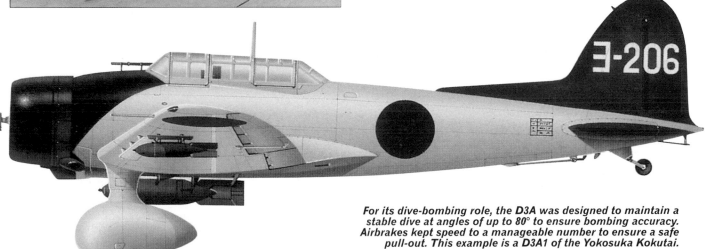

For its dive-bombing role, the D3A was designed to maintain a stable dive at angles of up to 80° to ensure bombing accuracy. Airbrakes kept speed to a manageable number to ensure a safe pull-out. This example is a D3A1 of the Yokosuka Kokutai.

Arado Ar 196

In many ways the 'eyes of the Kriegsmarine', the Arado Ar 196 had superb water- and flight- handling characteristics. During its early career its heavy armament made it the scourge of lumbering enemy maritime patrollers, although this situation was steadily reversed as the war progressed.

Fighting floatplane

Although it exerted only a minor influence on World War II, the Arado Ar 196 was nevertheless an important type. Evolving through a number of float configurations, the aircraft soon entered service, replacing the venerable He 60.

The first shipboard aircraft of the resurrected German navy was the Heinkel He 60, a conventional biplane. All such aircraft had to be stressed for catapult launching, possibly while the ship was rolling or pitching in a heavy sea, and for subsequent recovery by crane after alighting on the water. The main task of the He 60 was short-range reconnaissance, but coastal patrol, the rescue of downed aircrew and even the local close support of ground forces (for example in anti-partisan operations) were all to become important secondary duties.

By 1936 it was clear that the He 60 was becoming outdated. Heinkel was invited to produce a successor, but the resulting He 114 proved to have extremely poor hydrodynamic and seakeeping qualities and to be deficient in other respects. After prolonged testing and

The first and second prototypes of the Ar 196 had conventional twin floats, while the third, fourth and fifth prototypes (for the B-series) had a single main float on the centreline, with stabilising floats under the wings. The unarmed second prototype is shown here undergoing a catapult launch.

modification of the He 114, it was decided, around October 1936, to issue a fresh specification in order that the Focke-Wulf company or Arado Flugzeugwerke could offer a better product. Focke-Wulf produced a conventional biplane in the shape of the Fw 62, but the Arado offering was a monoplane, with (surprisingly) a low-mounted wing.

First prototypes

The Kriegsmarine and Reichsluftfahrtministerium agreed that the aircraft should be powered by a BMW 132K nine-

One early success was the capture of the British submarine HMS Seal by two Ar 196s of 1 Staffel/Küstenfliegergruppe 706. The vessel was damaged by a mine and its crew surrendered after the Ar 196s launched an attack with cannon-fire and bombs.

cylinder radial engine of 960-hp (716-kW) output – virtually the same as the engine of the He 114. It was further stipulated that prototypes had to be produced with twin floats, and a single central float and small stabilising floats under the wingtips. The two rival companies quickly submitted drawings and costings and the Ar 196 was judged to be the more attractive

option. Two prototypes of the Fw 62 were ordered as an insurance, but four of the Ar 196 were called for. With works numbers 2589-2592, the first two (Ar 196 V1 and V2) were A-series aircraft with twin floats, while V3 and V4 were B-series machines with a central float. All were registered as civil aircraft (respectively D-IEHK, IHQI, ILRE and OVMB).

The first prototype Ar 196 shows the twin-float layout that became the standard. The horn balance on the rudder was discarded on the V2, which was otherwise very similar to the V1.

In some respects the prototypes were interim aircraft. Their engines were of the 880-hp (657-kW) BMW 132Dc type, driving a Schwarz two-bladed propeller. As originally built, the first aircraft had twin exhaust pipes which were led round under the left side of the fuselage. Later, the standard arrangement consisted of twin shorter pipes discharging equally to left and right of the ventral centreline. The cowling fitted the engine tightly, with blisters over the valve gear, and cooling was controlled by trailing-edge hinged gills. Overall, the aircraft needed very little modification, the only visible change between the first two prototypes being the elimination of the balance horn at the top of the rudder, a slight increase in fin area and small changes to the water rudders on the floats. The V1 was also later fitted with the three-bladed VDM constant-speed propeller that was made standard.

The second and third prototypes, V2 and V3, were similar apart from the latter's different float arrangement. V4, however, was fitted with more streamlined stabilising floats, with a simpler arrangement of struts. It was also the first Ar 196 to be equipped with armament, comprising a 20-mm MG FF cannon in each wing, fed from a 60-round drum which left a blister in the underside. Moreover, it had a single 0.312-in (7.92-mm) MG 17 machine-gun on the right of the forward fuselage with its muzzle firing through the forward ring of the engine cowl, and a small container on the underside of each outer wing, just outboard of the cannon, for a single SC 50 (110-lb/50-kg) bomb.

The four seaplanes were carefully evaluated at Travemünde in 1937-38, but it proved difficult to decide which was the preferred float arrangement. The central float was considered preferable in operations from choppy water, but the stabilising floats could easily dip into the sea during take-off, resulting in pronounced asymmetric drag. In the event, although a further B-series prototype was built (the V5, D-IPDB), it was decided to standardise on the twin-float arrangement and this was used on the 10 Ar 196A-0 pre-production aircraft which were delivered from the Warnemünde factory from November 1938.

Conventional design

The Ar 196 was conventional in structure. Its wing was a two-spar all-metal stressed-skin component, which carried slotted flaps and Flettner tabbed ailerons. The wing was arranged to fold to the rear, undersurface outermost, around a skewed hinge very close to the root; folding the wings necessitated disconnecting the wing/float bracing struts. The fuselage was constructed around a strong

Bordfliegerstaffel 1./196 and 5./196 were the two units responsible for providing aircraft for naval vessels, based initially at Wilhelmshaven and Kiel-Holtenau, respectively. This aircraft is seen on board the heavy cruiser Prinz Eugen.

framework of welded steel tubes with light formers and stringers. These supported a skin which was of light alloy from the engine firewall to the rear cockpit, and of fabric from thence to the tail. The tail was a stressed-skin structure, but with the movable surfaces covered with fabric. The floats were of Alclad light alloy. Fuel was carried in two 66-Imp gal (300-litre) tanks, one in each float, with the feed pipes running up the forward struts. The latter also incorporated protecting rungs, forming a ladder up which the crew or servicing personnel could climb to the engine or cockpit.

Armament

The crew comprised a pilot and observer/gunner. The latter normally faced aft and, as there was no fuselage tank, the seats were arranged close together. A continuous glazed canopy covered the cockpits, the pilot having a section sliding to the rear and the observer a sliding portion which originally could be completely closed. In the production versions, the rear cockpit could not be totally enclosed, but wind deflectors avoided any discomfort and this cockpit canopy arrangement made it easier to aim the rear armament which, in the initial Ar 196A-1 version, comprised a single 0.312-in (7.92-mm) MG 17 machine-gun with seven 75-round saddle-type magazines. The forward-firing armament was omitted, while the two SC 50 bombs were retained. The engine was changed for the definitive BMW 132K, driving a Schwarz three-bladed propeller with no spinner. A great deal of operational equipment was added in the production A-1 version, including catapult spools (the structure being locally strengthened) and large smoke canisters in the floats, the latter also containing emergency rations, extra ammunition and flares in the aft section.

From the start, the Ar 196A was extremely popular. Not only was its performance adequate, and its handling superb (both on the water and in the air), but it was very reliable and had an excellent view from the cockpits, despite the low-mounted wing.

The Ar 196 was designed to meet a requirement to replace floatplanes aboard large ships of the Kriegsmarine. Here, one of the prototypes is tested aboard ship. In operation, the aircraft was catapulted into the air for take-off, and hoisted back on board the ship from the water after a sortie.

Eyes of the Kriegsmarine

*The Ar 196 served in all coastal areas of Hitler's Europe and was also the standard aircraft carried aboard major surface warships of the German navy, the largest of which (**Bismarck** and **Tirpitz**) carried four each.*

Operational for most of the war, the Ar 196 proved relatively successful, hunting in most European theatres and chalking up some notable successes along the way.

Deliveries of the first 20 A-1s commenced in June 1939. These aircraft – among the first to go to sea – were assigned to Bordfliegerstaffel 1./196 and 5./196, and mounted on the catapult of the pocket battleship, *Admiral Graf Spee*. This sailed for the South Atlantic in mid-August 1939 and, on 13 December of that year, encountered three (much less powerful) cruisers of the Royal Navy. Captain Langsdorff should perhaps have launched his brand new seaplane, which could then have directed the fire of the ship's 11-in (280-mm) guns as it steamed out of the range of the British cruisers. Instead, the German battleship closed with the British vessels, and suffered crippling damage.

As luck would have it, the very first salvo from the British ships struck the *Graf Spee*'s catapult and destroyed its Ar 196A-1 – the aircraft that might have reversed the outcome of the encounter.

Subsequently, additional Ar 196s replaced the He 60 in shore units as well as aboard all the Kriegsmarine's major surface warships. The very severe winter of 1939-40 delayed flight-testing from

Warnemünde, but the 20 A-1s were followed from November 1939 by the Ar 196A-2 version. This was intended for a wider spectrum of duties than just shipboard reconnaissance. Operating from shore bases, it was expected to range over the North and Baltic Seas looking for shipping to harass and hostile

Right: The Ar 196 V3 differed from its predecessors solely in the arrangement of its float undercarriage. Later models (see below) featured low-drag twin floats.

Below: Ar 196s were active over most European waters, from Norway to the Mediterranean. This Ar 196A-3 belonged to 4./Bordfliegergruppe 196, which was operational in the Adriatic in 1943.

aircraft to destroy, and it was fitted with forward-firing armament. The MG 17 was installed in the right side of the nose (as in the V4 prototype), and two MG FF cannon were also fitted, in an improved installation which left the wing undersurface undisturbed, the ammunition drum causing only a modest blister in the top of the wing. The pilot was expected to use the MG 17 more often than the cannon, the latter's existence giving him a feeling of superior-

ity, safe in the knowledge that the Arado could probably shoot down any hostile aircraft likely to be encountered over the open ocean.

New variants

In 1940 the factory delivered 98 Ar 196s, this total including the first of 24 of a version designated Ar 196A-4. This replaced the A-1 on board warships, and differed in having forward-firing armament and also the additional FuG 16Z radio. A further change to this variant was that the Schwarz propeller was replaced by a VDM pattern with a spinner, as fitted to the modified V1 prototype. The V4 was also slightly stronger, for harsh shipboard use.

On 26 May 1941 the battleship *Bismarck* launched its Ar 196A-4 in an attempt to destroy or drive away the RAF Coastal Command Catalina flying-boat that was looking for the battleship as it raced for a home port. The A-4s did not succeed, and the 'Cat' called up Swordfish torpedo aircraft which, by crippling the *Bismarck*'s steering gear, sealed the ship's fate (it was sunk on 28 May).

However, on 5 May 1940 two A-2 seaplanes from

A number of Ar 196s were captured by the Allies and this example, with the Air Ministry number 92 and serial VM748, was evaluated by the Marine Aircraft Experimental Establishment during 1945.

1/Küstenfliegergruppe 706, based at Aalborg in Denmark, spotted a British submarine, HMS *Seal*, which had been damaged by a mine in the Kattegat. Unable to dive, the submarine had to lie helplessly on the surface while an A-2 (flown by Lt Günther Mehrens) attacked with cannon and two bombs.

When a second A-2 joined in, the submarine's crew surrendered. Mehrens alighted by the vessel and took the submarine's commanding officer back to Aalborg.

Definitive A-3 variant

Production in 1941 comprised 97 Ar 196s, almost all being of the definitive Ar 196A-3 sub-type, which incorporated a few further structural changes and additions to the equipment. Production in 1942 totalled 94 A-3s and, between July 1942 and March 1943, a further 23 were delivered from SNCA du Sud-Ouest at Bougenais (St Nazaire). The parent factory delivered 83 seaplanes in 1943, nearly all being of the final main production model, the Ar 196A-5. This had a much

more effective rear armament, comprising an MG 81Z twin-gun installation, with automatic mass balance and no fewer than 2,000 rounds in a continuous pair of belts. The MG 81 fired at 1,800 rounds per minute per gun. Other changes included the FuG 25a radio, and later the FuG 141, as well as the FuG 16Z. Cockpit instrumentation was improved and there were other minor changes.

In summer 1943 the Fokker works at Amsterdam began to build the A-5 version, producing 69 by the time production ceased there in August 1944. At Warnemünde, production was terminated in March 1944, after the delivery of 22 of the A-5 version, bringing the total production of all versions to well over 500, including the 10 A-0s and five prototypes.

Almost all of this considerable total operated from shore bases, mainly with Seeaufklärungs-gruppen (SAGr) which were often partly equipped with the BV 138 flying-boat. Two of the chief units were SAGr 125, based initially in the Baltic and later at Constanza for operations

over the Black Sea, and SAGr 126, based on Crete and at other locations for operations over the Eastern Mediterranean and Balkans. Other units included SAGr 128, which operated over the western part of the English Channel and the Bay of Biscay, and SAGr 131 which operated off the west coast of Norway until the autumn of 1944. Further Ar 196 seaplanes flew over the Black Sea with the 101st and 102nd coastal reconnaissance squadrons of the Royal Romanian air force, as well as with the 161st coastal squadron of the Bulgarian air force. Most of these operations had ceased by the late summer of 1944 as a result of the westward movement of the Eastern battlefront.

In 1940-41 Arado also built a small number of Ar 196B-0 seaplanes with the single central float configuration. Otherwise similar to the A-2, the B-series was for a time on the strength of Bordfliegerstaffel 1./196 at Wilhelmshaven. An Ar 196C variant was also planned, which would have been improved in equipment and in streamlining, but this was never built.

Ar 196A-5

This A-5 served with 2./SAGr 125 in the Eastern Mediterranean and Aegean during 1943, alongside the Blohm und Voss BV 138. The unit later became 4./SAGr 126, under the control of Luftwaffenkommando Südost.

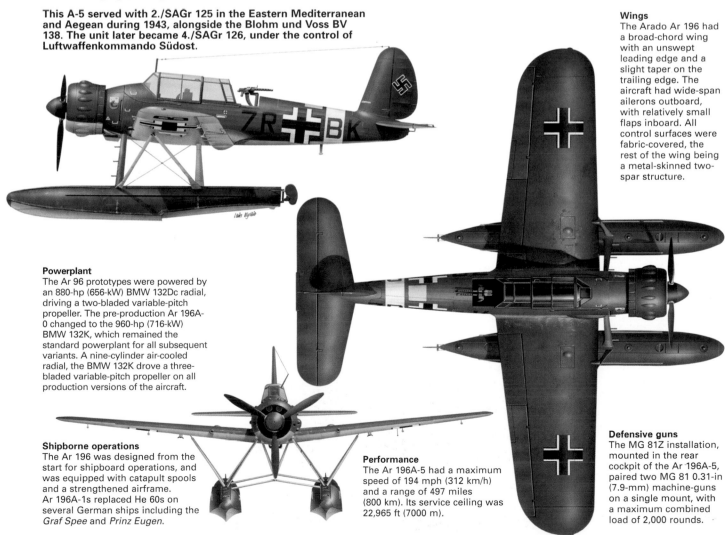

Wings
The Arado Ar 196 had a broad-chord wing with an unswept leading edge and a slight taper on the trailing edge. The aircraft had wide-span ailerons outboard, with relatively small flaps inboard. All control surfaces were fabric-covered, the rest of the wing being a metal-skinned two-spar structure.

Powerplant
The Ar 96 prototypes were powered by an 880-hp (656-kW) BMW 132Dc radial, driving a two-bladed variable-pitch propeller. The pre-production Ar 196A-0 changed to the 960-hp (716-kW) BMW 132K, which remained the standard powerplant for all subsequent variants. A nine-cylinder air-cooled radial, the BMW 132K drove a three-bladed variable-pitch propeller on all production versions of the aircraft.

Shipborne operations
The Ar 196 was designed from the start for shipboard operations, and was equipped with catapult spools and a strengthened airframe. Ar 196A-1s replaced He 60s on several German ships including the *Graf Spee* and *Prinz Eugen*.

Performance
The Ar 196A-5 had a maximum speed of 194 mph (312 km/h) and a range of 497 miles (800 km). Its service ceiling was 22,965 ft (7000 m).

Defensive guns
The MG 81Z installation, mounted in the rear cockpit of the Ar 196A-5, paired two MG 81 0.31-in (7.9-mm) machine-guns on a single mount, with a maximum combined load of 2,000 rounds.

Arado Ar 234

Development

The Luftwaffe's second jet in service and the world's first jet bomber, the Arado Ar 234 showed great potential but was produced too late and in too limited a number to save the Third Reich.

Post-war aviation literature is littered with instances of worthy, even excellent aircraft which have been over-shadowed by their more illustrious contemporaries. One obvious example is Handley Page's Halifax, which has long been eclipsed in print by the legendary Avro Lancaster. On the German side, mention the words 'Luftwaffe' and 'jet' and the Messerschmitt Me 262, the world's first jet fighter, immediately springs to mind. Although equally innovative and revolutionary, the Arado Ar 234 – the first operational jet bomber in the world – invariably comes a very poor second.

This undeserved 'also-ran' had begun life late in 1940 as Project E.370. The aircraft was Arado's response to a request from the *Reichluftfahrtministerium* (RLM) for a high-speed reconnaissance aircraft to be powered by two of the new turbojets then being developed by BMW and Junkers. Of clean and simple aerodynamic design, E.370 (soon to be redesignated the Ar 234) mated a narrow fuselage to shoulder-mounted wings, below which would be slung the two jet engines. With the bulk of the fuselage occupied by fuel tanks (dictated by the RLM's requirement for a range in excess of 1,243 miles /2,000 km), there was no space for an orthodox undercarriage. Arado therefore proposed two alternative, and equally novel, solutions. The first plan was to combine a centre-line retractable bogie comprising nine pairs of small wheels (reminiscent of the company's earlier Ar 232 Tausendfüssler (Millipede) battlefield transport design) with outrigger skids below the engine nacelles. The second suggestion saw the complex fuselage bogie arrangement replaced by a combination of jettisonable take-off trolley and centrally-mounted main landing skid. Presumably as the lesser of two evils, the latter option was selected to equip the

For take-off, the Ar 234A sat on a large trolley that featured a steerable nosewheel and main wheel brakes for taxiing. During the first flights of the V1 prototype, the trolley was jettisoned at altitude, but was subsequently released on the runway.

first production model, the Ar 234A.

The first two airframes were completed during the winter of 1941-42, but another year was to pass before Arado took delivery of its first pair of Junkers Jumo 004 turbojets. Even these were pre-production power plants suitable for static tests only – Messerschmitt's Me 262 took first priority in flight-cleared engines. In the event, it was 15 June 1943 before the company's chief test pilot, Flugkapitan Selle, lifted off in

Above: This captured aircraft is an example of the major production model, the Ar 234B-2. The projection above the cockpit is a periscope sight which could serve the two optional 20-mm rear-firing cannon, or give the pilot his only view aft of the aircraft.

The Ar 234B-2 was far more versatile than its predecessor, the Ar 234B-1, being capable of bombing, pathfinding or reconnaissance missions. This model is equipped with Rauchgeräte take-off assistance rockets outboard of the engine nacelles.

Above: The Ar 234 was involved in Deichselschlepp or 'air trailer' trials which were aimed initially at providing the aircraft with an expendable long-range tank. This 616-Imp gal (2800-litre) tank was to be attached to the aircraft by means of a semi-rigid tube which acted as a fuel feed pipe.

A highly modified Fiesler Fi 103 (V-1 flying bomb) formed the basis of the Ar 234's towed fuel tank in the Deichselschlepp configuration. The engine, guidance system and warhead of the missile were removed and a rudimentary wheeled undercarriage added.

the first prototype Ar 234 V1 from Rheine airfield for its maiden flight. Six further A-series airframe prototypes were constructed. Of these, two were to serve as test-beds for the projected four-engined Ar 234C variant (the V6 had four BMW 003A turbojets in individual nacelles; the V8's power plants were in paired nacelles under each wing), while the V7 formed part of the Ar 234B development programme.

By now, it was recognised that the Ar 234A's landing skid constituted a serious operational flaw. Once safely back on the ground, the aircraft could not move under its own power but would have to remain immobile until recovered by a special low-loader. This rendered it dangerously vulnerable to ground-strafing Allied fighters – a growing menace as the war neared its final 12 months.

Further variants

The first B-series prototype – the V9, first flown on 10 March 1944 – overcame the above problem by featuring a fractionally larger fuselage cross-section, with wheel wells occupying much of the space formerly taken up by the central fuel cell. The main wheels, fitted with large, low-pressure tyres to compensate for

the narrowness of track, retracted forwards and inwards. The new nosewheel retracted aft into a well behind the pilot's ejector seat. Other prototypes followed, powered both by the Junkers Jumo 004 and the BMW 003.

On 8 June 1944, the first of 20 pre-production Ar 234B-0s took to the air. These lacked the ejection seat and cabin pressurisation of the V9, but had provision for two cameras. The Ar 234B-1 reconnaissance aircraft was essentially similar, but had the added refinement of an autopilot and provision for drop tanks as standard. The major production model was the Ar 234B-2. This was a far more versatile machine, produced primarily as a bomber capable of carrying a maximum bombload of 3,300lb (1497 kg). It was also completed to various other equipment standards including reconnaissance (Ar 234B-2/b), pathfinder (Ar 234B-2/l) and

long-range (Ar 234B-2/r) versions. The final proposed variant of the B-series, the B-3 bomber, was abandoned in favour of the four-engined Ar 234C model.

The first C-series prototype was the V19, which undertook its maiden flight on 30 September 1944. No fewer than eight separate variants of the 'C' were planned, but only a handful of the earliest versions (up to and including the multi-purpose C-3) had

been completed by the war's end. At the cessation of hostilities, the number of prototypes that had been built or were under construction had risen to 40, the last 10 of these being intended for the D-series, which was to be powered by two Heinkel-Hirth HeS 011 turbojets. The prolific Arado design team was also already working on plans for an Ar 234E Zerstörer (heavy fighter) version, the Ar 234F – a scaled-up model, and an Ar 234P night-fighter. It was estimated that the performance of the last of these variants, the three-seat P-5, would be only slightly inferior to that of the Me 262B-2a.

The Ar 234 was an extremely worthy aircraft and, had it been produced in greater numbers, it may have proved to be more than a mere annoyance to the Allies.

Above: The Ar 234's need for more power resulted in the installation of four BMW 003A turbojets instead of the two Junkers Jumo 004Bs – the aircraft received the new designation of Ar 234C.

Right: A captured Ar 234B, named Snafu 1, sits on the ramp awaiting testing. Many 234s were captured, often in a relatively pristine condition.

Ar 234
Service history

Above: An Ar 234 taxis past a Ju 188. The world's first jet bomber, the Ar 234 also flew valuable reconnaissance missions over Europe.

Left: Operating over Britain in the high-altitude reconnaissance role, the Ar 234 was virtually immune to interception. Here ground crew load a camera into the rear fuselage camera bay.

Arado's Ar 234 was undoubtedly an exceptional aircraft and it was fortunate for the Allied forces that only a small number became operational.

The first two Arados to see front-line service were the V5 and V7 proto-types, which were despatched to Juvincourt, near Reims in France, in the immediate aftermath of the Normandy landings. Initially, only one arrived (the other having to return to Oranienburg with engine trouble), and even this had then to wait more than a week for its specialised ground equipment – most notably the take-off trolley – to follow on by rail.

It was not until 2 August 1944, therefore, that Oberleutnant Erich Sommer took off on the world's first jet reconnaissance sortie. In three parallel runs, each lasting about 10 minutes and completely with-

out opposition, he succeeded in photographing almost the entire Allied lodgement area from Avranches to Caen. That day also finally saw the arrival of Oberleutnant Horst Gîtz in the other Arado. During the next three weeks, the two pilots carried out 13 further missions.

Although their presence had remained totally undetected, the two jets were soon caught up in the general German withdrawal from France. After brief sojourns in Belgium and Holland, the tiny detachment arrived back in Germany on 5 September. Their new base, Rheine, was to be the centre for Western Front jet reconnaissance operations.

Hitherto, the Arados had been subordinated to a High

Command experimental Staffel. Now Gîtz and Sommer were each to set up their own small semi-autonomous Kommandos. Still rarely mustering more than a couple of serviceable aircraft apiece, both the Sonderkommando Gîtz – also known by the code-name of Kommando 'Sperling' (Sparrow) – and Sommer's Kommando 'Hecht' (Pike) could now at least enjoy the benefit of operating Ar 234Bs fitted with undercarriages.

First casualty

By the end of October 1944, the Arados had flown some two dozen sorties, a number of them over the United Kingdom. Late in January 1945, the two Kommandos were disbanded, all available photographic Ar 234s then being incorporated into three long-range reconnaissance Staffeln: 1.(F)/33, 1.(F)/100 and 1.(F)/123. These continued to fly over the UK, and it was after

one such sortie over Hull on 11 February that Hauptmann Hans Felden of 1.(F)/123 was shot down by an RAF Tempest as he was about to land back at Rheine. This was the first reconnaissance Ar 234 to be brought down by an enemy fighter after more than six months of operational service. The last recorded mission over the British Isles was carried out shortly before the end of the war by a 1.(F)/33 machine, then based at Stavanger in Norway.

Meanwhile, following the disbanding of his Kommando 'Hecht', Erich Sommer had set up Kommando Sommer (consisting of three aircraft) which he took to northern Italy in February 1945. Here it would remain, finally being stationed at Campoformido, outside Udine, at the time of surrender of all Axis forces in the area two months later. Even smaller was the Oranienburg-based Kommando Bisping, an experi-

A rocket-assisted Ar 234 roars into the air leaving a smoky trail behind it. Rauchgeräte units were employed to assist in short take-offs, and braking parachutes were used to reduce landing runs.

Arado 234s line up awaiting another mission during the Ardennes counter-offensive of December 1944–January 1945. The Ar 234s were used for pinpoint attacks on the advancing Allied positions.

mental night-fighter unit. It was composed of two modified Ar 234B-2s fitted with nose radar and ventral gun pack, and carried a second crew member shoe-horned into the rear fuselage. After Hauptmann Bisping was killed in a take-off accident on 23 February 1945, the detachment was renamed the Kommando Bonow. As the new commander (and sole operational pilot) of the unit, Hauptmann Kurt Bonow spent the last 10 weeks of the war chasing Mosquitos in the night skies of Berlin with a singular lack of success.

First jet bomber raid

It was as a bomber, however, that the Ar 234 made the most impact on the Allies. The first, and only, Kampfgeschwader selected for conversion to the Ar 234B-2 jet was Oberst Walter Storp's Ju 88-equipped KG 76. On 18 December 1944, the unit's 9. Staffel, under the command of Hauptmann Dieter Lukesch, was transferred forward to Munster-Handorf to support the Ardennes offensive which had been launched some 24 hours earlier. Hampered at first by the same bad weather which was keeping Allied air power firmly anchored to the ground, the world's first jet bomber sortie did not take place until 24 December, when Lukesch led nine of his Arados, all armed with a single 500-kg (1,100-lb) SC 500 bomb, to attack the rail yards at Liège. The raid was a complete success and all returned, with the only damage being a minor wing scrape due to a failed undercarriage.

Just over a week later, 9./KG 76 participated in the New Year's Day attack on Allied airfields, six machines striking Gilze-Rijen. During January, further missions were flown against Liège, Bastogne and Antwerp. In February, the remainder of Major Hans-Georg Butcher's III. Gruppe was declared operational. But it was all too late – lack of fuel was imposing severe limitations. Activity flared up again early in March after the Americans captured the bridge across the Rhine at Remagen. The third Gruppe of KG 76 was sent in five times in the space of a week to try to destroy the bridge, and lost five aircraft in the process. It was to be the Arado's final operational appearance. Over the next eight weeks, I. and II./KG 76 also completed their conversion to the new jet bomber – just in time to surrender them to the victorious Allies.

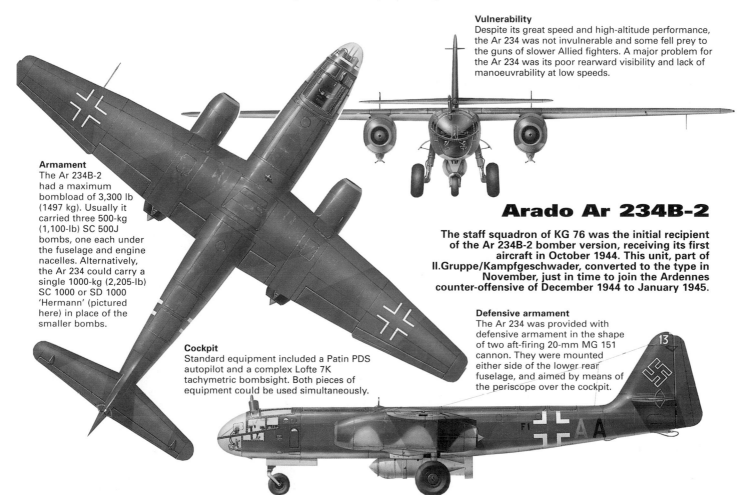

Vulnerability
Despite its great speed and high-altitude performance, the Ar 234 was not invulnerable and some fell prey to the guns of slower Allied fighters. A major problem for the Ar 234 was its poor rearward visibility and lack of manoeuvrability at low speeds.

Armament
The Ar 234B-2 had a maximum bombload of 3,300 lb (1497 kg). Usually it carried three 500-kg (1,100-lb) SC 500J bombs, one each under the fuselage and engine nacelles. Alternatively, the Ar 234 could carry a single 1000-kg (2,205-lb) SC 1000 or SD 1000 'Hermann' (pictured here) in place of the smaller bombs.

Cockpit
Standard equipment included a Patin PDS autopilot and a complex Lofte 7K tachymetric bombsight. Both pieces of equipment could be used simultaneously.

Arado Ar 234B-2

The staff squadron of KG 76 was the initial recipient of the Ar 234B-2 bomber version, receiving its first aircraft in October 1944. This unit, part of II.Gruppe/Kampfgeschwader, converted to the type in November, just in time to join the Ardennes counter-offensive of December 1944 to January 1945.

Defensive armament
The Ar 234 was provided with defensive armament in the shape of two aft-firing 20-mm MG 151 cannon. They were mounted either side of the lower rear fuselage, and aimed by means of the periscope over the cockpit.

13

The first Whitleys off the production line were Mk Is, powered by 810-hp (604-kW) Armstrong Siddeley Tiger IX radials.

Armstrong Whitworth
Whitley
Early night-bomber

One of the mainstays of RAF Bomber Command during the early years of World War II, the Whitley was also adapted for other roles, including maritime patrol, glider-towing and paratroop training.

The Whitley was already obsolete on the outbreak of war, and yet formed a crucial part of Bomber Command's night-bomber force – it was used intensively during the difficult early days of the conflict. The type was then used by Coastal Command and the airborne forces, adding to its reputation and laurels, before more modern aircraft could take over. The aircraft was subsequently withdrawn from use and quickly forgotten, and not one single aircraft remains extant today.

The Whitley was designed to meet a 1934 specification, and the prototype (derived from the AW.23 transport project which flew in 1935) made its maiden flight on 17 March 1936. The Whitley's slab-sided fuselage, massive wing and anachronistic-

looking tail unit, which combined inset twin fins and a low-set tailplane, were reminiscent of an earlier generation of bombers, although the aircraft (the RAF's first all-metal bomber) was actually astonishingly modern. The traditional tubular framework was replaced by a monocoque of rolled, pressed and corrugated light alloy, while great efforts were made to ensure ease of manufacture, with a low parts count and standard sections being used wherever possible.

Robust and resilient

The construction methods used produced a strong and robust airframe, and during the war, the aircraft would prove remarkably resilient, and extremely tolerant of battle damage. It also allowed develop-

This No. 78 Sqn Whitley Mk V is finished in the overall black applied to aircraft engaged in night raids over Germany during the early months of the war. Aircraft from No. 78 Sqn were among those on the first Bomber Command raid on Berlin.

Below: The Whitley was notable as the first British bomber to carry heavy defensive armament, the type introducing a manually-operated four-gun tail turret. (The example shown carries a camera gun.) From the Whitley Mk IV, the turret was powered.

Left: Merlin-engined Mk V G-AGDY was one of 13 used by BOAC on routes to Malta and Sweden during 1942-43.

Below: Among the new roles found for the Whitley was glider-towing. This 1943 view shows a No. 21 Heavy Glider Conversion Unit Whitley Mk V towing a Horsa aloft from RAF Brize Norton. The Whitley's use as a glider tug was confined to training; operational Horsas were towed by Halifax bombers.

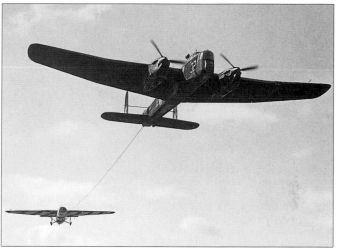

ment to be remarkably quick, and although conceived and 'commissioned' after the Wellington and Hampden, the Whitley appeared first, with the prototype being designed, built and flown within 18 months. The most striking features of the new aircraft were its broad-chord wing and very high angle of incidence – a feature adopted to give a shorter landing run, with less 'float', before the provision of flaps. This gave the Whitley an unusual nose-down attitude in flight, contributing to the type's pugnacious air.

No. 4 Group re-equips

By the time the prototype made its first flight, the RAF had already ordered an initial batch of 80 aircraft, deciding that the aircraft would form the back-bone of the heavy bomber force during the expansion. The type entered service with No. 10 Sqn at Dishforth on 9 March 1937, and progressively re-equipped all the squadrons of No. 4 Group (Nos 7, 51, 58, 77, 78, 97, 102, and 166 Sqns). On the outbreak of war, the Group was the world's only specialised night-bomber force, and was soon committed to 'nickels' (leaflet-dropping sorties) far into the Reich, starting with a mission to the Ruhr on the first night of the war. On 1-2 October, Whitleys became the first RAF bombers over Berlin, although on that occasion they dropped nothing more lethal than paper. They would later range even further, 'nickelling' both Prague and Warsaw. But as the Phoney War came to an end, Whitleys were heavily involved in more aggressive actions. On

19-20 March, 30 Whitleys were involved in a raid against the seaplane base at Borkum, drop-ping the first deliberate bombs on German soil. And on 11-12 May the first bombs delib-erately dropped on the German mainland were unloaded on a railway facility at Munchen Gladbach by Whitleys and Hampdens. Adding to its tally of 'firsts', the Whitley launched the first raid on Italian targets, cross-ing the Alps to strike Turin and Genoa on 11 June (the day after Mussolini declared war), landing in the Channel Islands to refuel! The aircraft was also used for the first bombing raid on Berlin, on 25-26 August 1940.

The Whitley served on in Bomber Command until 27/28 April 1942, when No. 58 Sqn flew the type's last bombing mission (against Ostend). By then, many of Bomber Command's aces had 'cut their teeth' on the Whitley, including Cheshire, Mahaddie, Pickard and Tait.

Coastal Command

The Whitley had joined Coastal Command in late 1939, with the temporary loan of a number of Bomber Command Whitley squadrons for convoy escorts and ASW sweeps. The Command gained its own Whitleys in late 1940, eventually re-equipping three squadrons and gaining Whitley Mk VIIs with ASV radar. These scored the first ASV U-boat kill of the war, sinking *U-206* on 30 November 1941. The aircraft remained in service with Coastal Command until July 1943.

The Whitley enjoyed even greater success supporting the

Airborne Forces, both dropping paratroops and towing gliders. Bomber Command Whitleys were used for Operation Colossus on 10-11 February 1941, dropping paratroops who destroyed the Acquedetto Pugliese, and for the Bruneval raid (Operation Biting) on 27-28 January 1942, dropping the teams which captured, dismantled and recovered a German Wurzburg radar.

Parachute training

Whitleys were used by the Parachute Training School at Ringway, by No. 21 Heavy Glider Conversion Unit, and by the training units of No. 38 Wing (Nos 295, 296, 297 and 298 Squadrons). These contin-ued flying operational leaflet-dropping sorties (in addition to their glider-towing duties) until as late as the summer of 1943, and the type remained active until late that year.

The Whitley was also used by the agent-droppers of Nos 138

and 161 Squadrons at Newmarket, Stradishall and Tempstord.

Armstrong Whitworth produced some 1,814 Whitleys, the vast majority of them (1,466) Merlin X-powered Mk Vs with a slightly stretched fuselage and revised fin shape. The basic Mk I was a rare beast, with only 34 built, and most of those had or were retrofitted with the dihe-dral wing associated with later variants. A total of 46 Mk IIs was powered by Tiger VIII engines with two-speed super-chargers, and the 80 Mk IIIs had a Heyford-style ventral dustbin gun turret.

Other variants included the GR.Mk VII (a Mk V for Coastal Command with six crew, increased fuel and ASV radar), and the Merlin IV-engined Mk IV and the Merlin X-engined Mk IVA. These aircraft introduced a powered Nash and Thomson rear turret, mounting four 0.303-in (7.7-mm) machine-guns.

RAF Coastal Command operated three squadrons of Whitley Mk Vs and VIIs for over three years. Z9190 was among the aircraft equipping No. 502 Sqn, the unit credited with the first successful ASV-assisted U-boat attack in November 1941.

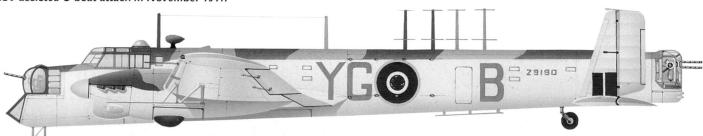

Avro Lancaster

Two Lancasters remained in airworthy condition 50 years after the end of World War II. This aircraft, PA474, was completed once hostilities had ceased, but has become the pride of the RAF's Battle of Britain Memorial Flight. In the late 1990s, it adopted the markings of No. 9 Squadron, a famous Lancaster unit.

A. V. Roe's Lancaster, designed under the supervision of Roy Chadwick, was to be the most successful of RAF Bomber Command's 'four-engined heavies' of World War II.

In response to the RAF's specification P.13/36 for a twin-engined medium bomber, Avro proposed and was contracted to produce the Rolls-Royce Vulture-engined Manchester Mk I which was to enter RAF service in 1940. However, the shortcomings of the complex powerplant meant that the Manchester's career would be a short one. In the heavy bomber category, the Handley Page Halifax was to be the RAF's preferred choice. Not to be outdone, Avro suggested that it could simply and quickly build an alternative – a four-engined Manchester derivative, the Manchester Mk III or Lancaster, as it was soon renamed.

New specification

Interested, the Air Ministry drew up a specification around the 'new' Avro design, requiring a 250-mph (402-km/h) cruising speed at 15,000 ft (4575 m) and a 7,500-lb (3405-kg) bombload capacity over a 2,000-mile (3218-km) range. The maximum range would be 3,000 miles (4827 km). The Manchester's large bomb bay, able to carry a variety of bomb types including a single 4,000-lb (1816-kg) 'Cookie', was retained.

A prototype flew on 9 January 1941. Impressed with its performance during testing, the Air Ministry cut Manchester production to just 157, ordering 454 Lancaster Mk Is instead. The first production example flew on 31 October 1941 and, on Christmas Eve, No. 44 Squadron at RAF Waddington became the first unit to receive four of the new bombers. On 3 March 1942 the type's first operational sortie – a mine-laying mission over the Heligoland Bight – was undertaken by the squadron.

Modifications

Throughout its service, modifications allowed the Lancaster to keep pace with the changing demands of the heavy bomber role. Defensive armament was improved and, most importantly, bombloads increased dramatically. The carriage of an 8,000-lb (3632-kg) 'Blockbuster' and, later, a 12,000-lb (5448-kg) bomb was soon necessary and, to cope with these new demands on the design, more powerful Merlin engines were fitted. In fact, most Lancasters were powered by Rolls-Royce's ubiq-

Above: Night after night, the RAF set about destroying Germany's war-making potential. This Lancaster delivers a 4,000-lb (1814-kg) bomb and incendiaries. Some aircraft carried special equipment; the two aerials on this machine were part of an ABC (Airborne Cigar) radio-jamming installation.

Right: From early 1944, daylight raids were being carried out on French targets in preparation for the D-Day landings.

1942, 91 Lancasters a month were being produced by five manufacturers in Britain and planning was well advanced for production in Canada.

From mid-1942 until VE-Day, the Lancaster had been RAF Bomber Command's main weapon in its nightly assault on German targets, equipping both the main force and Pathfinder Force (PFF). Of more than 7,300 Lancasters built, 3,345 were reported missing on operations, such was the intensity of their missions between 1942 and 1945, when 156,000 sorties were flown and 608,612 tons of bombs dropped. By March 1945, 56 squadrons were equipped with 745 examples of the type, another 296 serving with operational conversion units. Had the war continued, Lancasters would have joined the RAF's Tiger Force on sorties over Japan.

With the war over in 1945, most Lancasters were scrapped, but a few soldiered on, converted as Lancastrian airliners and freighters and as flying test-beds for new gas turbine engines. Others served as maritime reconnaissance aircraft with the RAF, and French and Canadian forces.

uitous Merlin, the exceptions being the small batch of Mk IIs with Bristol Hercules radial powerplants. All other production used the Merlin, although these were often American-built Packard Merlins, introduced during 1942.

Other changes concerned the aircraft's defensive armament – different turret designs were introduced, along with heavier-calibre guns. Some aircraft were fitted with 'Village Inn', the Automatic Gun-Laying Turret, which sported a small radar set to improve the gunner's aim.

Lower loss rates

Contemporary statistics show how Lancasters proved their worth; by July 1943, 132 tons of bombs were dropped for every Lancaster lost on operations. The corresponding figures for Bomber Command's other 'four-engined heavies' were 56 tons for each Halifax and 41 tons for each Stirling. Some aircraft survived to successfully complete more than 100 sorties.

Perhaps the best known of these raids was that on a series of dams in western Germany, on the night of 16/17 May 1943. Modified aircraft of No. 617 Squadron, each armed with a 9250-lb (4196-kg) mine, succeeded in breaching two of the three dams targeted in a daring low-level sortie.

'Tallboy'

In 1944, No. 617's Lancasters undertook raids using a streamlined 12,000-lb (5448-kg) 'Tallboy' bomb on Saumur railway tunnel and, with No. 9 Squadron, on the German battleship *Tirpitz*, anchored in a Norwegian fjord.

The heaviest bomb of all entrusted to the Lancaster was the 22,000-lb (9988-kg) 'Grand Slam'. With one of these giant bombs aboard, the suitably-modified aircraft had a maximum take-off weight of 72,000 lb (32688 kg), compared to the 57,000 lb (25878 kg) of the Lancaster prototype.

Only the Hurricane and Spitfire fighters were built at a higher rate than the Lancaster during World War II (though the Halifax production rate was higher than that of the Lancaster until mid-1943). By the end of

No. 207 Squadron, RAF, had been the first unit to operate the unfortunate Manchester, the Lancaster's predecessor. It soon re-equipped with the newer design.

The Canadian-built Lancaster Mk 10 served with the Royal Canadian Air Force well into the 1950s, mainly in the maritime reconnaissance role. This aircraft is one of three Mk 10-AR Arctic survey aircraft with nose-mounted radar. The RAF and French navy also operated maritime Lancasters after the war.

Manchester origins

A truly great aircraft in almost every way, the tragedy of the Manchester lay in its totally unreliable Vulture powerplant. The Manchester is best remembered as the forerunner of the immortal Avro Lancaster.

Bestowed with the looks and handling qualities of a truly fine aircraft, the Manchester was plagued throughout its development and brief service career by serious and recurring engine problems.

It is astounding to recall that the aircraft that was to evolve into the Avro Lancaster was designed to meet the requirements of Specification P.13/36, which said nothing about a long-range heavy bomber at all. Instead it called for a twin-engined medium bomber which could also fly dive-bombing, 'general-purpose' and reconnaissance missions. Moreover, in June 1936 when P.13/36 was drawn up, the Air Staff were excited at the possibilities of launching bombers by catapult.

Bumpy airfields

RAF airfields at that time were just fields, typically offering a was such a contrast that the Air Staff overlooked the cost of equipping the airfields and the sheer problem of launching one bomber after another. Nobody at that time had any conception that, six years later, Bomber Command would be mounting 'thousand-bomber raids'.

In the event, just two firms, Handley Page and A. V. Roe, were to build P.13/36 aircraft. The H.P.56 was well advanced when troubles with the chosen engine, the Rolls-Royce Vulture, caused it to be redesigned as the H.P.57, with four Rolls-Royce Merlins. This aircraft became the Halifax, which proved to be an extremely successful bomber.

Left: Production Manchesters were built by both Avro and Metropolitan-Vickers. This aircraft was the first Manchester built by the latter company. The photograph was taken on 22 December 1940 and this aircraft, along with 12 others, was destroyed that night when the factory was attacked by the Luftwaffe.

Below: The second Manchester prototype demonstrates the central fin that was fitted to improve directional stability. The fin fitted to production Manchester Mk Is was of much broader chord and greatly increased area.

bumpy take-off run of 1,500 ft (460 m). This was fine for the existing fabric-covered biplanes, but heavily loaded monoplanes simply could not get airborne – at least not with any worthwhile load on board. The eventual P.13/36 aircraft it was reckoned, could take off from a grass strip with a bombload of 1,000 lb (454 kg) and carry it for 1,000 miles (1609 km). However, if the aircraft were catapulted into the air (using huge catapults, much bigger than those on warships), it could carry 4,000 lb (1814 kg) for 3,000 miles (4828 km), or 8,000 lb (3629 kg) for 2,000 miles (3219 km). This

The Avro Type 679, however, retained the two Vultures and was named the 'Manchester' after the location of the company.

The Type 679 thrust Avro into the world of stressed-skin construction, with far greater weights and stresses, higher speeds and mind-boggling complexity. It succeeded brilliantly and, leaving aside the problem of its engines, the Manchester was by far the best British bomber to fly before World War II (the prototype flew on 25 July 1939).

The prototype had a span of 80 ft 2 in (24.43 m), which was fine for catapulting purposes, but meant that the aircraft needed a

very long conventional take-off run. By 1939, the catapult idea had faded into obscurity although, in August 1940, the first Avro Type 679 did undergo limited catapult trials at Farnborough. By this time, the span had been increased to 90 ft 1 in (27.46 m), and a third fin had been added to improve directional stability.

In this form, the 679 went into production as the Manchester Mk I, with deliveries starting in August 1940. Later, the tail was redesigned with taller fins and rudders and no central fin, the aircraft becoming the Manchester Mk IA. Other changes included a

Fraser-Nash F.N.7 mid-upper turret in place of a ventral turret, and modified ailerons and elevators with fabric covering.

Design error

Rolls-Royce had no spare capacity available for the rectification of the serious faults affecting the Vulture engine. The company showed no reluctance to cancelling the entire Vulture programme, but this would have meant the termination of the Manchester bomber as well, and possibly the loss of an airframe which showed great

potential for future development.

With the Manchester entering production, it was clear that the aircraft was not only stronger than its rivals, but also required less man-hours in its construction. It was also an exceptionally easy aircraft to maintain and repair.

In addition, the aircraft's huge bomb bay had been designed to accommodate torpedoes, which automatically gave it dimensions adequate for the 8,000-lb (3629-kg) light-case blockbuster 'Cookies', which had not been thought of in 1936 and which the other 'heavies' could not carry.

During 1941, this Manchester was flown from the RAF's test airfield at Boscombe Down. It was used to test the twin-finned Lancaster-type tail arrangement that would be adopted for the Manchester Mk IA and the Manchester Mk III.

Clearly, the Avro 679 was basically too good a design to lose, and the solution which sprung to mind was to follow Handley Page's example and fit extended outer wings carrying an extra pair of reliable engines. The obvious engine was the Merlin and, at the height of the Battle of Britain, A.V. Roe's chief designer, Roy Chadwick, produced drawings of two new four-Merlin aircraft derived from the Type 679.

Two new types

One was the Type 683, later named the Manchester Mk III and finally the Lancaster, and the other was the Type 685 York transport. The bomber naturally took priority – the first York would not fly until 5 July 1942.

In fact, neither the 683 nor the 685 would have come into being at all had it not been for a stroke of pure luck. Avro could produce an extended outer wing, but had no manpower to design an engine installation. Rolls-Royce had no design capacity either, but it so happened that – because of pressure for standard bolt-on 'power eggs' applied by Rolls' far-seeing Col L. F. R. Fell – a neat bolt-on Merlin XX package had already been put into production for the Beaufighter Mk II night-fighter. This came complete with under-slung radiator and seemed to be an ideal installation for the new Avro types. Urgent tests showed that this Beaufighter 'power-egg' was indeed just about perfect.

In three weeks the Avro designers drew the new outer wing and the prototype Manchester Mk III made a very successful first flight at Ringway on 9 January 1941. Only 18 days later it was at Boscombe Down, where it sent the official test pilots into raptures.

Manchester Mk I

This aircraft belonged to No. 83 Squadron, based at RAF Scampton, Lincolnshire in March 1942. At this time the aircraft had completed 10 operational sorties, as shown by the mission symbols on its nose. It was to fly a further four before being lost on its 15th mission, a raid against the Blohm und Voss shipyards at Hamburg. No. 83 Sqn was the first unit to use the formidable 4,000-lb (1814-kg) 'Cookie' bomb operationally.

Aerodynamic problems
Early tests showed that, with the nose turret rotated, the airflow along the fuselage sides was disturbed and the Manchester yawed violently. The problem was solved by installing a raised lip ahead of the tail turret and moving the nose turret's axis of rotation forwards by 2 in (5 cm).

Crew
A crew of seven normally operated the Manchester, comprised of a pilot, flight engineer, navigator, radio operator, bomb aimer/nose gunner, and two dedicated gunners. The mid-upper turret proved to be extremely cramped for its unlucky occupant, especially on long missions.

Mid-upper turret
When the order came to delete the ventral turret and replace it with a dorsal turret in the mid-upper position, Avro used one of the only modern power-operated turrets in production. The F.N.7 was already in production for the Blackburn Botha and in a lowered, more streamlined form, it was pressed into service on the Manchester.

Rolls-Royce Vulture
Both of the Manchester's three-bladed propellers was driven by a Vulture engine, theoretically rated at 1,760 hp (1312 kW) in service form. Consisting of two Vee-12 units mounted one above the other in an X-formation, the engines consistently failed to deliver their full power and were prone to a series of both minor and catastrophic failures.

Airframe strength
Designed to withstand both catapult launches and repeated dive-bombing attacks, the Manchester had an airframe of immense strength, which lent itself easily to modification into a four-engined configuration.

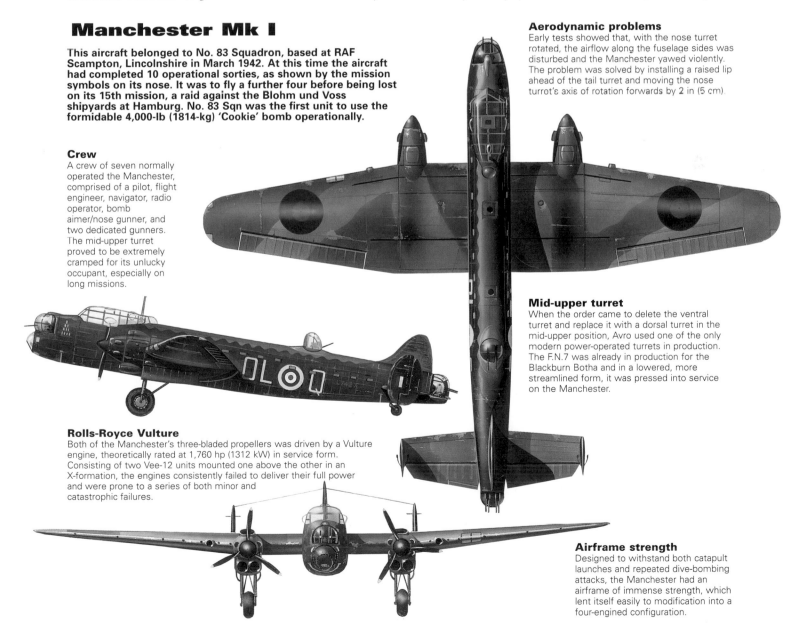

The Manchester's war

Precursor to the famous Lancaster, the Avro Manchester was ultimately a failure in front-line service, only operating for a short time before being gladly exchanged for its successor.

Shown in the camouflage scheme that was applied to No. 207 Squadron aircraft in early 1942, this Manchester Mk I features the mid-upper gun turret which was added in January of that year.

Plagued by engine trouble even before it reached an operational unit, the Manchester was destined to remain in front-line service for no more than 18 months. For No. 207 Sqn, the aircraft's first and longest-standing operator, these 18 months were some of the most arduous in its history.

No. 207 Sqn received its first Manchester Mk I on 10 November 1940. All those involved in the programme agreed that, due to the recalcitrant nature of its Rolls-Royce Vulture engines, the aircraft was far from ready for service. Nevertheless, with the Vulture engines derated to 1,760 hp (1312 kW) and its aircraft accordingly limited to a maximum take-off weight of 52,000 lb (23587 kg), the squadron began working up on the new bomber at RAF Waddington, Lincolnshire, under the leadership of Sqn Ldr Noel Challis Hyde. As soon as No. 207 began to fly the Manchester intensively, the unreliability of its underdeveloped Vultures became manifest.

In addition, it was soon discovered that the change in airflow, caused when the mid-upper gunner rotated his dorsal turret, led to a severe and potentially damaging vibration establishing itself in the central tail fin. Both the squadron and the manufacturer worked hard to bring the otherwise excellent aircraft up to an acceptable standard, a task made all the more difficult for No. 207 Squadron as it attempted to develop a new set of bombing tactics at the behest of Bomber Command.

These tactics involved a diving attack on the target, typically beginning at around 10,000 ft (3048 m), with bomb release at 5,000 ft (1524 m) – this had been detailed in the original P.13/36 specification for the Manchester. The in-service aircraft had grown considerably in weight, however, and these tactics proved a considerable threat to the bomber. Nevertheless, No. 207 Squadron continued its brave attempts to validate them, both in training and in action over enemy territory.

Manchester Mk I L7427/OL-Q (Q-Queenie) of No. 83 Squadron operated from RAF Scampton in December 1941. This aircraft was lost in a raid against the Blohm und Voss shipyards at Hamburg on its fifteenth mission.

Loaded with 500-lb (227-kg) semi-armour piercing (SAP) bombs, six Manchester Mk Is mounted the type's first combat mission on the night of 24/25 February 1941. The target was a cruiser of the 'Hipper' class, moored at the French port of Brest. The aircraft bombed successfully, even though their weapons lacked the destructive power necessary to penetrate the cruiser's deck, and all Manchesters returned to base.

However, one aircraft was lost on landing, although thankfully without injury.

Second unit

Coincident with this first Manchester raid, a second unit was established with the aircraft. A small cadre of machines and personnel from No. 207 formed the nucleus of No. 97 Squadron. As this new squadron began its work-up, No. 207 continued offensive operations, with five of its aircraft joining a sortie against Cologne on 27/28 February. A second mission against Brest on 3/4 March saw one Manchester destroyed by a German intruder within minutes of its taking off from Waddington.

April 1941 saw No. 207 re-equipped with a new standard of Manchester, featuring the F.N.7 dorsal turret, omitting the ventral 'dustbin' turret, and capable of dropping 2,000-lb (908-kg) SAP bombs. A joint operation between Nos 207 and 97 on 8/9 April marked the operational debut of the latter squadron and saw one aircraft fail to return

Almost all of the Manchester's in-service failings stemmed from its Vulture engines. This is Manchester Mk IA L7515 of No. 207 Squadron, which was based at RAF Waddington.

Above: As many Manchesters were lost to mechanical failure as to enemy action. As well as failing to deliver their promised power, Vulture engines were notoriously unreliable.

Left: The capacious bomb bay of the Manchester made the aircraft an excellent bomb-carrier. The Lancaster retained this bomb bay, giving it great flexibility, especially when compared to the Halifax and Stirling with their sectioned bomb bays.

from a raid against Kiel. By now, the squadrons could boast a strength of 40 aircraft, all of which were grounded on 13 April for engine modifications and alterations to allow the carriage of 4,000-lb (1816-kg) HC (High-Capacity) bombs. Berlin became the unlucky recipient of the first of these weapons on 8/9 May, courtesy of a No. 207 Sqn machine.

Five more squadrons

Just five more squadrons were equipped with Manchesters for front-line roles. No. 61 received its first in July 1941, along with No. 83 while, in 1942, No. 106 flew the Manchester from February, No. 50 from March, and No. 49 from May of that year. Such were the problems

facing the Manchester and such was the improvement offered by the imminently available Lancaster, that Nos 49, 50 and 106 Squadrons kept the aircraft on strength for just one, four and five months, respectively, and saw a minimum of combat with the type.

The remaining squadrons were less fortunate. With the improved Manchester Mk IA entering service, initially with No. 61 Sqn, operations continued. However, the improved handling of the Mk IA, thanks to its larger endplate fins and rudders and the omission of the central fin, combined with improved Vulture reliability, led to some optimism within the squadrons, especially as the aircraft was now modified to

accept its full design bombload of 14,000 lb (6350 kg).

In December 1941, attacks against Brest were resumed, with the Manchesters often hauling a bombload of 8,000 lb (3628 kg) to an altitude of 14,000 ft (4267 m) over the target. Naval intelligence suggested that the greatest symbols of German naval power, *Gneisenau*, *Prinz Eugen* and *Scharnhorst*, which had been berthed at Brest, were about to make a break for the open sea. Hence the port came in for increased attention from the Manchester units, with a mixed strength of 101 aircraft attacking unsuccessfully on 17/18 December.

A further 41 machines returned in daylight on 19 December, when a combination of ground fire and Luftwaffe fighters led to the loss of two aircraft from No. 97 Sqn. The raid was marginally successful, however, since damage inflicted to the gates of *Scharnhorst*'s dock kept the ship in port for a further month.

Break-out

When the *Gneisenau*, *Prinz Eugen* and *Scharnhorst* finally broke out of Brest on 12 February 1942, the Manchesters of Nos 61, 83 and

207 Sqns went after them. Poor weather conspired to prevent any bombs being dropped on target. *Gneisenau* was less fortunate two weeks later, when a Manchester raid on Kiel resulted in its being hit by a pair of 2,000-lb (908-kg) SAP bombs.

No. 207 gratefully relinquished its Manchesters for Lancasters in March 1942. Other squadrons continued Manchester operations, however, with F/O Leslie Thomas Manser carrying out one of the most meritorious. Flying as part of No. 50 Sqn's contribution to the first 1,000-bomber raid against Cologne on 30 May 1942, Manser's machine was hit by flak at the end of its bombing run. With the port Vulture in flames, Manser ordered his crew to leave the aircraft, as he held it straight and level to facilitate their escape. The aircraft, along with its gallant pilot, was seen to crash in flames. Manser received a posthumous Victoria Cross for his actions.

The final front-line use of the Manchester was made on 25/26 June 1942, when No. 83 Sqn contributed one aircraft to a raid against Bremen. Although it served on with a number of second-line units, the Manchester had disappeared from front-line RAF squadrons by the end of June 1942.

Coinciding with the entry into service of the Stirling, the new twin-engined Manchester joined the RAF in November 1940 but, by 1942, was ready for withdrawal.

Lancaster development

The need to carry heavier loads on the nightly raids over the Third Reich, deliver them more accurately, and survive the flight home, were the factors behind the steady development of the Lancaster.

The Lancaster shared many of the features of the aircraft from which it was developed, the ill-fated Manchester. In fact, the Lancaster prototype used a number of Manchester Mk I components, including the fuselage, centre-section and tail, along with the nose, tail and mid-upper gun turrets. New outer wing sections were fitted to incorporate the extra engines of the Lancaster. The three-fin tail was soon altered to a twin-fin layout, as on the Manchester Mk IA.

The first Lancaster Mk Is, of which 3,440 were built, entered service with No. 44 Squadron in late 1941. Certain modifications to the Lancaster were deemed necessary after an initial period of service. These included deletion of the ventral gun turret fitted to early production aircraft, a larger perspex bomb-aimer's blister in the nose of the aircraft, an increase in fuel capacity and, most significantly, changes to the aircraft's bomb support system to allow the carriage of an 8,000-lb (3632-kg) 'Blockbuster' bomb. Bulged bomb bay doors were fitted and later further internal changes were made to allow a 12,000-lb (5448-kg) bomb to be

carried. The maximum bomb load for the Lancaster was increased to 14,000 lb (6350 kg). To cope with these new demands on the design, more powerful Merlin engines were fitted. While the first Mk Is were equipped with Merlin XXs rated at 1,390 hp (1037 kW), later production aircraft had 1,610-hp (1201-kW) Merlin 24s, though these new Merlin variants did not bring a change in aircraft designation.

Radial-engined Mk II

Concerns regarding the supply of Rolls-Royce engines prompted the development of the Lancaster Mk II, first flown in November 1941. This differed from the Mk I in having more powerful Bristol Hercules radial powerplants. In all, 300 Mk IIs

Above: With Bristol Hercules radial engines fitted, the Lancaster Mk II was built as insurance against an expected shortage of Rolls-Royce Merlins for Mk Is. Performance was inferior and, after US Merlin production was secured, only 300 were built. The row of windows on the upper fuselage was also a feature of early Mk Is; they were deleted on later aircraft.

Top: The Lancaster prototype (BT308) is seen here with the Manchester tail unit with which it first flew. Unlike later aircraft powered by Merlin XXs, the prototype had Merlin Xs.

were built, but their speed and altitude performance were always inferior to those of the Mk I, the extra drag and fuel consumption of the Hercules outweighing their power advantage. Once

Merlin supplies were secured, repeat orders for Mk IIs were cancelled.

The engine supply problem was ultimately solved by setting up Merlin production overseas.

In preparation for bombing operations over Japan, as part of Tiger Force, Mk I aircraft were 'tropicalised' and painted white (to reflect the heat of the sun) as Mk I(FE)s. These aircraft would have been joined by newly-built Mk VII(FE)s, an example of which is seen here. Note the H₂S radome visible under the fuselage and the repositioned Martin mid-upper gun turret.

Two Lancasters, including HK541, were fitted with large 1500-Imp gal (6819-litre) 'saddle' fuel tanks to increase their range. Both were flown to India for trials with No. 1577 (SD) Flight in 1944.

Below: The ventral FN.64 barbette was aimed via a periscope from inside the aircraft but was soon deleted and its place taken, on many Lancasters, by an H₂S radar navigation aid. This left the Lancaster's belly exposed to attack from below by night-fighters, such as Bf 110s and Ju 88s equipped with Schräge Musik upward-firing guns.

In August 1942, the Lancaster Mk III was introduced, with American-built Packard Merlins, though these aircraft were, in most other respects, identical to the Mk I. In fact, it was not unknown for Mk Is to be re-engined with Packard engines in service (thus becoming Mk IIIs) and vice-versa.

Improved armament

The aircraft's defensive armament was also the focus of improvements. Various alternative Frazer-Nash mid-upper turrets were introduced, while some aircraft carried a Rose-Rice rear turret, armed with two 0.5-in (12.7-mm) Browning machine-guns in place of the usual quartet of 0.303-in (7.7-mm) guns. Towards the end of the war, other aircraft were fitted with the AGLT (Automatic Gun-Laying Turret) in the rear position. Code-named 'Village Inn', this incorporated a small radar set for automated aiming and twin 0.5-in (12.7-mm) Brownings.

By the end of 1942, Lancasters were being produced in Britain by Avro, Metropolitan-Vickers, Vickers Armstrong, Armstrong-Whitworth and Austin Motors. Production in Canada, by Victory Aircraft, of the Lancaster Mk X (essentially a Mk III with minor equipment changes) started the following year.

The first of these aircraft arrived in Britain in September 1943.

The Lancaster's load-carrying capability led to its modification for special weapon loads. These included Mk III (Special) aircraft equipped to carry the 9250-lb (4196-kg) 'Upkeep' mine (or 'bouncing bomb') used to destroy dams on the Ruhr in May 1943. The Lancaster Mk I (Special) was modified in 1944 to carry stream-lined 12,000-lb (5448-kg) 'Tallboy' bombs and 22,000-lb (9988-kg) 'Grand Slams'.

However, it was as the main weapon of Bomber Command's Main Force and Pathfinder Force (PFF) that the Lancaster was most utilised and best known. In the PFF (later No. 8 Group, Bomber Command) Lancasters were equipped with pyrotechnic flares for target marking and carried navigation and bombing aids, on occasions with extra crew members to operate them, with which to guide Main Force aircraft. From August 1943 many of the latter (though only those without bulged bomb bay doors) were equipped with H₂S, a navigation and target location radar carried in a prominent fairing under the rear fuselage. A Pathfinder unit, No. 635 Squadron, was equipped with a few examples of the Lancaster Mk VI in 1944, nine having been converted from Mk III standard. These machines were

fitted with Merlin 85s which, thanks to their two-speed, two-stage supercharging, boasted greatly improved performance at altitude. Radio countermeasures equipment was fitted to these machines, otherwise distinguish-able by the removal of their mid-upper and nose gun turrets.

Far East variants

The last wartime Lancaster variants were the tropicalised B.Mk I(FE) and B.Mk VII(FE), the latter boasting a repositioned Martin mid-upper gun turret and an FN.82 tail turret, both with 0.5-in (12.7-mm) machine-guns in place of the 0.303-in (7.7-mm) guns fitted hitherto. Both these variants would have joined the RAF's Tiger Force, equipping very-long-range bomber units for attacks on

Japan, had the war continued. In an attempt to improve the type's range for these missions, trials were carried out with large 'saddle' fuel tanks (which increased fuel capacity by 50 per cent) fitted to two Lancaster Mk Is. These aircraft were flown to India for testing in mid-1944. These were not the first Lancasters to reach the Far East; two aircraft had already flown to India in 1943 for tropicalisation trials and were additionally flown with Horsa and Hamilcar gliders in tow with a view to using glid-ers in the India-Burma theatre.

The final Lancaster variants were post-war conversions used for photo-reconnaissance (PR.Mk 1s), maritime reconnais-sance (GR.Mk 3s) and air-sea rescue (ASR.Mk 3s with airborne lifeboats fitted). Similar conver-sions were made of Mk 10s in Canada. These aircraft performed numerous tasks, from maritime reconnaissance to navigation training and drone direction. Many other machines served as testbeds for new turbine engines, armament or other equipment, while others were converted to airliners, known as Lancastrians.

With its turrets and other military equipment removed, the Lancaster served post-war as the basis for a 13-seat airliner. Though fast, and with a good range, the Lancastrian was expensive to operate. Some aircraft, as seen here, were converted to freighters.

The Augsburg raid

17 April 1942

The first bombing raid publicly linked with Bomber Command's new four-engined 'heavy', the Avro Lancaster, was one of the most daring of the war. Its object was the MAN diesel engine factory in Augsburg, Bavaria in 1942.

During the early months of his tenure as C-in-C of Bomber Command, Sir Arthur Harris ordered a number of experimental raids before settling on a largely night-time bombing campaign against the Third Reich.

One experimental raid was to be the first of any importance carried out with RAF Bomber Command's new four-engined heavy bomber, the Lancaster. Though successful, heavy losses were suffered, both in men and aircraft, but the raid proved that Bomber Command could reach into the depths of Germany and strike at the Third Reich's industrial heart. It was led by the experienced South African, Squadron Leader John Nettleton.

Diesel engine factory

The raid was to be made in daylight and at low level on 17 April 1942, against the MAN diesel engine factory at Augsburg. Twelve Lancasters were to take part, six each taken from those recently issued to Nos 44 and 97 Squadrons, the first squadrons equipped with the type, in December 1941 and January 1942, respectively.

On the days prior to the raid, crews undertook low-level flying training, part of which included a simulated raid on Inverness. Morale among personnel of the two squadrons was high as the nature of their training led them to expect that their target was to be the naval facilities at Kiel, a relatively 'easy' coastal target.

In fact, the destination was far more hazardous and far from the 'piece of cake' predicted, for Augsburg was 500 miles (805 km) from the French coast, in Bavaria, Germany. The actual target was a single building the size of a football pitch, set within a larger complex. Each aircraft was to carry a relatively light load consisting of just four 1,000-lb (454-kg) General Purpose bombs.

Take-off at 1400 hours

Taking off from Woodhall Spa and Waddington at 1400 hours, the dozen aircraft (in four sections, each of three bombers) crossed the French coast at low level to avoid detection by enemy radar. They would be over the target in the last light of day, which allowed them to return under the cover of darkness. Further assistance was provided in the form of diversionary raids by 30 Boston light bombers, and more than 700 fighter sorties over northeastern France. The latter were intended to keep the Luftwaffe's fighters occupied elsewhere as the Lancasters sped across France towards Germany in tight formation.

However, unbeknown to the Lancasters' crews, the Bostons'

Top: PA474, the well-known Lancaster operated by the RAF's Battle of Britain Memorial Flight, for several years carried the codes ('KM-B') of Sqn Ldr John Nettleton's No. 44 (Rhodesia) Sqn aircraft, flown during the Augsburg raid. Note the lack of a mid-upper turret, which was fitted later.

Below: A formation of early-production Lancaster Mk Is of No. 44 Sqn formate for an official photographer some time in 1942, though after the Augsburg raid.

Sqn Ldr Nettleton's Lancaster was this Mk I, serialled R5508. Note the ventral turret and rear fuselage windows, typical of an early-production aircraft. The Type 'A' fuselage roundel and grey code letters were also seen on early Lancasters, but were replaced from late 1942.

KM B R5508

raid had been brought forward some 20 minutes with the result that, as the latter left their appointed targets, the defending Bf 109s and Fw 190s returned to base before Nettleton's formation had cleared the vicinity.

Fighters attack

Spotted by a Messerschmitt pilot, the Lancasters were attacked and four of No. 44 Squadron's aircraft were shot down. In a few minutes, therefore, a third of the force had been lost, and there were still another 300 miles (483 km) to fly before the target area was reached.

Despite the losses, Nettleton refused to turn back, the eight aircraft pressing on to Augsburg, where the two remaining Lancasters of No. 44 Squadron dropped their loads; only one, Nettleton's aircraft, escaped to return home. By the time the two sections of No. 97 Squadron arrived over the factory, flak was heavy. Anti-aircraft fire quickly claimed one machine and, as the

last section dropped its bombs, a second Lancaster exploded in mid-air.

The five survivors, all damaged to varying degrees, now faced the frightening prospect of a return over hostile territory patrolled by Luftwaffe night-fighters. Fortunately, none appeared, the Lancasters landing in England just after 11.00 p.m.

Reconnaissance flights over the MAN factory revealed that severe damage had been inflicted, by the eight aircraft that managed to drop their bombs over the target. However, closer examination showed that, while 17 bombs had hit the vital engine assembly shop within the factory, only 12 had exploded.

What is more, the cost, in men and material, had been high. Of the 85 aircrew to have taken part in the raid, 49 were shot down – of these, 37 were killed, and 12 taken prisoner. Eight aircraft had been written off, one upon its return to base after the sortie.

On the other hand, Bomber Command had proved that it could reach distant targets in Germany and the Augsburg raid represented considerable propaganda value to the British public. The wider implications of the raid were serious, however. The choice of target was criticised by the Minister of Economic Warfare, Lord Selborne, for not being one of those recommended by the ministry for attack. Sir Arthur Harris replied that Augsburg had been on an approved list drawn up by the Chiefs of Staff and there the matter ended. This was not the last time that Harris's opinion was to clash with those of his colleagues.

In fact, Harris had considerable doubts about raids such as this. Valuable crews and aircraft had been lost on a mission that had been launched during the day (for tactical reasons) despite the fact that Bomber Command had already learned not to

send unescorted bombers on such sorties.

There were other lessons to be drawn from the events of 17 April, not least of which was the fact that the Lancasters' defensive rifle-calibre (0.303-in/7.7-mm) guns were inadequate against enemy fighters equipped with self-sealing fuel tanks.

Although it was soon overshadowed by the events of the following months and years, the Augsburg raid was a valuable test for the Lancaster, soon to become Bomber Command's most important type. It was also notable for the skill and courage of the Lancaster crews, still relatively inexperienced with their new aircraft.

For his bravery, determination and leadership not only in leading the hazardous raid, but also in nursing a crippled aircraft back to England, Squadron Leader Nettleton received the highest award for valour, the Victoria Cross, only to be killed on a raid in July of the following year. Many of the other surviving officers and men received Distinguished Service Orders, Distinguished Flying Crosses and Distinguished Flying Medals.

Above: Though carrying the same codes as Sqn Ldr Nettleton's aircraft on the Augsburg raid, Lancaster L7578 did not take part in the sortie and was, in fact, on strength with No. 97 Sqn.

Right: These No. 97 Sqn crewmen are some of those who returned safely from Augsburg. Apart from Nettleton's Victoria Cross, DSOs, DFCs and DFMs were distributed among the crew who survived the raid.

Chastise: the dams attack

Conceived by a famous engineer and led by a legendary pilot with hand-picked aircrews, the dams raid gave No. 617 Sqn its motto, 'After me, the flood'.

Dr Barnes Wallis had been heavily involved with the development of the R100 airship, and of the Wellesley and Wellington bombers. When the war started, he looked at ways of dealing the enemy such a telling blow that the conflict would be shortened. Accordingly, he studied ways of destroying the great dams of Germany – this would cause enormous flood damage and affect the supply of electricity, so vital to the German war machine. Early approaches to the Air Ministry were deflected but,

by 1943, he had amassed enough support within No. 5 Group for the creation of a special squadron with the initial purpose of attacking the dams.

Equipped with Avro Lancasters, No. 617 Sqn was formed on 21 March 1943 at Scampton from 'C' Flight of No. 106 Sqn, led by Wing Commander Guy Penrose Gibson. He was allowed to personally select his squadron's aircrew, who underwent intensive low-level training for the next two months – none of the crew knew what the target was to be or

Top: The Lancaster's bomb-bay was extensively modified to carry the 'Upkeep' bouncing bomb. Protruding out of the bomb bay are the two arms which held the bomb in place.

Above: Guy Gibson (at the top of the ladder) and crew board the Lancaster ED932/AJ-G before the attack on the Möhne dam. Neither Gibson nor any of his crew survived to the war's end.

what weapons were to be used.

The means of destroying the dams was Wallis's 'Upkeep' weapon. This was a rotating depth charge, weighing 9,250 lb (4195 kg) and containing 6,600 lb

(2994 kg) of Torpex explosive. The destructive power of the bomb depended on it being positioned next to the structure it was intended to destroy, meaning that a (relatively) small explosive load

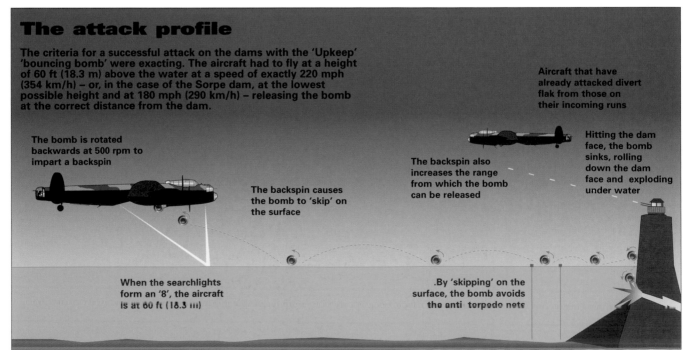

The attack profile

The criteria for a successful attack on the dams with the 'Upkeep' 'bouncing bomb' were exacting. The aircraft had to fly at a height of 60 ft (18.3 m) above the water at a speed of exactly 220 mph (354 km/h) – or, in the case of the Sorpe dam, at the lowest possible height and at 180 mph (290 km/h) – releasing the bomb at the correct distance from the dam.

Aircraft that have already attacked divert flak from those on their incoming runs

The bomb is rotated backwards at 500 rpm to impart a backspin

The backspin causes the bomb to 'skip' on the surface

The backspin also increases the range from which the bomb can be released

Hitting the dam face, the bomb sinks, rolling down the dam face and exploding under water

When the searchlights form an '8', the aircraft is at 60 ft (18.3 m)

By 'skipping' on the surface, the bomb avoids the anti-torpedo nets

OPERATION CHASTISE

The route taken by the Lancasters on the night of 16 May 1943 was designed to avoid concentrations of flak and night-fighters. The three dams targeted (Möhne, Sorpe and Eder) were located at the heads of reservoirs (shown on this map as being at the corners of the yellow triangle).

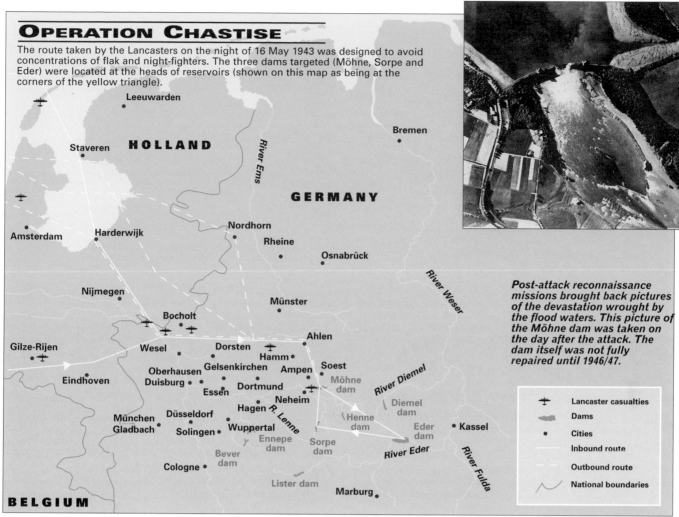

Post-attack reconnaissance missions brought back pictures of the devastation wrought by the flood waters. This picture of the Möhne dam was taken on the day after the attack. The dam itself was not fully repaired until 1946/47.

	Lancaster casualties
	Dams
	Cities
	Inbound route
	Outbound route
	National boundaries

---

would be effective against the massive structures. The great dams were protected by torpedo nets, which meant that either the bomb had to be dropped past the nets or a way of overcoming this obstacle needed to be found. Wallis's solution to the problem was the bouncing bomb, the inspiration for which came, he maintained, from seeing children skimming stones over water.

To achieve its aims, the weapon needed to be given backspin while still attached to the Lancaster, increasing the weapon's range on release and making it bounce on the surface of the reservoirs. Such a technique made the raid possible, but created its own problems. The distance between the aircraft and the dam had to be exact, as did the height of weapon release.

To carry the bomb, the Lancaster had to have several modifications. The bomb bay doors were removed and two arms were fitted, between which the bomb was carried. A belt rotated the bomb backwards at 500 rpm to impart the required backspin.

The difficult task of judging height at night over a flat surface was solved by fitting two search-lights to the Lancaster, which were arranged to form a figure of eight when the aircraft was at a height of 60 ft (18.3 m).

To judge when the aircraft was at the correct distance from the dam, a simple V-shaped tool, with two upright pegs on the extreme of each end, was used. This was held by the bomb-aimer at arm's length in the aircraft's nose and, when the pegs corresponded to a pre-determined feature such as the towers on the dams, the aircraft was at the correct distance.

The raids

The attacks were mounted on the night of 16 May 1943 as Operation Chastise. Leaving Scampton at 21.10 hrs, the first wave of bombers set out for the Sorpe dam. Lancasters 'E' and 'K' were shot down into the Zuider Zee on the way in, while 'H' lost its mine after hitting the sea and turned back. 'W' had its radio knocked out by flak and thus only 'T' attacked the Sorpe.

Gibson led the second wave in

'G', with six aircraft targeting the Möhne dam and the other three designated to attack the Eder. Taking off at 21.25 hrs, the flight lost Lancaster 'B' which was shot down near Rosendaal. The Möhne was attacked by 'G', 'P', 'M', 'A', and 'J'. The bomb belonging to Lancaster 'M' fell wide and the aircraft was shot down as it pulled away from its attack. The dam was breached by 'J' and the code word NIGGER was transmitted, signifying success. 'A' was forced to ditch on the way home. Of the Eder attack flight, Lancaster 'N' was successful in breaching the dam. 'Z' was shot down by flak, while 'L' managed to return to base.

A third formation acted as a mobile reserve. Of these, 'O' attacked the Schwelme dam by mistake, 'F' attacked the Sorpe without result, 'Y' headed for the Sorpe but could not find it, 'C'

went to the Lister dam and never came back, while 'S' was shot down and never traced.

Of the 19 aircraft sent out with 133 crew, eight aircraft failed to return and 53 aircrew died, three being taken prisoner. Gibson was awarded the Victoria Cross, and the squadron received 34 other decorations for this raid. The breaching of the Möhne and Eder dams resulted in widespread flooding and disruption to the industry in the Ruhr and the diversion of guards to the dams. No. 617 Squadron had made history on its first sortie.

A total of 23 Lancaster B.Mk IIIs was converted to be able to operate the 'Upkeep' weapon, of which 19 were used on the dams raid. This aircraft is thought to be one of those used to test the modifications undertaken by Avro. Surviving aircraft were returned to the standard configuration.

The lack of a nose turret and bomb bay doors reveal this Lancaster to be a B.Mk I (Special), which carried the largest and heaviest bomb ever used in anger.

617 Sqn special operations

After the dams attack, for which it had been formed, the decision was taken to reserve No. 617 Squadron for missions requiring specialised training or weapons.

The first mission for No. 617 Squadron after the dams attack was the bombing of the power stations at San Polo D'Enza and Aquata Scrivia. The attack was led by Squadron Leader G.W. Holden, who had replaced Guy Gibson, after which the squadron moved base to Coningsby in August 1943. No. 617 Sqn's first attack with the 12,000-lb (5443-kg) 'Tallboy' was on the Dortmund-Ems Canal, from which only three of the eight attacking aircraft returned. Holden and his crew were lost. His successor was the legendary Leonard Cheshire, later the founder of Cheshire Homes. No. 617 Sqn again changed base, moving to Woodhall Spa in the

second week of January 1944.

V-weapon sites were high on the list of targets for Allied aircraft and No. 617 Sqn's specialist weapons played a large part in this campaign. Eighteen aircraft bombed V-1 sites on 17 June 1944, attacking a concrete dome containing V-2 rockets at Wizernes the next day. Unsuccessful the first time, the squadron returned to Wizernes with 16 Lancasters and a pair of Mosquitoes on 24 June, dropping 'Tallboys' onto the 20-ft (6-m) thick concrete domes (this target was attacked three more times the following month). The V-2 store at Siracourt was attacked on 25 June using 17 Lancasters, two Mosquitoes, and a Mustang

Above: Conceived by Dr Barnes Wallis, the 22,000-lb (9980-kg) 'Grand Slam' 'earthquake' bomb was designed to penetrate deep into the target before exploding. The smaller version was the 12,000-lb (5443-kg) 'Tallboy'.

Left: No. 617 Squadron gained a reputation for its role in the destruction of bridges and viaducts. The Arnsberg viaduct was attacked successfully with six 'Grand Slams' on 19 March 1945.

flown by Cheshire and used as a low-level marker aircraft.

Photo reconnaissance had uncovered the site of the long-range V-3 gun (designed specifically for attacks on London) at Mimoyecque. The ferro-concrete structure was attacked on 6 July using 'Tallboys', again with Cheshire marking the target. After this raid, the last of his fourth

tour, he was ordered to rest – in fact, he never flew on operations again. Two months later, he was awarded the Victoria Cross.

Sink the *Tirpitz*

The next target was the pocket battleship *Tirpitz*, which was safely anchored in Norwegian waters, out of range of the heavily-laden, 'Tallboy'-carrying

Lancasters. To overcome this, No. 617 Sqn flew from Lossiemouth with No. 9 Sqn to Yagodnik in the Soviet Union. On 15 September, 28 Lancasters attacked the *Tirpitz* from a height of 11,000 ft (3353 m). One hit was recorded, although the attack was defeated by a smokescreen. The hit forced the Germans to bring the ship south to Tromsö, 200 miles (322 km) closer to Britain. On 12 November, 30 aircraft of Nos 9 and 617 Sqn left Lossiemouth and Milltown for Tromsö. Four 'Tallboys' dropped by No. 617 Sqn hit the *Tirpitz*, causing it to capsize. In the period of the campaign against the *Tirpitz*, No. 617 Sqn had also successfully breached the Dortmund-Ems Canal (on 17 September) and 13 aircraft

had raided the Kembs Dam on 7 October, destroying the dam gates and preventing the Germans from flooding the Rhine valley near Mulhouse.

U-boat pens

During February 1945, the squadron made daylight raids with 12,000-lb (5443-kg) bombs on U-boat pens at Poorteshaven, Ijmuiden, Hamburg and Farge. On 27 March 1945 the U-boat pens at Farge were hit by a pair of 'Grand Slams' and 'Tallboys', and then bombed by about 100 main force bombers. The 'Grand Slams' had breached the massive reinforced concrete roof of the structure.

On 14 March 1945, the 22,000-lb (9980-kg) 'Grand Slam' was used for the first time

when two aircraft attacked the Bielefeld viaduct, partially collapsing it. Five days later, six 'Grand Slams' were used to bring down a 40-ft (12-m) section of the Arnsberg viaduct, without incurring any aircraft losses. On 22 March, Nienburg Bridge was bombed by four aircraft (one with a 'Grand Slam') and destroyed. By comparison, a raid on the Bremen bridges undertaken on the same day by 102 aircraft of No. 5 Group with 'normal' munitions had no effect. On the following day, the Bremen railway bridge was the last of these targets to be attacked by No. 617 Squadron.

Final missions

Nos 9 and 617 Sqn set out to attack the warships *Prinz Eugen*

and *Lützow* in Swinemünde Harbour on 13 April, but the raid was abandoned because of cloud over the target. The attack was repeated on 16 April, using 18 Lancasters of No. 617 Sqn, which flew through intense flak. All but two of the aircraft were hit, although only one was lost (the last of the war for the squadron.) A near miss with a 'Tallboy' tore a large hole in the bottom of the *Lützow*, which sank. No. 617 Sqn's final target was the SS Headquarters at Berchtesgaden, on which four 'Tallboys' were dropped.

The squadron was slated to be part of the 'Tiger Force' Far East bomber fleet, the end of the war preventing it from playing its specialist role in that theatre of war.

Lancaster B.Mk I (Special)

No. 617 Squadron began to receive modified Lancaster B.Mk Is in the spring of 1944. These aircraft had bulged bomb bay doors in order to accommodate the 'Tallboy'. From March 1945, the squadron further modified its aircraft to enable them to carry the 'Grand Slam' – this required the complete removal of the bomb bay doors. A total of 33 of these B.Mk I (Specials) was produced, the first flying in February 1945.

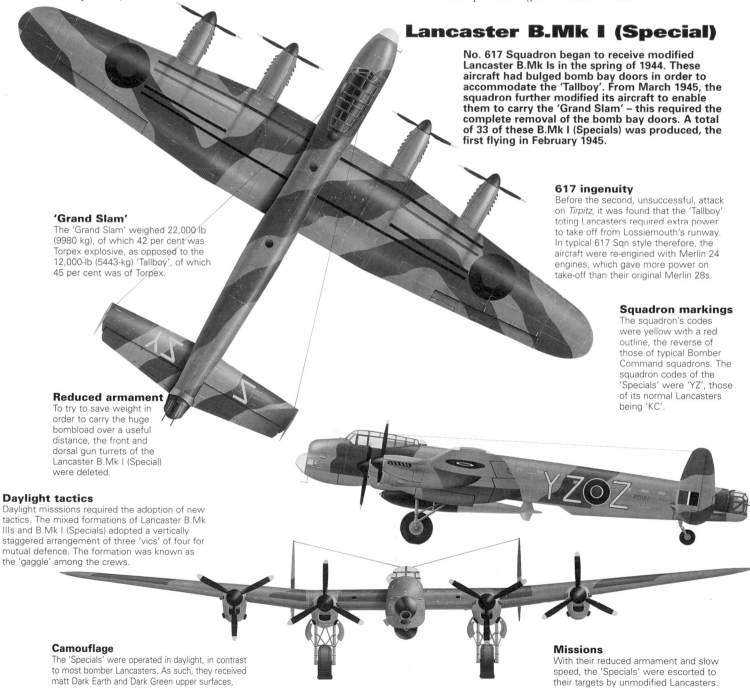

'Grand Slam'
The 'Grand Slam' weighed 22,000 lb (9980 kg), of which 42 per cent was Torpex explosive, as opposed to the 12,000-lb (5443-kg) 'Tallboy', of which 45 per cent was of Torpex.

Reduced armament
To try to save weight in order to carry the huge bombload over a useful distance, the front and dorsal gun turrets of the Lancaster B.Mk I (Special) were deleted.

Daylight tactics
Daylight misssions required the adoption of new tactics. The mixed formations of Lancaster B.Mk IIIs and B.Mk I (Specials) adopted a vertically staggered arrangement of three 'vics' of four for mutual defence. The formation was known as the 'gaggle' among the crews.

617 ingenuity
Before the second, unsuccessful, attack on *Tirpitz*, it was found that the 'Tallboy' toting Lancasters required extra power to take off from Lossiemouth's runway. In typical 617 Sqn style therefore, the aircraft were re-engined with Merlin 24 engines, which gave more power on take-off than their original Merlin 28s.

Squadron markings
The squadron's codes were yellow with a red outline, the reverse of those of typical Bomber Command squadrons. The squadron codes of the 'Specials' were 'YZ', those of its normal Lancasters being 'KC'.

Camouflage
The 'Specials' were operated in daylight, in contrast to most bomber Lancasters. As such, they received matt Dark Earth and Dark Green upper surfaces, with Ocean Grey undersides.

Missions
With their reduced armament and slow speed, the 'Specials' were escorted to their targets by unmodified Lancasters.

No. 83 Sqn, RAF was one of the first units to re-equip with the Lancaster Mk I, having earlier flown the ill-fated Manchester.

Operations: 1942
Before the big raids

The first Lancasters to arrive with an operational squadron appeared in the landing circuit at RAF Waddington on 24 December 1941, less than a year after the prototype had first flown.

It was No. 44 Sqn, then under the acting command of Sqn Ldr John Nettleton, which received the first Lancasters, the squadron being warned to have eight crews ready for operations within a month. The first Lancaster operation, on the night of 3/4 March, was a mine-laying sortie by four aircraft, each dropping four 2,000-lb (907-kg) sea mines in the waters off the north German coast; all four aircraft returned safely. Another four Lancasters were delivered to No. 44 Squadron by the end of the month.

By the end of January 1942, No. 97 Sqn (a former Manchester squadron) at Coningsby had also received half a dozen of the new heavy bombers. At dusk on 20 March six Lancasters, each carrying six mines, flew all the way to the Baltic, mining the waters off Swinemünde; again, no aircraft were lost to enemy action although, returning in poor weather, one aircraft was damaged in a forced landing. Thereafter, for several weeks, both of the above No. 5 Group squadrons were ordered to contribute small numbers of Lancasters to Bomber Command raids carried out over the continent.

The first real test of the aircraft was to be faced on 17 April 1942. On that day, following a number of low-level cross-country training flights, six Lancasters (flying about two miles apart) from each of the two squadrons set out in daylight to attack the MAN diesel engine factory at Augsburg, deep in southern Germany.

Although this daring raid was to prove costly in terms of men and machinery (seven out of 12 aircraft failed to return), and caused only limited damage to the target, the Lancaster had proved that it could reach deep into Germany, and so the propaganda value of the raid was considered to be immeasurable.

The number of Lancaster squadrons continued to increase and, by September, by dint of careful analysis of raid plots, the Lancaster 'standard' bombload for Main Force raids over German cities and towns was now established. It consisted of a single 4,000-lb (1814-kg) 'cookie' (an air-fused blast weapon), and 12 Standard Bomb Carriers each loaded with up to 236 incendiary bombs, giving a total maximum bombload of about 14,000 lb (6350 kg). The object of this mix was to collapse buildings by blast and then set fire to the wreckage with tens of thousands of incendiary bombs. For pinpoint attacks, the Lancaster could carry fourteen 1,000-lb (454-kg) HE bombs.

Nine squadrons
By October, there were nine fully operational Lancaster squadrons with Bomber Command's Main Force, and a tenth (No. 83) with No. 8 (Pathfinder) Group – formed two months previously. As if to emphasise the speed at which the Lancaster force was growing, Bomber Command launched a second spectacular dusk raid on the 17th of the month. In all, 88 aircraft from Nos 9, 44, 49, 50, 57, 61, 97, 106 and 207 Sqns were launched against the

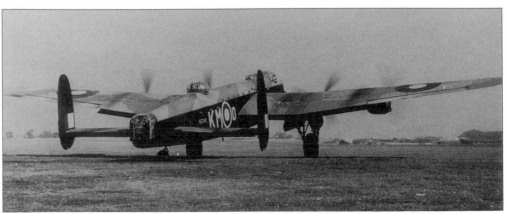

Awaiting its 4,000-lb (1814-kg) HC bomb, this Lancaster is shown with its load of Standard Bomb Carriers, each able to carry up to 236 4-lb (1.8-kg) incendiaries. During World War II, Bomber Command dropped over 80 million of these small bombs, of which almost 50 million were dropped by Lancasters.

Schneider factory at Le Creusot, 150 miles (241 km) south-east of Paris. Flying at low level once more, the main formation was accompanied by six other Lancasters (led by a certain Wing Cdr G. P. Gibson, commanding No. 106 Sqn), whose task it was to destroy the Henri Paul transformer plant, a few miles from Le Creusot. Among the bombloads of the whole force were 15 'cookies'. In contrast to the Augsburg raid, the Le Creusot attack (codenamed

Coded 'KM-O', R5740 was one of No. 44 Sqn's first Lancaster Mk Is. It was photographed in July 1942 at RAF Waddington.

Operation Robinson) was an outstanding success (one Lancaster was lost – probably as a result of dropping its bombs too low), and severe damage was caused to the factory.

The Capital Ship Bomb

Despite the raid's success, Air Chief Marshal Sir Arthur 'Bomber' Harris was set against such setpiece attacks as they deflected the growing weight of his Command away from his main task – that of bringing Germany to its knees by the systematic destruction of its towns, cities and war industries. During August 1942, despite misgivings by Harris, No. 106 Sqn had been ordered to prepare for a special attack on Gdynia in the Baltic where major ships of the German navy were believed to be anchored. A special weapon, the Capital Ship Bomb (CSB) had been developed for the sole purpose of sinking capital ships in harbour; indeed, the ability to carry this bomb had been a feature of the Lancaster's final design specification. The destruction of the German navy

had, after all, been the major strategic war aim of Bomber Command ever since it had been formed in 1936, although this was to change after the defeat of France.

On the night of 17 August 1942, three Lancasters of No. 106 Sqn, each carrying a CSB and led by a fourth (flown by Wing Cdr Gibson) with conventional bombs, set out to attack the enemy port. Owing to poor visibility and the difficulty of aiming a bomb possessing very poor ballistics, all the bombs missed their targets by a considerable distance. Harris lost no time in ensuring that the bomb was declared redundant.

Turin raid

By early December 1942, 13 Lancaster squadrons, most of which could launch about a dozen aircraft as a matter of course, were operational. In an extraordinary display of determination and skill, No. 106 Sqn had introduced into service the high-capacity 8,000-lb (3628-kg) blast bomb by carrying the weapon over the Alps

for an attack on Turin on the night of 28/29 November.

In its first year of operations the Lancaster had not only survived a bloody baptism of fire, but had also become the main weapon of Bomber Command. By the end of 1942, Lancaster crews were coming off the 'production lines' in Britain and Canada in fast-growing numbers. No. 5 Group was almost entirely equipped with Lancasters. It was now that the unit establishment of each squadron was increased from 18 to 24 aircraft, and re-equipment of a second Group began. Apart from the Vickers

Near-new Lancasters of No. 83 Sqn prepare to leave RAF Scampton for a raid on Bremen on 25/26 June 1942. The raid included the last operational Manchester sortie.

Wellington, all the former 'heavy' twin-engined bombers – the Handley Page Hampdens, Armstrong Whitworth Whitleys and Manchesters – were being withdrawn or had disappeared. The Stirling and the Halifax would suffer the same fate, although the process of discarding the Halifax as a heavy bomber took much longer. The major bomber battles were now to be addressed.

Above: The 6,800-lb (3084-kg) Capital Ship Bomb, as carried by Lancasters on the unsuccessful Gdynia raid, had a diameter of some 45 in (114.3 cm). Its shape gave it poor ballistic qualities, making accurate aiming virtually impossible.

Left: Lancaster Mk I ED593 Admiral Prune II provides the backdrop for this group photograph of No. 106 Sqn aircrew in 1942. This was the personal aircraft of the squadron's commanding officer, Wing Commander Guy Gibson (14th from left), later CO of No. 617 Sqn.

Lancaster invasion of Europe

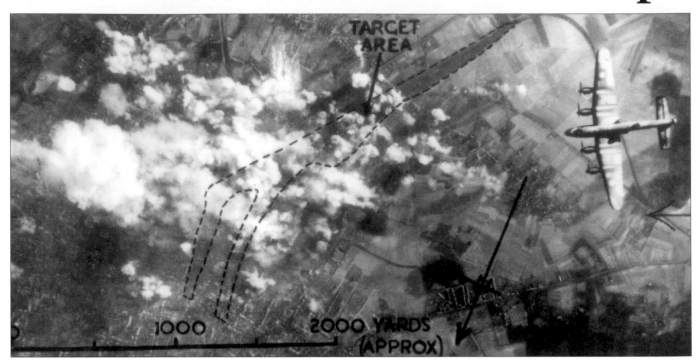

By 1944 the Avro Lancaster had firmly established itself as Bomber Command's most important asset. Prior to Normandy, the Lancaster squadrons began to step up their bombing campaign in France, with a series of daring raids designed to cripple the German war machine and the industry upon which it relied.

The air crews of Bomber Command must have breathed a sigh of relief with the end in sight of what would later be called the Battle of Berlin, and the switch to targets closer to home. Just over two months remained before the Allied armies would fight their way ashore in Normandy, and Harris was ordered to begin a series of assaults on railway marshalling yards in France, Belgium and western Germany. Ten raids were flown against the yards at Aulnoye, Rouen, Paris (Noissy, Juvisy and Ste Chappelle), Laon, Achères and Somain. Lancaster squadrons contributed 844 sorties against these targets, with the loss of 18 aircraft.

Coastal attack

In May the tempo was stepped up as the coastal gun batteries on the French coast also became a top priority. For security reasons, there could be no obvious concentration of effort against those in Normandy. The very heavy gun batteries at Calais, Cap Gris Nez, Merville, Mardyck, and Dieppe were bombed more than once, with those at Boulogne receiving a particularly heavy tonnage of explosives. Two heavy raids stand out from the others at

this time, the first being against the Paris-Juvisy rail yards. On the night of 18/19 April 1944, 202 Lancasters set out, all with maximum bombloads comprising 12,000-, 8,000-, 4,000-, 2,000- and 1,000-lb (5443-, 3629-, 1814-, 907- and 454-kg) high-explosive, demolition bombs. More than 92 per cent of bombs landed within the target area, and the entire complex, which measured about two miles (3.2 km) long and half a mile (0.8 km) wide, was obliterated. All the flyover bridges, sidings and through-tracks were hit repeatedly, and 80 per cent of the workshops were simply swept away. Few French civilians were hurt, probably as a result of forewarning the Resistance movement. The raid was marked by No. 617 Squadron, some of whose Lancasters carried the new 12,000-lb (5443-kg) bombs. One Lancaster was shot down and another crashed in England.

The other outstanding attack at this time was another all-Lancaster

Above: Pictured at Skellingthorpe in August 1944, this Lancaster Mk III of No. 61 Sqn (foreground) and Lancaster Mk I of No. 50 Sqn, had, at this time, flown 118 and 113 operations, respectively.

Top: 27 December 1944 witnessed the attack on the Rheydt rail marshalling yard. This photograph, taken at 15.00, shows the level of concentration of bomb bursts over the target.

raid, with 348 aircraft being despatched against the Wehrwuxcht depot at Mailly-le-Camp, about 20 miles (32 km) south-east of Paris. This was an enormous site for the maintenance of German armoured vehicles as well as a training establishment for Panzer personnel, and would be of vital importance

following an Allied invasion of France. Led and marked by the famous Leonard Cheshire (flying a Mosquito of No. 617 Squadron), the bombing had to be extremely accurate as the target lay alongside a French village, and was carried out from a relatively low altitude. The German night-fighter force reacted violently and shot down

Carried exclusively by No. 617 Sqn Lancasters, the 22,000-lb (9979-kg) 'Grand Slam' bomb is seen here during dropping trials, with a Lancaster B.Mk I (Special), identified by its deleted dorsal and nose turrets, and modified bomb bay.

Paris/Juvisy rail attack

These two reconnaissance photographs bear witness to the devastation of RAF Bomber Command's attack from 18-19 April, 1944. Targeting the Paris/Juvisy rail marshalling yards on the southern outskirts of Paris, Bomber Command's No. 5 Group aircraft comprised 184 Lancasters, and 18 additional lead and marking aircraft from No. 617 Squadron. The Lancasters carried demolition bombs ranging from 12,000 lb to 1,000 lb (5443 kg to 454 kg), accounting for virtually the entire track complex, all locomotive sheds and workshops, most of the cross-over rail bridges and more than half the rolling stock then in the yards. During the raids, No. 617's pathfinder Lancasters were supported by Mosquitoes, sweeping over the target at 400 ft (122 m) and laying red spot fires across the centre of the yard, prior to the Lancasters laying their bombs.

42 Lancasters (a loss rate similar to that of the raid on Nuremberg), but on this occasion the target was virtually destroyed. The main weapon used was the humble 500-pounder (227-kg), of which more than 4,000 fell in the target area. The relatively small number of 4,000-pounders (1814-kg) merely swept away the rubble.

Invasion support

Lancasters played an important part during the initial assault phase of the Normandy invasion landings, though not by delivering death and destruction. Instead, in an operation codenamed Taxable, eight Lancaster crews were briefed to simulate the approach of a seaborne invasion fleet about 100 miles (161 km) north-east of the Normandy beaches at night. By flying in line abreast, two miles (3.2 km) apart, each aircraft dropped bundles of Window for two minutes at a time before turning on to a reciprocal course (being obscured by its own Window); after a further set time each aircraft resumed its approach course to drop more Window. This blanket of Window, 16 miles (26 km) wide, would be seen by enemy radar, and appear to be a large mass of ships approaching the coast at approximately 4 kt (4.6 mph; 7.4 km/h). By dawn the Lancasters were on their way home and the sea would be seen to be empty of shipping. The ruse had the desired effect of confusing the Germans as to the main area of assault, thereby delaying the despatch of reinforcements.

Such was the very high standard of accuracy achieved by No. 617 Squadron that Air Vice-Marshal Cochrane, AOC-in-C of No. 5 Group, had come to regard Cheshire's Squadron as the Group's own pathfinder force, to such a degree that there were numerous occasions when the Group would constitute an entire 'Main Force' attack, with its own route and target marking; these were invariably the raids on which the emphasis was on accuracy and extensive demolition (as distinct from incendiary raids).

Three nights after the Normandy landings of 5-6 June 1944, No. 617 Squadron introduced a new weapon, the 12,000-lb (5443-kg) 'Tallboy' deep-penetration bomb, as 19 crews were ordered to attack the Saumur railway tunnel (a line carrying German reinforcements to the beachhead area). The tunnel was blocked with clinical accuracy and the rail tracks torn up for several hundred yards. One bomb penetrated the hillside into the tunnel, causing a huge volume of earth to collapse onto the track.

Back to daylight attacks

By gaining air superiority over Normandy, the Supreme Allied Commander could call on Bomber Command to bring its muscle to bear on the battlefield itself, and a number of attacks were carried out to 'carpet bomb' enemy defences, although these carried a considerable risk of hitting Allied forces 'in the fog of battle'. A number of Bomber Command attacks was flown against towns (not least Caen in Normandy itself), the object being to so bemuse the enemy troops as to enable armour to sweep in and overrun the shattered buildings. This tactic often failed, as it had done in Italy the previous year.

By no means were all the daylight attacks by Lancasters launched in direct support of the ground armies. After two unsuccessful attempts to sink the German battleship *Tirpitz*, anchored in Alten Fjord, Lancasters of Nos 9 and 617 Squadrons flew from Scotland to Yagodnik in northern Russia. On 12 November 1944, 31 aircraft took off from there for the final, successful attack. Several Tallboy weapons hit *Tirpitz* and capsized it.

The last great weapon to be carried by the Lancaster was the 22,000-lb (9979-kg) 'Grand Slam', another deep-penetration bomb. Very few of these were available before the end of the war, and all were carried by No. 617 Squadron, eventually destroying the Bielefeld viaduct and several other crucial bridges in Germany during the last few weeks of the war, as well as the massive U-boat shelters at Farge on the Weser river.

In daylight on 27 April 1945 115 Lancasters attacked the U-boat shelters target and, of the 12 Grand Slams dropped, two penetrated the 23-ft (7-m) thick concrete roof as others weakened the foundations with their shockwaves and whole areas of the structure collapsed.

At the end of the war, Bomber Command possessed 61 fully operational Lancaster squadrons, with an average of 26 aircraft each – a force capable of delivering 9,900 tons of bombs in a single raid, day or night and on any target in Germany. This figure does not even include the 30 Halifax squadrons. The fact that no such raid was ever ordered was a measure of Allied and, in particular, the RAF's sparing employment of air supremacy had the need to bomb Germany to its knees ever arisen. These facts are often overlooked when the subject of indiscriminate bombing is raised. Mistakes were made, such as Nuremberg (through incompetence) and the ill-judged bombing of Dresden, and the fog of war is often blamed. But Arthur Harris was ordered to destroy Germany's will to wage war, and the Lancaster was the weapon wielded to that end.

Operation Manna air drops of April and May 1945 provided Dutch citizens with much-needed food supplies. Towards the end of the war, the Lancaster was also used as a transport, carrying home 74,000 prisoners of war.

Lancaster variants

Far and away the most famous and effective British heavy bomber of World War II, the Avro Model 683 Lancaster was a remarkably stable design. Although produced in a number of variants, to all external appearances (and to most internal examination) these were virtually identical. Lancasters flew more than 156,000 sorties, dropping over 600,000 tons of high explosive and more than 50 million incendiary bombs.

B.Mk I

The prototype Avro Lancaster, which was converted from a twin-engined Avro Manchester airframe, first flew on 9 January 1941. Powered by four 1,145 hp (854 kW) Merlin XX engines, it was immediately recognised as an outstanding heavy bomber, and Avro's first order was for 1,070 aircraft. The first production aircraft took to the air in October 1941, and its initial operation took place with No.44 Squadron over the Heligoland Bight on 3 March 1942. Production demands were such that Avro's Chaterton and Yeadon factories could not cope with demand, and Lancasters were subsequently also built by Armstrong Whitworth at Coventry, Austin Morris in Birmingham, Metropolitan Vickers in Manchester and by Vickers Armstrong at Chester and Castle Bromwich. Total Lancaster

Mk.I production reached 3,425 out of a total of 7,377 Lancasters built. Initial bombload of the Mk.I was 4,000-lb (1814 kg) but the bomb bay was enlarged progressively to carry larger and heavier weapons, capacity increasing to more than 12,000 lb (5443 kg). In modified form the Lancaster B.Mk I was eventually able to carry the massive 12,000-lb (5443 kg) 'Tallboy' and the even larger 22,000-lb (9979 kg) 'Grand Slam' bomb. Lancaster B.Mk Is, together with the virtually identical B.Mk IIIs and Xs, ultimately equipped 59 Bomber Command squadrons during the War.

B.Mk II

Such was the success of the B.Mk I that there were fears that Merlin production would not be able to keep up with RAF orders for the new bomber. As additional insurance, the Lancaster B.Mk II was designed, powered by four Bristol Hercules VI or XVI radial engines. First flown in November 1941, the Mk II entered squadron service a year later. The Hercules-engined aircraft was an adequate machine, but it was slower than those powered by Merlins, had a lower ceiling and carried a smaller bomb load. Production ceased after a total of 301 were built, with the type remaining in operational service until its last mission in September 1944.

B.Mk III

The feared shortfall in Merlin production did not come about, thanks in part to the production lines set up by Packard in the United States. These were soon applied to the Lancaster, the resulting aircraft being known as B.Mk IIIs (below). Apart from some minor equipment changes and the addition of a slightly larger bubble for the bomb aimer, the B.Mk III was hardly different from the B.Mk I. More than 3,000 were completed. After the war a number of Mk IIIs were converted to air sea rescue configuration, the ASR Mk IIIs being equipped with large airborne lifeboats (right). These later became maritime reconnaissance machines, serving as GR.Mk 3s until 1954.

B.Mk VI

The Lancaster Mks IV and V were never built as such, being extensively redesigned machines intended to have increased range. They were later to emerge as the post-war Avro Lincoln. The Lancaster B.Mk VI was a less radical attempt to improve the performance of the big Avro bomber. Nine aircraft were converted by Rolls-Royce, being fitted with Merlin 85s or 87s in improved annular nacelles. With nose and dorsal turrets removed, they were used operationally on pathfinder duties by No.635 Squadron. Fitted with improved H2S radar bombing aids, they also carried early forms of electronic countermeasures designed to jam enemy radars. Although performance was superior to earlier Marks of the Lancaster, it was not enough to ensure production.

B.Mk VII

The final production version of the Lancaster was the B.Mk VII, which had an American-built Martin dorsal turret equipped with two 0.50-in (12.7-mm) heavy machine guns. The turret was mounted further forward than on earlier marks. They were powered by four Rolls-Royce Merlin 24s, the same engines that were fitted to late model Lancaster B.Mk Is. Construction of the Mk.VII totalled 180: a number of these were sent to the Far East where they operated with white-painted upper services. After the war a number of Mk VIIs were sold to the French Aéronavale. Modified with extra fuel tanks, they served as long range maritime patrol machines in North Africa and New Caledonia.

B.Mk X

To swell the output of production lines in the UK, Victory Aircraft in Canada was contracted to produce Lancasters under the designation B.Mk X. Powered by Packard Merlins, these were virtually identical to B.Mk I/IIIs. They were delivered by air across the Atlantic, armament being fitted on arrival in the UK. The first B.Mk X was handed over on 6 August 1943, and 430 aircraft were built before production was completed. Many of these aircraft were returned to Canada in 1945-46, and saw a considerable amount of post-war service. Some remained as bombers, but others became maritime patrol aircraft (Mk 10MR) or photo recce aircraft (Mk 10P, left). More than 20 were converted to ASR configuration, and three became Mk 10N navigation trainers (above). The last Mk 10 conversions retired from RCAF service in April 1964.

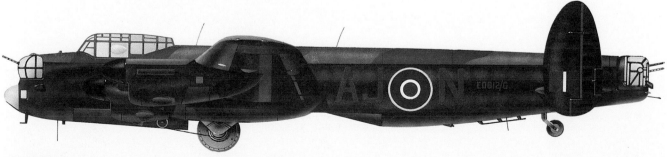

Specials

Although most Lancasters were similar in appearance, a number were extensively modified to perform special missions. The first, and most famous, were the B.Mk IIIs used in the Dams raid. Given the designation Mk. III (Type 464 provisioning), these had extensively adapted bomb bays designed to carry the 'Upkeep' bouncing bomb designed to destroy the Möhne, Sorpe and Eder dams. The engines were standard, as were the Frazer-Nash front and rear hydraulically operated 0.303-in (7.7-mm) calibre gun turrets. The mid-upper turret was deleted. These were followed by the Mk. I (Special), which was a B.Mk I designed to carry outsized bombs exceeding 12,000 lbs (5443 kg) in weight – 'Tallboys' and 'Grand Slams'. The front and mid-upper turrets were often removed to reduce weight and improve the centre of gravity. Other modified Lancasters included the Mk.I (FE) and the Mk.VII (FE), which were tropicalised and had extended range for Far Eastern use.

Bell P-39 Airacobra & P-63 Kingcobra

'Dear little Cobra'

Bell's P-39 and P-63 were unique among World War II fighters in their unorthodox powerplant installation. The Airacobra was also the first US Army single-seat fighter with tricycle landing gear.

In early 1935, executives of the Bell Aircraft Corporation had been present at a demonstration of the American Armament Corporation's T-9 37-mm cannon. Impressed by what they had seen, they instigated the design of a fighter which would include a T-9 cannon firing through the propeller hub.

This gun became standard on all production models except the US Army P-39D-1 and the export P-400. Early Airacobras also had two 0.50-in (12.70-mm) nose-mounted Colt machine-guns with 270 rounds each and four 0.30-in (7.62-mm) wing-mounted Colt machine-guns with 1,000 rounds per gun.

The decision to locate the cannon to fire through the propeller hub meant that the engine had to be mounted within the fuselage, directly above the rear half of the low-set monoplane wing.

With the engine situated far to the aft, a 10-ft (3-m) drive shaft, which passed beneath the cockpit floor, was required to couple the engine and propeller reduc-

tion gearing. The result was an aircraft fuselage that was rigid both literally and figuratively: engineers had few choices about where to put key features and the orthodox, semi-monocoque aft fuselage was literally 'stiff'. The US Army gave Bell no choice about incorporating tricycle landing gear – including a nose wheel that added 128 lb (58 kg) to the preponderance of weight up front. Nor did the army allow any choice about the four Colt wing guns, which eventually remained standard until the P-39Q model, even though they involved a weight penalty that exceeded their benefit.

The Allison V-1710 was a 1,100- to 1,300-hp (820- to 970-kW) liquid-cooled, 12-cylinder Vee-type inline engine equipped with an integral single-stage, single-speed supercharger. This engine, which also propelled the Curtiss P-40 Hawk series, was generally well-received in the field, although pilots and maintainers never quite forgave Bell for deleting the turbo-supercharger

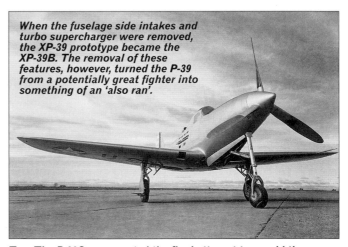

Top: The P-39Q represented the final attempt to mould the Airacobra into a world-class fighter. This is a P-39Q-20, most of which were built for the USSR and delivered without guns, although this example was destined for the USAAF and retained its armament.

on the Airacobra and thus hindering its higher-altitude performance.

First deliveries

At first designated P-45, the new fighter was ordered into production on 10 August 1939, the first contract being for 809 aircraft. Before the first of these was delivered, the designation reverted to P-39.

The US Army ordered 369 P-39Ds in September 1940, and initial deliveries began seven months later. The first operational unit to receive the type was the 31st Fighter Group, at

Selfridge Field, Michigan, P-39s being supplied to the 39th, 40th and 41st Fighter Squadrons.

British Cobras

The UK began to receive its first Airacobras in July 1941. The first aircraft, a P-39C, arrived on 3 July and was flying three days later. In August of that year, No. 601 Squadron began to exchange its Hawker Hurricanes for Airacobras.

However, RAF officers immediately grasped the significance of the decision to delete the turbocharger. RAF pilots found that the Airacobra had inadequate climb and high-altitude performance. The fighter was unacceptable for the fighting conditions to be found in the European Theatre. Only about 80 of the aircraft in the original order actually entered RAF service, and only with No. 601 Squadron, which gladly gave them up for Spitfires in March 1942. Britain eventually transferred a number to Russia and returned others to the USAAF (designated P-400).

On the day the US entered the war, the US Army had fielded a total of five pursuit groups equipped with 600 P-39D models: the 8th at Mitchell Field, New York; the 31st and 52nd at Selfridge, Michigan; the 36th in Puerto Rico; and the 53rd at MacDill Field, Florida.

Combat

The first combat mission by the Airacobra was flown by the 8th Fighter Group, which in March 1942 came to Australia, and thereafter to Port Moresby, New Guinea with 'D' models.

P-39s performed well in battle with the Japanese Zeros; heavier armour and increased firepower ensured that the USAAF aircraft often performed better in engagements. In the last major

air action at Guadalcanal on 17 June 1943, Airacobras tangled with dozens of Japanese bombers and fighters. Captain William D. Wells led a brace of Airacobras into a formation of 30 to 35 Aichi Type 99 carrier bombers and shot down four of them.

The P-39 was also called upon to act as a divebomber against Japanese ships, a role for which it had never been designed but at which, with proper techniques and tactics, it excelled.

P-39 and P-400 Airacobras found their way into US squadrons in North Africa. The American press gave some attention to the success of the Airacobra in prevailing over the Bf 109, and to the Bell fighter's role in knocking out tanks with its cannon – both almost certainly an exaggeration.

Most combat operations in the Airacobra were carried out by the Soviet air force in support of the Red Army. Intended primarily for close air support, the American-built fighter was also employed in other roles including air-to-air combat, where pilots often had opportunities to engage the Messerschmitt Bf 109 at low altitude. The 'Cobrastochka' ('dear little Cobra') performed better in Russian hands than American. Lieutenant Colonel Alexsandr I.

While the P-39 saw only limited in Europe and Africa, it was in the Pacific theatre that the Airacobra, along with the P-40, was the dominant fighter until 1944. These P-39s can be seen escorting a C-47 over New Guinea en route to Wau.

Pokryshkin became the second-ranking Soviet ace of the war with 59 victories, 48 of them in Airacobras. P-39s equipped the 9th Guards Fighter Division and the 16th Guards Fighter Air Regiment.

French forces received a total of 247 P-39K, P-39N and P-39Q Airacobras. Free French pilots first received P-39 Airacobras at Maison Blanche in North Africa

in May 1943 and a few days later claimed their first kill, a Dornier Do 217.

Some 4,924 P-39s were sent to the Soviet Union, of which 4,758 reached their destinations. A total of 9,529 Bell P-39 Airacobras was produced between 1939 and 1944. The USAAF reached a peak inventory of P-39 Airacobras in February 1944 with 2,105 aircraft on strength.

P-39Q Airacobra

The top-scoring Cobra pilot of any nation, and the second-ranking Soviet ace of the war, was Alexsandr Pokryshkin of the 9th and 16th GvIAPs. His overall score was 59 enemy aircraft, 48 of them destroyed while flying Airacobras. The third-ranking ace, Grigori Rechkalov, scored many of his 58 kills on P-39s. One of the P-39 aces, Mikhail Baranov (total score 28), brought down a Bf 109 over Stalingrad by chopping its tail off with his propeller in a *Taran* or ramming attack, having expended all his ammunition on three other 109s.

Cockpit door
One of the more unusual features of the Bell Cobras was their car-type entry doors, a feature only found elsewhere among wartime fighter aircraft on early models of the Hawker Typhoon. The jettisonable door unit was much the same as that fitted to an automobile, with the normal opening handle and a winding handle for opening the window.

Undercarriage
In the light of combat experience with the P-39, the nose undercarriage leg fork was strengthened, beginning with the P-39L model. This was a non-steerable, self-castoring unit. Undercarriage operation was electric, the gear taking 28 seconds to extend.

Markings
In common with most Soviet and Russian aircraft up until the very recent past, pinning down a unit assignment to a particular aircraft is almost impossible due to the lack of insignia specific to a particular squadron or regiment. The Guards badge on the pilot's door of this P-39 narrows it down to one of the Guards IAPs (Istrebitel'nyy Avia Polk – Fighter Regiments). They included the 16th,19th, 20th, 28th, 30th, 67th and 104th GvIAPs, most of which were awarded the coveted Guards status for combat performance while flying the Airacobra.

By the time the P-63 was ready for service, the USAAF was no longer interested. Apart from the Soviet air force, which took about three-quarters of total production, the Armée de l'Air received 114 P-63Cs. The few that remained in USAAF service after World War II were used as trainers.

Kingcobra
'Tank of the skies'

The Bell P-63 Kingcobra was a wholly new fighter design using the essential layout of the P-39 Airacobra and introducing the laminar-flow wing and taller tail tested on the XP-39E.

The USAAF ordered two XP-63 prototypes (41-19511/19512) in June 1941, powered by the 1,325-hp (988-kW) Allison V1710-47 engine located behind the pilot and driven by an extension shaft. The first machine flew on 7 December 1942, but was lost in an accident a few weeks later. The XP-63A (42-78015) was originally conceived as a Merlin engine testbed under the designation XP-63B, but became instead a third prototype powered by a 1,325-hp (988-kW) Allison V-1710-93. The XP-63A was actually the fastest Kingcobra built, attaining 426 mph (685 km/h) on military power at 20,000 ft (6096 m), but air combat was not to be the type's forte: the Kingcobra was envisaged for the ground-attack role and for export, primarily to the Soviet Union.

The production P-63A, 1,825 of which were built in numerous sub-variants with minor changes

in armament, armour and ordnance, was followed in 1943 by the P-63C with a 1,800-hp (1342-kW) Allison V-1716-117 engine with water injection. One P-63A (42-68937) was tested by the Royal Air Force as the Kingcobra Mk I (FR408).

Ventral fin

The first P-63C (42-70886) introduced a distinctive small ventral fin intended to improve lateral stability characteristics. The sole P-63D (43-11718) was configured with a bubble canopy and increased wingspan. The first P-63E (43-11720) with minor changes, was followed by 12 further examples before contracts for 2,930 were cancelled at war's end. One P-63F (43-11719) introduced the V-1710-135 powerplant and, while a second was cancelled, survived to be H. L. Pemberton's mount in the 1947 Cleveland Air Races with civil registration NX1719.

Ferried to the USSR via

Below: In this view of a P-63A (foreground) and a P-39Q the main external differences are clear. The Kingcobra was about 12 per cent larger than the P-39.

Above: The vast bulk of Kingcobra production went directly to the Soviet Union. These P-63As await delivery via the Alaska-Siberia ferry route.

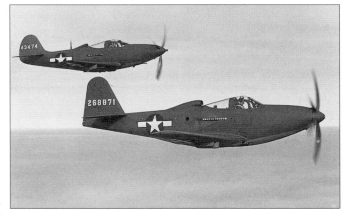

Alaska or Iran, the P-63 Kingcobra proved a potent attack aircraft and tank-buster. P-63s also served with Free French forces. The relatively few aircraft retained by the USAAF were used primarily for training, and none is thought to have seen combat. Post-war, five P-63Es were delivered to Honduras, but were used only briefly.

In 1945 and afterwards, P-63

Kingcobras were used as flying targets, painted bright red, piloted, and shot at by other fighters using frangible bullets. These 'robot' RP-63A and RP-63 aircraft were insulated with a protective covering of duralumin alloy, a bulletproof windscreen and canopy glass, a steel grille over the engine air intake, a steel guard for the exhaust stacks, and thick-walled,

Rebuilt from a P-63C, the P-63D tested a sliding bubble canopy intended for the P-63E-5 and was fitted with an M9 propeller hub cannon in place of the usual M10. It remained a one-off.

Tall vertical and enlarged ventral fins were tested on a pair of P-63Fs. Had the war continued, the P-63E-5, with bubble canopy and enlarged fin, would have been produced for Soviet use.

Laminar flow wing

Though there were obvious similarities in terms of layout and general design, the P-39 and P-63 were entirely different aircraft. The latter's enlarged vertical fin and four-bladed propeller were obvious visual differences, but perhaps more significant was the more efficient laminar flow wing.

Armament

The P-63 carried five guns: a single 37-mm M10 cannon in the propeller hub, a pair of 0.5-in (12.7-mm) machine-guns above the nose and a second pair of podded '50 calibres' under the wings. Each wing also sported an underwing stores rack, suitable for extra fuel or 500 lb (227 kg) of ordnance.

Final mission

The last mission by a French P-63 was flown on 30 April 1951. About 30 aircraft were lost to ground fire and accidents between 1949 and 1951.

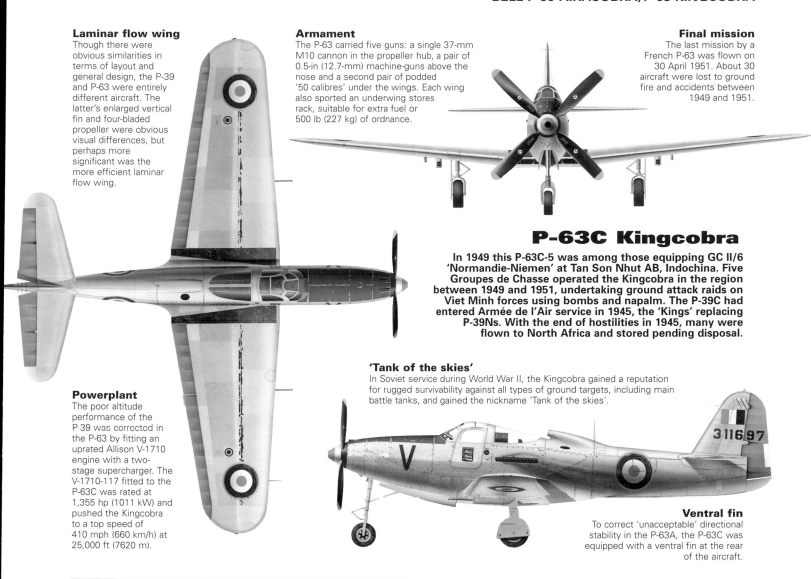

P-63C Kingcobra

In 1949 this P-63C-5 was among those equipping GC II/6 'Normandie-Niemen' at Tan Son Nhut AB, Indochina. Five Groupes de Chasse operated the Kingcobra in the region between 1949 and 1951, undertaking ground attack raids on Viet Minh forces using bombs and napalm. The P-39C had entered Armée de l'Air service in 1945, the 'Kings' replacing P-39Ns. With the end of hostilities in 1945, many were flown to North Africa and stored pending disposal.

'Tank of the skies'

In Soviet service during World War II, the Kingcobra gained a reputation for rugged survivability against all types of ground targets, including main battle tanks, and gained the nickname 'Tank of the skies'.

Powerplant

The poor altitude performance of the P-39 was corrected in the P-63 by fitting an uprated Allison V-1710 engine with a two-stage supercharger. The V-1710-117 fitted to the P-63C was rated at 1,355 hp (1011 kW) and pushed the Kingcobra to a top speed of 410 mph (660 km/h) at 25,000 ft (7620 m).

Ventral fin

To correct 'unacceptable' directional stability in the P-63A, the P-63C was equipped with a ventral fin at the rear of the aircraft.

With a roundel crudely applied over its USAAF 'star and bar', this P-39C-5 was among the 114 delivered to the Armée de l'Air. French Kingcobras all served abroad, mainly in Indochina.

hollow propellers. When a hit was scored by an attacking aircraft, a red light blinked to confirm impact, causing one RP-63A (42-69654) to be named *Pinball*. For more than 25 years an RP-63G (45-57295) has been on outdoor display at Lackland AFB, Texas. This unique piloted target was redesignated QF-63G in 1948, although the 'Q' prefix usually denotes an unmanned drone.

The sole XP-63H was converted from a P-63E to test new internal systems. Two P-63s without specific designations were modified to test the

V-shaped tail configuration more familiarly associated with the Beechcraft Bonanza. A sole P-63 was rebuilt with swept-back wings and test-flown by the US Navy as the L-39. A handful of standard aircraft was also used for various tests by the Navy, although the F2L designation was not taken up.

Although total Kingcobra production was a respectable 3,362 airframes, 2,456 being delivered to the Soviets, the type must be included among the second rank of wartime fighters and remembered as Bell's last great success in the fighter field.

Aerodynamic testbeds

Two P-63s (including P-63A-9 42-69606, below) were employed by Bell to test a 'vee-tail' configuration, while two other aircraft were fitted with swept-back wings and redesignated L-39. The second machine – L-39-2 (left) – was fitted with a wing intended for the X-2 supersonic aircraft.

Blohm und Voss
BV 138
The 'Flying Clog'

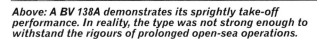

Above: A BV 138A demonstrates its sprightly take-off performance. In reality, the type was not strong enough to withstand the rigours of prolonged open-sea operations.

Top: The BV 138 matured into a reliable and useful patroller. The majority operated in Arctic waters from Norwegian bases, but this BV 138C operated in far more pleasant conditions, serving with 3.(F)/SAGr 125 at Constanza, on the Black Sea coast.

Known as 'die fliegende Holzschuh' (flying clog), the BV 138 was a stalwart of the Luftwaffe's coastal patrol and anti-convoy efforts in the hostile waters of the Arctic Ocean and North Atlantic.

The first flying-boat design to be built by Hamburger Flugzeugbau GmbH, under the direction of chief engineer Dr Ing Richard Vogt, was the Ha 138. Three prototypes of the original twin-engined design were each to have been powered by a different manufacturer's 1,000-hp (746-kW) engine for comparative evaluation, but development delays necessitated redesign to accept three 650-hp (485-kW) Junkers Jumo 205C engines. Almost two years after the completion of the mock-up, the first prototype (Ha 138 V1) took off on its maiden flight, the date being 15 July 1937. A

second prototype (Ha 138 V2), with a modified hull design, joined the test programme at the Travemunde centre in November, but the aircraft were quickly proved to be unstable, both hydrodynamically and aero-dynamically. Modifications to the vertical tail surfaces failed to improve the performance adequately and radical redesign was undertaken.

The result was the BV 138A, adopting the designation system of the Blohm und Voss parent company. The hull was much enlarged, its planing surfaces were improved, and the revised tail surfaces were carried by more substantial booms. The

prototype first flew in February 1939, and was followed by five more pre-series BV 138A-0 aircraft. Testing confirmed that there were still shortcomings in the aircraft's structure, and the BV 138A-04 was returned for further strengthening to become the first of 10 BV 138B-0s.

Into service

Meanwhile, 25 BV 138A-1s were constructed, as the need for coastal transport aircraft was pressing. The first two rapidly entered service with KGzbV 108 See for service in the Norwegian campaign and, soon after, 1./KüFlGr 506 equipped for service in the Bay of Biscay from October 1940, being rapidly joined by 2./KüFlGr 906. The BV 138A-1s proved troublesome in service, problems surfacing with the structure, engines and bow armament. Most of these were attended to in the improved BV 138B, which was fitted with more powerful Jumo

205D engines to overcome the weight increase.

The first BV 138B-1 flew in December 1940, and was a much better machine than its predecessor. Bow armament consisted of a 20-mm MG 151 cannon, and there was an MG 15 in an open position behind the central engine nacelle. A factory conversion (BV 138B-1/U1) increased the weaponload to six bombs or depth charges. The BV 138C-1 which followed had further airframe strengthening, a four-bladed propeller on the central engine (retrofitted to BV 138B-1s), an additional gun in the starboard side, fired by the radio operator, and a 13-mm MG 131 in the central nacelle position. The BV 138C-1/U1 was also available with extra armament capability. During 1942-43, a handful were converted to BV 138 MS standard, known as 'Mausi-flugzeug' (mouse-catching aircraft).

Above: The second prototype Ha 138 introduced a modified hull design, but this was insufficient to overcome the many aero- and hydrodynamic problems suffered by the type. A complete hull redesign resulted in the BV 138A production version.

Right: A key feature of the BV 138 was its bow turret, which in the mainstream BV 138B and C (illustrated) versions housed a single 20-mm MG 151 cannon.

In addition to operating from shore bases, BV 138s operated from seaplane tenders, some being modified with catapult points for launch. All aircraft could be fitted with assisted take-off rockets, and several sprouted FuG 200 Hohentwiel radar for shadowing convoys. The standard crew was five (six in the C-1), and the gun positions offered excellent fields of fire. Despite its early teething troubles, the BV 138 became an outstanding maritime patroller, offering long endurance and able to withstand a great amount of damage from either the enemy or the elements.

Norwegian operations

In early 1941 the two France-based BV 138A-1 units converted to the BV 138B-1 and were later reassigned to the Baltic. Meanwhile, Norway was becoming a principal operating location for the type, with the establishment of 2./KüFlGr 406 (later designated 3.(F)/SAGr 130), 3./KüFlGr 906, 1.(F) and 2.(F)/SAGr 130, and 1.(F) and

2.(F)/SAGr 131. From Norwegian bases, the BV 138s ranged over the North Atlantic and Arctic Oceans, shadowing and attacking convoys bound for Russia. In the course of such activities, BV 138s shot down a Catalina and a Blenheim. In northern waters BV 138s refuelled at sea from U-boats and, in a remarkable three-week deployment in the summer of 1943, operated from a base established on Novaya Zemlya (Soviet territory) by crews from two U-boats.

Further areas of operations included the Black Sea, where the BV 138C-1s of 3.(F)/SAGr 125 flew missions from Constanza until late 1944. In 1943, the type was assigned in numbers to the Biscay and Mediterranean theatres. 3./KüFlGr 406 (later 1.(F)/SAGr 129) operated from Biscarosse until 1944, while 3.(F)/SAGr 126 operated from Crete. This unit was transferred to the Baltic, and surrendered at the end of the war in Denmark. A few BV 138s were still serving in Norway to the end.

Above: A BV 138C of SAGr 130 makes a refuelling rendezvous with a U-boat in the Arctic Ocean. Note the hastily applied white distemper Arctic camouflage and the Hohentwiel search radar mounted between the engines.

Above: In addition to shore-based operations, BV 138s (like this mine-hunting BV 138MS) could be operated from seaplane tenders being craned on or off ship, or even catapult-launched.

Below: The BV 138A was hastily produced to provide coastal patrol aircraft for service in Norway and the Bay of Biscay. This aircraft, seen on its ground handling trolley at the factory, does not yet have the troublesome LB 204 bow turret fitted.

BV 138 MS

Although the majority of BV 138s served on standard coastal patrol duties, a small number were converted for mine-hunting tasks. This aircraft served with 6. Staffel/Minensuchgruppe 1 at Grossenbrode in the last year of the war.

Gun armament
The BV 138A was fitted with an LB 204 bow turret housing an MG 204 cannon, but both proved troublesome and were replaced in the BV 138B by a redesigned turret with a single MG 151. Additional guns introduced by the BV 138C-1 comprised a 13-mm MG 131 in the rear of the central engine nacelle and a single 7.9-mm MG 15 firing from the starboard hatch. The BV 138 MS aircraft had all gun armament deleted.

Mine-hunting equipment
The BV 138 MS was fitted with a circular degaussing loop made of dural. Onboard the aircraft, underneath the bow turret fairing, was an auxiliary motor which generated power for producing a strong magnetic field in the loop, sufficient to explode mines as the aircraft passed overhead.

Offensive armament
Offensive stores were carried under the wingroots. The BV 138C could carry up to six 110-lb (50-kg) bombs or four 330-lb (150-kg) depth charges.

Convoy patrol
A key role for the Norway-based BV 138s was surveillance of the convoys which plied between Britain and the Soviet Union. These operations were highly successful until the introduction of the Sea Hurricane in September 1942 forced the BV 138s to operate from much greater stand-off distances, enabling the convoys to often slip their shadowers.

Boeing
B-17 Flying Fortress

Introduction

The vast armadas of the US 8th Air Force, equipped mainly with the Boeing B-17, ranged far and wide over Germany and occupied Europe from 1942 to 1945. Bombing individual factories and other precision targets, they also whittled away at the fighter strength of the Luftwaffe in some of the largest and bloodiest air battles in history.

In 1934, the nature of the air battles to come could not have been foreseen. At that time, the only targets within the range of US bombers were in such unlikely places as Canada and Mexico. In the Depression, money was tight, and the new monoplane Martin Bomber appeared to be all that was needed.

But when the US Army Air Corps put out a request for a new multi-engined bomber, far-sighted engineers at the Boeing Airplane Company decided to interpret 'multi-engined' as meaning not two engines, but four. Admittedly, they did this mainly in order to achieve more height over the target, but it had the effect of making the Boeing Model 299 significantly larger than its rivals.

First flight

Design began in June 1934, and the prototype made a successful first flight on 28 July 1935. The main purpose of the new bomber was to defend the United States by bombing an invasion fleet (the only plausible kind of target) and it was the nature of this mission, rather than heavy defensive armament, that resulted in Boeing registering the name 'Flying Fortress' for the new aircraft.

With a number of changes,

Top: Camouflage began to disappear from 8th AF Fortresses from January 1944. These are 381st Bombardment Group B-17Gs.

Above: Clear weather meant that good visual bombing results were possible, but made the B-17s obvious targets for flak gunners. These B-17Fs of the 390th BG are seen over Amiens/Glisy airfield in France during 1943.

especially to landing gear, armament and engines (930-hp/694-kW) Wright Cyclones instead of 750-hp/560-kW Pratt & Whitney Hornets), test Y1B-17s were ordered and delivered to the 2nd Bombardment Group at Langley Field in 1937.

Turbocharging

The 14th aircraft was built as the Y1B-17A, its engines fitted with General Electric turbo-superchargers, which increased its speed from 256 mph (412 km/h) to 311 mph (500 km/h) and raised the operating height to well over 30,000 ft (9145 m).

When the B-17B entered service in 1939 (in the teeth of

US Navy opposition), it was the fastest, highest-flying bomber in the world, ideal for the USAAC which was perfecting the art of daylight strategic bombing with large formations of aircraft with heavy defensive armament.

In December 1941, the month in which Japan bombed Pearl Harbor, the first large-scale production B-17 was entering service. The B-17E was a visually different model, incorporating the lessons learned in World War II in Europe. Its most striking change was the much larger tail, with a giant dorsal fin and long-span tailplane giving better control and stability at high altitude. The armament was completely revised to substan-

Providing adequate forward-firing defensive armament was always a problem with the Fortress, but was finally addressed in the B-17G. This variant was fitted with four 0.5-in (12.7-mm) machine-guns in two turrets (chin and dorsal, each with two guns), and two manually-operated 0.5-in (12.7-mm) cheek guns.

In the chill of a February morning, ground crew at an 8th AF base at Framlingham, England stand by with fire extinguishers as a B-17G starts up prior to another daylight mission.

special Fortress variants appeared as the war progressed. Some 8th Air Force bomber aircraft were fitted with radar and electronic countermeasures equipment to improve survivability and bombing accuracy.

The YB-40 was a 1943 'escort fighter' conversion tested by the 8th Air Force. Armed with extra pairs of machine-guns and ammunition, and intended to fly in bomber formations, the YB-40 proved to be too heavy. Unable to keep up with the bombers, it was abandoned.

the 8th Air Force against targets in Germany.

Post-war, surplus B-17s found new roles, including air-sea rescue (equipped with an air-droppable lifeboat), airborne early warning (with a search radar installed) and drone launch/direction. 'Demobbed' aircraft flew as engine test-beds, crop sprayers and fire-bombers.

Probably the last Fortresses to be flown in anger were those secretly operated by the new state of Israel between 1947 and 1958. Other foreign air arms

New roles were found for surplus B-17Gs post-war. This SB-17 carries H₂X radar under its nose and an air-droppable lifeboat for rescuing downed airmen. The US Navy also operated B-17s as early warning aircraft (as PB-1Ws) fitted with search radar.

tially increase the aircraft's firepower. Further improvements in armour and equipment all helped to increase the gross weight to 54,000 lb (24494 kg), so that the cruising speed inevitably fell from 231 mph (372 km/h) to only 210 mph (338 km/h). Deliveries of this aircraft totalled 512.

The 'Mighty 8th'

With the B-17E and B-17F (the latter stressed to carry greater bombloads), the US 8th Air Force built up its strength in England. The first combat mission was flown on 17 August 1942 by 12 B-17Es of the 97th Bomb Group against a marshalling yard near Rouen.

This was the small beginning of the greatest strategic striking force ever created. It was to lead to a three-year campaign during the course of which 640,036 US tons of bombs were dropped on German targets, eventually achieving supremacy even over the heart of Germany in daylight, albeit at the cost of grievous losses.

By far the most numerous B-17 model was the B-17G, the final

result of bitterly won combat experience. As well as being fitted with better armament, most G-models had improved turbochargers which actually increased the service ceiling to 35,000 ft (10670 m). However, as these bombers were so heavy, the cruising speed fell to 182 mph (293 km/h). This increased the time during which the gigantic formations were exposed to attack by the German fighters but, conversely, lengthened the period in which the B-17 guns could destroy enemy fighters.

Boeing built 4,035 B-17Gs, Douglas turning out 2,395 and Vega (a Lockheed subsidiary) 2,250 – a total of 8,680. In total, 12,731 B-17s of all variants were built, of which 12,677 were formally accepted by the USAAF.

B-17 operations were not confined to northern Europe. The type also served with the USAAF in the Pacific and Mediterranean theatres, although the Fortress's contemporary, the B-24 Liberator, with its longer range, was the preferred type, especially in the Pacific.

Modifications and a number of

Reconnaissance and transport variants (the F-9 and C-108, respectively) were also used, though in comparatively small numbers. Perhaps the most unusual of the Fortress variants, however, was the BQ-7. This was a 'war-weary' airframe, filled with 10 tons of explosives and employed as a primitive form of guided missile on a limited (and potentially hazardous!) basis by

were also supplied with surplus American aircraft, mainly in South America.

A remarkable number of B-17s have survived, compared to other wartime bomber types, largely because they remained in use for so long after 1945. Of over 40 examples, 13 are in flying condition, a fitting memorial to the young men who flew the B-17 50 years ago.

Above: In spring 1941, a batch of 20 B-17Cs was assigned to the RAF, but these aircraft proved a failure in RAF service. However, the B-17F was used with more success by the RAF as the Fortress Mk II, and the B-17G as the Fortress Mk III, mainly with Coastal Command. The B-17G was also the chief heavy carrier of special electronics for the RAF Bomber Command's No. 100 Group.

Left: About 13 Fortresses were airworthy in 1998, including this aircraft, restored for the USAF Museum. Another 30 were displayed in museums.

This B-17B (38-211) was assigned to the Air Corps' Material Division at Wright Field. A distinctive feature of the B-17B and C was the location of the aircraft commander's blister, offset behind the cockpit.

B-17 Development

Boeing's Flying Fortress represented a quantum leap over earlier USAAC bombers then in service, although its development had met with fierce opposition from the US Navy.

When the US Army Air Corps (USAAC) put out a request for a new multi-engined bomber, a few far-sighted engineers at the Boeing Airplane Company decided to interpret 'multi-engined' as meaning not two engines (as had generally been the case before), but four. While they did this mainly in order to achieve more height over the target, it also had the effect of making the Boeing Model 229 significantly larger than its rivals. Design began on 18 June 1934, and the prototype made a very successful first flight in the hands of Les Tower at Boeing Field on 28 July 1935. The main purpose of the new bomber was to defend the United States by bombing an invasion fleet (the only plausible kind of target), and it was the nature of this mission, rather than the aircraft's heavy defensive armament, that resulted in Boeing eventually registering the name Flying Fortress.

On 20 August 1935, the impressive aircraft, unpainted except for USAAC rudder strips and the civil registration

NX13372, flew non-stop to Wright Field at an average speed faster than the maximum possible speed of its twin-engined rivals. On the first officially observed flight before the USAAC evaluation officers, on 30 October 1935, the great bomber took off, climbed too steeply, stalled and dived into the ground, where it burst into flames. The accident was caused entirely by the fact that someone had omitted to remove the external locks on the elevators and, although the immediate winner of the official trials had to be the Douglas B-18, the much greater potential of the Boeing bomber resulted in the placing of a service-test order for 13, designated Y1B-17, on 17 January 1936.

These aircraft had many changes, especially to the landing gear and armament, as well as the fitting of 930-hp (694-kW) Wright Cyclone engines instead of 750-hp (560-kW) Pratt & Whitney Hornets. In 1937, the machines were delivered to the 2nd Bombardment Group at Langley Field, which subse-

quently flew almost 10,000 hours with no serious trouble and did more than any other unit in history to solve the problems of long-distance bombing, especially at high altitude. A fourteenth aircraft was fitted with General Electric turbo-superchargers, which increased its speed as well as raising its operating height to well over 30,000 ft (9145 m).

Results with the B-17 (as the Y1B was called after its test period was complete) were so good that the USAAC fought for massive production numbers, in the teeth of opposi-

The Model 229, in 1935, epitomised the latest in aeronautical engineering, although it contained few features that were actually all-new. Built without a specific contract from the government, the bomber constituted a risk to the modestly-sized Boeing company.

tion from the US Navy. It even (with Boeing collaboration) planned a next-generation bomber, which eventually became the B-29. US Navy anger that the USAAC might take on a maritime role was so intense that production numbers

The first of the true production Flying Fortresses, the B-17B was delivered to the Air Corps on 29 July 1939. The service test period had revealed the need for a number of improvements to be made, and these included the redesign of the nose to eliminate the gimballed gun socket and to relocate the bombardier from his previous prone position. An enlarged rudder and flaps were fitted, as was a revised window layout.

Above: This B-17C is shown in India in mid-1942, having escaped from the advancing Japanese forces within the Philippines. Combat conditions brought a change of markings to the aircraft, with the conspicuous red centre of the US national marking being hastily deleted.

Left: This B-17D is from the 7th BG and is seen at St Louis during a stop on cross-country flight from Hamilton Field, California in early 1941, before the fuselage insignia were introduced.

had to be scaled down, and the production batch of the first series model, the B-17B, numbered only 39. These aircraft had numerous minor changes as well as a redesigned nose and large rudder, and were the first in the world to enter service with turbocharged engines. The B-17B entered service in 1939 and was the fastest, as well as the highest-flying, bomber in the world. The USAAC had, by this time, embarked on a major programme of perfecting long-range strategic bombing by day, using the massed firepower of a large formation to render interception hazardous. It was expected, because of the B-17's speed and height, that opposing fighters would be hard-pressed to keep up and would present an almost stationary (relative to the bombers) target that could be blasted by the fire from hundreds of machine-guns.

Greater power and speed

Boeing and Wright Field continued to develop improvements for the B-17 and, in 1939, an additional 39 were ordered under the designation B-17C. These were heavier, weighing 49,650 lb (19505 kg) compared to about 43,000 lb (19505 kg) for a B-17B, because of increased armour, self-sealing tanks, heavier defensive armament (with twin 0.5-in/12.7-mm guns above the fuselage and also in a new ventral 'bathtub', and twin 0.3-in/7.62-mm guns both in the nose and in new flush side positions), and extra equipment. Despite the greater weight, the fitting of 1,200-hp (895-kW) engines made this the fastest of all the versions, with a maximum speed of 320 mph (519 km/h).

In spring 1941, a batch of 20 was assigned to the RAF, following 15 months of negotiations which finally resulted in the aircraft being supplied in exchange for complete information on their combat performance (this was prior to the 1940 Lend-Lease Act). As RAF Fortress Mk Is, they had a disastrous and mismanaged career (primarily due to poor tactics) which dramatically reduced their numbers to a handful (about nine); these were transferred to Coastal Command and to North Africa.

Further extensive internal improvements, a new electrical system and engine-cowl cooling gills led to the B-17D, of which 42 were ordered in 1940. This was the model in service at the time of Pearl Harbor.

Despite its troubled development and poor combat record at the beginning of World War II, Boeing continued to refine and develop the Flying Fortress. USAAC generals had dictated that the B-17 would be the US's prime strategic bomber.

Right: Seen here on a pre-delivery test flight, AN528 became 'B-BAKER' (the first of two) for the RAF with No. 90 Squadron. It was lost on 4 June 1941 when it caught fire while running up on the ground at Polebrook.

Below: Thirty B-17s were on the ground at Pearl Harbor. This B-17C was one of the examples that were airborne during the attack, and was struck by cannon fire as it landed at Hickam. A flare storage box ignited and the aircraft caught fire, with the tail breaking off on the runway. Eventually, the bomber came to rest just short of the Hale Makai barracks. One passenger was killed.

Fortress variants

The Flying Fortress was, with the B-24 Liberator, the cornerstone of the Army's strategic bomber force. Improvements to successive variants introduced during World War II focussed on improved performance and defensive capability.

B-17C and B-17D

Further refinements to the B-17 were introduced in the B-17C (first flown in July 1940), 38 of which were ordered by the USAAC. The major outward change was the replacement of the fuselage side gun blisters with flush-fitting ports, while the bottom blister was replaced with a larger 'bathtub' housing. Extra guns, armour plating and self-sealing fuel tanks were among defensive changes, while uprated R-1820-65 engines increased top speed and range. (Twenty of these aircraft were later passed to the RAF as Fortress Mk Is, below). The otherwise similar B-17D (above) had engine cowling flaps, a revised electrical system and an extra crew member; 42 were built.

Model 299 prototype

Sometimes referred to as the XB-17, the Model 299 prototype was in fact a company-owned aircraft and carried a civil registration (NX13372). Powered by four 750-hp (559-kW) Pratt & Whitney Hornet radials, armed with eight 600-lb (272-kg) bombs and four machine-guns and with a crew of eight, the aircraft made its first flight on 28 July 1935. The design was not given an Army designation until January 1936; NX13372 was wrecked in an accident on 30 October 1935 and, therefore, was never known officially as the 'XB-17'.

B-17E, B-17F and B-17G

Known to Boeing as the Model 299-O, the B-17E (the first of which is shown above) was a major rework of the basic aircraft. Its tail surfaces were enlarged and redesigned to incorporate a large dorsal fin, while defensive armament was increased by the addition of two-gun powered turrets behind the cockpit and in the bottom of the fuselage, along with a two-gun manually-operated 'stinger' in the extreme tail. From the 113th aircraft the remotely-sighted belly turret was replaced by a manned Sperry ball turret, these later aircraft becoming the first Fortresses to action in the European theatre, in August 1942. (B-17Cs and Ds had been active against the Japanese since late 1941.) After 512 B-17Es came the first B-17Fs. These differed in having a larger Plexiglas nose assembly, fully-feathering, paddle-bladed propellers and other internal changes including, in late production aircraft, extra fuel capacity and a cheek-mounted gun either side of the nose. The B-17F (bottom left) was also the first Fortress variant built by sub-contractors; of 3,405 constructed, 2,300 came from Boeing's Seattle factory, while Douglas and Lockheed-Vega delivered 605 and 500, respectively. The last production Fortress variant was the B-17G, distinguished from the F-model principally in having a two-gun chin turret (bottom right), though there were numerous detail changes made during production. Like the B-17F, the G had a crew of 10 and was powered by four R-1820-97s rated at 1,200 hp (895 kW) at 25,000 ft (7620 m). By far the most numerous B-17, 4,025 Gs were built by Boeing, 2,250 by Vega and 2,395 by Douglas.

Y1B-17 (YB-17) and Y1B-17A

Thirteen improved Model 299B aircraft were ordered in January 1936, in order that the US Army could test the design in service. Briefly known as YB-17s, the Y1B-17s (one of which is shown, above, in 2nd Bomb Group service) were powered by four 1,000-hp (746-kW) Wright R-1820 Cyclones, had a crew of six and could lift 8,000 lb (3629 kg) of bombs. One additional airframe was flown in April 1938; this Y1B-17A had been originally intended as a static test airframe, but was made airworthy for use as a testbed for turbo-supercharged R-1820-51 engines.

B-17B

The Flying Fortress (a name coined by a local reporter who had attended the Model 299's unveiling on 17 July 1935) entered production as the B-17B (Model 299M). Powered by uprated 1,200-hp (895-kW) R-1820-51 engines, the B-17B also differed from the Y1B-17 in having a larger rudder and flaps, a redesigned nose which eliminated the 'greenhouse' gun turret and a belly bomb-aiming window. In addition, crew positions were revised and hydraulic brakes adopted. The first example made its maiden flight on 27 June 1939; in all, 39 were completed.

XB-38

Interested in ways of improving the B-17's performance, the Air Corps commissioned Lockheed-Vega to re-engine a B-17E in 1943 with liquid-cooled Allison V-1710 engines. First flown on 19 May 1943, the XB-38 proved to slightly faster and its range was much improved. However, as the aircraft was lost, as a result of an in-flight fire, less than a month after its first flight, a full comparison with a B-17 could not be made; two further examples were cancelled.

XC-108, YC-108, XC-108A and XC-108B

Four B-17s were converted as C-108 transport aircraft, with a reworked interior and most (if not all) guns deleted: B-17E 41-2593 became the XC-108 *Bataan* (pictured), a special personal transport for Gen Douglas MacArthur; B-17F 42-6036 was converted as a similar YC-108 VIP aircraft; the XC-108A was an experimental cargo aircraft converted from a B-17E; also converted from a B-17F, the XC-108B was an attempt to determine the feasiblity of modifying Fortresses as fuel tankers for use on the Burma-China 'Hump' route.

XB-40, YB-40 and TB-40

An experimental bomber escort, the XB-40 was a B-17F fitted with an extra twin-gun turret in the radio compartment position and a twin-gun chin turret under its nose. Its waist stations were also equipped with a pair of '50-calibers' in place of the usual single gun. Extra ammunition was carried in lieu of fuel and a bomb load. Though a further 20 B-17Fs were converted to an refined YB-40 standard (below), along with four as TB-40 trainers, the concept was abandoned after limited service in Europe showed that the extra weight carried by these aircraft meant that they could not keep up with B-17s flying light on the return leg of their bombing missions.

F-9, F-9A, F-9B and F-9C (RB-17G)

These designations were applied to over 50 B-17Fs and Gs converted as long-range reconnaissance aircraft, with cameras installed in the nose, bomb bay and rear fuselage. Sixteen F-9s (ex-B-17Fs) were followed by an unknown number of F-9As with a different camera fit. All of the latter were later redesignated F-9B after further equipment changes, this variant totalling 25 aircraft, including additional aircraft converted from B-17Fs. Ten B-17Gs were reworked as F-9Cs (briefly known as FB-17Gs), being redesignated RB-17Gs in 1948. In addition to the above, at least one so-called RB-17G is known to have been operated by the CIA in the Far East as late as 1957.

BQ-7 guided bomb

About 25 war-weary B-17s were converted as radio-controlled BQ-7 flying bombs in 1944. Carrying 20,000 lb (9070 kg) of explosive and enough fuel for a range of 350 miles (563 km), was taken-off by a two-man crew before being handed over to radio-control by another B-17, the two crew bailing out. Between 4 August 1944 and 1 January 1945 15 BQ-7s were launched against targets in Germany, to little effect.

Post-war & naval derivatives

PB-1 and PB-1W

The US Navy had received 48 B-17s towards the end of, and shortly after, World War II (and known as PB-1s from 31 July 1945). Post-war, 31 B-17Gs were acquired and fitted with AN/APS-20 radar for an anti-submarine search role (below). Designated PB-1W, these aircraft were later replaced by Lockheed WV-2s.

Other post-war variants

Other minor Fortress variants, most modified from B-17Gs, included: **CB-17G** (converted as transports), **DB-17G** (drone director conversion; initially designated CQ-4), **JB-17G** (two engine testbeds – including 44-85813, below right, with a Wright XT35 Typhoon turboprop – originally known as EB-17Gs), **MB-17G** (designation given to a later version of the BQ-7), **QB-17G** (target drone conversion, below, often operated in conjunction with DB-17G), **TB-17G** (crew trainer conversion), **VB-17G** (staff transport conversion), **QB-17L** (target drone conversion with TV transmitters fitted), **QB-17N** (QB-17L with TV transmitters deleted and guidance equipment modified), **DB-17P** (drone director for QB-17s), **QB-17P** (former DB-17Ps converted as target drones).

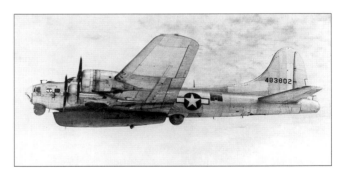

B-17H (SB-17G) and PB-1G

During 1945 plans existed for the conversion of about 130 B-17Gs to B-17H (above) and TB-17H standard, equipped with an airborne lifeboat and ASV radar for USAAF air-sea rescue duties. Only 12 B-17Hs were completed, becoming SB-17Gs in 1948. The US Coast Guard operated 17 similar aircraft as PB-1Gs, one of these aircraft (BuNo. 77254, below) being the last Fortress in US military service (other than target drones and directors), flying its last mission on 14 October 1959.

USAAF: European operations

Among **USAAF** aircraft, names tended to be patriotic such as Avenger of Yankee. Experience of combat operations, however, led to some definitely unofficial and more ambivalent nicknames such as **SNAFU** which was a B-17F.

Designed during the mid-1930s, the B-17 flew more than 290,000 sorties in the European Theatre of Operations and dropped in excess of half a million tons of bombs. Easy to fly, able to absorb a lot of punishment, yet only able to carry 4,000 lb (1814 kg) of bombs, the B-17 shared with, then eclipsed, the B-24 in the daylight bombing of the Third Reich.

The arrival of the United States into World War II required the establishment of the 8th Air Force in the United Kingdom, led by General Carl A. 'Tooey' Spaatz. General Ira C. Eaker, Commander of the subordinate VIII Bomber Command – and later to succeed General Spaatz – arrived during April 1942, followed on 29 February 1943 by the first of, eventually, thousands of B-17s.

First raids

The first raid was undertaken on 17 August 1942, by a dozen B-17Es of the 97th BG which attacked the railroad marshalling yards at Rouen, 35 miles (56 km) from the English Channel, without loss to themselves. Combat experience quickly led to the replacement of the B-17Es with the 'F', which had numerous interior changes, including self-sealing tanks. Having suffered to vindicate the concept of 'daylight precision bombing', in September 1942, the 8th's first three groups and a fourth sent directly from the US, were siphoned off to take part in the Allied invasion of North Africa. In exchange, four new groups arrived between September and late October, but throughout the rest of 1942 the 8th was unable to launch an attack on Nazi Germany proper.

'Round the clock' bombing

On 20 January 1943, at the Casablanca conference, General Eaker met Prime Minister Churchill and called for a 'round the clock' bombing campaign, with Bomber Command undertaking the night offensive, while

For returning bomber crews, the relief after a 12-hour mission was clear to see, but losses were horrific within the B-17 groups. At one time in mid-1943, the whole daylight bombing method was thrown into doubt.

the 8th Air Force bombed during the day. At the beginning of 1943, the 8th consisted of just six groups (four with B-17s and two with B-24 Liberators) each consisting of four nine-ship squadrons.

St Nazaire's U-boat base was the first target of 1943, bombed by 85 B-17s, while the first attack on Germany was launched on the 27 January against Wilhelmshaven using 55 B-17s, the primary target at Vegesack having been found to be under heavy cloud. The bombing was largely ineffective. During the next six months, the 8th tested its bombing theories on missions growing in size from 100 bombers

Clear weather gave good visual bombing results – but equally offered a good target for the enemy gunners. These B-17Fs prepare to drop on the leader's signal.

up to 300. Bomb damage was assessed by photographic missions, some flown by the F-9 reconnaissance version of the B-17. Escort fighters were introduced during the raid on 4 May 1943 on Antwerp, but the lack of range of the Republic P-47 Thunderbolt resulted in a gap in the protection on the long trips to the heart of Germany, where the Fortresses were most vulnerable to the German fighters.

'Blitz Week'

The first sustained aerial bombing against important industrial targets deep in the Reich, 'Blitz Week', started on 23 July 1943. By this time, Eaker had 15 bomb groups with well over 300 B-17s. On 24 July, 309 B-17s attacked targets in Norway, while 264 B-17s attacked Hamburg and

With fighters weaving overhead, 390 BG B-17Fs plough towards Germany. Contrails were a telltale sign of a bomber formation's position, but could disappear with a change in altitude of a few hundred feet.

Hanover the next day. Bad weather on 27 July prevented any missions, but on 28 July 302 B-17s attacked aircraft plants at Oschersleben and Kassel. 29 July saw 168 bombers attack Kiel, while 81 others bombed an aircraft factory in Warnemünde. Kassel was attacked on 30 July, by 186 B-17s. By the end of the month, the 8th had exhausted itself, having lost over 1,000 men and 105 B-17s to all causes during 'Blitz Week'. Strength had gone down from over 330 to 200 B-17s, requiring the first eleven days of August to rebuild lost strength. By mid August, the 8th Air Force was able to muster 16 B-17 groups. During September 1943, the first mission was flown using B-17s equipped with the H₂S or H₂X blind-bombing system as pathfinders.

Black week

From 8-14 October 1943, the 8th undertook four missions and lost 148 bombers. The first mission, to Bremen, was the first to use Carpet radio counter-measures. The Arado factory north of Berlin was visited on the 9 October, while the last major deep-penetration raid to take place, without escort 'all the way', occurred on 14 October, to the Schweinfurt ball bearing factory, and it paid a heavy price. The P-47 escort was 'bounced' early in the mission, forcing the majority to release their drop tanks. Of the 291 B-17s and B-24s that had set out, 60 were posted missing, 17 crashed or were written off on return and 121 had varying degrees of damage. Though long-range penetration missions were not abandoned, the tactics used where thrown into doubt.

This B-17F is from the 91st BG. This group led the infamous Schweinfurt raid on 17 August 1943. Memphis Belle, *which was among this group, became the first B-17 to complete the required 25 missions.*

Wing markings
The yellow tail markings of *Short Arm* denoted an aircraft of the 4th Combat Bomb Wing. The unit adopted yellow tail surfaces, for identification purposes, for a trial period after February 1945 and retained them until the end of the war.

Fighter escort
With the introduction of long-range fighters and, most notably, the P-51 Mustang in January 1944, bomber crews finally had air protection to Berlin and back.

B-17G Flying Fortress

Short Arm represents the definitive standard for a late-production Flying Fortress, as delivered to the 8th Air Force around the end of 1944 and, as such, combined all the refinements and experience incorporated from the earlier B-17Fs. The B-17G was one of the most heavily-armed bombers of the war, fielding up to 13 12.7-mm (0.50-in) machine-guns.

Late-war missions
The diminishing fighter opposition in the final months of the war allowed for the removal of some defensive guns as a weight-saving measure. This was a far cry from the initial daylight raids of by the B-17Es and B-17Fs, when Luftwaffe fighter opposition was intense.

Waist guns
The arrangement of the port gun forward and starboard gun further back became adopted as standard. The revised waist gun positions prevented 'fanny bumping', which was encountered on B-17Fs by gunners who complained that they had limited space in which to manoeuvre their guns during combat.

Group markings
In addition to the group identification letters, the 486th BG adopted three yellow bands around the fuselage and a red/blue chevron on the wings.

Tail turret
The 'Cheyenne' tail turret was introduced as a production item on late-build Douglas-built B-17s. It was said to give the gunner improved vision, sighting and traverse over the earlier-model turrets installed on B-17Fs.

USAAF: European operations

As fighter protection all the way to the target became a realistic proposition, the USAAF abandoned camouflage paint schemes. The transition from drab-finished aircraft to natural metal was slow, however, as aircraft were not stripped in the field and camouflaged machines only disappeared when they were lost or retired. Mixed formations were therefore a common sight.

Huge losses convinced USAAF leaders that the B-17 could not go to war over the Reich unescorted. With the advent of the P-51, however, the bombers could have 'little friends' all the way to Berlin.

The early Fortress missions were a steep learning experience for all concerned. With an increase in the size of the B-17 fleet, the availability of trained crews as the giant American war-machine geared up for all-out war, and the advent of the superb long-range Mustang escort fighter, 1944 was to be a critical year for the fortunes of the Europe-based B-17s.

Reducing losses
Despite the Fortress's strong defensive armament and the mutual support box formation that had been adopted, losses due to German fighters were relatively high. In order to improve the situation, several solutions were proposed. The use of head-on attacks by the German fighters resulted in the development of a nose turret for the Flying Fortress and this became a standard fit on the B-17G, which arrived in the European Theatre of Operations (ETO) during September 1943. Lockheed Vega developed the XB-40 and YB-40 escort bomber concepts – these aircraft

On 17 April 1945, over 1,000 B-17s and B-24s bombed railway bridges in the Dresden area and oil storage facilities in Czechoslovakia. The bridges were being used by retreating German forces.

were B-17s with extra guns and armour. Unfortunately, because of the extra weight, the B-40 could not keep up with the formation it was designed to protect and the idea was abandoned. It was the development and deployment of the long-range P-51 Mustang escort fighter, which could protect the bomber stream all the way to the

Napalm was occasionally used in the ETO from mid-1944. Nevertheless, it was not until 15 April 1945 that the weapon was used by the 8th AF. E-RAT-ICATOR is being prepared for that mission.

target and back, which was to be the greatest factor in reducing losses. The Mustang started to arrive in the ETO during last month of 1943.

Luftwaffe B-17s
Large numbers of aircraft were shot down over occupied territory and many were salvaged by the Germans. The Luftwaffe was able to put a number of crashed B-17s back into the air and used them for a variety of clandestine missions, such as dropping agents. One was used as a decoy, pretending to be a damaged American B-17 in need of

Having survived a strike against German synthetic oil plants and communications facilities, and almost reached their home bases, these B-17s entered dense cloud at relatively low level. The fiery aftermath of the almost inevitable collision is shown. There were no survivors.

Hound' missions. With the cessation of hostilities in Europe, a series of flights to take ground crews over the Ruhr was undertaken from 7 May 1945, giving them a chance to see some of the devastation caused by the bombers. While these flights were running, 'Revival' missions, the return of Allied prisoners of war from Germany and Austria, were also undertaken. Up to 40 former PoWs were crammed into each B-17.

Faded glory

The B-17 had helped to cripple the vital enemy war industries. Disruption caused by bombing, the dispersal of industry and the manpower and effort put into stopping the 'heavies' on the way to their targets had been a constant drain on the German war-machine. In all, 75 per cent of all the bombs dropped by the Eighth Air Force were done so after the Allies had landed on mainland Europe, and it was the B-17 and B-24 attacks against the oil and transport industries from May 1944 through to March 1945 which had brought the most benefit to the Allies.

At the end of the war in Europe, thousands of B-17s were returned to the United States, loaded with homeward-bound soldiers. The end of the war in the Pacific and the start of the nuclear age meant the cessation of the need for massive bomber formations of the type to which the European skies had grown accustomed. For the majority of B-17s that had fought in the ETO, only the melting pot awaited on return to America.

Since 1975, B-17G *Sally B* has been the only UK-based Fortress, a fitting tribute to the 3,219 B-17s that failed to return to base during European bomber operations.

A BIT O'LACE was assigned to the 709 BS of the 447 BG at Rattlesden, Norfolk, UK on 19 June 1944. The aircraft survived 83 missions to return to the US in July 1945.

support. Any American aircraft that came to help was then attacked. A trap was set for this aircraft, whereby one of the B-40 escort bombers was sent to the 'assistance' of the wounded aircraft, shooting it down when it was identified as hostile.

Against Berlin

On 6 March 1944 the B-17s of the US Eighth Army journeyed all the way to Berlin for the first time. In all, 474 bombers and their Mustang escort fighters flew to the German capital, facing a barrage of heavy flak and many Luftwaffe fighters. A total of 53 B-17s was lost, but it marked the beginning of the end for Germany. Any target could now be reached and bombed with the benefit of fighter escort.

BQ-7 flying bomb

Under Project Aphrodite, approximately 25 war-weary B-17s were converted to radio-control as BQ-7s. They were loaded with nine tons of high explosives, and used against heavily-defended German sites between 4 August 1944 and 1 January 1945. BQ-7s were actually put on course by a pilot, who then abandoned ship, control being passed to an accompanying aircraft. The project was not an outstanding success, partly due to the unreliability of the radio-control equipment.

D-Day and beyond

As D-Day approached, the B-17s were involved in tactical 'softening' raids on French communications facilities. By D-Day, the Allies had complete control of the air, and losses had been reduced. The summer bomber offensive saw the B-17s concentrating on oil, transport and military vehicle production centres and factories throughout the Third Reich. The number of B-17s available increased and the size of the formations rose accordingly. On 24 December 1944 more than 2,000 bombers, including 1,200 B-17s, bombed targets in Germany.

A total of 26 operational bombardment groups flew the B-17, including five groups that converted to the B-17 from the B-24 in late 1944. The number of B-17s with the Eighth Air Force in the ETO peaked in March 1945, when 2,367 aircraft were available. As the Allies advanced across Europe, the number of worthwhile targets available diminished.

Final missions

The final missions for the B-17s involved dropping food, rather than bombs, to the starving Dutch population, who were suffering from the effects of widespread flooding. These flights were known as 'Chow

Starving Dutch civilians were overjoyed to see cases of US Army rations cascading from the bomb bays of 8th AF Fortresses. This is a 569th Bomb Squadron, 390th Bomb Group aircraft.

Schweinfurt massacre

By the time the 1st CBW arrived back over its bases, it had lost 36 aircraft together with 371 crew members; 19 other B-17s were withdrawn from the combat-ready list for lengthy repairs.

Envisaged as an easy way to cripple the Reich's industrial base, the horror of the Schweinfurt raids had the opposite effect in virtually crippling the confidence and commitment of the USAAF. But in the American tradition, the USAAF never gave up.

The USAAF's 8th AF based in the UK was, by mid 1943, powerful enough to extend its operations deep into Germany. Planners targeted the German ball-bearing factories concentrated at Schweinfurt in southern Germany. The newly formed 1st Combat Bombardment Wing (Heavy) (CBW) was chosen for the mission in August 1943.

The original plan (Operation Juggler) called for the dispatch of 150 Boeing B-17Fs of the 4th CBW (Heavy) to bomb the big Messerschmitt factory at Regensburg-Prüfening and then to fly on to bases in North Africa.

These aircraft were to take off shortly before the 240 B-17s of the 1st CBW, which were to attack Schweinfurt. British and American Spitfires and P-47s would provide penetration cover as far as Brussels for the Regensburg raid, thereby attracting the great majority of enemy fighters into the air too soon to interfere seriously with the main raid on Schweinfurt. The German fighters would be forced to land and refuel at the critical time when the main force pushed through.

On 17 August, bad weather hampered operations, destroying these plans. Thick fog over the 4th CBW's bases delayed the Regensburg raiders. However, being based farther inland in the UK, where the fog persisted longer, the 1st CBW was unable to take off until 3 hours 30 minutes later. By this time the covering fighters were themselves on the ground refuelling.

By the time the 1st CBW

reached the Belgian coast, the enemy fighters had refuelled and were again on the alert. The leading box of 60 bombers was assaulted by successive waves of fighters from JG 26 and other units. Before the target was reached and bombed, this one box had lost 21 aircraft, and seven others had turned for home without bombing.

Subsequent reconnaissance disclosed that only two of the five vital ball-bearing plants had been significantly damaged. Postwar intelligence showed that bearing production was reduced by only 21 per cent, and then for not more than three weeks.

A second heavy raid was launched on 14 October by 291 B-17s. The leading 1st Division

American realisation that the raid had failed in its aims was reflected by the absence of any Distinguished Unit Citations among the 1st CBW's groups.

flew an almost direct route to the target, and the following 3rd Division followed a dogleg route in an attempt to confuse the enemy as to its eventual target. The former took the brunt of the German fighter reaction. Once

more 60 American bombers were lost to the Luftwaffe. On this occasion the bombing results were judged to be excellent, but unknown to the Allies the Germans had already disbursed their ball-bearing production.

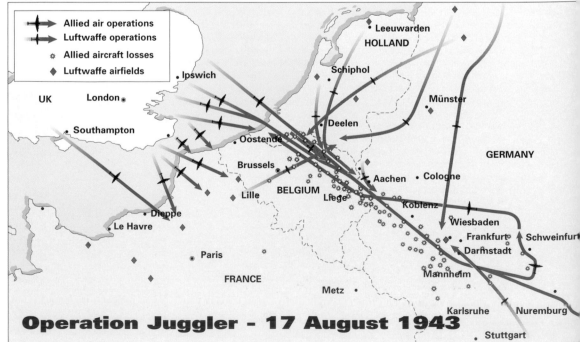

Allied air operations
Luftwaffe operations
Allied aircraft losses
Luftwaffe airfields

UK · London
· Ipswich
· Southampton
Leeuwarden
HOLLAND
Schiphol
Münster
Deelen
Oostende
Brussels
Lille BELGIUM Liège
Aachen · Cologne
GERMANY
Koblenz
Wiesbaden
Frankfurt Schweinfurt
Darmstadt
Mannheim
· Dieppe
· Le Havre
· Paris
FRANCE
Metz ·
Karlsruhe Nuremburg
Stuttgart

Operation Juggler - 17 August 1943

Having completed a bombing run against enemy supply lines in Tunisia, this B-17F (of the 414th Squadron, 97th Bomb Group) was hit by a German fighter with a dead pilot at the controls. The B-17 returned to base without any casualties aboard.

Mediterranean operations

Many students of air warfare are surprised to learn that there even was a 15th Air Force operating from Italy. The Axis countries had no doubts about the existence of the 'Thunder From the South'.

With no chance of an Allied landing on the European mainland in 1942, attention turned to driving the Axis forces from North Africa. In preparation for the landings, codenamed Operation Torch, the 12th Air Force (AF) was formed in the US. Entirely a paper organisation until its move to the UK in August, the new force set about creating the nucleus of a strategic bomber force by taking over the 97th and 301st BGs already established there. These two groups moved to Algeria, via Gibraltar, in time for the landings in November, and were followed by the 99th and 2nd BGs which had formed in the US. Together they formed the North African Strategic Air Force (NASAF) as part of the Mediterranean Air Command (MAC). The four groups took part in the Allied drive across North Africa, and were regarded as instrumental in the surrender without ground fighting in the last Axis stronghold in Africa, Pantelleria, in June 1943.

With North Africa secured, the heavy bombers were able to concentrate on softening up defences in southern Italy in preparation for the landings on Sicily. The first Allied air attack on Rome took place on 14 July and great care was taken by the 99th to avoid dropping any bombs on the Vatican City.

After Allied forces secured a foothold in Italy in the autumn of 1943, 12th Bomber Command was quickly re-established there. Allied advances northwards through Italy brought targets inside Germany within the range of B-17s based in the country. On 2 November 1943, the four B-17 groups of the 5th Wing and two B-24 groups of the 9th AF, were combined with two fighter groups to form the new 15th AF. On its first day of existence, the 15th flew a 1,600-mile (2575 km) round trip to bomb the Messerschmitt aircraft factory at Weiner Neustadt, Austria.

Once bases around Foggia in Italy became available, the 15th was able to reach targets in southern France, Germany, Poland, Czechoslovakia, and the Balkans, some of which were difficult to reach from England.

On 2 June 1944, in Operation Frantic, 130 B-17s bombed a rail yard at Debrecen, Hungary, and flew on to land at Poltava, Russia in the Ukraine. The bombing that day was excellent, and no flak or enemy fighters were encountered. This was the first of numerous shuttle missions to land on Russian soil and was deemed to be a success.

One of the most important achievements of the 15th AF was the reduction of the oil fields at Ploesti. In the spring and summer of 1944, the 15th AF opened a sustained campaign against these vital targets. Before the refineries around that city were shut down, following advances by the Red Army, their production had been reduced to a trickle.

The 15th AF destroyed half of all petroleum production in Europe, a good part of German fighter production, and crippled the enemy's transportation system over half of occupied Europe. The 15th flew 148,955 heavy bomber sorties and 87,732 fighter sorties, and dropped 303,842 tons of bombs on enemy targets in 12 countries, including major installations in eight capital cities.

The 15th, an outfit that the 8th AF referred to as 'minor leaguers,' had done a major-league job. This, in spite of the fact that the 15th had many fewer groups than the 8th AF.

As well as the Luftwaffe, the USAAF had to contend with poor operating conditions. The hostile climate increased routine maintenance on the Wright R-1820-97 Cyclone engines.

By 1944, nearly 60,000 airmen had flown missions to Ploesti alone. The missions expended some 13,000 tons of bombs, lost 350 heavy bombers, and left more than 3,000 airmen killed or captured.

Below: A B-17F returns to Biskra after raiding Tunis in December 1942 in support of US ground operations. The aircraft was lost in action over Palermo in April 1943.

British operations

AN530 was one of the original batch of 20 B-17C Fortress Mk Is to arrive in Britain. It commenced operations with No. 90 Squadron on 8 July 1941, taking part in a raid on Wilhelmshaven.

After an inauspicious debut, the B-17 slowly found favour within the RAF. While conventional RAF bombing missions were never the Fortress's forte, coastal support and special duties played an important part in the British B-17's war.

This view clearly shows the radar aerials fitted underneath the wings and above the nose of Coastal Command B-17F Fortress Mk IIAs. This aircraft was operated by No. 220 Squadron based at Ballykelly, Derry, Northern Ireland.

First flying in 1934, the Boeing B-17 soon found itself in demand from a beleaguered RAF embroiled in the war with Germany. Small-scale production in the USA allowed service trials to continue and, by the time the RAF found itself at war, Boeing was producing the B-17C variant, featuring heavier armament (10 machine-guns in all) and dispensing with the large lateral blisters but introducing a large ventral 'bathtub'.

Committed to the development of heavy bombers for night operation, the RAF was unsure that the B-17 would be useful for European operations, but was ready to put it to the test. In an unusual deal concluded in March 1940, the US government agreed to release 20 B-17Cs to Britain in exchange for detailed information on their operation in combat. Known as Fortress Mk Is, these aircraft arrived early in 1941 and were used to equip No. 90 Sqn based at West Raynham. Moving to Polebrook for operations, the squadron took the Fortress into battle for the first time on 8 July 1941, when three of the bombers attacked Wilhelmshaven.

The USAAC believed that the B-17s should be used in multi-ship formations to benefit from mutual defensive fire. The RAF missions, however, were flown mostly on an individual basis, operating in daylight at heights up to 30,000 ft (9144 m). By the end of September, 26 raids had been launched, totalling 51 sorties, but half of these had been aborted with no bombs dropped. Many difficulties were encountered, particularly with guns freezing up and with the operation of the Sperry bomb-sight (use of the more advanced Norden sight had been denied to Britain). Seven aircraft were lost.

The RAF concluded, not unreasonably, that the Fortress, at least in the form in which it was then operating, was unsuitable for the European theatre. A detachment of No. 90 Sqn was sent to Shallufa, Egypt – losing another Fortress Mk I in January 1942 – but was then redesignated No. 220 Sqn; the existing No. 220 Sqn, flying Hudsons in Coastal Command, moved to Polegate, took over the remainder of the Fortresses and took them to Northern Ireland to fly anti-submarine patrols. Joined there by the detachment from Egypt, No. 220 Sqn's strength grew to eight Fortress Mk Is, which remained in service until July. In preparation for operations with later marks of the Fortress, No. 206 Sqn, also in Coastal Command, briefly flew four of the Mk Is, and No. 214 – which would eventually specialise in radio countermeasures with Fortress Mk IIs and Mk IIIs – also used a couple of Mk Is for training.

The ignominious debut of the B-17 in Europe notwithstanding, the RAF sought the inclusion of substantial numbers of later, improved, models in the Lend-Lease programme, initially calling for 300 B-17Fs which it designated Fortress B.Mk II. In the event, only 19 of this batch materialised as the USAAF's needs had by this time become paramount and production could not keep pace with demand. They were preceded during 1942 by 46 Fortress B.Mk IIAs (of 84 requested), these being B-17Es from USAAF stocks. Differences between the B-17E and B-17F were minimal, but both represented a considerable improvement over the Fortress Mk I with two-gun dorsal and ventral ball turrets, and better mounts for the tail and beam guns. A longer rear fuselage with

Brand-new Fortress Mk Is are lined up in the USA awaiting delivery to the RAF. They have the ventral 'bathtub', which was inadequately armed with a single 0.50-in (12.7-mm) machine-gun.

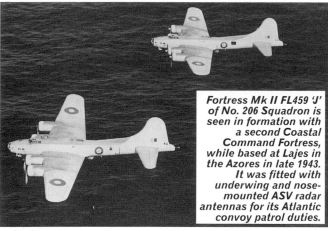

Fortress Mk II FL459 'J' of No. 206 Squadron is seen in formation with a second Coastal Command Fortress, while based at Lajes in the Azores in late 1943. It was fitted with underwing and nose-mounted ASV radar antennas for its Atlantic convoy patrol duties.

a large dorsal fin was a ready identification feature.

In the RAF, the new Fortresses were dedicated to Coastal Command service – designations changing to GR.Mk II and GR.Mk IIA – their long range and heavy armament making them especially suitable for overwater patrols. Already flying the Fortress Mk I, No. 220 Sqn was first to operate the Mk II/IIAs, from Ballykelly. It was soon joined by No. 206 Sqn at Benbecula and then by No. 59 Sqn at St Eval to cover the Western Approaches. In the hands of these units, the Fortresses made a major contribution to closing the mid-Atlantic 'gap' where U-boats were operating. To combat the U-boat, the Fortress relied upon the standard Torpex-filled Mk VII or Mk VIII depth charge, and the ASV Mk III radar, with its distinctive 'stickle-back' fuselage aerials and underwing Yagi aerials.

As part of No. 15 Group, the Fortress squadrons sank 10 U-boats between 27 October 1942 and 11 June 1943, the first success being scored by No. 206

Sqn. Both this unit and No. 220 Sqn then moved to the Azores and scored three more kills. With a decline in the U-boat threat, and the availability of Liberators and Sunderlands in larger numbers, other roles were found for the Fortress. In particular, No. 519 Sqn at Wick and No. 521 at Docking flew the type on long-range weather reconnaissance and No. 251 Sqn used it for ASR and met. work out of Iceland.

Another important role was found for the type when deliveries began to the RAF of the B-17G version, identified as the Fortress B.Mk III. From an initial batch of 60 deliveries in March 1944, 13 were diverted to the USAAF another 38 following later in 1944 and 1945. After appropriate modification, these aircraft were issued to No. 214 Sqn to operate in the new role of Special Duties in No. 100 Group, based at Oulton.

To allow this unit to begin training, 14 B-17Fs were transferred to the RAF from 8th Air Force stocks in the UK; these were designated Fortress Mk II(SD) after modification, matched by the Fortress

Mk III(SD) (B-17G). Externally, the modifications were visible by the variety of aerials required for the radio countermeasures role, with a number of different standards being adopted. The basic modification included a Monica Mk IIIA tail-warning receiver, a Jostle Mk IV VHF jammer, four Airborne Grocer AI jammers, Gee and Loran navigation aids and an H$_2$S navigation radar. Other jamming devices, such as the anti-V-2 Big Ben Jostle were introduced later. The H$_2$S scanner was contained in a large perspex fairing under the nose, replacing the chin turret of the standard B-17G bomber.

No. 214 Sqn flew its first operational sortie, with a Fortress Mk II(SD), on 20/21 April 1944. From then until the end of the war it flew more than 1,000 sorties, losing eight aircraft. In May 1945, No. 223(SD) Sqn at Oulton converted from B-24s to B-17s, but flew only four sorties. No. 1969 Flt, also at Oulton, provided conversion training on the Special Duties Fortresses.

The RAF promptly retired its Fortresses at the end of the war, with the survivors being scrapped in the UK.

Crew
Like most USAAF Fortresses, those of 100 Group carried a crew of 10, but its composition more closely reflected RAF heavy bomber practice. The crew consisted of pilot, flight engineer, bomb-aimer, two navigators, a special operator for the jamming equipment, and four gunners (two waist or 'beam', dorsal turret and tail turret).

Fortress B.Mk III(SD)

No. 100 (Special Duties) Group was formed in November 1943, to co-ordinate radar countermeasures (RCM) and other deception efforts within Bomber Command. Prior to this, diversionary and defence suppression efforts had been the responsibility of a variety of units spread across the Command, and were diverting an increasing number of bombers away from their prime tasks. This aircraft flew with No. 214 (SD) Sqn from Oulton.

No. 100(SD) Group
The group operated six squadrons of heavy bombers, including all the main four-engined types (sometimes mixed within squadrons), as well as 15 primarily equipped with the Mosquito. Other types used by 100 Group included the Beaufighter, Wellington and Defiant.

Aerials and equipment
The Fortresses and other bombers of No. 100 Group were festooned with aerials and radomes. Each of these was associated with an item of jamming or listening equipment. The principal aerials on this aircraft and their functions were (from nose to tail): **H$_2$S:** (chin radome) ground-mapping navigation radar. **Piperack:** (whip aerials above wings) radar jammer, particularly Air Intercept (AI). **Carpet:** (under mid-fuselage aerial) jammer directed at Würzburg GCI radars. **ABC (Airborne Cigar):** (large upper fuselage aerial) jammer for German radio (R/T) transmissions and homing beacons. A shorter aerial at this point signified a **Jostle** transmitter for jamming R/T across all six bands. **Window:** chute (below waist windows) for radar-deceiving chaff. **Airborne Grocer:** (either side of tail turret) jammer for AI radars. **Monica:** (between tail guns) tail warning radar.

Boeing
B-29 Superfortress

As well as the Boeing plants at Wichita and Renton, Bell Aircraft and Glenn L. Martin factories produced almost 900 Superfortresses. Here, newly-completed, Renton-built B-29A-5-BN 42-93869 cruises at altitude for a company photographer.

The first 'A-bomber'

No other aircraft ever combined as many technological advances as the B-29. Designed for a specific strategic task, it later spawned the double-deck Stratocruiser airliner and the KC-97 tanker/transport, and laid the foundations for the super-successful Boeing airliner series.

As well as being noteworthy for its technological advances, the B-29 also provided the Soviet Union with the starting block for the entire Tupolev heavy aircraft lineage, when US aircraft force-landed on Soviet territory at the end of World War II.

Even more amazing was that work on the Boeing B-29 Superfortress had commenced more than three years before the USA entered World War II, in October 1938. In one of his last acts before he was killed in a crash at Burbank, the US Army Air Corps Chief of Staff, General Oscar Westover, had officially established a requirement for a new superbomber to succeed the Boeing B-17, at a time when the B-17 itself was being denied funds by Congress. Despite a totally negative reaction from the War Department, procurement chief General Oliver Echols never gave up in his fight to keep the superbomber alive, and it had the backing of 'Hap' Arnold, Westover's successor.

Destined to remain with Boeing as a test aircraft for the duration of the war, the first of three XB-29 prototypes is readied for its maiden flight at Seattle on 21 September 1942.

The bomber was to be pressurised to fly very quickly at high altitude; the figures for speed (390 mph/628 km/h), range (5,333 miles/8582 km) and military load (up to 20,000 lb/907 kg) were staggering.

Design solutions

At the Boeing Airplane Company in Seattle there was, at least, experience of large pressurised aircraft, unlike all other companies. For most of 1939 the answer to conflicting design demands seemed to be to fit Pratt & Whitney's slim, sleeve-valve, liquid-cooled engines inside the wing, but newly-hired George Schairer soon pointed out that, as the biggest drag item was the wing, the best course was to make the wing as small as possible and

The B-29's pressurised forward section held seven of its 11 crew, namely the pilot, co-pilot, flight engineer, navigator, bombardier, radio operator and (if radar was installed) a radar operator.

not try to put engines inside it. (Thus began a basic philosophy which saw a sharp contrast between the Boeing B-47 and the British V-bombers, and which has continued to today's Boeing Models 757 and 767.) How does one pressurise a fuselage containing enormous bomb doors? The answer was to make the colossal bomb bays unpressurised and to link the front and rear pressure

cabins by a sealed tunnel. Chief engineer Wellwood Beall was first to crawl through the mock-up tunnel in January 1940.

By March 1940 the demands had increased, including 16,000 lb (7258 kg) of bombs for short-range missions, powered turrets, and far more protection including armour and self-sealing tanks. Weight had already leapt in stages from 48,000 to 85,000 lb

wing-loading was all against the designers, but using four monster Wright R-3350 Duplex Cyclones, each with not one, but two, of General Electric's best turbochargers and driving 16-ft 7-in (5.05-m) Hamilton Standard four-bladed propellers, the propulsion was equal to the task.

Fuselage structure

Behind the nose section were two giant bomb bays, from which an electric sequencing system released bombs alternately from front and rear to preserve the centre-of-gravity position. Between the two bays was a ring forming the structural heart of the aircraft and integral with the main wing box, the strongest aircraft part built up to that time. On the wing were four huge nacelles, which Schairer showed to have less drag than engines buried in a bigger wing. After four main gears had been studied, a way was found to fold simple two-wheel gears into the inboard nacelles. Fowler flaps were screwed out electrically to add 21 per cent to the wing area, fighting a wing-loading which, by September 1940, reached 71.9 lb/sq ft (351.1 kg/m²) and climbed to a frightening 81.1 lb/sq ft (396 kg/m²) by the time of the first combat mission.

Behind the wing the rear pressure cabin had three sighting stations linked to two upper and two lower turrets, each with twin 0.5-in (12.7-mm) machine-guns. The electric fire control was normally set so that the top station controlled either or both of the upper turrets, the side stations the lower rear turret, and the bombardier the forward lower turret, but control could be overridden or switched (because gunners could be knocked out in action). In the extreme tail was another gunner driving a turret with two 0.5-in (12.7-mm) guns and a 20-mm cannon. More than 2,000 B-29s were to be built before the tail turret went into production.

Immediately after Pearl Harbor, a colossal B-29 manufacturing programme was organised, with vast new plants set up across the nation.

(21773 to 38556 kg), and with the new requirements the design finally rounded out at a daunting 120,000 lb (54432 kg). With just 1,739 sq ft (161.55 m²) of wing, the wing-loading was going to be 69 lb/sq ft (336.9 kg/m²), about

double the figure universally taken in 1940 as the desirable limit. Test pilot Eddie Allen was happy that the Boeing Model 345 would be flyable (just) if it had the biggest and most powerful high-lift flaps ever thought of, in order to reduce take-off and landing speeds to about 160 mph (257 km/h), which was about double the equivalent speed of such familiar machines as the B-17 and Spitfire.

As the BEF was rescued from the beaches at Dunkirk, the new bomber was designated the B-29, and in August the US Army Air Corps provided funds for two (later three) prototypes. Work was rushed ahead, but nobody knew how to stop guns and propeller mechanisms from freezing at far more than 30,000 ft (9145 m), a height which Boeing was confident the aircraft could reach. The intense

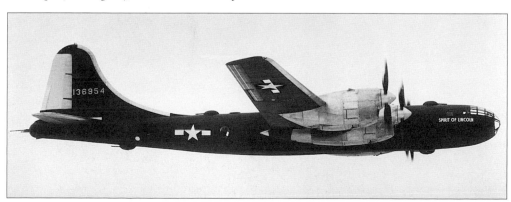

136954

SPIRIT OF LINCOLN

The B-29's first combat missions were flown from India to targets in Burma, raids in Japan from bases in China beginning shortly afterwards. In this dramatic photograph, B-29s of the 468th Bomb Group, 20th Air Force unload over a Japanese supply depot close to Mingaladon airfield near Rangoon.

This dispersal is on an island in the Marianas group – one of a number (including Saipan, Tinian and Guam) that played host to scores of B-29s during the last months of the war in the Pacific.

Superfortress at war

Elaborate planning was necessary to bring about production of the B-29 in adequate numbers when it was realised that the Superfortress was the only aircraft available with sufficient range to reach Japan.

Major B-29 components were made in over 60 new factories, the enormous nacelles – each as big as a P-47 – coming from a new Cleveland facility operated by the Fisher Body Division of General Motors. Final assembly was organised at three of the world's largest buildings: Boeing at Wichita, Martin at Omaha and Bell at Marietta. Later, yet another line was set up at Boeing Renton. All this had been organised before the Olive Drab XB-29 (41-002) had even flown, but from the first flight, on 21 September 1942 (initially using three-bladed propellers), it was clear that the B-29 was going to be a winner. It could so easily have been what test pilots then called 'a dog', and one of the firms delegated to build B-29s was convinced that Boeing's figures were far too optimistic and that the whole programme was a giant mistake. What made the B-29, by 1942 named Superfortress, now vitally important was that it was obviously going to be the only aircraft with the range to attack Japan.

To say that the good results of ship 41-002 were a relief would

be an understatement. Far more money ($3 billion) had been invested in the B-29 programme long before its wheels left the ground than in any other project in the history of any nation. At the same time, the technical snags were severe, and they multiplied. Many, such as powerplant fires and runaway propellers, were highly dangerous, and three months into the flight programme, the prototypes had logged just 31 of the 180 hours scheduled.

Complex and faulty

Even when the Superfortresses trickled and then poured off the lines, they were so complex that nobody in uniform fully understood them. All went to a modification centre at Salina, Kansas, where over 9,900 faults in the first 175, urgently needed for the new 20th Bomb Wing, were quickly corrected by a task force of 600 men in 'The Battle of Kansas'. Sheer manpower and the USA's mighty industrial power forced the obstacles out of the way, and the B-29s not only began racking up the hours but their baffled crews gradually learned

how to manage them, how to fly straight and level in a 'goldfish bowl' without continuously using instruments, and above all how to obtain something faintly resembling the published range with heavy bombloads. Air miles per pound of fuel were improved by exactly 100 per cent between January and March 1944. And the complex systems grew reliable in the ultra cold of 33,000 ft (10060 m).

On 5 June 1944 the first combat mission was flown from

Kharagpur, India, to Bangkok; the worst problem was an unexpected tropical storm. On 15 June the first of the raids on Japan was mounted, from Chengdu (one of many newly-bulldozed B-29 strips in China) to the Yawata steel works. The specially created 20th Air Force grew in muscle, and in October 1944 the first B-29s arrived on newly-laid runways on the Marianas islands of Tinian, Saipan and Guam, just taken from the enemy. The numbers grew swiftly as the mighty plants back home poured out B-29s and B-29As with 12 in (30 cm) more span and the four-gun front turret, while Bell added 311

Anti-aircraft fire and Japanese fighters claimed a number of aircraft. This machine made an emergency landing on Iwo Jima, having sustained battle damage. Unfortunately, it careered off the runway on landing and into the flight line, colliding with a P-51.

Defensive armament
Defensive armament consisted of pairs of 0.5-in (12.7-mm) machine-guns in four remotely-operated turrets and a manned turret in the tail. The latter also carried a 20-mm cannon and a camera to record results.

Powerplant
Four Wright R-3350-23 Duplex Cyclones rated at 2,200 hp (1641 kW) powered the Superfortress. Throughout its early career the R-3350 proved extremely troublesome, proving highly susceptible to fires. A large development effort by the manufacturer and in the field eventually solved many of the problems.

Bomb bay
Up to 20,000 lb (9072 kg) of bombs could be carried in two bomb bays situated either side of the wing centre-section. Bombs were usually carried in vertical stacks. The space between the bomb bays was used to mount the APQ-13 or Eagle BTO (bombing through overcast) radar in aircraft so-equipped.

B-29 Superfortress

The Big Stick was a typical Superfortress of the 73rd Bomb Wing – the first unit to assemble in the Marianas and comprising the 497th, 498th, 499th and 500th Bomb Sqns. A 500th BS aircraft, The Big Stick was based on Saipan in 1945.

B-29Bs with all armament stripped except that in the tail, making a considerable difference in reduced weight and complexity. The B-29B was made possible by the patchy fighter opposition, and many Superfortresses were similarly stripped in the field.

Moreover, the commander of the XXI Bomber Command, Major General Curtis LeMay, boldly decided to bomb Tokyo by night from low level, with a full load of incendiaries. There were many reasons for this, but the chief ones were that it promised much greater bombloads and the elimination of bombing errors attributable to jetstream winds. This policy, totally at variance with the idea of high-altitude day formations, resulted in the greatest firestorms the world has ever seen, and the biggest casualties ever caused by air attack. They were far greater than the 75,000 of Hiroshima, hit by the 20-kT Little Boy atom bomb dropped on 6 August 1945 from Colonel Paul Tibbetts' B-29 *Enola Gay*, or the 35,000 of Nagasaki hit by the 20-kT Fat Man dropped on 9 August from *Bock's Car*. The war ended five days later.

Only by the incredibly bold decision to go into the biggest multi-company production programme ever organised long before the first flight, did the B-29 manage to make so large a contribution to World War II. By VJ-Day more than 2,000 were actually with combat crews, and although 5,000-plus were cancelled days later, the manufacturing programme was slowed progressively, and did not close until May 1946, by which time 3,960 B-29s had been built. Hundreds were modified for different tasks, and many were launched on new careers as air/sea rescue aircraft, turbojet testbeds or tankers, which kept them busy for another decade or more. One hundred and eighteen B-29s and B-29As were converted as camera-equipped F-13 and F-13A reconnaissance aircraft to cover the raids on Japan from December 1944.

Above: As a B-29 of the 73rd Bomb Wing on Saipan is re-armed and 'bombed up', ground crew add their own personal messages to 2,000-lb (907-kg) bombs destined for targets in Japan.

Right: Perhaps the most famous B-29 of them all was Enola Gay, used to deliver the first atomic weapon to the Japanese city of Hiroshima. The 'circle R' on the aircraft's tail was a 313th BW marking.

Boeing P-26 'Peashooter'

Petite pursuit

America's first all-metal fighter to enter production, Boeing's 'Peashooter' was the last USAAC fighter to enter service with an open cockpit and fixed landing gear.

In 1931 the Boeing Airplane Company proposed a monoplane pursuit powered by the Pratt & Whitney R-1340 nine-cylinder air-cooled radial engine as the Boeing Model 248. A contract was issued by the US Army for three XP-936 prototypes, which would remain the property of the company for the period of an evaluation.

Construction started in 1932 and in only nine weeks the first was completed, with its first flight being made on 20 March, before its delivery to Wright Field. The second XP-936 was used as a static test airframe after

an initial assessment by the US Navy, while the final prototype was sent to Selfridge Field, Michigan, for evaluation by an active USAAC unit. The US Army was impressed with the new fighter and purchased the three prototypes from Boeing. They became XP-26s, later Y1P-26s and finally P-26s.

The all metal P-26 showed a good turn of speed compared to contemporary biplanes. With a 525-hp (392-kW) engine, the P-26 demonstrated a speed of 227 mph (365 km/h) at 10,000 ft (3050 m) while the biplane P-12E with a 500-hp

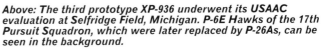

Above: The third prototype XP-936 underwent its USAAC evaluation at Selfridge Field, Michigan. P-6E Hawks of the 17th Pursuit Squadron, which were later replaced by P-26As, can be seen in the background.

Top: Seen flying above Hawaii in March 1939, this P-26C of the 19th Pursuit Squadron/18th Pursuit Group was based at Wheeler Field. By then, home defence P-26s were being replaced.

(373-kW) engine recorded 189 mph (304 km/h). Armament initially comprised of a pair of 0.3-in (7.62-mm) forward firing machine-guns, but provision was also provided for the carriage of up to 112 lb (51 kg) of bombs.

On 11 January 1933 the US Army ordered 111 examples of

an improved service version as the P-26A (Boeing Model 266). This order was later increased to 136. The production P-26A differed from the XP-936s in that it had an increased wing span, modified wheel spats, 600-hp (373-kW) Pratt & Whitney R-1340-27 in place of the R-1340-21, one or both of the 0.3-in (7.62-mm) guns replaced by 0.5-in (12.7-mm) calibre guns, the ability to carry either two 100-lb (45-kg) or five 30-lb (13.6-kg) bombs and, after an early production P-26A had overturned on landing, a strengthened headrest fairing. The first production P-26A was delivered on 16 December 1933 and upon entry to service the type gained the nickname 'Peashooter', because of its size

Having evaluated an XP-936, the three squadrons of the 1st Pursuit Group were the first operational unit to gain the 'Peashooter'. Each squadron was identified by a different coloured sash around the fuselage, these 94th PS aircraft using a red marking.

The 34th Pursuit Squadron/17th Pursuit Group operated the P-26A (illustrated) for just under a year, before re-equipping with the Northrop A-17 as the 17th Attack Group. This example has an underfuselage bomb rack.

and speed. It remained the fastest aircraft in service until the arrival of the Seversky P-35 and Curtiss P-36A in 1938.

Of the additional 25 aircraft ordered, two were powered by the R-1340-33 engine with fuel injection as P-26Bs (Model 266A), with the first flying on 10 January 1935. The rest, similarly engined and equipped, but initially without fuel injectors, were P-26Cs. Delivery started in February 1936, and the majority (if not all) were later fitted with injectors to become P-26Bs.

USAAC service

The first service user of the 'Peashooter' was the 1st Pursuit Group (comprising of the 17th, 27th and 94th Pursuit Squadrons) based at Selfridge Field, Michigan. The 27th and 94th gave up the type in 1938, but the 17th continued with the 'Peashooter' until 1941.

Second was the 17th Pursuit Group (34th, 73rd and 95th Pursuit Squadrons) at March Field, California, which used the aircraft from 1934 until it was assigned the attack role the following year. That year the 20th Pursuit Group (55th, 77th and 79th Pursuit Squadrons) at Barksdale, Louisiana became the last continental based group to receive the 'Peashooter'.

From 1938, P-35s and P-36s replaced the 'Peashooter' with home defence units and the P-26s were sent further afield. The 16th Pursuit Group, whose 24th and 29th Pursuit Squadrons were based at Albrook Field, Canal Zone, Panama, gained the type during 1938-1939, with the final squadron of the group, the 78th based at Wheeler Field on Hawaii, gaining the P-26 in 1940. Alongside the 16th group at Albrook Field, the 37th Pursuit Group's 28th, 30th and 31st squadrons used the aircraft from 1940. The 28th and 30th Pursuit squadrons passed on their

'Peashooters' to the 32nd PG, while the 31st Pursuit Squadron was still flying P-26s in 1942 - as the last American front-line operator. The 32nd Pursuit Group used the ex-37th group aircraft for a further year until the closing months of 1941.

Alongside the 78th PS/16th PG at Wheeler Field, Hawaii, was the 18th PG whose 6th and 19th squadrons operated 'Peashooters' between 1938 and 1941. The group re-equipped with the Curtiss P-40 before the Japanese attack on Pearl Harbor.

With an eye on the export market, Boeing produced the Model 281, which initially differed from the USAAC P-26A by the introduction of split landing flaps to reduce landing speed. These were later fitted to all USAAC aircraft.

Foreign users

Only twelve Model 281s were produced, with eleven going to the (Nationalist) Chinese to aid their fight against the Japanese and the final example to (Republican) Spain.

The first Chinese P-26 arrived in-country on 15 September 1934, the others arriving within fifteen months. They equipped

one pursuit squadron and achieved some successes against the superior Japanese forces, but a lack of spare parts eventually forced their retirement.

Ex-USAAC 'Peashooters' were sold to Guatemala and the Philippines. When Japan attacked the Phillipines the first Japanese aircraft to be shot down over the islands was credited to a 'Peashooter'.

Two withdrawn USAAC examples were sold to the Guatemalan Cuerpo de Aeronautica Militar in 1941 and these, along with other examples acquired from US units based in Panama, formed Guatemala's first fighter squadron. Six of these aircraft were still in service just after World War II and two even participated in a flypast (escorting a C-47) to celebrate the coming to power of Castillo Armas in July 1954.

Survivors

Two examples of the P-26 are known to have survived. One is located at The Air Museum 'Planes of Fame' at Chino Airport, California, and the second is on display at the National Air and Space Museum in Washington, D.C. Both aircraft are ex-Guatemalan examples that were returned to the United States in 1957.

Col Jesus Villamor poses on the wing of a P-26C of the Phillipines Army Air Force. These ex-USAAC aircraft had some local modifications made to ease operations from rough and ready bases. This example has modified spats.

Below: One of two surviving examples, the 'Planes of Fame' P-26A flew with the USAAC in Panama, and the Guatemalan air force, before being put on display in California.

Bristol **Beaufighter**

From fighter to 'Torbeau'

Above: Apart from night-fighting, the role with which the Beaufighter became most associated was that of maritime strike. Here, a No. 455 Sqn, RAAF Beaufighter Mk X, based in Scotland, releases all of its eight rockets at a seaborne target.

Left: R2052 was the first of four Beaufighter prototypes and initially flew six weeks before the beginning of World War II. Here it is seen in unpainted form around the time of its completion.

Developed as a private venture by the Bristol Aeroplane Company, the Beaufighter was a two-seat, all-metal fighter using components (wings, rear fuselage, tail unit and landing gear) from the Beaufort torpedo-bomber. This unlikely evolution, in fact, produced a highly successful aircraft.

First flown on 17 July 1939, the Beaufighter eventually equipped 52 operational RAF squadrons, giving outstanding service during World War II, in particular as a night-fighter and maritime strike aircraft.

In its original form, the Beaufighter Mk I was powered by two 1,400-hp (1044-kW) Bristol Hercules III radial engines and was capable of 309 mph (497 km/h) at 15,000 ft (4572 m) – some 26 mph (42 km/h) slower than the 335 mph (539 km/h)

expected of the aircraft. With this top speed inferior to that of the single-engined Hurricane, the Beaufighter was immediately judged unsuitable for the home-based day fighter role. But with Luftwaffe night-bombing raids on the increase, it was adapted to carry AI Mk IV radar as a night-fighter, replacing the makeshift Blenheim Mk IF.

First night-fighters

The Mk I's armament comprised four 20-mm cannon

in the forward fuselage and six 0.303-in (7.7-mm) machine-guns in the wings, the first radar-equipped examples entering service experimentally with Fighter Command in August 1940. The following month, five squadrons received Mk IFs, No. 604 Sqn scoring the first victory by a Beaufighter using AI Mk IV radar on the night of 19/20 November. By the end of 1941, AI-equipped Beaufighters were serving with 10 UK-based squadrons.

The German invasion of Crete in April 1941 highlighted the need for a long-range day fighter and prompted the deployment of the Beaufighter Mk IC (the 'C' indicating Coastal Command; the Mk I night-fighter was retrospectively redesignated Mk IF, for Fighter Command).

Mk ICs entered service with a detachment of No. 252 Sqn from Malta the following month.

Many were modified locally to carry two 250-lb (114-kg) or 500-lb (227-kg) bombs under the fuselage for ground-attack duties. Such was the success of the type in the Mediterranean and in Italy, that Coastal Command became the major Beaufighter operator.

The Beaufighter Mk II followed the Mk I into service, but was powered by Rolls-Royce Merlin XX engines, taken from Lancaster bomber production, as insurance against Hercules shortages. All were completed as Mk IIF night-fighters. The Beaufighter's distinctive 12°-dihedral tailplane, introduced to cure longitudinal instability in the climb, made its first appearance on the Mk II and became a standard feature of late-production Mk I and Mk II aircraft and all subsequent marks.

Beaufighters of Mks III, IV and V failed to see service. The

Above: Rolls-Royce Merlin-engined and AI Mk IV radar-equipped, this is the Mk IIF night-fighter prototype, also with an experimental dorsal fin which was later fitted as standard on the Beaufighter Mk X.

Right: No. 252 Sqn, RAF was the first Coastal Command unit equipped with Beaufighter Mk Is, from December 1940. On this example, the early straight tailplane may be seen.

Left: Crew pose with their torpedo-armed Coastal Command TF.Mk X, or 'Torbeau'. Note the four Hispano cannon ports in the lower fuselage and the nose-mounted strike camera. Beaufighters generally flew with two crew, although a third crew member could be accommodated to assist in torpedo-aiming.

Below: This late-production Beaufighter TF.Mk X is fitted with AI Mk VIII radar in a thimble nose radome, four rails for 60-lb (27-kg) rocket projectiles under each wing and the dihedral tailplane.

Mk III and Mk IV were so-called 'sports model' fighter variants of the Mk I and Mk II respectively, with slimmer rear fuselages. The Mk V reached prototype stage and was essentially a Mk II fitted with a four-gun Boulton Paul turret behind the cockpit. However, this ungainly conversion was rejected, the turret offering few benefits.

By mid-1941, as the Luftwaffe's night raids were scaled down, night-fighter units had begun intruder sorties over France and Belgium. Other aircraft were engaged in bomber escort duties, as decoys for German night-fighters. Soon a new Beaufighter variant began to appear.

In spring 1942, Coastal Command took delivery of Beaufighter Mk VICs, with 1,650-hp (1230-kW) Hercules VIs. The anti-shipping role was an increasingly important one, Beaufighters seeing action against shipping and submarines in the North Sea and Bay of Biscay, in

particular. However, as the Hercules VI produced peak power at a higher altitude, it was better suited to the night-fighter role. Thus, a fighter version, the Mk VIF (with AI Mk VIII radar), was issued to night-fighter units from March 1942. Mk VIFs were sent to the Far East where three squadrons operated the type in a night interdiction role, and two other squadrons took their aircraft to North Africa in the spring of the following year.

Torpedo-fighter Mk X

By the end of 1942, Mk VICs were being completed with torpedo-carrying gear, as Mk VIC (ITF) 'interim torpedo fighters', to replace Coastal Command Beauforts. The externally-mounted torpedo was first employed successfully from a Beaufighter on 4 April 1943.

To make the Beaufighter more suitable for these low-altitude operations, a Hercules-engined variant (the Mk XVII)

was developed to produce peak power (1,735 hp/1294 kW) at 500 ft (152 m). With these engines installed, the torpedo-carrying Mk VIC became the Beaufighter TF.Mk X torpedo-fighter; a strike variant of the Mk X without a torpedo-carrying capability was known as the Mk XIC.

Wing-mounted machine-guns had been deleted from Coastal Command Beaufighters to make way for extra fuel tanks, but production TF.Mk Xs featured a 0.303-in (7.7-mm) Browning or Vickers 'K' machine-gun, firing to the rear from the observer's position. Eight rockets or two 250-lb (114-kg) bombs under the wings, introduced on modified Mk VICs, became standard on the Mk X, the main production variant.

To help in finding targets, early examples carried air-to-surface vessel (ASV) radar; later aircraft had AI Mk VIII, adapted successfully for air-to-

surface use, and housed in a 'thimble' nose radome. It was the extra weight of the radar and weapons that prompted the fitting of a dorsal fin (originally tested on a Mk II to correct take-off swing) to improve the handling of an aircraft that was, by now, operating at weights 50 per cent higher than originally envisaged.

By early 1944, Beaufighter Strike Wings were harrying enemy shipping from bases in the UK, while other TF.Mk Xs were assigned to the South African squadrons of the Balkan Air Force. Though Mk Xs arrived in the Far East theatre before VJ-Day, their numbers were too small to have a significant effect on operations in the region.

Australian-built Mk 21s

The RAAF's urgent need for Beaufighters led to plans for a Hercules-engined Mk VII to be built in Australia. Fears that Hercules supplies could be interrupted resulted in the proposed Mks VIII and IX with Wright Double Cyclone engines but, in the event, the Hercules XVIII-powered Mk 21 entered service in 1944.

The last British-built wartime Beaufighter variant was to be the Mk XII, with wings strengthened to carry a 1000-lb (454-kg) bomb each, but suitable engines were unavailable. Instead, the new wings were incorporated into late Mk X production, the bomb racks additionally allowing the carriage of external fuel tanks.

Post-war, surplus Beaufighters were exported to Turkey, Portugal and the Dominican Republic, while the RAF's last examples were 35 Mk Xs converted as TT.Mk 10 target-tugs from 1948. The last of these aircraft was finally retired in Singapore in 1960, nearly 21 years after the type's first flight.

Left: A radar-equipped RAF Mk VIF, camouflaged for night operations, taxis along at an unknown airstrip.

Below: In all, 5,564 Beaufighters were built in Britain, and another 364 in Australia. The latter were Mk 21s, built by the Department of Aircraft Production at Fisherman's Bend, Victoria. This Mk 21 of No. 31 Sqn, RAAF was among those issued to the squadron from September 1944.

Fighter variants

Proposed by the Bristol Aeroplane Company as a day-fighter derivative of the Beaufort torpedo-bomber, the Beaufighter was overtaken by events and, with a top speed inferior to that of the RAF's Hurricane, was judged unsuitable for its intended role. However, not all was lost and the type soon gained an enviable reputation as a night-fighter.

Powered, in its original Mk I fighter guise, by a pair of 1,400-hp (1044-kW) Hercules IIIs, the production Beaufighter was capable of 309 mph (497 km/h) at 15,000 ft (4572 m). This disappointing performance cast doubts on the future of the Mk I as a production variant and prompted a search for solutions. Re-engining the type with Rolls-Royce Griffons or Hercules VIs was considered, but both powerplants were rejected as production of the former had been reserved for the Fairey Firefly and the improved Hercules engine was still two years from production.

Eventually, as a stopgap solution, the decision was taken to produce a Beaufighter powered by a pair of Rolls-Royce Merlin XXs, as fitted to the Lancaster Mk I. To speed development, an installation identical to that designed for the Lancaster was employed. The first Beaufighter Mk II, as the new variant was known, was ready in July 1940, though by this stage it had been decided to put both the Mk I and Mk II into production in similar numbers, totalling over 900 aircraft.

After the first 50 Mk Is had been completed an important change was made to the Beaufighter's armament. To the four 20-mm Hispano cannon mounted under the forward fuselage were added a further six machine-guns – 0.303-in (12.7-mm) Brownings mounted in the wings – four to starboard and two to port. With this fire-power the Beaufighter was to be the most heavily-armed of all the fighters to serve in the RAF during World War II.

Another armament variation was test-flown in the Beaufighter Mk V, two prototypes of which were converted from Mk IIs. This comprised a powered, four-gun Boulton Paul BPA.1 turret mounted behind the cockpit, which replaced the wing guns and a pair of cannon. Though intended for use against enemy bombers at night and tested operationally, the Mk V's armament offered little benefit and further reduced top speed. No further Mk Vs were produced.

First deliveries

The first Mk Is (known as Mk IFs from 1941 to distinguish them from the Mk ICs introduced in Coastal Command at that time) were delivered to the RAF on 27 July 1940. As Luftwaffe activity over the British Isles increased in the dark days of the summer of 1940, four RAF day- and night-fighter squadrons previously equipped with Blenheim Mk IFs were urgently issued with Beaufighters during September. A fifth squadron followed shortly afterwards and on 17 September No. 29 Sqn flew the first sortie by the type. In the event it was

night patrols in search of German bombers that occupied these units over the eight months of the 'night blitz' and before long all had become full-time night-fighter units.

All were eventually operating aircraft with AI Mk IV radar and it was No. 604 Sqn which scored the first victory by a Beaufighter using this equipment on the night of 19-20 November.

In this view of a No. 600 Sqn Beaufighter Mk VIF, in Italy some time after September 1943, its AI Mk IV radar (transmitting) antenna and four 20-mm cannon armament may be seen.

Home-based Beaufighter night-fighters were finished in overall matt black. This is a Merlin-engined No. 252 Sqn Mk IIF, with the original pattern 'flat' tailplane.

No. 307 Sqn was a Polish-manned night-fighter unit which re-equipped with Beaufighter Mk IIFs in August 1941, flying intruder sorties over France. No. 307 was the first 'foreign' RAF unit permitted to use aircraft fitted with the secret AI radar.

Above: Still equipped with AI Mk IV radar, the second Mk IIF prototype was used by Rolls-Royce as a flying testbed for its new Griffon IIB engine. Note the four-bladed propellers.

Below: The 'thimble' nose radome of this Beaufighter Mk VIF indicates an AI Mk VII or VIII centimetric radar installation. This radar set gave much improved performance. Note also the dihedral tailplane, introduced to alleviate low-speed instability.

(The pilot was Flt Lt John Cunningham and this was the first of 20 confirmed kills by the famed night-fighter ace.)

With the introduction of GCI (ground-controlled interception) radar stations, the AI-equipped Beaufighters became more effective and on 10 May 1941 – the night of the last major Luftwaffe attack on London – 14 bombers were destroyed.

American Beaufighters

Beaufighter night-fighters equipped four 12th Air Force, USAAF squadrons – the 414th, 415th, 416th and 417th – from 1943, in North Africa and, later, in Sicily, Italy and France. This tropicalised and AI Mk IV-equipped Mk VIF is typical of their equipment, which was retained until the arrival of the P-61 Black Widows in the Mediterranean shortly before VE-Day.

Merlin-engined Beaufighter Mk IIFs (also fitted with AI Mk IV radar) began to enter service in April 1941 and eventually nine night-fighter squadrons and a single ECM unit (No. 515 Sqn) in No. 100 Group, Bomber Command were so-equipped, joining an addi-tional four NF squadrons that had converted to the Mk IF. (In fact, Mk IIFs saw relatively little combat with the Luftwaffe and only two are known to have been lost in air combat.)

A distinctive feature of late-production Mk I and II aircraft was a tailplane with a 12° dihedral. This was introduced to cure a longitudinal instability problem especially noticeable at the low speeds associated with the climb and approach phases of a flight, and became a standard feature on the later Mk VI and Mk X aircraft.

Hercules VI for the Mk VI

The Hercules VI engine finally found its way into the Beaufighter Mk VI in early 1942. The new engine was rated for best operation at a higher altitude than the Hercules III, making it ideal for use in the fighter variant – the Mk VIF. The first of these machines was equipped with the same AI Mk IV radar as fitted to the Mk IF, but this soon gave way to the much improved centimetric AI Mk VII (and, in its full production form, Mk VIII) radar, installed behind a distinctive 'thimble' nose radome.

A Beaufighter Mk VI of the Fighter Interception Unit claimed the first victory by the new variant on 5 April 1942, Mk VIFs entering service with Nos 68 and 604 Sqns soon afterwards and re-equipping a number of former Mk IF and Mk IIF units, as well as squadrons new to the Beaufighter.

With less Luftwaffe activity over the UK, home-based units now began offensive night-time sweeps (code-named 'Rangers') over northern France, attacking road and rail transport, as well as undertaking escort and decoy work during Bomber Command raids over Germany.

1942 also saw the debut of the Beaufighter in the Far East, three RAF squadrons in India taking Mk VIFs into action in the interdiction role, striking at Japanese lines of communication in Burma and Thailand.

During the first nine months of 1943, No. 27 Sqn claimed 66 locomotives destroyed or damaged, 409 items of rolling stock destroyed, 123 ships and 1,368 sampans and other small river craft destroyed or damaged and 96 road vehicles destroyed, all for the loss of eight Beaufighters.

However, in this type of operation, losses were generally high, largely as a result of the low level at which attacks were made, plus the adverse weather and poor ground facilities that prevailed. One squadron lost 75 aircrew (killed or missing) – twice its full establishment – in 18 months.

Although examples of the Beaufighter Mk VIF remained in use in the Far East until VJ-Day, at home Beaufighter night-fighters began to be replaced by de Havilland Mosquitoes from 1943. This process gathered pace in 1944 and, by VE-Day, the Beaufighter night-fighter had disappeared from front-line RAF service in Europe.

'Coastal' variants

Against a typically Maltese backdrop, one of No. 272 Sqn's 'interim' Beaufighter Mk ICs (which retained wing-mounted machine-guns) taxis at RAF Luqa.

An urgent need for a maritime strike fighter for RAF Coastal Command spurred the development of Beaufighter variants with more range and the ability to deliver rockets and a torpedo, culminating in production of the TF.Mk X 'Torbeau'.

RAF Coastal Command introduced the Beaufighter in the spring of 1941 out of operational necessity. Fighting in the Mediterranean, in particular during the German invasion of Greece, led to an urgent requirement for a long-range fighter. To this end Bristol proposed a series of modifications to the Beaufighter Mk I for its new role, including extra wing tankage (50 Imp gal/227 litres in the starboard wing; 24 Imp gal/109 litres to port) in place of the fighter's machine-guns, a fully-equipped navigator's station in the fuselage and a D/F loop above the cockpit.

'C' for Coastal

Before the first of 300 Mk ICs (the 'C' standing for Coastal Command) were available, No. 252 Sqn took delivery of machines from a batch of 80 'interim' aircraft, each with a 50-Imp gal (227-litre) fuel tank in the front fuselage, in lieu of wing tanks. The squadron

moved to Malta in mid-May 1941 and to Egypt the following month, where it was joined almost immediately by another Coastal Command unit – No. 272 Sqn. Both units achieved considerable success against German and Italian shipping and shore targets and in November No. 272 Sqn supported Operation Crusader, attacking enemy airfields in the Western Desert. In four days of operations, 44 enemy aircraft were shot down or destroyed on the ground. Good use was made of local modifications which allowed the Beaufighters to carry a 250-lb (114-kg) or 500-lb (227-kg) bomb under each wing.

No. 603 Sqn joined the Desert Air Force in early 1943, while back in the UK, Nos 143, 235, 236, 248 Sqns operated Mk ICs briefly during 1941-42, mainly from bases in Scotland for convoy protection work. All four home-based units soon re-equipped with Mk VICs.

In the early months of 1942

Part of the Mediterranean Allied Air Forces, the Balkan air force was established in June 1944 to support the partisan army in German-occupied Yugoslavia. This Beaufighter Mk X, possibly of No. 39 Sqn, was one of its aircraft, based in Italy for offensive operations on the other side of the Adriatic.

Beaufighter production switched to the Mk VI, powered by 1,650-hp (1230-kW) Bristol Hercules VI engines. Of a total of 1,682 examples of this variant, constructed at three factories, 693 were completed as Mk VICs. The Mk VIC had a greater fuel capacity than the Mk VIF and soon began to

re-equip home-based Coastal Command units. Typical targets for these squadrons were shipping and submarines in the North Sea and Bay of Biscay and it was the anti-shipping role that provided the impetus for the development of the most numerous Beaufighter variant.

By 1942 the Air Staff was

Pictured on an Allied airstrip in Tripolitania, Libya, a Beaufighter Mk IC is run up prior to departing on another sortie against Axis shipping in the Mediterranean.

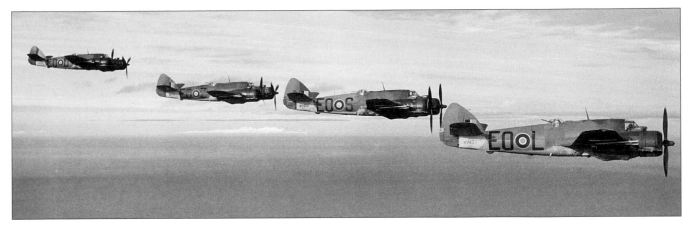

No. 404 Sqn, RCAF, flew Beaufighters from September 1942, receiving TF.Mk Xs, as seen here, in September 1943. From September 1944 it was one of the Banff Strike Wing squadrons and re-equipped with Mosquitoes just prior to VE-Day.

keen to find a replacement for Coastal Command's Beaufort torpedo-bomber, Bristol suggesting that the Beaufighter could be modified to carry a torpedo externally. The Air Ministry approved a trial torpedo installation on a Beaufighter Mk VIC and in May the suitably modified machine was dispatched to the Torpedo Development Unit at Gosport. Here, the installation

A pair of Coastal Command Beaufighters makes an RP and cannon attack on German shipping in the Heligoland Bight on 17 September 1944.

Below: No. 455 Sqn, RAAF was assigned to RAF Coastal Command and flew its last sortie with Handley Page Hampdens in December 1943. Converting to Beaufighter Mk Xs, it resumed operations in March 1944, undertaking attacks on shipping off the Dutch coast.

was shown to perform well and 50 'Beaufighter torpedo-fighters' were immediately ordered. These Beaufighter Mk VI(ITF)s featured bellows-type dive brakes developed by Youngman and fitted below the trailing edge of the outer wing panels, inboard of the ailerons. The first examples entered RAF service at the end of 1942 with No. 254 Sqn at North Coates, the new torpedo-fighters immediately taking on enemy convoys off the Dutch coast with 18-in (45.70-cm) torpedoes.

Definitive Mk X

The definitive torpedo-armed Beaufighter followed soon afterwards, the TF.Mk X differing from the Mk VI(ITF) only in being powered by different engines – Hercules XVIIs. These were effectively Hercules VIs modified, with cropped supercharger impellers, to produce more power at lower altitudes – 1,735 hp (1294 kW) at 500 ft (152 m).

In common with other Coastal Command aircraft, the Mk X was fitted with radar to aid target acquisition. Early aircraft had an ASV (air-to-surface vessel) set, but it was found that an AI.Mk VIII radar, as fitted to the Beaufighter Mk VIF fighter, was equally effective in an air-to-surface mode. Fitted in a 'thimble' nose radome, AI.Mk VIII replaced ASV on later production Mk Xs.

New armament was also introduced. For rear defence a 0.303-in (12.7-mm) Vickers 'K' machine-gun was installed in the observer's dorsal cupola; many Coastal Command Mk VICs were retrofitted with the same armament, while others were adapted to carry a 250-lb (114-kg) bomb or four 90-lb (41-kg) rocket projectiles (RPs) under each wing.

With the additional equipment as well as a torpedo, the Mk X's operating weight had crept up to a level some 50 per cent above the Beaufighter's originally projected weight. Handling suffered accordingly and the decision was taken to fit the TF.Mk X with a dorsal fin of the type flown experimentally on the Beaufighter Mk II fighter to cure take-off swing. Enlarged elevators were also provided on late production aircraft, the maximum take-off weight of which was some 25,400 lb (11522 kg).

Strike Wings

In all 2,205 TF.Mk Xs were built, plus 163 Mk XICs (basically Mk Xs without the torpedo-carrying provision). To take full advantage of the new aircraft, Coastal Command set up a number of Beaufighter Strike Wings, embracing RAF, RCAF, RAAF and RNZAF squadrons and operating from bases in Scotland and, later, eastern and southern England. From 1944 these units adopted new tactics for attacking shipping, whereby a wave of aircraft would use RPs to knock out AA guns in preparation for the second wave of the attack comprising torpedo-equipped aircraft. Thereafter, all aircraft would strafe the target with cannon and machine-gun fire and any remaining RPs.

Mk Xs also joined RAF and SAAF units in the Balkan air force for operations over Yugoslavia, where they enjoyed considerable operational success. A handful of aircraft arrived in the Far East with units redeployed from Europe, though their impact before VJ-Day was limited by their small numbers.

Bristol Beaufort

Showing the aircraft's substantial forward fuselage section which housed the crew, radio office, defensive armament and semi-recessed torpedo, this Beaufort Mk I (L9878) flew with No. 217 Sqn, Coastal Command.

Torpedo bombing twin

RAF Coastal Command's standard torpedo-bomber type from early 1940 until 1943, the Type 152 Beaufort was hampered early in its career by problems with its Taurus engines, but went on to serve well in the anti-shipping role from bases at home, in the Mediterranean and South West Pacific.

In 1935 the Air Ministry had issued two specifications, M.15/35 and G.24/35, which detailed requirements for a torpedo-bomber and a general reconnaissance/bomber, respectively. The latter was required to replace the Avro Anson and was to be met by the Bristol Type 149, which was built in Canada as the Bolingbroke. To meet the first requirement, for a torpedo-bomber, Bristol proposed an adaptation of the Blenheim, which was submitted to the Air Ministry in November 1935.

Single aircraft design

After sending off these details of the Type 150, the Bristol design team came to the conclusion that it would be possible to meet both specifications with a single aircraft evolved from the Blenheim, and immediately prepared a new design, the Type 152. By comparison with the Blenheim Mk IV, the new design was increased slightly in length to allow for the carriage of a torpedo in a semi-exposed position, provided a navigation station, and seated pilot and navigator side-by-side; behind them were radio and camera positions which would be manned by a gunner/radio operator. The Type

152 was more attractive to the Air Ministry, but it was considered that a crew of four was essential, and the accommodation was redesigned to this end. The resulting high roof line, which continued unbroken to the dorsal turret, became a distinguishing feature of this new aircraft, built to Specification 10/36, and named Beaufort.

Detail design was initiated immediately, but early analysis showed that the intended powerplant of two Bristol Perseus engines would provide

Above: The size of the 18-in (45.7-cm), 1,605-lb (728-kg) torpedo carried by Coastal Command Beauforts is readily apparent in this view. The blister under the nose of the aircraft housed a rear-facing 0.303-in (7.7-mm) Vickers machine-gun.

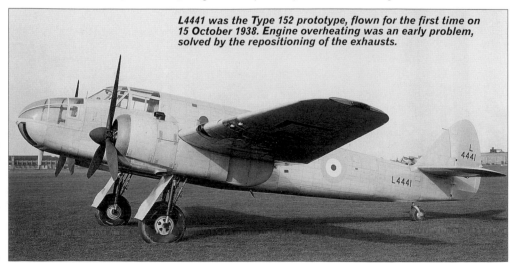

L4441 was the Type 152 prototype, flown for the first time on 15 October 1938. Engine overheating was an early problem, solved by the repositioning of the exhausts.

Right: The last Australian-built Beaufort Mk VIII, A9-700, flies near Sydney in 1944. All Beauforts built 'down under' were powered by Pratt & Whitney Twin Wasps, most of which were locally-manufactured. Note the ASV radar antenna under the wing.

Below: This view, from behind the pilot's right shoulder, shows the navigator at work at his chart table. To the left is the pilot's fixed gun sight, used to aim the twin Vickers guns in the nose of a Beaufort Mk I.

insufficient power to cater for the increase of almost 25 per cent in gross weight without a serious loss of performance. Instead, the newly developed twin-row Taurus sleeve-valve engine was selected for the Beaufort. The initial contract, for 78 aircraft, was placed in August 1936, but the first prototype did not fly until just over two years later, on 15 October 1938. Overheating problems with the powerplant and the need to disperse the Blenheim production line to shadow factories before the Beaufort could be built accounted for the delay.

Test-flying of the prototype revealed a number of shortcomings, leading to the provision of doors to enclose the main landing gear when retracted, repositioning of the engine exhausts, and an increase to two machine-guns in the dorsal turret. Continuing teething problems with the new engine delayed the entry into service of the Beaufort Mk Is, these first equipping No. 22 Sqn,

Coastal Command in January 1940. It was this unit which, on the night of 15/16 April 1940, began the Beaufort's operational career by laying mines in enemy coastal waters, but in the following month all aircraft were grounded until engine modifications could be carried out.

Australian interest

Earlier, the Australian government had shown interest in the Beaufort, and it was decided that railway and industrial workshops could be adapted to produce these aircraft. Twenty sets of airframe parts and the eighth production aircraft as a working sample were shipped out, but at an early stage the Australians obtained a licence from Pratt & Whitney to build the Twin Wasp, and these were to power all Australian-built Beauforts, which eventually totalled 700.

Australian production began in 1940, the first Australian Beaufort Mk V making its initial flight in May 1941. These were

generally similar to their British counterparts except for the change in engines and an increase in fin area to improve stability with the powerful Twin Wasp engine. In fact, engine and propeller changes accounted for most of the different variants produced by the Australian factories. These included the Beaufort Mk V (50) and Beaufort Mk VA (30), both with licence-built Twin Wasp S3C4-G engines; Beaufort Mk VI (60 with Curtiss propellers) and Beaufort Mk VII (40 with Hamilton propellers), all 100 being powered by imported S1C3-G Twin Wasps due to insufficient licence-production; and the Beaufort Mk VIII with licence-built S3C4-Gs. This last mark was the definitive production version, of which 520 were built, and had additional fuel tankage, Loran navigation system and variations in armament, with production ending in August 1944. Some 46 of the last production batch were subsequently converted to serve as unarmed transports; designated Beaufort Mk IX, this variant had the dorsal turret removed and the resulting aperture faired in. The powerplant rating of all the Australian versions was 1,200 hp (895 kW). The Beaufort was used extensively by the RAAF in the Pacific theatre, serving from the summer of 1942 until the end of the war.

The early trials of the Australian Beaufort Mk V with Twin Wasp engines induced the Air Ministry to specify this powerplant for the

next contract, and a prototype was flown in November 1940. The first production Beaufort Mk II flew in September 1941, and by comparison with the Beaufort Mk I revealed much improved take-off performance. However, because of a shortage of Twin Wasps in the UK, only 164 production Mk IIs were built before Mk Is with improved Taurus XII engines were reintroduced on the line. In addition to the powerplant change, this version had structural strengthening, a changed gun turret and ASV radar with Yagi aerials. When production of this version ended in 1944, 1,429 Beauforts had been built in Britain.

Mks III and IV

The final two Beaufort designations, Mk III and Mk IV, were versions with Rolls-Royce Merlin XX and 1,250-hp (932 kW) Taurus XX engines, respectively. Only a prototype Mk IV was built.

Beauforts were the standard torpedo-bomber in service with Coastal Command during 1940-43, equipping Nos 22, 42, 86, 217, 415 and 489 Sqns in home waters, and Nos 39, 47 and 217 in the Middle East. They were to acquit themselves well until superseded by the Beaufighter, and were involved in many of the early and bloody attacks against the German battle-cruisers *Gneisenau* and *Scharnhorst*, and the heavy cruiser *Prinz Eugen*, three vessels which often seemed to be invincible, at least to aircraft carrying conventional weapons.

The last 121 Beauforts built for the RAF were dual-control Mk II Trainers, powered by P&W Twin Wasp radials. The Mk II(T)s served as twin-engined instruction aircraft at Operational Training Units (OTUs).

Above: Seen here during trials at Martlesham Heath in 1935, the Bristol 142 Britain First was the result of a private order by the newspaper magnate Lord Rothermere, and it impressed the Air Ministry immediately.

Falling uncomfortably between older schools of thought and more modern concepts of military aircraft design, the Blenheim was a manoeuvrable aircraft for its time, but was quickly outmoded by faster and much more capable German bombers such as the Ju 88 and Do 17.

Bristol Blenheim
Battle of France bomber

Hailed at the time as the fastest light bomber in the world, the Blenheim was a fundamental part of the RAF's attack force, only to achieve disappointing results and heavy losses in combat.

Built in huge numbers, the Bristol Blenheim formed the backbone of the RAF's light, tactical home-based bomber force between 1938 and August 1942, lingering on rather longer (about another year) in North Africa and in India. Considered far superior to the other light and medium bombers available to the RAF on the outbreak of war in September 1939, the Blenheim was nonetheless entirely inadequate to face the threat posed by modern war, and especially that posed by the Luftwaffe.

A disappointing start

The aircraft suffered heavy losses, but represented the only realistic bomber option open to the RAF in the difficult first two years of the war. When first conceived (as a derivative of the Bristol 142 – itself derived from the 'paper' Bristol 135 – built as a high-speed transport for Lord Rothermere), the Blenheim was to have been 'faster than the fighters of the day', though this claimed advantage was lost as soon as the RAF received its first monoplane fighters.

Unfortunately, the Blenheim's speed was a function of a light and relatively flimsy structure, and of inadequate payload and range which were, in turn, a direct consequence of the RAF's insistence that its new bomber would be able to use much the same sort of grass airfield as the previous generation of biplane bombers. And the Blenheim's much-vaunted speed advantage was modest. The anachronistic-looking, single-engined Vickers Wellesley, for example, carried twice the bombload, had a longer range, the same defensive armament, and was only 12 mph (19 km/h) slower. And, with its geodetic structure, the Wellesley would probably have absorbed battle damage rather better than the Blenheim. Neither aircraft had adequate heaters, radios or blind-flying equipment – the features which would be so vital in a modern war in Europe – and neither of the aircraft had accurate bombsights or even effective bombs to drop!

In retrospect, it should have been obvious that the need was for a faster, tougher aircraft with better defensive armament, longer range and a heavier bombload – like the Blenheim's German and American contemporaries. Aircraft like the Ju 88 and Boston used massive two-row radial engines, and required longer, drier, smoother runways than the Blenheim, but they were equally fast, and much more 'survivable'. At the other end of the spectrum, if there was a place for a bomber carrying only a 1,000-lb (454-kg) bombload, then what was needed was a flexible aircraft like the Westland Whirlwind, which really was fast enough to be virtually safe from enemy fighters, and which had sufficient punch and performance to fight its way out of trouble. But the RAF had to go to war with the aircraft that it actually had, and not with what it could (or should) have had.

The RAF was initially no more than lukewarm about the Blenheim, and when large orders were placed, still regarded the aircraft as an interim type for the pre-war expansion, on which crews of the 'definitive' bombers could train and gain experience, and around which new squadrons could form. As a result, RAF orders for the original Blenheim Mk I reached an

Above: The superior performance and firepower of German fighters (like the Messerschmitt Bf 109E seen landing in the distance) made 'sitting ducks' of the Blenheims used in the early days of the war.

The Blenheim was used to much better effect as part of RAF Coastal Command than as a bomber, undertaking anti-invasion patrols, shipping escort and even attacks on Norwegian airfields. This six-ship formation of Mk IVFs is from No. 254 Squadron.

astonishing total of 1,415, to which were added 3,853 Blenheim Mk IVs and Bolingbrokes and even 942 of the hopeless Blenheim Mk Vs!

On the outbreak of war, the Blenheim equipped 24 front-line bomber squadrons (plus other units operating in the Army Co-operation and night fighter roles). Appropriately enough, it was a Blenheim which flew the RAF's first sortie of World War II (a reconnaissance mission of Wilhelmshaven), and played a major part in the 'Phoney War' campaign of leaflet-dropping and largely unproductive anti-shipping attacks, suffering a steady stream of losses.

But if losses were heavy in the first months of the war, they were even heavier during the Battle of France, although the Blenheim did perform better than the Fairey Battle. In all, 200 Blenheims were lost during the Battle of France. The Blenheims achieved little but the deaths of many of the cream of the pre-war air force, while the aircraft represented valuable production capacity which could have been devoted to more useful and potentially war-winning aircraft.

Multi-role Blenheim

Even after the Battle of France, Blenheims continued to fly dangerous day and night bombing attacks against targets in occupied Europe. There were 'Circuses' – whose aim was to drag enemy fighters into the air, and there were attacks against the invasion fleet being assembled in the Channel ports, and against German coastal shipping. Blenheims even mounted daylight raids against enemy fighter airfields and targets deep inside Germany, with predictable results. Sensibly, the aircraft should have been limited to night raids, but politically, the RAF had to be seen to be mounting offensive operations 'round the clock', whatever the cost.

No. 2 Group's Blenheim units began to re-equip with Venturas, Bostons and Mitchells at the end of 1942, and flew their last operations in August 1942. Coastal Command withdrew its last front-line Blenheims in September 1942, after two years of fierce and costly operations against enemy ships, U-boats and coastal targets.

By this time, the remaining Blenheim night-fighter squadrons had also re-equipped, having played a significant part in the development of night-fighter tactics and equipment (including the tactical employment of AI radar), albeit without amassing an enormous tally of kills.

Powerplant
A pair of Bristol Mercury XV radial piston engines, each rated at 920 hp (686 kW) powered the Blenheim Mk IV. The Mercury XV was introduced by the Blenheim Mk IV, and featured a 9-lb/sq in (62-kPa) boost for 3 minutes' 'combat time' when using 100 octane fuel, and providing a reserve of 30 mph (48 km/h) in an emergency.

Blenheim Mk IV

This Blenheim Mk IV of No. 59 Sqn is depicted as it appeared during the spring of 1940. No. 59 Sqn was at this time resident in France as part of the Advanced Air Striking Force, and was operational from Poix in the night reconnaissance role for II Corps. Following the German invasion, the unit returned to Andover in May 1940.

Asymmetric nose
The Blenheim Mk IV's nose was scalloped on the port side, ahead of the pilot, offering him a better forward view. The navigator sat ahead and to the right of the pilot, facing starboard towards his chart table.

Bombload
A maximum internal load of 1,000 lb (454 kg) could be carried by the Blenheim Mk IV, with a further 320 lb (145 kg) on underwing bomb racks. This was a major improvement over the Blenheim Mk I and the Battle.

Production
Blenheim Mk IVs superseded Blenheim Mk Is on the Filton production line in 1938, and were later built under sub-contract by Avro and Rootes. A total of 3,853 Blenheim Mk IVs and Bolingbrokes was built, in addition to the 1,415 Blenheim Mk Is. The Blenheim Mk IVF was built as a fighter derivative, carrying four 0.303-in (7.7-mm) Brownings in a ventral tray.

Defensive armament
Initially, the Blenheim IV had a single forward-firing Vickers K in the nose, with a single gun in the dorsal turret. This proved inadequate, and a new BI.Mk IV turret housing two belt-fed Brownings was added. Some Blenheims had a single Browning fitted under the nose to fire aft and below, but this was later replaced by a Frazer-Nash FN.54 turret housing two Brownings, aimed by the navigator.

Blenheim

Overseas operations

Outclassed by the Luftwaffe during the Battle of France, the Blenheim soldiered on in RAF service, both with Coastal Command units and in combat theatres farther afield, and with other air arms.

Above: The single Bolingbroke Mk III floatplane conversion was operated by No. 5 Sqn, RCAF, and performed anti-submarine patrols off Canada's east coast, alongside Canso flying-boats.

Top: The single turret-mounted Lewis or Vickers gun, as carried by these pre-war Blenheim Mk IVs, provided insufficient defence and was replaced by twin-gun Browning or Vickers installations.

As the pre-war expansion began, the RAF was as poorly equipped overseas as it was at home, despite the fact that many units overseas were actively engaged in colonial policing duties which often required them to fly operational sorties. Re-equipping such units with modern aircraft was therefore accorded a high priority, and the fifth Blenheim unit to form was actually No. 30 Squadron at Habbaniyah, Iraq, in January 1938. Once the Blenheim Mk IV started to enter service, many surplus Blenheim Mk Is were cascaded to overseas units and to other roles, and the remaining Harts and Hinds were relegated to training duties. By the time Italy entered the war (on 10 June 1940), the RAF in the Middle East included nine Blenheim squadrons, which immediately began operations against Italian colonial forces in

Libya. The poor showing by the Italians in North Africa prompted German intervention there and in the Balkans, and the Blenheim squadrons suddenly found themselves facing a sterner challenge. As Axis forces invaded Greece, Blenheims from the Middle East were heavily committed to the ill-fated campaign, not least since the Greeks actually refused British military assistance, except in the air. In Greece, the Blenheims flew in the fighter and bomber roles, and heavy losses were sustained. Most of the squadrons pulled out in April, and some were committed (from their Egyptian bases) to opposing the paratroop-led invasion of Crete. After the withdrawal from Greece, British forces in North Africa found themselves fighting on two fronts – against the Italians and newly-arrived German Afrika Korps in the

West, and then, in April 1941, against a German-backed coup in Iraq. This was supported by German aircraft operating from bases in Iraq and in Vichy French Syria.

Desert Blenheims

Blenheims were heavily committed to combat strafing and bombing enemy airfields. As the Iraqi operation reached its end, the Vichy High Commissioner in Syria asked Germany to withdraw its forces, fearing that their presence would provoke a British invasion. The

Germans left by 8 June, but this was too late to forestall the Allied invasion which began the next day. The Vichy forces resisted, and several Blenheims were shot down by their erstwhile allies, before the Vichy regime in Syria capitulated on 14 July. This victory allowed Britain to turn its full attention against the Afrika Korps, and Blenheims were used, especially from the beleaguered island of Malta, to interdict Axis shipping trying to resupply Rommel, and to attack German bases on Sicily. In North Africa, Blenheims were

Twelve of the 15 Bolingbroke Mk IV-Ws are pictured at the Fairchild plant at Longueuil, Montreal, displaying the revised nacelle contours dictated by the P&W Twin Wasp Junior engine.

Below: Built for company use, Bristol's Aquila-engined 143 could accommodate eight passengers and two crew. The 'convertible' 143F was offered to Finland as a multi-role military transport.

Above: The Bristol Bisley, designed to carry four Brownings in a solid nose, but pictured in unarmed prototype form, was designed as a short-range dive-bomber and low-level close-support aircraft.

used by the Free French, Greeks and South Africans. Blenheim Mk IVs were finally withdrawn from the Desert Air Force during mid-1942, and had all but disappeared by the time Montgomery fought and won the Battle of El Alamein in October 1942.

Torch and the Far East

As Blenheim operations in the Eastern end of the Mediterranean ended, the Blenheim Mk V made its debut in the West, with four squadrons supporting Operation Torch (the Allied invasion of North West Africa) in November 1942 and the subsequent operations. The Blenheim Mk V was hopelessly outclassed, and suffered appalling losses before being withdrawn in the spring of 1943, or relegated to coastal patrol duties. The last Coastal Patrol Blenheims were withdrawn (from No. 244 Squadron) in April 1944.

RAF Blenheims also saw extensive service in the Far East, with three India-based squadrons converting to the type in late 1939, and with two previously UK-based units moving out to Singapore soon after. The Blenheim's ability to operate from semi-prepared grass strips was extremely useful in the Far East, where facilities were frequently rather primitive. Four Blenheim squadrons were available when Japan invaded Malaya and Singapore in December 1941, but were wiped out in enemy air attacks and by enemy fighters after inflicting some cost on the advancing Japanese. A handful of aircraft escaped to Sumatra and finally to Java, where the last aircraft were destroyed before the surviving crews made their escape by boat.

As Japanese forces pushed through Burma, Blenheim units in India (reinforced by units rapidly despatched from the Middle East) began flying intensively in defence of India. Units were deployed into Burma and conducted a vigorous fighting retreat. The Blenheims proved very vulnerable to enemy fighters, but occasionally exacted a degree of vengeance. On one occasion, the gunner of a No. 60 Squadron Blenheim Mk IV damaged and drove off two Japanese aces (one with 10 kills to his credit) and then shot down Lt Colonel Kato, an 18kill veteran of the Sino-Japanese war.

When British and Indian forces began their 1942 offensive against Japan, Blenheims were at the forefront of the campaign, often escorted by Hurricanes. The aircraft hit hard at Japanese targets as the 'Forgotten 14th Army' pushed eastward, and then covered its withdrawal before the summer monsoon. New Blenheim Mk Vs were used in the following year's offensive, before being withdrawn from front-line squadrons in the late summer.

Blenheims remained in use in second-line roles, and one was used for a bombing attack on a Japanese airfield as late as 8 May 1944.

Support roles

In second-line roles (including pilot and aircrew training, calibration, survey, meteorological reconnaissance and even air ambulance), Blenheims remained in use in the UK, Middle East and Far East until the war's end, though the type was then immediately withdrawn from use and declared obsolete. The RAF had more than enough more modern Mosquitoes and Beaufighters to meet its post-war requirements, and the Blenheim disappeared.

In foreign hands, Blenheims saw brief service with the Greek, Yugoslav and Croat air forces before those nations succumbed to the Nazi juggernaut. The aircraft also saw more extensive service with the Romanian air force, fighting on the Axis side, under Luftwaffe control, until August 1944. The Blenheim also saw action with the Finns against the Russians. Finnish Blenheims were modified to carry Swedish-supplied bombs, and initially equipped a regiment at Immola, fulfilling bombing and reconnaissance duties. Later Finnish examples were licence-built by Valtion Lentokonetehdas at Tampere, which eventually produced 45 Mk IIs. Finland was the largest export operator of the Blenheim, and its aircraft survived the war and small numbers continued flying in non-operational roles, including target-towing, until 1958.

Above: Trained in the UK, the first Free French unit was formed in August 1940, before moving to North Africa in order to be part of Groupe Reserve de Bombardement 1 (GRB 1). In September 1941 GRB 1 was re-equipped and incorporated into the new 'Lorraine' Groupe.

Right: Turkey was the second-largest foreign operator of the Blenheim, with at least 56 aircraft delivered. Most were Mk Is, like these examples from the first batch received in 1937.

*Liberators, such as this **B-24D** which was involved in the first **Ploesti** raid, were called upon to undertake some of the most dangerous and demanding missions of the war due to their great endurance, ruggedness and survivability.*

Consolidated
B-24 Liberator
Introduction

Despite being overshadowed by the B-17, the B-24 Liberator was, in fact, built in greater numbers than any other American aircraft of World War II, a remarkable feat for so large a machine.

The Consolidated B-24 Liberator is one of the best-known bombers of all time. The four-engined 'Lib', instantly recognisable in flight by its ultra-narrow Davis wing, fought almost everywhere and did almost everything during World War II. Yet men who flew the B-24 Liberator feel relegated to the shadows, eclipsed by the smaller and older bomber to which the Liberator is always compared, the B-17 Flying Fortress.

Four companies and five factories produced the Liberator in greater numbers than any other military aircraft ever manufactured in North America. The B-24 carried more bombs and went farther than the B-17, and Liberators also flew photo-reconnaissance missions and hauled cargo. The aircraft were a vital part of the crowded Eighth Air Force offensive against Germany and were sometimes alone fighting in the vast expanses of the Pacific. It is true to say that the war in China would have been lost but for Liberators transporting precious fuel into China from India over the Himalayan 'Hump'.

A former Liberator pilot believes that the high-aspect 'fluid foil' wing patented by David R. Davis was the secret to success: "Without it", he says, "the Liberator wouldn't have been able to fly as far or as fast, nor carry as much as she did. Many of her virtues, as well as a good number of her faults can be traced directly to the wing: it gave the B-24 greater load-carrying capabilities than most other aircraft of her size, but also made her difficult to fly in formation. The wing helped make her faster but made her less manoeuvrable due to the

A 15th Air Force B-24 heads home from a bombing mission over Europe. It can be seen here flying through the vapour trails of preceding formations returning to their bases in southern Italy.

[high] wing loading. It allowed her to fly farther, which made the B-24 the logical choice for Asia and the Pacific where missions were carried out at extreme ranges, and led to her being the only heavy bomber to be used in all theatres." Furthermore, says this pilot, the unique wing lent "grace and beauty to what admittedly became, in later models, a rather homely-looking aircraft". Even those who loved this bomber were rarely able to find beauty in it. Some called it, jokingly, "the packing box the B-17 came in".

A waist gunner on a Liberator draws attention to a message meant for inquisitive enemy fighter pilots: "If you can read this, you're too damned close."

Above: Serving for just four years, the B-24 had a mixed press. Described by some as the saviour of the Allied air forces, others referred it as a 'widow-maker', an object of pilots' fears. Some said that it was versatile and unmatched, others that it was ungainly and underpowered. While all these claims have some basis in reality, the B-24 made an indelible contribution to the war, devastating Axis targets.

Right: A number of Liberators were captured by the Germans during the war, and used for surveillance, transport and testing duties.

Development

At the beginning of World War II, the United States realised the need for a bomber that could strike further, drop more munitions and survive more punishment than the B-17. Even before this – in January 1939 – Major-General Henry H. 'Hap' Arnold, Commander-in-Chief, Army Air Corps, had foreseen the need for a bomber that could exceed 300 mph (483 km/h), with a range of 3,000 miles (4828 km) and a ceiling of 35,000 ft (10668 m). Apart from its unique wing, the Consolidated bomber was distinguished by a tricycle undercarriage, twin rudder and fin assembly, and a big, slab-sided fuselage that seemed spacious when compared to other bombers.

In 1942, an AAF (Army Air Forces) training manual on the Liberator told student pilots that 'the B-24, when properly used, has no equal in any air force. It has proved itself capable of delivering tremendous blows against the enemy over extremely long ranges, under unfavourable weather conditions and against heavy enemy opposition. If the gunners are properly trained, they can create havoc among enemy fighters.'

Short life

The Liberator was not fully developed when the war broke out, and essentially obsolete by the time it ended. At one juncture, the industrial heartland that produced almost 100,000 aircraft in 1944 was turning out a new B-24 bomber every 51 minutes, but the bomber was built more for immediacy than for durability and would be gone from service in only a few years.

Some said that the B-24 was hard to fly, demanding the best of a skilled pilot. Despite its roomy interior, the Liberator could seem cramped and, at altitude, it was always cold. On their worst missions, Liberator crews were battered about inside their cramped confines, numbed by bone-chilling temperatures, and stalked by flak and fighters. Still, a 'Lib' would often survive battle damage and bring its crew home, sometimes with its controls so badly damaged that the aircraft had to land on autopilot. As one crew member, searching for the essence of the B-24 Liberator, put it very simply: "This was the workhorse of all the bombers."

The Liberator was well prepared for fighter attacks, armed with various combinations of .50-cal. (12.7-mm) and sometimes .30-cal. (7.62-mm) machine-guns. Because of its greater capabilities, it was usually assigned the toughest, longest missions. The Liberator was one of the few land-based bombers used in the Pacific theatre because it could handle the long flights with no emergency landing fields available.

Many decades after the war, the grandson of a Liberator flier, First Lieutenant Charles T. Voyles, summarised everything about this bomber that mattered to his family. Never mind the wingspan or the bombload, he said: "The most important aspect of the B-24 to me is that my grandfather and nine of his brothers-in-arms climbed into their 'plane, nicknamed the *Phantom Renegade*, 30 times and risked their lives. They left homes, jobs, wives and children to go half way around the world to fight for what they believed in. The B-24 symbolises the dedication of a generation that is quickly passing away."

Artwork on B-24s was both colourful and plentiful and helped to increase morale and team spirit. This tired B-24J, 44-40973, The Dragon and His Tail, was part of the 64th BS of the 43 BG in the Pacific theatre.

Development

A late January 1940 test flight sees the XB-24 flying with 'everything down' for the camera. With a wheelbase of just 16 ft (4.88 m) the need for a tailskid (just visible half way along the rear fuselage) is clear.

From LB-30 to PB4Y-2 Privateer

The B-24 was built in greater numbers than any other American type of the period. In order to produce a total of 18,482 LB-30s, B-24s, AT-22s and C-87s, plus 774 PB4Y-2s and RY-3s, between 1940 and 1945, one of the most complex production organisations was established, involving five factories run by four different companies – Consolidated, Douglas, Ford and North American.

The first members of the Liberator family to enter service were the six LB-30As (YB-24s). Without self-sealing fuel tanks they were deemed unsuitable for operational use and served as transports.

Consolidated's founder Reuben Fleet and design engineer I. M. 'Mac' Laddon approached the US Army Air Corps in January 1939, having been asked to create a new production outlet for the rival Boeing B-17. Consolidated had a counter-offer – to produce an aircraft infinitely better than the B-17. A period of frenetic work at Consolidated followed, culminating in the creation of a mock-up of the new and different bomber it wanted to build.

On 1 February 1939, the Army issued Type Specification C-212. This amounted to choosing Consolidated since any other aircraft manufacturer would have only three weeks to respond. On 21 February, the Army chose the Consolidated Model 32. A month later, the Army ordered a single XB-24 prototype (allocated the serial 39-556) with the proviso that it be flown by 30 December – a requirement that was just met.

The XB-24 was powered by Pratt & Whitney R-1830-33 Twin Wasp radial engines rated at 1,200 hp (895 kW) on take-off and 1,000 hp (746 kW) at 14,500 ft (4420 m).

The seven-place XB-24 had the first tricycle landing gear

flown on a large bomber. The nose wheel permitted faster landings and take-offs, thus allowing for a heavier wing loading on the low-drag Davis aerofoil. A bombardier's enclosure began the nose of the deep fuselage, which terminated behind twin rudders with a tail gunner's position. Armament included three 0.5-in (12.7-mm) guns and four 0.3-in (7.62-mm) hand-operated guns fired through openings in the fuselage sides, top, and bottom, and in a nose socket. The XB-24 could accommodate eight 1,100-lb (499-kg) bombs, twice the capacity of the B-17.

Uprated prototype

Eventually, this bomber would prove faster than its Boeing counterpart, too, but the prototype's speed was measured at only 273 mph (439 km/h) instead of the Army's specified 311 mph (500 km/h). So, on 26 July 1940 the Army ordered the prototype to be fitted with turbo-superchargers and leak-proof fuel tanks. The R-1830-41 Twin Wasp engines provided 1,200 hp (895 kW) at 25,000 ft (7620 m). Wing slots were deleted. This first ship in what was to be a long series was

redesignated XB-24B, and the reworked prototype flew on 1 February 1941. To confuse everyone forever, this airframe received a new serial number (39-680) and its original serial (39-556) was cancelled.

In March 1939, before the 'XB' ever flew, the Army ordered seven service-test YB-24 bombers with turbo-superchargers for high-altitude flight. Meanwhile, France, in dire need of warplanes, placed a June 1940 order for 139 export models,

known as the LB-30. When the French government collapsed the LB-30 production run was divided between Britain and the USAAF (US Army Air Forces).

Six of the seven YB-24s were completed as LB-30A aircraft for Britain and eventually operated as transatlantic ferry transports. The seventh YB-24 had armour and self-sealing fuel tanks and was accepted by the Army in May 1941. All seven of these bombers were identical to the 'XB' except for the deletion of wing slots and

The first major production Liberator variant for the USAAF was the B-24D, with the 3-ft (0.91-m) nose extension first seen in the RAF's Liberator Mk II (LB-30), and a powered tail turret.

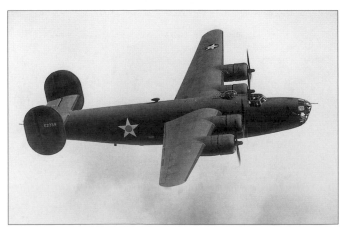

The B-24J was built in larger numbers than any other member of the Liberator family, and was the only model assembled by all five factories in the B-24 production pool. In all 6,678 were completed; this is a Consolidated San Diego-built example from 1944.

the addition of de-icing.

Dazzled by the promise of Boeing's stratospheric B-17, with its superb defensive armament and capacious cabin, the USAAC had initially ordered only 32 Liberators, while France and Britain (seeing the Liberator's incredible payload/range performance) ordered 139 and 114 respectively. The French order was overtaken by the Fall of France in June 1940, but production continued, since even the USAAF had become convinced as to the type's usefulness. "If the French can't take 'em, we will!" was the response.

The first Liberators in service were six LB-30As (with the 'LB' designation suffix standing for 'Land Bomber') diverted from the French contract to Britain in December 1940. The aircraft's lack of self-sealing fuel tanks was judged to be a major stumbling block to front-line service, so these aircraft (officially known simply as Liberators, but often referred to, inaccurately, as Liberator Mk Is) entered service with RAF Ferry Command in March 1941. Serialled AM258/AM263, some later went to BOAC.

First operational 'Libs'

The first truly operational Liberators were 20 'B-24A Conversions' (LB-30Bs) built for the USAAC but diverted to the RAF as Liberator Mk Is (AM910/AM929). These aircraft had self-sealing fuel tanks and the range performance that was needed to fight the growing U-boat menace, and 10 of the aircraft were therefore delivered to Coastal Command after modification by Scottish Aviation at Prestwick. RAF Bomber Command also received a number of the new aircraft, along with the first of 140 Liberator Mk IIs (LB-30s) allocated to the RAF, though 75 were requisitioned for the USAAF.

The USAAF's first actual B-24s were nine B-24A models (40-2369/2377) which were similar in appearance to the prototype but appeared in Olive Drab. Deemed inadequate for bombing duties, all nine examples were assigned to Ferry Command (later, the Ferrying Division of Air Transport Command) as transports.

Design evolution

The evolution of the Liberator design over time can be seen in a glance at the changing length and shape of the bomber's fuselage – or in a comparison of the fuselage length of various models. Virtually every 'Lib' boasted a Davis wing with a span of 110 ft 0 in (33.52 m) and a wing area of 1,048 sq ft (97 m²), but only the XB-24 and XB-24B had a fuselage length of just 63 ft 9 in (19.43 m). As the Liberator grew, the B-24C through XB-24F models were lengthened to 66 ft 4 in (20.21 m). Subsequently, the B-24G and all subsequent models were stretched further to a length of 67 ft 2 in (20.47 m). There were many advantages to increasing the length and volume of the fuselage, but crew comfort was not one of them.

After a handful of 'production shakedown' B-24Cs, the first B-24D was rolled out at San Diego on 22 January 1942. It was the B-24D variant which finally introduced a combat-ready bomber.

In all 2,696 B-24Ds were built and were followed by a small number of nearly identical B-24Es built by Ford and Consolidated-Fort Worth and assembled by Douglas. Similarly, the B-24G was a close relative of the D-model, but built by North American.

The first B-24H, which was also the first production Liberator with a factory-installed nose turret, was rolled out at Willow Run, Michigan on 30 June 1943. The B-24H model was probably the best-performing and best-liked Liberator, but was eclipsed in terms of production numbers by the B-24J – the definitive Liberator, with a new autopilot and bombsight. The B-24L and M, which followed the J-model and were in production at the end of the war, differed mainly in armament detail. The much improved, single-fin B-24N was cancelled after VE-Day.

Pre-dating the B-24N was the PB4Y-2 Privateer. This was another single-fin variant with a lengthened fuselage and engines designed to produce peak power at the lower altitudes at which this naval variant was expected to operate. Operational towards the end of World War II, Privateers were among the last members of the Liberator family to see operational use. lasting well into the 1960s.

Below: Huge numbers of B-24Ns – over 5,000 – were on order from Ford when VE-Day brought their cancellation. Much improved performance and stability were among this variant's advantages.

Above: Naval 'Liberator' development led to the 'Two by Four' – the PB4Y-2 Privateer. This was a lengthened derivative optimised for low-altitude maritime tasks and notable for its single fin.

Model 39/104 Liberator Liner

Consolidated designed the Model 39 as a private venture, in an attempt to interest the US Navy in a purpose-built transport based on the Privateer. Effectively a PB4Y-2 with a new fuselage 90 ft (27.40 m) long and 10 ft 6 in (3.20 m) in diameter, the Model 39 attracted immediate USN interest, 253 being ordered under the designation R2Y-1. However, upon completion the first Model 39 failed an inspection by the Navy; serious design flaws were cited and the production order cancelled. A single Model 39 (right) was completed and flown in April 1944, but remained a one-off. Convair attempted to market a 48-seat passenger derivative (the Model 104) post-war, but it failed to attract any orders.

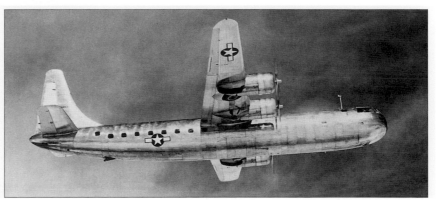

Ploesti: 1 August 1943

During July, practice flights against a mock-up target in the Libyan desert were followed by a full-scale dress rehearsal involving 175 Liberators.

The most important prelude to the subsequent formation of the Fifteenth Air Force was the 1 August 1943 low-level mission against Ploesti. Carried out by five American B-24 Liberator groups, the raid was launched from five bases around Benghazi, Libya.

Taking part were three B-24 outfits detached from the Eighth Air Force in England: the 93rd Bomb Group, 'Ted's Traveling Circus', commanded by Lieutenant Colonel Addison Baker, plus the 44th 'Eight Balls' and the 389th 'Sky Scorpions'. These groups had come from England (leaving the British Isles bereft of Liberators) and prepared for Ploesti with about 10 missions to other MTO targets in what was dubbed Operation Husky.

For the main event at Ploesti, the two Eighth Air Force groups joined 'KK' Compton's 'Liberandos' and the 98th BG 'Pyramiders' under Colonel John 'Killer' Kane, which was now also subordinate to Ninth Air Force. Kane was a spirited and volatile leader, much-admired, but a contrast to the quiet, experienced and much-loved Colonel Leon Johnson of the 44th group.

The Allies believed that sending heavy bombers against German oil production would strike a major blow and alter the course of the war. The AAF considered the B-24 Liberator to be the only heavy bomber for this mission. The aircraft could carry a greater bomb load than the B-17 Flying Fortress, was faster and had greater range. The B-24 was championed by Brereton, who was viewed as the brain – or, in the view of some, the culprit – behind the raid.

Tidal Wave

Some 179 Liberators made up the Tidal Wave – the formal name of the operation – which set forth from dust-strewn desert air bases around Benghazi. One aircraft crashed on take-off, and one flew into the sea. The lead

HALPRO – the Halverson Provisional Detachment

The MTO (Mediterranean Theatre of Operations) evokes many images, from the early Allied landings in North Africa to heavy bomber raids mounted from Italian air bases and aimed at the heartland of the Third Reich. To many, the term MTO means Fifteenth Air Force, created on 1 November 1943 to oversee the theatre's air operations. In fact, the B-24 and the American airmen who maintained and flew it were fighting in the Mediterranean much earlier, sometimes in squadron-sized units, sometimes in concert with other air forces, and for a period were part of Ninth and Twelfth Air Forces.

In June 1942, a specially-trained Liberator outfit equipped with 23 early B-24Ds reached the Middle East, commanded by Colonel Harry A. Halverson. The HALPRO unit, or Halverson Provisional detachment, was made up of members of the 98th Bombardment Group (Heavy) – the term will be abbreviated BG throughout – and was heading east with the intention of bombing Japan. After these B-24Ds reached

Fayid, Egypt, it became apparent that they were needed to combat German forces in the immediate vicinity, so they were kept in-theatre.

To HALPRO fell the honour of making the first USAAF bombing mission against German forces in Europe. It happened on the night of 11-12 June 1942, when 13 Liberators struck the oil refineries at Ploesti, Romania. It was a symbolic achievement but it is unclear whether the Liberators' bombs did much damage. Four of the bombers became the first US Liberator casualties in the theatre when they landed near Ankara, Turkey. Turkish technicians actually repaired and flew one of the bombers (B-24D-CF, 41-11596, *Brooklyn Rambler*) and it was eventually repatriated. As for Ploesti, the name of the place was to become synonymous with the Liberator – but only later.

Pictured are (left) B-24D 41-11603 *Malicious*, one of the original 23 aircraft allocated to HALPRO, along with (above) 41-11622 *Edna Elizabeth*. Held in Egypt for the June 1942 raid on Ploesti, these aircraft were to have been issued to the 10th Air Force in China for the bombing of Tokyo.

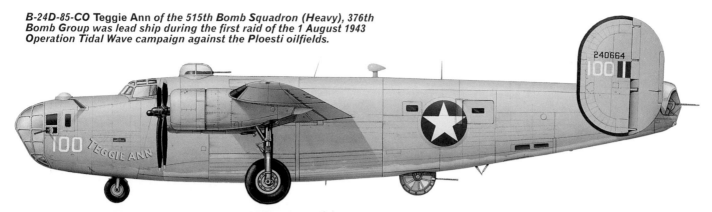

B-24D-85-CO **Teggie Ann** *of the 515th Bomb Squadron (Heavy), 376th Bomb Group was lead ship during the first raid of the 1 August 1943 Operation Tidal Wave campaign against the Ploesti oilfields.*

The Middle East edition of the Army newspaper **The Stars and Stripes** *carried this view of a Liberator, at low level over Ploesti on 1 August, on its 6 August 1943 front page.*

aircraft was attacked by a Messerschmitt Bf 109, jettisoned its bombs early, and crashed. No fewer than 10 Liberators had to abort and return to base, their engines fouled by the troublesome North African sand.

The strike force was to head north to Corfu, then swing to the northeast. At Corfu, the lead bomber, *Wongo-Wongo* (B-24D-120-CO 42-40563, 512th BS/376th BG), piloted by First Lieutenant Brian Flavelle, inexplicably began pitching violently. This Liberator stood abruptly on its tail in mid-air, shuddered, then dived suddenly straight into the sea. Radio

silence was being observed and no one knew what had happened. *Wongo-Wongo*'s wingman went down to investigate, found no sign of survivors, and ultimately had to abort and return to North Africa, carrying the deputy mission navigator. Contrary to myth, *Wongo-Wongo* was not carrying the lead navigator for the mission. For decades to come it would be reported, erroneously, that the loss of this Liberator led to the navigational problems which followed.

Navigational error

On approach to the target, the 376th BG mistook the IP (initial

point) at Floresti and turned south too soon. The 93rd BG followed but, thanks to second-thinking and prompt action by pilot Lieutenant Colonel Addison Baker and co-pilot Major John L. Jerstad in *Hell's Wench* (B-24D-120-CO 42-40994 of the 328th BS/93rd BG), the 93rd made another turn which took the group back in the direction of Ploesti. Among the trailing groups, the 389th flew northeast toward its target at Campina, 17 miles (27 km) north of the main refinery. Some confusion persisted as the 44th BG and 98th BG pressed on, but both reached the correct IP at Floresti and proceeded to their assigned targets.

Over the target, navigational mix-ups caused some of the refineries to be attacked by too many Liberators, others by two few. Dodging fighters and flak, many of the bombers flew into cables raised as barriers in their path by balloons.

Courage and heroism

Flying at low level, in gusting turbulence, confronting enemy fighters and gunfire – no one could doubt the courage of the Liberator crews who went against Ploesti, but decades later one of them would fume when the mission was included in a book about famous military blunders.

In war, success requires risk. The Ploesti attackers were going into nothing less than a fiery furnace. In the midst of the

inferno, the B-24 Liberator crews displayed incredible heroism. When *Hell's Wench* was hit by an 88-mm shell and several mortar rounds, Baker and Jerstad could have belly-landed in an open field but instead rushed at Ploesti's smoke stacks, trailing flames. 389th BG boss Colonel Leon Johnson lost nine aircraft from a 16-ship formation – his share was even worse than Brereton had predicted – but pressed his attack despite a sheer wall of German gunfire.

Despite potent defences and heavy losses, the Ploesti bombing inflicted heavy damage on the Romanian oil fields. A final tally showed that 179 Liberators took off, 14 aborted and 165 attacked. Of the B-24 losses, 33 were to flak and 10 to fighters. Some 56 Liberators were damaged. Eight aircraft recovered in Turkey. Of those B-24s which returned to North Africa, 99 recovered at their bases and 15 landed elsewhere. Some 532 American flyers died.

It will forever be debated how these bombings affected Germany's ability to fuel its combat forces, but no one doubted that the Third Reich was dealt a heavy blow by courageous American crews. Baker, Jerstad, Johnson, Kane and pilot Second Lieutenant Lloyd H. Hughes were awarded the Medal of Honor, all but Johnson and Kane posthumously. It was the only raid in history for which five Medals of Honor were awarded.

B-24D **Teggie Ann** *kicks up a cloud of dust at its Libyan base, while being run up before another mission. These aircraft were finished in a light shade known, unofficially, as 'desert pink' or 'tittie pink'.*

ETO/MTO operations

Liberators were performing anti-submarine duty in American and British hands, and fighting in the Pacific and Mediterranean theatres long before the Consolidated bomber became an important part of the Eighth Air Force in England – but the Eighth ultimately became the largest aerial armada ever assembled, and inevitably its achievements spawned more headlines and used more press ink than any of the other B-24 operators.

Above: B-24Ds of the 44th Bomb Group (H) taxi through the mud at a newly completed Shipdham airfield, prior to a practice mission. 'The Flying Eightballs' arrived in England in September 1942.

Inset above: Based in Italy, the 451st Bomb Group began operations with the 15th Air Force in January 1944. On 23 August the entire crew of this 725th BS B-24H was lost when the aircraft was attacked by Fw 190s after reaching its IP at 22,000 ft (6706 m) en route to Vienna. The aircraft caught fire and spiralled slowly earthwards some 5,000 ft (1524 m) before exploding. A lack of fighter escort was cited as the chief reason for the high losses sustained during 22/23 August; the 451st lost 15 aircraft.

The 'Mighty Eighth' had very humble beginnings, however. The US Army Air Forces were well ahead of most of the rest of the world in planning long-range bombing missions by huge, four-engined bombers, and even before the war, AAF officers envisioned putting 1,000 bombers in the sky at a time. But when General Ira Eaker went to England in 1942 to create the Eighth Air Force, he had five airmen with him. It was not Eaker, of course, but Major General Carl 'Tooey' Spaatz, who first commanded the Eighth Air Force (from 5 May 1942), but Eaker, who headed up Bomber Command under Spaatz before relieving him in the top job (on 1 December 1942), was the bomber boss in England from the start. It is unclear how Eaker viewed the Flying Fortress vs. Liberator controversy, but he clearly believed – wrongly, as it turned out – that a big bomber like the B-24 Liberator could fight its way to the target without help from any escort.

The founders of the Eighth Air Force came to England prepared to use B-17s, and the

B-24 Liberators that soon followed, to bomb German-occupied Europe by daylight. At first, they intended to do this with minimal or even no fighter escort. The Royal Air Force, whose Lancaster and Halifax crews already possessed considerable experience pounding the continent during the nocturnal hours, scoffed at daylight bombing. But nothing other than daylight bombing was seriously contemplated at Eighth Air Force headquarters at Bushey Park (codename Widewing), where Spaatz set up shop. Here, Spaatz established the 1st Bomb Wing (B-17s), then the 2nd Bomb Wing, which became the US parent unit for B-24 Liberator groups, beginning in September 1942 .The first of these was the 93rd BG, 'Ted's Traveling Circus', named for commander Colonel Edward J. ('Ted') Timberlake, Jr and flying from Alconbury.

Baptism of fire

The debut of the Liberator on the continent came on 9 October 1942 when the 93rd BG contributed 24 B-24Ds to the 108 bombers (the others

being B-17s) in a five-group assault against the French city of Lille. Timberlake led the Liberator force at the controls of his *Teggie Ann* (B-24D-5-CO Liberator 41-23754). Sergeant Arthur Crandall, a gunner of the 93rd BG, shot down an Fw 190 near Lille that day, in a B-24D

named *Ball of Fire* (apparently B-24D-1-CO 41-23667) piloted by Captain Joseph Tate. It was the first aerial victory for an Eighth Air Force Liberator.

The next Liberator group to reach England was the 44th BG 'Flying Eight Balls', arriving at Shipdham on 7 November 1942.

As the bombers' war over the Reich progressed, more sophisticated bombing aids were introduced. The lead aircraft in this formation of 446th BG B-24Hs is equipped with H₂S radar, installed in a 'trash bin' radome. This was tested by the 814th BS, 482nd BG in late 1943/early 1944.

Anti-submarine operations – USAAF and US Navy

The Anti-Submarine Command, USAAF was activated in October 1942, in response to the rise in shipping losses in the Atlantic. Prior to this units of the Eighth Air Force had undertaken ASW patrols in the Atlantic and a single squadron had been seconded to RAF Coastal Command. After the formation of a dedicated command, three groups were assigned the task of patrolling the Atlantic. By June 1943 a four-squadron group had been established in the UK for operations over the Bay of Biscay using B-24Ds; others were based in such locations as Newfoundland, Florida and Jamaica. The USAAF sank nine U-boats in the Atlantic up to August 1943; on 24 August Anti-Submarine Command disbanded, the entire ASW role being passed to the Navy.

By April 1943, PB4Y-1s of Fairwing (Fleet Air Wing) 7 in Iceland and Fairwing 15 in French Morocco were in operation in the war against U-boats in the Atlantic. During August two squadrons from the former and a single unit from the latter were transferred to RAF St Eval in Cornwall and by the end of the following month had flown 1,351 hours of ASW patrols over the Bay of Biscay, though two aircraft had been lost to Luftwaffe Ju 88s in the process. USN Liberators were also based on Ascension Island to cover the South Atlantic and later moved to San Miguel Island in the Azores, completing an umbrella of coverage over the Atlantic. By early 1944 10 USN VP/VPB units were equipped with Liberators; by the end of the war they had sunk, or had a hand in sinking, 13 U-boats in the Atlantic. Pictured is PB4Y-1 BuNo. 32032 of VB-103 (the first squadron to reach operational status in the Atlantic). Based at Dunkeswell, Devon, this aircraft was shot down on 12 November 1943, during an attack on *U-508*, which was sunk.

The group's first mission consisted merely of seven Liberators creating a diversion for an attack elsewhere by Flying Fortresses. The 44th was destined to participate in 343 missions between that date and 25 April 1945, a larger number of missions and more tons of bombs (18,980) than any other Liberator group save the 93rd. Over the course of the war, this group lost an extraordinary 192 Liberators and claimed 330

Luftwaffe fighters destroyed.

The Liberator was getting off to a slow start, with two squadrons from the 93rd BG briefly on loan to RAF Coastal Command for anti-submarine patrols in the Bay of Biscay. On 21 October 1942, 'Ted's Traveling Circus' launched 24 Liberators on an intended low-level raid against U-boat pens at Lorient, France, but because of 100 per cent cloud cover they were unable to bomb the target.

A mission to Brest by 12 Liberators on 7 November 1942 also produced little result, although it marked the first combat by the 44th BG, which launched seven aircraft in a diversionary effort.

On 13 December 1942, the 93rd BG was uprooted from England and sent off to North Africa. On this occasion, it was shifted to the 12th Air Force, although a later sojourn to the same region would place it under the purview of the 9th Air Force, to add its Liberators to the aerial bombardment of Axis supply ports. In North Africa, the men found primitive facilities, furious winds, rain, and mud. At one point, it was impossible to taxi a B-24D Liberator because the mud created such an obstacle. The 93rd BG eventually flew 22 missions over 81 days before returning to England. Another trip to North Africa lay in the future of 'Ted's Traveling Circus': soon after, the 93rd and 44th BGs were sent to North Africa for the Ploesti raid.

From May to September 1943, missions flown from England by the Eighth Air Force's B-24s were severely curtailed by the Ploesti raids. By the end of 1943 though, there were over 550 Liberators in Europe, there were almost three

times as many B-17s. USAAF policy since late 1942 was to concentrate all B-17s in England and the AAF's B-24 Liberators elsewhere – a goal that was not reached before the war ended. Sixteen bomb groups were in training in the US, for service with the 8th Air Force, though by the end of the year Liberator groups were flying diversionary raids for B-17 missions to main targets. Equipment included the new B-24H, with its factory-installed Emerson nose turret, which entered service in September.

MTO operations

The MTO (Mediterranean Theatre of Operations) evokes many images, from the early Allied landings in North Africa to heavy bomber raids mounted from Italian air bases and aimed at the heartland of the Third Reich. To many, the term MTO means 15th Air Force, created on 1 November 1943 to oversee the theatre's air operations. In fact, the B-24 and the American airmen who maintained and flew it were fighting in the Mediterranean much earlier, sometimes in squadron-sized units, sometimes in concert with other air forces, and for a period were part of the 9th and 12th Air Forces. By the end of the war there would be 15 Liberator groups in the 15th Air Force.

1944 and 1945

Both the 8th and 15th Air Forces continued to equip new groups with B-24s during 1944, the total number of Liberators in Europe totalling over 2,000 by April and peaking in August at 2,685. (Global B-24 strength reached its zenith at over 6,000 in front-line use the following month.) German fighter production became the focus of the Eighth's attacks in February (with the massed raids of 'Big Week') and in June came missions in support of D-Day.

By May 1945 there were 1,500 Liberators in service with the 8th and 15th Air Forces, though in the 8th the proportion of B-24s in use was slowly dwindling as they were replaced by B-17s. Weather was a problem for the 15th during spring 1945, limiting its ability to put large numbers of B-24s over targets. That said the 15th Air Force was to remain a major user of the Liberator until VE-Day.

*Bombs tumble from Ford-built B-24J **Urgin' Virgin** of the 491st BG's 853rd BS on the Vomag tank works at Plauen, Germany on 5 April 1945. Ford produced large numbers of B-24s.*

RAF 'Libs' at war

Liberator GR.Mk IIIs (and a single GR.Mk V) of No. 120 Sqn are serviced between sorties at RAF Aldergrove, Northern Ireland. Mk IIIs formed the backbone of Coastal Command's VLR squadrons until mid-1944.

Perhaps the most important of all the American aircraft that served with the RAF during World War II, the Liberator fulfilled three distinct roles – those of transport, bomber and overwater patrol.

Of 18,431 LB-30s and B-24s completed, some 2,340 came to Britain, although, as with several other important additions to Britain's armoury, it was French interest that brought the first Liberators to the UK. As late as April 1940, France had optimistically ordered 175 of the Consolidated bombers, under the designation LB-30MF (for 'Mission Francais').

This contract was taken over by Britain, resulting in the designation Liberator Mk II for 86 aircraft actually received by the RAF between August and December 1941 – the balance being taken over by the USAAC immediately following Pearl Harbor. The shortfall was made up in part, however, by the delivery between March 1941 and May 1942 of six YB-24s from USAAF stocks, which remained known as the Consolidated LB-30A (or sometimes simply as Liberators), and 20 'B-24A conversions',

(intended for the USAAF and also known as LB-30Bs) in April to August 1941, which became Liberator Mk Is. The six LB-30As, lacking armour and self-sealing fuel tanks, were used to open the ATFERO Atlantic Return Ferry Service, starting on 4 May 1941. Flying mail and cargo eastwards between St Hubert, Montreal, and Prestwick, Ayr, they performed the vital role of returning to Canada the ferry pilots who were regularly delivering Hudsons and other types to Britain via Iceland. A few of the Liberator Mk Is were also assigned to this role, and for training, while the remainder of this mark were developed for use by Coastal Command, which urgently needed aircraft with the Liberator's long range and striking power.

Entering service with No. 120 Squadron at Nutts Corner, the Liberator Mk Is were operational from 20 September 1941

'ZZ' codes identify this Liberator Mk VI as allocated to No. 220 Sqn. Derived from the B-24J, the GR.Mk VI of 1944 featured a retractable centimetric ASV radar set in the rear fuselage.

onwards, 15 of the 20 Mk Is serving with this unit at some time. To supplement the Liberator's offensive armament, a semi-retractable pack of four 20-mm cannon was developed in Britain to fit in the forward end of the bomb-bay, which could also carry four 500-lb (227-kg) and two 250-lb (114-kg) bombs, or up to six depth charges. The cannon were to be used to attack ships or submarines; defensive armament comprised single machine-guns in the nose and tail, and single or

paired beam guns. ASV Mk II 'stickleback' radar was added during the time the Liberator Mk Is were in service. The first recorded 'kill' of a U-boat by a Liberator Mk I of No. 120 Sqn came on 16 August 1942; there was another two days later, after which the Mk Is began to give way to Mk IIs and Mk IIIs.

The (ex-French order) Liberator Mk II introduced Boulton Paul four-gun dorsal and tail turrets, as well as the beam and nose guns – although turret production lagged behind

Nos 159 and 160 Sqns were the first RAF bomber squadrons to form on the Liberator Mk II (LB-30MF), both units seeing service in North Africa during 1942 before transferring to India. AL579 is believed to be a No. 159 Sqn aircraft, seen during July 1942, shortly after beginning day and night operations in the desert against targets in North Africa, Italy and Greece. Note the dorsal turret, fitted with a quartet of 0.303-in (7.7-mm) guns.

Above: AM929 was the last of the 20 LB-30Bs delivered to the RAF in August 1941. After trials at the A&AEE it was fitted with ASV radar and cannon and allocated to No. 120 Sqn, Coastal Command.

This Liberator Mk VI was assigned to No. 355 Sqn in India. Attacks on enemy airfields, harbour installations and shipping often involved round trips of over 2,000 miles (3219 km).

During 1944/45, No. 99 'Madras Presidency' Sqn flew Liberator Mk VIs on long-range sorties from Dhubalia, near Calcutta and, from July 1945, the Cocos Islands in the Indian Ocean.

aircraft deliveries and some Mk IIs operated without the dorsal turret. While some of the Mk IIs went to Coastal Command, delivery of this variant allowed Bomber Command to introduce the Liberator, earlier plans to issue Mk Is to No. 150 Sqn having been thwarted by Coastal's more urgent needs. At Kabrit in Egypt, No. 108 Sqn became the first to fly the Liberator as a bomber, in November 1941, while Nos 159 and 160 Sqns arrived at Fayid in June 1942 to join in the fight to stem the Axis advance into Egypt. A Special Liberator Flight was formed to support SOE operations in the Middle East, and No. 178 joined the fray early in 1943, staying on to receive Liberator Mk IIIs at the end of the year. Nos 149 and 160, meanwhile, took Liberator Mk IIs to India, where operations began in November 1942 – and it was from Indian bases that later marks would see most action. Some Mk IIs adapted in later life as transports became designated Liberator C.Mk II.

Deliveries to the RAF contin-

ued through Lend-Lease contracts, starting with 382 B-24Ds (of which 249 had initially been earmarked as a British Direct Purchase). These became Liberator B.Mk III or, when converted for Coastal Command, GR.Mk III (without ASV radar) and GR.Mk V (with ASV). Some were also converted for transport duty as C.Mk Vs. The B-24D versions all differed from the earlier models in having the dorsal turret (by Martin) moved forward to a position just aft the cockpit, and were the first of the Liberators to have exhaust-driven turbo-superchargers.

In Coastal Command, the Liberator GR.Mk IIIs and mostly, GR.Mk Vs served with Nos 53, 59, 86, 130 and 311 Squadrons over the North Atlantic and No. 354 in India. In the latter mark, ASV Mk III had been introduced, with aerial scanners in a chin fairing and a retractable ventral radome, providing a less drag-inducing addition than the ASV Mk II used in Liberator Mk IIs. Some Mk Vs also had their armament supplemented by

eight forward-firing rocket projectiles on racks each side of the forward fuselage.

Bomber role

In the bomber role, the Liberator B.Mk IIIs served wholly in the Far East, where Nos 159 and 160 Sqns were already flying the Mk IIs. They were joined in August 1943 by No. 355 in the offensive against Japanese targets in Burma.

Transport operations were continuing with No. 511 Sqn which, initially as No. 1425 Flight, had been using Liberator Mk Is and C.Mk IIs between the UK and Gibraltar, and by No. 45 Group, which had grown out of Ferry Command for the ATFERO operation and was to evolve into No. 231 Sqn. BOAC also flew several Liberators in support of the Transatlantic Ferry.

The Liberator B.Mk IV (and C.Mk IV) designations were applied to the planned Lend-Lease acquisition of the B-24E; none was delivered. Instead, the RAF received a total of 1,648 B-24Js which,

depending on role and equipment standard, became the Liberator B.Mk VI, C.Mk VI and GR.Mk VI. Some B-24G and H aircraft were also transferred in the field under the Mk VI designation. Late production B-24Js and a number of B-24Ls were known variously as B.Mk VIII, C.Mk VIII and GR.Mk VIII (and included the final 40 of what had been the original British purchase). Deliveries continued up to March 1945. The B-24J, which was the basis for the Mk VI, featured an Emerson nose turret, Martin dorsal and Sperry ventral 'ball' turret; after delivery, the British aircraft received a Boulton Paul four-gun rear turret and, in the GR versions for Coastal Command, were fitted with ASV in a ventral radome in place of the ventral turret. Starting in October 1943, No. 53 Sqn Liberators had an underwing Leigh Light installation, as did those of Nos 206 and 547 Sqns at a later point. While several squadrons continued to operate bomber Liberators in the Middle East, the great majority of the Mk VI and Mk VIII bombers went straight to the Far East, there to equip some 15 squadrons for the RAF's final campaign in Burma through 1944/45. From the Cocos Islands, eight Liberators of No. 99 Sqn and No. 356 Sqn mounted the RAF's last bombing raid of the war, on 7 August 1945.

Equivalent of the unarmed C-87 transport version of the Liberator that had been developed for and put into service with the USAAF, 24 Liberator C.Mk VIIs were delivered to Britain from June to September 1944, and were used by Transport Command's Nos 511, 246 and 232 Squadrons between the UK and the Far East. Finally, the RAF received 22 Liberator C.Mk IXs, these being the RY-3 version with a large, single fin and rudder.

Liberator C.Mk IX was the RAF designation for the RY-3 transport variant of the US Navy's Privateer. These were flown by No. 45 Group, Transport Command on routes between the UK, Canada and SEAC, via the Pacific.

B-24s in the Pacific and CBI

Among the first American aircraft lost during World War II was a B-24A, caught on the ground at Hickam Field, Hawaii, as the Japanese attacked Pearl Harbor on 7 December 1941. USAAF Liberators went on to play a prominent part in the Pacific and Far Eastern theatres.

By February 1942 the 7th and 19th Bomb Groups were operating repossessed British LB-30s in the Southwest Pacific, challenging Japanese convoys (with limited success) as they forged south. Often flying with B-17 Flying Fortresses, these aircraft pioneered the use of four-engined bombers in the Pacific theatre.

Meanwhile, in Alaska the 11th Air Force employed LB-30s and B-24Ds against Japanese forces heading for the Aleutians. By September 1942 the new 21st and 404th Bomb

Squadrons had moved out of the Aleutian chain and were based on the wind-swept island of Adak, within striking distance of Japanese targets.

In October, 10th Air Force India Air Task Force (IATF) Liberators made their first raids on Japanese targets in China and by the following month Liberators had joined the 5th and 7th Air Forces in the PTO. On the night of 22/23 December, 7th Air Force mounted an impressive 26-aircraft raid against Wake Island, staging through Midway from Hawaii.

During 1943 the B-17 was

Top: Seventh Air Force personnel watch one of their aircraft struggling off the runway on an island in the Marianas, heading for another Japanese target in the island-hopping war.

Above: B-24D Hell's Belle of the 400th BS, 90th BG, Fifth Air Force is pictured after scoring a direct hit on a 5,000-ton Japanese cargo vessel off the north coast of New Guinea in late 1942.

phased out in the Pacific as the decision was taken to concentrate Fortress deliveries in Europe. Thus the Pacific and China-Burma-India theatres became the preserve of the B-24 and by the end of the year the 5th, 7th, 10th, 11th, 13th and

B-24Ds destined for the PTO were modified with nose turrets during 1943. Betsy is a B-24D of the 321st BS, photographed in February 1944 during a mission to Wawak, New Guinea. The 'skull and crossed bombs' emblem on the tail is that of the 90th BG, nicknamed the 'Jolly Rogers' after the Group's commander, Colonel Arthur H. Rogers.

Left: B-24Ms of the 865th BS, 494th BG approach a target near Cebu City in the Philippines on 25 March 1945. Overall olive drab paintwork was abandoned in the PTO, for the reason that aircraft were seldom attacked on the ground and that, in the air, the camouflage was of little benefit. Paintwork also required maintenance, and ground staff were busy enough!

Below: B-24s of the 22nd and 494th BGs crowd the airstrip on Angaur Island, the Caroline Islands, December 1944.

14th Air Forces were all flying combat missions in Liberators. With more intensive use of the B-24 in combat, encounters with Japanese fighters became increasingly frequent and, with fighter escorts not always available, their vulnerability to attack became apparent, especially from head-on. It was during 1943 that B-24Ds destined for the Pacific were modified at USAAF depots, tail turrets being installed in the noses of these aircraft to discourage such attacks.

Other developments during 1943 included the use of radar to improve bombing accuracy, the 5th Bomb Group fielding 10 SB-24D 'Snoopers' from Guadalcanal.

Enter the B-24J

The B-24J, the most numerous Liberator variant, entered production in 1944, large numbers finding their way to the Pacific, followed by B-24Ls and B-24Ms. Key actions during the year included the ongoing effort to bomb the Japanese out of the island of Rabaul, an island in New Britain, east of New Guinea, so that a costly land invasion could be avoided. During January and February round-the-clock attacks, including night missions by B-24s, finally took the island out of the fight.

Further north the first raids by B-24s from Saipan on Iwo Jima (carried out by the 7th Air Force) took place during August while, on 26 December, Far East Air Force aircraft bombed the former American stronghold of Clark Field in the Philippines as the tide of the war continued to push the Japanese back.

In the CBI, USAAF B-24s carried out vital raids against Japanese supply routes in Burma and sowed mines in certain harbours and sea lanes to deny their use to the enemy.

If the PTO had a target for Allied bombing of equivalent importance to that of Ploesti in Europe, it was the formerly Dutch oilfields and refineries at Balikpapan, Borneo. These provided Japan with 35 per cent of its petroleum, including critical aviation fuel and had been a target for American B-24s since 1943. Naturally heavily defended, Balikpapan came under intense bombardment by the 5th and 13th Air Forces during 1944. In all, 433 tons of bombs were dropped by 321 Liberator sorties. Twenty-two B-24s were lost, but production from the refinery was significantly curtailed and valuable experience gained in long-range strategic bombing operations.

Azon guided bombs

1944 also saw the operational debut of a new weapon – the VB-1 Azon radio-controlled glide bomb. Dropped by specially modified 10th Air Force B-24s, the Azon comprised a standard 1,000-lb (454-kg) bomb fitted with steerable fins, a radio receiver and a flare so that the bombardier controlling the device could keep track of its decent.

It was first employed in the CBI in December against rail and road bridges, the Azon bomb enjoyed considerable success, paving the way for further development of what are known today as 'smart weapons'.

The number of front line B-24s in service in the Pacific peaked in May 1945 at 992. The island-hopping war had, by then, reached a point where mainland Japan was within reach of the Liberators of the Far East Air Forces (the 5th and 13th). So it was that the FEAF joined the B-29s in fire-bombing Japan into submission, joined by the aircraft of the 7th Air Force in July.

Above: This ferocious B-24L was photographed in Calcutta after VJ-Day. Its tail markings and sharkmouth indicate service with the 425th BS, 308th BG 'The Liberators of China', which had been based in China since early 1943.

Right: Ford modified over 200 B-24Js and Ls to C-109 standard as tankers to ferry fuel 'over the Hump' from India to China for use by B-29s bombing Japan. These aircraft typically carried twice the normal B-24 fuel load.

'Two-by-Four'

The US Navy's PB4Y-2 Privateer

In 1943 the US Navy began working with Convair on an optimised ocean patrol and ASW version of the Liberator. This first flew as the prototype XPB4Y-2 Privateer on 20 September 1943.

The 'Two-by-Four' as the type was to be known by its crews, incorporated the extremely tall single fin and introduced a completely revised fuselage, further stretched to 74 ft 7 in (22.73 m), 1,350-hp (1007-kW) R-1830-94 engines without turbochargers (superfluous at low altitudes), resulting in the cowlings being elliptical vertically instead of horizontally, and defensive armament of six pairs of 0.5-in (12.7-mm) guns (nose, forward dorsal, aft dorsal, left and right waist and tail). Fuel capacity was enhanced and the normal crew was increased to 11, with extensive radar, ASW and electronic-warfare equipment. There was provision for 8,000 lb (3628 kg) of bombs, torpedoes, mines or depth charges.

The Privateer entered service with the US Navy in January

1945, equipping VPB-118 and -119 on Tinian and Midway, respectively. The latter unit moved to Clark Field in the Philippines in March, flying bombing raids against occupied China from there until the end of the war. The following month VPB-118 moved to Okinawa to join the assault on Japan. In the meantime the first former PB4Y-1 unit to re-equip with the 'Two-by-Four' – VPB-106 – started its second tour in the Pacific. By the end of the war eight new Privateer squadrons had been formed, while 10 PB4Y-1 units had returned for a second tour, this time on the Privateer, or re-equipped on station. Training units in Hawaii and San Diego provided crews for these units.

April 1945 saw the first use of the SWOD-9 (ASM-N-2) Bat

Above: Erco ball nose turrets were a feature of most Privateers. In this view the type's lengthened forward fuselage, twin dorsal turrets, revised engine nacelles and radar antenna are also clearly evident, though the B-24 'family likeness' remains.

Above: Photographed in Shanghai in October 1945, 'X525' Our Baby (BuNo. 59525) is typical of wartime Privateers. This aircraft is known to have served with VPB-121 and -106.

Below: 'HA' codes on the tail of this aircraft are those of east coast-based patrol squadron VP-24, which operated P4Y-2s between 1947 and 1954. Note the 'Bat' glide bomb racks under its wings.

Left: A freight version of the Privateer – the RY-3 – was flown in 1944; 125 were ordered by the US Navy, though only 33 were completed before the end of the war. Of these, 26 were transferred to the RAF under Lend Lease, as Liberator C.Mk IXs, and four assigned to the Marine Corps for service as VIP transports.

Below and below right: The last Privateers in US Navy use were QP-4B target drones (designated P4Y-2K before 1962), employed for surface-to-air missile tests from 1952. The last example, BuNo. 59896, was destroyed on 16 January 1964.

Above: Nine Privateers were transferred to the United States Coast Guard for SAR duties, designated PB4Y-2G. Turrets were deleted and replaced with large observation ports.

guided glide bomb, two of which were launched from a Privateer of VPB-109, against shipping in Balikpapan Harbour, Borneo. PB4Y-2Bs carried two of the 1,600-lb (726-kg) devices on underwing pylons; before the end of the war in the Pacific, VPB-123 and -124 were also equipped to use the Bat and improved versions of the weapon remained in use post-war.

The last of 740 Privateers was not delivered until October 1945 and unlike the B-24 the Privateer remained in service after the war, being redesignated P4Y-2 in 1952. There were several post-war versions, including the P4Y-2S with improved ASW radar, the P4Y-2P photo-reconnaissance platform, the P4Y-2M weather reconnaissance aircraft (with a B-24D-style nose, a radome under the

forward fuselage and no armament), the P4Y-2G for the Coast Guard (with no armament and considerable modification), and the special 'ferret' electronic-warfare versions which, together with similarly equipped Martin P4M Mercators, carried out the Navy's Elint (electronic intelligence) missions during the post-war years.

One VP-26 PB4Y-2, operating from Wiesbaden over the Baltic on 8 April 1950, was shot down by a MiG-15, all 10 crew being killed. An unknown number of similarly-equipped aircraft were also made available to Nationalist China from May 1951 for reconnaissance duties. One of these aircraft is believed to have been shot down by a Burmese air force Sea Fury in 1961, having been caught dropping supplies to anti-Communist

Kuomintang guerrillas in the Shan State region of the country.

Korea and Indo-China

US Navy Privateers saw service in Korea, VP-772 flying the first of many 'firefly' flare-dropping missions for Marine Corps ground attack aircraft on 12 June 1951. Other USN P4Y-2S squadrons flew 'sampan patrol' maritime missions along the Korean coast for the duration of the 'police action'.

The most active fleet of Privateers outside the US Navy were those supplied to the French Aéronavale from November 1950. Initially allocated to Flottille 8F (renumbered Flottille 28F in 1953) at Tan Son

Nhut, 10 aircraft were supplied by the US and remained in the region until late 1955, flying bombing and reconnaissance missions throughout the French colonial war in Indo-China.

During 1956 the last French Privateers left the Far East for North Africa and further colonial tension. The aircraft were employed on patrol duties along the Algerian coast and the border with Tunisia, some night-bombing raids taking place on the latter tasking. The type was phased out by the Aéronavale in 1960, having been finally replaced by Lockheed P2V Neptunes.

Honduran transports

The only other operator of the P4Y was Honduras, which obtained at least three examples for use as transports in the 1950s. These may have been among the last Privateers in military service; the US Coast Guard retired its last PB4Y-2Gs in 1959 and the US Navy finally retired its last P-4s in 1964. The latter were QP-4B drones, converted by the Naval Air Development Center as targets for new missiles under development at the Pacific Missile Test Range at Point Mugu.

The Fuerza Aerea Hondurena's Privateer transports were serialled '792' (pictured), '794' and '796'.

'Super Privateer' fire-bombers

Hawkins & Powers Aviation Inc. of Greybull, Wyoming operates the last working PB4Y-2s – a group of five so-called 'Super Privateers' equipped with R-2600 engines salvaged from B-25 Mitchells. Fitted with superchargers, these engines give the much-improved performance needed for the demanding fire-fighting role. H&P's 'Super Privateers' have a 19,800-lb (8981-kg) payload, or 2,200 US gal (8328 litres) of retardant. Tanker '126' (N7962C) is pictured.

The first of the Lend-Lease Catalinas to enter RAF service were 170 Mk IBs (similar to PBY-5 standard). This example is fitted with ASV Mk II radar and was allocated to No. 202 Squadron, based at Gibraltar.

Consolidated PBY Catalina

Multi-role patrol 'boat

The greatest of all flying-boats, the Catalina proved to be one of the most versatile and enduring aircraft ever built. Active in all theatres of World War II, the PBY outlived its proposed replacement and earned its place in the annals of air warfare.

The Consolidated Catalina (known to its manufacturer as the Model 28) was one of the slowest combat aircraft of World War II; wags said its crews needed a calendar rather than a stopwatch in order to rendezvous with a convoy. Flown in 1935, it was no longer young even at the outbreak of war, and the US Navy had already ordered a next-generation flying-boat (the Martin PBM) to succeed it. But the well-loved 'Cat' happened to be rather hard to beat. In 1938 it had been recognised by the Soviet Union as superior to anything created by

their own designers, and it was built there under licence throughout the war. More than that, the original US machine blossomed forth in many new versions which, to the end of the war, outsold all the newer replacements. More Catalinas were built than any other flying-boat or floatplane in history.

Development

The genesis of the PBY, as the aircraft was known to US forces, lay in a 1933 requirement by the US Navy for a new long-range patrol flying-boat. At that time

the principal aircraft in this category was the Consolidated P2Y, designed at Buffalo by Isaac M. 'Mac' Laddon, a gifted seaplane engineer and a director of Consolidated Aircraft. To meet the new demand, he cleaned up the P2Y by giving it an almost cantilever wing, mounted above the shallow but broad hull on a central pylon housing the flight engineer. The wing differed from that of the P2Y by having a regular centre-section and tapered outer panels, all of stressed-skin all-metal construction (ailerons were fabric-skinned). A unique feature was that the wingtip floats were mounted on pivoted frames which could be retracted electrically so that in flight the floats formed the wingtips. The hull, likewise all metal, was quite different from that of most large 'boats in being all on one deck, with a broad semi-circular top. In the bow was a mooring compartment, and transparent

sighting window with a venetian blind giving sea water protection. The bow cockpit was a turret with large all-round windows in production aircraft, and a machine-gun above. Two pilots sat side-by-side in the wide cockpit, with large windows all round. Aft of the wing were left and right gunner's stations, each with a sliding hatch. Unlike the P2Y the tail was clean and simple, with the horizontal tail mounted well up the single fin. The powerplant switched from Cyclones to the new two-row Pratt & Whitney Twin Wasp, neatly cowled on the centre-section with cooling gills and driving Hamilton variable-pitch propellers.

With the massive order for 60, Consolidated had plenty of work to support its 2,000-mile (3220-km) move to San Diego in southern California, where the weather was fine throughout the year. In October 1935 the XP3Y made a non-stop flight of almost 3,500 miles (5633 km) from Coco Solo to San Francisco. It then went on to participate in the dedication of the giant new San Diego plant on 20 October, before returning to Buffalo to be modified to PBY standard with a broad rounded rudder, de-icer boots on all leading edges (with pull-out steps up the leading edge of the fin), full armament and combat equipment. It flew again in March 1936 and reached US Navy squadron VP-11F at the same time as the first production machines in October 1936. Unquestionably this was the best patrol flying-boat in the world at that time.

In July 1936 Consolidated received a contract for 50 PBY-2s with all four wing racks stressed to 1,000-lb (454-kg) loads and with 0.5-in (12.7-mm)

This PBY-1 is seen taxiing out, possibly at NAS Pensacola. A crewman is on the wing, waist hatches are open, and the pilot has full up-elevator and full left aileron. The biplane is an N3N Canary.

guns in the waist positions. In November 1936 an order followed for 66 PBY-3s with R-1830-66 Twin Wasps uprated from 900 to 1,000 hp (671 to 746 kW), and in December 1937 a contract followed for 33 PBY-4s, all but one with large bulged transparent blisters instead of lateral sliding hatches for the beam gunners and with 1,050-hp (783-kW) engines. Two more PBYs were sold in 1937 to explorer Dr Richard Archbold, who named them *Guba I* and *Guba II* (Motu word for a sudden storm). *Guba II* spent an arduous year in New Guinea, finally making the first flight across the Indian Ocean to survey the route known in World War II as the 'horseshoe route' on which hundreds of military and BOAC Catalinas were to fly. It then crossed Africa and the Atlantic, the first aircraft to circle the globe near the Equator. *Guba I* was sold to a Soviet expedition led by Sir Hubert Wilkins, flying 19,000 miles (30600 km) through the worst weather in the world, fruitlessly searching for S. A. Levanevskii, who vanished near the North Pole on 13 August 1937. So outstanding was the Model 28 in this work that the Model 28-2 was put into production at Taganrog on the Azov Sea as the GST (civil transport version, MP-7), over 1,000 being used in World War II with 950-hp (709-kW) engines in Polikarpov I-16-type shuttered cowlings and with Soviet equipment and armament.

British interest

Another Model 28-5 (PBY-4) was bought by the British Air Ministry and tested at Felixstowe as P9630, proving so outstanding that it was adopted as a standard boat for Coastal Command. Named Catalina Mk I – a name later adopted by the US Navy – the first RAF variant was similar to the latest US Navy type, the PBY-5 with 1,200-hp (895-kW) R-1830-92 engines, an order for 200 of

which had been placed on 20 December 1939. No flying-boat – in fact no large US Navy aircraft – had ever been ordered in such quantities, and the vast open-ended British orders called for massive extra capacity. British officials helped to arrange for licence-production by Canadian Vickers at Cartierville (Montreal) and Boeing of Canada at Vancouver. The San Diego plant also much more than doubled in size and was joined by a larger plant a mile down the road, building B-24s.

On 22 November 1939 Consolidated flew a PBY-4, rebuilt as the XPBY-5A with retractable tricycle landing gear. This excellent amphibian conversion was a great success and had only a minor effect on performance. The final 33 PBY-5s were completed as PBY-5As, and another 134 were ordered in November 1940. At the time of Pearl Harbor (7 December 1941), the US Navy had three squadrons of PBY-3s, two of PBY-4s and no fewer than 16 flying the new PBY-5. Before sunrise on that day, a PBY crew spotted the periscope of a Japanese submarine at Pearl Harbor, marked it with smoke and guided the destroyer USS *Ward*, which sank it – the first US shots of World War II – over an hour before the air attack began. By this time a further 586 PBY-5s had been ordered, and the export list had risen to 18 for Australia, 50 for Canada, 30 for France and 36 for the Netherlands East Indies. In 1942 another 627 PBY-5As were added, of which 56 were to be

OA-10s for the USAAF, used for search and rescue. The first Lend-Lease batch for the RAF comprised 225 non-amphibious PBY-5Bs (Catalina Mk IBs), 55 of which were retained by the USN, followed by 97 Catalina Mk IVAs, fitted in Britain with ASV Mk II radar. RAF Catalinas usually had a Vickers K (VGO) machine-gun in the bow and twin 0.303-in (7.7-mm) Brownings machine-guns in the waist blisters.

Pacific action

From the time of the devastating Japanese attack on Pearl Harbor, the Catalina was by far the most important US patrol aircraft. In the northern campaign along the Aleutians, many Catalinas had to make overloaded downwind take-offs in blizzards at

night, with ice over the windscreen. The PBY was the first US aircraft (other than the obsolete Douglas B-18) to carry radar. It fulfilled diverse missions including those of torpedo-bomber, transport and glider tug. Perhaps the most famous of all Catalinas were the Black Cat PBY-5A amphibians which, painted matt black, roamed the western Pacific from December 1942, finding Japanese ships of all kinds by radar at night and picking up Allied survivors from ships and aircraft in boats and dinghies. In addition to radar, bombs, depth charges and fragmentation grenades, the Black Cats often carried crates of empty beer bottles whose eerie whistling noise deterred Japanese gunners, making them look for what they imagined to be unexploded bombs.

The PBY-1's defensive armament comprised one 0.3-in (7.62-mm) machine-gun in the bow turret and one similar weapon in each waist position. A further 0.3-in (7.7-mm) machine-gun could be fitted in the tunnel position in the bottom of the hull.

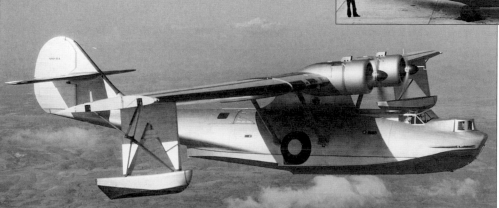

Above: The esteem in which the PBY was held is typified by this image of four US Navy patrol squadrons lined up in San Diego as part of the 1938 Warner Brothers film 'Wings of the Navy', starring Olivia de Havilland and George Brent.

Left: In November 1939 Consolidated first flew the XPBY-5A. This was converted with tricycle-type undercarriage from a PBY-4 and was the first of the amphibian variants (denoted by the 'A' suffix).

Late-war developments

Having proved itself as an exceptional patrol boat, the Catalina was adapted for a number of additional roles including those of night-bomber, mine warfare and air-sea rescue. Such was the demand for the aircraft that production was set up in four satellite plants.

Above: Built by the Naval Air Factory at Philadelphia, the PBN-1 Nomad introduced a taller rudder, enlarged fuel capacity and a hull with a longer clipper bow and extended afterbody.

Inset: This PBY-5A amphibian, equipped with British ASV (air-to-surface vessel) radar, was photographed while on patrol along the Aleutian Islands coast in early 1943.

By late 1941 the Cartierville plant was in full production. Canadian Vickers delivered 230 amphibians, ordered as PBV-1As, but actually passed to the USAAF as OA-10As, as well as 149 Canso I amphibians for the RCAF. Boeing, which came on stream later, built 240 PB2B-1s, mainly as Catalina Mk IVs for the RAF, RAAF and RNZAF, and 17 Catalinas and 55 Cansos for the RCAF. Yet another plant was brought into the programme in 1941 to produce its own improved models. The NAF (Naval Aircraft Factory) at Philadelphia had been the source of all US Navy flying-boat designs, and its experience enabled it to improve on 'Mac' Laddon's design in a way that could have been done by the parent company had it not been for the frantic demand for production. The NAF Catalina, the PBN-1, had a wing restressed for 38,000-lb (17237-kg) gross weight, with increased tankage, redesigned wingtip floats and struts, and a new hull with a longer and sharper bow, 20° step amidships, and rear step extended about 5 ft (1.52 m) aft. The most obvious of the changes was the tall vertical tail, with a horn-balanced rudder, and armament was generally increased to three or more 0.5-in (12.7-mm) machine-guns (only the ventral tunnel retained the rifle-calibre gun) with a rounded bow turret and improved continuous-feed magazines. Another change was a redesigned electrical system of increased capacity, with the batteries moved from the leading edge down to the hull.

The NAF itself delivered 138 PBN-1 Nomads, and Consolidated (by this time Convair) opened yet another plant at New Orleans to build the best Catalinas of all, the amphibious version of the PBN.

Ultimate 'Cat'

Called PBY-6A, this usually carried a centimetric radar in a neat pod above the cockpit, and the bow turret normally had twin 0.5-in (12.7-mm) guns. An order was placed for 900, but the end of the war cut this to 48 for the Soviet Union (which also received all but one of the PBNs), 75 as OA-10Bs for the USAAF and 112 for the US Navy. Fifty more were delivered by Boeing from Vancouver as PB2B-2s, designated Catalina Mk VI by the RAF.

Most of the Catalina's work up until mid-1942 involved long and arduous patrols of the many oceans and seas involved in the war. However, by September, the 'Black Cats' night bombing units had expanded and was organised as Fleet Air Wing 17 at

This PBY-5A amphibian is seen in the markings carried by the aircraft at the time of the US entry into World War II. After Pearl Harbor, a contract for a further 710 PBY-5As was placed, some of which ended up as part of the Lend-Lease agreement with the UK.

OA-10A Catalina

One of the more unusual aircraft handed over from the inventory of the US Army Air Force to the newly-formed USAF in October 1947 was this OA-10 of the Air Rescue Service. Built during the war by Canadian Vickers, it was one of a batch of 230 which served from early 1944 on several fronts and remained in the active inventory until at least 1954.

Flight deck
The pilot and co-pilot sat side-by-side on the flight deck and were provided with a roof escape hatch for emergency egress. The throttle and propeller controls were mounted within reach of both pilots in the overhead position.

Bow cabin
The nose section provided accommodation for one crew member, who performed, on the unarmed post-war OA-10, observer duties. The panel below the station was a blind which covered the flat-pane bomb-aiming window.

Radar
Situated above the cockpit was a centimetric surveillance radar which could be used to locate surfaced submarines or surface vessels. In the rescue role the radar could be used to detect stricken vessels or even floating aircraft.

Wing support
The wing was attached to the fuselage by a central pylon and four solid struts. The central pylon incorporated a step to allow easy access to the top of the wing and the engines.

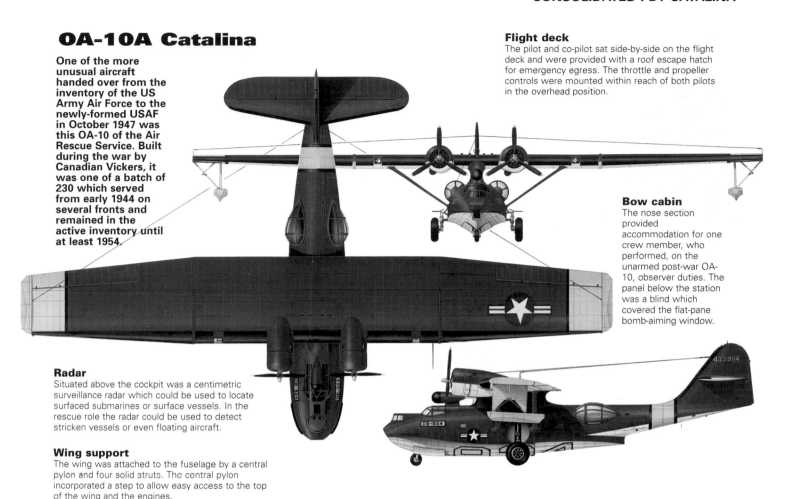

Brisbane, Australia. The vital anti-U-boat missions carried out in the North Atlantic began to decline in importance during 1943 as U-boat activity reduced and a number of PBY-5A units was deployed abroad, VP-83 and VP-94 deploying to Nata, Brazil.

US Navy Catalinas also operated from Morocco from November 1942, flying anti-shipping patrols and occasionally encountering German patrol aircraft such as Fw 200s and, in at least two instances, prevented attacks on Allied shipping.

The PBY had its twin Pratt & Whitney R-1830 Twin Wasp engines mounted on the high-set mainplane, well clear of the water. The wingtip floats retracted after take-off to form the outermost section of the wing.

One PBY-5A squadron, VP-63, became the first to be fitted with MAD equipment and operated from Pembroke Docks in the UK from July 1943. Engaged on anti-submarine patrols in the Bay of Biscay, the unit suffered losses arising from German fighter attacks. However, in January 1944 the unit moved to Morocco and, now equipped with 65-lb (29-kg) retro-rockets, had some success, including the sinking of U-boat U-761 in February 1944. Altogether, the US Navy PBYs made a significant impression on the war against the U-boats, sinking 20 of the 55 submarines claimed by US Navy aircraft in World War II.

'Dumbo' missions

The most popular role of the Catalina for other Allied aircrew was that of air-sea rescue. At first, the duty was completed by regular patrol squadrons, but efficiency was greatly improved with the introduction of special rescue squadrons. These consisted of USAAF detachments flying OA-10s and the USN's Air-Sea Rescue Squadrons whose Catalinas, by 1945, could carry specialised equipment such as droppable lifeboats. The Army Emergency Rescue Squadrons operated in the Mediterranean Sea, Pacific Ocean, Indian Ocean, Atlantic Ocean and English Channel. These missions and those of the Catalina were known by the codename 'Dumbo'.

Total production of all versions of the Consolidated Model 28 considerably exceeded 3,000. Of these, 2,398 were delivered by Consolidated Aircraft and Convair (the March 1943 name for the merged Consolidated and Vultee-Stinson companies). Some 892 were built by the NAF and by the two Canadian plants, and 27 were built in the Soviet Union.

RAF service

No. 209 Squadron flew this Catalina Mk I on general reconnaissance duties over the North Atlantic. Catalinas replaced the inadequate Saro Lerwick with this unit in April 1941, the squadron being based at Castle Archdale in County Fermanagh. From March 1942 the squadron patrolled the Indian Ocean, from bases in East Africa.

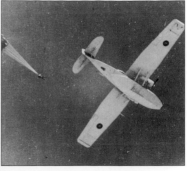

Above: Three Catalina Mk IBs were used to form No. 240 Squadron's Special Duties Flight, which operated on clandestine agent-dropping/ retrieval missions around the Burmese and Malayan coasts.

Although lightly armed and vulnerable to fighters, the Catalina possessed extraordinary endurance, and was consequently heavily committed to the Battle of the Atlantic against the U-boats.

Britain's first experience of the Consolidated flying-boat came with the arrival, in July 1939, of a single Model 28-5, acquired by the British Purchasing Commission in order to evaluate US hull design trends rather than the performance of the aircraft itself. Testing of this aircraft ended in February 1940 when it crashed and sank at Dumbarton. Another single example, a Model 28-3, was purchased in 1940 (named *Guba II*) from the explorer Dr Richard Archbold, and served briefly, from October to December, with No. 209 Sqn before passing to BOAC – thus

giving the RAF its first experience of the type at an operational level.

Meanwhile, the British Purchasing Commission had been busy ordering the Model 28-5, a total of 59 on direct contract being supplemented by 40 similar aircraft that had been ordered by France, but not delivered before the surrender. These 100 aircraft (including *Guba II*) took the designation Catalina Mk I; deliveries were spread from March 1941 to January 1942. They were preceded by seven similar Catalina Mk IIs, released by the USN for early delivery, from

January to April 1941. The RAF also received 17 Catalina Mk IIAs, this being the designation for 36 examples purchased by Canada in 1941, the others going to the RCAF and RAAF.

Full service use of the Catalina began in March 1941 with No. 240 Squadron stationed at Stranraer, closely followed by Nos 209 and 210. More than a year would pass before any of the squadrons could claim the destruction of a U-boat, but Catalinas from all three units took part in the discovery and shadowing of the *Bismarck* in the 24 hours before it was sunk, in May 1941, by ships of the British Home Fleet. A further squadron to use Catalina Mk Is, No. 413 (RCAF), formed in the UK in mid-1941 and moved to Ceylon in March 1942 to fly anti-submarine patrols over the

Indian Ocean. The advent of Lend-Lease arrangements allowed a steady build-up of the RAF's Catalina force, starting with the allocation of 225 Catalina Mk IBs (of which 55 were retained by the US Navy). These were basically similar to the Catalina Mk I but built to the PBY-5 standard, as were 97 Catalina Mk IVAs built by Consolidated and 200 Catalina Mk IVBs built by Boeing Aircraft of Canada. Not all of these allocated aircraft actually reached the RAF, there being some diversions to the RCAF (which called the aircraft the Canso), RAAF and RNZAF. In the RAF, the Catalina Mk I and Mk IV variants served in the Coastal Command squadrons already mentioned, being heavily committed to the Battle of the Atlantic and flying from bases in the UK, Gibraltar and Iceland.

Far East service

As more Catalinas became available, further squadrons were equipped: No. 202 was primarily Gibraltar-based; Nos 212 and 191 flew principally from Indian bases; and Nos 209, 259, 262, 265 and 270 were Africa-based. No. 205 Sqn, flying Catalina Mk Is from Singapore by October 1941, was virtually wiped out within three months, but later re-formed in Ceylon to operate Mk IVs with great success, alongside the Dutch-manned No. 321 Sqn. Because of its light defensive

A key innovation in the Battle of the Atlantic was ASV radar, which could spot a surfaced or snorkelling U-boat. This aircraft carries Yagi antennas for the system under its wings.

No. 210 Squadron was an early Catalina Mk I operator, based at Oban but with detachments at Reykjavik, Sullom Voe and Stranraer. It was a No. 210 aircraft which spotted and tracked the Bismarck on 26 May 1941, allowing the pursuing warships to close in and engage.

armament – six machine-guns in all – the Catalina was susceptible to attacking fighters and was therefore not best suited to patrols close to enemy shore bases. Its long range, on the other hand, permitted sorties of up to 20 hours' duration, allowing it to search far out to sea, although, with only four Mk VII or Mk VIII depth charges, pinpoint accuracy was needed to attack submarines successfully.

The effectiveness of the Catalina in the anti-submarine role was enhanced with the introduction of ASV radar, initially in the Mk II form with its array of Yagi aerials on the fuselage and beneath the wing. More effective was the ASV Mk III and, eventually, ASV Mk VI, with its dish scanner contained in a pod mounted above the cockpit. During 1943, No. 210 Sqn alone flew Catalina Mk IVAs with an underwing Leigh Light installation, but this displaced two of the depth charges usually carried, and therefore required the operation of aircraft in pairs, one with the light and one fully armed.

The Catalina's role was extended when No. 357 Squadron flew agents into and out of Burma and Malaya, and when No. 210 Squadron, flying from the Shetlands, flew similar sorties supporting clandestine Norwegian forces. In India, No. 628 Squadron was flying air-sea rescue and weather reconnaissance before the end of the war. This role led to the designation Catalina ASR.Mk IVB.

Amphibious 'Cat'

The advent of an amphibian version of the Catalina further enhanced its usefulness, although the RAF found less need for this type than did the US Navy and the RCAF. The adaptation was simple, with a nosewheel and mainwheels retracting into watertight bays in the hull. As the PBY-5A, the amphibious version entered US Navy service at the end of 1941 – by which time the RAF name had also been adopted by that service. The designation Catalina Mk IA was given to 14 of the amphibians bought by Canada, but these saw no service with the RAF. Through Lend-Lease, the RAF received 14 Catalina Mk IIIs, similar to the USN PBY-5A. These were used almost wholly in Iceland, in the hands of No. 119 Squadron and Norwegian-manned No. 330 Squadron. Another of the Norwegian squadrons, No. 333, also used Catalinas (Mk IVs) during the final months of the war in Europe. Two Catalina Mk IBs helped to maintain an important passenger, mail and freight link across the Indian Ocean from July 1943 to July 1945 in the hands of BOAC; three Mk IVs added for this service were, however, little used.

Final designations allotted to the Consolidated flying-boats were Catalina Mk V and Catalina Mk VI. The Mk V was reserved for Lend-Lease supply of tall-tailed PBN-1 versions, but none of these was in fact delivered. The Mk VI was another tall-tailed version, the PB2B-2 produced by Boeing Aircraft of Canada.

The RAF expected to receive 77 Catalina Mk VIs, but only 67 PB2B-1s had been built when production was terminated with the ending of hostilities, and only five of these actually reached Britain. They saw no service with the RAF, and were later transferred to the RAAF.

British 'Cats' at war

The pressing demands of the war saw all the early Catalinas assigned to the Atlantic theatre, but as sufficient numbers became available, RAF machines were dispatched to the Mediterranean and the Far East. BOAC flew a few to maintain vital passenger links.

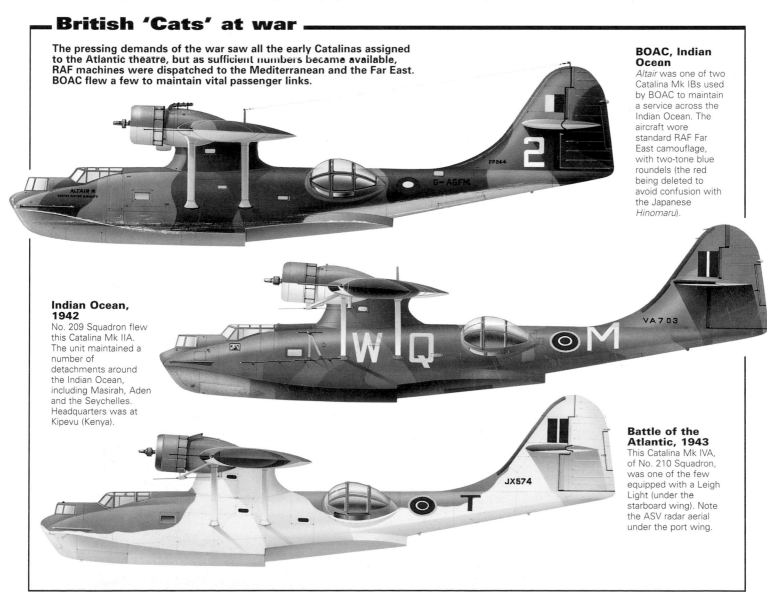

BOAC, Indian Ocean
Altair was one of two Catalina Mk IBs used by BOAC to maintain a service across the Indian Ocean. The aircraft wore standard RAF Far East camouflage, with two-tone blue roundels (the red being deleted to avoid confusion with the Japanese *Hinomaru*).

Indian Ocean, 1942
No. 209 Squadron flew this Catalina Mk IIA. The unit maintained a number of detachments around the Indian Ocean, including Masirah, Aden and the Seychelles. Headquarters was at Kipevu (Kenya).

Battle of the Atlantic, 1943
This Catalina Mk IVA, of No. 210 Squadron, was one of the few equipped with a Leigh Light (under the starboard wing). Note the ASV radar aerial under the port wing.

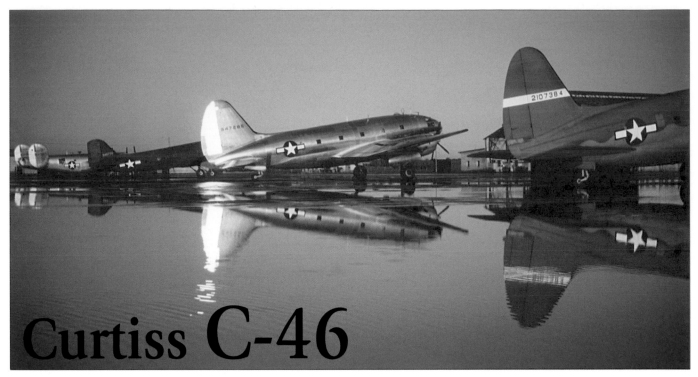

Curtiss C-46 Commando

Olive Drab and 'natural metal' Commandos share an unknown ramp with a C-47 and B-24. Like both the Skytrain and the Liberator, the Commando was produced in several factories.

In the shadow of the 'Gooney Bird'

The largest and heaviest twin-engined aircraft to see service in the USAAF, the C-46 was a derivative of the CW-20 airliner. Widely used in the Pacific and CBI, the Commando was also active in the Korean War.

The Curtiss C-46 Commando spent an eminently successful career in the shadow of the smaller Douglas C-47 Skytrain, and for years was plagued by rumours that it was a deathtrap. To some American veterans, what they remember about the C-46 is the aircraft exploding on take-off – due, they believe, to a flawed fuel system that was repaired only slowly and begrudgingly. The more familiar image of the C-46 is that of a mighty lifter, hauling much-needed war cargoes over the 'Hump' of the Himalayan mountain range into China. But there was another C-46, too, a pragmatic working aircraft that turned in excellent post-war service in places as disparate as Chile and Japan.

Development of the CW-20, later to become the C-46 and

Ground crew swing the port propeller of Polly the Queen before another mission from Chenyi, China. The C-46 became synonymous with operations in the CBI theatre, flying vital supplies 'over the Hump' into China.

the costliest project ever undertaken by Curtiss, began in 1936 under chief designer George A. Page. The goal was a new airliner, to replace the Curtiss Condor and other biplanes. The Douglas DC-3 was already producing revenue with American Airlines and other carriers, but the Curtiss aircraft promised to be larger and faster, powered by two 1,650-hp (1230-kW) Pratt & Whitney R-2800-17 Double Wasp 18-cylinder radial engines. Page's engineering team produced an aircraft with a cross-section of two circular segments, or lobes, intersecting at a common chord line, giving the mistaken impression of being a 'double decker'.

Twin-tail prototype

At Curtiss's St Louis, Missouri plant, the prototype – powered by a pair of 1,600-hp (1193-kW) Wright R-2600 Cyclone engines and distinguished by a cumbersome twin-rudder empennage – made its first flight on 26 March 1940,

piloted by Edmund T. (Eddie) Allen. Curtiss revealed the existence of the new aircraft on 11 April 1940, but the aircraft suddenly took on a new significance with the 7 December 1941 Japanese attack on Pearl Harbor. The military potential of the design had always been obvious, but now it became paramount. In fact, the prototype, soon refitted with a single fin, was impressed into USAAF duty as the sole C-55.

The prototype subsequently went to the British Overseas Airways Corporation (BOAC)

The appearance of the CW-20 was greatly improved by the fitting of a single tailfin in place of the twin fins with which the CW-20 prototype was equipped in its original guise.

Commandos were built in four factories – Curtiss facilities in Buffalo, New York (pictured), St Louis, Missouri and Louisville, Kentucky, plus the New Orleans plant of boat builder, Higgins Industries Inc.

and was used on Malta-Gibraltar runs until, lacking adequate spare parts, it had to be withdrawn from service and scrapped by October 1943.

Thus, the CW-20 was produced as the C-46 Commando, the USAAF (suffering from grave deficiencies in air transport) taking a liking to the aircraft's cavernous, double-bubble fuselage. The main compartment could accommodate (in addition to general cargo) 40 fully-equipped troops, up to 33 stretchers, five Wright R-3350 engines, or an equivalent tonnage in other freight. The C-46 was never easy to load, unload, or turn around quickly on a crowded ramp – the concept of 'roll-on, roll-off' transports, together with the word airlift, still lay in the

future. In September 1940 when the AAF ordered 200 C-46s, plans to pressurise the Commando had been dropped (at army insistence), minor engineering problems had been straightened out, and a wing fuel-leak problem had still not even been discovered.

First of over 3,000

By the time the first production C-46 reached the USAAF on 12 July 1942 – now, eight months into US participation in World War II – production had shifted to Curtiss's Buffalo, New York plant. The initial order for the streamlined transport was increased by a substantial number, the first step towards eventual construction of 3,181 Commandos. Adapting the aircraft for military use was a

slow process. Only after 25 aircraft had been built did Curtiss introduce the C-46A, with a large cargo-loading door, a cargo floor and fold-down seats along the cabin wall. While the design was being ironed out, Curtiss was re-adjusting its production plans. The company had constructed a new facility in Louisville, Kentucky which, unlike most buildings, was partly air-conditioned. Climate control was necessary to work with plywood, and Curtiss wanted to manufacture the all-plywood C-76 Caravan cargo aircraft. When the C-76 was abandoned, Curtiss shifted the C-46 programme to Buffalo, although a small number of aircraft was later built in St Louis. With the C-76 no longer a factor, Curtiss used Louisville as its major second source for C-46 Commando production.

The USAAF also planned to use Higgins Industries, Inc., of New Orleans, Louisiana, to build 500 C-46As and 500 C-76 Caravans. It was the discovery that sufficient alloy would be

available that made the all-wood C-76 superfluous, although in the end Higgins – busy manufacturing landing-boats – built only two C-46As, the first delivered on 1 October 1944.

'Stepped' windscreen

Curtiss turned out an XC-46B with 'stepped' windshield and different engines, the flush-windshield C-46D with double cargo doors, and only 17 C-46E models with stepped windshields and three-bladed Hamilton Standard propellers in place of the usual four-bladed Curtiss Electric models. The C-46F was an improvement on the more familiar Commando, and the sole C-46G and XC-113 models were used for engine tests. There were three XC-46L conversions with larger engines.

The operational career of the C-46 culminated in millions of pounds of supplies being brought to Allied forces, especially to the Chinese Nationalists who could be reached only by crossing vast mountain ranges from India. Fortunately, a few months after the type entered service, a 'fix' was found for the problem of leaking fuel in the wing fuel tanks – which occasionally caused a C-46 to blow itself to pieces. Marine Corps R5C Commandos performed yeoman cargo-hauling duties in the Southwest Pacific.

In post-war years, most C-46 Commandos became civilian air freighters, but the type remained on duty with the US Air Force and soon equipped a number of friendly air forces, including Nationalist China, South Korea, and Japan.

A Japanese official noted that the aircraft was attractive to his nation's air self-defence force because in the 1950s it was compatible with USAF Commandos still stationed nearby in Japan.

Above: Only 17 C-46Es, with the distinctive 'stepped' windscreen, were completed. A number was later passed to Nationalist China.

Right: In USMC service the Commando was designated R5C-1. Equivalent to the C-46A, 160 were built, remaining in use for several years post-war. Ten were used by the Coast Guard.

Commando in service

Most often associated with the airlift of supplies 'over the Hump' between India and China, the C-46 saw service in other theatres and in the Korean War. Some served in peacetime into the 1970s.

The Curtiss C-46 Commando is best known as the mainstay of the massive air transport effort undertaken from the Assam region of India to supply friendly forces in southwest China. Flying the 'Hump', as this treacherous crossing of the Himalayas became known, was a task fraught with peril for the C-46s and crews of Col Edward H. Alexander's India-China Wing of the Air Transport Command (itself part of the US Army Air Forces, or AAF).

The aircraft were loaded and flown under the most primitive conditions, their fuel pumped by hand from drums, the Assam airfields largely unpaved and transformed into quagmire by monsoons which poured down for half the year. On the 500-mile (804-km) Assam-Kunming route, C-46s had to haul cargoes over ridgelines looming at 12,000 to 14,000 ft

(3658 to 4267 m), even though ice began to form on the wings at 10,000 ft (3048 m).

In August 1942, using a few C-47 Skytrains, the AAF had been able to transport only 85 tons of cargo over the India-China route. By December 1943, with an identical number of C-46s, the figure had risen to 12,590 tons.

Short on spare parts, flying in unbearable wet and cold with minimal navigation aids, taking off at maximum overload weight, the C-46 crews were a lifeline to Chiang Kai-shek's Nationalist Chinese forces and Gen. Claire Chennault's 14th Air Force at a time when the Japanese were all around. Nor was the Commando excused from combat – Japanese fighters shot some down. Cpt. Wally A. Gayda shot down a Japanese fighter, apparently a Nakajima Ki-43 'Oscar', by firing a BAR (Browning Automatic Rifle)

Above: Though most often associated with the CBI theatre, the Commando saw some service in the ETO. C-46A 42-60956 was photographed in Italy.

Top: Commandos provided logistic support to units in the scattered island groups in the Pacific. This pair is seen in June 1944 on Saipan – soon to become an important B-29 base.

through his C-46 front-cabin window, killing the 'Oscar' pilot at close range.

Other theatres and wars

C-46s were widely used in other theatres. About 40 were delivered as R5C-1 Commandos for the US Marine Corps. They served initially with Marine Air Group 35 in the Southwest Pacific and showed themselves amenable to primitive island airstrips, often unpaved or paved

with pierced steel planking. The US Navy later used a handful of Commandos, including some R5C-1T trainers.

C-46s remained in AAF service after VJ-Day and played a vital role in the US Air Force's Troop Carrier Command. Some were employed in tests of glider-towing techniques, including hard tows with the gliders coupled close behind the tug. The C-46 was widely used to supply troops during the Korean War and some USMC R5C-1s were also in attendance.

Long-lasting Commandos pressed on with their USAF duties well past the 1950s. In addition, the USAF employed private operator CAT (Civil Air Transport) to fly civil-registered C-46s on military charter flights, including routine flights between Korea and Japan. A COIN (counter-insurgency) version of the C-46 was developed in the early 1960s for the USAF's 1st Air Commando Wing for

Paratroops of the US Army's 187th Regimental Combat Team pour from 437th TCW Commandos in a training exercise in Korea. C-46s partnered the Fairchild C-119 in the paradrop role.

Above: Passengers board a 437th Troop Carrier Wing C-46D at Iwakuni AB, Japan, for the long flight to Seoul. Previously based at O'Hare Airport, Chicago, the 437th was a Reserve unit.

Below: C-46D 44-77674 was photographed at Osan AB in June 1974, still in the service of the Republic of Korea Air Force. As late as 1999, Haiti was still believed to use a single example.

combat operations in South Vietnam. C-46s also operated in the Panama Canal zone and served with Air Force Reserve and Air National Guard units until June 1968, when the type was retired.

Japanese and Korean military services used the C-46 well past the 1960s and some were flown

on CIA (Central Intelligence Agency) supply missions in Laos by CAT and Continental Air Services. Risky and difficult missions were the order of the day, including paradropping supplies to anti-communist Hmong tribesmen in Laos' Plain of Jars. A C-46 civilian pilot on a CIA mission was held prisoner

by the communist Pathet Lao guerrillas for seven years.

The C-46 ended its principal military career in Southeast Asia, but it continued to serve with other air arms for years afterwards. In its second life, the C-46 became the rough-hewn stepchild of the commercial air world, hauling freight in many

countries and establishing a reputation for rugged service in Latin America. Denied its destiny as a luxury passenger liner by the outbreak of World War II, the Commando ended up in airline livery not as a liner, but as a sort of 'sky truck', doing heavy-duty work in distant lands.

Dispersed production

Three Curtiss plants at Buffalo, NY, Louisville, Kentucky and St Louis, Missouri were responsible for C-46 production. A handful was also completed by the Higgins Boat Company of New Orleans, Louisiana.

C-46D

All of the 1,410 C-46Ds were built at Curtiss' Buffalo, NY factory. They were primarily personnel transports, but had one additional cargo door on the starboard side of the fuselage. Phased into the end of Buffalo's C-46A production, the C-46D used the same R-2800-51 engines as the earlier variant.

C-46D Commando

Seen in the colourful markings of the Japanese Air Self-Defence Force (JASDF) in about 1973, this Commando was built as C-46D-20-CU 44-78495 and later became 51-1114. At this late stage of its career, the aircraft was being used for general transport and utility duties.

Powerplant
C-46s were powered by a pair of Pratt & Whitney R-2800 Double Wasp 18-cylinder, two-row radials rated at 2,100 hp (1566 kW). The Double Wasp also powered a number of other World War II types, including the A-26 Invader, B-25 Mitchell, B-26 Marauder, P-47 Thunderbolt and F4U Corsair.

Double-lobed fuselage
The C-46 was a conventional low-/mid-wing monoplane transport with a semi-monocoque fuselage. The double-lobed fuselage offered considerable benefits in terms of load-carrying capacity; the Commando could carry much bulkier loads than its contemporary, the C-47 Skytrain, thanks to its 2,300-cu ft (65.13-m³) main cargo compartment. Typical loads were 40 fully-equipped troops, 33 stretchers, five Wright R-3350 engines, or up to 15,000 lb (6804 kg) of cargo. Underfloor cargo capacity was also available.

Performance
The C-46A was able to reach 270 mph (435 km/h) at 15,000 ft (4572 m) and cruised at 173 mph (278 km/h). At the latter speed a range of 3,150 miles (5069 km) was attainable.

Fuel
Fuel was carried in tanks in the inner half of the wing, outboard of the engines. Total capacity was 1,400 US gal (5299 litres), to which could be added up to eight 100-US gal (379-litre) overload tanks in the main cargo compartment, for ferry flights.

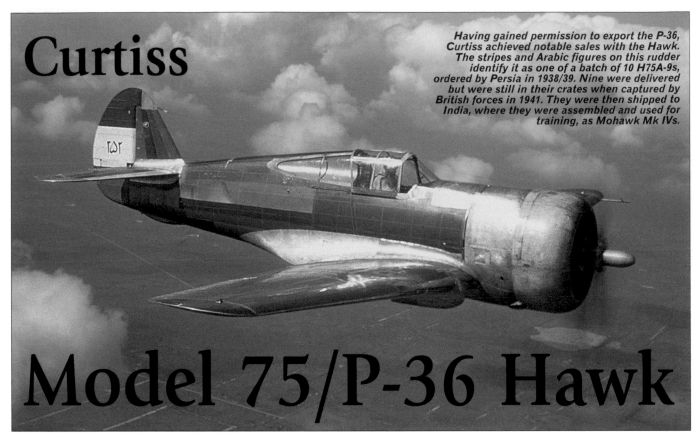

Curtiss

Having gained permission to export the P-36, Curtiss achieved notable sales with the Hawk. The stripes and Arabic figures on this rudder identify it as one of a batch of 10 H75A-9s, ordered by Persia in 1938/39. Nine were delivered but were still in their crates when captured by British forces in 1941. They were then shipped to India, where they were assembled and used for training, as Mohawk Mk IVs.

Model 75/P-36 Hawk

Curtiss's monoplane Hawk

Reintroducing the name Hawk for a Curtiss fighter, the Model 75/P-36 achieved only moderate success in American service. In the hands of European pilots, however – especially the Finns – the Hawk proved a worthy adversary.

In the summer of 1934, Curtiss-Wright's chief engineer Don Berlin created a fighter which he hoped would prove to be superior to its rivals. The Model 75 was a stressed-skin cantilever low-wing monoplane, fitted with hydraulically-operated split flaps and main landing gears which retracted directly to the rear, the wheels turning 90° to lie flat in the wing. The cockpit was enclosed by a sliding canopy, while on the nose was the new 900-hp (671-kW) Wright XR-1670 twin-row engine in a compact small-diameter cowling. The only traditional feature was the armament: one machine-gun of 0.50-in (12.7-mm) and one of 0.30-in (7.62-mm) calibre.

Sadly for Berlin, designers all over the world had similar ideas, and the US Army initially picked the rival Seversky IXP. Curtiss arranged for the decision to be postponed and, at a further competition in April 1936, offered the Model 75B, with the large-diameter Wright Cyclone R-1820-G5 and an improved cockpit with the rear fuselage scalloped to give a rear view. The US Army still preferred the Seversky, ordering its fighter as the P-35, but the Curtiss had some good points, so an order was placed for three further Model 75s designated Y1P-36, powered by the two-row Pratt &

Whitney R-1830 Twin Wasp driving the new Hamilton hydraulic constant-speed propeller. These were delivered in spring 1937, and the US Army test pilots were enthusiastic.

Meanwhile, Curtiss had also fought for export customers. Recognising that many air forces were not ready for all the new features, Curtiss quickly rebuilt the original 75B as a simplified export model called the Hawk 75, the most obvious change being the fixed landing gear.

The Hawk 75 proved a success from the start. Even the prototype was purchased by China, which bought 112 more, and other major customers included Thailand (with 23-mm

Madsen cannon in underwing gondolas) and Argentina. Meanwhile, following its good reception by Wright Field, the US Army Air Corps placed an order on 7 July 1937 for 210 P-36As – the biggest American fighter contract since 1918.

Basically, the P-36A was a perfectly sound aircraft, with good handling and manoeuvrability, although in terms of flight performance and firepower it was already outclassed by such European fighters as the Spitfire and Bf 109D. Moreover, from the start of its combat duty in the late spring of 1938, the P-36A was troubled by a host of problems which caused it to be repeatedly grounded.

While working its way through the contract for 210 aircraft, Curtiss made 81 major

Below: France received its first H75A-1s in December 1938 and, subsequently, over 300 A-2s, -3s and -4s followed. They were quickly thrown into action against the Germans, and the French Hawks, with their non-standard reverse throttle arrangement, gave valuable service up to the time of the armistice in June 1940. Examples can be seen here escorting British Fairey Battles.

Above: Although the Curtiss Model 75 failed to win the USAAC contest for which it was designed, it was successful in a further competition two years later, and became progenitor of a long series of fighters, widely used throughout the war. This is the original H75 in its second form, when fitted with a P & W R-1535 engine.

Advanced variants

It soon became apparent to the Curtiss engineers that the lifespan of the P-36 would be limited due to its R-1380 radial engine. It was therefore decided to modify the prototype Model 75/75B airframe so that it could be powered by the new 12-cylinder inline Allison V-1710-11. The resultant XP-37 became the first US aircraft to exceed 300 mph (483 km/h). The US Army was impressed by the potential of this new design and ordered 12

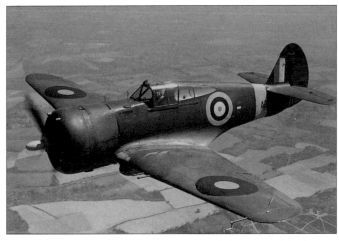

examples under the designation YP-37 (above). The YP-37 underwent constant modification but suffered numerous problems with its supercharger, preventing the type from reaching its potential – the remaining examples were retired from US Army service. The XP-42 (left) was operated by the US Army and NACA (National Advisory Committee for Aeronautics) to study the drag effects of radial engines. The XP-42 was delivered with a Pratt & Whitney R-1830-31 engine fitted with extensions to the propeller shaft and nose casing to give it a streamlined nose.

With the fall of France, it was agreed that Britain should take over all of the undelivered French Hawks. The RAF assigned them the name Mohawk, and the designations Mk I, II, III and IV (pictured) were allocated to the Hawk 75A-1, A-2, A-3 and A-4 respectively.

and minor changes to try to eradicate faults and improve the P-36's fighting ability. The XP-36B was temporarily fitted with a more powerful Twin Wasp. The P-36C designation was applied to the last 30 aircraft, which had the even more powerful 1,200-hp (895-kW) Twin Wasp R-1830-17, and an added 0.30-in (7.62-mm) calibre gun in each wing, whose spent cases were collected in prominent boxes under the wings. The XP-36D was the No. 174 aircraft, modified with two 0.50-in (12.7-mm) calibre fuselage guns and four 0.30-in (7.62-mm) calibre guns in the wings. The XP-36E was the 147th aircraft, fitted with new outer wings housing eight 0.30-calibre guns. The XP-36F

was the No. 172 P-36A fitted with underwing gondolas housing the Danish 23-mm Madsen cannon, each with 100 rounds, as used by Thai Hawk 75Ns. This reduced maximum speed from 311 to only 265 mph (500 to 426 km/h).

In March 1941 Curtiss-Wright rolled out the 1,095th and last of the radial-engined Hawk monoplane series. Among the late customers were China (Hawk 75A-5), Norway (75A-6), the Netherlands (75A-7), Norway again (75A-8), Peru (75A-8s redesignated P-36G) and Iran (75A-9). Most of the Hawk 75's combat experience was provided by French, Dutch, British and Finnish pilots. American Hawks were quickly relegated to a fighter training role in the Pacific.

In-service Hawks

Curtiss's Hawk managed to find itself fighting both for and against Axis forces during the war. In Finnish operations, Hawks notched up an amazing 190 kills against the Russians, somehow halting the Red advance. The Hawk's service with American forces, however, was limited to a few skirmishes with Japanese fighters in the Pacific.

P-36A
Operating in early 1940 with the 20th Pursuit Group, this P-36 has the group designator (PT) on the fin and the yellow cowling of the 79th Pursuit Squadron, whose insignia is on the fuselage side. Aircraft serial numbers were not prominently displayed; the '21' is the aircraft-in-group number.

Hawk 75A-3
With the fall of France, the Luftwaffe captured a number of examples of the Hawk and many of these were delivered to Finland. The Hawks were used to great effect in the war against Russia and this example was flown by 2Lt Kalevi Tervo, who achieved 15½ kills.

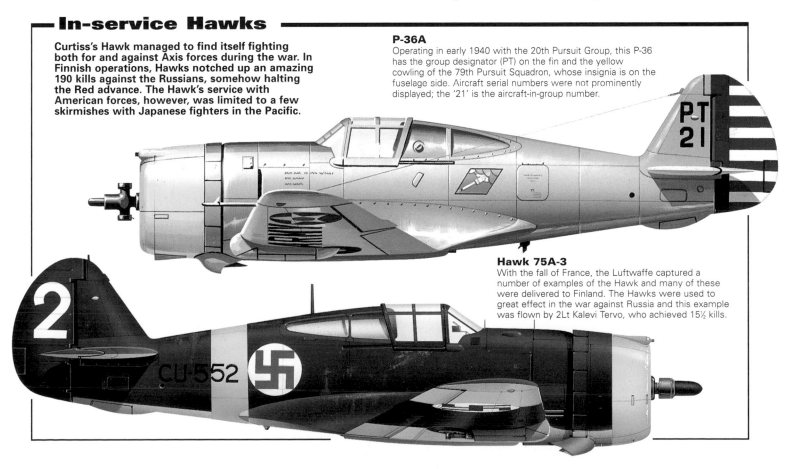

Curtiss

Displaying the short-lived red-bordered 'star-and-bar' insignia of July-September 1943, this Warhawk was photographed flying from Randolph Field. The serial number identifies it as a P-40E-1, a repossessed Kittyhawk Mk IA built for Lend-Lease to Britain; a P-40K-type fin has been fitted.

P-40 Warhawk family
Introduction

Although it was the most numerous American fighter at the time of Pearl Harbor, the P-40's development never kept pace with that of rival designs. Nevertheless, it compiled a creditable war record on many fronts.

In 1938, encouraged by the performance being demonstrated by European interceptors powered by liquid-cooled inline engines, the Curtiss-Wright Corporation decided to install a 1,160-hp (865-kW) supercharged Allison V-1710-19 in the then Wright radial-powered P-36A. The 10th production example (30-18), was retained the for the trial installation. Redesignated XP-40, this aircraft was first flown in October 1938 and evaluated at Wright Field the following May, in competition with the Bell XP-39 and Seversky XP-41. As originally flown, the XP-40 featured a radiator located under the rear fuselage, but was later moved forward to the nose, together with the oil cooler. In all respects other than the powerplant, the new aircraft

remained unchanged from the P-36A, being an all-metal, low-wing monoplane, whose main landing-gear units retracted rearwards into wings, the mainwheels turning through 90° to lie flush with the undersurfaces. Armament remained the paltry pair of 0.3-in (7.62-mm) machine-guns in the nose.

Although the other prototypes evaluated with the XP-40 later led to successful service fighters, the Curtiss-Wright aircraft was selected for immediate production and a contract was signed for 524 P-40s, worth almost $13 million – at that time the largest order ever placed for an American fighter. Production of 200 aircraft, known as the Hawk 81A, for the USAAC commenced in late 1939. Powered by the 1,040-hp (776-kW) Allison V-1710-33 engine, the aircraft was distin-

A prime example of evolution rather than revolution in fighter design, the Curtiss P-40 family was destined to serve widely throughout World War II. Its origin lay in the radial-engined P-36 Mohawk, the prototype XP-40 being the 10th P-36A, re-engined with an Allison V-1710.

guishable by the absence of wheel disc plates and by the positioning of the carburettor air intake above the nose. The first three aircraft served as prototypes (sometimes known as YP-40s) and subsequent machines were delivered to the 33rd Pursuit Squadron.

Production continued at Buffalo, NY with the P-40B (Hawk 81A-2). Some 131 were produced, introducing cockpit armour and an armament of four 0.3-in (7.62-mm) wing guns and two 0.5-in (12.7-mm) nose

guns. When Japan struck in December 1941 there were 107 P-40s and P-40Bs in the Philippines, but such was the measure of surprise achieved that only four managed to take off. Within four days the number of these fighters (flown by the 20th and 34th Pursuit Groups) had fallen to 22.

The RAF Tomahawk Mk IIA corresponded to the P-40B, and the majority of the 110 aircraft dispatched went directly to the Middle East. One hundred other Tomahawk Mk IIAs were diverted from RAF contracts to China for service with the American Volunteer Group.

The next variant was the P-40C (Hawk 81A-3), which introduced self-sealing fuel tanks; only 193 were produced for the USAAC, but this was the RAF's principal Tomahawk version, the Mk IIB. Out of a total of 945 produced under this designation,

The 33rd Pursuit Squadron, 8th PG, seen here at Langley Field, Virginia, was the first unit to convert to the P-40, deliveries of which began in September 1940. With newer P-40Cs, the 8th PG deployed to Iceland in 1941.

Above: The majority of the USAAC's Warhawks – mainly P-40Bs and Cs – served in the Pacific. Here, groundcrew service a Warhawk named Geronimo *from the 45th Fighter Squadron at Nanumea Island, east of the Solomons.*

Left: Considerable numbers of Kittyhawks supplied to the RAF under Lend-Lease were transferred to the RNZAF and RAAF (seen here) for service in the Pacific theatre.

21 were lost in transit at sea and 73 were delivered directly to the USSR. Due to its slow speed, when it arrived in North Africa late in 1941, the Tomahawk was found to be much inferior to the Messerschmitt Bf 109E and only marginally better than the Hawker Hurricane Mk I, and was therefore primarily used in the ground-attack role.

The P-40D (Hawk 87A-2) brought a major redesign of the nose with the introduction of the Allison V-1710-39 engine, which permitted the nose to be shortened by 6 in (15.24 cm).

The P-40E (Hawk 87A-3) was the first Warhawk (as the whole P-40 series was named in American service) to be produced in large quantities after Pearl Harbor. It accompanied the first American fighter squadrons to the UK in 1942, as well as those in the Middle East. Production totalled 2,320 on American contracts, plus 1,500 for the RAF as the Kittyhawk Mk IA.

Merlin tested

With dimensions approximately the same as those of the Allison V-1710, the Rolls-Royce Merlin was later selected for the P-40. During 1941, a production P-40D (40-360) was experimentally fitted with a Merlin 28, resulting in the designation P-40F (Hawk 87D); although the weight increased to 9,460 lb (4295 kg), the more powerful British engine raised maximum speed to some 364 mph (586 km/h) at 18,000 ft (5500 m).

The first 260 aircraft employed the same fuselage as the P-40E, but the progressive increase in the forward keel area had introduced a reduction in directional stability, so later P-40Fs featured a rear fuselage lengthened by 20 in (51 cm).

Produced in parallel with the last P-40Fs was the P-40K. With a marginally increased top speed of 366 mph (589 km/h), it had an edge over the Bf 109E in Europe and North Africa, and over the A6M Zero in the Far East. More power was added in the P-40M with the introduction of the V-1710-81 engine. Some 1,300 P-40Ks (originally intended for Lend Lease to China) and 600 P-40Ms were produced for the USAAF. RAF versions of the P-40F were the Kittyhawk Mks II and IIA, of which 330 were produced as an interim measure by converting USAAF aircraft. A total of 616 Kittyhawk Mk IIIs, equivalent to the P-40M, was delivered to the RAF.

Further variants

A number of other interim versions had meanwhile been produced or planned. Some 45 P-40Gs had been built, combining the Kittyhawk fuselage with RAF Tomahawk wings and six 0.5-in (12.7-mm) wing guns; all were retained by the USAAF. The intention in the P-40J was to use a turbocharged Allison, but the aircraft was not built owing to the introduction of the Rolls-Royce Merlin. The Packard (Merlin) V-1650-1 was fitted in the P-40L, of which 700 were produced for the USAAF in 1943, some of these aircraft having two guns, armour and some fuel removed to improve performance.

The definitive Warhawk was the P-40N, which entered production towards the end of 1943, commencing delivery to the USAAF in March the following year. Some 588 were also produced for the RAF, equivalent to the P-40N-20, as the Kittyhawk Mk IV.

In 1944, following the introduction of the Merlin in the P-51, there existed a heavy demand on spares for this engine, and so 300 P-40Fs and P-40Ls were converted to take the V-1710-81, their designations being altered to P-40R-1 and R-2, respectively. Finally, a small number of P-40Es and P-40Ns was converted to two-seat trainers under the designation TP-40N.

Warhawks of the USAAF served with many pursuit and fighter groups during World War II. They also provided the backbone of the USAAF's fighter defences, protecting the Panama Canal between 1941 and 1943, serving with the 16th, 32nd, 36th, 37th and 53rd Pursuit Groups.

It might be suggested that the P-40 remained in service with the USAAF in secondary war theatres in order to allow delivery priorities to be bestowed upon more advanced aircraft (such as the P-38, P-47 and P-51). However, the use of the Warhawk in main combat theatres, for which its production was prolonged as late as 1944 – by which time its performance was thoroughly pedestrian among fighters of the time – has never been satisfactorily explained, especially with regard to the large numbers built.

Be that as it may, many Tomahawks and Kittyhawks were also delivered against contracts for the RAF, RAAF, RCAF, RNZAF and SAAF; the relatively small number of squadrons so equipped is largely explained by the fact that a large proportion of the aircraft purchased by Britain were diverted to the USSR.

During the last two years of the war, the United States supplied 377 P-40s (mostly P-40Ns) to China, while in 1942 some P-40Es were delivered to Chile, and 89 P-40Es went to Brazil the following year.

Production of all Curtiss P-40s eventually totalled 16,802, including 4,787 built against British contracts.

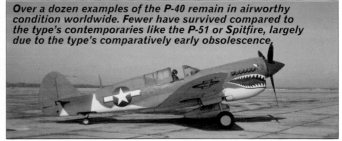

Left: Though France ordered Model 87s, none was delivered before the French surrender. These Armée de l'Air aircraft, seen at Algiers, are actually ex-USAAF P-40Fs, handed over in early 1943 for use in North Africa by Free French squadron GC II/5.

Over a dozen examples of the P-40 remain in airworthy condition worldwide. Fewer have survived compared to the type's contemporaries like the P-51 or Spitfire, largely due to the type's comparatively early obsolescence.

USAAF P-40s at war
China and the Aleutians

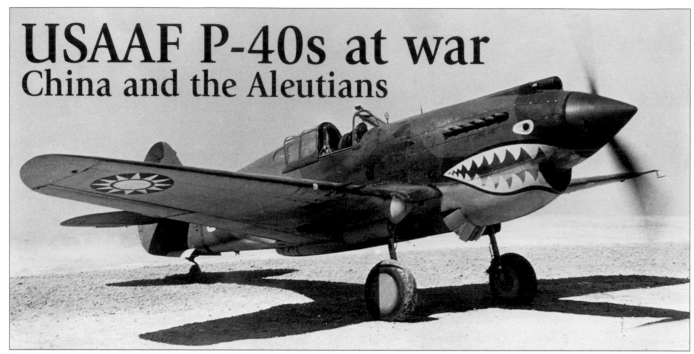

The first members of the Curtiss 81/87 Hawk family to see action in the hands of American pilots were those flown by the American Volunteer Group in China – the famous 'Flying Tigers'.

In late 1942, a stalwart band of American adventurers began preparations to defend Burma from the Japanese onslaught that had ignited World War II in Southeast Asia. They flew Curtiss 81A-1 fighters, better known to most Americans by their AAF (Army Air Forces) designation – P-40. These men were the 'Flying Tigers', alias the AVG (American Volunteer Group), headed by Gen. Claire Chennault, and they immediately began to demonstrate that, in the right hands, the Curtiss fighter could stand up to the best Japan had to offer.

One of the men who became an air ace with the AVG, David Lee 'Tex' Hill, claims that Japanese fighters were consistently overestimated and that the P-40 was too often belittled by those who did not understand it well enough. "You never wanted to dive with a Japanese fighter because he would claw his way up your butt and kill you every time," Hill said. "But at low and medium altitude, especially, the P-40 was as manoeuvrable as any Jap. And our aircraft were built with armour, self-sealing fuel tanks, and other protections for the pilot that Japanese fliers didn't have."

Hill's aircraft was a steel-and-fabric testimony to the state of the American aircraft industry at the beginning of the 1940s. The Tomahawk (later models would be dubbed Kittyhawk and Warhawk) typified American capabilities of the time and was a better fighter than has often been acknowledged. It was a solidly-built machine with twin 0.50-in (12.7-mm) machine-guns firing through its propeller and two 0.30-in (7.62-mm) guns in each wing. The Allison V-1710-C15 inline engine provided slightly in excess of 1,000 hp (746 kW) and the Tomahawk could cruise at 280 mph (450 km/h) with a maximum speed of 350 mph (563 km/h). In Burma and China, the 'Flying Tigers' – and their lineal descendants, the AAF's 23rd Fighter Group – often had to improvise for miss-

Above: Conditions in China were testing, especially away from the AVG's Kunming base. Dust in summer and mud in winter made operations difficult and crew accommodation was basic.

Above: Chinese personnel operated a servicing facility at Loiwing, where overhauls of AVG aircraft were carried out. In this view, a number of dismantled Hawk 81s awaits repair.

P-40Es arrived in the Far East in late March 1942 and were operated alongside the Hawk 81s until the AVG was dissolved in July 1942, becoming the 23rd Fighter Group, USAAF.

Below: Well wrapped up against the cold, a ground crewman looks on as a P-40K taxis over PSP matting at a base in the Aleutians. The aircraft is armed with six 0.50-in (12.7-mm) machine-guns and carries a 52-US gal (197-litre) drop tank.

ing parts and supplies, but mechanics generally found the P-40 series satisfactory to work on and maintain. This was an older fighter than the Mitsubishi A6M Zero, and was destined to be continuously improved throughout the war, but it was never as obsolescent or as cantankerous as its worst detractors claimed.

The first American overseas unit of P-40s in the Atlantic was the 33rd Pursuit Squadron, sent to Iceland on 25 July 1941 (all AAF units switched from 'pursuit' to 'fighter' nomenclature soon afterwards). In the UK, P-40s delivered to British orders were transferred to AAF squadrons fighting in North Africa. These aircraft were RAF Kittyhawks, with their British roundels overpainted and US serial numbers added. In Europe, American P-40s destroyed 520 enemy aircraft while losing 553 to all causes – a fine record for an aircraft that was considered inferior to the Luftwaffe's best.

The 'Flying Tiger' saga began when a freighter unloaded 100 civilian P-40 equivalents at Rangoon, Burma in August 1941. In September 1941 Chennault's AVG group of 100 pilots arrived with promises of $600 per month and a bonus of $500 for every Japanese aircraft destroyed. The first air battle involving the 'Flying Tigers'

occurred on 20 December 1941 (two weeks after Pearl Harbor) when P-40s flying out of Kunming, China shot down six enemy aircraft. On Christmas Day 1941, Duke Hedman became an ace by claiming his fifth victory while he and 18 colleagues – flying P-40s, characterised by a shark's mouth painted at the intake – shot down a third of an enemy formation without losing a single aircraft. Gregory 'Pappy' Boyington was another of the famous aces who flew along with Hill and others in the 'Tigers'.

Action in Hawaii

The two waves of attacks by Admiral Nagumo's Japanese task force at Pearl Harbor destroyed about 75 Warhawks on the ground. 1Lts George Welch and Ken Taylor took off from Wheeler Field to shoot down eight enemy aircraft. For his part in that action, Welch was invited to the White House by President Franklin D. Roosevelt. Welch ultimately scored 18 victories and became a well-known postwar test pilot.

On 8 December 1941, six hours after the Pearl Harbor strike, Japan attacked US forces in the Philippines. There, the principal fighter was the P-40B. "We are doomed at the start," wrote P-40B pilot Max Louk in a letter to his mother a few days

before the attack. He became the first American pilot to die in the Philippines when his P-40B ground-looped during a response to an air raid. There were 107 P-40s and P-40Bs in the Philippines, but such was the measure of surprise achieved that only four got airborne on 8 December, and within four days the number of these fighters (flown by the 20th and 34th Pursuit Squadrons) had plummeted to 22.

P-40s in the Aleutians

Apart from a handful of P-40D Kittyhawks that fought in North Africa, the P-40E Warhawk was the first version to reach AAF squadrons in significant numbers after Pearl Harbor.

In the Aleutians, Warhawks, including some led by Lt Col John Chennault – son of the 'Flying Tiger' leader – battled against horrendous weather and Japanese fighters simultaneously.

Ultimately, the P-40 flew in every theatre of war – a remarkable 13,143 of these fighters were built, including 8,410 for the AAF, although even higher numbers are frequently quoted in error – and gave good service. Unfortunately, it was overshadowed by more glamorous warplanes that came along during the war years. Curtiss, it seemed, lacked the imagination to change with the times, and the P-40 became the last aircraft to be built in large numbers by a company with a proud and historic name.

This Hawk 81-A2 was assigned to the 3rd Pursuit Sqn, American Volunteer Group and was based at Kunming, China in 1942. Its markings comprise the Chinese national insignia and the AVG's 'Flying Tiger' insignia and sharkmouth.

USAAF and Allied service

Blooded in China, Hawaii and the Aleutians, the USAAF's P-40s went on to serve elsewhere in the CBI theatre, in North Africa, the Mediterranean and Panama. As well as large numbers supplied to the RAF under Lend-Lease, others were made available to Commonwealth air forces and other Allied air arms.

USAAF Warhawks (the name became generic for all American P-40s) served on almost all fronts during World War II with many fighter groups. Among these were the 8th and 49th Groups of the Fifth Air Force in the Far East between 1942 and 1944, the 15th and 18th Groups of the Seventh Air Force between 1941 and 1944, the 57th and 79th Groups of the Ninth Air Force in the Mediterranean between 1942 and 1944, the 51st Group with the Tenth Air Force in India and China between 1941 and 1944, and the 27th and 33rd Groups of the Twelfth Air Force in the Mediterranean between 1942 and 1944.

Little noticed but important in deterring Axis ambitions, P-40 Warhawks guarded the vital Panama Canal between 1941 and 1943, serving with the 16th, 32nd, 36th, 37th, and 53rd Groups.

Known to the RAF and Commonwealth as the Tomahawk or Kittyhawk, the P-40 was also one of America's premier exports during World War II. Of 16,802 of these fighters built, 3,064 served in air forces outside the United States. No fewer than 23 countries flew the Curtiss fighter, but apart from its contribution to the British effort, the 'Hawk' series is especially well known for its contribution to other major US allies. Warhawks were essential to the Soviet Union and the Curtiss fighter was the most important fighter type of the war for Australia.

RAAF Kittyhawks

The RAAF took delivery of 848 P-40E, K, M, and N Kittyhawks between March 1942 and February 1945 for service at home and abroad. Australian pilots in North Africa also flew P-40B and C models bailed from the US.

Above: Rolls-Royce Merlin-engined P-40F-20s, repossessed by the USAAF from British Kittyhawk Mk II orders, are seen being flown off USS Chenango during Operation Torch, 29 November 1942.

Top: Towards the end of the war this P-40N-40 was finished in the markings of the 28 countries that ordered Curtiss-Wright fighters during (or immediately prior to) World War II.

Australia's top-ranking air ace, Group Captain Clive Caldwell, racked up 20½ of his 28½ aerial victories in Kittyhawks before graduating to the Supermarine Spitfire. Squadron Leader John Waddy's 15½ kills were all scored in Kittyhawks. Neither pilot ever claimed that early-model Kittyhawks were superior to late-model Mitsubishi A6M Zero fighters, but – like other flyers around the world – Australians found that the Curtiss fighter could give a good account of itself, even against Japan's best.

New Zealand, too, achieved considerable success, beginning with 44 Kittyhawks allocated from RAF allotments in the Middle East. While the RNZAF was building up strength, fighter

The USAAF had P-40s stationed in Hawaii in late 1943 for defensive patrols over the island group and its approaches. This P-40K is well camouflaged against air attack on a Hawaiian airfield.

Below: The RAAF fielded Kittyhawk-equipped squadrons at home and abroad. These No. 80 Sqn aircraft are seen on a offensive sortie against the Japanese whilst based in New Guinea.

No. 2 Sqn, SAAF Kittyhawks await their next sortie on a windswept desert airstrip in North Africa in 1942/43. These aircraft were largely employed in a fighter-bomber role. In mid-1943 they were replaced by Spitfire Mk Vs.

pilots cut their teeth on the Kittyhawk and fought with the type at some distinctly unpleasant places, like Guadalcanal. Only later in the war did the Vought Corsair eclipse the P-40 in RNZAF service.

The P-40 was, of course, the chosen mount of American volunteers, the Flying Tigers, who fought for China in 1941 and achieved success against the Japanese, even though desperately outnumbered. Although many of these men ended up in the US forces, the P-40 Warhawk also became an item of routine equipment with the Chinese Nationalist air arm.

South African service

South African fighter pilots joined their British colleagues flying early Tomahawks as low-level army co-operation warplanes and as ground attack fighters in North Africa. Many hundreds of other P-40Bs and P-40Cs went to the Soviet Union, China and Turkey.

The British-designed Rolls-Royce Merlin 28 engine went

into production in the USA in 1941 (built by Packard as the V-1650) and gave rise to the P-40F variant. Most Merlin-powered P-40s were exported to the Soviet Union.

Others were repossessed by the USAAF from RAF orders and served in North Africa. The Free French operated three squadrons of these aircraft after the end of 1942.

Despite the huge numbers of P-40s reaching the Soviet Union aboard Allied convoys, the Warhawk seems not to have made much of a mark as an air-to-air combatant in the Great Patriotic War. Air ace N. F. Kuznetsov scored many of his 36 aerial victories in a P-40K of the Northern Fleet Air Force in 1943 and was named a Hero of the Soviet Union, but many of Moscow's aces preferred their own country's fighters or the Bell P-39 Airacobra, which they

employed to good advantage. Finland, Germany and Japan are known to have evaluated captured P-40s.

NEIAF operations

A little-known P-40 operator was the Netherlands East Indies Air Force, which fought the Japanese in the region for most of the war, fielding a single squadron of the fighters. After VJ-Day the NEIAF fought Indonesian rebels, the P-40s remaining in use until 1949 – the last P-40s to see combat.

Above: Seven RNZAF squadrons flew Kittyhawks in the Southwest Pacific at various times. Here, a section of P-40s escorts a Lockheed Hudson during training in New Zealand. The RNZAF's 293 examples were mainly a mixture of P-40Es, Ks and Ns, though a single Merlin-engined P-40L was received in error and later replaced by a P-40M. The type was withdrawn at the war's end and most of the survivors scrapped.

Left: No. 120 Sqn, Netherlands East Indies Air Force fought the Japanese for much of the war. These P-40Ns were based at Biak, New Guinea.

FR241 was a short-tailed Kittyhawk Mk III of No. 250 Sqn, seen in the Western Desert in 1943/44. Though some units re-equipped with Mustangs, No. 250 Sqn was among those that soldiered on with the Curtiss fighter-bombers until the end of the war.

Tomahawk and Kittyhawk

The RAF's P-40s

Known as Tomahawks, the RAF's first P-40s were deemed unsuitable for a day-fighter role and saw limited service. However, the RAF's Kittyhawks, based on the P-40D and its successors, were used in large numbers in the Mediterranean, latterly as fighter-bombers in support of the British 8th Army.

Essentially, the aircraft known to the RAF as Tomahawks were examples of the original variants of the Curtiss P-40 (Model 81, or Hawk 81), the prototype of which had first flown on 14 October 1938 and had been the subject of a large order from the USAAC in April 1939.

Already flying the Hawk 75, France's Armée de l'Air was quick to order the improved Hawk 81A-1, with a contract for 230 in October 1939. Deliveries began in May 1940 and, with the French collapse imminent, the entire contract was taken over by the British Purchasing Commission, which also then placed an order for another 630 aircraft.

The first 140 of the Hawk 81A-1s were completed to the original French specification and, reaching Britain from November 1940 onwards, became Tomahawk Mk Is. However, as they lacked self-sealing fuel tanks and armour protection, they were judged unsuitable for use by RAF day-fighter squadrons.

Tactical reconnaissance

The same might have been said of their suitability for low-

Bearing the well-known 'sharkmouth' marking of No. 112 Sqn, these Tomahawk Mk IIBs were based in Egypt during 1941, flying fighter sweeps over the Western Desert.

level tactical reconnaissance and army co-operation duties, but this was the role to which the Tomahawk Mk Is were applied. With improved variants in the pipeline, the Mk Is were issued, for training and preliminary operations, to Nos II, 26, 171, 231, 239, 268 and 613 Squadrons of the RAF, and the UK-based Nos 400 and 403, RCAF Sqns. The first operation was flown by No. 26 Sqn from Gatwick in February 1941.

Next to appear was the Hawk 81A-2, designated Tomahawk Mk IIA by the RAF, which had a measure of armour protection for the pilot and self-sealing fuel tanks. A total of 110 was deliv-

Seen here are No. 414 Sqn, RCAF Tomahawk Mk IIBs. Britain released 100 of its Mk IIBs to the Chinese Nationalist government for use by the American Volunteer Group (AVG) 'Flying Tigers', and 195 were transferred to the Soviet Union in 1941; small numbers also went to the Egyptian and Turkish air forces.

ered, representing the conclusion of the original French contract and the first 20 of the British order. Deliveries proceeded through the early months of 1941 and then continued with the Tomahawk Mk IIB (with a British rather than US radio, oxygen equipment and the British-standard 0.303-in (7.7-mm) wing guns). An extra 300 of these were ordered to Hawk 81A-3 standard (broadly equivalent to the USAAC's

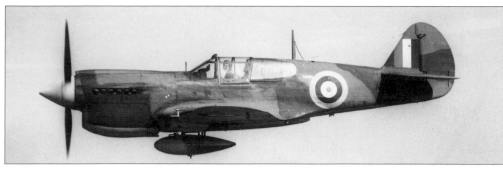

AL229 was among the first batch of Kittyhawk Mk Is delivered to the RAF. Though this aircraft is seen in standard northern European day fighter camouflage, the type saw no service in the theatre.

P-40C), with provision for a 43-Imp gal (197-litre) belly drop tank. Delivery of these aircraft in the second half of 1941 brought the total of Tomahawk Mk IIBs to 910 and of all Tomahawks to 1,160.

In the UK, the Tomahawk Mk IIA and Mk IIB supplanted the Mk I in Nos II, 26, 231, 239 and 241 Sqns and the two RCAF units. Of these, No. 239, at Gatwick, was the first to fly armed reconnaissance 'Rhubarbs' with the Tomahawk Mk II. With the availability of more aircraft, 300 Tomahawks were assigned for service in the Middle East, where No. 250 Sqn became the first to convert in May 1941, followed by No. 3 Sqn, RAAF and No. 2 Sqn, SAAF. The Tomahawk force in

North Africa grew, with the addition of Nos 112 and 260 Sqns, RAF, and Nos 4, 5 and 40 Sqns, SAAF providing the basis for the later introduction of the Kittyhawk into the area.

Hawk 87 – Kittyhawk

The Hawk 87A-2, with its Allison V-1710-39 engine (necessitating a redesign of the front fuselage and radiator) and much improved performance, especially at higher altitudes, was first ordered by the British Purchasing Commission in May 1940; the USAAC soon followed with an order for the basically similar P-40D. These aircraft had only four wing guns, but the Hawk 87A-2 and P-40E quickly followed, with six wing guns, and provision for a 500-lb (227-kg) bomb in place of a drop tank under the fuselage and, later, wing racks for two 100-lb (45-kg) bombs.

Britain's order was for 560 Hawk 87s, to be designated Kittyhawk Mk I. With the

advent of Lend-Lease, large quantities of later Hawk 87 variants were added to the RAF inventory, comprising 1,500 Kittyhawk Mk IAs, which were essentially the same as the Mk I and the P-40E-1; 330 Mk IIs, similar to the Packard Merlin-engined P-40F Warhawk; 616 Mk IIIs, of which 21 were P-40K-1 equivalents and the remainder P-40Ms; and, finally, 536 Mk IVs, similar to the P-40N.

Apart from examples brought to the UK for evaluation, all RAF Kittyhawks went straight to RAF and Commonwealth squadrons in the Middle East. Substantial numbers (over 350) of the British direct-purchase and Lend-Lease Kittyhawks were also transferred to the RAAF, RNZAF and RCAF, as well as to the SAAF. Others went to the Soviet Union and 81 were retained by the USAAF.

From early 1942 onwards, Kittyhawks replaced Tomahawks

in Nos 112, 260, 250 and 94 Sqns of the RAF, Nos 3 and 450 Sqns of the RAAF and Nos 2, 4, 5 and 11 Squadrons of the SAAF. No. 3 (RAAF) was the first squadron to convert to the Kittyhawk Mk I and commence operations, soon followed by No. 5 Sqn, SAAF, using Kittyhawk Mk IAs. Operating the Kittyhawks as fighter-bombers, these squadrons flew intensively in the Western Desert campaigns of 1942/43, responding to calls for close support from army units on the ground. No. 260 Sqn, RAF retained its Kittyhawks until August 1945, moving with them from North Africa to Italy, as did Nos 112 and 250 Sqns.

It is remarkable that, of the 16,802 Model 81/87 aircraft built, Britain purchased, or was allocated through Lend-Lease, no fewer than 4,702, or 28 per cent, of these aircraft. The operational success of the P-40s may not have justified such large-scale production, but there is no doubt that the RAF's Tomahawk Mk IIs and Kittyhawks did make a significant contribution to the ultimate success of the Allied forces in the Western Desert.

Above: No. 3 Sqn, RAAF flew both Tomahawks and Kittyhawks in North Africa and Italy. RAF and Commonwealth Kittyhawk units flew three or four bombing and escort sorties a day at the height of the North African campaign.

No. 260 Sqn Kittyhawk Mk IIIs (equivalent to the USAAF's short-fuselage P-40K-1) take off from a landing ground somewhere in Italy in early 1944. Interestingly, the rudder of 'HS-X' bears the remains of a USAAF serial number and the aircraft appears to lack an RAF identity.

Perhaps the best known of the RAF's P-40 squadrons thanks to its trademark 'sharkmouth' nose marking, No. 112 Sqn was an early operator of the 'Kittybomber', and was one of the most successful such squadrons, its P-40s using 250-lb (114-kg) bombs for ground-attack work. This Kittyhawk MK IV was based at Cutella, Italy, in early 1944.

Curtiss
SB2C Helldiver
War-winning dive-bomber?

A group of Helldivers heads out on another mission over the Pacific, with F6F Hellcats flying top cover. Though unpopular with pilots, the SB2C was the most successful Allied dive-bomber of World War II.

As the designated successor to the SBD Dauntless, the Helldiver proved initially disappointing, with little improvement in speed, and better range and load-carrying abilities spoiled by poor handling and low serviceability.

The Curtiss SB2C, one of the few members of the long and proud series of Curtiss dive-bombers to bear the name Helldiver, was intended to be a great war-winner to replace the ancient SBD. Unlike the Douglas product, created by Ed Heinemann working under John K. Northrop, the marvellous new Curtiss had a mighty new two-row engine, an internal weapons bay and a mass of fuel and new equipment all packaged into a tight space. After Pearl Harbor, it became the focus of a gigantic nationwide production

programme intended to blast the Japanese from the Pacific. The only thing wrong was the aircraft itself. To a man, the US Navy preferred the old SBD, which continued to be used in the forefront of the battle.

The SB2C was the creation of a group under Raymond C. Blaylock. As its designation reveals, the SB2C was planned as a scout bomber, for operation from US Navy carriers. The 1938 specification was extremely comprehensive and allowed little room for manoeuvre. The type had to be a stressed-skin

The XSB2C-1 prototype (BuNo. 1758) is seen here having sustained damage in an accident during test-flying in wintry conditions in February 1941. Although it was repaired, the aircraft was never tested by the US Navy before being destroyed after suffering an in-flight wing failure on 21 December 1941.

cantilever monoplane with an internal weapons bay beneath it. This bay had to take a 1,000-lb (454-kg) bomb and a wide range of other stores, and be closed by hydraulically-operated bomb doors. There had to be tandem accommodation for a crew of two, a large amount of fuel and comprehensive radio and other gear including a hefty camera in the rear cockpit. The structure had to be stressed for dive-bombing, and the aircraft had to be carrier-compatible, with folding wings, catapult hooks and an

arrester hook. The specified engine was the Wright R-2600 14-cylinder Cyclone.

Poor performance

Not unnaturally, the prototype XSB2C-1 came out looking rather like its rival, the Brewster XSMA-1 Buccaneer, and, if such a thing were possible, the latter was an even poorer aircraft than the Curtiss. In fact, the US Navy had such faith in the Buffalo-based company that it placed an order for 200 SB2C-1s before the prototype made its first flight

Assigned to a training unit in the US Navy, this Helldiver engages in a dive-bomb attack. Pictured is a 1,000-lb (454-kg) weapon, two of which could be carried in the capacious bomb bay.

on 18 December 1940. The single prototype, BuNo. 1758, had been ordered on 15 May 1939, and the big production order came on 29 November 1940. Thus, as 1941 dawned, Curtiss had a single prototype which occasionally flew, on the strength of which 14,000 workers were being hired for a vast new plant taking shape at Columbus, Ohio. Plans were already afoot for two further giant production programmes, at Canadian Car & Foundry at Fort William and Fairchild Aircraft at Longueil, Montreal.

Such confidence overlooked the fact that the SB2C was riddled with problems. Some were the normal ones of immaturity, affecting almost all the functioning items and particularly the R-2600-8 engine and 12-ft (3.66-m) Curtiss Electric three-bladed propeller. More serious were the deeper faults of the aircraft itself, which resulted in structural weaknesses, generally poor handling, shockingly inadequate stability (especially in yaw and pitch) and unacceptable stall characteristics.

Engine failure

Unfortunately, BuNo. 1758 crashed quite early, on 8 February 1941, the cause being engine failure on the approach. Like many aircraft of its day, the SB2C suffered violent changes in trim with application of flap, dive brakes, gear down or changes in engine power. But with a gigantic production programme fast taking shape, Curtiss simply had to carry on with flight-testing, so 1758 had to be rebuilt urgently. Almost every part was changed, the fuselage being about 1 ft (0.305 m) longer, the tail areas almost 30 per cent larger and numerous shapes subtly altered. Thanks to

combat reports from Europe, the fuel tanks in the fuselage and inner wings were made of the self-sealing type, local armour was added and the forward-firing armament changed from two 0.5-in (12.7-mm) guns above the cowling to four of these guns in the wings. The rear cockpit was redesigned with improved collapsible decking to improve the field of fire of the observer's single 0.5-in (12.7-mm) gun. Later, this gun was replaced by an armament of twin 0.3-in (7.62-mm) guns, each with no fewer than 2,000 rounds.

So enormous was the production scheme that it fell seriously behind. Curtiss had agreed to begin deliveries in December 1941, but by this time no production machine was even being assembled. Further changes had also been demanded, and another 900 Helldivers had been ordered for the US Army Air Force as A-25 Shrikes, with carrier gear deleted, pneumatic tailwheels and many other changes. Everyone worked hard to try to speed the programme, and eventually the first SB2C-1 was completed at Port Columbus in June 1942. Urgent testing of the first six production machines revealed that, in many respects, they were worse than the prototype, the great increase in weight (empty weight rose from 7,122 lb/3230 kg to some 10,220 lb/4636 kg) without change in the engine resulting in an aircraft being described at NAS Anacostia as 'extremely sluggish'. But, by this time, the trickle of production machines was fast building up, and to avoid political scandals some had to be delivered, so US Navy attack squadron VS-9 began to equip with SB2C-1s in December 1942.

*The final production Helldiver was the **SB2C-5**, with slightly increased internal fuel capacity (an extra 29 Imp gal/132 litres). More or less exact counterparts of most of the Columbus versions were built by the two Canadian companies.*

Subsequently production of the SB2C progressed through the many variants. Only the original order for 200 applied to the SB2C-1 model, and all of these were retained in the USA for training purposes. The SB2C-1A, which appeared in 1943, was the non-navalised A-25A after transfer to the US Marine Corps, with which many saw action, still painted in olive drab. The SB2C-1C introduced several armament improvements, including the option of removing the bomb doors and carrying a torpedo on an external truss, but little use appears to have been made of this. The major SB2C-1C change was to replace the four wing guns with two 20-mm cannon, each with 400 rounds loaded from above the wing. Immediately ahead of the magazines were extra 37.4-Imp gal (170-litre) auxiliary tanks, and at full load the SB2C-1C, the first model to go into action, was inferior in many performance respects to the old SBD.

A welcome small improvement in performance in the SB2C-3 resulted from fitting the more powerful R-2600-20 engine, its extra power being absorbed by an improved Curtiss Electric propeller with four blades and fitted with root cuffs. Certainly, by 1944, when the SB2C-3 appeared, the Helldiver was well established in service, and at least was becoming operationally effective, though crashes,

inflight break-ups and carrier landing accidents continued at the very top of the 'league table'. Everyone in the US Navy called this aircraft 'The Beast' and said its designation stood for 'Son of a Bitch, 2nd Class'.

Like most wartime programmes, production became a flood after most of the tougher fighting had been done, and the SB2C-4, which did not appear until summer 1944, was the most numerous version of all. From the pilot's viewpoint, the chief new feature of this model was that both upper and lower wing flaps were perforated, looking like a sieve. This had virtually no effect on their drag in dive-bombing, but did slightly reduce the tremendous tail buffet. Operational effectiveness was considerably increased in this version by strengthening the wing and providing for the carriage of either two drop tanks, two 500-1b (227-kg) bombs or eight 5-in (127-mm) rockets.

After the war, Helldivers did not vanish overnight. A few continued flying with the US Navy Reserves and with various test units until at least 1947, often being used to tow targets. Others were operated in the attack role by the French Aéronavale, the navies of Italy and Portugal and the air forces of Greece and Thailand. French Helldivers played a significant role in the war in Indo-China, which lasted until 1954.

Above: The US Army soon lost interest in the dive-bombing role and never used the A-25A in combat. The remaining examples were designated RA-25A and used as trainers and target tugs.

Right: Even before the Helldiver prototype had flown, the US Navy became interested in the potential of a floatplane version and at one stage the acquisition of 350 examples of such a variant was planned. The fifth production SB2C-1 became the XSB2C-2 floatplane for trials, but interest in the combat usefulness of such an aircraft quickly waned and no further development took place.

The crews of this pair of VB-1 SB2C-3s from aboard USS Yorktown (CV-10) take in some fresh air on patrol towards the end of their deployment during the summer of 1944. Note the gunners' pair of 0.30-in (7.62-mm) machine-guns in the rear cockpit of each aircraft.

Helldiver at war

Although it was, by far, the most successful Allied dive-bomber of World War II, the SB2C was never popular with its aircrew, despite its many accomplishments in the Pacific. SB2C was said to stand for 'Son of a Bitch, 2nd Class'!

Though deliveries of the first SB2C-1s were made to Scouting Sqn 9 (VS-9) from December 1942, two years after the prototype's first flight, another 11 months elapsed before the type was judged to be operationally effective and ready for combat.

In all, between 1943 and 1945, 30 US Navy bombing squadrons (these having merged with the scouting units) deployed Helldivers on combat cruises in the western Pacific from a mixture of 13 'fast' carriers and 12 of the newer, smaller 'Essex'-class carriers. These units were, in numerical order, VB-1 to VB-20, VB-80 through -88 and VB-94.

First operation

The first operational sortie by Helldivers was flown by VB-17, operating from USS *Bunker Hill*. Bombing 17's 'work-up' on the type during early 1943 had been far from encouraging. Several aircraft and crews were lost in accidents and it was even suggested that the squadron revert to the Douglas SBD for its combat cruise. However, this was resisted and, on 11 November 1943, VB 17's SB2Cs flew the second strike mounted that day against the big

Japanese base at Rabaul, New Guinea. In this, the type's first taste of combat, four aircraft were lost: one on take-off, one each to a Japanese fighter and flak and one to battle damage, shoved overboard after it had recovered to the carrier. Bombing 17's cruise aboard *Bunker Hill* ended on 4 March 1944 and by then, though an imperfect aircraft, the SB2C was tested and would be improved for a much expanded role in the Pacific war.

The First Battle of the Philippine Sea (the conquest of the Marianas) in mid-1944 involved five SB2C-1/-1C units, totalling 174 aircraft. The day after the 'Marianas Turkey Shoot' of 19 June (in which USN Hellcats claimed over 350 Japanese aircraft destroyed), a key raid was made on the Japanese fleet, with its seven remaining aircraft-carriers. Of 226 aircraft sent on the 300-nm (345-mile/555.5-km) sortie that afternoon, 52 were Helldivers, but although the attack was deemed a success, all but eight were lost. Returning in darkness, most ditched due to fuel starvation or were wrecked in landing accidents, for their pilots were not qualified for night-time deck

landings and had trouble locating their carriers.

By the time of the Battle of Leyte Gulf in the autumn of 1944, the SB2C-3 had replaced the SB2C-1. The Helldiver was well established in service, and at last was becoming operationally effective, though crashes, inflight break-ups and carrier landing accidents continued to place the SB2C at the very top of the accident 'league table'.

Given these problems and the creditable performance of the few remaining SBDs of VB-10 and VB-16 off Saipan in June, Vice-Admiral Marc Mitscher, commander of Task Force 58 in the Philippine Sea, considered re-equipping his other bomber units with the Douglas design,

Foreign Helldivers

Under Lend-Lease, 450 Helldivers were ordered for the Fleet Air Arm, to be built by Canadian Car & Foundry as SBW-1Bs, essentially similar to the parent company's SB2C-1C. Deliveries began at the end of 1943 but were suspended in 1944 after just 26 had been handed over – testing by the A&AEE had revealed unsatisfactory flight characteristics. Designated Helldiver DB.Mk I (below), these aircraft equipped No. 1820 Sqn briefly but saw no action, the unit disbanding in December 1944. The only other wartime user was the RAAF, which trialled a handful of ex-USAAF A-25A Shrikes, but declined the offer of more. Post-war, France (below right), Greece, Italy, Portugal and Thailand (right) flew Helldivers. The type's last combat sorties were from the French carrier *Arromanches* during the first months of the Indochina war, in 1954.

Powerplant

Wright's newly-developed two-row, 14-cylinder R-2600 Double Cyclone powered all SB2Cs, the Dash-3 having a 1,900-hp (1417-kW) R-2600-20 installed. This drove a Curtiss four-bladed, constant-speed, fully-feathering propeller.

Armament

The first production SB2Cs were fitted with two 0.50-in (12.7-mm) machine-guns in each wing, but after 200 had been completed this was changed to a single 20-mm cannon in each wing in the SB2C-1C. In the rear cockpit, a pair of 0.30-in (7.62-mm) machine-guns was fitted, while the internal bomb bay held 1,000 lb (454 kg) of bombs.

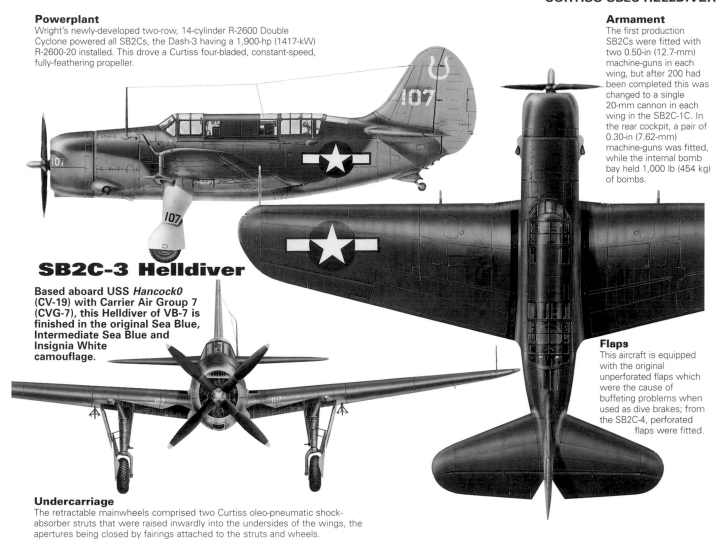

SB2C-3 Helldiver

Based aboard USS *Hancock0* (CV-19) with Carrier Air Group 7 (CVG-7), this Helldiver of VB-7 is finished in the original Sea Blue, Intermediate Sea Blue and Insignia White camouflage.

Flaps

This aircraft is equipped with the original unperforated flaps which were the cause of buffeting problems when used as dive brakes; from the SB2C-4, perforated flaps were fitted.

Undercarriage

The retractable mainwheels comprised two Curtiss oleo-pneumatic shock-absorber struts that were raised inwardly into the undersides of the wings, the apertures being closed by fairings attached to the struts and wheels.

but by July the Dauntless was out of production and he had no alternative but to persist with the Helldiver. In fact, the 'Dash-3' was to prove a very different aircraft to the earlier variants, with more power and improved handling characteristics.

The 'Beast' continued to serve in the US Navy's advance in the direction of Japan, eight Helldiver units (all equipped with SB2C-3s) participating in

Returning to USS Hornet (CV-12) from another strike on Japanese shipping in the China Sea, a Helldiver pauses while two TBF Avengers are cleared from the landing area.

the actions in Leyte Gulf in October, including the sinking of four Japanese carriers. Others undertook strikes against land targets on Formosa and the Philippine Islands, the latter during November in particular.

After Leyte Gulf, the requirement for dive-bombers aboard carriers in the Pacific had decreased and by February 1945 only 135 Helldivers were among the more than 1,000 aircraft with

TF.38 off the coast of Japan. However, the type still had a role to play and by the time of the invasion of Okinawa between April and June, 11 bombing units, equipped with SB2C-3s and -4s, were available. On 7 April, in the last major attack by the Allies on Japanese warships in the open sea, four of these Helldiver squadrons were among the elements that pursued, and eventually sank, Japan's much-feared battleship, IJNS *Yamato*.

On VJ-Day (15 August), nine Helldiver units, by then all flying SB2C-4s or -4Es, were in combat and a total of 48 USN squadrons was equipped with over 700 Helldivers.

'Leatherneck' Helldivers

Marine Corps Helldiver squadrons saw limited combat from June 1945, VMSB-244 (equipped with ex-USAAF A-25As) supporting US Army operations in the Philippines. Other 'Leatherneck' Helldivers saw service in the Marshall Islands, and by VJ-Day there were five USMC Helldiver units stationed west of Hawaii.

One of the lesser-known aspects of the Helldiver's service in the Pacific theatre is its air-to-air kill tally. Forty-four

confirmed and 14 'probable' victories were credited to SB2C crews. The top scorer was Lieutenant Robert Parker of VB-19 who shot down three Japanese fighters in late 1944 while flying from USS *Lexington*. Some carrier air groups transitioned suitable dive-bomber pilots to fighter duty, often with notable success. Sadly, Parker was killed on 5 November before he was given such an opportunity.

Initially greeted with enthusiasm, the Curtiss Helldiver did not outperform the Douglas Dauntless by as wide a margin as had been originally envisaged. In fact its greatest advantage over its predecessor was its folding wings, which allowed the embarkation of much larger dive-bomber complements aboard carriers.

A USN report of June 1945 concluded that 'when we needed the SB2C neither we nor it was ready', but it was all that the US Navy had. The aircrew's view of the Helldiver is perhaps summed up in an anonymously-penned ditty that concludes, "My body lies under the ocean; my body lies under the sea. My body lies under the ocean, wrapped up in an SB2C!"

With its pressurised cockpit, the Mosquito B.Mk XVI could fly at an altitude of 40,000 ft (12192 m). This aircraft was flown by No. 571 Squadron, which formed at Downham Market in April 1944 as a light bomber unit with No. 8 (Pathfinder) Group.

de Havilland DH.98 Mosquito

Introduction

The Mosquito was born in an uncertain fashion during the early months of World War II, with few real supporters. Within five years, however, it had become one of the RAF's most versatile and valued assets.

The all-wooden de Havilland Mosquito was possibly the most useful single type of aircraft produced by the Allies in World War II. It owed nothing to any official specification and was created in the face of often fierce opposition by officialdom.

Even after a prototype had been ordered, the limited nature of the programme (a mere 50 aircraft) caused it to be removed entirely from future plans three times after the Dunkirk evacuation. Each time it was daringly put back by a single believer, Patrick (later Sir Patrick) Hennessy, brought in from Ford Motors by Lord Beaverbrook to help run British aircraft production. Eventually, in November 1940, a single prototype at last took to the air.

Once that had happened, the fantastic performance of de Havilland's Mosquito soon silenced its official detractors.

The de Havilland Aircraft Company was famed chiefly for lightplanes and rather primitive mixed-construction light transports, but in 1936 it designed the aerodynamically superb (although technically disastrous) DH.91 Albatross airliner, with a structure entirely of wood. A few months later, work was started on a military derivative with two Merlin engines to meet the requirements of Specification P.13/36, but this was not accepted, largely because of the wooden structure which

The first Mosquito (W4050) was secretly built at Salisbury Hall, close to the Hatfield works in Hertfordshire. W4050 received an overall yellow colour scheme, and is seen here covered in tarpaulins in an effort to conceal the aircraft from prowling Luftwaffe aircraft.

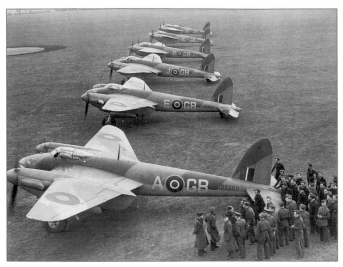

Pilots and ground crews crowd around a line-up of Mosquito B.Mk IVs at their home base of RAF Marham in late 1942. These light bombers of No. 105 Squadron had been on strength since November 1941 and were used for high-speed, long-range bombing raids. Their speed allowed them to fly without fighter escort.

was not taken seriously. Undeterred, the project staff under R. E. Bishop, R. M. Clarkson and C. T. Wilkins, continued to study a new high-speed bomber able to evade hostile fighters and thus dispense with gun turrets. The concept appeared to make sense. Doing away with turrets reduced the crew from six to two, comprising a pilot on the left with the navigator/bombardier on his right. Either could work the radio. Thanks to the scale effect, in that saving weight enabled the aircraft to be smaller and burn less fuel, it

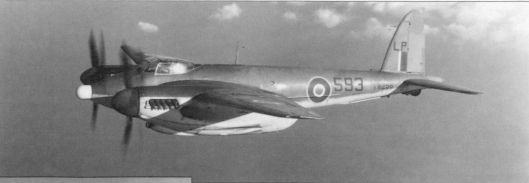

Right: The Royal Navy's Sea Mosquito TR.Mk 33 could carry a wide range of offensive stores, including an 18-in (457-mm) torpedo. It also had radar, four cannon and full carrier equipment. Prior to delivery of this fully-developed, Leavesden-built series, the Fleet Air Arm used 'hooked' Mk VIs.

Left: After the war the Royal Norwegian air force was one of the numerous foreign air forces that operated Mosquitoes. This FB.VI served with RNorAF No. 334 Squadron from Stavanger/Sola. The unit was originally B Flight of No. 333 Sqn, operating the same aircraft with the RAF strike wing at Banff, Grampian, in 1943.

was calculated that the twin-Merlin unarmed bomber could carry 1,000 lb (454 kg) of bombs 1,500 miles (2400 km) for a weight of just over 15,000 lb (6800 kg). In addition, with careful streamlining, the speed could reach almost 400 mph (655 km/h), almost double that of other British bombers.

Full-scale RAF service began with the B.Mk IV series II, the first definitive bomber version, which entered service with No. 105 Sqn of No. 2 Group at Swanton Morley in November 1941. Next came No. 139 Sqn at Marham. The first bomber mission was flown by just one aircraft – W4072 of No. 105 Sqn – at the end of the '1,000-bomber' raid on Cologne on 30-31 May 1942. After various ineffective sorties, a daring attack was made on Gestapo HQ in Oslo, but was thwarted by the performance of the bombs; one failed to explode inside the building, while three others went through the far wall before detonating. For the rest of the war, the original B.Mk IV made daring precision attacks throughout Europe from tree-top height.

Special missions

Mosquitoes proved highly effective in the photo-reconnaissance roles – the PR.Mk IV was a camera variant of the B. Mk IV series II. The FB.Mk VI fighter-bomber, with 2,584 examples completed, was built in the greatest numbers however. With two-stage Merlin engines, wing-mounted drop tanks and under-wing racks for two or more 250-lb (113-kg) bombs, which were later replaced by eight underwing rockets, the versatile FB.Mk VI ranged across Europe, hitting such point targets as the walls of Amiens prison, the Gestapo HQ at The Hague, Gestapo HQ at Copenhagen, and

numerous V-weapon sites. Indeed, the flexibility of the type was such that the Mosquito was not restricted to daylight operations. A host of night-fighter variants was produced, equipped with harpoon-like aerials, or bluff nose radomes.

Foreign operators

Many marks of Mosquito flew with all Allied air forces, including the Red air force and the USAAF, the latter using Canadian-built aircraft as the F-8 reconnaissance version. In addition to 10 civil Mosquitoes used by BOAC on high-priority services with cargo and passengers between the UK and Sweden (and occasionally other places), there were various later marks that did not see war service.

The heaviest and highest-performing of all versions were the closely related PR.Mk 34,

B.Mk 35 and NF.Mk 36. All had high-altitude Merlins and broad paddle-bladed propellers. The PR.Mk 34 was the longest ranged of all marks. A PR.Mk 34A made the last RAF's last operational Mosquito flight on 15 December 1955. There were also numerous Sea Mosquito variants, of which the most important was the radar-equipped TR.Mk 33.

The last of 7,619 Mosquitoes was VX916, a night-fighting NF.Mk 38, delivered from Chester on 28 November 1950. It was the 6,33st built in England; Canadian production totalled 1,076 and Australian 212. Post-war air forces using Mosquitoes included those of Belgium, China, Czechoslovakia, Denmark, Dominica, France, Israel, Norway, South Africa, Sweden, Turkey and Yugoslavia.

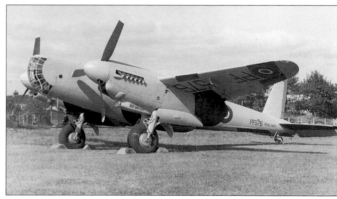

Right: The final incarnation of the Mosquito in regular service followed conversion for the target-towing role for the Royal Navy. Known as TT.Mk 39s, the aircraft were fitted with a 'glasshouse' nose which accommodated a cameraman, while the bomb bay housed an electrically-driven winch.

By various methods, only some of them legal, the infant Israeli air force (Heyl Ha'Avir) acquired real offensive muscle with Mosquito Mks IV, VI and NF.Mk 36. This colourful FB. Mk6 (post-war designation) was one of a batch bought at a knock-down price from the French Armeé de l'Air.

'Wooden Wonder' development

The genesis and development of the Mosquito occurred in an era in which Duralumin and other alloys had long since replaced wood and wire. This, however, did not stop Geoffrey de Havilland's British aircraft manufacturing company from developing an amazing twin-engined aircraft of wooden construction that would strike 'Moskitopanic' into the hearts of its enemies in World War II.

In 1934, in great secrecy, de Havilland produced three diminutive, streamlined DH.88 Comet low-wing monoplane racers, each powered by two 230-hp (172-kW) DH Gipsy Six R (Racing) engines. Wooden construction and stressed-skin covering not only reduced all-up weight but also hastened production. All three Comets took part in the 1934 London-Melbourne Centenary Air Race, which was won by DH.88 *Grosvenor House*, crewed by Tom Campbell Black and C. W. A. Scott. In 1935 two more DH.88 Comet Racers were built. This type ultimately played a crucial role in the development of the Mosquito. In the late 1930s these same manufacturing techniques were applied to the four-engined DH.91 Albatross commercial

monoplane. Mainly of wood and stressed-skin construction, it was capable of cruising at 210 mph (338 km/h)) at 11,000 ft (3353 m) and flew for the first time on 20 May 1937 at Hatfield. A total of seven of these beautiful aircraft was built.

Specification P.13/36

On 8 September 1936 de Havilland took an interest in Air Ministry Specification P.13/36, which called for a 'twin-engined medium bomber for world-wide use'. Further, it stated that the aircraft must have the highest possible cruising speed. Ideally, the new machine would be a medium bomber, general reconnaissance and general-purpose aircraft in one basic design, 'with possibly two 18-in [45.70-cm] torpedoes carried'. It would be armed with two forward- and

Above: On the day of the Mosquito prototype's first flight, 25 November 1940, Geoffrey de Havilland (with raised left hand) chats to DH colleagues in front of W4050.

Top: W4050 was retained by DH as a trials aircraft and made its last flight in around December 1943; a maximum speed of 439 mph (706 km/h) was attained in level flight. The aircraft survived the war and is today displayed at the de Havilland Heritage Museum.

two rearward-firing Browning machine-guns (remotely-controlled guns were another consideration), would have horizontal bomb stowage, in tiers if necessary, and would be suitable for outside maintenance at home or overseas. Notably, P.13/36

called for a top speed of not less than 275 mph (443 km/h) at 15,000 ft (4572 m) on two-thirds engine power and a range of 3,000 miles (4828 km) with a 4,000-lb (1814-kg) bombload.

De Havilland had bad memories of submitting competing designs to the military in the 1920s, when all of his ideas had been considered too revolutionary. DH therefore proposed a modified miniature version of the Albatross airliner design to

W4051, the PR prototype, was the second Mosquito completed at Salisbury Hall and the third to fly, after the fighter prototype (W4052), on 10 June 1941. W4051 became the first PR Mosquito to enter service with the RAF, at the PRU at Benson, Oxfordshire.

Below: Most Mosquitoes were crewed by a pilot and navigator. This B.Mk IV cockpit view shows the engine controls to the left, engine gauges to the left of the instrument panel and flying controls in the middle.

meet the specification. It could certainly carry a 6,000-lb (2721-kg) bombload to Berlin and back at 11,000 ft (3353 m). In April 1938 studies were conducted for a twin Rolls-Royce Merlin-engined version of the airliner. There was nothing radical about this, but what would the Air Ministry make of a wooden design being submitted to carry bombs 3,000 miles (4828 km) in war? On 7 July Geoffrey de Havilland sent a letter detailing the specification to Air Marshal Sir Wilfred Freeman, an old friend of de Havilland's from World War I, now the Air Council's member for Research and Development. Sir Geoffrey was to recall later in his autobiography, *Sky Fever*, that 'it only needed one meeting with this wise and far-sighted man to discuss our plans and get his full approval'.

In the event, the Merlin-engined Albatross lost out to the Avro Manchester and the Handley Page HP.56, both to be powered by two Rolls-Royce Vulture engines (although plans for the Vulture-engined HP.56 were scrapped in 1937). The loss of this contract was a blessing in disguise, for de Havilland now opted for a very radical approach to the design of a twin-engined bomber. DH proposed deleting armament altogether to save about one-sixth of the total weight of the aircraft; in turn, this would make production much easier and hasten service

delivery. Losing the armament (although chief designer, Ronald E. Bishop, did make provision under the floor for four 20-mm cannon) meant that the crew could be reduced to a pilot and a navigator only.

The Munich Crisis of 1938 provided much-needed impetus, and de Havilland proposed its unarmed, twin-engined wooden bomber with a crew of two. Speed would be the new bomber's only defence, so, predictably, the Air Ministry rejected the company's proposal. It wanted only heavily armed, conventionally built, all-metal bombers.

War with Germany was declared on 3 September 1939 and de Havilland saw no reason to modify its proposal, but, likewise, the Air Ministry saw no reason to accept it.

The fastest bomber

Eventually, and mainly due to Sir Wilfred Freeman's support, de Havilland's unarmed bomber proposal finally won acceptance. On 29 December 1939 the project received official backing, and on 1 January 1940 a single prototype of the unarmed bomber – the fastest in the world – powered by two Rolls-Royce Merlin engines, was ordered. On 1 March 1940 a contract was placed for 50 DH.98 Mosquito aircraft although, following the Dunkirk debacle of May 1940, there was no surplus capacity available for aircraft like the Mosquito. To save the project

altogether, de Havilland promised the Ministry of Aircraft Production that the 50 Mosquitoes would be delivered by December 1941.

W4050, the bomber/photo-reconnaissance prototype – referred to originally as E0234, the Company B-Class marking, and the first of three Mosquito prototypes – was built in strict secrecy at Salisbury Hall, Hertfordshire and assembled at nearby Hatfield. A team of nine designers, led by Ronald E. Bishop, handled the DH.98 design which, although constructed of wood, was far from straightforward. Techniques and processes used on previous DH designs could

not always be applied to the DH.98, which required higher load factors.

On 25 November 1940 W4050 made its first flight at Hatfield with Captain Geoffrey de Havilland, Jr, the chief test pilot, at the controls and John E. Walker, chief engine installation designer, in the right-hand seat. The aircraft flew like the pedigree machine it was and, once minor problems were eliminated during testing, the Mosquito proved to be a thoroughbred. Official trials at the A&AEE Boscombe Down in early 1941 confirmed that the aircraft met or exceeded de Havilland's speed and handling expectations.

The ultimate development of the PR Mosquito was the PR.Mk 34. This variant was the heaviest of all 'Mossies', with a gross weight of 25,500 lb (11567 kg) and a 1,255-Imp gal (5705-litre) fuel capacity that bestowed a range of some 3,600 miles (5794 km).

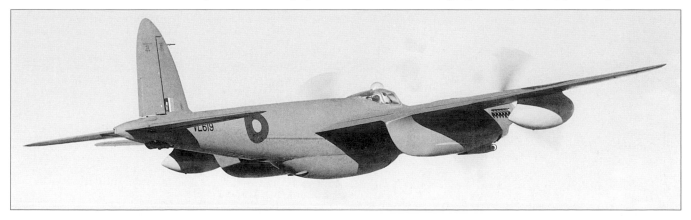

High-speed spies
Mosquito reconnaissance variants

Photo-reconnaissance Mosquitoes were the first of the 'Wooden Wonders' to enter RAF service and became one of the most important Allied reconnaissance platforms of World War II.

W4051, the photo-reconnaissance prototype, was the second Mosquito completed at Salisbury Hall and the third to fly, after the fighter prototype (W4052), on 10 June 1941. A delay had ensued when the fuselage originally intended for W4051 was used to replace that of W4050, which had fractured at Boscombe in a tailwheel-related incident. W4051 became the first of three PR Mosquitoes (used by the Photographic Reconnaissance Unit (PRU)) at RAF Benson, Oxfordshire.

On 13 July W4051 was flown to Oxfordshire by Geoffrey de Havilland and handed over to the PRU (later No. 1 PRU), where it became the first Mosquito to be taken on charge by the RAF.

W4054 and W4055 followed, on 22 July and 8 August, respectively. Beginning in September, No. 1 PRU received seven more production PR.Mk Is: W4056 and W4058-63 (W4057 became the bomber prototype, B.Mk V). Four of these (W4060-W4063) were later modified with increased fuel tankage for long-range operations, and two (W4062 and W4063) were tropicalised, leaving the UK for operational use in Malta and Egypt.

Camera fit

The standard contemporary Mosquito camera installation consisted of three vertical cameras – an F.52 20-in (51-cm) or 36-in (91-cm) high-altitude day reconnaissance camera, a

Above: W4051 was the last of the three Mosquito prototypes to fly, taking to the air for the first time on 10 June 1941. The following month, it was delivered to the PRU at Benson.

Top: The most numerous of the wartime Mosquito PR aircraft were the PR.Mk XVIs, developed in parallel with the B.Mk XVI. Here, a No. 681 Sqn example roars into the air, probably from Dum Dum in India, some time after February 1944.

K.17 survey and mapping camera with a 6-in (15-cm) lens, plus a single F.24 camera mounted in the lower fuselage. An F.24 Universal oblique camera was also fitted for day and night photography.

During tests of the new aircraft and its equipment on 16 September 1941, W4055's generator packed up over the Bay of Biscay, and with no power to drive the cameras, Sqn Ldr Rupert Clerke and Sgt Sowerbutts were forced to abandon the sortie. They were pursued by three Bf 109s but the PR.Mk I easily outpaced them at 23,000 ft (7010 m) and returned safely. Clerke and Sowerbutts made the first successful PR.Mk I sortie the next day, when they set out in W4055 for a daylight PR of Brest, La Pallice and Bordeaux, arriving back at Benson at 17.45.

By spring 1942 the PRU at Benson was in need of additional

PR.Mk Is, only nine having been built by that stage. During April to June 1942 four NF.Mk IIs – DD615, 620, 659 and W4089, all without long-range tanks – were diverted to the PRU, and in December two B.Mk IV bomber variants – DZ411 and DZ419 – arrived. Ground crew at Benson installed the three vertical and one oblique cameras aboard each of the machines and they were pressed into service.

PRU re-formed

On 19 October 1942 No. 1 PRU was re-formed at Benson as five PR squadrons, equipped with Spitfires, Wellingtons, Ansons and Mosquitoes. 'H' and 'L' Flights, by then based at Leuchars, were merged to form No. 540 (Mosquito) Sqn under the command of Sqn Ldr M J B Young, DFC. In the main, No. 540 Sqn photographed German capital ships in Baltic

The USAAF's first experience with the Mosquito was an unhappy one. The "Spook" was among the 40 Canadian-built bomber aircraft converted for the PR role and designated F-8. Hampered by their single-stage Merlin engines, they saw little, if any, use.

25th Bomb Group (R)

RF992/'R' is an aircraft of the 654th Bomb Sqn, 25th Bomb Group (Reconnaissance), 325th Photo Wing based at RAF Watton in March 1945. Tasked primarily with photo-reconnaissance, the squadron also operated a handful of aircraft modified as 'chaff bombers'.

Mosquito PR.Mk XVI

The 8th Air Force, USAAF operated the second-largest fleet of Mosquitoes during World War II, receiving 40 Canadian-built F-8s (which were not used operationally) and at least 80 PR.Mk XVIs. The latter carried out, from early 1944, photo- and weather reconnaissance and chaff-dispensing duties until VE-Day.

Powerplants

After its unhappy experiences with the F-8 (hampered by its engines and limited PR equipment), the 8th Air Force was keen to obtain a Mosquito that was up to the weather reconnaissance role envisaged for the 8th's Mosquitoes. The PR.Mk XVIs ultimately delivered were powered by the Merlin 72/73 and were equipped with a pressurised cabin and were therefore able to operate at altitudes up to 37,000 ft (11278 m).

Markings

Initially operated in standard RAF PRU Blue colours, 25th BG(R) Mosquitoes received red tail surfaces during August/September 1944 as a recognition aid, a number of aircraft having been mistakenly shot down by USAAF fighters unfamiliar with the type.

waters and North Germany, and later in the Mediterranean.

The first of five PR.Mk VIIIs, which began as B.Mk IV Series II aircraft with 1,565-hp (1167-kW) two-stage super-charged Merlin 61 engines, had begun to reach No. 540 Sqn late in 1942. Essentially, the PR.Mk VIII was intended to fill the gap until deliveries of the PR.Mks IX and XVI were made. The PR.Mk VIII had a greatly improved ceiling so that, for the first time, PR Mosquitoes could operate at high altitudes.

The first PR.Mk VIII sortie was on 19 February 1943 and No. 540 Sqn continued to carry out battle-damage assessment and target reconnaissance at such places as the experimental rocket

site at Peenemünde on the Baltic coast, and also successfully identified the existence of the V-1 flying-bomb and its dispersed launching sites.

Mk IXs and XVIs

No. 544 Sqn, meanwhile, continued to use Ansons, Wellingtons and Spitfire PR.Mk IVs in the PR and night photography roles over Europe, until, in April 1943, Mosquito PR.Mk IVs replaced the Wellingtons. In October, PR.Mk IXs completed No. 544 Sqn's re-equipment. This squadron had flown its first PR.Mk IX operation, a night sortie, on 13 September 1943, when Flight Lieutenant R. L. C. Blythe covered Vannes.

Production of PR.Mk XVIs began in November 1943, and 435 were eventually built. With 100-Imp gal (455-litre) drop tanks, the PR.Mk XVI had a range of 2,000 miles (3218 km). On 19 February 1944 a PR.Mk XVI brought back photos of Berlin, despite German fighters encroaching at 42,000 ft (12800 m).

Both these variants were developed in parallel with Mk IX and XVI bomber variants, the former a production derivative of the Mk VIII with two-stage Merlins (and therefore able to operate at higher altitudes), while the latter introduced cabin pressurisation which allowed even higher altitudes to be attained.

In March 1944 No. 544 Sqn received PR.Mk XVI Mosquitoes. No. 540 had to wait until July 1944 as some of the first PR.Mk XVI models to come off the production lines were urgently despatched to No. 140 Sqn, 2nd TAF, for reconnaissance and mapping duties as part of the build-up to the June D-Day invasion.

Mks IV, IX and XVI also saw service in the Middle East, while Mks IX and XVI were eventually despatched to the Far East after initial problems with the effects of humid tropical conditions, on the aircraft's largely glued wood structure, were overcome.

VLR Mk 34

In June 1945 the PR.Mk 34, a very long-range version of the Mk XVI, entered service. Based at the recently completed airfield at Cocos Island, it made reconnaissance missions to Kuala Lumpur and Port Swettenham. By the end of July some 25 sorties had been carried out by PR.Mk 34s from Cocos, with another 13 by VJ-Day.

PR.Mk 34s (plus a handful of B.Mk 35 bombers converted for night PR operations as PR.Mk 35s) operated with the RAF at home and abroad in the late 1940s and early 1950s.

The last RAF Mosquitoes in RAF service were PR.Mk 34As (with modified equipment) of No. 81 Sqn at Seletar, Singapore, which soldiered on until 15 December 1955.

Above: No. 544 Sqn Mosquito PR.Mk XVI NS502/'M' carries a 50-Imp gal (227-litre) tank under each wing. The use of external fuel tanks allowed longer round trips to be completed.

Right: The long-range PR.Mk 34 was a development of the Mk XVI, for use in the Far East. Entering RAF service shortly before VJ-Day, the Mk 34 remained in use until late 1955 when this aircraft, RG314 of No. 81 Sqn, made the last operational sortie by an RAF Mosquito, during Operation Firedog.

Night-fighter variants

De Havilland's Mosquito fighter prototype was sufficiently promising for the Air Ministry to pursue its development for the night-fighter role. The result was a separate family of heavily-armed, radar-equipped fighter aircraft that served with Fighter and Bomber Commands and the 2nd TAF.

Once the Air Ministry was finally convinced about sanctioning de Havilland's development of an unarmed twin-engined bomber, 50 aircraft were ordered to Specification B.1/40. As the design was required to be just as suitable for the fighter and reconnaissance roles, some of the aircraft would be completed for the latter tasks.

Night-fighter prototype

In fact, a night-fighter prototype (W4052) was the second Mosquito to fly, on 15 May 1941, just under six months after the first had flown. This, the F.Mk II, differed from the earlier machine in having strengthened wing spars to permit violent manoeuvring during air-to-air combat, four Hispano 20-mm cannon fitted under the fuselage

floor and four 0.303-in (12.7-mm) Browning machine-guns in the nose, a flat, bulletproof windscreen and an AI.Mk IV radar. Power came from a pair of 1,460-hp (1089-kW) Merlin 21s or 23s.

Of the first batch of 50 Mosquitoes, 21 were completed as NF.Mk II night-fighters, deliveries of these aircraft to front-line RAF squadrons beginning in January 1942.

The Mosquito fighter was the last of the three versions to enter service. No. 157 Sqn at Castle Camps was the first to be declared operational, in April. This was followed by No. 23 Sqn in July, which flew long-range intruder sorties over Northern Europe (to catch Luftwaffe bombers returning to their bases), before moving to Malta where it destroyed 17

Above: A frill-type Youngman airbrake was tested on NF prototype W4052. Other designs were also trialled, but all were abandoned – lowering the undercarriage was found to be just as effective.

Top: The matt black finish took as much as 23 mph (37 km/h) off the NF Mosquito's top speed and was soon abandoned. DD609 was the 10th machine from the second Mk II order, for 150 aircraft.

aircraft in its first three months on the island. For the intruder role, the aircraft flew without radar but with the 'Gee' navigation aid fitted, and were designated NF.Mk II (Special) – this variant was also known as the NF.Mk II (Intruder). In all, 466 NF.Mk IIs were built.

The next dedicated night-

fighter variant was the NF.Mk XII, which entered service with No. 85 Sqn (commanded by night-fighter ace, Wing Cdr John Cunningham) in February 1943 and introduced a new AI.Mk VIII centimetric radar. This was housed in a nose radome and necessitated removal of the machine-guns; the Mk XII and all later NF Mosquitoes (apart from the Mk XV) were armed solely with four cannon. All 97 Mk XIIs were converted from Mk IIs.

From the NF.Mk XII was developed the Mk XIII, a new-build aircraft based on the

Devoid of radar, the NF.Mk II (Special) was optimised for intruder operations. This aircraft is one of the No. 23 Sqn aircraft sent to Malta in late 1942. Note the hybrid day fighter camouflage/black finish.

Left: The Mosquito NF.Mk XII used AI.Mk VIII radar, housed in a thimble radome. Only 97 were delivered; all were conversions from NF.Mk IIs, the first entering service in early 1943.

Below: Extended wingtips were a feature of the high-altitude NF.Mk XV variant, a derivative of the pressurised B.Mk XVI bomber. The aircraft's armament was fitted in a pack under the fuselage.

FB.Mk VI fighter-bomber, with strengthened wings which allowed the carriage of 50-Imp gal (227-litre) external fuel tanks, and carried AI.Mk VIII radar. A total of 270 was delivered and, with the Mk XIIs, equipped 10 RAF units. An interesting modification made to 50 Mk XIIIs was the addition of a nitrous-oxide (N_2O) injection system to their Merlin engines to give more power for short periods at altitudes above 20,000 ft (6096 m), where speed and climb rate were in need of improvement. The other weakness affecting these variants was the performance of their radar. Thus, for the next Mosquito night-fighter variant, an American radar was substituted.

American SCR-720

Characterised by the 'bullnose' radome that contained the radar scanner for its US-built SCR-720 (AI.Mk X), the Mk XVII was another conversion of the original NF.Mk II. One hundred were so-treated, entering service in their revised form from early 1944. No. 25 Sqn scored its first victory with a

Mk XVII during February.

To offset increased drag caused by the new radome, the almost identical, but new-build, Mk XIX was the next variant, fitted with Merlin 25s rated at 1,635 hp (1219 kW). With either AI.Mk VIII or X radar, the Mk XIX entered service (in mid-1944) at a time when a number of other radar developments were coming on stream. These included a rear-facing radar code-named 'Monica' (a device which homed onto enemy IFF sets called 'Perfectos'), and 'Serrate', another homer that picked up German AI radar transmissions. Several Mosquito Mk XIX units used these devices to good effect, especially those engaged in bomber support duties, protecting Bomber Command's 'heavies' from marauding Luftwaffe night-fighters.

Wartime Mosquito NF development culminated in the NF.Mk 30, an AI.Mk X-equipped derivative of the Mk XIX. The Mk 30 differed from the former mark in two important respects. Firstly, it was powered by Merlin 70-series engines, equipped with two-stage

superchargers to improve performance at altitude. The second change was also brought about by the need to operate at greater heights – cabin pressurisation.

The first Mk 30s also entered service in mid-1944 and, by the end of the war, nine squadrons were equipped with the type, half of these flying bomber support sorties over Germany.

One member of the wartime 'Mossie' night-fighter family came outside the main line of development. To combat the expected use of Junkers Ju 86 high-altitude bombers over Britain during 1942, a pressurised Mosquito B.Mk XVI bomber was converted as the first NF.Mk XV. Fitted with extended wingtips, four-bladed propellers

driven by two-stage Merlin 61 engines, and finished in overall Deep Sky, the aircraft flew in its new guise in August 1942. Four B.Mk IVs were also converted to the new standard, but the Ju 86 threat failed to materialise and the aircraft were withdrawn.

Post-war developments

The RAF withdrew its last NF Mosquitoes – Mk 36s (Mk 30s with Merlin 113/114 engines), of which 266 were built – in 1953.

Foreign NF Mosquito operators included Belgium (Mk 30s), France (Mk 30s), Sweden (Mk XIXs, known locally as J 30s) and Yugoslavia (Mk 38s).

The Mk 38 was the last Mosquito night-fighter mark and featured British radar (AI.Mk IX), which resulted in the cockpit being moved 5 in (12.7 cm) forward. VX916, the last of 100 Mk 38s constructed, was completed in 1950 and was to be the very last of 7,619 Mosquitoes (of all marks) to be delivered.

Characterised by its 'universal' nose radome (housing AI.Mk X radar) and air intakes below its propellers (to feed the intercoolers of its two-stage Merlin engines), the NF.Mk 30 was the last Mosquito NF variant to see service during World War II.

Mosquito NF.Mk II

W4079 was one of the original batch of 50 Mosquitoes, 21 of which were completed to this NF.Mk II night-fighter standard. It was issued to No. 157 Sqn, the first Mosquito night-fighter unit, in June 1942.

Radar and armament
Mosquito NF.Mk IIs carried AI.Mk IV radar, with its so-called 'bow-and-arrow' nose antenna and two pairs of dipoles on each outer wing. Armament consisted of four Hispano 20-mm cannon in a pack under the forward fuselage, and four Browning 0.303-in (12.7-mm) machine-guns in the nose.

Fighter-bombers

This Mosquito FB.Mk VI was part of the station Flight at Banff and was photographed during the winter of 1944/45. It has 100-Imp gal (454-litre) underwing auxiliary fuel tanks fitted.

Were it a warplane of the 21st century, the versatile fighter-bomber Mosquito might be called a multi-role combat aircraft. More FB Mosquitos were built than any other variant.

In July 1942 the RAF's No. 23 Sqn began operations with the Mosquito NF.Mk II (Special). Devoid of radar, since it was forbidden to operate over enemy-held territory with AI radar at this time should the system fall into enemy hands, these aircraft flew intruder missions against Luftwaffe night-fighters and airfields. In addition however, some night-time raids against road and rail targets of opportunity were also flown and the Mosquito's considerable potential as a ground-attack aircraft had been realised.

The converted Mk IIs were only a stop gap however, and plans for an F.Mk II day fighter were dropped (except in Australia, where a single machine was built) as the FB.Mk VI was evolved. Based on the Mk II airframe, the Mk VI made its first flight in February 1943, the prototype being a converted Mk II. Great versatility and immense destructive potential were bestowed upon the FB.Mk VI by its weapons fit, which added up to 500 lb (227 kg) of bombs in the weapons bay, and a 250-lb (113-kg) bomb under each wing, to the four 20-mm cannon and four 0.303-in (7.7-mm) machine guns of the NF.Mk II.

Powered by 1,460-hp (1088-kW) Merlin 21 or 23 engines, the Mosquito FB.Mk VI Series I was built to the extent of 300 examples, before production switched to the FB.Mk VI Series II. This latter machine employed Merlin 25s rated at 1,635 hp (1219 kW) and boasted an internal bomb load of up to 1,000 lb (454 kg) and the ability to carry a 500-lb (227-kg) bomb, or auxiliary fuel tank, beneath each wing.

Prolific variant

Such was its versatility that the Mosquito FB.Mk VI became the most widely built of all Mosquito marks, a total of

Right: On a single sortie in June 1943, a No. 418 Sqn Mosquito FB.Mk VI crew destroyed two Luftwaffe bombers on the ground with gun fire, and with their bombs destroyed a train and a radio antenna.

Invasion stripes add to the menacing look of this Mosquito FB.Mk XVIII 'Tse Tse'. The barrel of its 57-mm gun can be seen beneath the nose. Many Mk XVIIIs had only two machine-guns to save weight.

On 12 August 1944 Nos 235 and 248 Sqns of the Portreath Strike Wing visited the Gironde Estuary near Bordeaux in their Mosquito FB.Mk VIs. Using bombs and rockets they sank two enemy minesweepers.

2,718 being built by Airspeed, de Havilland and Standard Motors. In Canada, three Mosquito FB.Mk 21s, based on the FB.Mk VI, were produced as the forerunners of two FB.Mk 24s and some 338 FB.Mk 26 fighter-bombers. De Havilland Australia was also a major Mosquito manufacturer, building 178 Mosquito FB.Mk 40s for the RAAF. These aircraft were based closely on the RAF's FB.Mk VI, and indeed their numbers were reinforced by 38 FB.Mk VIs in 1944/45, but were powered by US-built Packard-Merlin 31, or later 33, engines.

Ship killing

As a powerful, long-range fighter-bomber with the potential to carry a heavy weapons load, the Mosquito FB.Mk VI had all the makings of an excellent ship killer. Some means was required by which to give the aircraft heavier striking power and some degree of stand-off capability for this hazardous role and so the Mosquito FB.Mk XVIII was evolved and built to the extent of 27 examples. All four of the FB.Mk VI's 20-mm cannon were removed to make way for a 57-mm Molins automatic gun. Just 24 57-mm armour-piercing rounds were carried, fed into a breech that was positioned behind the cockpit. The weapon was somewhat temperamental and attacks had to be flown very precisely to avoid the lateral movements that were sure to cause the gun to jam.

Nevertheless, the FB.Mk XVIII was able to strike a target from as far as 5,850 ft (1783 m) out and proved a formidable weapon against its primary submarine targets, but also against ships and ground targets.

Although the 'Tse Tse' (Mosquito FB.Mk XVIII) Mosquitos were able to rack up impressive combat records in close co-operation with their escorting Mosquito FB.Mk VIs, a revolution in Mosquito anti-shipping operations came with the adoption of rocket projectiles (RPs). Four of these weapons could be carried beneath each wing in lieu of bombs or fuel tanks, the weapons initially being employed being those with 60-lb (27-kg) warheads used elsewhere by the RAF. The first operational firing of RPs by Mosquitos on the night of 21 October 1944 proved the effectiveness of the combination, but it was soon realised the penetrative qualities of the 60-lb (27-kg) weapon were insufficient to pierce the outer hulls of ships and a new rocket was developed.

Rocket-firing Mosquito FB.Mk VIs formed the backbone of the RAF's Banff Strike wing from late 1944 into 1945, the Wing playing havoc with German shipping around Norway and in the North Sea.

Elsewhere, the fighter-bomber Mosquitos were busy destroying important targets on the continent, many of them requiring precision bomb strikes, as well as scoring hundreds of kills in air-to-air combat.

Post-war, FB.Mk VIs were used in action against Indonesian extremists in Java and the type was also widely exported to countries including Czechoslovakia and New Zealand. The last RAF Mk VIs were retired in 1950.

Above: This Mosquito FB.Mk VI was photographed during RP trials with the A&AEE in November 1943. It carries the 60-lb (27-kg) warhead on its standard 3-in (7.62-cm) rockets.

Below: This aircraft was one of the Mosquito FB.Mk VIs delivered to the RAAF to cover a temporary shortfall in Australian production of FB.Mk 40 models.

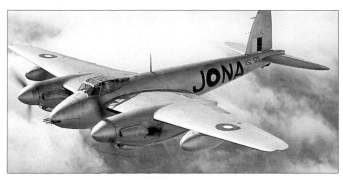

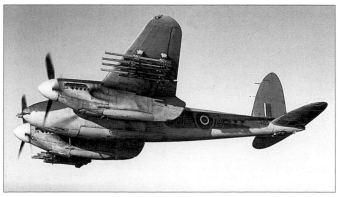

Above: Another Banff-based FB.Mk VI, of No. 143 Sqn, this time carrying rockets with the more streamlined 25-lb (11-kg) semi-armour piercing warheads to deal with ships' armoured hulls.

Bomber variants

Although RAF Bomber Command was initially hostile to the concept of an unarmed bomber, it was persuaded of the merits of de Havilland's high-speed design and ordered the DH.98 in large numbers.

On 21 June 1941, the Air Ministry instructed that, apart from five prototypes (one bomber, one photo-reconnaissance and three fighter), 19 Mosquitoes were to be PR models and 176 to be fighters. In July the Air Ministry finally confirmed that 50 more would be unarmed bombers. In addition to the construction totals agreed on 21 June, the Air Ministry further specified that the last nine aircraft (W4064-72), from the 19 originally ordered on 1 March 1940 as PR versions, could be converted to unarmed bombers also. These nine aircraft came to be known as the B.Mk IV Series I. W4072, the prototype B.Mk IV bomber, flew for the first time on 8 September 1941.

The 50 new-build B.Mk IV Series II bombers differed from the Series I in having a larger bomb bay to increase carriage to four 500-lb (227-kg) bombs instead of the Series I's four of 250 lb (114 kg); this was achieved by shortening the tail stabiliser of the 500-lb (227-kg) bomb so that four could be carried.

On 15 November 1941, at the No. 2 (Light Bomber) Group airfield at Swanton Morley, Norfolk, No. 105 Sqn finally saw the first of the revolutionary Mosquito Mk IV bombers, which had a maximum recommended speed of 420 mph (676 km/h) indicated – equiva-

lent to 520 mph (837 km/h) at 20,000 ft (6096 m).

Initially, No. 105 Sqn had to content itself with W4066, the first Mosquito bomber to enter RAF service, and three other Mk IVs; only eight Mosquitoes had arrived by mid-May 1942. However, No. 2 Group was anxious to despatch its 'wooden wonders' at the first available opportunity. No. 105 Sqn duly sent four Mosquitoes with bombs and cameras to 'harass and obtain photographic evidence' of the 'Thousand Bomber' raid on Cologne on 30-31 May – the Mosquito bomber's first operational sortie.

Second squadron

On 8 June, No. 139 Sqn was formed at Horsham St Faith using crews and Mk IVs from No. 105 Sqn. Its first operation on 25-26 June was a low-level raid on the airfield at Stade near Wilhelmshaven. On 1-2 July the squadron bombed the submarine yards at Flensburg in the first mass low-level strikes by Mosquitoes, but before long high-level raids in clear skies were the order of the day, and during July the first 29 'Siren Raids' were flown. Involving dog-leg routes across Germany at night at high level, they were designed to disrupt the war workers and their families and ensure that they lost at least two hours of sleep before their shifts

Above: Re-formed at Horsham St Faith on 8 June 1942, No. 139 Sqn became the second Mosquito bomber squadron, No. 105 Sqn having received its first aircraft earlier in the year. These are Mk IV Series II aircraft, with lengthened engine nacelles and shrouded exhausts.

Right: Mosquitoes soon joined Bomber Command's night offensive against Germany. Here, a Mosquito B.Mk IX of the Light Night Striking Force is run-up prior to a sortie.

the next day.

Nos 105 and 139 Squadrons moved to RAF Marham, Norfolk in September 1942. On the 19th, six crews flew the first Mosquito daylight raid to Berlin.

On 25 September four of the expert low-level raiders in No. 105 Sqn flew a long over-water mission to Oslo to bomb the Gestapo HQ and also to disrupt a rally of Norwegian fascists and quislings. The raid involved a round trip of some

1,100 miles (1770 km), and an air time of 4 hours and 45 minutes, making it the longest Mosquito mission to date. It was a remarkably successful assault, the first long-distance raid the Mosquitoes had flown and the first raid by the type reported to the British public.

The final large-scale daylight raid by Nos 105 and 139 Sqns was on 27 May 1943, and in June 1943 both squadrons were transferred to No. 8 (Pathfinder)

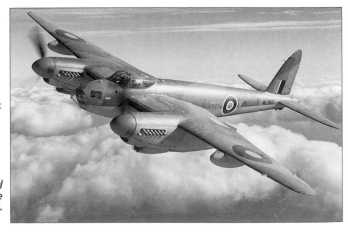

While the B.Mk IX, with its two-stage Merlin engines, allowed operations from higher altitudes, the B.Mk XVI (pictured) had the added benefit of cabin pressurisation. This is a No. 571 Sqn aircraft.

*Above: Mosquito B.Mk XX KB162, named **New Glasgow, Nova Scotia, Canada**, was one of the first two Canadian-built Mosquito bombers delivered to the RAF, arriving in August 1943. In all, over 500 Mk XXs and Mk 25s were delivered, the latter powered by Packard-built Merlin 225s.*

Below: Finished in an overall matt black paint scheme for night operations, this Mosquito B.Mk IV of No. 692 Sqn was among the first to enter service with its bomb bay modified to hold a 4000-lb (1814-kg) 'Cookie' HC bomb.

Group. This was under the command of Air Commodore (later Air Vice-Marshal) Don Bennett, who was committed to using Mosquitoes for pathfinding, and target-marking during night raids by the main force of Bomber Command 'heavies'.

No. 105 became the second Oboe squadron, after No. 109 Sqn which moved from Wyton to join No. 105 at Marham in July, and Bennett used No. 139 at Wyton (to which base the squadron moved in July 1943) as a 'supporting squadron' for the Oboe squadrons, to go in with the markers. (No. 8 Group Mosquito navigators used the Oboe high-level blind bombing aid. Oboe was to become the most accurate form of blind bombing used in World War II. Mosquito bombers of the PFF Group also used the navigational aid, Gee and, later, the radar navigational aid, H₂S.) A fourth Mosquito squadron, No. 627,

was established in November 1943 and, once the Mosquito force in No. 8 Group was further expanded in 1944, No. 139 Sqn led up to 150 of these aircraft in nightly attacks on Berlin.

Mk IXs and the LNSF

Meanwhile, by the summer of 1943, 'nuisance raiding' had become so effective that the Mosquitoes in No. 8 Group were now referred to as the Light Night Striking Force (LNSF). Earlier in the year the first Mosquito B.Mk IXs had entered service with No. 109 Sqn. Based on the PR.Mk IX reconnaissance variant, the B.Mk IX was powered by two-stage Merlin engines, allowing it to fly at higher altitudes.

By early 1944 suitably modified LNSF B.Mk IVs were capable of carrying a 4,000-lb (1814-kg) HC bomb, although it was a tight squeeze in the bomb bay. To accommodate this large

piece of ordnance, the bomb bay had been strengthened and the bomb doors redesigned.

No. 692, which became the fifth Mosquito squadron in No. 8 Group when it formed at Gravely on 1 January, was given the dubious honour of being the first Mosquito squadron to drop one of the 'Cookies', or 'Dangerous Dustbin' as it was known (because of its shape), over Germany. DZ647 released one during a raid on Düsseldorf on 23-24 February. 'Cookies' continued to be carried in modified B.Mk IVs and the B.Mk XVI high-altitude Mosquito, which had first flown in prototype form in November 1943, became operational in the spring of 1944.

The pressurised B.Mk XVI, with its bulged bomb bay and more powerful two-stage 1,680-hp (1253-kW) Merlin 72/73 or two 1,710-hp (1275-kW) 76/77 engines giving a top speed of 419 mph (674 km/h) at 28,500 ft (8687 m), was a much more acceptable 'Cookie-carrier'. No. 692 Sqn first used the B.Mk XVI operationally on 5-6 March, on a raid on Duisburg.

Earlier, on 1-2 February 1944, No. 139 Squadron – which had pioneered the use of Canadian-built Mosquitoes (Mk XXs, with single-stage Merlins) and which was operating a mix of B.Mks IV,

IX, XVI and XX – used H₂S for the first time, marking the target for a raid on Berlin.

In the 12 months from January to December 1944, apart from No. 692 Squadron already mentioned, five more Mosquito squadrons joined No. 8 Group, namely Nos 571, 608, 128, 142 and 162 Sqns, while in January 1945 the eleventh and final Mosquito bomber squadron, No. 163, was formed.

With the war in Europe reaching a conclusion, the Mosquitoes were repeatedly called upon to mark for the bombers in daylight. By late April, however, Mosquitoes were being used for more peaceful purposes, dropping leaflets over PoW camps in Germany and using Oboe to find 'targets' for food drops by RAF and USAAF heavy bombers over German-occupied Holland.

Altogether, No. 8 Group's Mosquito squadrons flew 28,215 sorties, yet they had the lowest number of losses in Bomber Command: just 108 (about one per 261 sorties), while 88 more were written off with battle damage.

The final Mosquito bomber variant, the Mk 35, first flew in 1945, but with the end of the war did not see any use until 1948, briefly equipping two Bomber Command and three BAFO units until replaced by jet types in the early 1950s.

Above: The last Mosquito bomber variant, the B.Mk 35, entered RAF service in 1948 with units in the UK and with the British Air Forces of Occupation in Germany. Replaced by Canberras and Vampires, these aircraft were retired in 1951-52. Here, aircraft based at Celle, West Germany are seen during an exercise in 1949.

Right: The need for a high-speed target tug led the RAF to contract Brooklands Aviation to convert 105 surplus B.Mk 35s as TT.Mk 35s, equipped to carry towed targets in their bomb bays. These were to be the RAF's last Mosquitoes, operated by Civilian Anti-Aircraft Co-operation Units until 1963.

Dewoitine D.520

Wartime chasseur

Its early development marred by official indifference, the D.520 was scarcely a match for the Bf 109, yet its pilots fought with great bravery and skill to bring the type respectability during the Battle of France.

In June 1936 Dewoitine established an autonomous design bureau under Robert Castello, and gave instructions to start project studies for a new fighter design, employing a 900-hp (671-kW) Hispano Suiza 12Y-21 engine and with a target performance of 311 mph (500 km/h). The design was rejected by the French air force authorities as they had already set their sights on a speed of 323 mph (520 km/h). Castello's design, now termed the D.520, on account of the speed demanded, underwent modification by a reduction of the wingspan and a change to the proposed new 1,200-hp (895-kW) engine being developed by Hispano-Suiza.

Despite further rejection of the design, this time on account of official preference for the MS.406, Dewoitine decided to persevere with detail design and building of two prototypes at

private expense, an initiative that was not rewarded by a government contract until 3 April 1938, by which time the first aircraft, the D.520.01, was nearing completion.

The first prototype's maiden flight was made by Marcel Doret at Toulouse-Francazals on 2 October 1938 with an Hispano-Suiza 12Y-21 engine driving a wooden fixed-pitch two-bladed propeller; after replacement of the twin under-wing radiators by a single central radiator and substitution of the early engine by an HS 12Y-29 engine with a three-bladed propeller, the D.520.01 achieved its design speed of 311 mph (520 km/h). The second prototype (D.520.02) with redesigned tail unit, cockpit canopy, strengthened landing gear and armament of one hub-firing 20-mm cannon and a pair of underwing machine-guns, was first flown on 28 January 1939.

Above: Marcel Doret is seen at the controls of the first D.520 on its second flight on 8 October 1938. The short fin gave the type the appearance of a racer rather than a fighting machine.

Top: After a heroic, yet ultimately futile, effort against the superior Messerschmitt Bf 109 during the Battle of France, the D.520 found itself fighting alongside its former enemy against Allied Forces in North Africa.

Only one other example, the D.520.03 with a Szydlowski supercharger in place of the Hispano-Suiza type previously fitted, had flown when war broke out in September 1939.

Due to the parlous state of their fighter equipment, the French authorities placed an order for 200 D.520s on 17 April 1939, delivery being demanded by the end of the year; subsequent contracts in June 1939, September 1939, January 1940, April 1940 and May 1940 increased the total

number on order to 2,200 D.520s (including 120 for the Aéronavale).

By the date (10 May 1940) on which the German attack in the West opened, 36 operationally-cleared D.520s had been issued to Groupe de Chasse I/3 at Cannes-Mandélieu. Non-operational aircraft had been delivered to GC II/3, GC II/7 and GC III/3 for use as conversion trainers.

Despite being scarcely ready for combat in its new fighters, GC I/3 was rushed to the

Below: In the post-war Armée de l'Air, the D.520 played a small part as a fighter trainer. At Fighter School 704 at Tours, several aircraft were given a second cockpit under the D.520DC designation.

Above: The extensive use of the D.520 by Luftwaffe fighter schools was an expression of the desperation faced by that service late in the war. Accident rates among the young students were high.

Below: There were several experimental D.520s, including the HD.780 floatplane, the D.521 with a Merlin engine and the D.550 racer. This is the D.520Z, with revised cooling system and new undercarriage.

Above: Several Dewoitine D.520s survive, including this example owned by the Musée de l'Air. It is on loan to the Aéronavale Museum at Rochefort, having been repainted in 1AC colours.

combat zone and was in action for the first time on 13 May. The D.520 scored many victories during the brief battle for France, against both the Germans in the north and Italians in the south.

By 25 June a total of 437 D.520s had been completed at Toulouse. Of these aircraft, 351 had been taken on charge by the Armée de l'Air and 52 by the Aéronavale; 106 had been lost either in combat or in accidents. Of the remainder, 153 were located in the unoccupied zone of France, 175 were flown to North Africa by surviving pilots of the French air forces and

three were flown to England.

As the Germans initially forbade the deployment of any D.520 unit in the unoccupied zone of the French mainland, many of the surviving aircraft provided the equipment in North Africa. In April 1941 the German Armistice Commission in France gave the SNCASE organisation (which had absorbed the Toulouse factory) a contract for 550 D.520s. A total of 349 of these had been completed by the end of 1942, including 197 aircraft powered by the 820-hp (612-kW) Hispano-Suiza 12Y-49 engine driving Chauvière propellers.

Meanwhile, D.520s had taken part in operations against the Fleet Air Arm during the Syrian campaign of 1941. At the time of the Allied landings in North Africa in November 1942, Vichy forces included a total of 173 D.520s, of which 142 were combat-ready.

Axis service

The outcome of the Allied landings in North Africa was the German seizure of unoccupied France, and on 27 November 1942 the Vichy air force was demobilised. Of the 1,876 aircraft sequestrated by the Germans, 246 were D.520s. In

March 1943 SNCASE was ordered to complete the 150 unfinished aircraft; in little over a year this was accomplished, bringing the total to 905 D.520s.

From this time onwards the D.520 saw fairly widespread service with the Axis air forces, being used initially as a fighter trainer, but also to a limited extent operationally by Jagdgeschwader of the Luftwaffe on the Eastern Front. Sixty D.520s were delivered to the Italian Regia Aeronautica in 1942-43. A small number of D.520s was allotted to the Romanian air force, while 120 were supplied by Germany to the Bulgarian air force in 1943.

Following the liberation of southern France by the Allies in mid-1944 a French fighter group was formed in the Forces Françaises de l'Intérieur, equipped with D.520s. Named Groupe Doret after its commander Marcel Doret, it participated in attacks on remaining pockets of Wehrmacht forces.

When the French air force was formally reconstituted on 1 December 1944 Groupe Doret was redesignated GC II/18 'Saintonge' and equipped with 15 D.520s. Three months later GC II/18 re-equipped with Spitfire Mk VBs and the D.520s were passed on to GCB I/18 'Vendée' and to a training unit at Toulouse. Some 50 D.520s were recovered from the Germans during the final months of the war, and to these were added about 20 aircraft brought back from North Africa.

After the war in Europe ended, D.520s continued in service as fighter trainers. About a dozen aircraft were converted at unit level to two-seat configuration and termed D.520DC (Double Commande).

The last unit to fly the D.520 was the Escadrille de Présentation de l'Armée de l'Air (EPAA) 58. The escadrille was given seven D.520s (of which three were DC two-seaters); the last flight by one of these aircraft was made on 3 September 1953.

D.520

Widely regarded as the best fighter of French origin to emerge during World War II, the D.520's combat career consisted of two main phases. After the fall of France, large numbers were sent to North Africa, some being dispatched to participate in the 1941 Syrian campaign against British and Free French forces. Flying alongside Luftwaffe fighters, the D.520s were involved in the fight against the Allies during the Operation Torch landings of November 1942. After the Allied victory, many D.520 pilots elected to rejoin the Allied cause, including the Armée de l'Air's top World War II ace, Pierre Le Gloan, who had scored kills against the Germans and Italians in France, and against the British in Syria. He was killed in a crash in a P-39 on 13 August 1943.

Armament
By comparison with other French fighters, the D.520 was well armed with one Hispano-Suiza HS404 20-mm cannon with 60 rounds, and four wing-mounted 0.295-in (7.5-mm) MAC 1934 M39 machine-guns, each with 675 rounds.

GC II/7
This aircraft wears the black panther badge of the 4e Escadrille, Groupe de Chasse II/7, while the unit was based at Gabes, Tunisia in 1942, shortly before the Torch landings. The panther was inherited from World War I SPAD squadron SPA78.

Powerplant
Power for the D.520 came from either a Hispano-Suiza 12Y-45 engine or 12Y-49, rated at 850 hp (634 kW) and 820 hp (612 kW), respectively, and driving different propellers. Trials aircraft were fitted with the more powerful 12Y-51 (D.523) and 12Z-89ter (D.524) engines, although neither was adopted.

Markings
Vichy air force aircraft were adorned with bold yellow/red stripe markings as a means of identification.

D.520 over France
The D.520 fought with great distinction in the brief Battle of France. In the north there were notable victories against the Luftwaffe, including the shooting down of leading Luftwaffe ace Werner Mölders, while in the south D.520s scored easy kills over the Italians who entered the war on 10 June. Le Gloan became France's only 'ace in a day', shooting down four CR.42s and a BR.20 in a single sortie on 15 June.

Cockpit
The cockpit was set well aft, giving excellent downward vision in flight. However, taxiing could be tricky, requiring much weaving to retain a semblance of forward visibility.

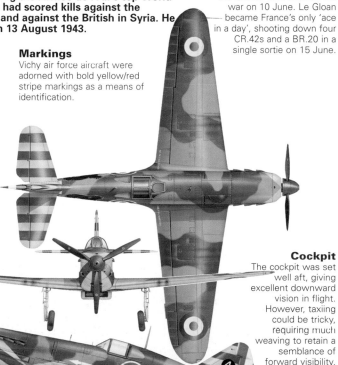

Dornier Do 17/215

The 'Flying Pencil'

Above: The Do 17Z-2 first appeared in 1939 and these two examples were among the last in front-line Luftwaffe service, fighting on the Eastern Front in 1942 with 15.(Kroat)/KG 53.

With poor defensive armament, the Do 17/215 proved vulnerable to enemy fighters in the bombing role. The aircraft did, however, achieve more success in the high-altitude reconnaissance and glider-towing roles.

Inevitably dubbed the 'Flying Pencil' due to its long, slender fuselage, the Do 17 was actually designed purely as a commercial aircraft, primarily a high-speed mailplane but capable of carrying six passengers. In this guise, the Do 17 V1 first flew in late 1934, being passed to Lufthansa for evaluation with the second and third prototypes in 1935. The airline found the passenger accommodation (a single two-seat cabin behind the flight deck, and an equally cramped four-seat cabin aft of the wing) completely impractical, and the prototypes were returned to Dornier. The type was saved from what seemed certain oblivion by a Lufthansa pilot, a former Dornier test pilot acting as liaison between airline and air ministry, who flew the aircraft and suggested that it had potential as a bomber, although he felt it lacked keel area. A fourth prototype was commissioned, with a bomb bay in the lower fuselage and with new twin endplate fins and rudders. This was followed by five similar prototypes, three of which introduced a glazed tip and bottom to the standard long nose and the last three of which

had an aft-facing gun position, with a single 0.31-in (7.9-mm) MG 15 fired by the radio operator, behind the flight deck.

The initial production model was the Do 17E-1, which was produced alongside the almost identical Do 17F-1, which was a dedicated long-range reconnaissance aircraft. Both aircraft had provision for a downward-firing MG 15 in a hatch just ahead of the bomb bay. In the E-1 this could accommodate up to 1,650 lb (750 kg) of bombs, although 1,100 lb (500 kg) was a more usual load, while in the F-1 it carried a pair of cameras.

Do 17F-1s were sent to Spain with the Légion Condor in the spring of 1937. They proved able to evade enemy fighters, as did the 20 Do 17E-1s which joined them in Spain.

The Do 17M and Do 17P were developed in parallel as replacements for the earlier Do 17E-1 and Do 17F-1. The 750-hp (562-kW) BMW VI 7,3 12-cylinder engines were to have been replaced by the same 1,000-hp (746-kW) Daimler Benz DB 600As that powered the Do 17 V8. Unfortunately, production of the DB 600A was

Dornier's Do 17 V1 fast mailplane caused much anxiety in Britain and France when it appeared in late 1934, as its military potential was obvious.

slow and engines were reserved for fighter production, so the Do 17M bomber emerged with 900-hp (675-kW) Bramo 323A-1 Fafnir nine-cylinder air cooled radials, while the Do 17P had the 865-hp (648-kW) BMW 132N, which gave the reconnaissance aircraft the required range. Armament was increased by the addition of a forward-firing MG 15, which could be clamped fore-and-aft and aimed by the pilot using a ring-and-bead sight, or used as a free gun by the navigator/bomb-aimer. Do 17Ms and Do 17Ps still in service in 1940 often had an extra pair of MG 15s added. Both versions had a bomb bay that was extended aft and

housed up to 2,205 lb (1000 kg) of bombs. The provision of a dinghy resulted in a change of designation to Do 17M/U1, while tropical filters resulted in the Do 17M-1/Trop and Do 17P-1/Trop.

Dornier Do 17Ms were exported to Yugoslavia as Do 17Kb-1 bombers, and Do 17Ka-2 and Ka-3 reconnaissance aircraft. All were powered by Gnome-Rhône 14 Na/2 radials and all had FN-Browning machine-guns (and some also had 20-mm Hispano Suiza 404 cannon) as defensive armament. They also had the original long glazed nose of the Do 17 prototypes. Twenty German-built aircraft were supplied, and licence-production began at the State Aircraft Factory in 1939. When German forces invaded in 1941, Yugoslavia had 70 Do 17Ks on strength, 26 being destroyed in the initial assault. Some survivors fled to Egypt (two briefly entering RAF service) and others were passed to Germany's new-formed ally, the Croatian air force, along with some surplus Do 17E-1s.

Above: Do 17E-1s and F-1s of 1. A/88 and 2. K/88 fought with the Légion Condor during the Spanish Civil War. They were utilised in the bombing and reconnaissance roles respectively.

Below: Seen in the winter of 1941-42, a Do 17Z from 7. Staffel III./KG 3 is bombed up by traditional methods on the Eastern Front. The unit converted to the Ju 88 early in 1942.

The Spanish Civil War showed that the Do 17 was vulnerable from below, and the cockpit had proved too cramped. The Do 17S (a high-speed reconnaissance aircraft that did not go beyond the prototype stage) and the Do 17U (a pathfinder version, of which three prototype Do 17U-0s and 12 production Do 17U-1s were completed) introduced a redesigned forward fuselage which increased the height of the cockpit, allowing the carriage of a five-man crew (two radio operators in the Do 17U) and a new lower-hemisphere machine-gun in a flexible mounting. The Do 17S and Do 17U were powered by the DB 600, but the Do 17Z-1 bomber, which shared the same forward fuselage, retained Bramo 323A-1 Fafnir radials. Underpowered with its full bombload, the aircraft was refined into the Do 17Z-2 by the introduction of 1,000-hp (746-kW) Bramo 323P engines with two-speed superchargers. The Do 17Z-3 was a dual-role reconnaissance bomber, with provision for a camera in the entry hatch, while the Do 17Z-4 was a dual-control trainer version, and the Do 17Z-5 a long-range over-water reconnaissance aircraft with flotation bags and extra survival equipment.

Some 212 of the 370 Do 17 bombers on strength on the outbreak of war between Britain and Germany were Do 17Z-1s and Z-2s, the rest being Do 17M-1s and a handful of Do 17E-1s. There were also 262 Do 17s serving with 23 Staffeln in the long-range reconnaissance role. The Do 17 participated in

the invasions of Poland and France (but not of Norway), and played a major part in the Battle of Britain, where it proved able to outrun most fighters in a shallow dive. Nonetheless, losses were heavy and defensive armament proved inadequate. The Do 17s made a number of spectacular low-level terrain-following mass raids, but several units began converting to the much superior Ju 88 even before the battle was over and, by the time Hitler launched Operation Barbarossa, only KG 2 remained fully equipped with the Do 17. Three Gruppen initially flew the Do 17 on the Eastern Front, the last being III./KG 3 which handed its aircraft on to Croatia, which continued to operate the type until transferred to anti-partisan duties in November 1942. Another 'foreign operator' was Finland, which received 15 Do 17Z-2s in early 1942, using the aircraft to replace Blenheims and keeping them operational until mid-1944.

New variants

Production of the Do 17Z was finally terminated in 1940, after 522 Do 17Zs had been delivered. The end of production did not spell the end for the Do 17, however. The single Do 17Z-6 Kauz was a dedicated night intruder created by grafting the cannon-nose of a Ju 88C-2 to the airframe of a Do 17Z-3. This gave the aircraft a forward-firing armament of three MG 15 machine-guns and a 20-mm MG FF cannon. The similar Do 17Z-10 Kauz II had an entirely new, purpose-designed

nose with four MG 15s and a pair of MG FFs, as well as a Spanner Anlage IR detector. The crew of the Z-6 and Z-10 was reduced to three, with the engineer loading the MG FFs and the radio-operator firing the aft-facing machine-guns.

The Do 215 designation was applied to the Do 17Z to cover a proposed export version for Yugoslavia. Prototypes were demonstrated with Gnome-Rhône (Do 215 V2) and DB 601A (Do 215 V3) engines, the DB 601-powered version attracting a Swedish air force order as the Do 215A-1. Embargoed before delivery, the 18 aircraft were modified on the production line for the long-range reconnaissance role and were delivered to the Luftwaffe as Do 215B-0s and Do 215B-1s. Dornier was ordered to continue production of the aircraft for the Luftwaffe, and produced a succession of sub-variants. The unbuilt Do 215B-2 was a bomber, while the Do 215B-3 designation covered two aircraft supplied to Russia. The Do 215B-4 had different camera

equipment and was converted to night-intruder configuration as the Do 215B-5. Unlike the original Kauz II, the Do 215B-5 was adapted to carry the FuG 202 Lichtenstein BC AI radar, paving the way for the fitting of radar to the Bf 110 and Ju 88 night-fighters. The Do 215 had disappeared from front-line service by the middle of 1942, although four were transferred to Hungary.

The last Luftwaffe 'Flying Pencils' served as glider tugs for the DFS 230 until the end of the war, despite steady replacement by more powerful Heinkel He 111s towing larger Gotha Go 242 gliders. They participated in one of the Schleppgruppen's final operations, the re-supply of Budapest in early 1945. In early 1943, the Do 17 glider tugs had enjoyed their finest hour towing DFS 230 gliders to resupply and eventually evacuate German forces in the Kuban bridgehead. By the end of the war, however, numbers had dwindled to the extent that only one captured Do 17 was taken on charge by the Allies for evaluation.

Above: This Do 215B-1 was converted on the production line for Luftwaffe use. It was configured for long-range reconnaissance and served with 3. Aufkl.St./Ob.d.L. at Stavanger in April 1940.

Left: KG 2 was the only Do 17 unit to remain in the West after the invasion of the Soviet Union. This aircraft is seen when assigned to Stab/KG 2 (the wing staff unit) in 1940.

Dornier Do 217

The bombers

Drawing heavily on the Do 17 design, Dornier produced a bigger, heavier bomber in the shape of the Do 217. Although it was overshadowed in its primary role by the He 111 and Ju 88, it nevertheless proved able to carry some of the more exotic weapons fielded by the Luftwaffe, and proved adept at anti-shipping strikes. It also provided the basis for a heavy night-fighter family.

Above: It was the complete reworking of the fuselage, introduced by the V9, which gave the Do 217 its distinctive appearance and respectable bombload. The Do 217E was the first bomber version and in its later sub-variants could launch Hs 293 guided bombs.

In 1937 the RLM had called for an enlarged Do 17Z with much heavier bombload and considerably greater fuel capacity, able to accept any of a range of engines, and equally capable at level- or dive-bombing. First flown in August 1938, the Do 217 V1 was powered by 1,075-hp (802-kW) DB 601A engines but, despite its similar appearance to the Do 17/215, it was a totally new design. It soon showed that it was less pleasant to fly, and in fact crashed, but development continued.

Prototypes flew with Junkers Jumo 211A and BMW 139 engines before the big BMW 801 was used in the Do 217 V9 prototype of January 1940. By this time, handling was acceptable, the leading edges of the fins being slotted, but the unique dive-brake, which opened like a giant cross at the extreme tail, caused endless difficulty. In mid-1941, after wing brakes had been tried and several aircraft lost, the RLM abandoned its stance that the heavy Do 217 had to be a dive-bomber.

The first aircraft into service was the batch of eight Do 217A-0s, built for the reconnaissance role and serving with Aufklärungsgruppe Ob.d.L. Delivered to this special unit in the spring of 1940, the aircraft undertook clandestine reconnaissance missions in the winter over the Soviet Union, in preparation for the invasion of that country. The equivalent Do 217C bomber did not enter service, and the A-0s remained the only examples of the 'thin-body' 217s to see service.

In early 1940 the V9 prototype appeared, this being a radically modified bomber with a much deeper fuselage throughout its length. Entering service in late 1940, the Do 217E-1 was the first 'deep-body' model, able to carry the massive bombload of 8,818 lb (4000 kg), of which 5,550 lb (2517 kg) was inside the bomb bay. A handful to fly, but still a most effective bomber, the Do 217E-1 had a hand-held 20-mm MG FF in the nose, used by KG 40 against ships in the Atlantic, and seven MG 15s. The Do 217E-2 introduced the EDL 131 electric dorsal turret with the excellent MG 131 gun, a hand-aimed MG 131 being in the ventral position, a fixed MG 151/15 firing ahead and three hand-aimed MG 15s completing the defence, although R19 (the 19th in the Rüstsätze series of field kits) added twin or quadruple MG 81

Below: As originally designed, the Do 217 retained the slim, pencil-like fuselage of the Do 17/215, as displayed here by the fourth prototype. This was the first of the series to feature armament, and was powered by Jumo 211 engines.

Below: Seen in late 1942, this Do 217E-4 served with II./KG 40. This group had been the first to put the Do 217E into action, employed on anti-shipping duties against the British. Note the lateral-firing MG 15 in the aft portion of the flight deck.

A Do 217E-2 runs up for a night sortie. In the bombing role the Do 217's finest hour came during Operation Steinbock, the January 1944 'reprisal' raids against southern Britain.

machine-guns firing aft from the tailcone. Other Rustsätze added barrage cable-cutters and various weapon kits, by far the biggest of which hung two Hs 293 anti-ship missiles under the wings, with Kehl/Strassburg radio command guidance link. The first operational missile carrier was the Do 217E-5, flown by II./KG 100, which went into action with increasingly devastating effect against British ships from 25 August 1943.

Do 217E in service

Kampfgeschwader 2 was the only wing to be totally equipped with Do 217Es, and for most of its career operated from bases in the Netherlands against Britain, taking part in the 'little Blitz' in 1944. KG 40 had been the first operator of the Do 217E, beginning anti-ship operations in the spring of 1941 but giving up its Dorniers in 1943. In April 1943, II./KG 100 was equipped with the Do 217E-5/Hs 293 combination, while III./KG 100 operated the Do 217K-2/FX 1400. Other units which operated the type were I. and III./KG 66 for bomber operations, and Versuchskommando/KG 200, which flew the type's last operational sortie on 12 April 1945 when Do 217E-5s launched Hs 293 glide bombs against bridges over the Oder.

The next major bomber version was the Do 217K-1, which began to come off production in about October 1942. It was similar to the later E variants, and it was likewise intended for night bombing. The only significant changes were the fitting of BMW 801D engines, giving a maximum power of 1,700 hp (1268 kW), and a redesign of the forward fuselage. There had been nothing particularly wrong with the original cockpit of the Do 17Z/215/217E, but Dornier – influenced by Junkers' development of the Ju 88B/188 – developed a nose similar to that of the He 177, with the front glazed part continued up to the top of the fuselage. This had the slight drawback of making the pilot look ahead through distant Plexiglas on which he tended to mis-focus his eyes, especially when the panes reflected lighted parts of the cockpit.

Initially, the K-1 had MG 81Z twin 0.31-in (7.92-mm) guns in the nose, two single MG 81s firing to the sides/rear, an MG 131 in the dorsal turret and another MG 131 in the rear ventral position. Later, two more MG 81s were added, firing to the sides. It was possible to fit the R19 installation of one or two MG 81Zs, firing astern from the tailcone, but it was more common to have the R25 installation of a Perlon dive-bombing parachute. Few K-1s were built, and at least one was fitted with underwing racks for no fewer than four LT F5b torpedoes.

'Fritz-X' carriers

At 37,147 lb (16850 kg), the Do 217K-2 was the heaviest of all production 217s. It was specifically developed to carry the FX 1400 radio-controlled heavy bomb, the He 111H having been found not really suitable for the task. The massive bombs, also known as 'Fritz-X', were slung on special racks under the inner wings. An extra fuel tank of 255-Imp gal (1160-litre) capacity was fitted into the forward bomb bay. To carry the greatly increased weight, the outer wings were extended in span from 62 ft 4 in to 81 ft 4 in (19 to 24.80 m), and handling and overall performance remained satisfactory. Almost all K-2s had the R19 fitting of twin MG 81Z guns (four in all) in the tail, and some even had an MG 81Z firing aft from the tail of each engine nacelle.

The K-2's greatest day was 9 September 1943. Major Bernhard Jope's III./KG 100, based at Istres, made a concerted assault on the Italian fleet as it sailed to join the Allies. The greatest battleship, *Roma*, took two direct hits and blew up and sank within minutes. Its sister, *Italia*, limped to Malta with 800 tons (726 tonnes) of water on board. Later, the powerful bombs, each weighing 3,461 lb (1570 kg), crippled or sank many other ships. Some were launched by Do 217K-3s which, instead of having the FuG 203a Kehl I/FuG 230a Strassburg guidance link, had the FuG 203c or 203d Kehl IV with which the bomb-aimer could guide either FX 1400 or the smaller Hs 293A winged bomb.

The Do 217K-2 and similar K-3 specialist 'Fritz-X' carriers were easily identified by their long-span wings, necessary to lift the weight of two giant FX 1400 bombs.

The other production Do 217 family was the M bombers. Structurally, these were similar to earlier versions; in fact, the first Do 217M was merely a K-1 fitted with Daimler Benz DB 603A liquid-cooled engines, each of 1,850 hp (1380 kW). The M-1 went into production almost straight away, being very similar to a K-1 except for having slightly better performance at high altitude.

Not many were built, the need for night-fighters being more pressing, but one achieved notoriety on the night of 23 February 1944 when it made a perfect belly landing near Cambridge (and was soon flying in RAF markings), the crew having baled out over 62 miles (100 km) away, near London.

Even at light weights, height could not be maintained on one engine and, as with all the Do 217s, the feeling was that there was too much aircraft for the available wing area and installed power.

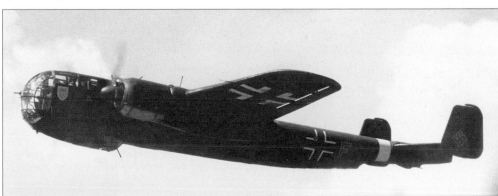

Above: DB 603A engines powered the Do 217M-1, but otherwise it was similar to the K-1. Not many were built, and most were employed on the sporadic cross-Channel bombing raids of 1943-44. A single M-5 was built (Hs 293) and a single M-11 (FX 1400).

Left: The BMW 801D-powered Do 217K-1 introduced a redesigned forward fuselage which did little to improve the aircraft in any significant fashion. This aircraft wears the badge of Luftflotte 2 on the side of the nose.

Night-fighters

Following some success with night-fighting Do 17s and 215s, Dornier fitted a new nose to its Do 217 bomber to produce an interim night-fighter variant. Procured in only small numbers, the type was regarded as unpopular by the Nachtjagdwaffe, and achieved only moderate success.

With the Do 217E sub-types, Dornier introduced the much heavier Do 217 family into service, and all subsequent models proved adequate but generally (and, in the case of the Do 217K-2, severely) underpowered. Despite this, and the absence of the 2,000-hp (1491-kW) engines that were desperately needed, Dornier proposed in early 1941 to develop a night intruder fighter version. The main, and obvious, change in the Do 217J night-fighter was the nose. Instead of a multi-pane Plexiglas nose for a bomb aimer, the J-1 had a 'solid' nose in which were installed four 20-mm MG FF cannon and four 0.31-in (7.92-mm) MG 17 machine-guns. The E-2's aft defensive armament, comprising an MG 131 dorsal turret and a hand-aimed MG 131 in the ventral position, was retained unchanged. The J-1 was operational from February 1942.

Crews liked its firepower and endurance, but found it a rather heavy brute which was sluggish when fast manoeuvres were called for (not often) and which needed bigger airfields than most of those that were available. More serious was the lack of airborne radar,

Right: Few wartime aircraft packed a harder punch than the Do 217 – this N-2 shows the four-cannon, four-gun nose armament, as well as the antennas for the FuG 212 Lichtenstein C-1 radar.

Below: Following the radarless Do 217J-1 night intruder was the FuG 202-equipped J-2, which entered service in small numbers in late 1942.

although in 1941-42 most night-fighter pilots were far from convinced that such new gimmicks were worth having.

Radar fighter

Dornier has no record of the first flight of a Do 217J-2, with FuG 202 Lichtenstein BC radar, but it was probably in the spring of 1942. The J-2 was a definitive night-fighter, not an intruder, the bomb bays being eliminated. The J-2 was lighter than previous Do 217 versions, and despite the 'mattress' of radar antennas the flight performance was almost the same as before. Only small numbers were built, and few combat missions were flown before 1943. Despite its later suffix letter, the corresponding

Daimler Benz night-fighter, the Do 217N, flew as early as 31 July 1942, the DB 603 engine installation having been designed in 1941. Production Do 217N-1s began to reach the Luftwaffe in January 1943. By this time, critical feedback about the 217J had been going on for many months, and the NJG (night-fighter wings) crews were

High-altitude bombers

Various related Do 217 aircraft which never entered service were all intended for flight at high altitudes. First to be started, as a contender for the 1939-40 Bomber B requirement, was the Do 317. This was to be basically a 217 with DB 604 engines, each with four banks totalling 24 cylinders and giving a maximum power of 2,660 hp (1984 kW) each, and with a four-seat pressurised cabin in the nose. In 1940 this was dropped and some of its features used to assist development of the Do 217P, which had a similar-pressure cabin but was powered by two DB 603B engines supercharged by a large two-stage blower and intercooler in the rear fuselage, driven by a third engine, a DB 605T. The first Do 217P flew in June 1942, and there were plans for a production Do 217P-1 reconnaissance aircraft with almost the same extended outer wings as the K-2 (raising service ceiling to an estimated 53,000 ft/16154 m), but this was abandoned.

Meanwhile, in late 1941, the Do 317 was resurrected, and in early 1943 the first 317 began flight testing. This was planned in two versions. The Do 317A was a broadly conventional high-altitude bomber with DB 603A engines, outwardly having much in common with the 217M apart from an odd tail with triangular vertical surfaces. The next-generation Do 317B was to have had extended wings of 85-ft (26-m) span, huge DB 610 double engines each of 2,870 hp (2141 kW), and defensive armament comprising a remotely-controlled 20-mm MG 151 in the tailcone and three twin-gun turrets, two of them remotely controlled. Eventually, the Do 317 also ground to a halt, but five of the Do 317A series prototypes were modified as unpressurised launch aircraft for the Hs 293A radio-controlled missiles. Redesignated as Do 217Rs, they saw combat duty with III./KG 100 at Orléans-Bricy in 1944. At 39,021 lb (17770 kg), they were the heaviest of the whole 217/317 family to fly, although, had they gone ahead, the 317A and 317B would have been much heavier still.

The ungainly underfuselage excrescences of the Do 217P-0 belied the fitment of a third engine, used to drive the pressurisation system. Note the heavily framed cockpit area.

Triangular endplate fins characterised the Do 317 V1 although it was otherwise a pressurised Do 217M. The few completed were redesignated Do 217R and used as unpressurised Hs 293 carriers.

Left and below: The DB 603 A engine fitted to the Do 217N addressed some of the performance shortfalls of the Do 217J, but the type remained underpowered and sluggish. This pre-delivery aircraft has the stanchions fitted for mounting radar antennas.

disappointed to find that the N-1 incorporated none of their mostly obvious recommendations. This was largely because the RLM, and Erhard Milch in particular, disallowed any modifications that would reduce output or increase costs.

By mid-1943, however, Dornier had switched to the N-2, and also produced the U1 conversion set with which existing night-fighters could be modified. The chief changes were to remove the dorsal turret and lower rear gun gondola and to add wooden fairings. The reduction in drag and removal of some 2.2 tons (2 tonnes) of weight raised flight performance to a useful level, maximum speed at medium heights exceeding 310 mph (500 km/h). With the devastating armament of four MG 151s and four MG

17s firing ahead, and four more MG 151s firing at 70° upwards, the Do 217N-2 was a vast improvement over the J-1, and soon appeared with the FuG 220 Lichtenstein SN-2 radar.

By 1944, Do 217Js and Ns were scattered over a vast area of Germany and the occupied countries, serving with around 10 Gruppen, as well as with I./NJG 100 on the Eastern Front.

The 217's devastating armament could easily down bombers when they were found, but the sluggish nature of the Do 217 meant that it could often not complete intercepts. It was frequently employed as a fighter controller, using its radar to steer nimbler Messerschmitt Bf 110s on to targets. Oversized crosses were added under the wings as the unfamiliar shape of

the Dornier in German skies led to many being shot down by 'friendly' night-fighters and flak.

In mixed-type groups, the Do 217s were normally assigned to the most junior crews, while the experienced fliers favoured Bf 110s or Ju 88s. Perhaps the only expert to favour the type

was Rudolf Schönert, who pioneered the use of *schräge Musik* armament on three Do 217s while serving with NJG 1 early in 1943.

Only 364 Do 217Js and Do 217Ns were delivered, and they had faded from the NJG front line by mid-1944.

Powerplant
The Do 217N was powered by the Daimler Benz DB 603A, rated at 1,750 hp (1305 kW) for take-off and 1,850 hp (1380 kW) at 6,890 ft (2100 m). Flame-dampers were routinely fitted.

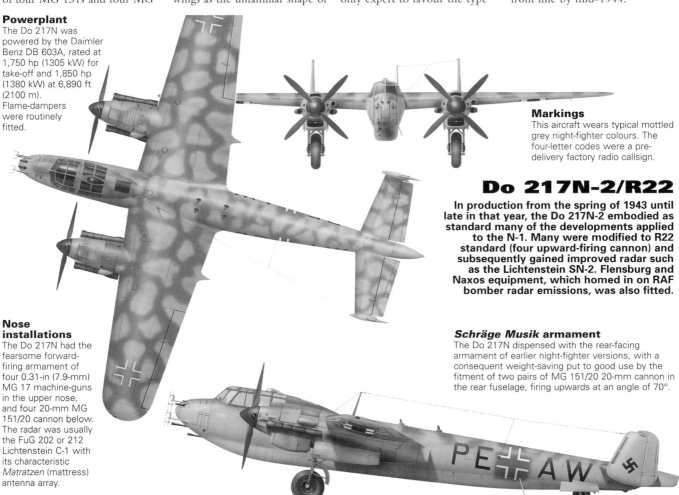

Markings
This aircraft wears typical mottled grey night-fighter colours. The four-letter codes were a pre-delivery factory radio callsign.

Do 217N-2/R22

In production from the spring of 1943 until late in that year, the Do 217N-2 embodied as standard many of the developments applied to the N-1. Many were modified to R22 standard (four upward-firing cannon) and subsequently gained improved radar such as the Lichtenstein SN-2. Flensburg and Naxos equipment, which homed in on RAF bomber radar emissions, was also fitted.

Nose installations
The Do 217N had the fearsome forward-firing armament of four 0.31-in (7.9-mm) MG 17 machine-guns in the upper nose, and four 20-mm MG 151/20 cannon below. The radar was usually the FuG 202 or 212 Lichtenstein C-1 with its characteristic *Matratzen* (mattress) antenna array.

Schräge Musik armament
The Do 217N dispensed with the rear-facing armament of earlier night-fighter versions, with a consequent weight-saving put to good use by the fitment of two pairs of MG 151/20 20-mm cannon in the rear fuselage, firing upwards at an angle of 70°.

This A-20G-20 served with a unit of the Ninth Air Force, which took its place alongside the Eighth Air Force in operations in the ETO, and flew more than 100,000 combat missions in the run-up to D-Day.

Douglas
DB-7/A-20/P-70 Havoc/Boston

Rows of Bostons and Havocs line up at the Douglas plant, awaiting delivery to the RAF and USAAF. The US aircraft wear the original USAAF 241102-K insignia which was worn until 28 May 1942.

US service

Blooded in battle in every theatre of war, sighted on every continent, the Douglas Havoc/Boston was one of the most popular aircraft of the war despite its undramatic and average capabilities.

When they fashioned their Model 711 in 1938, designers Jack Northrop and Edward Heinemann of Douglas at El Segundo, California, had not even been told that the US Army wanted twin engines, let alone tricycle gear, on an attack aircraft. The contract they won for a prototype was a reluctant one, and the snub-nosed, scoop-bellied machine, driven by twin Pratt & Whitney R-1830C 1,100-hp (820-kW) engines, which made its first flight on 6 October 1938, gave little hint of the type's promise, its life

being all too brief before a fatal crash on 23 January 1939.

By January 1940, when the Armée de l'Air began operating the type with its 19th and 32nd Air Groups, initially in Morocco and later in metropolitan France, the UK was interested in the machine and the US Army had placed an order. For the remainder of its career there was confusion and overlap between the company team DB-7 and the

USAAF designation A-20, and between the popular names Boston and Havoc. Many RAF machines officially had both names, the UK's involvement beginning with a 20 February 1940 contract for 150 aircraft, soon raised to 300 and eventually totalling 781; the type became the DB-7B Boston Mk III to distinguish it from the 200 French and 18 Belgian DB-7 Boston Mk Is and 249 French DB-7A Boston Mk IIs diverted to the UK after the fall of France.

Crew positions

Though armament, intended mission and modifications varied widely, the Boston/Havoc twin-engined, shoulder-wing

monoplane was fixed in its essential configuration virtually from the beginning. Pilots transitioning from 'tail-draggers', and so new to tricycle gear, sat high and comfortable and proceeded straight down the taxiway with a commanding view, the cockpit being located forward of the propeller arc for this reason.

With Heinemann's improvements following the Model 7B prototype came, too, a handicap which would remain with the

These A-20Bs operated with the 84th Bomb Squadron, 47th BG, at Mediouna in Morocco in December 1942. Large patches of brown were applied over the original Olive Drab to provide makeshift desert camouflage.

Left: Examples of the DB-7B were already in service with the Armée de l'Air in France by the time the first A-20 for the USAAC left the Douglas plant at El Segundo in 1940. This is the first A-20A to be completed.

Below: This dramatic picture captures the A-20 doing what it did best – low-level bombing. Such raids were used to devastating effect against a range of Japanese targets in the Pacific theatre. Here, a G4M 'Betty' can be seen having escaped the Havoc's wrath. Note also the crashed fighter at the base of the tree in the foreground and parked Zeros to the right.

Boston/Havoc series: because of the narrowness of the fuselage, each crewman was fixed in his own position, unable to exchange places with the others. Injury or death to the pilot would require the nose bombardier and dorsal gunner to bail out.

The essential design was conventional, with a slender, aluminium alloy, semi-monocoque fuselage and a single-spar, aluminium-alloy wing with fabric-covered control surfaces. Armament varied, but the basic design called for fixed forward-firing machine-guns in various combinations, while the rear gunner operated a pivoted 0.303-in (7.7mm) machine-gun in both dorsal and ventral locations, each stocked with 500 rounds of ammunition. Two tandem bomb-bays could accommodate a load of 1,200 lb (544 kg) of bombs, a typical machine having two vertical racks for six 100-lb (45-kg) bombs. Up to 2,000 lb (907 kg) could be carried over shorter distances.

While the initial aircraft were snapped up by France and the UK (including 16 ordered by Belgium), other purchasers came later, including the USAAF with its order for the A-20 Havoc. The USAAF A-20, A-20A and A-20B Havocs saw little action, although numerous A-20Bs ended up in Soviet colours. Some of the earliest Havocs built were converted as P-70 night-fighters. All El Segundo and Long Beach production transferred to Douglas' Santa Monica, California, facility in 1941, where the A-20C model emerged, powered by two 1,600-hp (1193-kW) R-2600-23 engines.

It was the A-20C which arrived in England in June 1942 with the USAAF's 15th Bomb Squadron, seeing action over the Continent and later in North Africa. This and other squadrons

soon began to acquire the A-20G solid-nose model, which dispensed with a bombardier in favour of nose armament eventually comprising six 0.5-in (12.7-mm) guns. The similar A-20H model had 1,700-hp (1268-kW) R-2600-29 engines.

Pacific action

In the Pacific, Havocs first saw action when they came under fire in the December 1941 Pearl Harbor attack. Modified A-20As with heavy nose armament were used for low-level strafing in New Guinea. Against the Germans, Havocs ranged across North Africa, then began striking targets in Sicily and on the Italian mainland. USAAF Havocs fought on in Normandy and across Europe to Berlin, although the more advanced Douglas A-26 Invader replaced the Havoc in some squadrons by VE-Day.

The final major operational variants of the Havoc were the USMC A-20J and A-20K, which returned to a glazed nose of a new and more streamlined, frameless type. Some A-20Ks were painted all-black for night interdiction missions. Representative operators in the European theatre of operations included the 47th, 409th, 410th and 416th Bomb Groups, and in the Pacific the 3rd, 312th and 417th Bomb Groups. The last Havoc built (7,385 by Douglas, 140 by Boeing) rolled off the Santa Monica production line on 20 September 1944.

The Havoc had in many respects the feel of a single-seat aircraft, and could indeed be taken 'upstairs' by the pilot alone. The aeroplane needed a full take-off roll, but having attained 110 mph (177 km/h),

it fairly leaped from the runway. The landing gear retracted very quickly because of the hydraulic accumulator, and the initial rate of climb was impressive. Once aloft, the machine manoeuvred with great agility and, with its high top speed of around 335 mph (539 km/h), was in every respect a first-rate performer.

British success with this aircraft type as a night-fighter may have inspired the USAAF's decision to convert early A-20 Havocs to the P-70 night-fighter standard. Seizing the opportunity offered by the availability of British air intercept radar, the first A-20 (39-735) was modified to XP-70 standard in 1942. A further 59 A-20 aircraft were converted to P-70s, while 13 A-20Cs received the P-70A-1 nomenclature and 26 A-20Gs were designated P-70A-2. Further conversions were the sole P-70B-1 and a small number of P-70B-2s.

Throughout the P-70 programme, various attempts were made to refine and develop the night-fighting capability of

the aircraft, but while these were going on, Northrop was designing its own twin-engined night-fighter from the ground up, and in the end the P-61 Black Widow offered considerable performance advantages over the P-70. The P-70 was used primarily for training, although a few saw combat in the Pacific.

The 'foto' reconnaissance designation F-3 was applied to camera-carrying Havocs after a proposal for an 'observation' derivative, the O-53, was cancelled. The potential of the Havoc as an intelligence-gathering platform, especially because of its good performance at low altitude, was obvious. Once 'bugs' were worked out of the photo-reconnaissance configuration, 46 A-20J and A-20K aircraft were modified to become F-3As. The relatively small number of F-3A reconnaissance craft actually saw a disproportionate employment in battle, and one Havoc was the first Allied aircraft to touch down at Itazuke air base in Japan following the 15 August 1945 surrender.

On occasion, the A-20G/Hs with the Fifth Air Force had their heavy, forward-firing armament supplemented by two clusters of three rocket-launching tubes below each wing, as can be seen on this A-20G of the 90th Bombardment Squadron in New Guinea.

RAF operations

A Boston Mk III unloads its internal load of four 500-lb (227-kg) bombs from medium altitude. Many attacks were made at very low level, under the radar, for which the four-gun nose armament was useful.

Initially used as the Havoc, as a night-fighter and nocturnal intruder, the Douglas DB-7 saw greater RAF service as the Boston in the light bomber role, scoring notable successes in cross-Channel raids and in the Mediterranean theatre.

The first Boston Mk IIIs were shipped to the UK in the autumn of 1941 and employed by No. 2 Group as Blenheim replacements. Some were converted for intruder duties.

Built as a private venture by the Douglas Aircraft Company, albeit with the encouragement of the USAAC, the Model 7B provided the basis for a family of versatile light attack bombers that would serve throughout the war with several Allied air forces. First flown on 26 October 1938, it was followed by the more definitive DB-7 prototype on 17 August 1939, by which time production orders had been placed by both the USAAC and the French Armée de l'Air.

French orders were placed for 100 in February 1939, 270 more in October 1939 and finally 480 in May 1940, embracing several different versions. The first of several British Purchasing Commission orders were placed

in February and April 1940, for 300 DB-7Bs, for which the name Boston was selected. By May 1940, three French escadrilles were working up on the Douglas twins, but only about 70 aircraft were actually on French territory at that time. With the collapse of France a few weeks later, all outstanding orders, and those aircraft in the delivery pipeline, were taken over by Britain.

Because of the piecemeal manner in which they were acquired – some at the factory, some from shipments already at sea and some flown to Britain from France by escaping Armée de l'Air crews – the number of earlier (ex-French) Bostons in the RAF is uncertain. Those with R-1830-S3C-G engines

and single-stage superchargers took the designation Boston Mk I and probably totalled only 20. They were not considered suitable for front-line duty, and were employed for conversion training, also being known as Boston Trainers. The DB-7s with R-1830-S3C4-G engines and two-stage superchargers were Boston Mk IIs and totalled 183. Having arrived in Britain, they were brought up to minimum RAF standard,

with modified throttles and British 0.303-in (7.7-mm) machine-guns – two dorsal and two in the nose.

Night-fighting Havoc

Considered unsuitable for use as bombers, the Boston Mk IIs in the RAF became Havoc Mk I night-fighters, while 100 ex-French DB-7As became Havoc Mk IIs, distinguished by longer nacelle tails. Conversion work was undertaken at the Burtonwood Aircraft Repair Depot near Liverpool, the main facility for erecting aircraft brought in from the United States. With flame-damped exhausts, matt black paint, additional armour, eight

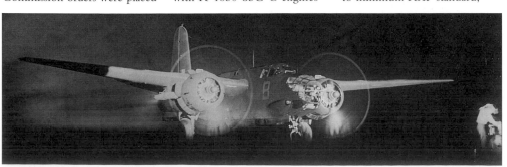

In the intruder role the Havoc was armed with the standard four gun nose armament and a single Vickers 'K' gun on a Fairey high-speed mounting.

All of the DB-7 Boston Mk IIs were converted into Havoc Mk I night-fighters or intruders. This machine was operated by No. 23 Squadron on intruder duties from April 1941.

machine-guns in the nose and AI Mk IV or Mk V radar, Havoc Mk Is were operating with No. 85 Squadron by March 1941, followed by Nos 25 and 600 Sqns. No. 23 Squadron, meanwhile, began using Havoc Mk Is that retained the original nose transparencies, dorsal guns and three-man crews for night intruder operations. These aircraft were known for a time as the Moonfighter, and then Havoc Mk IV before becoming the Havoc (Intruder), and were also used in the intruder role by No. 605 Sqn.

About 20 of the night-fighters were also modified as the Havoc Mk I (LAM) and used by No. 93 Sqn to operate, albeit with scant success, with the Long Aerial Mine, a weapon trailed on a 2,000-ft (610-m) length of wire in the path of enemy raiders. This variant was

also known as the Havoc Mk III or Havoc Mk I (Pandora). Other Havoc Mk Is, and 39 of the Havoc Mk IIs, were fitted in the nose with a 2,700 million-candlepower Helmore/GEC searchlight and, as the Havoc Mk I (Turbinlite), were used by 10 flights (later, squadrons) to operate alongside Hurricane night-fighters and attempt to illuminate enemy raiders. The other Havoc Mk II night-fighters were fitted with a 'solid' nose containing 12 machine-guns, and operated with AI Mk V radar but no dorsal guns. The planned introduction of a four-cannon armament led to the designations Havoc Mk IIC-B and Havoc Mk IIC-D, indicating belt feed or drum feed, respectively, but no such conversions reached the squadrons, and may not have been made at all.

Britain's 'own' Boston deliveries began in the early summer of 1941, introducing the Boston Mk III light bomber, in which role it entered service later that year as a Blenheim replacement in No. 88 (Hong Kong) Squadron, followed by No. 226 Sqn. Flying intensively to attack a variety of targets, including Channel shipping, these squadrons were joined in due course by No. 107 and No. 342 (Free French) 'Lorraine' Sqns. The first attack against a land target was made on 12 February 1942, and was followed by a daring low-level raid on the Matford works at Poissy. From November 1942 Boston Mk IIIs were sent to North Africa to bolster the light bomber force.

The inventory of Boston Mk IIIs was increased by the 480 French-ordered DB-7Bs, these being similar to the British version, with R-2600-A5B engines, a lengthened nose (compared with the Boston Mk I and Boston Mk II) and the broad fin first seen on the Boston Mk II. They had a crew of three, four 0.303-in (7.7-mm) guns in the nose and two each in dorsal and ventral positions.

With some of the planned French DB-7Bs eventually being

diverted to serve with the USAAF, Britain actually received 568 Boston Mk IIIs. Almost identical were 200 Boston Mk IIIAs supplied through Lend-Lease, from October 1942 onwards, and a further 55 that were 'swapped' for RAF Spitfires while passing through the Middle East en route to the Soviet Union. The Boston Mk IIIA was equivalent to the USAAF A-20C and had greater fuel capacity than the Boston Mk III.

Two squadrons, Nos 605 and 418 (RCAF), used the Boston Mk III (Intruder), carrying a ventral tray with four 20-mm cannon and having an overall black finish like the Havoc night-fighters. Also painted black for night operation were three Boston Mk IIIs fitted with Turbinlites and designated Boston (Turbinlite).

Power turrets

Final Lend-Lease supplies to Britain comprised 169 Boston Mk IVs and 90 Boston Mk Vs, the equivalent, respectively, of the USAAF A-20J and A-20K. These both had a Martin electric dorsal turret with two 0.50-in (12.7-mm) machine-guns, in a widened rear fuselage, and could carry four 500-lb (227-kg) underwing bombs. The A-20J/Boston Mk IV had R-2600-23 engines, and the A-20K/Boston Mk V had -29 engines; in virtually all other respects the types were similar.

The Boston Mk IV and Mk V were used in North Africa and the Mediterranean area to supplement Boston Mk III/IIIAs already being flown there by Nos 13, 18, 55 and 114 Sqns of the RAF, alongside Nos 12 and 24 Sqns (SAAF). Bostons remained a useful component of the RAF right up to the end of the war, participating in the D-Day landings by laying smoke screens, and serving with Nos 88 and 342 Sqns in the 2nd TAF until April 1945.

Above: Two South African squadrons, Nos 12 and 24, were in the thick of the Mediterranean fighting, flying Boston Mk IIIs. Along with RAF Boston units, they were instrumental in clearing the Axis from Africa and Sicily.

Right: BZ403 was the fourth of 165 A-20Js delivered to the RAF as Boston Mk IVs. These capable aircraft had power-operated turrets and could carry, as here, four bombs under the wings in addition to the internal load.

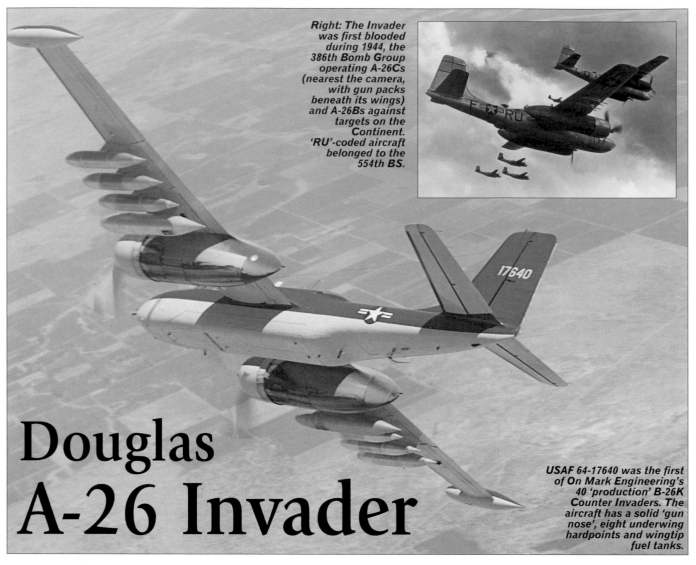

Right: The Invader was first blooded during 1944, the 386th Bomb Group operating A-26Cs (nearest the camera, with gun packs beneath its wings) and A-26Bs against targets on the Continent. 'RU'-coded aircraft belonged to the 554th BS.

Douglas A-26 Invader

USAF 64-17640 was the first of On Mark Engineering's 40 'production' B-26K Counter Invaders. The aircraft has a solid 'gun nose', eight underwing hardpoints and wingtip fuel tanks.

Long-serving warrior

The Invader fought in more wars than any other aircraft type. Americans flew it in World War II, Korea and Vietnam, while other air arms took the A-26 to war in Indo-China, Algeria, Biafra, Cuba, the Congo, and a dozen other conflicts.

France made good use of the B-26 in colonial wars in Indo-China and Algeria. The firepower housed in the nose of a B-26B – eight 0.5-in (12.7-mm) machine-guns was ideal for ground strafing.

If it does not spring instantly to mind as among the most important of American combat aircraft, the A-26 was, at least, a remarkably durable and potent light bomber that lasted four decades or more.

Designed as a replacement for the A-20 Havoc, the prototype XA-26 (42-19504) took to the air on 10 July 1942. Three variants were initially envisaged: the XA-26 (later A-26C bomber with a glazed nose for the bomb-aimer), the A-26A night-fighter with radar and four ventral 20-mm cannon, and the XA-26B with a solid gun-nose for the ground-attack role. The night-fighter version was short-lived (though the French air force later resurrected a night-fighter Invader in the 1950s), but bombers began to churn off the Douglas production lines at Long Beach, California and Tulsa, Oklahoma.

Different noses

The A-26B had six 0.5-in (12.7-mm) machine-guns in the nose (later increased to eight), remotely controlled dorsal and ventral turrets, each with two 0.5-in (12.7-mm) guns and up to 10 more 0.5-in (12.7-mm) guns in underwing and underfuselage packs. Heavily armoured and able to carry up to 4,000 lb (1814 kg) of bombs, the A-26B, with its maximum speed of 355 mph (571 km/h) at 15,000 ft (4570 m) was the fastest Allied bomber of World War II. Some 1,355 A-26Bs were followed by 1,091 A-26C machines with a bomb-aimer's glazed nose.

Rushed into combat with the 553rd Bomb Sqn at Great Dunmow in England by September 1944, and soon also operating in France and Italy, the Invader was flying air-to-ground missions against the Germans before all of its bugs had been ironed out. Pilots were delighted with its manoeuvrability and ease of handling, but the A-26 began life with a needlessly complex and fatiguing instrument array, a weak nose gear that collapsed easily, and an early cockpit canopy that was difficult to hold in the 'open' position for bail-out. Time and attention resolved these problems, and A-26 pilots took pride in mastering a demanding but effective bombing machine.

Left: Operations by Invaders of the US 5th Air Force played a significant part in the Korean War. This aircraft is about to make a belly landing after being hit by small arms fire.

Below: These Armée de l'Air Invaders – a B-26B (nearest the camera) and a B-26C of GB I/19 'Gascogne' – are seen during Operation Picardie in Indo-China during 1953.

In the Pacific war, the Invader also progressed from an inauspicious beginning to respectable achievement. With its 2,000-hp (1491-kW) Pratt & Whitney R-2800-27 Double Wasp piston engines and a sea-level speed of no less than 373 mph (600 km/h), the Invader was a potent anti-shipping and ground-attack weapon, but crews in the PTO did not immediately take to it. In the belief that the new machine was unsuited for low-level work, the 5th Air Force commander, General George C. Kenney, actually requested not to convert from the A-20 to the A-26. But conversions went ahead, the A-26 also replacing B-25 Mitchells in some units. The A-26 served with the USAAF's 3rd, 41st and 319th Bomb Groups in operations against Formosa, Okinawa and Japan itself.

At war in Korea

The North Korean assault on South Korea on 25 June 1950 followed by massive Chinese intervention in November, created a war of relatively short distance and intense battlefield environments where the durability and load-carrying capability of the B-26 Invader (as it had been redesignated in 1947) were all-important. The B-26 proved effective against tanks and truck convoys and was later unleashed on more general, high-altitude bombing missions. Solid-nosed B-26B and glazed-nosed B-26C Invaders also flew night intruder missions against Communist rail lines and other targets. The USAF's 3rd, 17th, 47th and

452nd Bomb Groups flew B-26 Invaders in the bulk of Korean operations. The 67th Tactical Reconnaissance Wing flew RB-26C aircraft, with their dorsal turrets removed, on photo-recce missions. In Korea, the Invader performed well in all regimes, including low-level strikes, and scored several probable air-to-air kills against Chinese MiG-15s.

The most important foreign user of the Invader was the French Armée de l'Air, which had up to 180 B-26B, B-26C and RB-26C aircraft, most of them committed to the Indo-China war. France's 1946-54 struggle with Viet Minh forces tested the B-26 Invader under crude, difficult tropical conditions, culminating in the siege at Dien Bien Phu where Invaders bombed and strafed Communist forces in the surrounding hills. French pilots liked the Invader for its toughness, firepower and handling characteristics. They flew B-26s again in their 1956-62 conflict in Algeria.

A 1961 survey found Invaders in no fewer than 21 countries, mostly in Latin America, but also in the Congo and Indonesia. Apart from being a total fiasco, the Bay of Pigs invasion in Cuba was the only instance when B-26 Invaders fought each other, CIA-backed exiles battling members of Castro's air arm.

Flying the Invader

Piloting the A-26 Invader was an experience. "It was graceful, potent and extremely unforgiving," says Lieutenant-Colonel Clifford Erly, who flew the A-26C with the 416th BG in the European theatre. Wide-track, tricycle landing-gear gave the A-26 excellent ground-handling characteristics. On take-off, it tended to "eat up runway," says Erly, especially with a full ordnance load, "but once you rotated and started to climb out, there was no ambiguity about it." A revised instrument layout made the aircraft easy to handle and the Invader's tall single tail assured responsiveness in turns.

"Once rid of the bombs it was a real fighter," says Erly. "Not only were we almost as fast as any fighter, we were almost as manoeuvrable. We had studies showing that at some altitudes under some conditions, we could turn inside a Bf 109. I never heard of a fighter successfully engaging an A-26 because we had the choice. We could run away from him in the straight-away or we could turn and fight..."

Several companies offered executive transport conversions of surplus Invaders, including L. B. Smith and On Mark Engineering. The latter company developed the Marksman, seen here.

The USAF Invader's swansong – Vietnam

In 1962, the US supplied B-26B and RB-26C Invaders to South Vietnam, where they were flown in combat by American crews and with South Vietnamese markings. Wing stress problems, resulting in the loss of one airframe and its crew when a wing was literally ripped off, brought an end to B-26 operations in Vietnam in early 1964. However, the US Air Force had decided that the type could have a rebirth if low-hour airframes could be converted for the special combat conditions of the South East Asia war. The On Mark Engineering Company, one of several firms which had also produced executive transport versions of the B-26, made the conversion and produced a virtually new machine, the YB-26K, first flown in production form in May 1964.

The B-26K was outwardly similar to the Invaders which had come before it, but on the inside it was a new aircraft. The fuselage was remanufactured and had the twin turrets removed, while the wings were rebuilt and strengthened, the tail section was enlarged, and new Pratt & Whitney R-2800-52W engines with reversible propellers and feathering controls were installed. The YB-26K had eight underwing hardpoints and six wing guns in addition to the nose guns. Wing guns were deleted on the 40 B-26K machines which followed, all but one of which had solid noses. While the camouflaged B-26K was being tested at Edwards AFB, California, in the Congo and in the Panama Canal Zone, the USAF completely obfuscated the situation by redesignating the 40 B-26K aircraft (63-17630/17679) as the A-26A. The A-26A (B-26K) was moderately successful in the conventional strike role in South Vietnam and was used for 'black covert' operations by the USAF's 609th Special Operations at Nakhom Phanom AB, Thailand as late as 1970.

Douglas C-47 Skytrain

Introduction

Built in huge numbers, the C-47 has a history unlike that of any other military aircraft, fulfilling roles as diverse as paratroop-dropping, air ambulance, gunship and electronic warfare and, after 60 years, the aircraft remains in service around the world.

A military mission was the last thing on the minds of Douglas Aircraft Co. officials when they observed the maiden flight of the DC-3 airliner on 17 December 1935 – a day that was also the 32nd anniversary of the Wright Brothers' first powered flight.

Although the Great Depression had brought economic depriva-tion to much of the Western world, airline travel was burgeoning, and the DC-3 design seemed likely to revolu-tionise commercial aviation. Yes, there were signs that a war might be brewing in Europe, but polls showed that most Americans wanted to stay out of it.

By the time Germany invaded Poland in September 1939, the DC-3 was fast becoming a famil-iar sight, cherished by pilots who flew it and by passengers who

were enjoying a new standard of travel. But the US Army was modernising, too. Already flying numerous military versions of an earlier Douglas transport, the US Army now saw a military version of the DC-3 not as unthinkable, but as inevitable. The first was the C-41A, a command trans-port with VIP accommodation and military communications gear. This military derivative of the DC-3 reached Wright Field, Ohio in late 1939 and so began the extraordinary saga of a remarkable series of aircraft, most of them known initially as C-47s.

There is a strong likelihood that, at this moment, a C-47 is flying in military attire some-where in the world today, a full six decades later, on the eve of a new century. No other aircraft can match the military equiva-

Early production C-47-DL Skytrains from the Long Beach factory are seen here towing Waco Hadrian troop-carrying gliders on a wartime training flight in the United States.

lent of the DC-3, with its many names – Dakota, C-47, and R4D are only the most familiar – for versatility, dependability and longevity.

Wartime roles

Some military DC-3s dropped paratroops, or operated on pontoons, or were stripped of engines to become gliders. A few (in Vietnam) became gunships with a fully-fledged combat role. But the majority of the military DC-3s that served in World War

II, Korea, Vietnam, and else-where were 'trash-haulers', the endearment bestowed by American airmen on those aircraft which carry people and cargo from point A to point B.

General Dwight Eisenhower called the C-47 one of the four most important wartime weapons. In later years, military C-47s tackled every chore from electronic spying to Antarctic exploration. In 1949, new life was breathed into the basic design with the Super DC-3,

Above: The last Dakota in active British military service was ZA947, operated by the RAE. It was used for trials of low-speed sensing equipment, RPVs and parachutes from 1984 before being transferred to the Battle of Britain Memorial Flight in 1993.

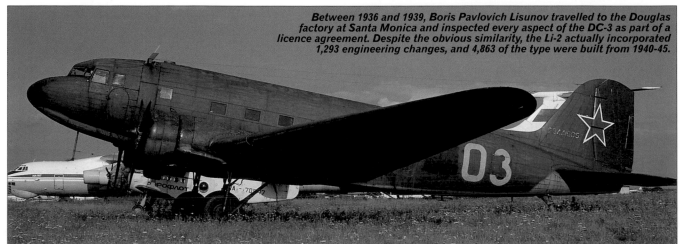

Between 1936 and 1939, Boris Pavlovich Lisunov travelled to the Douglas factory at Santa Monica and inspected every aspect of the DC-3 as part of a licence agreement. Despite the obvious similarity, the Li-2 actually incorporated 1,293 engineering changes, and 4,863 of the type were built from 1940-45.

Entering service in World War II with four squadrons, the Dakota served in the Royal Australian Air Force for over 50 years. Post-war service included active operations in the Malaya campaign and the Korean War.

which became the R4D-8 or C-117D in military garb.

Studies show that the DC-3 is one of the 'most recognised' aircraft in history, together with the Supermarine Spitfire, Boeing 747, and a handful of others. In military service as in civilian life, the aircraft was so sensible, with so many features that were right. The many versions of the Pratt & Whitney R-1830 Twin Wasp radial piston engines delighted maintenance men and performed so brilliantly that it has become almost a crime to say anything unkind about the DC-3.

Minor flaws

Still, there were flaws. As troop-carrying pilots realised during the Normandy invasion, minor changes in the design would have vastly improved cockpit visibility. For military use, it took several attempts to arrive at the right size and shape for a cargo door. The military DC-3 was docile and forgiving, and could be flown easily, even after suffering battle damage, but pilots and crews were often irritated by the little things, such as a window suddenly popping out, as happened frequently. For all its qualities, the C-47 lacked the 'roll-on, roll-off' capability of wartime gliders and was often difficult to taxi and park because of its tail-dragger configuration.

It is natural to dwell on the freaky stories about the military DC-3 that stand out in legend. In Burma, one of the aircraft lost a starboard wing. The wing from an earlier DC-2 model was attached and this asymmetrical flying machine became the 'DC-2½', flying quite effectively for a brief time. Also in the China-Burma-India theatre, a C-47 pilot shot down a Japanese Mitsubishi A6M Zero ('Zeke') by poking a Browning automatic rifle into the slipstream and blazing away. The stories touch us all, but they overlook the fundamental achievement of this aircraft – again, carrying people and cargo.

The US Army's Air Transport Command (ATC) used C-47s, together with other transports, to haul supplies across the Atlantic and over the fabled Himalaya 'Hump' into China.

Paratroop transport

In a different command, C-47s and C-53s of troop carrier squadrons took part in all major airborne assault operations, including those in Sicily, New Guinea, Normandy, southern France, and the bridges at Nijmegen and Arnhem. Under the post-war Military Air Transport Service (MATS), military versions of the DC-3 breathed life into the besieged German capital during the 1948 Berlin Airlift. C-47 and C-117 variants remained in US service well into the 1960s.

The US Navy and Marine Corps' R4D series was one of the best-known military versions of the DC-3 and remained in service from the 1942 New Guinea campaign through the Vietnam fighting of the late 1960s. Some of these aircraft were given an important job as VIP transports for embassies in overseas locations. If imitation is the sincerest form of flattery, the military DC-3 was complimented when carbon-copy variants were produced in the Soviet Union (Lisunov Li-2) and Japan (Mitsubishi L2D3).

Not conceived for a military role, yet adaptable to diverse military missions, the DC-3/C-47/R4D, in the end, became one of the classics in the annals of warfare.

Dubbed 'Puff the Magic Dragon', a small number of C-47s was converted as AC-47 gunships during the Vietnam War. They were armed with three rapid-firing 0.3-in (7.62-mm) Miniguns on fixed mountings on the port side of the cabin.

The Honduran air force is one of a number of Central American and Caribbean air arms which still operates the C-47 (the others being the Dominican Republic, El Salvador, Guatemala and Haiti).

At war with the USAAF

With longitudinal seats along the sides of the cabin for 28 troops and a port-side passenger door, the C-53 Skytrooper was a troop transport version of the C-47. A relatively small total of 404 C-53s was built for the USAAF.

Developed from the DC-3, the C-47 was undoubtedly the most important Allied transport aircraft of the war. The aircraft went wherever Allied troops served, adding casualty evacuation, paratroop-dropping and glider-towing to its basic transport role.

The initial production version of the DC-3 for the USAAF was the C-47, of which 953 were built at Long Beach, and the basic structural design remained virtually unchanged throughout the entire production run. Of all-metal light-alloy construction, the cantilever monoplane wing was set low on the fuselage, and was provided with hydraulically operated, split-type trailing-edge flaps. The fuselage was almost circular in cross-section and the tail unit was conventional but, like the ailerons, the rudder and elevators were fabric-covered. The landing gear comprised semi-retractable main units which were raised forward and upward to be housed in the upper half of the engine nacelles, with almost half of the main wheels exposed. The C-47's powerplant comprised two Pratt & Whitney R-1830-92 Twin Wasp engines, supercharged to provide an output of 1,050 hp (783 kW) at 7,500 ft (2285 m), and each driving a three-bladed constant-speed metal propeller. The crew consisted of a pilot and

co-pilot/navigator situated in a forward compartment, with the third member, the radio operator, in a separate compartment.

The all-important cabin could be equipped for a variety of roles. For the basic cargo configuration, with a maximum load of 6,000 lb (2722 kg), pulley blocks were provided for cargo-handling, and tiedown rings to secure cargo in flight. Alternative layouts could provide for the transport of 28 fully-armed paratroops, accommodated in folding bucket-type seats along the sides of the cabin, or for 18 stretchers and a medical team of three. Racks and release mechanism for up to six parachute pack containers could be mounted beneath the fuselage, and there were also underfuselage mountings for the transport of two three-bladed propellers.

The first C-47s began to equip the USAAF in 1941, but initially these were received only slowly and in small numbers. This was due to the establishment of the new production line at Long Beach which, like any other, needed time to settle down to

routine manufacture. With US involvement in World War II in December 1941, attempts were made to boost production, but in order to increase the number of aircraft in service as quickly as possible, DC-3s already operating with US airlines, or well advanced in construction for delivery to operators, were impressed for service with the USAAF.

Large-scale production

As Douglas began to accumulate contracts calling for the production of C-47s in thousands, it was soon obvious that the production line at Long Beach would be quite incapable of meeting requirements on such a large scale, so a second production line was established at Tulsa, Oklahoma. The first model to be built at Tulsa was the second

production version, the C-47A, which differed from the C-47 primarily in the provision of a 24-volt, in place of a 12-volt, electrical system. Tulsa was to build 2,099 and Long Beach 2,832 of the type, 962 of them being delivered to the RAF, which designated them Dakota Mk IIIs. Last of the major production variants was the C-47B, which was provided with R-1830-90 or -90B engines that had two-stage superchargers to offer high-altitude military ratings of 1,050 hp (783 kW) at 13,100 ft (3990 m) or 900 hp (671 kW) at 17,400 ft (5305 m) respectively. These were required for operation in the China-Burma-India (CBI) theatre, in particular for the 'Hump' operations over the 16,500-ft (5030-m) high Himalayan peaks, carrying

Prior to receiving the first purpose-built military C-47s, the USAAF operated various derivatives of the DC-2 and DC-3 civil airliners, designated C-32/33/34/38/39/40/41.

Hundreds of paratroopers (28 per aircraft) drop in tight sticks behind C-53s of the USAAF. During World War II, more paratroops were dropped from USAAF C-47s and C-53s than from all other Allied aircraft combined.

Right: A jeep trailer is loaded aboard a 9th Troop Carrier Command C-47A at an English airfield on D-Day, 6 June 1944. The loading of such items through the fuselage door was awkward and time- consuming – one of the less favourable features of the C-47 design.

desperately needed supplies from bases in India to China. Long Beach built only 300 of the model, but Tulsa provided 2,808 C-47Bs plus 133 TC-47Bs which were equipped for service as navigational trainers.

The availability of such large numbers, in US service, meant that it was possible to begin to utilise the C-47 on a far more extensive basis. The formation in mid-1942 of the USAAF's Air Transport Command saw the C-47's wide-scale deployment as a cargo transport, carrying an almost unbelievable variety of supplies into airfields and airstrips described as 'primitive'. Not only were the C-47s carrying in men and materials, but they were soon involved in a two-way traffic, serving in a casualty-evacuation role as they returned to their bases. They were thus carrying out the three primary missions for which these aircraft had been intended when first procured: cargo, casualty evacuation and personnel transport.

However, their employment by

the USAAF's Troop Carrier Command from mid-1942 was to provide two new roles, arguably the most important of their deployment in World War II. One role was as the carrier of airborne troops; the first major usage in this capacity came with the invasion of Sicily in July 1943, when C-47s dropped something approaching 4,000 paratroops.

Troop transport

The other important role originated with the C-53 Skytrooper version, built in comparatively small numbers as the C-53/53B/ 53C/53D. These were more nearly akin to the original DC-3 civil transport, without a reinforced floor or double door for cargo, and the majority had fixed metal seats to accommodate 28 fully-equipped paratroops. More importantly, they were provided with a towing cleat so that they could serve as a glider tug, a feature soon to become standard on all C-47s. It was in this capacity that they were operated conspicuously in both USAAF

and RAF service during such operations as the first airborne invasion of Burma on 5 March 1944 and the D-Day invasion of Normandy some three months later. In this latter operation more than 1,000 Allied C-47s were involved, carrying paratroops and towing gliders laden with paratroops and supplies. In the initial stage of this invasion, 17,262 US paratroops of the 82nd and 101st Airborne Divisions and 7,162 men of the British 6th Airborne Division were carried across the English Channel in the greatest airlift of assault forces up to that time. Not all, of course, were carried in or towed by C-47s, but these aircraft played a very significant role in helping to secure this first vital foothold on European soil: in less than 60 hours, C-47s alone airlifted more than 60,000 paratroops and their equipment to Normandy.

Other C-47 variants of World War II included the XC-47C, prototype of a projected version

to be equipped as a floatplane or, as was the prototype, with convertible amphibious floats. While this version was not built as such by Douglas, a small number of similar conversions was made by USAAF maintenance units for service in the Pacific. Douglas was contracted to build 131 staff transports under the designation C-117, these having the airline-standard cabin equipment of a commercial DC-3, plus the improvements which were current on the C-47. Their numbers, however, had reached only 17 when VJ-Day brought contract cancellation.

The requirement for a large-capacity, high-speed transport glider, to be towed by a C-54, resulted in an experimental conversion of a C-47 to serve in this role under the designation XCG-17. Tests were moderately successful, but no production aircraft were built, however, as a result of changing requirements.

British paratroops from the Allied 1st Airborne Army board a USAAF C-47A on 17 September 1944 as part of Operation Market Garden, the airborne assault on Eindhoven, Nijmegen and Arnhem. Over 1,500 Allied aircraft participated in the assault on that day.

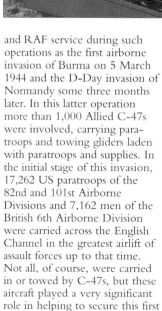

Above: This Dakota Mk III of No. 257 Squadron, with the unit's Pegasus artwork on the nose, is seen flying over the Greek islands near Missolonghi on its way back to its base at Araxos in October 1944.

Left: The C-47/Dakota was the Allies' most important transport aircraft of the war, being particularly effective in the paradropping role. During the first day of Operation Market Garden, 15,000 paratroopers were dropped from the type.

Dakota at war

As the war turned in favour of the Allies during 1941-42, the RAF found itself desperately short of modern transport aircraft. Salvation came in the form of the excellent Douglas C-47, named Dakota by the British, which went on to serve in every theatre.

A progressive evolution of the DC-1 and DC-2, the DC-3 (or DST, Douglas Sleeper Transport) first flew on 17 December 1935. While production proceeded apace for a variety of airlines, the US military was quick to place orders (having already bought DC-2s) and, once America was at war, also impressed large numbers of the civil transport under several different 'C for Cargo' designations.

The RAF's first experience of the DC-3 was obtained with some of these impressed aircraft (as well as some similarly ex-civil DC-2s). From April 1942 onwards, 10 of these aircraft – which were known in British service as DC-3s and, later, Dakotas with no mark number – were flown out from the US to India. They subsequently served with No. 31 Squadron, becoming engaged in operations in Burma, including support for the first Wingate expedition in 1943.

Lend-Lease 'Daks'

Meanwhile, provision had been made for Britain to receive substantial numbers of the Douglas twins through Lend-Lease; eventually, the total would grow to more than 1,900, from wartime production of just over 10,000 military examples in three US centres. The Lend-Lease aircraft were desig-

nated in four variants, comprising the Dakota Mk I, equivalent to the USAAF C-47; Dakota Mk II, equivalent to the C-53; Dakota Mk III, being the C-47A; and Dakota Mk IV, the C-47B. Of these versions, the Dakota Mk II, known as the Skytrooper to the USAAF, was the dedicated troop and para-troop transport, having a 26-in (66-cm) door in the port side of the rear fuselage, rather than the Dakota Mk I's double door for freight loading, and 28 troop seats.

The 'basic' Dakota had Pratt & Whitney R-1830-92 radial engines, bucket-type seats along the cabin walls and a gross weight of 29,300 lb (13290 kg). The Dakota Mk III differed, primarily, in having the 12-volt electric system of the Mk I changed to a 24-volt system; and the Dakota Mk IV switched to R-1830-90 or -90B engines with high-altitude blowers and extra fuel capacity, making it suitable in particular for the China-Burma-India theatre. Totals delivered to the RAF were 51 Dakota Mk Is; four Dakota Mk IIs (of 40 planned); 950 Dakota Mk IIIs; and 894 Dakota Mk IVs. These Lend-Lease totals were swelled by some 20 transfers from USAAF stocks towards the end of the war, for particular needs that arose 'in the field'; these included an additional Dakota Mk I and four more Dakota Mk IIs.

An RAF Dakota approaches at low level to 'hook' an American-designed Waco glider during training. This technique was used to recover the valuable gliders in Burma during the second Chindit expedition in the spring of 1944.

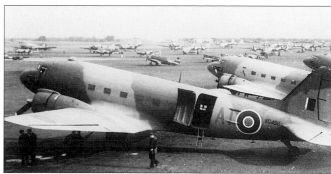

Left: Seen parked at Bari, Italy, in 1944 is a line-up of No. 267 Squadron Dakota Mk IIIs. The airfield was heavily utilised by both USAAF and RAF aircraft during the campaign in Italy.

Below: This No. 233 Sqn Dakota Mk III (named Kwicherbichen UK) is seen returning from Normandy with wounded servicemen on 1 August 1944. On 13 June 1944 two Dakotas from this squadron were the first Transport Command aircraft to land in France after D-Day.

Squadrons flew Dakotas on supply flights to Europe for the final few months of the war.

Further afield, the work of Nos 31, 117 and 216 Squadrons in the Middle East has already been mentioned. Also in Egypt, No. 267 Sqn was among the first unit to fly Dakotas, operating throughout the Mediterranean theatre.

Far East operations

Dakotas also played an important role in the fight against Japan, several squadrons receiving the Douglas aircraft in India. At Lahore, No. 194 Sqn received its first two Dakotas at the end of May 1943 and joined with No. 31 Squadron to support the Chindit incursions into Burma. No. 62 Squadron from 1943 and No. 52 from 1944 both flew Dakotas from Indian bases, including flights over 'the Hump' into China, and two RCAF squadrons, Nos 435 and 436, were similarly engaged from 1944. Further squadrons were in the process of working up on Dakotas in India when the war came to an end, but the type was destined to remain in service with the RAF for several more years – notably with No. 216 Squadron at home and No. 267 Squadron in the Malayan conflict.

The Lend-Lease Dakotas began to arrive in Britain in February 1943. Several of the earliest Mk Is went immediately to the British Overseas Airways Corporation (BOAC) to operate the route from the UK to Gibraltar and Africa, in RAF camouflage but with civil registrations replacing the military serial numbers. Other early users of the Dakota Mk I, supplemented by Dakota Mk IIIs in 1943, were No. 216 Squadron in Cairo, for use on the regular run between Egypt and West Africa, and casualty evacuation from the Western Desert; No. 117 Squadron, taking part in the invasion of Sicily; and No. 31 Squadron, to continue the supply missions in Burma started

with DC-3s. Furthermore, in the UK, No. 24 Squadron began to standardise on the Dakota in April 1943, giving up a miscellany of short-range aircraft in order to fly regular services to Gibraltar and other destinations – a service in which it was soon joined by No. 511 Squadron.

D-Day landings

No. 24 Squadron was one of several Dakota squadrons supporting the D-Day landings. In this it was joined by Nos 48 and 271 Squadrons at Down Ampney and Nos 512 and 575 at Broadwell, these being heavily engaged in dropping paratroops and towing Horsa gliders for the Normandy landings and later at Arnhem and the Rhine crossing.

For a re-supply mission to Arnhem, the pilot of a Dakota Mk III of No. 271 Sqn, Flt Lt D. S. A. Lord, DFC, was awarded a posthumous Victoria Cross. Formed in the UK too late for D-Day, No. 437 Sqn, RCAF, also participated in Operation Market Garden to Arnhem. Nos 147 and 525

Right: British paratroops of the First Allied Airborne Army prepare to drop from an RAF Dakota near the Dutch town of Arnhem on 17 September 1944 as part of Operation Market Garden.

Below: Dakotas from No. 271 Squadron, part of No. 46 Group based at Down Ampney, are unloaded at an airstrip in Belgium in 1945 after bringing in supplies from the UK.

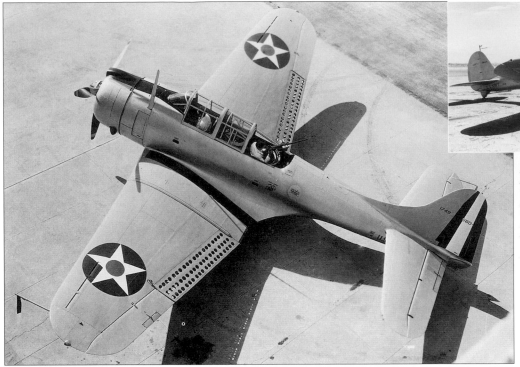

Above: The sole Northrop XBT-2 (BuNo. 0627) was effectively the Dauntless prototype, but was modified considerably before entering production as the SBD. The XBT-2 was powered by a 1,000-hp (746-kW) Wright XR-1820-32; known later as the Cyclone, this engine would power all subsequent SBDs.

Left: Prominent in this view of a production USMC SBD-1 are its perforated dive flaps. All 57 SBD-1s were delivered to the Marines in 1940. The USN's first aircraft were SBD-2s, delivered in 1940-41.

Douglas SBD Dauntless

El Segundo's scout

Underpowered, vulnerable, lacking in range and exhausting to fly for any length of time, the Douglas SBD Dauntless bore its fair share of derogatory appellations. But it was a war-winner, playing a vital part in the early battles of the Pacific, and went on to sink a greater tonnage of Japanese shipping than any other aircraft.

During the Battle of Coral Sea on 7 May 1942 the airwaves were cluttered with radio transmissions, and anxious crewmen aboard USS *Lexington* and *Yorktown* could not tell how the battle was going until a clear voice blasted through: "Scratch one flat-top! Dixon to carrier. Scratch one flat-top!" Lieutenant Commander Robert E. Dixon, commander of Bombing Two (VB-2), was reporting the sinking of the Japanese carrier *Shoho* with 545 of its crew after a 30-minute battle at the cost of only three US aircraft – a triumph for the SBD-2 and SBD-3 models of the Dauntless, to be exceeded only during the pivotal Midway

battle a few weeks later.

The dive-bomber turned the tide of war at the Battle of Midway on 4 June 1942. But to the men involved, the extent of their success may not have been immediately evident: their aircraft had a low power-to-weight ratio, giving it only fair climbing and manoeuvring characteristics and their arming systems malfunctioned, at times pitching their centreline-mounted, 500-lb (227-kg) bombs uselessly into the sea.

Launched from Admiral Chester Nimitz's carrier groups to seek out those of Admiral Isoroku Yamamoto, they were becoming short of fuel, running out of daylight and were stretched to the limits of range

and endurance when they came upon the enemy fleet and attacked. Lieutenant Commander C. Wade McClusky, Commander Max Leshe and the other Dauntless fliers from squadrons VS-5 and VB-3 on USS *Yorktown*, VS-6 and VB-6 on USS *Enterprise*, and VS-8 and VB-8 on USS *Hornet* lost 40 of their 128 dive-bombers.

But when they swarmed

down from the late afternoon sun to send the *Kaga*, *Akagi*, *Hiryu* and *Soryu* to the bottom of the sea they reversed the trend of the Pacific conflict. Few other aircraft types can lay claim to have so altered history as the Dauntless dive-bomber, 5,936 of which were produced before the end of World War II.

The Dauntless owes its origin to the low-wing, two-seat tandem Northrop BT-1 dive-bomber of 1938, and to the superb design work of Jack Northrop and of the mild-tempered but brilliant Edward H. Heinemann. When the El Segundo, California manufacturer became a division of Douglas Aircraft with Jack Northrop's January 1938 departure, a development of the BT-1, known as the XBT-2, was being

SBDs of scout squadron VS-6 are seen over USS Enterprise in October 1941, two months before Pearl Harbor. VS-6 and VB-6 were the first USN units to be equipped with the Dauntless.

Carrying a centreline bomb, a VS-41 SBD heads for the North African coast during Operation Torch, November 1942.

The crew of an unarmed SBD enjoy the fresh air as they fly over Enterprise (foreground) and Saratoga during a patrol off Guadalcanal in late 1942.

tested, but seemed to offer only limited potential. Heinemann's design team reworked the sole XBT-2 (BuNo. 0627), powering it with the 1,000-hp (746-kW) Wright XR-1820-32 engine which would become the world-famous Cyclone, driving a three-bladed propeller. The tail of the aircraft was redesigned following extensive wind-tunnel tests, and the XBT-2 was redesignated XSBD-1. Accepted by the US Navy in February 1939, while parallel work was under way on the Curtiss SB2C Helldiver, the SBD was to become the standard by which all other carrierborne dive-bombers ('scout bombers' in the jargon of the time) would be judged.

Its tailplane riddled with bullets from a Japanese fighter or flak, an SBD returns to its carrier, some time during early 1942.

On 8 April 1939 Douglas received an order for 57 SBD-1 and 87 SBD-2 aircraft. The SBD-1, with the definitive fin and rudder shape for the Dauntless type, was armed with two forward-firing 0.30-in (7.62-mm) guns in the engine cowling and a single 0.30-in (7.62-mm) gun for the radio-operator/gunner, who sat with his back to the pilot. Not yet fully cleared for carrier operations, the SBD-1 was earmarked instead for the US Marine Corps and was delivered in 1940. The SBD-2 model, which differed in having self-sealing, rubber-lined, metal fuel tanks and two additional 65-US gal (246-litre) tanks in the outer wing panels, was delivered to US Navy squadrons between December 1940 and May 1941.

Dive-bomber success

The fall of France, punctuated by the scream of descending Stukas, impressed the Washington authorities with the value of the dive-bomber and a further 174 SBDs were ordered as the SBD-3. The SBD-3 variant had a second 0.3-in (7.62-mm) gun for the rear crewmen, improved armour and electrical systems, and bladder-type, self-sealing fuel tanks. By now, the familiar Dauntless shape was established: the not ungraceful machine had a maximum speed of 252 mph

(406 km/h) in level flight, going up to 276 mph (444 km/h) in a dive; a range of 1,225 miles (1971 km) with, or 1,370 miles (2205 km) without, a bombload; and a service ceiling of 27,100 ft (8260 m).

The next model of the Dauntless was the SBD-4, delivered between October 1942 and April 1943. The SBD-4 had improved radio navigation aids, an electric fuel pump and an improved Hamilton Standard Hydromatic constant-speed, fully-feathering propeller. A total of 780 was built before production at El Segundo shifted to the SBD-5, powered by an improved R-1820-60 engine delivering 1,200 hp (895 kW); 2,965 examples of this variant were produced between February 1943 and April 1944, one of which became the XSBD-6 with installation of a 1,350-hp (1007-kW) Wright R-1820-66, the 'ultimate' Cyclone. Some 450 SBD-6s were built.

By late in the war, the Dauntless had been supplanted in the dive-bomber role by the more advanced Curtiss SB2C Helldiver, though this troublesome aircraft never won the recognition accorded to the SBD. The Dauntless was relegated to less glamorous anti-submarine patrol and close air support duties. The SBD also served with no fewer than 20 Marine Corps squadrons. Many hundreds of SBDs were retrofitted with Westinghouse ASB radar, the first to be used by the US Navy.

These SBDs are seen aboard USS Yorktown (CV-10) during the carrier's 'shake down' cruise in the Atlantic during April/May 1943. USS Ranger (CV-4) is in the background.

Dauntless undaunted

A carrier air group aboard a typical US Navy carrier usually comprised two squadrons of fighters, one of torpedo-bombers and two Dauntless squadrons – one in the bombing role and one for the scout mission. These were designated VB and VS squadrons, respectively. The scouting mission had been conceived before it was clear that American carriers would have the protection of radar and, in practice, there was little distinction between the two squadrons; scouting pilots trained and prepared for dive-bombing missions in just the same way as their colleagues in the VB squadrons. Here, a pair of VB-10 aircraft approaches USS Enterprise around the time of the assault on Truk in 1944.

Although the SBD gave sterling service in the US Navy and RNZAF, its USAAF career (as the A-24 Banshee) was less than successful and the type was also rejected by the RAF.

The pilot of an SBD-6 Dauntless found himself sitting high upfront in a machine of all-metal construction with fabric-covered control surfaces. His cantilever, low-mounted wing had a rectangular centre section with outer panels tapering in chord and thickness to detachable wingtips. The 'Swiss cheese' pierced flaps and dive-brakes, above and below the trailing edge of the outer wings and below the trailing edge only of the centre section beneath the fuselage, together with the 'multi-cellular' construction of the wing itself, were hallmarks of the design's indebtedness to Jack Northrop. The oval Duralumin monocoque fuselage was built in four sections, and the crew was housed beneath a continuous transparent canopy with a bullet-proof windshield and armour

plate. A swinging bomb cradle, with a maximum capacity of 1,000 lb (454 kg), was centred beneath the fuselage, and a bomb rack was mounted under each outer-wing section.

Forgiving machine

Flying the Dauntless, pilots found it a forgiving machine of few vices, although it had a troublesome tendency to stall in tight turns. On dive-bombing missions the pilot approached his target at 15,000 to 20,000 ft (4570 to 6095 m), took position almost directly overhead, pulled up the nose, and deployed upper and lower dive flaps. He then 'rolled in', the Dauntless accelerating less rapidly than might be expected while plummeting at over 70°. Using the Mk VIII reflector sight which, from the SBD-5 model on, had replaced the earlier extended telescope

Seen in the Pacific, this SBD-5 carries an array of bombing mission symbols and, under its port wing, an ASB antenna. The Dauntless was the first carrierborne USN type to be equipped with radar.

(this had a tendency to fog over in a dive as a result of temperature changes), the pilot aimed his bombload literally by pointing his aircraft at the target. His bomb release was a red button marked 'B' on the top of the stick, and he could drop his

ordnance singly or in salvo.

US Navy legend has it that pilots were prone to 'target fascination', which could lull them into failing to pull out of the dive in time. With its bombload gone, the Dauntless pulled out quite handily, with an easy

These 531st Fighter-Bomber Sqn, USAAF A-24Bs are seen on Makin Island in the Gilbert Islands, southwest Pacific.

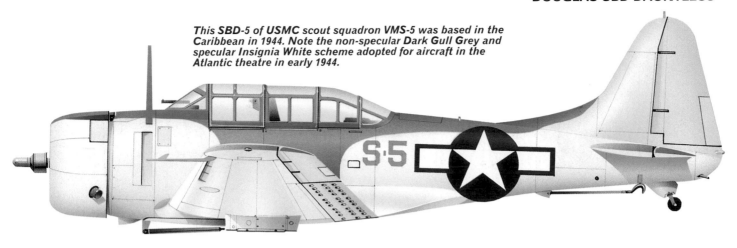

This SBD-5 of USMC scout squadron VMS-5 was based in the Caribbean in 1944. Note the non-specular Dark Gull Grey and specular Insignia White scheme adopted for aircraft in the Atlantic theatre in early 1944.

USMC SBDs, each carrying centreline and underwing bombs, head for a Japanese target on the island of Rabaul in 1944. Dauntless production ended on 22 July 1944, the type being supplanted by the Curtiss SB2C Helldiver.

motion on the stick. The machine generally handled well in normal flight and the pilot's visibility was excellent, both when level and when descending for a tricky landing on a carrier deck. Few aircraft were tougher or more reliable, the Dauntless often coming home with severe battle damage.

In the USAAF, where it was

An Aéronavale SBD-5 of Flottille 4 takes off from the deck of one of the two French carriers stationed off Indo-China (probably Arromanches in 1947-48) during fighting with the Viet-Minh.

officially given the name Banshee but still called Dauntless, this aircraft type seemed unglamorous from the beginning. In January 1941 the USAAF placed an order for 78 A-24s, similar to the US Navy's SBD-3 but for the deletion of carrier landing equipment. In addition, 90 SBD-3s from a US Navy contract were modified to land-based standard and delivered to the USAAF as the SBD-3A ('A' for Army). Eventually, the USAAF ordered 100 A-24As identical to the SBD-4, and 615 A-24Bs equivalent to the SBD-5 but manufactured at the Douglas plant in Tulsa.

Banshees in service

A-24s served with the 27th Bombardment Group at New Guinea and with the 531st Fighter Bomber Squadron at Makin. USAAF pilots, however, could not outmanoeuvre aggressive Japanese fighters. Where the rear-seat gunner had been highly effective in the US Navy machine – one US Navy crew shot down seven Mitsubishi Zeroes in two days – he was less potent aboard the A-24. Casualties were so high that the type was quickly withdrawn from front-line service. Since US Navy pilots at Coral Sea and Midway had demonstrated the

ability to handle themselves against the Zero, the US Army's less satisfactory performance with the Dauntless is usually attributed to the inexperience and lower morale of its flight crews.

In July 1943, No. 25 Squadron of the Royal New Zealand Air Force received 18 SBD-3s from US Marine Corps inventory. Later to receive 27 SBD-4s and 23 SBD-5s, the RNZAF squadron fought at Bougainville. Another foreign user of the Dauntless was France, which equipped two units of the Free French navy, Flottille 313 and Flottille 4B, with A-24s and SBD-3s at Agadir, Morocco, in the autumn of 1944. Dauntlesses went into operation in metropolitan France against retreating German forces and fought in dwindling numbers until VE-Day. Flottilles 3 and 4 operated SBD-5s over Indo-China during 1947-49; the type was finally retired by the fighter school at Meknes in 1953.

The UK obtained nine SBD-5 aircraft and named them Dauntless DB.Mk I. By this time (1944), however, the type was regarded as underpowered and slow. British pilots also found the Dauntless fatiguing, noisy and draughty. There was never to be general agreement about the type's vulnerability to fighters; the Pacific War indicated that it was not unduly vulnerable, but RAF test pilots considered that it was. The British machines were evaluated extensively, but it was too late for the Dauntless to have an operational career in British service. In American service, where the A-24 was redesignated F-24 in 1947, an unpiloted QF-24A drone and its QF-24B controller aircraft (both rebuilds with 1948 serial numbers) kept the Dauntless type in service until 1950.

A few A-24Bs found their way, post-war, into the hands of the Mexican air force, which was apparently the last user of this type, employing it until 1959.

Above: With the end of World War II, FAA use of the Rolls-Royce Griffon-powered Barracuda Mk V was confined to training and trials units – Nos 700, 778 and 783 Sqns. Late production aircraft differed from this example in having a taller, pointed rudder. Note the ASV radar pod under the wing.

Left: Its Fairey-Youngman flaps extended, this early production Mk I demonstrates the type's dive-bombing ability.

Fairey Barracuda

Tirpitz-bomber

Aircrew converting from antiquated Swordfish and Albacore biplanes to the Barracuda must have thought their new mount an extremely complicated machine. It was more streamlined than its predecessors although, with landing gear down and a full radar array, its appearance was distinctly odd.

The Barracuda originated with Specification S.24/37, to which six companies (Bristol, Blackburn, Fairey, Hawker, Vickers and Westland) tendered designs, and an order for two prototypes to be built at Hayes was placed with Fairey in July 1938. The original engine selected was the 1,200-hp (895-kW) Rolls-Royce 24-cylinder 'X' engine, but when the makers stopped work on the new engine in favour of Merlins, Peregrines and Vultures, the decision was

taken to use the 1,300-hp (969-kW) Merlin 30 in the Barracuda Mk I.

The first prototype flew on 7 December 1940, and differed from later aircraft in having an Albacore-type tail unit with low-set tailplane on top of the fuselage. Flight testing showed that the Fairey-Youngman flaps at negative angle created an air wake which caused tail buffeting, loss of elevator effectiveness and vibration at high speeds. The result was a redesigned tail in which the tailplane was

strut-braced high up on a taller, narrower fin.

Large flaps were provided to give additional wing area when set in the neutral position, and for take-off, these were lowered by 20° to increase lift. In the landing configuration they were lowered to provide maximum drag, while for diving attacks

they adopted a negative angle of 30°. Prototype testing soon confirmed the vast performance increase of the Barracuda over its biplane ancestors: speeds of 269 mph (433 km/h) were reached in level flight at 9,000 ft (2745 m) in 'clean' configuration, and this was reduced by about 20 mph (32 km/h) when an underslung torpedo was carried. In this condition, the Barracuda prototype could climb at 1,100 ft (335 m) per minute.

Priority construction of fighters and bombers inevitably slowed work on the prototype, until the Admiralty intervened with the Ministry of Aircraft Production and managed to arrange for full production of aircraft for the Royal Navy to be reinstated.

Deck-landing trials

The second prototype flew with the new tail unit on 29 June 1941. In the meantime the first prototype, on loan to No. 778 Sqn, had carried out deck-landing trials aboard HMS *Victorious* on 18/19 May 1941,

Differing from the Mk I in being powered by a more robust 1,640-hp (1223-kW) Merlin 32, driving a four-bladed propeller, the Barracuda Mk II was the first major production variant. Here, an early example is seen with the type's primary weapon, a 1,620-lb (735-kg) torpedo.

The *Tirpitz* raids

Launched on 3 April 1944, the Fleet Air Arm's strikes against *Tirpitz*, anchored in Kaafiord in northern Norway, were intended to neutralise the threat posed by the battleship to the Russian convoys. Six Royal Navy aircraft-carriers gathered for the raid, comprising 42 Barracudas from four squadrons aboard HMS *Victorious* and *Furious* and 80 escorting fighters. Taken by surprise, *Tirpitz* received 15 direct hits from 500-lb (227-kg) and 1,000-lb (454-kg) bombs dropped by Barracudas; only three of the latter and a single fighter were lost. Here, a Barracuda is shown returning to its carrier after the raid. Further strikes were made on *Tirpitz* during May, July and August.

Below: In order to hasten production, four companies were engaged in building the Barracuda. Of the 2,602 finally completed, 1,192 were built by Fairey, 700 by Blackburn, 692 by Boulton Paul and 18 by Westland. In this view of a Mk II, some of the unique features of the Barracuda are evident, including the navigator's window below the shoulder-mounted mainplane, the Merlin 32's shrouded exhaust and the high-set tailplane.

following which it was returned to Fairey for the new tail to be fitted. Handling trials at the Aircraft & Armament Experimental Establishment at Boscombe Down commenced in October that year, but some unserviceability and modifications delayed completion of the aircraft until February 1942.

Overweight

It was at this point that a problem arose which was to remain with the Barracuda for the rest of its career – it was overweight. Strengthening of the airframe and addition of equipment not included in the original specification played havoc with the take-off and climb performance. The result was that, after the first 30 production aircraft had been built, subsequent aircraft, known as Barracuda Mk IIs, had the 1,640-hp (1223-kW) Merlin 32 engine installed, this providing an increase of some 30 per cent in rated output over the earlier powerplant. No changes were made to the airframe of the Mk II, but a four-bladed propeller was substituted for the three-bladed version of the Mk I.

The Mk II, ordered in quantity, was the main production version and other companies were selected to build the type, these including Blackburn, Boulton Paul and Westland. By November 1941, 1,050 Barracudas had been ordered, but Westland was to build only five Mk Is and 13 Mk IIs before the remainder of its order (for another 232) was cancelled to allow the company to build Supermarine Seafires.

Barracudas built by Blackburn and by Boulton Paul began to enter service in spring 1943 and, although additional orders were placed, some of these were cancelled with the end of the

war in Europe. In all, 1,688 Mk IIs were built, plus 30 Mk Is and two prototypes.

The Barracuda Mk III was evolved to take a new ASV radar installation, with a blister radome beneath the rear fuselage. The prototype, converted from a Boulton Paul-built Mk II, flew first in 1943. Following orders placed that year, production of this version began in early 1944 alongside Mk IIs. A total of 852 Mk IIIs was manufactured by Boulton Paul and Fairey.

Griffon-powered Mk V

The final production variant was the Barracuda Mk V (the Mk IV being an unbuilt project), and this differed considerably in appearance, although the basic structure was unchanged. The shortfall on power of the Merlins available in 1941 made the designers consider alternatives, and the decision was taken to use a Rolls-Royce Griffon. Initial development was slow and

the first Griffon-powered aircraft, converted from a Fairey-built Mk II, did not fly until 16 November 1944.

In its production form, the Barracuda Mk V had a longer, squarer wing than earlier versions, enlarged fin area to counteract the greater torque of the 2,030-hp (1514-kW) Griffon 37, and increased fuel capacity. However, this development had come too late and, of the 140 Mk Vs ordered, only 30 were delivered before the end of the war brought cancellation of the outstanding balance.

The Barracuda's operational service life began when No. 827 Sqn received 12 Mk IIs on being reformed at Stretton, Cheshire, on 10 January 1943. Its companion squadron, No. 810, was re-equipped the following month and, by January 1944, there were 12 Barracuda squadrons, first into action being No. 810 from HMS *Illustrious* in September 1943, during the

Allied landings at Salerno, Italy. However, it was on 3 April 1944 that the type made its mark when 42 aircraft dive-bombed the German battleship *Tirpitz*, inflicting heavy damage.

The Barracuda squadrons of HMS *Illustrious*, Nos 810 and 847, introduced the type to the Pacific theatre in April 1944, supporting US Navy dive-bombers in an attack on Japanese installations in Sumatra. Barracudas flew from small escort carriers on anti-submarine patrols in European operations, using rocket-assisted take-off gear from the short decks. Most squadrons were disbanded soon after VJ-Day, or re-equipped with other aircraft, and after some shuffling within squadrons the last Barracudas in front-line service were replaced in 1953 by Grumman Avengers.

The Mk Vs never entered front-line service, being used for training and other second-line duties until 1950.

Though hastily retired after VJ-Day, the ASV radar-equipped Barracuda Mk III re-entered front-line service in 1947, equipping No. 815 Sqn at Eglinton, Northern Ireland. These were to be the last Barracudas in front-line FAA service and were finally replaced by Grumman Avengers in 1953. In this view of two Mk IIIs, their ASV radomes are clearly visible below the rear fuselage.

Fairey Firefly

Though it adhered to the Royal Navy's long-standing insistence that its day-fighters had two crew, the Firefly was to be the last aircraft of this type to see FAA service. With yellow undersides, as applied to prototype and trials aircraft, this machine was the seventh Firefly Mk I off the production line.

Robust FAA fighter

When the Fairey Firefly entered squadron service in late 1943, the Fleet Air Arm at last had a robust, well-armed, two-seat fighter. While it lacked the outright speed of a single-seater, it had a high cruising speed, good deck landing characteristics and, in the hands of a good pilot, could more than hold its own against its single-seat counterparts.

At a Tender Design Conference on 5 January 1940, when the single-seat and two-seat naval fighter projects originating from the Air Ministry Specifications N.8/39 and N.9/39 evolved into N.5/40F, a dramatic change in Admiralty policy towards naval aircraft had taken place. After only a short spell at war, the Royal Navy had recognised that the performance of fighters operating from carriers would only be enhanced if the amount of equipment carried by these aircraft was drastically reduced. Performance would be paramount in the new range of aircraft being ordered and destined for introduction with front-line units within two years. The aircraft then in service were for the most part unsuitable and/or obsolete, often being adaptations of RAF aircraft. British naval aircraft in 1940 left much to be desired.

The original specifications of

1939 had called for a two-seat 'front gun' fighter (i.e., with forward-firing guns) and for one with a turret, like the Blackburn Roc or Boulton-Paul Defiant. The turret fighter was a non-starter, considering its weight and recent RAF combat experience of the Defiant. The 'front-gun fighter' (N.8/39) eventually became the Firefly, while N.9/39 was revised to become a single-seat version of the two-seater, with the turret deleted.

Fairey submitted a design that could be adapted to fill both specifications, which were then combined as the two-seat N.5/40F, written around what was to become the Firefly.

The Firefly's wings, folded manually for stowage below decks on a carrier, were turned upward from a pivot on the rear spar and then rearwards to lie alongside the fuselage.

In order to get the new aircraft into service within two years, it was recognised that the usual process of testing prototypes and development aircraft would have to be revised. After various submissions, the new Rolls-Royce Griffon engine was selected to power the new fighter. The Griffon had been given the go-ahead in December 1939 and was designed from the beginning to provide high power

at low altitude – ideal for a naval fighter. Initially, it gave 1,735 hp (1295 kW) at sea level but later versions were capable of over 2,100 hp (1567 kW).

Initial Firefly production centred around 200 aircraft – two prototypes, 11 development machines and 187 production aircraft, though in the event, the two prototypes became four and at least 15 other Fireflies were used to speed development.

Firefly prototype Z1826 is seen at the Great West Aerodrome (now part of London's Heathrow Airport) around the time of its first flight there on 22 December 1941.

Below: A Firefly Mk I of No. 1770 Sqn, the first FAA Firefly unit to take the type into action, is seen landing after a sortie in the Pacific theatre. Note the Youngman area-increasing flaps, fully extended for landing, and underwing rails for rocket projectiles.

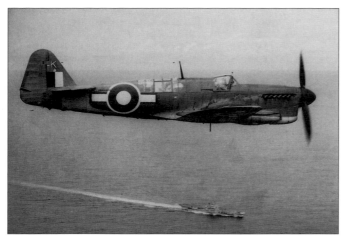

Above: Much of the action seen by Firefly units was in the Pacific theatre. This No. 1772 Sqn aircraft is seen over HMS **Indefatigable** *shortly before VJ-Day.*

The first works drawings to enable production to begin at Fairey's Hayes, Middlesex factory were issued to shop floor staff in March 1941. The Ministry of Aircraft Production (MAP) followed the first order for 200 with an additional 100, and then in May 1942 added a further 300. The MAP was looking for 50 Fireflies per month until, at least, the end of 1944. There were many changes to the numbers of the different marks ordered as the war progressed; for instance, on 28 April Fairey was informed by the MAP that the programme was 300 Mk Is, 100 NF.Mk IIs and 200 Mk IIIs. By August this had been changed to 500 Mk Is, 200 NF.Mk IIs and 100 Mk IIIs, and by October it was 350 Mk Is, 350 NF.Mk IIs and 100 Mk IIIs.

Such were the plans for the Firefly that a whole new range of squadron numbers was allocated, the first one, No. 1770, forming up at Yeovilton on 1 October 1943. The second unit, No. 1771, was formed at Yeovilton on 1 February 1944, followed by No. 1772 at Burscough on 1 May 1944. Plans to equip three others – Nos 1773, 1774 and 1775 – were scrapped after VJ-Day.

First action – *Tirpitz*
No. 1770 Sqn, embarked in HMS *Indefatigable*, was the first to see action, in strikes against the *Tirpitz* in mid-July 1944. The unit was given the task of flak suppression, a difficult one in the confines of a fjord, and at least one aircraft was lost to AAA.

The squadron then sailed to Ceylon (now Sri Lanka) to join the British Pacific Fleet. On 1 and 7 January 1945, No. 1770 attacked the Japanese-held oil refineries at Pangkalan Brandan, Sumatra using rocket projectiles (RPs). Lt D. Levitt shot down a Ki-43 Hayabusa on 4 January, drawing first blood for the Firefly in air-to-air combat. Another was shot down and shared by Sub-Lts Stott and Redding. Two more Hayabusas fell to the 20-mm cannon of No. 1770 on 24 January when RP strikes were made against refineries at Palembang. The Fireflies, leading the strike, had to fly through balloon barrages and intense flak. It was to prove an excellent debut for the new fighter and on 29 January three more Hayabusas were shot down by the Fireflies of No. 1770 Sqn.

Moving up to the Admiralty Isles as part of Task Force 57, the Fireflies were to the fore in strikes on Japanese airfields on Miyako, only 230 miles (370 km) southwest of Okinawa. On one occasion, four of the squadron's Fireflies escorted a USN Martin Mariner flying-boat to pick up ditched aircrews near the Sakashima Gunto islands. Spotting five Mitsubishi Ki-51 'Edna' dive-bombers heading for Okinawa, the Fireflies set off in pursuit, shot down four and left the other smoking.

Further strikes were made before the BPF withdrew to Australia to replenish. No. 1770 Sqn was disbanded. In the meantime, No. 1771 in HMS *Implacable* carried out air strikes against targets in the Caroline Islands and its Fireflies became the first FAA aircraft to fly over the Japanese mainland. It was joined in July by No. 1772, which had replaced No. 1770 aboard *Indefatigable*. With the end of the war in sight, No. 1772 was given the task of locating POW camps and dropping Red Cross supplies.

Firefly night-fighter variants

A night-fighter variant of the Firefly was envisaged early on in the aircraft's development, but development of the NF.Mk II night-fighter (below) proved problematic and was ultimately a failure. Placing extra night-fighter equipment (AI Mk X radar) in a radome under each wing leading edge led to centre-of-gravity problems. With the additional weight of associated equipment installed in the observer's cockpit, a plan to insert an extra 15-in (38-cm) bay in front of the firewall only aggravated the problem. The Mk II was directionally unstable and the initial plan for 100 Firefly night-fighters looked decidedly shaky. The Mk II's unsuitability as a carrier night-fighter was confirmed after trials aboard HMS *Ravager* when the trials aircraft crashed. The NF.Mk II was abandoned in June 1944 when it was realised that, with relatively small changes, the FR.Mk I could be adapted to provide the FAA with a night-fighter. The Mk II order, by now increased to 328 aircraft, was reduced to the 37 committed on the production line; some of these were later converted to NF.Mk I standard (right). The key to the change was the availability from the United States of AN/APS-4 radar, or ASH (Air-to-Surface H) as it became known in the FAA. ASH replaced AI Mk X and its compactness – it weighed only 200 lb (91 kg) – allowed it to be

contained in a streamlined transmitter/receiver pod mounted beneath the nose. The changes were quickly introduced on the production line and NF.Mk Is were produced concurrently with the FR.Mk I.

With the availability of NF.Mk Is, No. 746 Squadron formed up at Lee-on-Solent on 23 November 1942 as a naval night-fighter interception unit. Initially it operated Fulmars but started to receive Firefly NF.Mk Is in May 1943. This unit provided aircraft and crews to operate from RAF Coltishall in Norfolk, intercepting Heinkel He 111s over the English Channel and North Sea that were releasing V-1 flying bombs against British targets. Although quite a number of these night sorties were flown, no Firefly ever shot down an He 111. The first dedicated naval night-fighter squadron was No. 1790 formed at Burscough on 1 January 1945, followed by Nos 1791 and 1792 at Lee-on-Solent on 15 March and 15 May, respectively. Although No. 1790 joined the Pacific Fleet, it was too late to be used operationally. No. 1791 was soon disbanded but No. 1792 undertook trial flights investigating whether future night-fighter tactics favoured single-seat or two-seat aircraft. In the event, the two-seat Firefly was chosen, but instead of specific squadrons being formed, a flight of four Firefly NF.Mk Is was attached to existing units operating from carriers. Known as 'Black Flights', they moved from squadron to squadron.

Seen overflying the newly-commissioned HMS Ark Royal in early 1939, this Swordfish Mk I is from No. 820 Squadron. The unit had become the first squadron to deploy aboard the carrier in January of that year.

Fairey Swordfish

Fairey's 'Stringbag'

Archaic in appearance even when it first flew, the venerable Swordfish was the Fleet Air Arm's premier torpedo-bomber at the outbreak of World War II and was destined to become a naval legend.

Having arrived at a stage of World War II when a biplane, other than the odd small-span Avro Tutor or de Havilland Tiger Moth, was a very rare sight, the appearance of a large and noisy biplane in the circuit created more than average interest. Despite appearances, this beautifully ugly aircraft was no anachronism, for the Fairey Swordfish, as it was named, had then a still vital role to play in World War II. This was a role for which it was so well

engineered that it fought in the battle against the Axis from the very first moment of that conflict until victory for the Allies in Europe had been assured. In so doing, the Swordfish outlived and outfought aircraft which had been designed to replace it in service, and during this period created a record of machine achievement in association with human courage that makes pages of the Fleet Air Arm's history a veritable saga. Approaching obsolescence in 1939, the

Originally referred to as the Fairey T.S.R.II, the prototype Swordfish, K4190, was designed to Specification S.15/33 and given the Fairey works no. F2038. During flight tests the T.S.R.II exceeded the specified performance demands.

K5972 was a Swordfish Mk I from the initial Fairey-built production batch. It is seen in the markings of No. 823 Squadron, embarked on HMS Glorious in 1936.

Swordfish prepare for take-off from the flight deck of HMS Eagle off Mombasa in April 1941. The aircraft are from Nos 813 and 824 Squadrons, which carried out anti-submarine patrols. On 6 June 1941, Swordfish from these squadrons found and sank the U-boat supply ship, Elbe.

Swordfish had originated from Fairey's private- venture T.S.R.I biplane of 1933. When this was destroyed in an accident during September of that year, its progress had been sufficiently worthwhile to warrant further development. When, therefore, the Air Ministry issued its Specification S.15/33, which called for a carrier-based torpedo-spotter-reconnaissance aircraft, Fairey submitted its layout for the improved T.S.R.II on which the design office had been working. This was to become the prototype of the Swordfish (K4190), first flown on 17 April 1934.

Modified wings

It differed from the T.S.R.I in having a changed upper wing, slightly swept, to compensate for a fuselage which had been lengthened to overcome the stability problems that had led to the loss of the T.S.R.I. Other changes brought the inclusion of an additional wing bay, and modification of the tail unit. Subjected to intensive testing, both in landplane and alternative floatplane form, the type was ordered into production in April 1935 with a first contract for 86 aircraft, to be named Swordfish.

Initial production

The initial Swordfish Mk I, built to Air Ministry Specification S.38/34, was powered by a 690-hp (515-kW) Bristol Pegasus IIIM radial engine, driving a three-bladed, fixed-pitch metal propeller. The two-bay biplane wings were of all-metal construction, fabric-covered, with ailerons on both upper and lower wings, the biplane configuration and its structural integrity maintained by robust interplane struts, flying and landing wires. For shipboard stowage, the wings could be folded about rear spar hinges.

The tail unit was entirely conventional, with a strut-braced tailplane, and fin and rudder of metal construction with fabric covering. The fuselage, with two open cockpits to accommodate the pilot forward, and crew of one or two aft, was also of metal construction, but covered by a combination of light alloy panels forward and fabric aft. Landing gear was of the fixed tailwheel type, with the individual main units each having an oleo shock-absorber.

These were easily exchanged for an alternative float landing gear, consisting of two single-step light alloy floats, each provided with a small rudder to simplify directional control on the water.

Armament comprised one synchronised forward-firing 0.303-in (7.7-mm) Vickers machine-gun, one Vickers 'K' gun or Lewis gun in the aft cockpit, and mountings to carry one 18-in (0.46-m) 1,610-lb (730-kg) torpedo beneath the fuselage. Alternative weapon loads of the Mk I included one 1,500-lb (680-kg) mine, or two 500-lb (227-kg) bombs beneath the fuselage plus two 250-lb (113-kg) bombs on underwing racks, or one 500-lb (227-kg) bomb beneath the fuselage and one 500-lb (227-kg) bomb beneath each wing.

Swordfish Mk Is began to enter service with the FAA in July 1936, equipping first No. 825 Squadron as a replacement for the Fairey Seals which had first been allocated to squadrons some three years earlier. Next to go, before the end of 1936, were the Blackburn Baffins which had seen little service with Nos 811 and 812 Squadrons before their replacement, and also the Seals of No. 823 Squadron. When, in 1938, the Blackburn Sharks of Nos 810, 820 and 821 Squadrons were superseded (although they had seen even less service than the Seals), the FAA's torpedo-bomber squadrons had become equipped exclusively with the Swordfish.

At the beginning of World War II the Fleet Air Arm had 13 squadrons operational with the Swordfish, 12 of these squadrons at sea aboard the carriers HMS *Ark Royal, Courageous, Eagle, Furious* and *Glorious*, but the 'phoney' start to the war meant that these aircraft saw virtually no fighting until the beginning of the Norwegian campaign in 1940. This, of course, was beneficial rather than detrimental to the Swordfish cause, giving all squadrons ample time in which to work up to a state of perfection. It was to prove of immense value when, on 11 April, torpedo-carrying Swordfish went into action for the first time from the carrier, *Furious*. Two days later, a catapulted Swordfish from HMS *Warspite* sank submarine *U-64*, the first U-boat sinking of the war to be credited to the FAA.

Blackburn's 'Stringbag'

Fairey's production commitments were such that the growing contracts for Swordfish were becoming embarrassing, so continued construction was left in the capable hands of Blackburn Aircraft at Brough, Yorkshire, a company which had been concerned primarily with the design and manufacture of naval aircraft from its earliest days. Only a single example was built by Blackburn in 1940, but in the following year a total of 415 was produced.

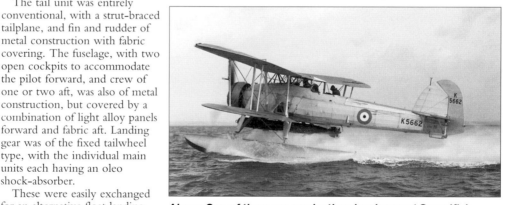

Above: One of three pre-production development Swordfish, K5662 was assembled as a floatplane and is seen here, equipped with a torpedo, during flight trials with the MAEE.

Left: The Swordfish's principal weapon was a single 1,610-lb (730-kg) torpedo slung beneath the fuselage. Although relatively slow and unmanoeuvrable, the aircraft proved to be superbly stable on the crucial torpedo run.

Right: Shore-based, carrier-based and even catapulted from warships, the Fairey Swordfish was an effective torpedo-bomber. The aircraft could also carry mines or bombs and, later in the war, eight 60-lb (27-kg) rockets.

Wartime service

A batman brings a Swordfish in to land on HMS Smiter in April 1945. Batmen led a dangerous life on carriers, frequently making use of the back-up net. Their job was made more hazardous by the narrowness of the escort carrier deck.

During World War II the Swordfish was involved in some of the most celebrated air attacks, most notably the assault on Taranto harbour. However, heavy Swordfish losses in the torpedo-attack role led to the type's redeployment in ASW operations, under the guidance of the RAF's Coastal Command.

In 1940 came the supreme triumph of the Swordfish – the memorable assault on the Italian fleet at anchor in Taranto harbour. The attack, made by 21 Swordfish on the night of 11 November 1940, was launched in two waves, with an hour's interval between them. All the aircraft had long-range tanks in the rear cockpit and, of the total, four carried flares for target illumination, six had bombs, and 11 were armed with torpedoes. The first flares were dropped at 23.00, the aircraft of the initial wave going in through a protective umbrella of barrage balloons and coming under intense light and heavy fire. In spite of the conditions, targets were being hit, and only one Swordfish was lost. The second wave also lost one of its number, but was able to launch a concerted attack. A reconnaissance flight the next day confirmed the devastation. It was realised that the Italian navy had been dealt a shattering blow: three battleships were damaged severely, two of them under water; a cruiser and two destroyers had been hit; and two

auxiliary vessels had been sunk.

In the short space of one hour, the balance of naval power in the Mediterranean had irrevocably shifted, confirming the belief of prophets such as the USA's 'Billy' Mitchell by demonstrating the potential of a force of 'obsolescent' aircraft to eliminate a naval fleet without any assistance from surface vessels.

The last of the great torpedo attacks made by these aircraft came in 1942, when a futile attempt was made to prevent the German battle-cruisers *Gneisenau* and *Scharnhorst*, accompanied by the heavy cruiser *Prinz Eugen*, from making good their escape eastwards through the English Channel. Almost as a last resort, six Swordfish of No. 825 Squadron, led by Lieutenant Commander Esmonde, were detailed to make a torpedo attack, but as they approached the battleships with their escorting destroyers and umbrella of fighters overhead, it was clear to the crews that their task was hopeless. Despite such odds, however, Esmonde led his men into the attack. Immediately,

Above: From August 1942, Swordfish carried out tremendous work, escorting convoys to Russia. The stressful conditions in which the Swordfish were operated, by day and night, cannot be stated enough. This aircraft runs up on the frozen deck of HMS Fencer in 1944.

Below: Throughout the war, British aircrews often trained in the safety of Canadian airspace. The adverse weather conditions necessitated the addition of a canopy for the crew.

Swordfish Mk II

Although fairly anonymous in being devoid of serial number, Royal Navy ship and squadron markings, this Swordfish is shown in a typical 1940-1 (the period of the Battle of Taranto) colour scheme.

Powerplant
Early production Mk IIs retained the Pegasus IIIM engine which delivered 690 hp (514 kW), but later examples were fitted with the more powerful, 750-hp (560-kW) Pegasus XXX.

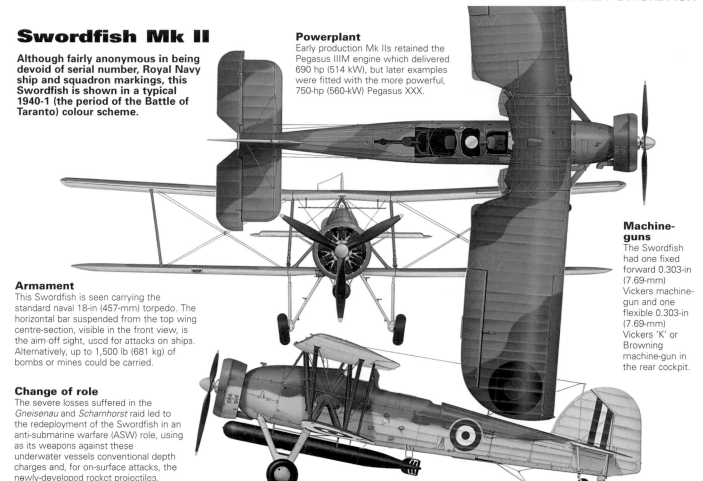

Machine-guns
The Swordfish had one fixed forward 0.303-in (7.69-mm) Vickers machine-gun and one flexible 0.303-in (7.69-mm) Vickers 'K' or Browning machine-gun in the rear cockpit.

Armament
This Swordfish is seen carrying the standard naval 18-in (457-mm) torpedo. The horizontal bar suspended from the top wing centre-section, visible in the front view, is the aim-off sight, used for attacks on ships. Alternatively, up to 1,500 lb (681 kg) of bombs or mines could be carried.

Change of role
The severe losses suffered in the *Gneisenau* and *Scharnhorst* raid led to the redeployment of the Swordfish in an anti-submarine warfare (ASW) role, using as its weapons against these underwater vessels conventional depth charges and, for on-surface attacks, the newly-developed rocket projectiles.

they were met by a concentrated hail of anti-aircraft fire, and were attacked from all angles by the defending fighters. Not a single Swordfish survived, and it was a miracle that five of the 18 crew members were rescued. All were subsequently decorated and the gallant leader, Esmonde, was posthumously awarded the Victoria Cross, the first to be given to a member of the FAA.

This experience gave confirmation, if any were needed, of the fact that it was no longer a practical proposition to deploy the Swordfish on torpedo attacks. Such operations called for a long, accurate approach if the weapon was to be successfully launched, but such an approach also provided the enemy with an excellent oppor-

This Blackburn-built Swordfish Mk II is seen on a training sortie with a practice bomb beneath the starboard wing. The Mk II had a strengthened lower wing allowing a greater weapons load.

tunity of destroying its attacker.

This led to development of the Swordfish Mk II, which entered service in 1943, and differed from the earlier version in having the lower wing strengthened and metal-skinned so that it could carry and launch rocket projectiles. The Swordfish Mk II was followed in the same year by what was to prove the final production version, the Swordfish Mk III, which mounted a radome carrying a scanner for its ASV (Air-to-Surface Vessel) Mk X radar between the landing-gear main units; in other respects it was generally similar to the Mk II. There were, in addition to the three main production versions, a few examples converted from Mk IIs and provided with an

enclosed cabin for operation in the much colder Canadian waters, these aircraft having the designation Swordfish Mk IV.

These changes were to bring new life to the old warrior which, at the peak of its deployment, equipped no fewer than 26 squadrons. Even at the beginning of 1945, nine front-line squadrons were still operating their Swordfish successfully. The advent of the rocket projectile into the armoury of the Fleet Air Arm had been the responsibility of the Swordfish, which carried out suitability trials before the weapon was accepted as standard. With rockets and mines, these aircraft were to achieve unbelievable success in ASW operations, a highlight coming in September 1944 when Swordfish aboard the escort carrier HMS *Vindex*, then employed in escorting a convoy to north Russia, sank four U-boats in a single voyage.

RAF service
The RAF also found the Swordfish valuable for maritime operations. In April 1940 No. 812 Sqn was assigned to RAF Coastal Command control, subsequently flying successful day and night mine-laying sorties in the English Channel and the North Sea. The squadron's Swordfish were also active in the Battle of France, making daylight bombing raids on enemy-held ports. Two regular

RAF squadrons also operated the type. In October 1940 No. 202 Squadron in Gibraltar received float-equipped Swordfish Mk Is and operated these on offensive patrols in the Straits of Gibraltar until January 1942. The other RAF unit to be equipped with the type was No. 119 Squadron which, operating Swordfish Mk IIIs from bases in Belgium, flew successful sorties in the North Sea against midget submarines between January and May 1945.

Production ended in 1944, after Fairey had built 692 and Blackburn 1,699, for a grand total of 2,391. On 21 May 1945 No. 836 Squadron, the last first-line Swordfish squadron, was officially disbanded. Even then, the Royal Navy was reluctant to lose such a doughty warrior, and odd examples were to remain in use for several years.

In a remarkable career, this valiant biplane had achieved a record that will remain indelibly endorsed in the history of air warfare, and especially that of the FAA. In five years of hard-fought war it had served as a torpedo-bomber for the British fleet, as a shore-based mine layer, as convoy protection from escort carriers, as a night-flying flare-dropper, as a rocket-armed anti-shipping and ASW aircraft, as well as for training and general utility duties.

Raid on Taranto

As the Swordfish approached Taranto, anti-aircraft and machine-gun fire rose to meet them. Four hours later, all except two aircraft were safely back aboard HMS Illustrious. They had left Taranto in chaos. The Italian battleships Cavour, Littorio and Duilio had all been successfully torpedoed.

Carried out by two FAA squadrons on 11 November 1940, the attack on Taranto was the first major victory for naval airpower in history and arguably the Royal Navy's most successful action of World War II.

An attack on the major Italian naval base of Taranto had actually been considered in 1938, when war was becoming inevitable. In 1940, the strike plans were dusted off and updated.

The main Italian fleet consisted of six battleships, consisting of two of the new Littorio-class and four of the recently rebuilt Cavour- and Dulio-class vessels, plus five cruisers and twenty destroyers, all based at Taranto.

Attacking the Italian fleet at anchor required high quality and up-to-date intelligence and reconnaissance, not merely to determine what ships were present but also to know their positions. The British strike force would also have to move silently in order to achieve surprise.

The plan specified a night attack to reduce losses, and so Swordfish crews were put

through a rigorous schedule of training for night flight and combat. The mission was scheduled for 21 October 1940, but was delayed to 11 November because of other naval duties and commitments.

A few days before the mission, the carrier HMS *Eagle* ran into trouble with its fuel systems. Several Swordfish were transferred to the carrier HMS

Illustrious, which then sailed from Alexandria, Egypt.

Aerial reconnaissance on the morning of 11 November indicated that five Italian battleships were in Taranto harbour, with three cruisers at dock protected by anti-submarine nets. The sixth battleship was seen to enter the harbour later that day.

By 20.00 hrs that evening, the *Illustrious* and its escorts were in position, 171 miles (275 km) from the port. Twelve Swordfish were fitted up for the first wave of the attack: six carried torpedoes, four carried bombs, and two carried a combination of bombs and flares. Most of the rear gunners were left behind, since an additional fuel tank

took up their position.

The first Swordfish took off at 20.35 hrs, and by 21.00 hrs, they were all in the air and on the way. Just before 23.00 hrs, the two flare-droppers split from the formation. One put a line of flares over the harbour from 7,500 ft (2,300 m) and then bombed an oil storage depot. The strike aircraft attacked in two groups; the flight leader's plane was hit by flak and went down, but multiple hits were scored on several of the battleships.

In the meantime, a second wave had taken to the air about 30 minutes after the first. The second wave consisted of five aircraft armed with torpedoes, two armed with bombs, and two

Shortly before 21.00 hrs on 11 November 1940, 12 Fairey Swordfish biplanes began a 171-mile (275-km) flight to Taranto. Ahead of them lay a two-hour flight in a bitterly cold, open cockpit before they launched an attack on the Italian fleet.

armed with flares and bombs. One had to turn back because of a technical problem, but the other eight arrived at about midnight and repeated the performance of the first wave, slamming torpedoes into the sitting battleships under the glare of the flares. However, another Swordfish was lost to ensuing flak.

All the aircraft, except the two that had been shot down, were back on board the *Illustrious* before 03.00 hrs that morning. Aerial reconnaissance conducted two days later indicated that one Cavour- and one Dulio-class

battleship were heavily damaged and beached; one Littorio battleship badly damaged; two cruisers and two destroyers badly damaged; and two auxiliary vessels sunk.

It was a brilliant action, inflicting massive damage on the Italian fleet with minimal losses to the British. The Italians withdrew their fleet to the north, effectively removing it from the game board. The successful raid on Taranto suggested to Japanese planners that they might be able to imitate the same tactics for their own purposes - at Pearl Harbor.

The value of the attack on Taranto lay in its demonstration of the sheer economy of a well-planned carrier strike, the further moral ascendancy of the Royal Navy and the withdrawal of all Italian heavy units to points further north.

Fiat CR.32

Rosatelli's masterpiece

After the Anschluss of March 1938, Austria's CR.32s were absorbed by the Luftwaffe; some of the 45 examples delivered are seen here in Luftwaffe markings.

155ª Squadriglia, 3º Gruppo, 6º Stormo 'Diavoli Rossi' (Red Devils) had re-equipped with CR.32s by early 1936.

Essentially a refined derivative of the CR.30 with reduced overall dimensions, the CR.32 was one of the outstanding fighters of the 1930s. Entering service in 1934, it saw action in Spain and Africa.

Celestino Rosatelli designed the first member of the CR family in 1923, the CR.1 being followed by a series of biplane fighters for the Regia Aeronautica. By the early 1930s the CR.30 was in service and it was this aircraft that served as the basis for the CR.32. An unequal span biplane with Warren-type interplane bracing, the CR.32 had a similar light alloy and steel structure and was powered by the same 590-hp (440-kW) Fiat A.30RA 12-cylinder inline engine. First flown on 28 April 1933, the fighter carried an armament of two 0.303-in (7.7-mm) or 0.5-in (12.7-mm) Breda-SAFAT machine-guns, mounted above the engine and firing through the propeller arc.

The first 16 production examples were delivered to China before the first of 291 (including prototypes) was delivered to the Regia Aeronautica from March 1934. The Chinese aircraft, ordered in 1933 and armed with a pair of Vickers machine-guns, were soon in combat with Japanese fighters and gave a good account of themselves, performing rather better against Japanese types than the Curtiss Hawk biplanes equipping most Chinese fighter units in the mid-1930s.

Hungary also received a batch of CR.32s, 76 aircraft being delivered during 1935/36 as fighter-trainers. These too saw action, as Hungary invaded the remnants of Czechoslovakia in March 1939.

Further deliveries to the Regia

CR.32s in pre-war service

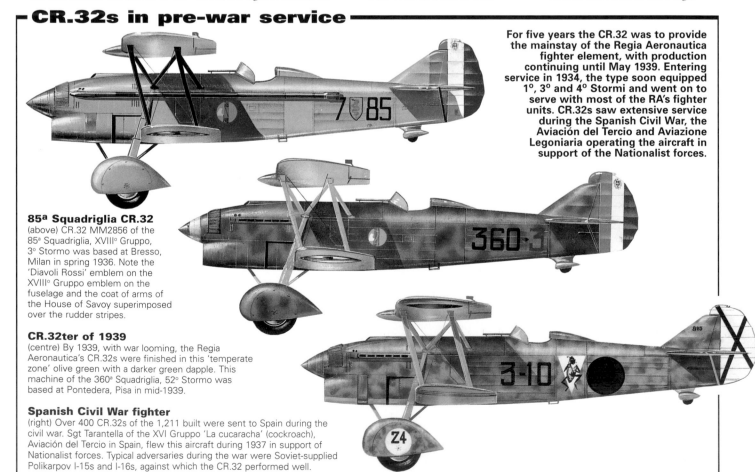

For five years the CR.32 was to provide the mainstay of the Regia Aeronautica fighter element, with production continuing until May 1939. Entering service in 1934, the type soon equipped 1º, 3º and 4º Stormi and went on to serve with most of the RA's fighter units. CR.32s saw extensive service during the Spanish Civil War, the Aviación del Tercio and Aviazione Legoniaria operating the aircraft in support of the Nationalist forces.

85ª Squadriglia CR.32
(above) CR.32 MM2856 of the 85ª Squadriglia, XVIIIº Gruppo, 3º Stormo was based at Bresso, Milan in spring 1936. Note the 'Diavoli Rossi' emblem on the XVIIIº Gruppo emblem on the fuselage and the coat of arms of the House of Savoy superimposed over the rudder stripes.

CR.32ter of 1939
(centre) By 1939, with war looming, the Regia Aeronautica's CR.32s were finished in this 'temperate zone' olive green with a darker green dapple. This machine of the 360ª Squadriglia, 52º Stormo was based at Pontedera, Pisa in mid-1939.

Spanish Civil War fighter
(right) Over 400 CR.32s of the 1,211 built were sent to Spain during the civil war. Sgt Tarantella of the XVI Gruppo 'La cucaracha' (cockroach), Aviación del Tercio in Spain, flew this aircraft during 1937 in support of Nationalist forces. Typical adversaries during the war were Soviet-supplied Polikarpov I-15s and I-16s, against which the CR.32 performed well.

Aeronautica followed, though the next 283 aircraft were of the CR.32bis variant, powered by an improved, 600-hp (447-kW) A.30RAbis engine and fitted with an extra pair of 7.7-mm machine-guns, mounted in the lower wings (though these were often removed in service, to save weight). A single bomb rack beneath the fuselage was able to carry a 220-lb (100-kg) bomb.

CR.32bis in service

The balance of CR.32bis production – 45 aircraft – was delivered to Austria, where it was absorbed into Luftwaffe fighter units in 1938 before being handed over to the Hungarian air force.

Meanwhile, it was the CR.32bis that entered service in Spain in August 1936, several Italian Stormi of the the Aviación del Tercio (later Aviazione Legoniaria) equipping with the type to fly in support of Nationalist forces.

The next production variant was the CR.32ter, which again differed mainly in terms of its armament, with only a pair of 12.7-mm guns installed. Fewer of this version were completed; just 103 were built, all serving in Spain with the Aviazione Legoniaria and Spanish Nationalist air force.

Finally, the most numerous CR.32 variant was the CR.32quater of which 398 were completed, bringing total production to 1,212. This was a lightweight vesion of the CR.32ter, with the same armament as the latter. Again, a number served in Spain, 105 with the Aviazione Legoniaria and 27 with the Spanish air force. Venezuela also acquired 10 and Paraguay an unknown number, believed to be about four. The remainder was delivered to the Regia Aeronautica.

Spanish production

After the end of the Spanish Civil War, remaining Italian aircraft were handed over to the Spanish air force. So impressed with the CR.32 were the Spanish that a local production line was established, Hispano Aviación building 100 aircraft under the local HA-132-L Chirri designation. Some of these remained in use into the early 1950s as C.1 trainers.

In Italian service the CR.32 soldiered on into World War II, 324 remaining in use when Italy declared war in June 1940.

Though by then obsolete, the type saw service in Libya, mainly in the ground attack role, and in East Africa.

Several attempts were made to improve the CR.32's performance before these were abandoned in favour of an all-new design – the CR.42. The CR.33 was powered by a 700-hp (522-kW) Fiat A.33 RC.35 engine and first flew in 1935. Only three were built.

The CR.40 was a parallel development of the CR.32, but differed markedly. Powered by a 525-hp (391-kW) Bristol Mercury IV radial, it had an upper 'gull' wing and first flew in 1934. The CR.40bis which followed had a 700-hp (522-kW) Fiat A.59 radial installed, but its performance, like that of the CR.40, was disappointing. More promising was the CR.41, effectively a CR.40 powered by a 900-hp (671-kW) Gnome-Rhône 14Kfs. Though successfully tested in 1936/37, the CR.41 came too late, development of the CR.42 having commenced.

Fiat CR.42 Falco

Strengthened by its achievements in the Spanish Civil War, the Regia Aeronautica believed that there was still a place for a highly manouevrable biplane fighter as late as 1938.

Thus Celestino Rosatelli developed the CR.42 Falco (falcon), which completed its first flight on 23 May 1938. Building on experience with his earlier fighter designs, including the CR.32 and experimental CR.40 and CR.41, Rosatelli retained the unequal-span wing configuration in the new aircraft's metal structure with a mixed fabric and light alloy covering. A wide-track main landing gear unit incorporated oleo-pneumatic shock absorbers and had strut and wheel fairings. An important departure was the use of a radial engine, the 840-hp (626-kW) Fiat A.74 R1C.38 being selected and installed in a long-chord cowling. Armament comprised single SAFAT-Breda 0.303-in (7.7-mm) and 0.5-in (12.7-mm) machine-guns mounted above the engine.

After a successful series of tests, during which the new fighter demonstrated a maximum level speed of 274 mph (441 km/h) at 20,000 ft (6096 m), a fast climb rate and a minimum speed of 80 mph (129 km/h), the Ministero dell'Aeronautica placed its first order for 200 examples. These began to leave Fiat's Turin factory in February 1939 and by the time production ceased in late 1942, 1,781 had been completed.

Making its operational debut during the brief 14-day campaign against southern France in 1940, the Falco went on to see extensive service in North Africa, though it suffered at the hands of the Allies. By the time of the Italian surrender on 7 September 1943, 113 aircraft remained on strength, 64 of which were serviceable.

The salient features of the CR.42 are evident on this early example.

Falco in service

The night-fighter Falco variant was the CR.42CN (Caccia Noturna), equipped with exhaust flame dampers, a radio and small underwing searchlights. This is a 300ª Squadriglia example.

In service in North Africa, the Falco proved robust and reliable, but was soon bested by the Allies' monoplane fighters. However, in the fighter-bomber role the CR.42 remained in use until VE-Day.

Deliveries to the Regia Aeronautica had begun in 1939, three Stormi having been equipped with Falcos by the time war had broken out in Europe in September 1939. Given that its fighter arm was also equipped with five Stormi of Fiat CR.32s and single Stormi of both the Fiat G.50 and Macchi MC.200, it may be seen that the Falco was a significant type for the service.

By 10 June 1940, when Italy entered the war, 143 had been delivered to units in Italy, 110 of these having been brought up to a state of front-line readiness. These aircraft equipped three Stormi, while two further Stormi in Libya and a pair of Squadriglie in East Africa were also equipped with the biplane fighter. A total

of 330 had been delivered in all; 290 of these were available for service.

Operational debut

The type's operational debut came during the brief two-week campaign in southern France in June, four Gruppi providing escort for Fiat BR.20 bombers attacking air bases and coastal targets. Strafing runs were also made, though stiff Armée de l'Air opposition was met. Both sides made inflated victory claims though, in fact, the victory/loss ratio on both sides was small.

1º Stormo, based in Sicily, was also active early on, escorting bombers on raids over Tunisia, while further north a Stormo comprising CR.42s and G.50s was sent to Belgium (accompa-

Right: Typical of the fate that befell many CR.42s fighting in the Western Desert, this Falco appears to have suffered at the hands of Allied fighter-bombers.

nying two Stormi of BR.20s and a squadriglia of CANT Z.1007bis bombers) to support the Luftwaffe in the Battle of Britain. Any thoughts that its comparatively light losses during the French campaign could be repeated soon vanished, as the Regia Aeronautica struggled with inclement weather, a lack of radios and superior RAF opposition. By April 1941 these units had all returned to Italy, where the CR.42 was in demand for use in the Mediterranean theatre.

In fact it was in North Africa that the Falco saw the mostwidespread use, though over the following months it became clear that it was no match for the Tomahawks and Hurricanes fielded by the RAF in the

Western Desert. Two Gruppi with CR.42s in Libya (designated CR.42AS, for Africa Settentrionale, or North Africa) were particularly active between June 1940 and February 1941, at the forefront of the offensive that culminated in the conquest of Sidi Barrani. For most of this

Experimental variants

In 1940 the CMASA company, a Fiat subsidiary with factories in Marina di Pisa, built a prototype ICR.42 (right), a twin floatplane version of the land fighter. The new machine had an empty weight of 4,070 lb

(1846 kg) and a loaded weight of 5,335 lb (2420 kg), some 273 lb (124 kg) heavier than the land plane. Though its top speed was only 5 mph (8 km/h) slower than that of the standard CR.42, the ICR.42 did not proceed past prototype stage. Another one-off aircraft was the CR.42B (left), an experimentally re-engined machine with a Daimler-Benz DB.601 inline engine installed. This had a designed top speed of 323 mph (520 km/h), but the airframe was considered unsuitable for the modification and this variant, plus a projected version with retractable landing gear, was abandoned.

Above: Regia Aeronautica CR.42s, some of them having been resprayed in a more appropriate camouflage scheme, are seen over the Mediterranean during May 1942.

Below: 85ª Squadriglia was one of the three squadrons making up 18° Gruppo, which joined 56° Stormo in Belgium during 1940, for operations over the English Channel.

period the most challenging opposition faced by Italian fighters came from RAF Gloster Gladiators, though during 1941 the Allies went on to the offensive and the Hawker Hurricane began to enter service.

Meanwhile, Falcos based in Sicily escorted the first Axis raids on Malta and, at the end of October 1940, the war against Greece began. The Italian invading force including a Gruppo of CR.42s, the aircraft and their pilots performing well against inferior and ill-equipped Greek pilots during operations over difficult terrain and in bad weather. The Regia Aeronautica lost 29 aircraft of all types in the Greek campaign, claiming 160 kills in return. The conquest of Crete which followed also saw the Falco in action, escorting Luftwaffe Ju 87 dive-bombers, though by the end of the year

the Falco had been replaced in the Aegean by the G.50.

Ethiopian operations

Operations by those Regia Aeronautica units equipped with CR.42s in Italian East Africa (formerly Ethiopia) were hampered by the long supply chain from Italy, especially once the Royal Navy blockaded the territory after Italy declared war. An air bridge was set up but by June 1941 the risk of interception, bad weather and a lack of radio facilities had taken their toll. During November the last two Falcos left in use were destroyed by the South African Air Force.

Back in North Africa, the CR.42 was being pressed into service as a fighter-bomber, carrying a pair of 200-lb (90-kg) bombs for the first time in combat after the reconquest of

Libya in May 1941. Three Stormi were eventually equipped with these aircraft and saw constant use until the end of 1942 and the final Allied advance on El Alamein. Typical targets were camps, vehicles and air bases, some sorties being flown at night.

By January 1943 there just 82 Falcos left in North Africa; these were evacuated to Italy and used to attack Allied convoys between Gibraltar and Malta, though their effectiveness was limited by the small size of the bombs they carried.

Night-fighter

Though superseded as an interceptor and with marginal capability as a fighter-bomber, the CR.42 remained in use until VE-Day. The role of night-fighter had been added to the

Falco's repertoire as early as October 1941, when a Gruppo of CR.42CNs (for Caccia Noturna, or night-fighter), equipped with exhaust flame dampers, a radio and a pair of small underwing searchlights, was established.

The unit saw only limited success, though it scored a number of victories over RAF bombers attacking industrial targets in northern Italy during 1942/43. After the Italian surrender a handful were employed by the Luftwaffe in the north of the country, undertaking night anti-partisan sorties.

Others flew south and saw service with the Allied ANR as trainers, a few of these machines remaining in service in the post-war AMI. At least one example was fitted with a second cockpit for the role.

Foreign Falcos

Fiat received a single pre-war order for CR.42s from Belgium and during World War II delivered aircraft to Hungary and Sweden. The Luftwaffe also operated a handful after Italy's surrender.

Belgium
(below) Ordered in September 1939, the first of 34 Falcos were delivered in March 1940, equipping 3ᵉᵐᵉ Escadrille de Chasse. Thirteen of these aircraft were destroyed by Ju 87 dive-bombers during the German invasion; the survivors playing little or no part in the fighting.

Hungary
Fifty CR.42s were exported to Hungary in late 1940. These equipped two 1st Fighter Regiment squadrons at home (above) and, later, in the Soviet Union (below).

Sweden
(below) The largest CR.42 export order comprised 72 aircraft for Sweden, delivered during 1940/41. A number were used as target tugs post-war.

Germany
(below) Based in the Rimini area for night harassment and anti-partisan duties in early 1944, this Falco was assigned to 2.Staffel, Nachtschlachtgruppe 9.

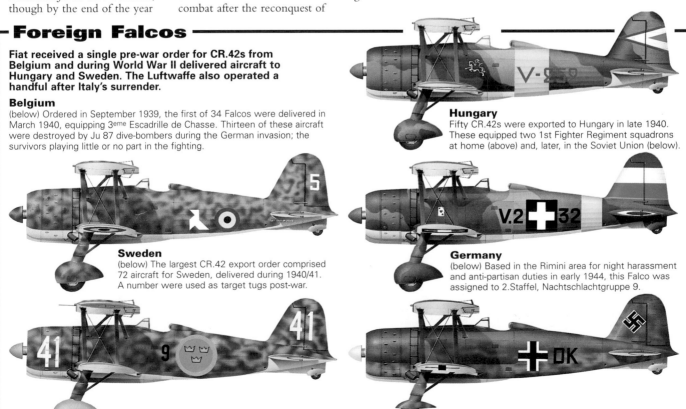

Shortly after the fall of Paris to the German Blitzkrieg in 1940, this Storch landed in the Place de la Concorde, demonstrating its excellent STOL characteristics.

Fieseler Fi 156 Storch

German STOL classic

All over northern Germany, one finds gigantic nests atop the chimneys of country houses. The nests are made by storks, which, despite their great size, have to be able to take off and land vertically. It was appropriate that, when Gerhard Fieseler won the contract to supply the Luftwaffe's multi-role army co-operation aircraft, he should have called the type the Storch.

Fi 156 V4 (the fourth prototype), D-IFMR, had ski undercarriage and a drop tank fitted for test purposes.

Fieseler, together with chief designer Reinhold Mewes, specialised in what today are called STOL (short take-off and landing) aircraft. In most of his company's aircraft (except the V-1 flying bomb), he could approach the airfield at 9,845 ft (3000 m) and then descend vertically to a soft landing, provided

there was a slight breeze.

In summer 1935, Fieseler, Mewes and technical director Erich Bachem designed the ultimate in practical STOL aircraft – the Fieseler Fi 156. It was no mere exercise, and was seen to fill numerous roles, both in civil life and for the recently disclosed Luftwaffe. It was a

three-seat, high-winged machine, powered by the excellent 240-hp (179-kW) Argus engine and with the wing liberally endowed with slats and flaps. Its stalky landing gear arrangement was well suited to

cushioning arrivals at unprecedented steep angles. Fieseler manufactured three prototypes

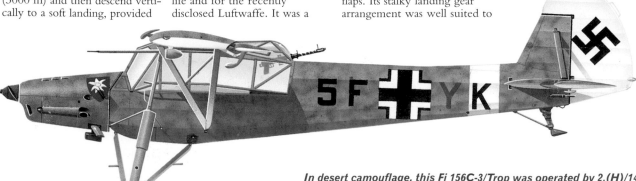

In desert camouflage, this Fi 156C-3/Trop was operated by 2.(H)/14 under Afrika Korps orders for tank-spotting duties. The Storch's excellent all-round visibility and slow-flying characteristics made it ideal for the task.

A factory in liberated Czechoslovakia briefly built the Fi 156 prior to the Communist takeover, as the Mraz K.65 Cap. These aircraft are seen in northern Bohemia in 1957, apparently in use as glider tugs.

with fixed slats: the Fi 156 V1 to V3. The V1 (D-IKVN) flew on or about 24 May 1936, with a metal ground-adjustable propeller. The V2 (D-IDVS) had a wooden propeller, and the V3 (D-IGLI) had military equipment. Their performance was so impressive that the RLM (air ministry) ordered further prototypes and preparations for series production. The first production version was the Fi 156A-1 utility and liaison machine. By mid-1937, the company had flown the ski-equipped V4, the military V5 and 10 Fi 156A-0 pre-production machines. One of the latter, D-IJFN, put on a dazzling show

at the Zürich meeting in July. The Storch repeatedly demonstrated full-load take-offs after a ground run of never more than 148 ft (45 m), and a fully-controllable speed range of 32-108 mph (51-174 km/h).

Deliveries begin

Deliveries to the rapidly growing Luftwaffe began in late 1937, one or two Fi 156C-1s being supplied to virtually every Gruppe in the Luftwaffe for general liaison duties. The Fi 156C-2 (armed with a 0.31-in/7.92-mm rear-firing gun) also had a vertical reconnaissance camera, and was crewed by a pilot and an

observer/gunner, either of whom could work the radio. Optional fits included skis and attachments for a stretcher.

Russian copy

By 1939, Fieseler was able to send a few Storchs to Finland and Switzerland. Presentation examples were given to the Italian Duce, Benito Mussolini, and after a non-aggression pact in summer 1939, to Stalin. The latter was so impressed that he instructed Oleg K. Antonov to produce a copy (no licence was sought). Antonov had no experience with steel-tube fuselages, neither did he have any As 10C engines, but he very quickly produced an excellent copy – the OKA-38 Aist (stork) – powered by the MV-6 engine derived from the 220-hp (164-kW) Renault six-cylinder inline. The OKA-38 was adopted for production as the ShS (*Shtabnyi samolyet*, staff aircraft), but the factory was overrun by German troops before deliveries began in summer 1941.

In North Africa the long-range Fi 156C-5, with provision for an underfuselage drop tank or camera installation, was employed. From late 1941, the Fi 156D-1 was produced alongside the Fi 156C – the new series having most of the right side hinged to facilitate rapid loading and unloading of stretchers. Yet another version, which appeared in 1941, was the Fi 156E. The new variant included tandem-wheel, tracked landing gears to reduce damage and write-offs caused by taxiing over ruts and small obstructions.

Fieseler was increasingly required to produce Bf 109 and Focke-Wulf Fw 190 fighters, but nevertheless managed to deliver 484 Storchs in 1942. An additional 121 came from a new Morane-Saulnier production line at Puteaux in France.

Production transfer

Subsequently, all Storch production was transferred from the overburdened Kassel works. Kassel delivered its last Fi 156 in October 1943. It sent the jigs and a few key workers to the Benes Mraz factory at Chocen – what the Nazis called the Bohemia-Moravia Protectorate (Czechoslovakia). All subsequent Storch deliveries were to come from Puteaux or Chocen, total Luftwaffe acceptances amounting to about 2,871.

Many hundreds of Storchs were built after the war in both France and Czechoslovakia. Chocen-built aircraft were known as the Mraz K.65 Cap after the war. Production ended soon after the Communist takeover in 1948. The Puteaux designations were Morane-Saulnier M.S.500, M.S.501 and M.S.502: the M.S.500 resembled the standard Fieseler Fi 156C series; the M.S.501 looked like the Soviet Antonov OKA-38 in having a Renault 6Q inverted inline engine; and the most important version, made in substantial numbers, was the M.S.502 Criquet with a Salmson 9Abc radial. The radial seemed to suit the 'Cricket' admirably, and it had a long career with the Armée de l'Air and the Aéronavale. Another important user was the Swedish air force, whose S14 versions from Germany were supplemented by post-war French examples. Several Storchs, from various sources, were put on the British civil register, and many examples, most of them built post-war, are still flying in several countries.

The badge on the cowling of this Storch identifies it as an aircraft belonging to the 1st Wüstennotstaffel in North Africa. Field Marshals Rommel and Kesselring both used Storchs early in the war, later preferring the faster Focke-Wulf Fw 189.

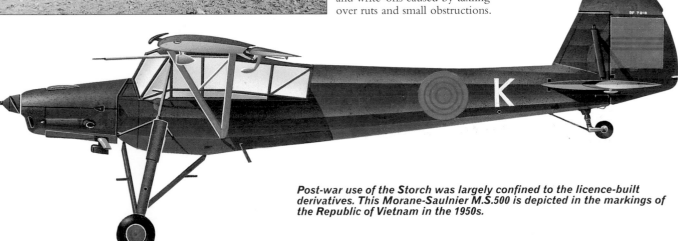

Post-war use of the Storch was largely confined to the licence-built derivatives. This Morane-Saulnier M.S.500 is depicted in the markings of the Republic of Vietnam in the 1950s.

Stork in combat

The Fi 156D-1 was the main air ambulance variant, equipped with two hatches in the starboard side to admit a stretcher case. Here, the patient is transferred to a Ju 52/3m somewhere in Tunisia in 1943.

From the start of World War II the Storch went, literally, everywhere the German army went. Despite audacious missions in full view of the enemy, it suffered amazingly few losses, its front-line life being (it was said) 10 times as long as that of the Bf 109 fighter.

From the outset, it was obvious that the Fi 156's outstanding STOL (short take-off and landing) qualities could be put to great military effect. Apart from the obvious roles of liaison and observation, the type was tested at an early stage for a variety of other tasks, including smoke-laying, coastal patrol (carrying a single depth charge) and for supply-dropping.

However, it was in its primary army-support role that it found fame. The immensely strong undercarriage and STOL qualities allowed the Storch to land just about anywhere; an attribute which endeared it to army commanders who used the Fi 156C-1 version just as they would have used a Jeep.

More importantly, the Storch became the eyes of the Wehrmacht, flying ahead of the troops to report on enemy positions. Artillery fire correction was another important role. Despite the adoption of the faster and better equipped Focke-Wulf Fw 189 for the short-range reconnaissance role, the armed Fi 156C was nevertheless used for this task throughout the conflict, its main attribute being its ability to operate from the very spot where the commander was situated. Reconnaissance Fi 156s served with the Nah-(Heeres-) Aufklärungsstaffeln (short-range army reconnaissance squadrons), and carried a single camera, either in the rear of the cabin or in a drum between the main undercarriage legs.

Air ambulance

Another wartime role of great importance was that of medical evacuation, for which the Fi 156D was developed. Retaining the single aft-firing gun, this variant had a large starboard hatch and revised glazing to allow the carriage of a litter. As well as evacuation of casualties from the front line back to field hospitals, Fi 156Ds made many daring rescues under fire – a role known today as CSAR (combat search and rescue). Medevac-configured Fi 156s were allocated primarily to the Wüstennotstaffeln, and first began to see service in this role during the battle for France in the summer of 1940.

Fi 156s starred in the North Africa campaign, especially the Fi 156C-5, which had a tropical dust filter and provision for a long-range tank, (the latter proving of great value in a theatre where the battle was fought at considerably greater distance than others). On the Russian front the Fi 156 was one of the few Luftwaffe aircraft which proved able to keep operational through the worst of the weather and most difficult ground conditions. So far as is known, the Storch did not fly night harassment missions with weapons on the Russian front – unlike thousands of Luftwaffe biplane trainers (many having the same As 10C engine) – but it

Perhaps the most famous of Storch 'users' was Erwin Rommel; he used the Storch throughout the North Africa campaign as his personal transport.

Below: A captured Storch is seen on a British beach while under test. Alongside is the equally ungainly but far less successful Stinson L-1 Vigilant. Many captured Fi 156s served with RAF units as hacks.

An Fi 156 drifts in to land on a farm track on the Russian front in 1942. To the Storch pilot this constituted no obstacle at all: they regularly operated from much shorter, much rougher strips. The aircraft is from the Kurierstaffel of the Luftwaffe headquarters.

the Führerbunker in a Storch, flying by night over the entire encircling Soviet armies and landing amid piles of rubble and under enemy fire. Hitler formally invested von Greim, who was then flown out again by the brilliant woman test pilot. She was the last person to escape from beleaguered Berlin, and the return trip should, on any rational basis, have been impossible.

During the war at least 47 Storchs, nearly all of them Fi 156C-3/Trop or C-5/Trop versions, were taken on charge by front-line RAF squadrons in the Mediterranean theatre. In the final few months of the war, more examples came into the hands of Allied units in north-western Europe.

By May 1945 further unde-stroyed examples had been captured in Germany, and a surprisingly high proportion escaped immediate destruction. The British MAP (Ministry of Aircraft Production) carried out a formal evaluation of VX154, which numerically confirmed its outstanding qualities. Among more than 60 Storchs taken formally on RAF charge was VM472, the personal aircraft of Field Marshal Montgomery, in preference to an Allied type.

nevertheless took part in many exciting actions.

Special missions

Certainly the most remarkable 'James Bond'-type mission of the entire war (which received little publicity because it was by the losing side) took place on 12 September 1943. Italy had reached an armistice with the Allies, and the former Fascist dictator, Mussolini, had been taken prisoner. Most of the country was at once taken over by the German army, and Hitler ordered SS Haupsturm-führer

Otto Skorzeny to find Mussolini and rescue him. Eventually Skorzeny located Mussolini; held in the hotel on top of the pinna-cle of the Gran Sasso in the Abruzzi mountains, accessible only by cable-car. He organised a rescue using a Focke-Achgelis Fa 223 Drache helicopter, but at the last moment this was unser-viceable. Undeterred, Skorzeny went in a Storch, landed on the tiny terrace at the back of the hotel, reached the former dicta-tor and, severely overloaded, took off over the sheer edge. Almost equal in excitement was

one of the very last missions ever flown by a Luftwaffe Storch. On 23 April 1945, Hitler received a communication from Reichsmarschall Hermann Göering, previously his closest aide, which made him furious. He immediately dismissed Göering as C-in-C of the Luftwaffe (Göering having escaped from Berlin to safer climes), and appointed instead Generaloberst Ritter von Greim. He sent a message from his bunker to Berlin-Gatow calling for von Greim, and Flugkapitän Hanna Reitsch brought him to

Powerplant
Early Storch aircraft were powered by an Argus As 10C eight-cylinder, air-cooled engine of inverted-Vee configuration, rated at 240 hp (179 kW). This was replaced in mid-Fi 156C-3 production by the improved As 10P.

Fi 156C-3 Storch

Ungainly, spindly, even gawky – such adjectives come to mind when viewing the Storch, yet the aircraft became the standard by which all other wartime army co-operation/observation types were measured. Beauty is in the eye of the beholder, and there can have been few more beautiful sights to a badly wounded Wehrmacht soldier than a Storch ambulance landing beside him.

Cockpit
The C-3 normally flew with a crew of two: pilot and an observer, the latter doubling as gunner. The glazing was bulged outward to give excellent downward visibility.

Propeller
The second prototype Fi 156 was tested with a variable-pitch metal propeller, but all other Storch aircraft had a wooden, fixed-pitch Schwarz propeller.

Low-speed surfaces
The low speed qualities of the Fi 156 were provided by full-span leading-edge slots and large slotted inboard flaps, allied to a high-lift aerofoil section. The ailerons were slotted and enlarged to ensure roll authority at speeds down to 32 mph (51 km/h).

Undercarriage
The Storch's STOL capability was enhanced by its strong undercarriage. The energy-absorbing oleos could easily withstand the high vertical sink-rate imposed by very steep approaches.

Defences
Against enemy fighters, the Storch's incredible low speed and agility rendered it one of the most difficult of aerial targets – if flown well. Nevertheless, it was given a single 7.9-mm MG 15, firing through the rear canopy to fend off any fighters which managed to get behind the aircraft.

Focke-Wulf
Fw 189 Uhu
Eagle Owl

Everything about the Fw 189 was slender, especially the wings and tail booms. Despite this, it was an immensely strong aircraft, able to take large amounts of battle damage. The latter was a vital asset in the low-level, over the battlefield environment in which the Uhu operated.

When the Luftwaffe issued a demand for an advanced armoured reconnaissance aircraft, Focke-Wulf produced the Fw 189, a radical design with twin engines and a clear nacelle, giving all-round visibility.

In the mid-1930s, aircraft technology was making rapid progress. The standard reconnaissance aircraft of the Luftwaffe was the He 46, a fabric-covered biplane, and its replacement, first flown in autumn 1936, was the Hs 126, a stressed-skin monoplane. But even the 126 could be seen to be an interim type. In February 1937 the air ministry issued a specification for a more advanced aircraft with a crew of three, all-round vision and high performance.

It was a challenge, and produced one conventional response, the Arado Ar 198, and one unconventional one, the Focke-Wulf Fw 189. Whereas the Arado was a single-engined mid-wing monoplane, notable only for having extensive glazing on the underside of the fuselage as well as on top, the Fw 189 had an almost completely glazed central nacelle, twin engines and twin tail booms.

The conservative officials favoured the Arado, considering both of the unconventional aircraft designs in some way inferior, if not actually faulty. Gradually they began to see the advantages of the notion of a completely glazed crew nacelle with, if necessary, an all-round field of fire for defensive guns. Moreover, Focke-Wulf's designers, led by Kurt Tank and (for the Fw 189) E. Kosel, pointed out that different kinds of nacelle could be fitted for various purposes.

The Arado, initially the favourite of the air ministry staff, never progressed far, but in this case it was because the prototype was a complete disappointment. In complete contrast, the

Fw 189 proved to be an excellent aircraft in all respects. The V1 (first prototype) was flown by Dipl Ing Tank in July 1938, and he was delighted with it. He called it Eule (Owl), although the Luftwaffe was to call the type the Uhu (Eagle Owl) and the official media dubbed it *das Fliegende Auge* (the Flying Eye).

Conventional structure

In fact, apart from the twin-boom configuration, which never caused any of the feared problems, the Fw 189 was quite conventional. The all-metal stressed-skin structure had a smooth flush-riveted exterior. The chosen engine – and nobody ever regretted it – was the Argus As 410A-1, an inverted-Vee with 12 air-cooled cylinders. Very smooth at 3,100 rpm, and easy to start even in a Russian winter, this engine proved very reliable, although the 189 could be flown perfectly well on one. A single fuel tank of 24-lmp gal (110-litre) capacity was in each tail boom just

Inset: The first V1 prototype took to the air in July 1938, with Kurt Tank himself at the controls. The aircraft, registered D-OPVN, differed little from the production aircraft which followed.

behind the landing-gear bay.

The central nacelle hardly changed from V1 to the last aircraft built (apart from two totally different versions described later). Basically a stressed-skin structure, almost the whole of it was covered with flat Plexiglas panels, with some roof panels and those in the pointed tailcone being curved. The pilot sat well forward on the left, with pedals projecting on beams ahead of the floor. On the right, slightly further back, was the seat for the navigator. He could face ahead and manage the floor-mounted camera(s), or take photos with a hand camera or the GV 219d optical bombsight. Alternatively, he could swivel his seat round and aim the dorsal gun(s). The third crew member; the flight mechanic, had little to do apart from keep an eye out for interception from the rear.

From the outset, the mainstream Fw 189 was to be the A-series, as described. The V1 differed from production

With a completely redesigned fuselage nacelle, the Fw 189B was intended as a five-seat trainer. Ten of the Fw 189B-1 production aircraft were delivered before Fw 109A production began.

Below: V6 was completed as the first true Fw 189C prototype; it was essentially similar to the V1b, but incorporated variable-pitch propellers and armament in the centre section of the wing. This comprised of two 20-mm MG FF cannon and four MG 17 machine-guns. A pair of MG 81s protected the rear.

Above: Supremely versatile and universally popular, the Uhu was essentially a low-altitude aircraft, befitting its tactical reconnaissance role. The ride was extremely smooth, while the extensive glazing gave good visibility although forward vision was impaired by refraction from the sloping panels.

machines only in such details as the propellers and in having single-leg main gears. The V2, flown only a month later in August 1938, was armed with two MG 17 machine-guns in the wingroots and three MG 15s. Four ETC 50/VIIId racks under the outer wings could carry 110-lb (50-kg) bombs or chemical containers. Via additional prototypes, the pre-production Fw 189A-0 was completely defined by the beginning of 1939 but, rather to Tank's chagrin, the Luftwaffe expressed the view that there was no need for such an aircraft and that the Hs 126A-1 and B-1 were perfectly adequate. All the company could do was press ahead with other versions but eventually, in spring 1940, permission was given to build 10 A-0s. At about the same time, the inadequacies of the Hs 126 were becoming obvious in the campaign in the west, and Focke-Wulf was told to carry on beyond the A-0s with production A-1s for front-line service. This was reinforced by the excellent service evaluation by the Aufklärungsstaffeln (H) and, quite suddenly, from being unwanted, the Uhu became a high-priority aircraft.

Focke-Wulf frantically tooled up to build the A-1 in series, but became increasingly overloaded, mainly because of the Fw 190 fighter. As a second source, the Aero factory at Prague Vysocany was swiftly tooled up, and in the course of 1941 the Czech plant

delivered 151 Fw 189s, compared with just 99 from the parent company at Bremen. It was obvious that the invasion of the Soviet Union, begun on 22 June 1941, was going to need all the Fw 189s that could be produced, so a major part of French industry was taken over by Focke-Wulf, and the Fw 189 production jigs were sent to France from Bremen. Breguet made outer wings at Bayonne, but most of the other parts were made by SNCASO, including the centre-section and nacelle at Bordeaux-Bacalan, booms and tail at Rochefort, and other parts at Bordeaux-Begles. Assembly and flight test was at Bordeaux-Mérignac.

In mid-1941 production switched to the Fw 189A-2, in which the single MG 15s were replaced by the neater and faster-firing MG 81Z twin installations. Small numbers were also made of the A-3 dual-control trainer, supplemented by a few A-0 and A-1 aircraft brought up to A-3 standard. Although a few A-0s reached the 9.(H)/LG 2 training unit in 1940, the *Fliegende Auge* was hardly seen in front-line units until 1942. Then it became truly important, progressively replacing the Hs 126 in Luftwaffe and related units, and also serving with units of the Slovakian and Hungarian air forces.

It proved to be a reliable, capable and tough aircraft, on at least two occasions surviving Soviet ramming attacks

and frequently fighting off hostile fighters. In late 1942 small numbers were delivered as A-4 close-support and reconnaissance aircraft, with extra armour and with the forward firing MG 17s replaced by 20-mm MG FFs. Out of the 864 aircraft produced in France, a few were built for the North African campaign with desert survival equipment and sand filters, and two A-1s modified for use as staff transports for Generalfeldmarschall Kesselring and General Jeschonnek. An additional 30 A-1s were modified as night-fighters, serving with I/NJG 100 and with NJG 5.

Fw 189C

In the winter of 1938-39, the original V1 prototype had been rebuilt with the planned armoured nacelle, becoming the V1b, flown in spring 1939. The pilot could hardly see out and, far from being able to aim his MG 15, the gunner had hardly any vision at all. In any case, the handling of the V1b was poor and performance unimpressive.

In early 1940, Focke-Wulf flew the rebuilt Fw 189 V6 as

the Fw 189C prototype, with the revised engines and landing gear of the 189A-0, an improved armoured nacelle offering better visibility to both crew, upgraded armament of two 20-mm MG FF cannon plus four MG 17s firing forwards, and a twin MG 81Z firing aft. In the event, although the Hs 129 was far from satisfactory, it was picked for production mainly because of its smaller size and lower cost.

Although the As 410 was an excellent engine, Focke-Wulf continued to investigate options with more power. The Fw 189E was to have been powered by the same French GR14M 4/5 radial of 700-hp (522-kW) as fitted to the production Hs 129B; SNCASO designed and carried out a single conversion, but this sole 189E crashed en route to evaluation in Germany in early 1943. Greater success attended the Fw 189F, an A-2 powered by 600-hp (447-kW) As 411MA-1 engines as used on the Si 204D. This caused no problems, and the final 17 aircraft made at Bordeaux in 1944 were Fw 189F-1s.

Slovakia and Hungary were supplied with the Fw 189, this being an Fw 189A-2 of the latter's Hungarian 3/1 Short-Range Reconnaissance Squadron (Ung.N.A.St). It was subordinated to Luftflotte 4 at Zamocz, eastern Poland, in March 1944.

Focke-Wulf Fw 190

Introduction

These Fw 190A-0s, seen on the Focke-Wulf test line in the summer of 1941, include a 'small-wing' aircraft (left) and two 'large-wing' machines. In the event it was the latter configuration that featured on production 190s.

When the Focke-Wulf Fw 190 first appeared in the skies over the northern coast of France in the summer of 1941, it was certainly the most advanced fighter in front-line service in the world. The *Würger* (or 'Butcher Bird'), as it was known, was, for a while at least, faster and more manoeuvrable than anything the Allies could put up against it.

Conceived in 1937, contemporaneously with the Hawker Typhoon, to replace the first generation of monoplane interceptors (in the Luftwaffe's case, the Messerschmitt Bf 109), the Fw 190 was tendered with two alternative engines, the Daimler-Benz DB 601 inline and the BMW 139 radial, the latter being selected to power the prototype on account of its assumed higher power potential. The first prototype was flown on 1 June 1939.

The Fw 190 was a small, low-wing monoplane with retractable undercarriage. Its seemingly bulky radial engine was faired into a slim fuselage and a clear-view cockpit canopy provided an excellent view for the pilot. The aircraft was all-metal, with a stressed duralumin skin and sat on a wide-track undercarriage, which provided much improved ground handling compared to that of the Bf 109.

After the BMW 139 was abandoned the Fw 190A entered production with the BMW 801 14-cylinder radial with fan-assisted cooling. The first nine pre-production Fw 190A-0s featured small wings of 161.46 sq ft (15.00 m²) area, but the definitive version had larger wings of 196.99 sq ft (18.30 m²) area.

Service trials at Rechlin went ahead in 1940 without undue problems, although pilots suggested that the proposed armament (four 0.31-in/7.92-mm MG 17 machine-guns) would be inadequate in combat. Production of 100 Fw 190A-1s was completed at Hamburg and Bremen by the end of May 1941, and these were powered by 1,600-hp (1194-kW) BMW 801C engines which bestowed a top speed of 388 mph (624 km/h). The following month the first combats were reported with RAF Supermarine Spitfire Mk Vs, showing the German fighters to be markedly superior, albeit lacking in firepower.

Cannon armament

However, the early criticisms had already led to the Fw 190A-2 version, with two wingroot-mounted synchronised 20-mm MG FF cannon and two MG 17 guns. With a speed of 382 mph (614 km/h), this up-gunned version still had the edge over the Spitfire Mk V.

As the RAF desperately sought to introduce an answer to the Fw 190, production of the German fighter was stepped up. Thus by the time the RAF was ready to introduce its new Spitfire Mk IX and Typhoon fighters to combat over the

Dieppe landings in August 1942, the Luftwaffe could field some 200 Fw 190As in opposition.

Unfortunately, not only had the RAF underestimated the number of Fw 190s available, the British were also unaware that a new version, the Fw 190A-4, had appeared with a top speed of 416 mph (670 km/h), and that a bomb-carrying variant, the Fw 190A-3/U1, was in service. A reconnaissance version of the Fw 190A-3 was first flown in

March 1942 on the Russian Front and Fw 190A-4/Trop ground-attack fighter-bombers appeared in North Africa during 1942. Before the end of that year Fw 190A-3/U1 and A-4/U8 fighter-bombers had embarked on a series of daylight low-level 'tip and run' attacks against cities and ports in southern England, forcing Fighter Command to deploy disproportionately large resources to counter the threat.

Further variants followed,

An immaculate line of Schlachtgeschwader I Fw 190F-2s pictured at Deblin-Irena in Poland waiting to move off to the front. Several of the aircraft wear the Mickey Mouse badge.

The Fw 190 soon took on a fighter-bomber role, initially in France and later in North Africa and on the Eastern Front. These Fw 190Fs of II Gruppe, Schlachtgeschwader 1 have bomb racks fitted.

including aircraft equipped with rocket-launchers for use against the growing bomber fleets operated by the USAAF. Other versions carried improved gun armament, extra fuel tanks and even torpedoes.

These were followed by a new fighter variant, the Fw 190A-6, in its standard form with reduced wing structure weight, armed with four fast-firing 20-mm guns inside the wings in addition to the two MG 17s in the nose. The arrival of the Spitfire Mk IX in Fighter Command and its threat to the air superiority of the Fw 190A led to the development of the Fw 190B series, with the GM-1 power-boosted BMW 801D-2 engine and pressure cabin, and the DB

603-powered Fw 190C, but development snags saw both types abandoned.

The Fw 190D, with 1,770-hp (1320-kW) Junkers Jumo 213A-1 inline engine and annular radiator in a much-lengthened nose proved very successful after it had first flown in May 1944. The first production Fw 190D-9s (widely known as 'Dora-9s' in the Luftwaffe) joined III/JG 54 in September 1944, Dora-9s equipping most Luftwaffe fighter units during the last months of the Third Reich, as the Luftwaffe struggled against overwhelming odds.

Fighter-bombers

Also introduced, in the spring of 1944, was the Fw 190F (*Panzer-Blitz*) armoured assault aircraft, while the Fw 190G fighter-bomber actually entered service long before the Fw 190F. The first of these aircraft were sent to North Africa following the Torch landings in November

Designated Ta 152 in honour of Focke-Wulf designer Kurt Tank, the Ta 152 (here in Ta 152H form) was destined for limited service in the closing stages of the war.

1942, though the majority served on the Eastern Front.

Mention must also be made of the Ta 152 (its designation finally reflecting Kurt Tank's design responsibility for the whole series). Various prototypes of this 'long-nose' derivative of the Fw 190D series were produced, but it was the Ta 152H-1 version with one 30-mm and two 20-mm guns and a maximum speed of

472 mph (760 km/h) at 41,010 ft (12500 m) that was selected for operational service; only a handful had been completed when the war ended.

Over 20,000 built

Fw 190 production assumed impressive proportions with no less than 20,087 (including 86 prototypes) being produced during the 1939-45 period and a peak daily production rate of 22 aircraft per day being reached early in 1944. Many Luftwaffe pilots achieved remarkable combat feats on the type. Pride of place must go to Oberleutnant Otto Kittel, the Luftwaffe's fourth highest scoring pilot, of whose 267 air victories some 220 were gained in Fw 190A-4s and Fw 190A-5s. Other very high scorers in Fw 190s included Walter Nowotny, Heinz Bär, Hermann Graf and Kurt Buhligen, all of whose scores included more than 100 victories gained with the guns of the aptly-named 'Butcher Bird'.

This aircraft (now part of the RAF Museum's collection at Hendon, London) is an example of the Fw 190F-8/U1 dual-control conversion trainer – one of a handful converted for the role.

Development aircraft

By early 1940 the Fw 190 V1 prototype had a conventional propeller and spinner and was coded *FO+LY*. The '01' on its tail was an abbreviated form of its Werk-Nummer (construction number) – 0001.

Fw 190 V1, V2 & V5

By careful design Kurt Tank hoped to achieve for his new fighter a combination of high performance, simplicity of operation, high structural integrity and ease of maintenance under combat conditions.

To achieve the performance he needed for his new fighter, Tank chose the most powerful German air-cooled radial then available. In contrast to British and other German high speed fighters of the period which used inline engines, Tank chose an air-cooled radial engine because these were far more rugged and less vulnerable to battle damage than their inline equivalents. He selected the 18-cylinder BMW 139 radial which developed 1,550 hp (1156 kW) during bench tests.

Apart from the use of the radial engine and an unusual ducted spinner arrangement the layout of Tank's new fighter was entirely conventional. It was a low-winged monoplane with the nose-mounted engine driving a tractor airscrew. At the time this was considered the optimum layout for a high performance fighter aircraft. The low wing provided a convenient housing for the retractable undercarriage, allowing the undercarriage legs to be kept short, and it did not restrict the pilot's vision in the upper hemisphere. From his own flying experience, Tank knew the importance of a good all-round view and he designed a frameless bubble canopy to fit over the cockpit. In later years

these clear-view canopies became fashionable for fighters, but in 1938 the idea was novel.

Handling

If the new fighter was to be successful it would have to handle well in the air. The key to achieving this was to make the control surfaces large enough to provide the necessary forces, and balance them with great care both statically and dynamically. Tank and his design team did a lot of work to achieve a crisp control response from the aircraft's elevators and ailerons. The rudder forces were less critical, because a pilot can exert a far greater force through the legs than through the arms. The flying controls in most aircraft at that time employed a system of wires, pulleys and bell cranks. With use the wires stretched and introduced 'play' into the system. Tank opted for a novel system using rigid rods instead of wires to connect the control stick to the control surfaces, so overcoming that problem.

In another far-sighted decision, Tank stressed the undercarriage and other areas to take greater loads than the aircraft's initial all-up weight warranted. He believed that once the aircraft entered service, the need to improve performance and mili-

The Fw 190 V1 takes shape in Focke-Wulf's experimental shop at Bremen during early 1939. Note the Fw 189 Uhu under assembly in the background.

tary effectiveness would inevitably lead to it putting on more weight. The structure had to be strong enough to accom-

modate these changes.

In the summer of 1938, the Luftwaffe Technical Office accepted Tank's proposals for the

Fw 190 V1's ducted spinner

To smooth the airflow around the radial engine and reduce cooling drag to a minimum, Kurt Tank designed a novel type of ducted spinner that would fit around the nose of the aircraft. However, the Fw 190 V1's BMW 139 engine was plagued by overheating troubles, even after a cooling fan was fitted. In an attempt to improve matters the aircraft's ducted spinner was replaced with a normal-type spinner. Although that failed to solve the problem of engine overheating, it was noted that the reduction in performance was negligible. The extra weight and complication of the ducted spinner was unjustified and it was abandoned. These drawings show the configuration of the Fw 190 V1 with the ducted spinner (top) and with a conventional spinner.

Engine problems – BMW 801 replaces 139

By April 1939 the Fw 190 V1, the first prototype, was in the final assembly stage and work on the V2 was well advanced. In the mean time, however, the BMW 139 had run into difficulties with overheating when running at full power. By then the company could offer a better engine, its new BMW 801 14-cylinder radial. This had the same diameter as the BMW 139, and in its developed form it was expected to offer an additional 150 hp (112 kW). The BMW 801 was somewhat heavier than the BMW 139, however, and to install it in the Fw 190 required a redesign of the forward fuselage and the restressing of the airframe. Officials at the Technical Office felt that the improvement in performance justified these changes and agreed to fund them, however.

Following that decision the Fw 190 development programme was revised. The V1 and V2 initial prototypes would be completed and flown with the BMW 139 engine as originally planned. The V3 and V4 prototypes, then in the early stages of construction, were cancelled. Work had yet to begin on the V5 prototype and this would have the revised airframe and it would be the first Fw 190 fitted with the BMW 801. In April 1940 the V5 (below), the first prototype with a BMW 801 engine, joined the Fw 190 test programme. With the additional weight of the new engine and the strengthened structure necessary to take it, the V5 weighed about 1,400 lb (635 kg) more than V1. Test pilot Hans Sander recalled:

"The eighteen cylinder BMW 801 was heavier than the BMW 139, which meant that a stronger mounting was necessary to support it. To compensate for this increased weight in the nose the fuselage had to be redesigned, with the cockpit moved back a little to keep the centre of gravity in the right place. This caused a deterioration in the pilot's field of vision forwards and downwards but it did confer one great bonus: since the engine and the cockpit were now further apart, at last one could fly in the new fighter without having one's feet gently roasted!"

With that extra weight the wing loading rose significantly and the Fw 190 V5 handled less well than the earlier prototypes. To restore the fighter's previous handling it was fitted with a new wing 20 per cent greater in area and with the span increased to 34 ft 5½ in (10.51 m). To maintain the correct dimensional relationship between the wing and tailplane, the span of the latter was increased too.

Fitted with new wing and tailplane surfaces, the V5 resumed test flying in the summer of 1940. With the extra engine power and the larger wing, Sander found that the fighter's rate of climb and its general handling were greatly improved. Officials at the Technical Office now asked that all Fw 190s not yet in an advanced stage of construction be fitted with the larger wing.

In these views of the prototype several features that did not find their way into the production Fw 190 are visible, including the ducted propeller and folding undercarriage doors.

Fw 190 V5, the fifth aircraft, was the first to be fitted with the BMW 801 engine, necessitating enlargement of its wing. Here it is seen in its earlier V5k form (for 'kleine Flügel', or small wing).

new fighter and ordered the construction of three prototypes. With that order the aircraft received its official designation: from now on it was known as the Focke-Wulf Fw 190.

In the workshops at Bremen the construction of the first two prototypes moved ahead rapidly. In the spring of 1939 the company received an order for an additional, fourth, prototype to speed development. Before the first prototype had flown the company received instructions to set up an assembly line to build 40 pre-production aircraft.

During May 1939 the Fw 190 V1 commenced its taxiing trials. By the end of the month these had been completed and the fighter was ready to fly. On 1 June test pilot Hans Sander took the prototype into the air for the first time. Throughout the flight he kept close to the airfield, and he took the new fighter in a spiral to about 6,500 ft (2000 m) to get the feel of the controls.

"I made a couple of high speed runs to see how she handled close to her maximum speed, then turns at different speeds and noted the stick forces that were necessary. Aerodynamically, she handled beautifully. The controls were light, positive and well balanced and throughout the initial flight I never once had to make use of the tailplane trim. I suppose most test pilots would have made at least a roll in the new aircraft, but I did no aerobatics during the maiden flight of the Fw 190; I was quite happy to leave such fancy flying until later in the test programme, when I knew a little more about her."

During that initial flight the BMW 139 engine demonstrated its propensity to overheat. It had been intended to fit a 10-bladed, engine-driven cooling fan on the front of the engine, but this was not ready in time and the V1 made its first flight without it. Soon after take-off, Sander became uncomfortably hot and began to sweat profusely – one disadvantage of the bubble canopy was that it could not be opened in flight to cool the cockpit, because that would have caused excessive turbulence to the airflow over the tail. Next, potentially lethal exhaust fumes started to seep into the cockpit.

Sander clamped on his mask and for the remainder of the flight he breathed pure oxygen.

Another, smaller, problem was that the undercarriage up-locks failed to engage properly. When Sander pulled *g* the main wheels sagged a little way below the wings and the red "undercarriage unlocked" lights illuminated in the cockpit. The problem with the undercarriage up-lock was soon cured and the application of additional sealant around the cockpit prevented the ingress of exhaust fumes.

Faster than the Bf 109

During speed trials conducted at the Luftwaffe test establishment at Rechlin the new fighter clocked a maximum speed of 369 mph (594 km/h) in level flight. Service test pilots praised its handling characteristics, which were significantly better than those of the Bf 109.

In October 1939 the V2 made its first flight. This aircraft was the first to carry armament, a Rheinmetall Borsig MG 17 0.31-in (7.9-mm) machine gun in each wing root. The V2 joined the V1 in the test programme, and Hans Sander and his colleagues systematically explored the aircraft's flight envelope. During the autumn of 1940, the first aircraft in the pre-production batch of 40 Fw 190A-0s started to emerge from the factory at Bremen. The first seven pre-production aircraft had the smaller wing and tailplane, the eighth and subsequent aircraft employed the enlarged surfaces. By now, the Focke-Wulf factory at Marienburg, the Arado factory at Warnemunde and the AGO factory at Oschersleben were tooling up to build the new fighter in quantity.

In mid-1942 C-in-C RAF Fighter Command, Air Chief Marshal Sir Sholto Douglas, wrote a strongly worded letter to the Under Secretary of State for Air, Lord Sherwood. Douglas complained that his force had lost the technical edge it had once had over the Luftwaffe and went on to say: "There is....no doubt in my mind, nor in the minds of my fighter pilots, that the Fw 190 is the best all-round fighter in the world today." These views show early examples of during testing, including small- and big-wing Fw 190A-0s at Rechlin during the summer of 1941 (left), the first of the large-wing aircraft (Werk-Nummer 0015, above to right of picture) with other early Fw 190As and the 18th and last Fw 190A-0 (below).

Into service, 1941/42

In March 1941 Oberleutnant Otto Behrens assumed command of Erprobungsstaffel 190 based at Rechlin-Roggenthin. The unit received six pre-production Fw 190A-0s and its brief was to test the new fighter under service conditions.

The pilots and ground crews assigned to the Erprobungsstaffel were drawn from II. Gruppe of Jadgeschwader 26, and the latter unit was earmarked to receive the first production Fw 190s when these became available.

During early service trials the Fw 190A-0 exhibited a number of serious shortcomings. The new BMW 801C engine suffered from overheating, though not to the same extent as the BMW 139. The engine's automatic fuel control system also gave trouble. For a given throttle setting, this automatic system should have established the optimum relationship between aircraft altitude, fuel flow, fuel mixture, engine revolutions, supercharger gear selection, propeller pitch setting and ignition timing. The system did not work reliably at first, but a string of modifications over a long period reduced the problems to an acceptable level.

In June 1941 the first four production Fw 190A-1s emerged from the Marienburg factory and by August, monthly production had reached 30 aircraft. The first two aircraft off the Arado/Warnemunde production line were delivered in August, and the first two from the AGO/Oschersleben plant followed in October.

By the end of September 1941 the Luftwaffe had accepted a total of 82 Fw 190A-1s. One Gruppe, II./JG 26 based at Moorseele in Belgium, had re-equipped with the new fighter and deliveries had started to III./JG 26 based at Liegescourt in northern France.

Besting the Spitfire Mk V

Even after it began flying combat missions the Fw 190 continued to suffer from engine overheating. Sometimes this led to fires in flight and, following losses to this cause, an edict was issued forbidding pilots to fly over the sea beyond gliding range from the coast. Despite that difficulty the Fw 190 proved a formidable adversary. In the months that followed, the RAF learned to its discomfort that the new German fighter had the edge in performance over its best fighter then in service, the Spitfire Mk V.

During the autumn of 1941 the Fw 190A-2 replaced the A-1 on the production lines. Powered by the improved BMW 801C-2 engine, this version was fitted with two Mauser MG 151 20-mm cannon in place of the MG 17 machine-guns in each wing root. Yet even with the new armament the Fw 190 was considered inadequately armed to attack enemy

bombers. As a result several A-1s and A-2s were retrofitted with two additional Oerlikon MG/FF 20-mm cannon in the wings, firing outside the propeller disc.

By the end of the 1941 more than 200 Fw 190s had been delivered to the Luftwaffe. Early in 1942 the A-3 replaced the A-2 in production, powered by the BMW 801D-2 engine giving 1,700 hp (1268-kW) at take off. The fighter's armament was stan-

dardised at the four cannon and two machine-guns as carried by the retrofitted A-1s and A-2s. Soon after the A-3 entered production, the FuG 7 HF radio was replaced with the more effective FuG 16 VHF set.

By the late spring of 1942 JG 2 and JG 26 had re-equipped with the Fw 190. Between them these units mustered about 260 of these formidable fighters. The engine troubles that had plagued

This Fw 190A-0 was employed as a test airframe for the Fw 190A-3/U3 fighter-bomber variant, the U3 factory modification providing an ETC 250 bomb rack for an SC 250 bomb.

Below: Fw 190 V8 (alias the first large-wing Fw 190A-0) was test flown with racks for SC 50 50-kg (110-lb) bombs. Where these were fitted to Fw 190A-3/U3s the wing-mounted MG/FF cannon were retained.

Near the end of June 1942 a German pilot became disorientated during a combat with Spitfires over western England and mistakenly landed this Fw 190A-3 at Pembrey in south Wales. So the RAF secured an intact example of this important fighter. At the time of the capture, however, this version of the Fw 190 had been superseded in production by the A-4. The latter's BMW 801D-2 engine carried the MW-50 water-methanol injection system which boosted power for short periods at low and medium altitudes.

the Fw 190 earlier had largely been cured. With the embargo on overwater flights lifted, German pilots were able to exploit the fighter's capabilities to the full and engage the enemy with greater confidence.

The Fw 190 pilots' more aggressive mood manifested itself on 1 June 1942, when the RAF mounted operation Circus No. 178. Eight bomb-carrying Hurricanes attacked a target near Bruges in Belgium. Seven squadrons of Spitfire Mk Vs from the Hornchurch and Biggin Hill Wings provided close escort while four squadrons from the Debden Wing provided target support. Positioned by radar some 40

Fw 190s of I. and III./JG 26 attacked the raiding force from out of the sun during its withdrawal. The Debden Wing took the force of the attack and lost eight Spitfires in rapid succession, including that flown by its commander. Five Spitfires limped home with battle damage. No Focke-Wulf suffered serious damage during the encounter.

During this period there were experiments using Fw 190s in the fighter-bomber role, to mount tip-and-run attacks on targets along the south coast of England. The two Jagd-geschwader in the west each operated a Staffel with specially modified Fw 190A-3s and A-4s. These aircraft had the MG/FF cannon removed from the outer wing positions, and had a rack to carry an SC 250 250-kg (550-lb) or SC 500 500-kg (1,100-lb)

bomb under the fuselage.

During the spring of 1943 the Fw 190A-5 entered production. This had the engine mounting lengthened by 15 cm (just under 6 in) to give improved handling. A few months later this version was superseded by the A-6, with heavier armour and fast-firing MG 151 20-mm weapons in place of the MG/FF cannon in the outer wing positions. Towards the end of the year the Fw 190A-7 entered production, with a pair of 0.5-in (12.7-mm) Rheinmetall MG 131 heavy machine guns replacing the weapons mounted above the engine. The Fw 190A-8, produced in greater numbers than any other version, had several detail improvements over the A-7 and was designed to accept a larger range of field modifications than its predecessors.

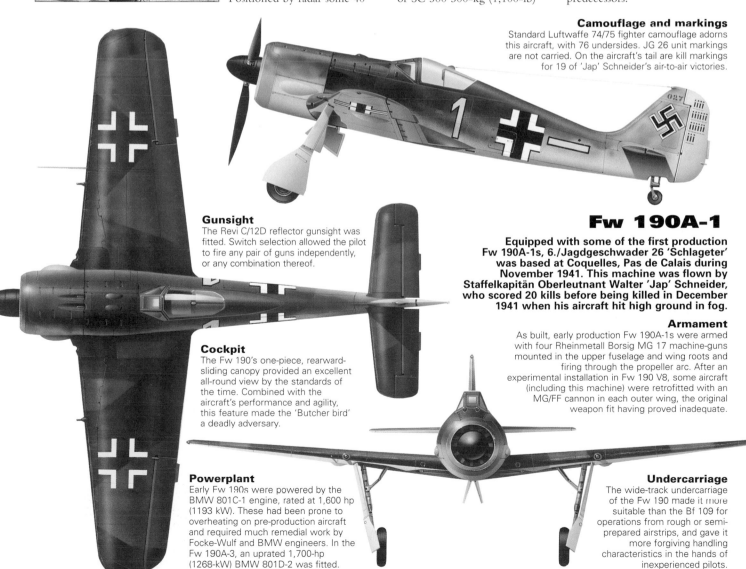

Camouflage and markings
Standard Luftwaffe 74/75 fighter camouflage adorns this aircraft, with 76 undersides. JG 26 unit markings are not carried. On the aircraft's tail are kill markings for 19 of 'Jap' Schneider's air-to-air victories.

Gunsight
The Revi C/12D reflector gunsight was fitted. Switch selection allowed the pilot to fire any pair of guns independently, or any combination thereof.

Fw 190A-1

Equipped with some of the first production Fw 190A-1s, 6./Jagdgeschwader 26 'Schlageter' was based at Coquelles, Pas de Calais during November 1941. This machine was flown by Staffelkapitän Oberleutnant Walter 'Jap' Schneider, who scored 20 kills before being killed in December 1941 when his aircraft hit high ground in fog.

Armament
As built, early production Fw 190A-1s were armed with four Rheinmetall Borsig MG 17 machine-guns mounted in the upper fuselage and wing roots and firing through the propeller arc. After an experimental installation in Fw 190 V8, some aircraft (including this machine) were retrofitted with an MG/FF cannon in each outer wing, the original weapon fit having proved inadequate.

Cockpit
The Fw 190's one-piece, rearward-sliding canopy provided an excellent all-round view by the standards of the time. Combined with the aircraft's performance and agility, this feature made the 'Butcher bird' a deadly adversary.

Powerplant
Early Fw 190s were powered by the BMW 801C-1 engine, rated at 1,600 hp (1193 kW). These had been prone to overheating on pre-production aircraft and required much remedial work by Focke-Wulf and BMW engineers. In the Fw 190A-3, an uprated 1,700-hp (1268-kW) BMW 801D-2 was fitted.

Undercarriage
The wide-track undercarriage of the Fw 190 made it more suitable than the Bf 109 for operations from rough or semi-prepared airstrips, and gave it more forgiving handling characteristics in the hands of inexperienced pilots.

Left: This Staffel of Fw 190Fs, probably belonging to Schnellkampfgeschwader 10, was photographed at the airfield at Deplin-Irena near Warsaw. Ground-attack units rotated through the airfield to conduct training missions with live ordnance on the nearby bombing range prior to being deployed to the front.

Below: This illustration provides a close-up view of the Fw 190's fuselage bomb rack, loaded with an SC 250 general purpose bomb, and of the barrel of the starboard wing root cannon.

Fw 190F & G

Designed as a replacement for the increasingly vulnerable Ju 87, the Schlact Fw 190s proved to be among the most capable attack aircraft of World War II, being heavily armed and armoured, and proved more than able to mix with the best Allied fighters in air-to-air combat.

From the summer of 1942 the overstretched Luftwaffe could no longer secure air superiority over the main battle fronts. The Junkers Ju 87 dive-bombers, the mainstay of the ground attack force, now suffered serious losses if they were caught by enemy fighters.

The initial answer was to re-equip some units with fighter variants of the Fw 190 – A-4s or A-5s – fitted with a bomb rack under the fuselage to carry a weapon load of up to 1,100 lb (500 kg). The improvisation worked well at first, but on the Eastern Front the increasingly ferocious ground fire caused serious cumulative losses to ground attack units. On Fw 190 fighter versions armour was positioned to protect the pilot from rounds coming from almost exactly ahead or almost exactly behind. During ground attack operations return fire might come from any direction in the lower hemisphere, however. Thus the Luftwaffe issued a requirement

for a specialised ground attack variant of the Fw 190 with armour tailored for this role.

The result was the Fw 190F fitted with curved plates of steel armour 5 mm thick along either side of the cockpit, and along the underside of the fuselage from the front of the engine cowling to behind the cockpit. To compensate for the additional weight, the two outer wing 20-mm cannon were removed. The first Fw 190Fs were delivered near the end of 1942.

The Fw 190G, developed in parallel, was an extended range fighter-bomber variant with fittings to carry a drop tank under each wing. To compensate for that additional weight, the G variant had the machine-guns removed from the fuselage leaving it with just two 20-mm cannon in the wing roots.

Into combat

The F and G versions were well received by those who conducted their operational eval-

uations. Pilots appreciated the much improved armour protection which enabled the aircraft to survive hits from small calibre weapons. At the same time, these fighter-bombers retained the performance to look after themselves if engaged by enemy fighters. Both versions were ordered into mass production.

By May 1944 the Luftwaffe had a total of 881 Fw 190s serving with combat units of which 387, nearly half, were F and G variants assigned to ground attack or fighter-bomber units.

Typical of the ground attack

units serving on the Eastern Front in the summer of 1944 was III. Gruppe of Schlachtgeschwader 3. Based at Idriza in western Russia with the F version, it was heavily embroiled when the Red Army launched its major offensive in August. One of the pilots, Leutnant Werner Gail recalled: "Our task was to do all we could to delay the thrusts, to give the German ground forces time to improvise defensive positions to stop the rush. Wherever there was a hole in the front, it was our job to try to plug it."

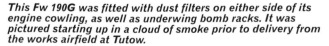

This Fw 190G was fitted with dust filters on either side of its engine cowling, as well as underwing bomb racks. It was pictured starting up in a cloud of smoke prior to delivery from the works airfield at Tutow.

Armour plating

Armour plating and laminated glass was fitted to the F and G ground attack variants of the Fw 190, in addition to that carried by the fighter versions, combined to protect the pilot against rounds fired from anywhere in the lower hemisphere.

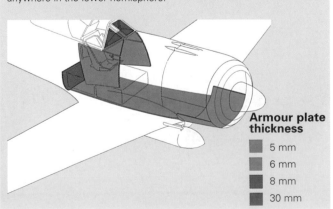

Armour plate thickness

- ▮ 5 mm
- ▮ 6 mm
- ▮ 8 mm
- ▮ 30 mm

These Fw 190F fighter-bombers belonged to Schlachtgeschwader 2, and were operating from the airfield at Sopoc/Puszta in Hungary in January 1945.

"Our Focke-Wulfs were armed with two 13-mm machine-guns and two 20-mm cannon, which we used for strafing attacks. The bombs we used during these operations were mainly the SC 250 and SC 500 and also SD 2, SD 4 and SD 10 bomblets carried in large numbers in containers.

"When we found enemy units moving forwards unopposed, as a matter of policy we concentrated our attacks on the soft-skinned supply vehicles; these were relatively easy to

knock out with machine-gun and cannon fire and we knew that without frequent replenishments of fuel the tanks spearheading the advance would not get far. If the enemy armoured units were actually in contact with our ground forces, however, then the tanks themselves were our main target."

Against tanks or armoured vehicles the usual tactic was to run in at speeds of around 300 mph (483 km/h), about 30 ft (9 m) above the ground, and release the bomb as the vehicle

disappeared from view beneath the engine cowling. Dropped in this way, an SC 250 would either smash straight into the tank or ricochet off the ground and then hit the tank. The bombs were fused to detonate one second after impact to give the aircraft time to get clear of the blast and fragments. After releasing their bombs the Fw 190Fs used their cannon and machine-guns to strafe soft-skinned vehicles or troops in the area.

During the Red Army offensive the pace of operations

by the Gruppe was very high, with pilots sometimes flying as many as eight sorties per day. On average these sorties lasted about half an hour. If the aircraft caught advancing Russian units that had outrun their flak cover, they could inflict a great deal of damage.

However, if the Russians had proper flak cover the Gruppe might take serious losses. At the beginning of April 1945, less than a month before the war ended in Europe, the Luftwaffe had 1,612 Fw 190s on strength. Of these 809, just over half were F and G ground attack versions.

The Fw 190F and G variants were arguably the most effective ground attack aircraft fielded by any nation during World War II. Yet although the units equipped with these machines could mount a powerful punch, like the rest of the Luftwaffe, they were overwhelmed by the strength of opposing forces.

Weapon trials
Weapons trialled on the F-8 included the SG 113A Förstersonde installation of two downward-firing 77-mm recoiless anti-tank guns in each wing.

External stores
A single SC 250 bomb on a centreline ETC 250 bomb rack, along with four SC 50 (50-kg; 110-lb) bombs on ETC 50 racks under the wings was a fairly standard bomb load for the Fw 190F. Alternatively, an ER 4 adaptor could be added to the fuselage rack, allowing, as here, the carriage of four SC 50s in this position.

Fw 190F-8

This machine was on the strength of 1./Schlachtgeschwader 2 'Immelmann', based at Varpalotta, Hungary during the summer of 1942. At this time the Schlacht units of Luftflotte 4 were engaged in ferocious combat with Russian forces as the Germans retreated through Romania and Hungary, while USAAF P-51s, on long-range missions out of bases in Italy, were also just beginning to enter the fray.

Canopy and fuselage bulges
Based on feedback from Schlacht pilots in combat, the F-8 was fitted with a bulged canopy for increased visibility. Being based on the Fw 190A-8 and retaining that variant's 0.51-in (13-mm) fuselage guns, the F-8 had the two bulges associated with these weapons ahead of its armoured windscreen.

Sub-munitions
Another common store was the AB 250 cluster bomb. This could deploy up to 144 SD 2 'butterfly bombs', or 30 of the larger SD 4 and 17 of the larger still SD 10 sub-munitions.

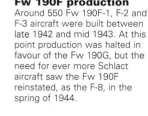

Fw 190F production
Around 550 Fw 190F-1, F-2 and F-3 aircraft were built between late 1942 and mid 1943. At this point production was halted in favour of the Fw 190G, but the need for ever more Schlacht aircraft saw the Fw 190F reinstated, as the F-8, in the spring of 1944.

Fw 190C, D & Ta 152

In 1942 Kurt Tank, test pilot and designer, set about rectifying the Fw 190's loss of performance at altitude. The end product was the impressive Ta 152H, but a more immediate result was the Fw 190D, one of the best Luftwaffe fighters.

While the Fw 190 was the best fighter in the world at around 15,000 to 20,000 feet (4572 to 6096 m), at higher altitudes its performance fell away rapidly. The arrival of the Spitfire IX in Fighter Command and its threat to overturn the Fw 190's combat dominance led to the development of the Fw 190B series with the GM-1 power-boosted BMW 801D-2 engine and pressure cabin. Trouble with the latter however, led to the abandonment of this version in 1943 after four Fw 190B-0 prototypes had been produced.

Above: The prototype Fw 190D-0 'DU+UC' (werk nr. 170003) was a conversion of an Fw 190A-7, incorporating the rear fuselage stretch but retaining the original fin and guns.

Left: Always regarded, by Kurt Tank, as a stop-gap until the fully developed Ta 152 was available, the Fw 190D proved to be one of the best Luftwaffe fighters of the war.

Fw 190C

The second of the high altitude projects was the Fw 190C series, of which five prototypes were completed with DB 603 inline engines, annular radiators, Hirth 9-2281 superchargers and four-bladed propellers. Technical problems and political opposition to the use of the DB 603 led to the demise of the Fw 190C early in 1944. However, the C led to the development of the Fw 190Ra-4D (Ta 153), which was later abandoned, and the Fw 190Ra-2/3 (Ta 152).

The Fw 190D 'Dora'

The third avenue of development for the Fw 190 was the Fw 190D, with a 1,770-hp (1320-kW) Junkers Jumo 213A-1 engine (originally developed for bombers) and an annular radiator in a much-lengthened nose (necessitating increased fin and rudder area). Destined to be a medium level fighter, the D was originally planned to have a pressurised cockpit. In the winter of 1943-44 a number of Fw 190A-7s was converted into D-0s, retaining the original armament of four MG 151 cannon in the wings and two MG 17 machine-guns in the fuselage. The difference between these and the D-9s (so designated because they followed the Fw 190A-8s in production was a broader fin, the MW-50 injection system for boosting the engine and a change of armament. The Fw 190D-9 took to the air at Langenhagen in May 1944, and was cleared for production in about mid-June

1944. The first production Fw 190D-9s joined III/JG 54 in September 1944, to defend the jet base of Kommando Nowotny. The next Gruppe with the Fw 190D-9 was Major Karl Borris's I/JG 26. The aircraft soon became known as 'Dora-9s' in service.

Fw 190D sub-variants

Other versions of the Fw 190D were built, but none saw action. Among them was the Fw 190D-10 with a single 30-mm MK 108 cannon located between the engine cylinder banks and firing through the propeller hub. The Fw 190D-12/R21, a ground-attack version of the hub-gunned Fw 190D-10, with MW50 water-methanol injection, was

almost certainly the fastest of all Fw 190s with a top speed of 453 mph (730 km/h) at 36,090 ft (11000 m). The D-11 featured the Jumo 213E engine and a pair of MK 108 cannon in the outer wings; the D-13 replaced the hub-mounted Mk 108 of the D-10 and 12 with an MG 151 machine-gun; the Fw 190D-14 was a new build fighter with the DB 603 engine; and the D-15 was a conversion of the Fw 190A-8 to use the same engine.

Overwhelming odds

'Dora-9s' equipped most of the Luftwaffe's fighter units during the last fateful months of the Third Reich, but in combat with Allied types, particularly P-51s and Spitfire XIVs, were frequently overwhelmed. The Luftwaffe's problems centred on a shortage of fuel, which allowed only small formations of fighters to get airborne. For instance, when JG 6 (commanded by Major Gerhard Barkhorn, an ace with 301 kills) took delivery of 150 brand-new Dora-9s in April 1945, it could only fly patrols of four aircraft at a time, against the

Long-span wings gave the final variant of the Fw 190/Ta 152 family, the Ta 152H, a superb high-altitude performance. Fortunately for the Allies, only a few made it into action.

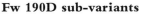

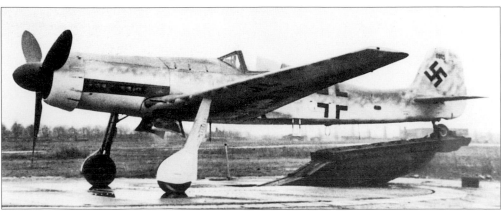

The Fw 190 V18 was one of the C-series prototypes, featuring a Daimler Benz DB 603 turning a four-bladed propeller, and a massive supercharger in a ventral fairing.

massed wings of Allied fighters. However, such was the performance of the D-9, that captured examples were pressed into use by the Russians.

The ultimate 'Fw 190'

The Ta 152 ('Ta' reflecting Kurt Tank's overall design responsibility) was developed from the Fw 190C and the abandoned Ta 153 proposal. It was a 'long-nose' derivative of the Fw 190D series, retaining the hub-firing 30-mm gun but introducing improved electrical systems.

Originally two versions were to be developed simultaneously, the Ta 152H high-altitude fighter powered by the Jumo 213E-1, and the Ta 152B with the Jumo 213C. Prototypes of the Ta 152H were tested from late June 1944, and the first 20 pre-production Ta 152H-0s were constructed during October/November 1944. With a wing span extended to 47 ft 4½ in, they could reach 472 mph (760 km/h) at 41,000 ft (12500m). The Ta 152H-1 with one 30-mm and two 20-mm guns was selected for operational serv-

ice, but only about a dozen aircraft of this type had been completed and delivered to JG 301 by the time the war had ended.

The Ta 152B fell by the wayside, but with the Jumo 213C replaced by the DB 603 as the Ta 153C-0 short span fighter, it entered production as the C-1, the C-2 (with improved radio equipment) and the C-3, which featured revised armament. A two-seat conversion trainer, the Ta 152S-1, and a reconnaissance offshoot, the

Ta 152E were projected but never built. Only 26 prototypes and 67 pre-production and production Ta 152s were completed by the war's end.

Survivors

Post-war interest in the Fw 190D/Ta 152 saw several examples shipped to the UK and USA. In the US three Fw 190Ds survive – an Fw 190D-13 at the Champlin Fighter Museum, an Fw 190D-9 at the USAF Museum and a stored Ta 152H-1 with the National Aerospace Museum. The Luftwaffen Museum in Germany has a D-9 for restoration, which was recovered from Lake Schwerin in 1993. Other examples may survive in Russia.

Fw 190Ds captured by the Soviet forces were put to good use. Acquired in East Prussia, these examples fought with at least one regiment of the Baltic Fleet air force in the summer of 1945.

Powerplant
The installation of the Jumo 213A-1 12-cylinder inverted Vee piston engine necessitated an increase in forward fuselage length. The new section was surrounded by a ring of armour with a thickness of 0.43 in (11 mm).

Armament
Basic armament was two MG 151 cannon in the wing roots with 250 rounds per gun. Other cannon could be fitted in the wings. A centreline bomb rack could take one 1,102-lb (500-kg) bomb.

Fw 190D-9

Belonging to the Geschwaderstab (wing staff) of Jagdgeschwader 2 'Richthofen' based at Merzhausen in December 1944, this Fw 190D-9 was tasked with home defence, in particular the interception and destruction of American daylight bombers.

Performance
At normal weight, the D-9 had a maximum speed of 426 mph (686 km/h) at medium altitude, dropping to 357 mph (575 km/h) at sea level. Its speed and diving abilities made it a formidable opponent.

Markings
The chevron and two bars signified a 'Major beim Stab', a major on the wing staff. The yellow-white-yellow bands were applied to JG 2 aircraft as this was one of the units tasked with the 'Defence of the Reich'.

In combat
Without the intended cockpit pressurisation system, the D-9 operated primarily at lower altitudes. German combat pilots found the aircraft to be superior to the Fw 190A in speed and climb performance, although it had an inferior rate of roll.

Weapons

The Fw 190 was one of the most versatile single-engined aircraft of World War II. Together with the Ta 152, numerous different variants were produced to enable the aircraft to perform in a huge variety of air-to-air and air-to-ground roles.

Above: **Jagdbomber mit vergrösserter Reichweite (Jabo-Rei)** *was the official designation for the extended range Fw 190 fighter-bomber. This Fw 190G-3 carries a single 500-kg (1,102-lb) SC500 bomb and a pair of 300 litre (66 Imp gal) fuel tanks. Fixed armament was reduced to just two* **MG 151** *cannon.*

The Fw 190A-4/R6 **Pulk-Zestörer** *carried a pair of WfrGr 21 mortars under the wing. The shells were designed to break up Allied bomber streams so that waves of conventionally-armed following interceptors could attack the individual bombers.*

The Fw 190 was generally smaller than contemporary British and American fighters. Despite this modest size, it was remarkably heavy, and yet was to prove capable of carrying a diversity of weapons and other equipment, including full-size naval torpedoes and the 1800-kg (3,968-lb) SC1800 bomb. The reason for this capability was a combination of sheer structural strength, large ground clearance, strong wide-track landing gear and brute engine power; but designer Kurt Tank continued to express astonishment at the Fw 190's ability to carry anything and fly almost any mission.

This versatility was expected to be achieved by building special versions, such as the Fw 190E for photo-reconnaissance. In the event it was achieved much more effectively by mass-producing a series of basically similar aircraft, plus *Umrüst-Bausätze* (factory conversion sets) and *Rüstsätzen*

(field conversion sets). In general, most of these conversion kits could be attached to any Fw 190 subtype, though there were many exceptions and some special weapon fits had to be built in a factory or major maintenance unit. The Fw 190 was probably adapted to carry more types of armament than any other aircraft in history.

Fighter-bomber

Typical of early *Umrüst* installations were the Fw 190A-3/U1 with the mainwheel-bay doors removed and a fuselage rack added to carry a bomb of 250 kg or 500 kg (551 lb or 1,102 lb), or four 50-kg (110-lb) bombs; the A-3/U3 with a 250-kg fuselage rack and wing racks for four 50-kg bombs; and the A-3/U4 with two Rb 12.5/7x9 reconnaissance cameras in the rear fuselage. Some of these loads were accompanied by removal of the MG FF cannon.

In spring 1942 production switched to the A-4 variant. Among various A-4 fits was the A-4/U8 *Jabo-Rei* (long-range fighter-bomber) which could carry various combinations of bombs and tanks including a 300-litre (66 Imp gal) drop tank and two 250-kg bombs. The A4/R6 was fitted with a WfrGr 21 tube at a nose-up angle under each wing from which could be launched 210-mm (8.27-in) rocket 'mortar shells' intended to break up bomber formations. On 14 October 1943 waves of R6-equipped Fw 190s inflicted over 50 per cent casualties to B-17s over Schweinfurt.

In April 1943 the A-5 went into action. It was designed from the outset to be compatible with the full range of *Umrüst*, namely: U1/3/4/8 as described; the U2 night *Jabo* with anti-glare shields, flame dampers, and racks for 250-kg bombs and two tanks; the U9 with two MG 131 fuselage

guns, two MG 151 in wing roots and two MG 151s under the outer wings; the U11 with two 30-mm MK 103/108s replacing the MG FFs; the U12 with MG FFs replaced by the R1 pack under the wing, each with two MG 151 weapons; the U13 with 500-kg fuselage bomb rack and wing mounts for faired-in drop tanks; the U14 with a rack for the LTF 5b torpedo, bigger fin and longer tail-wheel leg; the U15 which was similar to the U14 but for LT 950 guided torpedo provision; and the U17 with wing racks for four 50-kg bombs.

Bomber destroyer

While production kept increasing dramatically - 1,878 in 1942, 3,208 in 1943 and 11,411 in 1944 - development of the basic A-series continued, and was joined by minor variations (notably the F and G). The A-6 was regarded as a peg on which to hang the U and R kits, and the MG FF

The Fw 190A-5/U12 deployed six MG 151/20 E cannon. The additional weapons were mounted under the wing in two WB 151/20 pods with two guns in each pod. Two aircraft were built.

Above: Fw 190A-5/U14 was adapted to carry an LTF 5b torpedo mounted on the under-fuselage ETC 502 rack. The type had an enlarged fin and heightened tail wheel strut to eliminate the possibility of ground contact by the torpedo.

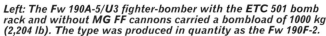

Left: The Fw 190A-5/U3 fighter-bomber with the ETC 501 bomb rack and without MG FF cannons carried a bombload of 1000 kg (2,204 lb). The type was produced in quantity as the Fw 190F-2.

Below: The Fw 190A-5/U11 ground-attack aircraft deployed two 30-mm Rheinmetall-Borsig MK 103 cannon mounted in streamlined underwing pods. This particular armament conversion was standardised as the Rüstsätz 3 (R3).

cannon was deleted. Only about 80 examples of the A-7 were built, which replaced the MG 17s with 13-mm MG 131s, causing a shallow bulge ahead of the windscreen.

By contrast the A-8, an A-7 plus the MW50 boost system, was made in larger numbers than any other version (about 8,000). It was able to carry every type of U and R kit, and three were modified into A-8/U1 tandem two-seaters with dual controls to speed the conversion of Ju 87 pilots to the Fw 190. In addition a handful of S-5 and S-8 two seaters was converted from the A-5 and A-8. A-8s were used to test *Doppelreiter* long-range tanks

above the wings; the SG 116 installation comprising a row of three 30-mm guns set to fire almost vertically at bombers; the SG 117 with seven 30-mm barrels; and the X-4 wire-guided anti-bomber missile.

Jabo-Rei

From late 1942 production concentrated on the Fw 190F. This was a sub-family intended for close-support, and it swiftly became the replacement for the Ju 87 in *Schlachtflieger* units. Originally it was an A-4 with provision for heavy and varied bombloads, extra armour and stronger landing gear, and with the MG FFs deleted. In

mid 1943, when some 550 F models had been delivered, production switched to the G-series *Jabo-Rei* (long-range fighter-bomber). The most numerous F variant was the F-8, with 13-mm fuselage guns. Examples were used for the testing of over 40 experimental weapons including the SG 113 (pairs of 77-mm recoilless barrels firing upwards from each wing); BV 246 stand-off glide bomb and BT 400, 700 and 1400 (the numbers denoting the weight in kg) '*Bomben-Torpedo*' weapons for use against ships and concrete bunkers.

The Fw 190G family retained only the inboard MG 151 guns, but had the Fw 190F's armour and landing gear plus a PKS 11 autopilot. Most had a power boosting system for low-level operations and either MW50 engines or the bulky and heavy GM-1 nitrous oxide system for boosting power at high altitude. All had provision for two 300-litre wing drop tanks.

By early 1945 G-1s, G-3s and G-8s were carrying bombs of 1000 kg (2,204 lb), and on 7 March 1945, massive SC1800 bombs were first used against the Remagen bridge over the Rhine.

On their own initiative, the Luftwaffe's Eastern Front Schlachtflieger units tested the WfrGr 28/32 in the anti-tank role. The 280-mm (11-in) projectile achieved disappointing results.

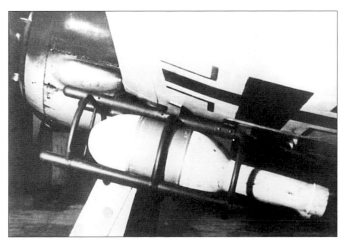

Above: This Fw 190 carries the effective AB 250 cluster weapon. The canister split in two while in flight, scattering over 100 SD-2 2-kg (4.4-lb) 'butterfly bomb' sub-munitions.

Left: This Fw 190F-8 displays a twin SG 113 Forstersonde missile launcher. Firing was performed automatically using magnetic field detection, when the plane flew over a tank. The system was inaccurate and trials were abandoned.

Focke-Wulf Fw 200 Condor

for propaganda purposes.

In early 1938 the Fw 200 V1 was fitted with extra tankage and re-painted as D-ACON *Brandenburg*. Tank had specially secured the RLM (air ministry) number 200 for propaganda purposes, and the V1 now became the Fw 200S (special). On 10 August 1938 it took off from Berlin-Tempelhof in the hands of Flugkapitäne Henke and von Moreau. It made a remarkable non-stop flight against headwinds to Floyd Bennet airport, New York, covering the estimated 4,075 miles (6558 km) in 24 hours 55 minutes. On 28 November 1938 the same aircraft and pilots flew via Basra, Karachi and Hanoi to Tokyo, in a total elapsed time of only 46 hours 18 minutes. On the return, in a way never publicly explained, D-ACON ran out of fuel on the first leg and ditched near Manila.

Condor in the Far East

While in Japan, the Fw 200 created great interest. By this time the Bremen factory was in production with what was envisaged as the standard version, the Fw 200B. Export sales were eagerly sought, five being ordered by Dai Nippon KKK of Japan.

There was a secret additional contract from Japan which called for a long-range reconnaissance version for the Imperial navy. Tank was eager to build this, because he was convinced such a machine could be useful to the Luftwaffe. He therefore picked the Fw 200 V10, the B-series prototype, for conversion. This was fitted with 60 per cent more fuel in fuselage cabin tanks, provision for over 4,409 lb

Military development

Designed as a four-engined long-range airliner, the Fw 200 was adapted to fill a Luftwaffe requirement for a maritime patrol aircraft. Only built in small numbers, the Fw 200's effect on Allied shipping earnt it the sobriquet 'Scourge of the Atlantic'.

In contrast with the belief that the Germans are painstakingly methodical, it must be remembered that the Nazis planned carefully for World War II as a Blitzkrieg (lightning war) without considering the possibility that it might last for years. A deliberate absentee from the Luftwaffe's ranks was a large long-range bomber and ocean reconnaissance aircraft. To some degree this oversight stemmed from the death in 1936 of General Wever and his replacement as Luftwaffe chief of staff by Kesselring, but it was basic policy to concentrate on twin-

engined tactical bombers (among other things, Goering could boast to Hitler of the hundreds built). So, the Luftwaffe showed only cursory interest when the Focke-Wulf Fw 200 V1 (first prototype) flew on 27 July 1937.

In fact, the Fw 200 was the best long-range airliner in Europe, if not in the world. It resulted from discussions held by Dipl Ing Kurt Tank, technical director of Focke-Wulf Flugzeugbau of Bremen, and the board of DLH (Deutsche Lufthansa), the state airline, in the spring of 1936. For some time Tank had wished to design

a modern long-range airliner to beat the Douglas DC-3 and replace the Junkers Ju 52/3m as the chief DLH equipment on trunk routes. What Tank finally decided to build was a four-engined aircraft with unprecedented range, able to fly the North Atlantic non-stop. This had been far beyond the capability of any previous payload-carrying aircraft, and Tank's objective was primarily

This is believed to be the first photograph taken of a Condor in flight. It shows the Fw 200 V1 climbing out of Bremen on its first flight on 27 July 1937; at this time it had not been painted.

Below: The Focke-Wulf Fw 200 V3 Immelmann III *was flown by the Luftwaffe as the personal transport of Adolf Hitler in this non-standard colour scheme.*

Above: The initial production maritime patrol model for Luftwaffe service was the Fw 200C-1. This picture clearly shows the ventral gondola and forward dorsal blister toting MG 15 machine-guns.

(2000 kg) of cameras, flares, markers, dinghies and other mission equipment, and also with three 0.31-in (7.9-mm) MG 15 machine-guns, one in a small dorsal turret above the trailing edge and the others firing to front and rear from a ventral gondola offset to the right. There was no bomb bay.

Military requirement

In spring 1939 it suddenly looked as if Hitler's gambles might not win for ever, and that a war was a near-term prospect. Luftwaffe Chief of Staff Jeschonnek ordered Oberstleutnant Edgar Petersen, a very experienced pilot, to form a squadron which could sink ships out in the Atlantic, on which the obvious enemies, France and especially the UK, would depend during a war. The problem was that there was no suitable aircraft. The intended machine, the Heinkel He 177, was years from combat duty. The only answer seemed to be the 'Japanese' Fw 200 V10.

As in the case of the Ju 52/3m, Dornier Do 17 and several other types, the RLM was faced with botching up a combat aircraft from a commercial transport. The Fw 200 was fundamentally unsuited to its new role because it had been designed to operate at lighter weights and at civil load factors. The airframe would henceforth have to operate from rough front-line airstrips with heavy loads of fuel and weapons, and in combat would certainly have to 'pull g' in tight turns or dive pull-outs, and all at low level in dense air. The Bremen stressmen did what they could to beef up the structure, but this consisted of a few local reinforcements. Ideally they should have started again, but the proposed Fw 200C-series was almost immediately accepted when it was offered in August 1939. A pre-production batch of 10 Fw 200C-0 aircraft was ordered just after the start of the war, and by agreement as many as possible were modified from B-series transports already on the line. The first four had to be delivered as Fw 200C-0 transports. Their only modifications were to introduce twin-wheel main gears, long-chord cowlings with gills and various internal equipment items. All four were delivered just in time for the invasion of Norway in April 1940.

The remaining six Fw 200C-0s were given the locally reinforced structure and simple armament comprising three MG 15s, one in a small (almost hemispherical) turret behind the flight deck, one in a rear dorsal cockpit with a fold-over hood and the third fired from a rear ventral hatch. An offensive load of four 551-lb (250-kg) bombs could be carried, two hung under the enlarged outer nacelles and the others on racks immediately outboard under the roots of the outer wings. Production continued immediately with the Fw 200C-1, which was planned as the definitive version although it still had a weak structure, very vulnerable fuel system (especially from below), no armour except behind the captain's seat and many inconvenient features. The main addition to the Fw 200C-1 was a ventral gondola, offset as in the Japanese Fw 200 V10 but longer, in order to provide room for a weapons bay (which was normally used to carry a cement bomb with 551-lb/250-kg ballistics to be dropped as a check on bombsight settings). At the front of the gondola was a 20-mm MG FF aimed with a ring-and-bead sight, used mainly to deter any AA gunners aboard enemy ships. At the rear was an MG 15, replacing the previous ventral gun. The only other change was to replace the forward turret by a raised cockpit canopy with a hand-aimed MG 15 firing ahead.

The normal crew numbered five: pilot, co-pilot and three gunners, one of the last being the engineer and another the overworked radio-operator/navigator. There was plenty of room inside the airframe, and all crew stations had provision for heating and electric light, but from the start the crews of Petersen's new maritime unit, Kampfgeschwader (KG) 40, were unhappy with the Condor's structural integrity and lack of armament. There is no evidence any Condors were delivered to any prior combat unit, as sometimes stated, but only to the transport Gruppe already mentioned. KG 40 was henceforth to be the sole major Fw 200C operating unit.

Airframe shortage

There were never to be enough Condors to go round. Focke-Wulf was well aware of the demand, and organised dispersed manufacture at five plants with final assembly at Bremen and Cottbus, and also by Blohm und Voss at Finkenwerder. Moreover, because of high attrition, KG 40 never had full wing strength and seldom had more than 12 aircraft available. Indeed, more than half the aircraft delivered in the first year suffered major structural failure, at least eight breaking their backs on the airfield.

Condor in service

Alongside the four modified B-series Fw 200s operated in the transport role by KGrzbV 200, the sole combat operating unit for the type was KG 40. After service in Denmark during the spring of 1940 KG 40 moved to Bordeaux-Mérignac which was to be its main base until it had to evacuate in the autumn of 1944.

Fw 200C-0
In 1940 the Luftwaffe received four Fw 200C-0 transports. These were not only the first batch of military Condors delivered, but also the first with long-chord cowls, three-bladed propellers and twin-wheel main undercarriage. X8+BH is shown during Stalingrad supply duties with KGrzbV 200 in January 1943.

Fw 200C-6
This Fw 200C-6 of 9./KG 40 is fitted with nose-mounted antennas for the FuG 200 Hohentwiel radar, (used mainly for blind bombing) and carries a pair of Henschel Hs 293A radio-guided missiles underwing.

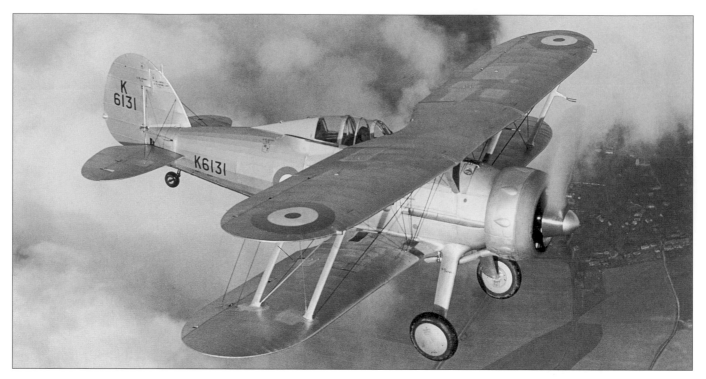

Gloster **Gladiator**

Above: A total of 231 Gladiator Mk Is was produced for the RAF, the last 28 aircraft being delivered into storage as attrition replacements. This is the third production example, seen shortly after completion.

Development

Somewhat overrated and largely sentimentalised as a result of myth rather than actual achievement, the Gladiator stands in history as the RAF's last biplane interceptor. It served just prior to World War II, as the era of the classic monoplane fighter was dawning.

One of the most far-sighted of all RAF fighter specifications was F.7/30 of 1930. It was intended to end the design stalemate imposed by rigid conservatism and perpetuation of the two-gun, single-bay, radial-engined biplane interceptor formula, epitomised by the Bristol Bulldog, which had entered service two years previously. The urgent need to decide on a successful contender for F.7/30 was soon satisfied by the introduction of the Kestrel-powered Hawker Fury which, though still armed with the traditional twin Vickers guns, entered service with a fairly respectable top speed of 207 mph (333 km/h).

When eventually finalised, F.7/30 suggested use of the Rolls-Royce Goshawk steam-cooled V-12 engine, a four-gun armament and a top speed of 250 mph (402 km/h). This unwieldy

This view of Gladiator Mk I K6129 shows two of the major differences between the Gladiator and the earlier Gauntlet – flaps fitted to both the upper and lower wings, and an enclosed cockpit.

engine died a natural death in 1934, and it was then that the Gloster Aircraft Company decided to pursue an F.7/30 design as a private venture.

Radial-engined designs

The company had been persevering with a radial-powered two-bay biplane design family, the SS.18 and SS.19, since 1928, and by 1933 the SS.19B with a 530-hp (395-kW) Bristol Mercury IVS2 appeared as the Gloster Gauntlet prototype. In the event, the Gauntlet entered service in 1935 with a maximum speed of around 230 mph (370 km/h). It remained the

RAF's fastest fighter for two years, despite its air-cooled radial, and was exceptionally popular among its pilots.

By 1934 the Air Ministry was aware of the significant advances likely to be achieved by the forthcoming Hawker Hurricane and Supermarine Spitfire monoplane fighters, then no more than paper projects. Faced with a likely three-year gap before their service debut, the Ministry determined on a final resolution of the F.7/30 specification, if only as a stopgap.

Tendered as little more than a sideline, the Gloster design – in effect a single-bay adaptation of the Gauntlet with flaps on upper

The Gladiator prototype, K5200, differed from production aircraft in having an open cockpit. In this view, the starboard underwing 0.303-in (7.7-mm) Lewis machine-gun blister may be seen.

and lower wings and single-leg cantilever landing gear – easily disposed of most of the opposition, whose field comprised one-off oddities and 'specials' wholly compromised by the out-of-favour Goshawk III. Indeed, the Gladiator prototype (K5200), designated SS.37, had a top speed approaching the magic 250 mph (402 km/h) specified when it first flew in September 1934. Two Lewis guns mounted below the lower wings, each with 97 drum-fed rounds, complemented the twin Vickers Mk V guns on the sides of the nose.

Modern fighter shortage

Leaving aside the fortunes of the Hurricane and Spitfire, both of which suffered six-month delays in service introduction, the situation facing the RAF in 1935 (the first year of perceptible expansion) was one of shortage of modern aircraft, particularly fighters. The Bulldog (two guns and a top speed of 174 mph/ 280 km/h) still equipped more squadrons than any other fighter, while the Gauntlet and Fury equipped six further squadrons.

And, despite similarity with the Gauntlet, the Gladiator's entry into service with RAF Fighter Command (No. 72 Sqn at Tangmere) did not take place until February 1937, the same year that No. 111 Sqn received its first Hurricanes.

Production deliveries quickly accelerated and, by the end of 1937, eight fighter squadrons had received Gladiators, more than 200 Gladiator Mk Is having been completed. Browning 0.303-in (7.7-mm) machine-guns had been intended from the outset for the fuselage installation, but as a result of delays with the weapon (and priorities afforded to the Hurricane), the first 23 Gladiators retained the Vickers Mk V guns in the nose and drum-fed Lewis guns under the lower wings. The next 37 aircraft had universal gun mounts which allowed the retrofitting of Brownings with 600 rounds per gun although, in the event, the gun adopted for the wings was the Vickers 'K' gas-operated weapon with 400 rounds.

The re-equipping of Fighter

Command with the Gladiator continued in 1938, Nos 25 and 85 Sqns taking deliveries in June. Meanwhile the first deployment of Gladiators had taken place in the Middle East, No. 33 Sqn receiving Gladiator Mk Is (and some Gauntlets) at Ismailia, Egypt, in February as No. 80 Sqn sailed from the UK for the same airfield in April. Thereafter, use of the Gladiator by home-based front-line squadrons slowly dwindled as the Hurricane and Spitfire arrived in service. Gladiator Mk Is were replaced by Mk IIs and the earlier version was shipped out to Egypt to allow the formation of new fighter squadrons. By the end of 1938 the first Auxiliary Air

Force Sqn, No. 607 (County of Durham), was flying Gladiator Mk Is at Usworth.

Gladiator Mk II

The type's service with RAF squadrons had disclosed the unsuitability of the Mercury IX/Watts two-bladed wooden propeller combination, with its rough running and over-speeding in the dive. For some months in 1937, a Gladiator Mk I with a three-bladed, fixed-pitch, Fairey Reed metal propeller had been returning promising test results. The upshot was a switch to the Mercury VIII or VIIAS, which drove this propeller in the other-wise similar Gladiator Mk II.

Gladiator production, includ-ing one prototype, around 200 examples sold abroad, and a small batch of Sea Gladiators built for the Royal Navy, totalled 747 aircraft. A handful survives in museums, while a sole example is maintained in airworthy condition in the UK.

RAF Gladiators at war

Though popularly regarded as an emotive relic of the era of the biplane interceptor, the Gladiator's true merits are often overestimated. When put in the correct perspective of early wartime deficiencies, it can be seen as struggling in a desperate combat environment that had overtaken its capabilities and, though bravely flown, it suffered accordingly.

Above: Cheerful pilots and their No. 615 Sqn Gladiator Mk IIs, part of the Air Component of the British Expeditionary Force, are seen in France in 1939/40. In fact, the BEF's Gladiators had an unhappy time, suffering heavy losses in the face of experienced Luftwaffe pilots flying modern fighter aircraft.

Top: No. 239 Sqn operated Gladiator Mk IIs and Westland Lysanders from Hatfield upon its re-formation in September 1940. Camouflage had first appeared on Gladiators when the RAF was put on alert during the Munich Crisis of 1938.

At the beginning of World War II in September 1939 only four home-based fighter squadrons (Nos 603, 605, 607 and 615) were still equipped with Gladiators. In the following month, however, No. 141 (Fighter) Sqn at Grangemouth, No. 151 at Acklington and No. 263 at Filton were re-formed (after being disbanded after World War I) with Gladiators as temporary equipment.

In November Nos 607 and 615 Sqns were sent to France as part of the Air Component of the British Expeditionary Force, and were just beginning to re-equip with Hurricanes when the German attack in the West was launched on 10 May 1940. Completely outmatched by the modern German aircraft, the Gladiators suffered heavily before the squadrons struggled home to southern England to complete their changeover to Hurricanes and participate in the Battle of Britain.

Gladiators to Norway

No. 263 (Fighter) Sqn had in the meantime been preparing to sail to Finland to assist that nation in the 'Winter War' against the USSR. The war ended before the squadron sailed, and it was to Norway that No. 263 Sqn was sent at the end of April 1940 to cover the first British forces in their defence of the area around Andalsnes against the German invasion. Operating from the frozen Lake Lesjaskog, the Gladiators flew a number of defensive patrols before the lake was bombed, and all were destroyed. The pilots returned to the UK where the squadron was given replacement Gladiators and ordered to return to Norway, this time in defence of the expedition to Narvik in the far north in May. On this occasion the squadron gave an excellent account of itself: one pilot, Flying Officer Jacobsen, destroyed at least five German aircraft in a single sortie. However, unable to support an expeditionary force so far from home bases, the British withdrew from Norway at the beginning of June, and it was during the return voyage aboard HMS *Glorious* that No. 263 Sqn lost all its aircraft and all but two of its pilots when the carrier was sunk by the German battle-cruisers *Scharnhorst* and *Gneisenau*.

During the Battle of Britain No. 247 Sqn was formed from the Fighter Flight, Sumburgh, with Gladiators and sent south to Roborough to protect Plymouth but, although it flew many patrols, the squadron was never in action during the great battle.

Middle East service

It was in the Mediterranean and Middle East that the Gladiator saw the most action. When Italy entered the war in June 1940 Gladiators were serving with Nos 33 and 80 Sqns in Egypt, and with No. 94 Sqn at Aden, representing the most modern equipment available in

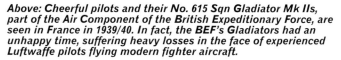

After being superseded in Fighter Command by more modern aircraft, Gladiators went on to equip two of the RAF's meteorological squadrons. This 'ZK'-coded machine was among those with which No. 521 Sqn carried out weather flights over the United Kingdom as late as April 1945.

Camouflaged to avoid detection from the air, this Gladiator Mk I of No. 263 Sqn is seen during the ill-fated Norwegian campaign of 1940. None of the No. 263 Sqn aircraft shipped to Norway survived to return to the UK; the original aircraft were lost on Lake Lesjaskog, while those sent in May 1940 were lost when HMS Glorious was sunk after evacuation in June.

the theatre. The former pair fought with excellent effect against the paltry Italian forces in the Western Desert during Marshal Graziani's abortive invasion of Egypt, the Gladiator proving fairly evenly matched against the Italian Fiat CR.42. No. 94 Sqn likewise operated with success in the defence of Aden and later supported the British Commonwealth army in its destruction of the Italian empire in East Africa.

Outclassed in Greece

During the ill-fated Greek campaign, Gladiators of Nos 80 and 112 Sqns participated and held their own against the Regia Aeronautica until the intervention of the Luftwaffe when, once again, they were outclassed.

Scarcely any survived to return to Egypt at the end of the campaign. During the Iraqi revolt of 1941 No. 94 Sqn, which had come north to Egypt to re-equip with Hurricanes, was hurriedly moved with its Gladiators to Habbaniyah where it joined in the successful defence of the RAF base; a few Gladiators of No. 112 Sqn subsequently took part in the invasion of Syria. Gladiators continued to serve in the

Western Desert throughout 1941, but finally disappeared from first-line service when, in January 1942, No. 6 Sqn at Wadi Halfa re-equipped with Hurricanes.

In second-line duties the type continued to fly with Nos 520 and 521 (Meteorological) Sqns (at Gibraltar and in the UK, respectively) until 1945, and for a couple of months in 1942 with No. 123 Sqn at Abadan, Iran, on army co-operation work.

Maltese Gladiators

In Malta, where the Royal Navy stored a number of replacement Sea Gladiators, the approach of war in 1940 prompted the assembly of four of these and, flown by volunteer pilots, they started defensive patrols over the island when hostilities broke out. Contrary to popular myth, the Navy's Sea

Gladiators represented the island's sole air defence for only 10 days (11 to 21 June) when the Italians flew three small, half-hearted raids. They do not appear to have destroyed any enemy aircraft during this period, although they probably served to upset the Italian bombing accuracy, for little damage was caused. Thereafter, some Hurricanes, which were staging through Malta on their way to North Africa, were impressed into service for defence of the island. Certainly, the names *Faith*, *Hope* and *Charity* were never applied to the Sea Gladiators during this period, being the product of a Maltese newspaper some months afterwards. Three of the Sea Gladiators that survived joined the Hurricanes to form No. 261 Sqn on 1 August, but this unit was disbanded five months later.

Left: When Italy entered the war, No. 33 Sqn in Egypt began fighter patrols over the desert. Seen here is one of its Gladiator Mk Is, bearing 'NW' codes. Note the tropical filter fitted to the main carburettor air intake, beneath the engine.

Sea Gladiators

An important adaptation of the Gladiator Mk II took place at the end of 1938 with the appearance of the Sea Gladiator. Initial trial installation of naval equipment had been carried out on Gladiator Mk Is K6129 and K8039, resulting in the conversion of the first 38 Gladiator Mk IIs (N2265-N2302) to become Sea Gladiators (Interim), and a further 60 as full-standard Sea Gladiators. These differed from the RAF's Gladiator Mk II in being equipped with catapult spools, an arrester hook, dinghy stowage (between the landing gear legs) and two additional Browning guns, each with 300 rounds, in the upper wing. Sea Gladiators first embarked in HMS *Courageous* with No. 801 Sqn in May 1939. N5519/'R' was one of the four aircraft flown by RAF pilots of the Malta Fighter Flight during June 1940, until the arrival of Hawker Hurricanes.

Foreign operators

Gloster Aircraft achieved notable successes in its efforts to export the Gladiator, making sales to air forces in Europe and further afield. Other Allied air forces received ex-RAF aircraft during World War II.

China – Gladiator Mk I

China ordered 36 Mk Is in October 1937 after war with Japan broke out. Delivered by sea to Hong Kong, the aircraft were assembled at Kai Tak by Gloster engineers with a view to flying the machines to their future base at Tien Ho. However, diplomatic pressure was brought to bear, which saw the aircraft crated once more and shipped by train and junk to Canton for delivery. A handful was immediately re-assembled at Tien Ho, despite Japanese air attacks, but the remainder of the first 20 machines did not fly until late 1937/early 1938. Upon completion, all were flown some 300 miles (483 km) out of reach of Japanese bombing, to a new base where training could be undertaken without interruption. Some of the remaining 16 aircraft were assembled at Tien Ho, these machines assisting in the defence of Siuchow later in 1938.

Finland – Gladiator Mk II

Thirty ex-RAF aircraft were supplied to the Finnish air force between December 1939 and February 1940 and went on to take an active part in the defence of southern Finland during the Winter War with Russia. A number of pilots scored kills while flying Gladiators, many of which were fitted with skis for operations from snow and ice. By the time of the armistice with Russia in September 1944, about five remained in use with a reconnaissance unit.

Gladiator Mk II GL-256 was flown by Cpl Ilmari Joensuu of 2/LLv 26 at Ruokolahti during February 1940. 'Pitkä-Jim' ('Long Jim') Joensuu scored four kills in this aircraft during February 1940, achieving ace status in August 1941 while flying a Fiat G.50.

Greece – Gladiator Mk I/II

Greek businessman Zarparkis Homogenos bought a pair of Mk Is (costing £9,400 complete with spare parts and ground equipment) in January 1938 and presented them to the Royal Hellenic Air Force. In 1940 additional aircraft were transferred from RAF stocks, comprising 13 aircraft that had served with Nos 33 and 80 Sqns, RAF and four from reserve stocks in the Middle East.

Belgium – Gladiator Mk I

Belgium's first Gladiators were delivered on 12 September 1937, 22 aircraft joining the country's air force. Licensed production by Avions Fairey was discussed by Gloster Aircraft and the Belgian government, but never materialised. By the time of the German invasion in May 1940 the Belgian air force had just 15 serviceable Gladiators, which were quickly overwhelmed by the invading forces.

Egypt – Gladiator Mk I/II

During early 1939 the Royal Egyptian Air Force received 18 ex-RAF Gladiator Mk Is modified to Mk II standard. A number of these aircraft was later returned to the RAF for use by Meteorological Flights. In 1941 a further 27 Mk IIs were transferred to the REAF.

Iraq – Gladiator Mk I/II

Nine Mk Is were transferred to the Royal Iraqi Air Force during 1940-42, though some of these aircraft were later returned. An additional five ex-RAF Mk IIs joined the IAF in March 1944 as attrition replacements and at least two of these were still in use in 1949, based at Mosul.

Ireland – Gladiator Mk I

The Irish Army Air Corps received four new Mk Is in 1938, these aircraft having been ordered the previous year. Delivered by air, they served until 1941 and represented the first of a number of British aircraft types acquired as part of an Air Corps re-equipment programme.

Lithuania – Gladiator Mk I

Within days of the Latvian order (see below), Lithuania ordered 14 aircraft from Gloster. These Gladiator Mk Is were test-flown at Hucclecote and then dismantled for shipping during October and November 1937. Re-assembly took place at air bases at Vilna and Kaunas. After the seizure of Lithuania and Latvia by the USSR, Gladiators are known to have flown in Russian markings.

Latvia – Gladiator Mk I

A Latvian air mission visiting the UK in March 1937, with the aim of buying British aircraft, went to Gloster's Hucclecote factory and was shown the Gladiator. Evidently impressed, it placed an order for 26 Mk Is on 27 May, this representing the first export order for the type. These were fitted with Vickers Mk VM 0.303-in (7.7-mm) machine-guns, the completed aircraft being shipped to Latvia between August and November. The air mission's purchases, valued at £120,000 and including three Hawker Hinds ordered in January 1938, were funded by a State-run lottery!

Norway – Gladiator Mk I/II

Norwegian interest in the Gladiator can be traced to April 1937, discussions centring around an initial purchase of six complete aircraft and the establishment of licensed production in Norway. This plan was later changed to provide for the supply of 12 aircraft, though after six Mk Is had been delivered, in July 1938, the contract was revised again. The remaining six machines were to be Mk IIs diverted from Air Ministry contracts (the last Gladiators built, in fact). Armed with 0.30-in (7.62-mm) Colt machine-guns, all these aircraft took part in the defence of Oslo against the Luftwaffe. Although all were lost in the air or on the ground (two, at least, breaking through ice on the lake from which they were operating), they destroyed at least four enemy aircraft.

South Africa – Gladiator Mk II

The South African Air Force evaluated Gladiator Mk I K7922, from No. 72 Sqn, RAF, in January 1939. In April 1941 a further 11 aircraft were transferred to the SAAF and were issued to Nos 1, 2 and 3 Squadrons for both training and operational flying in the Middle East and East Africa.

Sweden – Gladiator Mk I (J 8) and Mk II (J 8A)

The Royal Swedish Air Force undertook an expansion in the late 1930s which included the purchase of 55 Gladiators. These comprised 37 Mk Is (known locally as J 8s), powered by 640-hp (477-kW) Bristol Mercury engines driving Watts two-bladed wooden propellers, delivered from June 1937, and 18 Mk IIs (J 8As) with 740-hp (552-kW) Mercury VIIs and three-bladed metal props, delivered in 1938. Ten aircraft were held in reserve, while the remainder were issued to the three squadrons forming No. 8 Fighter Wing. These aircraft saw action in January 1940 when a Swedish volunteer force joined the Finnish air force in the war with Russia. A number of aircraft was equipped with locally-designed ski undercarriage and bomb racks and, though the aircraft were operated in harsh winter conditions against a numerically superior enemy, only three Swedish machines were lost. Sweden's Gladiators were withdrawn from front-line use in spring 1941.

Portugal – Gladiator Mk II

Portugal's aircraft were ordered in February 1939 and, as an early delivery was requested, 15 Mk IIs were diverted from an Air Ministry contract. Though interest was expressed in a further 30 aircraft, a follow-up order never materialised.

Gloster Meteor

Britain's first operational jet

Britain's first and only operational jet combat aircraft of World War II was Gloster's extraordinary Meteor, which would go on to serve front-line RAF squadrons for a further 17 years.

The only Allied turbojet-powered aircraft to see action during World War II, the Gloster Meteor was designed by George Carter, whose preliminary study was given Air Ministry approval in November 1940 under Specification F.9/40. Its twin-engined layout was determined by the low thrust produced by the turbojet engines then avail-

Above: Trials with axial-flow Metro-Vick F.2 engines were carried out by Meteor prototype DG204/G from November 1943 to April 1944. Unlike other Meteors, the engine nacelles were mounted below the aircraft's wing.

Top: In May 1945, as World War II in Europe was drawing to a close, the Meteor Mk IV began to reach RAF units. The aircraft was distinguishable by the long-chord engine nacelles housing the Derwent IV turbojet.

able. On 7 February 1941 an order was placed for 12 prototypes, although only eight were actually built. The first of these was fitted with Rover W.2B engines, each of 1,000-lb (4.5-kN) thrust, and taxiing trials were carried out at Newmarket

No. 616 Squadron Meteor F.Mk I/IIIs are seen here at RAF Colerne prior to the unit moving to Europe in January 1945. The squadron had been the first to equip with the Meteor in July 1944.

Above: Seen on the PSP at B.158/Lübeck, Germany in the spring of 1945, this No. 616 Squadron Meteor F.Mk III is finished in standard day-fighter camouflage.

Left: The second Meteor variant to see wartime service was the F.Mk III, examples of which were operational with No. 616 Squadron in January 1945. A flight of F.Mk IIIs was sent to Belgium in an attempt to draw Me 262s into combat and, as a recognition aid, they were painted white overall.

Right: The first Meteor F.Mk I, EE210/G, became the very first Meteor 'export' when, in February 1944, it was loaned to the USAAF for evaluation at Muroc; Britain received a Bell YP-59A Airacomet in return.

Heath, commencing in July 1942. Delays in the production of flight-standard engines meant that the fifth airframe, with alternative de Havilland-developed Halford H.1 engines of 1,500-lb (6.75-kN) thrust, was the first to fly, this event taking place at Cranwell on 5 March 1943.

Modified W.2B/23 engines then became available and were installed in the first and fourth prototypes, first flight dates being 12 June and 24 July respectively. On 13 November the third prototype made its maiden flight at Farnborough, powered by two Metrovick F.2 engines in underslung nacelles, and in the same month the second aircraft flew, initially with Power Jets W.2/500 turbojets. The sixth aircraft later became the prototype F.Mk II, with two 2,700-lb (12.15-kN) thrust de Havilland Goblin engines, and was flown on 24 July 1945. It had been preceded by the seventh, used for trials with a modified fin, rudder, and dive brakes, and flown on 20 January 1944. The eighth, with Rolls-Royce W.2B/37 Derwent Is, was flown on 18 April 1944.

Early production

Twenty Gloster G.41A Meteor Mk Is comprised the first production batch, these being powered by W.2B/23C Wellands and incorporating minor airframe improvements, including a clear-view canopy. After a first flight on 12 January 1944, the first Mk I was delivered to the United States in February, in exchange for a Bell YP-59A Airacomet, the first American jet aircraft. Others were used for airframe and engine development, and the 18th later became the Trent-Meteor, the world's first turboprop-powered aircraft, which was flown on 20 September 1945. The Trent was basically a Derwent engine provided with reduction gearing and a drive shaft that turned a five-bladed Rotol propeller of 7-ft 11-in (2.41-m) diameter, necessitating the introduction of

longer-stroke landing gear to provide tip clearance. Each engine delivered 750 hp (559 kW), with a residual thrust of 1,000 lb (454 kW).

Into service

The first operational jet fighter squadron was No. 616, based at Culmhead, Somerset, which was equipped with Spitfire Mk VIIs when its first two Meteor F.Mk Is arrived on 12 July 1944. On 21 July the squadron moved to Manston, Kent, receiving more Meteors on 23 July to form a detached flight of seven. The first operational sorties were flown on 27 July, and on 4 August, near Tonbridge, Flying Officer Dean destroyed the first V-1 flying-bomb to be claimed by a jet fighter, using the Meteor's wingtip to tip it over into a spin after the aircraft's four 20-mm cannon had jammed. On the same day, Flying Officer

Roger shot down a second V-1 near Tenterden.

Conversion to Meteors was completed towards the end of August, and the autumn was spent preparing for operations on the continent. From 10-17 October, however, four Meteors were detached to Debden, to take part in an exercise with the USAAF 2nd Bombardment Division and 65th Fighter Wing, to enable defensive tactics against the Luftwaffe's Messerschmitt Me 163 and Me 262 fighters to be devised. The first Meteor F.Mk IIIs were delivered to Manston on 18 December, and on 17 January the squadron moved to Colerne, Wiltshire, where the remaining Mk Is were replaced. On 20 January 1945 one flight of No. 616's Meteors joined No. 84 Group, 2nd Tactical Air Force in Belgium, and in March No. 504 became the second Meteor F.Mk III unit to operate

on the other side of the English Channel.

The Meteor F.Mk III, the second and last mark to see operational service during World War II, had increased fuel capacity and a sliding bubble canopy in place of the sideways-opening hood of the Mk I. Fifteen F.Mk IIIs were completed with Welland engines and 265 with Derwents, some in lengthened engine nacelles. Derwents also powered the Meteor F.Mk IV, later examples of which were modified by a 5-ft 10-in (1.78-m) reduction in wingspan. Of 657 built, 465 were supplied to the RAF, enabling Meteor F.Mk IIIs to be passed to auxiliary units.

On 20 September 1945 a Meteor F.Mk I, converted with Rolls-Royce Trent engines, became the world's first turboprop-powered aircraft. The machine was converted back to standard Mk I configuration in late 1948.

Grumman
F4F/FM Wildcat

Pugnacious feline

Despite a difficult birth, the Wildcat had established itself as the US Navy's premier fighter by the time the US entered World War II. In the dark early days of the Pacific War, the Wildcat and its heroic pilots held the seemingly invincible Japanese at bay.

With US naval aviation heavily reliant on biplanes in the 1930s, the introduction of monoplane designs was bound to meet with scepticism from traditionalists. Add to this a series of teething troubles, and the Grumman-designed F4F Wildcat would appear to have stood little chance of success. In reality, it went on to become one of the most effective and successful of carrierborne fighters.

It was known universally as the Grumman Wildcat, although most were not built by Grumman and many in foreign use were known as Martlets. It is best remembered in the hands of outnumbered American pilots pitted against the Mitsubishi Zero in 1942-3, although its combat debut had come in the hands of the British when a naval pilot from HMS *Audacity*

shot down a four-engined Focke-Wulf Fw 200 Condor near Gibraltar as early as 20 September 1941. It was the fighter used by Lieutenant Edward (Butch) O'Hare of squadron VF-42 from the USS *Lexington* who shot down five Mitsubishi G4M bombers in five minutes near Rabaul on 20 February 1942, becoming the US Navy's first ace of World War II and earning the Medal of Honor. Yet O'Hare, for all his achievement, was one of only two men to win this medal while flying the Wildcat.

Battle-winner

All things to all men, the Grumman Wildcat (7,815 of them built before VJ-Day, most by the Eastern Division of General Motors corporation) has one principal claim to fame that no other American aircraft can

Above: In prototypical form, the XF4F-2 (BuNo. 0383) exhibited the more barrel-like appearance of its predecessors, the F2F and F3F. Note also the rounded tailfin, with its leading edge perpendicular to the fuselage.

Top: The portly Wildcat should have been no match for the better performing and more manoeuvrable Zero, yet its ruggedness, better guns and the innovative tactics of its pilots carried the day.

make: it was the fighter flown by US Navy and US Marine Corps airmen in the dark hours at Pearl Harbor, Coral Sea and Wake Island, and at Guadalcanal when the first hints appeared that the war might be turned against an until-then unbeaten Japanese enemy. The Wildcat never outperformed the Zero, but it won battle after battle nonethe-

less, and when those battles were over, the war had turned in the direction of an Allied victory.

Like many great aircraft, the Wildcat was almost not built at all. A 1936 US Navy requirement for a new carrier-based fighter went not to Leroy Grumman's well-established Bethpage, Long Island, firm but to the forgettable Brewster Aeronautical Corporation for its XF2A-1 Buffalo. The F2A-1 thus became the US Navy's first operational monoplane fighter, but US Navy planners were so sceptical of its promise (wisely so) that they authorised one prototype of Grumman's competing biplane design, the

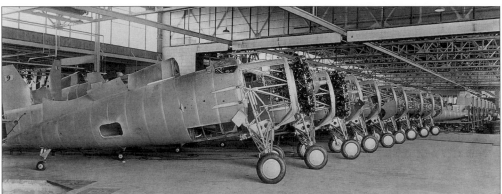

The bulk of Wildcat production was undertaken by General Motors, though early examples (these are Martlet Mk Is for the Fleet Air Arm) were built at Grumman's Bethpage plant.

Two flights of Wildcats are seen during a training sortie. The use of sound formation tactics enabled US Marine Corps and Navy pilots to overcome the agility advantages of the A6M Zero.

Still exhibiting early-war markings, this F4F-4 was assigned to VF-41 aboard Ranger. In November 1942 the squadron went to war during Operation Torch, the Allied landings in North Africa.

XF4F-1. Later, the biplane proposal was shelved and on 28 July 1936 an order was placed for a prototype Grumman monoplane fighter, the XF4F-2.

First flown by company pilot Robert L. Hall on 22 September 1937 and almost immediately moved to NAS Anacostia, Washington, DC for tests, the XF4F-2 was powered by a 1,050-hp (783-kW) Pratt & Whitney R-1830-66 Twin Wasp engine and was able to demonstrate a maximum speed of 290 mph (467 km/h). Of all-metal construction with a riveted monocoque fuselage, its cantilever monoplane wing set in mid-position on the fuselage and equipped with retractable tail-wheel landing gear, the XF4F-2 proved to be marginally faster than the Brewster prototype in a 1938 'fly-off' evaluation at Anacostia and Dahlgren,

Virginia. It also outperformed the Seversky XFN-1, a derivative of the USAAC's P-35. But speed was the XF4F-2's only advantage over the Brewster product, and the latter was ordered into production on 11 June 1938.

Hidden potential?

Clearly, the US Navy believed the XF4F-2 had hidden potential, for it was returned to Grumman in October 1938, together with a new contract for its further development. The company introduced major improvements and changed the type's company designation from G-18 to G-36 before this prototype flew again in March 1939 under the designation XF4F-3. Changes included the installation of a more powerful version of the Twin Wasp (the XR-1830-76 with a two-stage

supercharger), increased wingspan and area, redesigned tail surfaces, and a modified machine-gun installation. When tested in this form the XF4F-3 was found to have considerably improved performance. A second prototype was completed and introduced into the test programme, with a redesigned tail unit in which the tailplane was moved higher up the fin, and the profile of the vertical tail was changed again. In this final form the XF4F-3 was found to have good handling characteristics and manoeuvrability, and a maximum speed of 335 mph (539 km/h) at 21,300 ft (6490 m). Faced with such performance, the US Navy ordered 78 F4F-3 production aircraft on 8 August 1939.

The name 'Wildcat' was in use in US service from 1 October 1941. The first F4F-3 Wildcat for the US Navy was flown on 20 August 1940, and at the beginning of December the type began to equip US Navy squadrons VF-7 and VF-41. Some 95 F4F-3A aircraft were ordered by the US Navy,

powered by the R-1830-90 engine with single-stage super-charger, and deliveries began in 1941. An XF4F-4 prototype was flown in May 1941, incorporating refinements which resulted from Martlet combat experience in the UK including six-gun armament, armour, self-sealing tanks, and (above all) folding wings. Delivery of production F4F-4 Wildcat fighters began in November 1941, and by the time that the Japanese launched their attack on Pearl Harbor a number of US Navy and US Marine Corps squadrons had been equipped. As additional Wildcats entered service, they went to sea aboard the carriers USS *Enterprise* (CV-6), USS *Hornet* (CV-12) and USS *Saratoga* (CV-3), being involved with conspicuous success in the battles of the Coral Sea and Midway, and the operations at Guadalcanal, and were at the centre of all significant actions in the Pacific until superseded by more advanced aircraft in 1943. They also saw action with the US Navy in North Africa in late 1942 during Operation Torch.

Wildcat at war

The Wildcat first saw action in US hands with US Marine squadron VMF-211 at Wake Island. The first carrier-launched US Navy F4F kill, scored by Lt(jg) 'Bill' Rawie, was achieved on 1 February 1942, launching an illustrious career for the stubby fighter.

Pearl Harbor survivor
This F4F-3A was one of two VF-6 aircraft to survive a disastrous friendly-fire incident. USS *Enterprise* dispatched six Wildcats to Ford Island, Hawaii, in the wake of the Japanese attack. Confused and shell-shocked US anti-aircraft gunners opened up on the landing aircraft. This aircraft, flown by Ensign James G. Daniels, and one other, survived the onslaught.

Santa Cruz ace
During the Battle of Santa Cruz on 26 October 1942, Ensign George L. Wrenn flew this VF-72 F4F-4 from USS *Hornet* to engage Japanese aircraft attacking the US fleet. He shot down five Nakajima B5N 'Kates' during the sortie. *Hornet* was sunk during the attack, and Wrenn had to recover aboard *Enterprise*.

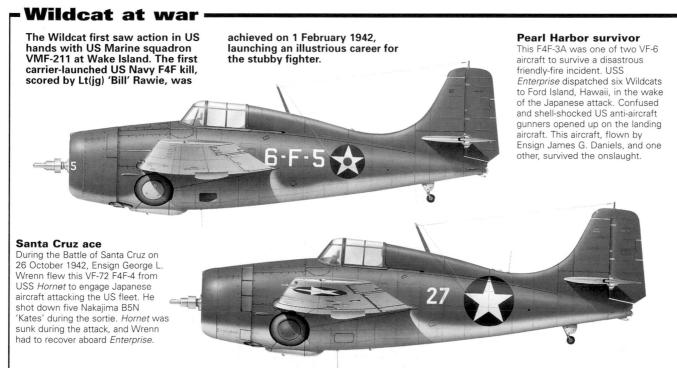

F4F in action

The Grumman F4F Wildcat was the mainstay of the US Navy and US Marine Corps fighter squadrons in the first two years of World War II, and served with distinction right up to the end of the conflict.

Wildcats served in the front line through to 1945. These Eastern-built FM-2s are being launched from the escort carrier USS Makin Island for the attack on Iwo Jima in March of that year.

The first Wildcat pilot to win the Medal of Honor belonged to US Marine squadron VMF-211, which lost nine F4F-3s on the ground during the 7 December 1941 attack on Pearl Harbor and seven more on the ground at Wake Island the next day. On 9 December two VMF-211 pilots from Wake teamed up to shoot down a Japanese bomber, the first American Wildcat 'kill'. Before Wake was overwhelmed, Captain Robert McElrod achieved a direct hit on a Japanese destroyer with a bomb dropped from his Wildcat, sinking the ship but losing his life in the process. He was awarded the Medal of Honor posthumously.

Guadalcanal

Wildcat-Zero dogfights at Wake, Coral Sea and Midway are the stuff of legend. But to many men, the Wildcat's finest hours came in the heat, stench and muck at Henderson Field on Guadalcanal, where the United States mounted its first major offensive of the Pacific War.

Major John L. Smith's VMF-223, the 'Rainbow' Squadron, was launched from the escort carrier USS *Long Island* on 20 August 1942 and landed at the recently-captured Henderson – "a bowl of black dust or a quagmire of mud" according to its official history. The next day, the squadron was strafing Japanese troops at the Tenaru river. On 24 August, accompanied by five USAAF Bell P-39 Airacobras, VMF-223 intercepted 27 Japanese aircraft, shooting down 10 bombers and six fighters. Captain Marion Carl, who was to become the first US Marine ace of the war, scored three of the kills. Smith became the third Wildcat pilot to rate the Medal of Honor after McElrod and 'Butch' O'Hare.

It was hard enough simply piloting the Wildcat. Its stalky landing gear gave it dubious ground-handling characteristics, and it could be 'mushy' when agility counted most. The cockpit was poorly designed – there was a violent draught if the hood was slid open in flight and the pilot's seat was cramped and too low relative to the location of his head and his need for outside visibility.

Fighting Zeros

But the F4Fs bad points were nothing compared to the problem of fighting the Mitsubishi Zero. American pilots learned one rule early in the war: never dogfight with a Zero if you can possibly avoid it. They sought instead to smash through a screen of Mitsubishis and attack the enemy's big bombers directly. At times, a brace of Zeroes could be lured into an overshoot, making it easier to break through to the enemy bombers.

At Guadalcanal, the bombers would approach in Vee formations more than 20 strong, and the Wildcats aimed to dive on the bombers to destroy some, diving away before the Zeroes pounced. These hit-and-run tactics forced the Japanese pilots, who were operating a long way from their bases, to waste precious fuel.

Once the dogfighting started a Wildcat pilot had to depend on his wingman to shoot the enemy off his tail. 'Lone wolves' rarely survived very long, although some individual Wildcat pilots excelled. Major John L. Smith

Above: July 1943: a Marine Corps Wildcat is wheeled out of a crushed coral revetment on Palmyra Island, a tiny atoll about 1,250 miles (2000 km) south-west of Hawaii. Palmyra was a staging post on the US Navy's Central Pacific drive to Tarawa, Kwajalein and beyond.

Left: It took a good pilot to handle a slow-moving Wildcat. Merely landing the easily-stalled machine on a pitching carrier deck amounted to a supreme achievement.

The Wildcat was small enough to be used to great effect from escort carriers: these FM-2 Wildcats were phtographed while escorting a torpedo bomber from USS White Plains in June 1944.

was credited with downing 19 Japanese aircraft and Major Marion Carl with 18 and a half. One of the more intriguing tests involving the Wildcat was a 1942 effort in Philadelphia to evaluate the idea of fighters being towed by bombers, to serve as long-range escorts. The idea recurred throughout the 1940s, although it was never tried in actual operations. The Wildcat was an ideal candidate because its three-bladed Curtiss Electric propeller could be easily

feathered and the engine restarted in flight. A hook-on and break-off system was devised to enable the Wildcat to be towed from an attachment point beneath the wing; the Wildcat pilot could connect and disconnect at will. In May 1942, an F4F was towed by a Douglas BD-1 (the US Navy version of the A-20 Havoc) and later two Wildcats were towed by a Boeing B-17 over a 1,200-mile (1930-km) eight-hour course.

The system worked. The

Wildcat pilot could remain idle while his aircraft flew effectively as a glider, its range thus being limited only by the endurance of the tow aircraft. But no practical application of the arrangement was ever made.

The final production variant built by Grumman was the long-range reconnaissance F4F-7 with increased fuel capacity, camera installations in the lower fuselage, and no armament. Only 21 were built, but Grumman also produced an additional 100 F4F-3s and two XF4F-8 fighter prototypes.

Licence production

With an urgent need to concentrate on development and production of the more advanced F6F Hellcat, Grumman negotiated with General Motors to continue production of the F4F-4 Wildcat under the designation FM-1. Production by

General Motors' Eastern Aircraft Division began after finalisation of a contract on 18 April 1942, and the first of this company's FM-1s was flown on 31 August 1942. Production totalled 1,151, of which 312 were supplied to the UK.

Ultimate Wildcat

At the same time, General Motors was working on an improved version, the FM-2. This was a production version of the XF4F-8 prototype. Its major change was the installation of a 1,350-hp (1007-kW) R-1820-56 Cyclone 9 radial engine. A larger vertical tail was introduced to maintain good directional stability with this more powerful engine, and airframe weight was reduced to the minimum. A total of 4,777 FM-2s was built, the most numerous variant by far. Many served aboard the massive force of escort carriers built between 1943 and 1945, while 370 of them were supplied to the British. The last aircraft built by Grumman was delivered in May 1943, while Eastern Aircraft continued to build FM-2s until August 1945.

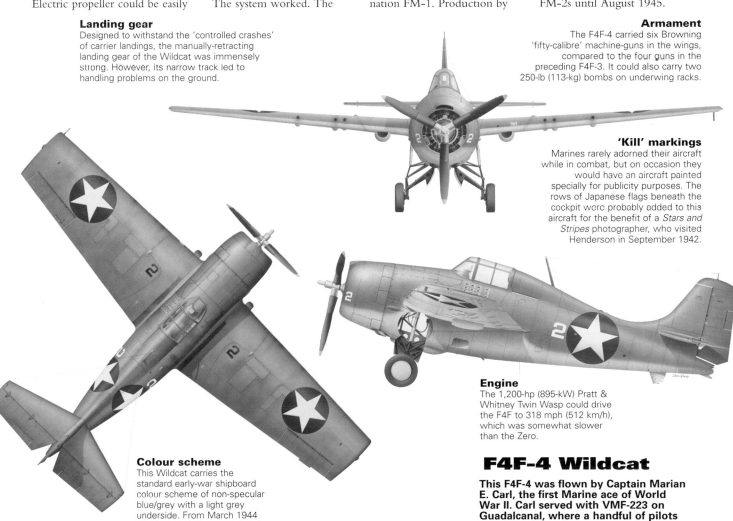

Landing gear
Designed to withstand the 'controlled crashes' of carrier landings, the manually-retracting landing gear of the Wildcat was immensely strong. However, its narrow track led to handling problems on the ground.

Armament
The F4F-4 carried six Browning 'fifty-calibre' machine-guns in the wings, compared to the four guns in the preceding F4F-3. It could also carry two 250-lb (113-kg) bombs on underwing racks.

'Kill' markings
Marines rarely adorned their aircraft while in combat, but on occasion they would have an aircraft painted specially for publicity purposes. The rows of Japanese flags beneath the cockpit were probably added to this aircraft for the benefit of a *Stars and Stripes* photographer, who visited Henderson in September 1942.

Colour scheme
This Wildcat carries the standard early-war shipboard colour scheme of non-specular blue/grey with a light grey underside. From March 1944 US Navy aircraft were painted all over in a much darker gloss sea blue finish.

Engine
The 1,200-hp (895-kW) Pratt & Whitney Twin Wasp could drive the F4F to 318 mph (512 km/h), which was somewhat slower than the Zero.

F4F-4 Wildcat

This F4F-4 was flown by Captain Marian E. Carl, the first Marine ace of World War II. Carl served with VMF-223 on Guadalcanal, where a handful of pilots proved to have the measure of the Japanese. He amassed a tally of 16.5 victories in Wildcats, to which he later added two kills while flying F4U Corsairs.

FAA Martlets & Wildcats

Delivered in September 1940, Martlet Mk I BJ513 was one of the French Cyclone-powered G-36A aircraft. In October it was issued to No. 759 Sqn, the Fleet Fighter School at RNAS Yeovilton.

Before deliveries of the Navy's F4F-3 Wildcats could begin, both France and the UK had placed contracts for the Grumman G-36A and G-36B, respectively. In the event, all were delivered to the British.

Developed in competition with the Brewster XF2A-1 (Buffalo) to provide the US Navy with its first single-seat fighter monoplane, the XF4F-2 flew for the first time on 2 September 1937. To overcome some early problems, particularly associated with the Pratt & Whitney R-1830-SC-G Twin Wasp engine, this prototype was extensively revised as the XF4F-3 and flown on 12 February 1939 with an improved R-1830. The first US Navy contract was placed in August 1939.

Fixed-wing variant

The French order for 81 plus the equivalent of 10 complete airframes in spares, was for a fixed-wing carrier-based version, with an armament of two 7.5-mm Darne guns in the fuselage and four in the wings; the powerplant was a Wright R-1820G-205A engine. Britain's order for 109 was for a folding-wing version with the R-1830-S3C4-G engine and British or US machine-guns. None of the G-36As had been dispatched by the time France collapsed; consequently, Britain took over the full quantity of 91 (in the event the 'spares' were provided as completed aircraft after 10 of the earlier deliveries were lost at sea when en route). These fixed-wing aircraft were given the British designation Martlet Mk I, being delivered with four 0.5-in (12.7-mm) wing guns but none in the fuselage. The first examples reached the UK in August 1940 and No. 804 Sqn at Hatston was nominated to be the first to fly the new aircraft – replacing Sea Gladiators. Combat initiation followed on 25 December 1940

Wildcat Mk VI JV677 was flown by Lt Cdr Bird, CO of No. 882 Sqn aboard HMS Searcher in March 1945. Bird led No. 882 in one of the last productive actions involving FAA Wildcats, downing one of four Bf 109Gs claimed by the unit off Norway in March 1945.

with the destruction of a Junkers Ju 88 off Orkney.

The British-ordered Martlet Mk IIs began to arrive in the UK in April 1941, but the first 10 were 'non-standard' with fixed wings and were redesignated Martlet Mk III in July 1941 as a result. The definitive folding-wing Mk IIs were delivered between August 1941 and early 1942, 36 to the UK and 54 direct to Karachi or China Bay for service in the Far East.

Martlet Mk IIs were urgently needed for service aboard the small escort carriers, and No. 802 Sqn took the new type to sea for the first time in July 1941 in HMS *Audacity*, and in HMS *Argus* in August. The following month, the squadron was again in Audacity escorting a convoy to Gibraltar and claimed the destruction of an Fw 200 Condor. The whole squadron was lost, however, when Audacity was sunk by a U-boat

Below: The Martlet name was dropped in January 1944 in favour of Wildcat. Here a No. 898 Sqn Wildcat Mk V lands aboard HMS Searcher during convoy escort duties in the north Atlantic.

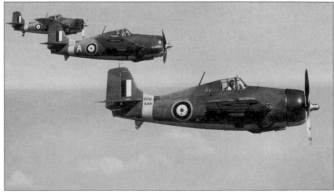

Above: Delivered from a French order, the Wright Cyclone-powered Martlet Mk Is first entered FAA service with No. 804 Sqn in July 1940, replacing Sea Gladiators.

Below: This No. 805 Sqn Martlet Mk III, serving with the RN Fighter Unit during 1941/42, was one of the F4F-3As intended for the Greek air force, and still carries a USN Bureau Number on its rear fuselage. For service in the desert it has been sprayed with a coat of Middle Stone paint.

Above: For improved handling the General Motors-built FM-2 had a taller tailfin. Known to the British as the Wildcat Mk VI, this variant entered Royal Navy service shortly after D-Day.

in December 1941. For the next two years, the Martlet Mk IIs saw intensive service, flying at various times with 10 different FAA front-line squadrons from as many as nine different carriers. Among these were Nos 890 and 892 Sqns, which worked-up at NAS Norfolk in the summer of 1942 using 16 (or more) F4F-3s temporarily on loan from the US Navy. These Martlet squadrons were engaged, in particular, in providing air cover for Arctic convoys to Murmansk in 1942/43.

Martlet Mk IIIs

Another batch of Martlets passed into British service in the Middle East in April 1941, and like the 10 fixed-wing aircraft in the UK, were given the designation Martlet Mk III. These came from a batch of (95) F4F-3As that were folding-wing aircraft with R-1830-90 engines with single-stage two-speed superchargers (whereas the F4F-3 had a two-stage version of the R-1830). The first 30 F4F-3As were released by the US Navy for use by the Greek Air Force, but were still at sea when Greece fell, and were consequently offloaded at Gibraltar and taken over by the Royal Naval Fighter Unit that was then flying from land bases in the Western Desert, particularly in the hands of No. 805 Sqn. In the Western Mediterranean, No. 806 Sqn was aboard HMS *Indomitable* for Operation Pedestal in August 1942 and Nos 882, 888 and 893 Squadrons supported the Operation Torch landings in Algeria. Martlet Mk IIs in the hands of Nos 881 and 882 Sqns aboard HMS *Illustrious* appeared in the Indian Ocean for the first time in May 1942, when Operation Ironclad was mounted to take control of Madagascar.

Passage of the Lend-Lease act allowed Britain to receive further batches of Martlets, starting in mid-1942 with 220 Martlet Mk IVs. Designated F4F-4B by the USN for contractual purposes, these had the Pratt & Whitney R-1830 Twin Wasp engine, folding wings and six 0.5-in (12.7-mm) machine-guns in the wings (all earlier marks having had only four wing guns).

In January 1944, the US Navy name Wildcat was adopted in place of Martlet, applied retrospectively to all earlier mark numbers. Britain then received 312 Wildcat Mk Vs, which were built by Eastern Aircraft Division of General Motors as the FM-1 and differed from the Mk IV in having only four wing guns (but with a greater quantity of ammunition). Finally came 370 Wildcat Mk VIs, these being also Eastern-built (as the FM-2), but powered by the Wright R-1820-56 Cyclone engine, and having a taller fin and rudder. The later Wildcats were fitted to carry,

underwing close in to the fuselage (i.e., inboard of the wing fold), two 250-lb (113-kg) bombs or two 48-Imp gal (220-litre) drop tanks. Trial installations were made of a six-rocket installation under the wings, using either British Mk I rails or US Mk V zero-length launchers, but these weapons were not used operationally on Wildcats.

Major contribution

Having been reinforced with Lend-Lease deliveries, the British Wildcat force was able to make a major contribution in the Battle of the Atlantic, with a dozen squadrons aboard the escort carriers from April 1943 until September 1944. Their objective was to fly defence sorties and to strafe surfaced U-boats. In a generally similar role, four other squadrons flew from escort carriers in the Indian Ocean but, both there and in the Atlantic, the Wildcats were largely out of service by the time the war ended.

British Wildcats at war

Though the Fleet Air Arm produced some 14 aces, very few scored five or more kills on any one FAA type. Lt C. C. Tomkinson was the most successful on the Martlet/Wildcat, claiming 2½ victories over Vichy aircraft over Madagascar in May 1942.

Martlet Mk II AM974/'J'
Another of the more successful Martlet pilots, Sub-Lt B. J. Waller of No. 881 Sqn shared in three victories (over a Vichy French Potez 63 and a pair of MS.406s) off Madagascar in May 1942. His squadron was based aboard HMS *Illustrious*.

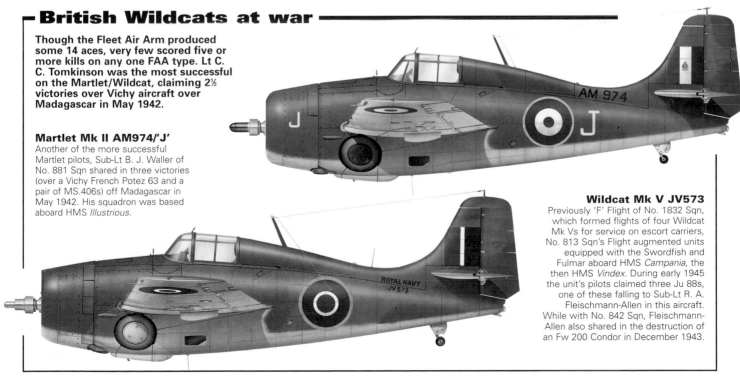

Wildcat Mk V JV573
Previously 'F' Flight of No. 1832 Sqn, which formed flights of four Wildcat Mk Vs for service on escort carriers, No. 813 Sqn's Flight augmented units equipped with the Swordfish and Fulmar aboard HMS *Campania*, the then HMS *Vindex*. During early 1945 the unit's pilots claimed three Ju 88s, one of these falling to Sub-Lt R. A. Fleischmann-Allen in this aircraft. While with No. 842 Sqn, Fleischmann-Allen also shared in the destruction of an Fw 200 Condor in December 1943.

Grumman F6F Hellcat

Left: A radar-equipped F6F-5N night fighter and three F6F-5 Hellcats pose for the camera. Dozens of Hellcat pilots became aces and the leading ace, Commander David McCampbell, scored 34 kills and received the Medal of Honor.

Below: After successful strikes on Truk, F6F-3 Hellcats land on the USS Enterprise. Hellcats destroyed some 6,000 enemy aircraft during World War II and have been credited with almost 75 per cent of the US Navy's air-to-air victories.

Proving to be an outstanding fighter with the US Navy during World War II, the Grumman-designed F6F Hellcat was mass-produced at a rate unequalled by any other aircraft manufacturing programme and went on to turn the tide against the attacking Japanese hordes.

The bright blue, spirited Grumman F6F Hellcat is rarely named on any shortlist of aviation's greatest flying machines, but that is only because the Hellcat has never been given the credit it deserves. Not as fast as a Mustang, not as manoeuvrable as a Zero, lacking the peppiness of a Yakovlev, and by no measure as advanced as the Vought F4U Corsair – which had begun its life on the drawing board at an earlier date – this sturdy and functional product of the 'Grumman Iron Works' did nothing more than

to turn the tide of the Pacific air war.

The Hellcat was one of the few aircraft to need minimal changes during flight test and development, moving quickly from drawing board to combat. This is how one naval aviator described the creation of the Hellcat: "A questionnaire was sent to all Navy and Marine Corps pilots in mid-1942 asking them what they would like in the way of design, manoeuvrability, horsepower, range, firepower, and the ability to operate off an aircraft-carrier.

The naval aviation people went to Grumman and presented them with what they learned; thus was born the F6F Hellcat." The questionnaire was very real, and it meant a lot to hard-pressed naval personnel aboard carriers at sea that their opinion was being sought, but in fact this occasion was the improvement of the basic Hellcat design rather than its beginning. In truth, the Hellcat had been designed after the Japanese attack on Pearl Harbor (on 7 December 1941) had brought

the US into the war. Nor was the Hellcat, as is often claimed, a direct response to Japan's Zero. The Hellcat owes its origin to Grumman company model proposals in 1938 to improve the XF4F-2 Wildcat. However, after considering modifications to this design, engineers decided instead to begin work on a new aircraft – the F6F Hellcat.

Heavyweight fighter

Literature has described the Vought F4U Corsair as 'back-up' insurance against the Hellcat when, if anything, the reverse was true: Grumman forged ahead to ensure that the Navy had a high-performance fighter if the Corsair was delayed. The Corsair did run into developmental problems and, accordingly, the Hellcat was the first to fly from carriers. The latter was intended to be a heavyweight and had enormous strength to enable it to survive against Japanese fighters armed with cannon. However, many thought that the Hellcat was the right aircraft with the wrong

This F6F-5 awaits launch aboard the USS Bennington, poised for more action against Japanese targets. Almost all the major air combats in the Pacific from 1943 were dominated by the Hellcat.

*Above: Finished in the **US** Navy's 1943 scheme of non-specular blue-grey graduating to a light grey-blue around the base of the fuselage, these F6F-3s bear the markings of Navy Squadron **VF-8**. Hellcats continued to serve with the Navy until 1954, after which they were used for several more years in the target drone role.*

Right: The only other operator of the F6F during the war was the Fleet Air Arm, flying the type over Norway, the Mediterranean and the Far East. The unusual way in which the undercarriage folded backwards into the wings is well illustrated in this view.

engine. The initial production version of the Hellcat needed changes because of this, although these were only minor. In an era in which American industry was unchallenged as the world leader, there were other problems involved in building the Hellcat, including inadequate plant space at Bethpage. In spring 1942, therefore, Grumman bought up thousands of steel girders from New York city's dismantled Second Avenue 'el' (elevated railway) and World's Fair pavilion to help build a new Bethpage plant.

Grumman and the Navy improved the Hellcat as the war progressed, in much the way that any aircraft receives improvements over time. In the case of the Hellcat, however, there was little to improve and changes were minimal. At one juncture, an improved windshield resulted from US Navy complaints that dust was accu-

mulating between the curved windshield and the bulletproof transparent plate. In what might have represented a bigger change to the Hellcat, consideration was given to fitting the aircraft with a bubble canopy, but the idea was rejected because it would have dramatically decreased the aircraft's production rate.

So, although there were six variants in the Hellcat series by the end of the war, the fighters were so similar that it was all but impossible to tell them apart. All in all, a total of 12,275 Hellcats were manufactured by Grumman between June 1942 and November 1945.

Hellcat at war

The F6F first saw combat in the Pacific in 1943 and was soon involved in island-hopping campaigns in which many dozens of Navy fighters routinely battled similar numbers of Japanese aircraft. Hellcats are not usually remem-

bered for fighting in Europe, but they did see limited action during Allied landings in southern France in 1944. In one celebrated air engagement, three Heinkel He 111 bombers were downed by F6Fs. The Hellcat was flown by the Navy's top Pacific aces; Captain David McCampbell, the Navy's all-time ace of aces (with 34 kills), shot down nine aircraft in a single mission on

24 October 1944.

Early plans for licence production of the Hellcat by Canadian Vickers never bore fruit, and the only foreign user of the Hellcat during World War II was Britain, which had once planned to name the aircraft the Gannet. Among the many actions carried out by British Hellcat pilots were strikes against the German battleship *Tirpitz*.

*Above: The 10,000th Hellcat, an F6F-5, was delivered to VFB-87 aboard the **USS** Ticonderoga in May 1945. During construction, a bucket was hung upon its tail and used by Grumman workers for the collection of money for the squadron; $700 was collected in all.*

Left: At least 120 ex-USN Hellcats were supplied to France's Aéronavale for use in Indo-China, and survivors later served in North Africa.

F6F Hellcat

From Bethpage to the Pacific

Above: The second Hellcat prototype was completed as an XF6F-3 with a Pratt & Whitney R-2800-10W engine and minor airframe modifications. The aircraft first flew on 30 July 1942, and was joined in September by the original prototype, re-engined to the same standard. Note the propeller spinner, omitted from production aircraft.

Left: Gear down, an early production F6F-3 poses for the camera. The first production Hellcats were issued to VF-9 aboard the aircraft-carrier USS Essex and went into action in the Pacific on 31 August 1943.

The most important fighter to operate from the US Navy's carrier fleet during World War II, the F6F underwent remarkably little development, wartime production consisting of just two major variants.

Grumman's F6F Hellcat was one of those rare aircraft that was right from the very beginning. Rarely in history has the first prototype of a new warplane rolled out of the factory been refined to such perfection that only minor problems showed up during flight test and development, enabling the aircraft to move quickly from drawing board to combat. The

Hellcat is best remembered today as the big, powerful fighter that wrested control from Japan's vaunted Mitsubishi A6M5 Zero, but it should also be remembered as a kind of aeronautical miracle – a flying machine almost without flaw.

The Hellcat owes its origin to Grumman plans in 1938 to install a 1,500-hp (1119-kW) Pratt & Whitney R-1830 Twin Wasp radial engine in a derivative of the XF4F-2 Wildcat. In fact, the plans were short-lived. Engineers rejected this design and, instead, moved boldly to create a wholly new fighter initially built around the new and promising 1,700-hp (1268-kW) Wright R-2600-10 Cyclone 14 radial.

From the start, the Grumman engineers on Long Island drew from a decade of experience in building carrier-based fighters, thought constantly about the demanding rigours of operations from flat-top decks, and sought to achieve power, strength and durability. The result was a conventional, low-wing, 'tail dragger' fighter using all-metal construction with flush-riveted skins. The Hellcat's wings had outer panels that folded for stowage aboard ship. Standard armament comprised six 0.50-calibre (12.7-mm) Browning machine-guns located

This Grumman photograph, dated 10 March 1943, shows one of the XF6F prototypes next to another product of the 'Ironworks', the TBF Avenger. With the proliferation of Grumman designs during World War II, production was often contracted out. While all Hellcats were built by Grumman, most Avengers were in fact TBMs, built by a division of General Motors.

Left: Brand-new Hellcats await collection outside Grumman's Bethpage, Long Island plant. Originally it was intended that Canadian Vickers build the F6F-1 (as the FV-1), but plans did not proceed and the F6F-3 became the first production version, beginning in 1943.

Below: Over half of the 12,275 F6Fs built were F6F-5s; around 900 became FAA Hellcat Mk IIs.

in the wings. The fuselage and tail were conventional in structure and very similar to those of the earlier F4F Wildcat.

An evaluation by the US Navy of Grumman's design proposal resulted in an order dated 30 June 1941, covering two prototypes. Between them, these aircraft test-flew four different engine types, permitting their competitive evaluation of the flight envelope. The other three engine types were the R-2600-16, the more reliable, 2,000-hp (1491-kW) Pratt & Whitney R-2800-10 Double Wasp, and the R-2800-27.

Hellcat myth

One myth from the wartime years is that the Hellcat – which was a beautiful aircraft as well as a robust one – was the first American combat craft designed after the US entered the war; in fact, many aspects of its design were determined before Pearl Harbor. In the early days of US involvement in the conflict, Americans used the word 'Zero' to refer to any Japanese fighter (including the Japanese army's Ki-43 Hayabusa or 'Oscar') and headlines spoke of the supremacy and invulnerability of the Zero and the woefulness of American

combatants, especially the carrier-based Brewster F2A Buffalo and Grumman F4F Wildcat. The true Zero – the Mitsubishi fighter – was a superior warplane but had some weaknesses, including lack of armour for pilot and fuel system.

Although the size and shape of the Hellcat were finalised before the US entered the war, Grumman engineers did, in fact, have access to considerable information about the capabilities of Japanese fighters. It was difficult to hit a Zero, but a single hit would bring it down. It was much harder to set a Hellcat afire, or wound its pilot, or disable its hydraulics, because the F6F design was sturdier and stronger.

Also persistent is the myth that the less-celebrated Vought F4U Corsair was a 'back-up' insurance purchase by the US Navy in case the bold Hellcat design should fail. In fact, it was the other way around: Grumman conceived, designed, built and tested the Hellcat to give the US Navy an option in case the much earlier Corsair was delayed. The Corsair did fall foul of developmental problems and the Hellcat flew combat missions from carriers at an earlier date.

Hellcat variants

The new fighter was a heavyweight and had enormous strength to enable it to survive against Japanese fighters armed with cannon. The first all-silver XF6F-1 made its first flight on 26 June 1942. The initial production version of the Hellcat, the F6F-3, powered by an R-2800-10 (or -10W with water injection), introduced a propeller without spinner hub, and minor changes to the engine cowling.

In an era in which American industry emerged as the world

leader, there was inadequate factory space at Grumman's Bethpage, New York plant. In spring 1942, Grumman bought up thousands of steel girders from New York city's dismantled Second Avenue 'el' (elevated railway) and World's Fair pavilion to help construct a new building to handle increased production.

The company continued to develop the Hellcat and turned out the XF6F-4, powered by the R-2800-27 Double Wasp, and later used to test 20-mm cannon armament.

The F6F-5 made its first flight on 5 April 1944. This was the definitive version. F6F-5 variants were powered by R2800-10Ws with water injection and became the final production version of the Hellcat. Numerous sub-variants of all Hellcat models were used as night-fighters and for photo-reconnaissance.

The XF6F-6 appellation went to a pair of production F6F-5 Hellcat fighters modified to handle the R-2800-18W engine with a four-bladed propeller, the only version so-equipped.

Above: The night-fighter variant of the F6F-5, the F6F-5N, of which well over 1,000 examples were produced, carried an AN/APS-6 radar in a pod on the starboard wing. Late-production F6F-5Ns had 20-mm cannon fitted to increase kill probability during night sorties.

Right: Two XF6F-6 prototypes were converted from incomplete F6F-5 airframes, fitted with a 2,100-hp (1566-kW) R-2800-18W radial driving a four-bladed propeller. Plans to produce the variant beginning in September 1944 were cancelled due to the engine being required to power the better-performing F4U-4 Corsair.

Hellcat into combat

Landing aboard USS Yorktown (CV-10) in spring 1943, the Hellcat's similarity to the earlier F4F Wildcat is readily apparent. Introduced into the USN fleet in January 1943, the Hellcat saw action against the Japanese within seven months.

The F6F first saw combat on 31 August 1943, with the Pacific Fleet. US Navy warplanes from several carriers went into action near Marcus Island, and Lt Richard Loesch of squadron VF-6 scored the first aerial victory to be credited to a Hellcat.

Putting this fine combat aircraft into battle quickly and effectively was a tribute to the American industrial machine and to the US Navy's administrative talents. Will Carroll, a naval aviator who had his baptism with an F6F-3 (BuNo. 04940) on 15 April 1943, remembered "There was no instructor. At the runway's end, you were cleared for takeoff. You pushed the throttle forward and the airplane threw your head against the headrest. That's what kind of plane it was."

Carroll never left the US, but logged hundreds of hours in the Hellcat with ferry squadron VRF-1, the indispensable outfit that delivered F6F fighters from the Grumman plant to the fleet. He recalled that the F6F was "always a little troublesome to get going, with its shotgun starter", in contrast to the hand crank on the F4F Wildcat. Carroll noted that the compact Hellcat "was much bigger than it looked, with its 14-ft [4.26-m] propeller".

Thanks to ferry flights by Carroll and others, Hellcats joined the Pacific island-hopping campaign. There was no false start. F6F Hellcats achieved success after success in the Solomons, Gilberts, and Marshalls, including the bloody Marine invasion of Tarawa in the Marshall Islands.

The American press had claimed early in the war that the Mitsubishi A6M Zero was almost unbeatable. However,

while it had superb manoeuvring ability and cannon armament, the Zero offered its pilot little protection and could not sustain battle damage and continue to fight. The bigger, heavier and more powerful Hellcat was more robust, and its pilot was protected by armour lacking in the Zero.

The Hellcat had gone from drawing board to combat with few design changes and was without question one of the finest fighters in the world; at last, an American pilot could triumph over the Zero, confident in the performance of his own aircraft. The Hellcat was not perfect, however. Its visibility could have been better, and the aircraft had a tendency to weathercock on the ground unless the tail wheel was locked. Its main landing gear provided such little clearance that, at

some angles of attack, the propeller would strike the ground (or carrier deck), with catastrophic results.

Yet the superiority afforded by the Hellcat was beyond dispute. On 5 October 1943, Ensign Robert W. Duncan of VF-5 scored a 'first' when he became the first Hellcat pilot to shoot down two Japanese Zero fighters in a single engagement,

a feat that would often be repeated. In an air battle of enormous proportions near Kwajalein on 4 December 1943, 91 Hellcats tangled with 50 Zeros and shot down 28, with a loss of just two F6Fs.

The Hellcat showed its worth as a night-fighter in February 1944 when F6F-3Ns from VF(N)-76 began to fly combat missions from the decks of

Above: With the details of his target displayed on the deck crew member's board, this VF-1 'Tophatters' pilot – flying from USS Yorktown on 19 June 1944 – prepares to embark upon a 'Marianas Turkey Shoot' mission over the Philippine Sea.

Left: Deck crew prepare VF-83 Hellcats aboard USS Essex (CV-9) off Ie Shima in April 1945. Pilots of VF-83, the most successful F6F unit during Okinawa operations, accounted for 122 enemy aircraft between 1 April and 23 June 1945.

Left: The Royal Navy's HMS Emperor launched Hellcats for the 1944 Tirpitz strikes. The Emperor's Nos 800 and 804 Squadrons achieved, between them, 8½ aerial victories.

Below: This F6F Hellcat is pictured aboard USS Randolph in March 1945. The first Hellcat ace and double ace, 'Ham' McWhorter, flew similar striped-tailed VF-12 Hellcats from the Randolph. McWhorter's full wartime tally was 12 aircraft.

Above: USS Enterprise (CV-6) flew the Hellcats of VF-20 during 1944. Claiming 135.16 victories between 10 October and 30 November 1944, the unit was one of the most successful in the Leyte theatre. The Battle of Leyte Gulf involved nearly 550 F6Fs.

Below: VF-12 Hellcats are pictured leaving USS Randolph (CV-15) for a raid on Japan in July 1945. Air Group 12 was something of a 'crack' fighter unit, with its ranks embellished by former VF-9 'Fighting Nine' aces, including McWhorter, Armistead M. Smith, Reuben Denoff, John M. Franks and Harold Vita. By the end of the Pacific war, Randolph was carrying the Hellcats of VF-16.

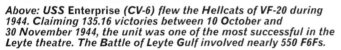

Until the summer of 1944, USN Hellcats wore, almost exclusively, a two-tone blue camouflage scheme, with gloss white undersides. This was gradually replaced by an all-over Dark Sea Blue scheme.

'Essex'-class carriers. VF(N)-77 and -78 soon followed and the three squadrons racked up an impressive record of nearly two dozen night kills. It became the practice for four Hellcat night-fighters to operate with each VF (fighter squadron) aboard a carrier. Several additional night-fighter squadrons also participated in Pacific fighting and at least five Hellcat pilots became aces during the nocturnal hours.

F6F-3N night-fighters belonging to Marine Corps squadron VMF(N)-534 began combat operations from Guam in August 1944. The following month, VMF(N)-541, also equipped with F6F-3Ns, arrived on Peleliu. Initially, the US Marines achieved few results in their efforts to take the night back from the Japanese – though it is difficult to measure the deterrent effect that night operations clearly had – but in later months the story changed.

As for continuing day-fighting, on 17 and 18 February 1943, during carrier strikes on Truk, Hellcats from 10 squadrons destroyed 127 Japanese aircraft in the air and 86 on the ground. "There was metal flying around", remembered Marine Cpt. M. P. Curphey, "but the Hellcat handled well at low altitude and you could line up and shoot at 'em without having to make a lot of complicated adjustments." On 29 and 30 March 1944, Hellcats from no fewer than 11 aircraft-carriers shot down 150 Japanese aircraft in and around Palau.

The Hellcat was flown by every US Navy ace in the Pacific. Captain David McCampbell became the navy's all-time ace of aces, with 34 kills. As skipper of carrier air group 15 aboard USS *Essex* (CV-9), McCampbell shot down nine aircraft in a single mission on 24 October 1944.

Although it was a superb aircraft in an aesthetic sense, the F6F Hellcat must have been a disappointment to purists keen on studying individual aircraft markings. Although US Navy and Marine combat units painted an individual number (technically called a 'side number') or a number/letter code on every aircraft, few opportunities were offered for artists to show their creativity and the aircraft, for the most part, were indistinguishable from each other.

Notable exceptions were the F6Fs of VF-27 aboard USS *Princeton* which boasted a variation on the sharksmouth design, the shark complete with glaring eyeballs.

Hellcats are not usually remembered for fighting in Europe. The big Grumman fighter did, however, see limited action against the Third Reich. During Allied landings in southern France in 1944, at least two squadrons from USS *Tulagi* (CVE-72) and USS *Kasaan Bay* (CVE-69) provided air cover, strafed and bombed, and shot down three Heinkel He 111 bombers. Thereafter, both vessels and Hellcats were reassigned to the Pacific. It was a difficult war out there, in the ocean expanses around Japan – and the Hellcat's job was not yet finished.

Left: June 1944, and a Hellcat is stowed on the deck of the USS Hornet (CV-12), after a raid on the Marianas. Popularly known as 'the Turkey Shoot', 1944's Marianas operations were codenamed Operation Forager.

Hellcat ascendancy

The F6F produced more US aces than any other aircraft, and gave rise to the greatest number of aces from a single engagement. No fewer than seven men achieved ace status in the 'Marianas Turkey Shoot'.

Medal of Honor recipient Captain David McCampbell (with 34 kills), described by a wingman as having 'hands of magic', used typical, colourless fighter-pilot talk to describe the remarkable performance offered by the Grumman F6F Hellcat. He referred to it as "a satisfying performer and a stable gun platform". With greater endurance and survivability than Japan's famous A6M Zero, the Hellcat was able to stay in the fight, slug it out, and return safely to the carrier. McCampbell was pleased when the F6F-5 variant arrived

on the scene, providing a limited air-to-ground capability, including rails for the launching of 5-in (127-mm) HVARs (high-velocity aircraft rockets).

Other leading US Navy aces were LCr Cecil Harris with 24 kills, LCdr Gene Valencia with 23, and LCdrs Alex Vraciu and Pat Fleming with 19 each. Vraciu, of squadron VF-6, flew both the F6F Hellcat and the F4U Corsair.

In a little-publicised experiment, the US Navy developed a unique catapult that made it possible to launch a Hellcat from the below-decks hangar of an

aircraft-carrier, without using an elevator to bring it up to the deck. The 72-ft (21.94-m) H-2 catapult was tried on four carriers, USS *Yorktown* (CV-5), *Enterprise* (CV-6), *Wasp* (CV-7), and *Hornet* (CV-8). This effort to ease congestion on the main deck of the carrier was demonstrated in the combat zone with no difficulty, but plans to convert six more 'Essex'-class carriers to this installation were abandoned.

Hellcats fought across the Pacific and were in action at Saipan, Iwo Jima and Okinawa. During fighting at Okinawa, three Marine squadrons, VMF(N)-533, -542, and -543, accounted for 68

Above: VF-15's Lt Bert Dewayne Morris, Jr (Hollywood movie star Wayne Morris), is seen aboard the USS Essex in 1944. During the Leyte occupation from October to November 1944, VF-15 led the field with 140.5 kills.

Japanese aircraft shot down during night battles. Improved Japanese fighters such as the Nakajima Ki-84 'Frank' and Kawanishi N1K1 'George' appeared to have a chance of challenging the Hellcat more effectively than the Mitsubishi Zero. They were too few and too late, however; the Americans now had not only a better warplane but overwhelm-

The scene aboard the USS Enterprise in November 1943, as Lt Walter L. Chewning, the catapult officer, climbs aboard an F6F-3 to rescue Ensign Byron M. Johnson (later an ace, with eight kills) of VF-2, near the Gilbert Islands.

The take-off flag launches this VF-16 F6F from USS Lexington, during an attack on the Marshall Islands in November 1943. USS Yorktown is in the background, with VF-5 aboard.

Right: The USS Yorktown's flight deck on 5 October 1943 is occupied by the F6F-3s of VF-5. Cdr Jim Flatley leads the line-up, on the day the USN returned to the skies over Wake Island after a long absence, and claimed a total of 17 Zeros in 24 hours.

Below: The scene at Betio islet as a VF-1 F6F-3 lands in November 1943, in the shadow of a Zero hulk. One of the main aims of the Tarawa assault was the capture of the Betio airstrip; days later, VF-1 staged 24-hour CAS missions for US marines from there.

ing numerical superiority.

In late 1944, Marine squadron VMF(N)-541 moved to Leyte in the Philippines, where it claimed 22 aerial kills and five Japanese aircraft destroyed on the ground in a six-week period ending on 11 January 1945. A number of Marine day-fighter squadrons at this time were training with air-to-ground rockets in preparation for action in Europe against V-1 rocket bomb launch sites, but these units were instead shifted to the Pacific.

Other US Marine squadrons that flew the Hellcat in combat from the decks of escort carriers included VMF-351, -511, -512, -513 and -514. A US Marine photo squadron, VMD-354, flew F6F-5P Hellcats at Guam late in the war. With Japan resorting to kamikaze attacks in the Philippines and at Pearl Harbor, the US Navy established VBF (fighter-bomber) squadrons in addition to its traditional VFs, giving each aircraft-carrier an added fighter capability. Both F6F Hellcats and F4U Corsairs equipped these squadrons, which had limited success in countering the kamikazes.

Early plans for licence-production of the Hellcat by Canadian Vickers never bore fruit. The only foreign user of the Hellcat during World War II was Britain, which had once planned to name the aircraft the Gannet. In all, 1,177 Hellcats reached the Fleet Air Arm: 252 F6F-3s became the Hellcat Mk I in British service and began arriving in May 1943; 849 F6F-5s and 76 F6F-5Ns became Hellcat Mk IIs. Some of the latter mark were modified by Blackburn Aircraft for a limited air-to-ground capability, while others had cameras installed for the photo-reconnaissance role.

British operations

On 3 April 1944, British Hellcat pilots of Nos 800 and 804 Squadrons covered strikes against the German battleship *Tirpitz*, anchored in Kaafjord, Norway. While operating from the carrier HMS *Emperor*, Hellcats also covered a convoy to Gibraltar in June 1944 and, like their American counterparts, covered Allied landings in southern France in August 1944.

The British Hellcats operated throughout the East Indies, Malaya, Burma, and in the final assault on Japan. On 29 August 1944, first blood was drawn when British Hellcats aboard HMS *Indomitable* covered air strikes in the Dutch East Indies. By the end of 1945, the last FAA Hellcats had been retired from front-line service.

A total of 12,275 Hellcats was manufactured by Grumman between June 1942 and November 1945, the largest number of fighters ever produced at a single factory. The Grumman F6F Hellcat was designed, built, tested, entered into service, put into combat, and brought home faster than any of the other major American combat aircraft.

Below: F6Fs return from an attack on Formosa, with one aircraft recovered on the flight deck, and another taking a wave-off. During the Formosa operations of 1944, the US Fast Carrier Force faced 350 Japanese aircraft on the island, half of them fighters.

Above: VF-16 pilots pictured aboard USS Lexington, CVAG-16, during a period of anti-submarine patrols in November 1943. The third top-scoring F6F unit of 1943 (55 kills), its pilots wear standard life-preservers, with dye marker pouches and flare rounds.

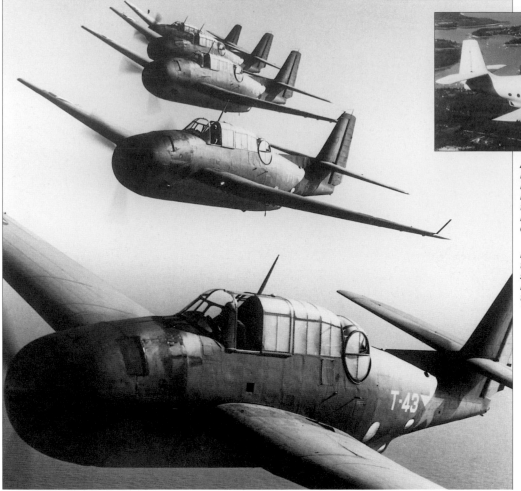

Above: The first XTBF-1 is seen here in flight over Long Island in the latter half of 1941. A number of changes was made to the aircraft in its brief career, most notably the addition of a dorsal fin at the base of the tail.

Left: This picture depicts five of the first TBF Avengers to enter squadron service. The national markings and camouflage date the photograph as post-May 1942 and pre-February 1943.

Grumman TBF Avenger

Development

For over 50 years Gruman has provided some of the world's best carrier-based aircraft, typified by generous wings, amiable handling and such strength that the company is colloquially known as 'The Iron Works'. No aircraft better exemplifies Grumman than the Avenger, chief torpedo-bomber of the Pacific war in 1942-45.

On the Avenger's first combat mission, on 4 June 1942, six new TBF-1s thundered off into the Battle of Midway. Only one came back, and that had the pilot flying a shattered aircraft on the trimmers, one crewman injured and the other dead. This seemed almost a repetition of what had been happening with the previous-generation Douglas TBD-1 Devastator, which was simply not survivable in World War II. In fact, nothing could have been further from the truth, and the Avenger was to be one of the great winners of the conflict.

When Douglas had produced the TBD in 1935 it had been as modern as the hour, with all-metal stressed-skin construction, enclosed cockpits and retractable gear. As early as October 1939, however, it was clear that a single 900-hp (671-kW) engine was inade-

quate for the ship-based torpedo-bomber mission, and in that month the US Navy began organising plans for an industry competition for a replacement aircraft. The key to the development lay in the existence of such powerful engines as the Pratt & Whitney R-2800 and the Wright R-2600 and R-3350. Grumman was well placed to win what was certain to be a major programme.

The US Navy's stipulations were no pushover, however, and the numerical requirements for mission radius with particular weaponloads could only just be met. In an intensive five weeks at the turn of 1941 the engineering team, under chief experimental engineer Bob Hall, roughed out the shape that was later to be called 'The Pregnant Beast' or, more kindly, 'The Turkey'. That portly fuselage, giant angular wing and distinc-

tive tail could only have come from Grumman, but what might not have been expected were the internal weapons bay and the gun turret. Project engineer R. Koch was first to decide on an internal bay, partly because this fitted in with the lower rear defensive gun position. There was no problem with the pilot, who sat in lofty state in a roomy and comfortable cockpit above the leading edge, where his view was perfect. The other two crew were less obvious.

A door on the right side aft of the wing gave access to the rear fuselage, which was packed with equipment, flares, parachutes and ammunition. At the lower level the bombardier was provided with a folding seat from which he could either man the lower rear machine-gun, a Browning of 0.3-in (7.62-mm) calibre, or face forward and aim the aircraft for medium-altitude level bombing.

Radar installation

During development in 1942 radar was introduced to the US Navy, and the Westinghouse ASB radar became standard equipment on some versions. Another common fit was the APG-4 'Sniffer' low-level auto-bombing radar which used a dipole Yagi array, toed out at 40° under each outer wing. The radar viewing scope was ahead of the bombardier, whose compartment thus became somewhat crowded. The radar scope was, in fact, directly under the turret, which in itself was an innovation where the US Navy was concerned (though a turret had been fitted to a few other single-engined attack types such as the Soviet BB-1/Su-2).

The US Navy had specified a

Above: A flight of TBFs makes a textbook torpedo attack with box-tailed Mk XIII weapons in the summer of 1942. The Mk XIII torpedo was less than ideal for the Avenger as it could not be dropped above 100 mph (161 km/h) or 120 ft (37 m).

Seen overflying the ASW ship USS John A. Bole, this pair of TBM-3E Avengers carries the midnight blue livery of the late 1940s. Although not specifically anti-submarine variants, they were assigned to the shore-based squadron, VS-25.

Above: As the largest single-engined aircraft to serve in World War II, the Avenger represented a massive step-up in capability and complexity compared to the TBD Devastator.

turret, to mount a single 0.5-in (12.7-mm) gun, and Grumman handled the development in-house. Although almost everything on the TBF was hydraulic, it eventually found itself with an electrically-driven turret, chiefly because the job was assigned to Oscar Olsen whose entire background (mainly with General Electric) had been electrical. He was aware of the problems caused by flight manoeuvres which could impose totally different loads on different parts of the turret

mount ring. The best answer appeared to Olsen to be the Amplidyne form of control, which can govern both the torque and speed of an electric motor with great precision. He was thus able to equip the turret with synchronised motors which, no matter what the attitude of the turret or aircraft might be, always gave fingertip gun-pointing accuracy.

Landing gear

In contrast, most of the other movable items were hydraulic,

Converted from TBM-3Es, the TBM-3W2 'hunter' entered service with VS squadrons in 1950-51 and operated in conjunction with TBM-3S 'killers' in the anti-submarine role.

including the massive main landing gears (which could take a bone-crushing arrival at 16 ft/ 4.88 m per second vertical velocity onto a hard deck), the folding outer wings, the big split flaps and the double-fold bomb doors.

Leroy Grumman himself had hit on the wing fold only a year earlier, and this feature was first applied to production models of the F4F Wildcat then just coming off the line. He had foreseen the clearance problem caused by conventional upward-hinged wings on carrier hangar decks, and so experimented with two partly unfolded paperclips stuck into the sides of a draughtsman's soap-eraser. Eventually he got the two clips at just the right skewed angle so that the 'wings' folded neatly alongside the 'body'. In the folded position the upper surfaces faced outwards. For the big TBF power-folding was essential; no crew of men could have handled such wings, loaded with radar, tanks and rockets, on a pitching deck. The only other item driven electrically was the giant sting arrester hook, normally housed inside the rear fuselage, but extended on rails by a cable and pulley track when needed.

Weapon fit

As well as the two rear guns, a 0.3-in (7.62-mm) gun was mounted high on the right side of the nose, firing through the propeller disc. It was always considered good practice to give

the pilot a gun, not only to improve morale, but for sound offensive reasons. Though the bombardier could aim bombs from altitude, it was the pilot who managed torpedo attacks, using the illuminated torpedo sight on the left side of the coaming. Ahead, he had merely a ring-and-bead sight for the gun, though this could also be used for dive-bombing, the bombardier then being a mere passenger. The main gears could be extended as airbrakes to hold dives to about 300 mph (482 km/h), though the controls became exceedingly heavy and a great deal of effort and fast re-trimming were needed both in the dive and the pull-out.

The first of two XTBF-1 prototypes, BuNo. 2539, made a highly successful maiden flight on 1 August 1941. The pilot, as with most experimental Grumman aircraft at the time, was the chief experimental engineer himself, Bob Hall. He had only recently been fished from the ocean after deciding that the XP-50 was no longer a safe place in which to stay, and he found the XTBF-1 a welcome contrast, seemingly as safe as houses with the trusty 14-cylinder Cyclone tumbling lustily ahead of his feet. Grumman was fast becoming overloaded with work and was well into the construction of Plant 2, a complete new factory twice as big as the first. Here would be built the 286 TBFs ordered 'off the drawing board' in December 1940.

The deck of the 'Independence'-class carrier USS Belleau Wood burns fiercely after being hit in a kamikaze raid in October 1944, repairs taking three months. Earlier, in June of that year, the carrier's Avengers had contributed to the sinking of the Japanese carrier, IJNS Hiyo.

Avenger goes to war

After a disastrous start to combat operations at Midway, the Avenger went on to be the Allies' most important torpedo-bomber of the war. The aircraft later also proved deadly when armed with conventional bombs and air-launched rockets.

After an initially successful flight trial period, trouble for the TBF project came out of the blue. On 28 November 1941 the XTBF-1 was flying in the hands of Bob Cook and engineer Gordon Israel. Near Brentwood, about 10 miles (16 km) east of the Bethpage plant, they found that the bomb bay was burning fiercely. (The only cause anyone could think of was an electrical fault.) Cook and Israel parachuted out, and the flaming torpedo-bomber dived into some woods. This did not damage the programme, and by

this time the US Navy had changed its order for 286 to an open-ended contract which was to last until 31 December 1943, 2,291 aircraft later (and with even bigger numbers built by others).

On an unseasonably hot Sunday morning, 7 December 1941, all was bustle at Bethpage as, amid colourful ceremony, the vast new Plant 2 was dedicated. Spotlighted in the middle was the

gleaming new second prototype XTBF-1, which was to be the priority product. Suddenly the company vice-president, Clint Towl, was called to the telephone by the public address system. He picked up the instrument to be told, "The Japs have attacked Pearl Harbor; we're at war." Towl prohibited any announcement, and the public began to go home; then, when the last of the thousands had gone through the gate, the plant was locked and searched for any saboteurs. It was to be a secure place for the next four years; and the TBF was appropriately named the Avenger.

By this time Plant 2 was

already full of production TBF-1s, and the number one off the line, BuNo. 00373, flew on 3 January 1942. So few engineering changes had been needed that, by the end of six months, another 145 had been delivered, with half of US Navy squadron VT-8 already nearing the end of its conversion course at NAS Norfolk, Virginia. From here the six new TBFs were flown, with 270-US gal (1022-litre) tanks in the bomb bays, right across the USA and over the 10-hour ocean sector to Pearl Harbor. Their ship, USS Hornet, had already departed, so they rumbled on all the way to Midway Island. It was here that all six aircraft were shot to pieces; it was perhaps the only occasion on which the TBF came off second-best. From that time on it was to be the destroyer not only of the Japanese navy, but also of Hitler's U-boats.

Long legs

With the normal internal load of a Mk XIII-2 torpedo or four 500-lb (227-kg) bombs, and full internal fuel of 335 US gal (1268 litres) in three wing tanks, the TBF-1 could attack targets up to 260 miles (418 km) distant. It was always pleasant to fly, though spinning was prohibited. When flown with determination by a strong pilot it could almost turn like a fighter. Quite early in production it was decided to increase the forward-firing armament, the TBF-1C having the 0.3-in (7.62-mm) nose gun replaced by two of 0.5-in (12.7-mm) calibre in the outer wings, each with 600 rounds. These are included in the Grumman total of 2,291, no breakdown being possible. This total also includes 395 TBF-1Bs, which were fitted with British radio and several other different equipment items for the Fleet Air Arm.

Altogether, the British received no fewer than 921 Avengers (the original British name Tarpon being dropped), which equipped 33 first- and second-line squadrons. These served on literally dozens of carriers, numerous UK bases and many other shore stations from Canada to Ceylon and the Far East.

USMC Avengers taxi out at Piva for a strike. The Allied foothold on Bougainville was subject to occasional assault by the Japanese and the attentions of 'Pistol Pete', a naval gun hidden in the mountains.

Left: In addition to bombs and rockets, the Avenger was cleared to drop less deadly cargo. Here, a load of food, water and ammunition is parachuted to the First Marine Regiment, cut off from its supplies by muddy roads at Shuri Castle.

Below left: In the closing months of the war, Allied air power was overwhelming. Here, an assortment of Avengers from the Essex air group bombs the Japanese mainland.

New producer

In December 1941 the urgent need for TBFs made it essential to find a second-source producer. General Motors had five plants on the east coast (Tarrytown, Linden, Bloomfield, Trenton and Baltimore), which were without work. Quickly they were organised into a powerful team called Eastern Aircraft Division, and they tooled up to build not only Wildcat fighters under the designation FM, but also Avengers, the latter being designated TBM. By December 1943 the 1,000th Eastern TBM had been delivered, and the final total by VJ-Day from this builder was no fewer than 7,546 in more than 20 variants. Most were of the TBM-3 type, with more power and an external arrester hook, often with no turret and in all cases with provision for outer-wing rockets or drop tanks. The Dash-1D (TBF and TBM) and the TBM-3D and -3E had the RT-5/APS-4 search radar, operating at 3-cm wavelength,

in a pod well outboard on the right wing.

Thus, by the end of the war, 9,836 Avengers had been produced, including small numbers of many special variants, of which perhaps the most significant was the Project Cadillac testbed, first of the TBM-3W series – in November 1946 this became the first aircraft to fly the APS-20 surveillance radar in a giant 'Guppy' radome. After 1945 the dominant model was the TBM-3E, used both with and without a turret, and supplied under the Mutual Assistance Program to many friendly navies, including those of Canada, France, the Netherlands and, later, Japan (the country against which most Avengers had fought!). In the US Navy and also in Britain the anti-submarine Dash-3S served in hunter/killer pairs with the Dash-3W and -3W2 with 'Guppy' radars and triple fins until June 1954, several utility models going on for years longer.

TBF-1 Avenger

This illustration shows one of the first TBF-1 Avengers to come off the Grumman production line at Bethpage early in 1942, bearing the number 25. Only about 200 examples were delivered with the national insignia as shown; the insignia was revised in June 1943 with the addition of a red border with white bars.

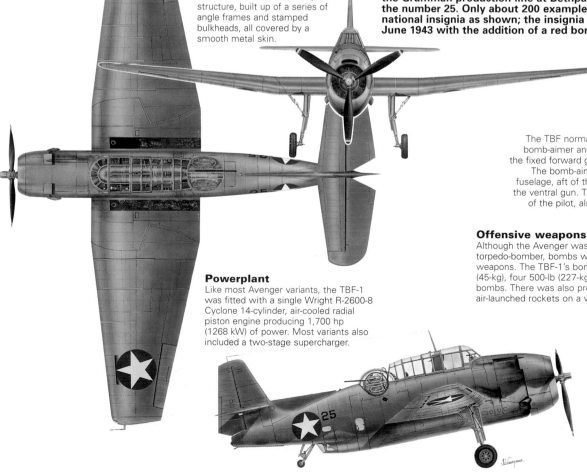

Fuselage
The chunky fuselage had an oval-section, semi-monocoque structure, built up of a series of angle frames and stamped bulkheads, all covered by a smooth metal skin.

Powerplant
Like most Avenger variants, the TBF-1 was fitted with a single Wright R-2600-8 Cyclone 14-cylinder, air-cooled radial piston engine producing 1,700 hp (1268 kW) of power. Most variants also included a two-stage supercharger.

Avenger crew
The TBF normally had a crew of three – pilot, bomb-aimer and radio operator. The pilot fired the fixed forward guns and released the torpedo. The bomb-aimer's position was in the lower fuselage, aft of the bomb bay; he also operated the ventral gun. The radio operator, who was aft of the pilot, also served as the turret gunner.

Offensive weapons
Although the Avenger was designed as a torpedo-bomber, bombs were by far its primary weapons. The TBF-1's bomb bay could carry 12 100-lb (45-kg), four 500-lb (227-kg) or two 1,000-lb (454-kg) bombs. There was also provision for 5-in (12.7-cm) air-launched rockets on a variety of mountings.

Undercarriage
The cantilever undercarriage oleo legs were hinged at the extremities of the centre section and were raised outwardly into recesses in the undersides of the outer wing-sections, and the tailwheel was fully retractable.

FAA Avengers saw service in the Pacific from mid-1943. This aircraft is seen overflying **HMS** Indomitable *in late May 1945, during strikes on Sakishima. No. 857 Sqn operated Avengers from the deck of* **Indomitable.**

FAA/RNZAF service

Two other Allied air arms operated the Avenger during World War II – the British Fleet Air Arm and the Royal New Zealand Air Force. Both services used the type almost exclusively as a bomber.

Destined to become the principal torpedo-bomber used by the US Navy and, eventually, the FAA, in the Pacific war theatre, the Avenger was truly an example of 'the right aircraft at the right time'. Its design originated from a Bureau of Aeronautics requirement circulated in March 1939, and the prototype XTBF-l first flew on 7 August 1941. Production contracts had by then already been placed, and the first combat mission was flown on 4 June 1942. Early experience was inauspicious, but problems were successfully overcome and production demands led to a second source being provided by Eastern Aircraft Division, set up by General Motors. British Avengers came from both Grumman and Eastern Aircraft production.

Delivery of the Grumman torpedo-bombers to the Royal Navy began in August 1942, the name Tarpon Mk I being allocated; this was changed to Avenger TR.Mk I in January 1944 to conform to US Navy nomenclature. (Tarpon is a species of fish – the FAA's aircraft naming policy of the period specifying names of marine animals and fishes for torpedo-spotter types.) Provided through Lend-Lease, the 627 Mk I aircraft were US Navy TBF-1B or TBF-1C models; the -1B designation was specific to the Lend-Lease version of the TBF-1, while the -1C had extra fuel in a bomb-bay tank and underwing tank provision, plus two 0.5-in (12.7-mm) wing guns.

Tarpon enters service

No. 832 Squadron was selected to put the Tarpon into service, embarking for the US in December 1942 to equip at NAS

The Fleet Air Arm had little, if any, use for the Avenger's torpedo-carrying capability. Here, two American 500-lb (227-kg) bombs await loading aboard a No. 854 Sqn aircraft before a raid on Japanese positions at Surabaya, Java.

Norfolk. To help overcome an initial shortfall of aircraft, the US Navy transferred 25 TBF-1s for use by this squadron for the first few months of 1943, and they were in action from May onwards, making a sweep in the Coral Sea that month and then operating from USS *Saratoga* to support the landings in the Solomons. Returning to the UK in HMS *Victorious*, No. 832 Sqn was at Hatston with British Tarpon Mk Is by September 1943, but soon returned to the Far East, which would continue to be the principal area of operations for the Avenger.

Below: This Avenger TR.Mk II of No. 856 Sqn traps aboard **HMS Premier** *in late 1944. This unit was involved in operations off Norway and in escorting convoys to Russia.*

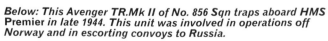

Above: Avenger Mk I J2159 carries a No. 852 Sqn code and was probably photographed in early 1944. Formed at Squantum, Massachusetts, No. 852 served aboard the Canadian carrier, **HMCS Nabob.**

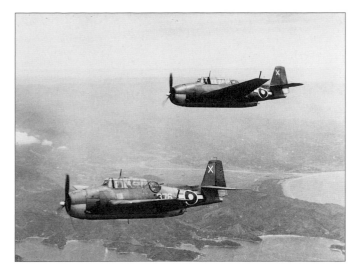

Avenger Mk IIIs of No. 848 Sqn aboard Formidable (as indicated by the 'X' tailcode) set out to bomb a kamikaze base sometime in 1945. No. 848 Sqn's aircraft carried '3xx' aircraft numbers.

Kiwi Avengers in the Pacific

The only nation other than the US and UK to receive Avengers during World War II was New Zealand. The RNZAF initially ordered 68 aircraft, but this was cut to 48, comprising six TBF-1s and 42 TBF-1Cs. After training in New Zealand and with VMTB-32 at Espiritu Santo, two units (Nos 30 and 31 Squadrons) flew combat from Bougainville between March and July 1944. Eight TBFs were lost to Japanese anti-aircraft fire and many others were damaged. During May, 22 sorties were flown by US pilots in the RNZAF TBF-1Cs. Sixteen aircraft were returned to the USN in October 1944 and nine to the Fleet Air Arm in September 1945. The aircraft below, NZ2505, was one of the six TBF-1s delivered to the RNZAF in 1943. Their inferior performance meant that they were confined to New Zealand and used for conversion training.

Meanwhile, Nos 845, 846 and 850 Squadrons of the Fleet Air Arm had all re-equipped on the new torpedo-bomber in the US, at Quonset, Norfolk or Squantum. Nos 832 and 845 participated in the major attack on the Japanese naval base at Surabaya in May 1944. Before the war ended, further FAA squadrons were operating in the Far East, including Nos 820, 849, 854 and 857 with the British Pacific Fleet aboard HMS *Indefatigable*, *Victorious*, *Illustrious*, *Indomitable* and *Formidable*. On 24 July 1945, Avengers of No. 848 Squadron from *Formidable* made the first attack by British warplanes on the Japanese mainland.

Home waters

Nearer home, Avengers flying from escort carriers and home bases flew anti-submarine patrols and mine-laying sorties. Escort duty was performed on convoys to Russia, and, in the build-up to D-Day, Avengers flew anti-shipping strikes in the English Channel from April 1944 onwards.

The FAA inventory of Avenger Mk Is was supplemented, from mid-1944, by delivery of 108 Avenger TR.Mk IIs, these differing from the Mk Is only in that they came from the Eastern Motors line as TBM-1 or TBM-1Cs.

Finally came 50 Avenger TB.Mk IIIs, which were TBM-3E versions with the R-2600-20 engine in place of the earlier -8, and APS-4 radar in an underwing pod. Planned delivery of 130 more Mk IIIs was cancelled with the end of the war, but delivery was made to the UK of 76 reconditioned ex-US Navy Avengers; these, however, went straight into storage and saw no service.

Defensive armament

As well as the two wing-mounted 0.50-in (12.7-mm) machine-guns, the TBF-1C had a single 0.30-in (7.62-mm) 'stinger' gun in the 'tunnel' at the rear of the radio compartment. The turret, rotated electrically, mounted a single 0.50-in (12.7-mm) gun on the left side.

TBF-1C Avenger

NZ2518 was flown by Flight Lieutenant Fred Ladd of No. 30 Sqn, RNZAF at Piva, Bougainville, in 1944. Ladd, a well-known post-war civilian aviator and Grumman amphibian pilot, was a non-drinker and could think of nothing more insulting than having beer poured over oneself; this gave rise to the design known as 'Plonky', the flying beer barrel with the open tap. The aircraft was taken over by No. 31 Squadron on 25 May, having been hit by AA fire.

Markings

The insignia adopted by the RNZAF in the Pacific theatre were an interesting hybrid of British and US styles. Red was removed from the RAF-style roundels of aircraft destined for the Pacific during 1942, and the white bars appeared from late 1943 at the behest of the US forces in an attempt to make Allied aircraft more identifiable as such. Fin-flashes remained three-colour, but were narrowed to minimise the area of red.

Offensive weapons

Although the Avenger was designed as a torpedo-bomber, bombs were by far its primary weapons. The TBF-1's bomb bay could carry 12 100-lb (45-kg), four 500-lb (227-kg) or two 2,000-lb (907-kg) bombs. There was also provision for 5-in (12.7-cm) rockets on a variety of mountings, although they, like torpedoes and depth bombs, were not used by RNZAF Avengers.

TBF-1C

The TBF-1C could be distinguished from the initial production TBF-1 by the absence of the 0.30-in (7.62-mm) machine-gun on the left upper cowling and its replacement by a pair of 0.50-in (12.7-mm) guns, one mounted in each wing.

Handley Page Halifax

The second heavy

It was not until July 1941 that the British public was given information about the existence of the Handley Page Halifax bomber. The announcement followed a successful attack on the German battleship Scharnhorst at La Pallice. The initial Halifax raid was made on 10/11 March by aircraft from No. 35 Squadron, the first Halifax unit.

Second of the four-engined heavy bombers to enter service with the RAF, in November 1940, the Handley Page Halifax was one of the famous triad, comprising the Halifax, Avro Lancaster and Short Stirling, which mounted Bomber Command's night-bombing offensive against Germany.

Although it entered service more than a year ahead of the Lancaster, the Halifax was always somewhat overshadowed in the bombing role by the achievement of the Avro design. The Halifax, however, was to score over the Lancaster in its multi-role capability for, in addition to its deployment as a heavy night-bomber, it was equally at home when employed as an ambulance, freighter, glider-tug, personnel transport and maritime reconnaissance aircraft.

The origin of the Halifax stemmed from an Air Ministry requirement of 1935 for a twin-engined bomber, for which Handley Page submitted a design identified as the HP.55. This proved to be unsuccessful, Vickers instead being awarded a contract for what was to appear in mid-1942 as the Warwick. About a year later the Air Ministry issued a new specification, P.13/36, which called for a medium/heavy bomber to be powered by a 24-cylinder engine known as the Vulture, which Rolls-Royce then had under development. Design proposals from Avro and Handley Page (HP.56) were selected for proto-type construction, that from Avro leading initially to the Manchester, which was to fly with the high-powered but underdeveloped Vulture engine. Presumably, Handley Page had

an ear rather closer to the ground than Avro, for the company soon had grave doubts that the Vulture engine would emerge as a reliable production powerplant; it therefore set about the task of redesigning the HP.56 to take four Rolls-Royce Merlins instead. It was, of course, no easy task, but while the overall configuration was not greatly changed, the HP.57 design which was submitted to the Air Ministry for approval was for a considerably larger and heavier aircraft. On 3 September 1937 Handley Page was awarded a contract for the manufacture of two prototypes of the HP.57, with construction beginning in early 1938. When the first of these was nearing completion, it was realised that the company's airfield at Radlett, Hertfordshire, was too restricted for the first flight of such a large aircraft. It was therefore decided instead to use the nearest non-operational RAF airfield, which was at Bicester in Oxfordshire, and it was from there that the first flight was made on 25 October 1939.

As then flown, the HP.57 was a mid-wing cantilever mono-

L7245 was the second prototype Halifax and was fitted with representative armament. This included two 'floor' guns, a nose and tail turret. It first flew on 18 August 1940.

plane of all-metal construction, the wing featuring automatic leading-edge slots. These were to be deleted on production aircraft, however, as the Air Ministry required that the wing leading edges should be armoured and provided with barrage balloon cable-cutters. Handley Page slotted trailing-edge flaps were fitted, and the large-span ailerons were fabric-covered. The tail unit comprised a large high-mounted tailplane and rudder assembly with twin endplate fins and rudders. The fins of the prototypes and of production aircraft built until early 1943 were of triangular shape, the apex facing forward. The fuselage was a deep, slab-sided, all-metal structure with considerable internal volume, and it was this feature which was to provide the later versions with a multi-role capability.

Crew accommodation

Accommodation was provided for a crew of seven, including three gunners to man nose, beam and tail positions, but

armament and turrets were not fitted for these early flights. Landing gear was of the retractable tailwheel type, and the powerplant comprised four Rolls-Royce Merlin engines. For its primary role as a bomber, a variety of weapons could be carried in a 22-ft (6.71-m) long bomb bay in the lower fuselage, supplemented by two bomb compartments in the wing centre-section, one on each side of the fuselage.

An interesting feature of this design was its method of construction, each major unit breaking down into several assemblies. The wing, for example, comprised five sections, and the very considerable thought which had been given to this system of fabrication was to pay enormous dividends in subsequent large-scale production, and in the simplification of transport, maintenance and repair. The second prototype made its first flight on 18 August 1940, followed just under two months later by the first production example, by then designated

Flight Sergeant D. Cameron and his crew pose in their damaged No. 158 Squadron Halifax. The damage was caused by a 'friendly' bomb which hit the aircraft during a mission from RAF Lisset in 1943. After being repaired, the aircraft was returned to service.

Halifax Mk I, and this was powered by 1,280-hp (954-kW) Rolls-Royce Merlin X engines. Armament of these early production aircraft consisted of two and four 0.303-in (7.7-mm) machine-guns in nose and tail turrets respectively. The full designation of the first production version was Halifax B.Mk I Series I, and these began to equip the RAF's No. 35

Squadron during November 1940. It was this unit that, in early March 1941, was the first to use the Halifax operationally, in an attack on Le Havre, and a few days later the Halifax became the first of the RAF's four-engined bombers to make a night attack against a German target, when bombs were dropped on Hamburg. The Halifax was used for the first

time in a daylight attack against Kiel on 30 June 1941, but it did not take long to discover that the aircraft's defensive armament was inadequate for daylight use, and by the end of 1941 the Halifaxes were used only by night in the bombing role.

This resulted in the provision of better armament for later versions, but there were two variants of the Mk I to appear before that: the B.Mk I Series II was stressed for a higher gross weight, and the B.Mk I Series III had standard fuel capacity increased by almost 18 per cent. Late-production examples introduced Merlin XX engines, which, although having the same take-off rating as the Merlin X, provided 1,480 hp (1104 kW) at their optimum altitude. Early deployment of the Halifax had confirmed that this new four-engined bomber had much to offer, but although contracts for large-scale construction very quickly exceeded the productive capacity of the Handley Page factories at Cricklewood and Radlett,

pre-war plans had been made for alternative sources of supply. The establishment of four new production lines was made easier by the unit method of construction which had been adopted for the Halifax; the first of these sub-contract aircraft to fly, on 15 August 1941, came from the English Electric Company, which had earlier been involved in manufacture of Handley Page's Hampden medium bomber. The other three lines were those of Fairey at Stockport, Rootes Securities at Speke and the London Aircraft Production Group. This last organisation saw rear fuselages being built by Chrysler Motors, forward fuselages by Duplex Bodies and Motors, inner wing sections by Express Motor and Body Works, and outer wing sections by Park Royal Coachworks; the extensive works of the London Passenger Transport Board saw the construction of many components and fittings, final erection and testing at Leavesden.

Halifax B.Mk I

The Halifax served with the RAF's Bomber Command through to VE-Day. The aircraft illustrated, L9530, was one of the very first batch (L9485-L9534) to be produced and was delivered in the winter of 1940-41. It carries the markings of No. 76 Squadron, Bomber Command, based at RAF Middleton St George.

Armament
The Halifax B.Mk I was fitted with Boulton Paul power-operated turrets in the nose and tail, housing two 0.303-in (7.7-mm) Browning machine-guns in the nose and four in the tail. Two Vickers 0.303-in (7.7-mm) 'K' guns could be aimed by hand through beam hatches. The maximum bombload consisted of six 1,000-lb (454-kg), two 2,000-lb (907-kg) and six 500-lb (227-kg) bombs, all carried on racks in the fuselage bomb bay.

Fiery end
No. 76 Sqn was the second unit to fly the Halifax Mk I operationally. L9530 was shot down during an attack on Berlin on 12/13 August 1941. Except for the front and rear gunners, the crew parachuted clear and became POWs.

Unusual construction
One of the Halifax's unusual features was the use of split assembly for its construction. Separate sections, such as the outer wings, rear fuselage, tail units and cockpit/nose, were manufactured independently, making it possible for more people to be involved and for the components to be constructed more quickly. Although the first 50 Halifaxes had leading-edge wing slots, the Air Ministry requirement to fit barrage balloon-cutters in the front of the wings necessitated deletion of the slots on subsequent aircraft.

Squadron service
This early-production Halifax Mk I has the squadron markings 'MP' of No. 76 (Bomber) Squadron and the individual letter 'L'. The unit was first equipped with the type at RAF Linton-on-Ouse on 1 May 1941, moving to RAF Middleton St George a month later.

Powerplant
As an early-production Halifax Mk I, this aircraft was powered by four 1,280-hp (954-kW) Rolls-Royce Merlin X in-line engines, driving three-bladed, constant-speed, compressed wood propellers, giving a top speed of 265 mph (426 km/h). After the 75th aircraft, 1,390-hp (1037-kW) Merlin XXs were fitted, although other airframe modifications still restricted performance. It was not until the Halifax B.Mk III, re-engined with four 1,615-hp (1204-kW) Bristol Hercules XVI engines and de Havilland Hydromatic propellers, that there was a marked improvement in speed to 282 mph (454 km/h).

Later service

Always treated as 'second best' to Avro's Lancaster, the Handley Page Halifax was the backbone of Bomber Command for many difficult months. After a poor early career, the 'Halibag' was developed into an effective bomber and was successful in roles never envisaged by its designers.

The Halifax Mk I was followed into service by the B.Mk II Series I, which introduced a Boulton Paul twin-gun dorsal turret, and an increase of 15 per cent in standard fuel capacity; the engines, initially Merlin XXs, were later changed for the Merlin 22 of equal power output. These changes, plus others introduced after the prototypes had made their first flights, had resulted in a steady increase in gross weight. As there had been no surplus engine power from the outset, the result was that operational performance was being eroded by enhanced operational capability. This can be accepted during wartime conditions provided that the rate of attrition remains fairly constant. In the case of the Halifax Mk II, the dorsal turret represented 'the last straw', and steps were taken immediately to improve the performance of these aircraft.

The resulting B.Mk II Series IA had a performance increase of some 10 per cent in both maximum and cruising speeds, which had been achieved by efforts to reduce both weight and drag. The nose turret was deleted, the nose acquiring a streamlined Perspex fairing; the dorsal turret was replaced by one which housed four instead of two guns, but which had a shallower profile and created less drag; the aerial mast, fuel jettison pipes, and all possible equipment were deleted; new engine cooling radiators enabled the cross-sectional area of the engine nacelles to be reduced; the astrodome was of improved aerodynamic form; fuselage length was increased by 1 ft 6 in (0.46 m); and the Merlin 22 engines were later changed to Merlin 24s which offered 1,620 hp (1208 kW) for take-off. News of these impending changes brought in-service adoption of those improvements which could most easily be introduced by squadron personnel. These included removal of the nose turret, dorsal turret and fuel jettison pipes, although only some aircraft had all of these modifications: the resulting Halifaxes were known as the B.Mk II Series I (Special). A later change introduced retrospectively to all aircraft then in service involved replacement of the triangular fins by larger units of rectangular shape. This came after extensive testing – following

The topside of a nearly-new Halifax B.Mk II shows the original short wingspan and Merlin engines of the early Halifaxes, features which combined to give poor altitude performance and thus high loss rates. The Halifax's reputation never really recovered, despite continual improvement.

some inexplicable losses of fully-loaded aircraft – had shown that it was possible for the Halifax to enter an inverted and uncontrollable spin.

The last major production version was the Halifax B.Mk III, the first of the bombers to introduce Bristol Hercules VI or XVI radial engines, which offered 1,615 hp (1204 kW) for take-off. Wingspan was also extended by 5 ft 4 in (1.63 m), the resulting increase of 25 sq ft (2.32 m²) in wing area improving the aircraft's operational ceiling. The first of the production Mk IIIs flew on 29 August 1943, and when this version entered squadron service in February 1944 it was found to have definite performance advantages.

Other bomber versions included the B.Mk V which, in Series I (Special) and Series IA variants, was virtually identical to the equivalent B.Mk IIs except

Left: The Halifax proved more suited to the military transport role than the Lancaster and nearly 100 C.Mk VIII conversions – with a capacity for 8,000 lb (3630 kg) of freight – were completed.

With the increase in daylight missions from mid-1945, distinctive tail markings were introduced to help unit coherence in close formation. Halifaxes wore particularly colourful tails, such as the red trellis pattern on this No. 346 (Free French) Sqn B.Mk VI.

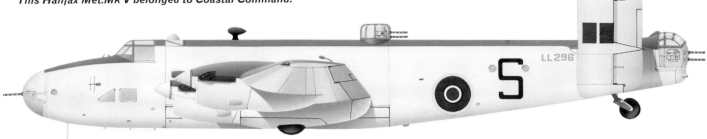

Coastal and Bomber Commands operated a number of specially modified Halifaxes. To gather meteorological information, they were equipped with a dedicated meteorological observer's station and their mission was collecting air- and sea-level pressure readings. This Halifax Met.Mk V belonged to Coastal Command.

for a change from Messier to Dowty landing gear. The B.Mk VI, with Hercules 100 engines which could develop 1,675 hp (1249 kW) for take-off and 1,800 hp (1342 kW) at 10,000 ft (3050 m), was virtually the last of the bombers, for the B.Mk VII was essentially the same, differing only in a reversion to Hercules XVI engines as the Hercules 100 was in short supply. Both the Mk VI and VII had a pressurised fuel system, plus small-particle filters over the engine intakes, as it had been envisaged that they would be used in the Pacific theatre after the war in Europe ended.

From the time of their introduction into operational service, Halifax bombers were in continuous use by Bomber Command, equipping at their peak usage no fewer than 34 squadrons in the European theatre, and four more in the Middle East. Two flights were in early use in the Far East and, following VE-Day, a number of squadrons operating with Halifax Mk VIs flew their aircraft out for co-operation with the Allied forces fighting in the Pacific theatre. The Halifax was involved in the first Pathfinder operations in August 1942; was the first RAF aircraft to be equipped with the highly secret H2S blind-bombing radar equipment; was extensively involved in daylight attacks on German

V-1 sites; and between 1941 and 1945 flew 75,532 sorties, during which 227,610 tons (231263 tonnes) of bombs were dropped on European targets.

Non-bomber Halifaxes

The Halifax was also operated by nine squadrons of the RAF's Coastal Command for anti-submarine, meteorological and shipping patrols. The aircraft were converted from standard bombers and specially equipped, taking the designations GR.Mk II, GR.Mk V or GR.Mk VI according to the bomber version from which they were derived. Similarly, RAF Transport Command acquired C.Mk III, C.Mk VI and C.Mk VII Halifaxes as casualty, freight and personnel transports. Little known in wartime was the work of Nos 138 and 161 (Special Duties) Squadrons which used the 'Halibag' in dropping agents and/or supplies into enemy territory.

One other vital use of the Halifax was by the Airborne Forces for, under the designations A.Mk III, A.Mk V and A.Mk VII, equivalent bomber versions were converted to serve for the deployment of paratroops or as glider-tugs. The Halifax was, in fact, the only aircraft capable of towing the large General Aircraft Hamilcar glider, a capability

Airspeed Horsas and General Aircraft Hamilcar gliders are seen lined up at RAF Tarrant Rushton shortly before D-Day. Halifax Mk V glider-tugs of Nos 298 and 644 Squadrons are prepared on either side of the runway to tow the gliders to their destinations.

first proven in February 1942. Soon after that date the Halifax tug made its operational debut when two Airspeed Horsas were hauled across the North Sea to attack the German heavy water plant in south Norway. Halifaxes subsequently towed Horsas from Britain to North Africa in preparation for the invasion of Sicily, and were involved in this action as well as in airborne forces operations in Normandy, at Arnhem and during the final crossing of the Rhine.

The last Halifaxes

Although withdrawn from Bomber Command immediately after VJ-Day, the Halifax GR.Mk VI continued to serve with Coastal Command after the war, as did the A.Mk VII with transport squadrons at home and overseas. Post-war versions included the C.Mk VIII which

could accommodate an 8,000-lb (3629-kg) detachable cargo pannier beneath the fuselage, and the A.Mk IX troop-carrier and supply-dropper for use by airborne forces. When production of these two versions ended, amounting to some 230 aircraft, a total of about 6,200 Halifaxes had been built, and examples remained in RAF service until early 1952.

Overseas, the Halifax remained in service somewhat longer. Pakistan's No. 12 Squadron retired its examples in 1954 while Egypt's aircraft survived long enough to be destroyed by strafing during the Suez campaign of 1956.

This Handley Page masterpiece acquired the affectionately bestowed nickname of 'Halibag', an affection which most probably stemmed from its punishment-absorbing, 'get-you-home' durability.

Above: After the war, one of the several Halifax VIs flown by the RAF Empire Radio School at Debden, RG815 Mercury, became famous when it flew 25,000 miles (40233 km) on a worldwide demonstration of radio and radar aids and equipment. The three-month tour included visits to Iraq, India, Singapore and Australia.

Right: The Halifax flew its final sortie in RAF squadron service on 17 March 1952, when the last GR.Mk VI of No. 224 Squadron returned home from Gibraltar. The type was declared obsolete during that same year.

Handley Page

The Hampden was used in a number of roles throughout the war including leaflet dropping missions, day- and night-bombing, minelaying and torpedo bombing.

Hampden/Hereford

The 'Flying Suitcase'

Designed along with the Vickers Wellington to Air Ministry specification B.9/32, the Handley Page Hampden and Hereford were the result of a unique but flawed approach to pre-war bomber design.

In 1932, the British Air Ministry issued a requirement for an experimental twin-engined day bomber under the specification B.9/32. Bristol, Gloster, Handley Page and Vickers began preparations to design an aircraft to meet the requirement, the former two dropping out to pursue other projects, the Vickers design (developed into the Wellington) being accepted along with the four-seat Handley Page H.P. 52.

Designed by Dr. Gustav. V. Lachmann, a former German Air Force pilot (rather ironically in view of later events), the H.P. 52 was highly original in its approach to the specification,

with tapered wings and, most distinctively, the rear half of the fuselage tapering into a slim boom carrying the twin-tail empennage. This cut down significantly on the weight of the aircraft, and enabled the crew to be brought together in a compact group in the deeper front fuselage, the width of which was a mere 3ft. It was this that led C.G. Grey, founder and editor of *The Aeroplane*, to remark after seeing the type, that "it looks like a flying suitcase", a name which stuck. The wing was mounted above the bomb-bay, with most of the taper on the trailing edge, and dihedral from root to tip of 2° 45', which

The H.P. 52 prototype, K4240, was finished in a glossy grey-green colour scheme for its first public appearances at the RAF Display at Hendon and the SBAC show at Hatfield, both in July 1936.

was later increased to 6° 30' to improve lateral stability. The H.P.52 was originally to be fitted with a pair of Bristol Pegasus IV engines, but the two-speed supercharging Pegasus XVIII was chosen in January 1935 as a replacement. Turrets were to be fitted in the nose and front fuselage at the trailing edge.

The H.P.52 and H.P.53

The all-green H.P.52 prototype, K4240, took off from Radlett for its first flight on 22 June 1936, with test pilot Major J.L.B.H. Cordes at the controls, and after testing it became apparent that the type would be more than adequate to fulfil its original specification, i.e. to carry a heavy load over a long distance at high speed. The H.P.52 could outrun the Wellington, and was almost as agile as the Blenheim, leading the Air Ministry to place an

order for 180 of the type on 29 January 1937, under the specification B.30/36. On the same day, specification B.44/36 was issued to cover production of 100 examples at Short & Harland in Belfast, fitted with 1,000-hp (746-kW) Napier Dagger engines. These machines were to be designated H.P.53, the prototype of which was the second H.P.52, L7271, and which was first flown on 1 July 1937.

Up until this point, the Air Ministry had been unable to agree on a name for the aircraft, although the strongest contender seems to have been 'Huntley'. After much discussion the names 'Hampden' and 'Hereford' were decided on for the H.P.52 and H.P.53 respectively. By August 1938, the build-up of the RAF was in full-swing and an additional order for 75 to be built at Warton, and 80 in Canada was

The cockpit of the Hampden looked much more like that of a single-seat fighter than a medium bomber, with its flat central windscreen and single fixed Browning gun on the port side, although the pilot was often uncomfortable on long missions.

Left: The H.P. 53 Hereford differed from the Hampden in having Napier Dagger VIIII engines, which proved somewhat troublesome to both ground and aircrew.

Below: No 489 Sqn of the Royal New Zealand Air Force operated Hampdens from Leuchars between March 1942 and December 1943 in the torpedo-bomber role.

placed with Handley Page.

Deliveries of the first RAF Hampdens took place in September 1938 to No. 49 Squadron at Scampton, Lincolnshire, and by the time the war broke out a year later, ten squadrons were operating the type, mainly in the daylight reconnaissance role. Although the Hampden offered excellent handling qualities and almost fighter-like manoevrability, its shortcomings were exposed early on, when five out of 11 Hampdens from No 144 Sqn were lost to German fighters on a reconnaissance mission over the Heligoland Bight area on 29 September. Crew fatigue was common due to the cramped accommodation and the aircraft's defensive firepower was totally inadequate, leading to the decision to operate the Hampden thereafter under the cover of darkness. The Hereford fared no better, the Napier engines proving unreliable, with a tendency to overheat on the ground and cool too quickly in the air, the high-pitched exhaust note making missions even more uncomfortable for the crews. In March 1940, Hampdens were used for 'Nickels' (long-range sorties) into Germany, for navigational experience and propaganda leaflet dropping.

With the advent of the air-droppable magnetic sea-mine, the Hampden was to find itself an effective niche as a mine-layer, and by the end of 1940, No 5 Group of Bomber Command had flown over a thousand mine-laying sorties in German and German-controlled coastal waters with Hampdens. After this success, attempts to re-employ the Hampden on daylight missions proved disas-

trous, forcing No 5 Group's AOC, Air Commodore Arthur Harris to insist on doubling the rear defence fire-power of the vulnerable Hampden. 12 Hampdens of Nos 61 and 144 Sqns took part in the first raid on Berlin by RAF bombers on the night of 25-26 August 1940, and continued to operate in the night-bombing offensive until September 1942, when the last sortie by a Hampden for Bomber Command was carried out over Wilhelmshaven by the Royal Canadian Air Force's No 408 Sqn.

Torpedo-bomber

Although the Hampden had become obsolete as a standard day- or night-bomber, its previous success as a mine-layer led to it being tested at the Torpedo Development Unit at Gosport. The trials were a success, the type adapting well to carrying one Mk XII torpedo in the bomb-bay, which was modified by removing the centre bomb-doors, and fixing the previously hinged side-flaps. The mainframe ahead of the ventral gunner's fairing also had 12 in (30 cm) removed from its base, and the type was redesignated the Hampden TB. Mk I. In April 1942, TB. Mk Is of No. 144 Sqn were transferred to Coastal Command, along with No. 455 Sqn RAAF, both squadrons re-training at Leuchars using sand-filled concrete pipes to simulate torpedoes, which were launched against dummy targets off the Isle of May.

Detachments from both squadrons were sent to protect convoy operations in northern

This picture illustrates well the narrow fuselage of the Hampden, and why it was known as 'The Flying Suitcase'.

Russia, where they often found themselves taking pot-shots from their trigger-happy Russian allies. The squadrons' Hampdens were handed over to the Russians after the completion of the operation in October 1942, the crew returning to the UK by sea. Hampdens were replaced by Bristol Beaufighters when the 'Torbeau' strike wings were formed in 1943, and 200 of the type were ferried to Canada by RAF Transport Command for

use as crew trainers. Hampdens were also used for meteorological reconnaissance under the designation Hampden Met. Mk I, until the end of 1943.

Two Hampdens were fitted with Wright R-1820 Cyclone engines, and given the designation H.P. 62 Hampden Mk II, but the powerplant was never adopted for service. By the time of its retirement, just under 1,500 Hampdens and 152 Herefords had been built.

In September 1938, a sole Hampden was supplied to Sweden and operated by Flottilj 11 from Nyköping under the designation P.5. It was sold to SAAB in November 1945, registered as SE-APB, and used as an electronics test-bed until November 1947.

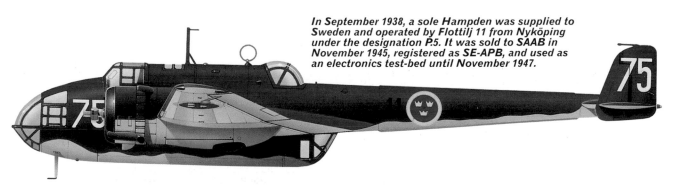

Hawker Hurricane

Overshadowed by the Spitfire, the Hurricane was slower, less manoeuvrable and half a generation older in terms of technology. What mattered was that it was available in numbers and could be adapted to a variety of roles. In terms of victories over enemy aircraft alone, it is undoubtedly the most successful of all British fighters.

Four months before the Spitfire, the Hawker F.36/34 prototype took to the air for the first time on 6 November 1935. Within a month, it had exceeded 300 mph (482 km/h) in testing. By the time war was declared in September 1939, 497 of these aircraft – the RAF's first monoplane fighter – had been completed.

Thrown into action in France in support of the British Expeditionary Force, Hurricane Mk Is suffered heavy losses, but the fact remains that Hurricanes destroyed enough enemy aircraft to make it the most successful British fighter ever built.

At home and abroad

Refined with a variable-pitch Rotol propeller and metal-skinned wings, the Hurricane came into its own during the summer of 1940. It was available in larger numbers than the Spitfire and, by virtue of its simple construction, was better equipped to sustain battle damage from Luftwaffe fighters. More

Above: Soon hard-pressed in the fighter role, the Hurricane was quickly adapted for ground-attack duties, equipped with bombs and rockets. Fitted with twin Vickers 40-mm cannon, the Hurricane took on a 'tank busting' role. So-equipped, the Mk IID, of which 300 were built, entered service in the Western Desert in mid-1942.

docile, and more forgiving of the novice pilot, the Hurricane was less difficult to fly in poor weather and, in addition, better suited to night operations.

It has been said that the Hurricane served in more theatres than any other combat aircraft of the war, from the Eastern Front to North Africa, Iraq and the Far East. With Spitfires hard-pressed in operations from bases in the British Isles, it was the Hurricane

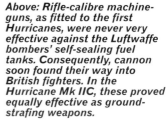

Above: Rifle-calibre machine-guns, as fitted to the first Hurricanes, were never very effective against the Luftwaffe bombers' self-sealing fuel tanks. Consequently, cannon soon found their way into British fighters. In the Hurricane Mk IIC, these proved equally effective as ground-strafing weapons.

Left: Mk I L1550 was the third production Hurricane delivered to the RAF. No. 111 Squadron at RAF Northolt was the first unit to equip with the type in January 1938, and helped to defend south-eastern England in 1940.

Below: Patrolling Hurricanes look for 'trade' in the skies over the English Channel. Without the Hurricane, which outnumbered the Spitfire by three to two in Fighter Command, the RAF would have been unable to defend the British Isles in the summer of 1940.

that was shipped abroad to provide air cover and support for ground forces.

These aircraft not only equipped RAF units overseas, but were also supplied to the Allies. More than 2,800 were shipped to Russia directly from the UK alone; others came from Canada and RAF stocks in the Middle East. After Russia, the Indian Air Force received the largest batch of Hurricanes, over 200 reaching the sub-continent in 1943.

While it lacked the development potential of the Spitfire, the Hurricane was nonetheless progressively improved to take advantage of engine enhancements and the demands of new roles. The Mk II introduced a Merlin XX powerplant with two-stage supercharging and, in successive sub-variants, heavier armament. Many of the latter changes helped to refine the design for the ground-attack role which grew in importance as the Hurricane's shortcomings as an interceptor became more apparent when faced with increasingly modern German opposition.

Bombs and cannon

The Mk IIB, fitted with no fewer than 12 machine-guns, was the first Hurricane mark to carry bombs and gained a suitable nickname – 'Hurribomber'. In common with other British fighters, the Mk IIC gained 20-mm cannon armament, and the Mk IID was equipped with a pair of 40-mm Vickers 'S' guns, ideal for anti-tank work.

The other important weapon associated with the Hurricane was the rocket projectile. This

appeared on the Mk IV, a dedicated ground-attack aircraft able to carry a variety of underwing stores, including the 40-mm cannon under a so-called 'universal' wing. Most served in the Mediterranean and CBI theatres.

Night-fighter/intruder operations and tactical reconnaissance were among other roles carried out to a lesser extent by suitably-modified Hurricanes, both at home and overseas.

The Royal Navy, lacking suitable fighter designs of its own, was forced to adapt both the Hurricane and Spitfire for ship-borne use, mainly aboard convoy escort carriers. Neither was particularly suitable, but the Sea Hurricane proved more robust than its fragile Seafire counterpart.

After hostilities ceased, Hurricanes found new export customers, including Portugal, Ireland and Iran. For the latter, a unique, two-seat trainer variant was developed. The RAF, meanwhile, quickly withdrew its remaining Hurricanes from front-line service after 1945.

Britain's saviour

That the Hawker Hurricane occupied a vital place in

Britain's history cannot be denied, no less seminal than the introduction of the dedicated fighter in World War I. Put simply, the Hurricane saved Great Britain in 1940; it was the right aircraft, at the right time, and flown by the right pilots. No-one can deny the excellence of the Supermarine Spitfire, nor that it was one of the great fighting aircraft of World War II.

Yet, outdated though the Hurricane may have appeared by comparison, its simplicity of concept and operation was such that it could be – and was – despatched to any of the danger spots that spread like cancer during those first three years of

the war when events threatened to engulf the Allied nations with disaster.

Flying not only in the great Battle of Britain, but in France, Norway, the Middle East, the Balkans, Malta, El Alamein, Singapore, and off the North Cape, the Hurricane – often arriving two years before the first Spitfires – was able to make its unique contribution to the ultimate victory. When the final analysis was compiled, it transpired that Hurricanes had, by a wide margin, destroyed more enemy aircraft in air combat during World War II than any other Allied fighter and, in fact, more than all other British aircraft put together.

After 1945, most Hurricanes were simply scrapped. Obsolete compared to late mark Spitfires, their usefulness in the post-war RAF was limited. For this reason, few have survived and only a handful of airworthy examples may be seen today. One of these is the last Hurricane built – PZ865. A Mk IIC completed in 1944, it was retained by Hawker, named Last of the Many, and registered G-AMAU. In 1972, it was donated to the RAF's Battle of Britain Memorial Flight, with which it continued to fly in 1998.

Hurricane development

These uncoded aircraft were captured on film shortly after delivery, but not before a squadron badge had been applied to their tailfins and the CO's aircraft (second from left) had gained a squadron leader's pennant below its canopy.

Sydney Camm's Interceptor Monoplane represented a technological quantum leap for a service still committed to biplane fighters. As well as being a monoplane, the new design had eight wing-mounted guns and was powered by an engine that had yet to receive official approval.

It was the adoption of the American Colt machine-gun, rebarrelled for 0.303-in (7.7-mm) ammunition and licence-built in Britain by BSA as the Browning, that allowed the Hurricane's armament to be wing-mounted. Vickers guns fitted to earlier types were prone to jamming and needed, therefore, to be mounted above the engine and accessible to the pilot.

When Lord Trenchard retired on 1 January 1930, his successor at the head of the RAF, Sir John Salmond, initiated an urgent reappraisal of Britain's fighter defences. Trenchard had built up the RAF's bomber force, but had given little thought to the protection of its bases. The interceptor fighter had been the major casualty of Trenchard's tenure of office.

1918 design formula

RAF fighters in 1930 still kept to the design formula of 1918. They were fabric-covered single-seat biplanes armed with a pair of synchronised Vickers guns firing through the propeller, and possessing a top speed of less than 200 mph (322 km/h).

Unfortunately, Salmond's plans to overhaul the RAF's fighter force coincided with a period of economic depression in Britain. Defence appropriations were severely curtailed. For years the aircraft industry had been starved of substantial production contracts whose proceeds could underwrite significant research, a vicious circle that became all too evident when the first of the new fighter requirements, Air

Ministry Specification F.7/30, was issued. This demanded an interceptor fighter, predominantly of metal construction, with armament doubled to four guns, and a top speed of at least 250 mph (402 km/h). Implicit in the requirement was the growing realisation that the days of the biplane fighter were, or should be, past. The hotch-potch of

prototypes that resulted from this specification only served to demonstrate, however, just how sterile the industry had become. The Gloster Gladiator biplane was declared the winner and was awarded substantial production contracts during the mid-1930s.

The threat of war

Meanwhile, events in Europe were lending urgency to the need to strengthen the RAF's fighter arm. The Bristol Bulldog biplane (top speed, 174 mph/ 280 km/h) was still the principal aircraft of the interceptor

The Hawker Interceptor Monoplane prototype K5083 is seen prior to its first flight in 1935. Note the light cockpit canopy structure, the lower hinged wheel doors and absence of armament.

Left: The Hurricane saw its first significant combat in the defence of France in 1940. No. 87 Squadron was among the units committed to the Advanced Air Striking Force during the Battle of France. This photograph shows the squadron's Hurricanes 'somewhere in France' in March 1940. Most of the aircraft still have fixed-pitch two-bladed propellers, though the second machine has one of the newer de Havilland three-bladed examples.

Below: The lack of a suitable engine, with a useful power-to-weight ratio, was the main handicap facing potential fighter manufacturers in the early 1930s. Rolls-Royce's Merlin filled this gap and found its way into the prototypes of both the Hurricane and Supermarine's Spitfire. Supercharging was the key to the engine's performance, especially at altitude.

squadrons, although the exquisite but expensive Hawker Fury (207 mph/333 km/h) equipped three élite units.

Foremost among the many difficulties faced by the aircraft manufacturers was the lack of a British engine of adequate power – or, more exactly, with a high power-to-weight ratio. By the early 1930s Rolls-Royce was the recipient of very large contracts for its Kestrel engines, and had been in a financial position to fund the private development of a very powerful racing engine (the Type R) which went on to power the 1931 Schneider Trophy-winning S.6B. It was the development of this special engine that led almost directly to the creation of the PV.12 in 1934, combining the reliability of the Kestrel with the higher power-to-weight ratio of the racing engine.

Deep-seated prejudice

Once the Air Staff's deep-seated prejudice against the monoplane fighter had been overcome, Sydney Camm, Hawker's chief designer, and others, turned their attention to the evolution of just such an aircraft, powered by the new PV.12 engine.

In order to achieve early production deliveries, Camm favoured an airframe which followed the traditional Hawker construction methods, using a

No. 79 Squadron ground crewmen are seen here during summer exercises in 1939. No. 79 flew Hurricanes from November 1938, later taking them to the Far East where they saw considerable action until replaced by Republic Thunderbolts in July 1944. Visible in the cockpit is the ring and bead type of sight fitted to early production aircraft.

Warren box-girder primary structure with wooden frames and stringers, the whole being fabric-covered. In any case, converting the Hawker production facilities to undertake state-of-the-art metal monocoque manufacture (as used in Supermarine's Spitfire) would have been problematic in the short term at least.

At first known simply as the Interceptor Monoplane, Camm's new design was accepted for prototype manufacture late in 1934, and a dedicated specification, F.36/34, was written around the design proposals. The

contract for a prototype was signed with Hawker on 21 February 1935.

Prototype flown

The Hawker F.36/34 prototype, K5083, was first flown by P.W.S. ('George') Bulman at Brooklands on 6 November 1935, four months before the first Supermarine Spitfire, but several months after the German

Messerschmitt Bf 109 prototype made its debut.

The first production Hurricane Mk I flew on 12 October 1937, 1,000 examples having been ordered by the RAF. No. 111 Squadron was re-equipped with the type in December, followed by No. 3 Squadron the following March. By the time war was declared, 16 squadrons flew the RAF's first monoplane fighter.

Hurricane Variants

As well as the main production Hurricane variants, there were a number of interesting 'one-off' aircraft worthy of note. The Mk III, the 'missing' variant in the model sequence, was a Packard Merlin-powered version for UK production that failed to materialise because of an engine shortage.

Mk IA (early production)

Changes made to the prototype in order to prepare it for series production included a larger radiator, a strengthened cockpit canopy, armoured windscreen, simplified undercarriage doors and a fixed tail wheel.

Mk IA (late production)

Metal-skinned wings, a longer propeller spinner and a three-bladed, variable-pitch propeller were among the features introduced in the late-production Mk IAs. The variable-pitch propeller improved take-off and climb performance, as well as top speed.

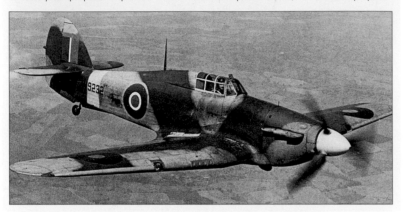

Mk IIA

While most Mk II production examples were cannon-armed, the first 100 or so were completed with the eight-gun 'A' wing to speed delivery in the closing weeks of the Battle of Britain.

Mk IIC

In all, 4,711 Mk IICs were built before production ended in September 1944. By far the most widely deployed of the Hurricane variants, the Mk IIC featured the four-cannon wing and bomb racks.

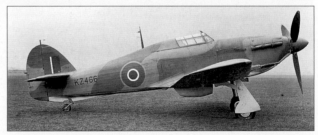

Mk IIB

With 12 Browning 0.303-in (7.7-mm) machine-guns, the Mk IIB had firepower equivalent to that planned for the Typhoon. Mk IIBs were the first Hurricanes to be equipped with bomb racks, as so-called 'Hurribombers', able to carry a 250-lb (113-kg) bomb under each wing.

Mk IV

Originally known as the Mk IIE, the Mk IV featured the so-called 'universal' wing, able to be equipped with 20-mm or 40-mm cannon, bombs or rocket projectiles (RPs). Indeed, on occasions No. 6 Squadron aircraft in Greece are known to have carried two rockets and a single 500-lb (227-kg) bomb on one wing, balanced by two more RPs and a single 40-mm 'S' gun on the other!

Mk IID

Introducing the 40-mm Vickers 'S' gun to the Hurricane's repertoire, the Mk IID was built in relatively small numbers (300) and served almost exclusively overseas, principally in the Western Desert and the China-Burma-India theatre. The 40-mm cannon was designed primarily for use against armoured targets.

Mk V

A dedicated ground-attack variant intended for service in Burma, the Mk V featured a 1,700-hp (1268-kW) Merlin 32 engine driving a four-bladed Rotol propeller, giving a top speed of 326 mph (525 km/h) at 500 ft (152 m) and an all-up weight of 9,300 lb (4218 kg). However, the engine was plagued by overheating problems, despite being fitted with a larger radiator. Only three prototypes were built.

Tactical reconnaissance variants

From late 1940, Hurricanes of both Mks I and II were locally modified with cameras in their lower rear fuselages. This Tac R.Mk II(FE) was first employed in the Middle East and was later flown to India.

Mk X

Having manufactured 200 Mk Is, Canadian Car & Foundry Ltd. (CCF) went on to produce the Packard Merlin-engined Mk X and Mk XI. The Mk XI was intended for RCAF service, though in the event most were shipped to Russia.

Mk XII

The Mk XII was the main Canadian production variant and was built with 12-machine-guns, four-cannon and 'universal' wings, while a few Mk XIIAs had eight-gun wings. This RCAF aircraft served with No. 1 OTU.

Ski Hurricane

A number of Canadian-built Hurricane Mk XIs were fitted with fixed ski undercarriage to enable flying to continue from snow-covered airfields in Canada. Most Canadian Hurricanes fitted with the American Hamilton Standard propeller flew without spinners.

Sea Hurricane Mk IA

This designation was applied to 'Hurricats' deployed from catapult-equipped merchant ships (CAM-ships). Once merchant aircraft carriers became available, these aircraft (converted from Hurricane Mk Is) were used for training.

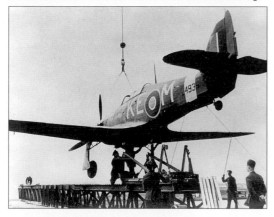

Sea Hurricane Mk IB/IC

Converted from Hurricane Mk Is, IIs, Xs and XIIs the approximately 260 Sea Hurricane Mk IBs had catapult spools and an A-frame arrester hook fitted for Fleet Air Arm operations from merchant aircraft carriers (MAC-ships) – merchantmen converted as makeshift aircraft carriers for convoy escort duties.

Sea Hurricane Mk IC/Mk IIC

Intended for use by the FAA's main fighter units aboard the Royal Navy's fleet carriers, the Sea Hurricane Mk IC (right) was a Hurricane Mk I conversion with cannon armament, while the Sea Hurricane Mk IIC was effectively a 'navalised' Hurricane Mk IIC.

Slip Wing Hurricane

As a comparatively simple aircraft, the Hurricane lent itself to experimental work, including studies into laminar-flow wings and 'towed fighters'. Perhaps the most unusual of these resulted in the Hillson F.H.40, or Slip Wing Hurricane. The 'auxiliary' upper wing surface allowed take-offs from short runways (after which it was jettisoned) and could also be used as an extra fuel tank for ferry flights.

Persian two-seat trainer

A two-seat Hurricane was first mooted in 1940, in a study by Hawker Aircraft into potential replacements for Harvard and Master trainers. Shelved during the Battle of Britain, the idea later attracted interest from Persia (now Iran), which ordered two examples for delivery in 1947. Excessive turbulence in the rear cockpit resulted in the fitting of a canopy shortly after delivery.

European operations

The Hurricane's first year at war

The Hurricane's first test came in the early months of World War II, when RAF units took the type to France. Before long, they had retreated across the English Channel, where they awaited their sternest challenge yet – the Battle of Britain.

The first Hurricanes had been delivered to No. 111 (Fighter) Squadron at Northolt a few days before Christmas 1937, and production accelerated rapidly in 1938, so that half a dozen squadrons were flying the new fighter by the end of the year, with four of them being regarded as operational.

By the outbreak of war, Hurricanes were operational with 16 home-based RAF squadrons, of which four were immediately sent to France, two with the Advanced Air Striking Force and two with the air component of the British Expeditionary Force (BEF).

Fighter backbone

The 12 remaining squadrons provided the backbone of Fighter Command, with five more squadrons due to become operational by the end of 1939. By that time, the Hurricanes coming off the production line were fitted with metal-covered wings and possessed either D.H. variable-pitch or Rotol constant-speed three-bladed propellers. As the early-production Hurricanes were replaced by later aircraft, they were

issued to a number of training units, now under tremendous pressure to increase the supply of pilots to the squadrons. Fortunately, the Hurricane proved to be a relatively viceless fighter and the Miles Master proved an excellent partner in the fighter training programme.

While the situation in France remained relatively quiet for the first eight months of the war (owing to Germany's adventures elsewhere), war had broken out between Russia and Finland, the latter having previously been equipped with British biplane fighters. It was originally intended to send a squadron of Gladiators to assist Finland in its fight, but the intended squadron was instead committed to Norway when that country was attacked by Germany.

Finnish Hurricanes

A number of Hurricanes (mostly early, ex-RAF examples) was shipped to Helsinki and arrived in time to see some

action before the war ended. One Hurricane squadron, No. 46, was eventually sent to northern Norway to cover the Allied forces around the northern port of Narvik, shipped aboard the carrier HMS *Glorious*, and subsequently took a fair toll of German aircraft, though it was soon obvious that it would be impossible to sustain the ground forces at such a distance from Britain. An evacuation was ordered and, after giving what air cover it could, No. 46 Squadron landed back aboard *Glorious*. The carrier was attacked by German battlecruisers during the voyage home and was sunk with almost all hands; the commanding officer and one other pilot of No. 46 Squadron were rescued. All the Hurricanes went down with the carrier.

By then, however, the German offensive in the West had burst on France and the Low Countries on 10 May 1940. The Allied forces were simply not equipped to match the German blitzkrieg tactics. There were too few Hurricane squadrons to contest German air superiority over the battlefield, and casualties among RAF aircraft were exceptionally heavy. The few Belgian Hurricanes were committed to

Pilots scramble to their No. 601 Squadron Hurricanes to meet Luftwaffe bombers on their way to British targets in 1940. Hurricanes outnumbered Spitfires by three to two during the Battle of Britain.

battle under suicidal conditions and almost all were destroyed, either in the air or on the ground.

Air Marshal Sir Hugh Dowding sent four more Hurricane squadrons to France, but it was immediately obvious that any further reinforcements would simply be wasted. Two of the squadrons were ordered to cover the withdrawal westwards by the remnants of the BEF, while the others were brought back to join home-based Spitfires in defending the beaches of Dunkirk during the great evacuation between 26 May and 3 June. By the time France capitulated in mid-June, the Battle of France and the Low Countries had cost Fighter Command 386 Hurricanes (out of RAF aircraft losses of 477). Yet, such had been the increasing rate of Hurricane production that not only were these losses made good within a fortnight, but deliveries to the training units had been maintained. The loss of 200 pilots was another matter.

A No. 501 Squadron Hurricane Mk I is seen here being speedily refuelled and rearmed at Béthéniville during the first days of the blitzkrieg on France. To the right is the pilot (in white overalls), probably reporting to the squadron's Intelligence Officer.

18 August 1940 was one of No. 501 Squadron's worst days during the Battle of Britain. In just two minutes in the afternoon, the squadron lost four of its Hurricanes, including these two aircraft, to one Luftwaffe pilot – Oberleutnant Gerhard Schöpfel of III./JG 26.

Battle of Britain

In July the Battle of Britain opened with Hurricanes equipping no fewer than 26 squadrons, compared with 17 of Spitfires, eight of Blenheim fighters and two of Defiants. The progress of the Battle of Britain is too well-known to do more than outline the part played by the Hurricane.

The overall tactic followed was to order the Hurricanes against German bombers, while Spitfires would tackle any fighter escort provided. Inevitably, the RAF pilots were outnumbered and Dowding always had to allow for the possibility of simultaneous attacks in the north and south, and had to deploy his numerically inferior number of fighters accordingly.

Eagle Day

Fortunately, the Luftwaffe attacked on all fronts on only one occasion, the famous 'Attack of the Eagles' on 15 August. Due to superb management of resources, skill and gallantry by the RAF pilots, the German attacks were blunted and their aircraft losses were far greater than those of the defenders. Hurricane pilots destroyed more enemy aircraft than all other defences combined (other RAF fighters, anti-aircraft guns and balloons), by a ratio of more than three to two.

By the end of the Battle, the number of Hurricane squadrons had, in fact, increased by three, one Canadian, one Polish and one Czech squadron each having become operational. Within two months, five more would have joined the defences (including the first 'Eagle squadron', No. 71, manned by American volunteer pilots).

The improved Hurricane Mk IIA had started to re-equip four squadrons and soon the 12-gun Mk IIB would join Fighter Command.

Moreover, during occasional night-defence sorties during the summer battles, the Hurricane had proved a more effective night-fighter (being simpler to fly and to land at night) than the Spitfire, with the result that several of the Hurricane day squadrons were deployed as night-fighters and intruders during that autumn.

Not all the Hurricanes in action during the opening months of the war were RAF machines. This Belgian Mk I was one of a small batch delivered during 1939 and put up against the German blitzkrieg. Many were shot down by Luftwaffe Bf 109s.

Powerplant
Rolls-Royce Merlin IIs, rated at 1,030 hp (768 kW) at 16,250 ft (4953 m), powered early Hurricane Mk Is.

Armament
Eight 0.303-in (7.7 mm) Colt-Browning machine-guns, mounted in the wings, equipped the first production Hurricanes. A total of 2,660 rounds was carried.

Fabric-covered wings
As an early-production aircraft, L1630 has fabric-covered wings. Metal wings were introduced on the 481st Hurricane.

BEF Hurricane Mk IA

No. 87 Squadron was in action in France between September 1939 and May 1940, engaged primarily in escorting Lysanders of No. II Squadron. Both units suffered heavy losses.

Camouflage and markings
L1630 carries the standard Dark Earth and Dark Green RAF fighter camouflage of the day, with 'Black and White' undersides, as adopted after the 1938 Munich Crisis.

Fixed-pitch propeller
No. 1 Squadron's first Hurricanes sported wooden, two-bladed, fixed-pitch propellers. These were later replaced with newer aircraft with three-bladed, variable-pitch airscrews, the older aircraft being passed on to No. 73 Squadron.

Hurricane operations
Northwest Europe and Russia, 1940-44

Loaded with a pair of of 250-lb (114-kg) bombs, a 12-gun Hurricane Mk IIB of No. 402 Sqn, RCAF is seen during training prior to the beginning of daylight cross-Channel fighter-bomber sorties in late 1941.

Following the Battle of Britain, Fighter Command went on the offensive, the RAF's fighter and light bomber forces, including Hurricane Mk IIs, being charged with attracting the Luftwaffe of western Europe into the air. Enemy aircraft could then be destroyed by the RAF's more modern and capable fighters such as the Spitfire.

It was acknowledged that the Hurricane, owing to its outdated construction, would have to be phased out of operational service early in the cross-Channel offensive, and shipped overseas. At this time, the Spitfire was not only still running behind delivery schedules but was itself, in its Mk II version, inferior to the Messerschmitt Bf 109F, which entered service early in 1941. The new Spitfire Mk V was entering service with Fighter Command, which was rashly determined to standardise on this version for many months to come.

Hurricane Mk IIs

In the event, however, the Hurricane was to continue in service until the end of the war. The Hurricane Mk II entered service at the end of the Battle of Britain, and in its Mk IIB form, with 12-gun armament, was quickly found to be a surprisingly effective fighter, particularly in 'Rhubarb' operations – *ad hoc*

sweeps by small numbers (often only pairs) of aircraft – which seldom attracted enemy fighters into the air. The Hurricanes were therefore able to search for and destroy relatively large numbers of mainly second-line enemy aircraft; they also engaged in growing numbers of freelance attacks on enemy airfields.

By May 1941 the number of Hurricane-equipped squadrons in Fighter Command had in fact increased to 35, the former fighters now undertaking night intruder attacks in addition to their daylight sweeps. The Hurricane had already proved to be much more suitable in the night roles than the Spitfire, its wide-track undercarriage bestowing much simpler landing characteristics. Indeed, a number of Hurricane units were tasked exclusively with night operations. The Hurricane Mk IIB fighter-bomber variant, which could

Posed in the moonlight, this No. 85 Sqn Hurricane Mk I was among those given a night-fighting role in an effort to counter the night blitz by the Luftwaffe. Intended as a stop-gap until dedicated radar-equipped night-fighters became available, the Hurricane's successes were few.

carry a pair of 250-lb (114-kg) (later 500-lb/227-kg) bombs, was an ideal night intruder, particularly in operations against German night bomber bases in France and the Low Countries.

Late in 1941 the four-cannon Hurricane Mk IIC started equipping Fighter Command, this version being the most widely-

employed sub-variant of all. The Mk IIC was almost universally confined to night intruder work, although, if a Spitfire escort could be provided, the aircraft was flown on bombing sweeps by day. It played an active part in the Dieppe landings of August 1942.

The Hurricane IIB and IIC survived in front-line operational

The Battle of Britain over, the RAF's Hurricane units re-formed and went onto the offensive. These aircraft equipped No. 174 Sqn, a dedicated fighter-bomber unit based at Manston in May 1942.

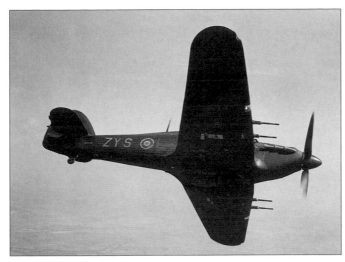

service over northern Europe until late in 1943, though in rapidly dwindling numbers as the more effective Typhoon assumed the ground attack role in preparation for the coming invasion of Europe. With its withdrawal from combat operations, the Hurricane was increasingly relegated to training and communications work. A special courier unit, the Air Despatch Letter Service Squadron, formed with Hurricanes in the latter stages of the war to carry despatches between Belgium and London, was typical of the type of work undertaken.

Increasingly, the Hurricane carried out coastal patrols and convoy escort during the last 18 months of the war and was widely used for fighter affiliation training, being flown in mock attacks on bombers to provide training for gunners.

Hurricanes for Russia

The German attack on Russia which opened on 22 June 1941 was followed by an immediate pledge by Winston Churchill that Britain would do everything it could to send military materiel to assist its new ally. This quickly took the form of sea convoys, heavily laden with all manner of weapons, military vehicles and aircraft. The Hurricane featured in these supplies in larger quantities than any other aircraft from Britain, no fewer than 2,952 such fighters being despatched between August 1942 and the end of the war. The majority of these were shipped aboard the famous North Cape convoys, and several hundred also reached Russia via the Middle East, being carried by rail from the Persian Gulf to Baku on the Caspian Sea.

Many of the early aircraft on the North Cape convoys were in fact Hurricane Mk Is, re-engined with Merlin XXs and dubbed Mk IIs, even though they had already flown many hours with Fighter Command during 1940! The majority, however, were Hurricane IIBs – originally intended for shipment to the Middle East, complete with tropical air filters, only to be hastily thrown into combat over the snow-covered wastes of northern Russia.

The first arrival, on 1 September 1941, of Hurricanes in Russia by sea were those of No. 151 Wing (Nos 81 and 134 Squadrons, RAF), hurriedly formed in Britain in order to train Russian personnel to operate the British aircraft.

Soviet naval pilots

Despite some suspicion among the Russians that the Hurricanes were not of the latest type, they quickly became firmly attached to the aircraft, appreciating the ease with which it could be flown. Several German aircraft were destroyed by the RAF pilots before the two squadrons returned home, having left their Hurricanes behind. It is believed that most of the aircraft which reached Russia during the first three or four months were subsequently flown by Russian naval pilots, occasionally against the Finns, but more frequently in defence of ports used by the Russian Baltic Fleet. Although at least three Russian regiments were equipped with Hurricanes – probably mostly during 1942 – the aircraft came to be widely used as advanced trainers, the Mk IIC being a particular favourite on account of its heavy armament.

Surviving records show that the Russians were particularly anxious to receive the Hurricane Mk IID anti-tank variant during 1944, but this need proved difficult to satisfy; the RAF had not planned to use this version in the invasion of France that year (the Typhoon having become the ideal close-support aircraft), and almost all the available Mk IIDs and anti-tank Mk IVs had been or were being shipped to the Mediterranean and the Far East. Eventually 60 Mk IIDs and about 30 Mk IVs were put on trains at Basra in the Persian Gulf and sent to Baku, having been taken off a convoy to Bombay. Whether these aircraft were used operationally by the Russians during the tank battles of the final offensive into Germany is not known.

In reality, the anti-tank Hurricane was seldom able to destroy German tanks, but was effective against German and Italian armoured troop carriers.

Cannon-armed Hurricanes played a significant role in the defeat of the Axis powers in North Africa. Nevertheless, the first, third and fourth aircraft of this five-ship formation from No. 94 Squadron have had their outboard cannon removed to reduce weight.

Hurricanes in the Middle and Far East

After the Hurricane's vital contribution to the Battle of Britain, the aircraft went on to achieve further success in the Middle and Far East, gaining a fearsome reputation as the ground-attack 'Hurri-bomber'.

Stung into action in May 1940 by the imminent defeat of France, the Air Ministry made hurried arrangements to fly Hurricanes to the Middle East while there were still airfields in the south of France, where the aircraft could refuel before flying on to Malta and Egypt. Accordingly, on 10 June, the day on which Italy entered the war, 12 Hurricanes set course from Boscombe Down (with a Blenheim which carried a navigator) for southern France. However, while attempting to land, all but three of the fighters and the Blenheim crashed due to obstruction of the runway. The remaining three Hurricanes reached Malta a day later, having obtained fuel in Tunisia.

Several batches of very old Hurricanes were carried to the Mediterranean aboard aircraft-carriers during the remainder of 1940, being flown off when within range of Malta. Another reinforcement route was opened in September of that year, Hurricanes being carried by sea to Takoradi on the Gold Coast, where they were assembled and flown the breadth of Africa and then north to Egypt. Many of the early aircraft had not been fitted

with carburettor dust-filters, and these aircraft were almost worn out by the time that they arrived at their destination. By October, however, there were enough serviceable Hurricanes to equip one squadron and, shortly afterwards, No. 73 Squadron arrived from the UK, having flown up the Takoradi route.

The build-up of Hurricanes in the Mediterranean was slow to begin with and, with the onset of the Greek campaign, it was only possible to provide a total of three and a half squadrons for the Western Desert and Greece. All were Mk Is and, by February 1941, all new arrivals were tropicalised either in the UK or at

Takoradi. The big filter reduced the maximum speed, but still the aircraft proved more than a match for the Italian aircraft encountered over the desert and in Greece. When, however, the Germans joined the Balkan campaign, the Hurricanes began to suffer losses and, after giving a good account of themselves in Crete, the few survivors were withdrawn to Egypt.

By March 1941 the first Hurricane Mk IIAs were arriving, and these managed to hold their own, even after the arrival of the Luftwaffe's JG 27 with Messerschmitt Bf 109Es, although casualties were sometimes high. During the East African campaign against the Italians, a dozen or so Hurricanes were 'milked' from the Takoradi route and put to good use against the generally poor-quality Italian aircraft.

By June 1942 most of the old Hurricane Mk Is in the Middle

East had been withdrawn to training units or converted to reconnaissance fighters; the latter was, at the time, a conversion unique to the Middle East, but was later also undertaken in the Far East, and involved the installation of a fan of three vertical and oblique cameras in the Hurricane's lower fuselage, just aft of the wings. The Mk I was replaced by the Hurricane Mk IIC with four 20-mm cannon, and the Mk IID anti-tank aircraft with two 40-mm guns, the former version becoming a useful night-fighter in the theatre, and the latter joining the IIBs as fighter-bombers over the desert. The IIDs received their baptism of fire at Bir Hakim and later gained many successes against Axis armour during the Battle of El Alamein and the long advance through Cyrenaica, Tripolitania and Tunisia in 1942. No. 6 Squadron retained its anti-tank Hurricanes until the end of the war, fighting on through Sicily, Italy and the Balkans. It eventually received Hurricane Mk IVs which were flown with 40-mm and 20-mm guns, bombs, rocket projectiles, or combinations of these stores, with drop tanks often added.

Hurricanes were also flown by a dozen squadrons during the Torch landings in November 1942, being joined by Sea Hurricanes and Canadian-built Mk Xs.

Far East operations

Hurricanes were reaching the Middle East in a steady flow at the end of 1941, when Japan struck in Malaya, immediately threatening the safety of Singapore. Hurricane Mk IIBs (equipped for the tropics) arrived in the Far East by carrier, having been diverted from their original destination in the Middle East.

It was too late, however, and although these fighters fought with great courage during the final stages of the battle for Singapore and over Java and Sumatra, they fought to extinction. Other Hurricanes had been

Armed with a pair of Vickers 'S' 40-mm guns, the Hurricane Mk IID was particularly effective against Axis tanks and armoured vehicles. Five squadrons operated this variant in the Middle East theatre from April 1942.

Powerplant
The Mk IIC was fitted with a 1,280-hp (955-kW) Rolls-Royce Merlin XX, the additional power compensating for the extra weight of the airframe compared to the Mk I. The engine was coupled to a Rotol RS5/2 or /3 three-bladed constant-speed propeller.

Fuselage
The fuselage, like that of all Hurricanes, was a fabric-covered box structure of round-section steel and duralumin type, wire-braced, and connected by wooden stringers attached to 11 tapering metal frames.

Hurricane Mk IIC

Based in Egypt during 1942 with No. 94 Squadron, this Mk IIC carries the normal camouflage for RAF fighters in the theatre – Dark Earth, Middle Stone and Azure Blue. The unit served in the Middle East and Mediterranean throughout the war before disbanding in Greece in April 1945.

Operational career
At the height of its deployment in northern Europe (December 1941-January 1942), Hurricane Mk IICs equipped 30 Fighter Command squadrons; at about the same time, they also equipped 10 squadrons in the Middle East and, later, 21 squadrons in Southeast Asia.

The MacRobert fighters
HL851 was one of three Hurricane Mk IICs donated by Lady Rachel MacRobert of Douneside and Cromar in memory of her three sons who had all been killed flying with the RAF in the early part of the war. *Sir Roderick* was named after her eldest son, Baronet Roderick, who went missing over the Kiruk-Mosul oilfields in Iraq on 20 May 1942. The others were *Sir Iain* (HL735) and *Sir Alasdair* (HL844). In addition, Lady MacRobert donated a further Hurricane which served elsewhere and a Stirling bomber, *MacRoberts' Reply*.

Filter
Tropicalised Hurricanes were fitted with Vokes filters to protect the ventral radiator and oil cooler from sand and dust. They proved equally useful on aircraft operating from the primitive non-tropical airfields of northern Russia.

Armament
Mk IICs were armed with either Oerlikon or Hispano 20-mm cannon, with a capacity of approximately 364 rounds. HL851 later had its outboard guns removed to save weight.

diverted to Rangoon in Burma, where the Japanese were also advancing. This time, however, the Hurricane pilots were confronted by fighters of the Japanese army; these were of poorer quality, with the result that a fairly heavy toll was taken of the invaders. More importantly, more Hurricanes survived to provide air cover for the subsequent British retreat northwards through Burma, the main difficulty being the lack of adequate airfields and landing strips.

With the inevitable loss of Burma, all future Hurricane reinforcements to the Southeast Asian theatre were disembarked at Indian ports and in Ceylon. The Hurricane Mk IIBs were widely used in the two Arakan campaigns, usually as fighter bombers, but also providing fighter cover and escort for bombers. During the sudden Japanese naval attack against Ceylon, Hurricanes, joined by Fleet Air Arm Fulmars, took a significant toll of the enemy carrierborne aircraft, though with fairly heavy losses. Nevertheless, the Japanese losses were more significant as, with no replacements available within a thousand miles, the attack on Ceylon was halted; moreover, the loss of naval fighters rendered the naval task force more vulnerable when brought to action later by the Americans.

By April 1943, there were already 14 Hurricane squadrons – equipped mainly with Mk IIBs

The first Hurricanes arrived in Asia in January 1942 and, as the war progressed, were committed increasingly to ground-attack operations such as this attack on the Tiddum Road, Burma, in 1945.

and IICs, but also with the first of a growing number of Mk IIDs, which were found to be particularly effective against Japanese tanks and armoured vehicles. Of these squadrons, seven were operating over the Burma front or providing air defence of Calcutta, three were deployed for the defence of Ceylon and four were resting or re-equipping with Hurricane Mk IICs and IIDs. In 1944, as the tide finally turned

A tropicalised ground-attack fighter, the Mk IV was fitted with a universal wing, allowing the carriage of a wide range of stores such as rocket projectiles (seen here), bombs, 20-mm or 40-mm guns and drop tanks.

against the Japanese, the number of operational Hurricane squadrons fell to 11, all but two of them being in Nos 221 and 224 Groups, with headquarters at Imphal and Chittagong. Most were now equipped with Mk IVs. During the final advance, low-flying Hurricanes, frequently armed with rockets, were in constant action, bombing bridges and river traffic and taking a heavy toll of Japanese light tanks, personnel carriers and troop concentrations. Having played a key part in the battles of Imphal and Kohima in the north, the Hurricanes served on until the end of the Burma campaign.

Foreign operators

The British government approved the export of Hurricanes to several countries prior to World War II and supplied aircraft to a number of states friendly to the Allied cause. Further sales, of surplus RAF aircraft, were also made post-war.

South Africa

Seven Hurricane Mk Is (right) were released by the Air Ministry and shipped to South Africa after requests for new aircraft made in mid-1938. These equipped No. 1 Sqn at Pretoria but none survived to see war service. After the outbreak of war, No. 1 Sqn was joined by four other units equipped with Hurricane Mk Is and IIs for service in North Africa. Post-war, a few Mk IIBs and IICs returned to South Africa, but they survived only a few months before being written off.

Pre-war orders

Yugoslavia

An order for 12 Hurricane Mk Is was placed in 1938, the first two examples being delivered in December. A second order for a further 12 Mk Is followed soon afterwards, deliveries of these aircraft beginning in February 1940. At about the same time, a licence agreement was negotiated for the production of Hurricanes in Yugoslavia by PSFAZ Rogozarski of Belgrade and Fabrika Aeroplana I Hidroplana of Zenun. At the time of the German invasion of the Balkans in April 1941, the Yugoslav air force had some 38 Hurricanes on strength (top right), including 15 locally-built examples. Within a week most had shot down or destroyed on the ground. Post-war, the Hurricane Mk IVs (bottom right) of the Yugoslav-manned No. 351 Sqn, RAF, were handed over to the Yugoslav Partisan Air Force, with which they saw a short period of service.

Romania

Romania ordered 12 Hurricane Mk Is (below) in late 1938 and, although all were delivered, Romania's signature of the Axis Tripartite Treaty with Germany meant that they are unlikely to have seen action. When the Romanian air arm was modernised by Germany in 1940, the Hurricanes were probably relegated to second-line duties.

Poland

Poland was the last country to place an order for Hurricanes before the war, requesting one aircraft for evaluation, with options for another nine. Though the first aircraft left Britain in July 1939, followed by the other nine machines in September, evidence regarding their final destination suggests that they may not have reached Poland and may have either returned to Britain or been shipped to the Middle East!

Belgium

In March 1939 Belgium ordered 20 Hurricane Mk Is (below), the first three of which were delivered the following month. Meanwhile, Avions Fairey secured a licence to build another 80 aircraft, equipped with four 0.5-in (12.7-mm) machine-guns in place of the standard eight 0.303-in (7.7-mm) guns. However, delays meant that the 20 aircraft completed before the German invasion in May 1940 retained the eight-gun armament.

Canada

The RCAF's first Hurricanes were 20 British-built Mk Is, shipped across the Atlantic in late 1938 with a view to training pilots for RAF Hurricane units. Eventually, Canadian Car and Foundry Co. was contracted to build Hurricanes, principally for the RAF and Fleet Air Arm. The first of 1,451 Canadian-built aircraft (left) was delivered in 1940 and, while most were shipped abroad, the RCAF retained some examples (including a number of Mk Xs) for defensive duties.

Wartime deliveries

Australia

Hurricane Mk I V7476, believed diverted from a shipment en route to Takoradi, was taken on charge by the RAAF. Finally finished in an overall silver with Southeast Asia Command (SEAC) markings, the aircraft was given the Australian serial A60-1, though this was never carried; the aircraft was eventually abandoned at RAAF Point Cook.

Egypt

No. 2 Sqn, Royal Egyptian Air Force, manned in the main by Egyptian pilots, received around 20 tropicalised Mk IIBs and IICs in 1944 and flew them alongside the Desert Air Force in North Africa until January 1946. A few remained in REAF service in the years following World War II.

Turkey

Turkey's first Hurricanes were a batch of 24 Mk Is delivered during September and October 1939. In the mid-war years, as part of a large batch of aircraft supplied by the Allies in an attempt to encourage Turkey to withstand Axis overtures, ex-RAF Mk IIs were supplied, including HV608, a tropicalised Mk IIC (below), seen shortly after delivery in January 1943.

France

France's Aéronavale acquired 15 Sea Hurricane Mk IICs and XIIs (all ex-Fleet Air Arm and tropicalised) in 1944 and 1945. A few remained airworthy until early 1946.

Soviet Union

The best information available suggests that 2,952 Hurricanes were supplied to the Soviet Union from 1941 by both Britain and Canada, including 1,557 Mk IIBs (pictured) and 1,009 Mk IICs. Most were new aircraft shipped from Britain, though several hundred were supplied from RAF Maintenance Units in the Middle East and transported by rail across Persia to units defending Russia from the advancing German army.

Post-war sales

Ireland

Ireland obtained at least 19 Hurricane Mk Is and IICs by various means during World War II, including '93' (below), which crash-landed in the Republic during the Battle of Britain. Two were later exchanged with Britain for three older examples and during 1943/44 seven Mk Is and six Mk IICs (bottom) were delivered. A handful remained in service until 1947.

Portugal

The wartime Azores Agreement, signed by Portugal and Britain to allow the latter access to military bases in the islands, guaranteed the supply of several batches of aircraft to the Portuguese. Among these were 40 surplus Hurricane Mk IICs (left), refurbished by Hawker, and delivered post-war with a large stock of spare parts. These, the first Hurricanes exported after World War II, remained in Portuguese service as late as 1951, latterly equipping the Lisbon Fighter Defence Flight.

Finland

Finland took delivery of a dozen Hurricane Mk Is (pictured) in February 1940, during the country's Winter War with the Soviet Union. The combatants had signed an armistice before the aircraft could be reassembled and placed in service. However, with the renewal of hostilities in 1941 (the Continuation War), 11 aircraft saw some use, though this was limited by a complete lack of spares.

India

No. 1 Sqn, Royal Indian Air Force, became the first Indian Hurricane unit to become operational, equipped with some of the 106 aircraft issued to the RIAF in late 1943. Eight RIAF units were eventually equipped with the type, a few serving into 1946 before being replaced by Tempest Mk IIs.

Captured aircraft

Aircraft inevitably fell into the hands of the enemy on both sides. Tropicalised RAF Hurricane Mk I V7670 arrived in the Middle East in about January 1941, only to be captured intact (and presumably flown) by advancing German forces. The above photograph was taken after the Hurricane's recapture during Operation Crusader towards the end of the year.

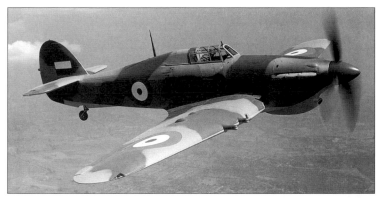

Persia (now Iran)

Persia ordered 18 Hurricane Mk Is in 1939, but owing to delays in the development and testing of tropical air filters, only one was shipped before the outbreak of war and one other in 1940. Neither had a filter fitted and, with the uncertainties of wartime, delivery of the balance of the order was delayed until after the war. However, it transpired that, during the war, 10 aircraft were transferred from the RAF to the Persian air force and these were joined by 16 Mk IICs (above) and two two-seat aircraft in 1946/47.

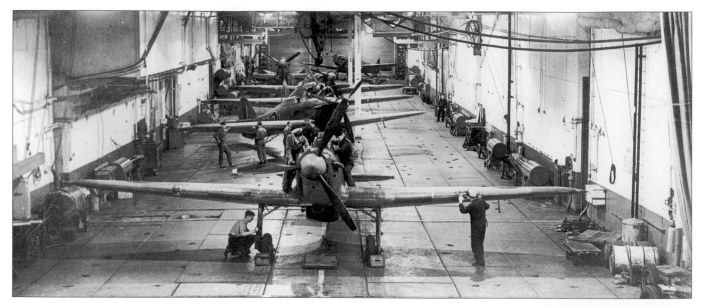

Hurricanes at sea
The FAA's Sea Hurricanes

The use of the Hurricane as a naval fighter may be considered to have been a case of necessity being the mother of invention, as the Fleet Air Arm found itself without a modern interceptor. The resulting Sea Hurricane was the FAA's first single-seat, carrierborne, monoplane fighter.

The type first took off from a carrier at the height of the Norwegian campaign in May 1940 when, faced with providing air cover for an Allied Expeditionary Force (far out of range of any Allied airfield), the Air Ministry ordered No. 46 Sqn, RAF to Narvik aboard the carrier HMS *Glorious*. The Hurricanes were standard Mk Is and the pilots had no experience of operating from a flight deck. Yet the aircraft were successfully flown off to operate from the Norwegian airfield at Bardufoss, well inside the Arctic Circle. After a frustrating period flying defensive patrols against fleeting attacks by German aircraft, the squadron landed back on *Glorious* for the journey home, only to be lost when the carrier was sunk by German warships;

only two of the pilots survived. Also at the time of the Narvik campaign, Hawker was asked to investigate the practicability of equipping the Hurricane with floats, but this venture was abandoned when Norway collapsed.

Sea Hurricane

This operation occurred at a time when the Fleet Air Arm was equipped with Sea Gladiator biplanes and the dual-role Skua fighter/dive-bomber; the two-seat Fulmar was about to enter service although, with a top speed of 280 mph (451 km/h) and manoeuvrability much akin to that of the related Fairey Battle, few observers were very optimistic as to its value as a modern fighter. It was not until the need arose to send Hurricanes to Malta, and RAF

pilots (again untrained in carrier flying) achieved success in flying their aircraft off a carrier while still in the Mediterranean during September 1940 that the Admiralty began to authorise trials with a view to ordering a dedicated adaptation of the Hurricane as a fleet fighter. The first Hurricanes were transferred from RAF Maintenance Units to Admiralty charge the following month and, in December, FAA pilots were undergoing training on redundant Hurricane Mk Is, whose only concession to naval operations was the inclusion of a naval radio. They were nevertheless restyled as Sea Hurricane Mk Is and repainted in two-tone grey.

Meanwhile, following the sinking of the 42,000-ton (42674-tonne) *Empress of Britain*, attention was focused on the possibility of equipping merchant ships with catapults from which Hurricanes might be launched on the appearance of an enemy maritime bomber. Thus were borne the Fighter Catapult Ships and Catapult Aircraft Merchantmen (CAM-ships), the Hurricanes being fitted with catapult spools, and designated

Above: This war-weary Sea Hurricane Mk IB of No. 760 Sqn (part of the Fleet Fighter School in 1941/42) started life as an RAF Hurricane Mk I, delivered in 1939/40.

Top: Five Sea Hurricane Mk IBs of No. 768 Sqn (part of the Deck Landing Training School) and a solitary Supermarine Seafire are seen below decks aboard HMS Argus, probably during 1943. Hastily derived from the RAF's Hurricane, the naval variants lacked folding wings, thereby limiting the number able to operate from smaller aircraft-carriers.

Sea Hurricane Mk IAs. Manned by volunteer RAF and FAA pilots, these Hurricanes sailed with Atlantic convoys and later the famous North Cape convoys. Their pilots were faced with the likelihood of being catapulted from their ship while far out of range of the nearest land, with no carrier available to land on at the end of their sortie; they then underwent the ordeal of baling out near the convoy in the hope of being picked up. Combat successes were rare for these catapult fighters but, after the first few victories, the enemy pilots were noticeably more circumspect when attacking a convoy that might possess fighter defences.

The Merchant Ship Fighter Unit at Speke, in effect the

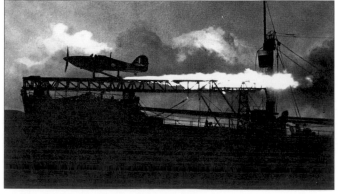

A long tongue of flame shoots from the rockets attached to the sled under Sea Hurricane Mk IA V6756/'NJ-L' aboard CAM-ship Empire Tide.

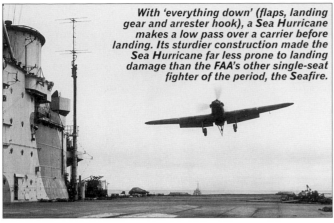

With 'everything down' (flaps, landing gear and arrester hook), a Sea Hurricane makes a low pass over a carrier before landing. Its sturdier construction made the Sea Hurricane far less prone to landing damage than the FAA's other single-seat fighter of the period, the Seafire.

Above: Sea Hurricane Mk Is of No. 801 Sqn are seen being serviced on the deck of an 'Illustrious'-class fleet carrier, about mid-1942. These aircraft were heavily engaged in the Malta convoy battles of 1941/42.

controlling unit of the catapult Hurricanes (and a few Fulmars), represented a 'specialist' branch, independent of the FAA, which was responsible for offensive air action by naval ships, and the air defence of the fleet at sea. The catapult Hurricanes were therefore independent of Fleet and escort carrier operations, which began shortly before the end of 1941 when Sea Hurricane Mk IBs entered service with No. 801 Squadron of the FAA aboard HM carriers *Argus* and *Eagle* and with No. 806 Sqn in HMS *Formidable* – the latter two being fleet carriers. Their Sea Hurricane Mk IBs were equivalent to the RAF's Hurricane Mk I, but were equipped with deck arrester hooks to enable them to operate from carriers at sea. These aircraft were later joined by Sea Hurricane Mk ICs, which were similar but armed with four 20-mm cannon. This version was appreciably slower than the previous Sea

Hurricanes as it was powered by the old Merlin III (unlike the similarly-armed RAF Mk IIC which was powered by the Merlin XX). Nevertheless, the Sea Hurricane Mk IC was regarded as an excellent bomber destroyer and a number of German Focke-Wulf Fw 200 convoy raiders were destroyed by these fighters.

Four-cannon Mk II

The next Sea Hurricane version was the four-cannon Mk IIC which was, in effect, similar to the the RAF's Mk IIC but fully equipped with catapult spools and deck hook. These were heavily involved in the defence of the famous Operation Pedestal convoy to Malta in August 1942, intended to revitalise the island prior to the crucial battle of El Alamein in the Western Desert. This convoy consisted of just 14 merchantmen, but was escorted by no fewer than four fleet carriers,

two battleships, seven cruisers and 24 destroyers. Aboard the carriers were 39 Sea Hurricanes of Nos 801, 880 and 885 Sqns and 31 Fulmars and Martlets of four other squadrons. HMS *Eagle* was torpedoed and sunk in eight minutes with the loss of all but four of No. 801 Sqn's Sea Hurricanes (which were airborne and later landed on *Indomitable* and *Victorious*). The same evening, the Axis air forces began attacks on the convoy, a total of some 500 aircraft being based for the purpose on airfields in Sicily. Both *Victorious* and *Indomitable* were hit and badly damaged by bombs and only the former – now packed with the 47 surviving fighters – remained in action. When the convoy reached Malta, only five of the merchant ships had survived, but they proved just sufficient to sustain the island. Losses among the fighters amounted to eight in combat and 35 on HMS *Eagle*, while enemy records show that 31 German and Italian aircraft were destroyed by the fighters and the ships' defences.

The introduction of escort carriers into the North Cape convoys marked a turning point in the fortunes of this traffic to northern Russia, these small carriers being merchant ships with their former superstructure replaced by a flight deck. Although of relatively small size, these decks were adequate for

the operation of Sea Hurricanes and a few Swordfish torpedo-bombers. From the outset, the convoys began to fight back, not only against German air attacks on the ships, but against the shadowing Fw 200s. Without information on the whereabouts of the convoys, the Luftwaffe was at a serious disadvantage, and losses among the convoys declined sharply.

Canadian manufacture

Sea Hurricanes were also manufactured in Canada and served with the Royal Canadian Navy from late 1942 onwards. During the Torch landings of November that year, Canadian Sea Hurricane Mk Xs and XIIAs bearing American star insignia, with FAA pilots flying from Royal Navy escort carriers (HMS *Dasher*, *Biter* and *Avenger*), provided much local air defence for the landings, their principal opponents being aircraft of the Vichy French air force. Shortly afterwards *Avenger* was torpedoed and blown up with the loss of almost its entire crew and all its Sea Hurricanes.

The Mk XII remained in front-line service with the FAA almost until the end of the war, these fighters being sent out to the Pacific. Here, No. 835 Sqn, as part of the 45th Naval Fighter Wing, continued to operate from HMS *Nairana* until August 1945.

Above: In atrocious seas, a Sea Hurricane takes a battering from the elements. CAM-ship sailings on North Atlantic convoy escort duty were suspended during the winter of 1941/42, as it was thought that the weather would not allow the launching of Sea Hurricanes.

Right: Carrying the 'LU' code letters of the Merchant Ship Fighter Unit, a pair of Sea Hurricanes is ferried to a CAM-ship anchored in the Mersey.

Hawker Typhoon

With bomb racks empty, this Typhoon rolls in to commence a strafing pass over a German convoy. Mounted on each wing are two 20-mm Hispano cannon, each with 140 rounds; these were used to devastating effect prior to, and immediately after, the D-Day landings.

Inset: Two rows of exhausts distinguished the Vulture-engined Tornado from the Typhoon. P5224 was the second prototype, sporting a Typhoon-type 'chin' radiator and was followed by a single Avro-built production example.

The Typhoon was intended as a pure fighter, but it failed to make the grade. Instead, it brought a whole new concept to air warfare as the originator of what we today term 'close air support'. Typhoons were on hand as Allied forces advanced towards Berlin.

Before Hawker's Hurricane entered service (in late 1937), its manufacturer was already working on the next generation of interceptor for the RAF, powered by a new type of engine which promised to deliver twice the power of a Rolls-Royce Merlin.

In January 1938, a new specification (F.18/37) was issued, calling for a replacement aircraft for both the Hurricane and Spitfire with, above all, a top speed in excess of that of contemporary bomber types, i.e. over 400 mph (644 km/h) at altitude. Its armament was to

consist of no fewer than 12 0.303-in (7.7-mm) Browning machine-guns.

Hawker's early interest was rewarded with a contract for two designs, each of which would have two prototypes. One of these was powered by Rolls-Royce's new X-configuration Vulture, the other by a Napier powerplant – the H-type Sabre. Both engines were large 24-cylinder designs expected to produce around 2,000 hp (1491 kW).

Both airframes were all-metal, with tubular framework for the front half of the fuselage and an

alloy monocoque at the rear. An equally robust one-piece wing was supported by a sturdy wide-track undercarriage. The main differences between the two aircraft were necessarily related to their differing engines. The first Vulture-engined machine (named Tornado) had a Hurricane-type ventral radiator, while the Sabre-engined Typhoon had the characteristic 'chin' radiator arrangement.

As Vulture development was proceeding at a faster pace, the Tornado was the first to fly, on 6 October 1939, the first Typhoon following some four and a half months later. Orders were placed for 500 Tornados, 250 Typhoons and another 250 of whichever type proved the most successful. Though both were dogged by engine reliability problems, plan-

ning went ahead for production by Gloster Aircraft (Typhoon) and A. V. Roe (Tornado).

Winds of change

Meanwhile, the first flight of the second Typhoon, delayed by the Battle of Britain, finally took place on 3 May 1941. This aircraft incorporated a number of improvements, including four 20-mm cannon in place of the machine-guns and a larger fin and rudder to improve directional stability. Progress was such that a production Typhoon flew later that month – the first of 110 Typhoon Mk IAs, equipped with machine-guns due to a shortage of cannon feed mechanisms. All subsequent Typhoons (3,205 in all) would be cannon-armed Mk IBs. Meanwhile, the Tornado was cancelled, dogged

The first major order for 250 Typhoon Mk Is was placed in 1939. The fourth Typhoon Mk IA was typical of the first 110 aircraft of this order, in being machine-gun armed.

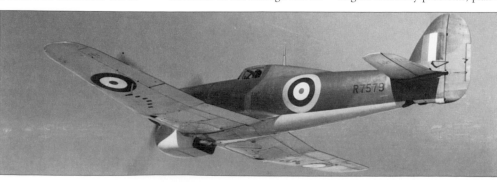

Right: Armed with eight rocket projectiles, this early Mk IB demonstrates a typical Typhoon warload. The worn paintwork is clearly evident even at this early stage and is a testimony to the Typhoon's demanding low-level mission.

Below: Uncluttered by external stores, this Typhoon Mk IB displays the clean lines of the aircraft. Aerodynamic refinements visible here are the 'teardrop' canopy and faired-over cannon barrels, both of which contributed to a welcome increase in maximum speed.

by serious engine failures; only one production example was ever completed.

In September, tactical trials with the Typhoon commenced. Comparative flights with a Spitfire Mk VB revealed a top speed which was 40 mph (64 km/h) faster at 15,000 ft (4572 m) and faster still at lower altitudes. While the Typhoon was less agile than the smaller, lighter Spitfire, it was felt that its speed would make up for this deficiency.

The first service examples were delivered to No. 56 Squadron that same month (and were operational from May 1942), but soon a number of problems, some minor but others more serious, became apparent. The first to manifest itself was

carbon monoxide leakage into the cockpit, blamed for a fatal crash in November. Though cockpit sealing was improved, the fumes were never fully eradicated and Typhoon pilots from then on always flew with their oxygen masks in place.

Poor rearward visibility was improved by replacing the solid fairing behind the cockpit with a transparent version. This preceded the design of an entirely new 'teardrop' canopy, eventually introduced on production aircraft (and retrofitted to some existing machines) from September 1943.

Potentially more serious was the unreliability of the aircraft's Sabre engine, which had been prone to failure from its earliest days. This was attributed to deformed sleeve valves (which caused engine seizures); a solution was not found until mid-1943, when serviceability finally improved.

For a while the entire Typhoon programme looked likely to be cancelled. By late 1942, the daylight bomber threat had evaporated and the performance of the Typhoon left much to be desired. Not only was its engine unreliable and down on

power, but the aircraft lacked manoeuvrability and speed above 15,000 ft (4572 m), largely due to its thick wing section and high wing loading. (The Typhoon Mk II was planned to have a new, thinner wing and entered service as the Tempest Mk V in April 1944.)

Typhoon vs the Fw 190

However, in its favour, the Typhoon was very fast and surprisingly agile at low level. From September 1942, several Typhoon squadrons were stationed in the south of England to intercept Luftwaffe fighter-bombers making 'hit and run' raids. Interceptions often finished up at low level, where Typhoons frequently caught and overhauled the Fw 190s that had been causing the RAF so much trouble on such raids over the autumn months.

These successes kept the Typhoon in service while frantic attempts were made to cure its shortcomings. It was during this period, however, that a Typhoon was fatally lost after its tail separated from the fuselage in flight. Other similar crashes followed, forcing Hawker to quickly devise a strengthening modification for the joint between the fuselage and empennage.

This failed to completely eliminate the problem and eventually elevator flutter was identified as the actual cause. The ultimate cure was the fitting of an enlarged Tempest-type tailplane.

Drive into Europe

Clearly useful at low level, the Typhoon gained a bomb-carrying capability in late 1942. The aircraft of two squadrons were equipped to carry two 250- or 500-lb (113- or 227-kg) bombs, or two 1000-lb (454-kg) bombs from mid-1944. From 1943, Typhoon squadrons became increasingly involved in offensive missions over occupied Europe. The weapon most associated with these Typhoon sorties was the rocket projectile (RP), introduced in October 1943. Normally, four were carried under each wing, the most common type having a 60-lb (27-kg) high-explosive/ semi-armour piercing head. Initially, Typhoons were to carry RPs interchangeably with bombs, but as swapping bomb racks for RP rails was time-consuming, squadrons soon specialised either in RP or in bomb delivery. By D-Day, the Typhoon was the main close support type within the RAF's 2nd Tactical Air Force (TAF), with 20 squadrons equipped. As such, it played a vital role in the invasion of occupied Europe until VE-Day.

Typhoon variants were few. A radar-equipped NF.Mk IB nightfighter was tested successfully and three standard Mk IBs were tropicalised and saw service in the Middle East; neither was adopted for widespread use. A third version was the FR.Mk IB fighter-reconnaissance version (with three cameras in the port wing), a number of which were converted during 1944 and served until the end of the war in Europe.

Left: The immense size of the Typhoon can be appreciated when compared to the RAF personnel standing on the wing of this example. RAF pilots were initially highly sceptical of the aircraft as a fighter interceptor, but as a ground attack platform the machine excelled.

This weatherbeaten Typhoon with the new sliding canopy was MN363, aircraft 'Y' of No. 247 Sqn (which, two years later, was the first unit to be equipped with the Vampire Mk I). It is seen, with its invasion stripes and rockets, operating from an advanced base at Colombelles in June 1944. By this time, many Typhoons had the four-bladed de Havilland propeller.

Early operations

After more than a year of testing the Typhoon in factory trials and squadron operations, the aircraft was greeted with little enthusiasm by its pilots. Unreliability and frequent engine and structural failures meant that the Typhoon's future hung in the balance.

In September 1941, the first Typhoon unit – Duxford-based No. 56 Sqn, commanded by Sqn Ldr 'Cocky' Dundas – traded its Hurricanes for Typhoon Mk IAs. In January 1942, Spitfire-equipped No. 266 Sqn followed suit, with No. 609 Sqn (also a Spitfire squadron) joining the fold in April. Both these squadrons were based at Duxford with No. 56, the three units together forming the Duxford Typhoon wing.

To these highly successful squadrons, the Typhoon, despite its impressive straight-line speed and heavy armament (comprising twelve 0.303-in/7.7-mm) machine-guns), was to be treated with some suspicion for it weighed twice as much as a Spitfire and lacked the lines of the Supermarine fighter. In fact,

before long, teething problems were to appear – problems that took the lives of a number of pilots before solutions were found.

Operational status

In the meantime, under the enthusiastic leadership of Wing Cdr Denis Gillam, progress was being made in bringing the Duxford Typhoon wing to full operational status. This was reached on 28 May when a No. 266 Sqn aircraft was scrambled to investigate an intruder (which turned out to be a Spitfire). Over the following weeks further scrambles took place, though encounters with enemy aircraft were few. Sweeps over occupied France were also undertaken, often in support of 'Circus' raids by RAF bombers.

The first Typhoon victory came on 9 August, when two aircraft from No. 266 Sqn caught a Junkers Ju 88 off the coast of Cromer. Three days later the wing saw its first major action, carrying out three sweeps in support of Operation Jubilee, the ill-fated Dieppe landings.

Before long the Typhoon's shortcomings, in terms of its manoeuvrability above 15,000 ft

This No. 193 Sqn aircraft is an early production Typhoon Mk IB, as it would have appeared in service during 1942. The 'car door' entry to the cockpit, heavily-framed canopy and three-bladed propeller were typical of early Typhoons.

(4572 m), were clear. The Typhoon was not being used to its best advantage, given that it had been designed as a bomber

The most successful method of identification were these underside bands, introduced in late 1942 and used until early 1944 (and not to be confused with the differently arranged AEAF bands, applied to Allied aircraft before D-Day).

Above: Confusion with the Luftwaffe's Focke-Wulf Fw 190, with which the Typhoon shared a similar planform, led to the latter's adoption of various identification markings. Yellow wing stripes were tested from September 1942, though these were abandoned in favour of the white-painted nose, shown here, from November. This proved extremely unpopular with pilots, who felt that it drew more fire than it averted!

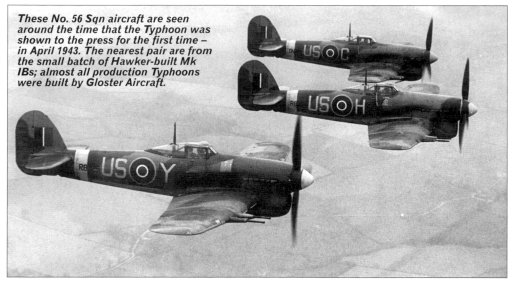

These No. 56 Sqn aircraft are seen around the time that the Typhoon was shown to the press for the first time – in April 1943. The nearest pair are from the small batch of Hawker-built Mk IBs; almost all production Typhoons were built by Gloster Aircraft.

destroyer and bombers were no longer a daytime threat. Accordingly, new roles were defined for the aircraft, taking advantage of its blistering low-level performance, including a top speed of close to 400 mph (644 km/h).

In September 1942, the Duxford wing and two of the three new Typhoon squadrons which had been equipped during the late summer – Nos 257 and 486 Squadrons – were stationed along the south coast to deal with the Luftwaffe Fw 190 and Bf 109 fighter-bombers which had proved almost invulnerable to Spitfires during their nuisance attacks on coastal towns. The aircraft were Typhoon Mk IBs, equipped with four Hispano 20-mm cannon in place of the Mk IA's machine-guns. Mk IBs had also replaced the earlier aircraft in original 'Tiffie' squadrons by this time.

The move south was a great success and by mid-1943 over 60 German raiders had been destroyed, including more than 40 Fw 190s. The interceptions often ended with a chase at zero feet across the Channel, which left the Luftwaffe pilots little option but to crouch behind their armour plate and push the throttle to the firewall. The Typhoon could overhaul even the vaunted Fw 190 'like a train' (as one Typhoon pilot described it in his combat report).

Fighter-bombers

In September 1942 the first two Typhoon fighter-bomber squadrons, Nos 181 and 182, had been formed; their aircraft were equipped to carry a pair of 250- or 500-lb (114- or 227-kg) bombs under each wing. Throughout 1943 they were joined by a steadily increasing number of specialised bomber squadrons which set about attacking airfields, factories, railways, harbours and shipping in and around occupied France, Belgium and the Netherlands. Towards the end of 1943,

'Noball' raids hit V-1 launch sites as a matter of priority.

By the end of the year, no fewer than 18 squadrons of Typhoons were operating, mostly as fighter-bombers. With the major problems that had plagued the Typhoon's Sabre engine overcome and the incidence of tailplane failures much reduced, the Typhoon became the premier ground attack aircraft for the 2nd Tactical Air Force. The latter was being formed to provide air support for the British and Canadian armies in the forthcoming invasion of Europe. However, although a handful of squadrons was still able to demonstrate the Typhoon's excellence as a low-level fighter, its days in the role were numbered.

Rocket projectiles

In October 1943 another new weapon was added to the Typhoon's armoury – the rocket projectile (RP). Having already seen action with Hurricane and Swordfish squadrons, the RP was particularly effective in partnership with the Typhoon, whose stability and high speed made it the ideal accurate delivery platform. At first, the rockets were considered interchangeable with bombs, depending on the target, but the high groundcrew workload required to make the change soon dictated the specialisation of Typhoon squadrons as either bomb- or rocket-equipped. Both weapons were used extensively in the campaign against 'Noball' sites, and then in May 1944, in the campaign to cripple the German coastal radar system before the Allied invasion of occupied France.

By D-Day, the RAF fielded 20 squadrons of Typhoons (including Commonwealth units), some of which were among the first over the beachhead. Operation Overlord and the months of fighting in occupied Europe that followed were to be the Typhoon's finest hour.

Flt Lt Walter Dring was photographed with his No. 183 Sqn aircraft at Gatwick in April 1943, when the squadron was engaged in offensive sweeps across the Channel. Note the bomb rack, just visible under its starboard wing.

Below: Tested at the RAE in May 1943, this NF.Mk IB remained a one-off. Fitted with AI.Mk IV radar, the night-fighter proved successful in trials, but was abandoned in favour of the Mosquito.

Above: A rocket-equipped Typhoon, possibly of No. 257 Sqn, prepares to leave its base in England for a raid on a German radar station near Boulogne. Note the clear-view sliding cockpit canopy, introduced in late 1943.

D-Day and Falaise

As the defeated German army retreated across Europe, Typhoons of the 2nd Tactical Air Force delivered devastating attacks from the air. Despite heavy losses due to 'flak', pilots pressed home attacks with rockets, bombs and cannon-fire.

A s soon as Allied troops landed on the beaches in Normandy on 6 June 1944, 18 Typhoon squadrons (11 RP-firing and seven bomb-carrying) were available to support the assault. As a prelude to the Allied landings, Typhoons of No. 98 and 609 Squadrons had attacked and destroyed an enemy radar station at Dieppe/Caudecote on 2 June; this installation would have given the Germans advance warning of the invasion fleet. The first call for help on 6 June

This sight was to become all too familiar to retreating German troops trapped on the ground. Following a request from Allied troops, a Typhoon unleashes its load of RPs at an enemy gun emplacement. The momentum of the RPs upon impact was equivalent to that delivered by the broadside of a naval frigate.

came at 07.34 hours when the 21st Army Group requested an attack on HQ 84th Corps at Château La Meauffe, near St Lô, and a squadron of 'Bombphoons' was dispatched, whereupon it destroyed the target, killing most of its occupants. Three days later, on 9 June, Typhoons of Nos 174, 175 and 245 Squadrons destroyed the Joubourg radar installation which virtually over-looked the beachheads in Normandy. Upon returning to England, the Typhoon squadrons were placed on alert, where they were available for direction by each Royal Navy HQ ship, anchored offshore, in case special targets needed attention. Another nine squadrons were on hand to attack military HQs, defended localities and enemy gun batteries.

Two others, No. 137 and 263 Squadrons of Air Defence of Great Britain (ADGB), operated over the English Channel (one at each end) to engage enemy naval vessels, in particular, E-Boats, which (it was anticipated) would be attempting to enter the area to attack Allied landing craft. On D-Day squadrons took off prior to the landings, searching for fast patrol boats. Throughout the day Typhoons attacked German targets, often at the request of friendly troops on the ground. There had been two surprises during the daylight hours – the lack of expected fierce Wehrmacht response and rein-forcement, and the almost complete absence of the Luftwaffe, although Typhoon pilots had enough targets to keep themselves busy. On the after-noon of 7 June, a call for aerial

By far the most potent weapon available to the Typhoon was the 60-lb (27-kg) high-explosive rocket projectile (RP). RAF armourers are seen here preparing RPs, while a Typhoon from No. 175 Squadron awaits its next sortie in late-September 1944.

support came from the British 61st Brigade for its attack on Port en Bessin. Not long after this, reports were received of Allied troops being bombed, but investigations revealed that it was Typhoon drop tanks, and not bombs, that were landing among them. Typhoon pilots had released the cumbersome tanks in an effort to increase aircraft speed before striking the targets around the port.

As the Allied armies broke out of the northern perimeter in France, more Typhoons operated close to the advancing forces, and a new tactic – the develop-ment of close-air support – was devised. Typhoon pilots were instructed to maintain a standing patrol, or 'cab rank' at about 10,000 ft (3048 m) over the battle area; the aircraft would then be called down by an RAF officer accompanying the land forces to strike any convenient target with guns, bombs and rockets as the need arose. This method was greatly appreciated by Allied troops embroiled in the numerous firefights within

Above: US infantry run for cover down a French country lane littered with the wreckage of German vehicles. For troops fighting on the ground, the ability to call upon air support whenever required (weather permitting) was instrumental in winning the hedgerow fighting around Normandy.

Left: This Typhoon IB is pictured undertaking RP trials with the A & AEE, later it was to return to combat with No. 183 'Gold Coast' Squadron, which operated Typhoons from November 1942 until June 1945. This particular example, EK497, was shot down on 1 January 1945 by a USAAF P-51, killing its pilot, Flying Officer D. Webber.

the maze of narrow lanes of the Normandy countryside.

Beach-head break-out

From mid-June, Typhoon squadrons began operating from advanced temporary airfields in France, some very close to the front line. From the French fields, clouds of dry dust were hurled into the aircrafts' radiators and engines, necessitating their withdrawal for repair and the rapid fitment of special filters. Few German fighters tackled the Typhoons, but some of them encountered German ground fire which caused serious damage and accounted for most losses, leading to a rapid turnover of aircraft. Many battle-damaged Typhoons returned to England for attention at civilian repair

centres run by Marshall's Flying School at Cambridge and Taylorcraft Aircraft at Rearsby, Leicester. Following the landings, the weather remained consistently poor for air operations, and it was thought that this would cloak enemy ground movement and the expected counter-attack by German Panzer units. But a foothold had by now been gained, over 5 miles (8 km) deep in some places. Typhoon squadrons of the 2nd Tactical Air Force (TAF) would have to help ensure that the German army was pestered by night and day.

Typhoon's finest hour

With the Allies having consolidated their beachhead, the march across Europe began in

earnest. The Typhoon squadrons of the 2nd Tactical Air Force were instrumental in this advance by virtue of their tactical air support role. There was to be no greater test of their ability than at Falaise, northern France. With the swiftly-moving American armoured forces sweeping up from the south, and British and Canadian forces in the north, a beaten 7th German Army was trying to extricate itself before being cut off and surrounded by the Allied armies. Its only means of escape was through the town of Falaise, where there remained a small

gap between the Allied lines. Throughout early August, Typhoons poured a hail of rockets, bombs and cannon-fire into the narrow lanes, decimating the retreating German army as it tried to escape through the Falaise Gap. Typhoon losses during August 1944 reached an all-time high, with more than 90 losses sustained during that month.

For the remainder of the war, Typhoons were to provide the Allied armies with a devastating aerial attack platform from which to strike targets across occupied Europe.

A Hawker Typhoon Mk IB built by Gloster Aircraft wears the markings exhibited by No. 198 Squadron between mid-1943 and D-Day. On 10 April 1943, No. 198 flew its first 'Rhubarb' fighter-bomber sortie against targets of opportunity across the Channel, moving to France in July 1944.

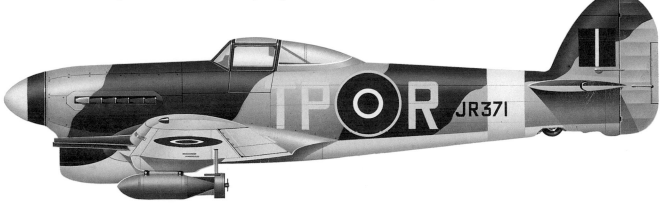

Tempest: Storm over Europe

No. 501 Squadron received the Tempest Mk V in August 1944. During this month it absorbed the FIU and became the only Tempest unit specialising in night operations against the V-1 flying-bombs.

A product from the drawing board of Hawker's prestigious designer, Sir Sydney Camm, the Tempest was built to remedy the problems of the earlier Typhoon. The resulting design proved to be the RAF's best low-/medium-altitude fighter and was particularly successful in countering the 'flying-bomb' threat.

Early in the development of the Typhoon, performance limitations had been linked to the wing section. In March 1940 investigations into thinner-section wings commenced and the profile of the wing was changed into a semi-elliptical form similar to that used on the highly successful Spitfire. The new aircraft, to be designated Typhoon Mk II, had an extended nose section to house an additional fuel tank (compensating for the lower fuel capacity in the thinner wing), a new undercarriage unit and, most significantly,

was to be powered by the latest version of the Napier Sabre engine, the Mk IV. Camm intended to move the radiator from beneath the nose to the wing leading edges, producing a far more streamlined design with less drag.

However, by spring 1942, serious shortcomings with the Napier engines fitted to the Typhoon were casting major doubts over future development, and alternative powerplants were examined. With the Rolls-Royce Vulture out of the running, the only alternatives were the Rolls-Royce

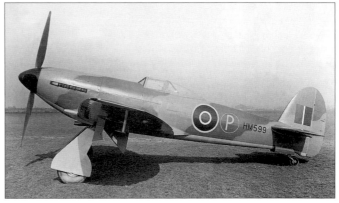

The Tempest Mk I was an exceptionally clean design and offered significantly greater performance than the Mk V. Official dislike of wing-mounted radiators ended its development.

Griffon and Bristol Centaurus. By the autumn of 1942, it was decided that five different powerplants were to be looked at and, at this point, the aircraft's name was changed from Typhoon

Mk II to Tempest. Although the 'new' aircraft differed from the Typhoon in a number of significant ways, the decision to change the name was also influenced by the poor reputation of the

Above: HM595 was the prototype Mk V. Converted from a production Typhoon, it is seen here late in the development programme with the 'bubble-canopy' and new tail arrangement.

Right: With a total of 21 V-1s, 10 aircraft kills and five DFCs, these No. 486 Squadron pilots were among the top Tempest exponents. From left: Stafford, Taylor-Cannon, Eagleson and Evans.

Seen fresh from the Hawker factory at Langley, this Tempest Mk II was fitted with bomb racks and was delivered to the A&AEE at Boscombe Down in September 1945 for weapons trials with 1,000-lb (454-kg) bombs.

Typhoon at this time.

The five differently-powered Tempests were allocated the following mark numbers: Mk I (Sabre IV and wing-mounted radiators); Mk II (Centaurus IV); Mk III (Griffon IIB); Mk IV (Griffon 61); and Mk V (Sabre II as fitted to production Typhoons). Delays in the development of the Sabre IV and Centaurus along with airframe modifications for the installation of the Griffon ensured that the Mk V was available long before the others. The Mk V prototype (HM595) was a basic Typhoon airframe fitted with the new wing. Testing proved that the new design handled well and showed improved performance over the Typhoon in terms of speed and rate of climb. The lengthened nose affected stability and an enlarged tail fin with a dorsal fillet was fitted, followed by the much improved one-piece sliding canopy.

Development of the other marks were not so successful. The Griffon-engined variants were abandoned as Griffon production had been largely earmarked for Spitfires. The Sabre IV-powered Mk I eventually flew in February 1943, but concerns over the engine coupled with official distrust of wing-mounted radiators ended the project. Development of the Mk II was to be continued as a long-term project.

The first production Tempest Mk V Series I flew in June 1943 armed with two long-barrelled Hispano Mk II cannon (later Series II aircraft were fitted with the short-barrelled Hispano Mk V and were equipped to carry drop tanks). Testing of production aircraft was carried out by the A&AEE and the AFDU, and the Tempest's excellent fighting ability at low/medium altitude was readily apparent. With a few minor modifications – such as the fitting of spring-tab ailerons to increase the rate of roll – the Tempest Mk V was accepted by the RAF for operational service.

The first operational mission was flown by No. 3 Squadron in April 1944. This unit was joined on operations in May by No. 486 Squadron, RNZAF and these two units began working-up for expected combat during the D-Day invasion. In the event, the Tempests did not see combat until 8 June when No. 3 Sqn, led by Wing Commander Roland Beamont, encountered seven Bf 109Gs. Three were downed for no loss, proving the Mk V's ability in combat.

Priorities for the two Tempest squadrons were changed in mid-June as the first V-1 flying-bombs were launched at the UK. The first of these missiles – codenamed 'Divers' – was spotted by a No. 3 Sqn Tempest on 13 June and, three days later, the two units joined other high-performance fighter squadrons in ADGB (Air Defence of Great Britain). Positioned at Newchurch, the Tempests downed their first V-1 on 16 June, commencing an amazing sequence of 'kills'. By the end of the first week, the two squadrons had destroyed 150 V-1s.

V-1s were also launched at night and the FIU (Fighter Interception Unit), equipped with a small number of Tempest Mk Vs, was dispatched to Newchurch to deal with the threat. The unit was highly successful with one of its pilots – Flt Lt Berry – achieving 52.5 kills. At the beginning of July, No. 56 Sqn joined the Newchurch Wing in the daytime effort against the V-1 and, by the end of August, the V-1 attacks had subsided. In this time, the Newchurch Wing claimed 632 'kills' and this total, along with 86.5 'kills' by the FIU, made the Tempest by far the most significant aircraft in countering the V-1s.

Tempest Mk Vs also made a valuable contribution with the 2nd TAF in Europe. With its heavy armament, the Tempest proved to be excellent in the ground-attack role and, in the last seven months of the war, the seven squadrons operating with the 2nd TAF built up a formidable reputation and an enviable kill/loss ratio.

Over 250 enemy aircraft were downed in combat as well as hundreds more destroyed on the ground. The Tempest Mk V proved itself to be one of the most effective Allied warplanes of the late-war period.

Development of the Tempest Mk II continued through 1944 with the first production example being delivered to the A&AEE in May 1944. Deliveries began early in 1945 but with the war in Europe drawing to a close it was decided to adopt the design for service in Asia.

Trials were relatively successful but in the event the war had ended before the Tempest Mk II could be tested in combat.

Above: Wearing invasion stripes, two Tempest Mk Vs depart for a fighter sweep over northern France. The aircraft could outperform both the Bf 109G and Fw 190A at low/medium altitude.

Below: MW742 was from the first production batch of Tempest Mk IIs and was one of many stockpiled at Maintenance Units in the final months of war, awaiting transfer to the Far East.

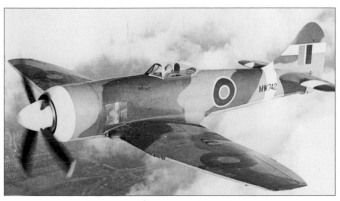

Seen at Newchurch in the spring of 1944, No. 486 Squadron, RNZAF was to become, along with No. 3 Squadron, one of the RAF's most successful units against the V-1 flying-bombs.

In March 1938 45 He 111Es were sent to the Legion Condor in Spain, where they joined He 111Bs. They operated throughout the remaining months of the Civil War, flown by both German and Spanish crews.

Heinkel He 111

Pre-war variants

Developed to fill both airliner and bomber requirements, the He 111 was a major part of the Luftwaffe's expansion in the 1930s, and became the backbone of the bomber force. Early variants saw action in Spain and the early wartime campaigns.

Designed under the leadership of Siegfried and Walter Gunter in response to demands at the time of the Luftwaffe's secret birth for a fast airliner capable of minimum adaptation for the bombing role, the He 111 was in effect a twin-engined, scaled-up version of the He 70 Blitz that had entered Luft Hansa service in 1934, retaining its elliptical wing and tail surfaces. Powered by 600-hp (448-kW) BMW VI 6,0 Z engines, the first prototype was flown at Marienehe by Gerhard Nitschke on 25 February 1935, being followed by the second less than three weeks later. The third prototype, forerunner of the

He 111A series bomber version, showed itself to possess a performance better than many then-current fighters.

As six 10-seat He 111C-0s entered service with Luft Hansa during 1936, the first of 10 military He 111A-0s were being evaluated at Rechlin but, owing to inadequate engine power when carrying a warload, were summarily rejected, all 10 aircraft being sold to China.

Anticipating the problem of power shortage, Heinkel produced the He 111B, of which the pre-production He 111B-0 series was powered by 1,000-hp (746-kW) Daimler-Benz DB 600A engines. Despite a considerable weight increase,

Unregistered, the He 111a first prototype took to the air from Heinkel's plant at Rostock-Marienehe on 25 February 1935, flown by Gerhard Nitschke. It was completed in bomber configuration.

this version returned a top speed of 224 mph (360 km/h). By the end of 1936 the first production He 111B-1s with 880-hp (656-kW) DB 600C engines appeared and, following successful trials, joined 1./KG 154 (later renamed KG 157), KG 152, KG 155, KG 253, KG 257 and KG 355. Thirty He 111B-1s were also shipped to Spain to provide the bomber force of K/88 of the Legion Condor fighting in the Civil War. The He 111B-2 was

produced in 1937 with 950-hp (709-kW) DB 603CG engines.

Few examples of the He 111D-0 and D-1, with 950-hp (709-kW) DB 600Ga engines, were built as a result of a shortage of this engine, and in 1938 production switched to the He 111E with 1,000-hp (746-kW) Junkers Jumo 211A-1s. Some 200 of these aircraft were produced, and they proved capable of lifting a 4,409-lb (2000-kg) bomb load – roughly

The first in-service bomber variant was the He 111B, delivered to KG 154 in late 1936. The type reached Spain in February 1937, first going into action with Kampfgruppe 88 on 9 March.

The He 111F introduced a new wing with straight, tapered edges, thus greatly easing manufacture. Turkey bought 24 He 111F-1s, which were delivered in 1938 and served until 1946.

Fifty-eight of the 75 He 111B/Es sent to the Legion Condor survived the Civil War. They remained in Spain, operated by the Spanish air force's 14th and 15th Regiments. A handful, like this He 111E-1, were in use until the end of the 1950s.

Having switched to the Jumo 211 engine for the He 111D, E and F, Heinkel returned to the DB 600 for the He 111J, 90 of which were delivered to the Luftwaffe in the summer of 1938. A few were still on charge at the outbreak of World War II.

similar to that of the RAF's much slower Armstrong Whitworth Whitley Mk III heavy bomber.

Straight-winged bomber

Meanwhile, efforts had been made to simplify the He 111's wing structure for ease of production, and a new planform with straight leading and trailing edges had appeared on the

Having first been tested on the He 111 V8, the rounded profile nose was first applied to He 111P production, which also introduced DB 601 power. This group of He 111P-1s is from III./KG 255. He 111Ps saw action during Germany's early wartime campaigns.

seventh prototype. This wing was introduced into production with the He 111F, which emerged from the shops of Heinkel's new showpiece factory at Oranienburg in 1938; powered by 1,100-hp (821-kW) Jumo 211A-3s, 24 He 111F-1s were sold to Turkey, while the Luftwaffe's version was the F-4. The He 111G series comprised nine examples, of which five (powered variously by BMW 132Dc and BMW 132H-1 radials and DB 600G inlines) were delivered to Lufthansa and the remainder went to Turkey as He 111G-5s. Produced simultaneously with the He 111G series, the He 111J series was

developed as a torpedo-carrying version, of which about 90 were produced, but in fact served as a normal bomber with the Kriegsmarine-allocated KGr 806 in 1939.

Hitherto, all He 111s had featured a conventional 'stepped' windscreen profile but, following the appearance of the eighth prototype in January 1938, the He 111P adopted the smooth nose profile with extensive glazing that so characterised the aircraft thereafter. This design incorporated a nose gun mounted offset to port, and a small hinge-up windscreen to improve the pilot's view during landing. The He 111P series entered production before the end of 1938, the type joining KG 157 in the following April. Although this series was intended as an interim version pending arrival of the He 111H, it survived in Luftwaffe service long after the outbreak of World War II in 1939.

He 111 at war

By September that year the He 111H was well established with operational units, the Luftwaffe deploying 400 such

aircraft compared with 349 He 111P series, 38 He 111E series and 21 He 111J series aircraft. Of this total of 808 aircraft, 705 were serviceable on the eve of Germany's attack on Poland. In that fateful campaign the Heinkels of KG 1, KG 4, KG 26, KG 27, and II/LG1 were in constant action, starting with raids far beyond the front line, but as the Poles fell back towards Warsaw, were launching devastating bombing raids on the Polish capital.

Owing to the lack of suitable airfields, only three He 111-equipped units (KG 4, KG 26 and KGr 100) operated in the Norwegian campaign, the other Geschwader deploying in readiness for the German attack in the West, which opened on 10 May 1940. Four days later, 100 Heinkels of KG 54 attacked Rotterdam – a raid now known to have occurred owing to the fact that a recall message was not received by many of the bombers, whose radio operators were already manning their guns; as it was 57 aircraft dropped 97 tons of bombs in the centre of the city, killing 814 Dutch civilians.

Commercial variants

Although Heinkel concentrated on developing the He 111 as a military bomber, it also worked on airliner versions. The second prototype, the He 111c (D-ALIX *Rostock*), was completed to airliner standard, and was subsequently operated by Luft Hansa. The He 111 V4 fourth prototype was also a civilian machine, as were the six He 111C-0s (below) which entered Luft Hansa service in 1936. Used primarily on the *Blitz-Strecken* fast services between German cities, they were found to be uneconomic, but flew on until the outbreak of war. Four further machines entered Luft Hansa service under the He 111G designation, two powered by the BMW VI 6,0 ZU engine and two fitted experimentally with BMW 132H-1 radials. Most of Luft Hansa's He 111C/Gs were taken over by the Luftwaffe.

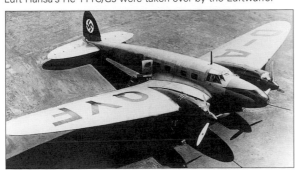

Above: An He 111C overflies some of the Luft Hansa fleet, including the He 111c.

Right: Named Augsburg, this is the He 111 V14, which served with Luft Hansa as an He 111G.

He 111H

A squadron of He 111H-16s maintains a tight formation while returning from a sortie on the Russian front. The H-16 was the third 'standard' production model (following the H-3 and H-6), and was powered by the Jumo 211F-2 engine.

Fitted with Jumo engines, the He 111H became the definitive version of the Luftwaffe's standard bomber. Many sub-variants were produced, and it served from 1939 to the end of the war.

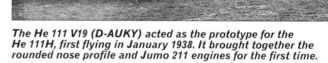

The He 111 V19 (D-AUKY) acted as the prototype for the He 111H, first flying in January 1938. It brought together the rounded nose profile and Jumo 211 engines for the first time.

By the beginning of the Battle of Britain the He 111H had almost entirely replaced the He 111P series. The airframe was essentially unchanged, but the powerplant was the Jumo 211. From the outset, the He 111H, with its 270-mph (435-km/h) top speed, proved a difficult aircraft to shoot down (compared with the Dornier Do 17), and showed itself capable of weathering heavy battle damage. The 17 Gruppen flying the He 111H during the battle operated an average strength of about 500 (compared with He 111P series aircraft, of which some 40 served in the reconnaissance role with the Aufklärungsgruppen), losing some 246 of their number in air combat in the course of the four-month battle. Among the outstanding attacks by He 111s were those by KG 55 on the Bristol aircraft factory on 25 September, and the same unit's devastating raid on Supermarine's factory at Southampton the following day.

The majority of the He 111Hs employed during the Battle of Britain were He 111H-1s, -2s, -3s, and -4s, the latter two initially powered by 1,100-hp (821-kW) Jumo 211D engines. Perhaps the main significance of their losses lay in their five-man crews, whereas the other bombers, the Ju 88 and Do 17, were crewed by only four.

The next variant to join the Kampfgeschwader was the He 111H-5, which incorporated additional fuel tanks in place of the wing bomb cells, and featured two external racks each capable of lifting a 2,205-lb (1000-kg) bomb; its maximum all-up weight was increased to 30,985 lb (14055 kg). He 111H-5s were widely used during the winter Blitz of 1940-41, these aircraft carrying the majority of the heavy bombs and parachute mines to fall on British cities in that campaign. The He 111H-5 could also carry a single 3,968-lb (1800-kg) bomb externally.

Torpedo-bomber

The He 111H-6 came to be the most widely-used of all He 111s, entering production at the end of 1940. With provision to carry a pair of 1,687-lb (765-kg) LT F5b torpedoes, this version was armed with six 0.31-in (7.9-mm) MG 15 machine-guns and a forward-firing 20-mm cannon, and some aircraft featured an MG 17 or remotely-operated grenade launcher in the extreme tail. Despite their torpedo-carrying ability, most He 111H-6s were used as ordinary bombers, the first unit to fly torpedo-equipped He 111H-6s being I./KG 26, flying these aircraft from Bardufoss and Banak in northern Norway against the North Cape

convoys from June 1942 onwards and participating in the virtual annihilation of the convoy PQ 17.

The He 111H-7 and He 111H-9 designations covered minor equipment alterations in the He 111H-6, while the He 111H-8 featured an outsize balloon fender designed to deflect barrage balloon cables to cutters in the wing tips; these were found to be of little use so surviving He 111H-8s were later converted to glider tugs, as He 111H-8/R2s. The He 111H-10 was similar to the He 111H-6 but included a 20-mm MG FF cannon in the ventral gondola and *Kuto-Nase* cable cutters in the wings.

Following the successful use of He 111Hs as pathfinders by KGr 100, this role featured prominently in subsequent development of the aircraft, the He 111H-14, He 111H-16/R3 and He 111H-18 being specially fitted with FuG Samos, Peil-GV, APZ 5 and FuG Korfu radio equipment for the task; He 111H-14s were flown on operations by Sonderkommando Rastedter of KG 40 in 1944.

As the He 111 was joined by such later bombers as the Heinkel He 177 Greif, Dornier Do 217 and others, it underwent parallel development as a transport; the He 111H-20/R1 was fitted out to accommodate 16 paratroops and the He 111H-

This black-painted He 111H is seen during the night Blitz of London. The He 111H later proved to be a good platform for the pathfinder mission, with sophisticated navaids.

Above: From the He 111H-5,racks allowed the type to carry large weapons externally. This KG 26 He 111H-6 is seen with an SC 1800 3,968-lb (1800-kg) bomb.

Left: Armourers load two practice LT F5b torpedoes on to an He 111H-6. Although mainly used as a bomber, this variant achieved spectacular success in the anti-ship role while operating with KG 26 in Norway. H-6s were also used for trials of guided weapons such as Fritz-X and BV 246 Hagelkorn.

20/R2 was equipped as a freight-carrying glider tug. Nevertheless, bomber versions continued to serve, particularly on the Eastern Front where the He 111H-20/R3 with a 4,410-lb (2000-kg) bomb load and the He 111H-20/R4, carrying 20 110-lb (50-kg) fragmentation bombs, operated by night.

Perhaps the most outstanding, albeit forlorn, of all operations by the He 111H bombers and transports was that in support of the Wehrmacht's attempt to relieve the German 6th Army at Stalingrad between November 1942 and February 1943. As the entire available force of Junkers Ju 52/3m transports was inadequate for the supply task, He 111 bombers of KG 27, KG 55 and I./KG 100 joined KGrzbV 5 and KGrzbV 20 (flying an assortment of He 111D, F, P and H transports) and embarked on the job of flying in food and ammunition to the beleaguered army. Although the bombers were occasionally able to attack Russian armour, bad weather severely hampered the supply operations, and by the end of the Stalingrad campaign the Luftwaffe had lost 165 He 111s, a sacrifice from which the Kampfgeschwader never fully recovered.

He 111H-2

The aircraft depicted here, Wk Nr 3340, 'Yellow B' of 9./KG 53 'Legion Condor' is shown with the wing bars carried (for fighter identification and station-keeping) during the big Luftwaffe daylight raids on London during Sunday 15 September 1940 – the climax of the Battle of Britain. The three white panels have always been said to indicate the III. Gruppe of a *Geschwader*, although so many anomalies exist as to throw doubt on this assumption. This aircraft was in fact damaged in action on that day and force landed at Armentiers with two wounded crew members; recent computerised research suggests that it was probably attacked by Spitfires of No. 66 (Fighter) Sqn.

Structure
The wings were built around a two-spar structure, which carried through the fuselage fore and aft of the bomb bays. Interspar fuel tanks were situated inboard and outboard of the engine nacelles. The rear fuselage was largely empty, providing stowage space for the master compass and emergency dinghy.

Powerplant
The He 111H was the Jumo 211-powered version intended for parallel production with the DB 601-powered He 111P. The first H-0/H-1 aircraft had the Jumo 211A-1 rated at 1,010 hp (753 kW) for take-off, but the H-2 introduced the 1,100-hp (820-kW) Jumo 211A-3.

Accommodation
The standard crew was five. The pilot sat back in the glazed section, offset to port. The navigator/bombardier sat alongside for take-off, but for operations moved forwards to the extreme nose. In the rear was the radio operator/dorsal gunner. Two further gunners were carried, to operate the weapons in the beams and ventral gondola, which was known to the crew as the '*Stertebett*' (death-bed).

Armament
The He 111H-2 introduced better defensive armament in the form of five MG 15s, firing through beam hatches, from the dorsal turret and rear of the ventral gondola, and from the Ikaria spherical mounting in the nose. Many aircraft were field-modified with an additional MG 15 in the right upper nose glazing, while the H-3 introduced a 20-mm MG FF in the forward part of the gondola. The next major model, the H-6, often featured an MG 17 in the tailcone. The bombload was carried internally in two ESAC bays, either side of a gangway which led from the forward to the aft crew compartments. The standard load was eight 551-lb (250-kg) bombs, carried vertically with the nose uppermost. The H-4 and H-5 introduced external bomb carriage, the internal bays being used for extra fuel if required.

Heinkel

Right: An He 162A-1 shows the turned-down wingtips first introduced on the V3 to overcome excessive dihedral problems. The A-1s were manufactured in parallel with the prototypes, the latter being regarded as A-0 pre-production airframes.

He 162 'Salamander'

Volksjäger

Conceived in the dying throes of the Third Reich, the He 162 'Salamander' was intended as one massive last-ditch effort to fend off the Allies. However, for the Nazis, this diminutive jet was too little, too late.

Autumn 1944 saw Hitler's Germany being reduced to rubble under the onslaught of continuous Allied bombing raids. Desperate measures were needed and strong Nazi officials began to take over the decision-making processes. Under the overall control of Albert Speer's armament ministry, Party Leader Karl-Otto Saur devised a *Volksjäger* (people's fighter). This was to be small (not over 4,410 lb/2000 kg when loaded), simple, jet-propelled and therefore able to outpace and outmanoeuvre the hordes of Allied fighters. It was to be armed with one or two 30-mm guns, be easy to maintain and make absolutely minimum demands on skilled labour and scarce materials.

The requirement was issued on 8 September 1944 and was immediately studied by all the leading aircraft manufacturers. Some, like Messerschmitt and Focke-Wulf, along with the outspoken fighter ace Adolf Galland, derided the project, claiming the idea was unfeasible and unrealistic. To go into mass production with such an unproven aircraft, which would be flown by inexperienced Hitler Youth, and adopt a policy that maintenance did not matter – as unserviceable or damaged fighters could be replaced by new ones – was unsound, and could detract from the war effort. Instead, they argued for greater effort in Me 262 produc-

tion, but their protests fell on deaf ears.

By 15 September, the proposals had been whittled down to the Blohm und Voss P.211 and the Heinkel P.1073. On every count, the P.211 was the better aircraft but, by sheer effort, Heinkel forced through its P.1073 so that, on 24 September, it received the go-ahead not only from Saur, but also from Göring.

Programme begins

After stormy meetings, the final go-ahead was granted on 30 September, with a planned initial output of 1,000 aircraft per month. The programme was given the name Salamander, while Heinkel called the aircraft itself *Spatz* (sparrow), the designation being given as He 162. The appellation 'Salamander' for the aircraft was never popularly used by the Germans – rather, it was bestowed by the Allies when they learned of the project name. The design could hardly have been simpler; the streamlined fuselage was a light-alloy, semi-monocoque structure of circular section, with a moulded plywood nose. The cockpit had an upward-hinged clear canopy and cartridge-actuated ejection seat while fuel was housed in a 153-Imp gal (695-litre) tank amidships. Wheels and brakes were taken from the Bf 109G

Above: This He 162A-2 was allocated to 3. Staffel/JG 1 at its Leck base in May 1945. By this time, the 50 aircraft had been reorganised into one single Gruppe, Einsatz-Gruppe I./JG 1; many pilots from other fragmented units at Leck were absorbed by this new Gruppe.

and the chosen engine was a BMW 003 turbojet, attached directly above the high-mounted wing by three bolts.

The 'Salamander' programme, centred on Heinkel's factory at Vienna-Schwechat, initially produced 10 prototypes, He 162 V1 to V10, which were also considered as the He 162A-0 pre-production batch. The planned He 162A-1 production fighter was to be mass-produced by a growing number of factories and sub-contract plants. The biggest factories, such as Heinkel Nord at Rostock-Marienehe, Junkers at Bernburg and the Mittelwerke in the Herz mountains – which used cheap slave labour – were to build up to 1,000 aircraft each per month, with total monthly production in all factories reaching 6,000. The entire 'Salamander' programme was run by a special organisation called Baugruppe Schlempp, which was headed by Heinrich Lübke.

The first prototype made its maiden take-off on 6 December 1944 and reached

Above: Production aircraft did not differ greatly from this, the first V1 prototype, except for turned-down wingtips, enlarged ailerons and compound taper on the trailing edge near the wingroot. The V1 had only been flying for four days when it broke up in mid-air.

Right: Considerable numbers of Heinkel He 162s were captured by the Allies in varying degrees of repair and some still exist in museums. This aircraft was flown on 26 flights by the British RAE at Farnborough. It was restored for display at RAF St Athan.

its maximum speed of 522 mph (840 km/h). Upon landing, the V1 was discovered to have suffered some structural damage as a result of the use of acids in the construction of the aircraft; moreover, a shortage of time had meant that substitute adhesives, in the shape of a phenol-based FZ-film, had been rushed in. On 10 December, with a large audience consisting of Luftwaffe, RLM (air ministry) and Nazi party officials who had all come to watch the potential saviour of Nazi Germany, the V1 flew from Schwechat airfield with test-pilot Flugkapitän Peter at the controls. While making a low-level pass over the airfield, the entire leading edge broke away from the right wing. In the ensuing violent roll and yaw, the right aileron and wingtip also separated before the aircraft crashed.

To show confidence, the first flight of the V2 prototype was made by the Schwechat technical director, Dipl.-Ing Franke. He explored the limits of the flight envelope, discovering unacceptable lateral and directional instabilities, especially in tight left-hand turns. As a result,

the tail was slightly enlarged and the wingtips were tilted downwards at an anhedral angle of 55°.

From the outset, there had been arguments over the armament. The requirement was for one or two 30-mm guns such as the MK 108, but the design team found it impossible to house more than 50 rounds per gun, whereas if the high-velocity 20-mm MG 151 was substituted, each gun could have 120 rounds. The V1 prototype had therefore been designed with the 20-mm guns, but the RLM insisted on the V2 having two MK 108s and, in early January 1945, trials were conducted with these weapons. The resulting vibration was judged to be unacceptable and, although MK 108s were fitted to the V6 aircraft, the Heinkel engineer's opinion was vindicated and the production He 162A-2 was standardised with the MG 151, each with 120 rounds.

By February 1945 approximately 100 aircraft had been completed, including over 20 prototype and development machines, and the gigantic production programme was

One of the four 'Salamanders' transported to Britain was 120072, which made four evaluation flights from Farnborough after the war. On the last of these, the aircraft broke up in a roll, killing the pilot.

getting into its stride. However, there was no parallel gigantic programme to train pilots. In 1944 the Luftwaffe's once mighty force had been devastated by Allied fighters and bombers and hardly any skilled pilots (so-called *Experten*) were left. One of the greatest was Obstlt Heinz Bär (220 victories) who, at the end of January 1945, was posted from the command of JG 3 to activate the vital Erprobungskommando (special test unit) 162 at the Luftwaffe's central test establishment at Rechlin.

In spite of the great urgency for a suitable aircraft, the Luftwaffe insisted on checking that the He 162A-2 could serve as a fighter. A few days later, on 6 February, I./JG 1, the first Gruppe of the Luftwaffe's

premier (at least numerically) fighter wing, handed its Fw 190s to II.Gruppe and began converting to the He 162 at Parchim. Subsequently, II./JG 1 also converted, but in the dying weeks of the Third Reich, chaos and fuel shortages were just two factors preventing effective operations. Plans had gone ahead for an entire year's intake of Hitler Youth, irrespective of flying aptitude, to carry out brief training on gliders, and then proceed directly to the He 162. At the same time, Heinkel was scheming further variants of the He 162.

However, while all this was happening, the Allied forces were overrunning Germany and any further plans for the He 162 were consigned to history.

He 162A-2 'Salamander'

The Heinkel He 162 was the product of a rushed attempt to mass-produce a fighter that would stem the Allied advance. However, the speed of the development process resulted in many structural and aerodynamic shortcomings. This He 162A-2 was assigned to 3. Staffel, Einsatzgruppen I./JG 1, and was the personal aircraft of Staffelkapitän Oberleutnant Erich Demuth. It carried his 16 victory marks on the tail, although these had been gained on other aircraft.

Configuration
Experts predicted that the He 162's unusual top-mounted engine would suffer airflow problems (which to a great extent did not occur), but did not foresee the pitch instability which made the aircraft so tricky to fly and fight in.

Powerplant
The He 162A-2 was powered by a single BMW 003E-1 or E-2 axial-flow turbojet, rated at 1,764 lb st (7.8 kN) with a 2,028-lb st (9.02-kN) emergency rating available for periods of up to 30 seconds. The pre-production aircraft had been powered by the BMW 003A-1, while some prototypes flew with the BMW 003R, combined with the 1,764-lb st (7.8-kN) BMW 718 liquid-fuel rocket. Shortages of BMW 003s led to the investigation of the Jumo 004D as a possible alternative, and this engine was installed in two prototypes.

Service history
Although it is likely that He 162 pilots saw some action, no encounters with Allied aircraft have been confirmed. This is mainly due to the fact that the fighters were still awaiting official approval for combat when the war ended.

Performance
The He 162A-2 had a maximum speed at normal thrust of 490 mph (789 km/h) at sea level or 520 mph (837 km/h) at 19,685 ft (6000 m). This speed could be increased for short periods with a burst of extra thrust. The range at full throttle was 385 miles (620 km) at 19,685 ft (6000 m).

Heinkel He 177 Greif

An audacious British operation saw this He 177A-5/R6 being taken from the Luftwaffe airfield at Blagnac. The machine was tested in autumn 1944 and into 1945. Officially named Grief (Griffon), the He 177 proved almost as dangerous to its crews as it did to the enemy, and it was generally considered a poor machine by its British test pilots.

The 'flying lighter'

Nicknamed *Luftwaffenfeuerzeug* 'flying lighter' because of its tendency to catch fire, the He 177 was the Luftwaffe's only operational strategic bomber.

During 1936, the Reichsluftminsterium (RLM) in Berlin offered its support to the development of a 'Ural-bomber' programme with two rival types, the Do 19 and Ju 89. Neither came to anything however, and the 'Ural-bomber' was cancelled in 1937. It was replaced by a requirement called 'Bomber A' which it was hoped would lead to a better aircraft.

Ernst Heinkel AG was given the job of designing and building 'Bomber A' and Projekt 1041 was started in late 1936. Under Technical Director Hertel, the gifted Günter brothers planned a bomber incorporating many radical new features. Designated He 177 by the RLM, the new bomber was marvellously clean aerodynamically. The fuselage was tube-like, with a glazed nose and a gun position in the glazed tail-cone. The mid-mounted wing had high aspect ratio, and under it was room for a large bomb bay. Clearly, power had to come from four engines of about 1,200 hp (895 kW) or two of 2,400 hp (1790 kW), but Germany had no 2,400-hp engines. Boldly, in part-

nership with Daimler-Benz, Heinkel produced the DB 606 double engine, which comprised two DB 601 inverted-V12 engines mounted side-by-side and joined through a common gearbox to a single propeller. Two of these were to power the new heavy bomber, clearly offering lower drag and better manoeuvrability than four separate engines. To reduce drag further it was planned to augment the engine cooling by using surface radiators, as had been pioneered on the He 100 and the He 119 floatplane, which also employed DB 606 power. There were to be four main landing gears, one retracting inwards and another outwards under each engine to lie in the wing ahead of the main spar. Defensive armament was to be installed in four remotely controlled turrets.

By early 1939, when the V1 first prototype was taking shape, it was reluctantly concluded that the surface radiators were impractical. Much larger, circular units were therefore mounted around the front of each double engine, increasing drag, which demanded

During Operation Steinbock, experienced He 177 crews found that by entering enemy airspace at 29,527 ft (9000 m), and attacking at full power and in a shallow dive at about 435 mph (700 km/h), they stood a chance of avoiding interception.

extra fuel which meant increased weight, in a vicious circle.

A dive bomber?

The RLM then decreed that this big bomber had to be able to make steep 60° dive attacks, which resulted in a considerable increase in structural weight, further reducing performance and also requiring the addition of large underwing dive brakes. To slow the landing of the overweight aircraft full-span Fowler flaps were adopted, the outer portions coming out from under the ailerons. Again there were problems because the wing had not been stressed for the large lift and drag loads of the flaps.

The V1 made its maiden flight on 19 November 1939. Despite being unarmed it failed to come anywhere near the 'Bomber A' performance requirements, but it

handled reasonably well, and there was little indication of the trouble that was to follow.

Seven further prototypes were built, each heavier than its predecessor. Vertical tail area was increased, triple bomb bays were incorporated, various types of defensive armament fitted (low-drag remotely controlled guns were replaced by conventional turrets or hand-aimed guns) and ceaseless efforts made to try to eliminate the most serious problem, which was the frequency of engine fires. V2 suffered flutter and disintegrated, V4 crashed into the sea and V5's engines caught fire at low level, the aircraft flying into the ground and exploding.

In 1939 30 He 177A-0 pre-production aircraft were ordered, plus five from Arado. These had many changes, including a redesigned nose for a crew of five, armament comprising a 0.31-in (7.92-mm) MG 81 in the multi-pane hemispherical nose, a 20-mm MG FF in the front of the gondola, a twin MG 81Z at the rear of the gondola, a 0.51-in (13-mm) MG 131 in the roof turret and a hand-aimed MG 131 in the tail. During production the

Almost all He 177 sub-types had an MG 151/20 in the front of the gondola and a second in the tail, aimed by a gunner who sat under a Plexiglas bulge under the rudder. In the case of the KG 40 A-3/R1 illustrated however, the forward weapon is an MG FF cannon.

Here the third pre-production aircraft demonstrates its hefty main landing gear during a take-off roll. Vicious swinging on take-off was common.

dive brakes were removed and there were many other changes, but the most urgently needed concerned the powerplants.

With hindsight, it seems that many features of the DB 606 installation might almost have been deliberately arranged to give trouble. The oil scavenge pumps were oversized, and at heights over 19,685 ft (6000 m) the oil tended to aerate and foam, leading to breakdown in lubrication, seizures and fires. Almost always the oil dripped on to the white-hot exhaust manifold serving the two inner banks of cylinders, and radiant heat from this frequently ignited oil and fuel that collected in the bottom of the cowling. Many fires resulted from fuel leaks from the high-pressure injection pumps and rigid piping.

Production system

Over 25 of the 35 A-0s were destroyed from various causes, and the rest were used for crew training at Ludwigslust. All 130 production He 177A-1s were made by Arado, using 2,700-hp (2014-kW) DB 606 engines, and incorporating only a few of the dozens of planned improvements. The aircraft could carry very heavy bomb loads however, and Hitler urged it be brought into service, to range far beyond the Eastern Front at night and to escort U-boats and blockade runners in the North Atlantic.

At last, in October 1942, Heinkel began delivering the improved He 177A-3, but found it hard to build more than five per month. The A-3 retained the DB 606, although it had been hoped to fit the 3,100-hp (2312-kW) DB 610 (made up of a pair of DB 603s). However, the engines were mounted further forward, the exhaust system was redesigned and many other dangerous features were altered. To balance the engines the rear fuselage was extended and a second dorsal turret was added. Like the A-1, the A-3 was produced with different Rustsätze armament sets.

Heinkel built 170 A-3s, following which, from February 1943, it and Arado delivered 261 He 177A-5s. In the final year of war this became the chief operational version. Features of the A-5 included a strengthened airframe, shorter main-gear legs, normal ailerons, and racks under the forward fuselage and outer wings for three Hs 293s, or two Hs 294s or two FX 1400 bombs.

Bombing London

Heinkel and Arado together delivered no fewer than 565 He 177A-5s. By far the most important Luftwaffe units to use the He 177 were KG 40 and KG 100, the former being concerned chiefly with the Battle of the Atlantic with the Hs 293 and both taking part in Operation Steinbock, the revenge attacks on London in the early weeks of 1944. The effectiveness of the Steinbock missions was low however – on 13 February 1944, 2. and 3./KG 100 set off for England; 14 aircraft taxied out, 13 took off, eight soon returned with overheated or burning engines, four reached London but only three came back.

There were many sub-variants made in small numbers, including a handful modified with a 50-mm BK 5 anti-tank gun under the nose. Later the A-3/R5 was fitted with a 75-mm gun, but only five such aircraft were built. Several were flown with an electrically powered tail turret with two MG 151/20 guns, and the planned He 177A-6 was to have either this turret or one with four MG 81s. The six A-6s had pressurised cabins, as did the A-5/R8, the latter being a single aircraft with remotely controlled barbettes in the chin and tail locations. One of the last of the numerous development prototypes, the V38 (basically an A-5), was stripped down and prepared to carry 'the German atomic bomb' in a single gigantic bomb bay. The He 177 Zerstörer was intended for destroying heavy bomber formations with a battery of 33 rocket launch tubes, while the last version to get into limited production was the extended-wingspan A-7. It was intended to have 3,600-hp (2686-kW) DB 613 engines, but these were not ready. It carried extra fuel, and intensely interested the Japanese who considered building it under licence with four separate engines. Heinkel's own similarly-configured He 277 never had official approval and only a string of prototypes was built.

He 177A-5/R2 Greif

This machine hailed from the 4. Staffel, II Gruppe of Kampfgeschwader 100, during the time the unit was based at Bordeaux-Mérignac, France, in 1944.

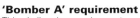

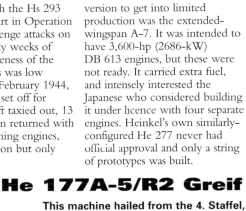

'Bomber A' requirement
This challenging requirement, which ultimately led to the He 177, demanded a maximum speed of 540 km/h (335 mph) and the ability to carry a 2000-kg (4,410-lb) bomb load over a radius of 1600 km (995 miles) at a cruising speed of 500 km/h (310 mph).

Powerplant
The He 177A-5 standardised on the DB 610 engine (coupled DB 603s) as opposed to the DB 606 (coupled DB 601s) of the earlier variants. Despite tests with one aircraft which had identified and fixed 56 potential causes for engine fires, these problems continued. It was felt that to incorporate the modifications would have severely disrupted the production lines.

Offensive weapons
Weapons carried by the He 177A-3 included the Hs 293 radio-controlled missile and, in the A-3/R7 and all A-5 versions, a range of anti-ship torpedoes, including the LT 50 glider torpedo.

Fire risk compounded
In addition to the fire risks associated with the He 177's oil and fuel systems, the engines of the A-1 were installed so tightly up to the main spar that there was no room for a firewall. The piping, electric cables and other services were also jammed in so tightly that, especially when soaked in leaking fuel and oil, the fire risk was absolutely awesome.

A-5 advantages
The main advantage of the A-5 was that it introduced the more powerful DB 610 engine, and as the weights were only fractionally heavier than those of the first versions the performance was improved, especially in ceiling.

Camouflage
The He 177s of KG 40 and KG 100 wore a variety of overwater camouflage, this example being standard for most of KG 100's aircraft.

Heinkel He 219 Uhu

Heinkel's Owl

This early prototype represents something of a mystery. It has the lengthened sharp nacelle tails associated with the production He 219, as well as production-standard enlarged tail surfaces. It has an unstepped fuselage, but appears to lack armament, and is not fitted with radar or operational equipment. It may be the He 219 V11.

Revolutionary for its day in terms of its innovative design, the Heinkel He 219 Uhu was arguably the finest German night-fighter to see combat during World War II. Despite the promise that the Uhu offered, however, its career was to be hindered by political meddling and production problems.

A post-war view of an He 219 serves to illustrate several characteristic features, including the stalky nosewheel which turned through 90° and retracted to lie flat beneath the cockpit.

Ernst Heinkel AG was one of the largest aircraft firms in Hitler's Germany and was highly experienced in producing combat aircraft. In mid-1940 the Rostock-Marienehe head office had surplus design capacity, and this was put to use in creating a number of projects, one of which was Projekt 1064. This was the building of a *Kampfzerstörer*, literally a bomber-destroyer but meaning a multi-role fighter, attack, reconnaissance and even torpedo aircraft. It incorporated many new features, including a tandem-seat pressurised cockpit in a rather serpent-like nose, a shoulder-mounted wing, giant underslung engine nacelles housing the twin-wheel main units of its tricycle landing gear, twin tail fins and remotely-controlled defensive gun barbettes. The design was just what the

Luftwaffe needed, but Projekt 1064 was looked at unfavourably because it used so many radical innovations. On top of this, the project was never requested officially and thus it was filed away and forgotten.

Fighting a lone battle to build up the Luftwaffe's vital night-fighter force was General der Nachtjägd, Josef Kammhuber. He failed to obtain a truly advanced night-fighter designed specifically for the job but eventually, after a meeting with Hitler, he was granted 'special powers' enabling the development of Projekt 1064, now designated He 219, to be commenced. At the same time, Focke-Wulf received a contract to develop a night-fighter, the Ta 154 Moskito. Problems with the aircraft's wooden construction, however, meant that the Moskito saw only limited operational service.

First flight

Heinkel's design was good enough that the first prototype, designated He 219 V1, required only minor modifications before its first flight on 15 November 1942. Although the aircraft was

This underside view of an He 219A-0 with an unusual single black wing shows to advantage the type's ventral armament tray. This accommodated either a cannon or machine-gun arrangement.

susceptible to yaw/roll stability problems, this was rectified by extending the fuselage and enlarging the tail surfaces. There then began a series of alterations to the armament and equipment that became so complex that the German air ministry (RLM) asked whether the resulting 29 different variations of armament could be reduced in number to ease confusion. Adding to these development problems were the repeated Allied air raids that twice destroyed virtually all the He 219 production facilities at Rostock in March and April 1942. These raids prompted Heinkel to distribute the production of the He 219 to a number of different sites. Fuselages were constructed in Poland, before being transported to Germany to join the sub-assemblies that were being supplied by numerous small factories.

Competition and comments

It was estimated that, by August 1942, there would be an operational wing of He 219s. However, by 1 April 1943, there was the sum total of just five prototypes. One of these prototypes undertook a series of trials against a Ju 88 which led to a highly biased report against

the He 219. Despite this unfavourable and unjustified criticism, the He 219 received an initial production order for 127 aircraft.

Political problems still surrounded the development of the He 219, resulting in another series of fly-offs between a Ju 88 and a Do 217N. Both opposing aircraft were to withdraw from the trials as the exceptional performance of the He 219, now known as the Uhu (owl), became clear.

The initial pre-series He 219A-0 was delivered from late May 1943 in He 219A-0/R1 and R2 sub-types; each housing either four MK 108s or four MK 103s, respectively, in its belly trays. The pilot had a two-pronged control column, partly to ease handling and partly to carry more switches and triggers. Guns were fired by the right hand, the top button firing the fuselage guns and the front trigger those in the wings. A further addition to at least one He 219A-0 was a compressed-air ejection seat for both occupants, the first in service in the world. So advanced was the design that Heinkel was looking ahead to the time when the He 219 would be jet-propelled. This explained the choice of nosewheel-type landing gear.

Initial deliveries went to I/NJG 1 at Venlo, on the Dutch frontier. The first combat mission was flown by Major Werner Streib who was determined to show what the aircraft could do. This mission took place on the night of 11/12 June 1943, He 219A-0 G9+FB shooting down five RAF heavy bombers. Upon returning, however, Streib misjudged his approach and crashed, although both he and his navigator were unharmed.

Mosquito kills

Despite this outstanding achievement, the He 219 was still the victim of criticism from within the higher ranks of the Luftwaffe. Nevertheless, these early prototypes flew six sorties over the next 10 days, accounting for the loss of a further 20 RAF heavy bombers, including six Mosquitoes. The capability of the Owl could no longer be ignored, but the network of plants now producing He 219 sub-assemblies could simply not deliver the quantity of aircraft required. Whereas the basic plan was for 100 aircraft to be delivered monthly, actual acceptances hardly ever exceeded 12 aircraft per month. Moreover, confusion reigned supreme due to the number of sub-variants of the aircraft, the result of the continual development of the design.

Deadly jazz

Although there was a succession of sub-types for the He 219, few were to achieve production status. However, certain features had become standard such as longer nacelles, the deletion of the rear-firing gun (except on the He 219A-5/R4), the installation of powerful FuG 220 Lichtenstein SN-2 radar with huge *Hirschgeweih* (stag's antlers) dipole aerial array, FuG 220 tail-warning radar, the ejection seat and, last but not least, the *schräge Musik* (jazz) armament. This consisted of two oblique upward-firing guns which could be brought to bear slightly behind and below the enemy bomber. Comprising two MK 108 cannon, each with 100 rounds, these could be directed at the bomber's vulnerable underside, with dire consequences for the RAF crew.

By mid-1944, the RLM officials had realised that their sceptical view of the He 219 Uhu was misguided, and emergency full-scale production of the aircraft was now ordered. However, the He 219 was never produced on the scale that it should have been as, by this late stage of the war, production was concentrated on the emerging jet fighters. The He 219 was never to equip any unit except I/NJG 1, and the number of aircraft in this night-fighter unit was trivial, often just two or three examples being delivered per month. In addition to these production problems, RAF night-fighting Mosquitoes were now acting as intruders, intercepting the He 219s during Allied bombing raids and only adding to the depletion rate of the Heinkels.

By January 1945, I/NJG 1's establishment was up to 64 aircraft, and total deliveries of all versions had reached 268. There were also about 20 development aircraft modified to operational standard, and a further six were assembled from replacement components and spares.

There is no doubt that the He 219 Uhu was an exceptional design which, in a more ordered situation, could have been developed for many roles with telling effect, as was the case with the RAF's Mosquito. The mass of sub-types merely diluted the main production effort, and the consistent failure of Daimler-Benz and Junkers to deliver the hoped-for engines killed the advanced versions that would have kept the He 219 in front.

In Allied hands

Following the ending of World War II, at least 10 He 219s were captured intact by the USAAF and RAF. Allied pilots were not as enthusiastic about the aircraft as their Luftwaffe counterparts; many found the Uhu to be underpowered, particularly on take-off. This He 219A was test-flown from Freemans Field in the United States before being scrapped. One He 219 survives intact, but unrestored, as part of the US National Air and Space Museum collection.

He 219A-7/R2

This particular example served with Stab I/NJG 1 based at Münster, Germany in June 1944, flown by Hauptmann Paul Forster. The sole night-fighter unit to be equipped with the Uhu, which was delivered in various configurations, I/NJG 1 suffered from the fact that He 219s were in constant short supply. Nevertheless, the unit achieved good results against the RAF's night-bombers.

Undercarriage

The He 219's tricycle undercarriage was an extremely novel feature on a Luftwaffe aircraft. A combination of a single nosewheel (which rotated as it retracted aft) and twin pairs of mainwheels gave superb take-off and landing characteristics.

Radar

The initial production aircraft (the first 12 He 219A-2/R1s) were fitted with the FuG 212 Lichtenstein C-1 with four small antenna arrays on the nose. On subsequent A-2s, a single antenna was fitted for the C-1, with four large *Hirschgeweih* antennas for the new FuG 220 Lichtenstein SN-2. Some A-5s omitted C-1 radar, and often had the SN-2 antennas in a slanted arrangement to reduce interference. The A-7 added the newer FuG 218 Neptun radar to Lichtenstein SN-2.

Alternative roles

One of the reasons for Generalfeldmarschall Erhard Milch's hostility to the He 219 was that he saw it as being unable to perform any other role. Heinkel accordingly designed the He 219A-3 three-seat fighter-bomber and the He 219A-4 long-span high-altitude recce aircraft, which were produced at the expense of the night-fighter.

Armament

The He 219A-2 abandoned the rearward-facing MG 131, which was not fitted again, except to the He 219A-5/R4 which had a stretched forward fuselage and a new three-man cockpit. All He 219s had a pair of 20-mm MG 151 cannon in the wingroots, and provision for two 30-mm MK 108s in an upward-firing *schräge Musik* installation. Contents of the ventral tray varied, with two MG 151s, two MK 103s or two MK 108s in the A-2, two MK 108s in the A-5 and a choice in the He 219A-7 – two MK 103s and two MG 151s (A-7/R1), two MK 103s and two MK 108s (A-7/R2), two MK 108s and two MK 151s (A-7/R3) or two MK 151s (A-7/R4).

Left: An Hs 123 in typical pose, turning to dive on a target. In fact the Henschel biplane was more widely employed in the close support role, in which its ability to absorb damage from ground fire was greatly appreciated.

Below: Before production came to an end, two further versions were proposed and prototypes produced. Pictured is the Hs 123 V5 D-INRA, intended as the first Hs 123B. This version had an uprated BMW 132K engine, a three-bladed, variable-pitch propeller and a reworked long-chord engine cowling.

Henschel Hs 123

Dive-bombing biplane

Though only intended as an interim design, pending the arrival of a more modern, monoplane dive-bomber, the Hs 123 was, nevertheless, an important type during the Blitzkrieg and on the Eastern Front, latterly in the close support role.

In 1934 the Luftwaffe issued a two-stage requirement for a dive-bomber. While the second phase would be filled by a new technology design, the first phase highlighted immediacy as the main goal. Henschel and Fieseler were asked to develop the first-phase aircraft both teams choosing the BMW 132A-3 radial engine for their designs. Both designs flew in early 1935, the Hs 123 V1 showing a marked superiority over the Fi 98 from the outset of flight trials.

The Hs 123 V1 was an ungainly biplane, featuring a wide-chord NACA-style cowling, unequal-span wings and virtually no interplane bracing, most of the loads being borne by

two large outward-canted struts. The V2 prototype introduced a shorter-chord, narrower cowl with 18 fairings to house the valves. The V3 was similar except for substituting a two-bladed, variable-pitch propeller for the three-bladed adjustable-pitch unit of the preceding aircraft. All three went to Rechlin for trials, where two were lost within three weeks. Both had shed the upper wing, and so hasty strengthening of the centre-section struts was introduced from the V4 prototype onwards. With this modification the V4 demonstrated adequate performance, including pulling out of dives at near-vertical angles.

First deliveries of production Hs 123A-1s were made in the

summer of 1936, the initial unit being Stukagruppe I./162 'Immelmann'. Power came from a BMW 132Dc and armament consisted of two MG 17 machine-guns in the upper fuselage decking. A 250-kg (551-lb) bomb was carried on a crutch which swung forward from between the main wheels, and four 50-kg (110-lb) bombs could be carried on wing racks.

Close support debate

Back in Germany, the Ju 87 had started to replace the Hs 123 with the Stukagruppen in 1937, and the Hs 123 was diverted to the close support units, equipping two of the five to form. Debate was raging in the Luftwaffe over the respective merits of the dedicated dive-bomber and the close support aircraft. The dive-bomber protagonists won, and the Ju 87 was also given a close support role, signalling the end of production for the Hs 123. Two variants built in prototype form were the Hs 123B with a BMW 132K engine under a long-chord cowling, and the Hs 123C which had additional machine-guns under the wings and an armoured headrest with a sliding hood. The latter feature was adopted by service Hs 123As.

In late 1938, after the Sudeten crisis had passed, the close

support units were officially disbanded. Nevertheless, one (Schlachtfliegergruppe 10) survived the axe and was incorporated into Lehrgeschwader 2 as II (Schlacht)./LG 2. In September 1939 it was the only front-line Hs 123 unit, all other aircraft having been passed to training units.

II (Schlacht)./LG 2 was in the lead air assault against Poland on 1 September 1939 that opened World War II. Armed with 50-kg bombs on the wing racks and the MG 17 guns, the Hs 123s flew just feet above the heads of the Polish cavalry brigades for 10 days. More effective than the armament was the terrifying noise of the BMW radial, which was every bit as effective at dispersing mounted columns as explosives. So effective was the Hs 123 in the lightning Polish campaign that plans to re-equip II (Schlacht)./LG 2 were immediately reversed.

Belgium and France

For the unit, the next target was Belgium, supporting the 6th Army as it smashed through from 10 May 1940. The first action was to ward off Belgian sappers attempting to destroy bridge crossings over the Albert Canal. Sweeping through Luxembourg and the Ardennes, Hs 123s were soon in France, and by 21 May were the most forward based Lufwaffe unit when they reached Cambrai. With victory in France achieved, II (Schlacht)./LG 2 was withdrawn to Germany for

The Hs 123 V1 is seen as flown in early 1935, with a smooth, long-chord, NACA-type cowling enclosing its 650-hp (485-kW) BMW 132A-3 nine-cylinder radial engine.

Spanish Civil War and post-1945 service

Five Hs 123A-1s were despatched to Spain for combat evaluation (and validation of the Luftwaffe's dive-bombing tactics in general), but from their debut in the Civil War during early 1937 they were mainly used in a ground attack role. In this they proved remarkably successful, flying close support over the battlefield despite the lack of any communications with ground forces. Spain acquired all five aircraft, and ordered another 11, the 16 aircraft equipping Grupo 24 of the Nationalist air force. Known as the Angelito in Spanish service, the Hs 123A remained in use in Spain until the late 1940s.

Luftwaffe mechanics carry out engine work on an Hs 123A-1. Production examples employed a BMW 132Dc engine, which benefited from fuel injection and a higher power output.

re-equipment with the Bf 109E, but the Hs 123 had by now built a legendary reputation for its ability to absorb battle damage, and the Gruppe only partially equipped with the Messerschmitt fighter.

After a spell in the Balkans from April 1941, the unit joined the fight against the Soviet Union, operating on the southern front. It was incorporated into the newly-formed Schlachtgeschwader 1 and again proved the considerable capability of the Hs 123 in the close support role. Armed with either four SC 50 bombs, twin 20-mm MG FF cannon or containers each bearing 92 SC 2 anti-personnel bombs under the wings, and with a fuel tank on the centreline, the Hs 123 proved so effective and dependable that there were calls even as late as 1943 for its reinstatement into production. When conditions were so wet that other aircraft could not take off from the quagmire-like advanced fields, Hs 123s could get aloft once the wheel spats had been removed.

Without new production aircraft to swell the ranks, attrition slowly took its toll on the Hs 123, which ended its days in mid-1944, the remaining aircraft having been grouped in II./Schlachtgeschwader 2.

This Hs 123A-1 of Schlachtgeschwader 1 sports the Infanterie-Sturmabzeichen emblem of the close support units on its forward fuselage. Four SC 50 bombs are carried under its wings.

Hs 123A-1

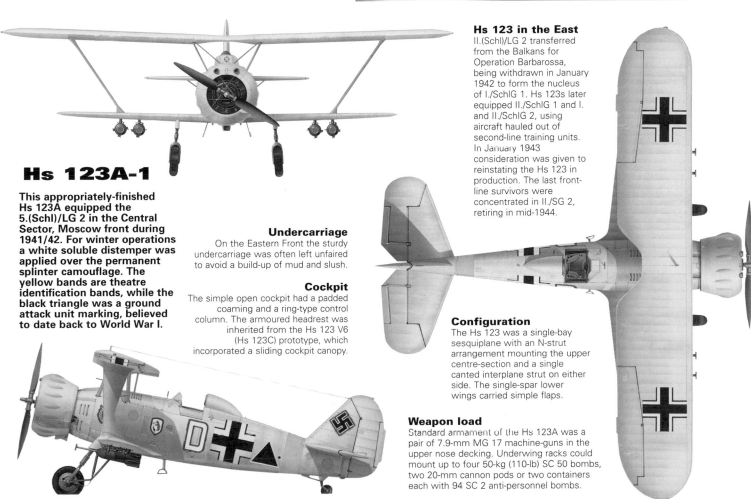

This appropriately-finished Hs 123A equipped the 5.(Schl)/LG 2 in the Central Sector, Moscow front during 1941/42. For winter operations a white soluble distemper was applied over the permanent splinter camouflage. The yellow bands are theatre identification bands, while the black triangle was a ground attack unit marking, believed to date back to World War I.

Undercarriage
On the Eastern Front the sturdy undercarriage was often left unfaired to avoid a build-up of mud and slush.

Cockpit
The simple open cockpit had a padded coaming and a ring-type control column. The armoured headrest was inherited from the Hs 123 V6 (Hs 123C) prototype, which incorporated a sliding cockpit canopy.

Hs 123 in the East
II.(Schl)/LG 2 transferred from the Balkans for Operation Barbarossa, being withdrawn in January 1942 to form the nucleus of I./SchG 1. Hs 123s later equipped II./SchG 1 and I. and II./SchG 2, using aircraft hauled out of second-line training units. In January 1943 consideration was given to reinstating the Hs 123 in production. The last front-line survivors were concentrated in II./SG 2, retiring in mid-1944.

Configuration
The Hs 123 was a single-bay sesquiplane with an N-strut arrangement mounting the upper centre-section and a single canted interplane strut on either side. The single-spar lower wings carried simple flaps.

Weapon load
Standard armament of the Hs 123A was a pair of 7.9-mm MG 17 machine-guns in the upper nose decking. Underwing racks could mount up to four 50-kg (110-lb) SC 50 bombs, two 20-mm cannon pods or two containers each with 94 SC 2 anti-personnel bombs.

In the event only two units received Hs 129B-3/Wa aircraft for operational use, in the winter of 1944/45. Though the Panzerabwehrkanone 40 gun drastically cut performance and agility, one shot could knock out the biggest Soviet tank.

Below: With the 75-mm PaK 40L anti-tank gun fitted, the Hs 129B-3/Wa dispensed with the twin MG 17s machine-guns normally fitted. The huge PaK 40L fired 26 7-lb (3.2-kg) shells.

Henschel Hs 129

Luftwaffe tank-buster

The Henschel Hs 129 was the only aircraft of World War II – and, apart from the A-10 Thunderbolt II , virtually the only fixed-wing aircraft in history – to be designed explicitly for destroying hostile armour.

Apart from the Soviet Sturmovik, which was a more versatile armoured attacker, the Allies had no aircraft in this class. All the RAF had were a few Hurricanes fitted with 40-mm guns, which by comparison were totally inadequate. Yet Hitler's Germany completely failed to foresee how crucially important the Hs 129 would become, and there were nothing like sufficient numbers to make much impact on the tide of Soviet armour in 1944-45.

In April 1937 the Technische Amt issued a specification for a close support aircraft, to carry at least two 20-mm cannon and to have two low-powered engines and the smallest possible size, with armour and 75-mm glazing around the crew.

Henschel, which proposed a neat single-seater, was chosen over Focke-Wulf, which had suggested using a modified version of the Fw 189. Comparative testing was hampered by the fact that both aircraft were disastrous. In the end, what tipped the scales in favour of the Hs 129 was that it was smaller and cost only about two-thirds as much as the Focke-Wulf rival. The decision was taken to go ahead with eight pre-production Hs 129A-0 aircraft, and these were all deliv-

ered by the time the Blitzkrieg was unleashed in Western Europe on 10 May 1940. They were put through prolonged trials and evaluation programmes and some later equipped the Schlachtflieger training Staffel at Paris-Orly.

Basically, the Hs 129 was a completely conventional aircraft with a simple, stressed-skin structure. The wing, with all the taper on the trailing edge, carried hydraulically driven slotted flaps, and was built as a centre-section integral with the fuselage and two bolted outer panels. The 465-hp (344-kW) Argus As 410A-1 air-cooled inverted V-12 engines driving Argus automatic controllable-pitch propellers were almost identical to the installations used in the Fw 189, which was already in production. Fuel was housed in a single cell in the fuselage and a tank in each wing inboard of the nacelles.

It was obvious to Chief Engineer Dipl Ing Fr. Nicolaus that a much better aircraft could be built, using more powerful engines. His team accordingly prepared drawings for the P.76, a slightly larger aircraft to be powered by two 522-kW (700-hp) Gnome-Rhône 14M radials, large numbers of which had become available following

The Hs 129A-0 pre-production aircraft were powered by the underpowered Argus As 410A-1 inline engine. After disastrous service trials, the Hs 129As were relegated to training.

the defeat of France. It was decided, however, that too much time would be lost in tooling up for a bigger aircraft, and so the final compromise was merely to modify the existing Hs 129A to take the bigger and more powerful French radial engines. Remarkably few modifications were needed, but in one respect the resulting Hs 129B did incorporate a major improvement. The cockpit was modified with large slabs of armour glass to give much better vision, although possibly at the expense of slight increase in

vulnerability.

Overall, the Hs 129B was a great improvement, although it was still a poor performer. It was slower than the Ju 87D, had a much shorter range and was nowhere near as agile or pleasant to fly, despite continual tinkering with the flight controls which resulted in the addition of fast-acting electric trim tabs.

Operation Barbarossa

After the invasion of the Soviet Union in June 1941, the Hs 129B was put into immediate production with high priority. A

With its gun blast troughs faired over, this is the second Hs 129B-0 pre-production machine. The Hs 129B was an improvement over the Hs 129A, but still lacked speed and agility.

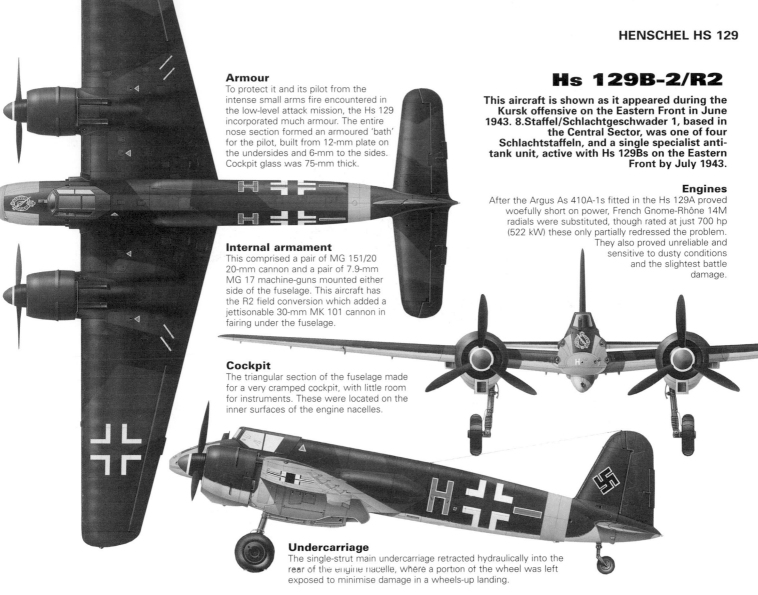

Hs 129B-2/R2

This aircraft is shown as it appeared during the Kursk offensive on the Eastern Front in June 1943. 8.Staffel/Schlachtgeschwader 1, based in the Central Sector, was one of four Schlachtstaffeln, and a single specialist anti-tank unit, active with Hs 129Bs on the Eastern Front by July 1943.

Armour
To protect it and its pilot from the intense small arms fire encountered in the low-level attack mission, the Hs 129 incorporated much armour. The entire nose section formed an armoured 'bath' for the pilot, built from 12-mm plate on the undersides and 6-mm to the sides. Cockpit glass was 75-mm thick.

Internal armament
This comprised a pair of MG 151/20 20-mm cannon and a pair of 7.9-mm MG 17 machine-guns mounted either side of the fuselage. This aircraft has the R2 field conversion which added a jettisonable 30-mm MK 101 cannon in fairing under the fuselage.

Cockpit
The triangular section of the fuselage made for a very cramped cockpit, with little room for instruments. These were located on the inner surfaces of the engine nacelles.

Engines
After the Argus As 410A-1s fitted in the Hs 129A proved woefully short on power, French Gnome-Rhône 14M radials were substituted, though rated at just 700 hp (522 kW) these only partially redressed the problem. They also proved unreliable and sensitive to dusty conditions and the slightest battle damage.

Undercarriage
The single-strut main undercarriage retracted hydraulically into the rear of the engine nacelle, where a portion of the wheel was left exposed to minimise damage in a wheels-up landing.

late change was to replace the MG FF cannon by the much harder-hitting MG 151, occasionally in the high-velocity 15-mm form but usually in 20-mm calibre, with 125 rounds each.

The first pre-production Hs 129B-0 was delivered at the

Below: Due to the cramped conditions in the cockpit, the Hs 129's Revi C 12/C gunsight was mounted outside, ahead of the windscreen.

end of 1941, but Henschel suffered many severe problems and delays which seriously held back the build-up of the planned Schlachtgeschwader force. Modifications were continually having to be introduced to rectify faults, equipment and parts were late on delivery, and the planned output of 40 per month was not attained until mid-1943. The first Staffel, 4./SchG 1, had a depressing experience in the push for the Caucasus in mid-1942, while at the end of the year the next unit, 4./SchG 2, suffered a series of disasters in North Africa and was eventually evacuated with no aircraft.

During 1943 the tempo of Hs 129B effort increased greatly, but difficulties in production and

high attrition made the actual build-up of SchG units a frustrating process. On the other hand, the combat effectiveness of the aircraft increased considerably with the fitting of the modification kits, most notably the addition of a huge 30-mm MK 101 gun under the fuselage, with 30 shells. This had a lethal effect against all armoured vehicles except main battle tanks, and even these were sometimes vulnerable when attacked from the rear. Other add-on loads included an internal camera, a battery of four MG 17 machine-guns or various loads of small bombs, especially boxes of 8.8-lb (4-kg) SD4 hollow-charge bomblets which had considerable armour-penetration capabilities.

The massive build-up in Soviet strength with thick-skinned tanks contrasted with the faltering strength of the SchG units. The overriding need was for more powerful anti-armour weapons; one of those chosen was the huge PaK 40 anti-tank gun of 75-mm calibre. At a range of 3,280 ft (1000 m), the shell could penetrate 5¼ in (133 mm) of armour if it hit

square-on. Installed in the Hs 129B-3/Wa, the giant gun was provided with 26 rounds which could be fired at the cyclic rate of 40 rounds per minute, so that three or four could be fired on a single pass. Almost always, a single good hit would destroy a tank, even from head-on. The main problem was that the PaK 40L was too powerful a gun for the aircraft. Quite apart from the severe muzzle blast and recoil, the sheer weight of the gun made the Hs 129B-3/Wa almost unmanageable, and in emergency the pilot could sever the gun's attachments and let it drop.

Limited production
Total production amounted to only 870, including prototypes. Because of attrition and other problems, the Hs 129 was never able to equip the giant anti-tank force and its overall effect on the war was not great. Towards the end, in autumn 1944, operations began to be further restricted by shortage of high-octane petrol, and by the final collapse only a handful of these aircraft remained.

With an engine and other parts removed, the carcass of this derelict Hs 129 gives an idea of its simple construction and diminutive size. Note the small single-seat cockpit.

Ilyushin Il-2/10 'Bark'/'Beast'

Il-2s depart from a forward base on a combat mission, probably in 1942. These early aircraft are ShVAK-armed single-seaters except for the one in the foreground which is fitted with VYa cannon (possessing longer barrels than the ShVAK).

Shturmovik

Outside Russia, the Il-2 and Il-10 remain, somewhat unbelievably, less well-known than other World War II types, although they were built in greater numbers than any other military aircraft in history.

During the 1930s, the Soviet Union placed great importance on creating survivable close-support and attack aircraft. Coupled with this was the fact that the Soviets possessed the world's best air weapons, including large-calibre guns, heavy recoilless cannon, hollow-charge, armour-piercing bombs and similar warheads fitted to air-launched rockets. From the beginning of the decade, a succession of heavily armed attack aircraft appeared and in 1935 the Kremlin issued a requirement for a BSh (*Bronirovanyi Shturmovik* or armoured attacker) aircraft,

specifically intended to knock out armoured vehicles and ground strong-points. By 1938 the OKBs of Sergei V. Ilyushin and Pavel O. Sukhoi were set in head-on competition. Both designers adopted a conventional low-wing, single-engined configuration, but Ilyushin's was ready much sooner, in the spring of 1939. Designated TsKB-55, with the service designation

BSh-2, it was powered by a large 1,350-hp (1007-kW) AM-35 liquid-cooled engine, and seated the pilot and radio operator/rear gunner/observer in tandem. The wing, hydraulic flaps and tail were of light alloy, but the lower part of the fuselage was made up of 1,543 lb (700 kg) of armour which covered the

underside of the engine, coolant pipes, radiator, fuselage tanks and cockpits. Four 0.3-in (7.62-mm) guns were mounted in the wings outboard of the main landing gear legs, with a fifth in the rear cockpit, and four compartments in the centre section housed up to 1,323 lb (600 kg) of bombs.

Right: Pictured in 1944, these Il-2M3 two-seaters can be seen over the Eastern Front which, by this time, had been pushed beyond the frontiers of the Soviet Union and into countries such as Poland and Romania.

This Il-2M3 demonstrates the not-unusual decision to remove the rear cockpit canopy to give the gunner a free field of fire. It was also common for the gunner to have twin UB guns, though with reduced ammunition. The slogan 'mstitel' painted on the side means 'avenger'.

Right: The neat lines in which these Il-2s are drawn up (there are more than 65 illustrated) suggest that this was a formal occasion following the defeat of the Germans. The dedication 'Chapayev' painted on the fuselages may relate to a person or to the many towns of that name (which may have paid for them).

Left: Stalin threw his weight behind the Il-2 project. When production delays were occurring, he said that "The Red Army needs the Il-2 as it needs air or bread...this is my final warning."

Crash programme

Ilyushin was dissatisfied with the poor armament, and in tests the TsKB-55 showed, as predicted, poor stability. An improved second prototype, with the centre of gravity shifted slightly forward and with a larger tailplane, flew on 30 December 1939, but NII (State) testing in the summer of 1940 considered the good features outweighed by poor stability, range and general performance. Ilyushin therefore launched a 'crash programme' which in four months produced the TsKB-57. This was fitted with the 1,600-hp (1194-kW) AM-38, had an extra fuel tank instead of a rear cockpit, thicker and better distributed armour, two of the wing guns replaced by 20-mm ShVAK cannon and new underwing rails for eight RS-82 rockets. This was a much better machine, which reached 292 mph (470 km/h) and had good agility. Very large-scale production was then put in hand at three factories: in Moscow, at Fili to the north and at Voronezh to the south.

When the Germans invaded on 22 June 1941, 249 had been delivered and a few were in service, but this was far below target. By October, the Moscow and Fili plants had to be closed and their tooling and workers evacuated far to the east, the chief new production centre being at Kuybyshyev. But output was slow to build up, and Stalin sent a telegram to the factory directors telling them that their performance was 'an insult'. In early 1942 the ShVAK guns were replaced by the much harder-hitting 23-mm VYa.

Later in 1942 the designation changed to Il-2M2 with the introduction of the 1,750-hp (1306-kW) AM-38F engines which improved all-round performance, even with an increase in armour to 2,094 lb (950 kg). Losses to fighters were severe, however, and it was not practical to provide adequate armour against fire from above and behind. Despite Stalin's reluctance to sanction any further modifications, Ilyushin was authorised to produce prototypes with a rear gunner, and these flew in March 1942. The gunner had a 0.5-in (12.7-mm) UB with 150 rounds and, differing from the original TsKB-55, was separated from the pilot by the amidships fuel tank.

Production was eventually sanctioned in October 1942 as the Il-2M3 – this new two-seater was in action on the Central Front by the end of the month.

Streamlining

Losses were immediately sharply curtailed, while casualties among Luftwaffe fighters increased. Production by this time was running at close to 1,000 per month, despite the introduction of a succession of minor changes which were mainly aimed at improving performance, which had fallen to a maximum speed of 251 mph (404 km/h). Thus, almost every part that could be better streamlined was modified, if this could be done without disrupting production. By mid-1943 maximum speed had improved to 273 mph (439 km/h) despite the continuing growth in weight.

Part of the weight growth was due to increased armament, which benefited from the superb products of the air weapon design staff. Most important was the new family of 1.45-in (37-mm) guns, unrelated to earlier weapons of this calibre and firing high-velocity ammunition fully capable of penetrating Pzkpfw V (Panther) and Pzkpfw VI (Tiger) tanks, except in a head-on attack. Additional types of bombs could be carried in the wing cells, while underwing loads were expanded to include the large (5.2-in/132-mm calibre) RS-132 rocket and boxes of 200 small PTAB anti-armour bombs.

In 1942 the first dual-control Il-2 appeared. Several more were produced by field conversion, and by 1943 small numbers were factory-built as the Il-2U, most with reduced armament. Another field modification resulted in the Il-2T torpedo-carrier which, with the greatest ease, carried a 21-in (533-mm) torpedo. Altogether, at least 36,163 Il-2s had been built when production switched to the Il-10 in August 1944. By that time, monthly acceptances were running at the record level of 2,300, almost 16,000 being delivered in the first eight months of 1944 – the figure for the whole of 1943 had been 11,200. Whereas previously it had been difficult to gather Il-2s to form a trained regiment, by 1944 they were operating in corps strength, as many as 500 being committed at a time on a single localised area and generally leaving no vehicle able to move. The usual method of attack was a 'follow-my-leader' orbit which gave a long firing run from the rear of heavy armour, while individual aircraft dropped cluster or anti-armour bombs. To the Soviet forces the Il-2 was commonly known as the *Ilyusha*, but to the invaders it was soon the *'schwarz Tod'* (Black Death).

In 1943 the first foreign units began to receive Il-2 equipment. Subsequently, an estimated 3,000 were supplied to Polish, Czech, Yugoslav and Bulgarian regiments, while large numbers were supplied to China and North Korea in the post-war era. Several countries, including Poland and Czechoslovakia, applied their own local designations, while many Il-2s were modified in various ways with different equipment, weapons or a rear fuselage of fabric-covered welded steel tubes.

This Il-2M3 was serving at the end of World War II with the 3rd Attack Regiment (Szturmowego Pulk) of the 1st Mixed Air Corps, one of the first non-Soviet units to be equipped with the aircraft.

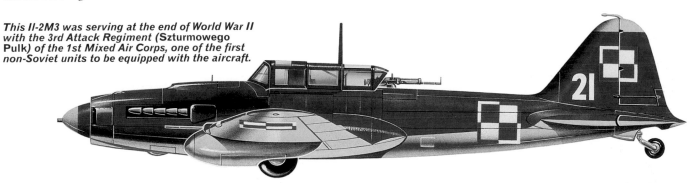

Operations, 1941-45

A vital component in the Soviet fight back against the Germans, the Il-2 served in huge numbers. It was joined later in the war by the improved Il-10, but it was the Il-2 which remained supreme.

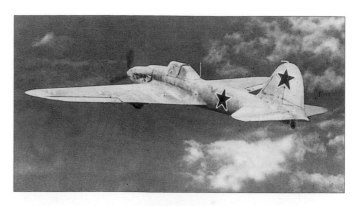

On 29 December 1940, Ilyushin flew its CCB-55P prototype for an improved single-seat attack aircraft based on a series of prototypes that had first flown on 30 December 1939 as the BSh-2. The CCB-55P underwent state tests until March 1941, emerging as an outstanding attack aircraft and by the time its designation had been changed to Il-2 in April 1941, the type was already in production at the GAZ-18 factory. Indeed, so impressed were the Soviet authorities with the Il-2, that Ilyushin was awarded the Stalin Prize 2nd class. Such favour was not to last however, since production fell well below targets and by December 1941, with production still running at no more than one aircraft per day, both Ilyushin and the manager at GAZ-18 had

received 'last chance' warnings from Stalin, insisting that matters must be improved.

However, production aircraft were reaching front-line units, the 4th Light Bomber Polk being the first unit to receive the Il-2. The new monoplane replaced the unit's R–Zet biplane attack aircraft and the transition proved a difficult one, with many pilots crashing their Il-2s. Nevertheless, once mastered, the Il-2 was proving its devastating worth in combat.

Vulnerability

While pilots were full of praise for the type's attack capabilities, they were less happy with its defensive capabilities. In an ideal world the Soviet fighter force would have been on hand to escort the Shturmoviks as they went about their work, but in the period 1941-42 this was just

Ilyushin's Il-2 protected its pilot and major systems with large amounts of armour. In its single-seat form however, it was vulnerable to fighter attacks from behind.

not possible and Il-2s fell in droves under the guns of the massed ranks of highly experienced and battle-hardened Luftwaffe fighter units.

Il-2 production continued into 1942 regardless of these problems, although some units were

modifying aircraft in the field with a second crew member and rear-firing machine-gun to provide a measure of defence. In May 1942, permission was finally granted for this modification to be incorporated on the production line, even though it meant a

Above: This early Il-2 was captured and repainted in Luftwaffe markings. The German advance forced Il-2 production out of European Russia and into factories in the Urals and Siberia.

Right: While bombs and rockets were more usual Il-2 loads, the aircraft was also employed on leaflet-dropping missions, most likely dropping bundles of leaflets from its bomb bays.

Below: From mid-1941, Il-2s were equipped for the use of the RS-132 rocket on the production lines, although RS-82 weapons are being carried by aircraft '8' in this winter 1941/42 shot.

temporary fall in output. The Il-2M two-seaters that now emerged were further improved by a new armour manufacturing process which meant that the aircraft could be built more quickly and that the armour was of a consistent weight and configuration.

The battle for Stalingrad

By January 1943, a more powerful Am-38-engined Il-2M was available for the Battle of Stalingrad, this aircraft maturing as the ultimate Il-2M3. The year also saw the aircraft reaching new levels of combat efficiency and production reaching new heights. An example of the former is offered by the action at Kursk, where the Circle of Death tactic proved particularly effective against German tanks. On 7 July 1943 Il-2M3s attacked in huge numbers, destroying some 70 of the 9th Panzer Division's tanks in just 20 minutes, while in subsequent actions two hours of constant attacks wiped out 270 of the 3rd Panzer Division's and caused

almost 2,000 casualties, while the 17th Panzer Division was almost annihilated in just four hours when 240 out of its 300 vehicles were destroyed. To keep up with the ferocious pace of operations, production was consistently reaching 1,000 Il-2s per month, with a number of factories contributing aircraft. In fact, of the 35,000 Soviet combat aircraft built in 1943, 25 per cent were Il-2s and construction of each machine was taking on average, just 37.90 per cent of the time taken per aircraft in 1942.

Acts of individual bravery were legion among Il-2 crews, not least that displayed by Senior Lieutenant Koratevitch and Lt Bykov, who were posthumously awarded Gold Stars for ramming a German ship in the Baltic on 19 November 1943.

Considerable ingenuity was also displayed by the Il-2 community. In preparation for a Soviet attack on German positions in Rumania, the Il-2M3s of the 9th Mixed Air Corps were used to drag steel grappling

hooks on lengths of cable through German field telephone wires. The consequent disruption in Wehrmacht communications led to the arrival of a fleet of liaison vehicles, which was immediately set upon and destroyed by the lurking Shturmoviks.

1944 and beyond

When the last of 36,163 Il-2s rolled off the production lines in August 1944, it represented the final machine of almost 16,000 built that year, at a peak rate of 2,300 per month. Production had stopped in favour of the much improved Il-10. These aircraft soon began to reach training units, and by October 1944, the first examples were serving on the front-line. The new machine was immediately a success, proving even more capable than the legendary Il-2, with its comparative ease of

maintenance and better performance in combat. Nevertheless, the Il-2 was still available in huge numbers and although the Il-10 fought through to the end of the war and saw action over Germany as the Soviets closed on Berlin, its was the faithful Il-2 that bore the brunt of the continued Soviet offensive against the Nazis.

Perhaps the ultimate task given to the Il-2 was to deliver the surrender demand on the German Army Group South Ukraine, an ultimatum that was accepted. Indeed, Stalin probably gave the best summing up of the importance of the Shturmovik's contribution to the Soviet war effort against the German invader, when, in a message sent to factory workers in December 1941 in a effort to spur them to extra effort, he said that, "The Red Army needs the Il-2 like air, like bread...."

Variants

One of the symbols of the Red Air Force during World War II, the Il-2 Shturmovik was steadily developed after a problematic start, and matured to form one of the great ground-attack fighters.

Early production

By the time the Il-2 designation had been applied, the *Shturmovik* was already in production. Early deliveries were made to the 4th Light Bomber Polk, but the initial service of the Il-2 was dogged by problems. Many aircraft were lost in the hands of inexperienced pilots, and the lack of a rear gunner resulted in severe attrition on the Eastern front from June 1941. Furthermore, the Il-2's glued joints and rear fuselage were prone to failure, this being rectified through the introduction of angled steel strengtheners. Firepower was increased from mid 1941, with the addition of RS-132 rockets (in place of RS-82s) and a pair of VYa-23 guns in place of the earlier ShVAKs.

Prototypes

Design work on the BSh-2 (*Bronirovannii Shturmovik* - armoured assaulter) single-engined attack aircraft began in 1938. Given the go-ahead by Stalin in early 1938, development work was hindered by Sergei Ilyushin's crash-landing of his AIR-11 in April. Despite this, and problems with the incorporation of shaped armour to the airframe, the first example was flying by the end of 1939. Manufacturer's tests were completed in March 1940, after which the aircraft were handed over to the LII (flight research institute). Performance of the fledgling Shturmovik was not impressive, and Ilyushin decided to pursue a faster single-seat version, the CCB-57, which was flown in October 1940. The VVS was convinced that a close-support aircraft without a gunner would be practicable, as it would be escorted into battle by friendly fighters. The CCB-57 replaced the rear (radio operator/gunner's) cockpit with an additional fuel tank, and introduced an AM-38 engine in place of the BSh-2's AM-35. An improved single-seater, the CCB-55P (above) flew in December 1940, and introduced two bomb cells in each of the wings, short-field landing gear and other minor changes. Numerous refinements had been made by April 1941, by which time the aircraft had become known as the Il-2.

Later production

Vulnerability to enemy fighters attacking from behind, and a lack of Soviet fighter units to offer protection in 1941-42 led to many Il-2's being converted to two-seaters on the front line. In response Ilyushin developed the Il-2M in May 1942, which added a backseater aft of the fuel tank that was situated behind the pilot. At least five different canopy arrangements were produced, and the gunner was provided with a UBT rear gun. At this stage armour was standardised at 990 kg (2,183 lb) as welding techniques were improved. Armour was applied in a variety of thicknesses, ranging from 4-mm (0.15-in) to 12-mm (0.47-in). Despite the shortfall in performance when a second crew

member was added (230 mph/370 km/h at sea level compared to 246 mph/396 km/h at sea level for the Il-2), the Il-2M was a success in combat. A more powerful AM-38F engine (which could run on motor fuel) was introduced in July 1942, with an output of 1,720-hp (1283-kW) compared to the original 1,550-hp (1156-kW) AM-38. The Il-2/AM-38F (also known by the designation Il-2 Tip 3) had an optional two-tier rocket installation, permitting the carriage of 32 RS-82s. New *strelkoi* (swept) outer wings were also added, with a 15° taper, after this installation had been tested by the LII in December 1942. The aircraft was available in numbers over Stalingrad by January 1943. The last series production Il-2 variant was known as the Il-2M3, which in 1944, its final year of production, introduced an all-dural structure as standard.

Il-2/M-82

In September 1941 an Il-2 was tested with a radial engine installation. The 1,400-hp (1044-kW) Shvetsov M-82 14-cylinder radial engine (later designated ASh-82) was chosen for the Il-2, using cylinders derived from the two-speed supercharged M-62. The M-62 (ASh-62) was itself ultimately derived from the Wright R-1820 Cyclone which had been licensed by the Soviets in 1934. Although the M-82 engine was generally reliable, the Il-2 installation left a lot to be desired and the project was ultimately abandoned. The ASh-82, however, went on to enjoy greater success, as it was employed by the An-2, and undergoing licensed production itself in both China and Poland.

Il-2M with 37-mm guns

From 1943 onwards a number of Il-2M3s were equipped with underwing 37-mm automatic anti-tank guns. Each with 50 rounds, these NS-OKB-16 weapons were capable of penetrating the PzKW VI Tiger. The introduction of the heavy-calibre guns necessitated the deletion of rocket and bomb armament, however, they were supplemented by by two ShVAKs and one UBT gun. The 37-mm weapons proved particularly effective during the battles at Kursk in 1943.

Trainers

The Il-2U (or UII-2) dual-control trainer had its armament reduced to a pair of ShKAS, together with two RS-82 rockets and two FAB-100 bombs in order to undertake weapons training. The 7.62-mm ShKAS gun was originally installed in the first prototype aircraft (two in each wing) but had been supplemented by the 20-mm ShVAK, and later the 23-mm VYa-23 with a higher muzzle velocity and greater penetration power. The Il-2U (left) was followed by the Il-10U (UII-10), which unlike the Il-2U, was produced alongside the single-seat Il-10 from the outset. The Il-10U was normally unarmed except for a pair of ShKAS and inherited the cockpit canopy of the Il-2U. After 1950 Il-10U production was continued by Avia in Czechoslovakia, as the BS-33. Post-war many Il-2/10s were used as bomber crew trainers. The Il-10M in particular served as a gunnery trainer for prospective Il-28 rear gunners.

Il-8

Following a conference at the Kremlin in January 1942, Ilyushin began work on a number of new Il-2 variants including the Il-1 single-seat fighter, the Il-8, Il-10 and the scaled-down Il-16. The Il-8 (above) of 1944 was the least radical of the redesigns, with a more powerful AM-42 engine (rated at 2,000 hp/1491 kW) within an aerodynamically refined cowling which was taken from the Il-1. The Il-8 featured a four-bladed propeller with anti-icing, oil cooler radiators set within the wing roots and an improved belly radiator installation. New landing gear comprised single air/oil shock-absorbing struts which retracted rearwards and were fitted with large low-pressure tyres. Armour plating was similar to that of the Il-2, but extended rearwards in order to protect the otherwise vulnerable radio operator/gunner. The Il-8's two-seat cockpit was situated further forward than that of the Il-2, and armament comprised two VYa-23 and two ShKAS in the wings and one rear-firing UBT. The Il-8 was rejected in favour of the Il-10.

Il-10

The Il-10 'second generation' Shturmovik utilised the airframe of the Il-1, and as such had little in common with the Il-2 beyond its basic configuration. Overall construction was of light alloy, with armoured panels inherited from the Il-8. An AM-42 engine and three-bladed propeller were also installed. Rearwards retracting landing gear and the crew compartment were taken from the Il-8 and an improved weapons bay was added. Ultimate armament comprised either four NR-23 cannon or two 37-mm NS-OKB-16 and two ShKAS. Large access doors allowed rapid re-arming of the guns, and a new gunner's cupola was provided with a 150-round 20-mm B-20EN cannon, and enhanced protection, visibility and headroom. Factory tests were followed by trials from June 1944, and the Il-10 proved superior to both the Il-8 and the rival Su-8. Ordered into production in August, the Il-10 arrived on the front line by October. Production continued post-war in both the USSR and in Czechoslovakia as the B-33 from 1950.

Il-10M

A major redesign resulted in the Il-10M, the central feature of which was an all-new single structure wing. This had a structural joint between the centre section and the outer panels and one-piece flaps running from the ailerons to the centreline. Span and wing area were only marginally increased, but the fuselage was slightly longer than that of the Il-10 and the vertical tail, although similar in appearance, was redesigned. These features were informed by the design of the Il-20 multi-role attack aircraft, elements of which were effectively scaled-down to arrive at the Il-10M. Typical armament comprised four NR-23 cannon in the wings (with 600 rounds) and a single B-20EN in a remote-control rear turret. A single aircraft undertook trials at Monino fitted with an RD-1X3 rocket motor mounted under the rudder and an additional ventral strake under the rear fuselage. This installation was intended to allow short-take off operations from unprepared airstrips.

Junkers Ju 52/3m

'Tante Ju'

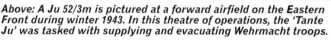

Above: A Ju 52/3m is pictured at a forward airfield on the Eastern Front during winter 1943. In this theatre of operations, the 'Tante Ju' was tasked with supplying and evacuating Wehrmacht troops.

Originally used as passenger- and freight-carrier for Germany's national airline, Lufthansa, the Ju 52/3m evolved into an excellent military transport, receiving its baptism in the Spanish Civil War.

Fairly widely recognised as the world's most efficient national airline at the end of the 1920s (while others struggled to survive the Depression), Deutsche Lufthansa flew highly competitive services throughout Europe. It used a heterogeneous fleet of aircraft, largely comprising designs progressively developed from Professor Hugo Junkers's original J 1 all-metal monoplane of 1915. The great majority of these early aircraft (the J 10, F 13, A 20, F 24, W 33, W 34, Ju 46 and Ju 52) were single-engined, low-wing monoplanes, but in 1924 there appeared a three-engined airliner, the G 23, powered by a 195-hp (145-kW) Junkers L 2 and two 100-hp (75-kW) Mercedes engines. It is thought that, as a result of

Versailles Treaty restrictions imposed on German aircraft manufacture, this prototype was produced at Junkers's Fili factory near Moscow; production of about nine aircraft (as well as that of the much more numerous G 24) was subsequently undertaken in Sweden. The G 24, usually powered by three 280-310-hp (209-231-kW) Junkers L 5 inline engines, served in numerous configurations and with a number of airlines, including Lufthansa, which retained it in service until 1933-34.

The Junkers concern enjoyed a busy year in 1926, with two new designs (the G 31 tri-motor transport and the W 33/34) being the most important to fly. The former was a beefier version of the successful G 24, and the latter an

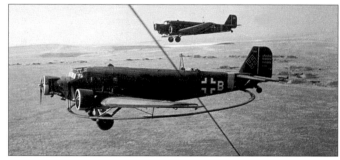

The Ju 52/3mg6e mine-clearance aircraft of the Minensuchgruppe were used extensively in the Mediterranean, equipped with large dural hoops below the fuselage, energised by an auxiliary motor in order to explode Allied mines.

excellent single-engined transport which was built in large numbers. Almost at once, the Junkers designers embarked on a new, but considerably enlarged, single-engined transport, the Ju 52, which embodied the cumulative experience of earlier designs and was primarily intended for freight-carrying. Like its predecessors, it was of standard Junkers all-metal construction with corrugated,

load-sustaining duralumin skinning, and featured the patented Junkers full-span double wing. Five aircraft were built, of which four underwent development with various powerplants in Germany and one (CF-ARM) went to Canada. The first aircraft flew on 13 October 1930. Despite its single engine (usually of around 780-825 hp/582-615 kW), the Ju 52 was able to carry 15-17 passengers when required. However, the following year the Junkers design team, under Dipl Ing Ernst Zindel, undertook work to adapt the Ju 52 to feature three 525-hp (392-kW) Pratt & Whitney Hornet nine-cylinder radials, and the prototype of this version, the Ju 52/3m

Seen here on a makeshift landing strip in Libya in June 1942 alongside a Bf 110, the Ju 52/3m proved itself equally at home in North African desert operations as in the frozen wastes of the Eastern Front.

Pictured in Poland in 1939, these ambulance-configured Ju 52/3ms comprised part of the 547 Ju 52/3mg3e and 3mg4e aircraft available to the Luftwaffe's Transportverband at this time.

(Dreimotoren, or three-motor), made its maiden flight in April 1932. Subsequent deliveries were made to Finland, Sweden and Brazil, as well as to Deutsche Lufthansa. Ultimately, Ju 52/3ms flew with airlines in Argentina, Austria, Australia, Belgium, Bolivia, China, Colombia, Czechoslovakia, Denmark, Ecuador, Estonia, France, Great Britain, Greece, Hungary, Italy, Lebanon, Mozambique, Norway, Peru, Poland, Portugal, Romania, South Africa, Spain, Switzerland, Turkey and Uruguay. Powerplants included Hispano-Suiza, BMW, Junkers Jumo, Bristol Pegasus, Pratt & Whitney Hornet and Wasp engines. Commercial Ju 52/3ms delivered to Bolivia were employed as military transports towards the end of the Gran Chaco war of 1932-35.

Civil service

From late in 1932, Ju 52/3ms were delivered to Lufthansa, with D-2201 *Boelcke* and D-2202 *Richthofen* inaugurating the airline's Berlin-London and Berlin-Rome services before the end of that year. In due course, no fewer than 230 Ju 52/3ms were registered with Deutsche Lufthansa, continuing to fly commercial services to Spain, Portugal, Sweden, Switzerland and Turkey almost to the end of World War II. Despite the stringencies of treaty restrictions imposed on Germany since 1919, clandestine adventures had continued, by which potential military personnel had undergone training in foreign lands, particularly the USSR. When, after its walk-out from the disarmament talks in 1932, Germany set about the covert establishment of a military air force, it fell to such aircraft as the Ju 52/3m to provide the basis of its flying equipment, and in 1934 the first military version, the Ju 52/3mg3e, appeared.

The Ju 52/3mg3e was an attempt to produce a bomber version quickly and without unduly interrupting the highly profitable commercial production line. Powered by three 525-hp (392-kW) BMW 132A-3 radials, this version normally carried a bombload of 1,321 lb (600 kg) comprising six 220-lb (100-kg) bombs, and featured a dorsal gun position and a ventral 'dustbin', each mounting a single 0.31-in (7.92-mm) MG 15 machine-gun. Deliveries of the Ju 52/3mg3e to the new Luftwaffe totalled 450 in 1934-5, the first unit thus equipped being Kampfgeschwader 152 'Hindenburg'. In 1937 this Geschwader's IV Gruppe was redesignated KGrzbV 1; this designation (Kampfgruppe zur besonderen Verwendung, or bomber group for special operations) was roughly comparable to the RAF's 'bomber transport' category, and was intended to reflect a dual role of bombing and military transport duties. It thereby perpetuated the originally intended function of the Ju 52/3m. In the event, Ju 52/3m-equipped KGrzbV seldom, if ever, engaged in bombing operations during World War II.

Rough-field operations

Operations from Germany's poorly-surfaced military airfields had resulted, in 1935, in the introduction of the Ju 52/3mg4e with a tailwheel in place of the tailskid, and by 1938 this version was being standardised in the KGrzbV. In March that year, at the time of the Austrian Anschluss, German troops were carried forward by KGrzbV 1 and 2 in a massive show of strength – the former based at Furstenwalde with 54 aircraft, and the latter at Brandenburg-Briest. By the time Germany was ready to crush Poland, the Luftwaffe's Transportverband possessed an inventory of 552 aircraft, of which 547 were Ju 52/3mg3e and Ju 52/3mg4e aircraft (the balance being two obsolete He 111 transports, a Junkers G 38, a Ju 90 and an Fw 200). Losses in the month-long campaign in September amounted to 59 Junkers Ju 52/3ms, all but two to ground fire or flying accidents. In the course of 2,460 flights, the aircraft carried 19,700 troops and 1,600 tons (1451 tonnes) of supplies.

Spanish Civil War – a baptism of fire

When, on 18 July 1936, the Spanish Civil War broke out and Germany quickly aligned itself with Franco's right-wing Nationalists, 20 Ju 52/3ms (including one Ju 52/3m Wasser floatplane) and six Heinkel He 51s were sent to Spain, absorbed into the Legion Condor under the command of General Hugo Sperrle the following November. Initially used as transports, the Ju 52/3ms were employed on night flights, bringing 10,000 Moorish troops from Tetuan, Morocco to Spain. Thereafter, they were employed in three bomber *Staffeln* of Kampfgruppe 88, and flown in raids on Republican-held Mediterranean ports and in support of the land battle for Madrid. By mid-1937 they were deemed obsolete in the bombing role, and were largely replaced by Dornier Do 17s and Heinkel He 111s. Nevertheless, the Ju 52/3m continued in the role of both bomber and troop transport until the end of the war, in both German and Spanish Nationalist colours. Pictured on the left are injured members of the Legion Condor being loaded aboard a Ju 52/3m as German soldiers returned home from León, Spain in May 1939. Below is shown a Ju 52/3m from 2./K 88 in bomber configuration. Of the Ju 52/3m's performance in Spain, Hitler stated: "Franco ought to erect a monument to the glory of the Junkers [Ju 52/3m]. It is this aircraft that the Spanish Revolution has to thank for its victory."

Right: The first task for the Ju 52/3m of the Luftwaffe contingent in Spain was the transportation of Moroccan troops to the war zone from 29 July 1936. This is a Ju 52/3mg3e of Kampfgruppe 88 in late 1936.

Left: As well as serving with the German Legion Condor, the Ju 52/3m was supplied to the Spanish Nationalist forces, like this Grupo de Bombardeo Nocturno 1-G-22 example in early 1938. In Spanish service, the aircraft was nicknamed 'Pava' (turkey).

Wehrmacht workhorse

Although it was the best transport type the Luftwaffe possessed, the Ju 52/3m was slow, lacked manoeuvrability and defensive armament and was an easy target for marauding Allied fighters.

During the Aegean campaign and operations on the Eastern Front, the Ju 52/3m was often a 'sitting duck' and suffered unsustainable losses. However, the aircraft's reliability and ability to operate in all conditions ensured that it remained vital to the German war effort.

In the relatively swift and clinically organised invasion of Norway in 1939, the number of Ju 52/3ms available had risen to 573, equipping all four Gruppen of KGzbV 1, and KGrzbV 101, 102, 103, 104, 105, 106 and 107 – an average of 52 aircraft in each Gruppe. A small number of twin float-equipped Ju 52/3m Wasser aircraft was also employed in the Norwegian campaign, alighting in the fjords to disembark troops, engineers and supplies. A new version, the Ju 52/3mg5e with provision for alternative wheel, float or ski landing gear, had been introduced, powered by three 830-hp (619-kW) BMW

132T-2 engines. Among the operations undertaken by Junkers in Norway was the capture by airborne forces of Stavanger-Sola airport and the Vordingborg bridge. A total of 29,000 men, 259,300 Imp gal (1180000 litres) of aviation fuel and 2,376 tons (2155 tonnes) of supplies were airlifted during the campaign, for the significant loss of 150 aircraft.

Assault in the West

Prior to the conclusion of the Norwegian campaign, the majority of Ju 52/3ms was being withdrawn back to Germany in preparation for Operation Yellow, the great assault in the West. As a result of losses in Norway, the number of Junkers available was only 475, to which was now added 45 DFS 230 assault gliders, the whole transport force being commanded by General Putzier. Because of the need to conserve the Ju 52/3ms for a likely air assault on the UK, the Luftwaffe's transports were largely confined to airborne attacks in the initial stage, and it was against the Netherlands and Belgium that most of these were

Ju 52/3mg7e

This Junkers Ju 52/3mg7e belonged to 2./Staffel, KGzbV 1, based at Milos, Greece, in May 1941 immediately prior to the invasion of Crete. By the end of the operation, more than 170 Ju 52/3ms had been lost or seriously damaged and German paratroops were never again able to mount a major airborne operation, so heavy were their losses.

Controls
The mechanical controls used chain links and pulleys. The tail (rudder and elevator) controls ran under the cabin floor to the rear, with the aileron controls splitting off and running along the inside of the trailing edge of the wing structure.

Corrugations
The Ju 52/3m was an all-metal aircraft, covered mainly with corrugated duralumin skinning. The skin was load-bearing, and the corrugations gave it immense strength for little weight penalty. Corrugation was a feature of many early Junkers designs.

Tail unit
Both tail and tailplane were built, like the wing, on a multi-spar structure. The elevators (and ailerons) featured distinctive balancing horns to lighten control forces.

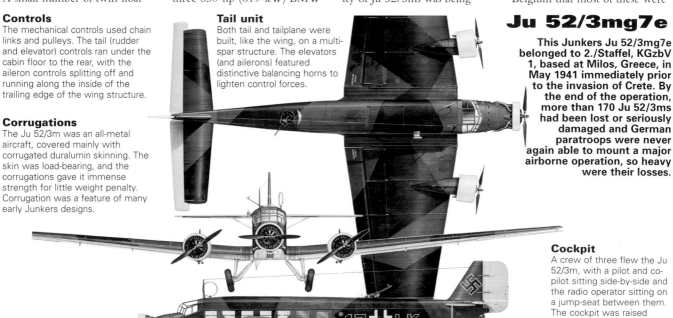

Cockpit
A crew of three flew the Ju 52/3m, with a pilot and co-pilot sitting side-by-side and the radio operator sitting on a jump-seat between them. The cockpit was raised above the level of the main cabin door.

Camouflage
This was the standard camouflage for Luftwaffe Ju 52/3ms, consisting of upper surfaces with a dark/light green splinter pattern and light grey undersurfaces. Aircraft operating in winter on the Eastern Front had soluble white distemper applied over the standard paint to camouflage them against the snow. This aircraft has yellow theatre markings on the rudder, wingtips, elevators and engine cowls.

Wing
A feature of Junkers designs of the period was the detached flap/aileron assembly, positioned below and behind the main wing structure. The ailerons drooped at low speed to act as partial flaps which, together with the normal slotted inboard flaps, gave the type tremendous STOL capability. The entire wing could be detached from the fuselage and was attached by eight ball-and-socket joints.

Minesweeping role

In addition to its transport and training roles, the Ju 52/3m was modified for the task of minesweeping and formed the principal equipment of six Minensuchstaffeln during 1940-44. Several variants (including the Ju 52/3mg4e, g6e and g8e) were converted and received the suffix MS to indicate their Minensuche (mine-search) role. The majority of Ju 52/3m (MS) aircraft had a large Dural hoop fitted beneath the wings and fuselage, which was energised by an auxiliary motor in the fuselage. The aircraft were particularly active in the Mediterranean where groups of three aircraft would explode Allied mines by flying a magnetic sweep over suspected areas.

launched, in particular on the Moerdijk bridges and on Rotterdam's Waalhaven airport. Large numbers of Ju 52/3ms were employed in each attack, and losses, mainly from anti-aircraft gunfire, were extremely heavy; in the five days that it took the Wehrmacht to crush the Netherlands, no fewer than 167 Junkers were totally destroyed, and a similar number badly damaged. By the end of 1940 a total of 1,275 Ju 52/3ms had been delivered to the Luftwaffe, of which some 700 aircraft had already been struck off charge.

New versions

After the collapse of France, no further major operations involving the use of Ju 52/3ms were launched until the advance by German forces through the Balkans in April 1941. By then, a number of new versions had appeared, namely the Ju 52/3mg6e, which was similar to the Ju 52/3mg5e but equipped with improved radio, and the Ju 52/3mg7e with automatic pilot, accommodation for up to 18 troops and wider cabin

doors; it also featured provision for two 0.31-in (7.92-mm) machine-guns to fire through the cabin windows.

Despite its ultimate capture, Crete proved a disaster for the Transportverband. Assigned to the task of an airborne invasion of the island, the 493 Ju 52/3ms and about 80 DFS 230 gliders were intended to attack in three waves. However, as a result of confusion on the ground caused by dense clouds of dust, there were numerous collisions and delays, so that what had been planned as an attack concentrated in time and area degenerated into widespread confusion and dissipated effort. German casualties were more than 7,000 men (of whom about 2,000 were paratroopers) and 174 Ju 52/3ms, representing more than a third of the Luftwaffe's available transport force. It has often been said that the Balkan campaign was a lost cause for the Allies, yet the heavy losses inflicted on this vital enemy assault arm proved of immense importance when Germany launched Operation

Barbarossa less than two months later. Henceforth (apart from isolated instances of commando-type operations), the use of air transport was confined within the Luftwaffe to logistic supply and evacuation. On the opening day of Barbarossa, the Luftwaffe could field no more than 238 serviceable Ju 52/3ms, a far cry from the numbers available in 1939 and 1940.

Eastern Front

The nature of warfare on the Eastern Front quickly determined the role to be played by the Ju 52/3m, with 'scorched earth' tactics employed by the retreating Russians demanding considerable dependence by the Wehrmacht on air supplies. Production of the Ju 52/3m increased to 502 in 1941, 503 in 1942 and 887 in 1943. New versions continued to appear: the Ju 52/3mg8e dispensed with the wheel spats (found to be a hindrance in the quagmire conditions on the Eastern Front), but included a 0.51-in (13-mm) MG 131 gun in the dorsal position, while some

aircraft had 850-hp (634-kW) BMW 132Z engines; the Ju 52/3mg9e, which appeared in 1942, featured strengthened landing gear to permit a take-off weight of 25,353 lb (11500 kg) and was equipped to tow the Gotha Go 242 glider; the Ju 52/3mg10e was a naval version with provision for floats; and the Ju 52/3mg12e had 800-hp (597-kW) BMW 132L engines. Only one other version reached the Luftwaffe (late in 1943), namely the Ju 52/3mg14e with an MG 15 machine-gun mounted in a streamlined position over the pilot's cabin.

It may be said of the Ju 52/3m that its star shone brightest in adversity from 1942. In February of that year, when six German divisions were trapped at Demyansk, the Luftwaffe performed the prodigious task of sustaining 100,000 troops, and in three months delivered 24,300 tons (22045 tonnes) of materiel, airlifted 15,446 men into the pocket and evacuated 20,093 casualties; the cost of this effort was a loss of 385 flying personnel (including Major Walter Hammer, commanding KGrzbV 172) and 262 aircraft. Far greater disasters befell the German armies at Stalingrad and in North Africa, and in a single raid on Sverevo in the dreadful winter of 1942-43, 52 Junkers were destroyed by Russian bombers. In the final attempts to assist (and eventually to evacuate) the Axis armies in Tunisia in April 1943, the Luftwaffe lost 432 transport aircraft, almost all of them Ju 52/3ms, in less than three weeks.

German forces in North Africa relied heavily on supplies and reinforcements delivered by Ju 52/3ms. These aircraft are seen in April 1941 shortly before the German invasion of Crete which saw the Ju 52/3m in its other major role – as a paratroop assault transport.

Junkers Ju 87
'Stuka' dive-bomber

Few aircraft have ever caused such terror, to seasoned troops and helpless civilians alike, as the ugly Junkers Ju 87 dive-bomber. Widely known as the Stuka, from the German word for dive-bomber (Sturzkampfflugzeug), the Ju 87 also sank more ships than any other aircraft type in history.

A pair of Ju 87R-2s of 2./StG 3 is pictured returning from a patrol in the Mediterranean in early 1941. The Med was a region in which the 'R' was repeatedly used against British convoys. The aircraft carry 66-Imp gallon (300-litre) drop tanks under their wings.

The technique of dive-bombing was familiar in World War I, but no aircraft designed for the job existed until the 1920s. One of the first was the Junkers K 47, of which two were flown in 1928 with Jupiter engines, and a further 12 with Pratt & Whitney Hornet engines were later sold to China. Extensive research was carried out on the K 47s and revealed that a 90° dive is the most accurate, although such a dive demands a strong aircraft and a resolute pilot, as well as the existence of an indicator of dive angle. At this time, many who later were to head Hitler's Luftwaffe became convinced of the importance of a dive-bomber as a central weapon in an air force dedicated to the close support of ground forces.

When plans for new combat aircraft for the Luftwaffe were made in 1933, the immediate need was met by a trim biplane, the Henschel Hs 123, while Junkers continued to work on the definitive Stuka. The design staff under Hermann Pohlmann adopted the same configuration as that of the K 47, a single-engined low-wing monoplane with prominent fixed landing gear and twin fins and rudders. This was later changed to a conventional single-fin design during development as, during an early dive test, the twin fins collapsed and the aircraft crashed. Another change was to the powerplant; the prototype had originally flown with a British built Rolls-Royce Kestrel engine, but this was later changed to a German-built Jumo 210Ca when the Stuka entered Luftwaffe service in 1937.

Into combat

Stukas were first to see action with the Légion Condor in Spain, where the type proved outstandingly effective. Despite the Stuka's remarkable combat debut, however, Junkers continued to refine and improve the design. One notable addition was to fit sirens – called 'Trumpets of Jericho' – to the landing gears. As the aircraft entered its dive, the flow of the wind through the sirens would cause them to screech and so strike extra terror into people near the target.

By mid-1939, Stuka production had reached up to 60 a month, and these improved 'B' models were soon in combat supporting

The Ju 87 V4 is seen in its original form, with smooth cowling side panels, and before the rearmost windows of the canopy were installed.

Above: A Ju 87A-2 serving with StG 165 in 1938 displays a not-uncommon variety of camouflage finish – usually obtained by switching the basic colours and splinter pattern. The red tail banner and white circle behind the Swastika were soon eliminated on operational aircraft, as illustrated.

Left: Flanked by a 500-kg (1,102-lb) SC500 bomb, this Ju 87B Stuka is seen parked on a Greek airfield during the continuation of the Blitzkrieg campaign through the Balkans. This was the last campaign in which the Ju 87 was able to demolish its targets while encountering little opposition.

Above: The water-soluble white distemper used as snow camouflage by Luftwaffe aircraft in Russia weathered rapidly, becoming heavily stained by exhaust gases. Here, five Ju 87Ds from an unidentified Geschwader turn in for an attack against Soviet armour.

Above: German troops watch as a flight of Stukas return from a mission. Stukas flew in support of Rommel's Afrika Korps, providing close-air support throughout the early years of the campaign in North Africa.

Hitler's blitzkrieg across Europe. Stukas flew the first combat mission of World War II when three B-1s took off on 1 September 1939 to attack the Dirschau Bridge over the Vistula river, some 11 minutes before the Nazis declared war on Poland. Later, Stukas were to prove equally effective in the campaign against Poland, sinking all but two of Poland's warships and attacking numerous troop concentrations.

Alongside the developing ground-attack models, Junkers proposed the Ju 87C, equipped with folding wings and hooks, and incorporating many other changes to enable the type to be used aboard the carrier *Graf Zeppelin*, which was ultimately never completed. Other models were to feature overwing-mounted personnel pods to serve as transport aircraft.

Having wrought havoc throughout Europe in the first year of World War II, over Britain Stuka losses were to prove unacceptably heavy. At the height of the Battle of Britain – from

13-18 August 1940 – RAF Spitfires and Hurricanes shot down 41 Stukas, with the result that, from 19 August, the aircraft were withdrawn from attacks against UK targets.

The Stuka had been designed on the basis of good fighter protection by Bf 109s and Bf 110s and, in such conditions, it had demonstrated its devastating effectiveness. However, the Luftwaffe's inability to achieve air superiority over the UK caused huge losses to be suffered by Stuka units.

Basic design

By early 1941 what was to become the definitive Stuka variant, the Ju 87D, had entered combat on the Eastern and North African Fronts. The entire aircraft was refined to reduce drag, the most visible improvement being the deletion of the large radiator intake and its replacement with a smaller armoured design.

No longer viewed as purely a dive-bomber, Stukas were increasingly used as close-support aircraft, dropping bombs within 330 ft (100 m) of friendly troops. Other roles extended to glider-

towing, anti-partisan attacks and general utility transport with a diversity of loads.

Developed from the Ju 87D were a succession of sub-variants, including the '-5' with extended wingtips to counter the increasing weight of the Ju 87D versions; the '-7' night variant (reflecting the increasing peril of day operations) with long exhaust pipes extending back across the wing to hide the exhaust flames; and the Ju 87D-8 which was the last version in production. The total number of Stukas built by late September 1944 – when almost all aircraft production other than fighters had been terminated – is generally accepted as 5,709.

The Ju 87 was widely used by all the Axis air forces, including those of Italy, Hungary, Slovakia, Romania and Bulgaria, although it was with the Luftwaffe that the aircraft achieved its well-deserved reputation.

Even at the outbreak of war, the Ju 87 was recognised as a somewhat dated design, but this fact was masked by its fantastic successes. Like so many other long-serving Luftwaffe types, it continued to be operated long beyond its original termination of production date, due to the lack of a replacement aircraft. Ju 87 crews, like those of the Messerschmitt Bf 110 and He 111, were subjected to flying combat missions in an outdated aircraft, and so the results achieved stand as a testament to the skill of the crews and the durability of the Ju 87 Stuka.

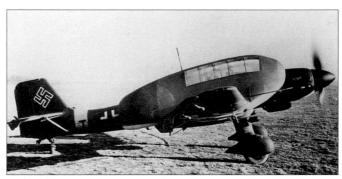

Above: A Ju 87D-3 is seen with experimental personnel transport pods overwing. They seated two passengers in tandem, and were designed to be released in a shallow dive, descending to the ground on the end of a massive parachute.

Left: The Ju 87G-1 anti-tank aircraft was the last Ju 87 variant to become operational (apart from the Ju 87H trainer). Converted from earlier Ju 87Ds, the aircraft were adapted to carry a pair of massive Flak 18 (Bk 3,7) 37-mm cannon pods under their outer wing panels.

This was the gunner's eye view during the pull-out after an attack by his I./StG aircraft on a target on the outskirts of Warsaw. Smoke can be seen rising from the explosion of the aircraft's bomb.

Poland, Norway and the West

The term 'Stuka' was a contraction of 'Sturzkampffugzeug', meaning 'dive-bomber'. But during the early part of World War II, that term referred to just one aircraft – the Junkers Ju 87.

Until the advent of the air-to-surface guided weapon, the steep-diving attack was the most accurate method for delivering bombs on defended targets. At the beginning of World War II, horizontal bombers carried crude bombsights that gave poor results. They released several bombs with an interval between each, which landed in a long 'stick' with hopefully one or two hitting the target. However, most of the bombs landed too far away from the target to cause any damage.

The steep-diving bomber offered a better solution. Small and relatively cheap, it carried only a few bombs. Yet a well-trained dive-bomber pilot could place half of his bombs inside a circle of 82-ft (25-m) radius , centred on the aiming point (for a horizontal bomber, the circular error from a single bomb was two or three times greater). Thus, against a pinpoint target, a

dive-bomber attacking with a few small bombs was considerably more effective than a horizontal bomber attacking with several larger bombs.

The Ju 87 was designed without compromise as a dive-bomber. The fixed undercarriage gave the aircraft an outdated look, but it was there for good reason. Typically, the pilot commenced his attack from around 10,000 ft (3048 m). In the 80° dive, the combined drag from the undercarriage and the underwing dive brakes prevented speed building up too rapidly. That made the aircraft a stable aiming platform throughout the dive – lasting about 15 seconds – enabling the pilot to centre the target in his bombsight and hold it there. The Ju 87 had a propeller-driven siren mounted on each undercarriage leg, and during the dive its wailing scream was profoundly demoralising to those on the ground. The pilot released his bombs at 2,200 ft

Above: Armourers prepare to load a 550-lb (250-kg) high-explosive bomb on the fuselage rack of a Ju 87. The standard weaponload for the dive-bomber was one of these weapons under the fuselage, and four 110-lb (50-kg) bombs under the wings.

Below: Ju 87B-2s of I. Gruppe of Stukageschwader 77 are pictured at their camouflaged field landing ground at Courcelle near St Quentin, between missions during the campaign in France.

Above: The Junkers Ju 87 was a rugged aircraft, and was brought back safely to base with all manner of battle damage. Oberleutnant Hartmann of 3. Staffel Stukageschwader 77 picked up this severe wing damage over Warsaw.

Left: German paratroops wave a greeting to a Stuka during the invasion of Holland. These lightly armed troops relied on the dive-bombers to provide heavier support.

(671 m), and the aircraft pulled out of the dive automatically. The airframe was specially stiffened to enable it to perform the sharp pullout manoeuvre without over-stressing the structure. At about 1,000 ft (305 m) the Stuka bottomed out, safely out of reach of small arms fire and splinters from the exploding bombs.

In action in Poland

On 1 September 1939, German forces invaded Poland. To support the offensive, the Luftwaffe committed all nine of its Ju 87 Gruppen, a total of 319 dive-bombers. During the first two days, Ju 87s attacked several airfields and aircraft factories. The Polish air force was too small and its equipment too outdated to cause serious interference. The Luftwaffe quickly established air supremacy, and the Ju 87 established a reputation for hitting targets with great accuracy.

After the first two days, the Luftwaffe switched its main effort to supporting the army. Although several published accounts have stated otherwise, Ju 87s rarely flew close air support operations – that is to say, against targets in close proximity with friendly ground forces. For an accurate diving attack the Ju 87 pilot needed to see his target from 10,000 ft (3048 m)– nearly two miles vertically. Few battlefield targets were so clearly visible. The dive-bombers were at their most effective against well-defined targets in the enemy rear areas, for example bridges, rail targets, supply depots and barracks.

On 27 September 1939 the Polish government capitulated. The Stuka emerged from its first great test with glowing endorsements, having played an important part in speeding the

German victory.

The period of relative calm after the fall of Poland ended on 9 April 1940, when German forces invaded Norway. Only one Stuka unit took part in that campaign, I Gruppe of Dive-Bomber Geschwader 1, but it proved very effective. That morning the unit sent 22 aircraft to dive-bomb shore batteries at Akershus and Oskarsborg, guarding the entrance to Oslo Fjord.

During the weeks that followed, the Norwegian and Allied forces were squeezed further and further into the north of the country. By early May their position was untenable, and the evacuation began. Stukas delivered several attacks on warships covering the withdrawal, and sank three destroyers and an anti-aircraft sloop.

On 10 May 1940 it was the turn of France, Holland and Belgium to suffer blitzkrieg attacks. Initially, almost all the 380 available dive-bombers were concentrated against Holland and Belgium, ready to provide close air support for the German airborne troops landed at several points. It was not the most effective way to use the Stukas, but there was no alternative. The airborne troops were lightly armed, and relied on the Stukas to provide their heavy punch.

Leutnant Otto Schmidt of 3 Staffel, Dive-Bomber Geschwader 77, took part in one such action on 10 May. His Staffel sent nine Stukas to hit a Belgian army position near the Albert Canal, to support glider-borne troops attacking the nearby fortress at Eban Emael. It seemed to Schmidt that the return fire was inaccurate, but when his Staffel landed, two aircraft were missing.

Schmidt's Staffel flew three

further missions that day, once against Veldrezelt and twice against Antwerp. Returning from the last mission, a Stuka was seen to drift out of formation, lose height and smash into the ground. There was no indication of enemy action; possibly, carbon monoxide fumes had leaked into the cockpit and rendered the crew unconscious-ness. These losses were a severe blow to the Staffel. In Poland it had lost only one crew, whereas in the new campaign it had lost three on the first day.

Into France

As advancing German ground forces linked up with each pocket of airborne troops, the battle in Holland was won. Then the focus of operations shifted to the city of Sedan in northern France, to support the main German thrust. Advancing Panzer columns reached the Meuse River on 13 May, and preparations began for an assault crossing. That afternoon dive-bombers flew some 200 sorties, and twin-engined bombers flew 310 more, to neutralise French infantry and artillery positions along the south bank. Meanwhile, German infantry-men crossed the river in assault

boats and established defensive positions on the far side. Their bridgehead quickly expanded, and engineers threw pontoon bridges over the Meuse. Tanks streamed across the river, commencing an armoured thrust that would end at the English Channel.

Reverting to their more usual targets in rear areas in the weeks to follow, the Stukas were in action on every day the weather allowed. Sometimes, crews flew as many as four missions per day.

By the final week in May, the Allied forces in northern France were falling back on the port of Dunkirk, and the evacuation operation began on 27 May. In a bid to thwart the operation, the Luftwaffe launched concentrated attacks on the port. Royal Air Force Spitfires and Hurricanes fought to blunt the attacks, but the bombers caused severe damage to ships and harbour installations.

One of those engaged over Dunkirk, Hauptmann Helmut Malilke of Dive-Bomber Gruppe 186, recalled, "I was not too worried about heavy flak over the port, but the light flak was dangerous especially if it was situated on the target. In that case the gunners were presented with an easy target. On 1 June a Spitfire tried to shoot me down, but almost certainly it ran out of ammunition before it could do so. So the pilot curved around, moved into formation alongside me, saluted and pulled away for home. It was an act of chivalry that could never have happened in Russia..."

The evacuation operation ended at dawn on 4 June 1940, having lifted nearly 340,000 British and French troops. The Stuka's reputation now stood at its pinnacle. Only Great Britain remained unsubdued, and now the dive-bomber units prepared to assist in its downfall. However, when pitted against stronger and more determined defensive fighter opposition during the Battle of Britain, the Stuka's fortunes were dramatically reversed.

Officers of StG 77 examine the damage they have inflicted on a French vehicle column. The attack occurred near Auxerre, in a typical Ju 87 mission during the German blitzkrieg.

Battle of Britain

This Stuka of StG 77 failed to pull out of its dive after it was hit by an RAF fighter during the action on 18 August 1940. The aircraft crashed at West Broyle, near Chichester.

Very lucky to be alive! Unteroffizier Karl Maier, a Ju 87 gunner, returned from the attack on Thorney Island on 18 August after suffering eight hits from machine-gun bullets. In each case, they caused only flesh wounds.

Until June 1940 the Stukas, operating in skies where the Luftwaffe held air superiority, could hit their targets without serious interference from the enemy. That was about to change, however.

The Battle of Britain opened in July 1940, with small-scale attacks on convoys of coastal shipping passing through the English Channel. Typical of these scrappy air actions was the engagement on the afternoon of 13 July. Half a dozen Junkers 87s from Stukageschwader 1 attacked a convoy off Dover. Eleven Hurricanes of No. 56 Squadron broke up the attack, inflicting damage on two Stukas. No ship was hit. Escorting Messerschmitt Bf 109s then intervened, however, and shot down two Hurricanes.

Largest convoy action

In the weeks to follow, the pace of the air fighting slowly accelerated. Then, on 8 August, the Luftwaffe mounted its heaviest convoy attack. Convoy CW9, with 18 freighters and a naval escort, was heading west along the Channel towards Weymouth. That morning, small forces of dive-bombers tried to reach the convoy, but in each case patrolling Spitfires and Hurricanes drove them away. Then, at mid-day, the Luftwaffe launched a far heavier attack. Fifty-seven Stukas, escorted by Bf 109s, hit the convoy as it passed off the Isle of Wight. As the Messerschmitts fought a furious battle with RAF fighters, the dive-bombers attacked the slow-moving ships. Several vessels suffered damage, and two were left sinking. Then, later in the afternoon, the Luftwaffe sent in 82 more dive-bombers to finish off the surviving ships. Again, there were violent air combats with the escorting Messerschmitts, but by the end of the action Convoy CW9 had almost ceased to exist. Seven vessels had been sunk, six more suffered serious damage and one took light damage. Only four reached Weymouth without damage. During the day's actions the Luftwaffe had lost 28 aircraft.

Nine Ju 87s were lost and 10 returned with varying amounts of damage. For its part, the RAF lost 19 Spitfires and Hurricanes.

On 12 August formations of Stukas hit targets in southern England in force for the first time. Their objectives were the radar stations at Pevensey, Rye, Dover, Dunkirk (in Kent) and Ventnor. The station at Ventnor was knocked out of action for some weeks, but following repairs the other stations were all back in action the next day.

'The Hardest Day'

The largest Stuka attack of all during the Battle of Britain took place on 18 August, 'The Hardest Day'. Early that afternoon a force of 109 Junkers Ju 87s, drawn from all three Gruppen of Stukageschwader 77 and I.Gruppe of StG 3, set out to attack the airfields at Gosport, Ford and Thorney Island and the radar station at Poling. One hundred and fifty Messerschmitt Bf 109s provided protection for the force.

Radar stations along the south coast of England observed the approach of the raiders and five

The Stukas usually delivered their attacks with great precision. This German reconnaissance photo shows fires burning at the airfield at Ford, after the attack on 18 August.

Above: Men of 'Dad's Army' (the Home Guard) stand alongside a Ju 87 of II./StG 77 which made a forced landing on Ham Manor Golf Course near Angmering on 18 August 1940.

A Ju 87 of StG 77 is pictured after it nosed-over on landing at its base in Normandy. Such accidents were not uncommon when the Stukas operated from hastily prepared airfields.

from Nos 43 and 601 Squadrons charged into the dive-bombers.

Oberleutnant Johannes Wilhelm heard the radio warning of approaching enemy fighters. He glanced around his Stuka and saw nothing, so he concentrated on holding position in formation. His gunner, Unteroffizier Anton Woerner, squinted into the sun looking for the assailants, but could see none. Then, appearing as if from nowhere and with guns belching fire, the Hurricanes came flashing through the German formation. Wilhelm saw three or four British fighters roar past in rapid succession. To one side, a Stuka burst into flames and slid out of formation. Then a loud crash and a shudder announced that Wilhelm's Stuka had been hit. Oil streamed over the canopy, blotting out everything outside. More disconcertingly, the cockpit filled with smoke; the aircraft was on fire. Wilhelm rolled the Stuka on to its back and shouted "Raus!" (get out). Each man slid back his canopy, released his straps and tumbled clear of the stricken dive-bomber. For them, the war was over.

Those Ju 87s that survived the initial encounter now entered their dives, with their assailants buzzing angrily around them.

Once in the dive, the Stuka was a difficult target. Flight Lieutenant Frank Carey, who led the Hurricanes of No. 43 Squadron in this action, later commented: "In the dive they were very difficult to hit, because in a fighter one's speed built up so rapidly that one went screaming past him. But he couldn't dive for ever ..."

Under attack

After emerging from their attack dives, the Ju 87s headed out to sea in a gaggle. As he pulled out of his dive after attacking Thorney Island, Oberleutnant Otto Schmidt noticed an enemy fighter closing in rapidly. He wondered why his gunner had not opened fire, and when he looked back he realised why. The unfortunate man was slumped lifeless in his seat. In concentrating on his attack, Schmidt failed to notice that his own aircraft had come under fire. He pushed the Stuka into a screaming sideslip and the British fighter shot past.

As the surviving dive-bombers headed south, one by one the attacking British fighters ran out of ammunition and broke off the chase. The nearest friendly territory was 70 miles (113 km) away, and Stukas with battle damage and dead or

wounded crewmembers had a difficult sea crossing. Feldwebel Gunther Mayer-Bothling returned with blood streaming from a head wound, a dead gunner, scarcely any working instruments, no compass, part of the rudder shot away, the cabin awash with engine oil and two 110-lb (50-kg) bombs jammed on the rack under the port wing. Oberleutnant Karl Henze flew home at 100 mph (161 km/h), after damage to the hydraulic system prevented retraction of the dive brakes. Oberleutnant Helmut Bruck landed in France with 130 bullet holes in his Stuka, but not a scratch on himself or the gunner. But, without question, the luckiest man that day was gunner Unteroffizier Karl Maier: he was hit eight times by machine-gun rounds, but suffered only flesh wounds.

Of the four Stuka Gruppen engaged in the attack, Ist Gruppe of StG 77 bore the heaviest losses: of the 28 Stukas it put up, 10 had been shot down and five returned with damage. Hauptmann Herbert Meisel, the Gruppe commander, was among those killed. The other three Gruppen suffered relatively light losses: a total of six aircraft shot down and two damaged.

As usual, the Stukas had hit their targets with great precision, and scarcely a bomb had fallen outside the designated target areas. Ford airfield would remain out of action for several

weeks. The airfields at Thorney Island and Gosport continued in use, though at reduced efficiency. The damage to Poling radar station was quickly repaired and the equipment was soon back on the air.

Achilles heel

The action on 18 August 1940 was the first real setback suffered by the Stuka. It highlighted the major weakness of this aircraft, one that would be demonstrated repeatedly as the war progressed. Without doubt, the Ju 87 was a highly effective attack weapon, but only when it could operate without interference from enemy fighters (or when the target was not well protected by anti-aircraft guns). If those conditions were not met, the dive-bombers would take heavy losses.

If the planned invasion of England went ahead, the Stukas would represent the only effective anti-shipping force to counter the might of the Royal Navy. It was therefore important to preserve the dive-bomber force. For that reason, the Ju 87s were now withdrawn from the Battle, and would play little further part in it.

Although it had been blooded over England, the Ju 87's career was far from over. When Hitler launched the invasion of the Soviet Union, the Stuka would again play a vital role.

This Ju 87B-2 was operated by Stab III./StG 77, based at Caen, France, in August 1940. The Gruppenstab emblem on the forward fuselage was the family crest of the Kommandeur Hauptmann Helmuth Bode.

Eastern Front

The Stuka units suffered their first reversal of fortunes during the Battle of Britain, but in terms of casualties this would be nothing compared to the long, grinding war of attrition on the Eastern Front that began in June 1941.

Operation Barbarossa, the all-out attack by German forces on the Soviet Union, opened on 21 June 1941. Eight Stuka Gruppen, with 324 aircraft, were in position to support the start of the onslaught.

An indication of the power of their attacks may be gained from the Air Fleet 2 report on 4 October, five days into an offensive to seize the Baltic coast. That day, the dive-bombers flew 48 sorties against rail targets, 202 in support of Panzer units advancing near Bryansk and 152 sorties to support troops advancing near Vyazma.

After an easy start, the Stuka units began to suffer heavy cumulative losses in aircraft and crews. Hauptmann Otto Schmidt, who flew with StG 77, explained: "At first things were easy in Russia and we had few losses to either flak

or fighters. Gradually, however, the Russian gunners gained experience in dealing with our diving attacks. They learned to stand their ground and fire back at us, instead of running for cover as others had done before. And when that happened our losses began to mount, especially in view of the large number of sorties we flew. A further strain was caused by the knowledge that if one was shot down on the enemy side of the lines and captured, the chances of survival were minimal." When replacements in aircraft and crews failed to keep up with losses, Ju 87 units were forced to operate at below their established strengths.

Harsh conditions

The Russian winter brought additional problems with heavy snowfalls, long spells of low cloud and poor visibility. For the remainder of the first winter,

Above: The crew of a Ju 87 of I./StG 5 check the security of a wing-mounted, 550-lb (250-kg) high-explosive bomb on their aircraft before departing on another mission.

Top: Ju 87Ds of I./StG 5 en route to a target near Leningrad. Each aircraft carries two AB 500 cluster-bomb containers under the wings and an SC 250 bomb under the fuselage.

the Stuka units played only a small part in the fighting.

When the ground dried after the spring thaw, the German blitzkrieg resumed with its previous ferocity. In 1942 the initial German thrust was in the south, to seize the Crimean peninsula. The assault on the important naval base at Sebastopol opened on 2 June. To support it, the dive-bomber units moved to

forward airstrips within 10 minutes' flying time of the city. Otto Schmidt explained: "During the operations over the Crimea the bodily strain was great, but the mental strain was not. There was little flak and no fighter opposition. For us the most difficult time was when the infantry wanted us to drop each bomb individually, to keep the enemy heads down and send up great clouds of chalk dust to screen our troops as they worked their way forwards. From our point of view that meant carrying out five separate diving attacks per sortie. Since we flew several sorties each day, that placed considerable strain on the

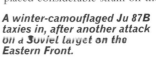

A winter-camouflaged Ju 87B taxies in, after another attack on a Soviet target on the Eastern Front.

The Ju 87 'Gustav' tank-busting aircraft featured two 37-mm, high-velocity cannon mounted under the wings. These modified anti-aircraft guns were effective in piercing the relatively thinly armoured rear parts of Soviet tanks.

body." The outnumbered and outgunned Soviet troops were squeezed into a progressively smaller pocket, until resistance ended on 3 July.

Then the German army moved on to its next objective, Stalingrad. At the end of August, spearhead units reached the outskirts of the city. Stukas and twin-engined bombers pounded targets to support the ground assaults. The bitter contest dragged on through October, with both sides feeding fresh divisions into the battle.

In November the winter arrived, bringing snow, freezing rain and low cloud. Now, the Soviet army launched its counter-offensive. Late in November, under cover of fog, reinforced army groups to the north and then the south of the city launched powerful attacks.

This is a Stuka pilot's view of the target – one of the forts at Sebastopol – obtained during an 80° dive. The bombs from the aircraft in front can be seen exploding on the target.

The Soviet thrusts threatened landing grounds used by the Stukas, forcing units to make panic evacuations, with aircraft taking off under fire from Soviet artillery or tanks. Unserviceable aircraft, ground equipment and quantities of stores and fuel had to be abandoned. During this period the Luftwaffe threw every available combat aircraft into action in its desperate attempts to slow the Soviet advance. However, due to the poor weather, these efforts had little effect.

On 23 November the claws of the Soviet pincer snapped shut, trapping 22 divisions of the German 6th Army in the pocket. Hitler demanded that the Luftwaffe supply the forces by air, but from the start the airlift was a forlorn enterprise. A few Stukas operated from the pocket until the last airstrip came under threat

from Soviet forces, at which point they withdrew. On 2 February 1943 the last units in the pocket surrendered. The German army had suffered its first major defeat of the campaign.

Anti-tank 'Gustav'

The need for an effective tank-busting aircraft on the eastern front led to the development of the Ju 87G, or 'Gustav'. This aircraft carried two 37-mm, high-velocity cannon under the wings, and in the spring of 1943 a batch of Ju 87Ds was modified for the new role.

The main German offensive in 1943, Operation Citadel, was aimed at the central front near Kursk. Every available Stuka unit, a total of some 360 Ju 87 'Doras' and a dozen or so 'Gustavs', moved into position to support the attacks.

The offensive commenced on 5 July, and in the days to follow dive-bomber crews flew up to six sorties per day. Bomb-carrying Stukas attacked targets in the Soviet rear areas, while 'Gustavs' attacked enemy tanks caught in the open. Then, despite powerful air support, the German armoured thrusts became bogged down in the Soviet defences. On 23 July, with the last of his reserves fully committed, Hitler ordered his army to move on to the defensive. The offensive against Kursk, the last all-out German onslaught on the Eastern Front, had failed to produce the hoped-for decisive victory.

In the autumn of 1943 the Luftwaffe tactical support units underwent a reorganisation. All Stukageschwader were redesignated as Schlachtgeschwader (Ground Attack Geschwader). Also, ground attack Fw 190Fs began replacing the Ju 87 'Doras'. As each Geschwader re-equipped, it retained one Staffel of Ju 87 'Gustavs' to provide a tank-busting capability.

On 23 June 1944 the Red Army unleashed its long-

prepared summer offensive, with powerful thrusts at several points on the central front. By then, the Luftwaffe had withdrawn several fighter Gruppen to bolster the air defences of the homeland. Less than 400 single-engined fighters remained to cover the entire Eastern Front. The Soviet air force fighters supporting the offensive outnumbered their opponents by five to one. Moreover, the programme to re-equip Stuka units with Fw 190s had slipped badly and it was only half complete. Lacking fighter escorts, the remaining Ju 87 units took heavy losses whenever they operated by day.

Heavy losses

At several points the German defences collapsed. Luftwaffe dive-bombers and ground attack units made desperate, but futile attempts to slow the thrusts, incurring severe losses. Low-flying Ju 87 'Gustavs' destroyed many Soviet tanks that had broken through the defences and outrun their anti-aircraft gun protection.

By night, individual Ju 87s flew nuisance raids over the enemy rear areas. Although these operations inflicted some damage and reduced movements to a snail's pace, they failed to have any decisive effect. The Soviet offensive finally petered out in mid-October. In places, the Germans had been pushed back 300 miles (480 km), having been ejected from the whole of the Soviet Union.

The last of more than 4,000 Ju 87s came off the production line in September 1944, but the type continued in service. In April 1945, the last month of the war, 125 Ju 87 'Doras' and 'Gustavs' remained with front-line units. The type had flown operations from the first day of the war until the last, and it fully deserves its reputation as one of the truly great military aircraft of all time.

This Junkers Ju 87B, flown by the commander of III./StG 77, Major Helmut Bode, is seen on its way to attack Sebastopol in June 1942.

Junkers Ju 88

The Ju 88A formed an important part of the Luftwaffe's triumvirate of medium bombers, seeing action in this role in every German campaign of the war. The good performance and manoeuvrability of the type rendered it more survivable in the face of fighter opposition than the Do 17/217 or He 111.

The Ju 88 V1 first prototype featured large chin radiators for the DB 600 engines, removed on subsequent aircraft. Here, the aircraft is seen with an aft-facing test camera installation above the cockpit.

With the exception of close dogfighting, it is difficult to think of any military duty in World War II for which the Ju 88 was not adapted. The original missions were level- and dive-bombing, but to these were added night-fighting, intruder, anti-ship, reconnaissance, anti-armour, and many more.

Versatility was the last thing considered at the start of the Ju 88 programme. By 1935 the RLM (German air ministry) was doubting the viability of a multi-role aircraft and issued a requirement for a simple *Schnellbomber* (fast bomber) which could fly at 500 km/h (311 mph) carrying a bombload of 1,765 lb (800 kg). Junkers went flat out to win the competition, even hiring two designers from the USA who had pioneered stressed-skin construction (even though Junkers had, by that time, already moved on from its traditional corrugated skin structures). In early 1936 two proposals were tendered, with twin (Ju 85) and single (Ju 88) fins. The Henschel Hs 127 and Messerschmitt Bf 162 were also offered.

Work on the Ju 88 began in May 1936, leading to the first flight of the prototype (D-AQEN) on 21 December, with Flugkapitän Kindermann at the controls. The V1 was powered by two Daimler-Benz DB 600Aa 12-cylinder engines, each rated at 1,000 hp (746 kW), housed in annular cowlings which gave the engines the impression of being radials.

Initial trials proceeded smoothly, the V1 demonstrating a good turn of speed and fine handling. It was lost in a crash in early 1937, shortly before the second prototype, D-AREN, flew for the first time on 10 April. This retained DB 600 power, and differed in only minor detail from the V1.

Jumo power

However, the third prototype (D-ASAZ) was considerably altered. Firstly, it was powered by Junkers' own Jumo 211A engine, of the same power output. It also introduced a raised canopy line to permit the installation of a rear-firing 0.311-in (7.9-mm) MG 15 machine-gun. It also had a more rounded rudder of greater area and a bombsight added in a blister under the nose. The performance of the V3 was very impressive, to the point that three more prototypes were ordered and plans drawn up for a massive dispersed production effort, involving not only Junkers plants at Schönebeck and Aschersleben, but also involving Arado, Dornier, Heinkel, Henschel and Volkswagen factories. Final assembly would be at Junkers-Bernburg and by other companies

Above: The V3 was the first Ju 88 with Jumo power, and the first to have gun armament in a raised cockpit. Note the bombsight fairing under the nose, offset to starboard.

Left: The V4 introduced the 'beetle eye' nose glazing, which consisted of 20 flat panels. The long engine nacelles, which reached nearly as far forward as the nose, led to the nickname 'die Dreifinger' (three-finger).

Speed record

Although initially completed as a standard bomber prototype, the Ju 88 V5 (D-ATYU) was modified for speed record work as part of Germany's propaganda effort. With ventral cupola removed, cockpit glazing lowered and a solid, pointed nose added, the V5 achieved a 621-mile (1000-km) closed-circuit speed record, carrying a 4,409-lb (2000-kg) payload at 321.25 mph (517 km/h) in March 1939. In July it set another record by carrying the same load for 1,243 miles (2000 km) at 311 mph (500 km/h).

Sporting the four-bladed propellers also fitted to the Ju 88A-0 series, the V6 was an important prototype in that it introduced the remarkable single-strut mainwheel undercarriage. The wheels rotated through 90° during retraction to lie flat at the rear of the slimmer nacelles. Shocks were absorbed by the Ringfeder system, which employed a series of high-tensile steel rings of tapered profiles. These expanded radially under compressive loads, bounce being prevented by the friction as the rings pushed their way apart.

(notably Arado at Brandenburg).

Changes specified for the Ju 88 included the addition of a fourth crew member, increased armament and dive-bombing capability. The first two requirements were incorporated in the V4, which flew initially on 2 February 1938. This incorporated the characteristic 'beetle eye' crew compartment with ventral bomb-aiming cupola, which had a rear-facing MG 15 at its aft end.

The Ju 88 V5 (D-ATYU) was similar, but introduced 1,200-hp (895-kW) Jumo 211B-1 engines. This aircraft was then modified for speed record attempts. D-ASCY, the V6, was considered as the first pre-production aircraft for the Ju 88A bomber, featuring four-bladed propellers for the Jumo 211B-1s and a redesigned main undercarriage/engine nacelle arrangement. The similar V7 followed on

27 September 1938, after which came the V8 and V9, which introduced dive-bombing capability through the use of slatted divebrakes housed in the wings outboard of the engine nacelles. The final prototype was the V10, which tested external bomb carriers between the fuselage and the nacelles.

A batch of 10 pre-production Ju 88A-0 aircraft followed the prototypes, these incorporating the divebrakes and bomb carriers. All had four-bladed propellers, initially at least. They were issued to a specially-formed unit, Erprobungskommando 88, from March 1939, this unit being charged with service evaluation, the development of tactics and the provision of a nucleus of crews for the first operational unit.

Into service

This first unit, I. Gruppe/Kampfgeschwader 25, was formed in August 1939, shortly before redesignation as I./KG 30 on 22 September. At the same time a training unit, the Lehrgruppe-88, was established at Greifswald.

Ju 88s were considered operational early enough to just see action during the last days of the Polish campaign. I./KG 30 flew the type's first mission on 26 September 1939, and continued in operation to the final fall of Poland on 6 October. Among

its inventory were several of the pre-production Ju 88A-0s, interspersed with full-production Ju 88A-1s. These differed little from the earlier aircraft, but reverted to three-bladed propellers, setting the basic configuration for all subsequent bomber aircraft.

The crew of four were all housed forward of the wing, the pilot sitting offset to port, with the bombardier behind and to starboard. From this position he could access the ventral cupola for bomb-aiming. Behind the pilot sat the flight engineer, facing rearward so that he could operate the upper gun. Alongside him, but lower, was the radio operator, who could squeeze into the rear of the cupola to operate the ventral gun. The pilot operated a single MG 15 mounted in the starboard side of the windscreen.

As a result of initial combat experience, the A-1's defensive armament was soon increased. The ventral position was revised to accommodate two MG 15s, while further weapons were fitted to fire laterally from the cockpit sides. The maximum bombload consisted of 28 110-lb (50-kg) bombs carried in the two internal bays, with four 220-lb (100-kg) bombs carried externally. Maximum speed was a creditable 280 mph (450 km/h).

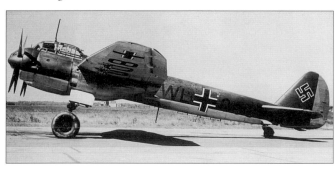

Above: This is one of the 10 Ju 88A-0 aircraft, completed with four-bladed propellers. Visible under the wing is the airbrake.

Left: Production of the Ju 88 was undertaken at a massive level from the outset. This is the scene at Aschersleben, where Junkers built fuselages before shipment to Bernburg for final assembly. Other Junkers plants were Halberstadt (wings) and Leopoldshall (tails).

Believed to be the fourth production aircraft, this Ju 88A-1 is seen at Bernburg, with a Ju 86G in the background. The aircraft has yet to be fitted with its defensive armament.

Bomber versions

Of all the theatres in which the Ju 88 fought, the one most closely associated with the type is the Mediterranean. This Ju 88A-4 displays the white fuselage band worn by all Axis aircraft in the theatre.

Ju 88 bombers served in all theatres of Germany's war, gaining a reputation for survivability in the face of enemy fighters. Development as a bomber resulted in a large array of sub-variants.

Backbone of the Luftwaffe's Kampfgruppen, the Ju 88A bomber entered service with KG 30 in September 1939. The initial Ju 88A-1s differed little from the Ju 88A-0 pre-production aircraft. As a new combat aircraft, it suffered from its fair share of problems, chiefly concerning the undercarriage and divebrakes. These were swiftly rectified. The A-1 spawned three sub-variants, the A-2 with Jumo 211G-1 engines (of similar power to the A-1's Jumo 211B-1s) and attachments for jettisonable rocket packs for boosted take-offs, and the A-3, which was a dual-control variant for conversion training. The Ju 88A-9 was a tropicalised A-1.

What was to become the definitive bomber variant, the Ju 88A-4, began development in early 1940 and was to be powered by the more powerful Jumo 211F and 211J engines. At the same time, the Junkers engineers added a further 5 ft 4¼ in (1.63 m) in wingspan to improve load-carrying, changed the ailerons from fabric to metal covering, and beefed up the main undercarriage.

However, the new powerplant was not ready in time, so the A-4's airframe was married to the original A-1 engines to create the A-5. It was this

version which saw widespread use during the Battle of Britain. The A-5 was further developed as the Ju 88A-7 dual-control trainer, Ju 88A-10 tropicalised bomber and the A-6 anti-balloon aircraft. The latter was produced specifically for the attacks on Britain, much of which was heavily defended by barrage balloons. The A-6 employed the *Kuto-Nase* device, a fender running from wingtip to ahead of the nose, with a balloon cable-cutter. The Ju 88A-6 was intended to scythe through the balloon groups, clearing the way for following bombers. In the event the *Kuto-Nase* ate perilously into the aircraft's performance, rendering it vulnerable to fighters. Most

had the equipment removed and served either as standard bombers or as anti-shipping aircraft (Ju 88A-6/U).

Ju 88A-4s appeared in large numbers from late 1940, the first aircraft having Jumo 211F-1 engines rated at 1,350 hp (1007 kW) before the definitive Jumo 211J-1 (of the same power) was installed. The armament was improved through the substitution of 7.92-mm MG 81

*Above: The **Totenkopf** (death's head) badge identified **KG 54**, which operated this Ju 88A-5 on standard bomber duties. After action in the Battle of Britain, **KG 54** served in Russia, before returning to the West in 1944 for nocturnal raids on Britain.*

*Below: The main undercarriage of a Ju 88A-4 rotates as it retracts on take-off from a Sicilian base. Note the carriage of four **SC 250** bombs on the external racks. A further 10 **SC 50**s could be carried internally.*

Ju 88B – bug-eyed bomber

Appended to the original proposals for the Ju 88 bomber was a further proposal for the Ju 88B, which featured a deeper and more extensively glazed cockpit section. This offered good visibility with reduced drag. The concept was initially shelved, but was resurrected in early 1939 when the RLM ordered Junkers to pursue the Ju 88B as a low-priority programme, specifying the use of BMW 139 (later BMW 801) radial engines. Based on the Ju 88A-1, a single prototype (D-AUVS) was built, first flying in early 1940. Ten pre-production Ju 88B-0s followed, based on the Ju 88A-4 airframe. The variant was not ordered into production to avoid disruption to the Ju 88A lines, but some of the Ju 88B-0s were converted for reconnaissance and used operationally by the Aufklärungsgruppe des Oberbefehlshabers der Luftwaffe, the air force high command reconnaissance unit. One was subsequently used as a development aircraft for the Ju 188.

Above: A trio of Ju 88A-4s from III./LG 1 is seen over the Mediterranean in 1942. The aircraft have the bulged rear canopy glazing which allowed easier firing of the twin MG 81 defensive guns.

Right: This is one of the Ju 88B-0s operated by the Aufkl./Ob.d.L on reconnaissance tasks. With its new front fuselage and BMW 801 radials, the B offered better performance than the A.

machine-guns instead of the MG 15s. Other armament configurations included a single 13-mm MG 131 installation. The glazing was bulged from mid-1941 to provide more room for the gunner. Internally, the A-4 dispensed with the forward bomb bay in favour of more fuel, and bombloads were

usually carried on the four external racks inboard of the engine nacelles (two 1,102-lb/500-kg bombs or four 551-lb/250-kg bombs).

All subsequent variants were based on the A-4 airframe, the third major bomber production version being the Ju 88A-14. This was similar to the A-4 but

had improved armour protection for the crew and 20-mm MG FF cannon in the gondolas of some aircraft. Other variants based on the A-4 included the A-8 (a few early aircraft with balloon cable-cutting equipment), A-12 and A-16 (dual-control trainers) and the A-15. The latter had the ventral gondola removed and a bulged wooden bomb bay fairing accommodating 6,614 lb (3000 kg) of weapons.

In the desert A-4s were tropicalised locally (designated A-4/Trop) or built as such (A-11). A number of aircraft were modified as Ju 88A-13s for low-level close air support with

dive-brakes deleted, extra cockpit armour and up to 16 forward-firing guns, including podded weapons carried on the wing racks. Finally, some bombers were modified for the carriage of two LT F5b aerial torpedoes under the wings as the Ju 88A-4/Torp, and others were built to this standard as Ju 88A-1/s.

Operational history

KG 30's Ju 88As were involved in the fighting over Denmark and Norway in 1940, and the type also saw action in France. However, it was the Battle of Britain that marked the first large-scale use of the type, serving with KGs 1, 4, 30, 51, 54 and LG 1. In early 1941 Ju 88s were serving in the Mediterranean, performing attacks on Malta and against Allied shipping. Anti-shipping operations were also conducted from French bases into the Atlantic. Virtually all of the Ju 88A units saw action on the Russian Front during the long campaign, usually alternating with Mediterranean service. By 1945 a few aircraft were still in service with KGs 26 (Norway) and 66 (specialist pathfinder unit), and LG 1 (Belgium and northern Germany).

Ju 88As also flew with the air arms of Finland, Hungary, Italy and Romania as part of the Axis cause, although Finland and Romania flew their aircraft against the Germans in the last months of the war. Another air arm to turn the aircraft on its former masters was that of France, which in 1944/45 flew Ju 88A-4s left behind by the retreating Luftwaffe.

Left: This Ju 88A-10 is from the Geschwaderstab (staff flight) of Lehrgeschwader 1. Tropicalised aircraft were fitted with sand filters for the engines, sunblinds in the cockpit and desert survival packs. As in the West, anti-shipping was the primary activity of the 'Dreifinger'.

Anti-ship attack

The Ju 88 was an effective anti-ship platform, notably in the Mediterranean and around the Norwegian coast. The Ju 88's finest hour came in July 1942, when Ju 88As flying with III./KG 30 inflicted severe damage against the ill-fated convoy PQ 17 taking arms to Russia. Ju 88s were modified to carry torpedoes, while others had radar. Both versions had a reduced three-man crew.

Left: The Ju 88A-17 and A-4/Torp were dedicated torpedo-carriers, with a pair of PVC racks under the wings.

Right: For the anti-shipping mission some Ju 88s carried FuG 200 Hohentwiel search radar. The Wellenmüster disruptive wave pattern was oversprayed.

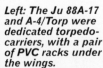

Fighter versions

Although not entering large-scale production until the autumn of 1943, the Ju 88 fighter variants were to be of enormous importance to the Luftwaffe, both as ground-attackers and in the nocturnal war against the RAF.

With its good speed and agility, the Ju 88 was recognised from the outset as having considerable potential as a heavy day- or night-fighter. However, such was the priority afforded to Ju 88A bomber production that fighter development was undertaken only on a limited basis. Furthermore, the Luftwaffe believed that it already had an excellent heavy fighter in the Messerschmitt Bf 110.

In the summer of 1939 the Ju 88 V7 was modified to a trial Ju 88C *Zerstörer* configuration with three MG 17 machine-guns and a single 20-mm MG FF cannon firing through the nose panels. Subsequent trials proved the Ju 88 to be a stable gun platform, ideal for the long-range intruder and anti-shipping roles.

Meanwhile, Junkers had schemed a *Zerstörer* model (Ju 88C-1) based on the Ju 88B, powered by BMW 139 radials (later switched for the more powerful BMW 801). Junkers was instructed to proceed slowly with this variant, but in the event the BMW 801s were needed for Fw 190 production, and the first fighter variant became the Ju 88C-2 which returned to the trusty Jumo 211 engines.

A small number of Ju 88C-2s was built, converted from Ju 88A-1 airframes with a solid nose, armour and retention of the aft bomb bay. They served on anti-ship duties with

Zerst./KG 30 and, from July 1940, on night intruder missions over England with II./NJG 1. This very limited service continued until October 1941, when the Ju 88C-2s transferred to the Mediterranean. Around this time the Ju 88C-4 was introduced, built as a fighter from the outset and based on the long-span airframe and Jumo 211F/J powerplant of the Ju 88A-4. Armament was increased by two MG FF cannon mounted in the ventral gondola (able to be replaced by cameras for armed reconnaissance), while podded guns could be carried under the wings. The C-3 and C-5 designations covered trials aircraft powered by BMW 801s.

In early 1942 the major C version entered production, the C-6. This featured better armour but was otherwise similar to the C-4. The importance of the Ju 88 fighter began to increase from this juncture, beginning with KG 40's anti-shipping oper-

Above: Essentially a Ju 88C-6b with BMW 801 radial engines, the Ju 88R-1 was distinguished by its more curved engine nacelles. This aircraft landed at Aberdeen on 9 May 1943, allowing the British a close look at the FuG 202 Lichtenstein B/C radar (not fitted here).

Left: Converted from the second pre-production bomber, the Ju 88C V1 had a crude gun installation which poked through metal panels in the 'beetle-eye' nose.

ations from France, which also encompassed attempts to intercept aircraft being ferried at night to North Africa. In late 1942 the first radar-equipped Ju 88C-6b aircraft began to appear, equipped with FuG 202 Lichtenstein B/C radar for night-fighter work. Shortly after this, the Ju 88R-1 made its debut, this being a C-6b but powered by BMW 801MA radials (the R-2 was similar except for BMW

Above: The day-fighter Ju 88C-6 packed a heavy punch in the form of three MG FF cannon and three MG 17 machine-guns.

Below: On the Russian Front the Ju 88C-6 was employed primarily as a train-buster, notably during the first half of 1943. The solid gun nose was often painted with mock glazing to confuse enemy fighter pilots into thinking it was a regular bomber. This one served with 4.(Zerst.)/KG 76.

The C-6b and C-6c were the first true night-fighter (as opposed to night intruder) variants. This C-6c has the pair of upwards-firing schräge Musik cannon which could be fired into the unprotected belly of a bomber (albeit only from close range).

801D engines). In early 1943 day-*Zerstörer* Ju 88C-6s assumed an important train-busting role on the Russian Front. In late 1943 the Ju 88C-6c night-fighter was introduced, with FuG 220 Lichtenstein SN-2 radar that could 'see' through the Window (chaff) dropped by RAF bombers. By this time, fighter production had been afforded top priority, with the result that around 3,200 Ju 88Cs were produced. The final variants were the Ju 88C-7a *Zerstörer* with a central cannon tray replacing the offset gondola, similar C-7b with wing bomb racks, and the C-7c with BMW 801 engines and MG 151/20 cannon in the nose.

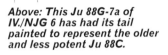

Above: This Ju 88G-7a of IV./NJG 6 has had its tail painted to represent the older and less potent Ju 88C.

Right: In later variants (like this G-7a) the Hirschgeweih (stag's antlers) antennas of the FuG 220 were canted to reduce interference. The bulge above the cockpit housed FuG 350 Naxos Z, which homed on H₂S radar emissions.

Definitive night-fighter

Although it continued to serve until the end of the war, it was obvious from the summer of 1943 that the Ju 88C-6c was straining to maintain performance under the increasing burden

The ultimate night-fighter was the Ju 88G-7c, which had FuG 340 Berlin N-1a radar. This set was the first German airborne radar to have a dish antenna, and was derived from the RAF's H₂S radar. The latter had been acquired in December 1942.

of equipment it was expected to carry. Accordingly, a BMW 801-powered Ju 88R-1 was modified as the Ju 88 V58, with the larger, angular fin tail surfaces of the Ju 188 and fitted with an armament of six MG 151/20 cannon (two in the nose and four in a ventral tray). The production Ju 88G-1 version dispensed with the nose cannon, as these blinded the pilot when fired, and was fitted from the outset with FuG 220 radar. It also featured FuG 227 Flensburg, a wing-mounted antenna array

which homed on the Monica tail-warning radar of RAF bombers. G-1s entered service in early 1944.

Following was the G-4, which standardised on equipment retro-fitted to G-1s, and the G-6a, which had BMW 801G engines. Upward-firing MG 151/20 cannon were often fitted, as was a rear-facing FuG 220 radar to provide tail warning. The G-6b designation covered aircraft provided with FuG 350 Naxos Z homing antennas.

Jumo 213A engines provided the power for the Ju 88G-6c, distinguished by a forward row of cooling gills on the cowling and flame dampers covering the exhaust stubs. The upward-firing

cannon were moved forward and internal fuel capacity was reduced to maintain centre of gravity.

By the end of 1944 the Ju 88G-7 was entering service in tiny numbers, powered by Jumo 213E engines with MW 50 water-methanol boosting, slightly increased fuel capacity and the ability to carry a single drop tank. Four primary radar installations were flown in G-7s, beginning with FuG 220 in the G-7a. The G-7b initially featured FuG 228 Lichtenstein SN-3, but when this was jammed by the Allies the FuG 218 Neptun VR radar was substituted, this featuring a *Morgenstern* (morning star) antenna often partially enclosed in a wooden nosecone. The final night-fighter version was the G-7c, with FuG 340 Berlin N-1a radar. Only about 10 of these reached combat.

To make full use of their capabilities, Ju 88Gs were routinely used as fighter controllers, guiding less well-equipped Bf 109s and Bf 110s towards their target. In late 1944 several Ju 88Gs were switched to day ground-attack sorties in a futile effort against the onrushing Red Army.

Long-range *Zerstörer*

The Ju 88G-10 was developed as an ultra long-range heavy fighter, based on the standard Ju 88G but with an additional 9-ft (2.74-m) fuselage section aft of the wing for increased fuel capacity. Power came from the Jumo 213A-12 engine. Very few were completed, and all were redirected to the Mistel programme. When mated with an Fw 190A-8 (itself with extra tanks), the result was the Mistel 3C or S3C trainer.

Reconnaissance and attack versions

The prototype Ju 88P carried a KwK-39 cannon, inclined slightly downward to decrease the dive angle needed to aim it.

As the war progressed, the basic Ju 88 airframe was developed for a wide range of tasks. Photographic reconnaissance was an obvious duty for the aircraft, but it was also fielded as a dedicated anti-armour weapon, long-range ocean patroller and high-altitude pathfinder.

During summer 1942 the Red Army, fighting for its life against the Germans, introduced the T-34 tank in huge numbers, and immediately the tide began to turn against the Wehrmacht. A weapon to destroy Soviet armour became of paramount importance. Junkers was instructed to investigate fitting large-calibre weapons to the Ju 88 as part of the ongoing work undertaken by the Versuchskommando für Panzerbekämpfung (anti-tank trials command), which was also testing weapons on the Bf 110, Hs 129 and Ju 87. Initially, the 'Ju 88N' was proposed, a Ju 88C carrying a Nebelwerfer (a six-barrelled recoilless shell weapon). This showed no promise, so Junkers turned to the 75-mm KwK-39 Kampfwagen-Kanone.

A Ju 88A-4 was modified with its ventral gondola removed and the weapon mounted in a huge fairing, which extended a long way aft to house a rearward-facing defensive position with an MG 81Z twin 0.311-in (7.92-mm) machine-gun installation. Designated Ju 88P V1 and nicknamed 'die dicke Bertha' (Fat Bertha), the aircraft first flew in the summer of 1942. Firing

Below: In an attempt to overcome the poor firing rate of the Ju 88P-1's gun, the P-2 and P-3 (illustrated) employed a pair of BK 3,7 weapons – an airborne version of the 37-mm Flak 38 gun.

trials demonstrated the promise of the concept, although the extra drag and weight made the aircraft extremely unwieldy. It would be highly vulnerable in the face of enemy fighters, so the entire cannon fairing was fitted with explosive bolts so that it could be jettisoned as a whole. The KwK-39 had to be hand-loaded, with the result that only two rounds could be fired on each pass.

Production Panzerjäger

Nevertheless, a small number of Ju 88P-1s was built, featuring a solid nose and improved armament in the shape of the 75-mm PaK 40 or BK 7,5 cannon, which had electro-pneumatic loading. The P-1s, flown by the Panzerjagd-kommando Weiss (named after its leader, Major Otto Weiss), entered service in early 1943 on the southern sector of the Russian Front. The Ju 88P unit later became Panzerjagdstaffel 92. Several successes were achieved, but service was generally unsatisfactory due to the low rate of fire of the cannon and vulnerability of the aircraft.

Smaller calibre weapons were introduced in further Ju 88Ps, beginning with the Ju 88P-2 which introduced a pair of 37-mm BK 3,7 cannon,

mounted offset to port. The P-3 was similar, but with additional crew protection, while the Ju 88P-4 introduced a smaller and less draggy fairing, housing a single 50-mm BK 5 cannon.

P-2s and P-4s were evaluated as bomber-destroyers, by both day and night, but the sluggish performance rendered the type virtually useless in this role.

Reconnaissance

When the Luftwaffe entered the war, the Dornier Do 17P was its principal long-range reconnaissance platform. The Ju 88A offered far better performance, and specialist reconnaissance versions began to enter service in summer 1940 under the Ju 88D designation

Above: In addition to the anti-tank weapons of the Ju 88P, cannon also appeared on Ju 88s in the form of the 20-mm MG FF carried by some Ju 88A-14s for anti-shipping duties. This installation required the removal of the bombsight.

Right: The 75-mm BK 7,5 (modified PaK 40) was a lethal weapon when employed correctly. Unfortunately, it could also be detrimental to the carrier due to its massive muzzle compression. Despite the long muzzle brake, it was not unknown for the Ju 88's nose to be crumpled or its propellers bent by the blast.

Left: The lack of a bombsight fairing on this aircraft suggests that it is a Ju 88T-1, the reconnaissance version of the high-performance Ju 88S. A small number was delivered from early 1944, surviving to the end with at least three units.

Right: This Ju 88D-5 carries drop tanks under the wings. Note the standard three-camera installation with two Rb 50/30s and one Rb 75/30.

(preceded by a few Ju 88As modified for the purpose). They were based on the Ju 88A-4 airframe and, like the bomber, were to have been powered by the Jumo 211J-1 engine. Like the bomber variants, the first aircraft appeared with earlier engines, and were therefore equivalents of the Ju 88A-5.

For the reconnaissance role the forward bomb bay was replaced by a fuel tank and the divebrakes and wing racks removed. Cameras were mounted in a heated central fuselage bay, with corresponding windows in the lower fuselage side. A few pre-production D-0s were built, leading to the first major production version, the D-2. This reinstated the wing

racks for the carriage of drop tanks on long-range missions. Many were tropicalised as D-2/Trops, retrospectively redesignated as D-4s.

Power for the D-2 came from the Jumo 211B-1, G-1 or H-1, but when the Jumo 211J-1 became available, production switched to the Ju 88D-1, which was virtually identical apart from the uprated engines. Tropicalised versions were produced as the D-1/Trop and the D-3.

The reconnaissance aircraft retained a crew of four, but defensive armament was reduced to just three MG 15 machine-guns. The camera installation of most D-1s and D-2s comprised a high-altitude Rb 50/30 and low-altitude Rb 20/30. Some

D-2s had a three-camera installation, and this became standard fit for the Ju 88D-5, produced alongside the D-1. Around 1,500 Ju 88Ds were built, and the variant saw widespread service in all theatres. In addition to the Luftwaffe, it served with Hungary and Romania.

In the spring of 1944 the Ju 88D was replaced in production by the Ju 88T, a reconnaissance derivative of the Ju 88S and similarly lacking the ventral gondola. A few Ju 88Ts served in the reconnaissance role until the end of the war.

The stretched 'H'

One unusual reconnaissance variant was the three-man Ju 88H-1, a strange machine

which married the wings of the Ju 88G-1 fighter (complete with BMW 801 radial engines) and the camera-equipped fuselage of the Ju 88D-1. The fuselage was considerably stretched fore and aft of the wing, resulting in an elongated machine which could accommodate considerable extra fuel, giving a range of 3,200 miles (5150 km). FuG 200 Hohentwiel radar was fitted in the nose, and the ventral gondola was replaced by a small fairing, housing fixed forward-firing WT 81Z 7.92-mm twin gun armament. Ten were built and were used for reconnaissance over the Atlantic. A similar number of Ju 88H-2s was built, this being a *Zerstörer* version with six 20-mm MG 151 cannon in place of the radar.

Above: The Ju 88S was distinguished by its smoothly curved nose glazing, replacing the flat-pane 'beetle eye' arrangement of earlier bombers. The production aircraft also lacked any forward-firing or ventral armament, apart from the few S-2s produced which had two aft-firing 7.92-mm MG 81s added in the rear of the underfuselage weapons pannier.

Ju 88S – high-altitude pathfinder

To improve the Ju 88's performance, notably at high altitude, Junkers developed the Ju 88S. The first prototype, flown in late 1942, introduced a curved glazed nosecone and BMW 801 radials, and was followed by a batch of similar S-0s. In late 1943 the first Ju 88S-1 appeared, featuring BMW 801G radials with nitrous oxide boost, ventral gondola removed (although a fairing for the bombsight was retained), gun armament reduced to just one 13-mm MG 131, and a three-man crew. With a top speed of 379 mph (610 km/h), this variant entered service with I./KG 66, which employed it as a pathfinder and on single-aircraft specialist bombing missions. Subsequent versions were the Ju 88S-2 with turbo-supercharged BMW 801TJ engines and a wooden ventral pannier replacing the bomb bays and racks, and the Ju 88S-3 which was similar to the S-1 but with Jumo 213 engines. Only a few were built during 1944 before the project was terminated.

This Ju 88S-1 served with I./KG 66 on pathfinder duties from Dedelsdorf in 1944/45. It was equipped with the Y-Gerat radio beam equipment and wears nocturnal camouflage. The unit also operated Ju 88As, Ju 188s and Do 217s.

Junkers Ju 90/290
Giant from Dessau

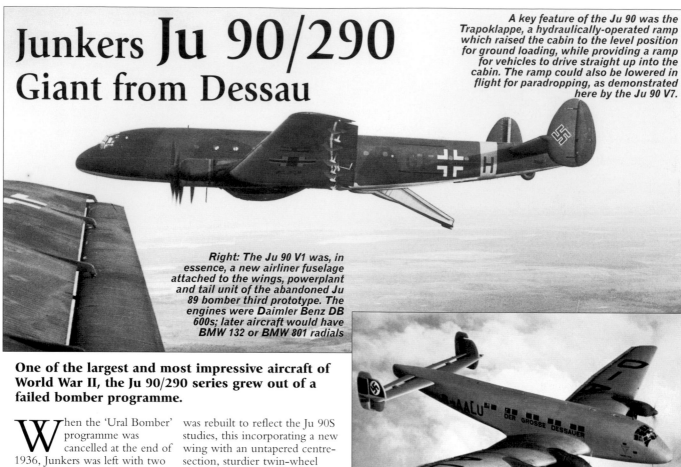

A key feature of the Ju 90 was the Trapoklappe, a hydraulically-operated ramp which raised the cabin to the level position for ground loading, while providing a ramp for vehicles to drive straight up into the cabin. The ramp could also be lowered in flight for paradropping, as demonstrated here by the Ju 90 V7.

Right: The Ju 90 V1 was, in essence, a new airliner fuselage attached to the wings, powerplant and tail unit of the abandoned Ju 89 bomber third prototype. The engines were Daimler Benz DB 600s; later aircraft would have BMW 132 or BMW 801 radials

One of the largest and most impressive aircraft of World War II, the Ju 90/290 series grew out of a failed bomber programme.

When the 'Ural Bomber' programme was cancelled at the end of 1936, Junkers was left with two examples of the Ju 89 heavy bomber, and components for a third. The company obtained permission to mate the wings and tail assembly with a new fuselage optimised for transport. The result was the Ju 90 V1 (D-AALU – *der grosse Dessauer*), which made its first flight on 28 August 1937, this to be followed by three prototypes and 10 Ju 90B-1 production airliners.

The V2 (D-AIVI) and V3 (D-AURE) flew during early 1938, following the crash of the V1 in February. The V3's career was also short, ending during route-proving trials for Deutsche Luft Hansa in December. Despite this inauspicious start, DLH confirmed their order for eight of the airliners, the other two being purchased by South African Airways, which specified Pratt & Whitney Twin Wasp engines. In the event, these two Ju 90Z-2s were never to be delivered to SAA, but those of DLH went into service from late 1938 onwards.

These aircraft were completed to the original design, with the Ju 89 wing featuring the Junkers 'double-wing' flap arrangement. However, in early 1939, the V4

was rebuilt to reflect the Ju 90S studies, this incorporating a new wing with an untapered centre-section, sturdier twin-wheel undercarriage and enlarged and more elegant vertical fins.

In late 1939, Junkers spread its Ju 90 programme over three offices, Dessau retaining prototype construction and flight trials while Letnany in Czechoslovakia took on design, mock-up and static test work and Bernburg assumed production duties. In early 1940 the DLH aircraft were impressed into service with the Luftwaffe in the transport role, although later two were returned to the airline, while others went back to Junkers for participation in the Ju 90S (now called Ju 290) programme.

Developments in this direction had seen the V4 re-engined with the more powerful BMW 801 radial and the Ju 90 V7 fitted with an extended fuselage which not only gave the aircraft greater carriage potential, but also helped nagging yaw and centre of gravity problems. The Ju 90 V8 then introduced defensive armament in the shape of a dorsal turret, waist guns, tail gun and undernose gondola (one

forward- and one rearward-firing gun), for by now the type was being considered for the long-range maritime surveillance role. Finally, the Ju 90 V11 introduced angular fins, redesigned windows and wing. Although unarmed, it was now felt that the Ju 90S programme had been developed to the point that the aircraft could assume the designation Ju 290 V1.

Maiden flight

First flight of the aircraft occurred in August 1942, and immediate production began at Bernburg. Two Ju 290A-0 preproduction aircraft were first, followed by five Ju 290A-1s. Possessing similar armament to the Ju 90 V8, these aircraft were completed as transports and swiftly delivered to the Luftwaffe. So great was the need for transport aircraft, that even the Ju 290 V1 was impressed,

this and one of the A-0s dispatched quickly to help the relief of Stalingrad, where the V1 was lost and the A-0 badly damaged. At the same time, in January 1943, LTS 290 (later Transportfliegerstaffel 5) was established to operate the aircraft, plus survivors of the Ju 90 fleet.

Meanwhile, the need for a long-range maritime patroller was also great, and the Ju 290A-2 answered the call. Little was changed except for the addition of an aft dorsal turret, changes to navigation equipment and the addition of FuG 200 Hohentwiel search radar. Flying by the summer of 1943, the first example went to Rechlin for tests while two further machines were delivered to the newly-established Fernaufklärungsgruppe 5. Five Ju 290A-3s followed, these having low-drag Focke-Wulf gun turrets.

Five Ju 290A-4s were the next aircraft from the line, these introducing the Focke-Wulf turret in the forward dorsal position also. Armament for these comprised a single 20-mm MG 151 cannon. With A-2s, A-3s and A-4s in regular service, several operational shortcomings were noted, and these were rectified largely by the

One of the original Ju 90B-1s, then serving with LTS 290, comes under attack from RAF fighters in the Mediterranean. Noteworthy is the original wing, with kinked trailing edge and Junkers 'double-wing' flaps.

This Ju 290A-7 was captured intact by Allied forces and flown to the US for evaluation. The A-7 introduced a nose turret: in operational configuration it would have also featured search radar.

Ju 290A-5 version. Chief among these was the introduction of protection for the fuel tanks and heavy armour around the flight crew. The waist gun positions were improved and fitted with MG 151s in place of the MG 131 machine-guns used in earlier models. The crew complement went from seven to nine to provide more dedicated gunners.

The A-5 was the most numerous version with 11 examples, entering service in the spring of 1944 to general acclaim. 4./FAGr 5 formed around this time, but throughout its career the Gruppe rarely had even 20 aircraft on strength, totally inadequate for its taskings. This situation was further worsened by the withdrawal of three aircraft for special transport

duties. They were stripped of armour and armament at Finsterwalde and fitted with additional fuel tanks. So configured they left Odessa and Mielec for a non-stop flight to Manchuria with special cargo for the Japanese, before returning to Mielec with strategic materials that were in short supply in Germany.

Covert transports

Most of the Ju 290s, deprived of their true operational environment, were relegated to transport tasks. Perhaps with foresight, the patrollers had retained their Trapoklappe for emergency transport tasks, and this was used widely during the last year of the war. The clandestine unit I./KG 200 was a major

user, employing the type for long-range agent drops, the aircraft being hastily fitted with a trap-door in the lower fuselage.

Work had progressed on the maritime versions, the next development being the Ju 290A-7. This would have been a major type, with 25 aircraft laid down. It featured a bulbous glazed nose turret, which introduced another MG 151 cannon, raising total armament to one MG 131 and seven MG 151s. With Hohentwiel radar mounted above the glazed section, the Ju 290A-7 also introduced an offensive capability in the shape of pylons for Henschel Hs 293, Hs 294 or FX 1400 Fritz X anti-ship missiles. Production began shortly before FAGr 5's move from France, but only a few were completed at Bernburg.

Three Ju 290A-9s were also built – extended range patrollers with extra internal tankage and reduced armament to push the range to 5,157 miles (8300 km). Another aircraft built at this time was the sole Ju 290A-6, a pressurised personal transport for Hitler. Pressurisation was abandoned at an early stage, the aircraft being completed as a 50-seat transport.

One last A-variant deserves mention, this being the A-8 developed alongside the A-7. This differed principally in

The sole Ju 290A-6 was intended as a personal transport for Hitler. In April 1945 it made a flight to Spain, where it remained. For a few years in the 1950s it was flown by the Spanish air force.

adding two further dorsal gun positions (four in all) and a twin-MG 151 tail turret. Ten machines were laid down, but only two or three were completed before the Czech plant at Ruzyne was overrun by Soviet forces. However, the second pre-production aircraft was discovered mostly complete. Transported to the Letov factory, it was reassembled using other components from war spoils and flown in August 1946. Designated the L 290 Orel, it was offered to the Czech airline, which showed no interest. Although an Israeli buyer attempted to purchase the aircraft, it did not leave Czechoslovakia, and was finally scrapped in 1956 at Letnany.

Other versions of the Ju 290 were planned from late 1943 onwards, the most important being the Ju 290B bomber. Flying in the summer of 1944, it undertook flight trials in Czechoslovakia until March 1945. Before the Ju 290B-1 could enter production, the programme had switched to the B-2, which dispensed with the troublesome turrets and pressurisation. In fact similar to the A-8, no examples were completed before Ju 290 production was halted due to the lack of important materials. Left unbuilt were the Ju 290B MS for mine-clearing, Ju 290C transport/reconnaissance aircraft with redesigned loading ramp incorporating twin MG 151 cannon, Ju 290D bomber with Hs 293 control equipment and Ju 290E with internal bomb bays.

Ju 390 – the six-engined giant

The leader of the Ju 290 team, Dipl Ing Kraft, had realised that the Ju 290 could be easily scaled up by adding extra wing and fuselage sections, so early in 1942 work began on a six-engined enlarged version that could perform the transport, maritime reconnaissance or bomber role. Three prototypes were ordered to represent the three tasks and work began immediately, the V1 built at Dessau and the V2 at Bernburg. First flying in August 1943, the V1 (left) was powered by six BMW 801D engines, and had a wing span of 165 ft (50.30 m) and a length of 102 ft (31.1 m). The Ju 390 made extensive use of Ju 290A components, but added an extra set of main undercarriage units under the middle engines. These were used only to support the higher weights. The V1 was the transport prototype, and performed well, carrying a 22,045-lb (10000-kg) load over a distance of 4,971 miles (8000 km) at 205 mph (330 km/h). During 1944 it was sent to Prague-Ruzyne for flight refuelling trials, where it was to be used as a tanker for Ju 290As to extend their on-station time.

Meanwhile the V2 flew for the first time in October 1943, this having an even longer fuselage (110 ft 2 in/33.6 m). Equipped as a

maritime patroller, it had Hohentwiel radar and defensive armament (two dorsal turrets with MG 151, one MG 151 firing forward from the ventral gondola, one MG 151 in the tail, one MG 131 firing aft from the gondola and two MG 131s firing from lateral positions). As such it was delivered to FAGr 5 for evaluation in January 1944. After some short hops, its 32-hour endurance was put to the full during an Atlantic flight that took it from Mont-de-Marsan to within 12 miles (20 km) of the US coast near New York.

Bomber development centred on the Ju 390 V3, but this was a low priority due to Ju 290 production. Nevertheless, work continued on the Ju 390A bomber, powered by BMW 801E engines and featuring uprated armament including a four-gun turret in the nose and tail. Carrying its offensive load externally, the Ju 390A-1 was the subject of Japanese interest, the nation acquiring a manufacturing licence, but this proceeded no further.

Similarly, a high-altitude reconnaissance model with 181-ft 7-in (55.36-m) wing span was not built, and in the event the Ju 390 V1 and V2 remained the only examples constructed. Apart from the V2's remarkable flight across the Atlantic, the Ju 390 is best-remembered as the largest conventional aircraft ever built in Germany.

Junkers Ju 188

An improved '88

The Ju 188, basically a reworked Ju 88, incorporated many improvements over its predecessor. However, its late service entry due to the success of the Ju 88 meant that it had a brief and non-eventful war.

By the start of World War II, it had become clear to the Reichluftsfahrt-ministerium (RLM) that the Ju 88 was an outstanding aircraft and that any major redevelopment was unnecessary. However, since the Ju 88's inception in 1936, plans had been under way for a stretched Ju 85B and Ju 88B. In 1940, Junkers built a new crew compartment into the Ju 88B and, with the new 1,600-hp (1194-kW) BMW 801 radial engine, began flight testing. Apart from these changes, the aircraft was identical to its predecessor, the Ju 88A, and so the decision was made not to disturb Ju 88A production lines. The 10 Ju 88B-0 pre-production aircraft that had been built were modified as reconnaissance aircraft.

Work continued on a next-generation aircraft or 'Bomber B', but it soon became clear that the contenders – the Do 317, Fw 191 and Ju 288 – would not provide the Luftwaffe with the long-term aircraft it needed. Meanwhile, Junkers had continued to modify its Ju 88 and, in

September 1941, a new variant took to the air.

Changing design

The Ju 88 V27 had an airframe that resembled that of the Ju 88E-0 (a version of the Ju 88B-0 used for developmental purposes), but had extended outer wings, the new pointed tips increasing the span from 65.6 to 72.2 ft (20 to 22 m). The Ju 88 V44, flown in the spring of 1942, continued the improvements with an enlarged tail, the span of the tailplanes being increased and the fin and rudder being enlarged into an almost rectangular shape.

In October 1942, the decision was made to move staff from the Ju 288 and put full development resources into construction of the Ju 88 V44, now designated Ju 188 V1; by January 1943, a second prototype had flown. The RLM decreed that the initial production Ju 188A-0 should be a bomber, capable of both level- and dive-bombing, and fitted with the same slatted dive brakes and automatic pull-

out gear as the Ju 88A. Furthermore, to avoid delay due to engine shortages, the 181 would be powered either by the BMW 801 or the Jumo 213.

The first aircraft to leave the production lines were actually Ju 188E-0s and E-1s because they had BMW engines (the A was fitted with the Jumo 213). The E-0 and E-1 entered service with Ekdo d.Lw 188 and KG 6 in May 1943, the first operational Gruppe being I./KG 6, which began Pathfinder missions on 20 October 1943. By the end of the year, production of the Ju 188 was in full swing, with 283 aircraft having been built.

There were some differences between the initial production versions. While the A-1 and E-1 sub-types were both four-seat medium bombers with the same airframe, they had different

The BMW 801-powered Ju 188E series was delivered ahead of the Jumo 213-powered Ju 188A. This pre-production Ju 188E-0 was modified to act as a fast staff transport for General-Luftzeugmeister Erhard Milch.

dorsal turrets. The A-series had the EDL 151 with an MG 151/20 cannon, and the E-series had the originally proposed EDL 121 with the 13-mm calibre MG 131. In general, the A-series gave a slightly improved performance, especially when using the MW50 power-boosting system.

The A-3 version was a torpedo-bomber, able to carry two LT 1B or F5b torpedoes under the inner wings, and with a long bulge along the right side of the forward fuselage to accommodate the torpedo-aiming and steering gear. The equivalent BMW-engined version was the E-2 and this frequently had the dorsal turret omitted.

At the start of the programme, Junkers had proposed fitting the FA15 type of remotely-sighted and power-controlled tail barbette, housing an MG 131Z (twin 13-mm guns). This complex and weighty installation was flown in the Ju 188C-0, a converted A-0. However, poor aiming accuracy and reliability rendered the scheme worthless.

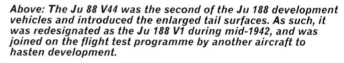

Above: The Ju 88 V44 was the second of the Ju 188 development vehicles and introduced the enlarged tail surfaces. As such, it was redesignated as the Ju 188 V1 during mid-1942, and was joined on the flight test programme by another aircraft to hasten development.

Top: A line-up of Ju 188D-2s of 1.(F)/FAGr 124 at Kirkenes, Norway. The Ju 188D-2 was intended primarily for the maritime strike and reconnaissance roles, and usually carried FuG 200 Hohentwiel radar.

The Luftwaffe's urgent need for a high-performance reconnaissance aircraft led to many Ju 188As being completed as Ju 188D-1 or D-2 aircraft. These had no forward-firing MG 151 cannon, only three crew, increased fuel capacity and a gross weight increased to 33,510 lb (15200 kg). These versions carried various arrangements of Rb 50/30, 70/30, NRb 40/25 or 50/25 cameras and the D-2 was invariably fitted with the FuG 200 radar for maritime operations. The BMW-powered equivalent was the Ju 188F-1 and F-2, the latter being the radar-equipped maritime aircraft.

To give the aircraft a defensive system behind the tail, the G-0 had a small manned MG 131 installation, but its arc of fire was poor. The G-2 bomber and the H-1 reconnaissance aircraft were then equipped with the FA 15 barbette but, by now, attention was turning to production of the superior Junkers Ju 388.

Combat experience

Junkers never did succeed in providing the Ju 188 with an all-round defensive armament. From the start of the Battle of Britain, it became obvious that the type

of fast bomber envisaged in the 1930s could not hold its own against modern Allied fighters.

In the autumn of 1943, work began on high-altitude Ju 188s with a pressurised crew compartment. Proposals were made for the Ju 188J *Zerstörer*, the 188K bomber and the 188L reconnaissance aircraft. This logical step was well received and in September 1943 Junkers was ordered to hasten these under a new 8-series RLM type number of 388 (thus these became the 388J, K and L). At the same time, Junkers was requested to use the same pressurised forward fuselage in the Ju 188S high-altitude intruder and 188T reconnaissance aircraft.

The S and T were to be devoid of defensive armament, relying on height and speed to avoid interception. Thus, they had an almost streamlined forward fuselage, the engines being Jumo 213E-1s fitted with GM-1 nitrous oxide power-boosting to give 1,690 hp (1260 kW) at 31,400 ft (9570 m). The S-1 could carry 1,763 lb (800 kg) of bombs internally and, with a full bombload, could reach 426 mph (685 km/h). The lighter T-1, with two large Rb cameras, could reach 435 mph (700 km/h) at the same height. Both variants

went into limited production from early 1944, but neither made a major impact on front-line units. In late 1944, the S-1 had its cabin pressurisation removed, and provision was made for the ground attack role. The new designation was Ju 188S-1/U and some went into action, usually with a crew of two.

From the outset, the Ju 188 enjoyed a reputation in the Luftwaffe which was, if anything, even greater than that of the Ju 88. It handled better, especially at high weights, and was able to make full use of the power of the BMW 801 and Jumo 213 engines. However, limited production – only 1,076 in all – meant that its impact was minor, most bomber versions operating in the anti-shipping

role from Denmark and Norway.

Even the reconnaissance aircraft accomplished little. No photographs were brought back of the prolonged and massive build-up of forces prior to D-Day, and reconnaissance flights over the British Isles were almost non-existent until the advent of the Arado Ar 234B in 1944.

After the war, the French Aéronavale, recognising the qualities of the type, used at least 30 overhauled, captured Ju 188Es and Fs in the land-based bomber role. They only had a short active life, but were subsequently used in valuable test programmes, including the development of advanced piston engines, turbojets and early guided missiles.

Torpedo-bomber versions of both A- and E-series aircraft were produced, this machine being a Ju 188E-2. Two 1,763-lb (800-kg) LT 1B or 1,686-lb (765-kg) LT F5b torpedoes could be carried beneath the wingroots, while guidance equipment was contained in a fairing on the side of the nose. FuG 200 radar was fitted.

Service
Only 1,076 Ju 188s were completed, compared to around 14,700 Ju 88s. They equipped just two complete Kampfgeschwadern (KG 6 and KG 2), and elements of three more (a few Staffeln from III./KG 26 and I./KG 66, and one Staffel from KG 200). The type also partially equipped elements of 10 Fernaufklärungsgruppen.

Maritime Ju 188s
Maritime versions of the Ju 188 included the torpedo-armed Ju 188A-3 and Ju 188E-2, and the reconnaissance-configured Ju 188D-2 and Ju 188F-2. All usually the FuG 200 unit.

Camouflage
This aircraft has pale blue-grey *Wellenmüster* sprayed over its standard green camouflage scheme. *Balkenkreuz* and *Hakenkreuz* are applied in outline form only.

Powerplant
As a reconnaissance derivative of the Ju 188A, the Ju 188D-2 retained the Jumo 213A-1 liquid-cooled 12-cylinder inline engines, rated at 1,766 hp (1316 kW) for take-off, or 2,240 hp (1669 kW) with MW-1 injection. The Ju 188 was designed so that the aircraft could be fitted with either Jumo 213 or BMW 801 'power eggs' on the production line, with no changes to the engine bearers.

Junkers Ju 188D-2

When it entered service, the Ju 188 was an immediate improvement over the Ju 88, yet it could have been in production much earlier, had the Ju 88's success not been so great. Relatively few Ju 188s entered service and they made little difference in a war that was already turning against Germany. Over half the aircraft went to reconnaissance units, for use either in an overland role, or as maritime patrollers with FuG 200 Hohentwiel radar. This is one of the latter, the exhaust stubs of the engine nacelles denoting a Jumo 213-powered Ju 188D-2. This example served with 1.(Fern) Staffel/Aufklärungsgruppe 124 at Kirkenes, Norway.

Crew
The Ju 188D-1 and D-2 saw the crew complement reduced from four to three, with the removal of the dedicated bomb aimer. This left the pilot, a flight engineer and a radar/wireless operator.

Wing
By comparison with the Ju 88B, the Ju 188 had a wing of greater span, with both wingtips and ailerons being extended outboard to give a distinctive pointed outline in plan view. The slotted dive-brakes of the V1 and V2 prototypes were omitted from production Ju 188 versions.

H8K2-L transport flying-boats had a crew of no fewer than nine: a commander, pilot, co-pilot, navigator/bow gunner, two radio operators, two flight engineers and rear gunner. Up to 64 passengers could be accommodated.

Kawanishi H8K 'Emily'

Long-range naval flying-boat

Though built in far smaller numbers than contemporary British Short Sunderlands and American Consolidated PBY Catalinas, the Kawanishi H8K was one of the outstanding flying-boats of World War II.

Soon after the first three Kawanishi H6K2s entered service in January 1938, the Imperial Japanese Navy issued a development contract to the company for a new large flying-boat to serve as a replacement for that aircraft, appreciating that it would be two or three years before a prototype would emerge. The estimate was fairly accurate, the Kawanishi H8K1 prototype making a first flight on the last day of December 1940 and while, like its predecessor, it was powered by four engines, in other respects it differed considerably. The high-set cantilever monoplane wing tapered in both chord and thickness from wing-root to wingtip and, served also to mount strutted and braced underwing stabilising floats at about two-thirds span. The hull was more conventional, losing the graceful lines of the H6K, and mounted at its rear was a tail unit with single fin and rudder.

Radial engine power

Power for the three prototypes and early production aircraft was provided by four Mitsubishi MK4A Kasei (Mars) 11 14-cylinder radial engines mounted in nacelles at the wing leading edge. Accommodation was provided for a crew of 10, and defensive armament comprised five 20-mm cannon in port and starboard blisters and in nose, dorsal and tail turrets, supplemented by three 0.303-in (7.7-mm) machine-guns in two side hatches and a ventral position. Comprehensive armour protection was provided and the bulk fuel tanks within the hull were partially self-sealing and incorporated a carbon dioxide fire-extinguishing system.

The H8K was, therefore, an advanced aircraft, and designed to a specification that called for a performance superior to that of the Short Sunderland. Not

Right: One of the largest aircraft of World War II, the H8K was of similar size to the RAF's Short Sunderland. In fact, the H8K's specification called for an aircraft to exceed the performance of the British flying-boat. The windows in the hull and angled nose cupola of this example indicate that it is the H8K1-L transport prototype.

Below: The first Kawanishi Navy Experimental 13-Shi Flying-Boat, prototype of the Japanese navy's H8K series, is seen here on an early test flight.

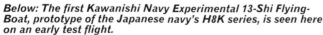

Above: In this view of the H8K prototype, the shorter nose of the aircraft is clearly evident. Interior high-speed taxiing and take off handling led to the major redesign of its hull.

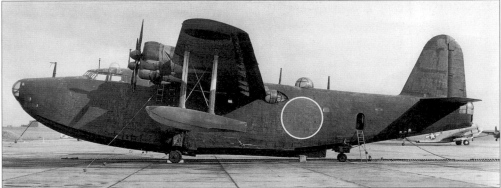

H8K2 426 was captured intact by the US Navy and test flown in the US post-war. Stored for many years this, the sole surviving 'Emily' was returned to Japan in 1979 for display.

surprisingly, Kawanishi was greatly disappointed with early tests which showed that the first of the H8K1 prototypes was dangerously unstable on the water. Modifications were begun immediately to rectify this situation, including an increase in hull depth of 1 ft 8 in (0.55 m). New tests showed a considerable improvement, and the second and third prototypes introduced the deeper hull and additional less major hull modifications, as well as an enlarged vertical tail-fin. Service trials conducted with the modified flying-boats showed acceptable water performance, still not as good as that of the H6K, but they demonstrated such a marked

improvement in flight characteristics that the navy had no hesitation in ordering the type into production in late 1941 under the designation Navy Type 2 Flying-Boat; this subsequently acquired the Allied codename 'Emily'. The type remained in operational use until the end of the war, by which time construction of all versions totalled 167.

More power and radar

The initial H8K1 production version (16 built), which was the same as the second and third prototypes, was soon superseded by the major series version, the H8K2 (112 built) which introduced more powerful Mitsubishi

MK4Q engines, a revised tail unit, more extensive armament and anti-surface vessel (ASV) radar. After being used for service trials, the original H8K1 prototype was given Mitsubishi MK4Q engines and converted to a transport role, then being redesignated H8K1-L; it was later developed as a production transport accommodating 29 to 64 passengers according to role, being powered by the MK4Q engines and having armament reduced to one 20-mm cannon and one 0.51-in (13-mm) machine-gun.

Ordered into production as the Navy Type 2 Transport Flying-Boat Seiku (clear sky), (naval designation H8K2-L), 36 examples of this variant were completed. Two early production examples were used as development aircraft for an

improved version with retractable wingtip floats and a retractable dorsal turret, being redesignated H8K3; they were later tested with 1,825-hp (1361-kW) Mitsubishi MK4T-B Kasei 25b engines under the changed designation H8K4, but no production aircraft were built. A transport variant, the H8K4-L, was also proposed.

As was the case with so many other Japanese types, production of the H8K was hampered by shortages of strategic materials in the latter stages of the war. Vital supplies were earmarked for the urgent building of fighter aircraft with which to defend Japan from the USAAF's bombers.

Operational debut

Early production aircraft entered service in 1942, the type's operational debut being made on the night of 4/5 March 1942, when two aircraft based at Wotje Atoll in the Marshall Islands, some 2,300 miles (3700 km) east of Pearl Harbor, were despatched to make a bombing attack on Oahu Island. This operation involved refuelling from a submarine at French Frigate Shoals in the Hawaiian Islands, and it seemed unjust that such an ambitious piece of planning was frustrated by heavy cloud cover over the target area.

Nevertheless, H8Ks proved highly effective and the type was deployed on bombing, reconnaissance and transport missions, its heavy defensive armament and comparatively high top speed making it a formidable adversary.

801st Kokutai H8K2

The Yokohama Kokutai was a typical H8K unit, operating from a variety of bases during the Pacific war, in such diverse locations as the Bay of Bengal, the Aleutians and the Solomon Islands. The unit was renamed 801st Kokutai in November 1942 and was the sole remaining Japanese naval flying-boat unit at the war's end.

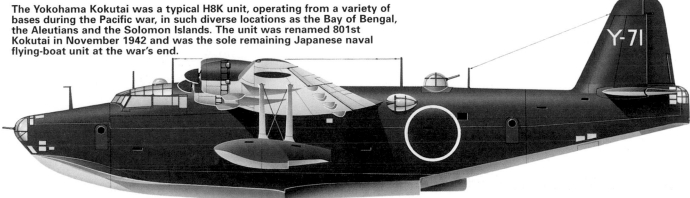

This Ki-61-I of the 37th Sentai was among those that fought in the last stages of the defence of the Philippines, before being forced to redeploy to Formosa and Okinawa in the last year of the war.

Kawasaki Ki-61 Hien

Germanic swallow

Heavily influenced in its design by a German engineer and powered by a licence-built version of a German in-line engine, the Ki-61 was unique among Japanese Army fighters of World War II.

Under the terms of the Treaty of Versailles Germany was forbidden to pursue the manufacture of military aircraft, with a result that young up-coming technicians sought employment overseas. Among the Germans who found employment in Japan was Dr Richard Vogt, under whose direction Kawasaki Kokuki Kogyo KK acquired the manufacturing rights of German liquid-cooled aircraft engines during the early 1930s. This association continued to flourish and in the late 1930s Kawasaki obtained the rights to build the Daimler-Benz DB600, and later the DB601. In April 1940 a Japanese team brought home drawings and a number of examples of the excellent DB601A 12-cylinder inverted-Vee liquid-cooled engine. After adaptation to Japanese manufacturing techniques, the first Kawasaki Ha-40 engine (as the licence DB601A was designated) was completed in July 1941, and four months later entered production as the 1,100-hp (820-kW) Army Type 2 engine.

Meanwhile, encouraged by the apparent superiority of European V-12 engine-powered aircraft, Kawasaki approached the Imperial Japanese Army with proposals for a number of fighter designs employing the new Ha-40 V-12

powerplant, and in February 1940 the Koku Hombu (Air Headquarters) ordered the company to undertake development of two aircraft, the Ki-60 heavy fighter and the Ki-61, a lighter all-purpose fighter. Priority was eventually afforded to the latter, emphasis swinging towards a preference for better performance at the expense of cockpit armour and fuel tank protection.

Design and manufacture of the prototype progressed swiftly, and this machine emerged from the Kagamigahara plant in Gifu Prefecture, north of Nagoya, in the same week that Japanese aircraft launched their great attack on Pearl Harbor in December 1941. Already a production line was being assembled, this confidence in the aircraft being confirmed by early flight trials with the prototype. Eleven additional prototypes were ordered and these introduced self-sealing fuel tanks

Ki-61-KAIs of the Akeno Flying Training School, the main home-based Hien training unit, are run up before another training sortie. KAI variants had strengthened wings and cannon armament.

which increased the wing loading to around 30 lb/sq ft (146.5 kg/m²), considerably more than Imperial Japanese Army air force pilots had generally experienced. Nevertheless the Ki-61 was popular among service evaluation pilots, who saw in its high diving speed an effective answer to American tactics of using a diving approach to combat. It was only after comparative trials in mock combat with a captured P-40E, an imported Bf 109E-3, a Nakajima Ki-43-II and a Ki-44-I that its superiority prompted the

Imperial Japanese Army to confirm a production order.

The thirteenth Ki-61, built from production tooling, was delivered in August 1942. Production accelerated slowly and by the end of the year 34 aircraft had been delivered under the designation Army Type 3 Fighter Model 1 Hien (Swallow), or Ki-61-I. Among these early aircraft two versions, the Ki-61-Ia and Ki-61-Ib, were produced; the former was armed with two 12.7-mm (0.5-in) Type 1 guns in the nose and two 7.7-mm (0.303-in) Type 89 guns

Although serving with the 3rd Chutai, 59th Sentai at Ashiya, Japan, in August 1945, this Ki-61-I Otsu (KAIb) carries an unusual hybrid of tail markings as a result of repairs to its rear fuselage and rudder. 22nd Sentai and Akeno Flying Training School markings are discernable.

Left: When first encountered over New Guinea, the Ki-61 was mistaken by American pilots for a version of the Messerschmitt Bf 109. A captured example undergoing evaluation is pictured.

Below: By Western standards the Japanese 53-US gal (200-litre) drop tank carried by all operational versions of the Ki-61 was a crude store, which reduced its maximum speed by around 50 mph (80 km/h) but increased the range of the Ki-61-II KAIa from 684 miles (1100 km) to 995 miles (1600 km).

in the wings, and the latter with four 12.7-mm (0.5-in) Type 1 guns. The first service unit to take delivery of the Ki-61 in February 1943 was the home-based 23rd Dokuritsu Dai Shijugo Chutai (independent squadron) for pilot conversion training. The fighter made its combat debut over the north coast of New Guinea a couple of months later with the 68th and 78th Sentai (groups), and proved itself a better match for Allied fighters than the Ki-43 (which it was replacing), principally on account of its superior diving speed.

Early problems

Problems were however already being encountered in New Guinea where the hot, humid conditions were causing engine boiling on the ground, necessitating fast taxiing over the inadequate field taxiways. In the field of armament the Ki-61 was

also undergoing improvement despite the lack of an indigenous 20-mm cannon in production in Japan. Instead, later Ki-61-Ias and Ki-61-Ibs were adapted in the factory to accommodate imported Mauser MG 151 20-mm guns in the wings; two such weapons, installed on their sides, replaced the customary machine-guns. Later, when the Japanese Ho-5 20-mm gun became available, Takeo Doi took the opportunity to strengthen and simplify the wing structure, and in the Ki-61-KAIc, which started appearing in January 1944, the Ho-5 cannon also replaced the fuselage machine-guns. Later still, the Ki-61-I KAId featured two 30-mm Ho-105 guns in the wings but a return to 12.7-mm (0.5-in) Type 1 machine-guns in the nose. The KAI versions also introduced a fixed tailwheel in place of the retractable wheel previously fitted, and underwing

store pylons – made possible by the strengthened wing. Through 1944 production was concentrated on the Ki-61-I KAIc, and production rates, hitherto relatively low, considerably improved, with the result that by January 1945 2,654 Ki-61s had been produced.

When the Hien appeared over New Guinea the Allies temporarily lost their air superiority, and there were even reports among American pilots that the Japanese were apparently using Messerschmitt Bf 109s. Once the combat tactics favoured by the Japanese pilots had been fully assessed Allied pilots were warned to avoid diving attacks, and in due course the Ki-61, whose top speed was, after all, not spectacular, was mastered. As deliveries of the Hien were stepped up in 1944 the type was encountered in much larger numbers during the Philippine campaign of 1944-5 and over Okinawa and Formosa.

The Ki-61-II

Faced with demands for better performance, Takeo Doi was urged to adapt his aircraft to accommodate the new 1,500-hp (1119-kW) Ha-140 V-12 engine, and the first prototype Ki-61-II with this powerplant was completed in August 1943. At the same time the new aircraft introduced a wing of increased area and a modified cockpit canopy providing the pilot with improved field of view. However, the Ha-140 engine suffered a spate of problems and a number of Ki-64-IIs suffered wing failures. Nevertheless the Ministry of Munitions ordered the Ki-61-II into mass production as the

Army Type 3 Fighter Model 2 in September 1944.

After completion of 11 prototypes (of which only eight were tested) the rudder area was increased to offset the slightly longer nose, and the Ki-61-II KAI reverted to the Ki-61-I KAI wings, thereby reducing the likelihood of further airframe failures. Provided the Ha-140 engine continued to function smoothly, the new fighter demonstrated a much improved performance, being capable of a top speed of 379 mph (610 km/h) at 19,685 ft (6000 m), and a climb to 16,405 ft (5000 m) in six minutes. The Ki-61-II KAI was produced in two versions, the Ki-61-IiIKAIa with two 20-mm guns in the nose and two 12.7-mm (0.5-in) guns in the wings, and the Ki-61-II KAIb with a total of four 20-mm guns. A total of 374 Ki-61-II KAIs were produced, but owing to persistent engine troubles relatively few of these ever reached operational units and never supplanted the earlier Ki-61-I KAIs. The Ki-61-II KAI was, however, the only Imperial Japanese Army interceptor fighter with adequate armament that could reach the operating altitude of the Boeing B-29 bomber, and was therefore probably responsible for the biggest share in the destruction (by fighters) of these large bombers. The Ki-61-II KAI was dealt its final death blow on 19 January 1945, when B-29s almost totally destroyed the Akashi engine plant where the Ha-140 engines were being produced, and some 30 other completed aircraft were destroyed on the ground before service delivery.

Ki-100 – nimble radial-engined derivative

Fortunately, expedients had been examined by which to circumvent the engine problems associated with the Ha-140 engines, studies that had begun as early as November 1944, two months before the catastrophe at Akashi. Kawasaki was instructed to adapt the Ki-61-II KAI to mount the 1,500-hp (1119-kW) Mitsubishi Ha-112-II 14-cylinder radial. Amazingly, this was accomplished in less than 12 weeks. The new aircraft, a converted Ki-61-II KAI redesignated the Ki-100, first flew in prototype form on 1 February 1945. For all its bulk the new radial installation, as a result of lower weight and therefore reduced wing and power loadings, produced much improved handling characteristics and only slightly reduced performance. Moreover, the radial engine had already acquired an excellent reputation for reliability. Accelerated flight tests were followed by an order to adapt all the engineless Ki-61-II KAIs, and 272 Ki-100-Ias were delivered to home-based fighter units between March and June 1945. In service the Ki-100 was hailed by pilots and groundcrew as the best and most reliable Imperial Japanese Army fighter of the war and at least a match for the US Navy's Grumman F6F Hellcats which, by then, flew in Japan's skies. As soon as the Ki-100's success was established, Kawasaki started building the new aircraft from scratch, production aircraft first appearing in May 1945, but heavy raids on assembly plants severely reduced deliveries. Ki-100-Is were flown by the 5th, 17th, 111th. and 244th Sentais, a total of 390 (including the 272 converted Ki-61s and 12 new aircraft produced at Ichinomiya) being delivered. Pictured is a Ki-100-Ib, which introduced a cut-down rear fuselage to improve the pilot's visibility.

These Lavochkin La-5FNs, operated by the 1st Czech Fighter Regiment, were photographed on 11 September 1944 immediately prior to a flight from Proskurov in the Ukraine to Stubno.

Lavochkin La-5/7

Lavochkin's masterpiece

When the La-5 appeared in service it was the first Soviet fighter with superior performance to the Bf 109G. The most widely used series of radial-engined fighters in the Soviet air force inventory, 9,920 were built during the Great Patriotic War, followed until 1946 by some 5,753 improved La-7 fighters in several variants.

Czech air force La-7s are seen post-war, parked alongside a captured Ju 290A-8 which was restored to flying condition in August 1946.

Semyon Alekseyevich Lavochkin, pioneer of *delta drevesiny* (a form of wooden construction based on the pressure-moulding of thin birch veneers with plastic resin adhesives), teamed up with V. P. Gorbunov and M. I. Gudkov to form LaGG OKB in 1938. From it came the LaGG-1 and LaGG-3, which, although less than ideal, were built to the extent of 6,528 examples.

Lavochkin and his partners subsequently tried to produce a better fighter, but neither Gudkov nor Gorbunov seemed to make progress. However, inspiration came from an official order of August 1941 to try out the newly-qualified Shvetsov M-82 radial. It was potentially more powerful, needed no liquid

coolant system, and promised a lighter and cleaner installation. Gudkov reckoned a poor fighter today was worth dozens tomorrow, and put an M-82 into a LaGG-3. The result was poor. Lavochkin saw that a great deal of care was needed in fitting the wide radial into the existing fuselage and also in maintaining the airframe's centre of gravity limits. He worked closely with Shvetsov to ensure that the best installation was achieved.

Unfortunately, Lavochkin had no great standing in the Soviet hierarchy. Yakovlev's reputation was much higher, so he was given sole charge of the previously LaGG-dedicated GAZ-153 plant and told to turn it over entirely to Yak-1 and Yak-7 production. Lavochkin, mean-

while, had been turned out of his manufacturing area at GAZ-31 at Tbilisi in Georgia, because the factory manager knew that Stalin had lost patience with Lavochkin's efforts and had no wish to damage his career by co-operating with him. Lavochkin therefore completed his design in a small hut out on the airfield.

La-5 emerges

The basic LaGG-3 airframe remained little changed, the wooden wing retaining its slats, fabric-skinned metal ailerons and three protected fuel tanks between the spars. The fuselage was mostly of birch ply, with metal around the engine nacelle. The cockpit was unchanged, due to Lavochkin's lack of staff

and facilities, and the urgency of the programme.

The prototype, loosely called LaG-5 because Gorbunov was still nominally with the OKB, was completed in the final days of 1941. However, the intense cold meant that it was March before the first flight could be completed. The LaG-5 performed well, with the potential for fine manoeuvrability, but it was difficult to fly on landing and take-off.

Towards the end of March 1942, the improved LaG-5 was put up for official state testing. Lavochkin's own test pilot thought that the LaG-5 was outclassed by the rival Yak-7/M-82, but the state's top test pilot, I. Ye. Federov, flew both aircraft and declared the LaG-5

Such was the airframe commonality that LaGG-3s laid down in the factories could be converted to La-5s by minor modifications and installation of the M-82 radial engine.

Seen wearing the Luftwaffe's Balkenkreuz and swastika symbols, this La-5 was captured by German forces on the Eastern Front during the winter of 1943-44.

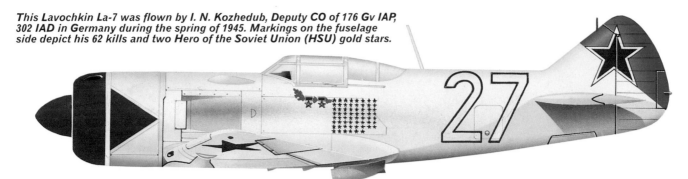

This Lavochkin La-7 was flown by I. N. Kozhedub, Deputy CO of 176 Gv IAP, 302 IAD in Germany during the spring of 1945. Markings on the fuselage side depict his 62 kills and two Hero of the Soviet Union (HSU) gold stars.

to be superior. After several days of testing and 'tweaking' by Federov and fighter pilot, A. I. Nikashin, the latter went to Stalin and reported that the LaG-5 was potentially as good as any fighter in the Soviet Union.

In April 1942 full-scale testing was underway and in July a priority directive was sent out ordering maximum-rate production of the new aircraft as the La-5, plus conversion of all incomplete LaGG airframes to take the radial engine. Within days dozens, and then hundreds, of engineers and mechanics appeared at Lavochkin's small hut, and he was given complete control of GAZ-21 at Gorki, previously the biggest of the LaGG factories, solely for the La-5. Teams were sent to dig incomplete LaGGs from the winter snow, fit ASh-82

engines (the M-82 was redesignated in honour of its designer at about this time) and fly them out.

Early aircraft suffered serious performance shortfalls due to shoddy workmanship. However, once these difficulties had been overcome, the aircraft began to take on Fw 190s and Bf 109Gs on equal terms.

Many improvements were gradually introduced, the most important being to cut down the rear fuselage and later to introduce the more powerful ASh-82F in the La-5F. Late in March 1943, Shvetsov produced the ASh-82FN (FN for directly-boosted), giving more power at all heights and, because it had direct fuel injection, no longer suffering engine cut-outs under negative *g*. The La-5, as the La-5FN, was now unmatched.

Perhaps the only serious shortcoming, apart from poor range and modest firepower, was the fighter's tricky handling on take-off and landing. Many La-5 trainer conversions had been completed in the field, but in August 1943 Lavochkin flew the factory designed La-5UTI. By this time, production had gradually been changing over to a fighter based on the La-5, but given sufficient improvements to

warrant the new designation La-7. The major difference lay in the adoption of a new wing with a substantial proportion of metal in its structure. The La-120 prototype for the La-7 was flown in November 1943, and fairly romped through its trials programmes. Production La-7s reached front-line units in spring 1944 and there were numerous wartime and post-war variants, including the La-7UTI.

A trio of La-5UTI (sometimes designated UTLa-5) two-seat trainers is photographed during a ferry flight from Zhitomir to Lvov. The second cockpit was inserted aft of the radio bay.

Propeller spinner
The spinner faired in the pitch-control mechanism and the propeller balance. On the front was a dog for the Hucks-type starter. The annular intake around the front of the engine was fitted with louvres to control the amount of air entering the powerplant.

Cockpit
The high setting of the cockpit provided the La-5 pilot with good all-round visibility apart from in front, as the long nose and supercharger trunking made taxiing difficult.

Gun armament
The La-5FN featured only two guns, these being 20-mm Shpital'ny-Vladimirov (ShVAK) cannon mounted in the upper fuselage decking and synchronised to fire through the propeller disc. Each weapon was provided with 200 rounds in tanks beneath the gun in the sides of the forward fuselage.

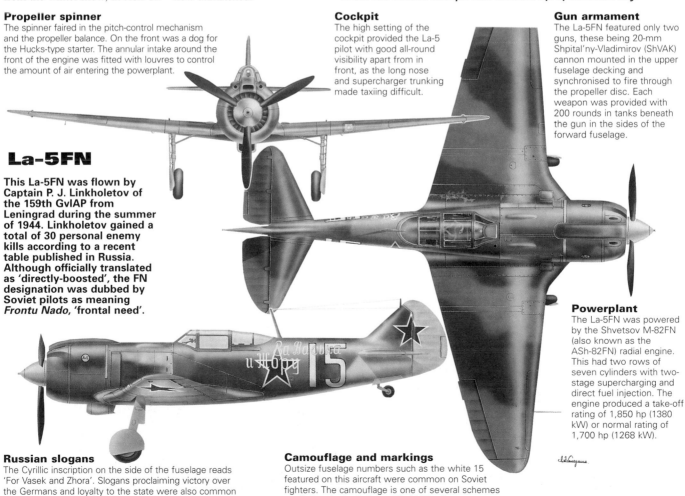

La-5FN

This La-5FN was flown by Captain P. J. Linkholetov of the 159th GvIAP from Leningrad during the summer of 1944. Linkholetov gained a total of 30 personal enemy kills according to a recent table published in Russia. Although officially translated as 'directly-boosted', the FN designation was dubbed by Soviet pilots as meaning *Frontu Nado*, 'frontal need'.

Powerplant
The La-5FN was powered by the Shvetsov M-82FN (also known as the ASh-82FN) radial engine. This had two rows of seven cylinders with two-stage supercharging and direct fuel injection. The engine produced a take-off rating of 1,850 hp (1380 kW) or normal rating of 1,700 hp (1268 kW).

Russian slogans
The Cyrillic inscription on the side of the fuselage reads 'For Vasek and Zhora'. Slogans proclaiming victory over the Germans and loyalty to the state were also common on Soviet aircraft of the era.

Camouflage and markings
Outsize fuselage numbers such as the white 15 featured on this aircraft were common on Soviet fighters. The camouflage is one of several schemes applied to the La-5 during World War II.

Lockheed Hudson

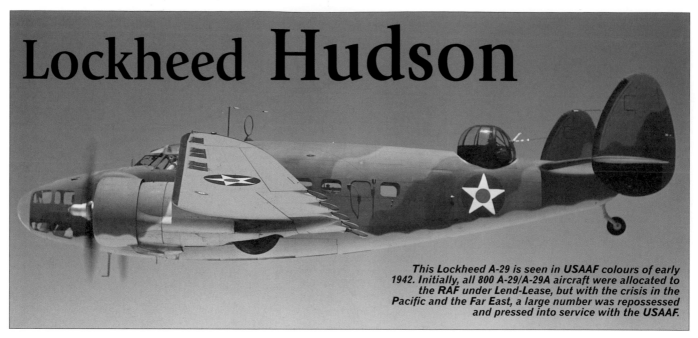

This Lockheed A-29 is seen in USAAF colours of early 1942. Initially, all 800 A-29/A-29A aircraft were allocated to the RAF under Lend-Lease, but with the crisis in the Pacific and the Far East, a large number was repossessed and pressed into service with the USAAF.

Maritime workhorse

Derived from the Lockheed Model 14 Super Electra airliner, the Hudson was designed to meet the requirements of the RAF and went on to be ordered in large numbers for use by Coastal Command.

In April 1938 the British Purchasing Commission visited the United States in search of good-quality American aircraft to bolster the strength of the RAF in its preparations for an inevitable war; the mission had $25 million with which to acquire its finds. At that time Lockheed engaged only 2,000 workers, and had eschewed the design of military types in favour of the commercial market. But in 10 days of frantic labour, the concern had cobbled together something that might whet the appetites of the Commission: this was nothing other than a mock-up of a Model L-14 provided with bomb-bay, bomb-aimer's panel and nose-glazing, and provision for various armaments.

RAF impressed

The British, with a need for a medium-range maritime patrol bomber for North Sea operations with RAF Coastal Command, were impressed. At the invitation of Sir Henry Self, the contracts director at the Air Ministry in London, Courtlandt Gross (brother of Robert Gross), travelled to the UK with Carl Squier, C. L. Johnson, Robert Proctor and R. A. van

Hake for consultations. The initial order for 175 Model B14s, now known as the Hudson, was signed on 23 June 1938, with provision for a maximum of 250 by December 1939; it was the largest military order gained by a US company to date. The first Hudson Mk I bomber took to the air on 10 December 1938, with the company, now numbering a workforce of 7,000, hard at work to fill the orders which rose in value, with additional orders for P-38s and B-34s, to an impressive $65 million.

First Mk Is arrive

Arriving by sea, the first Hudson Mk Is reached the UK on 15 February 1939. The type was powered by two 1,100-hp (820-kW) Wright GR-1820-

G102A Cyclones with two-speed Hamilton propellers. For reconnaissance duties the Hudson Mk I carried an F.24 camera, assorted flares and a bombload of up to 1,100 lb (499 kg) comprising either four 250-lb (114-kg) GP, SAP or AS, or 10 110-1b (50-kg) anti-submarine bombs; an overload of 12 112-1b (51-kg) Mk VIIc AS bombs could be carried, but in this event the bomb doors could not be fully closed. Modified with extra items at the

Lockheed-Vega subsidiary at Speke (Liverpool), the first Hudson Mk Is and Mk IIs were delivered to Wing Commander E. A. Hodgson's No. 224 Sqn at Leuchars, Scotland, in August 1939. Although less manoeuvrable than the lighter Avro Anson, the Hudson was considered by the squadron to be eminently suitable for its patrols over the North Sea as far as Norway, the Skaggerak and the German Bight. Cruising at 2,000 ft (610 m) at 190 mph

Below: Repossessed A-29s formate for the camera. Of 153 USAAF aircraft, 20 were diverted to the USN as PBO-1s. Note that these aircraft lack the Boulton Paul turret usually fitted to Hudsons.

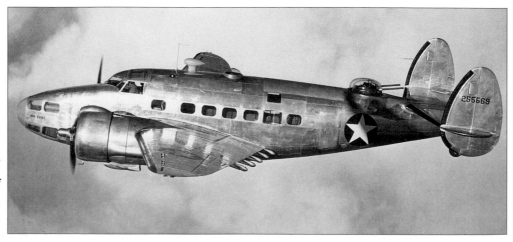

Right: The AT-18 gunnery trainer was equipped with a Martin turret, with a pair of 0.5-in (12.7-mm) machine-guns, and provision for target-towing. The later AT-18A was a navigation trainer.

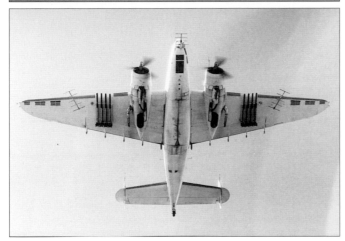

Above: No. 269 Sqn, Coastal Command, was an early recipient of the Hudson, replacing its Ansons with Hudson Mk Is from March 1940. The squadron was equipped with the Hudson until July 1945.

Left: Nos 517, 519, 520 and 521 Sqns, RAF performed a maritime reconnaissance role up to the end of the war. For air-sea rescue, No. 251 Sqn used Hudsons equipped to carry a lifeboat.

Above: This worm's eye view of a Hudson Mk VI gives an idea of the development that took place to boost the type's capability. Eight rocket projectile rails and ASV radar antennas are visible.

(306 km/h), a fuel consumption of 71 Imp gal (323 litres) per hour gave the Hudson an endurance of over six hours with 20 per cent reserves and a 570-mile (917-km) radius of action. Armament was light initially, and the twin 0.303-in (7.7-mm) nose guns, beam guns and the Boulton Paul Type 'C' Mk II turret were retrofitted during the autumn of 1939 and the spring of 1940.

The Hudson Mk II had Hamilton Standard Type 611A-12/3E50-253 constant-speed propellers, some structural improvements, and flush riveting and/or spot welding on exterior

Right: Post-war, surplus transport aircraft found a ready market. This former A-29, delivered to the RAAF during World War II, was bought by the proprietors of a Sydney morning daily newspaper.

surfaces for better aerodynamic performance. Only 20 were delivered to the RAF, followed by 428 Hudson Mk IIIs. The latter introduced the GR-1820-G205A engines in the Mk II airframe, and ventral and beam guns became standard. The first 187 became Hudson Mk III(SR) after the introduction of addi-

tional wing tanks, resulting in the subsequent 241 becoming Hudson Mk III(LR).

American designations

Following the introduction of Lend-Lease, the USAAC gave the designations A-28 and A-29 to Hudson variants for contractual purposes. Deliveries included 420 A-29s (and employed as bomber crew trainers) and 384 A-29As, the latter with convertible troop interiors. Those that entered RAF service were designated Hudson Mk IIIA and were similar to the Mk III(LR), but many of these Lend-Lease supplies went to Commonwealth air forces.

Further British contracts had already covered 30 Hudson Mk IVs, which switched to Pratt & Whitney R-1830-SC3G engines, and 409 Hudson Mk Vs, with these engines and all the definitive features of the Mk III. Through Lend-Lease, the RAF finally received 450 Lockheed A-28As, which it designated Hudson Mk VI.

Delivery of all these aircraft (and others direct to the RAAF, including the Hudson Mk IVA version) allowed the Coastal Command squadrons to maintain a high level of activity.

Those aircraft retained in the United States also performed

maritime tasks. USAAF A-29s not engaged in bomber crew training undertook anti-submarine patrols, and 20 went to the US Navy which designated them PBO-1. Some 24 of the US Army's A-29s were converted in 1942 for use in a photo-reconnaissance role, and were accordingly redesignated A-29B.

Transport variants

The designation C-63 was allocated by the USAAF to a projected cargo variant, but this was cancelled before any were built. The final variant procured by the USAAF was required as a trainer for air gunners, or as a target tug. These were generally similar to A-29As and were equipped with a Martin dorsal turret. Lockheed built 217 of them as AT-18s, followed by 83 AT-18As, as navigation trainers, with different internal equipment and the turret deleted. Three civilian Model 14s were impressed as C-111s.

Post-war, at least 36 Hudsons of various types found their way onto civil registers, especially in Australia and Canada, where they were employed as transports and aerial survey platforms. In the USA at least one aircraft was converted as a 'Hudstar' – a surplus AT-18 fitted with a Loadstar rear fuselage.

Hudson at war

Bristling with ASV radar antennas, machine-guns and rocket projectiles, this RAF Coastal Command Hudson Mk VI was ordered by the USAAF as an A-28A and delivered under the Lend-Lease agreement.

Allied sea patroller

Lockheed's plans for the Model B14 – a bomber version of the Model 14 Super Electra airliner – were dusted off in 1938 at the behest of the British Purchasing Commission, which was in the market for a new general-reconnaissance aircraft. The resulting Hudson went on to be an important maritime type in the opening years of World War II.

USAAF Hudsons performed a number of important second-line tasks, including crew training. These A-29Bs are photo-reconnaissance aircraft assigned to 'B' Flight of the 2nd Photographic Mapping Squadron. The aircraft are seen while being refuelled from drums at Manaos, Brazil. The unit spent much of 1942/43 mapping parts of South America.

One of the first Hudsons delivered to the RAF, Hudson Mk I N7217, was being flown by Flt Lt A. L. Wormesley of No. 224 Sqn on 8 October 1939, when its crew succeeded in downing a Luftwaffe Dornier Do 18D flying-boat of 2./KüFlGr 106, which they had caught during a patrol off Jutland.

N7217 was the first UK-based RAF aircraft to shoot down an enemy machine and the first aircraft of American manufacture

to destroy an enemy aircraft during World War II. Four months later another Hudson, this time from No. 220 Sqn, was instrumental in directing HMS *Cossack* and its boarding party to the Kriegsmarine prison ship *Altmark*, hiding in waters off Norway, thus helping to free a large number of captured British seamen. These incidents give an indication of the importance of the Lockheed Hudson to Coastal Command operations in the first three or so years of the war.

The first Coastal Command squadrons to re-equip with the Hudson flew regular patrols and anti-shipping sorties in the first year of the war, their effectiveness being much increased by the installation of ASV radar in early 1940.

Reconnaissance role

Elsewhere in the RAF during these early months of conflict, the Hudson served in a limited, but very important, reconnaissance role, the embryonic No. 2

Camouflage Unit (later the Photographic Reconnaissance Development Unit and No. 1 PRU, from July 1940) employing a handful of aircraft on top secret flights over occupied Europe, Germany and the USSR.

Meanwhile, from August 1940 Coastal Command's Hudsons had taken on an anti-submarine tasking, detachments from several units covering the Western Approaches from RAF Aldergrove in Northern Ireland.

Hudsons enter RAF service

The first of 350 direct purchase Hudson Mk Is entered RAF service with No. 224 Sqn, Coastal Command at Gosport in the summer of 1939. By the time war had broken out in September, No. 233 had followed suit and No. 220 was in the process of replacing its Avro Ansons with Hudson Mk IIIs. By March 1940 Nos 206 and 269 Sqns had joined the Hudson force, No. 320 (Dutch) Sqn following in October. Pictured (clockwise, from right) are aircraft equipping some of these early Hudson units: Hudson Mk V AM540 of No. 224 Sqn during 1941; presentation Mk III T9465 *SPIRIT OF LOCKHEED-VEGA EMPLOYEES* of No. 269 Sqn on detachment to Kaldadarnes, Iceland; a Hudson Mk I of No. 233 Sqn, which operated the variant until September 1941.

RAAF Hudsons of No. 8 Sqn were based in Malaya prior to the Japanese attack on the peninsula. In all, eight Australian Hudson squadrons were based in the region, Nos 1 and 8 Sqns bearing the brunt of the Japanese onslaught.

From March the following year a further detachment was based at Kaldardanes, Iceland and on 27 August 1941 a No. 269 Sqn machine damaged U-boat *U-570*. Its crew surrendered and the vessel was taken under tow, becoming the first U-boat captured by the RAF. Over the next two years RAF Hudsons took up ASW patrols from bases on the US east coast, the West Indies, Gibraltar, North Africa, Palestine, Italy and Corsica. While based in North Africa, No. 608 Sqn was reputed to have been the first unit to sink a U-boat using underwing rocket projectiles.

RAF Hudsons also undertook a limited number of bombing sorties, three Coastal Command units contributing a total of 35 Hudsons to RAF Bomber Command's second 1,000-bomber raid on Germany on 25/26 June 1942.

In the Far East six squadrons operated Hudsons in a variety of roles, including bombing, convoy escort and supply-dropping roles, but by May 1943, with Hudson production at an end, the type was becoming obsolete. Second-line roles were added to the Hudson's portfolio. Meteorological reconnaissance and air-sea rescue were two important roles, the latter necessitating the fitting of a Mk I air-droppable lifeboat to selected aircraft. Agent-dropping, operational training and transport duties were also undertaken (the latter by BOAC), though by April 1945 the Hudson had been withdrawn from RAF use, having been replaced by more capable types.

RCAF patrol aircraft

The first Commonwealth air force to operate Hudsons was the RCAF, which eventually received 248 examples of various marks. Four maritime/ASW units employed the type for patrol duties off the Canadian coast, though the most important role undertaken by the Canadian aircraft was training. Three Operational Training Units were among the units equipped, a No. 31 OTU Hudson notably damaging, and possibly sinking, a U-boat off Nova Scotia during a training sortie on 4 July 1943. Canada's last Hudsons, air-sea

rescue aircraft, were withdrawn in 1947; the last RCAF Hudson of all was struck off on 13 December 1948.

Following the RAF's lead, the Royal Australian Air Force ordered a batch of 50 Hudsons in late 1938. Under Lend-Lease a total of 248 aircraft was eventually supplied, the first entering service with No. 1 Sqn at Laverton, Victoria. By July, these machines were on their way to Singapore and by the time of the Japanese attack in December 1941, had been joined in the region by four other Hudson-equipped squadrons. A further three were in the process of type conversion in Australia.

Two squadrons in Malaya fought the Japanese before being forced to withdraw, but saw further action in the East Indies, Rabaul and New Guinea. In all, 11 RAAF Hudson units provided the main Allied bombing capability in the region until the autumn of 1943. They were joined, in late 1942, by Hudsons of the RNZAF. Five Kiwi bomber-reconnaissance squadrons were so-equipped and had initially been engaged in maritime patrols from bases in New Zealand, Fiji and New Caledonia. After joining the fight against the Japanese at Guadalcanal, No. 3 Sqn had some notable successes, including the RNZAF's first submarine 'kill' in April 1943.

New Zealand's Hudsons were later replaced by Venturas; the RAAF's machines were not finally phased out until 1949.

American service

Though over 1,300 Hudson carried USAAF serial numbers, most were Lend-Lease aircraft and only 153 actually saw service with the Army Air Forces. These A-29s were retained as interim patrol aircraft and issued to a number of bombardment and ASW squadrons on both US coasts. Their front-line service

was brief but included an incident in which German U-boat *U-701* was sunk, on 7 July 1942 – the first time a USAAF aircraft had sunk such a vessel. Before long the type had been withdrawn and joined the purpose-built AT-28s in the training role, while a handful were employed as transports and A-29B photo-reconnaissance aircraft.

The US Navy's use of the Hudson was even briefer and involved far fewer aircraft. Just 20 A-29s were passed to the Navy, these PBO-1s, as they were known, equipping a single squadron. VP-82 operated from Newfoundland and Rhode Island on Atlantic patrols beginning in October 1941.

On 1 and 15 March 1942 PBOs from the squadron notched up another significant achievement for the type, when they claimed the first two submarines sunk by US aircraft.

Brazil and China

Brazil declared war on Germany and Italy on 22 August 1942 and shortly afterwards received a batch of 28 A-28As to equip some of its Grupos de Bombardeio Medio (Medium Bombardment Groups).

Issued to the Grupo de Patrulha and flown from 12° Corpo de Base Aérea at Galeão, Rio de Janeiro, one of the machines managed to catch a surfaced *U-199* in the Atlantic on 31 July 1943. Though damaged by AA fire, the Brazilian crew managed to keep the U-boat on the surface until an FAB Catalina arrived and sunk the vessel.

China, which received 23 A-29s and three A-29A transports, made little use of its Hudsons, though it is believed that a number were employed on bombing duties against the Japanese in central China. However, most were written off in accidents.

Above: The first submarines sunk by the United States were claimed by US Navy patrol unit VP-82, equipped with PBO-1s – A-29s originally ordered by the British under Lend-Lease.

Left: The USAAF retained 153 Lend-Lease Hudsons, these A-29s (with a flexible 0.5-in/12.7-mm gun in place of the Boulton Paul dorsal turret) equipping bombardment and anti-submarine units.

An F-4 Lightning of the 3rd Photographic Reconnaissance Group banks towards the photographer, displaying the type's unique lines. The 3rd Group arrived at La Senia, Algeria, in mid-December 1942 and flew countless photographic missions in support of the Allied armies.

Lockheed
P-38 Lightning

Introduction

Unfairly overshadowed by its single-engined compatriots, the P-47 and P-51, Lockheed's Lightning was a formidable long-range fighter, proving hard-hitting, manoeuvrable and highly effective in all of the many theatres in which it served.

Fighter, bomber, night-fighter, reconnaissance aircraft, air ambulance, torpedo-bomber and even glider tug: there seemed to be no limit to the adaptability of the Lockheed P-38. It was one of the brilliant trio of 'pursuit' fighters produced by the USA during World War II, and the only one to remain in series production throughout the entire period of American participation in the war.

Originally conceived to meet a 1937 requirement for a high-altitude fighter, the Lockheed design team under H. L. Hibbard embarked on a radical twin-engined, twin-boom design, there being no engine available to meet

the performance demands stipulated by the air force in a single-engine layout. Known as the Lockheed Model 22, the design was accepted by the USAAC on 23 June 1937 and a single XP-38 prototype was ordered. This was flown by Lieutenant B. S. Kelsey at March Field, southern California on 27 January 1939. Two weeks later, the aircraft was flown across the continent in 7 hours 2 minutes with two refuelling stops, but was destroyed when it undershot on landing at Mitchell Field.

Following this outstanding performance, a batch of 13 YP-38 pre-production aircraft was ordered although the aircraft differed from the prototype by

First flown by Lieutenant B. S. Kelsey at March Field on 27 January 1939, the prototype XP-38 (37-457) promised to be an outstanding fighter from the outset, and its high-speed transcontinental dash made immediate headlines.

having Allison engines driving outward-rotating propellers in place of the prototype's inward-rotating examples. Armament configuration saw the introduction of a 37-mm Oldsmobile cannon and four machine-guns. Following testing with the early production batch, the USAAC placed a further order for 66 production examples, which were to be fitted with the origi-

nal armament configuration utilised on the XP-38 – one 23-mm Madsen cannon and four 12.7-mm Browning machine-guns. Despite the increasing numbers ordered, the aircraft remand largely within training units and it was not until the introduction of the fully combat-standard machine, the P-38D, in August 1941 that regular USAAF pilots conducted wide-scale mock combat with the type. America's entry into the war following Pearl Harbor was greeted by the availability of just 47 P-38s. Production was quickly a stepped up with the improved 'E' model, equipped with a revised armament and Curtiss Electric propellers. It was this variant that would allow the USAAF to achieve its first German kill of the war, when a Focke-Wulf Fw 200 Condor

P-38Hs were the first to have the bar added to the national insignia (illustrated). This factory-fresh example is seen on a test flight from Lockheed's Burbank facility in California, prior to delivery to the USAAF.

Below: Typical of the actions of the Far East Air Forces after the invasion of the Philippines had commenced, P-38s are seen attacking Japanese troops dug in near Ipo Dam, not far from Manila.

was downed within hours of the USA's declaration of war.

Meanwhile, the RAF had expressed an interest in the P-38 now known as the Lightning, and placed an order for 667 aircraft in March 1940. However, as a result of an American order banning the export of the turbo superchargers, the aircraft proved to have disappointing performance and the order was cancelled after only a handful had been delivered.

Lockheed continued to develop the Lightning further with the introduction of the 'F' model; this had an increased top speed and the provision of underwing racks for bombs or

torpedoes. It was this variant that equipped 27 squadrons of the USAAF in the Pacific theatre during 1943. And it was the drop tank-equipped version of a detachment from the 339th Fighter Squadron, 347th Fighter Group, that intercepted and destroyed the Japanese aircraft carrying Admiral Isoroku Yamamoto – this was at a distance of 550 miles (885 km) from the squadron's base.

European theatre

Meanwhile, the P-38 was in constant action in Europe and the Mediterranean, earning it the German nickname *der gabelschwanz Teufel* (the fork-tailed devil). Despite this name, the P-38 did not prove entirely suitable for combat with single-engined fighters of the Luftwaffe. This was learned at some cost during the first bomber-escort flights to Berlin from bases in England. Nevertheless, recon-naissance models of the Lightning developed alongside the fighter variants and mapped huge areas of occupied Europe, utilising their high altitude and speed to evade interception.

Shortcomings in the fighter-versus-fighter combat role proved largely academic at this time due to the build-up of P-47 and P-51 squadrons in Europe. Henceforth, the P-38 tended to be committed to ground-attack tasks in this theatre where it achieved great

Left: The final production model of the Lightning was the P-38M. It was developed following the poor performance of the P-70 in the Pacific against Japanese night attacks.

distinction during the build-up to the Allied invasion.

Pacific combat

Further improvements continued to be made to the Lightning, resulting in the P-38J and P-38L models; the most noticeable feature was the introduction of 'chin' fairings under the nose of the engines to enclose the intercooler intakes. Improved models continued to be delivered to all squadrons, but it was in the Pacific theatre (and particularly over the Pacific Ocean) where the Lightning's long-range ability on combat patrol was appreciated by USAAF pilots. By the end of 1944, P-38s were serving with a total of 34 squadrons in the western Pacific and Southeast Asia.

Two-seat night-fighter

Produced too late for the war in Europe, the P-38M was a two-seat variant. It was equipped with a primitive night interception radar, which was operated by a crewman seated directly behind the pilot in the

cramped elevated rear seat. Serving with the 5th Fighter Command, the radar-equipped night Lightnings saw only limited combat in the Pacific. During the final year of the war, the adaptability of the P-38 allowed the development of personnel pods, mounted on underwing racks, which were utilised for emergency casualty evacuation; other variants were tested as glider tugs.

Although the P-38 largely disappeared from front-line squadron use following the end of World War II, two further variants were developed. The XP-49 featured powerful Continental engines and a pressure cabin for high-altitude research. The XP-58 'Chain Lightning' – which was, in effect, an enlarged Lightning with an interchangeable nose and four-gun turret – was proposed as a ground-attack aircraft.

The variant model first flew in June 1944, but no requirement was issued by the USAAF and the aircraft was subsequently scrapped.

Exchanging their guns for a bank of cameras, reconnaissance Lightnings such as this F-5A provided Allied commanders with a wealth of photo-intelligence. Missions were flown at high altitude or, in some cases, at tree-top height.

Variant development

Production of the P-38 totalled 10,037 aircraft and covered seven major production variants and a number of prototypes. All were essentially similar, powered by a pair of Allison V-1710s.

Fighter variants

XP-38

The first of all Lightnings was the sole XP-38, serialled 37-457, which first flew on 27 January 1939. Powered by handed (inward-turning) Allison V-1710-11/-15 engines rated at 1,150 hp (858 kW) and fitted with GE B-1 turbochargers, the XP-38 had a very short life. During an attempt at the transcontinental speed record on 11 February, the aircraft was wrecked after losing power on approach to Mitchel Field, New York. Armament, though never fitted, was to have included a single 20-mm cannon and four 0.50-in (12.7-mm) machine-guns.

P-38D, P-38E

The small batch of 36 P-38Ds differed from the P-38 in having a low-pressure oxygen system, bullet-proof fuel tanks and a retractable landing light. All were redesignated RP-38Ds and employed as combat trainers. These were followed by the first major production aircraft – 210 P-38Es. Fitted with a 20-mm cannon, the P-38E (pictured) also boasted improved instrumentation and revised hydraulic/electrical systems. Still not combat-ready, most were 'restricted' as RP-38Es.

P-38F, P-38G

Comprising 377 US-ordered aircraft and 150 originally ordered by the British, the P-38F (right) was powered by 1,325-hp (988-kW) V-1710-49/-53 engines and had the same armament as the P-38E. Underwing racks (for tanks or bombs), desert equipment and 'manoeuvring flaps' were introduced during production. The similar P-38G (700 US ordered aircraft and 374 from British orders) had V-1710-51/-55 engines, improved oxygen equipment and a new radio. As with the P-38F, tank/bomb racks were added during production.

YP-38, P-38

A batch of 13 service aircraft followed the prototype, these YP-38s (as pictured, above) being powered by outward-turning Allison V-1710-27/-29 engines, again rated at 1,150 hp (858 kW). Fitted with GE B-2 turbochargers, the new engines also had new twin cooling intakes in place of the lip intakes of the XP-38; enlarged coolant radiators were also fitted either side of each tail boom. Armament was revised, a 37-mm cannon replacing the 20-mm weapon, while a pair of 0.30-in (7.62-mm) guns replaced two of the '50 calibres'. The first production Lightnings were 29 P-38s, which differed from the YPs in carrying four 0.30-in guns and a 37-mm cannon. Operational items, including armour and bullet-proof glass were also added, though in 1942 the P-38s were 'restricted' to non-combat status as RP-38s.

Lightning Mk I (P-322)

The USAAF's P-38s were preceded by a large order for 667 aircraft placed by the Anglo-French Purchasing Commission. These aircraft were powered by 1,090-hp (813-kW) V-1710-C15s, which were neither turbocharged nor handed, as both the RAF and Armée de l'Air wished to standardise on the Allison engine fitted to Curtiss H-81As (P-40s), also on order at this time. Given that air-to-air combat in Europe was expected to occur at medium altitudes, the lack of a turbocharger was deemed unimportant. Differences between the French and British aircraft were confined to cockpit equipment and armament. With the fall of France in June 1940, Britain took over the entire order, amending it to cover 143 Lightning Mk Is to the original specification and 524 Lightning Mk IIs with handed and turbocharged V-1710-F5L/-F5R engines. However, unsatisfactory testing at A&AEE Boscombe Down and a contract dispute with Lockheed resulted in just three Lightnings (one of which is pictured) being delivered. The remaining 140 were delivered to the USAAF as P-322s; all but 20 were fitted with handed Allisons and employed as operational trainers. Of the Lightning Mk IIs, only one was built and was used as a test airframe by Lockheed. The remaining British aircraft were completed as P-38Fs and Gs for the USAAF.

XP-38A (including P-38B, P-38C)

One P-38 was completed with an experimental pressurised cockpit, the extra weight of which was offset by the substituting a 20-mm cannon in place of the 37-mm weapon fitted in the P-38. Trials were flown during 1942, but the aircraft remained a one-off. The P-38B and P-38C were variants proposed by Lockheed in 1939; neither was built.

P-38H

Uprated 1,425-hp (1063-kW) V-1710-89/-91 engines powered the 375 P-38Hs, which also introduced automatic oil radiator flaps to solve a major engine overheating problem. In other respects the P-38H was essentially identical to the P-38G-10-LO, though it had B-33 instead of B-13 turbochargers.

P-38M

After the experimental conversion of a handful of P-38Fs and Ls as radar-equipped night-fighters, Lockheed developed the P-38M 'Night Lightning', a two-seat conversion of the P-38L, fitted with a podded AN/APS-6 radar. Seventy-five further conversions were ordered; the first of these were entering service as the war ended.

PR variants

F-4, F-4A

Ninety-nine P-38Es were completed as F-4 unarmed photo-reconnaissance aircraft (right), with four K-17 cameras in a modified nose. Most were retained as RF-4 trainers. The F-4A was a similar derivative of the P-38F; 20 were completed, though these, too, were redesignated as 'restricted' RF-4As in 1943.

P-38J, P-38L (including P-38K)

Lockheed adopted a new powerplant installation in the P-38J (below), the engines intercooler air intake being situated between the oil radiator intakes in a deeper 'chin' in the engine nacelle. The coolant scoops on the tailbooms were also redesigned, the new installation allowing a higher rating to be obtained from the same Allisons as fitted to the P-38H. In all 2,970 J-models were built, all but the first 10

having extra fuel tankage installed in the place formerly occupied by engine intercoolers. The final batch of 210 P-38J-25-LOs introduced two important innovations: power-assisted ailerons to improve roll rate and electrically-operated dive flaps. The latter were fitted to remedy airflow problems that had led to control loss in high-speed dives; they were also retrofitted to large numbers of earlier P-38s. The final production model was the P-38L, 3,923 of which were built (including 113 by Vultee). Essentially P-38J-25-LOs with uprated V-1710-111/-113 engines, P-38Ls had provision for carrying underwing HVARs and were equipped with strengthened bomb/tank racks. With the increased use of the Lightning as a light bomber, the P-38J and L could be fitted with 'Mickey' BTO radar (above left, on a P-38J) or a 'droop snoot' bombardier nose (above right, on a P-38L), both installations necessitating the carriage of an extra crew member. Some aircraft were fitted with rear seats and used as TP-38J and TP-38L trainers. The P-38K, combining a P-38G-10-LO airframe with V-1710-75/-77 engines and broad-chord propellers was a one-off.

F-5A, F-5B and conversions

A single P-38E was modified and 180 P-38Gs were completed as unarmed **F-5A**s, with a five-camera nose installation. The subsequent **F-5B** (pictured left, with a P-38J) which combined the camera installation of the F-5A with a P-38J-5-LO airframe and included a Sperry autopilot, was to be the last production PR Lightning, 200 of which were built. (Four were employed by the US Navy as **FO-1**s.) All subsequent F-5 variants were conversions of existing P-38s. These comprised the **F-5C**, a P-38J modified to F-5B standard, though with an improved camera installation. Around 123 of these aircraft are believed to have been modified in this way. The **XF-5D** was a one-off prototype (converted from an F-5A) of an armed two-seat PR aircraft, while the **F-5E** designation covered a total of 705 aircraft converted to F-5C standard from a variety of P-38J and P-38L airframes. The **F-5F** introduced a revised camera installation; an unknown number were created by converting P-38Ls. The final Lightning PR variant was the **F-5G** (above right), a P-38L derivative modified, in small numbers, with revised nose contours to provide more room for a wider range of cameras.

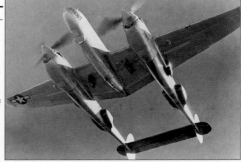

Europe and North Africa

Over Northern Europe the P-38 always struggled, but found itself far more suited to the climate and operations of the North African and Mediterranean theatres of operation.

Above: This pair of P-38Js were photographed as they left a British airfield for an escort mission into Germany. Both aircraft have 55-US gal (208-litre) drop tanks under wing.

Inset: Conditions in North Africa could be harsh, as demonstrated by this F-5A. Recce Lightnings, including the P-38G-derived F-5A, were always in great demand.

Lockheed's P-38 scored its first kill in the European theatre on 14 August 1942, when 33rd Fighter Squadron P-38Es flying from Iceland destroyed a marauding Fw 200. Soon after, the first Lightnings, indeed the first US fighters, to deploy direct to the UK, made the long transatlantic flight from the States. These P-38Fs of the 1st and 14th Fighter Groups reached the UK in the summer of 1942, the 14th flying the P-38's first operational missions from the UK late in July. Both Groups continued operations until being posted to the Mediterranean theatre for Operation Torch. Over North Africa the Lightning soon estab-lished itself as a formidable fighter, notching up victories at a high rate. In the MTO the Lightning proved its worth again and again, often at the forefront of operations thanks to its long range and heavy firepower.

Bomber escort

From mid 1943, the Lightning returned to combat operations from UK bases, escorting the heavy bombers of the Eighth Air Force on their strikes against Germany. With the P-47 not yet mature enough for full scale service, the P-40 having proved unsuited to operations over Europe and the P-51B not even near service, the P-38 was the fighter of choice for the impor-tant bomber escort role.

Unfortunately, the aircraft was always in short supply, since it was being built in fewer numbers than other American fighters. Its Allison engines were also notoriously unreliable in the cold and damp climate of Northern Europe, often leaving many of the meagre force on the ground due to failed power-plants. Nevertheless, the Lightning units were still able to down the Luftwaffe's Me 109 and Fw 190 fighters, although the fight was generally at the disadvantage of the US airmen and no one was sad to see the P-38 go.

The P-38's final ETO role was with the tactical Ninth Air Force, strafing and bombing targets from April 1944 in prepa-ration for D-Day.

Below: With their charges safely homeward bound, the Eighth's Lightnings were free to join their Ninth Air Force comrades in strafing targets of opportunity. Here a train is destroyed by an 'invasion stripe'-wearing Lightning.

Above: Lockheed technicians working in the UK developed the 'droop-snoot' version of the P-38J for use in the bomber-leader role. It entered service in April 1944. This machine was operating in Luxembourg on 4 October 1945.

Below: As soon as suitable landing grounds had been taken, Allied aircraft were moved onto the Continent. This Ninth Air Force P-38J is seen in Normandy on 14 June 1944.

CBI and the Pacific

In the skies over the Pacific and Far East, the Lightning suffered less from the reliability problems that had plagued it over Europe and deservedly gained a reputation as a foe to be respected.

Island runways in the Pacific could often be rough and were frequently carved out of the landscape by US engineers. Here an F-5B or F-5C approaches a strip which is most likely in the Marianas.

Having always struggled over Northern Europe, the P-38 was able to prove its true potential in the China-Burma-India (CBI) and Pacific theatres. The very first of the type's hundreds of kills was scored off the Aleutian Islands on 4 August 1942, when a pair of Kawanishi flying-boats was downed. The Lightning carried on scoring air-to-air kills right into 1945, many Japanese veterans declaring that it was among the type's most feared by their fighter pilots. US records justify this fear, for they show that in excess of 100 pilots achieved ace status in the CBI/Pacific theatres and more than 1,800 enemy aircraft were shot down.

In spite of the P-38's early promise, few of the fighters could be spared for the Pacific, since the majority of US resources was being directed at the war in Europe. Still, in early 1943, the Lightning was well placed to undertake one of the most audacious aerial operations of the war. In the aftermath of Guadalcanal, Japan's Admiral Yamamoto decided to make a tour of forward bases, while also boosting morale by his ever popular presence.

Taking out Yamamoto

US forces intercepted radio transmissions relating to Yamamoto's trip, including the fact that he would travelling in an escorted flight of 'Betty' bombers on 18 April 1943. Flying a long over-water leg at ultra low level, the P-38 force was able to avoid detection and destroyed Yamamoto's 'Betty', a blow to morale from which the Japanese never really recovered.

With the end of the campaign in North Africa, P-38 availability at last began to meet demand, with the result that some of the fighters could be spared for service in the CBI theatre. A number of P-38Gs was made available, both the aircraft and crews being sent straight from North Africa and first arriving in the summer of 1943.

CBI service

Flying air-to-air and dive bombing sorties from bases in China, the P-38s soon began taking a toll of Japanese warplanes. Continuing to fight through Burma, the CBI Lightnings scored their final victories in the spring of 1945.

With the Allies continuing their island-hopping campaign across the pacific, the USAAF's Lightning fighters were able to engage hordes of Imperial Japanese Army and Navy fighters, with a number of top aces emerging, the stars among which were 'Dick' Bong with 40 kills and Tom McGuire with 38. The last pilot to become a P-38 ace in World War II was Major George Laven, who downed an 'Emily' on either 26 April or 21 June 1945 in a P-38L, having scored his first kill, against a Japanese biplane, over the Aleutians in a P-38E in September 1942.

Top: Melba Lou, a P-38J, was photographed in Bengal in August 1944. CBI Lightnings retained Olive Drab over Neutral Gray camouflage long after the Pacific-based units had abandoned it.

Above: When Lockheed designed the P-38 it had no idea of its washing line role! The P-38's poor heating and ventilation system caused problems with the cold over Europe and the intense heat of the Pacific.

Below: Elsie, a P-38F, fell foul of a pothole on Dobodura, New Guinea, on 5 April 1943. The aircraft's four machine-guns and single cannon are clearly visible in the nose.

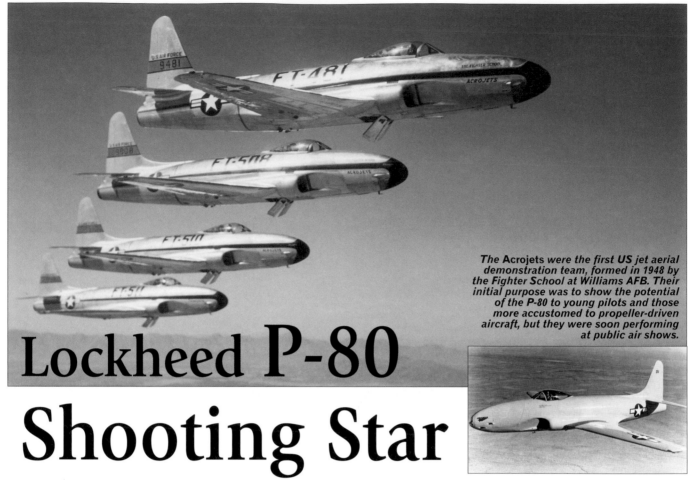

The Acrojets were the first US jet aerial demonstration team, formed in 1948 by the Fighter School at Williams AFB. Their initial purpose was to show the potential of the P-80 to young pilots and those more accustomed to propeller-driven aircraft, but they were soon performing at public air shows.

Lockheed **P-80**

Shooting Star

Introduction

America's first production jet fighter only just missed combat in World War II, but went on to form the backbone of USAF ground-attack forces in the early part of the Korean War. The Shooting Star was used in many test programmes and then evolved into the T-33 trainer and the F-94 fighter series.

To American combat pilots of the 1940s and 1950s, the Lockheed P-80 Shooting Star was a remarkable engineering achievement and a great aircraft to fling around the sky. To critics, the P-80 took the latest scientific advances and wasted them on a mediocre airframe that retained the shape, size and wings of a propeller-driven fighter (while others were developing jets with a sleeker shape, of a smaller size and with swept-back flight surfaces). "The P-80 was a great aircraft", says

1Lt Martin Bambrick, who flew the fighter in the late 1940s, "but we always wondered – what if the engineers had been more radical when they created it?"

Opinion was almost universal that the P-80 had few, if any faults – well, almost. In a hard-pressed operational setting, pilots and maintainers were furious that doors embraced the nose compartment. One flyer referred to this as a "bad feature" because the doors had a tendency to pop open in flight when a latch came loose,

rendering the P-80 almost uncontrollable. A hinge at the forward edge would have kept the doors closed in flight no matter what happened, but this remedy was never carried out. Pilots also criticised another design fault – the P-80's nose gear bay doors closed as the gear came up.

These were small complaints, however. By the time that the first Lockheed P-80 Shooting Stars became operational, victory was at hand and the Americans were seeing futuristic visions. Thus, in unveilings to

Differing significantly from the prototype, Lulu Belle, the XP-80A's main new feature was the General Electric I-40 engine, based on a Whittle design.

the press at Mitchel Field, NY and in Burbank on 1 August 1945, US Army Air Forces (USAAF) told the world that the Shooting Star had the "out-of-this-world appearance of a Buck Rogers spaceship" (referring to the comic-book and movie serial hero of the previous decade). By then, the P-80 was a proven aircraft, with a handful actually reaching Europe before

While bearing a strong resemblance to later Shooting Stars, the XP-80 was, in fact, a significantly different aircraft. The sound basic design of Lulu Belle was modified to incorporate a larger wing and tail surfaces, plus a detachable rear fuselage for engine access.

Apart from four aircraft that reached Europe prior to VE-Day, the first overseas P-80s were assigned to the 5th Fighter Group, under Colonel Horace Hanes. The unit received 32 Shooting Stars for its 38th FS at Giebelstadt, Germany, some of which can be seen here being towed through the streets.

Right: In the post-World War II period, the F-80 and the F-47 Thunderbolt, pictured here over the Bavarian Alps, constituted the major part of the USAF's offensive capability. Both aircraft were replaced by the F-84E Thunderjet.

Below: In a show no doubt designed to impress the Soviets, the 36th Fighter Group laid on this display of F-80Bs at Furstenfeldbruck. At least 72 aircraft can be seen, most with pilots and ground crew in attendance. The 36th FG was based at 'Fursty' from August 1948 to November 1952.

the war ended, although not in time to fight. This was all in marked contrast to the time when the P-80 had been conceived. Then, the war was being lost and the Americans were in a distant third place, behind the Germans and British, in the race to develop jets.

The saga had begun with a young engineer whose schoolmates had dubbed him 'Kelly' because he favoured green neckties, despite his Swedish ancestry. On 18 June 1943, Clarence L. ('Kelly') Johnson took stairs two at a time, vaulting up to the office of Robert Gross, Lockheed's president, at the company's headquarters in Burbank, California. In the office, Johnson found Gross and chief engineer Hal Hibbard. "Wright Field wants us to submit a proposal for building a plane around a British jet engine", Kelly Johnson told the two corporate leaders. "I've worked out some figures. I think we can promise them 180-day delivery. What do you think?"

At Johnson's behest, Lockheed established a goal of 180 days to first flight. This was an extraordinary goal. No fighter had ever been designed, developed and flown so quickly, certainly not one which used the revolutionary power of the jet engine.

Ironically, Lockheed could have started sooner. Back in

1939, Johnson's design team – later to be dubbed the 'Skunk Works' – had proposed a jet fighter. Engineers had drawn up plans on the drawing board for several versions, culminating in the model L-133-02-01, a futuristic canard design which would have been powered by two company-designed L-1000 turbojet engines (which existed only as a vague notion). But prewar indifference greeted Lockheed's model L-133. Meanwhile, isolationists were arguing that America should stay out of 'Europe's war', and the USAAF simply had no interest in it – at least, not yet.

But in late 1943, Johnson and his staff put together their new aircraft sooner than promised – in 143 days.

Design efforts

Kelly Johnson's team concocted an aircraft that appeared quite conventional, as if it might fly with either a jet or a reciprocating engine. In fact,

An idea of the low-level environment in which the F-80s operated in Korea can be ascertained in this view of a strike south of Pyongyang on 8 May 1952. As it releases its napalm tanks on a supply building and truck park, the F-80 is engaged by a gun position concealed in an embankment. The white blob beneath the aircraft is an AA shell.

the design was straightforward, but unorthodox. The XP-80 had straight wings and tail surfaces, and tricycle landing gear. The wing was a low aspect ratio, laminar-flow surface never before tested on a propeller-driven aircraft.

To their credit, engineers hashed out the P-80, and factory workers cut metal, before anyone at Lockheed had ever seen any kind of jet engine. The first powerplant, borrowed from Britain, became available only after the airframe was nearly completed. The AEF had been flying the Bell P-59 Airacomet with jet engines for many months, but this aircraft offered a performance far inferior to that of propeller-driven fighters, and few of the Lockheed personnel were ever to see a P-59. Fewer knew about Britain's Gloster Meteor, Germany's

Messerschmitt Me 262, or other early jet fighters which were becoming operational overseas.

The spinach-green XP-80, nicknamed *Lulu Belle* was taken aloft by pilot Milo Burcham for its first flight on 8 January 1944. By the war's end, two P-80s were in Italy, preparing for combat, two more had reached England, and no fewer than 16 were flying.

It was the beginning of a revolution. In years to come, the P-80 (to be redesignated F-80 on 11 June 1948) would set numerous flying records, go to war in Korea, and inspire the widely-used F-94 fighter and T-33 trainer. As the first practical, fully-operational jet fighter, however, the Shooting Star had already secured its place in history even before the arrival of the records, the fighting, or the offspring.

Lockheed

Ventura and Harpoon
Stop-gap bomber and Pacific whaler

The early success of the Hudson in operational service with the RAF induced Lockheed to initiate the design of a more advanced versions. These was based on the company's somewhat larger Model 18 Lodestar civil airliner.

In response to a request from the British, the Vega Corporation developed a military version of the Model L-18 series. This was employed by the RAF as the Ventura, by the US Army Air Force as the B-34 and B-37, and by the US Navy as the PV-1 patrol bomber.

The first of these flew on 31 July 1941. Its design had benefited from the company's manufacturing and British operational experience with the Hudson, so there were no major problems discovered during its flight test programme, and the first examples began to enter service with the RAF's No. 21 Squadron in October 1942.

Designated Ventura Mk I, the new aircraft differed from the Hudson in having a wider, longer and deeper fuselage, more powerful Pratt & Whitney engines each rated at 2,000 hp (1491 kW), the introduction of a proper ventral gun position with two 0.303-in (7.7-mm) machine-guns and, because of the more voluminous fuselage and greater engine power, a bomb bay able to accommodate a maximum bombload of 2,500 lb (1134 kg).

Venturas were first used operationally by RAF Bomber Command on 3 November 1942. On daylight missions over France and the Low Countries

Above: Under Lend-Lease 388 PV-1s were supplied to the UK. Designated Ventura GR.Mk V, the majority served with the Commonwealth air forces, including that of South Africa.

Top: Both the RAF and USAAF decided that the B-34 Lexington would be unsuitable for bombing missions against heavily defended targets. The type was then relegated to a training role.

Below: This Ventura Mk II (AJ206) underwent lengthy testing at Boscombe Down from June 1943. The Mk II was not up to standard for European combat operations and was withdrawn in 1943, many of the units being transferred to RAF Coastal Command.

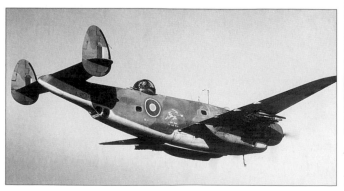

Above: Dated 25 January 1944, this photograph shows a PV-1 of the 1st Marine Air Wing at Bougainville, New Guinea. Note the fixed 'letter box' slots along the outer leading edge, a feature of all aircraft derived from the Model 14 transport.

Extending the wings and enlarging the tail of the PV-2 Harpoon improved handling and enabled heavier loads to be carried. However, flight performance suffered as a result. This was the first example, on test from Vega Aircraft at Burbank.

This view of an early PV-2 Harpoon emphasises the short nose, with the cockpit well behind the closely spaced engines. After 1945, many Harpoons were converted into PV-2T crew trainers, while others passed to friendly countries.

the Ventura faired badly against the dangerous Focke-Wulf Fw 190As of the Luftwaffe. Not for nothing did its unforgiving RAF pilots dub it 'The Pig'. During the summer of 1943 the type was withdrawn from No.2 Group, its place being taken by Mitchells and Boston Mk IIIA bombers. The Venturas were then transferred for operation with Coastal Command under the designation Ventura GR.Mk I and outstanding orders were cancelled.

The B-34s of the USAAF saw little action, while the B-37 (Ventura Mk III) saw none at all. However in the Solomons and South Pacific area, Ventura Mk IVs and GR.Mk Vs of the RNZAF enjoyed considerable success in action against the Japanese bastions at Kavieng and Rabaul. These last mentioned marks were known in the US Navy as PV-1s, of which 1,800 were built.

The PV-1 carried a crew of four or five. It weighed in at 20,197 lb (9161 kg) empty and 31,077 lb (14097 kg) gross. It was capable of a maximum speed of 312 mph (502 km/h) at 13,8700 ft (4205 m). Armament consisted of two forward-firing 0.5-in (12.7-mm) guns, two more of the same calibre in a Martin dorsal turret and two 0.3-in (7.62-mm) guns in the ventral position. Up to four 454-kg (1,000-lb) bombs could be stowed internally.

Harpoon

On 30 June 1943 the US Navy ordered an upgraded version of the PV-1 under the changed designation PV-2 and with the name Harpoon. While retaining the same general

appearance as the earlier Model 37, it differed in several respects. General configuration and powerplant was unchanged, but the wing span was increased by 9 ft 5 in (2.87 m), this giving a wing area of 686 sq ft (63.73 m2). Other changes included increased fuel capacity, greater fin and rudder area, and much improved armament. In the basic PV-2 this consisted of five 0.5-in (12.7-mm) forward-firing machine-guns in the nose and two flexibly-mounted 0.5-in (12.7-mm) guns in both dorsal

turret and ventral position, plus up to four 1,000-lb (454-kg) bombs carried in the bomb bay and two similar bombs carried externally. The final production version, of which 33 were built, had the designation PV-2D, and in these aircraft the nose armament was increased to a total of eight 0.5-in (12.7-mm) machine-guns.

The first flight of the PV-2 took place on 3 December 1943. Orders for the PV-2 totalled 500, and initial delivery of these to US Navy squadrons began in March 1944, for action from Aleutian bases. One of the aims of the increased wing span of this version was to provide considerably increased fuel capacity by use of the wing structure to form integral tanks, but great difficulty was experienced in making these fuel-tight. The first 30 aircraft were withdrawn from service and the integral tanks in the outer wings scaled off, the aircraft were then used in a training role with the designation PV-2C. The problem of the leaking outer tanks was beyond solution at that time, and all of the 470 production PV-2s had leak-proof fuel cells installed.

The PV-2 served primarily in the Pacific theatre as a patrol-bomber, until VJ-Day brought its withdrawal from front-line service. However, operated by US Navy Reserve units, the type remained in use for several years after the war.

A Lockheed PV-2 Harpoon in US Naval Reserve markings, with upper twin Colt 0.5-in (12.7-mm) machine-guns in the nose. The first of 69 delivered in 1944 went into service in March, with squadrons seeing action over the Kuriles. Production was eventually dropped in favour of the superlative P2V Neptune.

Slightly slower than the Hurricane, the MC.200 could however, turn inside all opposing fighters, while the Spitfire was the only Allied fighter capable of out-climbing it. First used operationally in Malta, the Saetta saw service in Greece, North Africa and Yugoslavia.

Macchi
MC.200/202/205
Saetta/Folgore/Veltro

Initial examples of the MC.200 were fitted with enclosed cockpit canopies, which offered a good all-round view and protection from the elements. Italian pilots, however, preferred open cockpits and this feature was later incorporated on all Saettas.

Italian thoroughbreds

Handicapped by design and industrial inadequacies, Italian wartime fighters were in general no more than mediocre. However, the Macchi MC.200, 202 and 205 were roughly comparable with the Hurricane Mk I, Spitfire Mk V and Mk IX respectively, though always deficient in gun armament.

It is unlikely that, in the mid-1930s, there was anyone in Italy better experienced to create a new single-seat fighter than Dr Mario Castoldi, chief designer of the Aeronautica Macchi company. Castoldi had adequately demonstrated his originality and attention to detail in the series of racing seaplanes developed by Macchi to compete in the Schneider Trophy contests. His MC.72 twice captured the world absolute speed record for seaplanes during 1934. The speed of 440.68 mph (709.209 km/h) established on 23 October of that year remains unbeaten in 2000.

Following the end of Italy's military campaigns in East Africa a programme was initiated to re-equip the Regia Aeronautica, the Macchi MC.200 Saetta (lightning) being designed by Mario Castoldi to meet the requirement for a new single-seat fighter. The resulting

prototype (M11 336) was flown for the first time on 24 December 1937 as a cantilever low-wing monoplane of all-metal construction. Power was provided by a Fiat A.74 RC.38 radial engine, an interesting change after the Fiat inline success in the Schneider Trophy contests. Italian engine manufacturers had now been instructed to concentrate on the development of radial engines. Castoldi would have liked to power the MC.200 with a high-performance inline engine, for he was concerned that the bulky radial would limit the performance of the new fighter, but he was to find a solution to this problem in the later MC.202.

Flight-testing of the two MC.200 prototypes was successful, one of them attaining a speed of 500 mph (805 km/h) in a dive. During 1938 the MC.200 won the fighter contest and was ordered into production with an initial contract for 99 aircraft, a

total of more than 1,100 being constructed eventually (about 400 were built by Macchi and the remainder by Breda and SAI-Ambrosini). Numbered among them were sub-variants that included the MC.200AS which was equipped for tropical operation, and the MC.200CB fighter-bomber with provision to carry a maximum 705-lb (320-kg) bombload or two underwing auxiliary fuel tanks. The single prototype of a developed version with a revised fuselage was built under the designation MC.201. It was designed to be powered by the 1,000-hp (746-kW) Fiat A.76 RC.40 radial engine, but had been flown only with the A.74 RC.38 of the standard MC.200

when development was abandoned in favour of the MC.202.

The MC.200 began to enter service in October 1939, by which time it had been given the name Saetta and, when Italy entered World War II in June 1940, about 150 had been delivered to the Regia Aeronautica. The first combat missions were flown as escorts for bombers/fighter-bombers attacking Malta in autumn 1940, and the type served subsequently in actions over Greece and Yugoslavia. The MC.200 saw extensive use in North Africa and a number was involved in operations on the Eastern Front during 1941-42. Following the Italian armistice with the Allies in September 1943, 23 of the Saettas were

An MC.200 flies low past a Spitfire on the airfield at Taranto in southern Italy. The aircraft was one of many Saettas surrendered to the Allies after the armistice with Italy had been signed.

MC.202 Folgore

Identified as an aircraft of the 22° Gruppo by the Spauracchio (scarecrow) device on the fuselage band, and as belonging to the 369ᵃ Squadriglia by its numerals, this mid-series MC.202 was based at Capodichino, Naples as part of the 53° Stormo CT (Caccia Terrestre) at the time of the invasion of Sicily in July 1943.

Performance
At 18,375 ft (5600 m), the MC.202 could achieve an admirable maximum speed of 373 mph (600 km/h). The aircraft's climb-to 16,405 ft (5000 m) time was 4 minutes 40 seconds and the service ceiling was 37,730 ft (11500 m). Range at maximum take-off weight was 475 miles (765 km).

Battle for Sicily
Throughout 1943, the Allies concentrated heavy attacks on Italy and southern Germany in preparation for the impending invasion. Folgores, with their light armament, had little or no effect on the heavily-armed US bombers and only achieved moderate success with head-on attacks. Some MC.202s even (unsuccessfully) dropped altitude-fused bombs. The massive Allied attacks destroyed over 1,000 Italian aircraft and the few remaining MC.202s could do little to oppose the Allies when they landed on 10 July. By the end of the month, all Italian fighter units had departed Sicily and the island fell in mid-August.

Undoubtedly one of the most graceful aircraft ever built, the MC.202 was also the best wartime fighter to serve in large numbers with the Regia Aeronautica.

Powerplant
Built alongside the MC.200 by Macchi, Breda and SAI-Ambrosini, early-series aircraft were powered by imported DB 601Aa engines until such time as Alfa Romeo had a licence-built version in production as the RA.1000RC.41-1 Monsone (monsoon). The Alfa Romeo engine delivered 1,075 hp (802 kW).

Armament
The MC.202 was armed with two 0.5-in (12.7-mm) Breda-SAFAT machine-guns in the nose, each with 360 rounds, and two 0.303-in (7.7-mm) Breda-SAFAT machine-guns in the wings, each with 500 rounds. This armament, however, frequently proved insufficient in comparison to that of Allied adversaries.

flown to Allied airfields in southern Italy, to be flown shortly afterwards by pilots of the Italian Co-Belligerent Air Force.

Folgore enters the fray
Mario Castoldi had been convinced from the earliest days of MC.200 flight-testing that full potential of the design would be achieved only by the installation of an inline engine. This opinion was confirmed during August 1940 when the prototype Macchi MC.202 (MM 445) was tested with an imported Daimler-Benz DB 601A-1 engine. The prototype first flew on 10 August 1940, and its initial trials were so impressive that it was ordered into production without delay. Generally similar in overall configuration to the MC.200, the

MC.202 Folgore (thunderbolt) introduced a new fuselage structure with an enclosed cockpit and similar wings, but retained the tail unit and landing gear of its predecessor. However, the single MC.202 prototype, which was basically a re-engined MC.200 airframe, was flown with a retractable tailwheel.

Because of the degree of commonality there was little delay in starting production, the first deliveries being made in the spring of 1941.

However, it was limited manufacture of Alfa Romeo's engine which restricted the number of MC.202s to a total of about 1,500 when production ended in 1943, and so the MC.200 continued to be manufactured simultaneously, instead

of being supplanted completely. Like its predecessor, the MC.202 was built in generally similar MC.202AS and MC.202CB tropicalised and fighter-bomber variants respectively.

Initial deliveries of production aircraft were made in

November 1941 to units operating in Libya. The Folgore also took part in actions against Malta and Allied convoys in the Mediterranean and, in September 1942, was deployed in some numbers on the Eastern Front, though its career in this theatre was somewhat inauspicious.

After having retreated across Libya in November 1941, the Italian Folgores gained air superiority over Tobruk, contributing to the taking of the town by Axis forces in June 1942.

Martin

B-26 Marauder

Development and early USAAF service

Dubbed the 'Widow Maker' after a series of early crashes, the B-26 went on to become one of the USAAF's most important medium bombers. By 1944 9th AF examples had the lowest loss rate in the ETO.

Above: Photographed soon after making its maiden flight on 25 November 1940, the first Marauder (40-1361) was built to a production contract but served as a prototype.

Top: 'PN' codes identify this B-26B as an aircraft of the 449th Bomb Sqn, 322nd Bomb Group. The 322nd was the first B-26 Group assigned to the European theatre.

During the last years of the 1930s the US Army Air Corps was singularly poorly equipped with medium bombers, dependence being laid almost exclusively upon the aged Douglas B-18 and Martin B-10, neither of which possessed the performance, bombload or defensive armament comparable with modern aircraft in service in Europe. When in January 1939 the AAC circulated among American manufacturers outline proposals for a new medium bomber, emphasis was given to high speed, long range and a bombload of 2,000 lb (907 kg), it being tacitly accepted that achievement of the characteristics would likely result in high wing-loading and therefore high landing speed and a lengthy take-off run.

Prepared by Peyton M. Magruder and submitted to the Air Board by the Glenn L. Martin Company on 5 July 1939, the Martin 179 design was adjudged the best of all competing tenders and, despite the highest-ever wing-loading of an aircraft intended for the AAC, was ordered into production immediately after the design had been accepted, an expedient prompted by the worsening international situation. With a five-man crew, the Martin 179 was to be powered by two 1,850-hp (1380-kW) Pratt & Whitney R-2800 Double Wasp radials in nacelles underslung from a shoulder-mounted wing of only moderate area. Two 0.3-in (7.62-mm) and two 0.5-in

(12.7-mm) machine-guns constituted the defensive armament, and the centre portion of the beautifully streamlined, circular-section fuselage featured an unrestricted bay to accommodate the bombload.

No prototype

Designated B-26, 1,100 aircraft were ordered in September 1939 and the first aircraft (40-1361) was flown by William K. Ebel

on 25 November 1940. There were no prototypes as such. The first 201 examples were powered by R-2800-5 engines and most were retained for experimental and training purposes, the latter proving to be a lengthy and somewhat hazardous procedure as a result of pilot unfamiliarity with the nosewheel type of landing gear and the high landing speed; at a gross weight of 32,000 lb (14515 kg) and wing area of 602.0 sq ft (55.93 m²), the wing loading was 53.2 lb/sq ft (260 kg/m²) and at a normal landing weight the touchdown speed was around 96 mph (154 km/h). The maximum

In the basic Olive Drab and Neutral Gray USAAF finish of 1942, this an early B-26, as indicated by the short wing span, short fin and small engine intakes.

This B-26B-50-MA served with the 558th Bomb Sqn, 387th Bomb Group, in the UK. The 387th BG flew only 29 missions with the 'Mighty 8th' before transferring to the 9th AF and moved to France in August 1944.

B-26B 42-95857 **Shootin in** *of the 556th Bomb Sqn, 387th BG releases its deadly load over a target in occupied Europe. The 9th Air Force made good use of the Marauder, supporting the Allied armies during and after the D-Day landings.*

bombload of 5,800 lb (2631 kg) far exceeded the original requirement, and the top speed of 315 mph (507 km/h) was the highest of all B-26 variants.

First deliveries

First deliveries to the AAF started in 1941, and during the second half of that year production switched to the B-26A which, introducing provision for optional bomb-bay fuel tanks, shackles for a 22-in (58.8-cm) torpedo under the fuselage and 0.5-in (12.7-mm) guns in place of the 0.3-in (7.62-mm) guns in nose and tail, had a maximum all-up weight of 32,200 lb (14606 kg). At the same time the electrical system was changed from 12 volt to 24 volt.

A total of 139 B-26As was built, and it was with this version that the 22nd Bomb Group (Medium) moved to Australia immediately after Pearl Harbor in December 1941; with extra fuel replacing part of the bombload these aircraft flew attacks against targets in New Guinea the

following April. In June that year torpedo-carrying B-26As went into action during the great Battle of Midway, as others of the 73rd and 77th Bomb Squadron attacked shipping in the Aleutians.

Production of the B-26A continued at the Baltimore, Maryland, factory until May 1942 when the first B-26Bs appeared. With a total of 1,883 built, the B-26B was the most-produced version. The B-26B-1 introduced increased armour protection, improved engine cowling shape (without propeller spinners), a ventral gun position and a twin 0.5-in (12.7-mm) tail gun position. These alterations increased the gross weight to 36,500 lb (16556 kg) without any change in powerplant, but in the B-2, -3 and -4 production blocks the engines were the uprated 1,920-hp (1432-kW) R-2800-41 or -43 version.

The B-26B-4 sub-variant introduced a lengthened nose-wheel leg as an attempt to provide increased wing incidence

While most Marauders were built at Martin's Baltimore plant, a batch of 1,210 B-26Cs was completed at the company's Omaha, Nebraska factory. These apparently unarmed examples appear to be training aircraft.

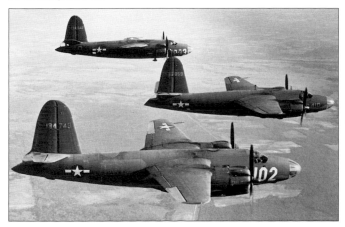

on take-off, and single 0.5-in (12.7-mm) beam guns replaced the ventral gun. The B-5 featured slotted flaps to improve landing approach handling. A total of 641 B-1s, -2s, -3s, -4s and -5s was produced.

Still the B-26 attracted harsh comment from the service, and the B-10 (and subsequent versions) featured a wingspan increased to 71 ft (21.64 m) to reduce the wing loading, but this was accompanied by yet further weight increases (to a gross weight of 38,200 lb/ 17328 kg) by the addition of four 0.5-in (12.7-mm) 'package' machine-guns on the sides of the nose, and a Martin-Bell power-operated tail turret. Far from being significantly reduced, the wing loading at all-up weight had advanced to 58.05 lb/sq ft (283.4 kg/m²) and the normal touchdown speed to 103 mph (166 km/h). As a means of limiting the critical speed and of improving lateral stability, the vertical tail was also increased in height and area.

The Baltimore plant produced 1,242 B-10s and their derivatives, and Martin went on to open a new facility at Omaha, Nebraska, late in 1942, where 1,235 B-26Cs (equivalent to the B-10 and subsequent blocks) were produced.

Wartime service

War operations by the B-26 during the USA's first 11 months of war were confined to the Pacific theatre but, in support of the campaign following the

'Torch' landings, the 17th, 319th and 320th Bomb Groups (Medium), comprising the 34th, 37th, 95th, 432nd, 437th, 438th, 439th, 440th, 441st, 442nd, 443rd and 444th Squadrons operated with the 12th Air Force in North Africa with B-26Bs and B-26Cs from December 1942, thereafter accompanying and supporting the Allied armies in Sicily, Italy, Sardinia, Corsica and southern France.

In northern Europe the B-26's early operations were disappointing. Following a partly successful baptism by the 8th Air Force's first B-26 group, the 322nd, in an attack on the Velsen generating station at Ijmuiden on 14 May 1943, a second attack by 10 aircraft led by Colonel Robert M. Stillman on the same target three days later resulted in the loss of the entire formation to flak, German fighters and collision. In recognition of the B-26's apparent vulnerability to ground fire, operations moved to medium and high altitudes. The Marauder's full potential was not realised, however, until it was assigned to the newly formed 9th Air Force at the end of 1943, when the aircraft assumed the role of medium-altitude strategic attack (albeit under fighter escort) against targets in preparation for the forthcoming invasion of Europe. By May 1944 the 9th Air Force operated eight B-26 groups, the 322nd, 323rd, 344th, 386th, 387th, 391st, 394th and 397th, comprising 28 squadrons.

The B-26G was the last Marauder variant built in any numbers; 893 were completed, the last in April 1945. Brandishing a fire extinguisher in case a back-firing engine catches fire, a Martin employee looks on as a test pilot prepares to start the port engine of 44-68144 from the final batch of 117 B-26G-25-MAs.

Marauder matures

By far more B-26Bs (and their Omaha-built equivalents, the B-26Cs) were built than any other Marauder variants. However, there were later developments, including the numerous B-26G.

Production of the B-26B ended at Baltimore in February 1944 with delivery of the last B-26B-55-MA. In addition, Martin produced 208 AT-23As for the USAAF, these being a target tug/trainer version of the B-26B without armour, guns or turret, but with a C-5 target winch. Omaha production ended in April 1944 with the B-26C-45-MO and 350 AT-23B target tug/trainers; 225 of the target tugs were delivered to the US Navy and US Marine Corps under the designation JM-1. The USAAF aircraft were redesignated TB-26s in 1944.

A single XB-26D was produced after modification of an early aircraft to test anti-icing systems, but the planned B-26E, with reduced weight and the dorsal turret moved forward to the navigator's cornpartment, was not built.

Two other production versions were produced. Both featured the long-span wings, and the wing incidence was increased by 3° 30'; this was

considered by most pilots to improve take-off and landing characteristics and certainly resulted in better approach handling, but sharply reduced the maximum speed to 277 mph (446 km/h). Production of the B-26F started late in 1943, with the first deliveries to the USAAF being made the following February. Some 300 B-26Fs were completed, of which 200 were delivered to the RAF under Lend-Lease as Marauder Mk IIIs (equivalent to the B-26F-2 and B-26F-6).

Numerous minor changes in equipment and fittings identified

the B-26G, of which Martin produced 893, with 150 purchased by the UK, also as Marauder Mk IIIs. Some 57 TB-26Gs were also produced in 1944, of which the last 15 went to the US Navy and US Marine Corps as the JM-2.

Final delivery

The final B-26 was delivered on 30 March 1945 for a total of 5,157 Marauders completed. (One other aircraft, the XB-26H, 44-28221, was produced to test the four-wheel bicycle landing gear planned for the Boeing B-47 and Martin XB-48 bombers.) Despite the problems stemming from the relatively advanced design philosophy, the B-26 had an impressive war record, including a total of

Right: This harrowing photograph shows an unidentified B-26 of the 12th Air Force after taking a direct hit from a flak shell during an attack on coastal guns in Toulon harbour. Operating at relatively low altitudes, medium bombers were particularly vulnerable to anti-aircraft fire and fighters.

Marauders saw considerable use in North Africa and, to a lesser extent, the Pacific before making their mark in the ETO. B-26B 41-18201 Sweet Sue was photographed while with the 12th Air Force in Tunisia during July 1943.

Below: Most Marauders were withdrawn soon after the end of World War II. These B-26C-25s are seen in a post-war salvage park. Removing the Marauder's engines caused a shift in centre-of-gravity towards the rear of the aircraft, with obvious results.

A total of 272 Marauders went to the US Navy, 225 of them designated JM-1s. These were former AT-23B target tugs employed in the same role by the Navy and Marine Corps. This USMC example is finished in yellow overall to aid conspicuity.

129,943 operational sorties flown in the European and Mediterranean theatres alone, during which B-26s dropped 169,382 tons of bombs, and their crews claimed the destruction of 402 enemy aircraft, while the loss of 911 aircraft in combat represented an overall loss rate of less than one per cent. The USAAF's B-26 inventory peaked in March 1944 when 11 groups were operational (comprising 43 squadrons), and 1,931 B-26s were on charge in the ETO alone.

When first introduced to service the B-26 cost $261,000, and by 1944 this had dropped to $192,000 (compared with $142,000 for a B-25). The B-26 was a robust aircraft whose semi-monocoque fuselage was constructed in three sections with four main longerons, transverse circular frames and longitudinal stringers; the centre-section, including the bomb bay, was constructed integrally with the wing section. The box-type wing structure, formed by two heavy main spars with heavy-gauge skin, was reinforced by spanwise members to provide torsional stiffness; the entire leading edge was hinged to the front spar to facilitate servicing. Only the rudder was fabric-covered. All units of the hydraulically-operated tricycle landing gear retracted rearwards, the nosewheel pivoting 90° to lie flat in the fuselage nose.

The seven-man crew included two pilots, navigator, radio operator, front gunner/bombardier, turret and tail gunners. The 11 0.5-in (12.7-mm) machine-guns (single nose gun, four in nose packs, two in the turret, two hand-held flexible beam guns and two in the extreme tail) were provided with a total of 3,950 rounds. The maximum bombload of two 1,600-lb (726-kg) bombs and a single 2,000-lb (907-kg) torpedo was seldom carried, most sorties being flown with eight 500-lb (227-kg) or 16 250-lb (114-kg) bombs.

Hasty withdrawal

The Marauder was quickly withdrawn by the USAAF after VJ-Day. Its handling 'qualities' put it near the top of the list for early retirement, the peacetime Army Air Forces preferring the more docile B-25 for training and the front-line medium bomber units having re-equipped with the Douglas A-26 Invader.

The last Marauder built was completed as the XB-26H Middle River STUMP JUMPER, used to test bicycle-type landing gear for the Boeing XB-47 and Martin XB-48. Note the strengthening applied to the aircraft's fuselage.

Warbird Marauders

Built in comparatively limited numbers compared to its contemporaries and quickly retired after the end of World War II, the B-26 has survived in only limited numbers. Just a handful of complete aircraft are known to exist, though all are static museum pieces or derelict hulks awaiting restoration. Two examples have flown in the 1990s, including Kermit Weeks' N4297J (40-1464), based at the Fantasy of Flight Museum in Florida. The other Marauder warbird was perhaps the most interesting survivor. TB-26C-20 N5546N (41-35071) was sold to United Airlines in 1946. Later purchased by Lelend H. Cameron, the aircraft was entered in the 1949 Bendix Trophy Race with the number '24' and named *Valley Turtle* (right). By August 1951 the aircraft was owned by the Tennessee Gas Transmission Company which contracted AiResearch Aviation Service to convert the machine as an executive transport (below). Uprated R-2800 engines, new three-bladed propellers and a dorsal fin were among the modifications made to the aircraft, which was equipped to seat 14-16 passengers. Between 1959 and 1967 N5546N

had several owners before finally being purchased by the Confederate Air Force. Restoration began in 1975, the aircraft flying again in 1984. Named *CAROLYN* (below), 41-35071 then joined the CAF's active display fleet but was wrecked in a fatal accident near Odessa, Texas on 28 September 1995.

Messerschmitt Bf 109

Introduction

Of the more than 30,000 Messerschmitt Bf 109s built during World War II, none remains airworthy, although several are undergoing rebuild to flying condition. This RAF-owned Bf 109G is now stored at the Imperial War Museum at Duxford, where it remains grounded following a landing accident in 1997.

Without doubt the most famous German aircraft of World War II, the fortunes of the Bf 109 mirrored those of the Luftwaffe itself: total dominance in the early victories, a long hard struggle to retain the superiority achieved, and final defeat in the face of overwhelming numbers.

When chief test pilot, Flugkapitän Hans 'Bubi' Knötsch, lifted the first prototype of a brand-new fighter from the runway of Messerschmitt's Augsburg-Haunstetten field in May 1935, he undoubtedly knew that the machine in his hands represented a quantum leap forward in fighter design technology. What he could not have foreseen was that a decade later, despite having suffered total defeat, it would be accorded a rightful place along-side the Spitfire and Mustang as one of aviation's true immortals.

Although the Bf 109A, as it was initially designated, was not the first single-seat fighter to combine an all-metal stressed-skin monocoque structure with a

Above: Leutnant Steindl, the Geschwader adjutant of JG 54, positions his Bf 109E-4B for a wingman's camera during a bombing mission to Stalingrad in spring 1942. The Jagdbomber (fighter-bomber) version of the Bf 109E stayed in front-line service long after the day-fighter version had been replaced by the Bf 109F and 109G.

low-wing cantilever monoplane configuration, it was the first to add to these a whole raft of extra refinements such as an enclosed cockpit, retractable undercarriage and the then radical combination of automatic leading-edge slots and slotted trailing-edge flaps.

Pioneering design

Messerschmitt's achievement in producing such a pure thoroughbred was all the more remarkable in that it was a first. Comparison is often made between the Bf 109 and its near contemporary, the Spitfire. But whereas the latter drew heavily on experience gained with the earlier Schneider Trophy high-speed racing floatplanes, the Bf 109 had no such illustrious forebears; its immediate predecessor was a four-seat light civilian touring machine.

Operational trials

The Bf 109 was without doubt the most advanced fighter of its time to enter service and

see combat. Four prototypes (V3-6) were sent to Spain late in 1936 for operational trials with the Legion Condor. They would be followed by 124 production machines. In an era of fighter biplanes whose design ancestry and tactics dated all too obviously back to World War I, the Bf 109 pilots in Spain rewrote the rule book. Foremost among them was the future fighter ace, Werner Mölders, whose Schwarm, or 'finger-four', formation was later adopted by air forces the world over.

The first major production model, the classic Bf 109E, or 'Emil', marked perhaps the early apogee of the entire 109 line. Not only will it forever be associated with the Battle of Britain, it was popular with the Luftwaffe pilots themselves. It embodied everything that the chief designer – Willy Messerschmitt – had sought to achieve before military necessity dictated the incorporation of

In Spain, Bf 109s were primarily used for bomber escort operations and low-level sweeps. The Messerschmitts proved vastly superior to the Republican fighters.

Above: During the early campaigns of World War II, the Bf 109 proved to be a formidable opponent when pitted against outdated French and Polish fighters. The few that were lost were mostly as a result of ground fire.

Left: Most of the Bf 109's actions were undertaken by day, but the type was impressed into action as a night-fighter. This is a II./JG 54 Bf 109F, flying in the early months of the war in Russia. Note the 19 victory bars on the rudder.

various lumps and bumps to house additional armament and equipment, and the bolting on of performance-sapping weapons packs.

If the Emil had a flaw – apart from the narrow-track under-carriage, which was a weakness in every one of the 30,000+ Bf 109s built – it was its lack of punch: at best, two 20-mm MG FF wing cannon and two fuselage-mounted 0.31-in (7.9-mm) MG 17 machine-guns. The aerodynamically improved Bf 109F, with its uprated DB 601N powerplant, did little to remedy the arma-ment situation. And, while many pilots appreciated the superior muzzle velocity and rate of fire of the single engine-mounted MG 151 cannon which had replaced the Emil's wing guns, others preferred to continue to fly the Bf 109E as long as conditions permitted.

Fighter for all fronts

The mid-war Friedrich had held its own on all flying fronts: the Channel, Mediterranean and Russia. It would fall to those who flew its successor, the Bf 109G, to pay the price for the Luftwaffe's failure to produce and make available an adequate replacement for a design which was already past its peak. By far the most prolific of all Bf 109 variants, the Gustav would soldier on under increasing pressure until the final collapse.

Development of the Bf 109G led to the Bf 109K-4 of October 1944, the final production version. Powered by the highly supercharged DB 605D engine, the K-4 was fast but, by this time, the design had lost most of the fine handling of its early predecessors. It was still a potent weapon: all it needed was fuel to power it and experienced pilots to fly it – both of which items were sadly lacking in the Luftwaffe during the final months of the war.

Post-war service

The ending of hostilities did not see the operational history of the Bf 109 draw to a close. Spain had investigated licence-assembly of the aircraft during the war and afterwards completed Bf 109s utilising its own Hispano-Suiza engines and, later, British Rolls-Royce Merlins (the same powerplant as used in its former wartime adversary, the Supermarine Spitfire). Known as Hispano HA-1112-M1Ls, the Spanish Bf 109s remained in service until the mid-1960s.

Further post-war use of the Bf 109 included a number of S-199 'Mezecs' (Czech-built Jumo 211F-powered 'Gustavs'), flown by Israel against the Egyptian air force in 1948-49. The fighter was disliked by pilots for its poor handling and was dubbed 'the mule' by those unfortunate enough to have to fly the aircraft in combat.

This Messerschmitt Bf 109G is operated by MBB Aircraft/Flugzeug-Union Sud in Germany. The aircraft is something of a hybrid machine, being a Spanish Hispano HA-1112 Buchón fitted with a German Daimler-Benz engine.

Bf 109 Early prototypes

First flying in 1935, the Bf 109 overcame official intransigence to become a classic fighter. The early prototypes demonstrated the type's superiority from an early stage in their development.

Top: D-IOQY was the third Bf 109 prototype, and the first to feature provision for engine armament. Powered by the Junkers Jumo 210 engine, the aircraft was one of three sent to Spain in December 1936 for combat trials.

Above: Designed for a 1934 tourist aircraft competition, the Messerschmitt Bf 108 introduced a large number of novel features. Many of these were used in the Bf 109 fighter design.

Work on the Bf 109 started in answer to an early 1934 requirement for a new fighter. Arado, Focke-Wulf and Heinkel were the main contenders, as they were established as the principal fighter manufacturers for the new Luftwaffe.

Messerschmitt was painfully aware of the antagonism towards his project, and seemed resigned to the fact that he would not win a production contract. He saw the emerging fighter as a means of incorporating the most modern features available in one airframe, rather than address the individual requirements of the customer.

To power the new fighter, the Junkers Jumo 210 was selected in the autumn of 1934, with the Daimler-Benz DB 600 as a possibility for the future. At around the same time, construction of the first prototype, the Bf 109a,

began. By May 1935, the aircraft was essentially complete, and was rechristened Bf 109 V1 (Versuchs) in line with newly-adopted German policy. Delivery of the Jumo 210 was delayed so, in a twist of fate to be fully realised five years later, the V1 was hastily fitted with a Rolls-Royce Kestrel VI engine rated at 695 hp (519 kW) for take-off.

Bearing the civil registration D-IABI, the V1 first underwent taxiing trials with the undercarriage locked together by means of a horizontal bar. Towards the end of May 1935 (the exact date is unknown), senior test pilot Hans-Dietrich 'Bubi' Knötsch lifted the Bf 109 from the Haunstetten runway for the first time. During flight trials at Rechlin, the V1 proved to be considerably faster and to offer better handling than the Heinkel He 112 V1, the Bf 109's main rival.

Construction of the next two prototypes proceeded during late 1935, and the Jumo 210A engine became available in October 1935 for fitment to the V2. Wearing a civil registration, D–IUDE, the V2 joined the flight trials programme in early January 1936.

Apart from the Jumo engine, which gave 680 hp (507 kW) for take-off, the V2 differed in only minor details from the V1,

although it was fitted with armament in the form of two 0.311-in (7.9-mm) MG 17 machine-guns in the fuselage upper decking, each weapon having 500 rounds. The V3 (D-IOQY) first flew in June, this aircraft having provision for a 20-mm MG FF/M engine-mounted cannon, with corresponding cropped propeller spinner.

Pre-production

Development proceeded with 10 pre-production aircraft, which were designated Bf 109B-0. All of these were assigned Versuchs numbers in the range V4 to V13, and were individually known as the Bf 109B-01, B-02 *et seq.* The

The historic V1 first prototype of the Bf 109 was hastily fitted with a Rolls-Royce Kestrel engine to get it into the air, while the intended Jumo 210 powerplant was readied. It was the only Bf 109 to fly with an upright, as opposed to inverted, engine.

Right: D-IALY was the first of the batch of 10 pre-production aircraft, and was designated Bf 109B-01. It had a Jumo 210B engine and was fitted with a pair of MG 17 machine-guns in the upper fuselage decking. The fixed-pitch propeller was replaced in later Bf 109B-0s by a VDM–Hamilton variable–pitch unit.

V4 (D-IALY) took to the air in November 1936, armed with two MG 17 machine-guns, and powered by a Jumo 210B providing 640 hp (477 kW) for five minutes and 540 hp (403 kW) in continuous running. Both the V5 (D-IIGO) and V6 (D-IHHB) flew in December and had three MG 17s. The third gun was mounted inside the engine block, firing through the spinner. These aircraft differed further by having variable-pitch VDM-Hamilton propellers in place of the Schwarz fixed unit of the early aircraft, and had new revised nose contours.

Combat evaluation

As a prelude of events to come, the V3, V4 and V5 were dispatched to Spain in December 1936 for evaluation under operational conditions. Although the aircraft achieved no significant success, much operational experience was gained which would smooth the full entry into service of the production Bf 109Bs a few weeks later. At the end of January 1937, the prototypes returned to Germany.

Development of the Bf 109 continued apace. The V3 was fitted with an engine-mounted MG FF/M cannon, but the installation posed vibration problems. In March 1937, the V7 (D-IJHA) first flew, featuring a VDM-Hamilton variable-pitch propeller and a Jumo 210G direct fuel injection engine with two-stage supercharger. The VDM propeller was introduced during the Bf 109B production run. However, the fuel injection engine, with the obvious benefits of maintaining full power with the aircraft in any attitude, was not available until the arrival of the Bf 109C, for which the V7 and V8 (D-IPLU) served effectively as prototypes. Both of these aircraft had repositioned oil cooler intakes. The V8 also tested wing-mounted MG 17 guns, as the fuselage-mounted weapons had proved troublesome. Both the V7 and V8 were subsequently fitted with the Jumo 210Ga engine.

The V10 had started life with a Jumo 210Ga but, in June 1937, was fitted with a Daimler-Benz DB 600Aa, giving 960 hp (716 kW) for take-off and 775 hp (578 kW) in continuous running. This engine also powered the next four pre-production aircraft (V11 to V14). The Benz engine was much longer and heavier, which caused a shift in the centre of gravity. This was offset by the redesign of the cooling system, which had a shallow radiator bath under the nose and two underwing radiators behind the centre of gravity. A three-bladed VDM propeller was fitted, and the aircraft, including its undercarriage, underwent considerable local strengthening to handle the higher weights and loads. The supercharger was aspirated through a prominent port-side intake.

Zürich races

So good was the Bf 109 that Germany sought a means of spreading propaganda about its latest fighter. The 4th International Flying Meeting, held at Zürich-Dübendorf between 23 July and 1 August 1937, was the perfect answer.

Five Bf 109s were dispatched to Dübendorf, comprising three Jumo 210Ga-powered aircraft – the V7, V8 and V9 – and two with the new Daimler-Benz DB 600A – V13 (D-IPKY) and V14 (D-ISLU). Ernst Udet flew the V14 in the 'Circuit of the Alps' race, but suffered an engine failure. The event was won by Major Hans Seidemann in the V8, covering the 228-mile (367-km) circuit in 56 minutes 47 seconds, at 241 mph (388 km/h).

The three Jumo-engined aircraft took the team prize for the fastest trio of aircraft round the same course, while Dipl.-Ing. Carl Francke won the dive-and-climb competition in the V13 and a four-lap, 31-mile (50-km) circuit race in the V8. Following the Zürich triumph, the BFW management strove for further international glory and, on 11 November 1937, Dr.-Ing. Hermann Wurster flew the V13 to gain the world landplane speed record, setting a mark of 379.38 mph (611 km/h) in four runs along a 1.86-mile (3-km) straight course at low level. The aircraft had been specially prepared with a boosted version of the Daimler-Benz DB 601 engine and featured an elongated, streamlined spinner, strengthened cockpit canopy and a polished skin to minimise friction.

Production of Bf 109B fighters led to initial deliveries in February 1937. The production line was soon transferred to Regensburg, leaving the Augsburg facility free to continue with development work.

This line-up shows Bf 109Ds fresh from the Focke-Wulf factory at Bremen. The D was built in parallel with the C during 1938, but was considered an inferior aircraft as its Jumo engine was equipped with a carburettor, rather than fuel injection.

'Bertha', 'Clara' & 'Dora'

The initial Junkers Jumo-engined Bf 109 variants began to enter Luftwaffe service in 1937 and were blooded in the Spanish Civil War of the following year, before giving way to the DB 601-powered 'Emil'.

As soon as the fighter competition had been won, BFW began tooling up at Haunstetten for Bf 109 production, the Bf 109B being the production version (the designations Bf 109B-1 and B-2 appear to have been retrospectively applied erroneously to aircraft fitted with the Schwarz and VDM propellers, respectively). The phonetic nickname 'Bertha' was given to the first production version. BFW was also involved in the licence-manufacture of other types, and with the potential of a major fighter contract it had already become obvious that the Haunstetten facilities were not adequate. Accordingly, the Messerschmitt GmbH company was established with a factory at

Regensburg, and production of the Bf 109B was soon transferred there. The design offices remained at Augsburg.

Meanwhile, development of the Bf 109 continued. The V3 was fitted with an engine-mounted MG FF/M cannon, but the installation posed vibration problems. In March 1937 the V7 (D-IJHA) first flew, featuring a VDM-Hamilton variable-pitch propeller and a Jumo 210G direct fuel injection engine with two-stage supercharger. The VDM propeller was introduced during the Bf 109B production run, but the fuel injection engine, with the obvious benefits of maintaining full power with the aircraft in any attitude, was not available until the Bf 109C, for which the V7

Though the definitive development of the Jumo-engined fighter, the Bf 109C-1 (pictured) was built in only small numbers. The C-1 was equipped with four MG 17 0.31-in (7.92-mm) machine-guns; a handful was retrofitted with a pair 20-mm calibre MG FF cannon, as C-3s.

and V8 (D-IPLU) served effectively as prototypes. Both of these aircraft had repositioned oil cooler intakes, although in the event the C model emerged with a deeper, redesigned radiator bath and oil cooler position as originally fitted to the B. The V8 also tested wing-mounted MG 17 guns, as the fuselage-mounted weapons had proved troublesome. These guns were to become standard on the Bf 109C-1. Both V7 and V8 were subsequently fitted with the Jumo 210Ga engine.

Daimler-Benz in the air

The V10 had started life with a Jumo 210Ga, but in June 1937 had been fitted with a Daimler-Benz DB 600Aa giving 960 hp (716 kW) for take-off and 775 hp (578 kW) in continuous running. This engine also powered the next four pre-production aircraft (V11 to V14). The Benz engine was much longer and heavier, which caused a shift in centre of gravity. This was offset by the redesign of the cooling system, which had a shal-

low radiator bath under the nose and two underwing radiators behind the centre of gravity. A three-bladed VDM propeller was fitted, and the aircraft had considerable local strengthening, including the undercarriage, to handle the higher weights and loads. The supercharger was aspirated through a prominent port-side intake.

By mid-1937, apart from 1./J 88 (and imminently 2./J 88), the Bf 109B was in service with I/JG 132 at Döberitz, II/JG 132 at Jüterbog-Damm and I/JG 234 'Schlageter' at Cologne, although none of these was at full strength. In November 1937 II/JG 234 at Düsseldorf began converting to the aircraft, and at the end of the year the first aircraft from a second source – Gerhard Fieseler Werke at Kassel – was delivered. The B model was not built in great quantities and was soon replaced in service by later variants. A few lingered on in Luftwaffe service until the early part of 1940, flying with the fighter schools.

On 4 December 1937 one of the first production Bf 109Bs which had been sent to the Legion Condor (6-15), force-landed out of fuel behind Republican lines. The aircraft was evaluated in Spain by a French mission, and flown by test pilot Capitaine Vladimir Rozanoff. Unfortunately, the (very favourable) report was suppressed for diplomatic reasons and this windfall proved of little practical significance.

Photographs of Bf 109Bs used for engine development, and fitted with three-bladed propellers were distributed for propaganda purposes.

Development after 1937 concentrated on the next production model, the Bf 109C 'Clara'. The V9 was fitted with 20-mm MG FF cannon in the wings in place of the MG 17s. The cannon were mounted further outboard than the MG 17s, and had 60-round drums inboard of the weapons. The breeches were covered by a blister fairing on the lower side of the wing. This armament was not adopted initially for the Bf 109C-1, which had two nose-mounted MG 17s with 500 rounds each, and two in the wings with 420 rounds each. The engine was the Jumo 210Ga with revised exhaust slots and the 'Clara' had the deeper radiator

bath. The C-2 was a projected model with a fifth MG 17 mounted in the engine but was not proceeded with. The C-3 was the designation of C-1s retrofitted at the factory with the wing-mounted MG FF cannon originally tested on the V9.

Deliveries began in the early spring of 1938, with I/JG 132 converting during the summer. A small number of C-1s was shipped to Spain, but production was very limited, the majority of the aircraft produced at the time being the Bf 109D 'Dora', which was built in parallel. This version entered service in early 1938 with I/JG 131 at Jesau, and many served subsequently with the heavy fighter units.

Retrograde 'Dora'

If anything, the 'Dora' was a retrograde step, for it reverted to the Jumo 210Da engine with carburettor. It did, however, have four-gun armament. For many years, the Bf 109D designation

was thought to apply to aircraft powered by the DB 600, but no production aircraft had this powerplant. The myth has been perpetuated in many publications to this day, and many photographs which have appeared as being Bf 109Ds were actually early Bf 109Es, while many labelled as 'Claras' were really 'Doras'.

Production Bf 109D-1s were also built at Erla Maschinenwerk in Leipzig and by Focke-Wulf Flugzeugbau at Bremen, second-source production kicking in during early 1938. In August 1938 a batch of five was sent to 3./J 88 in Spain, and the D-1 also attracted export orders from Hungary for three, to be used for evaluation purposes. Most potential customers were far more excited by the prospect of the forthcoming Daimler-Benz-powered version, although Switzerland took delivery of 10 Bf 109Ds for familiarisation prior to receiving the DB-powered Bf 109E.

The first of the Swiss 'Doras' was delivered on 17 December 1938, and the batch was fitted with locally-supplied 0.29-in (7.45-mm) machine-guns (480 rounds for fuselage guns; 418 for wing guns). The Swiss 'Doras' served alongside Bf 109Es until finally scrapped in 1949.

Bf 109B/C/D in service, 1937-40

The Bf 109 entered service in its initial Jumo-engined form in early 1937. All three Jumo-engined variants were still in front-line use at the outbreak of World War II in September 1939, though the Bf 109E was fast supplanting the Bf 109Bs, Cs and Ds.

Bf 109B
This Bf 109B of 6. Staffel of Jagdgeschwader 132 'Richtofen' was based at Jüterbog-Damm in the autumn of 1937. The black bar over the numeral '7' indicates an aircraft of II. Gruppe.

Bf 109C
A handful of night-fighter units was equipped with Bf 109Cs in 1939/40. This aircraft is a 'Clara' of 10. (Nacht.)/JG 77, an interim night-fighting Staffel based at Aalborg July 1940.

Bf 109D
By 1940 some early aircraft had been relegated to training tasks. This 'Dora' was one of the aircraft equipping Jagdfliegerschule 1 at Werneuchen in 1940. Unusually, the aircraft has ejector-type exhausts fitted.

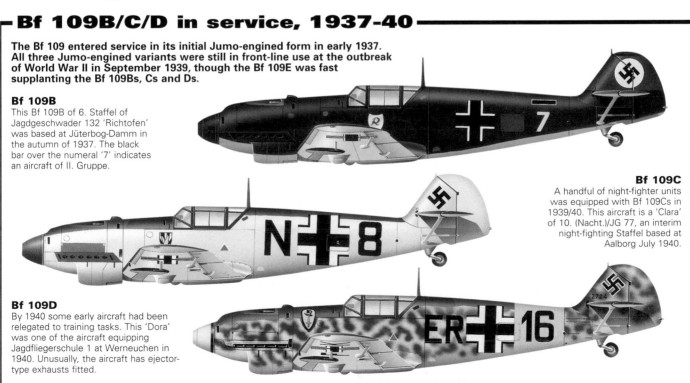

'Emil and T'

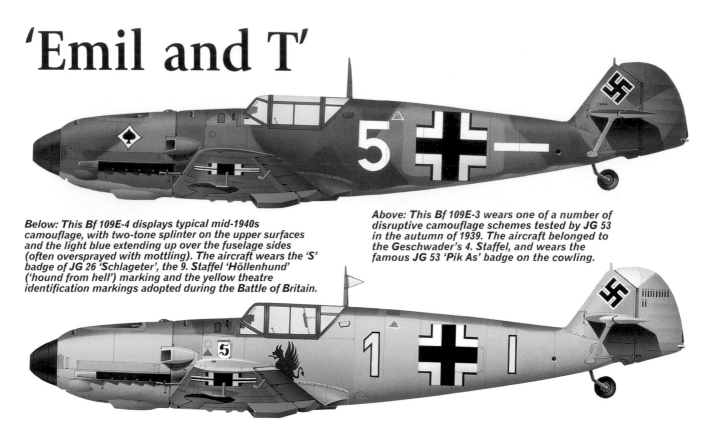

Above: This Bf 109E-3 wears one of a number of disruptive camouflage schemes tested by JG 53 in the autumn of 1939. The aircraft belonged to the Geschwader's 4. Staffel, and wears the famous JG 53 'Pik As' badge on the cowling.

Below: This Bf 109E-4 displays typical mid-1940s camouflage, with two-tone splinter on the upper surfaces and the light blue extending up over the fuselage sides (often oversprayed with mottling). The aircraft wears the 'S' badge of JG 26 'Schlageter', the 9. Staffel 'Höllenhund' ('hound from hell') marking and the yellow theatre identification markings adopted during the Battle of Britain.

In 1938, the excellent Bf 109 airframe was finally matched with the DB 601 engine, and a classic was born. Germany's early wartime successes were in no small way attributable to the Bf 109E 'Emil'.

Bf 109E 'Emils' started rolling from the production lines at the end of 1938, and it was this model which was to become perhaps the most famous of its breed. It had always been intended that the Bf 109 should be fitted with the Daimler-Benz DB 600/601 engine, but engine development had lagged behind that of the airframe, with the result that the early models were Jumo-powered. The first Bf 109 to have a DB 600 was the V10 and this became, in effect, the Bf 109E prototype. After a few DB 600-powered prototypes, the engine was switched to the DB 601A, which gave more power and, most importantly, had fuel injection. This allowed the engine to maintain power under negative *g*, a tactical advantage which the Bf 109E

enjoyed over the Supermarine Spitfire until 1941. Delayed by problems, production of the DB 601A finally got under way in late 1938.

With the DB 601A fitted, the Bf 109E-1 was an astonishing performer for its day and was without doubt the finest fighter in the world. Its armament remained the same as the Bf 109D, namely two MG 17 machine-guns in the upper fuselage decking and a pair of MG 17s in the wings.

Following close behind the E-1 was the E-3, which differed primarily by having 20-mm MG FF cannon in the wings instead of the MG 17 machine-guns. This was another tactical advantage which the Bf 109 would enjoy over its RAF rivals.

Initial 'Emil' deliveries went to Spain, the first of some 40

Just too late to see widespread action in the Civil War, Bf 109Es arrived in Spain in December 1938. The aircraft was nicknamed 'Tripala' on account of its three-bladed propeller.

Bf 109E-1s and E-3s arriving in December 1938. These formed the basis of the Spanish air force's fighter force throughout the war. Further early exports were made to Switzerland and Yugoslavia, to gain hard currency. During the

first half of 1939, the Luftwaffe fighter units rapidly transitioned to the new model (which was put into production at Messerschmitt-Regensburg, Erla, Fieseler and WNF) so that, by the outbreak of war, over 1,000 were on strength. The Bf 109E played only a small part in the Polish campaign but, where it did come up against Poland's inadequate P.7 and P.11 fighters, it downed them with ease. The 'Emil' also made a small contri-

I./JG 27 was the first Luftwaffe fighter unit to arrive in North Africa, preparing for operations in Libya in April 1941. At once, the tactical situation in the air changed: the Bf 109E easily outfought the Commonwealth Tomahawks and Hurricanes.

A Bf 109E-3 of II./JG 54 is seen in the standard pre-war dark-green camouflage finish. A key feature of the E-3 was the adoption of wing cannon, the slow rate of fire of this weapon being acceptable in the face of its considerable destructive power.

Bf 109T

German plans for an aircraft-carrier had seen the creation of a Bf 109B squadron in 1939 to begin training for eventual deployment afloat. The operational equipment was to have been the Bf 109T ('T' for '*Träger*' – carrier), a version of the Bf 109E-1 with extended folding wings, revised flaps and overwing spoilers. A batch of 10 Bf 109T-0s was built and these were extensively tested in anticipation of the Bf 109T-1 operational aircraft. When work on the aircraft-carrier *Graf Zeppelin* was completely halted in May 1940, the 60 Bf 109T-1s under construction were completed as Bf 109T-2s, stripped of carrier features but retaining the high-lift devices and extended wings. These were used as land-based fighters, employing their short-landing attributes to operate from bases with only short runways. Most of their career was spent in Norway, but they also formed the defence of Helgoland in the North Sea. They remained in operation until the end of 1944.

bution to the invasions of Denmark and Norway.

However, it was heavily committed in the battles over France and the Low Countries, and it was here that it built its invincible reputation. The attack on Britain followed soon after, during which the Bf 109E acquitted itself well. In the first days of the battle the Bf 109Es were employed in the *freie Jagd* role, able to hunt at will. The pilots could exploit the 109's legendary dive and climb performance to the full, while avoiding too many turning fights, where they were at a disadvantage compared to the Spitfire. Serious losses mounted only after the 109s were switched to bomber escort, following the failure of the Bf 110 to perform effectively in this role.

Experience in France and in the Battle of Britain led to a number of improvements.

Armour protection was improved and a new, heavily-framed canopy began to appear in mid-1940. The Bf 109E-4 appeared on the production lines, this version having wing-mounted MG FF/M cannon with an improved feed mechanism. The Bf 109E retained the capability to mount a cannon in the engine block, firing through the spinner, although this was not fitted in the field and later 'Emils' were built with solid spinners instead of the hollow units fitted earlier.

Range increase

In late August, the E-7 was introduced, with the ability to carry a drop tank under the centreline. Short range had always been the Achilles heel of the Bf 109, and was the chief reason that it had not been able to take part in the Scandinavian campaigns. The centreline rack could also be used to lift a 250-kg (551-lb) SC 250 bomb and, during the Battle of Britain, the type became increasingly used on 'Jabo' (fighter-bomber) sorties. Aircraft used for this role usually had a 'B' suffix applied to the designation (e.g. Bf 109E-1/B).

Small numbers of tactical reconnaissance aircraft were built as the Bf 109E-5 (with wing cannon removed and Rb 21/18 camera in rear fuselage) and the Bf 109E-6 (cannon retained and Rb 50/30 camera). The next major fighter version was the E-4/N, which employed a DB 601N engine and 96-octane fuel for greater power. A few Bf 109E-8s were built as fighters, with the uprated DB 601E engine, as were a very small number of the Bf 109E-9, a camera-equipped equivalent.

Following the end of the Battle of Britain, 'Emils' remained on alert in France to counter RAF cross-Channel operations, but the bulk were withdrawn to prepare for the attack on the Balkans. During the invasion of Yugoslavia, Luftwaffe Bf 109Es fought those of the Yugoslav air force.

Bf 109Es were committed to North Africa from April 1941 and, two months later, formed about a third of the fighter force gathered for the invasion of the Soviet Union.

In both campaigns the Bf 109 again proved to have mastery of the air, notably in the opening weeks of Barbarossa, when countless Soviet fighters fell to the guns of Bf 109Es and Fs. By the end of 1941, most Luftwaffe fighter units had converted to the Bf 109F, but the 'Emil' continued to fly with other Axis air forces for some time after. In the 'Jabo' role the Bf 109E survived at the front line well into 1943.

From July 1940, the Bf 109E was increasingly employed in the 'Jabo' role, carrying a single bomb on the centreline. Coastal shipping was the main target for such raids. This is a Bf 109E-7.

Bf 109F: fighting 'Friedrich'

Above: Early Bf 109Fs were distinguished by rounded wingtips and angular undercarriage bays. In a dive, the speed of the Bf 109F was superior to that of the RAF's Spitfire Mk V.

Left: A pilot removes snow from his aircraft during Eastern front operations in the winter of 1941/2. The Bf 109F spearheaded the German invasion of the USSR, destroying much of the VVS.

Appearing over the Channel in late 1940, the Bf 109F proved a worthy successor to the 'Emil', and went on to serve with Luftwaffe units in North Africa and the Eastern front in a variety of roles.

Arguably the finest of all Messerschmitt Bf 109 variants, the 'Friedrich' began life as a structured development of the Bf 109E. Intended to retain the superiority of the Bf 109 in the skies over Europe, the Bf 109F would couple developed versions of the DB 601 powerplant with improved handling, without losing the manoeuvrability of the 'Emil'.

Modifications
The new-look 'Friedrich' introduced a series of aerodynamic refinements, while maintaining the basic structure of its predecessor. A deeper, more streamlined cowling and larger spinner were the most immediately recognisable differences. Importantly, the Bf 109F carried a new wing, based on the E structure, but incorporating

reduced span and new wider-chord ailerons, as well as a low-drag radiator. In the tail, the 'Friedrich' carried a new retractable tailwheel and a reduced-size rudder. Following pilots' recommendations, armament was altered to include a single cannon firing through the engine hub, combined with two MG 17s in the upper fuselage decking. The removal of wing-mounted cannon would improve its roll-rate and manoeuvrability.

Prototypes
Four prototypes, as well as a batch of 10 pre-production machines, were assembled during 1940, with the prototypes employed in testing variants of the Daimler-Benz DB 601 engine. The first flight, taken in the summer of 1940, revealed the potential of the aircraft,

although the reduced wingspan appeared to hamper handling. This was restored in the third prototype, with the addition of detachable rounded wingtips.

Bf 109F-0 pre-production aircraft left the factory in the late autumn, with new wingtips and oil coolers. Problems with the development of the intended MG 151 cannon and DB 601E engine left the BF 109F-0 with the MG FF/M and the E's DB 601N. However, performance and manoeuvrability were improved in all respects, especially in terms of sustained turn and climb.

The first production F-1 models left the production lines in October 1940. Similar to the F-0, they carried a new supercharger intake, and were fitted to

operate on high-octane C3 fuel. Unfortunately, the machines, which were initially delivered to service evaluation units, suffered a spate of crashes, and were grounded. Eventually, the new brace-free tail unit was isolated as the cause and, to rectify the problem, remaining aircraft were fitted with external strengthening plates to improve control and rigidity.

Service entry
Some of the most experienced pilots based in France received the F-1 as early as October 1940, the first production aircraft being used by Werner Mölders of Stab/JG 51. Due to the earlier setbacks, the first F-1s entered quantity service in March 1941, with the first units to take on the

V24, the fourth prototype, introduced a streamlined cowling and an enlarged spinner. The engine-mounted cannon, absent from the Bf 109E, became standard on all later models.

Left: Following action during the assault of the Soviet Union (Operation Barbarossa), II./JG 27 flew its Bf 109Fs in support of North African operations from October 1941. The aircraft seen here served with 5. Staffel.

Below: These tactical reconnaissance-configured Bf 109F-4s are protected from the desert heat by sunshades. Small pipes behind the under-fuselage camera window ducted away excess oil to prevent fouling of the camera.

type *en masse* being the geschwaders of Luftflotte 3, JG 2 'Richtofen', and JG 26 'Schlageter'. Several other units later received examples, but due to the short production run, none operated the type as sole equipment.

The Bf 109F-2 was delivered concurrently, entering production in January 1941. These aircraft differed in carrying interim 200-round MG 151/15 cannon in place of the F-1's MG FF/M. Meanwhile, the RAF was introducing the Spitfire Mk V on the Channel front. This new variant proved well-matched to the 'Friedrich'; superior in turning circle, although inferior in terms of dive and climb.

Following the equipping of Channel-front units with the F, the next units to transfer to the new aircraft were those in Germany awaiting the assault on the USSR. Operations elsewhere in Europe relied on the earlier 'Emil'. By June 1941, the majority of Jagdgruppen units to be pressed into the opening attack of the Soviet Union had converted to the 'Friedrich'.

Eastern front

By midday on the first day of Operation Barbarossa, the VVS had lost 1,200 aircraft, 320 of which had been shot down, principally by the Luftwaffe's 'Friedrichs'. With their Spanish experience in mind, the Luftwaffe

pilots avoided tackling the nimble I-153s and I-16s in close-in fighting, opting for dive and climb tactics to scythe through the Soviet defences. The aerial superiority of the Fs against the Soviet air force paved the way for the following lightning ground advance toward Moscow.

On the Russian front, the 'Friedrich' pilots began gaining higher scores than their compatriots in Libya, with the veteran Mölders heading the list of aces. In the last half of 1941, the VVS offered little challenge to the Luftwaffe's finest, and several elite units were transferred to the important Mediterranean theatre. In 1942, the outnumbered F units still held their own in the air war, against the emergence of superior new Soviet types,

including the Il-2 battlefield support aircraft.

Southern operations

As the 'Friedrich' moved from strength to strength on the Russian front, the aircraft prepared to make an impact over the desert theatre of North Africa.

Reaching Libya in April 1941, the 'Emil' had an immediate impact against the RAF and, with the SAAF and RAF's adoption of the Kittyhawk Mk I, the Luftwaffe felt it necessary to introduce the 'Friedrich'. JG 27 swiftly converted, and filter-equipped Bf 109F-2/Trop and F-4/Z Trop fighters began to make their mark. Modified in the field, these aircraft quickly found ascendancy against opposing Kittyhawks and Hurricanes.

New F variants included the F-2/Bs equipped for bomb carriage; and the F-2/U1 sub-variant with 13-mm MG 131s in place of the MG 17s, flown by Adolf Galland of JG 26. Intended to introduce GM 1

nitrous oxide boosting, the Bf 109F-2/Z never, in fact, saw service.

At the end of 1941, the intended DB 601E engine became available, running on low-octane B4 fuel, and this first saw service with the F-3. Built in only small numbers, this variant was superseded by the definitive production machine, the Bf 109F-4.

The F-4 introduced the 150-round 20-mm MG 151/20 cannon, and the originally intended engine/armament combination had finally come to fruition. Other changes included new self-sealing tanks, additional armour, and streamlined internal tail strengthening.

The F was used only briefly as a fighter over the Channel before the appearance of the Fw 190, as emphasis switched to the Jagdbomber role. Nevertheless, the Bf 109F-4/B made its mark with hit-and-run attacks on shipping and coastal installations during 1942.

Above: Setting out for a mission across the Channel, this 10.(Jabo)/JG 26 Bf 109F-4/B carries a belly-mounted SC 250 bomb and related bomb insignia on the rear fuselage. The Jabostaffeln specialised in low-level surprise anti-shipping strikes against coastal targets.

Below: After crash-landing at Beachy Head in Sussex in May 1942, this Bf 109F-4/B 'White 11' was adopted by No. 1426 (Enemy Aircraft) Squadron of the RAF. Assigned the RAF serial NN644, the aircraft retained its original Luftwaffe Jabo markings.

Developing the 'Gustav'

In the Bf 109F Messerschmitt had produced one of the finest fighters of the war, but in the 'Friedrich' the Bf 109 had arguably reached the zenith of its development. However, without a suitable successor, the design had to be pushed further in the constant quest for speed and altitude performance. The result was the Bf 109G 'Gustav'.

Above: Bf 109Gs were often fitted with the Rüstsatz-1 kit which added an ETC 500 IXb bomb rack (for a single 500-kg/1,102-lb bomb) on the centreline. This Bf 109G-6 served with JG 3 'Udet'.

The first 'Gustav' – standing in the snow at Regensburg in the winter of 1941/42, VJ+WA was the first of three Bf 109G-0 pre-production aircraft. Of note is the heavily-framed canopy for the pressurised cockpit.

In mid-1941, as the Bf 109F was leading the German charge into Russia, development work was under way for a new version of the Bf 109, the G or 'Gustav', which would become the most numerous variant. Messerschmitt's work on the Bf 109G was by necessity of great haste, with the result that the aircraft was a minimum-change version of the 'Friedrich' with improved basic performance. By 1941 the greatest emphasis was being placed on speed, with handling and manoeuvrability considered to be of lesser importance. Also, the air battle, especially in the West, had moved continuously upwards, and the ability to fight at higher altitudes carried

increasing weight. Therefore, the Bf 109G was designed with a more powerful engine – the DB 605 – for greater speed and, at least initially, pressurisation.

Daimler-Benz's new DB 605A for the Bf 109G was closely based on the DB 601E, but introduced greater bore, higher permissible rpm and increased compression ratio. The result was an engine which produced 1,475 hp (1100 kW) for take-off. Although of similar overall dimensions, the engine was heavier, demanding a strengthening of the engine bearers and other parts of the fuselage structure. In turn, the extra weight required a beefing up of the main undercarriage. The engine installation required additional

cooling, and the G featured an enlarged oil cooler and four small additional airscoops just aft of the spinner.

Cabin pressurisation was provided by the expedient means of sealing the original Bf 109 cockpit enclosure without major redesign. The fore and aft bulkheads, walls and floor were all sealed, while the canopy and windshield incorporated rubber seals. The lower quarterlights which had characterised the earlier models were dispensed with, while the canopy had strengthened framing. The glazing was made of a sandwich, which incorporated a silica pellet to dry the air between the layers.

Construction of the first pre-production batch of three

Bf 109G-0s was undertaken at Regensurg in October 1941, but the DB 605A was not yet available. Accordingly, the G-0s were powered by the DB 601E, albeit with the G's revised cowling (minus the four small airscoops). The first production Bf 109G-1s introduced the DB 605A, and they began to leave the factories in the late spring of 1942, in parallel with the Bf 109G-2, which differed only in having the pressurisation equipment and GM-1 provision deleted. To confuse students of the Bf 109, many G-2s were built with some, or all, of the external airscoops which were associated with the G-1's pressurisation system. The unpressurised Bf 109G-2 was

One of the most common Rüstsätze applied to the Bf 109G was the R6, which added 20-mm MG 151/20 cannon in gondolas under the wings to produce the 'Kanonenboote' ('Gunboat'). These aircraft are both Bf 109G-6s, displaying the bulged cowlings over the MG 131 machine-guns which typified this sub-variant. The aircraft above served with I./JG 53 'Pik As' in Sicily, while the G-6/R6 at left flew with 13.(slowak)/JG 52 on the Russian front.

built in much larger numbers, and was soon in evidence in all theatres, notably on the Russian front where the first examples arrived in June 1942.

Chronologically, the next 'Gustav' variant was the G-4, which began to roll from the lines in October 1942. Like the G-2, it was an unpressurised multi-role fighter built in large numbers and equipping many units. Differences between it and its predecessor were small, the main one being the installation of a FuG 16Z radio in place of the FuG VIIa, with a resultant subtle change in antenna configuration. Early in the G-4 production run, larger main-wheels were introduced, which in turn led to the addition of bulges on the top of the wings. These bulges are believed to be the inspiration for the nickname 'Beule' ('bump') which stuck with the Bf 109G throughout the remainder of its life, although it has also been attributed to the gun fairings of the G-6. Not all G-4s had the wheel bulges, while several later and rewinged G-2s did.

Many G-4s were issued to reconnaissance units, some as Bf 109G-4/U3s with MW-50 water-methanol boosting. A specialist reconnaissance variant was the Bf 109G-4/R3, which was a long-range sub-variant with racks for two 66-Imp gal (300-litre) tanks under the wings

and a single Rb 50/30 or Rb 75/30 camera in the rear fuselage. The MG 17 machine-guns were removed and the muzzle troughs faired over. At least one G-4 was given a trials installation of three MG 151/20 cannon gondolas, with one mounted on the centreline.

Some time after the G-4 had appeared, the Bf 109G-3 entered service, in March 1943. This was a high-altitude pressurised fighter like the G-1, but featured the improvements of the G-4. Only 50 were built.

G-6 – the definitive '109

By mid-1942 the Bf 109G was being asked to perform an ever-increasing number of differing missions – no longer was it a pure fighter. To cater for this diversity of role without major disruption to the production lines, Messerschmitt introduced the Bf 109G-6, which was the most numerous variant, accounting for over 12,000 airframes. The principle behind the G-6 was to produce a basic fighter airframe which could accept any one of a number of conversion sets to equip it for its chosen mission. The aircraft could also accept a number of versions of the DB 605.

Persistent cannon malfunction problems encountered by the Bf 109Fs in the desert had given some cause for concern. While the MG 151/20 remained the

cannon armament of the G-6, the MG 17 machine-guns were replaced with the 13-mm Rheinmetall-Borsig MG 131 machine-gun, with 300 instead of 500 rounds per gun. The new weapon provided the Bf 109G with a reasonable weight of fire even if the primary cannon jammed. The muzzle troughs were moved further back, but the most obvious difference was the addition of large fairings over the spent case return feeds of this much larger gun.

Interspersed with the G-6 on the production lines were small numbers of Bf 109G-5s. They were essentially pressurised versions of the G-6. G-5s entered service in September 1943 and virtually all were assigned to units in the West or on home defence duties.

Conversion kits

As befitted its initial design concept, the G-6 (and G-5) was subject to a bewildering array of conversions and modifications. Many aircraft were fitted with either the GM-1 (U2) or MW-50 (U3) boost systems. Initially, the engine cannon remained the Mauser MG 151/20 with 150 rounds, but increasingly became the Rheinmetall-Borsig MK 108 30-mm cannon with 60 rounds as production of the weapon ramped up from mid-1943 onwards.

The heavier cannon was a

lethal weapon, with one hit sufficient to bring down any fighter. Fitment of the MK 108 was covered by the Umbausatz-4 designation. Other U designations also concerned armament: the U5 was an MG 151/20-armed aircraft fitted with MK 108s in wing gondolas, while the U6 was an aircraft with three MK 108s. These latter two schemes remained in the test phase only, and were never deployed.

Rüstzustände designations for the G-6 included the R2 and R3 tactical reconnaissance platforms, with camera installations similar to those of the G-4, while the standard range of Rüstsätze was available, including R1 (centre-line ETC 500 bomb rack), R3 (centreline drop tank) and R6 (underwing MG 151/20s).

Experience with the Bf 109G had shown that the GM-1 and MW-50 systems, while useful, were less effective than the provision of extra supercharging, leading to the installation of the DB 605AS engine.

This powerplant featured the supercharger which had been developed for the larger DB 603 and gave a maximum output of 1,200 hp (895 kW) at 26,250 ft (8000 m). The DB 605AS had a somewhat larger supercharger, requiring a complete redesign of the engine cowling. The result was a much cleaner cowling which dispensed with the characteristic bulges in favour of larger but more streamlined fairings.

First appearing in the spring of 1944, G-6/AS aircraft were produced as both new-build machines and by conversion of older airframes. Most were assigned to home defence duties, where their increased altitude performance was welcome. A few served with night-fighter units. A small number of G-5s also received DB 605AS engines, although at least some, if not all, lost their pressurisation capability in the process.

Pulk-Zerstörer

Several G-6s were armed with the Werfergranate 8⅓-in (210-mm) rocket. This was essentially a mortar, which lobbed an 88-lb (40-kg) warhead into the middle of bomber formations, hence the name (Pulk-Zerstörer = formation destroyer). Breaking up bomber boxes greatly reduced the effect of mutual defensive fire. The WGr-21 system was used with some success in defence of the Reich and over northern Italy.

Early combat

It was in Spain that Hauptmann Werner Mölders developed the Schwarm (literally, 'swarm') formation, subsequently adopted by the RAF and other air forces as the 'finger four'. The Schwarm comprised two mutually-supportive pairs – a leader and a wingman.

Willy Messerschmitt's new fighter was blooded in the skies of Spain, the Legion Condor introducing the type in support of the Republican forces. The Bf 109 passed this test with flying colours, and was now ready for the Blitzkrieg.

Production Bf 109Bs began leaving Augsburg in February 1937, with the famous Richthofen Geschwader, JG 132, earmarked as the first service recipient. However, events in the Civil War in Spain, where the nimble Russian Polikarpov I-15s and I-16s were enjoying superiority over the Heinkel He 51s of the Legion Condor, dictated that the new fighters were needed desperately overseas. Sixteen Bf 109Bs were shipped to Spain and reassembled in March 1937.

These 'Berthas' were powered by the uprated Jumo 210Da engine of 720 hp (537 kW), driving the original Schwarz fixed-pitch propeller. Armament was restricted to the two MG 17s with 500 rounds each.

2. Staffel der Jagdgruppe 88 was the first unit to get the Bf 109 under the command of Oberleutnant Günther Lützow, who was to achieve ace status in Spain and eventually lose his life in a Me 262 jet in April 1945 with 108 kills to his credit. By late April the Staffel was to all intents operational, but it was not until the fighting around Brunete began in July that 2./J 88 got into action. Assigned to provide escort to Ju 52 bombers and

reconnaissance aircraft, the Bf 109Bs soon became entangled with the Polikarpov fighters on the Republican side. Below about 10,000 ft (3050 m) there was little to choose between them, the I-16s enjoying greater manoeuvrability and the Bf 109s better speed and dive performance. At higher altitudes, the Bf 109s were virtually invincible, and it was swiftly learned that the large formations of Republican aircraft could be easily attacked from above and behind, picking off the rear echelons in uncatchable dives. The only recourse available to the Republicans was to lure the Bf 109s down low, but this was far from easy, and the Bf 109 immediately assumed an enviable reputation.

Combat successes

Although the Republicans claimed a Bf 109 kill as early as 8 July (almost impossible, as 2./J 88 was still many miles from the war zone), there were some losses, but there were far more victories, one of the first being credited to Leutnant Rolf Pingel, later commander of I/JG 26. The Messerschmitt's base at Avila became the subject of increasing Republican bombing raids, so that the Staffel had

Inset above: This Bf 109B-2 of the Legion Condor was flown by World War II ace Walter Oesau. Just visible on the tailfin are eight of the nine kills credited to Leutnant Oesau in Spain, the eighth being an I-16 downed on 15 October 1938. In December 1937 a Bf 109B was captured after landing, out of fuel, behind Republican lines. Though evaluated by the French, a favourable report remained top secret and was not made available to the French aircraft industry as might have been expected; an unfortunate oversight in light of later events.

Below: While the Bf 109 was frequently used in the ground-attack role in Spain, bombs were not carried by the fighter in this war, despite the impression given by this photo which shows bombs awaiting loading into He 111Bs. Bomber and fighter units frequently shared airfields in Spain.

to mount standing patrols and keep aircraft on alert to meet the intruders. No aircraft were lost on the ground, and by the end of July the battle of Brunete ended, allowing 2./J 88 to return to its previous base at Herrera.

In August 1937 the Nationalists launched an assault on the Santander front, accompanied by the Bf 109Bs which moved almost daily from small

strip to small strip. Almost total superiority was enjoyed through this campaign, and this was further heightened by the arrival of more aircraft in September, deliveries of Bf 109Bs eventually totalling 45. Jagdgruppe 88's 1. Staffel converted to the Bf 109 in September with Lützow transferring as commander. The end of the Santander campaign allowed the

This aircraft is one of the first Bf 109Bs which were sent to Spain to join the Nationalist cause. The Legion Condor had been having trouble with the nimble Polikarpov I-15s and I-16s until the Messerschmitt's better performance turned the tables against the Republicans.

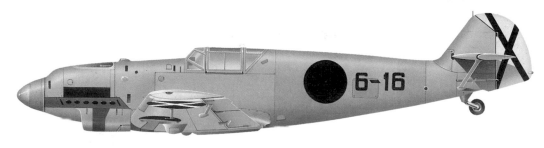

Above: Pristine Bf 109D-1s newly delivered to 2. Staffel of I./JG 132 'Richthofen' line-up at Döberitz during the summer of 1938. Note the early two-tone green finish and early style insignia.

This Bf 109E-1 of I/JG 20 is seen in August/September 1939, i.e. upon the outbreak of World War II. This Gruppe did not participate in the Polish campaign, remaining in eastern Germany on metropolitan defence duties around Dresden. In July 1940 I./JG 20 became III./JG 51 and the 'black cat' emblem was used by 8/JG 51.

Nationalists to concentrate on the southern front, with Madrid the eventual prize, and the two Bf 109 units headed south for a period of rest before turning on Guadalajara. Oberleutnant Wolfgang Schellmann arrived to take command of 2./J 88, his tally from Spain eventually totalling 12 kills.

Initial operations in Spain had more than proven the capabilities of the new fighter, and it had come through a stern test with flying colours, especially given the intensity of operations during the major campaigns and the extremely hot and dusty conditions encountered by ground crews.

'Clara' deliveries

In June, 3./J 88 was eventually withdrawn from the battle to begin its re-equipment with the Bf 109. Its commander, Oberleutnant Adolf Galland, returned home after his tour of duty and was replaced by one of the finest fighter pilots of all time: Oberleutnant Werner Mölders. Allowing partial re-equipment for the Staffel was the arrival in April of five Bf 109Cs, with four-gun armament. This coincided with the delivery to the Republicans of the four-gun I-16 Type 10. The air war continued, and, although the Bf 109 still had the upper hand, losses mounted. In early July, 3./J 88 returned to the fray, Mölders scoring his first kill, an I-16, on 15 July. At the end of the month the second Ebro campaign opened, heralding some of the fiercest fighting of the war. The Messerschmitts were heavily tasked with bomber support, the targets in the main being the bridges across the Ebro river which were usually repaired again the night following their daytime destruction.

In early August five Bf 109D-1s arrived, allowing 3./J 88 to reach full strength. It was during the second Ebro campaign that Mölders introduced the *vierfingerschwarm* formation. By doubling up the formation and adding longitudinal spacing, Mölders at a stroke vastly increased the flexibility of the formation. This was of inestimable value during fighter sweeps, and the 'finger four' became the basic formation of fighter tactics, used to this day.

With the delivery of the first DB 601s in late 1938, production of the Bf 109E-1 got under way. Due to pressing military needs and the political situation, some of the first 'Emils' went to Spain. Early production examples began arriving in Spain in late December, by which time the final offensive of the war had been launched. Fifty-five Bf 109Bs, Cs and Ds had already been sent to Spain, and 37 of these were still in service to support the Catalonian offensive, which opened on 23 December. Barcelona fell on 26 January 1939, after which the Bf 109s were then engaged in preventing Republican aircraft escaping south. The last combat sortie was flown on 27 March, and on 28 March the Republicans surrendered Valencia and Madrid to end the long, damaging war.

Around 200 German pilots had flown with Jagdgruppe 88, and the experience they had gained in Spain was to prove of inestimable value in the much larger conflict which loomed months away.

'Phoney War'

Throughout the spring and summer of 1939 the Jagdgruppen were transitioning to the new variant at fever pitch. During this rapid expansion, on 1 May, the Luftwaffe introduced a more streamlined unit designation system. On 1 September 1939, the Luftwaffe had 1,056 Bf 109s on strength, of which 946 were serviceable.

Despite this good strength, the Bf 109 was employed in only small numbers during the Polish campaign. These early months of the 'Phoney War' provided few opportunities for fighter versus fighter combat, but on the few occasions that the Bf 109E met either MS.406s or the Hurricanes of the advanced RAF force in France, the Messerschmitt proved far superior. Bf 109Es of JGs 1, 2, 3, 21, 26, 27, 51, 52, 53 and 54 soon established total air superiority over the Dutch, Belgian, British and French air forces. Only the Dewoitine D.520, available in small numbers, posed any serious threat to the Bf 109.

France finally capitulated in June 1940 and soon the Luftwaffe'a all-conquering fighter would meet its sternest test, against a determined RAF equipped, in part, with the Supermarine Spitfire.

Above: Pilots of III./JG 2 take a well-earned break – still in their flight overalls – at Signy le Petit during the advance across France, May 1940. Seated to the right is Feldwebel Willinger who, six months later, on 16 November, would be credited with JG 2's 500th victory, over an RAF Hurricane downed over Portsmouth.

Left: Bf 109E 'Yellow 9' is seen during the early stages of the Blitzkrieg campaign against France. Four kill markings are displayed, ahead of the swastika on the aircraft's tail.

Bf 109s of the Adlerangriff

Adlerangriff (attack of the eagles) was the code name for Germany's planned assault on the British Isles. Before it could be launched however, air superiority was vital and the Bf 109 was to play a crucial part in attempts to secure mastery of the air.

Following a month's lull in activity, during which only the three Gruppen of JG 51 Bf 109s remained in France to face the RAF, a slow but deliberate build-up of forces began on 12 July with the return of III/JG 3. At the end of July, JGs 26, 27 and 52 returned to France. Other Gruppen followed.

Although the Bf 109s had enjoyed air superiority over France, combat losses were still high, and one of the chief concerns was the lack of armour protection. In the summer of 1940 Bf 109E-3s began to appear with a heavily-framed

canopy and 8-mm seat armour. A further armour plate was provided over the pilot's head, attached to the canopy. The Bf 109E-4 rapidly replaced the E-3 on the production line, this variant differing by having the MG FF/M cannon in the wings. Essentially similar to the first 20-mm weapon, the new gun had an improved rate of fire. Ikaria-Werke studied a belt-feed for the MG FF, but in the event the trial installation was not flown until early 1941, and was cancelled. The Bf 109 retained the capability for an engine-mounted weapon, although problems with cooling and

A mixed 'Schwarm' – aircraft from all three component Staffeln – of Bf 109Es of I./JG 3 formates over the English Channel in September 1940. The Gruppe was based in Pas de Calais at this time.

vibration had meant they were not fitted. The hollow spinner was nevertheless retained in the fighter variants.

In late August 1940 the Bf 109E-7 began to arrive at fighter units. This differed from the Bf 109E-4 by having the capability to carry a 66-Imp gal (300-litre) jettisonable plywood fuel tank. The lack of range had been one of the main disadvantages of the Bf 109 during the French campaign, and would further embarrass the Jagdgruppen over England, limiting combat time to just a few minutes. In practice, the tank was prone to terrible leaks and suspected of a tendency to ignite. It was rarely used in action due to the suspicions of the pilots. The rack could also carry a single

SC 250 bomb.

Adlerangriff (attack of the eagles) was the grand name bestowed on the operation aimed at Britain, and 13 August was Adlertag (day of the eagles), the date of the major opening bombing assault. Prior to this there were a growing number of exploratory missions along the coast and several skirmishes ensued. The Jagdgruppen were still at about 80 per cent of their strength when they had launched the Western campaign, and on Adlertag their numbers comprised 805 serviceable Bf 109Es. They were divided between Luftflotte 2 in Belgium and the Netherlands, with the full Geschwaders JGs 3, 26, 51 and 52, together with the Stab and I./JG 54 fighter-bombers of 3./Erpro bungsgruppe 210, and Luftflotte 3 in France, which boasted JGs 2, 27 and 53.

In the initial onslaught on Britain, the Bf 109s enjoyed great success, largely because they were entrusted with an

Above: The 'yellow nose' seen on this JG 2 'Richthofen' aircraft, based at Le Havre/Octeville, became a common marking on Channel-based Bf 109s during the battle. Note also the 'wavy line' marking on the fuselage, indicating a III. Gruppe machine.

Below: 'Yellow 14' of 3./JG 2 was the aircraft of Leutnant Franz Fiby, a regular member of Helmut Wick's 'Schwarm', and was photographed early in the Battle of Britain.

Arguably the most famous casualty of the Battle of Britain was Helmut Wick. His Bf 109E is pictured in October 1940, with 42 victories marked on its rudder. He downed 56 aircraft in all before being shot down by a Spitfire the following month.

anti-fighter role which allowed the 'Emil' to fight in its best environment. Complete tactical freedom in the freie Jagd role allowed the Luftwaffe to exploit the dive and climb characteristics in picking off RAF fighters almost at will, and the fluid tactical formations devised in Spain by Mölders proved to be so much better than the rigid and predictable tight formations based on three-ship vics flown by the RAF. Begrudgingly, the RAF began to adopt the finger-four formation, with dramatically improved results.

Where the Luftwaffe was at a real disadvantage was in the poor performance of the much-vaunted Messerschmitt Bf 110, which was supposed to be escorting the bombers. The Zerstörer forces were cut to ribbons, and it became painfully obvious to the Luftwaffe commanders that the Bf 110 could no longer provide adequate protection for the bombers. Accordingly, the Bf 109 was switched from its fighter sweep role to close escort around the beginning of September, immediately denying the tactical freedoms enjoyed by the Messerschmitt pilots during the opening weeks of the battle. With its limited range, the Bf 109 could reach no further than London, while combat over the southern coast of England could rarely be maintained for more than 20 minutes at most.

This situation severely hampered the attempts of the Luftwaffe to defeat the RAF in the air, and, coupled with the decision to leave the bombing of RAF airfields and begin attacking the cities, marked a turning point in the battle. Hurricanes and Spitfires began to exploit the situation to the full, introducing more advanced tactics themselves to keep the rampant Bf 109s in check. Tied closely to the bombers, the Bf 109s could be easily out-turned by both Spitfires and Hurricanes, and, instead of being the hunters who struck at large formations in slashing manoeuvres from altitude, the German aircraft found themselves on the receiving end. Losses began to escalate.

Of course, the Bf 109 was still a most feared opponent, especially in the hands of experienced pilots of the Jagdgruppen who, under the tutelage of Spanish veterans such as Galland and Mölders, built upon their experiences over France to rack up impressive victory tallies. Mölders himself was the leading ace of the Battle of Britain, becoming the first pilot to pass 50 victories while serving with JG 51. Galland, flying with JG 26, was not far behind. Apart from its performance characteristics and experienced pilots, a key advan-

tage enjoyed by the Bf 109E was the 20-mm MG FF cannon, which proved to be devastating against the British fighters.

As the battle progressed, the Bf 109 units were reorganised to reflect their new-found encumberment. The fighter-bomber unit had been joined by I (Jagd)/Lehrgeschwader 2 with new Bf 109E-7s, and the Bf 109E-4/Bs of II (Schlacht)/LG 2. These units mounted several effective raids, although of little destructive effect.

31 October is recognised as the last day of the Battle of Britain. Since July the Luftwaffe had lost 610 Bf 109s, while RAF Fighter Command lost 631 Hurricanes and 403 Spitfires. Drained of energy by the bloody daytime battle of attrition, both sides withdrew from the fighter battle to attempt to recover their strengths, both in numbers of aircraft and from an emotional standpoint. Looked at from an objective, strategic standpoint, the battle ended inconclusively, although from the British perspective the fact that it, alone in Europe, had not succumbed to the might of the German military machine was seen as a great victory.

From a German point of view, the fact that it had not completely crushed the RAF was conversely seen as defeat. A vitally important corner in the course of the war had been turned.

Powerplant
The Bf 109E-4 was powered by a DB 601Aa 12-cylinder inverted-Vee engine with direct fuel injection. This feature allowed the 109 to perform negative-*g* manoeuvres without the engine cutting out.

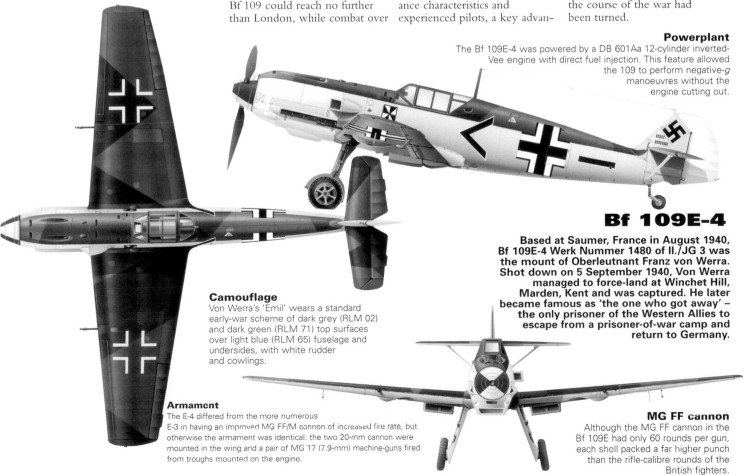

Bf 109E-4

Based at Saumer, France in August 1940, Bf 109E-4 Werk Nummer 1480 of II./JG 3 was the mount of Oberleutnant Franz von Werra. Shot down on 5 September 1940, Von Werra managed to force-land at Winchet Hill, Marden, Kent and was captured. He later became famous as 'the one who got away' – the only prisoner of the Western Allies to escape from a prisoner-of-war camp and return to Germany.

Camouflage
Von Werra's 'Emil' wears a standard early-war scheme of dark grey (RLM 02) and dark green (RLM 71) top surfaces over light blue (RLM 65) fuselage and undersides, with white rudder and cowlings.

Armament
The E-4 differed from the more numerous E-3 in having an improved MG FF/M cannon of increased fire rate, but otherwise the armament was identical: the two 20-mm cannon were mounted in the wing and a pair of MG 17 (7.9-mm) machine-guns fired from troughs mounted on the engine.

MG FF cannon
Although the MG FF cannon in the Bf 109E had only 60 rounds per gun, each shell packed a far higher punch than the rifle-calibre rounds of the British fighters.

Left: This scene gives some idea of the bitter conditions experienced by the Bf 109 units on the Russian front. The aircraft is a Bf 109F, seen some time in the winter of 1940/41.

Below: The ground attack units used the 'Emil' into 1943. This II./SchlG 1 Bf 109E-4/B is taking off from a dusty field in the southern sector in the late summer of 1942. Note the Mickey Mouse emblem used by the Gruppe and the black triangle used by Schlacht units.

Eastern Front

Throughout the bitter German campaign on the Russian front, the Bf 109 remained the Luftwaffe's principal fighter. It achieved success out of all proportion in spite of its meagre numbers.

While the Bf 109E had provided the main fighter equipment for the preceding German campaign in the Balkans, when Operation Barbarossa was launched against the Soviet Union on 22 June 1941, it was the Bf 109F which was the dominant type, although just 609 serviceable fighters were assembled for the task (plus 57 Bf 109 fighter-bombers).

The front was arranged into three sectors: Luftflotte 1 in the north was fully equipped with the Bf 109F (with I., II. and III./JG 54 'Grünherz'), Luftflotte 2 in the centre had both Bf 109Fs (with I., II., III. and IV./JG 51, I., II. and III. JG 53 'Pik As') and Bf 109Es (II. and III./JG 27), while in the south Luftflotte 4 had five Bf 109E Gruppen assigned and three F units (I., II. and III./JG 3).

Barbarossa was savage: by midday on the first day the massed air attacks by Luftwaffe aircraft had accounted for around 1,200 Red Air Force machines. Most were caught on the ground in bombing and strafing attacks, but around 320 had been shot

down, mostly by Bf 109Fs. The Polikarpov I-15 and I-16 opponents were very agile, but posed no significant danger to the Bf 109 pilots providing the Jagdflieger used the vastly superior speed, dive and climb performance of the Bf 109 to scythe through the Soviet formations.

During the first weeks of the Russian campaign the Bf 109s swept away any Soviet resistance in the air, paving the way for the Wehrmacht to reach nearly to the gates of Moscow. Personal tallies mounted quickly – none more so than that of Werner Mölders, Geschwaderkommodore of JG 51 and Germany's leading fighter pilot. His score surpassed that of von Richthofen in the second week of the campaign, and reached 101 on 16 July, at which point he was recalled to Berlin.

As with previous campaigns, the Luftwaffe operated in Barbarossa with virtually no reserves and with relatively few

aircraft, relying on tactical and technological superiority to carry the day. The situation was exacerbated by the withdrawal of Luftflotte 2 to the Mediterranean theatre in December 1941, taking with it several elite units. Despite the continuing successes in the air, attrition accounted for many aircraft, and the overly-complacent German industry struggled to maintain numbers at the front.

In June 1942 the first Bf 109Gs arrived in the east. Although this variant had lost many of the fine handling qualities of the E and F, it was more powerful and faster. This was just as well for the Luftwaffe, as the Jagdflieger were encountering numbers of Yak-1 and MiG-3 fighters, which were a great improvement on the Polikarpov fighters. By the end of the year the Soviet air force was fielding Yak-7 and Yak-9 fighters in greater numbers – aircraft which greatly redressed the balance between the opposing fighter forces.

Nevertheless, the German *experten* continued to score freely, especially in Jagdgeschwader 52: Hauptmann

Hermann Graf from 9./JG 52 passed 150 kills on 4 September (Major Gordon Gollob of JG 77 had achieved this score six days previously) and went on to notch up 200 on 2 October.

By the end of the year though, Hitler's dream of a rapid conclusion to Barbarossa lay in tatters. The Wehrmacht was bogged down at Stalingrad, and in the air the Luftwaffe was beginning to struggle in retaining its supremacy in the face of ever-growing numbers of well-flown and capable fighters.

Jabo and allies

For all the successes or otherwise in the air, it was on the ground where the war was really fought, and Jabo (fighter-bomber) duties occupied a large number of Bf 109 units during 1942/43, until specialised versions of the Fw 190 became available in numbers. Various Bf 109 reconnaissance versions were also used. Although the Bf 109E had disappeared from most front-line fighter units by the end of 1941, a few remained in the fighter-bomber role into 1943.

Other Bf 109Es were flown by Germany's allies in the east.

In the extreme north JG 5 was the main fighter unit, retaining its 'Emils' long after the units to the south had re-equipped with Bf 109Fs and Gs. The Gruppenkommandeur's markings identify this Bf 109E-7 as that of Günter Scholz of III./JG 5, seen in September 1942 while flying from Petsamo.

Bulgaria, Romania and Slovakia all flew 'Emils' on the southern sector, before acquiring Bf 109Gs. Hungary operated Bf 109Fs and Gs, while volunteer forces raised in Croatia and Spain flew as part of the Luftwaffe organisation.

For the Luftwaffe fighter units, the enemies grew in number and strength. Conditions in the east were often appalling: in winter the temperatures were so low that fires had to be lit under the '109 engines to heat up the oil sufficiently; in spring the frozen ground turned into a quagmire which bogged down all but a handful of aircraft.

Bf 109s were at the centre of all the major air battles throughout the campaign in the east. At Stalingrad JG 3 Bf 109s were among the last aircraft to leave the trapped German pocket. In the heavy fighting over the Kuban in March/April 1943 around 220 Bf 109s were assembled – the vast majority of the available strength in the whole eastern theatre. It was in these battles that, for the first time, the Jagdflieger failed to prevail over the Soviet forces.

The turning point

Attentions then turned to Kursk, where Bf 109s fought alongside Fw 190s in some of the war's biggest air battles, involving over 400 aircraft. Soviet opposition included the La-5FN, Yak-9 and Bell P-39Q. Although the Luftwaffe generally fared well in the air, Kursk was the turning point of the bitter war in this theatre, and the Wehrmacht faced a long and bloody retreat thereafter.

As the war progressed the

Above: Leutnant Jürgen Harder's Bf 109F-2 is seen on the opening day of Barbarossa. He was serving with III./JG 53 at the time and had just scored his first kill.

Right: In the autumn of 1942 JG 3's Bf 109s were supporting the Wehrmacht's advance on Stalingrad. Mud made operations difficult in this sector, as this II./JG 3 pilot found as he waded to his Bf 109G-2 'Kanonenboote'.

Red air force continued its meteoric growth in both numbers and capability. Towards the end of the war the Lavochkin La-7 and Yakovlev Yak-3 appeared – both superb at low level and more than a match for all but the best-flown '109s. Nevertheless, while junior pilots were being killed in growing numbers, the 'aces' kept on returning to their bases, and kept on scoring. Although it was an Fw 190 pilot (Nowotny) who was the first to reach 250, JG 52's Bf 109 *experten* were not far behind. Günter Rall hit the 250 tally on 28 November 1943, and Barkhorn followed in February 1944. Erich 'Bubi' Hartmann, who had only scored his first kill in November 1942,

had already passed 100 by 20 September.

In May 1944 the Germans were forced out of Crimea, the Bf 109s of JG 52 being evicted from their productive hunting grounds. The Soviet summer offensives on all fronts pushed the Germans back out of Soviet territory. By 1944 Axis pilots on the southern sector were also regularly encountering USAAF P-38s and P-51s from Italy.

Without doubt one of the biggest 'enemies' was the parlous state of the German aviation industry, which had not only failed to provide an adequate successor to the excellent Bf 109F of 1941, but could barely keep up the supply of new airframes to cover the mounting losses.

Throughout the entire campaign in the east the Jagdflieger operated with an astonishingly low number of serviceable aircraft. Mobility was the key to this dangerous game: units were moved around regularly to bring strength to bear where it was needed, leaving

skeleton forces behind to defend long stretches of front.

From a June 1941 high of over 600 serviceable Bf 109 fighters, the figures fell to 409 in July 1942, and to 260 in May 1943 (plus some Fw 190s), spread across a front from Lappland to the Caucasus. Even by January 1945, with the defence of the Reich reaching desperate proportions, Luftflotten 1, 4, 5 and 6 could only scramble together 329 serviceable Bf 109 fighters, while most of the Fw 190s had been switched to the West.

Although the war's direction had been reversed at Stalingrad and Kursk, the fortunes of some individuals continued to rise. By the end of the war Erich Hartmann had achieved 352 victories. Gerhard Barkhorn (301) and Günther Rall (275) also ran up massive scores with JG 52, which emerged at the end of the conflict with the staggering total of nearly 11,000 kills to its credit. It had flown the Messerchmitt Bf 109 in the east throughout.

Above: Strapping into his Bf 109G-6 is Gerhard Barkhorn, Kommandeur of II./JG 52. The aircraft was named after his wife, Christl, and in it he scored his 250th kill (out of a total of 301).

Right: A front-wide ban on unit markings from 1943 made individual aircraft assignments difficult to determine. These Bf 109G-6s in 1943/44 wear striking winter camouflage patterns.

North Africa and the Med

Bf 109G-6s of 7./JG 27 patrol over the Adriatic from their base in Greece. The nearest aircraft is unmodified, but the two furthest from the camera have tropical filters and the Rüstsatz-6 underwing gondolas for an MG 151/20 cannon. The latter fix was nicknamed the 'Kanonenboote' (gunboat).

When it arrived in North Africa, the Bf 109 enjoyed the same degree of supremacy as it had in the early days over Europe. However, the quantity and quality of Allied aircraft overwhelmed the small force.

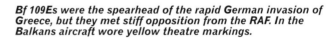

Bf 109Es were the spearhead of the rapid German invasion of Greece, but they met stiff opposition from the RAF. In the Balkans aircraft wore yellow theatre markings.

Although it was perhaps inevitable that the Messerschmitt Bf 109 would eventually be deployed in the Mediterranean theatre, it was due to Italian military failures that it arrived so soon. Firstly, the Italians could not shake the British from their fortress island of Malta. Secondly, the Wehrmacht was forced to intervene in the Balkans, and once Greece had fallen the Germans pushed on for Crete. Finally, the Italians were also suffering in the deserts of North Africa, and Germany again felt obliged to send some of its best forces to stabilise the situation.

February 1941 saw the first Bf 109s arrive in Sicily, 7./JG 26 being dispatched from its English Channel base to help the Italian effort against Malta. III./JG 27 was also deployed, and caused a considerable thorn in the British side until ordered to Greece in May to cover the campaign there.

The first Bf 109s in the desert were from the Stab and I. Gruppe of JG 27, equipped with Bf 109E-4/Ns. These fighters were hastily tropicalised in Sicily and deployed to Libya, where they set up camp at Ainel-Gazala on 19 April 1941 with a forward base at Gambut. Bf 109E-7 Trops were issued

soon after, this variant boasting a centreline rack for a bomb or drop tank. In June III./JG 27 was also deployed.

Flown by well-trained and motivated pilots, the Bf 109Es fared well against the Commonwealth opposition, which in turn found the Luftwaffe a most unpleasant surprise after the Regia Aeronautica. Among the 'Emil' pilots was a young officer of 3./JG 27 named Hans-Joachim Marseille, already a five-kill ace from the Battle of Britain.

In June 1941 7./JG 26 was deployed to Libya, but its unmodified aircraft suffered terribly from the dusty conditions experienced there, and it soon left.

Kittyhawk vs Bf 109F

In North Africa the RAF and SAAF introduced the Curtiss Kittyhawk Mk I. The Luftwaffe command feared that this new fighter would be a match for the Bf 109E, and demanded the urgent conversion of JG 27 to the Bf 109F. This process began in September 1941 with the arrival of II./JG 27. The other Gruppen swiftly converted.

A period of great ascendancy was enjoyed by the Jagdflieger, while the force itself grew with

the deployment of further units: JG 53 in December 1941, JG 3 in early 1942 and JG 77. These units brought with them Bf 109F-2s and F-4s, flown by battle-hardened veterans of the assault on the Soviet Union. With the exception of JG 27, there was considerable movement of units into and out of the theatre, and to and from Sicily.

Star of Afrika

Personal tallies also rose, and none more so than that of Marseille. Flying a Bf 109F-4/Z Trop marked as 'Yellow 14', the 'Star of Afrika' reached 101 kills by 18 June 1942. After an interlude in Germany, he returned to Libya as a Hauptmann to take

command of 3./JG 27. The additional burdens of leadership did not blunt his appetite for air combat: on 1 September he achieved the near-impossible task of shooting down 17 aircraft in one day. By the end of the month his total stood at 158. On 30 September he was killed during a bail-out attempt after his engine caught fire.

Marseille was flying a Bf 109G-2 Trop that day, the 'Gustav' having appeared in North Africa from late June 1942, in both G-2 and, following soon after, G-4 forms. The tropicalised 'Gustavs' had an umbrella stand fixed to the fuselage to protect the pilots from the sun as they sat in the cockpit

While the fighter force swiftly converted to the Bf 109F in the desert, ground attack units continued to use Bf 109Es. This is an E-4/B of III. Gruppe, Schnellkampfgeschwader 210.

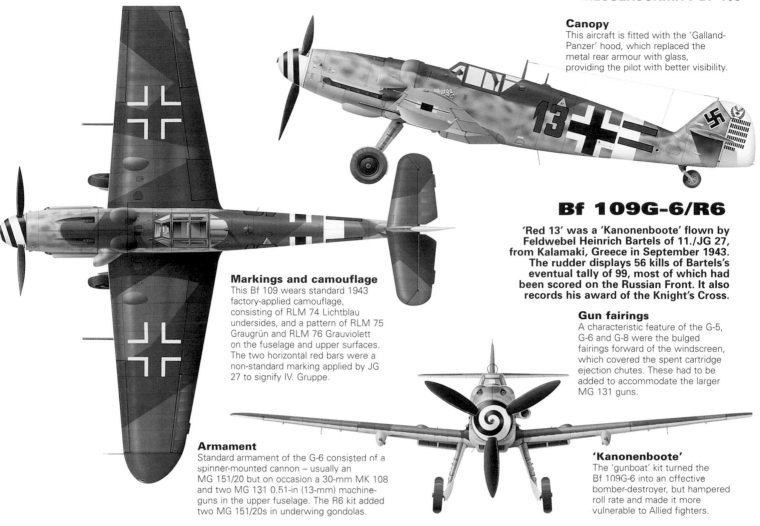

Canopy
This aircraft is fitted with the 'Galland-Panzer' hood, which replaced the metal rear armour with glass, providing the pilot with better visibility.

Bf 109G-6/R6

'Red 13' was a 'Kanonenboote' flown by Feldwebel Heinrich Bartels of 11./JG 27, from Kalamaki, Greece in September 1943. The rudder displays 56 kills of Bartels's eventual tally of 99, most of which had been scored on the Russian Front. It also records his award of the Knight's Cross.

Gun fairings
A characteristic feature of the G-5, G-6 and G-8 were the bulged fairings forward of the windscreen, which covered the spent cartridge ejection chutes. These had to be added to accommodate the larger MG 131 guns.

Markings and camouflage
This Bf 109 wears standard 1943 factory-applied camouflage, consisting of RLM 74 Lichtblau undersides, and a pattern of RLM 75 Graugrün and RLM 76 Grauviolett on the fuselage and upper surfaces. The two horizontal red bars were a non-standard marking applied by JG 27 to signify IV. Gruppe.

Armament
Standard armament of the G-6 consisted of a spinner-mounted cannon – usually an MG 151/20 but on occasion a 30-mm MK 108 and two MG 131 0.51-in (13-mm) machine-guns in the upper fuselage. The R6 kit added two MG 151/20s in underwing gondolas.

'Kanonenboote'
The 'gunboat' kit turned the Bf 109G-6 into an effective bomber-destroyer, but hampered roll rate and made it more vulnerable to Allied fighters.

A few Bf 109G-1 pressurised high-altitude fighters were deployed in November 1942, with JG 51 (fresh from Russia) and JG 53 (3. Staffel illustrated). The silica pellets between the double panes of the cockpit window were a tell-tale sign of this variant.

on strip alert.

In October 1942, Commonwealth forces achieved their epic victory at El Alamein and began to push back the Germans. In November the Torch landings on the Atlantic coast doubled the worries for Rommel. Fighter forces were still strong, and in the initial days after Torch, experienced German pilots found the inexperienced and over-confident US pilots easy game. However, the Americans brought excellent machines with them, and they learned fast. The Commonwealth, too, had sizeable

numbers of Spitfires in-theatre. Losses on the German side mounted and included many of the experienced leaders. The Allied net closed inexorably around the German power base in Tunisia, and on 13 May 1943 the Axis was expelled from North Africa.

Defending Sicily

Most of the Luftwaffe forces retreated to Sicily and Italy, pursued by the Allies. On 10 July the Allied invasion of Sicily began, opposed by the Bf 109G-6s of Stab and II./JG 27, II./JG 51 and

II./JG 77. Despite putting up a stout defence, sheer weight of numbers forced the day and the Bf 109 units pulled back to the Foggia complex. From here they opposed the Allied landings in Italy in September 1943, but the ensuing Italian surrender meant that Luftwaffe units withdrew to the north, where they were joined by I./JG 4.

By this time, however, the German High Command had largely lost interest in Italy, and felt that its Bf 109s would be more gainfully employed in the defence of Germany itself. Gruppen were gradually withdrawn during early 1944, and by the time Rome fell to the Allies on 5 June, only I./JG 4 and JG 77 remained on Italian soil. They, too, headed north before the end of the month.

Bf 109s continued to fight on in Italy, but not in Luftwaffe colours. The Regia Aeronautica had previously operated a few Bf 109F-4s and G-6s, which had fought in Libya alongside Luftwaffe aircraft. After the Italian surrender, several air force units continued to fly on the Axis side, organised as the Aviazione Nazionale Repubblicana (ANR). Former Bf 109 pilots were given new G-6s by Germany, the II° Gruppo Caccia Terrestre flying its first missions in June 1944. In January 1945 a second unit (I° Gruppo CT) was formed with Bf 109G-10s. Although the ANR efforts were ultimately futile, they were a continual nuisance to the Allies until the two Gruppi surrendered in northern Italy in April 1945.

Bf 109s also performed the tactical reconnaissance mission in the Mediterranean theatre. These camera-equipped Bf 109F-4s are from 1. (Fern)/Aufklärungsgruppe 122 based in Sicily.

Northwest Europe and the Reich

While two pilots hold a nonchalant discussion, groundcrew hastily push a 'Gustav' – possibly a G-6 – back into the treeline to keep it out of sight of Allied aircraft over Normandy sometime during July 1944.

From 1943 the Luftwaffe was on the defensive. In western Europe the 8th Air Force bombers embarked on a massive daylight campaign against the Reich. Bf 109s rose daily to defend the Fatherland.

On 27 January 1943 B-17 bombers flying from English bases raided German territory for the first time. The war against Germany had entered a new phase. At this time there were relatively few Luftwaffe fighter units in the West. JGs 2 and 26 were on the Channel Front, while JG 1 was in Holland and north Germany with Bf 109s.

As 8th AF attacks increased, the defences in the West and in Germany itself were strengthened by the withdrawal from the Russian front of several Bf 109 units, a process which was to gather pace throughout 1943 and 1944. New units were formed in the homeland, notably the anti-bomber specialists of Jagdgruppe 50, and JG 11, formed by the division of JG 1. The end of the fighting in North Africa released several units, including the crack I./JG 27, for duties in the West, while Bf 109 Gruppen in Italy withdrew into the southern Reich.

On 17 August 1943 the 8th AF launched its disastrous raid on Schweinfurt. Luftwaffe fighters, notably the Bf 109s of JGr 50, attacked the B-17s for most of the way from the Dutch coast to the target, accounting for 60 aircraft and damaging over 150. By September P-47s with drop tanks could cover the short-range raids, but a second mission to Schweinfurt on 14 October met with a similar fate as the first.

During 1943 the Jagdwaffe soon learned to bide their time until the fighter escorts turned back through lack of fuel. A new type of ace – the *Viermot Experte* (four-engine ace) – began to emerge, and the complex 'points' system by which decorations were bestowed was amended to reflect the 'glory' of bringing down a bomber. The Reichsverteidigung (RV – defence of the Reich) was organised for greater efficiency, with Gruppen assigned either a 'light' (anti-fighter) or 'heavy' (anti-bomber) role. Bf 109s were favoured for anti-fighter work, while the hard-hitting Fw 190 was the weapon of choice against bombers. Where only Bf 109s were available, many were given the 'Kanonenboot' modification which added 20-mm cannon under each wing to increase the weight of fire. Others adopted the Wfr 21 'Pulk-Zerstörer' (formation-destroyer) weapon, a 21-cm mortar tube under each wing. The projectile from this weapon was not primarily intended to bring down bombers, but rather to break up the tight defensive boxes flown by the USAAF.

In the heat of battle the distinctions between 'light' and 'heavy' roles, and the parts played by Bf 109s and Fw 190s, were soon lost. From available records there was no clear advantage of either type in fighting the bombers. However, a few high-ranking leaders are known to have kept one of each aircraft available, leaving their decision as to which one to fly until they knew if the opposition was mainly going to be fighters, in which case they would fly the Bf 109, or bombers.

Night-fighters

In March 1943 Bf 109s began operating as *wilde Sau* (wild boar) night-fighters, operating above the bomber streams and picking up targets silhouetted by flares,

Above: II./JG 11 was heavily involved in the early anti-bomber operations. This is a Bf 109G-1, a pressurised version, fitted with Wfr 21 'Pulk-Zerstörer' mortars under the wings. It was the mount of Oberleutnant Heinz Knoke of 5./JG 11, who had earlier experimented with bombs as a means of destroying bombers.

Right: JGs 2 and 26 each deployed a specialised high-altitude (11.) Staffel. These aircraft are improved pressurised Bf 109G-3s of 11./JG 2 in northern France during March 1943. JG 2 Fw 190s are also visible in the background.

I./JG 27 was one of the first units to reinforce the Western Front, arriving in France from the Mediterranean in early 1943. This photo, taken after the January 1944 application of the green RV band on the rear fuselage, shows a Bf 109G-6/R6 'Kanonenboot'.

searchlights or fires. The introduction of Window (chaff) by the RAF night bombers in July 1943 effectively blinded the German radars and the *wilde Sau* force was rapidly expanded to cover the shortfall, resulting in the creation of three new Jagdgeschwaders (JGs 300, 301 and 302), mostly equipped with Bf 109Gs, although in many cases the aircraft were shared with day-fighter units. In the summer of 1943, the *wilde Sau* aircraft achieved considerable success but the bad weather of autumn hindered their ability to recover safely to their airfields. These operations finally ended in March 1944.

By this time the daytime defenders were suffering greatly at the hands of the P-51, which had joined combat in January.

The Mustang had the range to escort the bombers all the way to the target, and the defence of the Reich grew more and more desperate. More units were brought in from the East but this posed its own problems, as the experienced veterans of this essentially low-level campaign had trouble adjusting to the high-altitude anti-bomber role, especially when faced with Mustang opposition.

Normandy

Defence of the Reich duties were put on hold when the Allies opened the second front on 6 June 1944. Eleven Bf 109 Gruppen were dispatched with haste to France, but they achieved little other than the decimation of their front-line strengths and by the end of

August, most had returned to more pressing matters in Germany.

In December Hitler launched a counter-offensive in the Ardennes, supported in number by Bf 109 units. They achieved some success, but the ground offensive ground to a halt. In its last major action, the Luftwaffe scraped together a considerable force of around 800 fighters for Operation Bodenplatte, which was aimed at the Allied airfields in Belgium and France. On 1 January 1945, Bf 109s and Fw 190s screamed across the Allied airfields but did not inflict the kind of damage that had been expected, while suffering over 200 losses.

After Bodenplatte the Bf 109 force was switched to the eastern front, leaving just JG 53 behind

in the west. The last major aerial action was fought on 14 January, resulting in yet further losses to the Luftwaffe. Although the Bf 109 continued to play a part, the final days of defence were largely entrusted to the Fw 190s and Me 262 jets.

One last act of desperate defiance was Operation Wehrwulf, the creation of a suicide ramming unit known as Sonderkommando Elbe. On 7 April it undertook its only mission, 60 stripped-down Bf 109s bringing down eight B-17s in ramming attacks.

In the end, it was a lack of fuel and experienced pilots which consigned the once-mighty Bf 109 fleet to inevitable defeat, an ignominious end to what was arguably the best fighter ever built.

One of the last units to operate Bf 109s in the west was JG 53. Here GIs examine the wreckage of a Bf 109G-14/AS of IV./JG 53 brought down near Saarlautern in January 1945.

Bf 109K features
The K was intended to rationalise the chaotic state of Bf 109 manufacture, which was producing large numbers of aircraft but in a bewildering array of sub-types. The K naturally sported many features of late-model 'Gustavs': Erla-Haube canopy, tall wooden tail and tall tailwheel. The parallel Bf 109G-10 programme remanufactured 'Gustavs' to a similar standard. One feature which distinguished the K from any G version was that its direction-finding loop was relocated further back along the spine.

Powerplant
The Bf 109K-4 was powered by a Daimler-Benz DB 605DM engine which, with MW-50 water-methanol boosting, produced 2,000 hp (1492 kW) for take-off. The installation of the engine required the addition of small bulges to the cowling on the sides behind the spinner.

Bf 109K-4

The Bf 109K-4 was the last variant to be built in any quantity, reaching the front line in October 1944. This aircraft flew with III./JG 53 and was based at Kirrlach in Bavaria in March 1945.

Armament
The K-4 was only fitted with three guns, all in the nose. Two were 13-mm MG 131 heavy machine-guns mounted above the engine, but the third was the devastating 30-mm MK 108 cannon, mounted in the engine block and firing through the spinner.

Undercarriage
The Bf 109K and G-10 introduced wider tyres to improve ground handling. These, in turn, required large fairings on the upper wing surfaces to accommodate them.

Markings
This aircraft is finished in a relatively rare finish of dark green/mid-green. The aircraft wears both its JG 53 'Pik As' badge and the black rear fuselage RV band.

Other WWII operators

Bulgaria

The Royal Bulgarian air force (VNVV) took delivery of 19 Bf 109E-4s (illustrated) in 1940. Subsequent deliveries of Bf 109G-2s, G-4s and G-6s from 1943 brought the total to 149, most serving with the two orliaks (regiments) of the 6th Iztrebitelen Polk (fighter division) based at Bozhouriste and Vrazhdebna. In the defence of the capital, Sofia, the Bf 109s fought mainly against USAAF bombers and their escorts operating from Italy, claiming over 50 kills but losing many aircraft on the ground in bombing raids. On 9 September 1944 Bulgaria joined the Allies, and the Bf 109s joined the fight against their erstwhile masters. At war's end over 100 late-model Bf 109Gs were given to Bulgaria, although the majority was handed on to Yugoslavia as war reparations. VNVV Bf 109 operations ceased in 1946.

Italy

Two squadrons of the Regia Aeronautica were supplied with Bf 109F-4s in early 1943, seeing brief service in North Africa. Bf 109G-6s arrived subsequently, shortly before the division of the air force into Axis and Allied camps. The pro-Axis Aviazione Nazionale Repubblicana fielded a squadron of Bf 109G-6s (illustrated) from September 1944 and one of Bf 109G-10s from January 1945.

Japan and the Soviet Union

In 1941 five unarmed Bf 109E-7s were sent to Japan (illustrated) for technical evaluation, although the Japanese were more impressed by the DB 601 engine. The Soviet Union also received a few Bf 109Es prior to the German invasion in July, as well as subsequently capturing others.

Croatia

The Croatian Legion was raised as a volunteer squadron for service with the Luftwaffe on the Russian front. Known as 15.(kroat)/JG 52 or the Kroat Jagdstaffel, the unit was initially equipped with Bf 109E-7s before converting to Bf 109G-2s in July 1942, and later to G-6s. Aircraft numbers dwindled to just four by February 1944. In late 1944, however, the unit re-equipped with Bf 109G-10s, and these flew on the Axis side until the last days of the war.

Finland

Finland received its first batch of 'Mersus', as the Bf 109 was called, in early 1943. Bf 109G-2 deliveries totalled 28, and these were followed by G-6s (illustrated), G-8s and G-10s for a total of 150. They served with HLeLv 24 and 34, and proved successful against the Russians. On 4 September 1944 an armistice ended the war against the USSR, although the Bf 109s lacked sufficient range to take part in subsequent Finnish operations against German forces in Lappland.

Hungary

As one of Germany's staunchest allies in the East, Hungary was supplied with Bf 109F-4s (illustrated) in October 1942, G-2s in early 1943 and G-6s in 1944. A large force, which peaked at nine squadrons, served alongside the Luftwaffe on the Russian front, and then in defence of Hungary itself as Allied bombers began to fly from Italy. Despite the Hungarian surrender in January 1945, the Bf 109 squadrons remained loyal to the Axis cause to the end of hostilities.

Romania

From early 1942, the Royal Romanian air force acquired 69 Bf 109E-4s (illustrated, with a Luftwaffe Bf 109E) for the Grupul 1 Vinatoare. Bf 109G-2s and G-6s were later supplied, operating both at home and on the Russian front. In August 1944 the air force joined the Soviet cause, at the same time acquiring ex-Luftwaffe G-10s and G-14s. The last was retired in 1948.

Slovakia

Two Slovak units received Bf 109E-7s (illustrated) in 1942, 11. Stíhací Letka defending Slovakia and 13. Stíhací Letka which operated on the Russian front as 13.(slowak)/JG 52. In early 1943 the latter unit received Bf 109G-6s, but was posted back to defend Bratislava in April 1944. After secret negotiations with the Allies, a handful of Bf 109s was involved in the national uprising of August 1944.

Switzerland

The Fliegertruppe took delivery of its first Bf 109, one of 10 D-1s, on 17 December 1938, paving the way for the supply of 80 Bf 109E-3s (illustrated) from April 1939. Other aircraft were added by internment of German machines (two Bf 109Fs and two Bf 109Gs), and the purchase of 12 Bf 109G-6s in May 1944. The aircraft were very active protecting Swiss neutrality (for which they were given large striped markings), including the shooting down of several German aircraft.

Spain

The Ejército del Aire initially acquired Bf 109Es (illustrated) when they were left behind by the Luftwaffe at the end of the Spanish Civil War. Bf 109F-4s were supplied in 1942, mainly to train pilots for the volunteer Escuadrón Azul, which flew in Russia as 15.(span)/JG 51. In 1942 Spain signed to licence-build 200 Bf 109Gs, but the engines were not delivered and the aircraft emerged as HA-1109/1112s.

Yugoslavia

Impressed with the Bf 109, the Royal Yugoslav air force ordered 100 E-3s in April 1939 for service with the 6th Fighter Regiment (illustrated), although only 73 were delivered. All were destroyed during the German onslaught of April 1941 – some at the hands of the Luftwaffe but most put to the torch to prevent them being captured. A few kills were achieved in reply. Towards the end of the war, Yugoslav partisan forces used Bf 109Gs in support of the Allied cause. The aircraft had either been left behind by the retreating Luftwaffe or brought in by defecting Croatian pilots.

Captured Messerschmitts

Many Bf 109s were captured by the Allies intact, or with only minor damage, and evaluated thoroughly. Several were captured during the fighting in North Africa, while others arrived in Allied territory after navigation errors or through forced landings. As the Allied armies progressed through Europe, more were recovered. The UK had over 20 intact aircraft at one time or another during the conflict.

Having made a wheels-up landing in Kent, this Bf 109E-3/B was repaired and extensively evaluated in the UK.

This Bf 109F-4 was captured by the Soviet Union, and presented as a gift to the USAAF. It arrived at Wright Field in March 1943.

Before the end of 1939 two Bf 109Es had been captured by France. This aircraft subsequently went to the UK for further trials.

Messerschmitt Bf 110
Zerstörer

Despite its successes in the early stages of the war, the Bf 110, with its high speed and heavy armament still found itself outclassed when faced with Spitfires and Hurricanes over the British Isles.

Having proved near-invincible during the Blitzkrieg campaign, the Bf 110 suffered desperately against the fighters of the RAF during the Battle of Britain. Soon, however, it would become the bane of Bomber Command in the night-fighter role.

Speed, acceleration and high manoeuvrability in the cut and thrust of a dogfight were the objectives laid before the fighter designers of all nations following the end of the war in Europe in 1918. Accordingly, it was the single-seat biplane, of high power:weight ratio and relatively low wing-loading, that held the position of pre-eminence in the world's air forces. Then came the monoplane revolution of the 1930s, with monocoque fuselages, retractable landing gear, cantilever tail units, and stressed single- or double-spar wings; the configuration of the fighter remained essentially the same, with armament and fuel tankage carefully restricted so as not to detract from speed and manoeuvrability. However, combat operations over the Western Front during 1917-18 had accentuated the need for fighters with extended range and endurance, and in particular for those with a combat radius of action that could enable them to accompany bombers on missions deep into enemy airspace, either as escort fighters or in order to gain air supremacy in an appointed area.

To design such an aircraft was considered to be well nigh impossible but, in 1934, the idea was resurrected. Whether the long-range strategic fighter concept was to be committed to offensive or defensive tasks is still a matter for argument. For the Luftwaffe at least, the requirement for this type, termed the *Zerstörer* (destroyer), was the pursuit and destruction of enemy bombers operating over the Reich, plus the additional ability to harass over a lengthy period as the bombers withdrew.

Lean design

Attending to the RLM specifications for the development of a heavy strategic fighter, the team at the Bayerische Flugzeugwerke AG (later Messerschmitt AG) started work on the project in the summer of 1935. With their wayward brilliance, they ignored much of the specification data and concentrated their efforts on the design of a lean, all-metal, twin-engined monoplane. Powered by two Daimler Benz DB 600A engines, the prototype Bf 110 V1 achieved a maximum speed of 314 mph (505 km/h) at 10,415 ft (3175 m), considerably in excess of that reached by the single-engined Messerschmitt Bf 109B-2 fighter. Of course,

The prototype Messerschmitt Bf 110 V1 first flew from Augsburg-Haunstetten on 12 May 1936, with Rudolf Opitz at the controls. Only four pre-production aircraft were built and their sleek design was very advanced for its day.

acceleration and manoeuvrability, as noted by the test pilots and later by those at the Erprobungsstelle (service trials detachment) on this and subsequent prototypes, in no way compared with those of lighter fighters. But Hermann Goering ignored the misgivings of the Luftwaffe regarding the

Messerschmitt Bf 110's potentialities, and ordered that production should proceed. The first pre-production model, the Bf 110B-01 powered by two Junkers Jumo 210Ga engines, first flew on 19 April 1938 in the wake of a major reorganisation of the Luftwaffe's units.

The shortage of Daimler Benz

As a way of destroying large formations of Allied bombers and for ground attack, a number of rocket launching methods was trialled on the Bf 110. This example tested the RZ65 rocket shell, which was fired from a battery of 12 2¾ in (73 mm) tubes mounted beneath the fuselage. The installation proved unsatisfactory and was ultimately abandoned.

Left: This Messerschmitt Bf 110B-0 fighter reveals the type's slim fuselage and graceful lines. Although the aircraft was hard put to stay the pace with the later single-seat Allied fighters, many German aces claimed high scores on the type. Too vulnerable as a day-fighter, the Bf 110 remained the mainstay of Germany's night-fighter force from 1940 to 1945.

Above: It was as a night-fighter that the Bf 110 finally found major success. There were over a dozen radar-equipped variants and their armament was steadily modified and upgraded. In one type, oblique firing 30-mm MK 108 cannon were successfully installed. Known as schräge Musik (slanting music or jazz), the cannon were located in the aft cockpit.

powerplants and the retention of the Jumo 210Ga engines conferred only a mediocre capability on the Bf 110B-1 series that emanated from the Augsburg production lines in the summer. Armed with two 20-mm Oerlikon MG FF cannon and four 0.31-in (7.92-mm) MG 17 machine-guns, the Bf 110B-1 had a maximum speed of 283 mph (455 km/h) at its rated altitude of 13,125 ft (4000 m); the service ceiling was 26,245 ft (8000 m). This version was the first to enter service, equipping a number of schweren Jagdgruppen (heavy fighter wings) in the autumn of 1938.

Early in 1939, the Messerschmitt Bf 110C-0 pre-production fighters were issued to the newly-formed Zerstörergruppen (ex-schweren Jagdgruppen); these featured the modified airframe that was to endure throughout the aircraft's lifetime, and were powered by the 12-cylinder, inverted-Vee direct-injection Daimler Benz DB 601A-1 engines rated at 1,100 hp (820 kW) at 12,140 ft (3700 m). The production Bf 110C-1s were highly effective long-range fighters, and the crews of I.(Zerst)/

Lehrgeschwader Nr 1, I./Zerstörergeschwader Nr 1 and I./ZG 76, who manned the new type, represented the cream of the Luftwaffe's fighter arm. Just before the outbreak of war, in September 1939, each Gruppe had two staffeln with Bf 110C-1s and a conversion unit with Bf 110B-3 trainers.

Zerstörer at war

The crews used their heavy aircraft well during the short campaign in Poland during September, flying top cover to the Heinkels and Dorniers and conducting sweeps at 19,685 ft (6000 m) and above; they quickly recognised the stupidity of entering turning matches with the nimble Polish PZL P.11c fighters, and adopted climb-and-dive tactics while maintaining good airspeed at all times. Oberst Walter Grabmann's I.(Z)/LG 1 (led by Hauptmann Schleif) downed five PZL P.11s over Warsaw on the evening of 1 September while covering the Heinkel He 111Ps of II./KG 1.

Already it was apparent that the Zerstörergruppen had eschewed what was probably the originally intended role, and were being employed on escort and superiority sorties against

enemy single-engined fighters. In theory, there was little wrong with the performance parameters of the Bf 110C-1: for its size and configuration, it was the finest heavy fighter extant. With a combat weight of 13,007 lb (5900 kg) it attained 336 mph (540 km/h) at a rated altitude of 19,850 ft (6050 m), faster than most contemporary Allied fighters, and only 20-30 mph (32-43 km/h) slower than its next opponents, the French Dewoitine D.520 and the British Supermarine Spitfire Mk I. But, in fighter-versus-fighter combat, snappy rates of roll and swift acceleration win the day, with maximum-rate turns being a factor of power, wing-loading and pilot strength.

Few problems were encountered by the Bf 110 pilots over Poland and Scandinavia, and their early success gave them a sense of security in the aircraft's abilities. Staunch opposition over France and southern England during 1940 destroyed much of that myth, however, for, while the Bf 110 could operate with relative impunity at high level, when it came down to fight with the nimble Spitfires and Hurricanes at medium level, often operating as a bomber escort, it found itself thoroughly out-turned and, as a result, was regularly shot down. At this time, other variants of the Bf 110, including fighter-bombers and extended-range fighters, made their appearance over Britain or in the Mediterranean

and North Africa. Bf 110 units were then unleashed against the Soviets, where they enjoyed mixed success. As the war progressed, the Bf 110 found itself more and more outclassed by the latest series of Allied aircraft and was gradually withdrawn from service in most theatres.

Night-fighter

However, there was one field in which the Bf 110 excelled, and that was as a night-fighter, performing in the defence of the Reich against enemy bombers. Successive series of aircraft were equipped with ever better radars, in particular the FuG 212 Lichtenstein C-1 and FuG 220 Lichtenstein SN-2. Many pilots chalked up a number of kills, in particular Major Heinz-Wolfgang Schnaufer, the last Kommodore of NJG 4 and a recipient of the Diamonds to the Knight's Cross, who claimed no fewer than 121 nocturnal kills during the war.

It should be remembered that few twin-engined aircraft, even those as legendary as the Mosquito, Kawasaki Ki-45 or Lockheed P-38 Lightning, could match the single-seat fighters of the day. Despite its failure as a dog-fighter, the Bf 110 should be remembered as a highly efficient and versatile all-purpose combat aircraft. And, in the Bf 110's original role, as bomber destroyer – particularly at night – it proved highly effective.

A Bf 110C-4b is seen after capture by the Desert Rats of General Montgomery's Eighth Army. The Bf 110 played an important role in the Western Desert, providing fighter-bomber support to Rommel's Afrika Korps.

A Bf 110C of 5./ZG 26 taxies out from its camouflaged revetment during the early stages of the Blitzkrieg in the west, May 1940. The aircraft's insignia includes a pair of badges on the nose: the white dog of II. Gruppe foremost, and the ace of spades (in red triangle) of 5. Staffel behind.

The early months
Bf 110 at war, 1939/40

Much feted before the war as the élite of the Luftwaffe, the Zerstörer force and its Messerschmitt Bf 110s achieved just enough success in the early German campaigns to keep the myth alive. However, the reality was to be cruelly exposed in the fighting of the Battle of Britain.

Photographed during the campaign in France during summer 1940, this 1./ZG 52 aircraft appears to have suffered a take-off or landing accident, as evidenced by the twisted prop blades.

Herman Göring regarded his Zerstörer (strategic fighter, literally destroyer) force as the cream of the rebuilt Luftwaffe, and the main weapon with which the air force would sweep aside opposition ahead of the victorious advance of the Wehrmacht.

When Hitler ordered the invasion of Poland, Göring ensured that all three Zerstörergruppen, comprising I./ZG 1, I./ZG 26 and I.(Z)/LG 1 would be committed to the opening assault. This force amounted to around 90 Bf 110Bs and Cs. One Gruppe covered each of the three axes of attack, and was initially used to escort He 111 and Do 17 bombers. Opposition to the raids was sparse, and the few dogfights

which developed generally went the Bf 110's way, although a few fell to Polish guns, exposing the weakness of the Bf 110 in fighter v. fighter combat in its first few engagements. With the Polish air force virtually nullified, the final days of the campaign were spent in train-busting and strafing the columns of retreating Poles.

Within days of the Polish invasion, RAF bombers began to make armed reconnaissance patrols and bombing attacks along the German North Sea coast, resulting in Bf 110s being sent to bolster the defence of the area after the end of the Polish campaign. They scored their first kill on 6 December.

On 18 December, in what became known as the Battle of the German Bight, Luftwaffe

fighters shot down 12 of a force of 24 Wellingtons, nine of the victories going to Bf 110s. This battle ended Bomber Command daylight bombing operations for good, although RAF bombers continued to make daylight patrols, providing sporadic fodder for the Bf 110s. Along the French border there were several skirmishes with fighters, mostly inconclusive, although the kill achieved by Leutnant

Werner Methfessel on 23 November 1939 made him the first Bf 110 ace, even though the veracity of the claim remains in some doubt.

110s up north

Two Zerstörergruppen were included in the Luftwaffe line-up for Operation Weserübung, the invasion of Denmark and Norway. I./ZG 1 accompanied the push into Denmark, meeting with little opposition, while I./ZG 26 had the difficult task of escorting Ju 52/3m paratroop transports to Norway. The trip was to be one-way only – there was insufficient fuel for the return – and they were ordered to land at the target airfields (Stavanger-Sola and Oslo-Fornebu) once the airfields had been secured. With fog hampering the operation, only two of eight aircraft reached Stavanger, while at Oslo only three of eight

Another I./ZG 52 aircraft (with the white dragon Gruppe badge on the nose), camouflaged by ground crew in preparation for an aerial attack. The airfield could be a captured French site, or I./ZG 52's 'jumping-off point' of Neuhausen ob Eck.

Left: A Schwarm of Bf 110Cs passes the Arc de Triomphe (bottom left) following the close of the campaign in France. Although retouched by the censor, these are V.(Z.)/LG 1 aircraft (L1 codes).

Below: A Rotte (two aircraft) of 5./ZG 26 demonstrates the efficacy of the new mottled camouflage scheme (on the foreground aircraft) compared to the earlier dark green scheme. The original German caption read: 'over England, October 1940' although the field pattern would suggest Europe.

arrived undamaged, two having been lost in fighting with Norwegian Gladiators. With southern Norway secured, the fighting shifted to the central sector, where the Bf 110's considerable range was put to good use, mainly against RAF bombers. The twin also put up a good fight against RAF Gladiators, although attrition in the harsh conditions was high. Bf 110Ds were deployed, with a ventral long-range tank, giving rise to the nickname 'Dackelbauch' ('dachshund belly').

Despite being ousted from Norway in early June, the British kept up attacks. On 13 June a force of Blackburn Skua dive-bombers attempted to attack the battle-cruiser *Scharnhorst*, but it was cut to ribbons by the Messerschmitt Bf 110s, with the result that the Royal Navy never again would procure dive-bombers.

Into France

On 10 May 1940 attentions turned to France, Belgium and Holland. Again, the Bf 110s were to spearhead the Blitz on enemy airfields, escorting bombers and strafing airfields. Nine Gruppen and three staff flights of Bf 110s were gathered for the campaign. In the initial attacks resistance was weak, with most opposition being caught on the ground. Only two Bf 110s were lost in the first day's fighting, but as the battle over France wore on, losses began to mount, especially to French and RAF single-seat fighters. Bf 110 pilots also scored freely, chiefly because the Allied opposition was flying obsolete equipment in many cases, and because the defences were uncoordinated.

As the campaign neared the Channel coast increasing numbers of RAF fighters were encountered, and Bf 110 losses increased accordingly. Spitfires extracted a heavy toll over the Dunkirk beaches, although on 31 May Bf 110s allegedly caught five of the British fighters and shot them all down. Despite the Zerstörergruppen's successes, by the time British forces completed their evacuation from Dunkirk in the early hours of 3 June, an unacceptably high figure of over 60 Bf 110s had been lost in the 3½-week campaign. The writing was clearly on the wall.

Decimation

And it was written in bold, capital letters. The Bf 110 was clearly outclassed in air combat with modern single-seat fighters such as the Spitfire. Its forward-facing armament was hard-hitting, but the sluggishness of the aircraft made it difficult for a pilot to bring the guns to bear against nimble opposition. Over France Bf 110 pilots soon learned to employ the defensive circle when faced with fighter opposition as their best chance of survival. A formation would turn into a circle, the guns of the following aircraft covering the tail of the one in front.

These tactics were often employed in the Battle of Britain when the beleaguered Bf 110s were faced with Hurricanes and Spitfires. In some cases the circle was used as a decoy to draw in the British fighters for attack by high-flying Bf 109s.

The battle itself was a disaster for the Messerschmitt twin. It began with the closure of the Channel to British shipping in which the Bf 110 played only a secondary part, yet enough to lose several aircraft to the RAF. The second phase opened on 13 August – Adlertag (eagle day) – and concentrated on RAF airfields. The theory was that the Bf 110s would fly ahead of the bombers to draw the RAF fighters into the air. By the time the bombers arrived, the defenders had either been severely mauled or run out of fuel and had landed to replenish, giving the bombers a free run at their targets. The appaling showing of the Bf 110 in combat ruined these plans.

'Only' 13 were lost on 13 August, but two days later nearly 30 were shot down. In the mistaken belief that RAF fighters were fully committed in the south of England, the Luftwaffe in Norway mounted a raid against the northeast. This was escorted by the cumbersome long-range Bf 110Ds, which were met by Spitfires and Hurricanes with the loss of seven. The bombers were widely dispersed and overall the raid was a disaster.

On 17 August another 15 Bf 110s were lost, and from that time the type's importance to the battle declined as Bf 109s assumed the bomber escort role on all but the long-range missions. This was not a tactical decision: it was simply due to the falling numbers of Bf 110s available. By the end of the month 120 had fallen, and by the end of September this figure had topped 200. The Zerstörergruppen had started the campaign with 237 serviceable aircraft.

An unidentified ZG 26 Bf 110C conducts a Freie Jagd (free hunt, roaming patrol) mission over southern England or France in summer 1940. The individual aircraft letter 'A' may mark this machine as belonging to the Staffelkapitän.

Mediterranean operations

Despite its severe mauling in the Battle of Britain, the Bf 110 could still play a useful daylight role in theatres where fighter opposition was weak. In 1941 that meant the Mediterranean.

Göring's vision lay in tatters. His much-vaunted Zerstörer force of Bf 110s had received such a drubbing over England in the summer of 1940 that only a handful of aircraft remained serviceable by the end of the Battle of Britain.

With hindsight, it can be regarded as pure folly to have thrown the Messerschmitt twin into combat against the RAF in such a way, and the fighting over France in May/June 1940 should have provided sufficient warnings to the Luftwaffe to have prevented its deployment over England. However, the Bf 110's excellent range and hard-hitting armament still had applications in many other roles and theatres.

At the end of the Battle of Britain such tasks were difficult to envisage, and the force was immediately withdrawn to coastal patrol duties in Norway, northern Germany and the Mediterranean. In the winter of 1940/41 many Bf 110 units were switched to the role of night-fighting, to which they proved well suited.

War in the Balkans

By April 1941 Hitler's aim was focussed on the Soviet Union, but to underpin his assault the southern flank of Europe had to be secured. When Italian forces had failed in their bid to invade Greece, Hitler was forced to act. Romania and Bulgaria capitulated readily, but Greece and Yugoslavia stood firm. Germany decided to crush both in a single act. Suddenly the need for a long-range day fighter rose again, and two Bf 110 units which had just been allocated a

Above: A Bf 110C scours the arid terrain of Crete for pockets of Allied resistance. Units involved in the May 1941 invasion of Crete included I. and II./ZG 76, both based at Argos, Greece.

Top: An 8./ZG 26 Bf 110C is pictured after the arrival of III./ZG 26 in North Africa in spring 1941. Although its cockpit and tyres are protected against the sun, it still carries European camouflage.

night-fighter role were reactivated as Zerstörergruppen for the Balkans campaign.

I./ZG 26 was installed at Szeged in Hungary, while II./ZG 26 was further south, at Krainici in Bulgaria. When the attack opened on 6 April, the northern unit escorted bombers on a devastating raid against Belgrade. During the course of these missions the Bf 110s encountered Bf 109s of the

Yugoslav air force, which shot down a number of the twins. In the south II./ZG 26 Bf 110s covered the Wehrmacht's advance into southern Yugoslavia, which then turned south into Greece. The Geschwader's III. Gruppe, resident in Sicily, also made a fleeting appearance in the campaign, staging through Italy to attack targets along the central Yugoslav coast. With the initial

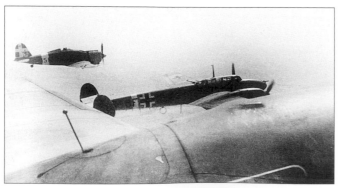

Emphasising Axis co-operation, this 2.(H)/14 Bf 110C (wearing temperate splinter camo) was being escorted by a 51° Stormo Fiat G.50bis of the Regia Aeronautica over Libya in early 1942.

Above: A replacement aircraft is prepared at III./ZG 26's North African airstrip, perhaps in 1942. At the extreme left of the photograph is an Italian CR.42 fighter-bomber, minus its wings.

Below: Two Bf 110-equipped tactical reconnaissance Staffeln operated in North Africa: 2.(H)/14, and 4.(H)/12, with crew from the latter seen here celebrating their 500th sortie in this theatre. Reconnaissance missions were flown by Bf 110E-3 and Bf 110F-3 models, which had one or two cameras mounted in the rear fuselage. They could also carry the enormous 198-Imp gal (900-litre) underwing tanks.

air opposition neutralised, the Bf 110s turned to ground attack, strafing targets of opportunity.

These duties also occupied the Bf 110s as the Wehrmacht smashed southwards through Greece. Here the Luftwaffe was fighting the RAF once again, but the Hurricane was the best fighter the British could muster, and many were destroyed on the ground. Nevertheless, the RAF exacted a toll from the Bf 110 gruppen, although there were losses on both sides. In the hectic air battles over Athens it is believed that a Bf 110's guns accounted for Squadron Leader Marmaduke 'Pat' Pattle, the RAF's highest-scoring pilot of the war with over 50 victories. By the end of April Greece was in German hands.

Merkur and Iraq

With Greece secure, the Germans next turned on Crete. Bf 110s from I. and II./ZG 26 were again involved, flying long-range attack missions from Argos. II./ZG 76 also joined the action in Operation Merkur. Many of the missions were aimed at Allied shipping, and the Bf 110s achieved some success against small vessels, but at considerable cost to groundfire. At the end of the campaign, all but one staffel returned to Germany.

That unit, 4./ZG 76, embarked on an unusual foray to Iraq. In early 1941 a coup led by Raschid Ali had installed a pro-Axis government in Baghdad. Britain responded by moving troops and aircraft into its garrisons, notably the airfield complex at Habbaniyah. The Luftwaffe formed the Sonderkommando Junck, a special formation of fighters, bombers and transports which were hastily painted with Iraqi markings. 4./ZG 76 and its dozen Bf 110s formed the fighter arm of this group, and staged through Syria to Mosul. From this base the aircraft set out to attack British positions, especially Habbaniyah, on 17 May.

For 10 days the Bf 110s attacked the British, losing several of their number in the process. Others were badly damaged in RAF counter-attacks on Mosul, and by 26 May all were unserviceable. The Germans were evacuated before Commonwealth forces overran Mosul. One of the Bf 110s, which had crash-landed near Habbaniyah, was repaired and test-flown by the RAF, named *The Belle of Berlin*.

North Africa

III./ZG 26 had been the first Bf 110 unit in the Mediterranean theatre, reaching Sicily in December 1940. Its aircraft often operated from Crete and in North Africa to allow them to protect the Axis sea lanes. They also supported raids against British forces on Malta and in the western desert. On such a raid, against Tobruk, Bf 110s from 8./ZG 26 scored their first kills over Hurricanes, albeit with one loss.

In mid-November 1941 the push eastwards by the Afrika Korps ground to a halt. In order to counter the inevitable Commonwealth counter-attack, all of III./ZG 26 was concentrated at Derna. From here it opposed the Crusader campaign, suffering heavily in the process. By January 1942, the Afrika Korps was moving eastwards once more, but only 7./ZG 26 remained in Africa, the other squadrons having withdrawn to re-equip and to engage on less demanding patrol work. By May 1942 the three staffeln were again back together at Derna.

Rommel's advance gathered momentum in the summer of 1942, and the Bf 110 units moved with it. As well as bomber escort duty, they were heavily involved in ground attack work, sustaining several losses to heavy groundfire. With Cairo tantalisingly close, the advance ground to a halt at El Alamein. At this point much of III./ZG 26 returned to Crete to resume its routine patrols.

From Cretan bases the Bf 110s encountered new opposition in the form of USAAF Consolidated B-24 Liberator bombers operating from Palestine. These proved to be worthy targets for the heavy-hitting Zerstörers, which were generally successful against the American 'heavies'.

Meanwhile, a few detachments of Bf 110s had remained in North Africa, but they could do little to prevent the long and weary retreat from El Alamein to Tunis, pushed and harried by Montgomery's Commonwealth forces. After the Torch landings in November, most Bf 110s retreated to Trapani in Sicily, from where they attempted to protect the air bridge of Ju 52/3m transports flying to Tunisia, as well as flying against USAAF B-17 Flying Fortresses which attacked Sicily. In this work they were joined by the Bf 110s of II./ZG 1, hastily rushed from the Russian front.

When Tunisia fell to the Allies in May 1943, the Messerschmitt Bf 110s retreated further, to bases around Rome. From here they attempted to intercept USAAF heavy bombers, but by July they returned to ground attack sorties, opposing the Allied landings in Sicily. Before the end of the month, III./ZG 26 was ordered back to Germany, so sparing it from witnessing the fall of Sicily.

Equipped with underwing bomb-racks, this Bf 110 Jagdbomber was abandoned by ZG 26 in North Africa. The aircraft wears the ZG 26 Geschwader badge on its nose (a stylised 'HW' standing for Horst Wessel, the Geschwader's official name, on an orange and black background). The presence of a Ju 87D suggests this photograph was taken in the later stages of the Libyan campaign.

Defending the Reich

Above: The Lichtenstein BC radar improved the chances of a Bf 110 finding a bomber at night, but it cut around 25 mph (40.2 km/h) from the top speed. The radar was blinded by Window (chaff).

Left: The night-fighter arm of the Luftwaffe was built upon the Bf 110. Until the Bf 110F appeared as the first night-fighter version, the night units used day-fighter Bf 110Cs, Ds and Es.

Night-fighter operations

Although it had proved ineffective against all but the weakest opposition in its original heavy fighter (Zerstörer) role, the Bf 110 nevertheless had great potential as a night-fighter.

In the early months of the war the Luftwaffe's small night-fighter arm relied totally on fighters retired from the day-fighter front-line. These included Heinkel He 51s, Arado Ar 68s and Messerschmitt Bf 109Ds. However, they were soon replaced by the Messerschmitt Bf 110, which was to become, at least numerically, the backbone of the Nachtjagdwaffe throughout the remainder of the war.

Hauptmann Wolfgang Falck, Gruppenkommandeur of I./ZG 1, oversaw the introduction of the Bf 110 to the night-fighting role. While based at Aalborg, Denmark, on Zerstörer duties in April 1940, Falck was convinced that his Bf 110s could intercept RAF bombers as they passed over at night, especially if the assistance of ground radar units could be recruited. Although initial unofficial trials resulted in no kills, the idea was proven.

Shelved during the fighting for France in May, Falck's night-fighting concepts were resurrected in June, and he was ordered to form Nachtjagd-geschwader 1 on the 22nd. NJG 1's I. and III. Gruppe were equipped with Bf 110Cs for the night defence of Germany and scored their first kill on 9 July 1940. From the outset, the Bf 110 proved particularly well-suited to the night-fighting role: it had the endurance to wait around for the bombers and the extra pair of eyes were often crucial in spotting targets. Its manoeuvrability and performance were more than adequate to tackle the bombers of the day. In deference to their new role, the Bf 110s were given a matt black paint scheme and received flame-dampers for the exhausts.

Operating in small areas with searchlight batteries and early warning from Freya coastal radar, the Bf 110s achieved few results initially. RAF bomber crews soon learned to circumnavigate the unusual isolated searchlight batteries where there was no flak. However, throughout 1941 and into 1942, the Kammhuber Line of searchlight batteries and Freya radars was extended to form a defensive chain strung across the usual bomber ingress routes, while many former Zerstörer Bf 110 units converted to the night-fighter mission. The Himmelbett system was introduced, dividing the Kammhuber Line into boxes. Each box had a searchlight battery, a Freya radar and two Giant Wurzburg radars, the latter used for tracking individual aircraft (one for the target and one for the Bf 110).

Several of the night-fighter units operated a handful of Dornier Do 17s or 215s. These heavy aircraft were too cumbersome to be successful as night-fighters, but they were the first to be fitted with Lichtenstein-A airborne interception radar. They were occasionally used to vector accompanying Bf 110s.

In early 1942 the RAF introduced new tactics of using dense bomber streams to swamp small sectors of the Kammhuber Line, this greatly affecting the ability of the Himmelbett system to work successfully. Development of Lichtenstein BC freed the night-fighter crews from the need to fly under close ground control, and in early 1942 the introduction of the equipment on Bf 110s coincided with an upturn in fortunes for the night-fighter force, but the precious radar sets were initially only fitted to the aircraft operated by night-fighting experts.

Upward-firing guns

More types joined the Nachtjagdgruppen in 1943, including the Do 217J, but it was the Bf 110 which remained the

These Bf 110G-4s on a daylight mission in the summer of 1943 are from 9./NJG 3. The original matt black night-fighter paint scheme gave way to various mottled light grey schemes from mid-1941. This photo was taken from the rear gunner's position.

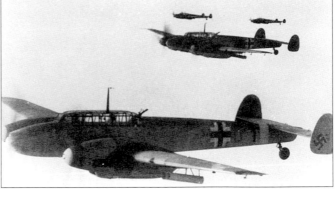

Left: In 1943 the Bf 110 was employed on daylight operations as well as night fighting. Radar was removed, as displayed by this 7./NJG 1 Bf 110G-2.

Below: When tackling bombers in daylight, some use was made of the underwing Werfergranate 21-cm mortar tube, which was dubbed the Pulk-Zerstörer (formation destroyer).

most numerous. Armament and equipment steadily improved, including the fitment of upward-firing *schräge Musik* cannon to some Bf 110s from May 1943. Lichtenstein radar became more common, but the RAF's introduction of chaff (Window) blinded the new radar.

Messerschmitt's twin was employed on Zahme Sau (tame boar) operations in which its radio equipment was used to home in on large areas of Window, narrowing the area for a visual search to commence. Bf 110 night-fighters also flew the more typical Wilde Sau (wild boar) mission, which involved a visual search only.

Losses mounted through the year, with many Bf 110s falling to Mosquito night-intruders,

which proved to be the great nemesis for the Nachtjagdwaffe.

On occasion Bf 110s were added to the roster of day-fighters opposing the US 'heavies' which were gaining strength in their operations, but the use of the Bf 110 by day was almost suicidal, and such operations came to an end in the winter of 1943/44.

Towards the end of 1943 the new FuG 220 Lichtenstein SN-2 radar became the main answer to Window, being able to 'see' through the chaff. This was added to most Bf 110s thereafter, which sometimes also carried the original Lichtenstein BC for short-range work. By the end of the war, some Bf 110s sported the FuG 218 Neptun radar with forward- and aft-facing antennas, although most ended the conflict

with FuG 220 Lichtenstein SN-2d, with its characteristic *hirschgeweih* (stag's antlers) aerials canted at 45°.

Although outclassed by the He 219, the Bf 110 remained at the forefront of night-fighter operations until the end of the war, usually working in mixed squadrons with Ju 88s and He 219s, which were rarely available in sufficient numbers to

equip whole units. In general, the unit's *experten* flew the newer equipment, while the regular squadron members flew the Bf 110s. There were, of course, notable exceptions, the greatest being Heinz-Wolfgang Schnauffer, Germany's leading night-fighter ace who gained 121 kills in Bf 110s and gained the nickname 'Ghost of St Trond' from Bomber Command crews.

FuG 220
The Lichtenstein SN-2b radar set used the larger set of antennas, and provided detection over a sector of 120° in azimuth and 100° in elevation. Its maximum range was around 1,312 ft (4000 m) but it could only work down to around 984 ft (300 m), which was often insufficient to visually acquire the target. The FuG 212 was carried to address this shortcoming.

Flame-dampers
An elaborate exhaust system was installed to prevent visible flames, which would give away the fighter's position.

FuG 212
The small, centrally-mounted antenna array was for the FuG 212 Lichtenstein C-1 radar, also known as the Weitwinkel (wide-angle). This provided target information at very close range, and was often used for the final moments of an intercept where the larger FuG 220 set could no longer function.

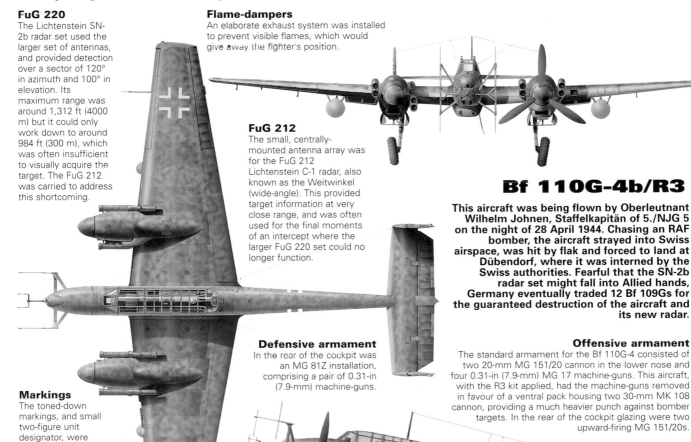

Bf 110G-4b/R3

This aircraft was being flown by Oberleutnant Wilhelm Johnen, Staffelkapitän of 5./NJG 5 on the night of 28 April 1944. Chasing an RAF bomber, the aircraft strayed into Swiss airspace, was hit by flak and forced to land at Dübendorf, where it was interned by the Swiss authorities. Fearful that the SN-2b radar set might fall into Allied hands, Germany eventually traded 12 Bf 109Gs for the guaranteed destruction of the aircraft and its new radar.

Defensive armament
In the rear of the cockpit was an MG 81Z installation, comprising a pair of 0.31-in (7.9-mm) machine-guns.

Offensive armament
The standard armament for the Bf 110G-4 consisted of two 20-mm MG 151/20 cannon in the lower nose and four 0.31-in (7.9-mm) MG 17 machine-guns. This aircraft, with the R3 kit applied, had the machine-guns removed in favour of a ventral pack housing two 30-mm MK 108 cannon, providing a much heavier punch against bomber targets. In the rear of the cockpit glazing were two upward-firing MG 151/20s.

Markings
The toned-down markings, and small two-figure unit designator, were typical for the period. Johnen's aircraft displayed 17 kill bars on the fin at the time of his forced landing: he had scored his 18th during the mission.

Eastern Front Zerstörer

In the fighting in the East the Bf 110 played only a minor part. Apart from the early days of the Barbarossa campaign, it was largely confined to ground attack duties.

By the time Hitler launched Operation Barbarossa, the invasion of the Soviet Union, on 22 June 1941, much of the Bf 110 Zerstörer force had already been transferred to the night-fighter role. A few Staffeln remained in the day Zerstörer role in the Mediterranean theatre. Consequently, few Bf 110s were included in the Luftwaffe line-up at the start of Barbarossa, although the units involved would see considerable action.

Zerstörer in the East

On the central sector were the Stab, I. and II./ZG 26, with a mix of Bf 110Cs and Es. Having taken part in the Balkans and Crete campaigns, they had returned to Germany briefly before staging to Suwalki in Poland, where they awaited the assault to begin. The 50 or so serviceable aircraft were part of VIII. Fliegerkorps, subordinate to Luftflotte II.

From their base in Poland, the two Gruppen and Stab flight of ZG 26 were involved in the massive opening assault on the Soviet Union. Little opposition was encountered in the air, as the Red Air Force fighters mainly operated at low level, way below the Bf 110's optimum fighting altitudes. Quickly the Bf 110's role became one of ground attack, including strafing and bombing runs against Soviet aircraft on their airfields. Over 1,000 Soviet fighters were destroyed on the ground on the first day alone, many the victims of Bf 110 attacks. As the Wehrmacht crashed into the Soviet Union, so the ZG 26 Zerstörers accompanied the army, providing attack support as it moved on. The Bf 110s were assigned to the northern push, moving bases several times to keep up with the rapidly advancing troops. The advance ended in late August, with the Germans close to Leningrad. On this front a stalemate had been reached, leading to one of the most vicious sieges of military history, and one of the most heroic defences of a city ever.

ZG 26 was engaged in fighting over Leningrad into the winter. Anti-aircraft fire was intense, and fighter opposition was more determined than it had

Above: '3U+GM' of 4./ZG 26 lands at a waterlogged field on the northern sector of the Russian front as the Germans advance toward Leningrad, autumn 1941.

Top: Oberleutnant Heisel, Staffelkapitän of 2./ZG 26 flying Bf 110C-1 '3U+KK', leads his unit low over Wilno, north-east Poland (formerly occupied by the Soviets), at the start of the campaign in the east in July 1941.

Only one Staffel of Bf 110s operated on the far northern (Arctic) sector of the Russian front, albeit under a succession of designations as the Luftwaffe's Arctic force evolved. Bf 110G '1B+AX' of 13(Z)./JG 5 is well wrapped up against the elements in tis view from the winter of 1943/44

Another 4./ZG 26 machine lands on the northern sector of the Russian front, autumn 1941. This aircraft lacks the usual yellow theatre band and '3U' code of ZG 26, but has white kill bars on its tailfin. Note also the II./JG 54 Bf 109Fs, which also supported the ground forces' advance on Leningrad.

been in the opening weeks of the campaign. Losses mounted accordingly, although generally the Luftwaffe maintained air superiority. Elements of I. and II./ZG 26 rotated back to Germany for rest and re-equipment, although a number were reassigned to the central sector, covering the fighting around Smolensk and Vitebsk.

In April 1942 I. and II./ZG 26 were finally withdrawn to Germany to be swallowed up by the growing night-fighter organisation, becoming I. and II./NJG 4 in the process. The last of the origi-nal Zerstörergruppen had escaped this fate once already: they had briefly carried NJG designations in April 1941, shortly before they were recalled for day operations over the Balkans.

'Fast bombers'

Schnellkampfgeschwader 210's two Gruppen of Bf 110Cs were assigned to Luftflotte II on the central sector, and they supported the Wehrmacht's drive towards Moscow. Its aircraft resplendent with a giant wasp marking on the nose (inherited from one of its fore-runners, 1./ZG 1), the

'Wespen-Geschwader' used its Bf 110s to make dive-bombing and strafing attacks on Soviet targets ahead of the advancing German troops. Air combat was mostly avoided, but the 'fast-bombers' gave a good account of themselves when attacked by VVS fighters. A number of pilots made *experte* status (10 kills or more) with this unit and its successor. By the end of the year the two Gruppen of SKG 210 had moved forward to Orel and Bryansk. In early 1942 the unit's title was changed to Zerstörergeschwader 1, although the mission remained the same.

Having been thwarted in its attempts to reach Moscow before the winter halted further progress, the German army prepared for a major offensive in the south, the objective being the oilfields in the Caucasus. The redesignated I. and II./ZG 1 were both involved in the push, supporting Army Group South. Progress was again rapid, the Bf 110 Gruppen reaching Rostov in the summer. In August they were within strik-ing distance of Stalingrad, and flew numerous missions to attack lines of communication into Stalin's showpiece city.

In September 1942 ZG 1 formed a night-fighting Staffel, known as 10.(NJ)/ZG 1. This achieved some success and produced an *experte* in the form of Oberfeldwebel Josef Kociok, who scored 21 night kills before being killed in September 1943. By this time the unit was semi-autonomous, and was known as Nachtjagdschwarm/Luftflotte 4.

As Soviet resistance at Stalingrad hardened, so the Bf 110s were increasingly used as anti-armour weapons, using dive attacks (sometimes with 2,204-lb (1000-kg) SC 1000 bombs) followed by strafing attacks. Aerial kills were scored, too, the highest-scoring pilot

being Oberfeldwebel Hans Peterburs with 18. Losses also mounted, a testament to the growing resolve of the Red Army to defend Stalingrad at all costs. ZG 1 retreated from Stalingrad to Rostov on 31 January 1943.

Soon after, in March, II. Gruppe returned to Germany before being sent to the Mediterranean. I./ZG 1 was transferred to the central sector of the front and, in June, was embroiled in the massive tank battle at Kursk. It was with-drawn to Germany at the end of July, to become I./ZG 26.

Arctic warriors

In early 1941 Jagdgeschwader 77, the resident Bf 109-equipped fighter wing in Norway, established a coastal patrol flight at Kirkenes with Bf 110s. This subsequently grew to squadron size, and was chris-tened 1.(Z)/JG 77. It had a dachshund badge, and was known colloquially as the 'Dackel-Staffel'. When the attack on the Soviet Union began, the unit was involved initially in escorting bombers as they attacked Russian ports in the Kola Peninsula, notably Murmansk. However, as in the other theatres, the Bf 110 turned mainly to ground attack duties. The good 'legs' of the type allowed it to range beyond Murmansk, striking at commu-nications lines to the south. In an area where Soviet fighter opposition was relatively weak, the Bf 110 crews fared well in air combat, even when faced with the RAF Hurricanes of No. 151 Wing which operated in northern Russia. One pilot, Feldwebel Theodor Weissenberger, scored 23 kills in this theatre before being posted to Bf 109s.

When JG 5 'Eismeer' took over as the parent unit from JG 77 in 1943, the Bf 110 Staffel was redesignated as 6./JG 5. It subsequently became 10. Staffel and, finally, 13. Staffel. By this time it was operating from Rovaniemi in Finland, and continued to do so until it was pulled out in February 1944. It returned to Norway and its original role of coastal patrols.

This Bf 110G, believed to be of 5./ZG 1, is pictured during the Gruppe's (i.e. II./ZG 1) brief deployment to Mamaia, Romania in April 1944. The Gruppe had been flying Defence of the Reich missions in southeastern Europe (Munich, Vienna and Budapest) since November 1943 and converted to Bf 109s (as III./JG 76) in July 1944.

Messerschmitt Me 163
Rocket fighter

In 80 years of air warfare there have been very few occasions when a nation has gone into battle with an aircraft so advanced in concept, that its enemies did not at first know how to tackle it. Such was the case with the Me 163, which was very small, agile and nearly twice as fast as most of its opponents.

The story started in 1926 when Dr Alexander Lippisch built his first tailless glider. Over the next decade Lippisch also became involved with rocket propulsion, so it was no great surprise when in 1937, he was asked by the research section of the RLM (German air ministry) to design an aircraft to test a new rocket motor, the 882-lb (3.92-kN) Walter I-203. This operated on a mixture of two liquids which reacted violently on meeting: T-stoff, consisting mainly of concentrated hydrogen perox-

ide, and Z-stoff, an aqueous solution of calcium permanganate. With such reactive propellants it was decided to sub- contract Heinkel to build a metal fuselage.

In the event, Heinkel never built the metal fuselage and early in 1939, Lippisch left the DFS (glider research institute) and teamed up with Messerschmitt. Willy Messerschmitt showed frosty disinterest, but Lippisch was allowed to carry on in strict security, with his own team, and in late 1939 decided that his preliminary research aircraft, the

Above: Two of the Me 163B prototypes, V6 and V18, were modified with prototypes of the HWK 509C-1 motor with main and cruising thrust chambers, to give much better flight endurance. Here the V6 blows steam through its propellant lines in the summer of 1944. Note the repositioned retractable tailwheel.

Top: An Me 163B-1a launching at Bad Zwischenahn, home of the trials unit Erprobungskommando 16, which accepted its first Me 163B during May 1944.

all-wood DFS 194, could in fact be powered by the rocket and not by the intended small piston engine. The machine was taken in early 1940 to Karlshagen, the test airfield at Peenemunde, where the I-203 rocket was installed. On 3 June 1940 famed glider pilot Heini Dittmar made a successful first flight, reporting superb handling. Later this flimsy machine, designed for

186 mph (300 km/h), reached 340 mph (547 km/h) in level flight, and also demonstrated fantastic steep climbs.

The Walter company had by this time developed the 1,653-lb (7.36-kN) II-203b RATO unit, and was working on a still more powerful motor. Lippisch was instructed to design a fast-climbing interceptor to use the latter engine, the short flight

This Me 163B-1a was flown to the UK in 1945 in an Arado Ar 232B-0. It was test flown as a glider in Britain, being towed to altitude by a Spitfire Mk IX, but crashed on 15 November. Parts of the aircraft were incorporated into the Me 163 subsequently exhibited at the Imperial War Museum.

endurance being no problem to a target-defence aircraft which could stay on the ground until enemy bombers were almost overhead. The designation Me 163B Komet was allocated.

Carefree flight

The first Me 163 was completed except for its motor at Lechfeld in March 1941, and was at once put through a programme of trials as a glider, towed off by a Bf 110. Dittmar again was enraptured at the handling, but the aircraft was such a good glider it consistently refused to land, and invariably almost went off the far side of the field. The maiden flight under power took place at Karlshagen on 13 August 1941, and although he did not intend to reach high speed, Dittmar was informed that the level speed as measured by ground instruments was over 497 mph (800 km/h). Soon speeds were exceeding 550 mph (885 km/h). On 2 October 1941, Dittmar was towed to over 13,125 ft (4000 m) by a Bf 110; he then cast off and started the motor. He accelerated, but suddenly lost control as the nose dropped violently. It was possibly the first occasion on which a human had approached the speed of sound, compressibility trouble being experienced at about Mach 0.84. The speed of 624 mph (1004 km/h) was 155 mph (250 km/h) above the official world speed record.

Getting airborne

Subsequent research led to a modified wing with large fixed slots over the outer leading edge, which rendered the aircraft spin-proof. Basically, the Me 163A could hardly have been simpler, but one feature was to endure into the production Me 163B and cause endless problems and catastrophic accidents. The Lippisch glider background made it seem normal to take off from a wheeled dolly, jettisoned once airborne, and to land on a sprung skid. In fact, the piloting difficulties were immense. If the

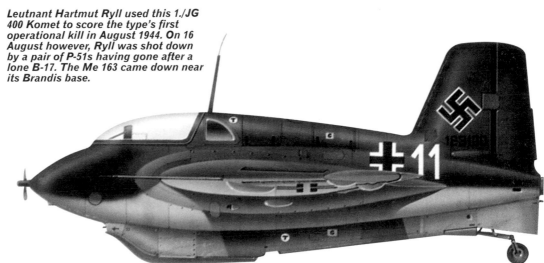

Leutnant Hartmut Ryll used this 1./JG 400 Komet to score the type's first operational kill in August 1944. On 16 August however, Ryll was shot down by a pair of P-51s having gone after a lone B-17. The Me 163 came down near its Brandis base.

aircraft was not dead into wind it would slew around and possibly overturn, the rudder being useless at low speeds. Any bump in the surface caused premature take-off or a bounce on landing. This combined with the totally unsprung, dolly causes spinal damage to pilots and the occasional explosion, due to the propellants being shaken up.

So tricky were the liquids that for the big R II-211 motor, which was made fully controllable, the Z-stoff was replaced by C-stoff (hydrazine hydrate solution in methyl alcohol). Although testing of the motors was twice punctuated by explosions which destroyed the entire building, work went ahead on the six Me 163A prototypes, 10 Me 163A-0 pre-production aircraft and 70 pre-production versions of the Me 163B interceptor. During 1941, procurement chief Ernst Udet had become an enthusiastic supporter of the project. His suicide in November 1941 did not help matters however, and there was no immediate need for such an aircraft, so priority remained low, and Walter continued to have severe and dangerous motor problems.

Gradually more people joined the programme, although Lippisch himself took up another

appointment. The Luftwaffe's Rudolf Opitz came to share the flying, while Dittmar stalled onto the poorly sprung skid and spent two years in hospital having his spine reassembled. On his first Me 163A flight Opitz almost met disaster, because he was far above dolly release height before he realised he was airborne. He kept the valuable dolly attached and landed back on it; by a miracle he did not swing and overturn. Opitz made the first Me 163B flight, albeit unpowered, from Lechfeld on 26 June 1942. Powered flights did not begin until 23 June 1943, when Opitz again had trouble, but managed to recover safely.

The Me 163's nose was full of radio and other items, including the generator driven by the small

Having only a skid undercarriage for landing, the Me 163 was recovered by the Scheuschlepper (illustrated).

windmill propeller, with access by hinging back the instrument panel. Armament comprised two cannon (one in the root of each wing between the spars). Compressed-air bottles cocked the guns, and gas pressure served most of the onboard auxiliary power services. The landing skid was hydraulically retracted on take-off, along with the neat steerable tailwheel. Retracting the skid automatically released the wheeled dolly, but this had a habit of bouncing up and smashing into the aircraft or even hooking on the front of the skid. If it failed to separate, a successful landing back on the dolly was not advised; it was only accomplished once. Even Hanna Reitsch tried it, following total hang-up, and she was severely injured.

The Wolf Hirth Segelflugzeugbau (glider works) built a run of 10 Me 163A-0 pilot trainers, fitted with the dangerously temperamental R II-203b motor and a large sprung take-off dolly. This particular A-0 was fitted with wooden underwing racks each carrying 12 of the R4M air-to-air spin-stabilised rockets.

Messerschmitt Me 210/410

Die 'Hornisse'

With its neatly cowled engines and purposeful nose contours, the Me 210 looked the part, but it was plagued with vicious and unpredictable handling qualities. This aircraft is one of those fitted with a longer rear fuselage, which largely cured the design's major faults.

Inset: The Me 210 V1 first prototype clearly showed its Bf 110 genes, although the twin tail was swiftly changed after the first few flights.

After a difficult gestation, the Me 210/410 emerged as a powerful *Zerstörer*, but only after a major redesign. In the latter part of its career, it came to be known as the 'Hornisse' (hornet).

In 1938, in a rare display of foresight, the Reichsluftfahrtministerium issued a requirement for a replacement for the Messerschmitt Bf 110 in the *Kampfzerstörer* role. The new aircraft would have to be able to undertake air fighting, ground attack, dive-bombing and reconnaissance. In the summer Messerschmitt was awarded a contract for its Me 210 design, with prototypes of the twin-engined Arado Ar 240 being ordered as a back-up. So great was Messerschmitt's reputation that various long-lead production items, such as wing spars, were ordered at the same time.

In design the Me 210 drew heavily on the Bf 110, although it introduced several novel features, such as the gun armament (two Mauser MG 151/20 cannon and two MG 17 machine-guns) being mounted beneath the cockpit floor either side of a small bomb bay, a very short nose giving the pilot an excellent view, and rear-firing armament consisting of two 0.51-in (13-mm) MG 131 guns mounted in barbettes either side of the rear fuselage. The barbettes were mounted on a rotating drum, and each gun could traverse through 90°. They were aimed by the observer, who sat in the rear of the bulged glazed canopy, facing aft. Power came from two Daimler Benz DB 601A-1s. Venetian blind-style airbrakes were mounted in the wings.

Disastrous tests

Dr Ing Hermann Wurster took the Me 210 V1 aloft for the first time on 5 September 1939. His report was damning: the aircraft was, in his view, unacceptable in terms of yaw and pitch handling to the point of being dangerous. With its reputation at stake, Messerschmitt immediately fitted a single large fin, but subsequent tests proved that there was only marginal improvement. However, production was already gearing up, and by 1941 Me 210A-0s and A-1s were issuing from the lines. No complete solution to the problems had yet been found, and production was terminated by March 1942.

However, that same month, an Me 210A-0 flew with a new, longer and deeper rear fuselage, slatted outer wings and other changes. A dramatic improvement was observed, and work rushed ahead to convert a number of existing aircraft, and those partially complete, to the new standard. These saw service with 16./KG 6 and III./ZG 1 in the Mediterranean theatre. A few Me 210Bs were completed as reconnaissance aircraft, while a handful was modified to serve as dual-control trainers. The Duna works in Hungary built Me 210C-1 and Me 210Ca-1 aircraft, powered by DB 605B engines. Production reached 267

Above: Heavily retouched, this photograph shows Me 210Ca-1s of the Hungarian air force. Fitted with the long rear fuselage and DB 605 engines, these proved very popular with the Hungarians.

Right: Me 210A-2s from the Stabsschwarm, III./ZG 1 fly low over the Tunisian countryside in 1943. Only a small number of units used Me 210s before the improved Me 410 entered service.

Above: Previously an Me 210A-0 pre-production machine, this is the Me 410 V1. The Me 410 introduced a new wing planform and DB 603A engines.

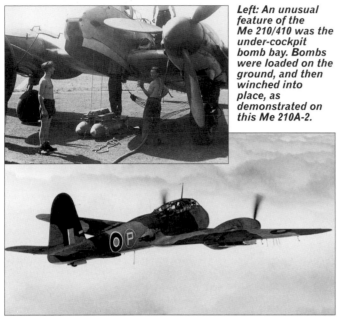

Left: An unusual feature of the Me 210/410 was the under-cockpit bomb bay. Bombs were loaded on the ground, and then winched into place, as demonstrated on this Me 210A-2.

At least six Me 410s were acquired for evaluation by the UK, this being an Me 410A-3 reconnaissance aircraft. Evident are the gun barbettes and the bulged canopy glazing.

before Duna switched to Bf 109G production.

Despite the resignation of Willy Messerschmitt over the 210 fiasco, the company continued development of the long-fuselage airframe. Uprated 1,850-hp (1380-kW) DB 603A engines were installed and a straight taper wing (instead of the 210's 5° leading-edge sweep-back) was tested. The results were good when trials began in autumn 1942, allowing production to start in January 1943. The 'new' aircraft was rechristened Me 410 in an attempt to hide its inglorious past.

Early production centred on the Me 410A-1 *Schnellbomber*, with the same armament as the Me 210A, and the Me 410A-2 *Zerstörer*. The Me 410B introduced the 1,900-hp (1417-kW) DB 603G engine. Various armament options were produced with an array of 'U' and 'R' suffixes. U1 aircraft had a camera in the rear fuselage for reconnaissance duties, while most others had variations of cannon armament, including 30-mm MK 103 or MK 108 weapons, up to six MG 151/20s, or in the U4 sub-variants a single BK 5 50-mm cannon. The B-2/U4 had the BK 5 and two MK 108s.

An unusual variant was the Me 410B-5, which could carry a torpedo under the port side of the fuselage. This version was used to test the Friedensengel glide torpedo, SB 800RS Kurt anti-ship rolling bomb, and the SB 1000/410 blast weapon. The B-5, and the cannon-armed B-6, were usually fitted with FuG 200 Hohentwiel radar for their anti-shipping duties.

For reconnaissance the Me 410A-3 and B-3 were developed, these sporting a two-camera installation in a deepened weapons bay under the cockpit. They were far more successful than the earlier makeshift U1 modifications, and operated with virtual impuntiy in all theatres apart from over England.

Anti-bomber role

By 1944 the Reich was being pounded by day and by night by Allied bombers. Me 410s were drafted in from their many other assignments to join the desperate fight against the day bombers. Many of the heavy cannon installations were made as a result of this switch of role. Anti-ship aircraft lost their scarch radar and joined the fray.

Enjoying a good turn of speed and heavy firepower, Me 410s brought down many USAAF 'heavies', although they, in turn, suffered badly at the hands of the escort fighters, which could easily outmanoeuvre and out-perform the heavy twins. Among the novel armament features tested in this desperate time for Germany was a rotary rocket launcher, based on the Wfr.Gr. 21 mortar tubes carried by Bf 109 day-fighters. The six-barrelled rotary launcher was mounted in the Me 410's weapons bay, with the lower tube exposed and angled upwards. Once lined up on a bomber, the pilot could fire all six rockets within two seconds. Initial trials nearly caused the loss of the fighter, but the system was refined to the point of being fielded in a handful of Me 410Bs, although the results remain unknown.

High-altitude models

The use of the Me 410 as a fighter spurred development for aircraft with better performance at high altitude, to operate in both day- and night-fighter roles. The Me 410C was planned with much longer wings, more powerful turbo-supercharged engines (DB 603JZ, Jumo 213E/JZ or BMW 801TJ) in annular cowlings, a stretched fuselage and revised undercarriage with twin mainwheels. Although the annular cowls and new undercarriage were tested by Me 410A/Bs, the C was cancelled.

In its place came the very similar Me 410D, which was to feature DB 603JZ engines and long-span wings, of which the outer panels were made of wood, and a revised nose section giving the crew an even better view. Problems with wood manufacture spelled the end of the Me 410D, to be replaced by the Me 410H.

This was in essence an Me 410B-2 with the addition of extra untapered wing panels immediately outboard of the engines. Span would have been around 75 ft (23 m). However, the first modification was never completed.

Above: Another captured aircraft was this Me 410B-6, which had previously been used for anti-ship duties by I./ZG 1 at Lorient. For this task the B-6 was armed with two 30-mm MK 103 cannon and two 13-mm MG 131 machine-guns. Noteworthy is the nose antenna array for the FuG 200 Hohentwiel search radar.

Left: Captured by US forces was this Me 410A-3. The 'F6' codes denoted use by 2.(Fern) Staffel/Auflklärungsgruppe 122, which operated from Sardinia on reconnaissance duties.

Messerschmitt Me 262 Schwalbe

Fighting 'Stormbird'

Young German gunners, huddled around their light 20-mm and 37-mm flak weapons, could be excused for a slight lack of attention to their task at their first sight of the Messerschmitt Me 262s on the snow-covered expanses of Rheine-Hopsten air base in 1944. In every sense the sleek, shark-like fuselage, mottled ochre and olive green and beset with razor wings from which hung the huge turbojets, was a portent of the future.

The noise, the high-pitched whine and howl of the Jumo 004B-1 turbines, the swirls of snow, the hot paraffin-tainted blast: all were of a different time. This was the present, however, and, beset by Allied air superiority on all sides, black-helmeted pilots, crouched forward in the narrow cockpits of their Messerschmitt Me 262A-2a fighter-bombers, code-named *Sturmvogel* ('Stormbird') by the Luftwaffe, anxiously scanned the overcast skies for the first signs of the diving Hawker Tempests, North American P-51s or Supermarine Spitfires, as they coaxed throttles

and jabbed brakes prior to take-off. Flak gunners trained their pieces along the approach paths, watched for the red Very lights that would bring them to instant action, and heard the thunder of the departing jets.

With such machines, how could Germany lose the war in the air? Such a thought must have raced through minds. The job of a flak gunner is humble, and he and his comrades could have had no insight into the extraordinary train of events and decisions that were instrumental in the denial in quantity of Germany's most potent air weapon of World War II. In the

Above: Four months after the Me 262A-1a fighter entered service, in April 1944, the Me 262A-2a (also known as the Me 262A-1a/Jabo) fighter-bomber entered the fray against targets in northern France. This example carries the usual pair of 551-lb (250-kg) SC 250 bombs; the A-2a differed from the fighter solely in having pylons and bomb-fusing equipment fitted.

Top: Seen at Lager-Lechfeld in the late summer of 1944, this Me 262A-1a was on strength with Erprobungskommando (EKdo) 262, the operational test detachment established in late 1943. Standing on the wing is believed to be Leutnant Fritz Müller, who later achieved ace status on the type, while flying with JG 7.

heady days of 1941, when the Messerschmitt Me 262 series was born, not one person in the Third Reich could foresee the desperate need for an outstanding aircraft with which to wrest

air supremacy from the hands of the enemy. The Heinkel concern was already deeply involved in the development of a fighter powered by the new reaction-turbine engines when,

Among a number of Me 262 variants that failed to see more than experimental service was the Me 262C-1a Heimatschützer I ('Home Protector I'), fitted with a rocket motor in the rear fuselage to boost climb rate. The C-1a could reach 38,400 ft (11704 m) in 4½ minutes. In V186 (pictured) Oberstleutnant Heinz Bär, CO of III./EJG 2 and one of the top scorers on the Me 262, scored a kill over a P-47 in early March 1945, shortly before the aircraft was destroyed on the ground by an Allied fighter sweep.

Above: The Me 262 was at its most vulnerable during take-off and landing; it was during this low-speed regime that Allied pilots claimed most of their kills over the fighter, though they needed to down the jet before it reached the protection of flak batteries protecting its base.

Below: An American GI guards the engineless remains of a Schwalbe, abandoned in a German forest in the last weeks of the war. By the end of April 1945 only JV 44 and III./JG 7 were still operational. JV 44 was finally overrun by US armour on 3 May.

on 4 January 1939, the Augsburg-based Messerschmitt AG received orders from the German air ministry (RLM, or Reichsluftfahrtministerium) to produce specifications for a similar type of aircraft. Two plans were drawn up by a team led by Dipl Ing Waldemar Voigt, one for a twin-boom configuration and the other for a pod-and-boom design. Neither of the two then-existing turbojet designs was considered to be powerful enough for a single-engined fighter, and as a result Voigt was forced to resort to the design of a twin-engined aircraft.

Heinkel had already turned to twin engines with the development of the promising He 280 series powered by the six-stage axial-flow BMW P.3302 engines, and Germany's first definitive jet fighter, the Heinkel He 280 V2 prototype, lifted off from Rostock-Marienehe's runway at 15.18 on 30 March 1941 with Fritz Schäfer at the controls. (Within six weeks of this maiden flight, the UK, too, flew its first jet aircraft: powered by a Whittle-designed W.1X centrifugal-type turbojet of 860-lb (3.82-kN) thrust, the Gloster E.28/39 took to the air on 15 May.) At Augsburg, work had proceeded slowly on the design

of what at first bore none of the hallmarks that graced the Heinkel product, or gave any hint of the fineness of line that was a characteristic of Messerschmitt's piston-engined fighters.

This ugly duckling, known as the Me 262 V1 was taken into the air for the first time on 18 April 1941, powered by a piston engine. The jet engines for the Me 262 V1 eventually arrived from Spandau in mid-November 1941, being BMW 003s each of 5.39 kN (1,213 lb) static thrust. On his first flight with the BMW 003s, Wendel suffered a double flame-out shortly after take-off and was forced to put the aircraft down with some damage.

Fortunately, an alternative to the touchy BMWs was available – Junkers' Jumo 004. By August 1941, the Jumo 004 was giving 1,323 lb (5.88 kN) static thrust, and many of the earlier problems had been cured. Jumo 004s were installed on the Messerschmitt Me 262 V3, first flown on the morning of 18 July 1942. Henceforth the fortunes of the Messerschmitt Me 262 were to rise at the expense of its nearest rival, the Heinkel He 280, which suffered a series of setbacks until its eventual cancellation in March 1943.

Service test pilots of the Erprobungsstelle (test establishment) at Rechlin showed interest in the Me 262 from its earliest days. The experienced Major Wolfgang Späte had already reported his enthusiastic findings when the General der Jagdflieger, Adolf Galland, flew the Me 262 V4 on 22 May 1943 and become unequivocal in his praise for this revolutionary aircraft. A production order for 100 followed at the end of the month.

In the meantime, on 17 August 1943 the US 8th Air Force's attack on Regensburg destroyed much of the embryonic Me 262 production lines, forcing Messerschmitt AG to move its jet

development centres to Oberammergau, near the Bavarian Alps. The delay occasioned by the move was increased by a chronic shortage in the supply of skilled labour, and production slipped by many months.

By the autumn of 1943, Germany was on the defensive in the USSR and Italy, and was being subjected to furious aerial assault by day and by night. Therefore, nobody could have been surprised when many senior commanders, including Hitler, mooted the concept of the Me 262 as a fighter-bomber as opposed to an interceptor, for the idea was tactically sound. The Me 262 could carry up to 2,205 lb (1000 kg) of bombs with uncomplicated conversion work completed within two weeks per unit.

So, from that day the Messerschmitt Me 262 was destined to play a dual role, that of a fighter-bomber and that of a pure air-superiority fighter. Neither the role nor the aircraft could by then have had any influence on the outcome of the war. It was too late to start a major production scheme, as oil and aviation kerosene, precious alloys, and skilled airframe and engine specialists were all at a premium. The Messerschmitt Me 262 had been recognised in its full potential, but too late in the war.

Over the period March 1944 to 20 April 1945, the Luftwaffe took delivery of 1,433 Me 262s, but for the Allies the impact of this fine aircraft was largely psychological. On inspection after the war's end, it was acknowledged that in design of airframe and engine the Messerschmitt Me 262 was years ahead of aircraft of other nations, and its secrets permitted the Russians and the Anglo-Americans to accelerate development of jet fighter and bomber aircraft to the magic of Mach 1.0 and beyond over the ensuing years.

Avia S.92 'Turbine'

Major components for the Me 262 were produced in German-occupied Czechoslovakia during World War II, the large Avia factory building airframe parts, while other dispersed facilities supplied, among other things, engine parts. By the end of the war a considerable stockpile of engines, airframes and other spares existed and it was decided that these would be used to produce aircraft for the newly reformed Czech air force. The Jumo 004B-1 engine was copied by Letecke, as the

M.04, while Avia continued its airframe work, producing an S.92 prototype, based on the Me 262A-1a (left). This aircraft made its first flight on 27 August 1946 and was followed by three CS.92 two-seat trainers (above) and a further three S.92s. The third of these latter machines was the first accepted by the air force, in 1947; by the early 1950s eight aircraft equipped the 5th Fighter Flight. Plans to develop the Me 262 (including fitting BMW 003 engines in place of the Jumo 004s and redesigning the fragile nosewheel undercarriage) and produce further aircraft for the Yugoslav air force were cancelled after the Soviet MiG-15 became available for local production.

Early development

The Me 262 V6, the first example to be equipped with a fully retractable tricycle undercarriage, achieved just 28 test flights between first lifting off on 17 October 1943 and its destruction on 9 March 1944.

Although design development of the Me 262 (as it was to become) had been initiated in the late autumn of 1938, the decision to employ BMW turbojet power plants caused major delays.

The world's first jet aircraft, the Heinkel He 178, first flew on 27 August 1939, five days before the outbreak of World War II. Heinkel followed this up less than two years later with the twinjet He 280, which first took to the air on 30 March 1941. Given these achievements, Ernst Heinkel was fully confident of being awarded a development contract, and subsequent production order, by the Reich Air Ministry. But for reasons of 'a technical nature' (plus, it was believed at the time, a certain amount of political manoeuvring) the order went instead to Professor Willy Messerschmitt, Heinkel's archrival in the jet fighter stakes,

When the first prototype Me 262 V1 finally took off on 18 April 1941 it was powered by a single nose-mounted Jumo 210G piston engine. A pair of 1,764-lb (7.85-kN) thrust BMW 003 turbojets were subsequently slung beneath the wings and the following year, on 25 March 1942, the V1 lifted off

with all three engines 'turning and burning'. The two BMW 003 turbojets promptly flamed out, however, and test pilot Fritz Wendel managed to complete only one circuit.

Meanwhile, two further prototypes (V2 and V3) had been completed with more powerful Junkers Jumo 004 A turbojets, and it was the Me 262 V3 which made the first all-jet flight on 18 April 1942 (only to be badly damaged in a crash just over three weeks later).

The V2 made its maiden flight on 1 October 1942. It too was to crash – during its 48th test flight on 18 April 1943, killing pilot *Flugkapitän* Ostertag. The V4, which first took off on 15 March 1943 and was destroyed in a crash on 25 July during flight number 51, was the last prototype to be fitted with a tailwheel. The Me 262 V5 was not only the first to be powered by uprated (1,984-lb; 8.83-kN) Jumo 004Bs, it was also the first to feature a (fixed) tricycle undercarriage.

In less than two months (from

The Me 262 V7 was the second pre-production aircraft, and compared to the Me 262 V6, introduced a new 'blown' canopy for all-round pilot vision and a rubber-sealed pressurised cockpit.

first take-off on 6 June 1943) the V5 racked up a total of 74 test flights before being damaged on 4 August. But, like the V3, it would be repaired and resume test-flying until finally being destroyed in 1944.

Final Prototypes

The final four of the original 10 prototypes were each employed in testing various armament, electrical and pressure systems. The history of the V7 was as brief as that of its immediate predecessor. It encompassed 31 test flights from first take-off on 20 December 1943 to write-off on 19 May 1944. In contrast, the V8, first flown on 18 March 1944 and the first machine to be fully armed, amassed a grand total

The Me 262 V1 is pictured with the Jumo 210G piston engine and BMW 003 turbojets, prior to its abortive first flight on turbojet power, which took place on 25 March 1942.

of 258 flights before a collapsed nosewheel brought its career to an end in October of that year. The last pair (V9, first flown 19 January 1944, and V10, first flown 15 April 1944) both survived their test programmes, despite suffering damage, and completed some 200 and 135 flights respectively.

In the closing months of the war two further prototype numbers were allocated to extensively modified production aircraft; both machines first flying in January 1945. The V11 embodied the glazed nose compartment intended for the A-2/U2 bomber variant. It carried out 22 test flights before crash landing on 30 March 1945. The Me 262 V12 was powered by two BMW 003R composite jet and rocket engines. The aircraft's one and only purely rocket-powered flight took place on 26 March 1945, just six weeks before the end of hostilities.

Me 262A

Only two Me 262A-1a/U4 aircraft were completed, each featuring a huge 50-mm Mauser MK 214A cannon protruding some 6 ft 6 in (2 m) ahead of the nose. Plans for a production version of this, which was to be known as the Me 262E-1, never came to fruition, although ground trials were conducted from 23 March 1945.

Although the Me 262 was originally envisaged as a high-speed interceptor fighter, Hitler's now famous intervention – demanding that the machine be employed instead in the fighter-bomber role – greatly complicated its operational development.

After completing ten prototypes, Messerschmitt next delivered 20 pre-production aircraft. These were followed by the first production models. Powered by two Jumo 004B turbojets, the maximum speed of the Me 262A-1a was 540 mph (870 km/h) at 19,680 ft (6000 m). Armament comprised four 30-mm MK 108 cannon grouped in the nose; the upper pair having 100 rpg, the lower pair 80 rpg.

This basic fighter version then gave rise to a number of sub-variants as attempts were made to up-gun the Me 262 (the MK 108 had a reportedly poor trajectory and was prone to jamming) and adapt it for other purposes. The Me 262A-1a/U1 had a battery of six nose-mounted cannon: two MK 108s, two long-barrelled 30-mm MK 103s, and a pair of 20-mm MG 151s. This model did not enter production, unlike the A-1a/U2 all-weather fighter (equipped with a FuG 125 'Hermine' radio homer), of which a small number were built.

The Me 262A-1a/U3 was an unarmed reconnaissance version, with a camera bay replacing the nose cannon. The last of the numbered sub-variants of the basic Me 262A-1a was the sole A-1a/U5, which upped the number of MK 108 cannon in the nose to six: two with 100 rpg, two with 80, and two with 65, with which Major Heinz Bär claimed a P-47.

Rocket armament

A number of rocket weapon arrangements were tested on late model A-1a aircraft with varying degrees of success, among them two tube-launched 210-mm WGr 21 mortars (carried on pylons beneath the forward fuselage) and batteries of 55-mm R4Ms, which were ripple-salvoed from 12 rails under each wing.

Small numbers of Me 262A-1a/U3 recce aircraft entered service. Modified fighters with cannon deleted, these could carry two Rb 50/30 cameras or an Rb 20/30 and an Rb 75/30 in a nose bay.

Two other A-1a variants are recorded on the production lists. The A-1a/Schul (school), a single-seat trainer intended for service as the A-4, and the A-1a/Jabo interim fighter-bomber. Lastly came the Me 262A-1b, a version fitted with less powerful (1,764-lb; 7.85-kN thrust) BMW 003A turbojets, only three of which were completed before the war came to an end.

It was while watching a demonstration of the latest Luftwaffe aircraft in November 1943 that Hitler enquired whether the Me 262 was capable of carrying bombs. Assured that this would be feasible – although it had not been planned – it was at the Führer's direct order that a dedicated fighter-bomber version was built.

The major difference between the Me 262-2a Jabo and the standard A-1a fighter was the deletion of the upper pair of nose cannon, and the addition of two pylons beneath the weapons bay, each capable of carrying a 250-kg (551-lb) bomb. This was later adapted for fighter operations to carry either jettisonable fuel tanks or rocket launchers.

The only known Jabo sub-variants were the A-2a/U1, two examples of which were completed to test the improved TSA bomb-aiming device, and the Me 262A-2a/U2, which featured a glazed nose section accommodating a prone bomb aimer. Again, only two test aircraft (including the V11 prototype) were built and flown.

The last two versions of the single-seat Me 262A series were the proposed A-3a, a heavily-armoured ground-attack machine, and the Me 262A-5a armed reconnaissance fighter.

In an attempt to improve bombing accuracy, the Me 262A-2a/U2 carried a gyro-stabilised Lotfe 7H bomb sight within a new wooden nose section, which contained a bomb aimer lying prone.

Operational history

'Green 3' was the Me 262A-1a/Jabo flown by Hauptmann Erich Mikat, Geschwaderadjutant of JG 7. The aircraft is armed with a pair of Wgr 21 rocket launchers on TEC bomb racks under the nose.

Over twenty operational units are known to have flown the Me 262A. They ranged in strength from complete *Geschwader*, like KG(J) 54, whose normal establishment numbered well over one hundred machines, down to units such as the *Kommando* Gladenbeck, a small detachment whose half-dozen aircraft included just one Me 262A.

KG 51 was one of the largest Me 262 operators, receiving almost 350 A-2a machines between September 1944 and the end of the war, a figure that reflects the high rate of attrition suffered by the unit.

One of the first units to be formed was, of necessity, a trials *Kommando* tasked with developing the tactics to be employed by Messerschmitt's revolutionary new interceptor fighter in operational service. *Ekdo* 262 was activated in December 1943; its pilots being mainly ex-*Zerstörer* personnel with many hours of twin-engined experience.

For much of its nine-month existence this unit was based at Lechfeld, close to Messerschmitt's Augsburg factory. Flying a mix of pre-production machines and early A-1a aircraft, the twenty-strong *Ekdo* 262 was credited with the destruction of 11 high-altitude Allied reconnaissance aircraft and one B-17. It lost three of its own number, all reportedly to technical malfunctions.

Three weeks before *Ekdo* 262 had come into being, Hitler had expressed his wish that the Me 262 be employed as a fighter-bomber. As a result, the first front-line unit to be selected for conversion on to the Me 262 was KG 51 '*Edelweiss*', a veteran bomber group. The process began in May 1944 with the re-equipment of 3./KG 51. Two months later, nine Me 262A-2a aircraft of this Staffel were despatched to France (as the *Eins.Kdo* Schenk) after the Allied invasion of Normandy. Its impact there was minimal, however, and in September the *Kommando* rejoined its parent unit.

Another bomber group, KG 54 '*Totenkopf*', began conversion to the Me 262 in September. By this time the *Führer* had reversed his decision, and the emphasis was now on using the Me 262 as a fighter again. Designated KG(J) 54 (indicating a bomber group employed in the fighter role), the '*Totenkopf*' unit was therefore equipped with the A-1a. It, too, suffered swingeing losses (over 225 aircraft destroyed or damaged) but was able to claim some 50 kills in return.

Two further units set up in autumn 1944 emphasized the return to fighter operations. *Kdo* Nowotny did not long survive the death in action of its famous leader, Major Walter Nowotny, on 7 November. III./EJG 2 was a specialised Me 262 fighter training wing which, at its peak, comprised some 30 instructors and 140 pupils. The former were responsible for most, if not all, of the unit's approximately 40 kills.

However, the overwhelming number of jet kills were claimed by the pilots of the Luftwaffe's one and only dedicated Me 262 fighter group, JG 7.

JG 7 may have been the most successful Me 262 jet fighter unit, but arguably the most charismatic was JV 44. Although claiming little more than a tenth of the former's number of kills, this unit, set up by the 'disgraced' Generalleutnant Adolf Galland in January 1945, attracted some of the most highly decorated Luftwaffe fighter pilots still surviving after more than five years of hostilities.

As the war in Europe drew to a close the only other unit of significance still operating the Me 262 was NAGr 6, although this tactical reconnaissance wing's complement of A-1a/U3s rarely reached double figures.

It was not aircraft availability, however, but shortage of fuel (and time) which prevented the planned conversion of four further bomber groups – KGs 6, 27, 30 and 55 – on to the Me 262A *Schwalbe* fighter.

In just six months, from activation in November 1944 until the final collapse of the Third Reich, JG 7 alone was reportedly responsible for shooting down some 500 Allied aircraft (predominantly of the USAAF). In the same period, however, it lost well over half of the 370 or more machines it had taken on strength.

Pilot accounts

The Me 262A was, without doubt, a revolutionary machine in an era of accepted piston-engined aerial warfare. Its performance represented a quantum leap forward; taking not only Allied aircrews by surprise, but sometimes its own pilots as well.

Hauptmann Georg-Peter Eder flew with the *Kdo Nowotny* before transferring to JG 7:

"My first kill on the Me 262 came about almost by accident, you could say. I had taken off in an attempt to intercept a high-flying reconnaissance Lightning. Ground-control vectored me on to the target faultlessly. Not that he was difficult to spot, for he was drawing a nice broad condensation trail in his wake.

"I approached out of the sun from behind and slightly above. When about 80-m [262-ft] distant I ducked into the condensation trail, casting a quick glance down to check my instruments and gun indicator lights. When I looked up again a split second later, the Lightning was filling my windscreen. I tried desperately to pull up above him, but it was too late. There was an almighty crash, and then he disappeared.

"I waited a few seconds, expecting a wing to fall off, or an engine to flame out. But nothing of the sort happened. Just a few nasty dents, but my crate continued to fly."

Once they were familiar with their new mounts, however, Me 262 pilots began to feel almost invincible, "We were no longer the hunted, but the hunters!" Leutnant Fritz Müller of JG 7 recalled:

"South of Dresden I found a solitary Boeing [B-17] flying at 7,500 m [25,000 ft] with an escort of four Mustangs trailing behind it at the same altitude. I overtook the Mustangs from below. They immediately gave chase, but my ASI showed me I had nothing to fear from that quarter.

"The Boeing was now curving slightly to the left, so my approach was made from some 10° to port and 5° above him. At about 1000 m [3,281 ft] his tail gunner opened fire. What happened next was over in seconds. From 300 m [984 ft] range my wingman and I let loose with a short burst of cannon fire. We observed about a dozen hits sparkling along the fuselage and between the Boeing's engines – and then we were past him.

"We pulled a wide circle, the Mustangs getting ever smaller behind us, and watched the end of the bomber. It went spiralling down for about 2,000 m [6,500 ft], large pieces flying off it, before exploding."

Cannon failure

But things did not always go so smoothly. Hauptmann Helmut Kornagel, *Staffelkapitän* of 7./KG(J) 54, was attacking a group of P-38s from 6-o-clock low, "when suddenly my cannon simply packed up. I was only able to escape the angry pack of fully alerted, wildly firing Lightnings by diving steeply away."

In the closing weeks of the war Me 262 fighters began to use R4M underwing rockets. Ex-*Zerstörer* pilot Oberleutnant Günther Wegmann, now of JG 7, took part in one such attack on US bombers west of Berlin.

"The effect of these rockets, salvoed at a range of about 400 m [1,312 ft], was devastating.

A 'veteran' Eastern Front **Experte**, *Major Theodor Weissenberger was made* **Kommodore** *of* **JG** *7 aged 30, assuming Johannes Steinhof's position. Following his appointment, Goering gave Weissenberger just 15 days to bring* **JG** *7 up to full combat strength.*

Ripped-open fuselages, broken-off wings, engines, scraps of metal of all shapes and sizes were tumbling around in the air. It was as though some giant hand was emptying an enormous ashtray in the sky!"

Meanwhile, the Me 262A-2a fighter-bombers of KG 51 '*Edelweiss*' were waging their own low-level war. Briefed to attack British armour located near the Reichswald forest, Otto Zappenfeld spotted 30 or 40 Allied fighters circling above the target area:

"No time for second thoughts. Check all systems – cannon and bombs armed and ready? Right – stand the machine on its nose and down we go! At 1200 m [4,000 ft] release the bombs. A sudden jerk and climb quickly away in a steep left-hand turn."

But it was all in vain. When American troops captured the Remagen bridge across the Rhine, the duty officer of KG 51 received an astonishing personal call from Reichsmarschall Goering odering that volunteers be produced to crash into the bridge, *kamikaze* style: "Only two would-be heroes volunteered. Fortunately the attack was called off. It was too late."

Left: Oberst Johannes 'Macki' Steinhof, who claimed six jet kills with **JG** *7 and* **JV** *44, was the original* **Kommodore** *of* **JG** *7 and evolved appropriate tactics for use against Allied bomber streams.*

Below: Erich Hohagen, seen walking in front of EJG 2 aircraft (including a two-seat trainer), briefly served as **Kommandeur** *of* **III./JG** *7. Already a 55-kill ace by the time he began flying the Me 262, after a suffering head injury he failed to score any jet kills.*

Nocturnal Schwalbe

The Luftwaffe's desperate attempts to stem the night-time Allied bomber offensive led to the development of the Me 262 two-seat night-fighter. Only small numbers were finished in time to equip the first and only jet night-fighter unit of World War II, Kommando Welter.

In the light of modern rigorous and intensive aircrew training programmes, it seems almost inconceivable that the Luftwaffe should have introduced into service a completely new and revolutionary fighter without making proper provision for training the pilots who were to fly it in combat. Yet such was the case during World War II.

Despite the huge advance in technology represented by the Me 262, and the fundamental differences in its flight and handling characteristics, single-seater piston-engined pilots were expected to solo on it after only a brief course of ground instruction and some 20 flying hours in a piston-engined twin (Bf 110 or Me 410) with its throttles locked in one position to simulate jet handling (the Me 262's Jumo engines were notoriously prone to flame-out at any sudden or violent throttle movement).

Fortunately for Allied bomber crews, only limited numbers of Me 262 two-seaters saw operational service. They arrived much too late to make any impact on the Luftwaffe's night-fighter operations.

This syllabus, barely adequate to begin with, suffered yet further cutbacks as Germany's situation worsened. Belatedly, it was realised that training would be greatly simplified if a suitable two-seater dual-control conversion trainer could be produced.

This resulted in the Me 262B-1a, which differed from the standard single-seater primarily in having a second seat for the instructor in the aft section of the lengthened cockpit. This seat displaced the rear main fuel tank and necessitated the introduction of a pair of auxiliary fuel tanks mounted side-by-side on so-called *Wikingerschiff* (Viking ship) pylons beneath the forward fuselage. Full dual controls were provided and the machine retained the standard single-seater nose-mounted armament of four 30-mm MK 108 cannon.

Limited numbers

Little more than a dozen Me 262B-1as were built, however, before an even greater need was identified, for an aircraft which could combat the growing number of high-speed RAF Mosquitos which were roaming the night skies of the Reich with virtual impunity. A series of trials carried out at Rechlin in October 1944 using an Me 262A-1a experimentally fitted with a FuG 220 Lichtenstein SN-2 intercept radar had proved sufficiently successful for the decision to be taken to adapt the Me 262B-1a trainers then under construction as interim night-fighters.

With a radar operator now occupying the rear seat, the conversion consisted mainly of the installation of a FuG 218 Neptun V search radar (with

It is believed that only 15 or so Me 262B-1a tandem two-seat trainers were converted into Me 262B-1a/U1 night-fighters. This example (Werk/nr 110306) was briefly operated in the defence of Berlin by the Kommando Welter. After the end of the war, it was transferred from RAF hands to the USAAF's Air Technical Intelligence unit. Led by Colonel Harold Watson, and known as 'Watson's Whizzers', the team collected intelligence on German aircraft projects.

This Me 262B-1a/U1 (Werk/nr 111980) was assigned to 10./NGJ 11, known more familiarly as Kommando Welter. 'Red 12' was operated from Burg bei Magdeburg until May 1945. After the end of the war, it was evaluated by an RAE team from Farnborough led by famed test pilot Captain Eric 'Winkle' Brown, RN.

Development of the Me 262B night-fighter went ahead despite a significant reduction in performance caused by the drag of its Hirschgeweih *(stag's antlers) antenna array. The 9/16-in (7-mm) diameter dipoles reduced top speed by around 30 mph (50 km/h).*

Me 262 two-seater operational history

The main recipient for the majority of the few Me 262B-1a trainers which were produced was III./Ergänzungsjagdgeschwader 2. This unit, roughly the equivalent of an RAF OTU, was based for much of its brief career at Lager-Lechfeld. It was responsible for the entire output of new Me 262 pilots for the Luftwaffe and, as such, was to have a planned establishment of 122 aircraft. In reality, it rarely mustered more than 30 Me 262s (known as *Schwalbe* or Swallow by its pilots) at any one time, only one or two of which would be B-1a two-seaters.

Some of the trainers did not even make it as far as Lager-Lechfeld. There were several crashes during ferry flights, including at least one fatality. Predictably, the combination of inexperienced pilots and unfamiliar – often unreliable – aircraft also produced its share of accidents during the training programme itself.

The only operational unit to fly the Me 262B-1a/U1 night-fighter was the Kommando Welter, which had been activated at Burg near Magdeburg early in November 1944 with just two Me 262A-1a single-seaters. The Kommandoführer, Leutnant Kurt Welter, who had served as a flying instructor until 1943, had since emerged as a leading exponent of *helle Nachtjagd*, a form of visual night-fighting sortie flown in conjunction with ground-based searchlights. He is believed to have scored the world's first nocturnal jet victory by downing a Mosquito on 27 November.

It was not until March 1945 that the Kommando Welter (which had chosen to ignore its official redesignation of 10./NJG 11 the previous month) received its first B-1a/U1 two-seaters; six examples were added to the similar number of A-1as being flown by the unit. While the single-seaters continued to hunt Mosquitos in the skies over Berlin, the two-seaters – being some 37 mph (60 km/h) slower – were now intended to infiltrate and attack the RAF's heavy bomber streams. It was a task in which they were singularly unsuccessful. It is believed that all 48 of the Kommando's kills (predominantly Mosquitos) were scored by the Me 262A-1a pilots. The two-seaters did, however, contribute two of their number to the unit's total of 11 losses: one aircraft suffered engine flame-out during an operational sortie in March, and the other was buried beneath a hangar roof in an Allied bombing raid on Lübeck-Blankensee airfield.

The Kommando had transferred to Lübeck on 12 April 1945 with just four machines after an earlier raid on Burg. This latest attack prompted another move. On 21 April they abandoned traditional bases, decamping to take up residence on the Lübeck-Hamburg autobahn. Hiding their remaining six aircraft (incredibly, they were still receiving replacement machines, even at this late stage in the war!) under the trees alongside the carriageway, they used a long straight stretch of autobahn near the Reinfeld interchange as a makeshift runway. The Kommando was on its last legs, though. On 7 May 1945 Hauptmann Welter led his half a dozen survivors (including two Me 262B-1a/U1 two-seaters) to Schleswig-Jagel for formal surrender to British forces.

attendant *Hirschgeweih* array) together with a FuG 350 ZC Naxos passive homing device for detecting the H$_2$S emissions of RAF bombers. Work was carried out at the Lufthansa facility at Berlin-Staaken, where the resident engineers' expertise proved invaluable in completing the handful of Me 262B-1a/U1 night-fighters thus produced.

Definitive version

Whereas the B-1a/U1 was simply a hurried adaptation of the two-seat trainer, design work had already begun on the B-2a, which was to be the definitive night-fighter version ready for service in mid-1945.

The Me 262B-2a featured a lengthened fuselage, resulting from the insertion of additional sections fore and aft of the tandem cockpits. The latter were fitted with an aerodynamically refined canopy. Increased fuel capacity provided longer patrol endurance, and the nose armament was augmented by two oblique upward-firing 30-mm *Schräge Musik* cannon immediately behind the rear cockpit. In order to increase range, provision was made for the B-2a to deploy a towed fuel tank (similar to the *Deichselschlepp* towed-bomb array tested on single-seaters).

The B-2a mock-up was ready for inspection on 7 December 1944 and, with only minor alterations, first flight was planned for 22 March 1945. In the event, this schedule slipped and the Me 262B-2a was not flown before the German surrender. Although a development report prepared for the occupying US forces in June 1945 declared the aircraft "ready for take-off," no maiden flight ever took place.

In the months leading up to Germany's final collapse, Messerschmitt had proposed more advanced variations on the basic night-fighter. Needless to say, none of them progressed beyond the drawing board.

Above: Only three two-seat Me 262s survive today. The best example is 'Red 8' (Werk/nr 110305), the only genuine Me 262 night-fighter to survive the war. It is on display at the Johannesburg War Museum, amazingly with its radar array and drop tanks intact.

Left: The Me 262 demonstrated Germany's clear technological superiority over the Allies. Messerschmitt proposed numerous advanced versions of the two-seat Me 262, including a turboprop version, and two- and three-seat swept-wing variants with HeS 011 turbojets.

Above: Seen here head-on is the Me 323 V1, prototype of the four-engined Me 323C series which was not put into production. The four GR 14N 48/49 engines did not provide sufficient power for take-off at full load and, although the Troikaschlepp was not essential, a powerful tug would still have been required.

Left: By 1943, the Me 323E-1 had become the standard model. It had greater fuel capacity, more armour and enhanced armament compared to previous variants.

Messerschmitt Me 321/323 Gigant

The Luftwaffe's giant

With the sudden realisation that existing assets would be insufficient to the task of invading Great Britain, the Luftwaffe ordered a giant aircraft to transport men, supplies and vehicles. The immense Gigant family dwarfed all other contemporary aircraft, but suffered innumerable problems, leading to its eventual demise.

The giant Messerschmitt Me 321 transport glider and its powered derivative, the Me 323, must be considered as one of Germany's most unusual designs during World War II. The basic type had its origin in the plan to invade the UK, following the fall of France, when the English Channel seemed to provide the only serious obstacle to an invasion. Since the RAF had proved that strenuous opposition would be mounted against any operation of this nature, speed in transporting equipment across the Channel was paramount, and a scheme was drawn up for the use of giant gliders to ferry tanks, guns and men.

Although Operation Sealion, as the planned invasion was codenamed, had been postponed by Hitler in October 1940, in favour of an all-out attack on the USSR, there was still an urgent need to continue design of the glider. In less than a week, a broad specification was drawn up, following which Messerschmitt and Junkers were given a mere 14 days for initial design studies to be submitted, each manufacturer also being instructed to acquire materials for the construction of 100 gliders.

It says much for the capability of the design teams that both met the deadline and were then instructed to double the initial order. The Junkers project, the all-wing Ju 322, was built only in prototype form and had such poor handling qualities that it was scrapped. However, Messerschmitt's design, the Me 321, was rolled out in 14 weeks from the programme go-ahead; at the time it was the world's second largest aircraft, with a wingspan of 180 ft 5¼ in (55.00 m). The cargo hold had a capacity of 3,814 cu ft (108 m³) and was 36 ft 1 in (11 m) long, 10 ft 10 in (3.3 m) high and 10 ft 4 in (3.15 m) wide. It had a capacity for loads of up to 44,092 lb (20000 kg), almost double its empty weight, and could carry an estimated 200 troops.

A jettisonable take-off dolly was used for flight-testing, with the aircraft landing on sprung skids. Up to eight 1,102-1b (5-kN) thrust hydrogen peroxide rockets, giving 30 seconds of power, could be attached to assist the take-off.

A Junkers Ju 90 was used as tug for the first flight on 25 February 1941, when the Me 321 was found to handle satisfactorily although, not surprisingly, the controls were heavy. The tug proved barely capable of hauling the glider, through a lack of power, and the twin-fuselage Heinkel He 111Z conversion then being undertaken had not been completed. Further tests were carried out using a triple tow by three Bf 110s, an extremely complex and dangerous operation which resulted in a number of accidents.

Into service

By late summer 1941 the Messerschmitt plants had delivered the first 100 Me 321A

The planned invasion of the British Isles, Operation Sealion, required heavy equipment to be airlifted with the first airborne assault. Although the invasion never took place, the Me 321 transport glider did reach production status.

Take-offs were a problem for the Me 321. There was no aircraft of sufficient power available in numbers to launch the glider and, following rather discouraging model tests, the Troikaschlepp was devised. This involved three Messerschmitt Bf 110s all pulling one Me 321, the centre tug having a towline 66 ft (20 m) longer than those of the others.

gliders and had begun deliveries of the Me 321B-1 with a wider flight deck to accommodate a pilot and co-pilot (the earlier versions had been for single pilot operation). As the gliders were delivered, units were formed, still with trios of Bf 110s, and moved to the Eastern Front where they performed several missions with varying success. It soon became apparent that a powered transport was required and Messerschmitt was therefore tasked with investigating this possibility. Meanwhile, the last of 200 Me 321s was delivered in early 1942, by which time the first He 111Z tugs had flown and proved satisfactory.

Messerschmitt converted the two prototype Me 321s as prototypes for the powered version, the Me 323C with four second-hand Gnome-Rhône radial engines and the Me 323D with six similar engines. The intention was that the Me 323C would be towed off the ground by a trio of Bf 110s and would then be able to cruise under its own power, whereas the Me 323D would not require tug assistance. Because of towing accidents, the Me 323D was chosen for production, and modifications were made to the design before manufacture began of a pre-series batch of 10 Me 323D-0 aircraft. Rocket-assisted take-off was still available and the production Me 323D-1 and Me 323D-2, which differed only in detail, could each carry a 21,495-lb (9750-kg) cargo load over 621 miles (1000 km). As a troop transport, each type could carry 120 soldiers with full equipment, and a detachable floor could be removed to accommodate 60

stretcher patients with medical attendants. What was considered to be heavy and adequate defensive armament comprised five 0.31-in (7.92-mm) MG 15 machine-guns in the nose and upper fuselage, with up to 10 MG 34 infantry machine-guns in the fuselage sides.

Production deliveries began in August 1942, and two months later two Ju 52/3m groups were re-equipped with these giant transports. In November the Me 323s began Mediterranean operations in support of the Axis forces in North Africa, and the first aircraft were lost shortly afterwards to British fighters. Operating in groups of up to 100 transports (together with Ju 52/3m aircraft) and with

fighter escort, the Me 323s at first enjoyed immunity from attacks, but gradually the Allied aircraft began to take their toll and in mid-April 1943 a formation of 16 Me 323s was attacked by RAF fighters and lost 14 of its number. The low speed of these giant transports and their inability to adopt evasive manoeuvres when attacked meant that it was essential to increase defensive armament, and the Me 323D-6 began this trend by uprating the five MG 15s to five 0.51-in (13-mm) MG 131 machine-guns. It was followed by the Me 323E-1 which introduced two HDL 151 gun turrets with a 20-mm MG 151/20 cannon in each, with an increase of two crew members to operate them; and the Me 323E-2 with the same armament, but which housed the MG 151/20s in low-drag EDL 151 gun turrets. However, these increases in armament

proved to be ineffective, and attempts were then made to increase performance, a number of Me 323E-2s being given six 1,350-hp (1007-kW) Junkers Jumo 21 1R engines, with the resulting conversion redesignated Me 323F-1. This also failed to reduce the vulnerability of these transports to any worthwhile degree, and plans to develop the Me 323E-2/WT with an armament of 11 cannon and four machine-guns, and the redesigned Gnome-Rhône-powered Me 323G, were abandoned. Me 323s were withdrawn from the Mediterranean theatre where losses were unacceptably high and transferred for use on the Eastern Front. Production ended in April 1944, after a total of 198 had been built, and it would seem that their operational deployment ended at about the same time or very shortly afterwards.

Multi-purpose giant

One of the few positive features of the Gigant family was its versatility in the type of cargo it could carry. Different combat zones called for different supplies; for example on the Eastern Front, horses were needed to pull guns and vehicles through the mud (below) and Me 323s transported the animals en masse to Russia. More than a whole company of infantry could be carried for the air assault role (top right) or a single vehicle like this SD KFz 251 (bottom right) could add weight to an armoured thrust.

The ultimate standard form of Gigant was the Me 323E-2; this is an E-2 of I./TG 5, which was desperately overworked on the Eastern Front from late 1943. This aircraft has a white stripe ahead of the tail instead of the expected yellow theatre band. The E-2 differed from earlier versions chiefly in defensive armament, the normal fit comprising two hand-aimed MG 131s low down in the front doors, another MG 131 firing aft from the radio compartment behind the cockpit, two 20-mm MG 151s in low-drag EDL 151 turrets behind the outboard engines, and four single MG 131s firing from front and rear beam positions.

Mikoyan-Gurevich

By the time Operation Barbarossa was launched in June 1941, the VVS had received 1,289 MiG-3s, though these aircraft formed only about 10 per cent of its front-line fighter force.

MiG-1/MiG-3

A dynasty is founded

Ever since the Korean War, the word 'MiG' has been synonymous with the Soviet Union and its military machine. During the Cold War the design bureau became, arguably, the most famous aircraft manufacturing organisation in the world. Less well known were the MiG OKB's first in-service fighter designs – the MiG-1 and MiG-3.

Originally known as I-200s, the first 100 aircraft (the third of which is seen here) were redesignated MiG-1 after their designers. Entering service in 1940, the production I-200 had a 391-mph (630-km/h) top speed.

Answering an urgent call for a high-altitude interceptor, aired at a January 1939 meeting at the Kremlin (attended by Stalin himself), Polikarpov OKB (Experimental Design Bureau) designers Artem Mikoyan and Mikhail Gurevich started work on Project 'K' – a new fighter to be powered by a Mikulin AM-37 engine and with a projected 670-km/h (417-mph) top speed.

With permission granted in November to proceed towards production, and Nikolai Polikarpov out of favour with the Communist hieratchy, Mikoyan and Gurevich were granted their own OKB. Work now proceeded apace, as a mid-April 1940 first flight deadline had been imposed; it was on 5 April that the first I-200 took

to the air. In the event the aircraft was powered by a proven 1,350-hp (1007-kW) AM-35A engine, as the AM-37 had been delayed by development problems, and within eight weeks the I-200 prototype had been flown to a new Soviet speed record of 403 mph (649 km/h) at 22,127 ft (6900 m).

Though its speed was exceptional – some 25 mph (40 km/h)

faster than other contemporary Soviet fighter prototypes – the I-200's handling gave cause for concern. With a particularly high wing loading, the aircraft had a tendency to stall and spin, lacked longitudinal stability and was not sufficiently manoeuvrable. Test pilots also complained of an unreliable side-opening canopy and poor brakes, poor visibility and inadequate cockpit ventilation.

Pilots disperse after listening to a speech on combat tactics given by Aleksandr Pokryshkin, the Soviet Union's third highest scoring ace (with 59 kills by the end of the war, 12 scored while flying the MiG-3) whose first taste of action came on the opening day of Operation Barbarossa. The 'parade ground' line-up of MiG-3s in the background (which also includes Lend-Lease Curtiss P-40s) was typical; the VVS lost many fighters in the opening bombing raids of Barbarossa because they failed to disperse their aircraft to minimise potential losses in such raids.

Above: Each of these MiG-3s carries RS-82 rockets under its wing. Up to eight could be carried, as an alternative to a pair of 100-kg (220-lb) FAB-100 bombs in the fighter-bomber role.

Right: "A Red Air Force landing ground camouflaged by nature" reads the caption of the official Soviet photograph. The MiG-3 was being withdrawn from front-line units as early as spring 1942.

Modifications were hastily carried out in an attempt to 'tame' the I-200 sufficiently to allow it to enter squadron service, and by the end of 1940 some 100 I-200s had been completed; 20 had been delivered to the VVS by the end of the year.

I-200 production

In production form, the I-200 was armed with a single UBS 0.50-in (12.7-mm) and a pair of ShKAS 0.30-in (7.62-mm) machine-guns, all mounted above the engine and synchronised to fire through the propeller arc. A bomb rack, able to carry a FAB-50 or FAB-100 bomb, was fitted beneath each wing and the aircraft's cockpit canopy was designed to open more easily in flight. With these changes weight increased slightly and the I-200's maximum speed dropped to 391 mph (630 km/h) but this was still faster than any of its contemporaries.

In service the handling of the I-200, redesignated MiG-1 from January 1941, was still of concern. The aircraft was difficult to control in various parts of the flight envelope, largely due to the fact that its centre-of-gravity was well aft. Feedback from service pilots prompted further modifications which culminated in an aircraft that was sufficiently different to warrant a new designation.

The MiG-3 had a new fuel tank beneath the cockpit to improve endurance, its engine was moved forward 3.94 in (10 cm) to help correct the c-of-g problems and the dihedral of its outer wings was doubled to 6° 30' to help improve handling. Despite all the work carried out to improve the aircraft, however, it remained a demanding machine to fly well. Soviet ace Aleksandr Pokryshkin described the MiG-3 as a "frisky, fiery horse" that would "run like an arrow" in the hands of an expe-

rienced pilot. It was also short on firepower, armed as it was with only three machine-guns, as per the MiG-1.

By March 1941 70 MiG-3s were being produced every week and were equipping air defense regiments at Moscow, Leningrad and Baku, front-line air force fighter regiments in border regions and units in the Northern Fleet and Black Sea Fleet air forces.

Barbarossa combat

On 22 June 1941 Operation Barbarossa, the German invasion of the Soviet Union, was launched and the Great Patriotic War had begun. The MiG-3 had already seen combat, however. Prior to the invasion, the Luftwaffe had begun preparatory reconnaissance flights over the Soviet border, using Junkers Ju 86P high-altitude aircraft. In early 1941 a Ju 86P was shot down by a MiG-3 and a second was forced to land – clearly the

Luftwaffe had no idea that a fighter with the altitude performance of the MiG existed.

MiG-1s and -3s were active from day one of Barbarossa and accounted for significant numbers of Luftwaffe aircraft, but as the air war with the Luftwaffe was largely fought at altitudes below 6,560 ft (2000 m), the MiGs had little opportunity to show their opponents what they could really do. Some attempt was made to use the aircraft as front-line fighters and for ground attack (equipped with RS-82 rockets), though this did not meet with much success. For the front-line fighter role several dozen aircraft were fitted with the uprated AM-38 engine (as installed in the Ilyushin Il-2 *Shturmovik*) to improve low-level performance.

However, by late 1943/early 1944 the MiG-3 had been effectively retired from the front line, though it remained in use in the air defence role until VE-Day.

With the inscription 'For Stalin!' below its cockpit, this MiG-3P was the mount of A. V. Shlopov of 6.IAP (6th Guards Fighter Regiment), 6.IAK PVO (6th Guards Fighter Aviation Corps, Air Defence Fighter force). Based at Moscow during the winter of 1941/42, the aircraft has an all-white finish with light-blue undersides. Note the podded UBK 0.5-in (12.7-mm) machine-guns under the wings – an attempt to overcome the type's lack of firepower.

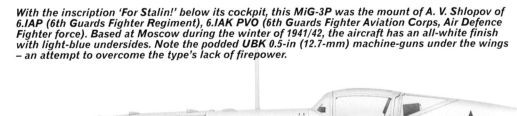

Though obsolete by the time of the attack on Pearl Harbor, the A5M had proved an effective type in the second Sino-Japanese war of 1937. Typical of the types over which the Mitsubishi type proved superior was the Soviet Polikarpov I-152.

Mitsubishi

A5M 'Claude'

Early carrierborne monoplane fighter

The Imperial Japanese Navy's first monoplane fighter, the A5M was one of the first carrierborne examples of an aircraft of this type in the world and saw considerable service over China during 1937/38.

In February 1934 the Imperial Japanese Navy drew up its specification for a new single-seat fighter, the requirements including a challenging maximum speed of 217 mph (350 km/h) and a rate of climb that would take it to 16,405 ft (5000 m) in only 6 minutes 30 seconds. Mitsubishi took up this challenge with a design team headed by Jiro Horikoshi, later to gain his place in aviation history for the remarkable A6M Zero, working against difficult odds to gain what was seen by Mitsubishi to be a potentially important contract.

All single-seat fighters then in service with the navy were of biplane configuration so the

The Imperial Japanese Navy maintained land-based kokutai as well as carrier-based units. These A5M4s are seen ashore some time in the late 1930s.

The '3' prefix in the tailcode of these A5M2s signifies allocation to the 12th Kokutai, a large composite unit which saw much action in China during 1938.

team's monoplane layout was seen as something of a gamble, especially as an earlier monoplane design from Mitsubishi had failed to gain the navy's approval. Horikoshi's design for the proto-type united an inverted gull wing to a narrow-section fuselage, the gull wing being chosen to allow the designers to combine a large-diameter propeller with main landing gear units that would be as short as possible. The tail unit was conventional, the powerplant was a 550-hp (410-kW) Nakajima Kotobuki (congratula-

tion) 5 radial engine, and the pilot was accommodated in an open cockpit directly over the wing.

Designated Mitsubishi Ka-14, it was flown for the first time on 4 February 1935 and demon-strated very quickly that it was more than capable of meeting the navy's requirements. In early tests a maximum speed of 280 mph (450 km/h) was recorded, and the climb to 16,405 ft (5000 m) was achieved in only 5 minutes 54 seconds. There were, however, aerody-

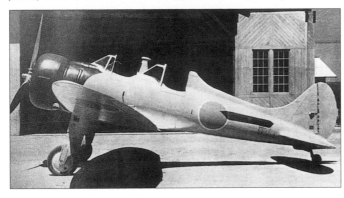

A5M variants built in limited numbers included the A5M2b (above), with an enclosed cockpit which proved unpopular with pilots, and the two-seat A5M4-K fighter-trainer (below).

namic shortcomings and so the second prototype was given a conventional cantilever low-wing with split trailing-edge flaps; at the same time a 560-hp (418-kW) Kotobuki 3 engine was installed. Four other prototypes were completed with varying powerplants, and it was with the low-wing configuration of the second prototype combined with a 585-hp (436-kW) Kotobuki 2 KAI-1 engine that the Mitsubishi A5M1 was ordered into production as the Navy Type 96 Carrier Fighter Model 1.

The A5M1 of 1936 was the Japanese navy's first monoplane fighter, the basic model being armed with two forward-firing 7.7-mm (0.303-in) machine-guns, but the A5M1a variant carried two 20-mm Oerlikon FF cannon. The A5M2 of 1937 was regarded as the most important fighter aircraft in the Navy's inventory during the Sino-Japanese War, the performance of the initial A5M2a being improved, by comparison with the A5M1, by installation of the 610-hp (455-kW) Kotobuki 2-KAI-3 engine; the ensuing generally similar A5M2b differed primarily by the introduction of more power, in the shape of the 640-hp (477-kW) Kotobuki 3, and early production aircraft had an enclosed cockpit. This did not prove popular with its pilots, and late-production A5M2b fighters reverted to an open cockpit configuration. Under the designation A5M3 two experimental aircraft were built and these, similar to earlier open-cockpit production aircraft, each had a 610-hp (455-kW) Hispano-Suiza 12Xers 'moteur canon' engine installed, with a 20-mm cannon firing through the propeller hub. Final production version was the A5M4 with the uprated Kotobuki 41 radial engine, and under the designation A5M4-K a total of 103 was

completed as tandem two-seat trainers. At the outbreak of war in the Pacific the A5M4 was then the Navy's standard fighter, but this situation was of only short duration for, when confronted by Allied fighter aircraft, the A5M's performance was soon found to be inadequate; by the summer of 1942 the type had been relegated to second-line duties.

The A5M had also come very close to being procured by the Japanese army, for the remarkable performance of the second prototype had resulted in a similar prototype being evaluated by the army under the designation Ki-18. Flown in competitive evaluation against the Kawasaki Ki-10-1 biplane then entering service it was found to be considerably faster but inferior in manoeuvrability. Two modified and re-engined Ki-18s were submitted for further testing under the designation Ki-33, but failed to gain an army contract.

Production of the A5M, which was allocated the Allied codename 'Claude', reached a total of 1,094, built by Mitsubishi (791), the Omura Naval Air Arsenal (264) and Watanabe (39). In the final stages of the Pacific war A5M4s and A5M4-Ks were used in a *kamikaze* role against Allied shipping.

A5M in service, 1938-42

The A5M saw its first combat in early 1937, the A5M2a variant joining the fray over China. The A5M4, with improved range, followed in 1938 and, although the type was to be progressively replaced by A6M2 Zeros from September 1940, delivery problems with the A6M meant that by the end of 1941 85 A5M4s were still in front-line use – 49 aboard aircraft-carriers and 36 with land-based *kokutai*. Their main contribution during World War II was in su\`port of landings on Mindanao, during which they flew from *Ryujo*. Others saw action in Malaya, the Bay of Bengal, the Dutch East Indies and New Britain, though by May 1942, had been withdrawn from front-line service.

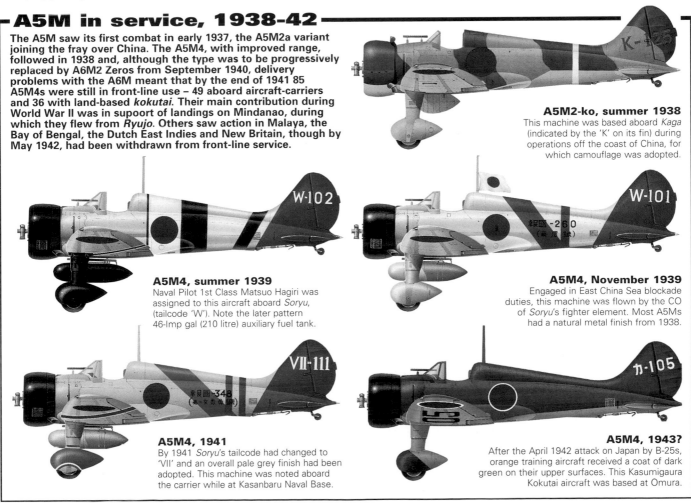

A5M2-ko, summer 1938
This machine was based aboard *Kaga* (indicated by the 'K' on its fin) during operations off the coast of China, for which camouflage was adopted.

A5M4, summer 1939
Naval Pilot 1st Class Matsuo Hagiri was assigned to this aircraft aboard *Soryu*, (tailcode 'W'). Note the later pattern 46-Imp gal (210 litre) auxiliary fuel tank.

A5M4, November 1939
Engaged in East China Sea blockade duties, this machine was flown by the CO of *Soryu*'s fighter element. Most A5Ms had a natural metal finish from 1938.

A5M4, 1941
By 1941 *Soryu*'s tailcode had changed to 'VII' and an overall pale grey finish had been adopted. This machine was noted aboard the carrier while at Kasanbaru Naval Base.

A5M4, 1943?
After the April 1942 attack on Japan by B-25s, orange training aircraft received a coat of dark green on their upper surfaces. This Kasumigaura Kokutai aircraft was based at Omura.

Mitsubishi
A6M Reisen 'Zeke'

Introduction

The Zero dominated the early years of the war in the Pacific. With its superb agility and exceptionally long range, it gave Japanese naval forces almost guaranteed air superiority. From 1943 the tide turned against the Zero, with the introduction of more capable Allied fighters.

The Mitsubishi A6M is perhaps more popularly known as the Zero or Zero-Sen, a contraction of its full designation (it was officially the Rei Shiko Kanjo Sentoki – Type Zero Carrier Fighter). The Zero is remembered as being one of the great fighters of World War II, though it was never the invincible and faultless aircraft demonised by Allied air forces during the early years of the war.

The A6M was certainly fast when it entered service, and extremely agile, but these undoubted attributes were achieved despite having relatively little engine power. Thus the designers of the Zero had to do everything possible to reduce weight, and this meant a structure so light as to make it vulnerable to even the lightest calibre enemy armament, with little armour and a relatively light punch.

Few aircraft in history had as much mystique built around them as the Zero. Following its combat success in China, and during the early stages of the Japanese campaign in the Pacific, Allied airmen became convinced that the Japanese fighter was invincible.

Allied intelligence scored a dramatic coup when an almost intact A6M2 force-landed in the Aleutian Islands in June 1942. It was shipped to NAS North Island in San Diego for thorough evaluation. At last, the myth of the Zero's invincibility had been broken.

While the Zero was fighting ill-trained Chinese airmen and similarly inexperienced volunteers, flying inferior fighters like the Polikarpov I-15 and I-16, it was almost unbeatable. But even during the early years of World War II, when folklore has it that the Zero was 'invulnerable', small numbers of aircraft were despatched by 'inferior' Allied types, including the Hawker Hurricane, the widely disparaged Brewster Buffalo, and even the unwieldy Bristol Blenheim bomber. Eight Zeros were shot down during the Pearl Harbor operation. Overall, the Zero did enjoy an impressive degree of superiority over Allied aircraft in the first few years of the war, and this was reflected by its highly favourable kill:loss ratio. The Zero won its reputation in these early encounters, and such was the measure of its early superiority that its reputation lasted long after the aircraft had lost its edge.

The Zero was never able to gain mastery over the Grumman F4F Wildcat, whose heavier armament and robust construction compensated for its slightly inferior performance and agility. Allied fighters had gained in weight (like the Zero), but

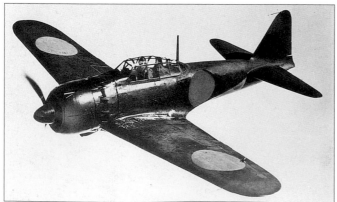

The Zero possessed a level of manoeuvrability which was far in excess of any contemporary Allied fighter. It could out-turn even the Grumman F6F Hellcat, but was hampered by poor diving ability and woefully inadequate armour protection.

Left: The A6M5 was an interim improved version which was built in greater numbers than any other Zero variant. Introduced in the autumn of 1943, it aimed to redress the balance of power against the F6F Hellcat.

Below: Riding on the Divine Wind. As the tide of the war turned against Japan, its military forces resorted to desperate measures – such as suicide bombers – to stem the Allied advance in the Pacific. A bomb-laden Zero taxis out during the Leyte operations in November 1944. Comrades cheer as this kamikaze pilot begins what is certainly to be his last mission.

engine improvements had brought about massive improvements in performance and agility. The Zero was being overtaken and would soon be thoroughly outclassed by almost all of its competitors. Thus, against the F4U Corsair and Spitfire, the Zero enjoyed only superior turn performance, and against the Grumman F6F Hellcat even this advantage was severely eroded at higher speeds. The superiority of the Hellcat over the Zero was most conclusively demonstrated at the Battles of the Philippine Sea and Leyte Gulf in 1944.

Design weaknesses

By the end of the war the Zero's weight had increased through essential improvements which addressed a handful of the type's weaknesses. Engine development had been slow, and performance improved very little between the first and last variants of the aircraft. In fact, the major late-war version, the A6M5, was actually slower than the A6M2, but was slightly faster climbing. This weakness was well recog-

nised even by the Zero's designers. Replacements for the Zero had been put in hand as early as 1940, but prototypes of more advanced aircraft like the J2M Reisen and A7M Reppu took many years to emerge, and proved disappointing when they did so. Thus, the Zero served on after it should have been replaced, and its abil-

ity to do so, in the face of increasingly superior opposition, was a tribute to the versatility and adaptability of the aircraft. The aircraft remained in very large-scale production until the end of the war, and some 10,449 were built, making it the most numerous of Japan's wartime fighters.

By the end of the war the Zero was teetering on the brink of complete obsolescence, fit only for Imperial Japan's last, desperate gamble – the *kamikaze* offensive. Today, the Zero is remembered for its early successes – and has gone down in history as one of the great classic fighters of the war.

Of nearly 10,500 Zeros built, just two examples survive in airworthy condition. The A6M5 (top) is currently operated by the Planes of Fame Museum in Chino, California, and retains its orginal Sakae engine. The remaining example (pictured below) is the Confederate Air Force's A6M2, which saw combat over the Solomon Islands with the 5th Carrier Division on the carrier Zuikaku. Ironically, it is now fitted with an American engine and propeller.

Operational history

Initially thought to be invincible, the Zero was soon discovered to be underpowered and underprotected. By 1945, it was hopelessly outclassed.

The preliminary specification that resulted in the Zero was issued in 1937. Later that year, it was revised in the light of combat experience gained by the Imperial Japanese Navy during the war with China. The new requirements called for a top speed of 270 kt (310 mph; 498 km/h), the ability to climb to 9,840 ft (3000 m) in three minutes 30 seconds, an endurance of eight hours, and an armament consisting of two 20-mm cannon and two 0.303-in (7.7-mm) machine-guns. At the same time, the aircraft had to retain the exceptional manoeuvrability of the A5M monoplane. This was a highly ambitious undertaking for Japanese industry and in 1937 seemed almost impossible to achieve. Nevertheless, the prototype A6M1 was transferred to its test airfield by ox-cart and

took to the air on 1 April 1939. By the standards of the time, the new Japanese fighter was among the most advanced in the world. However, in order for it to achieve the performance figures required by the IJN, the aircraft was as light as possible, with little in the way of armour for the pilot or fuel tanks. Its low weight also meant that relatively little engine power was required – the prototype featured a 780-hp (582-kW) Zuisei radial engine.

A second prototype soon followed, but the third example marked the change to the 950-hp (690-kW) Sakae 12 engine, which resulted in a change of designation to A6M2. It was this variant which would prove to be a formidable foe to Allied pilots during the early years of the war in the Pacific.

Above: This A6M2 was photographed shortly after the type's entry into service and was among those deployed to China as part of the 12th Combined Air Corps.

Right: Exceptional range enabled the Zero to roam far from the carrier battle group. This A6M2 is seen on the Hiryu prior to the attack on Pearl Harbor.

Into combat

Pre-production A6M2s of the 12th Rengo Kokutai (Naval Air Corps) were rushed to China for operational trials, where they proved remarkably successful against Soviet Polikarpov I-15s and I-16s. The type scored its first combat victory on 13 September 1940 and, by the end of the year, the single Zero squadron had claimed 59 victories without losing a single aircraft.

The surprise attack on Pearl Harbor initiated a run of successes

which enhanced the myth of the Zero's invincibility. A total of 105 A6M2 Zeros, flying from six carriers of the Imperial Japanese Navy, as escorts to the attacking Nakajima B5N2 torpedo and Aichi D3A dive-bombers, managed to shoot down a number of American fighters in two waves, with minimal losses.

During the subsequent Japanese advances of the war in the Pacific, the Zero proved able to dominate most of the Allied fighter types it encountered, and

▶ Zeros in service

First blooded in the skies over China in 1940, the A6M was Japan's premier fighter in the early years of the World War II, but began to be eclipsed by superior Allied types from 1943 onwards.

Mitsubishi A6M2 Reisen
The first production variant was the A6M2. This example sports late war camouflage, with dark green upper surfaces and grey undersides, and served with the 402nd Chutai (squadron) 341st Kokutai (naval air corps) at Clark Field in the Philippines in 1944.

341-S-51

Mitsubishi A6M3 Reisen
By 1942, production of the improved A6M3 variant was in full swing. This model featured a more powerful Sakae 21 engine with a two-speed supercharger and modified engine cowling. The aircraft pictured here, with pale green hastily applied over the standard light grey finish, was serving with the 251st Kokutai at Kyushu in late 1942.

UI-120

A6M5c Reisen 'Zeke'

Externally similar to the standard A6M5, the 5c variant featured improved armament in the form of two 13.2-mm (0.6-in) machine-guns outboard of the wing cannon. Only 93 A6M5c models were built.

Reduced range
As more powerful versions of the Sakae 21 engine were fitted and weights increased, so the range of the aircraft was reduced.

Japanese pilots
in 1941-42, the Imperial Japanese Navy boasted an elite force of well-trained pilots, many of whom had seen action in the skies over China. By 1945, most were dead, and the training of young recruits was inadequate. Many Japanese pilots were thus easy prey for Allied fighters.

Lack of armour
Throughout the war in the Pacific, a major shortcoming of the Zero was its inadequate armour. The A6M5 attempted to redress this by means of its self-sealing fuel tanks and improved pilot protection. The A6M5 also boasted thicker wing skins compared to the A6M3 and was thus able to attain higher dive speeds.

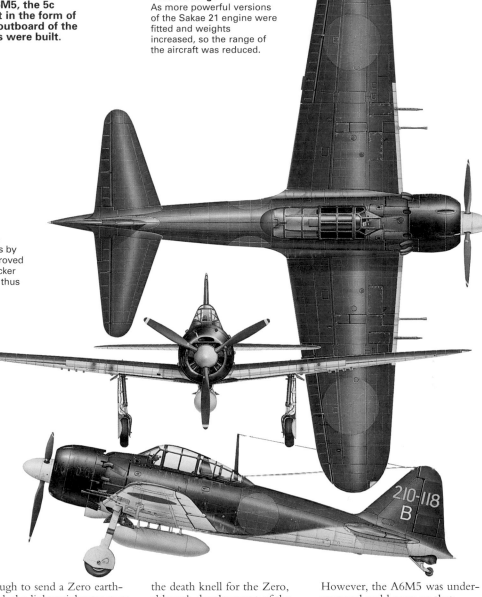

was flown by all the leading Japanese Navy pilots. In particular, one Flight Officer Saburo Sakai became Japan's leading ace of the war, running up an impressive tally of 64 confirmed kills. In a dogfight, aircraft such as the Brewster Buffalo, Curtiss P-36 and P-40, and the Hawker Hurricane proved no match for the agile Japanese fighter,

Shortcomings revealed

The Reisen had its drawbacks, however. Despite its astonishing manoeuvrability, the Zero was somewhat slow in a roll, and took time to accelerate in a dive. In 1942, a single A6M2, flown by Petty Officer Koga, was forced to land on a remote island, having been damaged during an attack on Dutch Harbor. The aircraft was captured virtually intact by the Americans and its shortcomings were revealed, notably its light construction and lack of power. The US began development of a new generation of fighters which would prove superior to the Zero in virtually all respects.

Meanwhile, the Japanese came up against the might of the US Navy during the Battles of the Coral Sea and Midway, where the Zero met its match in the tubby Grumman F4F Wildcat. The American fighter was slightly slower and less agile, but it featured pilot armour and self-sealing fuel tanks. In a dogfight, a few bursts from the guns of the F4F were often

enough to send a Zero earthward, the lightweight structure offering little, if any, protection from the Wildcat's shells.

Fighting improvements

The original A6M2 formed the basis of both the A6M2-N 'Rufe' floatplane fighter (built in small numbers) and the A6M2-K trainer. The fitting of a new engine, the 1,100-hp (820-kW) Sakae 21, resulted in the A6M3. This variant proved better able to cope with the Wildcat, but soon came up against the newly-developed Grumman F6F Hellcat, produced in response to the Zero. With a 2,000-hp (1491-kW) engine, the Hellcat was faster at all altitudes and was a sturdily-built and heavily-armed fighter. It would eventually sound

the death knell for the Zero, although development of the Japanese fighter continued.

Too little, too late

The supercharged A6M4 remained in prototype form only. The next production Zero was the A6M5, which was improved to offer a faster diving speed. Sub-variants of the basic type introduced armament improvements, and even featured self-sealing tanks and armour protection for the pilot.

However, the A6M5 was underpowered and heavy, so that performance was marginal at best – it proved no match for American aircraft and Zeros were shot down at an alarming rate. Its development culminated in the definitive variant, the A6M8, which finally gained a more powerful engine in the shape of the 18-cylinder, 1,340-hp Kinsei, but even this proved to be too little, too late and, by 1945, the Zero was unable to meet Allied fighters on even terms.

Right: By the time of the Solomon Islands campaign, most Kokutai were flying the Mitusbishi A6M3. Although this variant had a more powerful engine, it suffered from reduced range due to its smaller fuel capacity.

Mitsubishi G4M 'Betty'

The 'Flying Cigar' appellation is fully justified in this view of a G4M1. Built in larger numbers than any other Japanese bomber, the type saw considerable success in long-range bombing duties.

'Flying Cigar' – Genesis and early versions

So lightly protected that it was known to US fighter pilots as 'the Honorable One-shot Lighter', the G4M (codenamed 'Betty' by the Allies) tried to get too much range from too small an aircraft. Despite this, it was by far the most important Imperial Japanese Navy bomber, seeing action throughout the Pacific.

Probably the rock-bottom moment of World War II for the British was 10 December 1941, when the Japanese, whose aircraft were as all knew copied from Western designs but made of bamboo and rice paper, sank two of the Royal Navy's greatest warships (HMSs *Prince of Wales* and *Repulse*) by air attack. What could have done such a thing? The only answer seemed to be the ancient Yokosuka B4Y biplane torpedo bomber. Only later was it realised the great battleship and battle-cruiser had been sent to the bottom by Mitsubishi G3M and G4M long-range bombers. The latter was totally unknown to the Allies, because nobody had read the reports on it sent back from China; they had not read the reports on the Mitsubishi A6M fighter, either, and this was an even bigger shock.

In the context of the war in the Pacific a Japanese twin-engined bomber was unlikely ever again to be more than a thorn in the side of the Allies. At the same time a front-line force of more than 2,000 aircraft flown with immense courage and determination could hardly be ignored, and on occasion 'Betty' did inflict damaging blows. It must be remembered that this modest aircraft, with a much lower gross weight than (for example) a B-25 Mitchell, was used for missions which really demanded a four-engined 'heavy', a type that the Imperial Japanese Navy elected to develop too late to see service during World War II.

Development begins

Development of the G4M began with the issue, in September 1937, of a specifica-

Unbeknown to the Royal Navy at the time, the G4M made its debut against Allied forces when a number joined G3Ms in attacking and sinking Royal Navy battleships on 10 December 1941. Here IJN personnel load a torpedo aboard a G4M1.

tion (known as a 12-*shi* specification, because it was in the 12th year of Emperor Hirohito's reign) for a new long-range bomber to succeed the very successful G3M. The latter had gone into action over China in July, and had delighted navy officials by having a combat range in excess of 2,300 miles (3700 km).

Not unnaturally the Koku Hombu (navy air HQ) considered it would be possible to do even better, though it suggested that Mitsubishi should use just two engines of 1,000 hp (746 kW) each. Other numerical demands were a speed of 247 mph (398 km/h), a range with a 1,764-1b (800-kg) torpedo or similar bombload of 2,299 miles (3700 km) and all-round defensive guns needing a crew of seven to nine.

It was soon evident to Kiro Honjo, leader of the bomber design team at Kagamigahara, that the task could not be done on the stipulated power. It was

essential to use engines in the 1,500-hp (1119-kW) class, and the company's engine division happened to have a promising new two-row engine, the Kasei (Mars), that fitted the bill admirably. The rest of the aircraft almost designed itself, the general layout (especially the forward fuselage) being closely similar to the army's Ki-21 bomber produced at the company's main Nagoya plant. Where the new bomber, which was given the designation G4M, differed from most previous single-fin twin-engined machines was that there was a gun position in the extreme tail. As a result the rear fuselage did not taper in the usual way, and this gave rise to a most distinctive shape that immediately resulted in the G4M's popular name of 'Hamaki' (cigar). Aerodynamically it was perfectly acceptable, though Honjo was unable to achieve the long-span wing he wanted, for maximum range, and was forced for reasons

Though the much improved G4M2 was available from 1942, engine shortages kept its predecessor, the G4M1 (pictured), in production until early 1944.

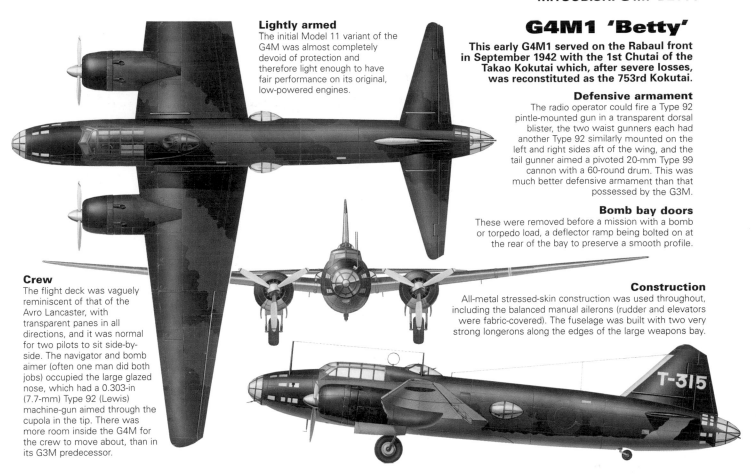

Lightly armed
The initial Model 11 variant of the G4M was almost completely devoid of protection and therefore light enough to have fair performance on its original, low-powered engines.

G4M1 'Betty'

This early G4M1 served on the Rabaul front in September 1942 with the 1st Chutai of the Takao Kokutai which, after severe losses, was reconstituted as the 753rd Kokutai.

Defensive armament
The radio operator could fire a Type 92 pintle-mounted gun in a transparent dorsal blister, the two waist gunners each had another Type 92 similarly mounted on the left and right sides aft of the wing, and the tail gunner aimed a pivoted 20-mm Type 99 cannon with a 60-round drum. This was much better defensive armament than that possessed by the G3M.

Bomb bay doors
These were removed before a mission with a bomb or torpedo load, a deflector ramp being bolted on at the rear of the bay to preserve a smooth profile.

Crew
The flight deck was vaguely reminiscent of that of the Avro Lancaster, with transparent panes in all directions, and it was normal for two pilots to sit side-by-side. The navigator and bomb aimer (often one man did both jobs) occupied the large glazed nose, which had a 0.303-in (7.7-mm) Type 92 (Lewis) machine-gun aimed through the cupola in the tip. There was more room inside the G4M for the crew to move about, than in its G3M predecessor.

Construction
All-metal stressed-skin construction was used throughout, including the balanced manual ailerons (rudder and elevators were fabric-covered). The fuselage was built with two very strong longerons along the edges of the large weapons bay.

G6M escort fighters

As the previous-generation G3Ms were met with much tougher resistance over China, notably from the American Volunteer Group, and the decision was taken to modify the G4M with heavy gun armament instead of bombs and send them in formation with the G3Ms. The result was that the first 30 production machines were G6M1s, or Type 1 Wingtip Convoy Fighters. The bomb bay was sealed, the dorsal gun removed, and the beam guns replaced by a single Type 99 cannon which could be swung on an arm to fire to either side. Two more Type 99s were mounted in a new ventral gondola, one firing ahead and the other to the rear. Thus four cannon could be brought to bear on attacking fighters, and the nose machine-gun was also retained. With a crew of 10 and 21 drums of ammunition the G6M1 was a sluggish performer, and cruising speed was actually slower than that of the G3Ms after the latter had dropped their bombs. Survivors were taken off operations and converted first as G6M1-K trainers and finally as G6M1-2L paratroop transports.

In this view of early G4M1s on a bombing mission, it is possible to see the space left by the deleted bomb bay door. Note also the gun blisters on the fuselage flanks.

of structural strength to use a strongly tapered wing of modest span (25 m/82 ft compared with a 20-m/5.6-ft length of fuselage).

Katsuzo Shima made the first flight on 23 October 1939. The new G4M was outstanding from the start, and the only visible change needed was to increase the height of the vertical tail. By 1940 Mitsubishi's Nagoya

factory was all set to build what in most respects (notably excepting the question of vulnerability) was the best twin-engine bomber of the day. But by this time the Koku Hombu had come to the questionable conclusion that the first aircraft off the line should be completed as escort fighters! In late 1940 production of the G4M1

Several identifying features of an early production G4M1 are visible on this example, including three-bladed propellers, an oval crew door in the rear fuselage and limited nose glazing.

bomber, or Type 1 Attack Bomber Model 11, at last got under way, 13 trials aircraft being followed by the first for the navy inventory in April 1941. By June 1941 the Kanoya Kokutai had become fully operational in China and completed 12 combat missions in that month. Another Kokutai went into action in August, and by the time of Pearl Harbor on 7 December 1941 the Imperial Japanese Navy had 120 G4M1s in its front-line inventory. Of these 97 were with the 21st and 23rd Air Flotillas on Formosa, while 27 Kanoya Kokutai aircraft were switched to the Saigon area to attack the British fleet. These were the aircraft which, with G3M2s, sank HMS *Prince of Wales* and HMS *Repulse*, opening attacks on the following day on US airfields in the Philippines. By 19 February 1942 Japanese forces had over-run a huge geographical area, and the G4M1s were bombing Darwin in northern Australia.

From early March 1942 the G4M1s hammered at Rabaul, Port Moresby and other New Guinea targets. Opposition by the scattered and initially demoralized Allies gradually stiffened, and even though the Allied fighters (initially Curtiss P-40Es of the No. 75 Sqn, RAAF) had a hard time against the A6M2s, if they got near a G4M the bomber went up like a torch. It had been known from the start that, to meet the severe range requirement, the G4M must lack armour and self-sealing tanks. As the situation appeared likely to get worse, the Model 12 bomber was quickly produced with various arrangements of rubber sponge and sheet to protect the tanks, and CO_2 extinguishers were added. The side blisters were replaced by flat gunnery windows, the tail gun was put in a blunter position with a large vertical wedge-shaped opening, and Kasei 15 engines were fitted to give better altitude performance, above the effective ceiling of 40-mm AA fire.

G4M2 and beyond

Within three months of the Pacific War starting, nearly 200 G4M1s had been lost, an unacceptable rate of attrition which led to the ongoing development of the 'Betty' until the end of the war.

The G4M2 introduced a number of improvements to the basic design, including more powerful Kasei engines and air-surface radar equipment. This improved 'Betty' was also developed as a launch platform for the Yokosuka MXY7 Ohka piloted suicide aircraft.

In the summer of 1942 Japan's industry was undamaged and highly responsive to front-line needs. The engine division's uprated Kasei 21 engine, using water-methanol injection for take-off and emergency power, and driving a four-bladed propeller, made it possible to plan a structurally redesigned G4M2 incorporating many improvements. The latter included a so-called laminar-flow wing and extra fuselage fuel which, with other changes, raised gross weight from 20,944 lb (9500 kg) to 27,558 lb (12500 kg). The tail was enlarged and all wing and tail tips were rounded. The nose glazing was increased and a flat bombsight window added. Two extra hand-aimed Type 92 guns were fitted in the sides of the nose, and the dorsal blister was replaced by a simple electrically rotated dorsal turret with a 20-mm Type 99 cannon, the gunner standing on a fixed plat-

form in the fuselage. The production G4M2 in July 1943 also at last had bomb doors, which slightly improved range.

Shortage of Kasei 21s kept the G4M1 in production, however, and it was in one of these that, on 18 April 1943, Admiral Isoroku Yamamoto, the great and inspiring leader of the Imperial Japanese Navy, planned to fly to Kahili, on Bougainville in the Solomon Islands for a general inspection of his troops. This trip to the Solomon Islands and the Bismarck Archipelago was the only part of Yamamoto's itinerary that was within range of American aircraft, and the need for secrecy was absolute. For some time, American Intelligence services had been able to decode Japanese messages, which were encrypted on a machine similar to the Enigma type being used by the Germans in the European Theatre. Occasionally crises arose in which to take action

might give the game away and prove that signals were being read, and Yamamoto's flight was just such an occasion. Eventually it was decided to go ahead with the plan, and the interception mission was flown brilliantly by Lockheed P-38s with extra-long-range tanks. The wreckage of Yamamoto's G4M1 still lies in the jungle where it fell.

New armament

In 1943 production at Okayama, a second source, switched to the G4M2, and both this and the Nagoya plant built the Model 22A with two 20-mm beam guns replacing the

Type 92s and the Model 22B in which the four cannon were all of the Model 2 type with belt feed. Later in the year the G4M2a began production with improved 1,850-hp (1380-kW) MK4T Kasei 25 engines and bulged bomb-bay doors. This had the previous armament variations, and in the Model 24C the central nose gun was changed for a 0.51-in (13-mm) Type 2, while at the very end of the year a proportion of all G4M production was fitted with ASV (anti-surface vessel) radar. By mid-1944 the G4M1 had been withdrawn from front-line units and was used primarily for train-

Above: The designers of Mitsubishi's 'Betty' made a grave mistake in not taking into account the possibility of aggressive fighter opposition, and the type's lack of self-sealing fuel tanks and armour-plating earned it the nickname 'Flying Lighter' from Allied fighter pilots.

Left: The G4M2 introduced a new laminar flow wing, methanol-water injected engines, revised armament and a fuselage fuel tank protected by layers of rubber sheet and sponge.

G4M 'Betty' combat colours

Numerically, the Mitsubishi G4M was by far the most important shore-based bomber in the Imperial Japanese Navy's inventory during World War II. Due to its lack of armour, the type was very light, giving enormous range but was also very vulnerable to enemy fighters.

Mitsubishi G4M1
This G4M1 flew with the 761st Koku-tai from Kanoya in southern Kyushu during 1943. Note the lateral gun blisters, which were replaced by flush glass panels on the G4M2. Note that this aircraft has had its entire tailcone end section removed to improve the gunner's field of fire.

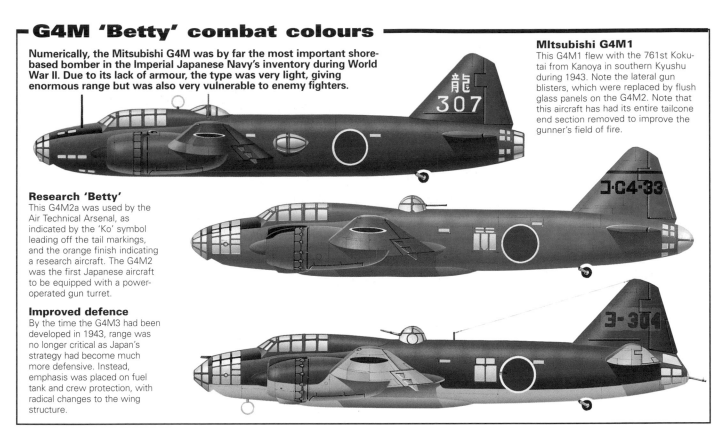

Research 'Betty'
This G4M2a was used by the Air Technical Arsenal, as indicated by the 'Ko' symbol leading off the tail markings, and the orange finish indicating a research aircraft. The G4M2 was the first Japanese aircraft to be equipped with a power-operated gun turret.

Improved defence
By the time the G4M3 had been developed in 1943, range was no longer critical as Japan's strategy had become much more defensive. Instead, emphasis was placed on fuel tank and crew protection, with radical changes to the wing structure.

ing, transport and maritime reconnaissance duties, though it is now known that at least 30 were expended in suicide missions later in the war. Indeed, such was the Allied superiority in the Pacific skies by late 1944 that in the final year of the war attrition on all G4M missions averaged 39 per cent, a totally unacceptable state of affairs for any air arm.

Cherry Blossom
In August 1944 navy officers suggested that the specially designed MXY7 Ohka (cherry blossom) piloted missile be

carried by modified G4Ms. A large number (certainly over 120) of G4M2a bombers was rebuilt with bomb doors removed and special attachments for the rocket-propelled aircraft. Redesignated G4M2e (Model 24J), these aircraft were much heavier than other versions, with poor handling characteristics when carrying the Ohka, making an easy target for Allied fighters. On the first major Ohka combat mission, on 21 March 1945, 16 G4M2es of the 721st Koku-tai headed in loose formation for the Allied fleet but all were shot down long before they got

within missile-launch range. The potentially devastating Ohka failed because of vulnerability of its carrier aircraft.

Final developments
By late 1942 Mitsubishi had in desperation started yet again with a redesign of the G4M to try to reduce vulnerability. The result was the G4M3, first flown in January 1944, with well protected tankage of reduced capacity in single-spar wings and plenty of crew armour. It also had a tail gun position which either resembled that of the Martin B-26 Marauder or ended in a completely open end giving increased field of fire. The fuselage was reduced in length, which shifted the centre of gravity further forward, necessitating the adoption of dihedral on the tail surfaces to restore the stability of the aircraft. The type was designated G4M3a Model 34A, which was developed in January 1945 into the final version of the long-serving 'Betty', the turbo-supercharged G4M3 Model 36, three examples of which were

still undergoing flight trials when the war ended. The under-achieving 'Betty' eventually served as an escort fighter, a bomber, a trainer, and a reconnaissance aircraft and flew on the front-line from the first day of the war until the very last.

These US Navy gun camera frames capture the last moments of a G4M2a that has not yet released its Ohka.

G4Ms in Allied hands
On 19 August 1945, four days after the cessation of hostilities, two all-white Mitsubishi G4M1s bearing green crosses (right) carried the Japanese surrender delegation led by Lieutenant-General Torashiro Kawabe to Ie-Shima on Okinawa, to decide the terms of the surrender of the Japanese, which was officially signed on the deck of the battleship USS *Missouri* on 2 September. In the immediate aftermath of the war, many Japanese types were exhaustively tested by the Allies, including a sole G4M2 (above) which was put through its paces by the Allied Technical Air Intelligence Unit (ATAIU) based in Singapore. A mixture of Japanese and Allied pilots under RAF supervision were used for the trials, which were conducted from an airfield at Tebrau in Malaya. The tests were concluded in March 1946.

Morane-Saulnier MS.406

This MS.406 escaped destruction at the hands of the Axis, and was serving with the 1er Escadrille of Groupe de Chasse I/2 at Nîmes in July 1940. On the fin it wears the badge of World War I Spad squadron SPA3, the 'Cigogne de Guynemer'. This version of the famous stork badge, with drooping wings, was worn by the squadron of the World War I ace Georges Guynemer.

French survivor

When Germany turned its Blitzkrieg on France in 1940, the MS.406 was the most numerous fighter available to the defenders. Thanks to the Swiss, this fighter design was amazingly still in service almost 20 years later.

The MS.405 designation covered the two prototypes and 15 pre-series aircraft. The pre-production aircraft, of which this is the 11th, incorporated successive improvements intended for the production MS.406 fighter.

Design of the MS.406 dates back to a September 1934 requirement issued by the Armée de l'Air for a modern single-seat fighter. The neat fighter was designed around a 642-kW (860-hp) Hispano Suiza 12Ygrs engine, and was unremarkable apart from being mostly covered in a stressed plywood/aluminium bonded skin. Armament consisted of one 20-mm cannon firing through the propeller hub, and a single 7.5-mm (0.295-in) machine-gun in each wing.

The first prototype of what was designated the MS.405 first

flew on 8 August 1935. Development was initially slow, and it was not until 20 January 1937 that the second prototype flew, powered by a 671-kW (900-hp) HS 12Ygrs engine, with which it turned in a top speed of 443 km/h (275 mph).

A pre-production batch of 15 further MS.405s was ordered, incorporating numerous improvements (including the HS 12Y31 engine from the fourth) intended for the production aircraft, which was to be designated MS.406. While most of the MS.405s were used for test and development purposes, a

few were pressed into service at the outbreak of war.

With all the developments installed, MS.406 production with the 642-kW (860-hp) 12Y31 engine got under way in late 1938, building up rapidly as war clouds loomed in Europe. Morane-Saulnier could not handle all of the 1,000 aircraft on order, so three separate divisions of the nationalised aircraft industry were set up to produce

MS.406s. The first production aircraft flew on 29 January 1939. By the time France declared war on Germany at 5 pm on 3 September 1939, the Armée de l'Air possessed 826 'modern' fighters, of which no fewer than 535 were MS.405/406s. Eleven were being produced daily.

Production continued at a rapid pace so that by the time the Germans launched their attack on France on 10 May

Right: The most potent derivative of the MS.406 was the Finnish Mörkö, which replaced the inadequate Hispano Suiza engine with a Klimov M-105P. The resulting aircraft was too late for wartime action, but served until withdrawn on 11 September 1948.

Below: Poland placed an order for 50 MS.406s, but they were taken back by the French at the port of Gdynia. These Armée de l'Air aircraft were flown by pilots who had escaped the German onslaught on Poland.

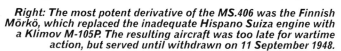

Left: Armament of the MS.406 consisted of a hub-firing cannon and two MAC 1934 machine-guns in the wings. The radiator was semi-retractable, and is seen here on a GC III/1 aircraft in 1940.

Below: France employed the MS.406 in Indochina in 1940. The aircraft had been diverted from a Chinese order and were without cannon, these weapons having already been delivered to the Chinese.

1940, the MS.406 inventory stood at 1,070 – more than all the other fighter types put together. Groupes de Chasse equipped with the type at the time were: GCs III/1, II/2, III/2 and III/3 in the northern zone (Zone d'Opérations Aériennes Nord – ZOAN), GCs I/2, II/6 and III/7 in the eastern zone (ZOAE), GCs III/6 and II/7 in the south (ZOAS) and GCs II/3 and I/6 in the Alps (ZOAA).

Naturally, the ZOAN units bore the brunt of the early fighting, in which the MS.406 was shown immediately to be inferior to the Messerschmitt Bf 109 in most respects, although it was pleasant enough to fly. However, the tenacity of the French pilots ensured that the German victory was no easy one, although the 175 kills credited to MS.406s were achieved at the expense of over 400 aircraft, with many others destroyed on the ground. As French units battled with the Luftwaffe in the north, the Italians struck through the Alps, and MS.406s were in the thick of the fighting. One of the last MS.406 units to form was the Aéronavale's Escadrille AC5, which had 11 ex-Armée de l'Air aircraft.

Export fighters

In the massive MS.406 building programme of 1939-40, sufficient aircraft were spared to sell 30 to Finland and 30 to Turkey. Further export orders for China (12), Poland (50), Lithuania (13) and Yugoslavia (20) remained undelivered or were seized back by the French authorities and redirected to the Armée de l'Air.

Morane-Saulnier had continued the development of the type with the aim of ironing out some of its problems and improving its performance, resulting in the MS.410. The semi-retractable radiator bath, which had caused immense problems in service, was replaced by a fixed unit, while the wing was redesigned to be lighter and to accommodate two belt-fed machine-guns in place of the single drum-fed weapon. In the event, 74 MS.406s were rewinged and modified to become MS.410s, although only five had been completed in time to see action against the Luftwaffe, and the remainder were modified under German control after the armistice on 25 June 1940. Over 50 more aircraft were completed for Finland, where the type was

heavily used in the Continuation War with the Soviet Union.

Surviving French aircraft were assigned to the Vichy government. Only one front-line MS.406 unit remained, most other aircraft being employed for fighter training purposes. When Germany occupied Vichy France in November 1942, 98 MS.406s were acquired and passed on to Finland (2), Croatia (44) and Italy (52).

Finland, having recognised that the MS.406 was underpowered, produced a variant known as the Mörkö (ghost). This used a Soviet-built Klimov M-105P engine, a supply of which had been captured by the Germans. A 20-mm MG 151 cannon fired through the propeller spinner.

The first flew on 4 February 1943, but by the time of the ending of the war with Russia, only two had been completed. Nevertheless, conversions (of both MS.406s and 410s) continued until 41 had been completed. Shortages of the MG 151 cannon led some 'Mörkö-Moraani' to be completed with 12.7-mm (0.5-in) Berezin UB machine-guns. The Mörkös were finally scrapped in 1952.

Swiss development

As early as September 1938 Switzerland had acquired one of the MS.405 pre-production aircraft (and a second in April 1939) to act as pattern aircraft for licence construction. The aircraft were dubbed MS.406H, and had the MS.405 airframe with the 406's 12Y31 engine. A total of 84 of these was built between 1939 and August 1940 by EFW as the D-3800. After front-line use as fighters they were used for advanced training, the last being scrapped in 1954. A more powerful aircraft was developed by Morane-Saulnier specifically for the Swiss. This was the MS.412, with a 783-kW (1,050-hp) 12Y51 engine. Development of the type was completed in Switzerland, where it was designated D-3801. The first flew in October 1940, and between 1941 and 1945 three factories (EFW, Dornier and SWS) produced 207. Another 17 were built up in 1947-48 from sub-assemblies left over from production.

D-3801s entered service in 1941 as fighters, but when their front-line days were over they were relegated to training duties and target-towing. The last one was withdrawn in 1959.

MS.406s are lined up in the south of France in the spring of 1940. As well as having the Germans to contend with in the north, France was also attacked by the Italians through the Alps. MS.406s fared better in this theatre than against the Luftwaffe.

Finnish 'Moraani'

Finland's first MS.406s were 30 aircraft delivered in February 1940, serving with Lentolaivue 28 at Naarajärvi. Too late to see action in the Winter War, they were heavily involved in the Continuation War, claiming 135 kills. The force was bolstered by 57 more aircraft, mostly MS.410s (illustrated). As well as fighter duties, they were used for train-busting and reconnaissance.

Nakajima

Armed with its standard anti-ship weaponload of one 1,764-lb (800-kg) torpedo, a B6N2 Tenzan rolls down the deck of a Japanese Imperial Navy carrier for a raid on Allied shipping in late 1944.

B5N 'Kate'/ B6N 'Jill'

Imperial torpedo-bombers

Used to devastating effect at Pearl Harbor the B5N 'Kate' was an important weapon in the initial stages of the Pacific War. However, by the time its replacement, the B6N, had entered service the tide had turned against the Japanese.

The B6N's first major action of the war began on 19 June 1944 with the great carrier-versus-carrier battles west of the Mariana Islands. The aircraft suffered heavy losses in air-to-air combat.

Nakajima's Type K prototype, first flown during January 1937, had been designed to meet an Imperial Japanese Navy requirement of 1935 for a single-engine carrier-based attack bomber. A cantilever low-wing monoplane with retractable tailwheel landing gear, the prototype accommodated a crew of three (pilot, radio operator and observer/bomb-aimer) all enclosed beneath a long 'greenhouse' canopy. To meet the requirement for carrier operations, this first prototype, powered by a 700-hp (522-kW) Nakajima Hikari 2 radial engine, had a large-area wing incorporating Fowler-type trailing-edge flaps and hydraulic folding, but fears that this might prove difficult to maintain at sea resulted in a second prototype with plain flaps and a manually-folded wing. It was this latter prototype, powered by a Nakajima Hikari 3 radial engine, that was ordered into production in November 1937 as the Navy Type 97 Carrier Attack Bomber Model 1, company designation Nakajima B5N1. Introduced into operational use during the Sino-Japanese War, the B5N1 was found to be an effective

tactical bomber providing support for ground operations. However, its limited defensive armament of a single 0.303-in (7.7-mm) machine-gun meant that it could only be operated with fighter escort. This was not of great importance when it was confronted by the standard fighters then equipping the Chinese air force. When, however, more effective fighters became available to the Chinese from Soviet sources, the B5N1 ceased to be a viable weapon and the development of a more effective version was initiated in 1939. When they were replaced in service by this 'improved' aircraft, the B5N1s were converted for use in the advanced trainer role under the designation B5N1-K.

Improved 'Kate'

Nakajima's developed B5N2, first flown in December 1939, was little more than a version with a far more powerful Nakajima Sakae engine, one which failed to have any significant effect on maximum speed. Nevertheless, the B5N2s which spearheaded the Japanese attack at Pearl Harbor provided adequate evidence of their capability, and it was not until they were

confronted by more advanced Allied fighters that their losses became unacceptable. Allocated the Allied codename 'Kate', the type soldiered along in first-line use until early 1944, then being transferred to serve effectively in maritime reconnaissance and anti-submarine roles. Some operated with anti-service vessel (ASV) radar, and a few anti-submarine warfare (ASW) aircraft were equipped with an early form of magnetic anomaly detection (MAD) gear. When production ended in 1943 a total of 1,149 had been built by Nakajima (669), Aichi (200) and the navy's Hiro Air Arsenal (280).

In 1939, the Imperial Japanese Navy drew up its specification for a carrier-based torpedo-bomber to supersede the Nakajima B5N. To meet the requirement Nakajima decided to use an airframe very similar to that of the earlier aircraft, differing primarily in its vertical tail surfaces. The navy had specified use of the Mitsubishi Kasei radial engine, but Nakajima decided to use instead its own Mamoru 11 radial engine of similar output. The first of two prototypes was

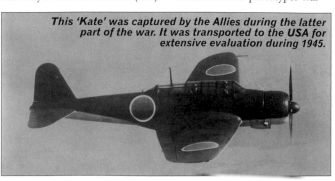

This 'Kate' was captured by the Allies during the latter part of the war. It was transported to the USA for extensive evaluation during 1945.

Left: Two late-production Nakajima B5N2s, with empty bomb racks visible beneath their wings, fly in a tight formation over the infamous 60,000-ton (60963-tonne) Japanese navy battleship Yamato.

Right: Designed like its predecessor, the B5N, for operations from carrier decks, the B6N2 Tenzan featured a wing which folded at mid-span for easy storage on and beneath the crowded decks of Japanese fleet carriers.

flown in early 1941, but flight testing revealed a number of problems, requiring revised vertical tail surfaces and strengthened arrester gear, and it was not until 1943 that the type entered production as the Navy Carrier Attack Bomber Tenzan Model 11, company designation Nakajima B6N1, incorporating a number of refinements as a result of extended flight testing. However, after only 135 production Tenzan (heavenly cloud) aircraft had been delivered a new crisis arose when Nakajima was ordered to terminate manufacture of the Mamoru engine, a step taken to allow greater emphasis to be placed on production of the widely-used Nakajima Homare

and Sakae engines. The company was now compelled to use the engine which the navy had specified originally, the Mitsubishi Kasei, but fortunately the adaptation of the B6N airframe to accept this powerplant presented no major difficulties. The resulting aircraft, which was also the major production version, had the designation B6N2 and differed only from the B6N1 by the installation of the Mitsubishi Kasei 25 engine; the B6N2a variant had the rear-firing 0.303-in (7.7-mm) machine-gun replaced by one of 0.51 in (13 mm) calibre.

When production ended, Nakajima had built a total of 1,268 B6Ns of all versions, this number including two modified

B6N2 airframes which had served as prototypes for a proposed land-based B6N3 Model 13. The powerplant had been the Mitsubishi MK4T-C 25c version of the Kasei engine and the strengthened landing gear had larger wheels for operation from

unprepared runways, but production did not start before the war ended. Allocated the Allied code-name 'Jill', the B6Ns saw intensive use during the last two years of the war for conventional carrier operations and, in the later stages, in kamikaze roles.

This 'Kate' wears the white 'surrender' colouring with green cross insignia, which indicated 'peaceful' intentions after the Japanese capitulation.

B5N2 'Kate'

At the outbreak of the Pacific War, the 'Kate' was the most advanced carrierborne torpedo bomber in the world. During the following 12 months, it delivered fatal blows to three separate US Navy aircraft-carriers and supported Japanese amphibious attacks throughout the region. By 1944, technical developments had rendered the aircraft obsolete and it ended its service in second-line units.

Armament
The inadequate defensive armament consisted of one flexible rear-firing 0.303-in (7.7-mm) Type 92 machine-gun. Offensive capability could comprise one 1764-lb (800-kg) torpedo or three 250-lb (551-kg) bombs.

Powerplant
The B5N2 variant was powered by one Nakajima NK1B 11 14-cylinder air-cooled radial piston engine driving a three-bladed constant-speed metal propeller.

Protection
The 'Kate' suffered from a failing common to many Japanese aircraft of the early part of the war, in that range and performance had been achieved at the expense of defensive armour and self-sealing fuel tanks.

Crew
The B5N2 had a crew of three in an enclosed cockpit, comprising a pilot and an observer/navigator who doubled as a bomb-aimer in the level-bombing role. Seated between the pilot and the radio operator, he could see the target by opening a pair of small folding doors in the floor of the fuselage. The radio operator also manned the single trainable machine-gun in the rear cockpit.

Performance
The B5N2 variant of the 'Kate' had a maximum speed of 235 mph (378 km/h) at 1,181 ft (360 m) and a cruising speed of 161 mph (259 km/h) at 9,845 ft (3000 m). The aircraft had a maximum range of 1,075 nm (1238 miles; 1992 km).

Markings
This aircraft was flown by a squadron leader in the Pearl Harbor attack force launched from the flagship of Vice Admiral Nagumo's fleet, the 36,500-ton aircraft carrier *Akagi*.

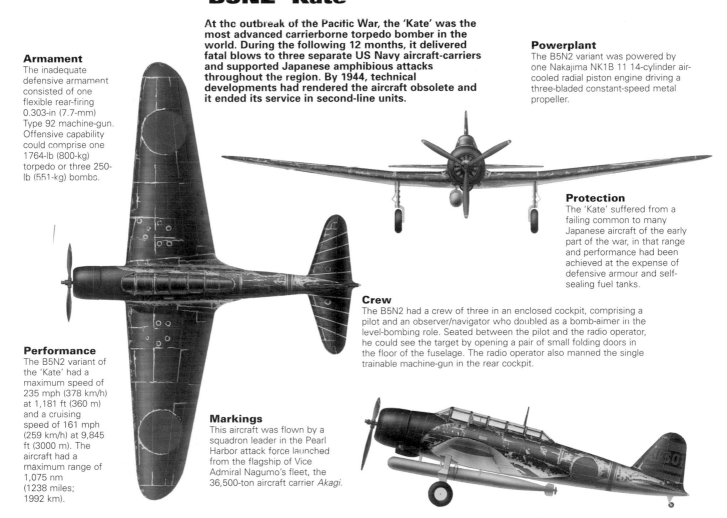

Nakajima Ki-43 Hayabusa

The Japanese puppet state of Manchukuo was supplied with Ki-43s for home defence. Here the Japanese equivalent of the British 'Hucks starter' is seen being employed to start a section of Hayabusas.

Peregrine Falcon

Lightly armed and powered, the Nakajima Ki-43-I was obsolescent at the time of its service debut over Malaya in December 1941. Yet this aircraft obtained a decisive advantage over Allied types during the first year of the war, and remained in production until the Japanese surrender, long after it had become totally outdated.

In the last days of peace in the Malay peninsula, the Commonwealth pilots assigned to RAF, RAAF and RNZAF squadrons in the region exuded confidence. Though their Brewster Buffaloes had been found hopelessly obsolete for first-line European service, they were lured into complacency by the ill-founded belief that their Japanese opponents were flying even more obsolete aircraft. However, they were soon to find that their Buffaloes were easily outmanoeuvred and outperformed by the Nakajima Ki-43-I Hayabusas of the Imperial Japanese Army.

Difficult gestation

First flown at the Ojima airfield in January 1939, the prototype had a difficult gestation period and was saved from oblivion only after a major redesign had corrected initial deficiencies. Preliminary design work was begun in December 1937 when the Koku Hombu (Air HQ) instructed Nakajima Hikoki KK (Nakajima Aeroplane Co Ltd) to design a single-seat fighter to

replace the Nakajima Ki-27 then just entering service. The specification emphasised manoeuvrability and called for a top speed of 500 km/h (311 mph), a climb rate of 5 minutes to 5000 m (16,405 ft), a range of 800 km (497 miles) and an armament of two 7.7-mm (0.303-in) machine-guns – rather uninspired requirements, with the exception of manoeuvrability, compared to those being drawn up in Europe at this time.

The design team elected to retain the wing planform and aerofoil of the Ki-27 for the new fighter, but adopted a longer rear fuselage to balance the heavier weight of the 925-hp (690-kW) Nakajima Ha-25 double-row radial driving a two-bladed fixed-pitch wooden propeller and retractable main landing gear.

Despite these improvements the three Ki-43 prototypes proved barely faster than production Ki-27s and were less manoeuvrable. After an unsatisfactory report by the Imperial Japanese Army test organisation at Tachikawa, the Koku Hombu seriously considered suspending

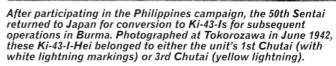

After participating in the Philippines campaign, the 50th Sentai returned to Japan for conversion to Ki-43-Is for subsequent operations in Burma. Photographed at Tokorozawa in June 1942, these Ki-43-I-Hei belonged to either the unit's 1st Chutai (with white lightning markings) or 3rd Chutai (yellow lightning).

further development. In the event, prudence prevailed and the design team was instructed to proceed with a major redesign and the construction of 10 service trials aircraft. The first of these aircraft was completed in November 1939 and introduced a refined and lightened fuselage, new vertical tail surfaces, a revised canopy improving vision to the rear, and a more powerful

version of the Ha-25 engine. The results of these changes proved satisfactory, and performance met revised and more demanding requirements.

An 1,100-hp (821-kW) Ha-105 engine, with a two-speed supercharger instead of the single-speed supercharger of the Ha-25, was tested on pre-production aircraft, as was an armament of two 12.7-mm

Shining under the Chinese sun, this Ki-43-II-Otsu of the 2nd Chutai (red diagonal tail stripe), 25th Sentai, proves that the application of green mottle over natural metal was less than effective.

Above: Bearing Chinese markings, this Ki-43-I-Hei (Ic) – the first flyable 'Oscar' to fall into Allied hands – was tested by US personnel who were impressed by its manoeuvrability, but noted a lack of protection and light armament.

Below: After Nakajima had built 10 prototypes of the Ki-43-III-Ko powered by the 1,190-hp (887-kW) Ha-115-II radial engine, this version entered production with Tachikawa. Few saw action and were easy prey for Allied fighters. Pictured is a 1st Chutai, 48th Sentai machine.

(0.5-in) machine-guns. The Ha-105 engine was not retained, but the heavier armament was adopted for late production versions, along with the provision for carrying two 200-litre (44-Imp gal) drop tanks beneath the wings. It was, however, the installation of 'butterfly' combat flaps which ensured the final acceptance of the Ki-43 as a service type, as with these flaps, the aircraft demonstrated exceptional manoeuvrability. Consequently, Nakajima was authorised in September 1940 to start production of the Ki-43-I as the Army Type 1 Fighter Model 1, three sub-versions being planned depending upon the availability of 12.7-mm (0.5-in) machine-guns (the Ki-43-I-Ko (Ia) had two 7.7-mm/0.303-in guns, the Ki-43-I-Otsu had one 7.7-mm/ 0.303-in and one 12.7-mm/ 0.5-in gun, and the Ki-43-I-Hei (Ic) two 12.7-mm/0.5-in machine-guns).

Service entry

Named Hayabusa (peregrine falcon), the new type entered service in June 1941. The Ki-43s were soon blooded in Malaya, besting the Buffaloes and more than holding their own against Hawker Hurricanes. In fact, most losses incurred during the first two months in combat were the result of operational causes, including fuel starvation and structural failures. The former problem was easily remedied when a sufficient number of drop tanks were delivered to these units, but the latter, which occurred even after initial production aircraft had undergone emergency strengthening at the Tachikawa Arsenal, required a redesign of the wing structure.

Within months of the type's entry into service, both the manufacturer and the army recognised that the Ki-43-Is performance was inadequate, with the exception of its superb manoeuvrability. Unfortunately, little could be done to increase speed or armament dramatically. Nevertheless, by substituting a 1,150-hp (858-kW) Nakajima Ha-115 engine (with a two-speed supercharger and driving a constant-speed three-bladed propeller), Nakajima was able to increase maximum speed to 347 mph (558 km/h) at 19,125 ft (5830 m) for the Ki-43-II prototypes. However, with the addition of 13-mm (0.51-in) head and back armour plating and a rudimentary form of self-sealing fuel tanks, the production versions of the Ha-115-powered Hayabusa could not do better than 329 mph (530 km/h) at 13,125 ft (4000 m).

In common with the Ki-43-II prototypes, the Ki-43-II-Ko, Ki-43-II-Otsu and Ki-43-II-KAI versions had wings of slightly reduced span and area with stronger spars. In addition, the underwing shackles, which during the course of the Ki-43-II-Otsu production were moved from aft of the main landing gear units to a position farther outboard, were strengthened to carry bombs of up to 551 lb (250 kg).

With the Imperial Japanese Army now fighting over a broad front from the Chinese mainland to the jungle of New Guinea, the increased production rates were still insufficient to make up for combat losses. Accordingly, the Koku Hombu instructed both its 1st Army Air Arsenal at Tachikawa and the Tachikawa Aeroplane Co Ltd to manufacture the Hayabusa. The Arsenal produced only 49 Ki-43-II-Ko fighters, but the latter company became the prime manufacturer of Hayabusas. The last Nakajima-built Ki-43 was delivered in September 1944; Tachikawa was still manufacturing the type at war's end.

Following the conquest of Malaya and the fall of Singapore on 15 February 1942, the very swift conquest of the Dutch East Indies saw the pilots of Ki-43-Is racking up impressive scores. On the Burma front, however, things soon became less easy for the Hayabusa pilots as they faced the experienced pilots of the American Volunteer Group. From then on the Ki-43, which was known to Allied personnel by the codename 'Oscar', found itself on the defensive, though Ki-43s nevertheless still bore a heavy burden in the defensive campaign fought by the Imperial Japanese Army during the last two years of the war.

More than any other type, the Ki-43 Hayabusa epitomised both the qualities and deficiencies of Japanese fighters of World War II. In a dogfight, it had no peer. However, from 1943 onward speed, heavy armament, and good protection were qualities of greater importance than manoeuvrability to success in air combat. Thus it is indeed quite remarkable that the Ki-43 became the only Japanese fighter aircraft to be used after the end of the war, when a small number of captured Hayabusas were operated in 1945-6 by the Indonesian People's Security Forces against the Dutch and by the French Groupes de Chasse I/7 and II/7 against Communist insurgents in Indo-China.

'Peregrine Falcon' plumage

Total production of all Ki-43 variants amounted to 5,919, including 3,239 by Nakajima and 2,631 by Tachikawa. The first examples entered IJA service in 1941.

Ki-43-I-Hei
Right: This aircraft was flown by the 64th Sentai during initial Japanese attempts to cut off China from Allied forces in India and Burma. The blue tail marking indicates an aircraft of the unit's headquarters Chutai.

Ki-43-II-Otsu
This colourful aircraft wears the markings of the leader of the Headquarters Chutai of the 77th Sentai, during operations in Burma in the winter of 1943/44. The unit was then flying escort missions for the bombers which sporadically operated against British installations in India.

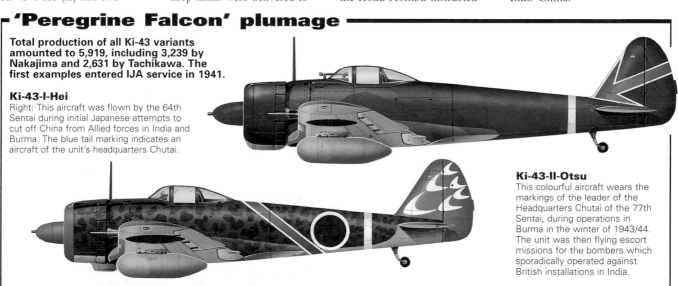

Nakajima Ki-84 Hayate

This is one of the initial pre-production batch of 83 Ki-84s, seen at Tachikawa in August 1943 from where it was flown by the Army Air Arsenal as a service trials aircraft.

Imperial hurricane

Nakajima's Ki-84 was the best mass-produced Japanese fighter of World War II. However, by the time it became widely available the Allies had already established supremacy in the air.

Long after fighter pilots in Europe and America had recognised the importance of armour, fuel tank protection and heavy armament, their Japanese counterparts still insisted on extreme manoeuvrability at the expense of these heavy items. The Koku Hombu (Air Headquarters) of the Imperial Japanese Army had, however, realised the need for those items considered unnecessary and too heavy by the aircrews. Accordingly, in 1940 it initiated the development of a successor to the Nakajima Ki-43, a lightly armed and unprotected fighter about to be placed in production. The newer type was to be

an adequately armed all-purpose fighter with limited armour and fuel tank protection, and was intended to be powered by the Kawasaki Ha-40 liquid-cooled engine, a licence-built version of the German-designed Daimler-Benz DB601A. To fulfil this requirement, two competitive designs were undertaken by Kawasaki Kokuki Kogyo KK (Kawasaki Aircraft Engineering Co. Ltd) and Nakajima Hikoki KK (Nakajima Aeroplane Co. Ltd). As Kawasaki had greater experience with aircraft powered by liquid-cooled engines, and as Nakajima was already fully occupied with the production of its Ki-43 and Ki-44 fighters, it was

This aircraft is one of the three Ki-106 prototypes built by Tachikawa late in the war. Although it looked exactly like a Ki-84, it was built entirely of wood in an attempt to save strategic materials.

the former's Ki-61 which was retained for further development and eventual production. Even though Nakajima's Ki-62 had lost the competition for Ha-40 powered fighters, the design team led by T. Koyama had gained valuable experience from the preliminary engineering of the Ki-62 and Ki-63, the latter being a proposed version to be powered by a 1,050-hp (783-kW) Mitsubishi Ha-102

radial. Koyama and his team were thus well prepared to submit a design in answer to a specification issued early in 1942 by the Koku Hombu. This specification called for an all-purpose, long-range fighter with a top speed of 398/423 mph (640/680 km/h) and capable of operating at combat rating for 1 hour 30 minutes at 250 miles (400 km) from base. A wing area of 204.5 to 226 sq ft

Ki-84-Ias of the 101st Sentai start their engines prior to a mass defensive action in the latter part of 1944. Along with the 102nd Sentai, the unit was embroiled in the defence of Okinawa, and enjoyed conspicuous success in raids on US airfields.

Left: Ki-84s served mostly in variations of dark green camouflage on the top and side surfaces, including considerable use of mottling to match local vegetation. The undersides were usually left as natural metal and the paint was prone to flaking off. All IJA aircraft wore large Hinomaru ('meatball') insignia.

Below: A section (shotai) of Ki-84-Ia fighters is seen departing Bofu airstrip during the Philippines campaign. The aircraft are carrying 44-Imp gal (200-litre) drop tanks under the wings.

(19 to 21 m²) and wing loading not exceeding 34.8 lb/sq ft (170 kg/m²) were recommended. Power was to be supplied by a Nakajima Ha-45, a version of the NK9A Homare (honour) 18-cylinder radial being developed for the Imperial Japanese Navy, and the specified armament was to comprise two 0.5-in (12.7-mm) Type 1 (Ho-103) machine-guns and two 20-mm Ho-5 cannon. In a marked departure from prior requirements for army fighters, the aircraft was to incorporate provision for armour and self-sealing fuel tanks. Drawing heavily on the preliminary design of the Ki-62 and Ki-63, the prototype of the new Ki-84 fighter was designed and built in 10 months, roll-out taking place at the end of March 1943. Of low-wing monoplane configuration, with conventional retractable landing gear and a three-piece canopy with rearward-sliding centre section, the Ki-84 flew for the first time from Ojima airfield in April 1943; two months later it was joined in the manufacturer's flight trial programme by a second prototype.

Engine improvements

Tests and preliminary service evaluation proceeded rapidly and smoothly, with few modifications required to prepare the aircraft for mass production. Several changes and improvements, as well as several versions of its powerplant (1,800-hp/ 1342-kW Ha-45-11, 1,825-hp/ 1361-kW Ha-45-12 and 1,900-hp/1417-kW Ha-45-21), were evaluated on Ki-84s from the large batch of service trials aircraft which were largely hand-built as Nakajima had not yet set up the required tooling. Few of these changes, however, were adopted for the production aircraft. The only significant ones to be incorporated on the assembly lines were the provision for two underwing drop tanks in place of the single ventral tank initially used, minor alterations of the shape and area of the vertical tail surfaces to improve control on take-off as the aircraft suffered from propeller-induced torque, and the replacement of the two large exhaust collector pipes (one on each side of the cowling) by individual ejector exhaust stubs. Service pilots, who by then had realised the need for armour, self-sealing tanks, and heavy armament, criticised only the heaviness of the elevators at high speeds and the mushiness of the rudder at low speeds. These, however, were minor complaints on an otherwise highly capable machine. Accordingly, as soon as Nakajima were able to make room in their Nos 1 and 4 airframe plants at Ota and Utsonomiya, the aircraft was placed in quantity production under the designation Army Type 4 Fighter Model 1A (Ki-84-1a). In addition, Ki-84-1s were to be built by Mansyu Hikoki Seizo KK (Manchurian Aeroplane Manufacturing Co. Ltd) in Harbin, Manchukuo. It was named Hayate (hurricane). Requiring 44 per cent less tooling than the lighter Ki-43 fighter, the Ki-84 was built in large numbers, with Nakajima delivering 3,288 production Ki-84s between April 1944 and mid-August 1945, and Mansyu adding 94 aircraft during 1945. These impressive production numbers do not reflect the great difficulties experienced by the Munitions Ministry and the contractors in implementing this ambitious programme: an insufficient number of skilled workers, aggravated by the drafting of civilian employees without regard to skills or to industry requirements, and the shortage of raw materials and poor standards of metallurgy, played havoc with the programme. Quality control, particularly in the manufacture of engines and specialised equipment (landing gear, radio, etc.), resulted in poor serviceability and numerous accidents. Even when not involved in accidents, the performance and reliability of production Ki-84s seldom matched those of the hand-built service trials machines. Moreover, in service these problems were magnified by the paucity of trained maintenance personnel and by the need to service the aircraft under primitive and often dangerous conditions.

For the Allies, however, this was a fortunate turn of events as, immediately upon entering service, the Hayate had proved to be a potent foe with performance closely matching that of the most advanced Allied aircraft (F4U, P-38J/L, P-47D, P-51D) and superior to such important types as the F6F Hellcat then equipping most US Navy carrier-based fighter squadrons.

Sizeable numbers of Ki-84s survived at the war's end, including these aircraft littering an Imperial Japanese Army base. The aircraft behind this machine is a Tachikawa Ki-55 'Ida' advanced trainer.

Formed in late 1944, the 102nd Hiko Sentai operated from Kyushu. In April 1945 it was thrown into the fray over Okinawa, attacking US units employed in supporting the amphibious landings. Okinawa was the last stepping stone before Japan itself.

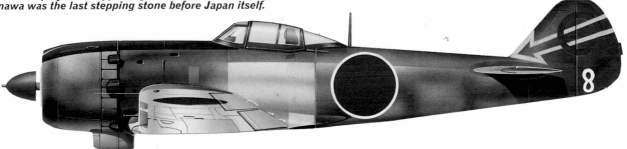

Into combat

This Ki-84-Ia was captured intact by US forces and extensively tested, eventually being returned to Japan for display in 1973. Notable features of the aircraft were the individual exhaust stubs and large oil cooler in a fairing under the engine.

Once in service the Ki-84 showed excellent combat characteristics, which led to it being feared by Allied pilots. However, such was the desperate situation in which Japan found itself the type was not developed fully, and while it matched Allied fighters, it could not tackle Japan's real enemy: the high-flying B-29 Superfortress.

The large number of service trials and pre-production aircraft which had been ordered enabled manufacturer's and service tests to proceed rapidly, with Ki-84s becoming available to form a service evaluation chutai (squadron) in October 1943, a mere six months after the prototype's maiden flight. However, another six months were required to set up the assembly lines, and the first Ki-84-Ia built with production tooling was not completed by Nakajima until April 1944. From then on the production rate was stepped up, with monthly deliveries going from 54 Ki-84-Is in April 1944 to a peak of 373 in December of that year, and averaging 200 aircraft per month.

The availability in quantity of the superlative Hayate came none too soon for the hard-pressed fighter sentais (regiments or groups) of the Imperial Japanese Army as, except on the Chinese front, they had lost the initiative. Moreover, their Kawasaki Ki-61s, Nakajima Ki-43s and Nakajima Ki-44s were no longer superior to most types of fighter aircraft then fielded by the Allies.

The Hayate made its operational debut in March 1944 when the 22nd Sentai, flying a mix of Ki-84-Ia and Nakajima Ki-44-II fighters from Hankow,

supported a Japanese ground offensive. Opposed mainly by obsolescent Curtiss P-40s flown by American and Chinese pilots, the 22nd Sentai pilots did much to establish the Hayate as a formidable foe possessing most of the virtues and few of the vices of earlier Japanese fighters. However, within five weeks of their debut, the Ki-84s of the 22nd Sentai had to be transferred to the Philippines where the next Allied offensive was anticipated to take place.

Philippines campaign

During the eight-month Philippine campaign, which began on 20 October 1944 with American landings at Tacloban and Dulag on Leyte, 11 sentais (the 1st, 11th, 22nd, 29th, 50th, 51st, 52nd, 71st, 72nd, 73rd and 200th) equipped with Ki-84s fought desperately in an effort to halt the Allied offensive. However, the Japanese forces were now on the defensive and their air units were operating under exacting conditions. Unfortunately for them, the outnumbered Hayates, which as a result of inferior workmanship often suffered from failures of fuel pressure and hydraulic systems, and from weak landing-gear struts, could not do enough to alter the course of events. The situation repeated itself when the 47th, 52nd, 101st

and 102nd Sentais were thrown in to repulse the American assault on Okinawa in April 1945. Even on the Asian mainland, where the Ki-84 (known to the Allies by the codename 'Frank') had first operated with success, the 13th, 25th, 64th, 85th and 104th Sentais were ineffective as by then their Hayates were opposed by numerically superior Allied fighters such as P-38J/Ls, P-47Ds and P-51Ds. The same fate befell the 20th Sentai, which flew Ki-84s from Formosa.

In the Japanese home islands, Hayates fared well in combat against the long-range P-47Ns and P-51Ds operating from Iwo Jima, and against the carrier-based aircraft of the US and British fleets. Against the high-flying Boeing B-29s,

Although the Hayate was primarily employed as a pure fighter, the two underwing shackles could each carry a 551-lb (250-kg) bomb for ground attack missions.

This battered Ki-84-Ia wears the Chinese national insignia on the fuselage, and is seen after capture. It had previously flown with the 22nd Sentai, which had been the first unit to take the Hayate into combat.

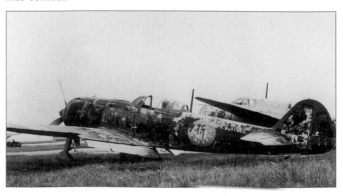

Above: A droptank-equipped Hayate is waved off on a mission. The tanks augmented internal fuel which was held in two inboard interspar tanks and two leading-edge tanks outboard of the cannon. Combined capacity was 109.4 Imp gal (480 litres).

Left: US Technical Air Intelligence Command fliers who tested this ex-11th Sentai Ki-84-Ia confirmed the type's reputation as an excellent fighter which could match most Allied types.

however, they were far from effective as their Ha-45 engine did not endow them with the necessary high-altitude performance. The need to produce the maximum number of aircraft, to re-equip as many sentais as possible and to make up operational and combat attrition in already established units, had meant that only limited priority was given by the Koku Hombu and the Ministry of Munitions to the development of more advanced versions. Whatever efforts could be spared were directed toward three development objectives.

Firstly, there was a need to reduce the use of alloys which were available only in limited quantities. Accordingly, a few Ki-84-II Hayate Kai aircraft, embodying wooden rear fuselage, certain fittings and modified wingtips, were built by

Nakajima, and three prototypes of the Ki-106, an all-wood version of the Ki-84-Ia, were produced by Tachikawa Hikoki KK (Tachikawa Aeroplane Co. Ltd). The aircraft were extremely heavy by comparison with the standard Ki-84, with the result that armament would have been reduced to just two 20-mm cannon if the aircraft had been adopted for production. The Ki-106 was intended to not only reduce the demand on strategic materials, but also to maximise the use of semi-skilled workers. Nakajima completed, but did not fly, a Ki-113 prototype partially built of steel.

Secondly, following heavy bombing of the Musashi plant in which Nakajima produced the Ha-45 engine, it became necessary to find a substitute powerplant for the Hayate. To

that end, Mansyu lightened and modified its fourth Ki-84-Ia airframe to take a 1,500-hp (1119-kW) Mitsubishi Ha-33-62 engine; designated Ki-116, the modified aircraft was undergoing tests at the time of Japan's defeat.

High-altitude fighter

The objective of the third line of Hayate developments was to obtain an aircraft with better high-altitude performance. The Ki-84-III was a straightforward adaptation of the basic airframe to take a turbo-supercharged Ha-45 Ru engine; the Ki-84R was a similar development to be powered by a Ha-45-44 with a mechanically-driven two-stage three-speed supercharger; and the Ki-84N and Ki-84P were proposed versions with 2,500-hp (1864-kW) Mitsubishi Ha-44-13 engines and increased wingspan and area.

During the last month of the war, while the Ki-84-I remained in full production along with a few Ki-84-IIs, plans were in hand for the production of the

Ki-84-III, Ki-106, Ki-113, Ki-116 and Ki-117 (redesignated Ki-84N).

In 1945-46 a captured Ki-84-Ia from the 11th Sentai was extensively tested in the Philippines and the United States, this evaluation confirming the high opinion in which the Hayate was held by Allied aircrews. Since then, this aircraft has been rebuilt twice before being returned to Japan in 1973 for permanent preservation, as a fitting tribute to an outstanding Axis warplane.

Total 'Frank' production amounted to 3,514 aircraft, including 3,416 aircraft built by Nakajima Hikoki KK (two Ki-84 prototypes, 83 Ki-84 service trials aircraft, 42 Ki-84 pre-production aircraft, 3,288 Ki-84-I and Ki-84-II production aircraft, and one Ki-113 prototype), 94 Ki-84-I production aircraft and one Ki-116 prototype built by Mansyu Hikoki Seizo KK, and three Ki-106 prototypes built by Tachikawa Hikoki KK.

For the Emperor

To the very last day of the war the Ki-84 remained a thorn in the Allied side, and exacted a heavy toll on naval fighters and light bombers. However, the B-29 'heavies' and their P-51 escorts operated with relative impunity at high altitude. As well as interceptor duties, Hayates were used as dive-bombers against Allied shipping, and a small number were expended in *kamikaze* attacks.

Formosa 'Frank'
Unpainted Ki-84s were relatively common by the end of the war. This aircraft served with the 29th Sentai on the island of Formosa in August 1945. The cobalt blue fin marking signified the HQ chutai.

Home defence
In August 1945, just as the war was ending, this Ki-84-Ia was assigned to the 1st Chutai of the 47th Sentai at Narumatsu. By this time the B-29s had nearly bombed Japan into submission, although it took two atomic bombs to force a surrender.

North American

B-25 Mitchell

This B-25G flew anti-submarine patrols from Orlando, Florida from 1943. Armed with a 75-mm cannon (as fitted to the M4 Sherman tank), the B-25G (and refined B-25H) served mainly in the Pacific and Mediterranean theatres.

Talented bomber twin

The B-25 struck back at Japan when the Allies were losing the war, fought in North Africa and the Mediterranean, became the first aircraft to carry a 75-mm cannon into combat and, in post-war years, trained tens of thousands of pilots and navigators. Mitchells also fought with the US Marine Corps, the RAF, and a dozen other combat arms.

The mainplane fitted to the first nine B-25s had a constant dihedral, which presented directional stability problems. All subsequent aircraft had a gull-wing, whereby the wing section outboard of the engines was horizontal. This is an early aircraft, which also sports one of several tailfin designs tested before the definitive tailfin configuration was decided upon.

Early development and flying of the B-25 (and its NA-40 predecessor) proceeded with few difficulties. The basic B-25 Mitchell, unchanged from start to finish, had a cantilever wing comprising a two-spar centre section which was permanently attached to the fuselage and contained integral fuel tanks and the engine mounts/nacelles, single-spar outer wing sections, and detachable wingtips. There was no

XB-25 experimental prototype. From 1940, these medium bombers began to join US Army squadrons and the Mitchell became one of the most readily-recognised aircraft of the war.

Doolittle's raid

On 18 April 1942, 16 B-25B Mitchells, each loaded with 2,000 lb (907 kg) of bombs, took off from the deck of the aircraft-carrier USS *Hornet* (CV-8). The aircraft were led by

The US Marine Corps operated large numbers of Mitchells, as PBJ-1s. Most early examples were PBJ-1Ds, many of which carried AN/APS-2 or -3 sea search radar in a ventral radome, as seen on this aircraft in action over Rabaul on 15 March 1944, the second day of USMC Mitchell operations.

Lieutenant Colonel James H. Doolittle on the 'Tokyo Raid', a daring low-level mission to bomb targets in Tokyo, Kobe, Yokohama and Nagoya.

It cannot be true, as one historian asserted, that the raid "broke the morale of Japanese civilians in Tokyo who had been propagandised into believing that their defences were impregnable" – most Japanese never learned about the raid, then or later – but the bold attack did boost American morale, and hinted at what the industrial juggernaut of the American heartland would do to the Axis powers.

Although the USAAF had only 183 Mitchell bombers in its inventory when the US entered the war, NAA's Kansas City

factory was to turn out an average of 165 Mitchells per month (D and J models) during 40 months of production. Inglewood, where the Mitchell began, kept pushing B-25s out of the front door long after it had committed much of its shop floor space to 10,000 California-built P-51 Mustangs.

When General George C. Kenney assumed command of the Southwest Pacific Air Force on 4 August 1942, he inherited only one unit of B-25 Mitchells, the 90th Bombardment Squadron, 3rd Bomb Group. Lieutenant Colonel Paul 'Pappy' Gunn, an officer under Kenney in Australia, teamed up with NAA field service representative Jack Fox to install guns in the noses of their Mitchells. At the same time, Kenney's officers developed skip-bombing techniques.

Gunn and Fox installed four 50-calibre (0.5-in/12.7-mm) machine-guns in the nose and a single gun in a blister pack on each side of the nose of a Mitchell, and loaded it up with

The B-25J was the major production Mitchell variant and was built with either a so-called 'glass nose' (seen here) or an eight-gun, solid 'strafer nose'. Exported examples reached 16 countries during and after the war. A47-44 is an RAAF example seen on a test flight over Brisbane in July 1945.

parafrag (parachute fragmentation) bombs, each a 23-lb (10-kg) fragmentation bomb with a proximity fuse and a parachute. The 3rd BG took the suggestions of Fox and Gunn and wrought havoc on the Japanese, fighting under hellish circumstances in New Guinea and the western Pacific, using a mix of B-25B, C and D aircraft with field-modified gun noses. By February 1943, Gunn, Fox and others at the Eagle Farm depot in Australia had produced 12 strafer bombers, which were taken into action by 90th BS crews under Major Ed Larner.

Desert Mitchells

After B-25C and B-25D models began to equip USAAF bomb squadrons during 1941, significant numbers of Mitchells started to appear in the Pacific, China and North Africa. In July 1942 Mitchells of the 12th BG joined Major General Lewis H. Brereton's Middle East Air Force (later Ninth Air Force) at Fayid, Egypt in time to participate in the battle of El Alamein that began on 23 October 1942. On 11 May 1944, Twelfth Air Force B-25s began Operation Strangle in central Italy, strafing and bombing supply routes along the Gustav Line,

culminating in the liberation of Rome on 4 July 1944.

Even without Kenney, Gunn or Fox (or, for that matter, the Marine pioneer who came a little later, Jack Cram), the merits of the B-25 Mitchell as a gun platform had been obvious to NAA engineers almost from the beginning. Following the one-off XB-25E and XB-25F aircraft which tested de-icing systems, it was inevitable that NAA would produce a Mitchell bomber with a 75-mm cannon in the nose. The XB-25G, B-25G and B-25H (and corresponding Navy/Marine Corps PBJ-1H) were flying artillery pieces. Virtually all of these cannon-equipped Mitchells went to the Pacific and China.

When the definitive B-25J model came along, it was produced in both glass- and solid-nosed variants. With eight 0.5-in (12.7-mm) machine-guns in the nose and more elsewhere, the solid-nose B-25J was in many respects the airborne arsenal that the cannon-equipped Mitchell was not.

The US Navy purchased Mitchells based on army models. Except for a handful of ships used for developmental work, the navy's entire allocation of 706 Mitchells (a figure which

The majority of the RAF's Mitchells were 'glass nose' B-25Cs and Ds, designated Mitchell Mk II and operated, for the most part, by No. 2 Group, Bomber Command over northwestern Europe.

includes 19 aircraft not actually delivered) was transferred to the Marine Corps under the designation PBJ-1.

Radar equipment

Marine Mitchells differed in several ways from their army counterparts. PBJ-1C and PBJ-1D aircraft had AN/APS-2 (later AN/APS-3) search radar installed in the lower belly. By the time they reached the South Pacific, PBJ-1Ds had both the belly radar kit and AN/APS-3 radar in a 'hose nose'. The nose-mounted radar apparently suited crews well for, when later PBJ-1Js arrived with the radar housed in a starboard wing pod, the Marines routinely moved it up front.

The Marine Corps had 16 Mitchell squadrons, nine of which saw combat in World War II. The first to reach combat, VMB-413, got as far as Hawaii aboard the escort carrier USS *Kalinin Bay* (CVE-68), then flew to the New Hebrides. Marine PBJs began combat operations

Post-war, several hundred B-25s were converted as pilot trainers for the USAF. This colourful aircraft is a TB-25J operated by the Flight Test Center at Edwards AFB in 1954.

with VMB-413 at Stirling Island on 14 March 1944.

As the war progressed, the Mitchell cemented its reputation as one of the finest ground-attack warplanes of the conflict. With a reduction in the air and ground threat as the war went on, many B-25s and PBJs became more lightly armed than when they had rolled out the factory door.

Numerous B-25G and B-25H Mitchells had their 75-mm cannons removed, sometimes being replaced with field-installed machine-guns.

Post-war transports

Upon victory in World War II, many B-25s and PBJs were stripped to become transports. Total production was 9,889 aircraft, including 920 which were earmarked for the RAF, although not all were delivered.

Wartime users of the Mitchell included Australia, Brazil, China, Great Britain, the Netherlands East Indies Air Force, and the Soviet Union. Post-war users included Argentina, Bolivia, Chile, Colombia, Cuba, Dominican Republic, Mexico, Peru, Soviet Union, Uruguay, and Venezuela.

USAAF B-25s at war

Probably the most famous of the Mitchell's many wartime exploits was the April 1942 raid on Tokyo and three other Japanese cities, led by Lt Col 'Jimmy' Doolittle. Here, one of the 16 aircraft that took part leaves USS Hornet.

On 18 April 1942, Americans struck back for the Japanese attack on Pearl Harbor. While nervous sailors watched, 16 North American B-25 Mitchell bombers took off, one after another, from the wooden deck of the carrier USS *Hornet* (CV-8).

Right: Two of the 16 B-25Bs that crowded the deck of USS Hornet on 18 April 1942 run their engines in preparation for the 'Tokyo Raid'. The aircraft were modified to carry extra fuel for the long mission.

Beginning with the lead aircraft flown by Lt Col James 'Jimmy' Doolittle, each bomber roared down the carrier deck, sank from view apparently to plough into the waves, then reappeared as it gained power and climbed – setting course for Tokyo.

Months earlier, in a gruelling test of men and equipment conducted in a Florida swamp, Doolittle had proven that the powerful B-25 bomber could take off in less than 500 ft (152 m). Now, Doolittle's bombers launched while still 800 miles (1287 km) from the enemy coast. The B-25s zoomed up to 1,500 ft (457 m), split up and pressed their separate attacks on Tokyo, Kangegawa, Kobe, Nagoya, Osaka, Yokohama, and the Yokosuka navy yard.

Most daring moment

The B-25 Mitchell had not been designed for a carrier-launched air strike on Japan, but the Doolittle raid was the B-25's most daring moment.

There were many others. The twin-engined medium bomber was named after air power pioneer Brig. Gen. William S. 'Billy' Mitchell who had shown in the 1920s that a bomber could destroy a battleship.

North American, which was new to the aviation industry and had never produced anything but a trainer, might have seemed an unlikely builder for one of the most important bombers of World War II. Indeed, when the prototype NA-40 was flown by celebrated test pilot Vance Bresse in 1940, it was very much an experimental aircraft, requiring extensive further development before the design was finalised. Ultimately, the B-25 Mitchell became a high-wing, twin-tailed, fast and powerful medium bomber that was familiar to a generation of pilots, maintainers, and observers.

The basic B-25 design was decided upon before Americans entered the war. Eventually, 9,889 B-25s emerged from North American factories in Inglewood, California and Kansas City, Kansas. They fought in almost every combat theatre.

341st Bomb Group

In the China-Burma-India (CBI) theatre, the B-25 was deemed so rugged that the 341st Bombardment Group could operate from dirt and grass airstrips, fly far behind unfriendly lines and strike Japanese supply centres at low level.

When General George C.

Kenney assumed command of the Southwest Pacific Air Force on 4 August 1942, he inherited only one unit of B-25 Mitchells, the 90th Bombardment Squadron of the 3rd Bomb Group. Lt Col Paul 'Pappy' Gunn, an officer under Kenney in Australia, teamed up with NAA field service representative Jack Fox, to install guns in the noses of their Mitchells. At the same time, Kenney's officers developed skip-bombing techniques – the dropping of a conventional explosive bomb which bounced across the top of the sea until it slammed into an

enemy ship. While the Mitchell as a big-gun platform has received plenty of attention, the Mitchell as a skip-bomber was,

Equipped with Mitchells, the 345th Bomb Group, Fifth Air Force, fought across the Pacific from New Guinea, through the Philippines to the Japanese home islands. Adopting the name 'Air Apaches' in July 1944, the unit specialised in 'strafer-bomber' tactics, in particular against Japanese shipping.

Above: On 3 February 1944 Fifth Air Force B-25s attacked this Japanese airstrip eight miles (12.9 km) west of Wewak, New Guinea, releasing 'parafrag' bombs over three Ki-61 'Tony' fighters.

Above: A section of 487th BS Mitchells gets airborne from Sousse, Tunisia. Of note are the RAF fin flashes on these aircraft, adopted as a recognition aid during Operation Torch, November 1942.

in fact, more important, but the risks were high. Skip-bombing involved approaching at low altitude against intense, accurate defensive fire from heavily-armed Japanese land bases and seagoing vessels.

Gunn and Fox installed four 0.50-calibre (12.7-mm) machine-guns in the nose and a single gun in a blister pack on each side of the nose of a Mitchell and loaded it up with 'parafrag' bombs – each a 23-lb (7-kg) fragmentation bomb with a proximity fuse and parachute. The 'parafrag' bomb detonated a few feet above the ground and inflicted widespread damage over a radius of 200 ft (61 m). The 3rd Bomb Group followed the suggestions of Fox and Gunn and wreaked havoc on the Japanese.

3rd BG strafer-bombers

The 3rd BG, commanded by Robert F. Strickland (who rose from first lieutenant to colonel in nine months in 1942), fought under hellish circumstances in New Guinea and the western Pacific, using a 'mix' of B-25B, C and D aircraft with field-modified gun noses. By February 1943, Gunn, Fox and others at the Eagle Farm depot in Australia had produced 12 strafer-bombers which were taken into action by 90th BS

crews under Major Ed Larner.

In the Pacific theatre, the B-25-equipped 345th Bombardment Group proved that it could strike at relatively long range, attack Japanese ships at wavecap altitude and survive direct hits from small-arms weapons.

Halfway around the planet, Mitchells attired in desert garb – a light, muddy colour scheme that could be called yellow – laboured in North Africa during some of the heaviest fighting of the war. Once North Africa was won and the war shifted to Italy, B-25s flew to war from Sardinia and Corsica. A bombardier in one of these units, Joseph Heller, later wrote an unusual book about his experiences – *Catch 22*.

About the only place where the Mitchell did not make a big hit was the European Theatre of Operations (ETO). A B-25C (42-53357) was flown to England in March 1943 to become the first aircraft in a combat group; when the idea was dropped, the bomber was assigned to Eighth Air Force headquarters as a 'hack'. Later, it flew 13 night photo missions over V-1 flying-bomb sites, but no B-25 Mitchell combat group ever flew from East Anglia, except in the post-war Hollywood film, 'Hanover Street'.

B-25C Mitchell

Based at Sfax, Tunisia, this aircraft was one of those equipping the 487th Bombardment Sqn, 340th Bombardment Group (Medium), Ninth Air Force, in August 1943. The 340th BG was the last combat unit to join the Ninth AF in the desert, in April, operating alongside another Mitchell-equipped group in the Ninth AF and two others in the 12th AF. Each group had a different system for identifying its aircraft, the 340th BG using an alpha-numeric combination where the numeral in the tailcode was the last digit of a constituent squadron's number and the letter was used to identify an individual aircraft.

Overseas deployment

The first Mitchells sent overseas were a batch of 48 B-25Cs ferried to Australia in March 1942 for the 3rd Bomb Group in New Guinea. As well as the Pacific and North Africa, B-25Cs saw service in the China-Burma-India theatre and in Europe with the RAF, which designated the aircraft Mitchell Mk IIs.

Improved B-25C

The B-25C incorporated changes to the Mitchell found necessary following combat experience with the earlier models. Extra armour, defensive armament and self-sealing fuel tanks were among the features added.

Uprated engines

Although the B-25C was fitted with uprated R-2600-17 engines, rated at 1,700 hp (1270 kW), the addition of new combat equipment, especially the dorsal turret, made the B-25C 38 mph (61 km/h) slower than the first B-25s.

Colour scheme

The first B-25s to arrive in North Africa wore standard USAAF Olive Drab over Neutral Gray colours. These soon faded in the harsh desert conditions and were replaced by the 'desert pink'/azure blue scheme depicted on this aircraft.

Mitchells at war

The definitive B-25J was built in both solid- and glass-nosed versions. Both types often served in the same unit; these are 47th Bomb Sqn, 41st Bomb Group aircraft, seen on Okinawa in July 1945. Both carry Mk 13 glide torpedoes.

'Strafers' and PBJs

Later Mitchell variants introduced new types of armament, like the M4 75-mm cannon, and included the definitive B-25J and naval PBJ-1. Most served in the Pacific and CBI theatres.

North American's brilliant chief, James H. 'Dutch' Kindelberger, was the moving force behind the new aircraft company's first bomber, the NA-40 of 1939. The 'one-of-a-kind' NA-40 was a shoulder-wing aircraft with tricycle landing gear. In natural metal, it was a shining, silvery machine. It became the NA-40B after an engine change which gave it a pair of 1,610-hp (1200-kW) Wright R-2600 Cyclone radial piston engines. The Cyclone was reliable and was later to win praise from mechanics who worked on it in every climate, often under primitive conditions with inadequate supplies and support. The final design of the B-25 bomber was not yet solidified, but the choice of powerplant never changed.

Based on its experience with the NA-40B, North American introduced its NA-62 design. US Army Air Forces quickly gave the new aircraft its B-25 designation and the name Mitchell followed.

For Americans it was still peacetime. Camouflage colours – the way in which most B-25s would later be remembered – were yet to come. Shining like a newly minted silver dollar, the first B-25 with its unpainted aluminum exterior took off from Los Angeles' Mines Field (the location of today's international airport) for its first flight on 19 August 1940.

The new aircraft had its wing changed from shoulder to mid position, the fuselage being widened to provide side-by-side seating for pilot and co-pilot/navigator in an improved enclosed cockpit. As test-flying progressed, a further change in the B-25 design produced a 'bent' or 'broken' dihedral wing which angled upward from the side of the fuselage but was level outboard of the Cyclone engines. Once this change to the wing had been made, few other changes were needed to make the B-25 Mitchell a fully operational combat machine. As the war

progressed, most changes to the B-25 involved its armament. In the end, the Mitchell bomber carried just about every combination of guns and bombs that pilots and engineers could imagine.

Cannon armament

After enterprising airmen in the combat zone had tried to instal heavy cannon in the nose of the B-25, North American created the XB-25G to test an M4 75-mm cannon weighing 760 lb (348 kg) with a mere 21 rounds. A lightweight version of the cannon was installed at the production line on production B-25H models, which also boasted 14 machine-guns. This firepower was especially potent during low-level raids on Japanese shipping.

Following the 'one-off' XB-25E and XB-25F aircraft which tested de-icing systems, it was inevitable that NAA would produce a Mitchell bomber with a 75-mm cannon in the nose. The XB-25G, B-25G, and B-25H (and corresponding USN/USMC PBJ-1H) were flying artillery pieces. Virtually all of these cannon-equipped Mitchells went to the Pacific and China. Unfortunately, the 75-mm cannon was not as effective as first supposed, in part because it required a crewman to

Above: The nose-mounted 75-mm M4 cannon first appeared in the B-25G, 400 of which were built at NAA's Inglewood plant and another 63 were converted from B-25Cs. The partly plated-over pilot's windscreen protected the glazing (and the pilot) from the cannon's flash and blast.

The B-25H differed from the G-model in sporting extra 0.50-in (12.7-mm) machine-guns in its nose, waist and tail positions. This USAAF example was based in India in 1945.

Above: Solid-nosed B-25Js carried a battery of eight nose-mounted 0.50-in (12.7-mm) machine-guns and 3,200 rounds of ammunition. These could be fitted 'in the field' to any B-25, but were only factory-fitted to the J-model. 43-27585 was photographed on Iwo Jima during June 1945.

Below: Some USN PBJ-1Ds were equipped with APS-2/3 sea search radar in a so-called 'hose nose' installation. Originally, a ventral radome was used and later aircraft (PBJ-1H and -1J) were built with a starboard wingtip-mounted radar pod. Many aircraft were modified with a 'hose nose' in the field.

reload it manually each time a round was fired. By the end of the war, many Gs and Hs had had their big guns removed and were performing effectively without them.

Definitive B-25J

When the definitive B-25J model came along, it was produced in both glass- and solid-nosed variants, although the latter has been largely ignored in Mitchell literature. With eight 0.50-in (12.7-mm) machine-guns in the nose and more elsewhere, the solid-nose B-25J was in many respects the airborne arsenal that the cannon-equipped Mitchell was not.

The US Navy purchased Mitchells based on US Army models. Except for a handful of aircraft used for developmental work, including one which operated aboard a carrier, the USN's entire allocation of 706 Mitchells (a figure which includes 19 aircraft not actually delivered) was transferred to the US Marine Corps under the designation PBJ-1. In a departure from usual USN practice, these were given a letter suffix corresponding to their US Army designations: PBJ-1C (B-25C), PBJ-1D (B-25D), PBJ-1H (B-25H), and PBJ-1J (B-25J).

USMC Mitchells differed in several ways from their US Army counterparts. Nearly all PBJs had a gun gas dispersion tube running along the lower fuselage from the bombardier's position back to a point in line with the cockpit windows. PBJ-1C and PBJ-1D aircraft had AN/APS-2 (later AN/APS-3) search radar installed in the lower belly, the location of a ventral, remotely-controlled turret in most US Army bombers. In the air, the pilot extended the scanner of this set to achieve a 360° sweep over a broad area of ocean. The pilot retracted the radome for ground clearance before landing. By the time they reached the South Pacific, PBJ-1Ds had both the belly radar kit and AN/APS-3 radar in a 'hose nose'. The nose-mounted radar apparently suited crews well, for when later PBJ-1Js arrived with the radar housed in a starboard wing pod, the Marines routinely moved it up front.

Early PBJ Mitchells, like early B-25s, had relatively small windows in the waist position on both sides, from which flexible machine-guns were routinely deployed. Marines squadrons flew Mitchells with the larger 'picture windows' that became standard on the B-25H and J to give better visibility and an improved field of fire for the gunners. At least one Marines squadron, VB-611, flew Mitchells with additional protection for the waist positions in the form of an armour plate fitted over the windows.

The USMC had 16 Mitchell squadrons, nine of which saw

combat in World War II. The first to enter combat, VMB-413, reached Hawaii aboard the escort carrier USS *Kalinin Bay* (CVE-68), then flew to the New Hebrides. Coinciding with a tragedy when two aircraft with full crews were lost, Marine PBJs began combat operations with VMB-413 at Stirling Island on 14 March 1944.

VMB-612 drew the special mission as a 'low-altitude night striking force using radar' and, under Lt Col Jack Cram, began operations at Saipan on 13 November 1944. The squadron suffered losses, moved on to Iwo Jima, became proficient with the 11½-in (29.2-cm) Tiny Tim rocket, and even suffered the loss of one of its Mitchells at the hands of over-enthusiastic F4U Corsair pilots.

As the war progressed, the Mitchell cemented its reputation as one of the finest ground-attack warplanes of the conflict. But with a reduction in the air and ground threat as the war went on, many B-25s and PBJs became more lightly armed than when they rolled out the factory door. Numerous B-25G and B-25H Mitchells had their 75-mm cannon removed, sometimes being replaced with field-installed machine-guns. PBJ-1Ds and Js of Marines squadron VMB-612 became the most lightly-armed Mitchells to fly actual combat missions, going into action with only a single tail gun.

The Marines lost 26 Mitchells in combat and an additional 19 in non-combat mishaps while in the combat zone.

Empire State disaster

The B-25 Mitchell is also remembered as the aircraft that crashed into the 79th story of the Empire State Building in New York City in dense fog on 28 July 1945, killing its crew of six and 13 occupants of the building.

Except for two variants, all Mitchells were manufactured by the NAA plant in Inglewood, California and thus properly had the '-NA' suffix, i.e. B-25C-NA. The exceptions were the B-25D and B-25J, all of which were built by NAA in Kansas City and thus properly had the '-NC' suffix, i.e. B-25J-NC. Total production was 9,889 aircraft, including 920 which were offset to the RAF, although not all were delivered to the RAF.

Back in the US, stripped-down early-model Mitchells were employed as trainers, under the AT-24 designation. 41-29811 was an AT-24A, converted from B-25D standard for multi-engine pilot training.

North American P-51 Mustang

Above: To many pilots, the best P-51 variant was the P-51B. When fitted with the British Malcolm hood, it was lighter, faster, and had crisper handling than the bubble-hooded P-51D. The Iowa Beaut was a P-51B-15-NA of the 354th FS, 355th FG.

Introduction

The P-51 Mustang was arguably the best operational piston-engined fighter ever built. With P-51s providing long-range escort, US heavy bombers could carry the war into the heart of the Third Reich with acceptable losses. Thus, the P-51 can justifiably claim its title as the fighter that won the war.

During World War II there were faster fighters than the P-51, more agile fighters than the P-51, fighters that packed a heavier punch, fighters that were more versatile and fighters that were built in larger numbers. Even among its US contemporaries, the Grumman F6F Hellcat turned more tightly, the Vought F4U Corsair was a better gun platform, and the Republic P-47 Thunderbolt was easier in a turning fight.

Few could claim that any other fighter was more important than the mighty Mustang, although an objective assessment might conclude that the Mustang had excessively high stick-forces, inadequate stall warning and vicious departure characteristics which severely constrained the aircraft's effectiveness.

The Mustang had a remarkable birth, being designed, built and flown (according to legend) in only 180 days. Even more remarkably, North American Aviation had originally been asked to produce Curtiss P-40s under licence for the RAF, and the young company had cheekily told the customer that it could design and build a superior fighter of its own design in the same timescale.

In its original form, the Mustang proved to be a superb performer at low altitude, and the early versions had successful careers as fighter-bombers and tactical reconnaissance aircraft. However, the performance of their Allison engines fell off dramatically at altitude, limiting the aircraft's usefulness in the pure fighter role. Even operating

The Mustang was flown by many of the United States Army Air Force's top-scoring aces in the European Theater of Operations. Exemplifying the breed was Captain Don Gentile, 336th Fighter Squadron, 4th Fighter Group, US Army Eighth Air Force, a remarkable fighter leader who scored 15.5 kills on Mustangs.

simply as a low-level fighter bomber and recce aircraft, the Mustang would deserve to be remembered as one of the great aircraft of history. But the success of the early Mustang was quite overshadowed by the achievements of the later versions.

The Mustang was entirely transformed through the replacement of its original engine by the Rolls Royce Merlin. The Merlin

Left: The Mustang's cockpit has been compared to that of a high-class sports car, and for general all-round comfort, visibility and ease of operation, the P-51 was rated as being the best American fighter of World War II. These factors were very important during long-range bomber escort missions, for Mustang pilots had typically been airborne for several hours before engaging in combat.

Below: A gaggle of P-51s is framed by the starboard engines of a B-29 Superfortress bomber. The Mustang's long range made it ideal for long overwater missions, but the demands of the European theatre were such that only relatively small numbers of P-51s served in the Pacific. As the bombing campaign against Japan was stepped up, three P-51D fighter groups based on Iwo Jima took on Japanese fighters, allowing the B-29s to strike freely against industrial, military and civilian targets, with devastating results.

conferred the high-altitude performance which had been so lacking, while other modifications improved the aircraft's armament and the pilot's all-round view. With their new powerplant, the later Mustangs out-performed any other USAAF fighter, and the type was built in huge numbers and urgently rushed into service.

Although the aircraft was used in every theatre, and for a variety of roles, the Mustang found its métier escorting USAAF

Precious Metal *is typical of the many modified racing Mustangs still competing regularly in the US. These range from simple engine tweaks to complete rebuilds. This aircraft features a Cavalier Mustang tail, along with a streamlined, low drag cockpit canopy.*

bombers during their daylight raids over the Reich. With the arrival of the Mustang, the bombers could be escorted all the way to their targets, by a fighter capable of meeting aircraft like the Messerschmitt Bf 109 and Focke-Wulf Fw 190 on even terms. This kept bomber losses to an acceptable level, and allowed the USAAF and RAF to continue the round-the-clock bombing attacks which eventually brought the Third Reich to its knees.

The arrival of the jets rendered the P-51 obsolete in the fighter role, while its liquid-cooled engine and belly-mounted radiator made it too vulnerable for ground attack duties. Post-war, many operators preferred P-47 Thunderbolts to the Mustang,

and it faded from the scene. However, it served briefly in the defence of the continental United States and played a major combat role during the Korean War.Into the early 1970s, Mustangs were still in action in low-intensity conflicts over Central America.

The Mustang's exploits during World War II were more than enough to win it a prime position in aviation's hall of fame. Today, P-51s continue to dominate the unlimited air-racing scene, and are the most popular and sought-after warbirds.

P-51 Mustang
Early development

The P-51 Mustang was designed and built for the RAF by North American, a company with no previous experience of fighter design. NAA achieved the remarkable feat of conceiving and flying the prototype NA-73X Mustang in just 186 days.

It seems supremely ironic that the genesis of the legendary P-51 Mustang was marked initially with complete indifference and even opposition from the service which eventually became its major operator, the US Army Air Force. In fact, the aircraft which became the P-51 was almost totally foreign in conception, design and even, for the first few years of its existence, military application.

By 1937, the growing possibility of war with Germany had led Britain and France to purchase aircraft from the United States. One of the companies approached was North American Aviation (NAA), whose NA-16

advanced trainer was ordered in substantial numbers by the RAF under the name Harvard.

Formed in 1934, NAA was a small team, with 75 employees. Located at Inglewood, Los Angeles, NAA had a skilled workforce, and ambitions – as well as the potential – to grow.

The team of British purchasers found only two US fighters which might be of some use to the Royal Air Force. Bell's P-39 Airacobra and Curtiss's P-40 Warhawk were not up to the standards of performance of the latest European fighters, but they were the best that America had to offer. They promised to be useful ground-attack machines, allow-

ing the precious Spitfires and Hurricanes to be used for air defence.

In 1939 Sir Henry Self of the British Purchasing Commission contacted NAA's President James H. 'Dutch' Kindelberger, and, in essence, asked if NAA could build P-40s for the RAF to augment the flow from Curtiss. NAA's obvious answer was, in so many words, "Yes, if we must, but we could design you a much better fighter ourselves."

The British purchasing team was briefed on NAA's proposed NA-73X by Kindelberger, Vice-President Lee (J. Leland) Atwood, Chief Engineer Ray Rice and a preliminary design team led by Edgar Schmued.

The fighter that was proposed was a totally new and uncompromised design. The legend persists that NAA cooked up the P-51 from scratch and created it at lightning speed. In fact, Atwood spent months working with the

Mustang development timescale

Contrary to the legend of the Mustang, the British Purchasing Commission never set specific deadlines for completion of the NA-73X prototype. NAA presented the British with a preliminary design less than four months after the blueprints were approved. The British suggested that a timescale of 120 days, from approval of drawings (or from the date of the order, according to some sources) to prototype roll-out (or first flight according to some), would be a good target, although this legendary timescale has since been misinterpreted and consequently denied ever since. Britain's request was made in April 1940, and the preliminary design was approved on 4 May. The British order was placed on 29 May. NAA also had to seek US Army Air Corps permission for its plant to be thus committed to a foreign contract. This was granted, but in return the Army requested that two examples of the NA-73 should be supplied, without charge, for testing at Wright Field. The only dates set forth in the contract were January 1941 for initial delivery and 30 September 1941 for completion – and both were comfortably met. Confident of a production order, NAA began producing tooling and

Quality workmanship is evident in the NA-73X prototype, seen here unpainted before its first flight.

collecting material as early as June, and when the initial order for 320 aircraft was signed three months later there was already the beginning of a production line. Just 186 days after its inception, the prototype NA-73X (NX19998) took to the air for the first time, on 26 October 1940. A legend had been born.

The RAF's fifth Mustang Mk I (AG349) poses with other American aircraft destined for the British war effort: a Curtiss Kittyhawk Mk I, a Lockheed Hudson and several Douglas Bostons. The location was RAF Burtonwood, an airfield where aircraft arriving by sea at the Liverpool docks were assembled and air-tested.

British and – at British insistence, because NAA had no fighter experience – with the Curtiss firm. Curtiss designer Don Berlin had created another sleek fighter called the XP-46 and Atwood was ordered by the British to secure all current data from Curtiss on P-40 developments, including this aircraft.

Some 78,000 engineering hours and 127 days went into the first prototype, which was rolled out, completely unpainted, into the sunlight at Mines Field in Los Angeles on 9 September, 102 days after the British order. So hastily had the new fighter been assembled that it had no engine (until 7 October). The 1,150-hp (862-kW) Allison V-1710-F3R engine was installed and ground running began two days later. With freelance test pilot Vance Breese, the NA-73X (registered NX19998) made a successful first flight on 26 October.

Delighted with the new fighter, Breese made four flights, after each of which minor modifications were made. The most important was to redesign the forward part of the radiator duct so that the inlet stood entirely away from the

underside of the fuselage ahead. The gap ensured that turbulent and sluggish boundary-layer air did not enter the radiator duct.

Development setback

From flight No. 5 Paul Balfour was to be the test pilot. Unfortunately, on his very first familiarisation flight, on 20 November, Balfour made an error in switching fuel feed and the engine went dead at a critical moment. The NA-73X piled up in an upside-down wreck, but Balfour was unhurt. The NA-73X was later repaired and resumed test flying, but the programme was seriously delayed by the accident. The NA-73X resumed flying on 11 January

1941 and continued to operate as part of the initial development programme until being retired on 15 July 1941. After Balfour, subsequent testing was headed by R. C. (Bob) Chilton.

US Army Air Corps (USAAC) interest in the NA-73X had been limited; the service thought that it had all the fighters it needed and had failed even to send a test pilot or an engineer to collaborate with NAA. As part of the USAAC's stipulation that NAA could commit itself to the foreign contract, the fourth and 10th production Mustangs off the line were duly delivered to Wright Field as XP-51s.

These were thoroughly evaluated by Army test pilots,

although no orders were initially placed by the service. Such testing proved valuable as it highlighted many teething problems, including a need for minor changes in the Mustang aileron design. The two XP-51s were later handed over to the RAF which in December 1940, having toyed with the name Apache, had decided to call its new fighter the Mustang.

The second aircraft – the first production Mustang, with British serial AG345 – did not fly until 1 May 1941, four months after NAA was contracted to begin deliveries. Moreover, a considerable amount of work remained to be done to bring the aircraft to an operational standard.

The Curtiss connection

The effect of the sale of data from the Curtiss XP-46 and the full magnitude of the Curtiss/Don Berlin contribution to the P-51 remain in dispute to this day. Claims that the Mustang was a copy of the XP-46 are somewhat facile, since the Curtiss aircraft shared only a similar radiator/oil-cooler configuration with the P-51, and did not have laminar flow wings. Moreover, development of the XP-46 lagged behind that of the P-51, and prototypes were not ready to fly until February 1941, some four months *after* the NA-73X. NAA's designers were able to avoid the mistakes made with the XP-46 and thus produce a more refined, more ambitious fighter.

41-038 was the first of two XP-51s pulled from RAF production for the US Army. It was delivered to Wright Field in August 1941 where it was thoroughly evaluated by Army test pilots. It later became the fourth RAF Mustang Mk I (AG348).

Left: Curtiss's XP-46 was a smaller but more heavily armed version of its previous P-40 design. Although NAA's designers had access to material on the XP-46, all claim to have made minimal use of this in creating the Mustang. The NA-73X and XP-46 were strikingly similar, but philosophically miles apart. The XP-46's poor performance soon consigned it to history.

The legend begins

Overshadowed by its later Merlin-engined cousins, the Allison-powered Mustang played a vital ground-attack role during World War II. Blooded first with the RAF, the aircraft went on to serve until 1945 with both the RAF and USAAF.

To say that the Mustang made a favourable impression on its arrival in Britain is a considerable understatement. In fact, the first Mustang to reach England was a test aircraft for which many were to follow. At all heights up to 20,000 ft (6096 m), it was faster than any fighter in service with the RAF. At 13,000 ft (3965 m), the speed was measured at 382 mph (615 km/h), and from 7,000 to 20,000 ft (2133 to 6096 m), the margin of speed over the Spitfire Mk V was always greater than 28 mph (49 km/h). The Mustang's rate of climb, acceleration, speed in a dive, stability, handling in all configurations, rate of roll, and radius of turn were all rated satisfactory to outstanding, and in one area – range – the Mustang 'rewrote the book'. While the Supermarine Spitfire had a range of some 400 miles (640 km) and an endurance of two hours, the Mustang could be flown by a pilot reasonably unfamiliar with the aircraft for some four to five hours, covering more than 1,000 miles (1600 km).

Minus Mustang

On the minus side, the Mustang's service ceiling at this time was limited to 30,000 ft (9288 m), and British pilots noted that camouflage paint slowed its maximum airspeed by some 8 mph (13 km/h). Furthermore, whereas the Spitfire could climb to 20,000 ft (6192 m) in seven minutes, the Mustang required 11 minutes. Both the Spitfire and Messerschmitt Bf 109 were deemed nimbler at higher altitudes than the Mustang, which weighed about a third again as much as a Spitfire.

Although faster than the Spitfire V, the RAF never regarded the Mustang as its primary air-to-air fighter. Most missions flown were ground-attack, in cooperation with the British Army.

The only major shortcoming, and it was a serious one, was that the Allison F3R engine was supercharged for optimum performance at low levels. Above about 13,000 ft (3960 m), performance fell away increasingly rapidly, so that at 20,000 ft (6096 m) the Mustang was overtaken by the Spitfire V. Of course, from about mid-1942, the forthcoming Spitfire IX promised to fly rings round both, while the latest Bf 109 and Fw 190 variants already could!

Although Army Co-operation Command's mission was low-level reconnaissance, the RAF had already found that this could usefully be combined with fighter sweep and fighter-bomber roles, and it was soon discovered that the Mustang I excelled at both. The aircraft was a match for any Luftwaffe Bf 109 or Fw 190 at low level, and could deliver bombs with formidable accuracy. By a remarkable chance, the first air-to-air victory credited to the Mustang was claimed by P/O Hollis H. Hills, an American volunteer (in the Royal Canadian Air Force) from the same state of California whence the aircraft came. He downed an Fw 190 during the ill-fated raids against Dieppe on 19 August 1942. He later joined the US Navy and flew Grumman F6F Hellcats. Several RAF reconnaissance pilots gained victories in the Mustang I, including Duncan 'Bitsy' Grant, who scored three victories. On one occasion, a pair of RAF Mustang Is downed five enemy aircraft on a single sortie.

Indian at war

Similar in appearance to the Mustang, the A-36 Apache went to war in April 1943, with the

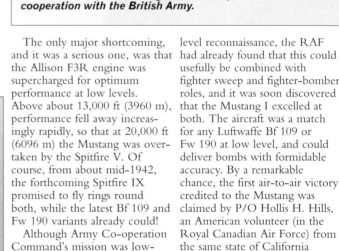

Left: Carrying M-10 smoke tanks (used to dispense smoke screens and tear gas), this trio of P-51As are seen on a practice mission.

Left: A-36A Apaches first went into combat in Africa in 1943. The aircraft were instrumental in the development of later Mustang variants

Left: Wearing the distinctive white stripes of the 1st Air Commando Group, these P-51A Mustangs were employed on attack duties over Burma in 1944. The Group Commander, Lt Col Cochran, is seen at the rear.

Below: British pilots found few undesirable features with the Mustang I, but at high altitudes the Allison powerplant was unable to deliver the performance to match the feared German Bf 109.

27th Fighter Bomber Group based at Rasel Ma in French Morocco. Here it was called the Invader, but the seldom-used official name was the Apache epithet originally rejected by the RAF for the Mustang. The first operational sortie was flown on 6 June 1943 during the mass fighter-bomber assault on Pantelleria. This island was captured and became the base for two A-36 groups during the assault on and invasion of Sicily. One of the pilots of the 27th Fighter Bomber Group, Lieutenant Michael T. Russo, became the only ace in the Allison-engined Mustang,

although several of his A-36 pilot colleagues also scored aerial victories (totalling 84 enemy aircraft). The other user of the A-36 was the 311th Fighter Bomber Group in India. The aircraft were used intensively and 177 were lost before the type was withdrawn, to be replaced by newer, younger airframes. The type's relatively brief service life should not camouflage the fact that it made a major contribution to the Allied war effort in both North Africa and Burma.

The first version bought by the Army for the fighter role was the NA-99, of which 310 were ordered in August 1942 as

P-51As. These were essentially A-36As without the dive brakes or fuselage guns, with the V-1710-81 (F20R) engine rated at 1,125 hp (843 kW) at 18,000 ft (5490 m) to give better performance at altitudes over 20,000 ft (6096 m). A new supercharger to further enhance low-level performance, and a new, larger diameter propeller,

were also fitted. Maximum speed rose to an excellent 409 mph (658 km/h) at 11,000 ft (3353 m), faster at medium altitudes than any other fighter then in service. The ammunition magazines were enlarged, two for 280 rounds and the others for 350 rounds but, as in the A-36A, the guns lay almost on their sides and the belt feed tended to jam under severe *g* loads. Of the 310 P-51As built, 50 went to the RAF as Mustang IIs. One example was tested at Boscombe Down, and demonstrated a best rate of climb of 3,800 ft (1158 m) per minute (at 6,000 ft/1828 m), with a full-throttle climb allowing the aircraft to reach 20,000 ft (6096 m) in 6.9 minutes and 34,000 ft (10363 m) in 24 minutes.

Early combat

Nearly all the USAAF P-51As served in the CBI (China-Burma-India) theatre and in North Africa. The first P-51A group was the 311th Fighter Bomber Group in India. USAAF P-51A operations began on Thanksgiving Day (23 November), 1943 in a mission in which eight P-51As from Chennault's 23rd Fighter Group escorted North American B-25 Mitchells attacking a Japanese airfield near Shinchiku.

When production of the Allison-engined Mustang ended, some 1,580 had been built. These remained in combat, operating in both European and CBI theatres until the end of hostilities. But it was later in the World War II that the Mustang would achieve legendary status through its British-built-Rolls-Royce Merlin engine.

Above: The Mustang was simply too slick for the dive-bombing role. To stay at slower, more controllable, speeds the RAF's only A-36 was fitted with mid-wing fence-style dive brakes, but pilots felt that the aircraft offered no major advantage over the Mustang I.

Mustang, the mount of legends

Pictured here is Colonel David 'Tex' Hill of Hunt, Texas, climbing into his P-51B Mustang while operating with the 23rd Fighter Group. 'Tex' learned the deadly art of aerial combat by operating with the American Volunteer Group in China, widely known as the 'Flying Tigers'. These pilots fought the Japanese prior to America's involvement in World War II, facing far superior numbers of enemy aircraft and a constant shortage of supplies. Remaining in China throughout the war, 'Tex' initially flew the outdated Curtiss Tomahawk before progressing through Allison- and Merlin-engined P-51s. Quickly emerging as a leading ace in the theatre, he achieved 12¹/₄ kills. He then celebrated his promotion to the rank of Colonel with six more victories.

The smooth finish of the Mustang's laminar-flow wings is clear on this brand-new production P-51B. The aircraft is powered by a Packard V-1650 engine, a licence-built version of Rolls-Royce's immortal Merlin. With this powerplant the performance of the Mustang was transformed, especially at altitude.

Merlin Mustangs

North American's Mustang and the Merlin engine were a match just waiting to happen. Mustang-protected Allied bombers could now be escorted all the way from Britain to Berlin.

The switch from the Allison to the Rolls-Royce Merlin engine in the P-51 Mustang was one of the most important steps in aircraft design during World War II. The move had been spurred by the urgent development of the Merlin 60 series, a new family of engines produced, in fact, for an aircraft that played little part in World War II, the pressurised, high-flying Wellington VI.

To gain power at the highest possible altitude, the Merlin was fitted with two superchargers in series, both on the same shaft geared up from the crankshaft. Due to the compression and the resultant heating of the air, an intercooler was inserted into the delivery duct of the engine. With the Wellington VI seeing only limited service, it was decided that the logical next step for the engine was for it to be fitted to the Supermarine Spitfire.

On 30 April 1942, when the Spitfire Mk IX was about to enter service, Rolls-Royce test pilot Ronald Harker, who had been involved in the development of the Merlin 66 engine, made a 30-minute flight in a Mustang IA. He found that the aircraft was everything he had been led to believe, with its outstanding low-level speed, unrivalled range and endurance, and a high rate of roll even at high airspeeds, something

the Spitfire lacked. He appealed immediately to Air Marshal Sir Wilfred Freeman for a Merlin-equipped Mustang, and five of the aircraft were prepared for conversion. They were to be powered by the Merlin 65 engine which, in comparison to the Merlin 66, had a lower full throttle height 21,000 ft (6400 m), but was more powerful at lower altitudes.

The conversion was authorised on 12 August 1942. It had been calculated that the fitting of a Merlin 60 series engine to a Mustang would result in an aircraft capable of around 441 mph (710 km/h) at 25,500 ft (7770 m). All five of the conversions were designated Mustang Xs, and the first aircraft to fly was AL975, which took to the air on 13 November 1942. The other aircraft flew shortly afterwards and, as a result, the British and American Merlin Mustang programmes merged.

Rolls-Royce planned to produce 500 Merlin Mk 65 engines to convert the RAF's Mustangs to Mk X standard. The difficulty was that there seemed to be nowhere that could carry out the conversions that was not already working around the clock. In any case, even with Merlins being produced at Derby, Crewe and Glasgow, and by the Ford Motor Co. at Manchester, another 500 could not be fitted

into the existing programme. In the USA, however, there was no such problem.

American Merlin

By this time, Packard was already building Merlin engines for Canadian-built Hurricanes, Lancasters, Mosquitos and the P-40F Kittyhawks. As soon as it became known that the two-stage Merlin 60 series was taking shape, Packard began discussions on expanding its licence to cover the series. The proposal was accepted and Packard began production of the Merlin. Additional orders were placed with Continental Motors.

Prior to this, in late 1941, North American Aviation (NAA) had heard about the two-stage Merlin 60 series engine, and had looked at the work that would be involved in switching to the British engine. The task appeared

simple and, on 25 July 1942, NAA received authorisation for the conversion of two aircraft to XP-78 standard, powered by Merlin 65 engines sent from Britain. The two aircraft, NA-101-37352 and -37421, went through a series of rigorous tests and modifications including the fitting of a new radiator.

The first conversion was 'about an 80 per cent job', with an improved but still interim radiator installation, and many other features that were far from final. By 30 November 1942, the aircraft had received the new designation of XP-51B. A second aircraft soon reached the same status. This retained its four 20-mm cannon, but had an engine installation of almost production standard, driving a specially-designed four-bladed Hamilton Standard propeller with a diameter of 11 ft 2 in (3.5 m). It

One of the early P-51Bs is seen in RAF camouflage and carries an RAF fin flash and serial number (FX883), although marked with the short-lived, mid-1943 US national insignia.

Re-engined and named the Mustang X, the five Merlin 65 trials aircraft each featured improved engine installations. The No. 2 prototype, AM203, with a smoother chin scoop, reached 422 mph (679 km/h) at 22,000 ft (6811 m).

Albuquerque, New Mexico, circled the city, and flew back. There was now no further need to look for a bomber escort, as the P-51B had just made a flight equivalent in distance to that of England to Berlin and back.

Entry into service

Under Lend-Lease, the RAF received 910 P-51Bs and P-51Cs, designated the Mustang Mk III. In USAAF service, 71 Bs and 20 Cs were fitted with cameras in the rear fuselage for the reconnaissance role. The Cs differed little from their B counterparts, the separate designation reflecting the fact they were built at a different manufacturing plant – Dallas, rather than Inglewood.

Surprisingly, the first Merlin-powered P-51Bs to become operational belonged not to the Eighth Air Force, which needed them for bomber escort, but to the Ninth Air Force, which was charged with air-to-ground responsibilities to support the expected invasion of occupied Europe. The 354th Fighter Group at Boxted was the first unit in the ETO to receive Mustangs. Although it remained under the control of the Ninth Air Force, the Group was immediately ordered to support bomber operations by the Eighth Air Force, and soon the P-51s began to prove themselves against the beleaguered Luftwaffe.

also had the definitive radiator duct, with a sharply sloping inlet standing further away from the belly ahead of it. It was at this point that the so-called Meredith effect, in which the radiator was made to give a major amount of propulsive thrust, first became obtainable.

USAAF/RAF interest

Even before the predicted performance of the conversion could be confirmed, the USAAF moved into top gear. In August 1942, 400 P-51Bs were ordered on the basis of NAA's predictions, before the XP-51B could make its maiden flight. Almost overnight, the Mustang changed from being just another tactical attack/reconnaissance aircraft into the most important fighter in the entire Allied inventory. The results of the manufacturers' tests and the USAAF's evaluation of the Mustang Mk X came in early 1943, in time for the production Merlin Mustang to take advan-

tage of what had been learned, and prompting the RAF to order a massive 1,000 P-51Bs as the Mustang Mk III.

So, as 1943 dawned, the Mustang programme suddenly expanded enormously. Engines were to be no problem, with massive production both from Packard at Detroit and Continental at Muskegon. NAA began to expand its already huge Inglewood and Dallas manufacturing plants.

By the end of January 1943, the production standard for the P-51B had been agreed. The airframe was redesigned to make full use of the power, while the wing racks were eventually cleared to carry bombs of 1,000 lb (454 kg) each, or a wide range of stores including drop tanks or triple rocket tubes. The engine installation was further refined with a rectangular filtered air inlet on either side of the carburettor duct, visible on each side of the cowling. The armament, similar

to that of the P-51A, was judged to be the best compromise between weight, firepower and duration of fire, the magazines holding a total of 350 rounds for each inboard gun and 280 rounds for the outer weapons.

One of the most significant developments was the decision to add a third fuel tank to the P-51B. Although the Mustang already offered superb range, which could be enhanced by the addition of drop tanks, the expansion of operations in both the European and Pacific theatres demanded that this range be increased still further. Calculations showed that a tank of 85 US gal (322 litres) could be fitted between the seat armour and the radio bay, giving an internal capacity of 269 US gal (1018 litres) or 419 US gal (1586 litres) with two drop tanks. The three-tank P-51B was sent to Wright Field and a flight was made with maximum internal and external fuel. The aircraft flew to

P-51B Mustang

Although not the first Mustang unit to see operational service (this honour lies with the RAF), the 354th Fighter Group – which comprised the 353rd, 355th and 356th Fighter Squadrons – adopted the name 'Pioneers' because

it was the first to take the Merlin-engined P-51B into front-line combat. On 13 December 1943, the 354th FG flew the longest mission of the war up to that date when it escorted B-17s to Kiel and back, a round trip of

1,000 miles (1609 km), an impressive achievement for a month-old unit. Then, on 16 December, while on escort over Bremen, the group shot down its first enemy aircraft, a Messerschmitt Bf 110.

Markings
Peg O'My Heart of the 354th FG was the mount of George Bicknell, and shows the earliest Ninth Air Force markings, before the introduction of white recognition bands on the nose and wings to distinguish the Mustang from the Messerschmitt Bf 109.

Range
The arrival of the Mustang marked the beginning of the end of the Third Reich. Bombers could now arrive at their targets with adequate cover as the P-51 was able to fly to Berlin and back, something that previous fighters had not been able to do.

P-51 Mustang
Allison-engined variants

As originally developed for the RAF, the P-51 Mustang was powered by the Allison V-1710 engine. This gave the type excellent performance at low altitude, and the early variants were therefore used primarily as tactical reconnaissance platforms, low-level fighters and ground-attack aircraft.

NA-73X Mustang prototype

This is the first ever Mustang, which wore the civil registration NX19988. It made its first flight on 26 October 1940 but on its fifth was damaged in a crash after the engine had quit unexpectedly. It was repaired and was back in the air in January 1941. A feature of the NA-73X was the curved windscreen.

Wing
NA-73X was the first aircraft to feature a laminar-flow wing, in which the maximum thickness of the wing was further back (chordwise) than on a conventional aerofoil section. The result was much smoother airflow over the wing and greater aerodynamic efficiency.

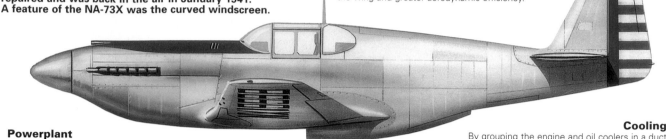

Powerplant
The prototype was powered by an Allison V-1710-F3R engine which developed 1,150 hp (862 kW). The first flight was delayed while North American waited for the government-furnished engine: V-1710s were in high demand for the Curtiss P-40 production effort.

Cooling
By grouping the engine and oil coolers in a duct under the central fuselage, drag was kept to a minimum. The duct was subsequently developed with a variable ejector flap at the rear, allowing the cooling system to add some useful propulsive thrust.

NA-73/NA-83: Mustang Mk I/XP-51

The first production examples were destined for service with the Royal Air Force, and were completed with V-1710-F3R engines driving a three-bladed Curtiss propeller. The first Mustang Mk I (AG345) flew on 1 May 1941, while the second aircraft (AG346) became the first to be shipped to England, arriving on 24 October 1941. The fourth and 10th aircraft were delivered to the USAAC for testing at Wright Field, becoming XP-51s in the process. Chief differences between the Mustang Mk I and NA-73X concerned the addition of armament in the form of four 0.50-in (12.7-mm) M2 Browning machine-guns, two in the nose and two in the wings. Outboard of the wing '50-cals' were two pairs of 0.3-in (7.62-mm) Browning machine-guns. Many Mk Is were subsequently fitted with an obliquely-mounted F.24 camera behind the cockpit (with two wing guns deleted). The first of 608 supplied to the RAF entered service with No. 26 Squadron in February 1942. The total of 620 actually built was completed by the two aircraft for USAAC evaluation and 10 dispatched to the Soviet Union. Shown below is the 13th aircraft (AG357), sporting the early-style 'fish-tail' exhaust stacks and equipped for trials with rocket projectiles.

NA-91: P-51/P-51-1/F-6A

The evaluation at Wright Field of the two XP-51s, while favourable, did not result in an immediate US order. President Roosevelt had signed the Lend-Lease Bill in March 1941, and subsequent UK military purchases were made under this arrangement. Among the first Lend-Lease contracts was one for 150 Mustang Mk IAs. Of these, the USAAC held back 57 aircraft, all but two being delivered to operational units under the designation P-51. These were then modified with a K-24 camera behind the cockpit and another facing downwards in the rear fuselage, receiving the new designation F-6A, although they were also known as the P-51-1. Flying with the 68th Observation Group in Tunisia, the F-6As carried out the first USAAF Mustang missions of the war. This aircraft sports a dramatic disruptive camouflage and displays a bulged window over the camera installation.

NA-91: Mustang Mk IA

Having acquired its first batch of Mustangs (Mk Is) through direct purchase, the RAF used the new Lend-Lease Act to acquire subsequent batches of aircraft, beginning with the Mustang Mk IA. Although Mk Is had scored several kills, early combat operations had demonstrated the need for heavier armament, especially for the ground attack role. Accordingly, North American developed the NA-91 with four Hispano-Suiza 20-mm cannon in the wings. These were mounted with the barrels projecting far ahead of bulky leading-edge fairings. For contractual purposes the 150-aircraft Mustang Mk IA batch was acquired by the USAAC under the P-51 designation, and in the event 57 of them were retained for American use. The remaining 93 were dispatched to the UK, the aircraft entering service in July 1942. Mustang Mk I/IAs flew primarily on low-level cross-Channel operations, flying armed reconnaissance missions, usually in pairs. The aircraft could usually out-pace Luftwaffe fighters, but ten were lost during the disastrous Dieppe raid in August 1942.

NA-97: A-36A

The first order for the Mustang from the US Army was not for a fighter version, but for the NA-97, subsequently designated A-36A and initially christened Apache. This aircraft was developed as a ground attack platform with dive-bombing capability. To that end the aircraft featured a bomb rack under each wing (in a different position from the P-51's bomb rack) capable of carrying a 500-lb (227-kg) bomb or a 75-US gal (284-litre) drop tank. The engine was an uprated V-1710-F21R (V-1710-87) which developed 1,325 hp (994 kW) at 3,000 ft (914 m). For the dive-bombing role the A-36A had slatted dive-brakes mounted above and below the wings which could hold the aircraft to about 250 mph (400 km/h) in a steep dive. In the event, the A-36's dive-bombing capability was rarely used in operations. A change in gun armament saw the deletion of the four rifle-calibre wing guns in favour of another pair of 0.50-in (12.7-mm) weapons, raising the total complement to six (two in the nose and four in the wings). In the field the nose guns were often removed.

A-36As went into service with the 27th and 86th Fighter Bomber Groups in Morocco, arriving in North Africa in April 1943. After seeing action in the final weeks of fighting in Tunisia the A-36 was then heavily employed during the softening up and subsequent invasion of Sicily, and then fought through Italy as part of the 12th Air Force. Following the type's successes during the invasions of Sicily and Italy, an attempt was made to change the official name of Apache to Invader. In service neither name was widely used, most personnel referring to it as the Mustang.

Shown above is an A-36A at Sousse in Tunisia, sporting the yellow-bordered pre-June 1943 national insignia and chordwise yellow identification bands on the wings. The aircraft below is the sole A-36A supplied for evaluation to the RAF, officially designated Mustang Mk I (Dive Bomber).

NA-99: P-51A/F-6B

Spurred on by good initial experience with the P-51/F-6A and the A-36A, the USAAF placed a further order for Mustangs in August 1942. The NA-99, designated P-51A by the Army, was a fighter version with ground attack capability. In reality, it differed little from the A-36A apart from deletion of the dive-brakes and the nose guns (which were often removed on A-36s, anyway). Thus armament was four wing guns of 0.50-in (12.7-mm) calibre, two supplied with 280 rounds and the other two with 350. The P-51A retained the wing racks for two 500-lb (227-kg) bombs or drop tanks. The major new feature of the P-51A was the V-1710-F20R (V-1710-81) engine, which was rated for medium-altitude performance (1,125 hp/843 kW at 18,000 ft/5490 m) and provided with a new supercharger which improved low-level performance. To cater for the extra power a larger-diameter propeller was fitted and combined with the new engine gave the P-51A a top speed of 409 mph (658 km/h) at medium level, making it the world's fastest fighter at the time of its debut.

P-51A production totalled 310, of which 260 served with the USAAF. Virtually all went to the 10th Air Force in the China-Burma-India theatre, where the lack of high-altitude performance was not so crucial. The first unit to be equipped was the 311th Fighter Bomber Group in India, but it was the 23rd Fighter Group which flew the initial combat operation on 23 November 1943. Thirty-five P-51As were converted to F-6B standard for reconnaissance, with two K-24 cameras.

Shown above is the 11th production example on a pre-delivery test flight. Below is the third P-51A which, along with the first production aircraft, was sent to Ladd Field, Alaska, for trials with a retractable ski undercarriage. This was intended for use in the Aleutians, but was not adopted despite the favourable results of the tests.

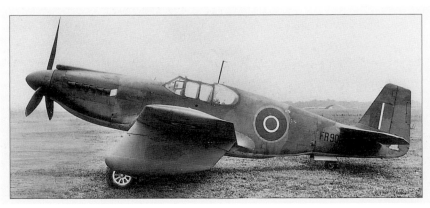

NA-99: Mustang Mk II

Of the total production of 310 P-51As, 50 (FR890 to FR939) were transferred to the Royal Air Force, with whom they served as Mustang Mk IIs. Most had camera installations fitted. Only two squadrons had the aircraft assigned: No. II (AC) between May 1944 and January 1945 and No. 268 from November 1944 to the end of the war in France, Holland and Germany. RAF Mustangs were used for a variety of tests, notably for rocket projectiles and the 40-mm Vickers 'S' gun (Mk Is), while this Mk II was tested by the A&AEE with oversize ferry tanks under the wings. The Allison Mustang remained in RAF operational service right up to the end of the war, its high speed making it a very useful tool in the TacR role.

P-51B/C briefing

Nowhere was the P-51B's extra reach more important than in escorting the 8th Air Force bombing raids deep into Germany. This 'Mighty Eighth' Mustang was a P-51B-1-NA of the 357th FS/355th FG, from Steeple Morden.

Fitting the Merlin into the Mustang created an instant classic, built in large numbers by Inglewood and Dallas as the P-51B and P-51C, respectively. The late production models, when fitted with the Malcolm hood, were arguably the best of the breed.

Testing with the two proto-type XP-78s (later rechristened XP-51B) had, by the end of 1942, shown a maximum speed of 442 mph (711 km/h) at 24,000 ft (7315 m). When the magic figure '442' was cabled to Washington, North American Aviation (NAA) received an immediate contract for 400 P-51B-1 fighters, to which the company assigned charge-number NA-102. P-51B procurement was completed by orders totalling 1,588 for the NA-104 models, called P-51B-5, -10 and -15. A further contract for 1,350 was placed with Dallas. These latter aircraft, called NA-103 and designated P-51C by the customer, differed only in very minor details, as did further blocks of P-51Cs with charge-number NA-111.

The first P-51B was initially flown on 5 May 1943, and the first P-51C followed on 5 August. In the course of production of the P-51B-10 and P-51C-1, the decision was taken to omit the olive-drab camouflage and deliver aircraft in natural metal finish. It had become an objective to try to bring the Luftwaffe to battle, rather than to try to hide from it, and the move saved weight, cost and drag. Camouflage was later reapplied to upper surfaces at field level, and was subsequently removed again after D-Day. RAF aircraft, however, stayed in day-fighter camouflage until almost the end of the war, when they followed suit.

The vital third fuselage tank, which provided the Mustang with sufficient range to reach Berlin and back, went into the final 550 P-51Bs, which became P-51B-7, and into P-51Cs which

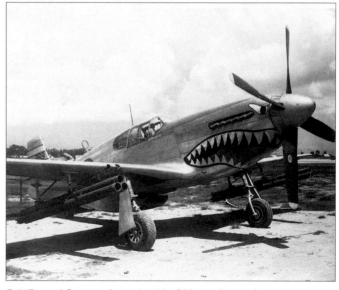

P-51Bs and Cs were important in China, where a heavy accent was placed on ground-attack duties. This P-51B is suitably equipped with 3-in rocket tubes on each wing. The shark's mouth markings were the trademark of the 26th FS/51st FG.

became Block 3 aircraft. It was retrofitted to many existing aircraft, and of course became standard on future production, but unfortunately the tricky handling at maximum aft centre of gravity resulted in an order to put only 65 US gal (54 Imp gal; 246 litres) in the fuselage tank. With later Mustangs this was still enough for escort missions to Berlin, however.

Uprated engine

In the course of production of the P-51B and C, several further modifications were introduced. The P-51B-15 and all P-51Cs from Block 5 onwards were powered by the V-1650-7

instead of the Dash 3. The latter was rated at 1,400 hp (1050 kW) at take-off, with a war emergency rating of 1,620 hp (1215 kW) at 16,800 ft (5120 m), whereas the Dash 7 engine gave 1,450 hp (1087 kW) for take-off and had emergency ratings of 1,695 hp (1271 kW) at 10,300 ft (3139 m) and 1,390 hp (1042 kW) at 24,000 ft (7315 m).

In AAF service, 71 Bs and 20 Cs were fitted with cameras in the rear fuselage for the reconnaissance role, becoming F-6C-NA or F-6C-NT, respectively. The usual fit was two oblique K24s, as in the Allison-powered F-6A, or a K24 and a K22. In each case the cameras

The two XP-51B prototypes were converted from RAF Mustang Mk IAs, and consequently were fitted with four 20-mm cannon. The second of the two, shown here, retained this armament throughout its test career.

Under Lend-Lease provisions the RAF received 274 P-51Bs and 636 P-51Cs, these becoming Mustang Mk IIIs. This rocket-armed aircraft is fitted with the Malcolm hood which dramatically improved visibility.

were immediately in front of the structural break ahead of the tailwheel, looking out to the left side.

One drawback of the early P-51B/C was its lack of armament, redressed part way through production by a neat three-gun wing installation devised by North American. The two outer guns each had 270 rounds, while

the inner gun had 400 rounds.

Two British companies made significant improvements to the operational effectiveness of the P-51B and C, F-6C and Mustang Mk III. Pytram Ltd mass-produced drop tanks which, although they held 90 Imp gal (108 US gal; 409 litres), were lighter than the metal kind, cheaper to produce and, dropped

by the thousand over Germany (output was 24,000 per month), did not provide the enemy with aluminium as they were made of impregnated paper. After having been familiar with the Mustang for three years the RAF belatedly decided that the cockpit canopy was 'not acceptable for European operations'. R. Malcolm Ltd devised a bulged aft-sliding hood

of blown Perspex which in a modest number of man-hours could replace the unsatisfactory hinged canopy. The result transformed the cockpit, not only giving extra space but most importantly effecting a dramatic improvement in view, especially to the rear and obliquely down to the front and over the sides. Many pilots expressed a preference for the Malcolm-hooded P-51B over the later bubble-hooded P-51D, especially insofar as visibility was concerned. Several Eighth and Ninth Air Force groups obtained Malcolm hoods for their P-51Bs and P-51Cs, but the modification was primarily a British one, and was unknown in the USAAF's Mediterranean and Far East squadrons.

Wing
The laminar-flow wing of the P-51B/C spanned 37 ft ½ in (11.29 m) with an area of 235 sq ft (21.83 m²). Subtle changes to the wing shape were introduced with the V-1650-7 engine. Standard metal drop tanks were of 62.5-Imp gal (284-litre) capacity but most aircraft in Europe carried the pressed-paper 90-Imp gal (409-litre) tank.

Powerplant
The P-51C-10 was powered by the Packard V-1650-7, a licence-built version of the Rolls-Royce Merlin 61. The P-51B/C introduced a refined engine installation with a rectangular filtered air inlet either side of the carburettor intake under the propeller. Exhaust gases were ejected through individual stubs projecting through a slim fairing.

Armament
Wing guns on the P-51B/C were restricted to four 0.5-in (12.7-mm) Browning MG53-2 guns. The inboard guns had 350 rounds while the outboard guns had 280. Later, a six-gun armament configuration was fitted.

P-51C-10-NT

Ina the Macon Belle was the personal mount of Lee 'Buddy' Archer, the highest-scoring of the African-American fighter pilots flying in a segregated Army. Having trained to fly at Tuskegee, Alabama, Archer was posted to the 332nd Fighter Group, part of the 15th Air Force in Italy. He is widely recognised as having at least five kills to his credit, but they were never officially recognised by the authorities, who credited him with just four Bf 109s. This was alleged to be a means of circumventing any potential aggravation that might have been caused 'back home' by having a black ace.

Personal markings
Archer's aircraft was initially known as simply *The Macon Belle*, but acquired its additional name when squadronmates discovered the name of his sweetheart. The 'hepcat' figure on the rear fuselage was applied as the rest of the squadron viewed Archer as a sophisticated 'city boy'.

Unit markings
By 1944, Mustangs were being delivered unpainted, providing the fighter groups and squadrons with a broad canvas. The 332nd FG employed red tails and red spinners, with red wingtips and code outlines. The 302nd Fighter Squadron used the red and yellow candy stripes and yellow elevator tabs as its squadron identifier.

332nd Fighter Group
The all-black 332nd FG comprised the 99th 100th, 301st and 302nd Fighter Squadrons. The 'Red Tails' had arrived in Italy for combat in February 1944, flying Bell P-39s. Transition to the P-47 was made in April and then to the P-51B/C in July. The 332nd FG ended the war flying P-51Ds.

P-51D/K
Variant briefing

This is one of the best photographs ever taken of P-51s on an operational flight in World War II. Three of the aircraft are P-51Ds, while furthest away is a P-51B with the original canopy. All the aircraft flew with the 8th Air Force's 357th Fighter Squadron, 361st Fighter Group.

By mid-1944 Mustangs were fast replacing other types of fighter in the USAAF. North American Aviation responded to the lessons of aerial combat by improving the Mustang still further, the D/K models offering better visibility and heavier firepower.

The Merlin-powered P-51B and P-51C possessed outstanding high-altitude performance that made them formidable adversaries to any enemy aircraft. Additionally, all Mustang variants had great range capabilities which exceeded those of most other fighter aircraft of World War II. However, as good as the Mustang was, there were several problems with the design, and complaints about two shortcomings in particular resulted in the development of the P-51D and K models.

Combat lessons

Firstly, the visibility from the original standard canopy was very restricted. In combat, the pilot who saw his adversary first had a decisive advantage, more often than not emerging as the victor. The second complaint about the Mustang was that the four .50-in (12.7-mm) calibre

machine-guns were not sufficient for the average pilot. Further they were subject to jamming, and this was partly because they were mounted at an angle.

To correct the visibility problem, two P-51Bs were modified with a cut-down aft fuselage section and a full bubble canopy. This provided excellent visibility around and above the aircraft. For more firepower, the number of machine-guns was increased from four to six. This was rather a simple matter, because the gun-bays in previous Mustangs had always been large enough for an extra gun in each wing. To reduce the chances of jamming, the guns were mounted upright instead of at a slant. Ammunition capacities for the guns were increased, and a K-14B gyro-computing gunsight replaced the reflector sight during the P-51D production run.

Because of complaints about the limited visibility of the standard framed canopy used on early Mustang variants, P-51B 43-12102 was modified with a cut-down aft fuselage and a bubble canopy. It was used as a test ship aircraft for what became the P-51D and P-51K.

A total of 6,502 P-51Ds was built at North American's plant in California, while an additional 1,600 were produced in Dallas, Texas. These Dallas-built aircraft were originally called P-51Es, but the designation was changed to P-51D before production began. This change dispensed with the practice of applying different model letters to aircraft according to which production line they had been built on. This had been the case for the identical P-51B and P-51C, and had caused immense confusion to NAA's suppliers.

Of the 1,600 P-51Ds built in Texas, 136 were fitted with cameras and redesignated as F-6D photo reconnaissance versions. In total, 8,103 P-51Ds were built, which exceeded by a wide margin the production numbers of any other Mustang variant.

Distinguishing the D

The P-51K was nearly identical to the P-51D and was built in Dallas, production for this version totalling 1,500. Of all P-51Ds and P-51Ks built in the US, 280 P-51Ds and 594 P-51Ks went to the RAF, where they were both called the Mustang Mk IV. Of the remaining 906 P-51Ks, 163 were completed as tactical reconnaissance aircraft, receiving the revised F-6K designation.

At least one P-51D (44-14017) was fitted with an arrester hook for carrier trials. These were undertaken by Lt R. M. Elder, USN, aboard USS Shangri-La (CV-38). The aircraft later became the ETF-51D, fitted with a P-51H tail. The Navy did not adopt the Mustang.

This P-51K-5-NT Nooky Booky IV was flown by Captain Leonard 'Kit' Carson of the 362nd Fighter Squadron, 357th Fighter Group. Carson was the top-scorer of the group, claiming 18.5 aerial victories (plus 3.5 more achieved by strafing). This K model was his fourth Mustang, and all bore the same Nooky Booky name.

The main difference between the P-51D and P-51K was the type of propeller used. Initially, the P-51D used the Hamilton Standard cuffed propeller that was 11 ft 2 in (3.41 m) in diameter. This contrasted with the P-51K which was fitted with an Aeroproducts uncuffed propeller of 11 ft (3.35 m) in diameter. The latter hollow-bladed propeller was to prove troublesome, and up to one in five were rejected due to vibration problems. Later in their service life, P-51Ds were fitted with an uncuffed Hamilton Standard propeller with blunt tips.

There were two types of canopies used on the P-51D and P-51K. One, with a continuous smooth curve, is usually associated with the D variant, while the other, with a higher profile and a noticeable increase in curvature near the aft end, is normally connected with the P-51K model.

Problems with directional stability were compounded by the cut-down aft fuselage area. To reduce this problem, a fillet was added between the leading edge of the vertical tail and the spine of the aircraft. Not only was this fillet added to production-line aircraft, but was also retrofitted to many Mustangs in the field, including a few P-51Bs and P-51Cs.

Into service

The P-51D and P-51K, as well as their camera-laden counterparts, began to enter operational service during the second half of 1944, when the air war over Europe was at its height. Their numbers increased rapidly during the last year of the war and, by the end of World War II, Mustangs had become the most numerous of all fighter types in service with the USAAF, and second only to the Republic P-47 Thunderbolt in terms of total numbers produced.

Having been replaced by faster jet types in service, this former USAF F-6K rests semi-derelict in the corner of an airfield. The rear fuselage-mounted camera windows are clearly visible.

Propeller
The P-51D and the Mustang IV used a cuffed Hamilton Standard four-bladed 24D50-87 hydromatic propeller, similar to that of the P-51B/C, with a diameter of 11 ft 2 in (3.41 m). A square-tipped version without cuffs appeared on very late production aircraft.

P-51D-15-NA

Alabama Rammer Jammer was flown by Lieutenant Arthur C. Cundy of the 352nd Fighter Squadron, 353rd Fighter Group. Cundy's aircraft wears typical 353rd FG markings with black recognition stripes. From November 1944 to March 1945 Cundy chalked up a tally of six enemy aircraft destroyed, including three shot down in this P-51D on a single day (2 March 1945). Cundy was killed on 11 March 1945 after a coolant leak led to an engine fire over the North Sea.

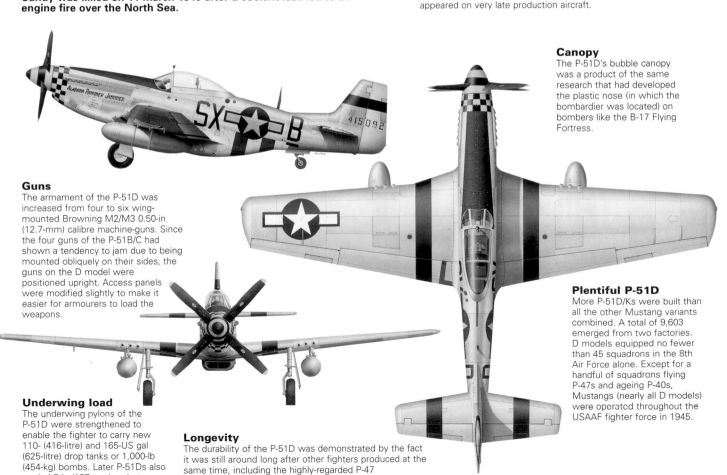

Guns
The armament of the P-51D was increased from four to six wing-mounted Browning M2/M3 0.50-in (12.7-mm) calibre machine-guns. Since the four guns of the P-51B/C had shown a tendency to jam due to being mounted obliquely on their sides, the guns on the D model were positioned upright. Access panels were modified slightly to make it easier for armourers to load the weapons.

Underwing load
The underwing pylons of the P-51D were strengthened to enable the fighter to carry new 110- (416-litre) and 165-US gal (625-litre) drop tanks or 1,000-lb (454-kg) bombs. Later P-51Ds also carried 5-in (127-mm) rockets.

Longevity
The durability of the P-51D was demonstrated by the fact it was still around long after other fighters produced at the same time, including the highly-regarded P-47 Thunderbolt, had disappeared from the inventory.

Canopy
The P-51D's bubble canopy was a product of the same research that had developed the plastic nose (in which the bombardier was located) on bombers like the B-17 Flying Fortress.

Plentiful P-51D
More P-51D/Ks were built than all the other Mustang variants combined. A total of 9,603 emerged from two factories. D models equipped no fewer than 45 squadrons in the 8th Air Force alone. Except for a handful of squadrons flying P-47s and ageing P-40s, Mustangs (nearly all D models) were operated throughout the USAAF fighter force in 1945.

Operational history
RAF Allison Mustangs

Initially disappointed with the high-altitude performance of the Mustang I, the RAF realised its formidable potential as a low-altitude, high-speed tactical reconnaissance and attack aircraft.

With the first production Mustang I having been retained by the USAAC, the RAF received its first aircraft, the second production machine, during October 1941. Shipped to the UK in a crate, the aircraft was reassembled and reflown for the first time on 24 October 1941.

Testing at the Aeroplane & Armament Experimental Establishment (A & AEE) soon revealed that the Mustang I comprehensively outperformed the Spitfire V in most respects. Similar results were found when flying against a captured Bf 109E, but above 20,000 ft (6096 m) the Mustang I lost its advantage, since its Allison F3R engine was supercharged for optimum performance at low levels.

Since the RAF intended to use the Mustang at low altitudes, any performance deficiencies were largely irrelevant, and the aircraft represented a major improvement over the Westland Lysanders and Curtiss Tomahawks that it was destined to replace.

Receiving its first Mustang Is in April 1942 and retaining them until January 1945, No. II Sqn initially flew photo reconnaissance sorties against radar stations on the French coast.

Europe. This reconnaissance mission along a section of the French coast set the trend for further armed reconnaissance sorties, during which pairs of Mustang Is searched for targets of opportunity. From March 1942, No. 26 Squadron became a leading exponent of these so-called Lagoon sorties, as it hunted for enemy shipping off the Dutch coast.

Rangers and Rhubarbs

By mid-1942, with the Mustang I in widespread service, the army co-operation units were flying regular overland sorties across Europe. These operations were generally of two types: either Rhubarbs, which involved as few as two aircraft attacking targets of opportunity, or Rangers, which used larger numbers of aircraft (often at squadron, wing or group strength) marauding over enemy-held territory, with the aim of wearing down the enemy's fighter defences. While a number of Mustangs were lost on these missions, enemy fighters rarely offered a great threat. Below 15,000 ft (4570 m), the Mustang could outrun the Bf 109F and was a match for the new Fw 190. In fact, the RAF lost more Allison-engined Mustangs to engine failure or flak than it did to fighters.

Disastrous Jubilee

Any information gathered on a tactical reconnaissance (TacR) mission was to be returned to base at all costs. Mustang pilots were discouraged from engaging enemy fighters and were to use their superior speed to escape. It was not until 19 August 1942, therefore, that the first Mustang I aerial victory was scored.

No. 400 Sqn arrived in the UK on 25 February 1940. From July 1942 the unit became a Mustang squadron, using the aircraft on combat sorties until replacing them with Spitfires and Mosquitos in 1944.

Mustangs across Europe

From January 1942, No. 26 Squadron of the RAF's Army Co-Operation Command was relieved to begin the replacement of its vulnerable Tomahawks with Mustangs. The squadron was soon joined by a number of other squadrons, all re-equipping for the army co-operation role.

By 5 May 1942, No. 26 was sufficiently proficient with its new aircraft to mount the first Mustang sortie to occupied

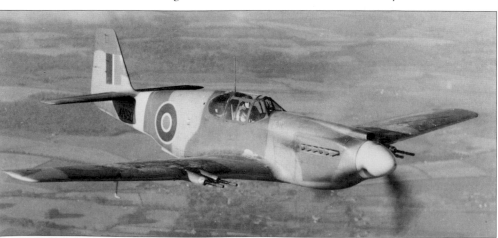

On the Mk IA, four 20-mm cannon replaced the four 0.303-in (7.62-mm) and two 0.5-in (12.7-mm) machine-guns in the wings of the Mustang Mk I. The two 0.5-in (12.7-mm) nose guns were deleted.

Mustang Mk I

AM101, the 364th Mustang I built for the UK, commenced operations with No. 26 Sqn from RAF Gatwick in January 1942. The aircraft was involved in Rhubarbs and Poplars (photographic reconnaissance along the French coast). On moonlit nights, No. 26 also carried out Rangers, mostly against rail targets, and the unit flew during Operation Jubilee.

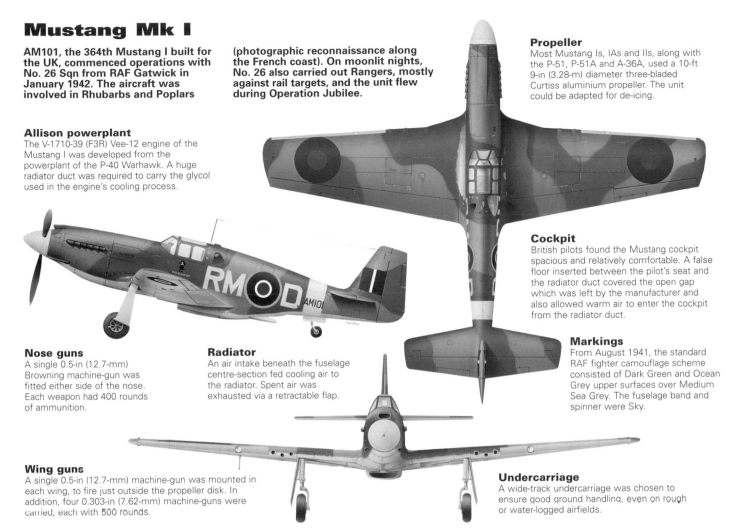

Allison powerplant
The V-1710-39 (F3R) Vee-12 engine of the Mustang I was developed from the powerplant of the P-40 Warhawk. A huge radiator duct was required to carry the glycol used in the engine's cooling process.

Propeller
Most Mustang Is, IAs and IIs, along with the P-51, P-51A and A-36A, used a 10-ft 9-in (3.28-m) diameter three-bladed Curtiss aluminium propeller. The unit could be adapted for de-icing.

Cockpit
British pilots found the Mustang cockpit spacious and relatively comfortable. A false floor inserted between the pilot's seat and the radiator duct covered the open gap which was left by the manufacturer and also allowed warm air to enter the cockpit from the radiator duct.

Nose guns
A single 0.5-in (12.7-mm) Browning machine-gun was fitted either side of the nose. Each weapon had 400 rounds of ammunition.

Radiator
An air intake beneath the fuselage centre-section fed cooling air to the radiator. Spent air was exhausted via a retractable flap.

Markings
From August 1941, the standard RAF fighter camouflage scheme consisted of Dark Green and Ocean Grey upper surfaces over Medium Sea Grey. The fuselage band and spinner were Sky.

Wing guns
A single 0.5-in (12.7-mm) machine-gun was mounted in each wing, to fire just outside the propeller disk. In addition, four 0.303-in (7.62-mm) machine-guns were carried, each with 500 rounds.

Undercarriage
A wide-track undercarriage was chosen to ensure good ground handling, even on rough or water-logged airfields.

Pilot Officer Hollis H. Hills of No. 414 Squadron, Royal Canadian Air Force (RCAF) was taking part in Operation Jubilee when he shot down an Fw 190. This triumph for the Mustang force was overshadowed by the loss of 10 aircraft among the 106 Allied aircraft lost during the disastrous operation. Operation Jubilee was designed to force the entire Luftwaffe strength in France and the Low Countries into battle, but was responsible for one third of the RAF's entire Mustang losses for 1942.

At home and in combat
As the end of 1942 approached, the Mustang squadrons were split between combat operations and training in the UK. Lagoons, Rangers and Rhubarbs, along with general TacR missions, continued unabated throughout the winter and into 1943. A number of squadrons, exemplified by Scotland-based Nos 63, 241 and 225, did not engage in combat operations, exercising intensively with army units in the UK, in preparation for Operation Torch in North Africa. Late in October 1942, No. 225 re-equipped with Hurricanes and left for North Africa. It was followed by No. 241 on 12 November. No. 63 remained at Macmerry, Scotland, often detaching aircraft to RAF Odiham, from where they flew missions over France.

Tactical Air Force
March 1943 saw the majority of the UK's Mustang I force based at Dunsfold, Surrey with No. 39 Army Co-Operation Wing. The wing consisted of Nos 400, 414 and 430 Squadrons, all of the RCAF. It was deeply involved in Operation Spartan, an exercise designed to test the mobility of army co-operation units under field conditions.

Mustang units were to experience a great deal of change as 1943 progressed. From July 1942, the Mustang IA with four 20-mm cannon had been arriving in the UK and during 1943 it began to replace the Mk I with a number of squadrons.

A more fundamental change was to occur on 1 June 1943, however, when Army Co-Operation Command was disbanded and the 2nd Tactical Air Force was established. Throughout late 1942 and early 1943, Army Co-Operation Command had exercised continuously with ground units, honing its close support and tactical reconnaissance techniques; the formation of 2TAF marked the final stage in the preparation of tactical airpower for the forthcoming invasion of Europe.

In addition, the Merlin-engined Mustang III was also becoming available and, with its superior performance, was quickly replacing earlier marks. The RAF's final Allison-engined Mustang, the Mk II, could accommodate two 500-lb (227-kg) bombs or fuel tanks underwing, but deliveries totalled just 50, since it was superseded by the Mustang Mk III.

Most RAF Allison Mustangs were fitted with an F24 reconnaissance camera. It was installed behind the cockpit, to shoot obliquely through the port-side rear cockpit glazing.

A-36As cruise over southern California. The markings carried by these aircraft date the photograph at between mid-1942 and mid-1943.

Above: This view of an A-36A clearly shows the air intake and nose-mounted 0.5-in (12.7-mm) machine-guns that helped to distinguish the variant.

Apaches & 'Invaders'
USAAF A-36A/F-6A/P-51A operations in World War II

While the RAF's Allison-engined Mustang Mk Is went into action for the first time in May 1942, the type was not to see USAAF service until almost a year later, and then only in a reconnaissance role.

From 1941 until the winter of 1943-44 the North American P-51 Mustang fought in combat around the world in a configuration which looked and behaved very differently from the bubble-hooded, Merlin-power P-51D that is so well-known today.

The Allison-powered Mustangs began with North American's prototype for the British, the NA-73X, powered by the 1,150-hp (858-kW) Allison V-1710-F3R engine and initially tested by veteran pilot Vance Breese who completed the maiden flight on 26 October 1940.

The fourth and tenth production examples of this new fighter to come off the line were delivered to Wright Field, Ohio, as XP-51s and evaluated by the US Army Air Corps.

Predictably, the NA-73X was "clean as a hound's tooth". The aerodynamics were as modern as the hour, the wing, fuselage and cooling system all being more advanced in design than any other fighter at that time.

Breese made four flights, after each of which minor modifications were made. From Flight No. 5 the test pilot was to be Paul Balfour. Alas, on his very first familiarisation flight, on 20 November, Balfour made an error in switching fuel-feed and the engine went dead at a critical moment. The NA-73X piled up in an upside-down wreck. The unhurt Balfour in due course was replaced by test pilot R. C. (Bob) Chilton.

RAF before USAAF

In December 1940, having toyed with the name Apache, the RAF decided to call its new fighter the Mustang and put it to work with Army Co-operation Command for tactical reconnaissance duty, because its Allison F3R engine was supercharged for best performance at low levels. No. 26 Squadron at Gatwick took delivery of its first Mustang Mk Is in January 1942.

The first P-51s to reach US Army Air Forces were 55 ships held back from the RAF's Lend-Lease Mustang Mk IA batch. They were retrofitted with two K.24 cameras in the rear fuselage for the tactical reconnaissance role, and were then officially designated as F-6As. In April 1943 they went to the 12th Air Force in Tunisia, where 41-137328 of the 154th Observation Squadron, 68th OG flew the first AAF Mustang mission of the war, a recce over Kairouan airfield.

Meanwhile, on 16 April 1942 NAA received the first contract to build aircraft specifically for the US Army. The contract covered A-36 dive bombers. The engine was the V-1710-87 (F21R), rated at 1,325 hp (988 kW) at 3,000 ft (914 m). Four 0.30-in (7.62-mm) guns were replaced by a single extra 0.5-in (12.7-mm) in each wing, making the gun armament six of the heavier calibre (four of them in the wings), and a rack was added under each wing for a 500-lb (227-kg) bomb. Airbrakes

A-36A Apache dive-bombers of two unidentified training squadrons (with red and yellow propeller spinners) are seen at a Stateside base. The aircraft wear the red-bordered US national insignia used only between June and August 1943.

Above: Cannon-armed 41-37324 is a P-51 (as opposed to a machine-gun-armed P-51A) repossessed from the batch of 150 NA.91s (Mustang Mk IAs) ordered by the RAF. In USAAF service most of these aircraft (55 in all) were modified to carry cameras and served as F-6A (or 'P-51-1') tactical reconnaissance platforms. The first members of the P-51 family to see USAAF service, a number served in North Africa with the 68th Observation Group.

P-51A Mustangs are seen in late 1943, during Air Proving Ground exercises in the US. Note the training squadron 'plane in group' number on the lead aircraft's nose.

Equipped with two bomb racks, able to carry a 500-lb (227-kg) bomb each, and dive brakes, the A-36A was a potent dive-bomber. In service in Italy from 1943, the type was nicknamed 'Invader'.

above and below the wings outboard of the bombs, opened to 90 degrees by a hydraulic jack to hold speed in steep dives to about 250 mph (400 km/h).

A-36 into service

The A-36A entered service over Sicily in June 1943 with the 27th Fighter Bomber Group based at Rasel Ma in French Morocco. The first operational sortie was flown on 6 June 1943, during the mass fighter-bomber assault on Pantelleria. This island was captured and became the

base for two A-36 groups during the invasion of Sicily. One of the pilots of the 27th Fighter Bomber Group, Lieutenant Michael T. Russo, became the only ace in the Allison-engined Mustang. The only other A-36 user was the 311th Fighter Bomber Group in India. A-36s were used intensively and 177 were lost before the type was withdrawn, to be replaced by newer, younger airframes.

P-51A fighter

The first version bought by the US Army as a fighter was the P-51A. This was an A-36A without dive brakes or fuselage guns, and with the V-1710-81 (F20R.) engine rated at 1,125 hp (839 kW) and fitted with a new supercharger which further enhanced low-level perform- ance. Maximum speed rose to a superb 409 mph (658 km/h) at 11,000 ft (3353 m).

Nearly all of the USAAF P-51As served in the CBI (China-Burma-India) theatre and in North Africa. The first P-51A group was the 311th Fighter Bomber Group in India.

12th AF A-36s in combat

Since the A-36 was a dedicated low-level attack aircraft and the Allison-engine lacked performance except at low altitude, it is remarkable that those units equipped with the A-36 and P-51A scored as many air-to-air victories as they did. These aircraft served with the 27th Fighter Bomber Group, 12th Air Force in Italy, 1943.

A-36A-1-NA 42-83803
42-83803/'B3' *PAT* was the mount of Lt Michael T. Russo of the 522nd Fighter Bomber Squadron. In December 1943, in this machine, Russo claimed the last three of his five kills (two Bf 109s and a Ju 52/3m) made while flying the A-36, becoming the only 'ace' to accomplish this feat in the dive-bomber or any other Allison-engined Mustang.

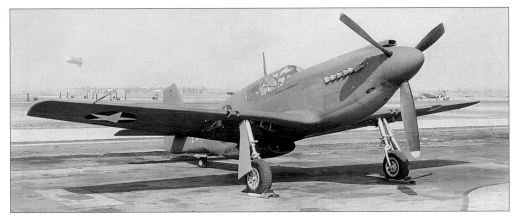

A-36A-1-NA 42-83901
Named *Dorothy Helen*, after the pilot's wife, this aircraft was flown by John P. Crowder of the 524th FBS. Crowder scored two victories while flying P-40s, but failed to add to his tally during the squadron's spell with A-36s. The 'star and bar' national marking with a red border was only used (at least, officially) between June and August 1943.

Famous for the 'sharkmouth' markings that adorned its Tomahawk and Kittyhawk fighter-bombers, No. 112 Sqn re-equipped with Mustang Mk IIIs in June 1944 and Mk IVs (pictured) in early 1945.

RAF Merlin Mustangs

Operational history

Merlin-engined Mustangs joined the RAF in early 1944 and saw service exclusively in the European and Mediterranean theatres, mainly in the escort and ground attack roles.

Though faster at low level than the RAF's most capable fighter type at the time of its introduction – the Spitfire Mk V – the Allison-engined Mustangs that entered service with the RAF in mid-1942 were never able to 'mix it' at altitudes over 25,000 ft (7620 m) with their fighter contemporaries in Europe. Thus, the RAF confined their use to army co-operation – a role in which they performed admirably until VE-Day.

However, with the installation of a supercharged Rolls-Royce Merlin powerplant, the Mustang was transformed and offered excellent all-round performance at altitude. Improved armament and stores-carrying capability and and exceptional range were additional features.

No. 65 Squadron

The RAF was quick to request the supply of the new Merlin-engined P-51B/C under Lend-Lease and received its first Mustang Mk IIIs, as they were designated, in late 1943. Fighter Command's No. 65 Sqn became operational on the type in February 1944 and, with Nos 19 and 122 Sqns, formed No. 122 Wing later that year. With these new aircraft, medium- and high-level escort sorties were flown, as well as cross-Channel ground attack missions. The formation of a second wing, No. 133, soon followed, comprising No. 129

Sqn and two Polish-manned units – Nos 306 and 315 Sqns.

'Trade' for these squadrons in the months leading up to D-Day comprised the provision of escorts for tactical operations across the Channel and for longer range anti-shipping strikes by Coastal Command on targets off the coasts of the Netherlands, Norway and Germany. For the latter role a seventh squadron, No. 316 (Polish) Sqn, was issued with Mustang Mk IIIs, beginning operations in April.

2nd TAF

Nos 122 and 133 Wings joined the 2nd Tactical Air Force in support of the Allied landings in Normandy on 6 June, after which sortie rates for the Mustang squadrons increased markedly. Typical targets were bridges, vehicles, marshalling yards and river traffic in France – there were few opportunities for air combat. As the Allied armies advanced, No. 122 Wing moved to France in late June, but plans for No. 133 Wing and No. 316 Sqn to follow suit were soon revised as another more pressing threat emerged.

Remaining part of Air Defence of Great Britain or ADGB (as the remaining units of the erstwhile Fighter Command became with the formation of 2nd TAF), the four UK-based Mustang Mk III squadrons joined Operation Diver – the defence of southern England

Above: No. 315 Sqn, RAF, was one of five Polish-manned squadrons to fly the Mustang. Equipped with Mk IIIs, the unit was largely engaged in anti-Diver and bomber escort work after D-Day.

Above: Like No. 315 Sqn, No. 19 Sqn received Mustangs in 1944, supporting the D-Day landings before being assigned a long-range escort role from stations in East Anglia.

Above: Stripped of its camouflage, this No. 93 Sqn Mustang Mk IV is seen in Italy during 1946. No. 93 Sqn exchanged its Spitfire Mk IXs for Mustangs in January, but disbanded at the end of the year.

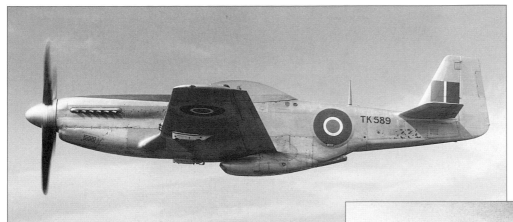

Left: Mustang Mk IVs TK586 and TK589 were P-51Ks and the first bubble-canopied Mustangs to arrive in the UK in 1944. Both were confined to trials work. Note the traces of TK589's USAF serial under its tailplane.

Below: A formation of RAF Mustang Mk IVs cruises over snow-capped Italian mountains in 1946. Most are No. 93 Sqn aircraft, though the 'GA'-coded machine carries the trademark 'sharkmouth' of No. 112 Sqn.

against V-1 flying bombs. Over the next few months, Mustang pilots did well against the V-1s, the Mustang Mk III being the third most effective type engaged in Diver, after the Spitfire Mk XIV and Tempest Mk V. Of the pilots that were credited with five or more V-1 kills (the so-called 'Diver' aces), 20 flew Mustangs and, of these, 13 were Polish nationals.

Meanwhile, by the autumn of 1944, 2nd TAF Mustangs had begun 'loco-busting' sorties against the Belgian and German rail networks, but these were short-lived. No. 122 Wing was about to re-equip with Typhoons, and its Mustangs returned to the UK as it was decided that the Mustang's long range could be put to better use elsewhere.

Nos 118, 126, 165, 234 and 309 Sqns in Fighter Command all converted to the Mk III and joined the other former ADGB units based in the UK in providing escorts for strategic daylight bombing sorties and pinpoint attacks by fighter-bombers on Continental targets.

They were joined by the RAF's first Mustang Mk IVs and Mk IVAs (P-51Ds and Ks – mostly the latter) from early 1945. These joined Mk III squadrons 'as required', rather than replacing the earlier aircraft *en masse*.

No. 611 'West Lancashire' Sqn was the first unit to re-equip completely with the Mk IV (having previously flown Spitfire Mk VIIs), becoming operational in March 1945, and was joined by Nos 441 and 442 Sqns, RCAF, the following month. All three undertook escorts of daylight bombing raids over Germany in the last weeks of the war in Europe.

Italy and the Balkans

The other theatre in which the RAF's Merlin Mustangs served was the Mediterranean. After the successful invasion of Italy, the four Curtiss Kittyhawk fighter-bomber squadrons of No. 239 Wing, RAF, received Mustang Mk IIIs between April and November 1943. Nos 112 and 260 Sqns (RAF), No. 3 Sqn, RAAF and No. 5 Sqn, SAAF, not only supported the Allied armies in Italy, but also flew long-range strikes across the Adriatic to assist the Yugoslav partisans. In June the Balkan air force was established to serve in the region and included No. 260 Sqn with Mustang Mk IIIs.

Strafing, bombing and escort missions kept No. 239 Wing busy as it supported the British Eighth Army's advance northwards through Italy, the Mustang units perfecting a 'cab rank' air support system whereby circling Mustangs were called in on a

Personalised codes were the preserve of wing leaders, 'JAS' being the initials of Wing Cdr J. Storrar, DFC and bar. The aircraft is seen in April/May 1945, while based at RAF Digby.

target by a forward air controller in an Auster AOP aircraft. Typical Mustang ordnance on these sorties included 500- and 1,000-lb (227- and 454-kg) bombs and, for the first time on an RAF Mustang, underwing rocket projectiles.

By the end of the year, RAF units of the Mediterranean Allied Air Forces had received 277 Mustang Mk IIIs and 46 Mk IVs, the latter serving as attrition replacements in a

theatre where losses to ground fire were high. Losses were so great that No. 249 Sqn was forced to re-equip with Spitfire Mk IXs in April, handing its remaining Mustangs to No. 213 Sqn.

After VE-Day, the last UK-based Mk IVs, with No. 64 Sqn, were replaced by de Havilland Hornets in 1946, while No. 213 Sqn in Cyprus traded its examples for Hawker Tempest Mk VIs in early 1947.

Polish 'Diver' ace

The Polish fighter squadrons in the RAF were among the most accomplished on the Mustang, carrying out a variety of roles ranging from long-range and tactical escort to ground attack to defensive tasks, in particular against the V-1 offensive. As well as amassing an impressive air-to-air kill tally, 13 Polish nationals were credited with five or more V-1 kills.

Flt Sgt W. Nowoczyn

Mustang Mk III FZ149 was Nowoczyn's mount with No. 306 'Torunski' Sqn during Operation Diver. Nowoczyn was the top-scoring Mustang pilot against the V-1, scoring 51 'Diver' kills. Many of the Mk IIIs engaged in these operations were polished in order to wring the last few knots of speed from the aircraft.

'Malcolm hood'

Most RAF Mustang Mk IIIs, at least in the European theatre, were fitted with R. Malcolm Ltd's 'bubble' cockpit canopy, as seen on this aircraft. Improving visibility considerably, the 'Malcolm hood' also found its way onto USAAF P-51Bs and Cs, but demand outstripped supply. The feature proved particularly popular with American pilots, some even preferring older machines with a 'Malcolm hood' to the P-51D.

USAAF European Theatre operations

Ferocious Frankie, a bomb-armed P-51D, was the regular mount of Major Wallace Hopkins, CO of the 374th Fighter Squadron, 361st Fighter Group.

The Mustang made its USAAF combat debut with the Ninth Air Force, operating in the tactical role, before the type's obvious utility as a long-range escort fighter was realised. After this it formed the backbone of the VIIIth Fighter Command, able to escort B-17s and B-24s all the way to their far flung targets, taking the war to the Luftwaffe's home defence fighters.

The first Mustangs delivered to the ETO wore prominent white recognition markings around the nose, wings, tailplanes and fin, to avoid confusion with enemy Bf 109s. The 355th Fighter Group retained the white nose as its unit marking after other groups adopted coloured noses.

Although the first Mustang Group in the European Theatre of Operations (ETO) was actually assigned to the Ninth Air Force for use in the tactical ground attack role, the unit (the 354th Fighter Group) was almost immediately transferred to the Eighth Air Force, as was the second Ninth Air Force unit, the 357th Fighter Group. The first P-51Bs arrived at Greenham Common in November 1943, and the 354th transferred to its operational home at Boxted later that month. The Mustang was the answer to the Eighth Air Force's prayers, in that it was a fighter with greater range and better high altitude performance than the otherwise excellent P-47, and with superior reliability to the P-38 Lightning.

While the potential of the new Mustang was apparent from the start, the new type did suffer its share of teething troubles, many of them related to the very low temperatures encountered at high altitude in a European winter. Guns froze, the coolant system leaked and spark plugs fouled, but these problems were relatively quickly overcome. The arrival of the Mustang in Europe had an immediate effect on the 4th Fighter Group at Debden, whose commander immediately pleaded for his Group to be re-equipped with the new type. Raised on nimble Spitfires, the pilots of the 4th had never liked the big and cumbersome P-47,

Above: The 353rd Fighter Group's **Danny Boy 2nd** came to grief on 29 December 1944. The Mustang in the air is equipped with 108-US gal (1083-litre) drop tanks.

Left: 'Don' Gentile, the leading Mustang ace of the 4th Fighter Group, walks away from Shangri-La, his personal P-51B. Gentile was initially rejected by the USAAC, and joined the RCAF, scoring his first victories as an Eagle Squadron Spitfire pilot.

The 4th Fighter Group had originally flown Spitfires, replacing these with lumbering P-47s, which the unit never really got on with. Mustangs proved more to the Group's liking, however.

but happily adapted to the smaller, more agile Mustang. The Group CO was attached to the 354th to gain experience, and flew on some of the first combat missions in December 1944, before returning to his own unit, which finally began flying combat missions with the new type at the end of February 1944.

The arrival of the Mustang had an immediate effect on the USAAF's ability to sustain its daylight bomber offensive - a high priority campaign for both political and military reasons - not least because it demonstrated America's commitment to taking the war direct to Germany's heartland. With the P-51 operating in the long range escort role, USAAF Bombers could finally be despatched against targets deep inside Germany (already being attacked by the RAF at night), allowing them to be attacked around the clock. The success of the Mustang was such that plans were soon put in place to equip all Eighth Air Force Fighter Groups with the type,

Both the Eighth and Ninth Air Force P-51 Mustang Groups engaged in perilous ground-strafing missions.

just as the decision was taken that all Bomber Groups would operate the B-17. At the same time, the Ninth Air Force would standardise on the Thunderbolt, and other Air Forces would trade their B-17s for B-24s. This programme promised huge improvements in logistics support, although, ironically, the Eighth's leading fighter outfit, the 56th FG, resisted all attempts to make it re-equip, and retained P-47s until the end of the War, while the Ninth Air Force held onto its few P-51 units. Despite this, the Mustang eventually equipped 12 Eighth Air Force Fighter Groups by May 1944, and 15 by the end of the year. The type also equipped three Groups from the Ninth Air Force, and a host of smaller recce formations. During the Summer of 1944, the Fighter Groups began converting to the new P-51D - immediately recognisable from its blown bubble canopy, but more significantly armed with six instead of four wing-mounted 0.50-in machine guns, and soon retrofitted with a K-14 lead-computing gunsight, which dramatically enhanced gunnery accuracy.

Armament
The P-51 packed a respectable punch, with six wing-mounted 0.50-in (12.7-mm) Browning machine-guns. This was rather less than the P-47 with its eight guns, and was lighter than the four 20-mm cannon armament of some later British fighters, but allowed a high rate of fire and relatively good combat persistence. The Mustang's gun was adequate against lightly-built fighter targets, if not for strafing armoured targets or for destroying larger aircraft.

P-51K Mustang

North American P-51K-5-NT Mustang 44-11622 (G4-C) Nooky Booky IV was assigned to Captain Leonard Kit Carson, the leading ace of the 357th Fighter Group, with 18.5 victories. The 357th was the top-scoring Eighth Air Force P-51 Group, notching up an impressive 609 kills.

Cockpit
The enormous bubble canopy introduced on the P-51D afforded the pilot an excellent all-round view. The cockpit was roomy and comfortable, making the aircraft ideally suited to the long-range escort role.

Ventral radiator
The liquid-cooled Rolls Royce Merlin relied on glycol coolant and an enormous radiator, fed by the P-51's distinctive belly air scoop. This made it somewhat vulnerable to ground fire. Despite this, P-51s were used in the ground strafing role to devastating effect, by both the Eighth and Ninth Air Forces.

Markings
The first P-51s delivered to the ETO were camouflaged, with Olive Drab topsides and Neutral Gray undersides. This eventually gave way to an unpainted natural metal finish. Unit markings, originally confined to two-letter codes also appeared, with each group adopting distinctive colourful nose markings, and with squadrons using coloured trim and/or rudders.

These P-51Ds of the 31st FG's 308th Fighter Squadron were photographed in 1944, wearing the distinctive red stripe markings of the Group. The second aircraft of the formation, 'HL-C', was flown by Capt. Leland Molland, who finished the war with 10.5 kills. 'HL-J' is being flown by Capt. Jack Smith who scored five kills.

P-51B/C/D in the Med

Four Fighter Groups flew the Merlin-engined Mustang in the MTO. In general, their missions were like those of their Eighth AF counterparts, escorting bombers into enemy territory.

In the Mediterranean theatre, the Merlin-engined Mustang did not arrive until April 1944, when two Twelfth Air Force Fighter Groups transferred to the Fifteenth Air Force and traded in their Spitfires for P-51Bs. Of these two groups, the 31st and the 52nd, the former was the first to see combat, when its aircraft escorted a force of B-24s raiding Ploesti from their Italian bases on 21 April.

'Checkertail Clan'

The 332nd and 325th FGs were also transferred from the Twelfth, with the 332nd being the last to receive Mustangs, when it swapped P-47s for P-51Cs in June 1944. On 18 May, the 52nd FG had flown its first escort mission, again to Ploesti, but this time in support of B-17s. The 325th FG, the 'Checkertail Clan', began flying the P-51B and C from Lesina, Italy, late in May 1944. Among its early missions was a Frantic shuttle mission to Russia, in which the Mustangs escorted B-17s bombing rail targets at Debrecen in Hungary.

History records that the all-Negro 322nd FG performed badly compared to the other MTO P-51 FGs. However, the Group was deliberately given fewer missions than the others in

an attempt to prevent its pilots from shining in combat. In fact, such was the prejudice against the black pilots that the Group's only ace was denied his fifth victory such that his ace status was never officially recognised.

P-51D in theatre

The 31st, 52nd, 325th and 332nd Fighter Groups in the Mediterranean theatre made the transition from the P-51B/C to the P-51D gradually, and in some squadrons not until early 1945. The definitive, teardrop-canopy Mustang made an enormous contribution during the final fighting in this region, including some truly marathon missions escorting bombers to their targets.

Although it faced even greater distances than the Eighth AF in England, the Fifteenth escorted B-17 and B-24 bombers on missions deep into Germany. It made the 1,500-mile (2414-km) round trip to Berlin on

25 March 1945. This mission, which involved all four fighter groups, saw Colonel William Daniel, commander of the 308th Fighter Squadron, 31st Fighter Group, prevail over a Messerschmitt Me 262, the first victory by Fifteenth Air Force P-51Ds over the German jet. That day, six others fell, including three claimed by the 332nd.

The P-51Ds of the Fifteenth had very colourful markings, which were extended over a larger surface of the aircraft in the winter of 1944-45. One of the most prominent was the 52nd's yellow empennage, which was stretched to cover the entire rear fuselage.

Right: Attitudes in the US were very much against the use of Negro combat pilots and when they were allowed to enter combat, it was as part of all-black fighter groups. The performance of these pilots, in terrible conditions, was superb.

Left: 'Bubbletop' Mustangs of the 325th (foreground), 332nd, 52nd and 31st FGs formate for the camera later in the war. Note the 332nd aircraft's lack of colourful markings.

P-51D 44-63995 was photographed as it was being unloaded from USS Sitkoh Bay for operations from Okinawa in February 1945.

P-51B/C/D Far East ops

While the P-51 performed admirably in a number of roles in the CBI and PTO, it was as an escort fighter that it made its most significant contribution to the air war in the Far East.

In most respects, the China-Burma-India theatre (CBI) was a backwater – located at the end of the logistics train where pilots and maintenance men struggled under primitive conditions, improvised without adequate supplies, and carried out gruelling sorties over long distance against an experienced and entrenched Japanese enemy.

US combat aircraft presence in the theatre began with the famous Flying Tigers, but the principal wartime formations were the Tenth and Fourteenth Air Forces. The 311th FG of the Tenth AF introduced the Mustang to the CBI with its A-36As and P-51As from October 1943. Soon, the 1st and 2nd Air Commando Squadrons and the 23rd Fighter Group appeared with Mustangs, including P-51B/Cs and P-51D/Ks, They were joined in the region by the 51st FG.

Unlike Europe, where the emphasis was on air-to-air action, the 23rd based at Kwelin, China, flew strafing and bombing attacks on shipping and land targets. On 8 December 1944, Mustangs successfully raided Hong Kong with 500-lb (227-kg) bombs.

In the Pacific, the Merlin Mustang did not enter combat until the very end of 1944, when the 82nd TRS of the 71st TRG took delivery of its first F-6D Mustangs. The Squadron was delighted with its new aircraft, which replaced P-39Ns for missions over the Philippines.

Attacking Japan

However, it was that tiny crag of rock, the island of Iwo Jima, invaded by US Marines on 19 February 1945, which eventually became home for a massive P-51 force. The Seventh Air Force had no Mustangs until the P-51Ds of the 15th Fighter Group began arriving at Iwo Jima's South Field on 6 March 1945, followed by the 21st FG, and (in late April) the 506th FG. Soon P-51 Mustangs, usually carrying two 165-US gal (625-litre) drop tanks, began escorting B-29 Superfortresses in the final campaign against the Japanese home islands. They also undertook long-range fighter and fighter-bomber sweeps.

"Mrs. Bonnie" was flown by Major William 'Dinghy' Dunham, Deputy Group Commanding Officer for the 348th FG. This P-51D, based at Ie Shima, eventually recorded all 16 of Dunham's kills.

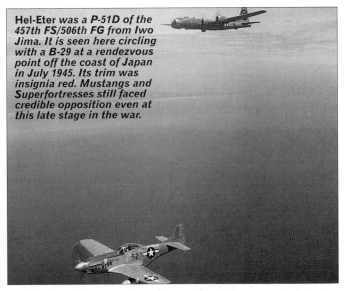

Hel-Eter was a P-51D of the 457th FS/506th FG from Iwo Jima. It is seen here circling with a B-29 at a rendezvous point off the coast of Japan in July 1945. Its trim was insignia red. Mustangs and Superfortresses still faced credible opposition even at this late stage in the war.

Depicted is an aircraft from the first batch of P-61As. The Black Widow had the makings of a superb night-fighter, but suffered from over-complicated design.

Northrop P-61 Black Widow

Nocturnal arachnid

The P-61 deserves its place in history as the first aircraft ever designed (rather than modified) for use as a radar-equipped night-fighter.

In spite of its odd looks, the first XP-61 proved to be a great flying machine when test pilot Vance Breese took it aloft for its first flight in May 1942.

In 1940 the USAAC was busy with a programme to convert A-20 bombers into P-70 night-fighters, keeping a close eye on the RAF's similar conversion of A-20s into Havocs. The USAAC knew about the British development of AI (airborne interception) radar and, in fact, 60 sets of this radar were shortly supplied for incorporation into the production P-70s, even though the USA was strictly neutral. Even more significantly, the Tizard mission, sent to the USA in August 1940, gave preliminary details of the most important single technical secret then possessed by the UK: the cavity magnetron. This totally new device was the key to the operation of radars on centimetric wavelengths (previous radars had wavelengths measured in metres) and enabled superior AI radars to be created. The amazing disclosure was made on 28 September 1940, and on 18 October the USA decided to go ahead at top priority with a world-beating AI radar and a fighter to carry it.

Radar success

Radar development work went ahead with a joint US/UK team, with astonishing rapidity. On 4 January 1941, the first microwave radar built in the USA was displaying a picture of the Boston skyline across the Charles River from a roof of the Massachusetts Institute of Technology. While the challenging radar needed the resources of all the chief companies in the emerging US electronics industry, the aircraft to carry it, which was launched three days later in a letter of 21 October 1940, was assigned to Northrop Aircraft. With the benefit of hindsight, while the SCR720 radar was unquestionably a war weapon of the very highest importance, the all-new night-fighter arrived late and was no better than a modification of (for example) the Douglas A-26 Invader for the same purpose. Indeed, the considered opinion of many experts was that it offered little that the night-fighter versions of the Bristol Beaufighter and de Havilland Mosquito had not been doing since 1941. Many who flew both the British aircraft and Black Widow considered the P-61 to be a first-class aircraft, whose only fault was the burden it placed on everyone concerned with its maintenance.

Hatching the 'Widow'

It was not meant to be like that. John K. Northrop expected to have the aircraft in production inside a year. From the start, the US Army insisted on a crew of

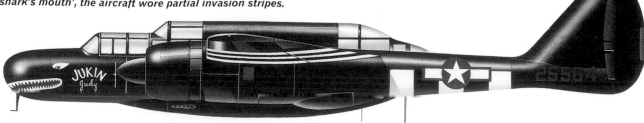

P-61A-5 42-5564, Jukin Judy, was flown by the 422nd NFS during its work-up period at RAF Scorton, Yorkshire. In addition to its 'shark's mouth', the aircraft wore partial invasion stripes.

Tabitha, a barbette-less P-61A-10-NO, was photographed while operating with the 425th NFS in France a few weeks after D-Day. The unit downed several V-1s which had been launched against southern England.

three, an exceptional all-round view and armament including a power-driven turret or turrets. Northrop's outline NS-8A proposal comprised a central nacelle with twinboom tail, and three crew in a row: pilot, radar/gunner above and behind – and thus able to use a gunsight directly ahead (as could the pilot) – and a gunner in the rear of the nacelle to cover the aft hemisphere. Four 20-mm cannon were to be mounted in the inboard wing or in the outer panels. In addition, there was to be a dorsal turret with four 0.5-in (12.7-mm) machine-guns and a ventral turret with two more such weapons.

At the NS-8A mock-up review board, on 2 April 1941, no fewer than 76 engineering changes were called for, the most serious being the relocation of the fixed cannon to the under-floor area of the nacelle, the ventral barbette being omitted. Countless other factors conspired to delay the programme, which had been designated XP-61 in December 1940, including arguments over the engine installation, structural materials, flight controls and tankage. In addition, Northrop's priority task of building 400 Vengeance dive-bombers did not help

matters. In September 1941 an order for 150 production P-61s was nevertheless placed, followed on 12 February 1942 by 410 more. This represented a backlog of over $26 million, about 26 times larger than anything Northrop had known before, and still the first proto-type was not ready.

Prototype problems

In early May 1942 the unpainted XP-61 (41-19509) was finally completed, and flown with generally excellent results. It was enormous for a fighter, with a wing area of 662.36 sq ft (61.53 m²), even larger than the wing of today's F-15, and with a crew area considerably more spacious than that of most medium bombers, despite the mass of controls and switchgear.

On 18 November 1942, the second XP-61 (41-19510) flew. It was painted in the gloss black which helped to give the fighter its name. Altogether it was a very fine machine, although there were enough major prob-lems to prevent the initiation of full production. The fuel system, tail unit and flaps were all modi-

fied. In late April 1943 the radar was installed and, by that time, 13 service-test YP-61s were visi-ble on the line. Tests with these aircraft showed that, when slewed to the beam position, the dorsal turret could cause severe tail buffet. Accordingly the turret was fitted to just the first 37 production P-61As. From the 38th the turret was omitted, but at least 10, and probably many more, of the remaining 163 P-61As had the turret installed after the buffet trouble had been eradicated. Problems continued to appear after the start of service deliveries to the 348th Night Fighter Squadron of the 481st Night Fighter Group in March 1944. The troubles were due almost entirely to the fact that there was so much to go wrong; for example, there were 229 design changes to the cannon installation alone between early 1942 and spring 1944.

First kill

The first P-61 'kill' was scored in the Central Pacific area on 6 July 1944. In the UK the first units were the 422nd and 425th NFS, which initially did little

more than classroom exercises, although by July both units were in business with 16 'Widows'.

In its first ETO (European Theater of Operations) actions, the P-61 succeeded in catching and shooting down nine flying-bombs. From August 1944 the 422nd and 425th NFS saw real action in deep intruder missions, bagging not only large numbers of locomotives, supply convoys and even the odd bridge, but also Bf 109s, Bf 110s, Me 410s, Fw 190s, Do 217s and various unidentified types. In Italy the 414th converted from the Beaufighter and, by January 1945, had chalked up five kills, but the 415th, 416th and 417th NFSs did not convert until later. In the Pacific, units were luckier, the 418th and 421st NFS seeing a lot of action from mid-1944, and in China the 426th and 427th NFS converted late in the year and flew mainly on ground attack with rocket tubes.

From July 1944 deliveries were of the P-61B version, which had the 2,250-hp (1679-kW) wet-rated R-2800-65 engine (this had been introduced on the 46th P-61A), four-gun dorsal turret and, from the B-10 block, four wing pylons each stressed for a tank or a 1,600-lb (726-kg) bomb. The P-61C introduced further uprated engines, but only a few were completed before the war's end. Certainly the best-looking of the whole family were the XP-61E fighter and F-15A Reporter reconnaissance aircraft, having slim nacelles and teardrop canopies. As for the P-61, 674 were built by VJ-Day and 706 altogether, and the P-61C did not pass from the scene until the 68th and 339th NFSs finally re-equipped in 1950.

Above: Northrop installed flaps over almost the whole span of the wing. The conventional ailerons were very small, but roll control was backed up when needed by four sections of differential spoiler on each wing. This enabled the P-61 to be amazingly agile considering its size and weight.

Right: Some 12 P-61Bs were transferred to the US Marine Corps for use as night-fighter trainers with the revised designation F2T-1.

Petlyakov Pe-2
Soviet 'Buck'

Above: With a second cockpit in place of the defensive gun position, the Pe-2UT (or UPe-2) retained a full bombing capability. These are Polish examples.

Top: The clean lines of the Pe-2 are clearly evident in this view of Soviet air force Pe-2FTs. Fighter escorts were seldom provided for Pe-2 bombers after 1942.

Comparatively unknown outside the land of its birth, the Pe-2 was the Soviet counterpart of the Mosquito, but made of metal. Indeed, it was built in considerably greater numbers than the British aircraft, and for as many different types of mission.

The Pe-2 was the one gigantic success of Vladimir M. Petlyakov who, from 1921, had worked at TsAGI, the national aerodynamic and hydrodynamic research centre. He became a leading expert in metal wing design, and in 1936 was appointed head of the ZOK experimental brigade to produce a large new bomber. This began life as the ANT-42, entered service as the TB-7 and finally, in World War II, matured as the Pe-8, honouring its designer. But Petlyakov had only 18 months on that programme, because in the Stalinist terror of 1937 he was one of the thousands arrested on trumped-up charges. Incarcerated in the CCB-29 special prison at GAZ (aircraft factory) No. 156, Petlyakov was told to organise a design bureau called KB-100, and to create the VI-100, VI standing for high-altitude fighter. The VI-100 was created from the proverbial clean sheet of paper to a higher standard (in aerodynamics, structure, and several aspects of systems and equipment) than anything previously extant elsewhere.

Stressed-skin structure

The VI-100's stressed-skin structure was superb, being faulted only on the score of complexity. All control surfaces were fabric-covered. The twin liquid-cooled engines were beautifully cowled and, as on many other Soviet twins of the period, the coolant radiators were inside the wings between the lattice spars. The radiators were fed by ducts from the leading edge and exhausted through flush shutter-controlled apertures in the upper skin, which were intended to give forward thrust. The engines had turbochargers for high-altitude power and drove constant-speed feathering propellers, which were totally unavailable in the UK at the time. Armament comprised four 20-mm ShVAK cannon in the nose, the backseater having a ShKAS machine-gun firing at 1,800 rounds per minute. Following US practice, the power services were totally electric, some 20 DC motors driving the landing gear, split flaps, radiator shutters, tank booster pumps, trim tabs, and many other items.

Piotr Stefanovsky and engineer Ivan Markov flew the first of two VI-100 prototypes on 22 December 1939, and took part in the 1940 May Day flypast over Red Square. The aircraft's top speed was an impressive 391 mph (630 km/h) at 32,810 ft (10000 m) but, before long, the decision was taken to expand the KB-100 bureau to handle a mass-production programme, not of the VI-100 but of a three-seat bomber derivative, the PB-100.

The Klimov VK-105 12-cylinder, liquid-cooled, inline engine that powered the Pe-2 was a derivative of the VK-100, a licence-built version of the Hispano 12Y of the 1930s.

The battle cry on the fuselage of this Pe-2FT reads 'Leningrad-Königsberg'. The aircraft is believed to have been attached to the 1st Air Army in the final weeks of the war, as it operated from bases in Poland against retreating forces in East Prussia.

A mock-up was approved on 1 June 1940 and two prototypes built.

The PB-100 prototypes differed from the VI-100 in many respects, including the fitting of dive brakes and detail changes to the airframe and wings. The engine turbochargers were first changed to the smaller TK-2 type and then omitted entirely. Back-to-back cockpits provided for the pilot and navigator/bomb-aimer, and aft of the fuselage tank was the new third crewman, who managed the radio and a lower rear gun.

An important engineering change was the installation of a hydraulic system (energised by electrically-driven pumps) to power such systems as the twin-strut main and steerable tail landing gears.

Standard bombload comprised four 250-kg (551-lb) FAB-250 bombs in the main bay. Six 100-kg (220-lb) FAB-100 bombs could alternatively be carried, with two additional FAB-100 bombs located in small door-enclosed compartments at the rear of the nacelles. With six internal FAB-100 bombs, it was also possible to carry four more FAB-100 bombs externally under the wingroots. Normal gun armament comprised two 0.3-in (7.62-mm) ShKAS machine-guns firing ahead and aimed by the pilot, plus a single ShKAS aimed by the navigator/bomb-aimer to the upper rear and another aimed by the radioman to the lower rear, in each case aiming by hand.

The initial production version was, in 1941, redesignated Pe-2 in honour of the lead designer, who was freed from detention in January of that year, and later awarded a Stalin Prize.

Various modifications naturally took place as a result of PB-100 flight trials, one being to give the pilot simple manual open/shut control of the dive brakes, replacing the complex AP-1 automatic dive control which modulated the brakes according to dive angle and airspeed. Crew armour was improved, the navigator/bomb-aimer was given a swivelling seat, and all five fuel tanks were made self-sealing and continuously inerted, at first by bottled nitrogen and later by cooled and filtered exhaust gas.

First production aircraft

The first aircraft came off the line in November 1940, and flew on 18 November. The VI-100 had been flown on skis, and the Pe-2 was also cleared to use skis which, like the normal wheeled gear, retracted backwards.

Very early in production the oil coolers were installed in improved low-drag ducts smoothly faired into the underside of the cowlings. For the remainder of the war the Pe-2 was constantly given small modifications to reduce drag, while the internal fuel capacity was also slightly increased. Production at GAZ-22 built up rapidly and, when Hitler struck on 22 June 1941, about 458 had been completed, of which at least 290 were with operational regiments, including the 24th BAP (bomber regiment) and 5th SBAP (fast bomber regiment). Though the Pe-2 was quite a demanding aircraft, it was immediately very popular and was commonly called 'Peshka', which means 'little Pe' as well as a pawn in chess.

The initial production engine was the VK-105RA, rated at 1,100 hp (820 kW); by 1943 the 1,260-hp (940-kW) VK-105PF or PF-2 became available, having previously been reserved for Yak fighters, and this powered virtually all the regular Pe-2 production aircraft to the end of the war.

The standard versions, the Pe-2 and Pe-2FT bombers, the Pe-2R reconnaissance aircraft, the Pe2UT trainer and the Pe-3bis fighter, accounted for a grand total of 11,427 aircraft when manufacture was stopped in early 1945, just before the end of the war in Europe (though later variants continued as prototypes and development aircraft).

Probably the most important variants were the Pe-2FT and Pe-2UT. The former, with initials meaning 'front-line request', replaced the navigator/bomb-aimer's hand-held ShKAS with a hard-hitting 0.5-in (12.7-mm) UBT machine-gun in an MV-3 turret.

Pe-2UT trainer

The Pe-2UT was the standard dual-control pilot trainer, with the instructor seated in an additional cockpit which replaced the defensive gun position and mid-fuselage fuel tank, and with a poor forward view. The first flew in July 1943, an unusual case of the trainer lagging far behind initial deliveries of the basic combat aircraft. The Pe-3bis was the only model built in quantity from a sub-family of fighter versions. Some retained the internal bomb bay, and a few even had underwing rails for the RS-82 or RS-132 rockets used in the low-level attack and anti-armour roles. Most, however, merely had the bombing equipment and third crew station removed, and instead added heavy gun armament such as one ShVAK, one UB and three ShKAS guns, or two ShVAKs plus two UB weapons.

Petlyakov's OKB retained several Pe-2s as development aircraft, and also the second production machine which was used as a hack to shuttle between Kazan and Moscow. On 12 January 1942 this aircraft caught fire in the air, and all on board, including Petlyakov, were killed. Stalin personally ordered a wave of arrests and interrogations to see who was responsible for killing 'this great patriot', whom he had only lately released from prison!

Left: Codenamed 'Buck' by NATO after the war, the Pe-2 was supplied to most of the Soviet Union's eastern European client states after World War II, including Czechoslovakia, the operator of this example. Note the folded dive brake, just visible under the wing.

Right: The Finnish air force received seven captured Pe-2s and a single Pe-3 from Germany. This example has a yellow theatre band, as carried by all German-allied aircraft on the Eastern Front. Only a single Finnish Pe-2 survived the war.

Polikarpov I-15/I-152/I-153

Following the restoration of six Polikarpov I-16s in Siberia, the first of which took to the air in 1995, the Alpine Fighter Collection, based at Wanaka in New Zealand, has sponsored the rebuild of three Chaikas. '10 Red' was the first example to be completed, and is pictured during flight testing in Russia in September 1997.

Pug-nosed seagull

Polikarpov's I-15 fought with great effect in a number of conflicts before spawning the equally effective I-152 and I-153. The I-153 must surely claim a place alongside Fiats CR.42 as one of the ultimate biplane fighters.

With a string of biplane fighter designs, most notably the I-5, and a spell in prison behind him, Nikolai Nikolayevich Polikarpov designed the I-15 for completion in October 1933. Powered by an imported 630-hp (470-kW) Wright R-1820 Cyclone radial piston engine, the I-15 featured a 'gull' configuration for its top wing. This distinctive feature soon gave rise to the nickname 'Chaika' (seagull).

The I-15 was based closely on the I-5 in terms of its construction, with a fabric and Dural-covered chrome/molybdenum steel alloy tube fuselage and fabric covered, wooden wings. It was designed to fit in with the new Soviet doctrine for air combat, which involved using a combination of highly manoeuvrable biplane fighters in concert with fast monoplane fighters. The monoplane part of this combination, the I-16, was also supplied by Polikarpov, earning him the nickname 'the king of fighters'.

Preparations for mass production of the I-15 began even before trials had been completed,

the aircraft entering service from late 1934 with an armament of two 0.3-in (7.62-mm) PV-1 machine-guns synchronised to fire through the propeller disc.

Unfortunately, development and production of the licence-built M-25 variant of the R-1820 was slow and while prototype and early production I-15s employed imported engines, the majority of production aircraft was fitted with the 480-hp (358-kW) M-22 engine, resulting in a drastic degradation of performance. This was especially the case when the optional underwing armament of four 22-lb (10-kg) bombs or chemical weapons containers was fitted; a

situation also exacerbated by the fitting of an extra pair of machine-guns in latter production machines.

Spanish combat

Although production of the I-15 continued through 1935 to the extent of some 384 aircraft, it was clear that high-ranking officials at the VVS (Soviet air force) were unhappy with the 'gull-winged' layout of the I-15 and Polikarpov only managed to avert the withdrawal of his

VVS Polikarpov biplanes

I-15 was the service designation of a design known to Polikarpov as TsKB-3. The TsKB-3 prototype was finished in a red scheme

and, following an accident, was replaced by a second prototype which wore a green over blue finish. A dark green over blue scheme

subsequently became standard for VVS I-15s.

I-15
This aircraft shows both the standard finish and Soviet national insignia typical of the mid-1930s. Early I-15s were plagued in service by problems caused by poor workmanship. Finish was generally below standard, with the main landing gears badly attached and, typically and most alarmingly, the wing skins showing a tendency to tear off in flight.

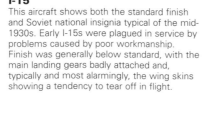

I-152
As on the TsKB-3, all variants of the I-15 and I-152 could have ski undercarriage fitted in place of the standard wheeled units. Note the distinctly different upper wing centre section shape of this aircraft when compared to the I-15 illustrated above.

fighter from service by a personal plea to Stalin.

In Spain however, the I-15 soon began to show its excellence during the Spanish Civil War. In addition to batches supplied by the Soviet Union, the Republican side built some 287 I-15s under licence, of which around 80 entered squadron service. Nicknamed 'Chato' (pug nose), the aircraft proved outstanding, proving near unbeatable in air-to-air combat until the arrival of Nationalist Fiat G.50s and Messerschmitt Bf 109s and a small number of 'Chatos' survived into the 1950s.

I-15bis & 'Super Chato'

In an effort to settle his doubters at the VVS, Polikarpov redesigned the I-15 without its 'gull-wing', resorting to a more conventional biplane layout for the I-15bis or I-152. An extra 600 rounds of 0.3-in (7.62-mm) ammunition (for a total of 2,600 rounds) was also catered for, as well as an underwing load of 331 lb (150 kg). These additions, along with a general structural strengthening exercise added to the new variants weight and, since the same engine was employed, an inevitable decline in performance was noted. Nevertheless, production began in 1937, although deliveries began only in 1938, after several modifications had been incorporated. A number of variations on the I-152 theme were mooted and even prototyped, but the performance of the I-15 in Spain had convinced the VVS of the qualities inherent in Polikarpov's original 'gull-wing' layout, and

Spanish 'Chatos' and 'Super Chatos'

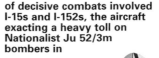

While the operational career of the I-15 in Soviet service was relatively brief, the type played a major role in the Spanish Civil War. A number

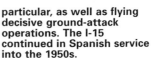

of decisive combats involved I-15s and I-152s, the aircraft exacting a heavy toll on Nationalist Ju 52/3m bombers in

particular, as well as flying decisive ground-attack operations. The I-15 continued in Spanish service into the 1950s.

I-15
This machine served as a trainer in Nationalist colours with the Ejército del Aire in the mid-1940s. Note the 'yoke-and-arrows' emblem of the post-war Nationalist forces. The aircraft may have served with the Escuela de Caza.

I-152
The Republican Fuerzas Aéreas flew this I-152 from Villajuiga in January 1939. When the war ended on 28 March 1939, some surviving airworthy Polikarpovs passed to the victorious Nationalists for continued service.

no further development of the I-152 was undertaken. Anxious to prove that the I-152 was a match for the I-15 in combat, the VVS despatched four squadrons of I-152s to China in November 1937. These aircraft fought alongside Chinese machines in the 2nd Sino-Japanese war, proving so successful that the Soviet high command became convinced of the efficacy of the biplane fighter and continued its development at the expense of monoplane fighters. A number of machines supplied directly to the Chinese proved less successful, probably due to a lack of pilot training.

Finland flew I-152s and I-153s against Soviet forces. 3/LeLv 6 flew I-153 Chaikas – like that illustrated – during the Continuation War, the unit's kills on the type including other Chaikas.

Late in 1938, Stalin authorised the supply of I-152s to the Spanish Republicans as attrition replacements for I-15s lost in combat. Three batches of 31 machines were sent, two of these batches being stopped at the French border. Those machines which did see combat marked little improvement over the I-15. After the war, 20 I-152s were presented to the winning Nationalist side by the French, these machines flying in the ground-attack role into the mid-1940s.

Soviet I-152s returned to combat over the Nomonhan plateau in the summer of 1939. The adversary was again Japan, and while the I-152 fought valiantly, it became clear that even with an I-16 escort, it was no match for the newer generation of Japanese monoplanes.

The final chapter in the I-152's colourful combat career saw these now hopelessly outdated biplanes facing the might of the Luftwaffe during Operation Barbarossa. The aircraft fought hard, but to little avail and was finally retired, after conversion to two-seat configuration, from the artillery-spotting role in the summer of 1943.

I-153 Chaika

In the ultimate expression of his biplane fighter line,

The Alpine Fighter Collection's I-153 restoration project has been aided by the availability of Shvetsov ASh-62IR radial engines (Polish-built as the ASz-62), the engine fitted to the Antonov An-2 utility transport. The ASh-62 is itself a modernised derivative of the I-153's original M-62.

Polikarpov strove to overcome the problem of increasing speed without installing a far more powerful – and therefore heavier – engine. Although I-153 engine power increased from the 750 hp (559 kW) of the M-25V fitted to the prototype, through the 800 hp (597kW) of the M-62 used in some later production aircraft and ultimately to the 1,100 hp (820-kW) of the M-63 which was introduced from December 1940, the better part of the I-153's improved performance came from the designer's reversion to his preferred 'gull-wing' configuration and the installation of retractable main landing gear.

Two I-153s may have been tested in Spain, but the type's first combat probably came against the Japanese over Mongolia. The Japanese soon came to terms with the new aircraft however, as did the Finns during their Winter and Continuation Wars against the USSR. Ironically, eleven captured I-153s also flew on the Finnish side, with some success. The Chaika's greatest trial came with the German invasion of the USSR however. In excess of one third of the fighters confronting the Germans in the western USSR were I-153s, along with a handful of I-152s. The aircraft gave a good account of themselves, flying as they were very much against the odds. As a testament to the prowess of their pilots and maintainers, a few I-153s fought through the Great Patriotic War to survive into 1945 as a fitting tribute to one of the world's last and greatest biplane fighters.

Polikarpov I-16
Monoplane fighter

Working from prison, Polikarpov did a stunning job in leading his team to create the I-16 fighter. Although obsolete by the time of Germany's invasion of the USSR, the little aircraft nevertheless gave a good account of itself.

Nikolai Nikolaaevich Polikarpov was the leading Soviet fighter designer before World War II, but his most successful designs had an unusual origin. Late in 1929, following a series of prototype crashes, Polikarpov and his assistants were accused of sabotage and imprisoned. This was not unusual in the paranoid world of Stalin's Russia, where almost anything could be twisted to be seen as counter-revolutionary activity.

While in custody, technicians and designers were expected to continue their work for the state, and the Polikarpov design team was no exception. They created the Polikarpov I-5, which was to become the standard fighter of its day. It was a traditional biplane of mixed construction, the fuselage being of welded steel tube and the wings mainly wood, with fabric covering overall. It was built in

Created at a time when other manufacturers were still producing biplane fighters with fixed landing gear, the Polikarpov I-16 was a landmark in fighter design.

substantial numbers, powered by the M-22 licensed version of the Bristol Jupiter, and gave good service. In his final months in detention, in early 1933, Polikarpov examined ways of improving the I-5 and in October 1933 the prototype Polikarpov I-15 biplane demonstrated

Above: One of the most unusual variants of the I-16 was the Sostavnoi pikiruyushchy bombardirovshchik – SPB or composite dive bomber – in which two bomb-armed I-16 Type 5s were hung beneath the wings of an ANT-6 carrier aircraft. In August 1941 the combination was tested in action against oil and communications targets in Romania.

Right: The Soviets failed to capitalise on the lead they gained in fighter design with the I-16, a fact which saw the type committed to actions in 1941 in which it was at a considerable disadvantage. Even so, the I-16's contribution to Russia's defence cannot be underestimated.

outstanding all-round handling, with the ability to complete a 360° turn in 8 seconds.

The Air Force Scientific Institute was already thinking of the future, however, and the Soviets were among the first to recognise that the day of the biplane was over. As a result, the design bureau came up with the Polikarpov I-16, intended to be the fast monoplane partner to the agile but slower I-15 family of biplanes.

Although of bizarre appearance, with a stumpy fuselage seemingly influenced by the Gee Bee racer of 1932, the I-16 was a landmark in fighter design. Though it had a traditional structure with semi-monocoque wooden fuselage and metal wings fabric-covered aft of the front spar, the I-16 was a clean cantilever monoplane with fully retracting landing gear, the first to go into military service.

Flown on the last day of 1933, the prototype had an imported Wright Cyclone engine, and early production (preceded by a few with the M-22 Jupiter) had the licensed M-25 version. Some of the later models had the improved M-62 or M-63 of up to 1,100 hp (820 kW). The first major production version was the Type 4, with the I-16 Type 10 of 1937 being built in the largest numbers.

A host of different armament schemes was used, most involving two or four ShKAS 0.3-in (7.62-mm) machine guns, but later aircraft were also armed with two ShVAK 20-mm cannon. The Type 29 carried a single Berezin UBK heavy machine gun mounted in the lower engine cowling in place of the inboard ShKAS guns. Many I-16s carried six or eight RS-82 rockets, while the I-16 Type 24 could carry bombloads up to 500 kg (1,102 lb) in weight.

In action the I-16 was tricky and tiring to fly, which also made aiming its guns a problem, but against this must be set what was perhaps the fastest roll of any fighter of the day and outstanding all-round performance and manoeuvrability. In Spain and in the fighting with Japan in 1938, it was a formidable opponent but by 1941 it was showing its age. In the first year fighting the Luftwaffe, thousands were shot down or destroyed on the ground.

Though it had many faults, the I-16 sustained a massive production programme. Although it was obsolete by the time of Operation Barbarossa in June 1941, it was kept in production until early 1942, the final total manufactured reaching 7,005 single seaters, plus at least 1,639 two-seaters (mainly UTI-4 trainers).

Even though it was thoroughly outclassed by German fighters, the I-16 continued in front line service until late in 1943. The 29th IAP (Istrebitel'nyi Aviatsionnyi Polk or Fighter Air Regiment) was one of the most heavily engaged units in the early months of the war, using its I-16s to attack German ground forces. It was the first air force unit to receive the Guards title, becoming the 1st Guards IAP during the defence of Moscow on 6 December 1941

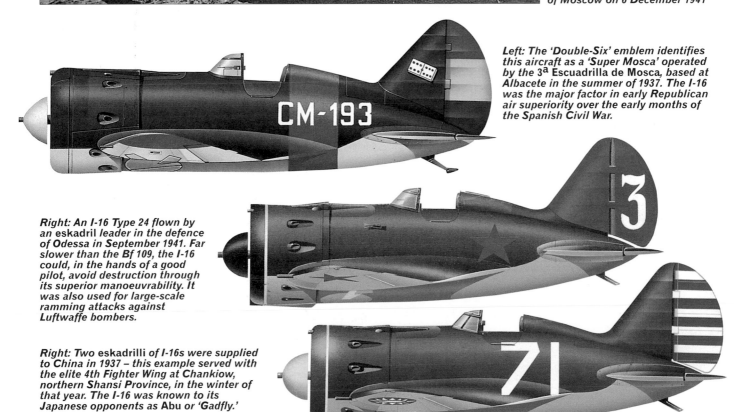

Left: The 'Double-Six' emblem identifies this aircraft as a 'Super Mosca' operated by the 3ª Escuadrilla de Mosca, based at Albacete in the summer of 1937. The I-16 was the major factor in early Republican air superiority over the early months of the Spanish Civil War.

Right: An I-16 Type 24 flown by an eskadril leader in the defence of Odessa in September 1941. Far slower than the Bf 109, the I-16 could, in the hands of a good pilot, avoid destruction through its superior manoeuvrability. It was also used for large-scale ramming attacks against Luftwaffe bombers.

Right: Two eskadrilli of I-16s were supplied to China in 1937 – this example served with the elite 4th Fighter Wing at Chankiow, northern Shansi Province, in the winter of that year. The I-16 was known to its Japanese opponents as Abu or 'Gadfly.'

Republic P-47
Thunderbolt
Introduction

As the heaviest single-engined piston fighter to reach large-scale service, the P-47 is acknowledged as one of the greatest ground-attack aircraft of World War II.

The big, roomy, powerful Republic P-47 Thunderbolt was produced in greater numbers (15,683) than any other American fighter. Yet its career was near an end as early as 1945. The Thunderbolt was one of the top-performing fighters of the war and enjoys a devout following of veteran pilots and vocal advocates. Yet the P-47 was always a paradox, a big

aircraft with an air-cooled engine even though the US Army Air Force (USAAF) believed in in-line engines, a superb high-altitude fighter that was often outclassed by other fighters at lower heights, yet was rugged and enduring in air-to-ground strafing and bombing missions.

The P-47 could dive at incredible velocity – giving rise to mistaken rumours that it could

Most early P-47 variants were of 'razorback' design, like those in this formation of six P-47Bs from the 56th Fighter Group in October 1942. The lead aircraft is flown by P-47 ace, Hubert Zemke.

Above: Fitted with eight 0.5-in (12.7-mm) machine-guns and capable of carrying bombs and rocket projectiles, the P-47N was an ideal weapons platform in the ground-attack role.

Right: Armourers of the 318th Fighter Group load and clean the guns of P-47N Thunderbolt Jane at Ie Shima in July 1945. The long range of the P-47N variant rendered it ideal for escorting B-29 Superfortress raids against the Japanese mainland.

approach or even exceed supersonic speed in the dive – but it was sluggish in a climb. In 'clean' condition, there was no better dogfighter, but P-47 pilots were often sent into action carrying hated bomb pylons that slowed the Thunderbolt and impeded its manoeuvrability.

Other Thunderbolt attributes were a comfortable cockpit, a low internal noise level, little vibration, and excellent control response. The large barrel-like nose did, however, protrude far ahead of the pilot, with the result that visibility downwards and to the front was obscured both on the ground and in flight. The firepower of the P-47 was a sight to behold and it was rated the 'best strafer' among US fighters. The aircraft could also withstand considerable combat damage and there was no more glorious an apparition than a P-47 returning safely to its home base after being riddled with hundreds of rounds of gunfire.

Francis Gabreski, Robert Johnson, Hubert Zemke and Neal Kearby were among the aces who flew the P-47 Thunderbolt and swore by it. Luftwaffe ace General Adolf Galland flew a P-47 and said that he initially felt that the cockpit was big enough to walk around in. But on internal fuel alone, the Thunderbolt lacked the 'legs' to enter the war and, even with drop tanks, it never possessed the

range of its slimmer, prettier rival, the P-51 Mustang. Some US officers in Europe thought that the Thunderbolt used up too much runway to take off, was difficult to pull out of a dive, and had weak landing gear. In the Pacific, however, 5th Air Force General, George C. Kenney, liked the performance of the Thunderbolt and requested that more fighter groups be equipped with the big machine.

Misconceptions were many. Contrary to myth, the P-47 Thunderbolt was not especially difficult to fly. It was not even difficult to land, although even a skilled pilot had to be careful not to flare and to bring the aircraft straight down for a solid, thumping reunion with the ground. Nor was it true, as lore had it, that the P-47 was effective only at high altitude – although its air-to-air prowess was greatest at the edge of the stratosphere.

Heavily armed

Contrary to another widely published mistake, the Thunderbolt was not nicknamed the 'Jug' because it was like a juggernaut. The 'Jug' appellation came about because the fuselage of the P-47 resembled an illicit container for home-made whisky.

The company that manufactured the Thunderbolt in Long Island was sometimes called the 'Republic Iron Works'. Founded by Russian immigrant, Major

Able to take considerable punishment and packing a hefty punch, USAAF P-47s played a vital role in crippling German supply and communication lines. This P-47 from the 406th FG flys through the explosion of an ammunition-filled road vehicle in June 1944.

Alexander P. de Seversky – who awarded himself the rank of major and published volumes about the preponderant role of air power – the company dropped Seversky's surname and became Republic just when the first P-47 was taking shape. It was another Russian settler, Alexander Kartveli, who led the engineering design team. Kartveli and his company believed in size and strength, and their aircraft were built accordingly. It was said that if a P-47 pilot could not defeat his foe any other way, he could taxi over top of the enemy and retract his gear. The sheer inertia of the 11,600-lb

(5261-kg) 'Jug' would do the rest.

As recently as 1990, an extract from a USAF history stated: 'The Thunderbolt first took shape in a sketch made by Kartveli on the back of an envelope. That was at an Army fighter-plane requirements meeting in 1940.'

The legend is heartwarming, but overlooks the step-by-step, 'building block' process whereby the Thunderbolt came into being after a progression of earlier pursuit types from the same shop, among them the lacklustre P-43 Lancer which saw limited action in the China-Burma-India theatre.

To exploit the enormous power of its corpulent R-2800 engine, the Thunderbolt mounted a massive 12-ft (3.65-m) four-bladed, controllable-pitch propeller and, in later models, employed 'paddle' blades that enhanced performance. Its supercharging system was the key to its success and was placed in the fuselage aft of the pilot, with exhaust gases piped back to the turbine and expelled at the rear – ducted air being returned to the engine under pressure. Despite teething problems, the system worked well, ensuring the superb reputation of the 'Jug' at altitude.

Five years after VJ-Day, when the US needed a prop-driven fighter for air-to-ground work in Korea, the Pentagon tried to find enough Thunderbolts for the job. By then however, the most widely-built American fighter was almost out of inventory, so the Air Force had no choice but to give the job to the less enduring and more fickle Mustang.

P-47 Thunderbolt pilots said, then and now, that their aircraft was superior and, on that occasion, there was no arguing with them.

Right: The fastest and heaviest of all wartime variants, the P-47N featured square-cut wingtips and four new fuel cells in the root of each wing. Its gross weight of 20,700 lb (9389 kg) was the highest for a piston-engined single-seat fighter.

Below: Over 800 P-47Ds were allocated to the RAF, under the Lend-Lease agreement, for operations in the Far East. This aircraft was one of four Thunderbolt Mk IIs which underwent operational trials in the UK.

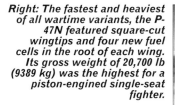

P-47 Development

After a protracted period of early development, Republic's promised world-beating fighter eventually emerged as the P-47 Thunderbolt, spawning a variety of combat-proven variants.

Built as a follow-on aircraft from the Seversky (later Republic) P-35A, the XP-41 and similar private-venture AP-4 resulted in the company winning a lucrative contract from the USAAC. Thirteen pre-production turbocharged YP-43s (developed from the XP-41) were ordered, the first being delivered in September 1940. Service trials progressed unhindered, but the aircraft revealed itself to be a generation behind the technology of the latest European designs. Consequently, Republic's improved Lancer, the P-43A (80 of which had been ordered as early as September 1939 as the P-44), was promptly cancelled in favour of an altogether improved design.

Enter the Thunderbolt

Although the USAAC had ordered 54 P-43s and 80 P-43As, these aircraft were only intended to bridge the gap until the arrival of Republic's next evolutionary machine, the P-47 Thunderbolt.

Originating in response to a 1940 USAAC requirement for a lightweight interceptor, the lineage of the resulting P-47 was clear, its forebears being the P-35, XP-41, P-43 and the abortive P-44. Alexander Kartveli, and the design team responsible for the P-35, also drafted the P-47.

A contract for the XP-47 prototype was awarded by the USAAC in November 1939, and Republic began development of the new fighter, powered by a 1,150-hp (858-kW) Allison inline engine. A further contract covered the construction of a lighter-weight derivative, the XP-47A. As aerial battle raged over Europe in 1940, it became clear that neither machine would be suitable for service, with no provision for heavy armour, eight-gun armament or self-sealing fuel tanks.

Republic's redesign

Kartveli announced a redesigned fighter, based upon a turbocharged Pratt & Whitney engine, that would offer both high performance, a heavy warload and armour. After USAAC evaluation, the design was given the go-ahead in September 1940.

Built around the 1,999-hp (1491-kW) Double Wasp, the P-47 required a propeller with a diameter of 12.2 ft (3.71 m), this

Top: Predecessor to the Thunderbolt, the P-43 Lancer high-altitude fighter conducted its final Army tests at Floyd Bennett Field, attaining sub-stratosphere altitudes on test flights.

Above: Eighty P-43As were ordered by the USAAC as re-engined Lancers intended as a stop-gap measure following the cancellation of the P-44, and prior to the introduction of the P-47.

Unlike the XP-47 and XP-47A, the XP-47B was not built in response to a USAAC specification for a lightweight fighter. As a result, Kartveli's team were free to develop a high-performance fighter with plenty of room for a large fuel and weapons load, and with an airframe that would be robust enough to survive over the European battlefield.

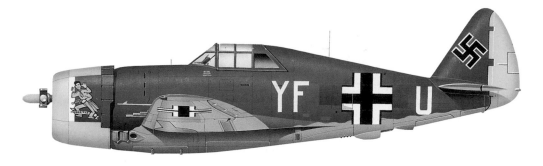

First flown by the 358th FS of the 355th FG on escort and ground-attack missions over France, this P-47D was captured and test-flown by Sonderkommando Aufklarugsstaffel 103 after the aircraft was forced to land in 1944. The machine flew with the Luftwaffe from Paris-Orly.

in turn dictating tall landing gear for ground clearance. When rolled out, Republic's new fighter revealed not only its enormous proportions, but a machine with a conventional all-metal structure. However, early flights in May 1941 highlighted numerous problems, and one prototype was lost in August 1942. By this time, orders for an initial batch of 773 aircraft had already been placed. Production P-47Bs, named Thunderbolt, began to be delivered to USAAF's 56th Fighter Group in June 1942. The later production machines featured a pressurised cockpit, as tested in the XP-47E.

Combat debut

When the 56th Fighter Group deployed to the UK in 1943, the P-47B had its baptism of fire. Unfortunately, it proved to be lacking in performance and manoeuvrability at lower levels, and was limited by its internal fuel capacity. The P-47Cs that followed the 171 B-models introduced rudder and elevator changes to increase manoeuvrability, water injection to increase power to 2,299 hp (1715 kW) and, most importantly, an external fuel tank to allow operations deep into continental Europe.

After the 602 P-47Cs, production turned to the most numerous model, the P-47D, also built by Curtiss-Wright (P-47G). A total of 12,956 aircraft were built on both production lines.

Early block numbers differed little from the P-47C, introducing better cockpit armour, wing strengthening, underwing pylons and additional fuel. The most significant change came after Block 25, when the P-47D was

Above: Seen in prototype form, the eventual P-47N was to be the final major production model of the venerable P-47 Thunderbolt series.

Right: Production versions of the Pacific-optimised P-47N could be distinguished by their underwing rocket launch stubs, clipped wings and dorsal fin fillet with antennae.

fitted with a high-visibility canopy, as on the Hawker Typhoon, and a reduced height 'cut-away' rear fuselage. These changes were debuted on the experimental XP-47K.

Later models

Following the P-47D series, of which a number was exported to the RAF in Burma as the Thunderbolt Mks I and II (with bubble-canopy), came a small

run of P-47Ms, a high-speed version of the P-47D airframe, to counter rocket-powered fighters and V-1 flying bombs.

Aside from production aircraft, a number of further experimental types was also developed. These comprised the XP-47F with laminar-flow wings, the XP-47H with its 2,299-hp (1715-kW) Chrysler inline engine, the radical high-powered lightweight XP-47J which led to the advanced XP-72

project and, lastly, the XP-47L with increased fuel capacity.

Last in the line of production variants, however, were the 1,816 P-47Ns for Asian operations. Utilising the airframe of the P-47D and the powerplant of the P-47M, and strengthened landing gear and wing as well as new wing fuel tanks, the P-47N had the range to escort XXI Bomber Command's B-29s on missions over the Pacific.

Following World War II, P-47Ns went on to serve with the United States Air National Guard into the early 1950s. Redesignated F-47N from June 1948, Thunderbolts in the ANG served with squadrons in Connecticut, Delaware, Georgia (128th and 158th), Hawaii, Massachusetts, Mississippi, Pennsylvania (146th and 147th) and Puerto Rico.

P-47 Thunderbolt
Variants

The P-47 Thunderbolt was constantly upgraded and modified to ensure that it could hold its own against its Axis opponents. A number of variants was therefore built, some superior to others, but all contributed towards making the P-47 a highly successful aircraft.

P-43A-1

Developed from the P-43 Lancer and fitted with a 1,200-hp (895-kW) engine, the P-44 had a top speed of 356 mph (573 km/h). It was armed with just four guns, but introduced the self-sealing fuel tanks that had been shown by the war in Europe to be vital to a fighter. A number of these aircraft were supplied to China, and elements of its design were incorporated into the P-47 Thunderbolt.

P-47D Thunderbolt

Almost identical to the P-47C-5 on the exterior, the early 'D' models had 'razorback' fuselages, but included internal refinements such as a redesigned exhaust gas duct for the turbo-supercharger, changes in the engine accessory compartment, a paddle-bladed propeller, and increased armour for the pilot. From the P-47D-25 onwards, a new teardrop canopy was added which defined the shape of future models and greatly increased visibility from the cockpit. The development of an external fuel tank also gave greater endurance. The extra tanks were first used in July 1943 when P-47Ds escorted US heavy bombers to the Germany/Holland border, the presence of P-47s surprising the Luftwaffe fighters when they tried to intercept the bombers. The RAF used the P-47D as Thunderbolt Mk I (razorback) and Mk II (teardrop).

P-47G, TP-47G

Thunderbolts built by Curtiss (rather than Republic) were given the designation P-47G although they were virtually identical to the Republic models. The first 20 built were similar to the P-47C, but after that, Curtiss built P-47D equivalents. Two P-47Gs were modified to become two-seaters, with the second cockpit forward of the first, and were thus designated TP-47Gs.

P-47B

Incorporating many elements of the XP-47B prototype, the P-47B was externally identical to its predecessor apart from a sliding cockpit hood, metal covered control surfaces and repositioned aerial mast. Its performance was much in line with original proposals although the aircraft was some 650 lb (295 kg) heavier than planned and consequently took 6.7 minutes to reach 15,000 ft (4572 m), rather than the predicted five. However, the top speed was 429 mph (690 km/h), around 30 mph (48 km/h) faster than predicted.

P-47C

With strengthened tail surfaces, an 8-in (20.32-cm) increase in length, new engine mounting and aerial mast, the P-47C was accepted into surface in September 1942. Despite these improvements, it soon found itself embroiled in a number of incidents, most notably power dives in which speeds of 500 mph (804 km/h) were exceeded. During these, the P-47C was in the grip of compressibility which meant that its controls would either be reversed or would not even work at all. In one dive, it was claimed that a P-47C had reached 725 mph (1166 km/h), although a speed of 100 mph (161 km/h) less than this is more realistic. The 'C' was the first Thunderbolt to be considered truly combatworthy and later versions of the 'C' incorporated design changes deemed necessary to overcome dive problems. Provision for fuel tanks, which were carried under the belly, was also made.

TP-47G

XP-47H

One of several experimental variants of the P-47, the XP-47H was used as a testbed for the Chrysler 16-cylinder 2,500-hp (1865-kW) XI-2220 engine. Only two such aircraft were converted in 1943, but it was not until July 1945, when hostilities in Europe had ceased, that the aircraft actually flew. Extensive rebuilding work had to be performed on the aircraft, but it was never seriously considered for anything but the testing of the ultimately unsuccessful Chrysler engine.

XP-47K/L

To give all-round vision for the pilot, Republic followed the trend of the time and installed a bubble canopy on a P-47D. Designated the XP-47K (illustrated), the rear decking was cut down and the radio equipment moved. These changes, introduced from the P-47D-25, gave the Thunderbolt a much slimmer and more streamlined form. Republic took another P-47D and gave it a new fuel tank (which held an extra 65 US gal; 246 litres), increased the oxygen supply (six oxygen cylinders were fitted instead of four) and made other minor improvements. The aircraft was given the designation XP-47L.

P-47N

Another modified 'D' model Thunderbolt began life as the XP-47N which was also equipped with the 'C' series Double Wasp engine, but the major alteration was the fitting of experimental wing inserts. These had been developed by Republic to increase fuel load, and further refinements resulted in the long-range wing which raised the fuel load from 370 US gal (1400 litres) to 500 US gal (1893 litres). The wing extensions improved the roll and turning radius of the P-47 and a number of P-47Ds were modified to utilise this new wing. A total of 1,816 P-47Ns was produced and deployed to the Pacific, where they provided an escort service to Boeing B-29 Superfortresses during long overwater missions. The P-47N, the last of the Thunderbolts, stayed in service long after the war, passing to the Air National Guard before being phased out in 1955, by which time it had been given the new designation of F-47N.

XP-47J

A lightweight Thunderbolt variant first built in 1943, the XP-47J showed great potential. It was fitted with an uprated Pratt & Whitney R-2800-57 'C' engine which was specifically designed to obtain higher output without causing an increase in weight. The close cowled engine also included a special fan to aid cooling and, with the inclusion of a larger propeller and more powerful supercharger, the aircraft reached the magical 500 mph (804 km/h) mark in August 1944. However, when tested by the AAF, its top speed was some 7 mph (11 km/h) slower and even this speed was unattainable when the aircraft was fully loaded. Another minus point was that Republic would have to have altered 70 per cent of its production line to accommodate the changes. The aircraft never made it into service.

P-47M,

The P-47M was a 'D' model Thunderbolt equipped with the 'C' series Double Wasp engine which was aimed at improving the aircraft's all-round performance. While other new systems proved somewhat unsatisfactory, the new engine gave a top speed of some 50 mph (80 km/h) more than that achieved by the 'D' model. This made the P-47M the fastest of all the Thunderbolts, an attribute that was useful for countering the threat of German rocket- and turbine-powered aircraft and V-1 flying bombs. Some 130 P-47Ms were built, preceded by three YP-47Ms. A number of P-47Ds were actually modified to be completed as P-47Ms and joined the 56th FG in the UK.

XP-72

Shortly after the Thunderbolt first flew, Republic turned its attention towards studying new high-powered radials from Pratt & Whitney. A mock-up was built of an aircraft with the radial buried in the fuselage aft of the pilot, driving the propeller in the nose through an extension shaft. However, the AAC never took up this unorthodox idea and a more conventional aircraft, the XP-72, was put forward which promised superior performance and used many P-47 components. The XP-72 was powered by the 3,000-hp (2238-kW) 28-cylinder Wasp Major engine and two prototypes were ordered in 1943. The first, equipped with a four-bladed propeller, flew in February 1944 and the second, with contra-rotating propellers, flew five months later. However, the new aircraft was much heavier than the P-47 and, in order to keep its weight down, mounted only six guns. It also had a very high rate of fuel consumption which restricted its range and the advent of the jet engine meant that its top speed of 490 mph (789 km/h) was soon overshadowed. A preliminary production contract for 100 aircraft was cancelled; the aircraft never entered service as, like the XP-47J, it would have taken too long to be converted from the Republic production line.

ETO Thunderbolts

The first Thunderbolts arrived in England in late 1942, to equip three fighter groups in the Eighth Air Force but it was as a fighter-bomber in the Ninth Air Force that the P-47 was to make its name in the European theatre.

Initially issued to the 4th, 78th and 56th Fighter Groups, these P-47Cs saw their first major action in April 1943 and proved worthy opponents for Luftwaffe Fw 190s. Though slower in the climb and less manoeuvrable than the German fighter, the Thunderbolt was faster in the dive and in a straight line.

However, teething problems abounded. Engine failures, in particular, led to the loss of a number of aircraft and it was not until the arrival of P-47Ds in April 1943, that the Eighth Air Force had a genuinely useful aircraft. The 'D' variant incorporated a number of engine modifications and increased armour for the pilot. Perhaps more importantly, it was the P-47D that was first modified to carry external fuel tanks, allowing the aircraft to accompany the Eighth Air Force's bombers further into occupied Europe.

Ten P-47 groups

By the end of 1943 the 'Mighty Eighth' had 10 fighter groups equipped with the P-47. It was intended that most of these groups would convert to the new P-51 Mustang – an aircraft more suited to the long-range escort role. It was the Ninth Air Force, newly reformed as the US contribution to the Allied air forces committed to support the forthcoming invasion of Europe, that was to become the largest operator of the Thunderbolt.

By May 1944, 13 of the Ninth's 18 fighter groups were equipped with P-47Ds. The Thunderbolt had found a new

Above: The 78th Fighter Group was among the earliest operators of the P-47 in the ETO. This 82nd FS 'bubbletop' P-47D is pictured in late 1944; note the vestigal AEAF stripes applied for D-Day.

Top: Early- and late-production P-47Ds served side-by-side until the end of the war in Europe. These are Ninth Air Force fighter-bombers of the 373rd FG flying from a French base in August 1944.

role as a ground attack and dive-bombing aircraft, its performance at low altitude making it an ideal aircraft for this new assignment.

The latest batches of P-47Ds, shipped from the US, were accordingly tailored for the new role. Engines were equipped with water injection to increase their power 'on the deck', new paddle-bladed propellers using this power more efficiently. Racks able to carry a 500-lb (227-kg) bomb were also fitted beneath each wing.

After D-Day the P-47 came into its own. US Army tank crews with VHF radios were able to summon bomb-carrying

aircraft to attack specific targets (in the same way that British forces called on 'cab rank' Typhoons of the RAF). From July 1944, these aircraft were also able to carry rocket projectiles.

By January 1945 the Eighth Air Force had just one P-47 group – the 56th – which was in the process of converting to the new P-47M. In the event, further engine problems meant that the new aircraft were not properly in service until April, but it remains a fact that the 56th FG was the highest-scoring group in the Eighth and the highest-scoring P-47 group in the USAAF.

A 'razorback' P-47 strafes an enemy airfield, damaging a captured Lioré-et-Olivier LeO 451 bomber in the process. This was a task at which the Thunderbolt excelled.

Left: Evansville-built P-47D-15-RA 42-23289 **Lady Ruth** *of the 19th FS, 318th FG is prepared for gun harmonisation after repairs at its base at Ie Shima in the Marianas, July 1945. The P-47D-15 introduced important improvements, such as wing pylons for the carriage of fuel or a 1,000-lb (454-kg) bomb, plus extra internal fuel tankage.*

Below: 19th Fighter Squadron personnel celebrate the unit's 70th kill at Ie Shima during July 1945. The 318th FS was the first group to receive the P-47N, in April 1945. The 'N' was faster than the late-model 'D' and had much improved range, thanks to its integral wing tanks.

At war with Japan

In mid-1943, the Thunderbolt, serving with the Fifth Air Force in the southwest Pacific, saw combat with the Japanese for the first time. The P-47 went on to equip a number of groups in the central Pacific and Burma.

The big Thunderbolt did not immediately endear itself to the Fifth Air Force. In the remote SWPA theatre, with its fuel supply problems, the P-47's heavy fuel consumption was less than desirable and agile fighter opposition, in the shape of 'Tony', 'Oscar' and 'Zeke' fighters, soon taught P-47s pilots not to engage them in a turning fight.

As in Europe the Thunderbolt suffered engine problems and was handicapped by its limited range but, once engine 'snags' had been ironed out and modifications made so that the aircraft would accept a belly fuel tank, the P-47 was able to take up a fighter-bomber role much as it would in Europe. By the end of 1943 three fighter groups were supporting the reconquest of New Guinea and the subsequent 'island hopping' campaign north to the Philippines.

China-Burma-India

In Spring 1944 the first USAAF P-47s were deployed to India for operations on the Burma front (where the type was also used in large numbers by the RAF). Beginning with the 80th FG, eight squadrons eventually flew the type. It spent much of its time in the fighter-bomber role and also protected C-46 and C-47 transports flying 'over the Hump' to China.

In the central Pacific, the Seventh Air Force had a single Thunderbolt-equipped group – the 318th – which was shipped to the Marianas islands from Hawaii in June 1944. These aircraft supported the invasions of Guam and Tinian and other islands in the Marianas. By April 1945 the group had reached Ie Shima, three miles (4.80 km) off the coast of Okinawa. Here it re-equipped with new P-47Ns. Four more groups equipped with P-47Ns arrived in the region in mid-1945, three at Ie Shima and one on the recently-captured island of Iwo Jima.

Though intended to provide escort for B-29s bombing the Japanese mainland, the New Thunderbolts saw little use in this role and were instead assigned to attack missions, bombing and strafing shipping and ground targets such as railways and airfields. The P-47N proved a reliable and effective aircraft and one that was more robust that the P-51 Mustang. Its main shortcoming was the long take-off run the aircraft required when fully loaded. Even though the runways on Ie Shima and Iwo Jima were 1½ miles (2.40 km) in length, P-47N pilots used very high power settings and considerable speeds in order to get airborne.

Five diagonal blue stripes were the well-known markings of the 1st Air Commando Group which, by the summer of 1944, was equipped solely with fighters and was mainly engaged in the forward support of troops.

British service

Famous for its exploits in the hands of USAAF pilots, the Thunderbolt also gave little-known, but valuable, service with the RAF in Asia. Using the aircraft's renowned 'punch' in the ground-attack role, the RAF's Thunderbolts harried the retreating Japanese during the last 12 months of war.

With a total production run of 15,683 examples, the Republic P-47 came second only to the Curtiss P-40 family in terms of US fighter production quantities during World War II. Within that total, the run of 12,602 P-47Ds singled out this particular variant of the 'Jug' as the most-produced of any single model of a US fighter. Perhaps surprisingly, therefore, RAF use of the Thunderbolt was relatively modest, deliveries totalling 825 and deployment being limited almost exclusively to the Burma theatre.

Influenced by early combat reports from the air war in Europe, Republic designers sketched in 1940 an advanced single-seat fighter that was characterised by its large size and great weight.

Brute force

The design philosophy dramatically contrasted with that of other companies that sought to achieve operational effectiveness through light weight. The XP-47B, first flown on 6 May 1941, was powered by the massive Pratt & Whitney twin-row air-cooled radial

Above: No. 134 Squadron re-equipped with Thunderbolt Mk I/IIs in August 1944 and commenced operations the following December. The squadron subsequently covered the Allied landings at Rangoon in April 1945.

Below: This early example of the Thunderbolt Mk I was delivered to the RAF in spring 1944. It was photographed carrying auxiliary fuel tanks, during tests with the A&AEE.

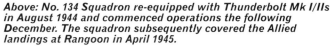

Below: Thunderbolts in Burma flew 'cab-rank' patrols, directed by controllers on the ground. With 500-lb (227-kg) bombs and heavy armament, they caused considerable damage to the Japanese ground forces and their long supply lines.

Above: RAF Thunderbolts flew operations exclusively in the Far East from 1944. White recognition bands were applied to prevent confusion with Japanese aircraft such as Nakajima Ki-84s.

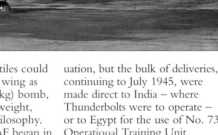

Below: The 'teardrop'-style canopy of the P-47D-25 Thunderbolt Mk II gave the pilot much improved all-round vision. The Mk II was involved in little air-to-air combat, concentrating instead on ground-attack.

Above: As Thunderbolt Mk Is arrived in the Far East during the latter half of 1944, they began to replace Hurricanes in the fighter-bomber role. These Thunderbolt Mk Is, carrying auxiliary fuel tanks, taxi past a squadron of Hurricanes.

engine, with a turbo-supercharger located under the rear fuselage, and weighed in at 12,000 lb (5443 kg). In the proposed production form, armament was to comprise eight wing-mounted 0.5-in (12.7-mm) machine-guns – following European trends – and weight would go up to 15,000 lb (6804 kg).

Lend-Lease

Initial USAAF orders covered the P-47B and P-47C versions, but the RAF had to wait for the P-47D before Lend-Lease supplies could begin. The P-47D designation covered several sub-variants that introduced progressive improvements: range was increased by use of a centre-line drop tank that could be replaced by a 500-lb (227-kg) bomb, while wing pylons could carry two tanks or two 1,000-lb (454-kg) bombs. Eventually, two

or three rocket projectiles could be carried under each wing as well as a 500-lb (227-kg) bomb, vindicating the heavyweight, high-power design philosophy.

Deliveries to the RAF began in mid-1944 and comprised 240 Thunderbolt F.Mk Is and 590 Thunderbolt F.Mk IIs (of a planned total of 1,098). The Mk Is were the so-called 'razor-back' variants with the original built-up rear fuselage into which the cockpit canopy faired, whereas the Mk IIs were the USAAF's P-47D-25 version with a 'bubble' canopy and cut-down rear fuselage. A few Thunderbolts came to the UK for test and eval-

uation, but the bulk of deliveries, continuing to July 1945, were made direct to India – where Thunderbolts were to operate – or to Egypt for the use of No. 73 Operational Training Unit (OTU) to train pilots destined to serve with the operational squadrons.

Into combat

The conversion of RAF squadrons in India (then flying Hurricanes) to Thunderbolts began in May 1944, and Nos 30, 79, 146 and 261 Squadrons were flying the Republic fighters by the late summer – by which time Thunderbolt Mk IIs were

already reaching all four squadrons. The first operational sorties were made on 14 September 1944 by No. 261 Squadron, when Mk Is and Mk IIs made an armed reconnaissance sortie over the Chudwin river; two days later No. 146 Squadron joined No. 261 Squadron in a bombing and strafing attack south of Imphal.

Nos 30 and 79 Squadrons went into operation over the Arakan, joined later by No. 135 Squadron. These became employed mostly on offensive reconnaissance and Rhubarb missions, but on 4 November, No. 30 Squadron was able to claim the first RAF Thunderbolt victory in an air-to-air engagement. Four more Thunderbolt squadrons were operational by the end of 1944 – three over the Arakan and one more in central Burma – and a final two Hurricane squadrons converted in March and April 1945. Action continued at a high rate through to the end of the war, and No. 60 Squadron continued to fly Thunderbolt Mk IIs in Singapore until October 1946.

These Thunderbolt Mk IIs of No. 30 Squadron were photographed during a patrol over Burma in late 1944. In January 1945, the squadron switched to the ground-attack role using bombs and napalm.

This P-47D-30 Thunderbolt Mk II belonged to No. 79 Squadron based at Wangjing, Burma in November 1944. It is adorned with the medium- and dark-blue national insignia adopted in Southeast Asia to avoid confusion with the red 'meatball' carried by Japanese aircraft.

Savoia-Marchetti

Spavieros were particularly active in the Mediterranean theatre of operations. These aircraft of 10º Squadriglia, 28º Gruppo were based in North Africa for much of 1941, before the unit converted to the CRDA Z.1007bis towards the end of the year.

SM.79 Sparviero
Tri-motored Sparrowhawk

Never wholly divesting itself of its commercial appearance, the Savoia-Marchetti SM.79 came to represent for wartime Italy what the Spitfire had meant to the British and the B-17 to the Americans. Superbly flown as a torpedo-bomber in the Mediterranean, it sank many Allied ships and, contrary to wartime propaganda, was a rugged adversary that proved difficult to shoot down.

As the seeds of the Axis partnership were being sown in Europe, and Germany's Lufthansa was being presented with dual-role bomber-transports for commercial operation, a similar philosophy was being pursued, albeit with less malice aforethought, in the other dictatorship.

Development of the commercial Savoia-Marchetti SM.79 was pursued along several paths: the SM.79C (C for *Corsa*, or race), the SM.79T (T for *Transatlantico*) and the twin-engined SM.79B.

Eleven SM.79Ts with additional fuel for prestigious transatlantic flights and five racing SM.79Cs were built, all with 1,000-hp (746-kW) Piaggio P.XI RC.40 radials. Among the outstanding achievements of these fine aircraft was their gaining of the first three places in the 1937 Istres-Damascus-Paris race, in which they beat the MacRobertson race winner, the DH.88 Comet G-ACSS, into fourth place. Early in 1938 three

SM.79s were flown from Rome to Rio de Janeiro, covering the 6,116 miles (9842 km) at an average speed of 251 mph (404.11 km/h). Further world speed-distance-payload records fell to SM.79s in 1938.

Development of the SM.79B as a commercial aircraft was short-lived, principally on account of the supposed public prejudice against twin engines on

the grounds of safety. However, after the prototype SM.79B flew in 1936 with two 1,030-hp (768-kW) Fiat A.80 radials, it became clear that the twin-engine layout was still being looked on with favour by some foreign air forces, and Savoia-Marchetti eventually sold four military examples to Iraq in 1938 (all of which were destroyed during the anti-British rebellion of 1941), and three to Brazil. Romania, on the other hand, adopted the SM.79B on a much larger scale, purchasing 24 in 1938 with 1,000-hp (746-kW) Gnome-Rhône Mistral Major radials, followed later by 24 more powered by 1,220-hp (910-kW) Junkers Jumo 211Da inline engines. Romania also

Prototype I-MAGO

When Alessandro Marchetti proposed a cleaned-up, high-speed eight-passenger development of his SM.81 early in 1934, ostensibly to participate in the forthcoming prestigious MacRobertson air race from England to Australia, it was immediately clear that in such an aircraft lay the basis of an efficient heavy bomber. In the event the commercial SM.79P (I-MAGO) was not completed in time for the great race, being flown at Cameri airport in October 1934, powered by three 610-hp (455-kW) Piaggio P.IX Stella RC.2 nine-cylinder radials. Deprived of the possible laurels of the 1934 race, I-MAGO went on to demonstrate its potential in a record-breaking flight from Milan to Rome in June 1935 and, soon afterwards, with three 750-hp (560-kW) Alfa Romeo 125 RC.35 engines (as shown in this view), established world records over 1000-km (621-mile) and 2000-km (1,243-mile) closed circuits with various loads; the following year, with 780-hp (582-kW) Alfa Romeo 126 RC.34 engines, I-MAGO raised its own record for carrying 2000 kg (4,409 lb) over 1000 km (621 miles) to 420 km/h (261 mph).

*'I-11' was one of the five **SM.79C** racing aircraft that achieved such great success in the 3,863-mile (6217-km) Istres-Damascus-Paris race of 1937, filling the first three places.*

Twin-engined variants: SM.79B & SM.79-JR

Though there was scant local interest in the twin-engined SM.79B on the grounds of safety, the type found buyers abroad and was soon in production in Romania by the late 1930s.

SM.79B
Four SM.79Bs were acquired by the Iraqi air force in 1938. Powered by a pair of Fiat A.80 radial engines, all were destroyed during the 1941 uprising against the British.

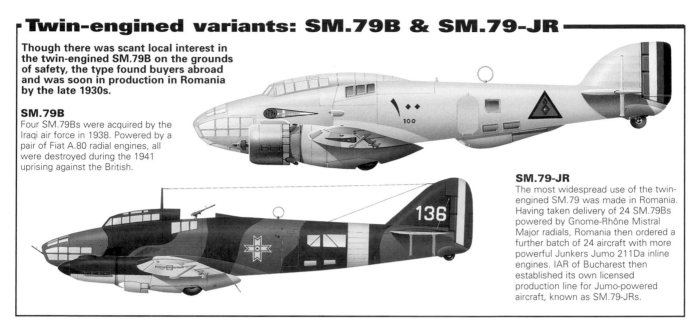

SM.79-JR
The most widespread use of the twin-engined SM.79 was made in Romania. Having taken delivery of 24 SM.79Bs powered by Gnome-Rhône Mistral Major radials, Romania then ordered a further batch of 24 aircraft with more powerful Junkers Jumo 211Da inline engines. IAR of Bucharest then established its own licensed production line for Jumo-powered aircraft, known as SM.79-JRs.

The twin-engined SM.79B was intended as an export variant and first appeared in 1936. The prototype (pictured) was demonstrated extensively in Europe, as well as Brazil and China.

negotiated to build the aircraft under licence (as the SM.79-JR) at the Bucharest plant of Industria Aeronautica Romana, these aircraft later serving as medium bombers with the Romanian forces on the Russian front in large numbers in 1942, while the earlier SM.79Bs were relegated to transport duties. The IAR-built SM.79-JR had a top speed of 277 mph (445 km/h) at 16,405 ft (5000 m), time to 9,845 ft (3000 m) was 8 minutes 40 seconds, and the service ceiling was 24,280 ft (7400 m).

Such was the early recognition of military potential in the SM.79 that the second prototype was completed in 1935 as a bomber. Construction was largely of wood, the three-spar low wing being built as a single unit with only 11 degrees of dihedral. The big fuselage was a welded steel-tube structure, the forward part being Duralumin and plywood-covered, and the rear section covered with ply and fabric. Two pilots were normally accommodated, and a single fixed forward-firing machine-gun (initially 0.303-in/ 7.7-mm, but later 0.5-in/

12.7-mm) was located over the cockpit. The bomb-bay, offset slightly to starboard, occupied the mid-fuselage, and aft of it was a ventral fairing containing the bomb aimer's station and a gunner with rear-firing 0.303-in (7.7-mm), later 0.5-in (12.7-mm) Breda-SAFAT machine-gun. Another machine-gun position was located at the rear of the prominent dorsal hump (which gave the SM.79 its service nickname *il Gobbo*, or the hunchback), and a single 0.303-in (7.7-mm) machine-gun in the rear fuselage could be swung from side to side to fire through beam hatches.

RA enthusiasm

From the outset the Regia Aeronautica test pilots expressed enthusiasm for the SM.79, and production orders were placed before the end of 1935. Early aircraft, SM.79-Is, with three 780-hp (582-kW) Alfa Romeo 126 RC.34 radials, entered service with the 8° and 111° Stormi Bombardamento Veloce (fast bomber groups) in 1936.

The introduction of the SM.79 (now officially named the Sparviero) into service with the Regia Aeronautica went ahead at full speed. By the beginning of World War II some 11 stormi,

each of four squadriglie (squadrons), were deployed with a total of 389 aircraft in Italy, Albania and in the Aegean. However, it was in a new role that the SM.79 was being examined. Given its geographical location athwart the Mediterranean, Italy had for some years worked to gain a justified reputation in torpedo warfare and technology, and in 1937 had conducted trials at Gorizia with an SM.79 carrying a single torpedo. Although these trials showed great promise, it was decided to pursue a dual torpedo installation, at the same time fitting more powerful engines, initially the 860-hp (642-kW) Alfa Romeo 128 RC.18 (this producing the prototype SM.84) and later the 1,000-hp (746-kW) Piaggio P.XI RC.40 radial. In the latter configuration the aircraft entered production as the SM.79-II, starting delivery to the Regia Aeronautica in 1940; later sub-variants were powered by 1,350-hp (1007-kW) Alfa Romeo 135 RC.32 18-cylinder radials, and also 1,000-hp (746-kW) Fiat A.80 RC.41 engines.

Towards the end of 1943 a new version of the Sparviero, the SM.79-III, began appearing in small numbers with torpedo gruppi of the Aerosiluranti. This version dispensed with the ventral gondola (the bomb-aimer's position being superfluous) and the forward-firing 0.5-in (12.7-mm) machine-gun was replaced by a fixed 20-mm cannon, the latter being fired as a 'Flak deterrent' during torpedo attacks.

The second SM.79 prototype was built from the outset as a bomber. The installation of a gun position above the cockpit gave the SM.79-I and its successors an even more pronounced 'humped back'.

Short Stirling

First of the 'heavies'

The Short S.29 Stirling was the RAF's first four-engined monoplane bomber to enter service, and the first to be used operationally in World War II. Ironically, since it was also the first to be withdrawn from service, it was the only one of the three bombers to be designed from the outset with four engines, both the Avro Lancaster and Handley Page Halifax originating as twin-engined projects.

Specification B.12/36 drew submissions from Armstrong Whitworth, Short Brothers and Supermarine, and two prototypes were ordered from each of the two latter companies. In the event, the Supermarine aircraft were destroyed in an air raid before completion, so Short's design was left with a clear field. An initial production order for 100 was given to Short's at Rochester, and another 100 were ordered from Short & Harland's new Belfast factory. It was decided to build a half-scale wooden research aircraft, powered by four 90-hp (67-kW) Pobjoy Niagara engines, to test the aerodynamic qualities of the design, and this flew at Rochester on 19 September 1938. It was later re-engined with 115-hp (86-kW) Niagaras and made well over 100 flights before being scrapped in 1943.

It was only natural that, as Britain's pre-eminent flying boat builder, Short should consider using the Sunderland wing design, but an Air Ministry requirement that the span should not exceed 100 ft (30.48 m), so

that the aircraft could be housed in standard RAF hangars, meant that the wing had to be shortened, and the Stirling's high altitude performance suffered accordingly.

Prototype wrecked

The prototype Stirling made its first flight on 14 May 1939, but was written off when a brake seizure caused the landing gear to collapse on landing; hardly an auspicious start to its career. Seven months later the second prototype flew, powered like the first with 1,375-hp (1025-kW) Bristol Hercules II engines. The first production Stirling, flown on 7 May 1940, had 1,595-hp (1189-kW) Hercules XIs, and deliveries to the RAF began in August 1940, when No. 7 Sqn at Leeming began to replace its Wellingtons with the first of the new four-engined bombers. The Stirling Mk I was 'blooded' on the night of 10/11 February 1941, when three aircraft from No. 7 Sqn attacked oil storage tanks at Rotterdam.

Stirling orders then stood at 1,500 aircraft, and contracts for

Above: A No. 149 Sqn crew confers with a meteorological officer prior to another sortie. Dorsal turret-equipped Stirling bombers generally carried a crew of six.

Top: A flight of No. 1651 Heavy Conversion Unit Stirlings flies over Little Thetford, Cambridgeshire on 29 April 1942. All three aircraft were subsequenly lost, aircraft 'G', in the centre, on a raid to Hamburg exactly three months later.

Below: Late-production Stirling Mk Is of No. 7 Sqn, fitted with Fraser-Nash FN.50 dorsal turrets are fuelled and prepared for operations at Oakington in 1942.

Below: This No. 7 Sqn Stirling Mk I was captured intact – barring the crudely repaired nose damage – by the Germans, and tested by the Luftwaffe's E-Stelle at Rechlin.

Above: A well-known Stirling of the early war years was MacRobert's Reply, a No. 15 Sqn aircraft donated by the MacRobert family and also bearing their coat of arms.

manufacture were extended to cover Austin Motors at Longbridge, Birmingham, and Rootes at Stoke-on-Trent; Stirling production eventually spread to more than 20 factories, but was initially very slow as priority had been allocated to fighter construction. Another factor which held up early production was the destruction of a number of Stirlings on the assembly lines, when the Rochester and Belfast factories were bombed in August 1940.

However, production eventually got into its stride, and by the end of 1941 more than 150 Stirlings had been completed. In service the Stirling was to prove popular with its crews and very manoeuvrable – a useful attribute when it was attacked by German fighters, and one which earned it the contemporary nickname 'the fighter bomber'. One Stirling of No. 218 Sqn, returning from a night raid in June 1942, survived attacks from four German night-fighters and destroyed three, before returning battered but safe to its base.

Canadian production

Plans to build Stirlings in Canada were made in 1941, but although a contract for 140 was placed it was later cancelled. This was to have been the Stirling Mk II, powered by 1,600-hp (1193-kW) Wright Cyclone R-2600 engines, and two prototypes were built as conversions from Mk Is. They were followed by three production aircraft, but this variant was not adopted as the supply of Hercules engines was proving sufficient for requirements.

New engines for Mk III

The Stirling Mk III had 1,635-hp (1219-kW) Hercules VI or XVI engines; apart from their minimal extra power, the main advantage of this power-plant was that it was far easier to maintain. The Mk III was given a new dorsal turret, of flatter profile, to replace the angular model of the Mk I, and some internal changes were made.

Stirling production peaked at 80 aircraft a month by mid-1943, and the last to be built as bombers were completed in the autumn of 1944.

As deliveries of the Halifax and Lancaster built up, so the Stirlings began to be withdrawn for other tasks. They had two main drawbacks: an inability to attain the operating altitude of around 20,000 ft (6100 m) achieved by the newer bombers, and a bomb bay which could not be adapted to carry the ever larger bombs that were being designed. Bomber Command's last operational Stirling sortie was flown by No. 149 Sqn, on 8 September 1944, and at the peak of their use 13 squadrons had been equipped in the bombing role (Nos 7, 15, 75, 90, 101, 149, 166, 199, 214, 218, 513, 622 and 623). Total production of bomber versions amounted to 1,759, of which 712 were Mk Is and 1,047 Mk IIIs.

Undercarriage
To shorten take-offs and landings the Stirling had very tall undercarriage to give the wing a sufficient angle of incidence to provide adequate lift. This made ground handling tricky.

Wings
Though stable in flight and surprisingly manoeuvrable, thanks to its high wing loading, the Stirling consequently had a poor operational ceiling when loaded. This was due to the aircraft's 100-ft (30.48-m) span wing, made necessary by the size of pre-war RAF hangars.

Wheels
The main wheels, the tyres for which were manufactured by Dunlop, were the largest fitted to an operational aircraft during World War II.

Bomb load
While a Stirling could carry as many as 25,500 lb (11567 kg) of bombs and deliver them over a short range, it was unable to accommodate the larger bombs that the Lancaster could accept.

Stirling Mk I Srs 1

The Stirling eventually equipped seven squadrons in No. 3 Group, RAF Bomber Command. No. 7 Sqn was the first of these receiving Stirlings in August 1940, the unit taking the new bomber on its first operation, to attack an oil storage depot at Rotterdam, on the night of 10/11 February 1941. N3641, coded 'MG-D', was the machine to join No. 7 Sqn.

Undercarriage retraction
The Stirling suffered from troublesome undercarriage retraction motors, which proved inadequate for the task.

Fuel
Seven fuel tanks in each wing held a total of 2,254 Imp gal (10247 litres) of fuel, sufficient to give a radius of action of 900 miles (1448 km) in favourable weather conditions.

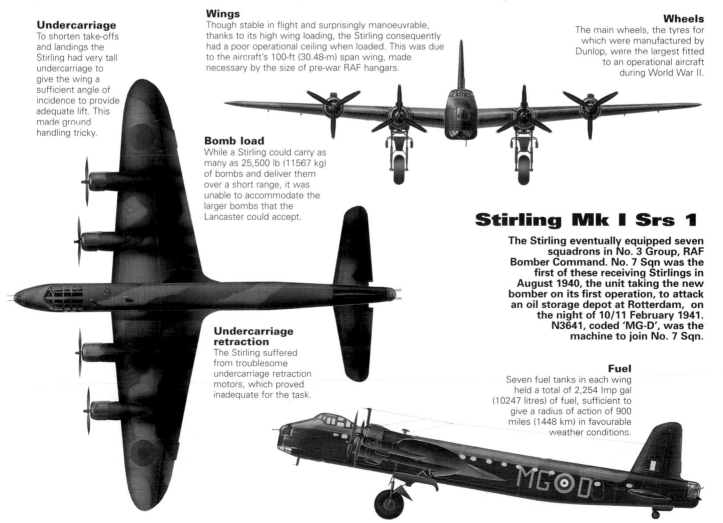

Transports and tugs

A Stirling Mk V of No. 46 Sqn conducts an air test during 1945. Note the propeller spinners, sometimes fitted, in conjunction with cooling fans, under the cowlings of Mk Vs to prevent overheating.

Official figures for the RAF Stirling bomber show that they made 18,440 sorties, dropped 27,821 tons (28268 tonnes) of bombs and laid 20,000 mines, for the loss of 769 aircraft. By mid-1943, however, the Stirling had been largely superseded, the type finding a new role as a transport and glider tug. Such was the success of the initial Mk IVs, converted from Mk III bombers, that the dedicated Mk V was built, with an eye for the post-war civil market.

EF506 was one of six Stirling Mk III bombers, from a batch of 150, converted to Mk IV standard for RAF Transport Command. Note the deleted dorsal turret and faired over nose. The nose turret was retained for defensive purposes.

From the beginning of 1944 the Stirling's main role became that of glider-tug and transport with RAF Transport Command, under the designation GT.Mk IV. Transport Command had hoped to obtain Halifaxes and Lancasters for these roles, but the former was only available in limited numbers and the latter not at all, for Bomber Command had priority.

Two Stirling Mk IIIs served as prototypes for the new version, and were first flown in 1943, one completed as a tug and the other as a troop carrier. Retaining the Mk III's engines, the Mk IV had nose and dorsal turrets removed and the apertures faired over. Glider-towing equipment was fitted in the rear fuselage, but although omitted from early conversions, the tail turret was retained in most Mk IVs.

Removing the turrets

improved ceiling and top speed, a loaded Mk IV glider tug operating at 60,000 lb (27215 kg) all up, some 10,000 lb (4536 kg) less than a Mk III bomber. In troop carrier mode, with tug equipment removed, take-off weight was as little as 58,000 lb (26308 kg) and a speed of 235 mph (378 km/h) could be maintained at 11,800 ft (3597 m).

Into service

Entering service with No. 299 Sqn on 23 January 1944, the Stirling proved efficient in its new role, also equipping Nos 190 and 620 Sqns at Fairford and No. 196 Sqn at Keevil. Operations began in January with hazardous night drops of supplies to Resistance forces in northern France. These were flown at low level, often through intense AA fire.

On D-Day Stirlings of all four

squadrons were engaged in towing Airspeed Horsa gliders to Normandy, and the type was also used for the airborne landings at Arnhem and the March 1945 attack across the Rhine. Other squadrons to use this version included Nos 138, 161, 171, 295, 570, 622 and 624.

Between D-Day and VE-Day, Stirling Mk IVs were continuously employed to fly fuel to fighter and light bomber units of the 2nd Tactical Air Force on the Continent. Each aircraft could carry 600 Imp gal (2728-litres) in 5-Imp gal (23-litre) cans.

As a glider-tug, the Stirling

Mk IV could cope with one Hamilcar or two Horsas in the assault role, or up to five Hotspurs on a ferry flight or for training. Less well known were the operations of Nos 138 and 161 (Special Duties) Sqns, flying for the Special Operations Executive (SOE) from RAF Tempsford. They had the task of supplying arms to the Resistance in occupied countries, and No. 624 Sqn engaged in similar work in the Mediterranean area (in particular over southern France in the build-up to invasion), operating from Blida in North Africa between July and September 1944.

Wearing recently applied 'invasion stripes', a Stirling Mk IV of No. 295 Sqn takes off from RAF Harwell with a Horsa glider in tow. The date was 6 June 1944 – D-Day.

Left: An elongated, faired-over nose was one of the main features of the Mk V. The propeller spinners were often removed in service.

Below: The Stirling Mk V could carry a pair of Jeeps, with trailers, or a single Jeep with a six-pounder field gun, trailer, ammunition and crew. These were loaded through a large cargo door on the starboard side of the aircraft.

Total production of the Mk IV was 321, including 120 conversions of Mk IIIs completed after their delivery, and a further 201 completed on the production line as Mk IVs. Small numbers of Stirling transports were also allocated to training units, including the Central Navigation School, which operated Mk IVs equipped with H₂S radar sets, during 1944.

The last production Stirling was the Mk V unarmed transport, first flown from Rochester in August 1944. It could carry up to 40 troops (20 if they were fully equipped paratroops), or 12 stretchers and 14 seated casualties. The lengthened nose hinged open, and there was a large loading door in the right-hand side of the rear fuselage with portable loading ramps. Two Jeeps with trailers, or a Jeep with a field gun, trailer and ammunition could be carried.

Production of the Stirling Mk V was undertaken at Belfast, and ended with the 160th aircraft, first flown on 8 December 1945. Stirling Mk Vs entered service in January 1945 with No. 46 Sqn, when it reformed at Stoney Cross in No. 47 Group, Transport Command. The following month No. 242 Sqn, also at Stoney Cross, received Mk Vs to replace its Wellington Mk XVIs.

First Mk V operations

Operations began on 17 February 1945, when No. 46 Sqn began training on a route to Maison Blanche, Algiers. The following month routes were extended to Castel Benito, Tripoli and India in April. From August the Azores were added to the list of destinations served by Stirling-equipped transport units. Trooping was an important tasking for these aircraft, regular trips being made between the UK and the Middle East, Iraq and India during 1945.

Other Stirling Mk Vs were issued to Nos 48, 158 and 299 Sqns and would have supported 'Tiger Force' in the Far East, had the war continued. The last examples in use were those of No. 46 Sqn, which were finally relinquished in March 1946 as Avro Yorks entered service – almost certainly the last Stirlings of all in RAF service. Post-war civil use, in a similar manner to the way in which Lancasters and Halifaxes were converted as airliners and freighters, failed to materialise.

Below: Mk V transport PK124/'Q', probably of No. 46 Sqn, is manoeuvred into position on the apron at Mauripur, Karachi. A former fighter squadon, No. 46 was reformed in January 1945 as a transport unit, flying freight schedules from the UK to India and Ceylon and, later, between Cairo West and Mauripur.

No. 196 Sqn Stirling Mk V PJ887, coded 'ZO-H', is shown as it appeared in early 1946, shortly after it entered service. Though it had operated in the Far East during World War II, No. 196 Sqn was flying mail runs on the Continent by 1946.

Short Sunderland

The 'Pig' that flew

Just as the Short S.23 C-class 'Empire' flying-boat marked a startling advance on all previous civil transport aircraft in Imperial Airways service, so its military derivative, the Sunderland, marked an equally great advance on marine aircraft in the RAF.

Sometimes nicknamed 'The Pig' by its crews, it was dubbed 'The Flying Porcupine' by Luftwaffe pilots who tried to attack it. When the last of these well-loved flying-boats was retired from the RAF on 20 May 1959, it had set a record of 21 years' continuous service in the same oceanic duty. It had also performed many other remarkable feats.

The Sunderland had its origins in a 1933 Air Ministry specification, R.2/33, calling for a new maritime reconnaissance flying-boat to replace the Short Singapore Mk III biplane then just coming off the production line at the Rochester works of Short Brothers. The same company's chief designer, Arthur (later Sir Arthur) Gouge, immediately began to prepare a tender to the new requirement. He was already well advanced with planning a new civil transport

flying-boat. Almost alone among British designers, Gouge realised that the all-metal stressed-skin monoplanes being built in the USA and Germany were superior aircraft; he designed the S.23 as a stressed-skin cantilever monoplane with a smooth skin and paid the greatest attention to the reduction of drag. It was an ideal basis for the new RAF 'boat, the S.25.

Gouge made his submission in 1934, the specified armament being a 37-mm Coventry Ordnance Works gun in a bow cockpit or turret and a single Lewis machine-gun in the extreme tail. Compared with the civil S.23, the military version had a completely new hull of much deeper cross-section, and a long nose projecting ahead of a flight deck quite near the wing. When construction was well advanced it was decided to alter the armament to a nose turret

with one machine-gun and a tail turret with four, a complete reversal of original thoughts on firepower. The shift in centre of gravity could only be countered by moving back the wing or altering the planform so that taper was mainly on the leading edge. The first prototype, K4774, now named Sunderland,

was completed with the original wing, basically similar to that of the C-class transport, and flown without armament by J. Lankester Parker from the River Medway on 16 October 1937. After preliminary trials it went back into the factory to have the 'swept-back' wing fitted, flying again on 7 March 1938.

Powered by 1,010-hp (753-kW) Bristol Pegasus XXII engines, more powerful than those of the civil machine, the Sunderland was far more capable in the maritime patrol role than

Above: The first S.23 prototype, K4774, rests on the slipway at Short's Rochester plant; its maiden flight took place on 16 October 1937. Later rebuilt to production standard, the aircraft remained at the MAEE until struck off in 1944.

Top: The second production Sunderland Mk I, L2160, is seen here during RAF trials in June 1938. Production aircraft differed from the prototype in having the slightly swept wing and outwardly-canted engines, both measures intended to restore the aircraft's centre-of-gravity after a powered rear turret was specified.

The Sunderland entered RAF service with No. 230 Sqn in Singapore in mid-1938. Four of the squadron's first aircraft were purchased for the RAF by the Federated Malay Sultanates and named accordingly by each of the Sultans; L2160, pictured, was named Selangor.

Though produced only in small numbers, the Sunderland Mk II (left) introduced important changes to powerplant and defensive armament. More significantly many Mk IIs were fitted with ASV Mk II radar, with its characteristic Yagi homing aerials under the outer wings and transmitter loops and dipole masts on the rear fuselage. W6050 (below) was the first example, seen here prior to its first flight in April 1941.

any previous RAF aircraft. Fuel was housed in six vertical drum tanks between the spars with a capacity of 2,025 Imp gal (9206 litres), later increased to 2,552 Imp gal (11602 litres) by four further cells aft of the rear spar. In the original Sunderland Mk I the normal crew was seven, accommodated basically on two decks with comprehensive provision for prolonged habitation, with six bunks, galley with cooking stove, workshops and stowage for a considerable quantity of equipment including four rifles and three spare propeller blades. At the upper level it was possible to walk aft from the two-pilot flight deck past the cubicles of the radio operator (left) and navigator (right) and through the deep front spar into the domain of the flight engineer, who had extensive instrument panels inside the wing centre-section.

The main offensive load, comprising up to 2,000 lb (907 kg) of bombs, depth charges, mines or other stores, was hung beneath the centre-section on carriers running on lateral tracks. In combat, large side hatches were opened beneath the wing and the weapons run out under the wings by a drive motor which cut out when the bomb carriages had reached full travel on each side. Defensive armament was concentrated in a Nash and Thompson FN.13 hydraulic tail turret, with four of the new Browning 0.303-in (7.7-mm)

guns. In the bows was an FN.11 turret with a single VGO (Vickers gas-operated) machine-gun with a winching system for retracting the turret aft so that the big anchor could be passed out through a bow hatch.

Despite its great bulk, the hull was well shaped and drag was actually lower than for the much smaller biplane Singapore Mk III. Wing loading was, of course, in the order of twice that common on RAF aircraft of the mid-1930s, but Gouge's patented flaps (which had broad chord and rotated aft about a part-cylindrical upper surface) provided increased area and added 30 per cent more lift for landing. Hydrodynamically, a new feature was the bringing of the planing bottom to a vertical knife-edge at the rear (second) step, thereafter sweeping the bottom line smoothly up and back to the tail. Flight-control surfaces were fabric-covered and driven manually, with no servotab assistance, but the Sunderland responded admirably to powerful control demands. A twin-wheel beaching chassis could be attached under the main spar and at the rear of the planing bottom.

Into service

RAF service began in June 1938 when the second production Mk I (L2159) was ferried out to No. 230 Squadron at Seletar, Singapore. About 40 were in service at the outbreak of war, and by late 1941 the total output of the Mk I had risen to

90, of which 15 were built by a second-source supplier, a works set up at the Denny shipyard at Dumbarton and run by Blackburn. From late 1939 until 1942 Sunderlands were camouflaged, though in their harsh environments paint flaked off rapidly. Early home-based units, such as Nos 204, 210 and 228 Sqns, plus No. 10 Sqn of the RAAF which arrived to collect its aircraft and stayed in the UK for the next six years, were intensively in action from the first day of the war. Successes against U-boats were at first non-existent, but rescues of torpedoed crews gave the aircraft a good reputation, starting on 18 September 1939 when two of No. 228 Squadron's aircraft had the whole crew of 34 from the *Kensington Court* in hospital an hour after their ship sank off the Scilly Isles.

By 1940 Sunderlands were being improved in various ways, notably by the addition of two VGO guns aimed from hatches at the rear of the upper deck on each side, with the front part of each hatch opening into the slipstream to give the gunner a calmer area for aiming. Other changes included the progressive addition of a second gun to the nose turret, replacement of the bracket-type de Havilland propellers by 12 ft 6 in (3.81 m) constant-speed propellers with spinners, the addition of pulsating rubber-boot de-icers to the wings and tail and, from October 1941, ASV Mk II radar which covered the upper rear of

the hull with matched dipole Yagi aerials in groups of four and added long dipole-equipped horizontal poles under the outer wings to give azimuth (homing) guidance. At the 150 mph (241 km/h) speeds which were hardly ever exceeded on patrol, these prominent arrays had little effect on performance.

Though the defensive armament was actually quite light, and contained no gun greater than rifle calibre, the Sunderland soon gained the great respect of the enemy. On 3 April 1940 a Sunderland off Norway was attacked by six Junkers Ju 88s, shot one down, forced another to land immediately, and drove the rest off. Later, another was attacked by eight Ju 88s over the Bay of Biscay and shot down three (confirmed by the convoy it was escorting).

Mk II production

In late 1941 production switched to the Sunderland Mk II, with Pegasus XVIII engines with two-speed superchargers and, in the last few examples of this mark, improved armament in a twin Browning nose turret, two more Brownings in an FN.7 dorsal turret on the right side of the hull at the trailing edge, and four Brownings in an FN.4A tail turret with ammunition doubled to 1,000 rounds per gun. Only 43 of this mark were produced, 15 of them at a third source, by the Short & Harland company at Queen's Island, Belfast (later the home of the parent company).

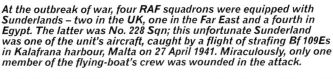

At the outbreak of war, four RAF squadrons were equipped with Sunderlands – two in the UK, one in the Far East and a fourth in Egypt. The latter was No. 228 Sqn; this unfortunate Sunderland was one of the unit's aircraft, caught by a flight of strafing Bf 109Es in Kalafrana harbour, Malta on 27 April 1941. Miraculously, only one member of the flying-boat's crew was wounded in the attack.

Supermarine Spitfire

Above: To meet an urgent Fleet Air Arm requirement for a modern carrier-based fighter in 1941, a navalised Spitfire, the Seafire, was produced, initially by converting land-based examples. The Seafire IIC variant, one of which is seen landing aboard HMS Indomitable, was one of the first variants built as such rather than by conversion – these variants did not have folding wings.

Below: The first of the Griffon-engined Spitfires to enter service, the Mk XII was the only variant to have the single-stage engine, asymmetric radiators and four-bladed propeller. This example is seen on a test flight prior to squadron delivery.

Introduction

By combining superb aerodynamics with one of the best aero-engines ever produced, R. J. Mitchell and his Supermarine team created a pure thoroughbred fighter which became a legend.

If asked to name a British aircraft of World War II, many people would pick the Spitfire. In production and front-line service throughout the war and the subject of constant development, this Supermarine design matured to become one of the greatest fighter aircraft of all time.

Supermarine's chief designer, Reginald Joseph Mitchell, had designed a monoplane fighter, the Type 224, in the early 1930s. However, this failed to win orders, the RAF preferring the Gloster Gladiator biplane. Mitchell then set about developing a new aircraft, the Type 300, this time as a private venture. An all-metal design (apart from its control surfaces), with a distinc-

tive elliptical wing plan-form, it was to be powered by Rolls-Royce's latest 12-cylinder engine, another private venture, appropriately known as the PV.12. Rated initially at 1,000 hp (746 kW), it offered an excellent power-to-weight ratio, and shared with Mitchell's airframe a great deal of development potential, something that was to be exploited to the full during the forthcoming war. In fact, it was the development of the PV.12 (soon named Merlin) and its eventual replacement, the Griffon, that was to be perhaps the most important catalyst in the Spitfire's development, as the engine lent itself to modification according to the different operational requirements placed on the aircraft.

Given the rapid development of monoplane fighter designs in Germany, it was clear to the RAF that it needed the new fighter for the home defence interceptor role. Impressed with the Type 300, soon renamed the Spitfire (much to the horror of Mitchell, who commented "It's the sort of bloody silly name they would give it!!"), the Air Ministry drew up a specification (F.37/34) around the design and ordered 310 production examples in June 1936. A prototype had flown in March 1936, and the first production Mk Is, fitted with a

Merlin II rated at 1,060 hp (791 kW) and armed with eight 0.303-in (7.7-mm) Browning machine-guns, reached No. 19 Squadron, RAF at Duxford in August 1938.

By the time war had broken out, a total of 1,960 Spitfires was

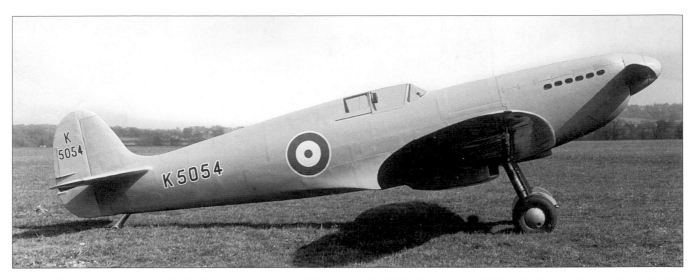

Above: The prototype Spitfire, K5054, first flew on 5 May 1936 from Eastleigh airfield near Southampton, with chief test pilot 'Mutt' Summers at the controls. Over the next three years, the aircraft accumulated about 260 hours' flying time. Its career finally came to an end on 4 September 1939, when Flt Lt 'Spinner' White was killed as the aircraft nosed over onto its back during a landing mishap. The aircraft was not repaired.

Right: Of the 20,000 Spitfires (of all variants) that were built between 1936 and 1948, over 200 survive, around 50 in an airworthy condition. Operating as a flying memorial to former Battle of Britain pilots is this Mk VB, owned by the RAF. The aircraft is displayed throughout the summer at airshows across the UK.

on order, of which 306 Mk Is had been delivered. The Spitfire saw action for the first time on 16 October 1939, when Nos 602 and 603 Squadrons engaged Luftwaffe bombers off the coast of Scotland. Both units were successful in downing German aircraft – the Spitfire's first aerial victories. Nineteen squadrons were operating the type by mid-1940; almost a third of these aircraft were lost to Luftwaffe fighters while covering the withdrawal from Dunkirk during May.

So began the production life of the Spitfire, which was to last 10 years and encompass an almost bewildering array of 22 variants. The aircraft filled not only the interceptor role, but also those of fighter-bomber and reconnaissance, and operated also as the carrierborne Seafire.

In all, more than 20,400 Spitfires were built, from the Mk I to the F.Mk 24, serving for more than 20 years. Not only were they operated by the RAF – which retired its last front-line examples in 1954, 'officially' withdrew the type in 1957, but returned a Mk XIX to service in 1963 to train Lightning and Javelin pilots

how to dogfight Indonesian Mustangs – but also by the air arms of at least 20 other nations. Neither was the type's war service limited to World War II. Burma, Egypt, France, India, Israel and the Netherlands all flew the Spitfire in anger during the 1950s.

If the Spitfire had a handicap, it was that it was designed as a home-based interceptor and, while it was fast, agile and possessed an excellent climb rate, it was short on range. This was something that the RAF had to live with and on which Supermarine expended much

effort trying to address. (While long-range variants were built, these were mainly specialised reconnaissance aircraft; once deployed overseas, Spitfire fighters and fighter-bombers were obliged to carry belly-mounted fuel tanks almost as a matter of operational necessity.)

It was the constant development of the Spitfire during the 1940s, born of necessity but facilitated by the brilliance of both the airframe's design, and that of its engine, that ensured the longevity of the Spitfire's production and service.

Above: The ultimate Spitfire – the Seafire FR.Mk 47 – served with several Fleet Air Arm squadrons in the Korean War, including No. 800 Sqn. The aircraft was involved mainly in ground-attack sorties, armed with rockets.

Right: Operating in the high-altitude photo-reconnaissance role, the PR.Mk 19s were the last variants to see active service with the RAF. It was not until July 1957 that the one remaining example, PS853, was finally retired.

Spitfire Mk I

As the first of over 20 distinct fighter variants of this most famous of all combat aircraft, the Spitfire Mk I was the equal of any fighter in 1940.

In early June 1936, Britain's Air Ministry placed an order for 310 examples of Supermarine's new Spitfire fighter, to be delivered at a cost not exceeding £4,500 excluding engine, armament and instruments. The significance of this order to the small Supermarine concern cannot be exaggerated and the circumstances were at that time unique. The Spitfire prototype K5054 had only just begun its acceptance trials at Martlesham Heath and no test reports had been issued at the time the order was placed. In a rare and inspired moment of foresight, the Air Ministry had put its faith in an unproven design, an act which was to have great significance in the global conflict then brewing.

Armour
As delivered, the first Spitfires had no armour protection for the pilot or fuel tanks. This was added as war approached.

Gas detection patch
The yellow diamond on the wing of this aircraft was a fabric patch treated with a chemical agent that would change colour in the presence of poison gas. Gas attack was a major fear in the early months of the war.

Canopy
The straight-topped canopy of the first Mk Is was replaced by the familiar 'blown' hood. This was done more to accommodate taller pilots than to improve visibility.

Armament
With its armament of eight 0.303-in (7.7-mm) machine-guns, the Spitfire Mk I had a lighter weight of fire (less 'hitting power') than the Bf 109E with its two cannon and two machine-guns. Cannon were trialled on the Mk IB but frequently jammed in combat.

Wings
Much of the success of the Spitfire was due to its thin and gracefully tapered wing. There was little room for larger weapons, however, and later marks gained bulges on the wing to allow for the ammunition drums of two or four Hispano cannon.

'Sailor's Spit'
This aircraft was flown by the South African ace Adolf 'Sailor' Malan during August 1940 when he was made commander of No. 74 Squadron based at Hornchurch. By the end of the year Malan had been credited with 18 victories.

Undercarriage
The narrow track of the main undercarriage made for tricky ground handling and led to many accidents. This was also true of the Bf 109.

Propeller
By the time of the Battle of Britain, almost all Mk Is had been fitted with de Havilland or Rotol constant-speed propellers. Earlier aircraft had Watts fixed-pitch or de Havilland two-pitch units.

Spitfire Mk I

Forever remembered for its part in the Battle of Britain, the Spitfire Mk I took on the deadly Messerschmitt Bf 109E in daily combat. This aircraft is typical of the configuration of Spitfires of the period.

Code letters
As with the black/white underside, the squadron code letter system was introduced as a response to the Munich crisis of September 1938. Before this, RAF fighters had worn a squadron badge or the squadron number as unit identification and were not individually coded.

SPECIFICATION
Spitfire Mk I
Type: single-seat interceptor fighter
Powerplant: one Rolls-Royce Merlin II or III rated at 1,030 hp (768 kW) at 16,250 ft (4953 m)
Performance: maximum speed 346 mph (557 km/h) at 15,500 ft (4724 m); maximum range 630 miles (1014 km); range at maximum cruising speed 415 miles (668 km); time to climb 6 minutes 51 seconds to 15,000 ft (4572 m); service ceiling 30,500 ft (9296 m)
Dimensions: span 36 ft 10 in (11.23 m); length 29 ft 11 in (9.12 m); height 12 ft 8 in (3.86 m); wing area 242 sq ft (22.48 m²)
Weights: empty 4,517 lb (2049 kg); loaded 5,844 lb (2651 kg)
Armament: eight Browning Mk II 0.303-in (7.7-mm) machine-guns

Underside colours
In April 1939 black and white undersides were introduced on fighters as a recognition feature. In June 1940 the undersurfaces were ordered to be painted in Sky. The black port wing reappeared for a brief period from November.

Almost two years elapsed before the flight of the first production Spitfire, K9787. By that time, the design had been refined and a huge new 'shadow' factory had been built at Castle Bromwich to handle the bulk of Spitfire production. This began with the second batch of 1,000 aircraft which was ordered in April 1939.

Unanticipated difficulties in expanding the aircraft production industry in general, plus problems with the new technology incorporated into the Spitfire, led to delays in the type's service entry. By August 1938, however, No. 19 Squadron, the first of dozens of

Above: Seen here before delivery, this Mk I went on to serve with No. 64 Squadron and was damaged in June 1940.

Above: The 48th production Mk I was modified by the Air Ministry for an attempt on the world landplane speed record. The blue and silver 'Speed Spitfire' was fitted with a 'sprint' Merlin engine, but never actually attempted the record flight. With the fall of France, Spitfires were needed in the front line and it was converted to the PR role.

Left: As war approached, many countries wanted to buy or licence-build Spitfires. Here a Mk I is demonstrated for French officers. One Mk I was delivered to France in late-1939.

Spitfire units in many countries, was fully equipped at Duxford.

In the last few months of peace, more squadrons formed. The aircraft gained the equipment it needed for fighting a modern war – notably, armour plate and variable-pitch propellers that allowed maximum engine efficiency in all flight regimes.

On 3 September 1939, when Britain declared war on Germany, the RAF had almost 11 fully equipped Spitfire squadrons. Slightly over 10 per cent of the 306 aircraft that had been delivered had been lost in accidents. Due to Air Chief Marshall Dowding's reluctance to send any of the precious Spitfires to France in May 1940, when the Luftwaffe was cutting through the air assets of the British Expeditionary Force, aircraft strength was husbanded so that 19 Spitfire squadrons were available at the beginning of the Battle of Britain in July.

Despite the introduction of improved marks, beginning with the Mk II during the Battle itself, the Mk I soldiered on in secondary and training units until virtually the end of the war. The Mk I also served as the basis for the first PR (photo reconnaissance) versions of the Spitfire. Of the many nations that showed interest in the Spitfire Mk I, including Finland, France, Greece, Norway, Sweden and even China, none was able to complete a sale before Britain's immediate needs precluded the possibility of exports. Portugal was an exception, taking delivery of several Mk Is during 1943, from a pre-war order for 15.

Left: The Spitfires of No. 19 Squadron are seen at Duxford five months before the outbreak of war. They exhibit many features found on the earliest aircraft, including protruding guns, fixed-pitch two-bladed propellers and a mix of 'flat' and bulged canopies.

Spitfire Mks II-IV
Fighting improvements

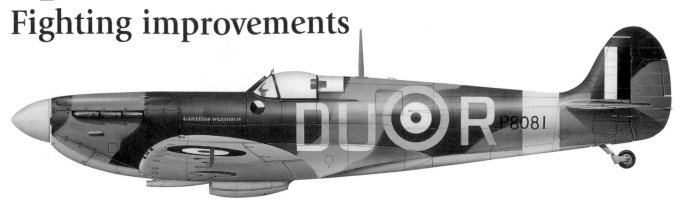

A lengthy process of evolution through combat experience saw the Spitfire mature, via the Mk II, into a fighter of legendary abilities.

A number of improvements were introduced to Spitfire Mk Is, both in service and on the production line. Late Mk Is featured three-bladed propellers for improved performance, along with an armoured windscreen and armour protection for the pilot and the forward fuel tank. This latter item was positioned immediately ahead of the cockpit and was protected by a 3-mm thick slab of light-alloy armour. Any increase in weight was compensated for by the aircraft's increased efficiency in combat and the additional performance provided by the new propeller.

From early 1940, IFF (Identification Friend or Foe) units had been fitted to Spitfires. This equipment transmitted a coded response when interrogated by British radar, identifying the aircraft clearly on screen.

Merlin XII into action

Car-manufacturer Nuffield was tasked with production of the Spitfire Mk II, in its huge Castle Bromwich factory near Birmingham. When the new aircraft began rolling off the line in June 1940, they incorporated all of the improvements embodied in the late Mk Is.

Externally, the two marks appeared very similar, the main difference being in engine type. The new machine introduced the Rolls-Royce Merlin XII, which produced some 110 hp (82 kW) of additional power, compared to the Merlin II or III of the Spitfire Mk I. Thus, the Mark II was able to demonstrate a slightly improved maximum speed and rate of climb.

Wing flexing

Both the Hawker Hurricane and the Spitfire had entered the Battle of Britain with an armament of eight 0.303-in (7.7-mm) Browning machine-guns. While proving adequate in combat against unarmoured aircraft, it soon became clear that these weapons were somewhat deficient in firepower when used against armoured machines. They lacked the power to punch through armour plating, or to puncture self-sealing fuel tanks. Cannon armament was seen as

Flight Lieutenant Adolphe Vybiral of No. 312 'Czech' Squadron flew this Spitfire Mk II from Ayr, Scotland during November 1941. Named GARFIELD WESTON IV, the aircraft wears the Ocean Grey/Dark Green over Medium Sea Grey camouflage that was introduced on production Spitfires from 16 August 1941.

Above: Still flying regularly with the RAF's Battle of Britain Memorial Flight, Spitfire Mk IIA P7350 is currently the oldest airworthy Spitfire. The machine is maintained and flown in pristine condition.

Below: An immaculate Spitfire Mk II demonstrates the type's graceful lines and its similarity to the Mk I. Neat fairings over each of the machine-gun muzzles in the leading edge and the underwing openings for the spent-cartridge ejection chutes are particularly noteworthy.

Above: Women's Royal Air Force (WRAF) ground crew work on Spitfire Mk IIAs of No. 411 (Canadian) Squadron at RAF Digby in October 1941. The unit was formed on Spitfires on 16 June 1941 and flew, successively, Mk Vs and IXs until disbanded on 21 March 1946.

the perfect remedy to this problem, and the French 20-mm Hispano Suiza Type 404 cannon, as used in the Morane MS.406 fighter, as the perfect weapon.

Early trials with Mark I Spitfires proved disappointing. Rigidly mounted in the MS.406, the cannon had worked well, but if fired from the wing of a Spitfire pulling *g* during a manoeuvre, the natural flexure of the wing caused the weapons to misfeed and jam. A number of engineering changes were introduced during the summer of 1940, solving the problem and allowing Supermarine to produce the Spitfire Mk IIB. This machine carried two of the 20-mm cannon and four machine-guns. On its introduction into service, all-Browning Mk IIs became IIAs. In a similar manner, Mk Is had become IAs when a few cannon-armed Mk IBs were produced.

A further Mk II variant appeared when about 50 aircraft were modified for use in the air-sea rescue role. Powered by the Merlin XX and retaining the

armament of the Mk IIA, these machines were designated Spitfire Mk IIC. Modifications to the rear fuselage enabled the carriage and dropping of canisters containing an inflatable dinghy and other emergency equipment.

Although more powerful, the Spitfire Mk II represented little advance structurally over the Mk I. The Mk III was therefore to mark the first major step forwards in Spitfire evolution. The internal structure was

redesigned and strengthened and a retractable tail wheel installed. Power was provided by the 1390-hp (1036-kW) Merlin Mk XX and the wings were clipped to a span of 30 ft 6 in (9.50 m). Orders for 1,000 Mk IIIs were placed, but the demand for Merlin Mk XXs to power the Hurricane, combined with the forthcoming availability of the Merlin 45-powered Spitfire Mk V, led to the cancellation of all Mk IIIs.

Only one true Mk III was completed (a second was converted from a Mk V) and this was flown for the first time, by Jeffrey Quill, on 16 March 1940. By September 1941, the wings had been returned to their normal span and the aircraft was employed by Rolls-Royce as a Merlin 61 testbed.

Griffon powerplant

On 8 November 1939, the Ministry of Aircraft Production expressed an interest in a Griffon II-powered version of the Spitfire. Rolls-Royce had developed the Griffon from its Type R Schneider Trophy-winning engines and it seemed to have the potential for greater power than the Merlin.

With the promise of improved all-round performance, the new Spitfire was developed as the Mk IV. A number of armament options were considered, including six 20-mm cannon, four cannon and four 0.303-in (7.7-mm) machine-guns or 12 machine-guns.

One prototype Spitfire Mk IV was completed and it demonstrated that the Mk IV was superior to the Mk V then in development, and all earlier marks. However, a new threat in the form of the Fw 190 led to the underdeveloped Mk IV being abandoned, in favour of the Merlin 61-powered Mk IX.

Just one Spitfire Mk IV was built and it is pictured here with a mock-up installation of six 20-mm Hispano cannon in the wings. A universal wing was proposed for the Mk IV, capable of mounting any of its specified machine-gun and cannon combinations with minimum modifications.

Spitfire Mks V-VI

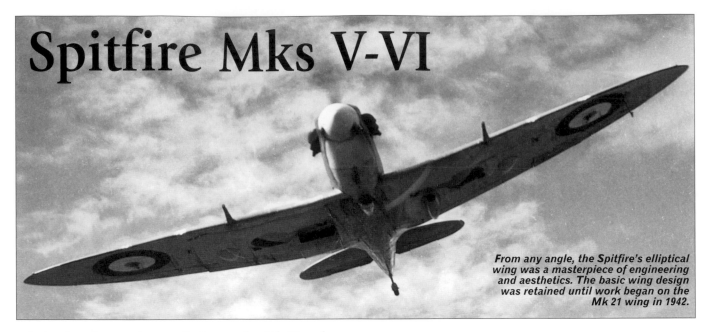

From any angle, the Spitfire's elliptical wing was a masterpiece of engineering and aesthetics. The basic wing design was retained until work began on the Mk 21 wing in 1942.

Introduced as a stopgap between the Mk II and Mk III, the Spitfire Mk V became one of the most successful marks of Supermarine's legendary fighter. It served in the UK and overseas as an interceptor and fighter-bomber.

Late in 1940, a Merlin 45 engine was installed in Spitfire Mk IA K9788, which was to act as the Spitfire Mk V prototype. Flight tests of the aircraft began in December and quickly proved that the new mark offered a significant increase in performance. Following a severe mishap to K9788, Rolls-Royce was ordered to convert a further 46 Mk I airframes to Mk V standard. The intention was that these machines would act as a stopgap measure before the Spitfire Mk III entered service, but the Mk V proved so successful that the Mk III, which was further from production status, was abandoned. Consequently, an order for 1,500 Mk IIIs was transferred to the Mk V.

Initial production Spitfire Mk Vs were powered by the Merlin 45 engine which was capable of producing 1,515 hp (1130 kW) at 11,000 ft (3353 m) using +16 lb (7.26 kg) of super-charger boost. Apart from the new engine, other changes from Mk II standard were relatively minor, and the new variant easily replaced the Mks I and II on the production lines. A large number of early Mk Vs were converted from Mk I airframes, with 100 Mk IAs becoming Mk VAs with eight 0.303-in (7.7-mm) machine-guns; most of the remaining Mk V conversions were VBs from Mk IB airframes with two 20-mm cannon and four 0.303-in (7.7-mm) machine guns. Throughout 1941 the production of Spitfires increased steadily, allowing a major expansion of the force. By the end of 1941, Fighter Command had 46 squadrons equipped with Spitfires, compared to 19 squadrons at the end of the Battle of Britain.

A stronger Spitfire

The initial production versions of the Spitfire V – the VA and the VB – used Mk I and Mk II airframes with the minimum of change necessary to accommodate the Merlin 45 engine. The extra weight of the new engine and additional items of equipment reduced the fighter's

Above: Three Spitfire Mk VBs were converted to floatplane configuration. The aircraft featured four-bladed propellers, increased fin area and a large ventral fin. Flown from the Great Bitter Lake in Egypt, the aircraft were not successful. The project was abandoned early in 1944.

Right: Spitfire LF.Mk VC AR501 is owned and operated by the Shuttleworth Collection. The machine was delivered to No. 310 (Czech) Sqn in July 1942 and made its first post-restoration flight in 1975.

strength factors, however. To restore them, the Mk V airframe was redesigned at several points to strengthen the structure. It was also fitted with the so-called 'Universal' wing, with provision to carry eight 0.303-in (7.7-mm) machine-guns, two 20-mm cannon and four machine-guns, or four 20-mm cannon. In practice, most aircraft carried the same armament as the Mk VB – two cannon and four machine-guns – although a few were fitted with four 20-mm cannon.

The new sub-variant, designated the Mk VC, appeared in October 1941, and as the war in the desert intensified the majority of Mk VCs were sent overseas to the Mediterranean, the Middle East and North Africa. The problems inherent in operations

under such harsh, sandy conditions had been foreseen and many Mk VCs were delivered with the Vokes filter fitted, while several Mk VBs were retrofitted. This bulky piece of equipment prevented sand entering the finely balanced and easily damaged Merlin engine. Later, a much smaller filter was developed by No. 103 Maintenance Unit, RAF, at Aboukir, Egypt, whose Aboukir filter caused dramatically less drag than the Vokes installation.

Spitfire Vs to Malta

As the campaign in North Africa progressed, the need arose for immediate Allied fighter reinforcements on the island of Malta. In answer to this requirement, Supermarine designed a 90-Imp gal (410-litre) drop tank to fit under the fuselage of the Spitfire. The first delivery of Spitfires to Malta took place on 7 March 1942, when 15 aircraft

A Merlin-46 powered Spitfire Mk VC, EE627, was flown to No. 602 Sqn on 19 October 1942. On 29 November it was passed to No. 29, before serving on three Operational Training Units (OTUs). The aircraft was struck off charge on 5 June 1945, having survived the war intact. As later marks were introduced, many of the surviving Mk Vs joined OTUs.

were transported from the UK aboard the aircraft-carrier HMS *Eagle*. The aircraft were able to take off for the final leg of their journey using the extra range offered by their auxiliary tanks. Before the end of the month, the carrier had completed two more delivery runs, bringing the total number of Spitfires that had reached the island to 31. The use of aircraft-carriers to deliver fighters to Malta was an enormously expensive business, however. Each

time these valuable warships put to sea, a major fleet operation was necessary to protect them.

At the request of the Air Ministry, therefore, Supermarine engineers began work on one of the most difficult challenges with which they were ever faced: to devise a way to extend the Spitfire's ferry range to 1,100 miles (1770 km), sufficient for it to fly from Gibraltar to Malta in a single hop. The solution was to fit a huge 170-Imp gal (772-litre) drop tank under

the fuselage, a 29-Imp gal (132-litre) auxiliary tank in the rear fuselage and an enlarged oil tank under the nose. For the flights, all non-essential equipment was removed from the fighter and its armament was reduced to two 0.303-in (7.7-mm) Browning machine-guns for self-protection.

During October and November 1942, 17 modified Spitfires set out from Gibraltar to make the lengthy flight to Malta; all except one made it. That distance was about as far as from London to St Petersburg, a remarkable feat for an aircraft originally designed as a short-range interceptor. Upon arrival on Malta, the fighters had the extra tanks removed and the rest of the armament fitted, to ready them for operations.

Australian failure

While the Spitfire Mk V was proving itself as an exceptional warplane in Europe and North Africa, the Royal Australian Air Force (RAAF) was less than satisfied. Operating against Japanese raiders from remote airfields which lacked the equipment to support sustained combat operations, the RAAF

suffered a shortage of spare parts and problems with the Spitfires themselves. The fighter had never previously operated in a true tropical environment close to the equator. On the ground, the aircraft had to face extremely high temperatures and high humidity. At altitude, the Spitfires encountered air temperatures lower than any they had previously encountered. Those very low temperatures caused repeated failures of the constant-speed units (CSUs). The CSU controlled the pitch of the propeller blades, continually adjusting their angle so that the engine ran at its most efficient speed of 3,000 rpm. At very low temperatures, the oil in the CSU was liable to congeal, causing the propeller blades to move into fully fine pitch. When that happened, engine rpm raced uncontrollably to around the 4,000 mark. With the Merlin threatening to shake itself to pieces, the pilot had to shut it down immediately. Then he had either to bail out or make a forced landing. Several Spitfires based in northern Australia were lost to CSU failures, and the problem was not solved until the RAAF received the Mk VIII.

Pressurized Mk VI

In order to counter a perceived high-altitude bomber threat, Supermarine developed the RAF's first operational pressurised aircraft.

After the Battle of Britain there were fears that the Luftwaffe might be about to introduce new bomber types able to attack from altitudes above 30,000 ft (9150 m). To meet this perceived threat, a high-altitude interceptor version of the Spitfire was developed, following pressurisation tests with a Spitfire Mk V. Based on the Mk V airframe, the Mk VI was the first RAF aircraft fitted with a pressure cabin to enter regular service. The 1,415-hp (1055-kW) Merlin 47 engine

fitted to this variant drove a four-bladed Rotol propeller and had an additional blower to supply air to the pressurised cabin, giving a pressure differential of 2 psi (13.79 kPa). Thus, when the fighter was at its maximum altitude of 37,000 ft (11280 m), the equivalent altitude in the cabin was 28,000 ft (8536 m). Special bulkheads fore and aft of the cockpit contained the cabin pressurisation, while the sealed canopy could be jettisoned in an emergency but could not be slid back in the traditional manner. The Mk VI also had an extended-span 'B' wing with pointed tips, giving an additional 6.5 sq ft (0.x6 m²) of wing area

and improved performance at extreme altitudes. From early 1942, the Mk VI began reaching Nos 616 and 124 Sqns but soon proved incapable of reaching the Luftwaffe's high-flying Ju 86P-2 reconnaissance aircraft. Six Mk VIs flown from Aboukir to counter similar enemy reconnaissance activity proved incapable of matching the altitude capabilities of locally modified Mk VCs. In addition, 12 aircraft were based in the Orkney and Shetland Islands, from which resting Fighter Command squadrons flew them against occasional German intruders. Only 100 Spitfire Mk VIs were built, all at Supermarine factories.

Above: The Mk VI featured distinctive extended wingtips, a modified cockpit structure and Merlin 47 powerplant. Although the Mk VI concept seemed promising, the aircraft proved to be a disappointment.

Right: Air was fed to the cockpit pressursation system via an air intake beneath the engine exhausts on the starboard side. The four-bladed propeller of the Mk VI helped distinguish it from the Mk V.

Spitfire Mks XII, XIV & XVIII

With the Rolls-Royce Merlin reaching the outer limits of its development potential, the Griffon – originating from a racing engine – was the logical choice to power the next generation of Spitfires.

As early as 1939, Supermarine had been looking at possible alternatives to the Merlin. Among them was the Rolls-Royce Griffon, a derivative of the 'R' racing engine fitted to Supermarine's pre-war S.6B floatplanes. With a capacity one third larger than that of the Merlin, the Griffon offered a sizeable increase in power, but accomplished this in an engine that was only 3 in (7.62 cm) longer than the Merlin and just 600 lb (272 kg) heavier.

A 'Griffon-Spitfire' prototype, the Mk IV, flew in November 1941. This was effectively a modification of the Merlin-engined Mk III, but fitted with a 1,735-hp (1294-kW) Griffon IIB. Impressed by the performance of the new aircraft, the Air Ministry ordered the Mk IV into production, with modifications, as the Mk XX, although its designation was to change to Mk XII before it entered service. The Spitfire Mk XII used what was essentially a Mk V or VIII airframe, with 'C' wing armament (usually four 20-mm cannon) and 'clipped' wingtips to improve roll rate. Its role was that of low-level interceptor, countering Fw 190 and Bf 109G fighter-bombers raiding coastal targets in southern England.

Mk XII enters service

One hundred Mk XIIs were built in all, the first entering service in February 1943 with No. 41 Squadron. No. 91 Squadron followed in April and was the only other unit so-equipped. As well as defensive

Top: No. 610 'County of Chester' Squadron, Royal Auxiliary Air Force, operated Spitfires throughout World War II and into the early 1950s, picking up Mk XIVs from January 1944. Its first Spitfires were Mk Is, which joined the squadron in 1939.

Above: The Spitfire Mk XII was essentially a modified Mk VC. This aircraft served with the RAF's first Griffon-Spitfire unit, No. 41 Squadron.

patrols, low-altitude sweeps over Europe were also undertaken.

While the Mk XII was the fastest fighter in the RAF at low level, its performance anywhere above medium altitude was inferior to that of the Merlin-engined Mk IX. Thus, the Mk XIV followed the Mk XII into service

in the spring of 1944 as another interim type, pending the arrival of the definitive 'Griffon-Spitfire' (the Mk 21). The Mk IV featured a Griffon 65 with a two-stage supercharger to improve performance at altitude, a strengthened fuselage, a five-bladed propeller and, initially, the four-cannon 'C' wing. A 'teardrop' canopy and the 'E' wing (with two cannon and two 0.5-in/12.7-mm machine-guns) were features of later production aircraft; many of these aircraft had 'clipped' wings. From the autumn of 1944, a considerable number were completed as FR.Mk XIVEs for the low-level

Looking very similar to a late-production Mk XIV, the Mk XVIII featured the Griffon 65 engine, 'teardrop' canopy and 'E' wing armament of the earlier mark. NH872 was the 11th production example.

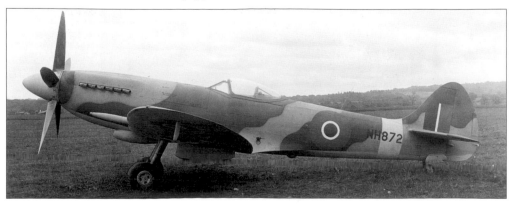

Based at Tan Son Nhut, French Indo-China, No. 273 Squadron operated FR.Mk XIVs briefly from November 1945.

tactical reconnaissance role, with an oblique camera installed behind the cockpit.

Nos 610, 91 and 322 Squadrons were the first units equipped with the Mk XIV, which entered service in the south of England in time to counter V-1 'flying bomb' attacks on London.

After D-Day, the Allied invasion of Europe in June 1944, the Mk XIV became the main air superiority fighter type employed by the RAF's tactical force in Europe (the 2nd Tactical Air Force) until the end of the war. Many also served as

ighter-bombers. Plans were in hand to ship Mk XIVs to the Far East, where the first examples arrived in June 1945 to re-equip No. 11 Squadron, but none were operational before the war ended. Mk XIV production reached 957, post-war operators including India, Belgium and Thailand.

Virtually indistinguishable from a late-production FR.Mk XIVE, the Mk XVIII featured the same Griffon 65 engine as the earlier mark, but had a strengthened fuselage and greater fuel capacity, the latter provided by two 31-Imp gal

(141-litre) fuel tanks in the rear fuselage. First flown in June 1945, the Mk XVIII was too late for war service, equipping No. 60 Squadron, RAF in Singapore from January 1947 and five other fighter squadrons in the Middle East and Far East.

Post-war Mk XVIIIs

However, Mk XVIIIs were to see action post-war. Aircraft of Nos 28 and 60 Squadrons, RAF carried out fighter-bomber sorties against guerillas during the first months of the Malayan uprising, until finally replaced by de Havilland Vampires in 1951.

Meanwhile, in the Middle East in early 1949, No. 208 Squadron's FR.Mk XVIIIs found themselves in air-to-air combat with Israeli Spitfire Mk IXs. In an infamous incident on 7 January, four of No. 208's aircraft were downed by aircraft of No. 101 Squadron, Israeli Air Force.

Altogether, 300 Mk XVIIIs were built, the final 100 to FR.Mk XVIII fighter-reconnaissance standard, with a single fuselage fuel tank and camera equipment. The only Mk XVIII operator other than the RAF was the Royal Indian Air Force, which received 20 after VJ-Day.

Five-bladed propeller
To absorb the extra power of the Griffon 65, the Spitfire Mk XIV sported a five-bladed Rotol propeller in place of the four-bladed example fitted to the Mk XII.

Spitfire FR.Mk XIVE

NM821 *Fochinell* was an FR.Mk XIVE of No. II (AC) Squadron, a tactical reconnaissance unit, based in Germany in September 1945 as part of the British Air Forces of Occupation (BAFO).

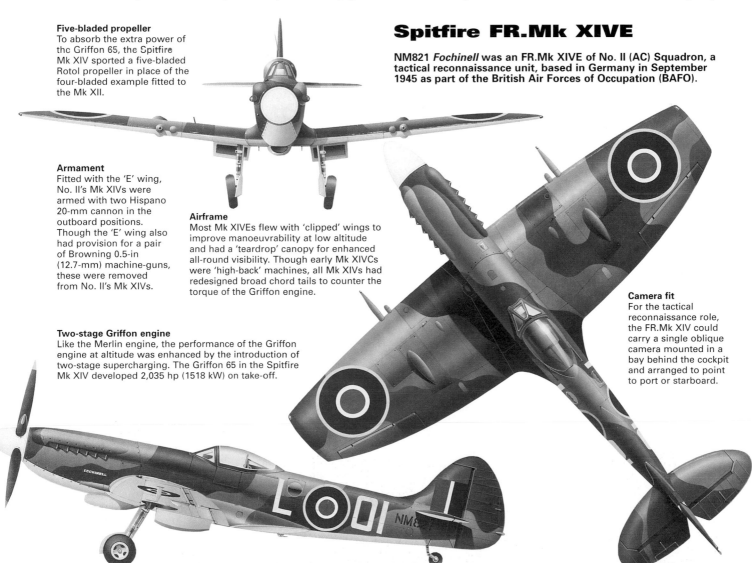

Armament
Fitted with the 'E' wing, No. II's Mk XIVs were armed with two Hispano 20-mm cannon in the outboard positions. Though the 'E' wing also had provision for a pair of Browning 0.5-in (12.7-mm) machine-guns, these were removed from No. II's Mk XIVs.

Airframe
Most Mk XIVEs flew with 'clipped' wings to improve manoeuvrability at low altitude and had a 'teardrop' canopy for enhanced all-round visibility. Though early Mk XIVCs were 'high-back' machines, all Mk XIVs had redesigned broad chord tails to counter the torque of the Griffon engine.

Two-stage Griffon engine
Like the Merlin engine, the performance of the Griffon engine at altitude was enhanced by the introduction of two-stage supercharging. The Griffon 65 in the Spitfire Mk XIV developed 2,035 hp (1518 kW) on take-off.

Camera fit
For the tactical reconnaissance role, the FR.Mk XIV could carry a single oblique camera mounted in a bay behind the cockpit and arranged to point to port or starboard.

The Spitfire PR.Mk IC introduced a further increase in range over the Mk IB, by adding a 30-Imp gal (136-litre) fuel tank under the port wing. This counterbalanced the two 8-in (20.3-cm) lens cameras in the flattened blister under the starboard wing.

The first PR variants

Of all the Spitfire models, the least-known are perhaps the photo-reconnaissance variants. Yet it was these aircraft that were the most important Allied strategic reconnaissance machines of the European theatre and, together with the Mosquito, made up the bulk of the Allies' camera-equipped assets.

Shortly before the outbreak of World War II, a young RAF officer, F/O Maurice 'Shorty' Longbottom, presented a report to the Air Ministry in which he outlined the way in which single, unarmed, high-speed aircraft, based on a fighter like the Spitfire, could be utilised in the strategic reconnaissance role, in place of traditional converted bomber types. Weight savings, gained by the removal of armament and other unnecessary equipment, would allow the fitting of extra fuel tanks to enable long-range sorties to be carried out.

Nothing was done about this suggestion until the RAF's Bristol Blenheims began to suffer heavy losses in the opening months of the war. The Air Ministry persuaded RAF Fighter Command to part with two of its precious Spitfire Mk Is, these becoming the first of a whole family of 'PR' Spitfires.

The first of these two Spitfire PR.Mk IAs – unarmed, with a 5-in (12.7-cm) focal length, vertically-mounted camera in each wing and painted light green – flew the inaugural Spitfire PR mission on 18 November 1939.

Taking off from a base at Séclin, France, the sortie photographed Aachen from 33,000 ft (10058 m). Although there were teething problems, the concept had been proven. The Spitfire was the ideal type and, most importantly, sustained a fraction of the losses of the RAF's Blenheim force on its early sorties.

Eight Spitfire PR variants, derived from early single-stage Merlin-engined Mk I fighter aircraft, were produced, the most widely used of which was the PR.Mk ID (PR.Mk IV), which served until 1943.

Spitfire PR.Mk IG

This aircraft, R7059, was built as a Mk I fighter and as such made its maiden flight from Eastleigh in February 1941. Converted the following month for the low-level reconnaissance role, as a PR.Mk IG, the aircraft was delivered to No. 1 PRU in May. Based with a detachment at St. Eval in Cornwall, the aircraft was engaged in low-level 'dicing' sorties over Brest harbour.

Powerplant
A mix of powerplants was fitted to the Mk I-derived PR Spitfires. The Types A and B were completed with Merlin IIIs, the Type C initially flew with Merlin IIs and XIIs, while the Type D was designed to take the Merlin 45/46. The Type G/Mk VII initially had a Merlin III fitted, though most were re-engined with Merlin 45s to gain the extra power.

Armament
For self-defence, the aircraft retained the fighter's armament of eight 0.303-in (7.7-mm) Browning machine-guns, mounted in standard 'A' wings.

Fuel
The two main fuel tanks, with a total capacity of 85 Imp gal (386 litres), were mounted behind the engine. In addition, this variant carried a 29-Imp gal (132-litre) tank in the rear fuselage immediately behind the cockpit.

Camera installation
The camera installation was located in the rear fuselage, aft of the additional fuel tank. The aircraft carried a 5-in (12.7-cm) focal length camera in an oblique mounting facing to port. In addition, the aircraft carried two vertical cameras, one with a 5-in and one with a 14-in (35.6-cm) lens, in the rear fuselage below the oblique camera.

Colours and markings
This Spitfire carried the very pale pink/off-white colour scheme developed by the PRU for aircraft photographing targets from below the cloud layer. During the early war period, the PRU had free rein to experiment with paint schemes, as evidenced by the non-standard colours used in the national markings and the positioning of the roundels on the upper surface of the wings. The aircraft carries the 'LY' codes of No. 1 PRU; no individual identification letter was carried.

Cockpit canopy
Bulged blisters on the canopy sides gave improved vision to the rear and below.

PR.Mk IA

Two Spitfire Mk IA fighters (N3069 and N3071) were converted to unarmed 'Type A' standard, with a 5-in focal length, vertically-mounted camera in each wing and a coat of light-green paint known as 'Camotint'. Here, N3071 is seen at Séclin, France on 18 November 1939, being run up prior to making the historic first PR flight.

PR.Mk IB

As the PR.Mk IA had its limitations – its 5-in (12.7-cm) camera did not produce sufficiently detailed pictures and the aircraft's range was limited – the PR.Mk IB was introduced in January 1940. Fitted with an 8-in (20.3-cm) camera and an additional 29-Imp gal (132-litre) fuel tank in the rear fuselage, the Mk IB also introduced what became known as 'PRU blue' paint. Few were produced; this aircraft (P9331) was operated by No. 212 Sqn in 1940.

PR.Mk IC (PR.Mk III)

The 'long-range' PR.Mk IC, deployed for the first time in March 1940, added a 30-Imp gal (136-litre) fuel tank in a blister under the port wing, balanced by the installation of two 8-in (20.3-cm) cameras in a similar position in the starboard wing. This work-stained machine, P9385, was converted to PR.Mk IC standard in 1940 and served with No. 8 OTU.

PR.Mk ID (PR.Mk IV)

The PR.Mk ID 'extra-super-long-range' aircraft of late 1940 had, as its description suggested, the greatest range. With a specially constructed wing housing a 114-Imp gal (518-litre) fuel tank, this Spitfire had two and a half times the total fuel capacity of a standard Spitfire Mk I fighter and was equipped with the same camera fit as the Mk IF. With this variant, much larger areas could now be covered by the PR units; sorties with the Mk ID took the aircraft to the Baltic, Norway and France's Mediterranean coast. Over 200 were built, the Mk ID becoming the most important PR type in 1941/42. This example, fitted with a Vokes tropical filter, served with No. 2 PRU, formed at Heliopolis, Egypt.

PR.Mk IE (PR.Mk V)

The need for close-up photographs, coupled with the additional requirement for an aircraft able to take photographs below the cloud base when weather conditions hampered high-altitude sorties, prompted the development of the PR.Mk IE in mid-1940. Low-altitude PR flying, known as 'dicing', required the use of an oblique camera in each wing, pointing outwards and downwards. Only one Mk IE (N3117, illustrated) is believed to have been produced.

PR.Mk IF (PR.Mk VI)

The quest for increased range led to rapid development of the PR Spitfires. The PR.Mk IF was introduced in July 1940, before the Mk ID. This so-called 'super-long-range' aircraft had a radius of action some 100 miles (161 km) greater than that of the Mk IC, thanks to a second 30-Imp gal (136-litre) blister wing tank. Two cameras (either 8-in/20.3-cm or 20-in/50.8-cm) were carried in the rear fuselage.

PR.Mk IG (PR.Mk VII)

The last PR Spitfire to be based upon the Mk I fighter, the low-level Mk IG differed from earlier aircraft in retaining eight 0.303-in (7.7-mm) machine-guns and sported only one extra fuel tank, the 29-Imp gal (132-litre) tank behind the cockpit. Three cameras were fitted: one oblique 5-in (12.7-cm) camera behind the cockpit and, below this, two vertical cameras of 5-in (12.7-cm) and 14-in (35.6-cm) focal lengths, respectively.

PR.Mk XIII

The armed low-level 'dicing' PR.Mk VIIs (Mk IGs) were replaced by the PR.Mk XIII from early 1943. This mark sported a Merlin 32 engine (producing peak power at just 2,500 ft/762 m), the same camera fit as a Mk VII and four 0.303-in (7.7-mm) machine-guns. The Mk XIII remained in use until the Spitfire FR.Mk XIV entered service in 1944.

An early production Spitfire PR.Mk XI is seen here in its element, at altitude. Most Mk XIs had the broad chord rudder with its characteristic pointed tip; this aircraft (converted on the production line from a Mk IX fighter) has the earlier-style vertical tail.

Spitfire Mks X, XI & XIX

The later PR variants

Steady improvements in the Luftwaffe's interceptors necessitated the development of new photo-reconnaissance Spitfires, able to fly faster and at higher altitudes. To this end new PR variants, derived from the latest two-stage Merlin- and Griffon-powered fighter models, were introduced.

The threat posed by the Luftwaffe's Fw 190As and Bf 109Gs that led to the introduction of the Merlin 60-engined Mk VIII and IX fighters prompted development of a similarly equipped photo-reconnaissance machine.

As an interim measure, a small batch of 15 PR.Mk IXs was converted from Mk IXs, with their armament removed and a pair of vertical cameras fitted in the rear fuselage. As these aircraft lacked the extra fuel tankage of purpose-built PR machines, they often flew with a 90-Imp gal (409-litre) drop tank under the fuselage.

PR.Mk IXs enter service

Entering service with No. 541 Sqn at Benson in November 1942, these machines were limited to operations over Western Europe, but restored the ability of the RAF's PR force to photograph defended targets without suffering major losses.

However, it was the arrival of the PR.Mk XI that gave the PR squadrons an aircraft that was not only capable of outflying Luftwaffe fighters, but combined this with sufficient range to reach targets in Germany.

Based on the Mk VIII fighter, but utilising the wing of the earlier Spitfire PR.Mk IV (Mk ID) with its leading-edge fuel tanks, the Mk XI could reach altitudes in excess of 40,000 ft (12190 m), 10,000 ft (3048 m) higher than previous reconnaissance versions. Two main fuselage fuel tanks, mounted behind the engine, carried 85 Imp gal (386 litres), while the wing tanks had a capacity of 132 Imp gal (588 litres). Like the PR.Mk IX, the Mk XI could utilise an external fuel tank to extend range still further though, on internal fuel only, the Mk XI had an impressive range of 2,300 miles (3700 km) – sufficient for a typical endurance of 5.4 hours.

Equipment consisted of an oblique camera behind the cockpit and two vertical cameras, of varying size, in a 'universal' mounting in the lower, rear fuselage. Later production

Rolling for the camera is this Mk XI of No. 541 Sqn, RAF. Notable are the 'invasion' stripes (dating the photograph at mid-1944, around the time of Operation Overlord, the Allied invasion of occupied Europe) and the two camera ports in the lower fuselage.

aircraft had provision to carry a small vertical camera in a blister mid-way along each wing.

In all, 471 Mk XIs were built from December 1942, replacing all the earlier, unarmed PR Spitfires, including those in the

Middle East. Others were sent to the Far East. In Europe, until the advent of the Luftwaffe's first jet fighters in early 1944, the Mk XI was virtually immune from interception.

The PR.Mk X followed the

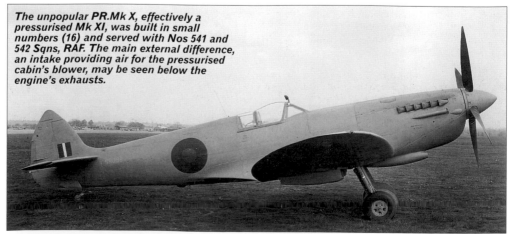

The unpopular PR.Mk X, effectively a pressurised Mk XI, was built in small numbers (16) and served with Nos 541 and 542 Sqns, RAF. The main external difference, an intake providing air for the pressurised cabin's blower, may be seen below the engine's exhausts.

Spitfire PR.Mk XI

Spitfire PR.Mk XI PL914 was on strength with the 14th Photographic Sqn, 7th Photographic Group, 8th Air Force, based at Mount Farm, a few miles from the main RAF PR base at Benson, near Oxford, England in 1944.

PR Spitfires in USAAF service
Without an equivalent American-built type capable of doing the job, the USAAF obtained a dozen Spitfire Mk XIs for pre- and post-strike photography of targets for the 8th Air Force's heavy bomber force.

Performance
The Spitfire PR.Mk XI had a top speed of 417 mph (671 km/h) at 24,200 ft (7376 m) and a ceiling of 44,000 ft (13411 m). Endurance was 5.4 hours, and range 2,300 miles (3700 km), enough to fly to Berlin and back from the UK.

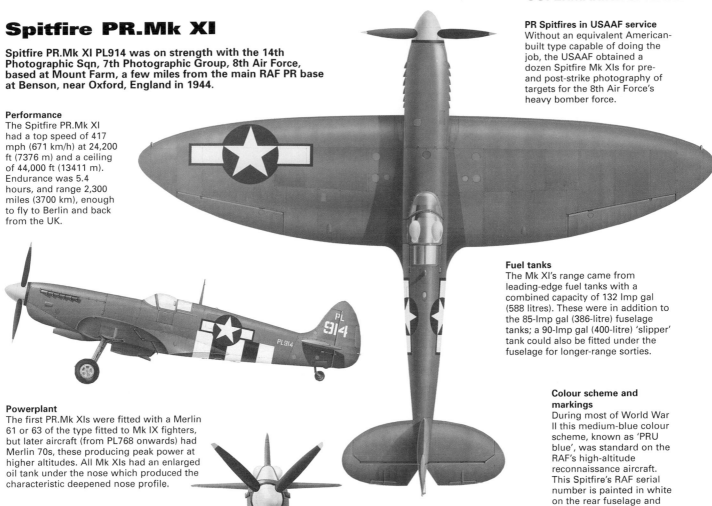

Fuel tanks
The Mk XI's range came from leading-edge fuel tanks with a combined capacity of 132 Imp gal (588 litres). These were in addition to the 85-Imp gal (386-litre) fuselage tanks; a 90-Imp gal (400-litre) 'slipper' tank could also be fitted under the fuselage for longer-range sorties.

Powerplant
The first PR.Mk XIs were fitted with a Merlin 61 or 63 of the type fitted to Mk IX fighters, but later aircraft (from PL768 onwards) had Merlin 70s, these producing peak power at higher altitudes. All Mk XIs had an enlarged oil tank under the nose which produced the characteristic deepened nose profile.

Colour scheme and markings
During most of World War II this medium-blue colour scheme, known as 'PRU blue', was standard on the RAF's high-altitude reconnaissance aircraft. This Spitfire's RAF serial number is painted in white on the rear fuselage and repeated on the tailfin. 'Invasion' stripes have been applied to the fuselage underside.

Camera installation
In 7th PG service, the Universal camera installation in the rear fuselage of a PR.Mk XI carried two 36-in (91.4-cm) focal length vertical cameras. If smaller cameras were carried, an oblique camera could be fitted behind the cockpit, to port or starboard.

Mk XI into service in 1943. Effectively a pressurised version of the Mk XI, only 16 examples were built.

In May 1944, the Griffon-engined PR.Mk XIX was introduced, with performance close to that of the Luftwaffe's Me 262 jets, the introduction of which had posed a potential threat to the PR force. Though based on the Mk XIV fighter, most Mk XIXs were pressurised (therefore able to reach altitudes above 45,000 ft/13716 m) and all had integral wing fuel tanks, as incorporated in the Mk XI

Carrying the '6C' codes of the Photographic Reconnaissance Development Unit, this PR.Mk XIX is seen post-war. India, Sweden, Thailand and Turkey also operated Mk XIXs post-war, while Denmark and Norway took delivery of Mk XIs.

and its predecessors. In all, 225 were built, for service in Europe, the Mediterranean and the Far East. Post-war, they formed the backbone (with de Havilland Mosquitoes) of the RAF's PR force until the advent of reconnaissance variants of the Meteor and Canberra.

After withdrawal from front-line use, a handful of Mk XIXs equipped the Temperature and Humidity (THUM) Flight at Woodvale until 1957, when the Spitfire was finally retired from regular RAF use. The final act came in 1963 as the Borneo confrontation was beginning.

Indonesian P-51 Mustangs were the RAF's potential opponents in the region, prompting the Central Fighter Establishment at Binbrook to bring a single Mk XIX out of retirement to train jet fighter pilots in the engagement of more agile piston-engined aircraft.

The RAF's last operational Spitfire, PR.Mk 19 PS888 served with No. 81 Sqn at Seletar, Singapore. Its last sortie was flown on 1 April 1954, to photograph areas thought to harbour Communist guerrillas during the Malayan Emergency.

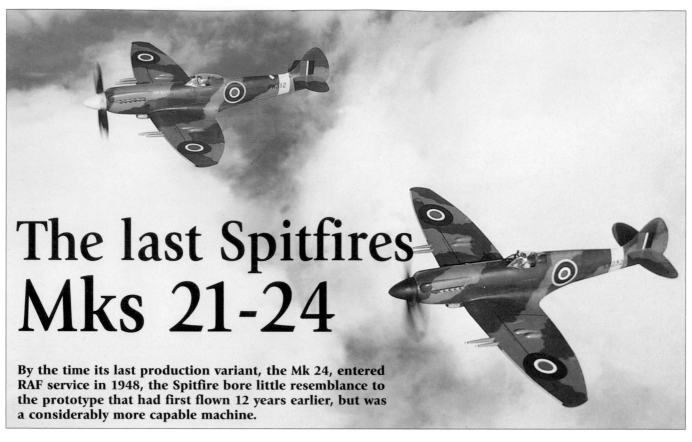

The last Spitfires Mks 21-24

By the time its last production variant, the Mk 24, entered RAF service in 1948, the Spitfire bore little resemblance to the prototype that had first flown 12 years earlier, but was a considerably more capable machine.

When the Rolls-Royce Griffon 60-series engine, as fitted to Spitfire Mks XIV and XVIII, became readily available in 1942, it became clear that significant changes to the Spitfire's airframe would be needed to exploit the new engine's power to the full.

The most important of these was a new, much stiffer wing. In fact, the wing fitted to production Mk 21s, with its larger ailerons and therefore a straighter trailing edge, was the first to differ in basic shape from that fitted to the Spitfire prototype back in 1936. A new name for the aircraft – Victor – was even considered, but not adopted.

Above: PK312, the first Spitfire Mk 22, retained a Mk 21 empennage, but was later equipped with an enlarged tailplane and tailfin.

Right: No. 600 (City of London) Squadron, Royal Auxiliary Air Force, was formed at Biggin Hill in 1946 – the first fighter unit within the RAuxAF. The following year, its first aircraft, Spitfire Mk XIVs, were replaced with Mk 21s, pictured. These aircraft had served with four regular RAF units between 1945 and 1947, then transferring to the RAuxAF, including Nos 602 (City of Glasgow) and 615 (County of Surrey) Sqns.

A Spitfire Mk 21 (foreground) formates with the Mk 22 prototype, PK312. Only the Mk 21 saw action during World War II, and though Mks 22 and 24 were operational in the late 1940s, the jet age had dawned and their service was short.

The first Mk 21 (a rebuild of the second Mk IV/XX prototype) flew in December 1942. This aircraft was a so-called 'interim Mk 21' with a Griffon 61 engine and standard Spitfire wings, though the latter had pointed tips and a revised structure with a thicker gauge skin for greater strength. Seven months later a 'full-spec' aircraft flew, with the new wing, extra wing fuel tankage and other changes, including an armament fit consisting of four 20-mm Hispano cannon. Power came from a Griffon 65 rated at

2,050 hp (1529 kW), over twice the rating of the Merlin 'C' engine installed in the Spitfire prototype six years earlier.

AFDU misgivings

Testing at Boscombe Down revealed a top speed of 450 mph (724 km/h) and was followed by orders for 3,400 production examples, the first of which flew in March 1944. Later in the year, however, the Air Fighting Development Unit was given one of the new aircraft for testing. Staffed with experienced fighter pilots, the

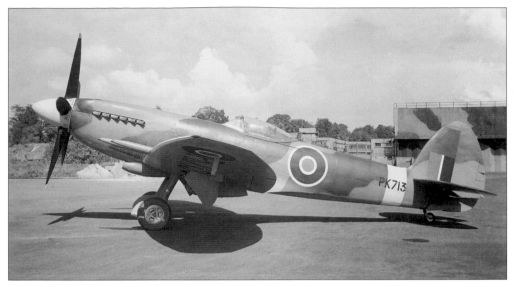

Unit produced a highly critical report on the machine's performance, citing directional instability as the Mk 21's main vice. So unhappy was the AFDU that it ended its report on the Mk 21 with the suggestion that 'no further attempts should be made to perpetuate the Spitfire family'.

Curing the snags in the new aircraft became a top priority,

although deliveries to No. 91 Squadron, RAF began in January 1945. Modifications to the aircraft's control surfaces were soon introduced (though it was recognised that an entirely new empennage would eventually be necessary to completely eliminate the problems) and, by April, No. 91 had received modified aircraft and was operational.

In all, just 120 Mk 21s were built, No. 91 Squadron being the only unit to operate the variant before VE-Day. Based at Ludham, Norfolk, the squadron (which had been one of the first to receive Spitfire Mk XIIs, back in 1942) undertook 154 sorties from 10 April. Most were armed reconnaissance sweeps, one of which saw the destruction of a German 'Biber'-class midget submarine. Two aircraft were lost to ground fire off the coast of the Netherlands, the unit's only Mk 21 losses.

Post-war operations

Nos 1, 41 and 122 Squadrons also flew the type post-war, though only briefly before they were disbanded or re-equipped. The Mk 21s were then transferred to Royal Auxiliary Air Force units, but all had been withdrawn from use by 1948.

The Mk 22, first flown in March 1945, differed from the Mk 21 only in having a cut-down rear fuselage and 'teardrop' cockpit canopy, changes that had not resulted in the issue of a new mark number in the past. Production examples featured the new, and long-awaited, tailplane and tailfin.

This variant had a longer production life than its predecessor, 278 being built. These aircraft equipped a single regular RAF unit (No. 73 Sqn in the Middle East) and 12 RAuxAF units until 1951. A number was then exported, to the air forces of Southern Rhodesia, Egypt and Syria.

A projected Mk 23 remained unbuilt. This was an attempt to build an aircraft with a wing conferring the advantages of the laminar flow wing (as fitted to the Supermarine Spiteful), with as few changes as possible. A Spitfire Mk VIII was flown with the new wing, but handling suffered and the aircraft's top speed was little more than that of a standard Mk VIII, so the project was abandoned.

The last Spitfires

The last aircraft to bear the famous Spitfire name was the Mk 24, 54 of which were completed, the last in February 1948. Externally the Mk 24 was no different from a late-production Mk 22. Internally, it had two extra fuel tanks in the rear fuselage and provision to carry underwing rocket projectiles. The last Mk 24s also had short-barrelled Hispano Mk V cannon.

One RAF squadron received the ultimate Spitfire – No. 80 Squadron based at Gütersloh in Germany. In July 1949, No. 80 moved to Hong Kong, flying Spitfires until January 1952 as the RAF's last Spitfire fighter unit. After withdrawal, the aircraft were handed over to the Hong Kong Auxiliary Air Force (with whom they operated until 1955).

Above: Here, the new wing designed for the Spitfire Mk 21/22/24 may be clearly seen, in this case fitted to a Mk 22. The longer ailerons, reaching nearly to the wingtip, are evident.

Right: Contra-rotating propellers were tested on several of the Mk 21/22/24 prototypes (this is a Mk 24). Still unreliable in 1945, they were not fitted to production Spitfires, though Fleet Air Arm Seafire FR.Mk 47s were so-equipped, post-war.

Mitchell's masterpiece
The F.37/34 prototype

After Supermarine lost the competition to design a fighter to Specification F.7/30, Reginald Mitchell redesigned the company's Type 224 submission around a new engine, the Rolls-Royce Merlin. In doing so, he drew on his experience as designer of some of the fastest floatplanes in the world – the Rolls-Royce-powered S.6 and S.6B. The result was the Type 300 prototype, K5054.

By the early 1930s Mitchell, the chief designer of the Supermarine Aircraft Company, had established a formidable reputation for creating high-speed floatplanes. His Supermarine S.5 had won the Schneider Trophy competition in 1927; his S.6 won it in 1929. In 1931 the Supermarine S.6B won the trophy outright for Great Britain and later raised the world air speed record to 407 mph (655 km/h).

This period saw rapid advances in aviation technology. The highly supercharged engine, the variable-pitch propeller, the streamlined all-metal airframe, the cantilever monoplane wing, the enclosed cockpit and the retractable undercarriage all appeared about this time. Each of them promised to improve aircraft performance.

Specification F.7/30

In 1931 the fastest fighter in the RAF was the Hawker Fury, which had a maximum speed of 207 mph (333 km/h) – about half as fast as the Supermarine S.6B. In its quest for a fighter with a better performance, in 1931 the Air Ministry issued Specification F.7/30. This called for an interceptor fighter with the highest possible rate of climb and the highest possible speed

above 15,000 ft (4573 m).

Seven companies entered the competition, resulting in five biplane and three monoplane fighters. Reginald Mitchell's first attempt at fighter design, the Supermarine Type 224, made its maiden flight in February 1934. A monoplane of all-metal construction and with a super-charged engine, it was conservative in appearance and retained a fixed undercarriage and open cockpit. Powered by a 680-hp (507-kW) Goshawk engine, its maximum speed was

Above: 'Spitfire' was the name suggested for the Type 224, built to Air Ministry Specification F.7/30. Hampered by its 680-hp (507-kW) Rolls-Royce Goshawk engine, the design lost out to a Gloster design that was to enter service as the Gladiator.

Top: By the time of its first flight in March 1936, the F.37/34 had been named 'Spitfire' and been finished in a high-gloss, blue-grey paint scheme. Its Merlin C engine developed 990 hp (738 kW).

only 228 mph (367 km/h). The Gloster SS.37, a classic fabric-covered biplane with a maximum speed of 242 mph (390 km/h), won the competition and later went into service as the Gladiator.

Once the Type 224 was flying, Mitchell saw several ways in which he could improve his design. He persuaded his company to provide initial financing for a more advanced

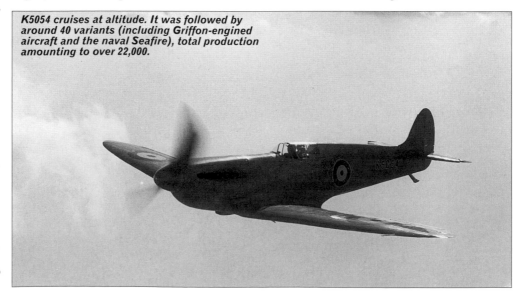

K5054 cruises at altitude. It was followed by around 40 variants (including Griffon-engined aircraft and the naval Seafire), total production amounting to over 22,000.

Left: K5054's first public appearance came at a display of Vickers types before 300 invited guests at Eastleigh on 18 June 1936. Other aircraft on show were K4049, the B.9/32 bomber prototype (later ordered by the RAF as the Wellington); K7556, a pre-production Wellesley bomber; and K5780, the ninth production-standard Walrus amphibian. In 1938, the Supermarine Aviation Works (Vickers) Ltd and its parent company, Vickers (Aviation) Ltd of Weybridge, were taken over by Vickers-Armstrong Limited.

Below: S.6B S1596 was the sister aircraft of the outright winner of the 1931 Schneider Trophy competition. It was flown by Flt Lt George Stainforth to a 407.5 mph (655.81 km/h) world absolute air speed record on 29 September 1931.

fighter, powered by the new Rolls-Royce PV 12 engine (later named the Merlin). The Air Ministry expressed interest in the projected fighter and drew up a new specification, F.37/34, to fund a prototype.

Floatplane myth

An oft-repeated myth has it that the Spitfire was 'developed from' the Supermarine racing floatplanes. This is simply not true. Mitchell certainly had learned a great deal about high-speed flight from his racing floatplane designs, but it is quite a different matter to say that the Spitfire was 'developed from' them. The two types of aircraft were intended for completely different roles. There was not a single component of any significance in the Spitfire that resembled its counterpart in the racing seaplane.

On 5 March 1936 the Supermarine F.37/34 made its

maiden flight from Eastleigh airfield near Southampton, with chief test pilot 'Mutt' Summers at the controls. From the start, it was clear that Mitchell's new fighter was altogether more effective than its predecessor. At the suggestion of the Vickers parent company, the new fighter was named the 'Spitfire'. We know that Reginald Mitchell had no part in the choice of that name. When the gifted designer learned of it he commented, "It's the sort of bloody silly name they would give it!"

The Spitfire became available just as the RAF had an urgent need for a high-performance modern fighter. In Germany the newly reformed Luftwaffe was building its strength rapidly. To meet the growing threat, in June 1936 the British government signed a contract for 310 Spitfires.

In July 1936 the prototype of the new fighter completed its initial service trials at Martlesham

Heath. Its maximum speed was 349 mph (562 km/h) at 16,800 ft (5122 m), and it could reach 30,000 ft (9145 m) in 17 minutes.

Gun freezing

Most aspects of the Spitfire's flight trials went smoothly. In December 1936 the prototype resumed flying after the installation of its armament of eight Browning 0.303-in (7.7-mm) machine-guns. It was at this time that the first and only serious problem with the new aircraft arose. Gun-firing trials at altitude revealed a tendency to

freeze in the cold temperatures found at 32,000 ft (9755 m). It took until October 1938, more than a year and a half after the problem was first revealed, to devise an effective system to prevent the guns freezing. Suitable gun heating modifications were accordingly introduced on the Spitfire production line.

With trials over, and the Spitfire entering squadron service, K5054 ended its days as a high-speed 'hack' and in test flying for the 'Speed Spitfire' project. In September 1939 it was wrecked in a fatal accident.

'Speed Spitfire'

The possibility of building a Spitfire for an attempt on the world landplane speed held by a Hughes H-1 at 567.115 km/h (353 mph) was mooted in the summer of 1937. To this end, the 48th Spitfire Mk I (K9834) was fitted with a modified airframe and a 2,160-hp (1611-kW) Merlin II (Special) and flown, as the 'Speed Spitfire', on 10 November 1938. The following month the record was raised to 611 km/h (380 mph) by the Messerschmitt Bf 109 V13 and, as the Air Ministry was convinced that the Heinkel He 100 V8 was about to reach 725 km/h (451 mph) (it reached 746.6 km/h (464 mph) in March 1939), the plans for a record attempt by the Spitfire were abandoned. Here it is seen in 'racing trim', with its more streamlined cockpit, a modified wing and a large, wooden four-bladed propeller. By the end of 1940 K9834 had been fitted with a standard Merlin and was a 'hack' aircraft with the Photographic Reconnaissance Unit at Heston.

On 22 March 1937, K5054 suffered its first major accident, when F/O Sam McKenna made a forced landing after experiencing engine trouble. By this time, the aircraft was fitted with a 1,045-hp (779-kW) Merlin F engine and eight Browning machine-guns. Six months later, after repairs (and the application of RAF day fighter camouflage), K5054 returned to the air. Two years later, on 4 September 1939, it suffered a landing mishap in which its pilot (Flt Lt 'Spinner' White) suffered fatal injuries. This time the aircraft was not repaired.

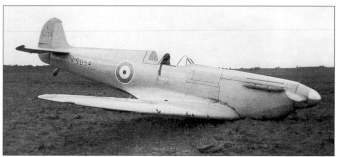

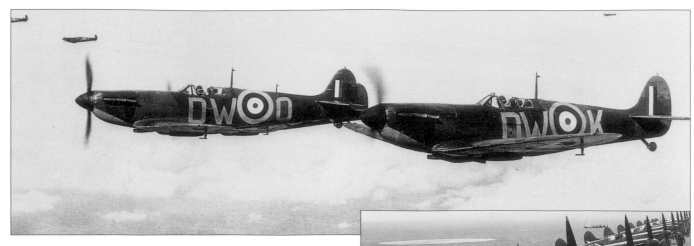

Operations
The early months

As Europe slipped inexorably towards war, Britain began to equip itself with the Spitfire, the aircraft that would become the very symbol of British defiance during World War II.

Top: Based at Gravesend in Kent and equipped with Spitfires, No. 610 Squadron was one of the RAF units that bore the brunt of Luftwaffe attacks during the Battle of Britain.

Above: May 1939 saw No. 19 Squadron's Press Day at Duxford. Of interest in this photograph are both the flat-topped canopies fitted to the second and fifth aircraft – the rest having the later bulged canopy – and the 'WZ' codes used by No. 19 during 1938 and 1939.

In August 1938, 29 months after the maiden flight of the Spitfire, No. 19 Squadron at Duxford was the first service unit to receive the new fighter. By December, it had its full complement of aircraft, and was followed by other squadrons that began to convert to the type.

By 3 September 1939, when Great Britain entered the war against Germany, the RAF had taken delivery of 306 Spitfires. Of these, 187 were serving with 11 Fighter Command squadrons (Nos 19, 41, 54, 65, 66, 72, 74, 602, 603, 609 and 611). A further 71 Spitfires were held at maintenance units, ready for

issue to replace losses. Eleven Spitfires served as trials machines, either with the makers or at service test establishments. One Spitfire was temporarily allocated to the Central Flying School, for use by those writing the Pilot's Notes on the aircraft. The remaining 36 Spitfires had been lost in accidents.

First blood

The Spitfire went into action against enemy aircraft for the first time on 16 October 1939. On that day, nine Junkers Ju 88s of Kampfgeschwader 30 attacked Royal Navy warships in the Firth of Forth. Nos 602 and 603

Squadrons, based at Drem and Turnhouse respectively, scrambled to engage the raiders. Flight Lieutenant Pat Gifford of No. 603 Squadron shot down one bomber, and Flight Lieutenants George Pinkerton and Archie McKellar of No. 602 Squadron destroyed another. Fighters of No. 603 Squadron engaged a further Ju 88

and shot out one of its engines, but it escaped out to sea.

In the months that followed, Spitfire units had sporadic encounters with individual German bombers, minelayers or reconnaissance aircraft. For the most part, however, this was a period of expansion of the force and of training for the battles to

Early Spitfire victor

Spitfire Mk Is and IIs served only briefly in front-line RAF service units, but they were responsible for achieving incredible victories against German forces which were often many times their size. From their first taste of blood over Scotland until their hour of glory over the south-east of England, they were a constant thorn in the German side.

Spitfire Mk I
Flt Lt George Denholm, a flight commander with No. 603 'City of Edinburgh' Sqn, was among the Spitfire pilots in action on 16 October 1939, the day of the first successful engagement by the RAF of a Luftwaffe bomber. On 17 March 1940, flying in this aircraft L1067, Denholm damaged a Dornier Do 17 before being shot down himself.

Poor armament
A drawback of the early Spitfires was their light armament. On several occasions, German bombers returned home after being hit by more than one hundred 0.303-in (7.7-mm) rounds, the ammunition used by early marks of the Spitfire.

Fighter Command lost 72 Spitfires while covering the evacuation of the Allied forces from Dunkirk. This wreck was photographed near Dunkirk on 6 June, after the end of the operation. Spitfires operating over Dunkirk suffered similar endurance problems to Bf 109s during the Battle of Britain.

come. By the beginning of May 1940, another eight squadrons (Nos 64, 92, 152, 222, 234, 266, 610 and 616) had received Spitfires, bringing the strength of the force to 19 squadrons.

The Spitfire was intended primarily to be a short-range home defence bomber-destroyer. In designing the aircraft, R. J. Mitchell had not intended that it should engage enemy fighters and, during the so-called 'Phoney War', it never had to do so. This came to an abrupt end during May 1940, however, when the German army launched its powerful Blitzkrieg offensive against France, Holland and Belgium.

Spitfire fighters mounted their first operation over Europe on 12 May 1940. Six aircraft of No. 66 Squadron, accompanied by a similar number of Defiants of No. 264 Squadron, flew from airfields in East Anglia on a sweep over Holland. The force engaged a Ju 88 and inflicted

some damage to it before it escaped inland. On the following day, the two units flew a similar patrol and, for the first time, Spitfires went into action against Messerschmitt Bf 109s. During a short but sharp engagement, four Ju 87s and a Bf 109 were shot down in exchange for five Defiants and a Spitfire.

The first encounter

The Spitfire first encountered German aircraft en masse on 21 May 1940. By then, the rapid German advance into Belgium and France had brought the war within range of the various Fighter Command units that were based in Kent.

In the days that followed, Spitfires and Hurricanes flew numerous sorties to cover the evacuation of Allied troops from Dunkirk. Both sides suffered losses during the fierce air battles fought above the port. When the evacuation ended on 3 June 1940, Fighter Command had lost 72

Spitfires – nearly one-third of this aircraft's front-line strength. It was as well the operation ended when it did, for the RAF had no choice but to accept this punishing loss

rate. As long as the evacuation continued, there could be no thought of abandoning the Royal Navy and the Allied troops to the mercies of the Luftwaffe.

Heritage of the first Spitfire squadron

No. 19 Squadron, RAF had always been a single-seat fighter squadron. Mustered from the nucleus of No. 5 Reserve Squadron, the unit was formed and equipped with BE.12s in June 1916. However, the BE.12s proved unsuitable for use as fighters and were replaced by Spad VIIs from December. In June 1918, Sopwith Dolphins were employed, serving until the unit was disbanded in 1919. No. 19 was based at Duxford, Cambridgeshire upon reformation in 1923, as a fighter flight attached to No. 2 Flying Training School. It achieved full squadron service on 1 June 1924, equipped with Sopwith Snipes. During the 1920s and 1930s, Grebes, Siskins, Bulldogs and Gauntlets were among the squadron's equipment before it became the first unit to fly the Spitfire from August 1938. No. 66 Squadron, formed at Duxford from 'C' Flight of No. 19, followed in November.

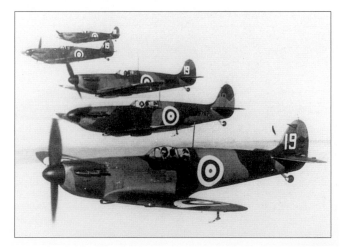

Below: During the first months of the war, the press frequently made visits to RAF fighter stations. This 'scramble', featuring Spitfires of No. 611 'West Lancashire' Squadron, was staged on 8 April 1940 at RAF Drem in East Lothian.

From perhaps the most famous sequence of photographs depicting Spitfires in action during the Battle of Britain, this view shows aircraft of No. 610 Sqn, based at RAF Biggin Hill, on patrol during June 1940. Lessons learned in combat are reflected in the loose line-astern formations flown by the two sections in this view.

Spitfires of the Battle of Britain

In recent years there has been controversy over the relative effectiveness of the Spitfire and the Hawker Hurricane during the Battle of Britain, the former having gained a reputation arguably out of keeping with the part it played in comparison to the more numerous Hurricane.

With their rifle-calibre machine-guns, both the Spitfire and Hurricane were deficient in fire-power when they engaged enemy bombers. During the large-scale actions, Spitfires and Hurricanes achieved victories approximately in proportion to the number of each type taking part. The Spitfire's superior performance and smaller size meant that it was less likely to take hits, however. In major actions the Spitfires suffered an average loss rate of around four per cent of those engaging, while Hurricane losses averaged around six per cent.

Due to their lower rate of attrition, the Spitfire units spent more days in action than those equipped with Hurricanes. On average, a Spitfire unit spent nearly 20 days in action during the Battle of Britain before it had to be withdrawn to re-form. That compared with under 16 days for the fully-engaged Hurricane squadrons (the four Hurricane units that played little part in the action are not included in this calculation). With more days in action, the individual Spitfire

units were able to gain more victories. The 19 Spitfire squadrons taking part in the Battle are credited with 521 victories, an average of just over 27 per unit. The 30 fully-engaged Hurricane squadrons are credited with 655 victories, an average of just under 22 per squadron. In combat, the average victory-to-loss ratio for Spitfire units was 1.8:1, while that for fully-engaged Hurricane units was 1.34:1.

Cannon-armed aircraft

It was during the Battle of Britain that the RAF was able to test its first few cannon-armed Spitfires. Great things were expected, but when No. 19 Sqn went into action in August 1940 the weapon's performance was abysmal. During combat on 16 August, both cannon functioned properly on only one out of the seven Spitfires that engaged the enemy. On 19 August it was none out of three, on 24 August it was two out of eight and on 31 August it was three out of six. Following these embarrassing failures, the squadron's commander, Sqn Ldr R. Pinkham, complained

The Browning machine-guns of Spitfire Mk I X4474 are hurriedly re-armed as a pilot straps in before another sortie. With the advent of the cannon-armed Mk IB, these machine-gun-equipped machines were known as Mk IAs.

to his superiors: "In all the engagements so far occurring it is considered that, had the unit been equipped with eight-gun fighters, it would have inflicted far more severe losses on the enemy. It is most strongly urged that until the stoppages at present experienced have been eliminated, this squadron should be re-equipped with Browning-gun Spitfires."

HQ Fighter Command accepted Pinkham's suggestion, and early in September the unit exchanged its cannon fighters for normal eight-gun Spitfires. The Hispano-armed Spitfire played no further part in the

Battle of Britain.

Because of these initial problems with the Hispano cannon, during the Battle the Spitfires and Hurricanes had to fight with a weapon that was inadequate against multi-engined bombers. There are several well-documented instances in which German bombers regained friendly territory after taking more than 100 hits from 0.303-in (7.7-mm) ammunition. To achieve that concentration of hits probably meant that at least two British fighters had fired most of their ammunition into the bomber from short range.

The alert section of No. 616 Sqn scrambles from RAF Kenley. Note the 'QJ' codes carried by these aircraft; for several months No. 616 Sqn confusingly identified its aircraft with these letters despite the fact that they had already been in use by No. 92 Sqn for some time. Confusion reigned at the time and the oversight has confused historians since!

'W-SH' is a No. 64 Sqn aircraft which appears to have suffered a wheels-up landing and is in the throes of repair – a task undertaken with some urgency given the shortage of aircraft.

The survivability of the German bombers was much enhanced by the self-sealing fuel tanks developed following combat experience in the Spanish Civil War. The light alloy tanks had a 0.39-in (1-cm) thick covering comprising alternate layers of vulcanised and non-vulcanised rubber. Surrounding the whole was an outer covering of leather. When a rifle-calibre round hit the tank it passed easily through this covering. When fuel started to leak through the hole, the petrol set up a chemical reaction with the non-vulcanised rubber, which caused the latter to swell and seal the hole. The carriage of fuel in self-sealing tanks saved many a German bomber from the fiery end that would otherwise have been its fate.

Had large numbers of cannon-armed Spitfires and Hurricanes been available to fight in the Battle, and had the cannon performed reliably, it is interesting to speculate how much more effective Fighter Command would have been. As it was, by resorting to 'overkill' on several occasions, the British fighters caused sufficiently heavy losses to the enemy bombers to force the Luftwaffe to abandon its daylight attacks on England.

Failings addressed

During the summer and autumn of 1940, work to cure the failings of the Spitfire's cannon installation continued at the highest priority. Only near the end of 1940, too late to play a major part in the Battle of Britain, were the problems finally eradicated. Yet even when the cannon did work properly, another problem remained. The 60-round magazine fitted to each Hispano weapon contained sufficient ammunition for only five seconds' firing. That was judged insufficient for normal air-to-air combat. Accordingly, the next batch of Spitfire Mk IBs carried a mixed armament of two Hispano cannon and four 0.303-in (7.7-mm) machine-guns. It proved a good compromise, and in November 1940 No. 92 Squadron re-equipped with the new variant. To differentiate these aircraft from the rest of the Mk Is armed with eight machine-guns, the latter were redesignated as Mk IAs.

In June 1940, after lengthy delays, the huge Nuffield factory at Castle Bromwich near Birmingham at last began large-scale production of the Mk II Spitfire. Externally, the new variant looked like the late-production Mk I, the main difference being the Merlin 12 engine developing an extra 110 hp (82 kW). The increase in power gave the Mk II a slight edge in maximum speed and climbing performance over its predecessor.

In August 1940 the first Spitfire Mk IIs were delivered to No. 611 Sqn, based at Digby. In the following month Nos 19, 74 and 266 Squadrons also received the new variant. The Mk II replaced the Mk I in several units, and the squadrons operating the newer variant concentrated in the south-east corner of England where the fighting was heaviest.

The initial batches of Spitfire Mk IIs were armed with eight machine-guns. Later, small numbers were produced with the two cannon and four machine-gun armament and designated Mk IIBs. As with the Mk I, when that happened the machine-gun-armed machines were redesignated as Mk IIAs.

In September 1940, X4179 – a Spitfire Mk IA – joined No. 19 Sqn, its former unit, No. 266 Sqn, having relinquished its early-mark aircraft in favour of Mk IIs.

Flt Lt John Dundas flew Spitfire Mk I R6690/ 'PR-Q' in August 1940. By 9 October he had claimed nine kills and was No. 609 Sqn's top-scorer of the Battle. His aircraft was a standard machine-gun-armed Mk I.

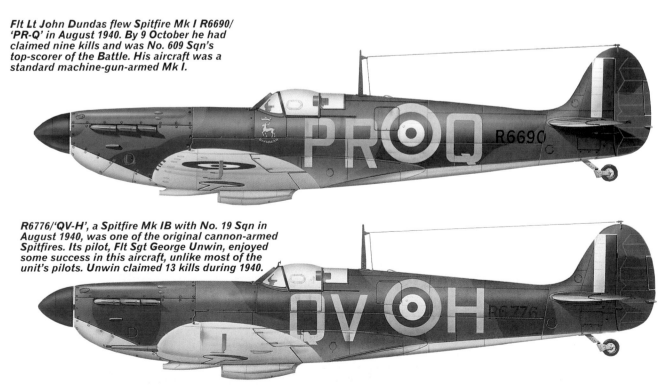

R6776/'QV-H', a Spitfire Mk IB with No. 19 Sqn in August 1940, was one of the original cannon-armed Spitfires. Its pilot, Flt Sgt George Unwin, enjoyed some success in this aircraft, unlike most of the unit's pilots. Unwin claimed 13 kills during 1940.

RAF Spitfires at war
Northwest Europe, 1941-45

Entering service from May 1941, initially with No. 92 Sqn, the improved Spitfire Mk V variant was among the RAF types to bear the brunt of cross-Channel operations. This is a No. 222 Sqn example, based at North Weald.

Early in 1941 RAF Fighter Command went over to the offensive. The new C-in-C, Air Chief Marshal Sir Sholto Douglas, termed the policy one of 'leaning forward into France' with the aim of drawing the Luftwaffe into action. The Spitfire was to play a leading role in the use of this new tactic.

On 9 January 1941 three squadrons of Spitfire Mk Is flew an offensive sweep over northern France. The German fighter controllers chose to ignore the incursion, however, and it passed off without incident. The lesson was clear: sweeps by fighters alone would not bring the enemy into action. Like Fighter Command in the Battle of Britain, the Luftwaffe did not feel the necessity to engage sweeps by fighters flying alone.

On the following day the RAF made a more ambitious attempt to draw German fighters into action. The new type of operation, codenamed Circus, was centred around six Blenheim bombers attacking an ammunition dump near Calais. Seven squadrons of Spitfires and four of Hurricanes, a total of 103 fighters, escorted the bombers. This time there were scrappy fighter-versus-fighter actions and a Hurricane and a Spitfire were destroyed. German fighters suffered no losses.

In the weeks that followed, the Circus operations became a regular feature. The most ambitious daylight incursion by the RAF during 1941 took place on 12 August. An attacking force of 54 Blenheims delivered a low-altitude strike on the electricity-generating plants at Knapsack and Quadrath in western Germany. Six squadrons of

Spitfires – Mks II, IIB and V – and one of Whirlwind twin-engined fighters, provided close escort during the initial phase of the penetration. Five squadrons of Spitfires flew down the bombers' route almost to the limit of their radius of action, orbited for five minutes and then headed for home. The withdrawal cover force comprised three squadrons of Spitfire IIs and three more operating the Mk II (Long Range) version. German fighter and flak units reacted vigorously to this bold incursion, shooting down 10 Blenheims and inflicting damage on several others. Four Spitfires were lost. Throughout 1941 the production of Spitfires increased steadily, allowing a major expansion of the force. From 19 Spitfire squadrons at the end of the Battle of Britain, Fighter Command moved to 46 squadrons equipped with Spitfires at the end of 1941.

The Mk IX in service

In July 1942, No. 64 Sqn at Hornchurch became the first unit operational with the Spitfire Mk IX. On 30 July, Flt Lt Donald Kingaby gained the first victory in the new variant. Although Kingaby's victory attracted little attention at the time, it marked a significant turning point for Fighter Command. It was the first occasion when the Spitfire had

No. 306 'Torunski' Sqn was a Polish unit based at Northolt in 1943 and engaged in daylight fighter sweeps over occupied Europe. Here some of the unit's aircrew pose with a Spitfire Mk IXC.

engaged the feared Fw 190 on equal terms. For the Luftwaffe, that engagement marked the beginning of the end of the air superiority it had established over northwest Europe nearly a year earlier.

Spitfires had their hardest day's fight, ever, on 19 August 1942. On that day British and

Canadian troops carried out amphibious landings at and beside the port of Dieppe in northern France. Forty-eight squadrons of Spitfires supported the landings, 42 with Mk Vs, two with Mk VIs and four with the new Mk IXs. These units flew 171 squadron-sized patrols totalling 2,050 sorties (out of a

No. 124 Sqn was one of the two Fighter Command units equipped with the high-altitude Spitfire Mk VI. Unfortunately the type proved unable to fight at altitudes above 35,000 ft (10668 m).

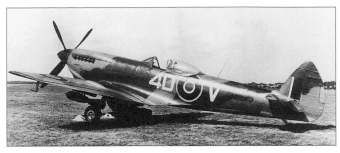

'Bombed up' for another sortie, this No. 74 Sqn aircraft is a good example of a late-production Spitfire Mk XVI in service as a fighter-bomber in Europe during 1945.

grand total of 2,600 sorties flown by all Allied aircraft involved in the operation). Also during that action, the Spitfire squadrons suffered their heaviest single day's loss ever: 59 aircraft lost to enemy action out of a total Allied loss of 97.

In the months that followed, many more home-based units re-equipped with the Mk IX, and it became the most-used fighter type in the theatre.

High-altitude action

Because of the continuing lack of a high-altitude threat to Great Britain, which had resulted in the Spitfire Mk VI seeing little action with the two squadrons the type equipped, production of the follow-up Mk VII had only a moderate priority. It was May 1943 before No. 124 Sqn at North Weald became operational with the variant. In August 1943 three Mk VIIs were based at Skeabrae in the Orkney Islands, to engage high-altitude reconnaissance aircraft attempting to photograph the fleet anchorage at Scapa Flow. In the spring of 1944, Nos 131 and 616 Sqns converted to the Mk VII. During the preparations for the Normandy invasion, their task was to prevent high-flying German reconnaissance aircraft from photographing the invasion ports. During the days immedi-

ately following the invasion, the Mk VII units provided top cover over the beachhead area. After a few days, the Mk VIIs operated in the same way as other Spitfire variants, carrying out low-altitude patrols and going down to strafe road and rail targets.

Soon after, the Mk VII's larger internal fuel tankage gave the variant a new lease of life as a bomber escort. The longest such mission was on 11 August, when No. 131 Sqn escorted Lancasters making a daylight attack on the submarine pens at La Pallice. That 690-mile (1110-km) round trip was close to the Mk VII's maximum radius of action, leaving little fuel to go into action if enemy fighters engaged the force.

Packard Merlin-engined Mk XVIs started to come off the production line at Castle Bromwich in October 1944. At the beginning of December, No. 403 Sqn based at Evère near Brussels was the first unit to exchange its Mk IXs for Mk XVIs. Other Mk IX units in the 2nd Tactical Air Force quickly followed and when the war in Europe ended, a total of 19 squadrons had re-equipped with this variant. In 1944, following the large-scale introduction into service of the Griffon-powered Spitfires and other high-performance new Allied fighter types, the Merlin-powered Spitfire units moved progressively from air superiority to fighter-bomber operations.

Griffon-engined Mk XIIs

In February 1943 No. 41 Sqn moved to High Ercall in Shropshire to re-equip with the Mk XII, the first of the Griffon-engined Spitfires to see service. In April the only other unit to receive the new variant, No. 91 Sqn, began its conversion. Both squadrons had previously operated the Spitfire Mk VB.

In April 1943, No. 41 Sqn

was declared operational and the unit moved to Hawkinge near Folkestone. From there it flew standing patrols in an attempt to catch enemy fighter-bombers making tip-and-run attacks on coastal targets. Initially, these operations had little success. The Spitfire Mk XII fired its guns in anger for the first time on 17 April, when F/O C. Birbeck strafed an enemy patrol boat. Later that day, Flt Lt R. Hogarth encountered a Junkers Ju 88 near Calais and shot it down.

With the lifting of the requirement to counter the fighter-bomber attacks, the two Mk XII units shifted to fighter sweeps and escort missions over enemy territory. Throughout the rest of the year, the two squadrons flew sweeps and escort missions over enemy territory.

The Spitfire Mk XIV, with its Griffon 61 boosted by a two-stage supercharger, went into production in the autumn of 1943 and by the following spring Nos 91, 322 and 610 Sqns had converted to the Mk XIV. All three units were fully operational in June 1944, when the Luftwaffe commenced its attack on London with the first of its V-1 flying bombs. As earlier Spitfire types had proved too slow to catch the 'doodlebugs', Mk XIVs were ordered to join in the 'diver' patrols. The first phase of the V-1 bombardment on London came to an end in September 1944. Following the end of that commitment, in October the first three Spitfire Mk XIV squadrons redeployed to airfields in France and Belgium. In following weeks, four more squadrons equipped with the new variant joined them: Nos 41, 130, 350 and 403 Sqns.

For the remainder of the war, the Spitfire Mk XIV was the RAF's primary high-altitude air superiority fighter type operating over northern Europe.

The 100 Griffon-engined Spitfire Mk XIIs proved highly effective at low and medium altitudes, countering hit-and-run raids by the Luftwaffe on English coastal targets.

Scafires in the Atlantic fleet

23 June 1942 saw the first Seafire Mk IICs reach an operational FAA squadron, No. 807 at Lee-on-Solent. Four other squadrons followed suit in the second half of 1942, all receiving Mk IICs, except No. 801 Sqn, which acquired Mk IBs and was to be the only front-line unit to be equipped with a full complement of the early Seafire variant. The next front-line unit to receive the Mk I (for operational use, rather than training) did not do so until the summer of 1943, when torpedo-bomber/ reconnaissance squadron, No. 842, acquired six examples with which to form a fighter flight. With most of the FAA's Seafire Mk IIs earmarked for use during the Salerno landings, Operation Avalanche, No. 842 Sqn was provided with Mk IBs withdrawn from training units in July, undertaking trade protection duties during the occupation of the Azores. No. 894 continued to operate Mk IBs until March 1944.

Seafire deployments during 1944 were diverse, encompassing land-based as well as carrier operations. Seafire units provided part of the escort for anti-shipping strikes off the Norwegian coast, in particular the well-known attacks on the German battleship Tirpitz mid-year. Prior to the Normandy landings (Operation Overlord) Seafire Mk IIIs of Nos 887 and 894 Sqns based at Culmhead provided a fighter escort for RAF Typhoons on cross-Channel fighter-bomber sorties and during the landings in June four FAA units, with shore-based Seafires and Spitfires, carried out gunnery spotting for naval guns offshore. During Operation Dragoon, the invasion of southern France in August, of nine American and British carriers taking part, four of the latter had Seafire units aboard. As well as combat air patrols, Seafires also made tactical reconnaissance and bombing sorties over the beachhead. The latter were performed by aircraft of No. 4 Fighter Wing, this being the first major use of the Seafire in the fighter-bomber role. Pictured is a Seafire Mk IB of No. 801 Sqn, the first FAA squadron to take the Seafire into action, aboard HMS Furious.

RAF Spitfires at war

As the Allies occupied Sicily and moved north through the Italian mainland, the RAF made use of captured Italian airfields. Pictured is a Spitfire Mk VC of No. 43 Sqn, at Comiso, Sicily.

Overseas service, 1942-45

Spitfire Mk Vs, the first examples of the type to be deployed overseas, were first shipped to Malta in March 1942. Later the Mk V and later Mk VIII were to see considerable overseas service.

Early in 1942 the Spitfire faced a new challenge. Britain's strategy in the Mediterranean hinged on the use of Malta as a base from which to interdict the Axis supply routes to Africa. Yet the besieged island was taking a fearful pounding from German and Italian bombers, and its continued survival was in question. Malta's main air defence comprised a small force of Hurricanes, which were no match for the Bf 109Fs that the Luftwaffe had deployed to the theatre.

The obvious solution was to deliver a number of Spitfire Mk Vs to the island, but there was no simple way of doing this. Malta lay 1,100 miles (1770 km) east of Gibraltar, far beyond the Spitfire's normal ferry range.

For the Malta delivery operation, Supermarine designed a 90-Imp gal (410-litre) drop tank to fit under the fuselage of the Spitfire. The first delivery of Spitfires to Malta took place on 7 March 1942, when 15 took off from HMS *Eagle* and flew to the island. The Spitfires arrived in the nick of time, for the Luftwaffe had stepped up its onslaught in preparation for the planned invasion of Malta. Heavily outnumbered, the Spitfires were pitchforked into a desperate battle for survival in which they took heavy losses.

Beginning in April 1942 the US Navy carrier *Wasp* joined *Eagle* on another 12 delivery trips, despatching a total of 385 Spitfires, all but 18 of which arrived safely.

Problems in Australia

Following those initial overseas deliveries of Spitfire Mk Vs to Malta, others went to units in Egypt. When Allied troops moved into northwest Africa in November 1942, Mk Vs of the RAF provided air cover for their advance. Southeast Asia was next to receive these fighters. In each of those theatres, the Spitfires' arrival enabled the RAF and its allies to secure air superiority.

The only war theatre where the Spitfire failed to live up to its high reputation was that of Australia. In January 1943, three squadrons of Spitfire Mk VCs arrived in the Northern Territory to provide a defence against attacks by Japanese aircraft. No. 54 Sqn was based at Darwin airport while Nos 452 and 457 Sqns went to the nearby airfields at Strauss and Livingstone.

The fighter had never previously operated in a true tropical

Right: Wg Cdr Ian Gleed leads a section of No. 601 Sqn aircraft in his capacity as OC No. 244 Wing. No. 601 Sqn had flown its Spitfires to Malta from USS Wasp in April 1942. Gleed, a 13-kill ace, was killed in April the following year, while flying the aircraft seen here, Spitfire Mk VB AB502. Note the personal 'IR-G' codes.

environment close to the equator. On the ground, the aircraft had to face extremely high temperatures and high humidity. At altitude, the Spitfires encountered air temperatures somewhat lower than any they had previously encountered. Those very low temperatures caused repeated failures of the constant-speed units (CSUs). Thus the Spitfire Mk V failed to quell the attacks on Northern Australia. By the time the fighter's failings became known and had been reported to its makers, the series of raids had come to an end. The Mk V's successor in that theatre, the Mk VIII, incorporated modifications which overcame the problems.

Mk IXs in the Med

Towards the end of 1942, the Luftwaffe moved a Gruppe of Fw 190s to Tunisia. Initially confronting Spitfire Mk Vs and fighters of lower performance, the German unit was for a time able to secure temporary air

Although the Spitfire Mk VIII had been earmarked for overseas service, the threat posed by Luftwaffe Fw 190s and delays in the delivery of the new Spitfires led to the use of Mk IXs in the Mediterranean theatre, from December 1942. These No. 241 Sqn examples are seen over Mount Vesuvius, Italy during 1944.

No. 81 Sqn was one of the first RAF units in the Far East to receive Spitfire Mk VIIIs, from late 1943. In all 10 squadrons in the CBI flew the Mk VIII, mainly in the fighter-bomber role.

Seafires in the Mediterranean

The FAA contributed seven carriers from Force 'H' to Operation Torch, the Allied landings in North Africa. Four of the carriers were equipped with Seafires from five squadrons. No. 880 Sqn, in HMS *Argus*, had 18 Seafire Mk IICs, No. 885 Sqn aboard *Formidable* had six Mk IICs, while Nos 801 and 807 Sqns (12 aircraft each) joined *Furious*, the former with a handful of Seafire Mk IBs. Finally, No. 884 Sqn joined the second fleet carrier, HMS *Victorious*, also with six Mk IIs. It proved to be an auspicious start to the Seafire's combat career; three enemy aircraft were shot down and another seven damaged, three of these in the air. In all, 160 sorties were launched, many in the Tac/R role, during which 21 Seafires (40 per cent of those available on 8 November) were lost. Only three of these were due to enemy action; most of the result of very poor visibility off the coast.

Operation Husky, the invasion of Sicily, again involved elements of Force 'H', including HMS *Indomitable* (with 28 Mk IICs of Nos 880 and 899 Sqns, and 12 L.Mk IICs of No. 807 Sqn) and *Formidable*, with five No. 885 Sqn Mk IICs in addition to 28 Martlet Mk IVs. The operation began on 10 July 1943, aircraft of Force 'H' flying daytime defensive patrols over its own ships and others passing through the area until the 15th. Sicily fell quickly and by 21 August Force 'H' was ready for its next task – the invasion of the Italian mainland, codenamed Avalanche. During this action *Formidable* and *Illustrious* (which had replaced the damaged *Indomitable*, and had No. 894 Sqn aboard, with 10 Seafire Mk IICs) were to provide protection for an inshore carrier force made up of *Unicorn* and four escort carriers (*Attacker*, *Battler*, *Hunter* and *Stalker*), all with Seafire L.Mk IICs aboard.

The final Allied invasion operation in the Mediterranean was Operation Dragoon, the landings on the south coast of France which began on 15 August 1944. Seven Royal Navy escort carriers supported the operation, HMS *Emperor*, *Pursuer*, *Searcher*, *Attacker*, *Khedive*, *Hunter* and *Stalker*. In addition to 75 Hellcat and Wildcat fighters, the carriers bore 97 Seafires L.Mk IICs, LR.Mk IICs and L.Mk IIIs. On the first day the Seafires were employed principally on defensive patrols over the landing area. It quickly became clear that the Luftwaffe was in no position to mount any sort of strong reaction against the landings. As a result, from the second day, the Seafire and other units reverted to flying armed reconnaissance missions ahead of the advancing Allied troops. Targets of opportunity, mainly road and rail traffic, were bombed and strafed. By 19 August the first airstrips were completed ashore, enabling land-based fighters to take over the air defence task. Despite low winds and occasional spells of poor visibility, the Seafire units suffered a relatively low accident rate during Dragoon. Pictured is a No. 880 Sqn Seafire Mk IIC aboard HMS *Indomitable* during 1943. The unit had covered the Torch landings in November 1942 and in July 1943 flew fighter patrols over Sicily.

superiority over selected parts of the battle area. Then, as over northwest Europe, the RAF countered by moving Spitfire Mk IX units into the area. No. 81 Sqn went into action with them in January 1943, followed soon afterwards by No. 72 Sqn. The Mk IXs quickly restored air superiority, and assisted in the tightening of the air and sea blockade of Axis supply routes from Italy.

Delayed Mk VIIIs

With the Mk IX available in large numbers, there was reduced urgency to get the fully engineered Mk VIII into mass production. The first Mk VIIIs appeared in November 1942, the entire production of Mk VIIIs going overseas, to units in the Mediterranean, Southeast Asia, southwest Pacific and Australia theatres. The need to ship the aircraft to those distant theatres further delayed the appearance of the variant in front-line service. The first unit to receive

Mk VIIIs, No. 145 Sqn based in Malta, became operational only in June 1943, just as the invasion of Sicily and Italy was launched. Numerous other units eventually converted to the Mk VIII, the variant being used increasingly as fighter-bombers, just as Mk IXs and XVIs were to be used in Northern Europe.

In Southeast Asia the first Mk VIIIs arrived toward the end of 1943. Nos 81 and 152 Sqns based at Alipore and Baigachi in eastern India converted to the new variant, soon followed by other fighter units in the theatre.

Initially, there was little air activity over the theatre. The Japanese Army Air Force was seriously overstretched and had to conserve its strength. The period of relative calm ended on 6 February 1944, when Japanese ground forces went on the offensive in the Arakan area. General William Slim, commander of the British 14th Army, ordered the 5,000 troops cut off at Sinzweya to stand firm

and, relying on the Spitfires to maintain air superiority, transport planes supplied the outpost until it could be relieved. Nos 67, 81 and 152 Sqns with Spitfire

Mk VIIIs moved to Ramu near the India/Burma border, from where they flew offensive patrols and escort missions. The siege of Sinzweya ended on 23 February.

Seafires east of Suez

Only during the final two months of the war against Japan, when experienced pilots operated the fighter from the large fleet carriers, was the Seafire at last able to demonstrate its real worth. Nos 887 and 894 Squadrons in Indefatigable, and Nos 801 and 880 Sqns in Implacable, performed particularly successfully during this period.

The most successful action in the Seafire's entire service career took place on 15 August 1945, the very day when hostilities ended in the Pacific. Eight aircraft from Nos 887 and 894 Squadrons escorted six Avengers to attack a coastal target in Japan. Between 12 and 14 A6M5 'Zeke' fighters ran in to intercept the force and a dogfight developed. In the ensuing action the Seafires claimed eight enemy fighters destroyed, one probably destroyed and two damaged. One Seafire was shot down

and another suffered damage. For their part, the Avengers delivered their attack and withdrew without loss.

East of Suez, the Seafire's lack of range was to prove an even greater handicap. Many fighter units re-equipped with American-built aircraft, but as insufficient numbers were available, the Seafire continued to serve. A small number of Seafires (Mk IICs equipping a flight of No. 834 Sqn aboard HMS *Battler*) were on trade protection duty in the Indian Ocean from October 1943 and towards the end of the year another squadron was added (No. 889 Sqn in Atheling with Mk IIIs). However, it was not until the beginning of 1945 that the FAA's striking power was concentrated in the Far East, with the Seafire Mk III eventually equipping eight squadrons east of Suez, aboard the escort carriers of the 21st Aircraft Carrier Squadron and the fleet carriers *Implacable* and *Indefatigable*. Notable actions for which the Seafires provided fighter cover included the the attacks on Japanese oil refineries in Sumatra in January and the occupation of Rangoon and Penang in May and August. In the Pacific during March/April, meanwhile, British Pacific Fleet Seafires (Nos 887 and 894 Sqns in *Indefatigable*) were in action over the Sakishima Islands. It was during this action that Seafires made their first combat claims in the Pacific and Sub-Lt Richard Reynolds of No. 894 Sqn became the FAA's first (and only) Seafire ace, downing three 'Zeros' to add to two BV 138s claimed off Norway. With the arrival of HMS *Implacable* (No. 38 Wing – Nos 801 and 880 Sqns), operations over Truk in the Caroline Islands in June saw Seafires in action once again and by August Seafires were flying over the Japanese mainland. Illustrated is a No. 807 Sqn Seafire Mk III from HMS *Hunter*, June 1945.

Deck crewmen hold down a Seafire as it is run up before a sortie from HMS Formidable. MB156/'O6-G' was a Seafire F.Mk IIC of No. 885 Sqn and was engaged in one of the Seafire's first combats, during the invasion of North Africa on 8 November 1942, in which its pilot shared in the destruction of a Vichy French bomber with another of No. 885's aircraft.

Seafire Mks I, II & III

By a wide margin the most effective British-built naval fighter of World War II, the Seafire was in reality, little more than a 'navalised' Spitfire. As such it was to gain notoriety as an aircraft apparently unsuitable for the rigours of carrier operations.

To some degree, the Seafire's reputation for being unsuited to carrier operations was deserved, for the Spitfire was a lightweight design never intended for naval service. However, in the absence of a more suitable aircraft (i.e., until the arrival of F4U Corsairs and F6F Hellcats), the Seafire served in significant numbers, taking part in major campaigns in Europe and the Far East.

The Fleet Air Arm decided as early as 1941 to adapt the RAF's excellent Spitfire fighter for carrierborne service. It seemed a logical step after the Hawker Hurricane had successfully made the transition to naval use, with catapult and carrier-based fighter

units, as the Sea Hurricane. The first trials to test the Spitfire's suitability were conducted in December, when a Mk VB, fitted with an arrester hook and flown by the CO of the RN Fighter School, Lt Cdr H. P. Bramwell DSC, made a series of landings aboard HMS *Illustrious*.

Seafire conversions

Sufficiently impressed, the Royal Navy ordered the conversion of another 165 Spitfire Mk VBs to Seafire Mk IB standard (the 'B' suffix indicating that the Spitfire Mk VB's 'B' wing armament was retained: two 20-mm Hispano cannon and four Browning 0.303-in machineguns.) As well as an arrester hook,

Above: Effectively the Seafire prototype, BL676 started life as a Spitfire Mk VB. Part of the new equipment fitted to the aircraft was an arrester hook, just visible under the rear fuselage. Redesignated a Seafire Mk IB, BL676 was reserialled MB328.

Below: MB293 was converted from F.Mk IIC to L.Mk IIC standard in 1942 and sent to the A&AEE for bombing trials. Intended for low-level operations, L.Mk IIs often had 'clipped' wingtips to improve roll rate, although this aircraft has standard tips.

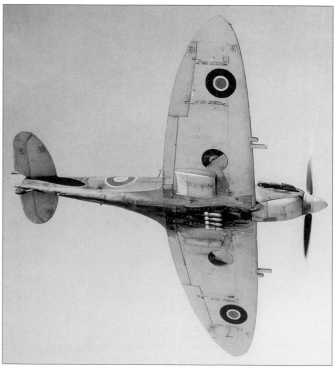

With the Mk IIC came the ability to be fitted with rocket-assisted take-off (RATO) gear. However, safety concerns and production difficulties meant that the latter was never used operationally during World War II.

Wing-folding allowed Seafire Mk IIIs to be stored below decks on board the smaller of the RN's carriers. Note that a double fold was necessary, such was the restricted space in carrier hangars.

these aircraft had slinging points, standard naval radios and IFF gear installed. The first Seafires entered service in June 1942 and were largely confined to training duties, though a few saw combat, mainly with No. 801 Sqn.

It was the Seafire F.Mk IIC that bore the brunt of early encounters with Axis aircraft. These entered service concurrently with the Mk IBs, but were new-build aircraft based on the Spitfire Mk VC with its stronger Universal or 'C' wing (usually with two cannon and four machine-guns – four cannon were rarely installed), a strengthened fuselage, catapult spools and fittings for RATO gear.

Five squadrons equipped with 54 Seafires were embarked on four RN aircraft-carriers in support of the Allied invasion of Morocco and Algeria in November 1942; in this they joined FAA Sea Hurricanes and Martlets covering the British landings. On the 8th, No. 807 Sqn from HMS *Furious* engaged Vichy French Dewoitine D.520s near La Senia, Sub-Lt G. Baldwin downing one of the aircraft – the Seafire's first air-to-air victory. After the first day, however, fighter opposition was almost non-existent and as land bases were established, the carriers withdrew.

May 1943 saw the introduction of the Seafire L.Mk IIC, a variant intended to improve climb rate and low-altitude performance. Fitted with a Merlin 32 engine (with a cropped supercharger impeller), a four-bladed propeller and, in some cases, 'clipped' wings (to increase roll rate), the first L.Mk IICs equipped No. 807 Sqn. This version also filled a secondary fighter-bomber role, carrying either a 250-lb (114-kg) or 500-lb (227-kg) bomb on a centreline rack, in place of the commonly fitted 'slipper' fuel tank.

Seafires were again in action covering the invasion of Sicily in May 1943, and played an important part in providing air cover for the beachhead during the landings at Salerno, on the Italian mainland, in September.

While no Seafires were lost to enemy action over Salerno, general loss rates were high. Of 106 aircraft deployed aboard the carriers, no fewer than 83 were wrecked or seriously damaged, largely due to the aircraft's fragile airframe and pilot inexperience. In all, 372 Seafire Mk IICs were built; this total included the low-level variants, all of which were conversions of F.Mk IICs.

Later in 1943, the first of about 30 examples of a tactical reconnaissance version, the LR.Mk IIC, entered service. Broadly equivalent to the RAF's Spitfire PR.Mk XIII, this variant sported one vertical and one oblique F.24 camera, although it retained its gun armament.

The major wartime Seafire mark was the Mk III, of which 1,263 were constructed. Developed in response to delays in the delivery of American aircraft, this variant introduced for the first time a manually-folding wing – this improved deck handling and allowed the use of the smaller hangar lifts found on some carriers. Built initially as the F.Mk IIIC (103 examples), most were completed with Merlin 55M 'low-level' engines as L.Mk IIICs, equipped for the fighter-bomber role. The production total also included 129 L.Mk IIICs completed as FR.Mk IIIs with a single reconnaissance camera installed. Mk IIIs were to see service in August 1944 during the invasion of southern France and later during attacks on the German battleship *Tirpitz*, but it was in the Pacific that the Mk III was to achieve its greatest successes.

Pacific operations

By 1945, eight Mk III units were aboard six carriers in the Pacific, where they provided cover for the invasion of Rangoon and Penang and escorted raids on Japanese oil refineries in Sumatra. In the final months of the war, experienced pilots from Nos 887 and 894 Squadrons aboard HMS *Indefatigable* and Nos 801 and 880 on HMS *Implacable* were particularly successful. In fact, the most successful actions in the type's entire wartime career took place on the final day of fighting (15 August), when eight aircraft intercepted by around a dozen A6M5 'Zeke' fighters, downed eight aircraft for a single loss.

Left: Such was the fragility of the Seafire and the inexperience of many FAA pilots, that a large number of sorties ended like this, with the hapless aircraft damaged, often seriously. This is a No. 807 Sqn L.Mk IIC aboard HMS Battler during the Italian landings in 1943.

Below: An F.Mk IIC prepares to make a three-point landing. Its long nose, finely balanced controls and an approach speed only slightly above stall speed made the Seafire a handful for pilots.

Seafire Mks XV & 17

In looking for a replacement for the Seafire Mk III, the FAA bypassed derivatives of the Merlin-powered Spitfire Mk VIII in favour of an aircraft based on the RAF's Griffon-powered Mk XII. Just too late for wartime service, the resultant Seafires of Mks XV and 17 were the Navy's only carrierborne fighters in the years immediately after World War II.

The Admiralty had been impressed by the potential of the Rolls-Royce Griffon, and its installation in a Spitfire airframe, from the earliest days of its development. Having already elected not to adapt the Spitfire Mk VIII, powered by the Merlin 60-series engine, because modifications to correct structural deficiencies would have resulted in unacceptable weight gain, the Navy chose instead to adapt the first Griffon-powered Spitfire variant, the Mk XII.

Designated Seafire F.Mk XV, the new naval fighter was a hybrid combining a Spitfire Mk VB fuselage, the Seafire

Mk III's folding wings, and the enlarged fin and rudder, wing-root fuel tanks and retractable tailwheel of the Spitfire Mk VIII. The powerplant was to be a Griffon VI, rated at 1,850 hp (1380 kW) at 6,250 ft (1905 m). Driving a four-bladed Rotol propeller, this bestowed a top speed of 383 mph (616 km/h) at 13,500 ft (4115 m). Armament was as for the Mk III (two cannon and four machine-guns), external stores including a 500-lb (227-kg) bomb or fuel tank on the centreline and two rocket projectiles under each wing.

The first of three Mk XV prototypes flew in 1944. Though it was the FAA's intention that

Above: Visible differences between the Mk XV and its predecessors included a broad-chord rudder, revised engine cowlings and large propeller spinner. SR449 was one of the 250 machines built by Westland; the remaining 134 were produced by Cunliffe-Owen Aircraft Ltd.

Top: Shown in the standard post-1948 Medium Sea Grey over Sky colour scheme, this Mk 17 served with No. 1833 Sqn, RNVR.

the Mk XV would replace the Mk III in the Pacific Fleet, the first examples did not reach an operational squadron (No. 801 Sqn, then in Australia), until September 1945. By the end of

that month three units were re-equipping with the new aircraft, but were too late to see action.

The FAA's only fighter

By the end of June 1946, Mk XVs had replaced the last of the remaining Seafire Mk IIIs and, with the disposal of American Lend-Lease aircraft, had become the Fleet Air Arm's sole carrierborne fighter type.

However, no sooner had the Mk XV entered service, than the new aircraft were banned from carrier operations after potentially dangerous problems arose with the Griffon VI engine. Take-off and landing reliability

NS493 was originally the third Mk XV prototype, but is seen here during 1945 after being modified as the first Mk 17, with a teardrop cockpit canopy.

Left: Visible on the underside of this Mk 17's port wing is the enlarged oil cooler intake introduced in the Mk XV. A more streamlined tropical air filter is also fitted under the nose. The stinger-type arrester hook may also be seen beneath the rudder.

Below: Seafire Mk 17s remained in service until the final days of FAA Seafire operation. No. 764 Sqn, a fighter training unit equipped with Mk 17s at RNAS Yeovilton (hence the 'VL' tailcode), was the last unit to fly Seafires, disbanding in late 1954.

were badly affected by a tendency for the engine's supercharger to malfunction at high engine speeds. It was early 1947 before a satisfactory modification was devised by Rolls-Royce. In the meantime, four Royal Navy aircraft-carriers put to sea without single-seat fighters aboard.

Shore-based operations continued. One unit, No. 807 Sqn saw service in northern Germany, based at Lübeck with the RAF's 2nd Tactical Air Force as part of the British occupation force.

In late 1944, the third Mk XV prototype was modified with a cut-down rear fuselage and a

tear-drop canopy, as first fitted to a Spitfire Mk VIII in mid-1943. Sufficiently impressed by the improved rearward visibility afforded by the new canopy, the Admiralty requested that the last 30 Mk XVs were completed by Westlands with this feature.

Improved Mk 17

The 384 Seafire Mk XVs were followed on the production lines by 232 FR.Mk 17s (Arabic numerals having replaced Roman in British designations from 1947), powered by the same Griffon VI engine. As well as the new canopy the Mk 17 sported a stronger, taller under-

carriage to improve propeller ground clearance – an important development as the Seafire had always been prone to 'pecking', where the propeller's tips struck the carrier deck when the aircraft was arrested on landing, causing propeller and engine damage.

A secondary benefit of this change was that higher take-off weights were permissible and more fuel and ordnance could be carried. Behind the cockpit,

Left: With his canopy open to facilitate his escape in the event of a ditching, a No. 800 Sqn pilot is catapulted from HMS Triumph in his Mk 17. The 50-Imp gal (227-litre) drop tank in the centreline position proved more reliable than the slipper-type tanks used hitherto on Spitfires and Seafires.

Below: Seafire Mk 17s of No. 800 Sqn (and Fairey Firefly Mk Is of No. 827 Sqn) are run up prior to operations from HMS Triumph in the Mediterranean in about 1948.

there were fittings for two vertical F.24 cameras or a 33-Imp gal (150-litre) fuel tank, while a 22½-Imp gal (102-litre) so-called 'combat' fuel tank could be carried under each wing, in place of rocket rails. A strengthened wing spar also allowed the carriage of a 250-lb (114-kg) bomb in this position.

Though no faster than the earlier variant, the Mk 17 represented an improvement over the former, by virtue of its greater combat radius and operational flexibility. The Mk 17 first entered FAA service in 1946, but deliveries did not begin in earnest until the following year. However, though the last examples were not completed until 1952, the Mk 17 only remained in front-line service until 1949, replaced by Hawker Sea Furies and Seafire Mk 47s. Reserve and training units then employed the variant into the early 1950s.

Exported Seafires

Though principally a Fleet Air Arm aircraft, the Seafire saw some limited foreign service. Twelve 'denavalised' Mk IIIs found their way into the Irish Air Corps service in 1947, while 48 refurbished L.Mk IIIs served aboard French navy carriers *Dixmude* (ex-HMS *Biter*) and *Arromanches* from 1948. These latter machines saw service in Indo-China before being replaced by Grumman Hellcats from 1950.

The only Mk XVs exported were 20 aircraft supplied to the Union of Burma Air Force in 1951. Prior to their delivery, these machines underwent reconditioning in the UK, this work involving substituting Spitfire Mk XVIII wings for the Seafire's folding wings and removing naval equipment. In UBAF service the Seafires served alongside Spitfires for four years.

The second step in the evolution of the definitive Seafire was the Mk 46, which introduced the Rotol contra-rotating propeller. LA542 was the second of just 24 examples completed.

Seafire Mks 45, 46 & 47

Combat swansong

Seafire development culminated in the FR.Mk 47, an aircraft far removed from R. J. Mitchell's F.37/34 Spitfire interceptor prototype of 1936, but destined to see combat just prior to its retirement.

The Fleet Air Arm's first Rolls-Royce Griffon-engined Seafires – the Mk XVs and Mk 17s – were a stop-gap, tiding fighter squadrons over until the Griffon 60 series engine, with its two-stage super-charging, was successfully married to a suitably redesigned Spitfire airframe.

The resulting Spitfire Mk 21, with its strengthened structure, including a redesigned wing, was ordered in large numbers by the RAF. Though the Admiralty was not entirely happy with the design, the new Spitfire was the only new fighter that not only approached its requirements for a naval aircraft, but was also likely to enter service within the next

three years. In 1944 it was decided to adapt the Mk 21 for naval use, as the Seafire Mk 45.

Mk 45 development

Modifications were few, confined to the essential equip-ment required to make the aircraft 'carrier-capable'. Newly converted, the first Mk 45 (TM379) took to the air in late 1944 and was followed, over the next 12 months, by a further 50 production examples, all built by Vickers-Supermarine.

Trials showed that the new 2,035-hp (1518-kW) Griffon 61 gave the Mk 45 a top speed of 380 mph (612 km/h) at sea level and 442 mph (711 km/h) at 20,000 ft (6096 m), as well as a

Looking little different from the Spitfire Mk 21 from which it was converted, TM379 was the Seafire Mk 45 prototype. Changes for naval service were confined to the addition of an arrester hook, slinging points and the substitution of a naval radio set.

much improved service ceiling and climb rate.

However, though these figures were impressive, the Mk 45 was purely a development aircraft and, as such, was never intended for front-line duties. Besides, trials had also revealed a number of performance traits that made

the aircraft unsuited to operation from aircraft-carriers.

The massive torque produced by the Griffon 61 and its five-bladed propeller caused a considerable swing on take-off, and once airborne the aircraft proved difficult to fly in a straight line. Moreover, its main-tenance requirements were some three times greater, in terms of man-hours, than those of the Seafire Mk III.

Second phase

Though often described as a naval version of the Spitfire Mk 22, the Seafire FR.Mk 46 represented more than a simple 'navalisation' of the RAF fighter.

Though it shared the Spitfire's

PS944 was the Mk 47 prototype. Here it demonstrates the manually folded wing that distinguished it from the Mk 46 and permitted service aboard RN carriers. Most Mk 47s had a powered fold mechanism.

Left: An early production Seafire Mk 47 snags the wire as it touches down on a Royal Navy carrier.

Below: This view of PS946, the third Mk 47, shows the new wing, of revised plan and profile, introduced on the Spitfire Mk 21 and fitted to all subsequent Spitfire/Seafire marks. PS946 was the first to be fitted with the Griffon 88 engine, with petrol injection.

cut-down rear fuselage (and bubble canopy) and 24-volt electrical system, the Mk 46 introduced important differences. A contra-rotating propeller and a new, taller fin and rudder (the latter taken from the Supermarine Spiteful interceptor) eliminated the swing and handling problems and, at a stroke, transformed the Seafire Mk 46 into a much more pleasant machine to fly.

Four cannon

Like the Mk 45, the Mk 46 was armed with four Hispano 20-mm cannon, could carry the same external stores as a Mk 17 and could be equipped with reconnaissance cameras. Fuel capacity was improved, the Mk 46 being able to carry a pair of so-called 'combat' underwing tanks of 22½-Imp gal (102-litre)

This fully-loaded Mk 47 carries a pair of 500-lb (227-kg) bombs and 135 Imp gal (614 litres) of external fuel, the latter in a pair of so-called 'combat' wing tanks of 22½-Imp gal (102-litre) capacity, and a centreline 90-Imp gal (409-litre) drop tank.

capacity. In the Mk 46, overall fuel capacity had risen to 228 Imp gal (1036 litres), almost twice the capacity of the original Seafire Mk IB, though it should be pointed out that its rate of fuel consumption was almost 50 per cent greater than that of the Merlin 45!

Only 24 Mk 46s were built for, without folding wings (still under development), these aircraft were unsuitable for carrierborne service. A number served ashore, with No. 1832 Sqn, Royal Navy Volunteer Reserve, but all had been withdrawn by 1951.

The ultimate Seafire development was the FR.Mk 47, the first example of which was flown in April 1946. Based upon the Mk 46, the Mk 47 introduced a deepened nose profile brought about by changes to the engine air intake. This was extended forward to a point just behind the propeller spinner, imparting a ram-air effect for improved supercharger performance.

The aircraft's Griffon 88 powerplant was equipped with a fuel injection system and its

wings were, at last, able to be folded – manually in the first 14 examples, but hydraulically in the remaining 76 of 90 Mk 47s built in total. Each wing was also strengthened to carry a 500-lb (227-kg) bomb.

The Mk 47 was able to carry both centreline and 'combat' drop tanks, while its flying surfaces were altered. Increases in the area of the tailplane and elevators improved the Seafire's handling.

Faster than most

Few production piston-engined fighters could match the Seafire 47's speed and climb rate and, though its cockpit design came in for criticism from pilots, the Mk 47 was considerably easier to deck land than its predecessors, partly due to its widened undercarriage track.

Seafires for front-line service finally appeared in early 1947, the last being delivered in 1949, by which time only one FAA squadron, No. 800, was

operational with the type at sea, other units having re-equipped instead with the superior Hawker Sea Fury.

That said, No. 800 Sqn's 19 months spent flying Mk 47s were far from uneventful. Embarked in HMS *Triumph* with the Far East Fleet, the unit took its Seafires into combat for the first time in attacks against Malayan insurgents during late 1949/early 1950. These shore-based sorties were followed, later in the year, by an extended period off the coast of Korea. Here, No. 800's aircraft joined those of the US 7th Fleet, flying over 300 patrol and attack sorties against Communist targets between July and September. *Triumph* returned home in November and No. 800 Sqn disbanded, bringing the Seafire's front-line FAA service to an end after eight years. A few Mk 47s lingered on with a training unit, but these were finally retired in 1954.

Seafires over Korea

The Seafire's last combat sorties were flown in 1950, when No. 800 Sqn FR.Mk 47s aboard HMS *Triumph* attacked shore targets in support of the retreating army of the Republic of Korea. VP461 is equipped with rocket-assisted take-off gear (RATOG) and carries a 500-lb (227-kg) bomb under each wing and a centreline 50-Imp gal (227-litre) drop tank.

Tupolev Tu-2

High-speed Soviet bomber

The Tu-2 was tailored to meet a requirement for a high-speed bomber or dive-bomber, with a large internal bombload, and speed similar to that of a single-seat fighter. Designed to challenge the Ju 88, the Tu-2 proved equally versatile, and was produced in torpedo, interceptor, and reconnaissance versions.

The requirement for Samolyet (aircraft) 103 was issued in 1938, and was known under the Tupolev OKB designation Tu-58. The resulting first prototype (ANT-58) was rapidly completed at factory N156, and made its first flight on 29 January 1941, piloted by Mikhail Nukhtinov. In tests the following June, the aircraft was found to possess outstanding performance, achieving a speed of 398 mph (640 km/h) at an altitude of 26,248 ft (8000 m).

Despite exceeding VVS requirements, the aerodynami-cally outstanding ANT-58 was hampered by AM-37 engines that were still at the developmental stage. The second prototype (ANT-59) introduced a series of refinements, and although early flights utilised the AM-37, the ASh-82 radial was eventually adopted, bringing a decrease in performance. Samolyet 103 production

began at Omsk in 1941, with the initial aircraft, the ANT-60 being based on the ANT-58. After only 19 of such aircraft had been built, the factory switched to construction of the Yak-1. The

Right: Andrei Nikolaevich Tupolev (in white hat), pictured visiting a front-line Tu-2 unit, developed the Tu-2, along with his design team, under prison conditions. Tupolev had been imprisoned in a Moscow jail in 1937 but was transferred to Bolshevo, where he worked at the Central Design Bureau N29 of the NKVD (TsKB-29) with other aviation specialists the following year. The full-scale mock-up of Samolyet 103 (the future Tu-2) was constructed from timber in a forest close to the prison.

Later production Tu-2s (throughout the war the Tu-2S designation was applied to production machines) featured numerous modifications compared to earlier aircraft. Early in production the cowling diameter was reduced (Block 20); small blisters added over the valve gear and a redesigned metal nose. By Block 50, the Tu-2 had been progressively equipped with windows for the ventral gunner, a new VUB-68 gun mount for the radio operator, an additional retractable landing light (all Block 44), improved Lu-68 ventral gun installation (Block 46), extended nose glazing, new straight-top canopy and new VUS-1 navigator's gun mount (Block 48).

Samolyet 103U was the second Tu-2 prototype, with a raised canopy and lengthened fuselage with accommodation for a fourth crew member, firing a ShKAS from a lower rear fuselage hatch. The 103U had provision for 10 RS rockets underwing.

Left: Modified from an early 103 in 1943-44, the Tu-2SBD (ANT-63) had all guns (except for a wingroot ShVAK) and dive brakes removed, and more powerful liquid-cooled engines installed in order to fulfil the role of a fast day-bomber.

Below: The five-seat Tu-2DB (ANT-65) long-range bomber introduced a long-span wing, supercharged (exhaust-driven) liquid-cooled engines and a twin-pilot cockpit, whilst retaining the Tu-2's weapons and bombload.

first ANT-61 was built in 1942, and differed only in detail from the ANT-60. After an enthusiastic reception during operational trials with the first series production aircraft (103VS), the 103S was ordered back into production at Omsk, under the new designation Tu-2S.

Tu-2S in service

The first ASh-82FN-engined Tu-2S began arriving with squadrons in early 1944, with 1,111 being delivered by the end of the war. Production continued post-war at Omsk (GAZ-125), bringing the total number of Tu-2s built (excluding other variants) to 2,257 by 1948, when construction ceased. Minor production variants, experimental aircraft or modifications (and not assigned individual factory designations) included the Tu-2M with more powerful ASh-83 engines (1945), the Tu-2/104 radar-equipped bomber interceptor (1944), UTB bomber trainer (1946) and the three Tu-2Sh Shturmoviks of 1944.

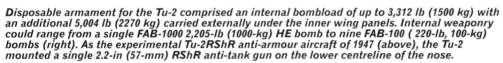

Disposable armament for the Tu-2 comprised an internal bombload of up to 3,312 lb (1500 kg) with an additional 5,004 lb (2270 kg) carried externally under the inner wing panels. Internal weaponry could range from a single FAB-1000 2,205-lb (1000-kg) HE bomb to nine FAB-100 (220-lb, 100-kg) bombs (right). As the experimental Tu-2RShR anti-armour aircraft of 1947 (above), the Tu-2 mounted a single 2.2-in (57-mm) RShR anti-tank gun on the lower centreline of the nose.

The Tu-2 recce bomber was produced as an 'in field' conversion from 1943. The aircraft carried three or four cameras behind individual ventral doors. In 1946, purpose-built reconnaissance variants appeared, comprising the Tu-2R (Razvyedchik) with standard airframe (left), and the Tu-2F (Fotorazvyedchik) with increased-span wings for high-altitude operations. The Tu-2R, a four-seat aircraft with long-range tanks and provision for cameras in fuselage bays, would have been assigned the designation Tu-6 had it been produced in quantity. Flown in October 1946 and tested until April 1947, the Tu-2R was also fitted with a radarom radar in a chin installation.

Vickers Wellington

A number of early bomber Wellingtons, including this Mk IA (N2887), underwent conversion as Mk XV interim transports for service with RAF Transport Command. Note that the defensive guns have been removed.

Bomber variants

An immensely strong warplane capable of surviving crippling battle damage, the Vickers Wellington was the Royal Air Force's most advanced bomber at the outbreak of World War II and was at the forefront of the British bomber effort for the first half of the war.

Building upon the experience gained from Barnes Wallis's geodetic structural concept, which had been used in the airframe of the Wellesley, Vickers adopted such a construction when tendering for a prototype contract to Air Ministry Specification B.9/32. This called for an aircraft capable of delivering a bombload of 1,000 lb (454 kg) and with a range of 720 miles (1159 km). These requirements were surpassed by the Vickers proposal, which was for a mid-wing medium day-bomber with two Rolls-Royce Goshawk engines and retractable landing gear, able to carry more than 4,500 lb (2041 kg) of bombs, and having a maximum range of 2,800 miles (4506 km).

The prototype B.9/32, with two 915-hp (682-kW) Bristol Pegasus X engines and a Supermarine Stranraer fin and rudder assembly, was completed at Weybridge in May 1936. It was first flown by Vickers chief test pilot, J. 'Mutt' Summers, on 15 June. Later that month, it was exhibited at the 1936 Hendon Air Display, with nose and tail cupolas covered to prevent details of its still-secret construction method being

revealed. After initial manufacturer's testing the aircraft was flown to the Aircraft and Armament Experimental Establishment at Martlesham Heath for official trials. Near there, on 19 April 1937, with tests almost concluded, the prototype crashed after elevator overbalance in a high-speed dive resulted in inversion and structural failure.

Significant orders

On 15 August 1936, however, the Air Ministry had placed an order for 180 Wellington Mk Is to Specification B.29/36. These were required to have a re-designed and slightly more angular fuselage, a revised tail unit, and hydraulically-operated Vickers nose, ventral and tail turrets. The first production Wellington Mk I was flown on 23 December 1937, powered by Pegasus X engines. In April 1938, however, the 1,050-hp (783-kW) Pegasus XVIII became standard for the other 3,052 Mk Is of all variants built at Weybridge, or at the Blackpool and Chester factories which were established to keep pace with orders.

Initial Mk Is totalled 181, of which three were built at

Above: The Vickers B.9/32 prototype K4049 made its maiden flight at Brooklands on 15 June 1936. After the aircraft crashed the following April, the Wellington underwent an almost total redesign.

Below: Destined for Bomber Command, these Wellington Mk I fuselages are seen in the erecting shop at Weybridge in 1939. The aircraft's geodetic, or 'basket weave', structure is clearly visible.

Below: A Wellington Mk III crew finalise its their route to the target before a raid over enemy territory. The fairing behind the cabin held the D/F loop which provided a bearing to any selected ground beacon.

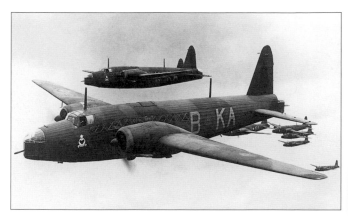

Above: A formation of Wellington Mk Is of No. 9 Squadron from RAF Stradishall is seen during exercises in 1939 prior to the outbreak of war. The squadron flew Wellingtons until August 1942, when it re-equipped with the Lancaster Mk I.

Chester. These were followed by 187 Mk IAs with Nash and Thompson turrets and strengthened landing gear with larger main wheels. Except for 17 Chester-built aircraft, all were manufactured at Weybridge. The most numerous of the Mk I variants was the Mk IC, which had Vickers 'K' or Browning machine-guns in beam positions (these replacing the ventral turret), improved hydraulics and a strengthened bomb bay beam to allow a 4,000-lb (1814-kg) bomb to be carried. Of this version 2,685 were built (1,052 at Weybridge, 50 at Blackpool and 1,583 at Chester), 138 of them being delivered as torpedo-bombers after successful trials at the Torpedo Development Unit, Gosport.

Many of the improvements incorporated in the Mks IA and IC were developed for the Mk II, powered by 1,145-hp (854-kW) Rolls-Royce Merlin X engines as an insurance against Pegasus supply problems. The prototype was a conversion of the 38th Mk I, and made its first flight on 3 March 1939 at Brooklands. Although range was reduced slightly, the Wellington Mk II offered improvements in speed, service ceiling and maximum weight, the last rising from the 24,850 lb (11272 kg) of the basic Mk I to 33,000 lb (14969 kg). Weybridge built 401 of this version.

With the Wellington Mk III, a switch was made to Bristol Hercules engines, the prototype being the 39th Mk I airframe with Hercules HEISMs, two-stage superchargers and de Havilland propellers. After initial problems with this installation, a Mk IC was converted to take two 1,425-hp (1063-kW) Hercules III engines driving Rotol propellers. Production Mk IIIs had 1,590-hp (1186-kW) Hercules XIs, and later aircraft were fitted with four-gun FN.20A tail turrets, doubling the firepower of the installation in earlier marks. Two were completed at Weybridge, 780 at Blackpool and 737 at Chester.

American engines

The availability of a number of 1,050-hp (783-kW) Pratt & Whitney Twin Wasp R-1830-S3C4-G engines, ordered by but not delivered to France, led to development of the Wellington Mk IV. The prototype was one of 220 Mk IVs built at Chester, but on its delivery flight to Weybridge carburettor icing caused both engines to fail on the approach to Brooklands, and the aircraft made a forced landing at Addlestone. The original Hamilton Standard propellers proved very noisy and were replaced by Curtiss propellers.

The fourth production

Wellington Mk I was the first to reach an operational squadron, arriving at Mildenhall in October 1938 for No. 99 Squadron. Six squadrons of No. 3 Group (Nos 9, 37, 38, 99, 115 and 149) were equipped by the outbreak of war, and among units working up was the New Zealand Flight at Marham, Norfolk, where training was in progress in preparation for delivery to New Zealand of 30 Wellington Mk Is. The flight later became No. 75 (NZ) Squadron, the first Dominion squadron to be formed in World War II. Sergeant James Ward of No. 75 later became the only recipient of the Victoria Cross while serving on Wellingtons, the decoration being awarded for crawling out on to the wing in flight to extinguish a fire, during a sortie made on 7 July 1941.

On 4 September 1939, the second day of the war, Wellingtons of Nos 9 and 149 Squadrons bombed German shipping at Brunsbuttel. Wellingtons in tight formation were reckoned to have such

outstanding defensive firepower as to be almost impregnable, but after maulings at the hands of pilots of the Luftwaffe's JG 1, during raids on the Schillig Roads on 14 and 18 December, some lessons were learned. Self-sealing tanks were essential, and the Wellington's vulnerability to beam attacks from above led to the introduction of beam gun positions. Most significantly, operations switched to nights.

Raid on Berlin

Wellingtons of Nos 99 and 149 Squadrons were among aircraft dispatched in Bomber Command's first attack on Berlin, which took place on 25-26 August 1940; and on 1 April 1941, a Wellington of No. 149 Squadron dropped the first 4,000-lb (1814-kg) 'blockbuster' bomb during a raid on Emden. Of 1,046 aircraft which took part in the Cologne raid during the night of 30 May 1942, 599 were Wellingtons. The last operational sortie by Bomber Command Wellingtons was flown on 8-9 October 1943.

This trio of Wellington Mk ICs is from No. 311 (Czechoslovak) Squadron which was based at RAF Honington in late 1940. This variant had beam machine-guns replacing the ventral turret.

Below: Characterised by the carburettor air intake scoop on the upper surface of the nacelle, the Wellington Mk III was powered by two Bristol Hercules XI piston engines.

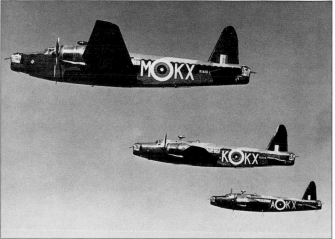

Maritime, training and transport variants

Though outmoded in the bomber role, the Wellington remained in use for the duration of World War II as a maritime patrol and transport aircraft. Training variants were in use as late as 1953.

Above: The RAF's last Wellingtons were the post-war T.Mk 10s employed as navigation trainers after refurbishment by Boulton Paul. All were converted from Mk X bombers, over 3,800 of which were completed. MF628 is served with No. 6 ANS in about 1949 and has since been preserved by the RAF Museum.

Maritime variants

Although as early as late 1941 Coastal Command had employed modified Wellington Mk ICs for torpedo and mine-laying work (initially attacking Axis shipping from Malta), it was during the spring of 1942 that the first true general reconnaissance Wellingtons entered service with RAF Coastal Command. These land-based maritime patrol and anti-submarine aircraft were **GR.Mk VIII**s, powered by Pegasus VIII radial engines (as on the Mk IC bomber) and the first 'Wimpies' to be equipped with ASV Mk II radar (with its associated lines of masts on the rear fuselage). Most were also equipped with a Leigh Light for night-time engagement of surfaced U-boats.

In all, 394 Mk VIIIs were built and were followed by 180 **GR.Mk XI**s and a batch of **GR.Mk XII**s. These differed from the earlier aircraft in being powered by Hercules VI and XVI radials, respectively, and carrying ASV Mk III radar in a 'chin' radome in place of the earlier Mk II set. The Leigh Lights fitted to these aircraft were retractable and installed in the rear fuselage; there was also provision for a pair of 18-in (45.7-cm) torpedoes. Both variants lacked a nose turret.

Two further variants, both powered by Hercules XVII engines, were also developed; the **Mk XIII** was equipped with ASV Mk II, while the **Mk XIV** – the last general reconnaissance Wellington intended for front-line service – was essentially similar to the Mk XII in terms of its equipment.

An unusual variant with a maritime role was the specialised Wellington **DWI** (for Directional Wireless Installation – a deliberately confusing cover designation), used successfully to counter an early German 'secret weapon' – the magnetic mine. Converted from Mk ICs, the DWI aircraft were equipped with a 48-ft (14.6-m) hoop housing a magnetic coil energised by a 47-hp (35-kW) generator carried in the fuselage. Entering service In January 1940, these aircraft were employed primarily in the Mediterranean theatre.

Above: This early Wellington GR.Mk VIII (HX419) would have traded its Bomber Command colour scheme for Coastal Command colours before entering service. The rear fuselage and underwing antenna for its ASV Mk II radar are evident.

Above and below: These views show examples of the Wellington GR.Mk XIV, equipped with a retractable Leigh Light, chin-mounted ASV Mk III and Hercules engines.

The Hercules-powered Wellington GR.Mk XIII (above) was equipped with ASV Mk II radar; some aircraft lacked a nose turret. NC606 (below) is a post-war Flying Training Command aircraft.

Below: This Wellington DWI was converted from a Weybridge-built Mk IC bomber and saw service in the Middle East.

Training variants

Two Wellington variants were employed as wartime training aircraft; both were equipped with radar. A number of Coastal Command Wellingtons carrying Air-to-Surface Vessel (ASV) radar were converted as radar trainers under the designation **Mk XVII**. The **Mk XVIII** was a new-build type, 80 of which were supplied to the RAF for the training of radar operators destined to join front-line Mosquito night-fighter units. Known later as T.Mk XVIIIs, these aircraft were equipped with a Airborne Interception (AI) radar in a nose radome.

The last Wellington to see service in the RAF was the **T.Mk 10**, a derivative of the Mk X bomber introduced in late 1942 and powered by the Hercules XVIII radial. The Mk X bomber, over 3,800 of which were built, served with 29 RAF squadrons, mainly in the Middle and Far East. With hundreds surplus at the end of the war, a considerable number were converted by Boulton Paul as training aircraft and issued to Air

Above: Completed in October 1945, Hercules-engined T.Mk 10 RP589 was the second-last Wellington completed. In all, 11,460 examples were completed over a period of eight years.

Navigation Schools; the last was retired in 1953. A number of additional aircraft were converted in the field by RAF units; these were designated **Mk XIX**.

Another little-known trainer variant was a derivative of the aborted **Mk VI** high-altitude bomber aircraft. A number were employed to train bomber crews in the use of the 'Gee' navigation aid.

Above: NC928 was a Hercules-powered Wellington Mk XVIII radar training aircraft. An AI radar set is housed in the nose 'thimble' radome. As training took place at night, the aircraft is finished in standard Bomber Command colours.

Above: After the Wellington Mk VI pressurised high-altitude bomber was abandoned, a number of the Rolls-Royce Merlin-engined aircraft were employed as 'Gee' trainers.

Left: Mk I L4340 was the 124th Wellington built and was originally intended for delivery to the RNZAF (as NZ302). However, with the outbreak of war the aircraft were offered to the RAF; this machine was converted as a C.Mk IA transport and served with BOAC and later No. 24 Sqn, the RAF's oldest transport unit, then based at RAF Hendon. Here the aircraft is depicted after modification, with faired-over turrets, 'NQ' squadron codes and the name Duke of Rutland.

Transport variants

RAF Transport Command employed two main Wellington versions – the **Mk XV** and **XVI**. Most were converted from Pegasus-engined Mk IC bombers rendered surplus by the re-equipment of Bomber Command units with more modern aircraft. Bomb doors were sealed and basic seating for 12 personnel fitted in the 'cabin'.

The Wellington Type 437 **Mk IX** was a one-off conversion of a Pegasus-engined Mk IA bomber as a specialised troop-carrying aircraft. Able to carry 18 fully-equipped troops or an equivalent load, the Mk IX had a range of 2,200 miles (3541 km).

Below: Like most Wellington Mk XVs and XVIs, this Pegasus-engined Mk XVI was converted from a Mk IC bomber. It had earlier served with Nos 115 and 305 Sqns and a number of OTUs before being converted to serve as a transport.

Above: Another No. 24 Sqn aircraft, N2990 'NQ-D' Duke of Cornwall is a C.Mk XVI transport. The nose and tail turrets are, in fact, painted on to disguise the fact that the aircraft is unarmed.

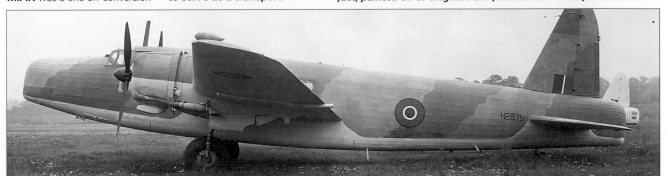

Vought

F4U Corsair
Introduction

The likely key to the Corsair's longevity was the combination of its superior air combat capabilities, a high top speed, the ability to absorb combat damage and a strong wing – all of which helped to produce a world-beating warplane.

The bent-wing F4U Corsair was the first carrier aircraft which could outfight not only the best Japanese fighters, but could also outperform other Allied aircraft. Many consider the Corsair to be the greatest piston-engined fighter ever built.

The Vought F4U Corsair enjoyed a unique place in naval aviation during World War II and afterwards. Any list of wartime 'greats' would have to include the blue, gull-winged F4U, but the Corsair can also claim numerous other achievements. Corsairs fought in Korea and were among the very last piston-engined fighters to come off a production line anywhere in the world. Furthermore, it was a Corsair that made the US Navy's first night-time, radar-guided interception.

The Corsair is perceived by some as a back-up to the superb Grumman F6F Hellcat. In fact, design work on the Corsair had begun before the idea of the Hellcat had taken shape in

anyone's mind and, in some ways, the Corsair was technically ahead of the Hellcat. However, the Corsair was seriously delayed in the early development stage and was late in appearing - reaching service only after engineers had grappled with infuriating flaws.

Although tardy and, at first, distrusted, the Corsair entered the war at Guadalcanal in February 1943 – early enough for pilots and maintenance men to experience some of the most gruelling conditions of the war.

The Corsair immediately took command of the sky. Japanese fighters had previously faced a serious challenge only when outnumbered American pilots coaxed more from their aging Wildcats than anyone had a right

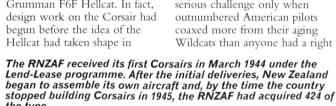

The RNZAF received its first Corsairs in March 1944 under the Lend-Lease programme. After the initial deliveries, New Zealand began to assemble its own aircraft and, by the time the country stopped building Corsairs in 1945, the RNZAF had acquired 424 of the type.

In service with the Confederate Air Force since 1969 is this Goodyear FG-1D Corsair (BuNo. 92468). It is one of about 12 Corsairs which remain in airworthy condition.

to expect. The Corsair gave these pilots speed, power, and decisive killing potential.

F4U Corsair pilots flew 64,051 combat sorties – 54,470 from land and 9,581 from carriers. They claimed the destruction of 2,140 Japanese aircraft for the loss of 189 Corsairs in air-to-air combat – a spectacular 11 to 1 kill ratio. The Corsair stayed in production long enough to be

the last propeller-driven fighter built in the United States.

When design work on the Corsair began in 1938 and a plywood mock-up was inspected at Vought's Stratford, Connecticut plant the following year, the US Navy could boast of a warplane built around the same powerful engine as the Army's P-47 Thunderbolt. To give the 13 ft 6-in (4.13-m) propeller ground

France received the last variant of the Corsair, the F4U-7, between 1952 and 1953. They were used operationally in Algeria and in Suez. Some examples were able to fire the early AS11 air-to-surface missile from pylons under the outer wing panels.

gull wing were strong and the Corsair was stressed for high manoeuvrability – a pilot with the right touch could fling it around the sky.

During the Korean War, an F4U Corsair shot down a MiG-15 jet fighter, no small accomplishment. The only US Navy ace from that war, a Corsair night-fighter pilot, was also the only ace not to fly the F-86 Sabre. When the final F4U-7 was completed on 24 December 1952, a total of 12,571 Corsairs had been built, including those manufactured by Brewster and Goodyear and AU-1 ground-attack variants. No other American fighter could come close to the Corsair's record of longevity on the production line.

Other service

In the postwar era, Corsairs became a frequent sight at open days, air shows, and air races. Among the best-known civilian Corsairs thrown into racing competitions at Cleveland in the 1940s and at Reno from the 1960s were examples of the more powerful, bubble-topped variant developed by Goodyear in the final days of World War II. Corsairs also served in a number of overseas air arms, and saw combat in the 1968 'Soccer War' between El Salvador and Honduras.

Vought further increased the capabilities of the Corsair with the F4U-5 which first flew on 4 April 1946. This particular example is an F4U-5N, a night-fighter, equipped with radar which can be seen in its underwing pod.

clearance without making the landing gear too stalky, designer Rex Beisel came up with the Corsair's distinctive, inverted gull wing which also reduced drag.

From testing to combat, the Corsair repeatedly proved itself a match for the Japanese Mitsubishi A6M Zero fighter, although it was heavier and was certainly more difficult to handle on the ground or in the runway pattern. The Corsair was as manoeuvrable as the Zero with better speed, range, and staying power, although visibility was to remain a problem through much of the Corsair's life.

The F4U Corsair pilot sat high and was tightly strapped into a narrow metal seat which had a liferaft and emergency supplies stowed underneath. The all-aluminium fuselage and inverted

Above: No fewer than 19 Fleet Air Arm squadrons received Corsairs, with a total of 1,977 being built for the Royal Navy. This Corsair Mk II's long-range underfuselage fuel tank has burst into flames, having come adrift following a heavy landing.

Left: F4Us line the deck of the USS Bunker Hill (CV-37), receiving minor maintenance before further combat. Problems – such as stalling and the tendency towards 'rudder kick' – had meant that the Corsair was not initially cleared for US carrier operations, although the FAA had already demonstrated its abilities.

Corsair development

Above: Only one prototype of the Corsair was built, a potentially risky decision, which proved disastrous when the XF4U-1 crashed on 11 July 1940, pushing the development process back by three months.

Left: The first production version of the Corsair, the F4U-1, differed somewhat from its prototype predecessor. It was the only Corsair with a framed or 'birdcage' canopy and early examples had a flat top and periscope.

Vought bucked the then-current trend for inline-engined fighters and, in the Corsair, produced an unconventional aircraft that went on to become one of the most successful fighters of World War II.

Design work on the Vought F4U Corsair began in 1938, along with work on two other fighters that were to be quickly forgotten as war clouds gathered: the lacklustre Grumman XF5F-1 Skyrocket and Bell XFL-1 Airabonita. The Airabonita, a 'taildragger' cousin of the P-39 Airacobra, performed so badly that one pilot called it a 'dog', and after the sole example crashed, the US Navy had no interest in building another. Grumman's twin-engined fighter was even less well-suited to combat, and its primary function was to appear in the popular 'Blackhawk' comic books during the war. Neither the Grumman nor the Bell designs gave the USN what it wanted – a carrier-based fighter with a performance up to that of land-based pursuit aircraft.

The first order for the Vought XF4U-1 was placed on 30 June 1938. A full-scale plywood mock-up of the XF4U-1, not noticeably different from the actual aircraft which followed, was ready for inspection at Vought-Sikorsky's Stratford, Connecticut facility as early as February 1939.

The XF4U-1 was the first US Navy warplane built around the 1,850-hp (1380-kW) Pratt & Whitney XR-2800-4 Double Wasp radial, the same heavyweight that powered the US Army's P-47 Thunderbolt. The Vought fighter had a propeller of 13-ft 4-in (4.13-m) diameter, wider than that of the Thunderbolt, but with three blades.

Rex Beisel, chief engineer on the design project and a veteran of service with the Curtiss and Spartan companies, searched for a way to give the big propeller ground clearance without making the landing gear too stalky or heavy. Beisel's solution was to design the aircraft so that the wing was gulled downwards, the inverted-gull configuration having the added benefit of reducing drag at the juncture of wing and body.

Armed with twin .50-in calibre (12.7-mm) machine-guns each in nose and wings, the natural-metal prototype Corsair had exactly the kind of practical undercarriage Beisel had sought, with wheels retracting backwards and swivelling by 90° flat into the wing. The inverted gull wing folded for carrier stowage, not to the rear as on the Hellcat, but upward as on most other shipboard aircraft.

The F4U Corsair design resulted from hard work by Beisel's team. Igor Sikorsky, contrary to some published accounts, was not involved in any way in the Corsair project, although the manufacturing firm was known as Vought-Sikorsky for a time. Beisel needed no help in creating a fighter which looked unorthodox when first seen because of its ingenious wing shape. The passage of time made the Corsair familiar and, to many, much loved.

The Corsair was heavier than the Japanese Zero, which became its principal adversary. It was as manoeuvrable, with better speed, range and staying power. Visibility was to remain a minor problem through much of the Corsair's life despite repeated changes in cockpit configuration, with only the final Goodyear F2G-1 variant acquiring the bubble canopy standard on US Army fighters. At Stratford on 29 May 1940, test pilot Lyman A. Bullard made the maiden flight of the new fighter, which was to be

The fighter-bomber version of the 'dash one' series of Corsairs, the F4U-1D was fitted with pylons which could carry bombs, napalm or external fuel tanks. This -1D, with its semi-bubble canopy, is preparing to make its first flight.

Above: To develop a high-speed, high-altitude Corsair, Vought took three XF4U prototypes and gave them R-2800-14W engines. This enabled them to reach speeds of 480 mph (772 km/h) and altitudes of 40,000 ft (12192 m). However, the variant did not offer an appreciable increase in performance over the F4U-4 and was therefore not adopted.

Below: The XF2G-1 was created as result of the desire to convert the Corsair into an effective interceptor that could defend the US fleets from Japanese attacks. The new variant was equipped with the R-4360 engine and could quickly climb to high altitudes to intercept Japanese reconnaissance aircraft. The new engine necessitated changes to the cowling of the aircraft, making it instantly recognisable. However, production of the Grumman F8F Bearcat meant that the (now) F2G-1 never entered service.

manufactured at Stratford throughout the war. Post-war, production of the Corsair would move to Dallas, following yet another company move.

Flight tests made it evident that the US Navy had a high-performing aircraft, but on its fifth flight the only prototype was caught with almost empty fuel tanks amid gathering rain squalls. Test pilot Boone T. Guyton made a courageous effort to save the valuable XF4U-1 on the exclusive Norwich golf course. Wet grass, however, caused the Corsair to slide and it slammed into trees, coming to a halt almost fully demolished, but with just enough space under the inverted fuselage for Guyton to get out. This proved an unexpected demonstration of the Corsair's toughness, for the machine was able to be repaired and reflown, but months were lost in the development programme.

When the silver prototype did get aloft once more, it reached a speed of 405 mph (652 km/h) on 1 October 1940 – faster, then, than any fighter in the world. Indirectly, this event helped elsewhere, for it contributed to the US Army's decision not to rely solely on liquid-cooled engines for fighters, and to proceed with the similarly-powered P-47 Thunderbolt.

On 30 June 1941, an order was placed for 584 F4U-1s. The attack on Pearl Harbor occurred within six months and the need for this shipboard fighter became much greater. Plans were established for Goodyear and Brewster to produce versions of the aircraft which became the FG-1 and F3A-1, respectively.

On 25 June 1942, the initial production F4U-1 flew with the 2,000-hp (1492-kW) Pratt & Whitney R-2800-8, lengthened fuselage, and cockpit moved back to make room for additional fuel. The engine consumed about 195 US gal (738 litres) of fuel per hour during normal-rated cruise, which was somewhat high. To increase the range of the new fighter, its 237-US gal (897-litre) internal fuel tank was supplemented by a 160 US-gal (606-litre) drop tank carried on the centreline.

USN delivery

Delivery to the US Navy occurred on 31 July 1942, one day after the first flight of the rival Hellcat, which had a similar engine. The F4U-1 was equipped with six .50-in calibre (12.7-mm) Browning M-2 machine-guns, 2,350 rounds of ammunition, 155 lb (70 kg) of armour, and the now-requisite self-sealing fuel tanks. Vought delivered 1,550 F4U-1 aircraft.

The F4U-1A became the next version, with more power and water injection. The main recognisable difference was the changeover from the Corsair's original 'birdcage' canopy to a totally new raised canopy shape which gave better visibility, had fewer frames to contend with, and was a prototype for the standard canopy shape in future aircraft in the series.

The F4U-1B, or Corsair Mk I for the Royal Navy, was identical to production F4U-1/ F4U-1As except that it had wingtips clipped by 8 in (20 cm) for stowage on smaller British carriers. This, incidentally, produced a craft which was more 'racer-like' in appearance.

The F4U-1C was built to the extent of a batch of 200, armed with four 20-mm M2 cannon. Arguments over whether machine-guns or cannon were more effective have persisted until recent times, when the latter emerged as the clear winner. The cannon meant that all that was required was to hit the opponent just once to assure that damage would be crippling, but many pilots preferred .50-in calibre (12.7-mm) machine-guns because they carried more rounds of ammunition.

The F4U-1D (and comparable FG-1D) introduced changes which included fittings for drop tanks, bombs and rockets. It marked the first time that the factory 'built in' a fighter-bomber capability for the Corsair, earlier F4U-1As and others being modified in the field. The -1D also incorporated the more powerful R-2800-8W engine with water injection which could be used for a maximum of five minutes in a combat emergency situation.

Vought produced 4,102 F4U-1Bs, -1Cs and -1Ds, including 95 Corsair Mk I and 510 Corsair Mk II fighters (differing only in cockpit design) for the Royal Navy and 370 for New Zealand.

The F4U had been conceived from the outset to serve aboard the USN's growing fleet of aircraft-carriers. CarQuals began on 25 September 1942 aboard USS *Sangamon* (CVE-26) with F4U-1 number seven, piloted by Commander Sam Porter. They showed that the Corsair was a bit too fast and that, again, visibility was a problem on final approach.

With the Hellcat coming along, the US Navy was reluctant to commit the Corsair to full-fledged carrier operations until its teething troubles could be resolved. When carrier operations were delayed, the Marine Corps, which operated most of its fighters from land, became the first user of the Corsair in combat in the Pacific.

Goodyear Corsairs

To increase production, in December 1941 Goodyear was named as the second contractor for the Corsair and the versions it built had slightly differing designations. The F4U-1 became the FG-1 (pictured), the F4U-1A became the FG-1A, and the F4U-1D became the FG-1D. They were essentially the same as their Vought counterparts and, from 1944 to 1945, Goodyear would actually produce more FG-1Ds than Vought's equivalent F4U-1D. During the course of the war, Goodyear manufactured a total of 3,941 Corsairs of assorted variants.

The final US version of the Corsair, the F4U-6 (later re-designated AU-1) was a dedicated ground attack variant. It had 10 wing pylons plus two centreline stations, and rockets or various bombs could be carried. The type served predominantly with the US Marines and the French Aéronavale, though the US Navy did have some examples.

Variants

The fighter that turned the tables on the Japanese in the Pacific War, the F4U Corsair was produced in formidable numbers from 1938 through to 1952. During this period, the Corsair progressed from its humble, yet effective, beginnings to become the powerful, missile-firing F4U-7 which fought the Vietcong in Indochina.

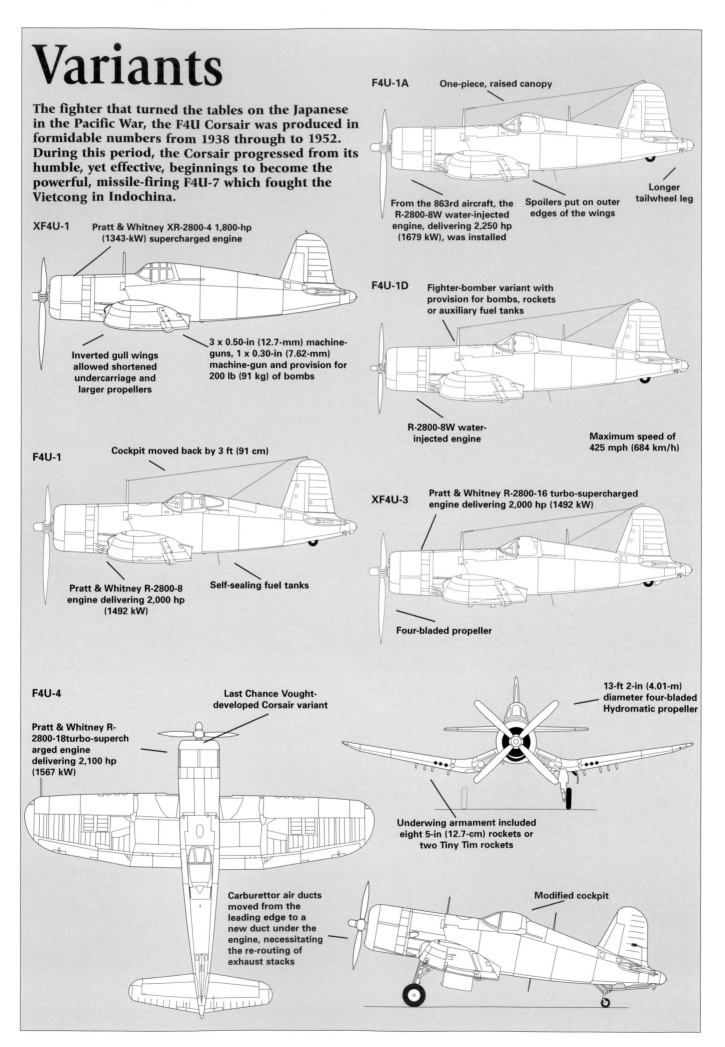

XF4U-1

Pratt & Whitney XR-2800-4 1,800-hp (1343-kW) supercharged engine

Inverted gull wings allowed shortened undercarriage and larger propellers

3 x 0.50-in (12.7-mm) machine-guns, 1 x 0.30-in (7.62-mm) machine-gun and provision for 200 lb (91 kg) of bombs

F4U-1

Cockpit moved back by 3 ft (91 cm)

Pratt & Whitney R-2800-8 engine delivering 2,000 hp (1492 kW)

Self-sealing fuel tanks

F4U-4

Pratt & Whitney R-2800-18turbo-supercharged engine delivering 2,100 hp (1567 kW)

Last Chance Vought-developed Corsair variant

Carburettor air ducts moved from the leading edge to a new duct under the engine, necessitating the re-routing of exhaust stacks

F4U-1A

One-piece, raised canopy

From the 863rd aircraft, the R-2800-8W water-injected engine, delivering 2,250 hp (1679 kW), was installed

Spoilers put on outer edges of the wings

Longer tailwheel leg

F4U-1D

Fighter-bomber variant with provision for bombs, rockets or auxiliary fuel tanks

R-2800-8W water-injected engine

Maximum speed of 425 mph (684 km/h)

XF4U-3

Pratt & Whitney R-2800-16 turbo-supercharged engine delivering 2,000 hp (1492 kW)

Four-bladed propeller

13-ft 2-in (4.01-m) diameter four-bladed Hydromatic propeller

Underwing armament included eight 5-in (12.7-cm) rockets or two Tiny Tim rockets

Modified cockpit

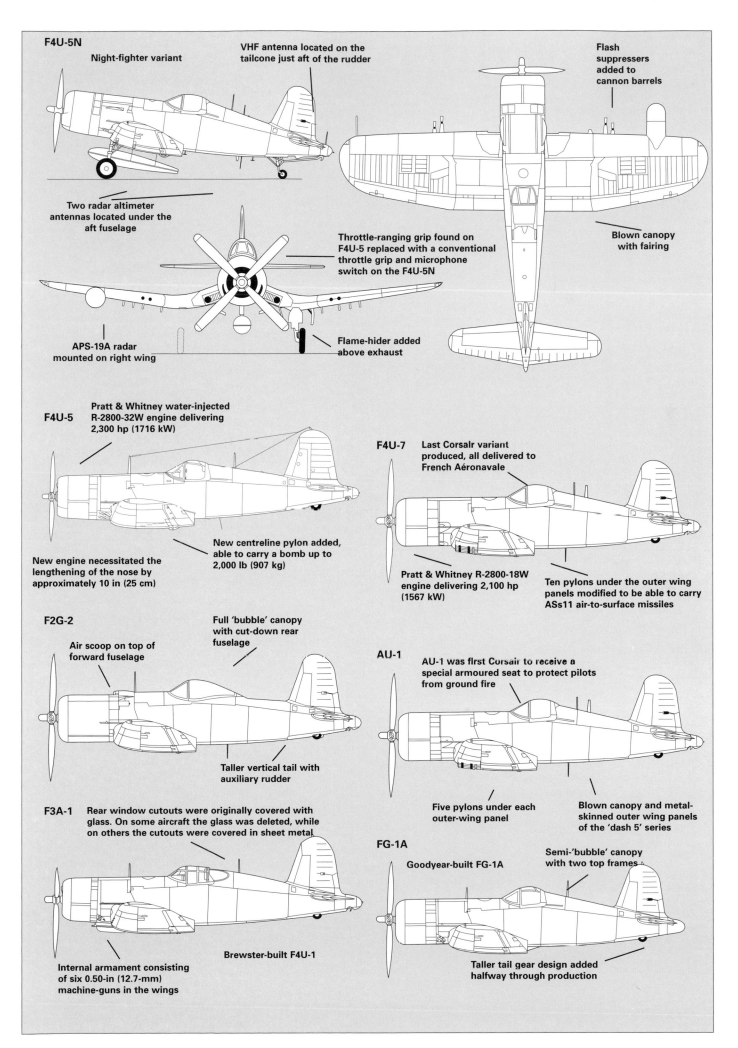

F4U-5N
Night-fighter variant

VHF antenna located on the tailcone just aft of the rudder

Flash suppressers added to cannon barrels

Two radar altimeter antennas located under the aft fuselage

Throttle-ranging grip found on F4U-5 replaced with a conventional throttle grip and microphone switch on the F4U-5N

Blown canopy with fairing

APS-19A radar mounted on right wing

Flame-hider added above exhaust

F4U-5
Pratt & Whitney water-injected R-2800-32W engine delivering 2,300 hp (1716 kW)

F4U-7
Last Corsair variant produced, all delivered to French Aéronavale

New engine necessitated the lengthening of the nose by approximately 10 in (25 cm)

New centreline pylon added, able to carry a bomb up to 2,000 lb (907 kg)

Pratt & Whitney R-2800-18W engine delivering 2,100 hp (1567 kW)

Ten pylons under the outer wing panels modified to be able to carry ASs11 air-to-surface missiles

F2G-2
Air scoop on top of forward fuselage

Full 'bubble' canopy with cut-down rear fuselage

AU-1
AU-1 was first Corsair to receive a special armoured seat to protect pilots from ground fire

Taller vertical tail with auxiliary rudder

F3A-1
Rear window cutouts were originally covered with glass. On some aircraft the glass was deleted, while on others the cutouts were covered in sheet metal

Five pylons under each outer-wing panel

Blown canopy and metal-skinned outer wing panels of the 'dash 5' series

FG-1A
Goodyear-built FG-1A

Semi-'bubble' canopy with two top frames

Internal armament consisting of six 0.50-in (12.7-mm) machine-guns in the wings

Brewster-built F4U-1

Taller tail gear design added halfway through production

Early wartime service

A series of unsuccessful take-offs and landings during suitability trials aboard USS *Sangamon* in September 1942 proved the F4U Corsair ill-equipped for carrier operations. As a result, the Corsairs saw its first combat with the Marines.

Whilst Grumman's F6F Hellcat was rushed into US Navy service from 1942, the potentially superior F4U-1 Corsair was met with official criticism. A variety of factors, including an unsafe deck landing speed, ineffectual shock absorbers, and the fact that the pilot was unable to see the flight deck during final approach, meant that the Corsair was not initially accepted for carrier operations.

Instead, all the first batches of F4U-1s were delivered to US Marine Corps units, mostly operating from narrow island airstrips in the Pacific, beginning with VMF-124. However, by the end of 1943, the Corsair had proved itself the premier air combat fighter in that theatre.

Guadalcanal debut

On 13 February 1943 VMF-124's Corsairs arrived in Guadalcanal and were used on the same day to escort B-24 bombers to Kahili airfield, 300 miles (483 km) away at Bougainville.

The following day, the unit embarked on a similar mission. The resulting action became known as the 'St Valentine's Day massacre' as fifty 'Zeke' fighters swooped down on the bomber formation, claiming two B-24s, along with four P-38s, two P-40s and two Corsairs on escort duty.

After an inauspicious start, the tables were quickly turned in favour of the Corsair, with the survivors of VMF-124 rapidly claiming 68 kills whilst suffering only four losses of their own aircraft.

Although the US Navy's VF-12 had received F4U-1s as early as October 1942, these were quickly replaced with F6Fs. The first Navy squadron to see action with the Corsair was VF-17, which began land-based F4U-1A operations in New Georgia in April 1943. In the 75 days of combat operations with the Corsairs, VF-17 destroyed 127 Japanese aircraft, producing 15 aces in the process.

Admiral C. W. Nimitz wired Vought in May 1943 with the announcement: 'The battles which are being waged daily in the South Pacific have already proved beyond doubt that the Corsair is a better plane than any version of the Japanese Zero.'

The first Marines Corsair ace was Lt Kenneth Walsh of VMF-124, the first Corsair pilot to be awarded the Medal of Honor, downing six 'Zekes' between April and May 1943.

The F4U-1D was developed in order to provide an attack capability for land-based Corsairs in the Pacific, but it was also the first model to deployed aboard carriers in large numbers, beginning in early 1945.

Above: A combat formation (two two-ship elements) of four Vought F4U-1 Corsair fighters of the celebrated Marines squadron VMF-124, 'Pappy' Boyington's 'Blacksheep', banks left over the island of Bougainville in the Solomons group.

Above: Corsair pilots scramble for their aircraft at Guadalcanal in early 1943. Aircraft '68' wears a field-applied three-tone scheme and modified national insignia. The glazed teardrop-shaped panel aft of the 'birdcage' canopy has also been sealed.

Above: A VMF-216 F4U-1A following battle damage sustained on a mission to Rabaul on 10 January 1943. VMF-216 claimed 27.33 victories (all on the Corsair), mostly on missions to Rabaul.

Left: F4U-1s return to USS Yorktown (CV-10) in October 1943. Early combat experience resulted in pilot requests for improved forward visibility, later corrected with the bubble-canopy F4U-1A.

Right: VF(N)-101 F4U-2s prepare to take off from USS Enterprise for an action against Truk in February 1944. VF(N)-101 was the first F4U-2-equipped USN unit to be based aboard a carrier.

Below: Early F4Us, such as this example seen at Torokina Point, Bougainville, in May 1944, were armed with three 0.50-in guns in each wing plus a pair of pylons stressed for loads of 100-lb.

'Whistling Death'

Above: A Marine Corps F4U-1D Corsair unleashes 5-in rockets at Japanese positions dug into the side of mountains on southern Okinawa during June 1945. The photograph was taken from a Lockheed F-5E, with a camera (and photographer!) mounted in a modified drop tank.

Performing superbly in the Battle of the Solomon Islands, the invasion of the Gilbert and Ellice and the Marshall Islands, the retaking of the Mariana Islands and the invasion of Iwo Jima and Okinawa, the F4U earned its Japanese title 'Whistling Death'.

Operated by 24 USMC squadrons and a further two Marines night-fighter squadrons- VMF(N)-311 and VMF(N)-532, the Corsair was ultimately also adopted in its intended role as a shipborne aircraft with the US Navy.

In April 1944, US Navy squadron VF-301 flew Corsairs in service trials aboard USS *Gambier Bay*, convincing the service of the practicality of a modified F4U for carrier service. The British Royal Navy had already adopted the Corsair as a carrier-based aircraft, and Marines examples had completed emergency landings aboard carri-

ers in the Pacific. Whilst awaiting the arrival of Corsair-equipped Navy units aboard their ships, two USMC squadrons, VMF-123 and -124 were the first to operate F4Us from an aircraft carrier, serving aboard USS *Essex* from January 1945, during the invasion of Okinawa.

Early Navy Corsair operators included VF-5, -10, -13, -14, -74, -82, -84, and night-fighter squadrons VF(N)-75 and -101.

Kamikaze interceptor

One role in which the Navy's Corsair excelled was the interception of *kamikaze* raiders,

which posed a threat to the US fleet's capital ships during the closing stages of the war.

During the Pacific war, Corsairs of US Navy and Marines units completed 65,041 missions, 54,470 of those being conducted from land airstrips, the remainder of 9,581 flown from carrier decks. Only 189 Corsairs were lost in aerial combat, in contrast to 2,140 enemy aircraft downed, a kill:loss ratio of 11.3:1.

Night-fighter

The F4U-2 was developed through the conversion of 34 F4U-1s, with the addition of an

AIA radar antenna in a radome on the leading edge of the starboard wing (resulting in the deletion of one gun). VF(N)-75 became the first Corsair night-fighter operator, flying its first Pacific mission in October 1943, and achieving its first confirmed kill the following month. VF(N)-101 was the second and only other Navy squadron to be equipped with the F4U-2. The only Marines night-fighter squadron to fly the F4U-2 during the Pacific war was VMF(N)-532, commanded by Maj. E. H. Vaughn, who also used their aircraft for night strafing attacks.

Above: F4U Corsairs are unloaded onto lighters at Guian Harbour, Philippines in May 1945 for transport to service units.

Left: These escorting FG-1Ds, seen from a USMC Avenger during an attack on Okinawa, belonged to VMF-323 'Death Rattlers'. The FG-1D was a Goodyear-built equivalent of the F4U-1D fighter-bomber, with provision for rockets, bombs or napalm.

Other Corsair operators

Three South American operators made good use of the rugged Corsair. Some of their aircraft eventually passed to warbird collectors, helping to swell the world's considerable airworthy Corsair fleet.

Honduras

The Fuerza Aérea Hondureña received a total of 20 Corsairs between 1956 and 1959. The first aircraft to arrive were F4U-5/-5N/-5NLs, with wing radomes but no radar-related cockpit equipment. The fleet was subsequently enlarged with ten older F4U-4s (illustrated). Honduras flew its Corsairs in the 1969 Football War with El Salvador, during which some of the latter's Corsairs were shot down. Honduras retired its F4Us in 1977-78.

El Salvador

El Salvador took 15 FG-1Ds as part of the Military Aid Sales programme in 1957. A further five machines, all grounded F4U-4s, were taken on charge by the Fuerza Aerea Salvadorena in 1959 as a source of spares. Two of the FG-1s were shot down by Honduran F4U-5Ns during the Football War. The last Salvadoran F4U mission was flown in 1971.

Argentina

Argentina also benefited from the Military Aid Sales programme when it received 10 F4U-5 and -5N aircraft in May 1956. The aircraft were for service with the Commando Aviacion Naval Argentina, and were supplemented by 16 F4U-5 and -5NL machines in 1957. Also included with this latter batch was a number of non-flying airframes for cannibalisation. Throughout their time with the Argentine navy, the Corsairs were shore-based at Punta de Indio, but were regularly operated from the carrier ARA *Independencia*.

F2G Super Corsair

Goodyear modified three of its FG-1A aircraft to XF2G-1 configuration, optimised for low-level combat. The aircraft had 28-cylinder, 3,000-hp (2237-kW) Pratt & Whitney R-4360-4 radial engines and canopy and fuselage modifications. The first was flown on 31 May 1944. Five F2G-1 land-based production aircraft were subsequently built, but a contract for 403 further machines was cancelled with the end of World War II. The type's naval equivalent, the F2G-2 was built to the extent of 10 examples before it suffered the same fate as the F2G-1 Corsair.

*Above: This **FG-1D** remains on strength with the Commemorative Air Force at Midland, Texas. It is owned by Colonel John Conrad and was built with Bu No. 92468.*

*Below: An ex-Aéronavale **F4U-7**, this machine was purchased by UK collector Lindsey Walton in 1981. Walton flew it until 1992 and it now flies in the US.*

*Below: Also based at Duxford, The Fighter Collection also has a 1945-vintage **FG-1D** on its books. The machine was delivered to the US Navy in the pacific during May 1945 and saw combat in the theatre before being passed to the Naval Air Reserve. It passed through a number of owners until eventually finding its way into the hands of Frank Tallman in 1960. Tallman flew as a stunt pilot for films and fell in love with the aircraft. He returned it to airworthy condition and flew it himself before selling it on. The Corsair passed to The Fighter Collection where it was flown in VF-17 markings until 1997. Since that time, it has flown in the colours of a British Pacific Fleet machine.*

*Below: Based at the Imperial War Museum at Duxford, Cambridgeshire, UK, the Old Flying Machine Company includes this **FG-1D** Corsair in its fleet. The machine was built in 1944 and assembled for service with the Royal New Zealand Air Force at Los Negros by 17 August 1945. With the war drawing to a close however, it seems likely that the aircraft only performed test flights with its new owners, being returned to New Zealand for storage. In 1949 it was purchased by a private owner and was eventually restored for static display early in the 1960s. In 1971 the aircraft was sold to an American owner, before being sold on again in 1973. A major restoration project now got underway and in 1982 the aircraft made its first post-restoration test flight. In 1989 it was sold to a British collector and in 1991 it joined the OFMC. It was originally operated in the RNZAF scheme illustrated below, but for the 2002 display season was repainted to represent an aircraft of US Navy squadron VF-17.*

*Bottom: This **F2G-1** won the Tinnerman Trophy Race in 1949, before being allowed to deteriorate in the hands of a number of owners. It was finally restored for a first public showing in 1999.*

*Below: Bu No. 92399, an **FG-1D** Corsair, had a long and varied career with the US Navy and a number of private owners before coming to the UK in 2000. The machine was on US Navy strength from July 1945 until 1964, before being sold for scrap with 1,450 hours. The aircraft was not scrapped however, continuing to fly in private hands until it crashed in 1969. Several owners and two restorations later, it was sold to the late Paul Morgan at Sywell.*

Legendary 'Lizzie'

Formed in 1939, No. 225 Sqn operated Lysander Mk IIs in the Army co-operation and air-sea rescue roles until re-equipping with Hurricanes in 1942. In this view the aircraft's stub wings, equipped to carry small bombs, are clearly evident.

Westland Lysander

Notable for its remarkable low-speed flying and STOL characteristics, the Lysander entered service in the army co-operation role in 1938. However, it is perhaps better remembered today for its exploits in flying Allied agents behind enemy lines.

Though already equipped with a single 0.303-in (7.7-mm) machine-gun in each wheel spat, this No. 16 Sqn aircraft carries an additional pair of Oerlikon 20-mm cannon. These were intended for use in attacks on German invasion barges, but though trialled were not adopted operationally.

B
ritish army co-operation aircraft used between the wars were largely conversions of existing airframes. In 1934, however, the Air Ministry issued Specification A.39/34, for a new aircraft to replace the Hawker Hector biplane which was then used for the purpose. In June 1935 Westland tendered for, and won, a contract covering two prototypes which the company designated P.8, the name Lysander being adopted

subsequently. The first prototype underwent taxiing trials at Yeovil on 10 June 1936, before being taken by road to Boscombe Down, where it made its first flight on 15 June, in the course of which it returned to Yeovil. Minor modifications were made and the prototype was shown at the SBAC Display at Hatfield at the end of June, and on 24 July it went to the Aircraft and Armament Experimental Establishment at Martlesham

Heath for a week to undertake handling evaluation.

A production order for 144 aircraft was placed in September, and the second prototype flew on 11 December 1936, spending much of its time at Martlesham Heath before going to India in 1938, for tropical trials with No. 5 Sqn. Deliveries to the RAF began in June 1938, when No. 16 Sqn at Old Sarum received its first aircraft to replace the Hawker Audax then in service. The School of Army Co-operation was also based at Old Sarum, and its pilots received instruction on the Lysander from squadron personnel.

Pre-war deliveries

During 1939, 66 Lysander Mk Is were completed: of these, No. 16 Sqn received 14, the School of Army Co-operation nine, while other deliveries were made to No. 13 Sqn at Odiham, No. 26 at Catterick and No. 4 at Wimborne, the Lysanders in all cases replacing Hawker Hectors. On the outbreak of war there were seven Lysander squadrons, the others being No. II, and the Auxiliary Air Force's Nos 613 and 614 Squadrons. By this time most of the home-based squadrons had replaced their

890-hp (664-kW) Bristol Mercury XII-powered Mk Is with Lysander Mk IIs. These had the 905-hp (675-kW) Bristol Perseus XII engine, which offered a slightly better performance at altitude. Many of the Mk Is were sent overseas, for service in Egypt, India and Palestine. A total of 116 Mk Is was followed on the production line by 442 Mk IIs, and it was with this

Huge spats, completely enclosing the wheels, and a metal three-bladed propeller (in place of a wooden two-blader) were fitted to the first Lysander prototype after its first flight in June 1936.

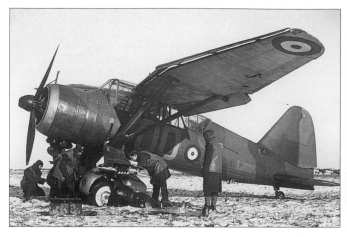

Below: The Royal Egyptian Air Force took delivery of 18 Lysander Mk Is in late 1938, the last of which is pictured. Other pre-war orders were received from France, Canada, Turkey and Ireland.

Not only did the Lysander suffer badly at the hands of Luftwaffe fighters during the Battle of France, but the weather also took its toll on servicability levels. This No. 13 Sqn Lysander Mk II has become bogged in soft ground at Mons-en-Chausseé.

latter mark that Nos II, 4, 13 and 26 Squadrons moved to France in 1940.

As the German attack began, No. 4 Squadron moved to Belgium, but such was the fury of the onslaught that 11 Lysanders were lost between 10 and 23 May, some being eliminated on the ground. One of the squadron's Lysander crews destroyed a Bf 110 during a running battle with six Messerschmitts and managed to return to base; on 22 May an aircraft of No. II Sqn accounted for a Henschel Hs 126 with its front gun and a Junkers Ju 87 with the rear gun. By then the end of French resistance was near, and the Lysander squadrons were withdrawn to the UK, although some sorties were still made over the battle area to drop supplies to Allied forces. One of these sorties was deci-

Westland P.12

Perhaps the oddest of a number of experimental Lysander derivatives was the P.12, seen here in July 1941. Employing a Delanne-type tandem wing configuration, the aircraft was an attempt to solve centre-of-gravity problems that had arisen when a gun turret was fitted behind the trailing edge of the wing. In the P.12 a mocked-up tail turret was fitted aft of the rear wing. The type did not proceed past the prototype stage.

mated when, of 16 Lysanders and Hectors sent out on a supply sortie over Calais, 14 aircraft and crews failed to return. In all, some 118 Lysanders and 120 crew members were lost over France and Belgium between September 1939 and May 1940, almost 20 per cent of the aircraft sent out from the UK. The type of army co-operation operation flown by these units was clearly outdated, particularly when air superiority had not been achieved. Accordingly, Lysanders were withdrawn from the UK-based squadrons, which began to re-equip in early 1941 with Curtiss P-40 Tomahawks.

In the East

Overseas, Lysanders had replaced Audaxes in No. 208 Sqn in Egypt in April 1939, and the squadron's new aircraft saw action in the Western Desert alongside Hawker Hurricanes of the same squadron which were being used for tactical reconnaissance. The squadron later took part in the Greek campaign, its Lysanders being replaced by Tomahawks in 1942.

No. 6 Sqn at Ramleh, Palestine, operated a variety of aircraft, and was using Hawker Hardies and Gloster Gauntlets when it received its Lysanders in February 1940. These were supplemented and later replaced,

in 1942, by various marks of Hurricane and Blenheim Mk IVs.

In September 1941 No. 28 Sqn at Ambala, India, was the first squadron in the area to receive Lysanders, replacing Audaxes. The squadron subsequently took its new aircraft to Burma, and operated in ground-attack, bombing and tactical reconnaissance roles before being withdrawn to India in March 1942; in December of that year it converted to Hurricanes, becoming a fighter squadron. The last squadron to use Lysanders in action was No. 20, in Burma during late 1943, before receiving Hurricanes as replacements.

SOE role

Although withdrawn from first-line service, Lysanders continued in operation as target-tugs, air-sea rescue aircraft and, least publicised at the time, with the Special Operations Executive. Nos 138 and 161 Sqns, using a mixed bag of aircraft which included Lysanders, maintained contact with resistance groups in occupied Europe, dropping supplies and agents, and bringing agents back to the UK. It was in these night operations in occupied territory that the Lysander really came into its own, being able to use its remarkable short landing and take-off capabilities to the utmost in the small fields marked out by the resistance. Lysander Mk IIIs and Mk IIIAs were used

for this work, 367 of the former and 347 of the latter being built, powered by the 870-hp (649-kW) Bristol Mercury XX or XXX engines.

Final production variant was the TT.Mk IIIA target-tug, of which 100 were built. Figures for total Lysander production vary, as a number of aircraft was cancelled, but around 1,650 were built, including 225 under licence in Canada.

Foreign sales

A batch of 26 Mk IIs was supplied to the Turkish air force, 20 to Egypt, six to the Irish Air Corps, nine to Finland, eight to Portugal and several to France. Three went to the USAAF, and others to the South African Air Force. Several Lysanders were used for experimental purposes, the most unusual being a tandem-wing conversion with twin fins and rudders and a Boulton Paul gun turret mock-up. This was intended as a home defence beach strafer, but fortunately was not needed. Another Lysander was fitted with a completely new wing designed by Blackburn. Intended for research purposes only, this Steiger wing was swept forward 9°, and used full-span slats and flaps to provide high lift. At the end of the war Canada was the only country to have a large Lysander population, some of which remained in service until the early 1960s.

Withdrawn from army co-operation duties in Europe, the 'Lizzie' found a new clandestine role in support of the SOE, where its STOL performance was particularly useful. This is a No. 161 (Special Duties) Sqn aircraft.

Yakovlev Yak-1, 3, 7 & 9

The lead aircraft in this Yak-9 formation carries insignia denoting both the Order of the Red Banner (forward) and that the aircraft belong to a Guard's Unit (aft). This machine was flown by M. V. Avdyeyev over the Crimea in May 1944.

Yakovlev's beauty

Over 36,730 single-engined Yak fighters were built. The type was crucial to the defence of the Soviet Union, but entered service, in Yak-1 form, as an under-developed and unforgiving warplane.

Hitler struck at the Soviet Union on 22 June 1941, at a time when the V-VS (Red Air Force) was least able to mount a defence. Almost all the main Soviet front-line types were obsolescent. Among the USSR's new fighter prototypes the best was probably the Yak-1, but even this fell into the same trap as the other Soviet fighters by having too few guns, and proving desperately difficult to fly by ill-trained pilots asked to operate such a 'hot ship' from rough airstrips of grass, mud or wooden planks. Despite this, the Yaks played a gigantic role in helping defeat the Luftwaffe.

Aleksandr S. Yakovlev had always wanted to design a fighter. His chance came in November 1938 when, with the effort on the Ya-22 fast bomber tailing off, his bureau received permission to work on a 'frontal fighter'. Design of this aircraft was initiated under the title Ya-26, the official designation being I-26 (I for *istrebeetel*, or fighter). Yakovlev had studied the Messerschmitt Bf 109 and Supermarine Spitfire at first hand, but had no experience with stressed-skin, all-metal structures and decided to stick

with traditional construction methods. He was already friendly with V. Ya. Klimov and agreed to use the latter's 1,350-hp (1007-kW) M-106-1 engine which was distantly derived from the Hispano-Suiza 12Y. By this time retractable landing gears were becoming less clumsy, and a good wide-track gear was designed, folding straight in ahead of the front spar. Pneumatic actuation was adopted, as it was for the Duralumin split flaps. For minimum drag the combined glycol radiator and oil cooler were

Yakovlev designed the I-26 with a wooden wing, a welded steel fuselage with mixed aluminium panel and fabric covering, and fabric-covered Dural control surfaces. The second I-26 prototype is illustrated.

located in a duct under the trailing edge of the wing, while the carburettor air intakes were at the wing roots. Armament comprised one 20-mm ShVAK cannon firing through the hub of the VISh-61 hydraulic propeller and two fast-firing ShKAS 7.62-mm (0.3-in) machine-guns above the engine, which had to be the 1,050-hp (783-kW) M-105 due to unavailability of the M-106.

When the first Ya-26 was almost complete the erection-shop workers called it Krasavits (beauty). It was then finished in the Yak OKB colour of bright

red, with the rudder striped red and white. Chief pilot Yu. I. Piontkovskii made a successful first flight, without guns or radio, on 13 January 1940, the wheeled gear working well from snow and ice. Sadly, the aircraft crashed fatally on 27 April, the cause being traced to a defect in its manufacture. By this time the future was assured, and with the V-VS designation Yak-1 the new fighter went into production at two factories, one being GAZ-301 adjoining the OKB on Leningradskii Prospekt in Moscow and the other GAZ-292 at Saratov. At about the time of the crash the second prototype had been about to fly, and this incorporated most of the numerous changes demanded for the Yak-1, including relocation of the oil cooler under the nose,

Lt Colonel V. F. Golubov flew this Yak-1 with 18 Gv.IAP at Khationki during the spring of 1943. Golubov was a superb pilot who finished the war with 39 kills, while the early Yaks were inferior warplanes thanks to their lack of development.

The inscription on this 37 Gv.IAP, 6 Gv.IAD Yak-1B read 'To the pilot of the Stalingrad Front Guards Major Comrade B. M. Yeremin, from the collective farm workers 'Stakhanov', Comrade Golovatov'.

Yakovlev's first UTI-26-1 two-seat prototype completed its initial flight on 23 July 1940. It entered official testing on 28 August 1940 and, like the I-26, had many faults.

dividing the carburettor air duct to inlets in the wing roots, making the fuselage wider behind the canopy, increasing the fin chord and making the tailwheel non-retractable.

Immature Yak

The second aircraft flew in the May Day parade and was put through NII official testing by P. M. Stefanovskii from 10 June 1940. By this time there was no question of rejection, but the Yak-1 was still immature. The most annoying fault was frequent fatigue failure of the aluminium fuel piping, which caused a few inflight fires. The pneumatic system was unreliable, guns frequently failed to fire and the sliding cockpit hood often jammed. The Kremlin also wanted higher flight perform-

ance, but what mattered above all else was sheer numbers, and 64 Yak-1s were delivered in the final weeks of 1940. By this time, Yakovlev's greatly expanded OKB was busy with improvements and derived versions, and in autumn 1941, with the relentless march of the German invasion, production had to be evacuated to GAZ-286 at Kamensk-Uralsk and, in late 1942, to GAZ-153 (previously a LaGG-3 factory) at Novosibirsk. Each plant introduced its own local changes; despite the need for standardisation and high output, a contemporary observer considered there were hardly any two consecutive aircraft that were identical! Among major changes aimed at reducing weight, from March 1942 some aircraft had

the two ShKAS replaced by a 12.7-mm (0.5-in) UBS (usually on the left), while a few had the weak armament of two UBS guns, one of them in place of the ShVAK. Simpler undercarriage leg fairings were introduced, along with improved wing-root inlets, retractable skis and ply decking behind the canopy, with side windows instead of the usual large curved sheet of Plexiglas. In all, loaded weight was reduced from around 6,431 lb (2917 kg) to 6,129 lb (2780 kg), with a corresponding increase in agility.

Improved Yaks

A much more difficult modification was designed under the 'Yak-1M' (Modifitsirovanny, modified) programme. The aim was to integrate the more powerful 1,260-hp (940-kW) Klimov VK-105PF engine into the lightened Yak-1 airframe, this engine becoming standard from June 1942.

Yak-1 pilot's had always struggled with the poor view available to the rear, and while part of the trouble was the rigid harness which prevented body rotation, it was clear that the canopy could be improved. The best answer was found by a front-line unit which boldly cut down the light secondary structure above the rear fuselage and fitted a transparent fairing behind the sliding hood. Pilot view was often poor in any direction because of the lack of uniformity in the Plexiglas mouldings used to form the canopy panels, but the new arrangement was adopted for production with the designation Yak-1B. Until this

time, many pilots had left the canopy open.

In addition to the production variants, there was a series of prototypes aimed at improving the Yak fighters. These included the I-28 (which also carried the designation Yak-3, but was not directly related to the aircraft produced during 1944 under the same designation), the I-30 (Yak-5) high-altitude interceptor and the I-33. These had various changes in airframe, engine/radiator installation and armament.

Yak trainer

In July 1940 a tandem trainer version of the I-26 had begun flight testing, and this quickly became a major programme. Though put into production initially as the UTI-26 trainer and two-seat liaison machine, it was recognised as being in many respects better than the Yak-1 fighter. The structure was simplified, the number of parts being reduced and the manufacturing effort greatly simplified. To maintain the centre of gravity with the armament removed and the extra cockpit installed, the radiator was moved forward under the wing. Small-scale production of the UTI-26 began in spring 1941, but the all-round ease of handling and simplicity of manufacture led to the idea of building a fighter version. In June 1941 therefore, the Yak-7M fighter was produced via the Yak-7UTI two-seater. The -7M was not adopted for service however, a refined Yak-7A instead entering production at GAZ-153 in January 1942. Between April and July 1942, GAZ-153 produced a further improved aircraft as the Yak-7B, with revised armament and powerplant. This aircraft suffered a number of drawbacks however, including low-quality cockpit transparencies, poor take-off performance and wing skins which tended to separate in flight. Around 350 Yak-7Bs were subsequently finished as reconnaissance fighters, with their machine-guns removed and a camera installed in the rear of the cockpit.

Entering front-line service over Stalingrad in August 1942, the Yak-7B was built to the extent of 5,120 examples, inspite of its quite serious inadequacies. Yak-7B problems which remained unsolved included massive engine oil loss and overheating.

Of the features trialled on the abortive Yak-7M, the Yak-7A (illustrated) retained only the 17.60-Imp gal (80-litre) rear-cockpit fuel tank. The rear cockpit area of the Yak-7A was enclosed by a simple hinged cover.

Bearing the inscription 'Little Theatre: Front' (i.e. donated by Moscow's Little Theatre for the Front), these Yak-9s are destined for the Eastern Front.

Below: A Yak-9B demonstrates its ability to deliver bombs. Four FAB-100s or a larger number of smaller anti-personnel weapons could be delivered by the variant, using underwing racks.

Yak-9/Yak-3
Dogfighters supreme

Yakovlev's family of single-seat fighters progressed from the Yak-7 to the Yak-9, but culminated with the superb, lightweight Yak-3 of 1944 – an aircraft that Luftwaffe pilots were warned to avoid in combat.

One of a sequence of famous wartime photographs, this view shows a pair of Yak-9s over the Crimea in 1944. Note the insignia of the Guards and the Order of the Red banner on the nose of '22'.

Towards the end of its production run, one batch of the simplified Yak-7 had wings with spars having aluminium-alloy webs and steel booms, while at least one machine had an all-metal wing. The change of material left more room for fuel, and pre-production examples were tested in action with designation Yak-7D and Yak-7DI (*dalnii istrebitel*, or long-range fighter), most having the Yak-1B rear-view canopy. These had a range exceeding 621 miles (1000 km), and by mid-1942 they had led to full production of a refined development, the Yak-9. This had improved radiator and oil-cooler ducts, revised rudder, redesigned metal-spar wings with improved ailerons and flaps and doped fabric over the ply skin, simple tabs bent by pliers on all control surfaces, improved gun installations, retractable tailwheel, new exhaust stacks (first used on late Yak-7Bs) and many minor changes. Usual armament comprised a ShVAK or MP-20 and one or two UBS, and there was provision for two FAB-100 bombs or six RS-82 rockets under the wings.

By May 1943 all the Yak factories had switched to Yak-9 versions. Notable variants included anti-tank models with centreline guns of up to 57-mm calibre (this and the 45-mm were too big for the small aircraft) and

the Yak-9B bomber with fuselage racks for four FAB-100 bombs carried 80° nose-up, or alternatively up to 128 PTAB 1,5 or 2,5 anti-personnel bombs. From mid-1943 the Yak OKB worked on the Yak-9U (*uluchshyennyi*, or improved) variants with numerous improvements to the airframe, fuel system and many other parts, including large oval engine air inlets projecting ahead of the leading-edge roots. Again there were many experimental models, including Yak-9P (*pushechnyi*, or cannon) versions with different arrangements including synchronized cannon in place of the machine-guns. This designation was often applied in Western accounts to the ordinary Yak-9U. Total output of series models totalled 16,769, with completion in late August 1945, of which over 3,900 were of the final Yak-9U models.

Yak-3 development

Back in late 1941 the Yak-1M search for a lightened Yak had led to a parallel development for the ultimate dogfighter for low/medium altitudes, and this was given the service number Yak-3 (already used for the Yakovlev OKB's own I-30 prototype). The urgent need for output and delay with the chosen VK-107 engine, resulted in this being abandoned, but in August 1943

Oleg K. Antonov (detached from his own OKB to help the vital Yakovlev team) picked it up again and pressed it forward. At least two Yak-1Ms were used to fly new Yak-3 features, one having the small 30.2-ft (9.2-m) wing and another having the revised fuselage with a fully retractable tailwheel, long and shallow radiator duct, streamlined oil cooler installation with inlet just below the spinner, new main gears with the leg fork on the inner side of the wheel (as in the original Yak-1) and low-drag frameless windscreen. Later changes relocated the oil cooler

to two ducts in the wing roots, fed by big root inlets as in the Yak-9, the engine being the PF-2 version as used in most Yaks after 1943. The first Yak-3 was sent for NII testing on 3 March 1944 (long after some Western accounts claimed the aircraft was in service!) and clearance for production was received in June. By this time GAZ-115 and GAZ-286 were tooled up to make the Yak-3 as well as the Yak-9, and GAZ-124 had reopened in Moscow, so that when production stopped in May 1945 a total of 4,848 Yak-3s had been delivered.

'Avoid combat with Yak fighters that do not have an undernose oil cooler intake' was the warning given to Luftwaffe fighter pilots on the Eastern Front. 'White 10' is an early production Yak-3.

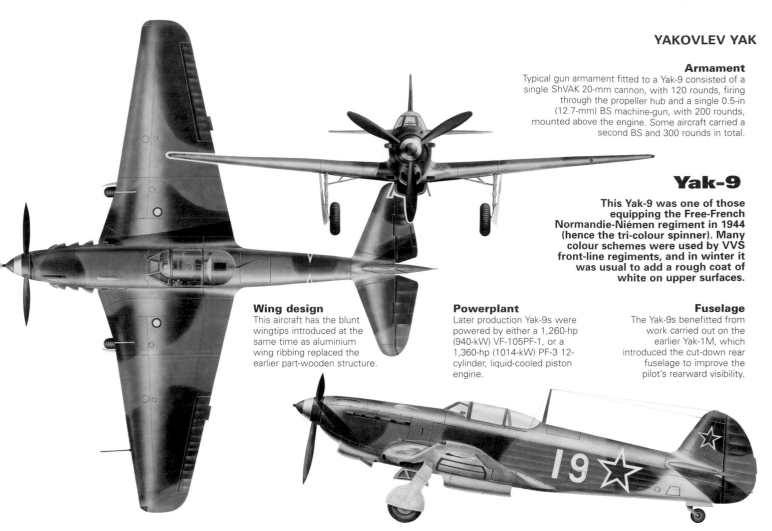

Armament
Typical gun armament fitted to a Yak-9 consisted of a single ShVAK 20-mm cannon, with 120 rounds, firing through the propeller hub and a single 0.5-in (12.7-mm) BS machine-gun, with 200 rounds, mounted above the engine. Some aircraft carried a second BS and 300 rounds in total.

Yak-9

This Yak-9 was one of those equipping the Free-French Normandie-Niémen regiment in 1944 (hence the tri-colour spinner). Many colour schemes were used by VVS front-line regiments, and in winter it was usual to add a rough coat of white on upper surfaces.

Wing design
This aircraft has the blunt wingtips introduced at the same time as aluminium wing ribbing replaced the earlier part-wooden structure.

Powerplant
Later production Yak-9s were powered by either a 1,260-hp (940-kW) VF-105PF-1, or a 1,360-hp (1014-kW) PF-3 12-cylinder, liquid-cooled piston engine.

Fuselage
The Yak-9s benefitted from work carried out on the earlier Yak-1M, which introduced the cut-down rear fuselage to improve the pilot's rearward visibility.

Normandie-Niemen regiment Yak-3s are seen shortly after the unit re-equipped with the new fighter type in July 1944. Yak-1s and Yak-9s had earlier equipped the Free-French squadrons.

Though it is believed no front-line Yak-3 had the intended VK-107 engine (though many experimental Yak-3s did) the basic aircraft soon established a tremendous reputation as the best dogfighter on the Eastern Front, on either side. There is a famous Luftwaffe signal telling pilots to 'avoid combat with any Yak fighter lacking an oil cooler under the nose', and when in August 1944 the French Normandie-Niemen Regiment was given the choice of any type of Allied fighter, it unanimously picked the Yak-3 and never had any cause to regret it. In 1945 this famed unit took its 42 surviving Yak-3s back to France.

Again, in the Yak-3 programme there were numerous experimental aircraft, not included in the production total. Fastest were the Yak-3B/108 with the VK-108 engine, which at full load reached 463 mph (745 km/h) and the Yak-3RD with a Glushko RD-1 booster rocket in the tail which reached 498 mph (801 km/h) whilst in a gentle climb. The best comment on one aircraft, the Yak-3T/57 with a 57-mm gun for tank-busting, is that it only flew once! It is worth mentioning that one variant, the tandem-seat Yak-3UTI trainer, went into production with the 700-hp (522-kW) ASh-21 radial engine and designation Yak-11. Moreover, the first Soviet jet fighter (though for political reasons kept on the ground until the rival MiG-9 was ready) was the Yak-15, which was almost a Yak-3 powered by an RD-10, the Soviet copy of the Jumo 004B, slung under the forward fuselage. This was finally allowed to fly on the same day as the first MiG-9 on 24 April 1946.

It is not easy for Western writers to assess the Yak fighters objectively. Certainly the VK series of V-12 engines, all originally derived from the Hispano-Suiza 12Y of 1934, fell well short of the British Merlin in specific power, and in particular in power at high altitude. Thus the fighters these engines powered were inevitably at a disadvantage at heights much above 20,000 ft (6095 m), and at all heights they were burdened by physically large engines in relatively small airframes. All the mass-produced Soviet fighters (the Yaks, the LaGGs and Las, and the MiGs) had wings with an area of some 184 sq ft (17 m²), compared with 242 sq ft (22.5 m²) for a Spitfire, 302 sq ft (28.1 m²) for a Hawker Tempest and 308 sq ft (28.6 m²) for a Republic P-47; thus they were cripplingly limited in the weight they could support whilst still having good power to manoeuvre.

But even this is only a small part of the story. The operating conditions on the Eastern Front were so appallingly harsh that only the toughest and simplest fighters could stay airworthy. Overall, the Yak family did more than any other group of aircraft to defeat the Luftwaffe.

'Yak-3M' and 'Yak-9U-M'

Interest from Western warbird operators in acquiring examples of Soviet aircraft from the World War II period prompted Yakovlev to build a number of all-metal replicas during the 1990s. These were powered by Allison V-1710 engines and sported modern instrumentation. At least 14 'Yak-3Ms' (pictured) were built before construction switched to the 'Yak-9U-M' in 1996. At least seven of these have been completed.

INDEX

Page numbers in *italics* refer to photographs and illustrations.

Tornado, Hawker 238–9
Triumph, HMS *479, 481*
Tu-2, Tupolev 482–3
Tupolev
    ANT-6 *424*
    Tu-2 482–3
Tupolev, Andrei Nikolayevich *482*
Typhoon, Hawker 43, 174, 231, 240–3, 244, 245, 429, 432

Unicorn, HMS 475

V-1 missile *see* Fieseler Fi 103
Vampire, de Havilland 129, 239
Ventura, Lockheed 77, 299, 308–9
Vickers
    Consolidated PBY Catalina 95, *97*
    Warwick 216
    Wellesley 76, *467*, 484
    Wellington 21, 37, 122, 123, 220, 344, 438, *467*, 484–7
    Wellington Mk I 484–5, *487*
    Wellington Mk II 485, *486*
    Wellington Mk III 485
    Wellington Mk VI 400, *487*
    Wellington Mk XVI 441
Victorious, HMS 154, *155,* 214, 215, 237, 475
Vietnam War
    A-26 Invader 142, *143*
    C-46 Commando 103
    C-47 Skytrain 144, *145*
von Greim, Generaloberst Ritter 171
Vought
    F4U Corsair 103, 111, 202, 205, 371, 385, 393, 394, 476, 488–97
    XF4U 490–1

Waco Hadrian *144, 148*
Wallis, Neville Barnes 32, 33, 34, 484
Warhawk *see* P-40 Warhawk, Curtiss
Warspite, HMS 159
Wasp, USS 208, 474
Welch, Lt George 109
Wellesley, Vickers 76, *467,* 484
Wellington, Vickers 21, 37, 122, 123, 220, 344, 438, *467,* 484–7
Wellington Mk I, Vickers 484–5, *487*
Wellington Mk II, Vickers 485, *486*
Wellington Mk VI, Vickers 400, *487*
Wellington Mk XVI, Vickers 441
Westland
    Fairey Barracuda 155
    Lysander 229, 498–9
    Supermarine Spitfire 155, 478, 479
    Whirlwind 76, 472
Whirlwind, Westland 76, 472
Whitley, Armstrong Whitworth 20–1, 37, 247
Wildcat *see* F4F/FM Wildcat, Grumman
Wilkins, Sir Hubert 95
Window radar-jamming 39, 339, 348, 349

XB-48, Martin 314, 315
XF4U, Vought 490–1
XP-41, Seversky 106, 428

Yakovlev
    Yak-1 294, 334, 482, 500–1, 502, 503
    Yak-3 335, 500–1, 502, 503
    Yak-5 501
    Yak-7 294, 334, 502
    Yak-9 334, 335, 502, 503

Yak-15 503
Yak-22 500
Yak-26 500
Yamamoto, General Isoroku 301, 305, 376
Yamato, IJNS 117
Yokosuka
    B4Y 374
    D4Y1 'Judy' 11
    MXY7 Ohka piloted missile 376, 377
York, Avro 25, 441
Yorktown, USS 11, 150, *151, 206, 209, 494*

Zero *see* A6M Reisen 'Zeke' (Zero), Mitsubishi